BUSINESS BANKRUPTCY

ASPEN CASEBOOK SERIES

BUSINESS BANKRUPTCY

Financial Restructuring and Modern Commercial Markets

Second Edition

ADAM J. LEVITIN

Professor of Law
Georgetown University Law Center

Published by Wolters Kluwer in New York.

Wolters Kluwer Legal & Regulatory U.S. serves customers worldwide with CCH, Aspen Publishers, and Kluwer Law International products. (www.WKLegaledu.com)

To contact Customer Service, e-mail customer.service@wolterskluwer.com, call 1-800-234-1660, fax 1-800-901-9075, or mail correspondence to:

Wolters Kluwer
Attn: Order Department
PO Box 990
Frederick, MD 21705

Printed in the United States of America.

1 2 3 4 5 6 7 8 9 0

ISBN 978-1-4548-9606-7

Library of Congress Cataloging-in-Publication Data

Names: Levitin, Adam Jeremiah, author.
Title: Business bankruptcy : financial restructuring and modern commercial
  markets / Adam J. Levitin, Professor of Law, Georgetown University Law
  Center.
Description: Second edition. | New York : Wolters Kluwer, [2019] | Series:
  Aspen casebook series | Includes index.
Identifiers: LCCN 2018024569 | ISBN 9781454896067
Subjects: LCSH: Business failures—Law and legislation—United States. |
  Bankruptcy—United States. | Corporate reorganizations—Law and
  legislation—United States. | United States. Bankruptcy. Chapter 11,
  Reorganization. | LCGFT: Casebooks (Law).
Classification: LCC KF1544 .L48 2018 | DDC 346.7307/8—dc23
LC record available at https://lccn.loc.gov/2018024569

About Wolters Kluwer Legal & Regulatory U.S.

Wolters Kluwer Legal & Regulatory U.S. delivers expert content and solutions in the areas of law, corporate compliance, health compliance, reimbursement, and legal education. Its practical solutions help customers successfully navigate the demands of a changing environment to drive their daily activities, enhance decision quality and inspire confident outcomes.

Serving customers worldwide, its legal and regulatory portfolio includes products under the Aspen Publishers, CCH Incorporated, Kluwer Law International, ftwilliam.com and MediRegs names. They are regarded as exceptional and trusted resources for general legal and practice-specific knowledge, compliance and risk management, dynamic workflow solutions, and expert commentary.

To Sarah for everything.
You deserve all the credit.

SUMMARY OF CONTENTS

CONTENTS

CHAPTER 28
Liquidation   567

   I. Abandonment   568
  II. Property Encumbered with Liens   569
 III. Distribution of Remaining Assets   570
     A. Compensation for Inadequate Protection   571
     B. Administrative Expenses of the Estate   571
       1. "Actual, Necessary Costs of Preserving the Estate"   571
       2. Reclamation Claims   572
       3. Prioritization of Chapter 7 "Burial Expenses"   573
     C. Employee Wage and Benefit Plan Claims   573
     D. Consumer Deposit Claims   575
     E. Tax Claims   575
     F. Late Claims and Punitive Claims   576
     G. Interest and Surplus to Equity   576
     H. Super-Super-Super-Priority Under Section 364(c)(1)   576
     I. Subordination Agreements   577
     J. Priority Summary   577
  IV. The End of a Chapter 7 Bankruptcy   578
     Problem Set 28   579

Part III.D
Reshaping the Bankruptcy Estate   583

CHAPTER 29
The Strong-Arm Power and Statutory Liens   585

   I. Avoidance Powers   585
  II. The Strong-Arm Power   586
     Official Committee of Unsecured Creditors for Tyringham Holdings,
       Inc. v. Suna Brothers, Inc.   588
 III. Statutory Liens   591
 IV. Preservation of Avoided Liens: The Sword of Gryffindor   592
  V. Avoidance Action Liability   593
     Problem Set 29   594

CHAPTER 30
Voidable Preferences and Setoffs   597

   I. Elements of a Voidable Preference   598
     A. Has There Been a Transfer on Account of an Antecedent Debt?   599
       In re Nivens   600
     B. Insolvency and the Preference Period   601
     C. Timing of a Transfer   602
     D. Has the Creditor's Position Improved as a Result of the Transfer?   603
  II. Preference Exceptions   604
     A. Contemporaneous Exchanges   604
     B. Ordinary Course Transactions   605

The aim of this book is to provide an overview of the modern financial restructuring process. In so doing, the book aims to revitalize the traditional bankruptcy course with a healthy dose of "bankruptcy realism." By this I mean that my goal is to provide a book that can be used to teach bankruptcy law as it actually lives in a broader legal ecosystem.

Bankruptcy realism has three components. First, it means teaching bankruptcy law as but one piece of the restructuring puzzle (even if it is the most important piece). My goal in this book is to broaden the scope of "bankruptcy law" as taught in law schools to include more than the in-court Chapter 11 restructuring process.[1] The traditional bankruptcy course is focused on big-B Bankruptcy lawyering, meaning representing either debtors or creditors in litigation in Chapter 11 cases (or in consumer bankruptcy cases in Chapters 7 and 13). The traditional bankruptcy course largely ignores the small-b bankruptcy lawyering, including the transactional work in Chapter 11 cases, as well as out-of court restructurings and bankruptcy-influenced transaction design.

The traditional big-B conception makes for a coherent class, but is, in my view, too narrow. It presents bankruptcy as a stand-alone process divorced from the non-bankruptcy world. I want students to come away from the course seeing how bankruptcy fits with non-bankruptcy restructuring. Chapter 11 is a very powerful tool, but it is not the only one in the restructuring toolbox. The importance of bankruptcy as a system can only be understood once one understands the legal limitations of out-of-court restructurings. At the same time, what is possible in out-of-court restructurings as a practical matter is shaped by the parties' knowledge of what could happen in bankruptcy. Accordingly, the law of out-of-court restructuring, including private contractual limitations in loan syndications and securitizations, the Trust Indenture Act, and exit consent solicitations are properly part of the bankruptcy course, rather than a topic for a corporate finance class.

A second component of bankruptcy realism is teaching bankruptcy law as including not just the actual restructuring of financially distressed companies, but

---

1. This broader vision of bankruptcy law is not just a Chapter 11 issue. In another book, I make a parallel move relating to consumer finance, which prior to the creation of the CFPB was largely the bailiwick of consumer bankruptcy scholars, who examined the consumer finance system through the bankruptcy system, in part because of the availability of rich empirical data. The creation of the CFPB should underscore that bankruptcy filing is an exceptional behavior for consumers. Most consumers in financial distress do not file for bankruptcy, and most consumers are not in financial distress at any given time. Instead, the consumer finance system needs to be examined holistically from the front-end, not from the back, and not just from a consumer perspective, but from consumer, business, and regulatory perspectives.

also transactions shaped by bankruptcy concerns. Thus, a second goal of this book is to introduce students to modern financial transactions and products that are shaped by bankruptcy law: asset securitization, repos and derivatives, syndicated loan structures and intercreditor agreements, intercompany guaranties, and leveraged buyouts. Just as small-b bankruptcy is properly part of a restructuring course, so too are transactions structures that are heavily driven by bankruptcy concerns.

In my experience, law students are desperately thirsty to understand complex modern financial transactions. They know that they'll encounter some, if not all, of these transactions in practice, and that law school is the only place they will get a systematic overview of the transactions. Unfortunately, despite the ubiquity of complex financing transactions, they receive no reliable coverage within the law school curriculum, yet they are vitally important to the world of practice students are preparing to enter. If these transactions are covered at all in law school, it is usually only passingly in secured credit or corporate finance classes. All too often, secured credit classes are hyper-focused on the details of UCC Article 9 at the expense of considering either actual deal documents or the dynamics of the modern lending marketplace, which no longer fits the model of local bank making a Main Street loan. To understand both mega- and middle-market lending, one needs to understand the transactional structure and institutional framework of these financial products.

The typical bankruptcy course touches on these transactions only to the extent necessary to explain bankruptcy law issues, such as the scope of the automatic stay or fraudulent transfers. This book gives these topics much more emphasis. The goal in this regard is to provide students with an introduction to what these products are and how they are shaped by bankruptcy law; this is not a text about financial product regulation. Because these transactions are all shaped by bankruptcy concerns, bankruptcy attorneys are often involved in these transactions, just as they are in out-of-court restructurings. Hopefully students will come away from this book with a sense of the broader world of what bankruptcy attorneys do and what bankruptcy law affects beside Chapter 11 itself.

The third component of bankruptcy realism is teaching the reality of modern business bankruptcy practice. Too often bankruptcy courses present a collection of restructuring principles and theories applied haphazardly to both consumer and business debtors without systematic treatment of bankruptcy practice's non-statutory features that are perhaps more important than statute in shaping restructurings. While there is "one Code to rule them all" the issues, economics, policies, and often statutory provisions involved in consumer bankruptcies are fundamentally different from those involved in business bankruptcies. The combined consumer-business bankruptcy course is the standard offering in American law schools, but I do not think it does a favor to either consumer or business bankruptcy to try to cover both topics in a single course. Both topics are sufficiently rich and complex to merit their own courses.

This book confines itself to business bankruptcies, and it attempts to provide a view of the Chapter 11 process that reflects the realities of modern Chapter 11 reorganizations. This is an aim that is intimately connected with understanding modern financial transactions and the institutional participants therein. Thus, topics such as bankruptcy sales, including sales procedures, valuation issues and methodologies, first-day orders and DIP lending agreements, and claims trading and responses such as lock-up agreements, are given more extensive and integrated treatment than in existing texts. I have attempted to incorporate excerpts from actual transactional documents as much as possible so that students actually get some experience reading these real documents. Likewise, I have tried to provide more "color" about what is really going on in bankruptcy cases through the use of case studies that position particular bankruptcy issues within larger transactional fights.

It's impossible to cover everything in a casebook of reasonable (or publishable) length, much less in a 3- or 4-credit course. Obviously some things have to get cut. Bankruptcy jurisdiction and international coordination didn't make it. Bankruptcy jurisdiction gets some attention regarding venue and jurisdiction over personal injury and wrongful death claims, but bankruptcy jurisdiction is largely a federal courts topic (although largely ignored by federal courts scholars). Chapter 15 coordination issues are again a set of jurisdictional issues. Executory contracts get shorter shrift than in other texts. They are covered, but I do not believe that a deep dive into the morass of section 365 is worth the coin. Likewise, all the twists and turns of section 547(c) get limited coverage, despite being beloved of law professors for creating exceptions to exceptions, thus providing great exam questions. A final area that gets scant attention are the issues relating to the retention and regulation of bankruptcy professionals. For a practitioner these are quite important, but they are largely quite unrelated to understanding the system of financial restructuring and the transaction structuring that occurs in its shadow.

Adam J. Levitin
August 2015

PREFACE TO THE SECOND EDITION

A lot has changed in the second edition of this book. The first edition was a learning experience. Hopefully the lessons learned are apparent in this second edition. The major changes in the second edition are:

(1) There is now a much clearer thematic structure to the book that emphasizes first the limitations on out-of-court restructuring and then the ways in which bankruptcy law addresses those limitations (although not always perfectly). This is reflected with the addition of chapters specifically on the limitations on out-of-court restructuring, and overview of bankruptcy, and a final chapter that looks at how bankruptcy addresses the problems identified in the first part of the book.

(2) The chapters have been reordered in three substantial ways. First, I have moved up the materials about operating in bankruptcy and avoidance actions. The structure of the book is now more in keeping with the traditional order of teaching bankruptcy topics. Second, there are number of new chapters with new material. Third, a number of chapters have been split in two, even as others have been consolidated.

(3) Almost all statutory materials have been removed from the text. There really is no replacement for a statutory supplement because it is too difficult to look up non-consecutively numbered statutory sections in the textbook. There are some statutory materials that have been kept, namely those that are unlikely to be in statutory supplements, such as the Trust Indenture Act and the Federal Rules of Bankruptcy Procedure.

(4) Numerous cases have been cut. Despite adding new material, reducing the length of the book has been a major goal. Cutting statutory materials also helped.

(5) Some problems have been cut, some new ones added, and some reordered or fine-tuned. Hopefully I have caught all the glitches in the problems. At the very least, all the problems have been field-tested at this point.

(6) There are more extensive materials on syndicated loans, including substantial excerpts from a syndicated loan agreement.

A few additional thank yous are called for in this second edition of the book. The book benefitted greatly from my participation in the Financial Lawyers Seminar in 2016 and from the input of Whitman Holt in particular. Thank you also to Ted Janger for bravely field testing some of the materials. My work with Bill Bratton on bond restructuring has helped improve the chapters on the Truth Indenture Act and exit consents. Alexander Cahuante, Julia Dimitriadis, Melanie Miller, and Kimberly Oh all provided helpful research assistance on other projects that have had spill-over benefits on this revision. Thank you also to Troy Froebe and Dena Kaufman for their work on editing this second edition.

My family continues to tolerate my interest in bankruptcy, and I am thankful for that. Isaac joined the family just after the first edition appeared, and while he does not yet understand what I am doing at the computer or in the office, I expect he will join his siblings in teasing me about "boring bankruptcy" and writing stories that feature sheriffs levying on anthropomorphic animals' property because of a failure to pay taxes. So to Sarah, Amalia, Kalman, and now Isaac: *mayne tifeste dankn.*

Adam J. Levitin
August 2018

ACKNOWLEDGEMENTS

I owe a debt of gratitude to many people for helping see this book to fruition. First, my teachers, without whom I would never have fallen in love with the world of credit and finance: Martin Bienenstock, Richard Levin, Mark Roe, and especially Elizabeth Warren. I was fortunate to have had such an extraordinary and inspirational group of teachers when I was in law school, and know that if I had not been assigned to Elizabeth's 1L Contracts class, my life would have been entirely different. My 1L section assignment is a serendipity I cherish, even if this book eschews of Elizabeth's approach to teaching consumer and business bankruptcy together. I hope she will see my approach as exactly the sort of a challenge a good teacher hopes to encourage in her students.

One of the joys of my job is how I get to keep learning, and colleagues have played no mean part in this. Bill Bratton provided the most generous mentoring to me when I joined Georgetown as a junior professor. Bill was the one who made me first aware of the Trust Indenture Act and its background without which the absolute priority rule never really made sense, and Bill's avuncular wisdom in regarding corporate finance and scholarly and institutional norms was invaluable. I hope I can pass it on. Bob Thompson not only took over Bill's office, but also picked up on all aspects of the mentoring with unmatched patience. He is a treasured colleague, and I am in his debt. David Kuney and Peter Friedman, both part of Georgetown Law's amazing roster of adjunct faculty, provided valuable suggestions, infused with the knowledge gained from practice.

My co-bloggers at Credit Slips, particularly Bob Lawless, John Pottow, and Stephen Lubben, have all been fantastic and good-humored sounding boards on a range of bankruptcy issues, as has Ted Janger, who has engaged me with enthusiasm ever since I was a pup on the academic job market. And my Georgetown colleague and co-blogger Anna Gelpern has been my kindred comrade and friend in the academy ever since we created our very own *Frankenstein*. As she knows, I'm still working on Marshal Budyonnii.

My colleagues from my brief time in practice at Weil Gotshal, particularly Rachel Erlich Albanese, Ronit Berkovich, Sara Coelho, Harvey Miller, Chris Mirick, and Andrew Troop, have continued to be resources for me, as has Emil Kleinhaus. I am grateful for their time.

Several research assistants have helped along the years in assembling the materials that are now in this book: Ari Dropkin, Robert Enayati, Grant McQueen, Galena Petrova, and Anna Sandor. I am grateful for their hard work, as I am for the help of my faculty assistants Cynthia Rockwell and Roger Bourcicot. Additionally, students at Georgetown and Harvard served as unwilling guinea pigs for draft versions of this book, and their feedback, and in some cases detailed line edits, helped improve the manuscript.

My editors at Wolters Kluwer have also worked to make this book a reality. In particular, Richard Mixter, Cindy Uh, and Tom Daughhetee helped shepherd this book to fruition. Comments from several reviewers also saved me from (at least some) embarrassing mistakes. Thomas Plank's detailed comments on securitization structures were particularly helpful. All mistakes are, of course, my own.

My mother and father (z"l), brother and sister, and in-laws have always supported and encouraged my curiosity, even if they might not understand my particular interest in bankruptcy, and that is love.

Finally, the deepest of thanks to my family. This book was written on Sarah, Amalia, and Kalman's dime. You endured my chatter about bankruptcy and finance with generous patience and love, tolerated my eccentricities, and inspired me in my work. You are my happiness and are indubitably without equivalents. *A hartsikn dank.*

BUSINESS BANKRUPTCY

PART I

FINANCIAL RESTRUCTURING AND THE MODERN COMMERCIAL LANDSCAPE

CHAPTER 1

LEVERAGE, LIQUIDITY, RESTRUCTURING

This is a book about financial restructuring. Businesses frequently run into financial difficulty, whether because of poor management, poor business models, or factors beyond the firm's control. When they do, they attempt to restructure their financial obligations so as to be able to continue operating and remain competitive. This restructuring may involve transactions that aim to increase a firm's assets or change the nature of those assets or to decrease the firm's debt or change the terms of that debt or some combination thereof. The particular transactions will depend on the firm and its circumstances. The parameters of what a firm can do to restructure, however, are determined in the first instance by law.

The law of financial restructuring is the main focus of this book, but this is not a book entirely about law. Law is an important constraint on restructuring, but not the only one. Business, economic, and political factors also shape restructuring, and to understand financial restructuring it is necessary to understand the law, business, economics, and politics involved. This book aims to situate the law of financial restructuring in this broader context. Thus, if you want to know what you're getting into here, consider this infamous description of a restructuring (also known as a corporate reorganization):

> A corporate reorganization is a combination of a municipal election, a historical pageant, an antivice crusade, a graduate school seminar, a judicial proceeding, and a series of horse trades, all rolled into one—thoroughly buttered with learning and frosted with distinguished names. Here the union of law and economics is celebrated by one of the wildest orgies in intellectual history. Men work all night preparing endless documents in answer to other endless documents, which other men read in order to make solemn arguments.[1]

The goal of this book is to present the spectacle of a corporate restructuring in all of its decadent, Bacchanalian glory and to leave you thoroughly buttered with learning and frosted with distinction. Before we get to the pageants, crusades, horse trades, and orgies, however, we need to start with the basic building block: debt.

---

1. THURMAN ARNOLD, THE FOLKLORE OF CAPITALISM 230 (1937). Arnold, a Yale Law School professor when he wrote these words, was previously the mayor of Laramie, Wyoming, and thus likely a man with some knowledge of horse trades, municipal elections, and graduate school seminars, at the very least. He went on to be the head of the Antitrust Division at the Department of Justice, a D.C. Circuit Court of Appeals Judge, and founding partner of the law firm now known as Arnold & Porter LLP.

I. DEBT

Debt makes the world go round. Consider a world without debt. There could only be contemporaneous exchanges—cash on the barrelhead. That might work for purchasing a case of widgets or Blackacre, but how would one purchase water or electricity? Or pay for law school? You might not think of your electric bill as "debt," but that's what it is, just like your credit card bill. Any non-contemporaneous exchange creates debt.

The modern world cannot function without debt. Without debt, there could not be delayed payment, and the purchasing power of individuals and firms would be limited to cash (or other assets) on hand. Debt enables non-contemporaneous exchanges, which allows individuals and firms to smooth their consumption, so that it is not always in thrall to their liquidity, meaning the precise amount of cash or other liquid assets on hand. Debt also allows individuals and firms to shift consumption from the future to the present. In other words, present consumption is being financed based on the promise of future ability to repay.

Often debt is voluntary, created by contract. Debt, however, is not always voluntary. Nor is it always certain or in a known amount. Some types of debt are created involuntarily, such as tort and tax liability. Other types of debt are voluntary, but contingent, such as guarantees and warranties. The debt only comes due if a particular event comes to pass. Yet other types of debt may be either voluntary or involuntary, contingent or non-contingent, but simply of an unknown amount. This is known as "unliquidated" debt. For example, if I negligently hit you with my car, I would owe you a debt—contingent upon a judgment against me—but until there is such a judgment and damages are awarded, the amount of the debt is unliquidated.

While debt can be helpful to a firm, it also poses risks, as it represents a fixed obligation that does not automatically adjust with a firm's performance. A company with too much debt is "overleveraged." The more debt ("leverage") a company has, the more money it must devote to paying the principal and interest on the debt. This is called debt service. Servicing debt requires liquid assets, typically cash. A solvent firm with illiquid assets may not be able to pay its bills as they come due. The assets may be difficult to sell or borrow against. By the same token, a firm that is insolvent according to its balance sheet (meaning that at that particular moment its assets are worth less than its liabilities) may still be able to meet its current obligations without difficulty.

Liquidity is a matter of ensuring that a firm's revenue and cash on hand line up with its expenses. This is often easier said than done. Firms sometimes have unexpected revenue shortfalls or greater than anticipated expenses. Both can result in a firm becoming illiquid. Firms also sometimes have sharp unexpected liquidity shocks—being hit with a large tort judgment, for example.

Illiquidity can quickly metastasize into insolvency (just as insolvency can result in illiquidity). An illiquid firm may look to borrow to obtain liquidity. Borrowing, however, merely pushes off the liquidity problem into the future. If future revenues are insufficient, the firm is now more heavily indebted and will be facing liquidity problems in the future. As a result, creditors and suppliers will be reluctant to deal with the firm, except on more onerous terms, creating a downward spiral of more and more debt and less and less revenue.

II. PATHS TO RESTRUCTURING

A. Balance Sheet Restructuring

If a company is insolvent on a balance sheet basis, what can it do to get back to solvency? There are a number of nonexclusive potential solutions.

1. Debt Forgiveness

Perhaps the most obvious solution is to deleverage the firm through a reduction of its debts. If a firm's debts are reduced, either voluntarily or involuntarily, the firm can be restored to solvency without any change to its operations or its assets. Creditors are likely to be reluctant to voluntarily forgive what is owed to them, unless they believe that some debt forgiveness will increase the likelihood of repayment on the remaining debt. They are also unlikely to voluntarily forgive debt unless other creditors make similar concessions. But not all debt forgiveness occurs voluntarily; bankruptcy is a process that can force debt forgiveness on unwilling creditors.

2. Retained Earnings

A second solution is for the firm to earn its way back to solvency. If the company has a good business model and is able to sell its goods/services at a profit, it should be able to work its way back to solvency over time by retaining its earnings. Not all companies have good business models, however, and even those that do may be looking at a very long time to earning their way back to solvency. If the time lag is too great, the company may find itself lacking the funds to undertake maintenance, research, and development, and may end up unable to compete profitably.

3. Sale of Non-Essential Assets

Accordingly, insolvent companies sometimes need to undertake other actions to regain solvency. A third solution would be to sell some of the company's assets (other than inventory held for sale). From an operational standpoint, this may be problematic if the assets are essential to the firm—it's a bit like burning the furniture to keep warm in winter. It might produce a short-term infusion of cash for the firm, but it may leave the firm denuded of critical assets at a later point. Non-essential assets can, of course, be sold for cash, but selling assets doesn't change the truth of the company's balance sheet, unless those assets are being sold for more than their book value. The sale of a $10 million drill press for $10 million in cash is just swapping one asset for another and doesn't affect a firm's balance sheet solvency, even if it does improve a firm's liquidity and thus its ability to meet its obligations as they come due, which might be enough to buy the firm time to regain solvency through retained earnings.

4. Borrowing

Thus, we come to a fourth solution—borrow money. As an initial matter, borrowing funds does not enhance a company's solvency, and over time it may reduce it. A $100 million loan will add $100 million to the company's assets, but also $100 million to the company's liabilities. The interest payments and fees will erode the company's assets further, thereby reducing the company's solvency, unless the loan can be put to good use increasing the company's operating profitability so as to offset the costs of the financing. If so, then borrowing has the same net effect as a sale of non-essential assets, in that it provides a liquidity injection that might buy time for the firm to earn its way back to solvency.

Even when borrowing is sensible in terms of improving the company's operating performance, it's important to ask who will lend to an insolvent firm? If the firm doesn't earn its way out of insolvency, then there will be fewer assets than liabilities, so the lenders will take a loss if they are all paid on a pro rata basis. A solution to this from a lender's perspective is to find some way of getting paid first, before other creditors. We'll cover a bunch of methods for doing so in the next chapter. For now, however, it is important to recognize that someone getting paid first necessarily means that someone else will be paid second (or last), and that means existing creditors may well object (and be able to prevent) any new contractual liabilities that have priority over them, whether by contract or through statutory protections.

5. Equity Sales

Finally, an insolvent company could regain solvency by selling additional equity shares. But who would want to buy the stock of an insolvent company? In a liquidation, equity gets paid after all creditors, so if the company remains insolvent, equity would likely get nothing. Until the firm has regained positive equity, all gains in firm value go to creditors. Once the firm regains positive equity, however, all gains in firm value go to the shareholders—but these gains will be divided between the new and the existing shareholders, who get to free-ride on the new injection of capital, while maintaining their proportional share of control rights (assuming a single class of stock).

To illustrate this point, we're going to need to play with some numbers. You should be prepared for the fact that this book will require some math from time to time, although nothing more than simple arithmetic. Restructuring is, on some level, all about getting the numbers to work, and just because you chose to go to law school doesn't mean that you are doomed to innumeracy.

So let's imagine an insolvent firm with assets of $80 and liabilities of $100, and with 100 shares of common stock. If an investor buys another 100 shares of stock for $30, the firm will now be solvent, having assets of $110 and liabilities of $100. The equity value of the company will be $10, which means that the new investor who has 50 percent of the now 200 shares of common stock will hold equity with a value of $5.

Who would ever pay $30 to get something worth $5? Only someone who thinks there is a reasonable possibility that the value of the firm will end up being substantially greater. In our scenario, the expected firm value would have to rise to $60 (a gain of $80) for the new investor to break even. Thus, let's say the investor thinks there's a 25 percent chance that the equity value of the firm remains a $10, a 25 percent chance it goes to $30, a 25 percent chance it goes to $60, and a 25 percent chance it goes up to 100. The expected value of the firm would be $(.25 \times \$10) + (.25 \times \$30) + (.25 \times \$60) + (.25 \times \$100) = \$50$. The new investor would have only half of that (or $25), which is less than the value of its investment ($30).

The point here is not that the numbers are impossible to make work; they're not. Instead, it's that the increase in firm value from the new equity investment has to first make up any insolvency *and then* be a multiple of the inverse of the new equity investor's share of ownership. That can be a tall order, and depending on the percentage of shares held by the new investor, the new investor may not have the ability to control or influence the firm's governance.

Accordingly, potential new equity investors are likely to want to (1) dilute or wipe out existing equity investors in terms of economic stake and (2) have substantial control rights to protect their investment. Consider how the previous example would work if the new investor had 90 percent of the firm's equity. The expected value of the firm would be $50, and the new investor's share would be 90 percent, or $45, making the $30 investment a good deal. Existing equity holders, however, are likely to be resistant to both, particularly if they believe that the firm's value will rebound.

B. Asset Sale Restructuring

Up to this point, all of the methods of restoring a firm to solvency—debt forgiveness, retained earnings, asset sales (of non-essential assets), borrowing, equity sales—involve keeping the firm intact as a going concern and simply playing around with its capital structure. But it is also possible to restructure a firm by treating it not as a capital structure, but as a constellation of essential assets. Those essential assets can be moved through a sale to a new firm that has a new (solvent) capital structure. The sale might be a voluntary sale, or it might be a forced foreclosure sale.

Either way, if the firm's essential assets are sold, either piecemeal or wholesale (thereby retaining their going concern value), the assets end up in the hands of a purchaser that has a different capital structure than the original firm. The original firm receives cash (or other consideration) for the assets. If the sale price is at fair market value, it does nothing to affect the solvency of the original firm. But now the assets have been moved from an insolvent firm, which might have difficulty maintaining the assets and using them competitively, to a solvent firm that can put the assets to better use.

A sale of essential assets can further be combined with a balance sheet restructuring; part of the consideration paid for the essential assets can be the assumption of liabilities of the old firm. The old firm, then, is left with fewer assets and fewer liabilities. Whether this renders it solvent depends on the specifics. Notably, the effect of the assumption can be significant upon creditors; if the asset purchaser that assumes the liabilities is solvent, but the old firm remains insolvent, then those creditors whose liabilities were assumed have effectively gained priority over those creditors whose claims were left behind with the old, insolvent firm.

C. Multiple Paths of Restructuring

What we see, then, are two basic methods of financial restructuring. The first is a restructuring of a firm's balance sheet, whether by reducing liabilities or increasing assets (including through provision of liquidity to allow the firm to generate retainable earnings). Such a restructuring of a balance sheet can occur voluntarily through negotiations between the debtor and some or all of its creditors outside of any judicial process. It can also sometimes be forced upon creditors involuntarily outside the judicial process using a device known as an "exit consent." But it can also occur in the context of bankruptcy, a judicial process that allows for both voluntary deals and involuntary restructuring of the balance sheet. Table 1.1 summarizes.

Table 1.1 Balance Sheet Restructuring Paths

	Nonjudicial	Judicial
Voluntary	• Workout	• Consensual bankruptcy plan confirmation
Involuntary	• Exit consent	• Cramdown bankruptcy plan confirmation

The second restructuring method is through a sale of essential assets to a new firm(s), with the old firm liquidating any remaining assets. The sale path can be accomplished voluntarily (meaning here with the debtor's consent) outside of bankruptcy or under bankruptcy's judicial process. But the sale process can also be accomplished involuntarily, whether through a foreclosure sale by a secured creditor outside of bankruptcy or through the judicial process in bankruptcy in a plan proposed by a party other than the debtor. Table 1.2 summarizes.

Table 1.2 Asset Sale Restructuring Paths

	Nonjudicial	Judicial
Voluntary	• Sale by debtor	• Bankruptcy sale (debtor plan or pre-plan sale)
Involuntary	• Foreclosure sale	• Bankruptcy sale (creditor plan)

The point you should see here—and keep in mind as a framework for what you will learn in this book—is that there are several different restructuring paths that a firm and its creditors can pursue simultaneously. Different paths have different benefits and drawbacks for debtors and creditors. The ability for debtors and creditors to credibly threaten to use one path over another affects the dynamic of restructuring—the terms that a creditor can get in a voluntary workout, for example, depend on what the creditor would likely get in a consensual bankruptcy plan, which in turn depends on what the creditor would get in a non-consensual bankruptcy plan (a process known as "cramdown") or in a reorganization undertaken through a bankruptcy sale and liquidation.

We will be learning about all of these different paths and their interactions, recognizing that some of them, primarily bankruptcy plans, are shaped by detailed statutory rules, while others are more constrained by economics and contract. The first part of this book deals with nonjudicial restructurings, while the remainder deals with judicial restructurings, primarily bankruptcy plan confirmation, which is a detailed statutory scheme. While the book's coverage is heavily balanced toward bankruptcy plan confirmation, do not assume that this balance of coverage reflects a firm's choices. Instead, it is a reflection of the amount of law involved, rather than the relative importance or use of different restructuring paths.

III. FINANCIAL RESTRUCTURING THROUGH BANKRUPTCY

Both overleveraged and illiquid firms need financial restructuring. Financial restructuring can take place outside of the judicial process, or it can take place in the courtroom. In both cases, however, the parameters of financial restructuring are shaped by law. Restructuring necessarily means changing the rights of at least some of a firm's creditors or equityholders. Creditors' and equityholders' rights are legal rights, and a firm's ability to change those rights is legally constrained. Sometimes the constraints come from private contract, and sometimes from public law.

This book addresses both out-of-court and in-court (bankruptcy) restructuring processes. The out-of-court restructuring process is not typically within the ambit of a "bankruptcy" course, which is focused on in-court restructuring, but the line between out-of-court and in-court restructuring is fluid, and the choice to restructure in bankruptcy is shaped by what is possible in out-of-court restructuring. Not all or even most financial restructuring occurs in bankruptcy. But bankruptcy sets the background against which all financial restructuring processes occur because if an out-of-court restructuring does not work, the usual alternative is bankruptcy. Thus, to really understand the value of the in-court bankruptcy process, one needs to understand the out-of-court process and its limitations.

Most of this book deals with in-court financial restructuring through the bankruptcy process. There's a simple reason for this—there is much more law governing in-court restructuring than out-of-court restructuring. After a few chapters covering some basics of modern financial markets, we will turn to considering what can and cannot be accomplished in a non-bankruptcy restructuring. That, in turn, will set us up to explore the bankruptcy system and understand what additional tools bankruptcy provides for restructuring.

Bankruptcy is a legal procedure for financial restructuring under judicial supervision. This means it is a process for legally altering, and sometimes eliminating, debt obligations. Conceptually, the process is not especially complicated. The debtor's assets are collected and then divvied up among creditors and shareholders according to a statutory scheme. Sometimes this division of assets is immediate (a liquidation), while sometimes it occurs over time (a reorganization). While the basic bankruptcy process is conceptually simple, the rules governing how it is to be done are complex and have major distributional implications. In the typical case, the debtor lacks sufficient assets to pay all creditors in full. Therefore, the manner in which the assets are divided determines which creditors incur losses and how large those losses are. Bankruptcy law has important distributional consequences, and knowing these consequences, contractual creditors adjust the terms of their dealings with debtors with an eye toward the possibility of a bankruptcy.

A. Bankruptcy Law

Bankruptcy exists solely as a matter of federal law. Article I, section 8, clause 4 of the U.S. Constitution gives Congress the power to enact "uniform laws on the subject of Bankruptcies throughout the United States." Congress enacted and repealed bankruptcy statutes throughout the nineteenth century in the wake of economic crises. From 1800-1803, 1841-1843, and 1867-1878, there were federal bankruptcy statutes of quite limited scope. In 1898, Congress finally passed a lasting bankruptcy statute, the Nelson Act. The Nelson Act has been amended several times, most notably in 1938 by the Chandler Act, part of the federal securities laws. The 1898 Nelson Act, as amended by the Chandler Act, is known as the "**Bankruptcy Act**."

The Bankruptcy Reform Act of 1978 enacted the basis for the current bankruptcy law, known as the "**Bankruptcy Code**," in distinction from the Bankruptcy Act. The Bankruptcy Code is codified as title 11 of the United States Code. The Bankruptcy Code has been amended several times subsequent to 1978, most notably by the highly controversial and contentious Bankruptcy Abuse Prevention and Consumer Protection Act of 2005 (BAPCPA, pronounced bap-SEE-pah).

The Bankruptcy Code is divided into chapters, all but one of which are numbered by odd numbers (which is to say they are oddly numbered). Some of the chapters are applicable to all bankruptcies:

- Chapter 1 (definitions, rules of construction, general provisions);
- Chapter 3 (administration of the bankruptcy case);
- Chapter 5 (the bankrupt's estate).

Other chapters of the Bankruptcy Code provide the specific procedures for different types of debtors:

- Chapter 7 (liquidation for individuals and businesses);
- Chapter 9 (municipal debt adjustment);
- Chapter 11 (reorganization for businesses and high asset individuals);
- Chapter 12 (reorganization for family farmers and fishermen);
- Chapter 13 (repayment plans for consumers and very small businesses);
- Chapter 15 (procedures for transnational coordination in transactional cases).

The chapters of the Bankruptcy Act were numbered with Roman numerals; they do not always correspond with the Arabic numerals used for the Bankruptcy Code's chapters. This book is concerned solely with business bankruptcy under Chapters 7 and 11 of the Code.

Bankruptcy is federal law, but it often involves state law inputs. This is because bankruptcy law does not generally create substantive rights. Instead, it is primarily a procedural mechanism for adjudicating rights that exist as a function of non-bankruptcy law. Thus, the inputs to bankruptcy are rights created by federal or state statutes or, more commonly, by state contract and tort law. That said, bankruptcy's procedures can significantly curtail or expand a creditor's ability to exercise their substantive rights, and bankruptcy law does itself sometimes specifically create new rights.

B. Bankruptcy Courts

Bankruptcy is a judicial process, meaning that the financial restructuring takes place under the supervision of a judge. A bankruptcy case commences in the bankruptcy court for the federal judicial district in which it is filed. The bankruptcy court is staffed by a set of specialized federal judges. Bankruptcy judges are not Article III judges, meaning they are not appointed pursuant to Article III of the Constitution by the President with the advice and consent of the Senate. Accordingly, bankruptcy judges do not have lifetime appointments and protected salaries. Instead, they are appointed for 14-year terms by the judges on the circuit courts of appeals.

Lack of Article III status creates some vexing jurisdictional limits on the bankruptcy court, but these limitations are really a federal courts problem, rather than a restructuring problem; there is nothing that requires bankruptcy cases to be heard before specialized non–Article III judges, and sometimes federal district court judges will "withdraw the reference" to the bankruptcy court and handle a case themselves. *See* 28 U.S.C. § 157(d). Accordingly, we will not delve into the jurisdictional complexities in this book.

The bankruptcy judge does not decide on the terms of the restructuring. Generally, the terms of a restructuring are the role of the debtor's lawyers and financial advisors, operating within the constraints of the Bankruptcy Code and the bargains they can strike in the shadow of the Code. The judge's role is to ensure that the proposed restructuring complies with the relevant legal requirements. Sometimes, however, this entails findings of fact, including making valuation determinations.

C. Bankruptcy Appeals

Bankruptcy appeals work differently from regular civil litigation appeals, both in terms of the structure of the appellate process, and the procedural rules governing appeals. Appeals from orders of the bankruptcy court may be taken, depending on the circumstances, to the federal district court for the district in which the bankruptcy court sits, to a Bankruptcy Appellate Panel (BAP) comprised of three bankruptcy judges, or to the circuit court of appeals. Generally, appeals go to either the district court or the BAP. Not all circuits have BAPs, however. The creation of a BAP is vested in the discretion of the circuit court of appeals for a circuit, and only the First, Sixth, Eighth, Ninth, and Tenth Circuits have chosen to adopt a BAP. For circuits with a BAP, an appeal may be heard by the BAP only if all parties consent to having the appeal heard by the BAP. 28 U.S.C. § 158(c). Appeals from the district court or the BAP are heard by the circuit court of appeals. 28 U.S.C. § 158(d)(1).

Appeals from the bankruptcy court's decisions may also be taken directly to the court of appeals with the consent of the court of appeals in certain limited circumstances, namely if the bankruptcy court or all parties to the litigation certify that there is no controlling decision for the circuit on the issue, that the issue involves a matter of public importance, that it involves a question of law requiring resolution of conflicting decisions, or that an immediate appeal would materially advance the progress of the case. 28 U.S.C. § 158(d)(2). Appeals from the circuit courts of appeal may be taken to the Supreme Court, which has discretionary jurisdiction and typically agrees to hear only a handful of bankruptcy cases each year (often involving technical and less-than-critical issues). As a result, the rulings of the circuit courts of appeals constitute the key body of bankruptcy case law.

Not only is the appellate route different for bankruptcy cases, but not all bankruptcy court rulings and orders are appealable. Orders are generally appealable only if they are a "final" order. 28 U.S.C. § 158(a)(1). The standard of what is a "final" order is less than clear, but it appears to involve an order that "resolves the litigation, decides the merits, settles liability, establishes damages, or even determines the rights of any party to the bankruptcy case." *In re Urban Broadcasting Corp.*, 304 B.R. 263, 269 n.13 (E.D. Va. 2004). Non-final, "interlocutory" orders are not appealable as of right, but the district court may also grant leave to hear appeals of interlocutory orders. 28 U.S.C. § 158(a)(2)-(3).

D. Financial vs. Operational Restructuring

Bankruptcy enables a firm to significantly reshape its capital structure—its assets and liabilities—but this reshaping is a *financial* restructuring. If the firm's problem is economic, rather than financial, bankruptcy does not provide a fix. Bankruptcy can provide some financial breathing room for a firm to undertake operational restructuring, and bankruptcy provides some tools that facilitate corporate organizational reforms, but bankruptcy does not provide legal tools for improving day-to-day operations. If a firm's problems are not financial, then financial restructuring in bankruptcy is unlikely to provide much help.

Adam J. Levitin
Bankrupt Politics and the Politics of Bankruptcy
97 Cornell L. Rev. 1399, 1444-1445 (2012)

. . . Bankruptcy is a remarkably successful tool for dealing with collective action problems, preserving going-concern value, ridding debt overhang, and providing social insurance. If a firm's problems are merely financial—that is, if the firm is overleveraged or illiquid but solvent—bankruptcy provides an excellent forum for reorganizing the firm's capital structure to preserve going-concern value or, if there is none, to provide for an orderly liquidation. Moreover, bankruptcy provides a backdrop against which private orderings can occur, both when the initial decision to extend credit is made and when outstanding debt needs to be restructured.

But bankruptcy isn't a panacea for all problems that enterprises face. Bankruptcy can cure financial problems, but not operational problems. Bankruptcy can extricate an enterprise from burdensome contracts and slough off extra leverage, but bankruptcy cannot fix a bad business model.

If a firm's business is selling whale oil, corset stays, bustles, flash bulbs, slide-rules, floppy disks, cassette tapes, 8-tracks, or books or CDs in a brick-and-mortar store, bankruptcy cannot help it beyond providing an orderly way to redeploy the assets and giving it a dignified funeral. At best, bankruptcy can buy an enterprise the financial breathing room to undertake an operational restructuring, but nothing in bankruptcy law—understood broadly, with a small "b" as any form of debt restructuring, not necessarily along the lines of the existing chapters of the U.S. Bankruptcy Code—can fix a bad business model.

In Chapter 11, bankruptcy provides a forum for creditors to make a collective decision about the viability of a firm. If creditors do not think that a firm's business model will work even as restructured, they can try to block a reorganization plan and liquidate the firm. The creditors' collective viability decision is only meaningful, however, because of the liquidation option, which gives them leverage to push for changes that they believe will enhance viability. Thus, while creditors cannot formally require price increases in a debtor firm's products in Chapter 11, they can functionally achieve this goal by refusing to vote for a plan that does not contemplate such a move, either explicitly or by providing for creditor control over new management—perhaps by transforming creditors into shareholders.

IV. WHY BANKRUPTCY?

Although the Constitution contains a bankruptcy power, it is far from intuitive that a country needs to have bankruptcy laws. Indeed, there were no bankruptcy laws for most of American history prior to the 20th century, and corporations were not eligible for bankruptcy until 1910. So why do we have bankruptcy laws? Several non-exclusive policy rationales exist for bankruptcy law. Much of it can be summed up by understanding federal bankruptcy law as a solution for the inadequacies of state law procedures for liquidating or restructuring businesses. State law liquidation and restructuring procedures suffer from information and collective action problems that can lead to the unnecessary destruction of value. State law procedures may also fail to facilitate a pair of important social policies: the fair allocation of losses within society and the provision of a fresh start to the debtor.

A. Addressing Information Problems

One rationale for bankruptcy is the avoidance of various informational problems for creditors that can frustrate out-of-court resolutions. Outside of bankruptcy, creditors' decision making may be suboptimal because of informational problems. Creditors may have incomplete information about the debtor and each other. Creditors may not know the extent of the debtor's obligations, the identity of other creditors, the extent and priority of their relative rights, or the motivations of other creditors. Some of the informational problems are simply factual ones—who are the other creditors and how much are they owed—but some are questions about relative legal rights. For example, suppose two creditors each think that they are entitled to recover first from the debtor. In such circumstances, it will be difficult to achieve a deal to restructure the debtor's obligations because the aggregate expectations of the creditors will exceed what the debtor can pay. This is an informational problem too, but of a different variety. Bankruptcy creates both a disclosure regime about the debtor and creditors and a system for adjudicating the extent and priority of creditors' rights in order to address these informational problems.

B. Addressing Collective Action Problems

Another prominent rationale for bankruptcy law is to address creditors' collective action problems that impede efficient resolution of debt problems. The chief collective action concern is a **race to the courthouse**. State law does not have a mechanism for coordinating creditors' collections (not least because the collections might be taking place in multiple jurisdictions). The result is a grab race as creditors compete to be the first to seize the debtor's assets. Bankruptcy consolidates all of the debtor's assets and all of the claims against them in a single national forum and stays creditor actions outside of the bankruptcy process. Per this rationale, bankruptcy is a procedural mechanism for the orderly and fair distribution of those assets.

Related to the race to the courthouse problem is the **firesale dilemma**. If numerous creditors seize the debtor's assets and sell them simultaneously, the result may be to flood to market with a particular type of asset, thereby depressing the asset's price and creditors' recoveries. A more orderly disposition of assets may maximize creditors' recoveries relative to a free-for-all liquidation.

A third collective action problem complicating out-of-court restructurings is free-riding. If one creditor makes concessions to the debtor, those concessions will redound to the benefit of other creditors, as the debtor will have more assets available relative to the obligations owed to those other creditors. Therefore, no creditor will want to make concessions to the debtor, unless other creditors make equal and ratable concessions, necessitating creditor coordination, which is in turn complicated by informational problems and transaction costs. Bankruptcy provides a number of mechanisms designed to reduce the free-riding problem through cost-sharing and ratable recoveries for similar creditors.

C. Preserving Going-Concern Value

Another rationale for debt restructuring regimes like bankruptcy is to enable the preservation of going-concern value in illiquid but solvent firms. **Going-concern value** is the value of an enterprise above liquidation value, or the difference between the value of the whole and the sum of its parts. Liquidation value only covers the value of assets; to the extent that human capital is key to the value of a firm, the firm's going-concern value will exceed its liquidation value.

Consider as an example a railroad that runs between New York and Washington, D.C. The railroad's assets include miles of track, locomotives and rolling stock, train sheds and maintenance facilities, stations, rights of way, intellectual property, and cash. The railroad as a whole is quite valuable—there are many people who want to take the train from New York to Washington, D.C., or vice-versa, or to and from points in between those cities.

Now imagine that the railroad is liquidated and sold off piecemeal. How valuable is a mile of track in rural northeast Maryland, between Baltimore, Maryland and Wilmington, Delaware? If that track doesn't connect with other track and there is no train to run on it? At that point, the track's value might even be negative because it can't generate income and may give rise to liability. The same is the case for the next mile of track, and the mile after that, etc. The track only becomes valuable when it is connected with other track and with stations. In short, the value of the whole is substantially greater than the sum of the parts. That difference is the railroad's going-concern value, which comes from the synergy of the assets combined in the firm.

If a firm is dismantled piecemeal, going-concern value can easily be lost. The destruction of going-concern value can hurt not just creditors, but also other, non-creditor constituencies, such as communities and purchasers, that benefit from the existence of the debtor as an operating entity.

A firm's going-concern value can be preserved if all (or at least substantially all) of the assets are transferred to another firm because the going-concern value resides in the constellation of assets, not in the vessel of the firm itself. It is often difficult, however, to undertake such a wholesale transfer of a firm's assets at state law because of procedural limitations, creditors' rights, and coordination problems.

Bankruptcy adds three things to this mix. First, it can provide a forum for creditors to make a collective decision about a firm's viability. Bankruptcy is an information-forcing process. It is also a process that forces creditor coordination by virtue of bringing all of the debtor's assets and all of the debtor's creditors together in a single forum. Armed with information and with the aid of bankruptcy's procedural facilitation, creditors can determine if illiquidity is because, or in spite, of insolvency and whether the firm should be reorganized or liquidated.

Second, if the firm is to be liquidated, bankruptcy provides a potentially superior liquidation process. A firm that liquidates at state law has to potentially deal with multiple, uncoordinated state-law liquidations. Bankruptcy enables a single, coordinated federal liquidation process that is not subject to most state law and contractual limitations. Moreover, the bankruptcy liquidation process takes place under the judicial aegis, so there is potentially more transparency and oversight to ensure fairness in the liquidation process.

Third, if the firm is to be restructured, bankruptcy offers a pair of powerful tools: a federal sales power and a federal plan confirmation order. Bankruptcy law includes a federal sales power that can override most state law and contractual limitations on asset sales. Likewise, a bankruptcy court may issue an order confirming a plan of reorganization notwithstanding many types of non-bankruptcy limitations on debt adjustments. Thus, bankruptcy substantially expands the legal toolkit for implementing transactions that preserve going-concern value even in the face of certain contractual and non-bankruptcy statutory rights and information and coordination problems.

It bears emphasis that the preservation of going-concern value is not just a matter of creditor interest. A firm's liquidation can impose transaction costs and spillovers. For example, what happens to a firm's employees if a firm liquidates? The employees might be able to find other employment, but would it be equivalent? And would they have to engage in a costly and disruptive relocation to take that employment? Preservation of going-concern value—keeping the debtor functioning as an operating enterprise—can also enable a "soft landing" to help protect noncreditor constituencies, such as vendors, retirees, and municipalities that depend on the debtor in their tax base.

D. Allocating Losses in Society

Bankruptcy is also a system for dealing with losses in a free-market economy. Some businesses inevitably fail and bankruptcy also serves as a mechanism for allocating losses from business failure. When a business isn't able to pay all of its obligations, who gets paid? The banks? The bondholders? The employees? The pensioners? The vendors? The tax authority? Victims of torts committed by the business? Equity holders?

If the decision were left up to the debtor, one might expect certain favored creditors to get paid and others not. Insiders would likely be paid. Contractual creditors with substantial bargaining power, such as banks, would likely negotiate in advance to ensure that they will be repaid. Involuntary creditors, such as tort victims and tax authorities, would likely remain unpaid. Bankruptcy law provides a system for allocating losses that attempts to impose a modicum of fairness. This is done by prohibitions on special treatment of insiders, various requirements aimed at ensuring that similar creditors are treated similarly (similar creditors must be treated the same and recover on a pro-rated basis), and various equitable remedies that police against overreaching behavior by creditors.

The starting point for bankruptcy law is that "equity is equality"—losses are to be spread on a pro-rated basis among creditors. This basic policy functions as a system of social insurance, which helps disperse the pain of economic losses caused by things such as unmanageable pension commitments, mass toxic torts, the dislocation of the brick-and-mortar retail market by e-commerce, the disruption of the taxi industry by Uber and Lyft, and the death of the Rust Belt economy. Rather than concentrating all losses on a particular group of creditors, the equity is equality principle means that losses are spread out among all creditors, effectuating a type of mutual insurance.

Although equity is equality may be the starting point of bankruptcy law, there are many exceptions. These exceptions mean that some legally favored creditor groups will recover more than others (and at the expense of others). This means that bankruptcy is a system for effectuating wealth transfers between different groups in society. A rule that ensures a greater recovery for shopping center landlords or the lessors of aircraft engines is effectively a subsidy of those industries through the Bankruptcy Code.

Ultimately, as a system of loss allocation, bankruptcy has upstream effects. Bankruptcy serves as the background term for all lending—a type of worst-case scenario for lenders to consider. As such, lenders lend with an eye toward what their position would be in bankruptcy: the more risk they have of losses in bankruptcy, the more they are likely to charge for the loan. Thus, bankruptcy law affects the availability and allocation of credit in the first place.

E. Providing a Fresh Start

The provision of human debtors ("natural persons") with a fresh start through debt forgiveness makes bankruptcy a type of social insurance against financial failure. Overleveraged individuals have limited incentives to increase productivity because the gains from their labor go to their creditors. Similarly, the earnings of overleveraged firms go to creditors, not owners. This possibility limits individuals' and firms' incentive to take risks lest they end up in eternal debt peonage. Moreover, an overleveraged debtor may be unable to obtain the financing to undertake profitable projects. A system for deleveraging the debtor thus avoids the deadweight loss when a firm forgoes profitable projects.

State law lacks the ability to provide debtors with a fresh start. The Contracts Clause of the federal Constitution, U.S. CONST. Art. I, cl. 10, prevents states from providing debtors with a discharge of debts. Federal bankruptcy law is not subject to the Contracts Clause. Bankruptcy law thus makes it possible to cure debt overhangs and return overleveraged individuals and firms to productivity through the ability to discharge debts, meaning to permanently enjoin acts to collect the debt.

V. CASE STUDY: THE CHRYSLER RESTRUCTURING

The last section of this chapter tells the story of Chrysler's 2007-2010 restructuring. Chrysler's restructuring had a number of controversial features, but at core it was wholly typical of the restructuring process in and out of court. The Chrysler story illustrates some of the issues at stake in a restructuring, shows what can and cannot be accomplished in an out-of-court restructuring, and the limitations of the bankruptcy process in resolving all issues.

A. The Leadup to Bankruptcy

Chrysler's April 2009 bankruptcy filing was a long time in the making. The 83-year old auto manufacturer, like its Detroit competitors GM and Ford (the Big Three Original Equipment Manufacturers or OEMs), had labor and employee benefits costs that were significantly higher than its other competitors (see Figure 1.1, above). In part this was due to the Big Three having more highly unionized labor forces. While Chrysler, GM, and Ford were able to negotiate significant concessions regarding current labor costs from United Auto Workers (UAW), the union representing its unionized employees, retirees, and surviving spouses, they were still faced with enormous retiree pension and health care costs, with health care costs alone estimated at $100 billion in 2007. The longer history of U.S. operations for the Big Three meant that they had legacy health and retirement benefit obligations for additional decades of employees.

Unlike GM and Ford, Chrysler was not a publicly traded company during its restructuring. In 1998, Chrysler had been purchased by the German auto manufacturer Daimler for $36 billion. Throughout Daimler's ownership, Chrysler struggled. Daimler continued to run Chrysler until August 2007, when it sold an 80% stake to the private equity firm Cerberus (named after the three-headed hound of the underworld in Greek mythology) for $7.4 billion. The sale price implied that entire Chrysler firm was now worth only $9.25 billion, a far cry from the $36 billion Daimler had paid. Daimler also agreed to guarantee $1 billion of Chrysler's pension liabilities and contributed $1.5 billion to financing the purchase.

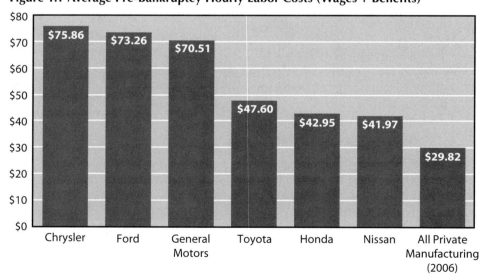

Figure 1.1 Average Pre-Bankruptcy Hourly Labor Costs (Wages + Benefits)[5]

5. James Sherk & Todd Zywicki, *Auto Bailout or UAW Bailout? Taxpayer Losses Came from Subsidizing Union Compensation*, Heritage Foundation Backgrounder #2700, June 13, 2012.

In the sale transaction, Cerberus purchased the stock of the Chrysler Holding LLC, a parent corporation that indirectly owned both the auto manufacturer Chrysler LLC and the affiliated financing company Chrysler Financial Services Americas LLC. Separately, a Cerberus subsidiary purchased Chrysler's sprawling Auburn Hills, Michigan headquarters complex—the third largest office building in the country, after the Pentagon and GM's Renaissance Center—from Daimler for $325 million.

Daimler did not receive most of the purchase price; instead much of the purchase price went into Chrysler entities themselves. Chrysler LLC received $5 billion of Cerberus's purchase price, while $1 billion went to Chrysler Financial Services. Daimler received only $1.4 billion. Daimler was so eager to be rid of its stake in Chrysler that it agreed to kick in another $675 million to pay down Chrysler's debts as part of the deal. Cerberus thought it could turn Chrysler around; unlike most private equity buyouts, Cerberus did not finance its acquisition of Chrysler through debt, but instead, used its own capital. The purchase was accompanied, however, by a new $10 billion financing for Chrysler.

Cerberus set out to make Chrysler lean and mean. First and foremost this meant dealing with labor costs. Under Cerberus's ownership, in October 2007, Chrysler also negotiated a new collective bargaining agreement with the United Auto Workers representing Chrysler's 48,000 unionized employees, and 78,000 union retirees and union surviving spouses. The agreement included major concessions from the UAW: Cost-of-living adjustments were suspended, overtime pay was limited, holidays were reduced, and future employees were to be hired on a different compensation scale that was 50% lower than existing workers. Most significantly, Chrysler and the UAW agreed to create a Voluntary Employee Beneficiary Association (VEBA) as a way of addressing its enormous retiree health care costs.

As part of renegotiation of a collective bargaining agreement, Chrysler agreed to fund the VEBA with cash and its securities in exchange for the VEBA assuming the future health care liabilities for Chrysler's UAW employees and retirees.[6] In other words, instead of Chrysler bearing the risk of rising health care expenses, the risk would be borne by the VEBA; Chrysler would settle its health care liabilities with a defined payment to the VEBA. The payments Chrysler was to make to the VEBA accounted for only 60% of its original pension and retiree benefit obligations. Thus, the UAW agreed to accept enormous concessions in order to keep Chrysler operating. From the perspective of Chrysler's unionized employees (about 60% of its labor force), a half loaf was better than no loaf at all. The deal was not an easy sell for the UAW; Chrysler's UAW members only narrowly ratified the deal. Days later, Chrysler announced 12,000 layoffs or 15% of its labor force. In the first year of Cerberus ownership, Chrysler shed 30,000 jobs or 38% of its labor force.

---

6. The VEBA was to be implemented as part of a settlement of a class action so as to bind all parties to the collective bargaining agreement. Order and Final Judgment, *International Union, United Automobile, Aerospace and Agricultural Implement Workers of America v. General Motors Corporation*, No. 07-cv-14074-DT (E.D. Mich. July 31, 2008).

Chrysler also did not have the funds available to fully fund the VEBA in 2007, even at the reduced funding level. Instead, Chrysler planned to continue funding the VEBA over time. Unfortunately for Chrysler, the market gods were not kind. 2008 was the worst year in over a decade for auto sales. Chrysler cut another 1,250 jobs in October 2008 and announced its intention to eliminate 25% of its salaried workforce. Going into 2009, Chrysler saw its cash position erode to dangerous levels, raising concerns that absent a major change in its financial fortunes, Chrysler would not be able to make its scheduled payments to its financial creditors.

Chrysler's need for cash rose at precisely the time that U.S. credit markets froze. Beginning in 2007, global credit markets began to constrict, driven by concerns over lenders' exposure to the mortgage market. Thus, in August 2007, along with the Cerberus purchase, Chrysler sought to obtain a new $10 billion credit facility from five banks, JPMorgan, Citigroup, Morgan Stanley, Bear Stearns, and Goldman Sachs. The five banks had planned to syndicate or collectively sell off pieces of the credit facility to investors such as hedge funds. The banks refused to close the financing because they did not believe that they could successfully syndicate the loan and feared being stuck with it. The loan only closed when Daimler and Cerberus agreed to purchase the riskiest $2 billion piece of the loan ($1.5 billion and $500 million, respectively), which was secured by a second lien, instead of a first lien on Chrysler's assets. Daimler thus had to finance its own buyout. Even so, the banks struggled to syndicate the remaining $8 billion, although individually some of the banks were able to sell off parts of the loan at steep discounts in the range of 63 cents on the dollar.

By the fall of 2008, global credit markets were totally frozen. The credit market freeze meant that consumers could not obtain financing to purchase cars, which severely impacted Chrysler's sales. Moreover, as consumers' own finances became more precarious, many held off on large-ticket purchases such as cars. Desperate for liquidity, in January 2009, in the last days of the Bush Administration, Chrysler received a $4.0 billion unsecured loan from the U.S. government as part of the Troubled Asset Relief Program for "financial institutions." Even this, however, was not enough to change Chrysler's financial position.

Chrysler began to explore a strategic alliance with Italian auto manufacturer Fiat, in which Fiat would purchase part of the company in exchange for access to technology and distribution channels. This proposed alliance still required at least $6 billion in additional funding, debt forgiveness from Chrysler's financial creditors, and major concessions from the UAW regarding wages and benefits and funding of the VEBA. As Chrysler worked to negotiate deals, its cash position continued to deteriorate, and the U.S. government indicated that it would only provide additional financing in the context of a bankruptcy.

B. The Bankruptcy

Chrysler had been desperate to avoid a bankruptcy throughout its restructuring process. Few believed that an auto manufacturer could survive a bankruptcy because consumers would not want to purchase cars from a bankrupt company because of doubts about whether warranties would be honored and replacement parts would be available if the company did not emerge from bankruptcy. Nonetheless, having exhausted its other restructuring options, Chrysler LLC and its subsidiaries—but not its parent company or its sister corporation financing arm, Chrysler Financial Services—filed for bankruptcy on April 30, 2009.

Chrysler LLC and its bankrupt subsidiaries promptly received an additional $4.5 billion debtor-in-possession (DIP) loan from the U.S. government to enable it to continue operating in bankruptcy. The loan was secured by a first lien on all of Chrysler's unencumbered assets and a junior (third) lien on other assets. Chrysler, however, had virtually no unencumbered assets, so the loan was functionally a third lien loan.

At the time of its bankruptcy filing, Chrysler had 38,500 hourly or salaried employees and 106,000 retirees or retirees' surviving spouses. Chrysler dealers employed another 140,000 people, and Chrysler's numerous parts suppliers had many thousands of more employees and retirees, all dependent on future business coming from Chrysler. Some 31 million Jeep, Dodge, and Chrysler owners depended on the ongoing availability of Chrysler parts, service, and warranties. And this for a company with only the fourth largest share of the U.S. new auto sales market (12.1%) in 2009.

While Chrysler was not the largest U.S. OEM, it was closely tied to its competitors (GM, Ford, and others) through shared suppliers. The failure of one of the Big Three could have possibly resulted in the failure of common suppliers. Many auto parts are "single-sourced," meaning that there is a single supplier of the parts. Re-sourcing parts often takes months or even years. Thus, the failure of a common supplier of single-sourced parts, say of drive shaft assemblies or brake assemblies, could result in a complete production shutdown of an OEM for months or years, resulting in its failure too. Thus, a liquidation of Chrysler posed a risk of far greater failures throughout the U.S. automotive industry, implicating hundreds of thousands of households' livelihoods, health care, and retirements.

It was against this backdrop that Chrysler proposed to enter into the central transaction in its bankruptcy, a sale of its "good" assets to a newly created entity ("New Chrysler"), with the "bad" assets remaining in the old company ("Old Car Co.") for liquidation.

Indiana State Pension Trust v. Chrysler LLC

576 F.3d 108 (2d Cir. 2009)

DENNIS JACOBS, Chief Judge.

. . . In a nutshell, Chrysler LLC and its related companies (hereinafter "Chrysler" or "debtor" or "Old Chrysler") filed a [planned] bankruptcy petition under Chapter 11 on April 30, 2009. The filing followed months in which Chrysler experienced deepening losses, received billions in bailout funds from the Federal Government, searched for a merger partner, unsuccessfully sought additional government bailout funds for a stand-alone restructuring, and ultimately settled on an asset-sale transaction pursuant to 11

U.S.C. §363 (the "Sale"), which was approved by the Sale Order. The key elements of the Sale were set forth in a Master Transaction Agreement dated as of April 30, 2009: substantially all of Chrysler's operating assets (including manufacturing plants, brand names, certain dealer and supplier relationships, and much else) would be transferred to New Chrysler in exchange for New Chrysler's assumption of certain liabilities and $2 billion in cash. Fiat S.p.A agreed to provide New Chrysler with certain fuel-efficient vehicle platforms, access to its worldwide distribution system, and new management that is experienced in turning around a failing auto company. Financing for the sale transaction—$6 billion in senior secured financing, and debtor-in-possession financing for 60 days in the amount of $4.96 billion—would come from the United States Treasury and from [the Canadian government]. The agreement describing the United States Treasury's commitment does not specify the source of the funds, but it is undisputed that prior funding came from the Troubled Asset Relief Program ("TARP"), 12 U.S.C. § 5211(a)(1), and that the parties expected the Sale to be financed through the use of TARP funds. Ownership of New Chrysler was to be distributed by membership interests, 55% of which go to an employee benefit entity [the "VEBA"] created by the United Auto Workers union, 8% to the United States Treasury and 2% to [the Canadian government]. Fiat, for its contributions, would immediately own 20% of the equity with rights to acquire more (up to 51%), contingent on payment in full of the debts owed to the United States Treasury and [the Canadian government].

At a hearing on May 5, 2009, the bankruptcy court approved the debtor's proposed bidding procedures. No other bids were forthcoming. From May 27 to May 29, the bankruptcy court held hearings on whether to approve the Sale. Upon extensive findings of fact and conclusions of law, the bankruptcy court approved the Sale by order dated June 1, 2009.

After briefing and oral argument, we affirmed the bankruptcy court's order on June 5, but we entered a short stay pending Supreme Court review. The Supreme Court, after an extension of the stay, declined a further extension. The Sale closed on June 10, 2009.

Figure 1.2, below, provides a summary view of the Chrysler sale transaction.

Figure 1.2 Chrysler Section 363 Sale Transaction

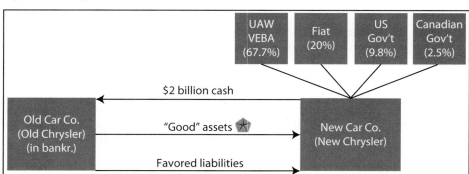

One of the most powerful tools offered by bankruptcy is the ability for the debtor to sell its assets "free and clear" of any liens or other interests. Normally when assets that serve as collateral for a debt are sold, the sale does not remove the lien from the asset absent the lender's consent. As a result, if the *seller* defaults on the obligation to the lienor, the lender can foreclose on the property in the hand of the *buyer*. The buyer is assuming the risk that the seller will fail to pay its debts secured by the collateral. Buyers will discount their purchase prices accordingly, so if the lien is for a greater amount than the value of the asset, the sale simply will not happen.

The bankruptcy "free and clear" sale power changes that. In a "free and clear" sale, the buyer takes the assets, but not subject to any creditors' liens or other third-party property interests, such as easements. Instead, the liens or other interests that had been on the assets are limited to the proceeds of the sale. If the sale proceeds are insufficient to pay off the lienholders or other creditors, then those creditors have to take the losses; they cannot look to the asset's buyer for any recovery beyond the purchase price paid for the assets, which is also all that the creditor could have recovered from foreclosing on the assets. The ability to sell "free and clear" means that a debtor's assets can be freed from liabilities that create a debt overhang problem and productively redeployed in the economy.

Free and clear sales are a standard part of bankruptcy practice and not controversial in and of themselves. Chrysler, however, did not simply undertake to sell its good assets free and clear of liens to New Chrysler. In addition, and as part of the sale, New Chrysler agreed to assume certain Old Car Co.'s liabilities. These assumed liabilities would become obligations of a rejuvenated operating company—while the unassumed liabilities would remain with the liquidating Old Car Co. This meant that the assumed liabilities could look to New Chrysler's future revenue for repayment, while the unassumed liabilities would be repaid from the "bad" assets and a small pool of cash transferred to the Old Car Co. as part of the sale transaction.

Figure 1.3, below, shows the capital structures of Old Car Co. and New Car Co. Notice which liabilities of Old Car Co. are assumed by New Car Co. They include some of Old Car Co.'s obligations to suppliers and warranties on existing vehicles. But most important, perhaps, was the assumption by the New Chrysler of its collective bargaining agreement with the UAW. The UAW agreed to the assumption of the collective bargaining agreement by New Chrysler and to significant concessions in the agreement (valued at around $1.3 billion), but the UAW's consent was contingent upon the VEBA receiving an ownership stake in New Chrysler and the completion of the bankruptcy sale.[7]

The effect of the selective assumption of liabilities was to favor some of Chrysler's creditors. Instead of a distribution that follows the "absolute priority rule," with

---

7. The concessions included 50% compensation cuts for new employees, thereby creating a two-tier wage system; the end of cost-of-living adjustments, annual wage increases, and layoff protection; the end of the "jobs bank" (a study hall where excess workers were paid for not working); elimination of overtime payment for work beyond eight hours and paid lunch breaks; mandatory Saturday work without overtime pay; and reduced prescription drug coverage (including elimination of coverage for erectile dysfunction medications).

Figure 1.3 Old Chrysler's and New Chrysler's Capital Structures

Old Chrysler (Old Car Co.)		New Chrysler	
Secured Debt		**Secured Debt**	
1st Lien (banks):	$6.9B		
2d Lien (equity loan):	$2.0B		
3d Lien (U.S. gov't DIP loan):	$4.5B	Gov't	$6.0B
Unsecured Debt		**Unsecured Debt**	
TARP:	$4.0B		
Trade:	$5.3B →	Trade	$5.3B
War./Dealer:	$4.0B →	War./Dealer	$4.0B
Pension:	$3.5B →	Pensions	$3.5B
UAW VEBA:	$10.0B	VEBA Note	$4.6B
Torts:	$??B		
		Shareholders' equity:	
	Equity: $ 0	VEBA:	67.69%
		Fiat:	20.00%
		US:	9.85%
		Canada:	2.46%

creditors paid in order of their seniority as determined ex ante by contract and statute, creditors' recoveries were a function of whether they were favored by New Chrysler, for whatever reason. In bankruptcy, a plan of reorganization requires absolute priority to be applied in the absence of creditor consent, as indicated by a vote of creditors in a complex voting mechanism. These same requirements, however, do not apply to an asset sale, at least as long as the sale is not functionally a reorganization plan. While absolute priority will apply to the distribution of the sale proceeds under a plan, it does not extend to other benefits in a sale, such as assumption of liabilities. All of these issues are examined in more detail in subsequent chapters of the book.

Figure 1.4, below, shows different creditors' claims against Old Car Co.; what they were to be paid in a liquidation under the absolute priority rule, both as a dollar amount and as a percentage of their claim; what the creditors received in New Car Co.; and the total they received from both Old Car Co. and New Car Co., both as a dollar amount and as a percentage of their claim. The key to understanding this figure is to compare the fifth column from left, showing the Old Car Co. liquidation proceeds as a percentage of the creditor's claim with the rightmost column, which shows the combination of the Old Car Co. liquidation proceeds and interest in New Car Co. as a percentage of the creditor's claim. When only the liquidation proceeds are considered, the distribution tracks with absolute priority—no one junior (as indicated by the priority ranking column second from the left) gets paid anything when those senior have not been paid in full. But when the interest in New Car Co. is added into consideration, the payments to different classes of claimants bear no relation to their priority ranking.

The Chrysler free and clear sale was approved by the Second Circuit in a highly controversial opinion, to which we will return in a later chapter when we consider bankruptcy sales. Irrespective of the formal legal issues in the case, however, it provides a stark picture of some of the competing policy concerns involved in bankruptcy.

Figure 1.4 Chrysler Bankruptcy Payments by Creditor Type

Claimant Class	Claimant Class Priority Ranking	Claim against Old Car Co.	Payment in Old Car Co. Liquidation	Payment in Old Car Co. Liquidation as % of Claim	Interest in New Car Co.	Payment in OCC Liquidation + Interest in New Car Co.	Payment in Old Car Co. Liquidation plus Interest in New Car Co. as % of Claim
1st Lien (bank syndicate)	1	$6.9B	$2.0B	29%	$0	$2.0B	29%
2d lien (equity loan)	2	$2.0B	$0	0%	$0	$0	0%
3d lien (US/Can. gov't DIP loan)	3	$4.5B	$0	0%	$6.0B note + 10% equity	$6.0B + 10% New Co. equity	≥72%
4th lien TARP loan (US gov't)	4	$4.0B	$0	0%			
Trade Creditors	5	$5.3B	$0	0%	$5.3B debt	$5.3B	100%
Warranty/Dealers	5	$4.0B	$0	0%	$4.0B debt	$4.0B	100%
Underfunded non-union pensions	5	$3.5B	$0	0%	$3.5B debt	$3.5B	100%
UAW VEBA	5	$10.0B	$0	0%	$4.6B note + 68% equity	$4.6B note + 68% New Co. equity	≥57%
Tort Creditors	5	$??B	$0	0%	$0	$0	0%
Equity	6	n/a	$0	n/a	0	0	n/a

C. Chrysler Dénouement

The bankruptcy sale was not the end of the Chrysler story. Chrysler roared back to profitability. Its sales, revenue, and perhaps most importantly cash on hand, were all up, and the firm was turning a profit again. Figure 1.5, below, shows the change in Chrysler's performance from 2008 to 2012.

The Chrysler reorganization was trumpeted in the media as a great success that saved many jobs. And it did. But for the bankruptcy restructuring Chrysler would almost surely have liquidated, costing not only jobs as Chrysler, but also potentially at its suppliers and perhaps even at other OEMs that shared suppliers.

Yet many jobs were also lost, just not quite as visibly. Chrysler closed a quarter of its dealerships—mainly independently owned—as part of the bankruptcy. Chrysler dealerships generally had very low sales volume compared with dealerships of other brands. While some of these dealers also did business in non-Chrysler vehicles and were able to shift employees, the closure of the dealerships inevitably resulted in significant job loss, just not of Chrysler employees, and therefore not included in the bankruptcy's toll. (It also meant that Chrysler owners sometimes had to travel significantly greater distances for warranty service on their vehicles.) The 789 dealerships that closed had employed around 40,000 employees.

Similarly, Chrysler's pre-bankruptcy downsizing is typically excluded from the cost of the Chrysler restructuring. From 2007-2009, Chrysler eliminated around 40,000 jobs (distinct from the 40,000 dealership jobs). While these jobs were not formally lost in bankruptcy, they were nevertheless lost as part of the restructuring process.

Figure 1.5 Chrysler Performance Metrics, 2008 vs. 2012[8]

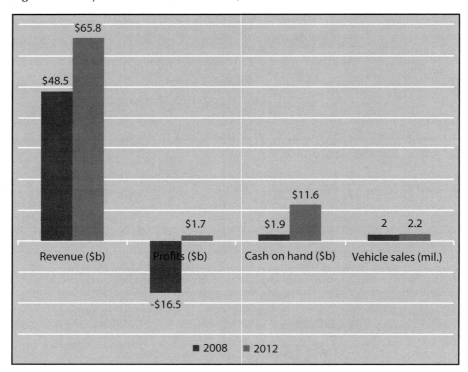

And what of the marriage between Fiat, UAW, and the governments? It turns out to have been somewhat rockier. The equity structure of New Chrysler was set up to reward Fiat for effective management. Fiat would receive an additional 5% of the equity of New Chrysler for achieving each of three milestones: commercial production of a new engine; $1.5 billion in annual revenue; commencing commercial production of a 40 mpg vehicle (the Dodge Dart). New Chrysler achieved all three of these milestones by 2012. This meant that Fiat acquired 35% of Chrysler without ever having contributed any cash for its stake.

After New Chrysler repaid its government debt (through a refinancing), Fiat was able to exercise a call option to increase its stake by an additional 16% for $1.2 billion. Additionally, Fiat bought out the U.S. and Canadian government stakes in Chrysler for $625 billion. Thus, by January 2012, Fiat had acquired 58.5% of Chrysler for $1.825 billion. The UAW VEBA held the remaining 41.5% of the company's equity.[9]

Fiat, however, also had a call option on part of the UAW holdings. Fiat had the option of purchasing five 3.3% stakes from the UAW holdings every six months at a strike price (the price at which an option is exercised) determined by a complex valuation formula. In mid-2012, Fiat attempted to exercise its call option, offering $139.7

8. Sharon Terlep *et al., Fiat Weighs IPO After Absorbing Chrysler*, WALL ST. J., Apr. 24, 2013, at B1.

9. *See* Chrysler Press Release, Jan. 5, 2012, *Chrysler Group LLC Completes Final Performance Event; Fiat S.p.A. Ownership Rises to 58.5 Percent; Fuel-Efficient Dodge Dart to Be Revealed at NAIAS on Jan. 9.*

million for the 3.3% stake. The UAW VEBA refused to accept the offer, claiming that it was not in good faith and not in compliance with the valuation formula. The UAW VEBA said that the proper exercise price was $342 million and that the valuation should not include the $4.5 billion note Chrysler owed the VEBA in its calculation of Chrysler debt, as it did not fall under the purchase agreement's definition of "borrowed money." Excluding the note would significantly increase the valuation of Chrysler: Fiat's valuation implied that it believed that Chrysler as a firm was worth $4.2 billion, while the VEBA's valuation implied the firm to be worth $10.3 billion. While Fiat later upped its offer to $198 million, implying a $6 billion valuation, the Fiat-UAW honeymoon was over.

Fiat sued the UAW VEBA in Delaware Chancery Court to enforce the option exercise. Complicating the valuation fight was that the VEBA's claim on Chrysler's equity value was capped at $4.25 billion as of January 1, 2010, but with the cap increased annually at a 9% compounded rate. If the value of the VEBA's position increased above the cap, any value was to accrue to the U.S. and Canadian governments under an Equity Recapture Agreement. Fiat, however, had purchased the Equity Recapture Agreement rights for $75 million, so the most the UAW VEBA could realize on the Chrysler stock in 2011 was $4.63 billion.

Meanwhile, the UAW VEBA was pushing for a Chrysler IPO, believing it could maximize the value of its stake by selling on the market instead of to Fiat. Chrysler hoped that the IPO would generate $5 billion, implying a firm valuation of $12 billion. In 2014, the equity recapture cap would have risen to $6 billion, so it would not have been an obstacle to Chrysler's recovery in an IPO. By September 2013, Chrysler went so far as to file securities registration documents in anticipation of an IPO. Meanwhile, Fiat indicated that it wanted to buy out the VEBA's entire position and merge Fiat into Chrysler, which was then the stronger of the two companies. To exert more leverage for a private sale rather than an IPO, Fiat threatened to end its alliance with Chrysler if the VEBA went through with an IPO.

In the end, the parties settled. Fiat and the VEBA agreed to a private sale of the 41.46% of Chrysler stock still held by the VEBA. Fiat paid the VEBA $1.9 billion, with another $1.75 billion paid by Chrysler in a stock buyback. Chrysler agreed to pay the VEBA another $700 million over four years. Thus, the VEBA received $4.35 billion, with an implied valuation of the firm at $10.5 billion, less than what the VEBA would have liked, but more than what Fiat wanted to pay. The result of the sale was a new, merged company, Fiat Chrysler Automobiles NV.

Ironies abound in this situation, as UAW and Fiat lived out the adage "marry in haste, repent at leisure." First, Fiat, the white knight, had to ultimately look to Chrysler to save its fortunes. Second, the UAW, which was the great beneficiary of the lack of a true market process in the bankruptcy sale, found itself eager for a market valuation for its shares. Indeed, from the UAW's perspective, being able to maximize the value of the Chrysler shares was especially important because the Chrysler VEBA is woefully underfunded.

Indeed, as of the end of 2011, the three UAW VEBAs (Chrysler, Ford, and GM) remained underfunded by $20 billion or 40% on an actuarial basis, and health care costs were significantly higher for UAW VEBA beneficiaries. The Chrysler sale proceeds presumably helped reduce the underfunding, but came nowhere close to closing the funding gap for a plan that is supposed to provide health care benefits for 80 years. In its first year of operation, the Chrysler VEBA increased co-payments and eliminated some prescription drug coverage. Annual deductibles for in-network care for family beneficiaries had risen from $340 in 2011 to $610 by 2014. Likewise, yearly out-of-pocket maximum payments for family beneficiaries for in-network care went from $570 in 2011 to $1,310 by 2014.

So who got what out of the Chrysler bankruptcy? The first lien debt got 29 cents on the dollar—roughly what the first lien debt was trading for in the secondary market around the time of the bankruptcy filing. Creditors' losses depended on whether they purchased at par or at a discount. The second lien debt—a loan from Chrysler's pre-bankruptcy owners, Cerberus and Daimler—got wiped out, as did Chrysler's pre-bankruptcy tort debt. Chrysler dumped a number of dealers, but those that it retained found their contracts honored by a financially stronger company, as did most suppliers. Chrysler also honored the pensions of its non-union employees and the warranties of its vehicle owners.

As for the rest of the players? Fiat managed to gain control of Chrysler for a surprisingly low price and may have ultimately saved itself from problems in its European operations.

The U.S. and Canadian governments avoided an even worse financial crisis and the concomitant political fallout. In the end, they did so for a relatively small cost: The U.S. government ended up losing $1.3 billion on its loans and investment in Chrysler, a small fraction of the economic harm that would have occurred had Chrysler completely liquidated.

Daimler took an enormous loss on its investment in Chrysler, having paid $36 million to buy the firm and then paying another $675 million to get out of 80% of its investment. To get out of the remaining 20%, Daimler agreed to relinquish its remaining equity stake in Old Car Co. LLC and to contribute $600 million to the VEBA in exchange for a release from its pension guarantee liability and various representation and warranty claims related to the 2007 stock sale. Additionally, Daimler received no recovery on its $1.5 billion portion of the second lien debt. Offsetting this is only the $1.4 billion Daimler received from Cerberus. One might roughly estimate Daimler's losses at around $37.4 billion, making Daimler perhaps the biggest loser in the Chrysler story.

Cerberus also took a bath on its Chrysler investment. Still Cerberus did not fare as badly as one might have thought. Recall that Cerberus had purchased the stock not of Chrysler LLC, but of its parent corporation, which did not file for bankruptcy. While the parent corporation's stock in Chrysler LLC was wiped out, the parent corporations' stake in Chrysler Financial Services was unaffected by the bankruptcy. Cerebus sold Chrysler Financial in 2010 to Toronto Dominion Bank for $6.3 billion. Accounting for the proceeds of the Chrysler Financial sale plus some of Chrysler Financial's assets that it retained, it lost only 10% of its original investment in the Chrysler family, a bad outcome to be sure, but far better than the 100% loss on the investment in the automotive company itself.

And the UAW ended up making major concessions, but managed to avoid catastrophe and ended up with something like what it had in 2007: reduced compensation, particularly for new hires, and a massively underfunded VEBA that is capable of meeting its obligations today, but perhaps not in the future. This was probably the best the UAW could have hoped for. The VEBA's funding shortfalls are a problem for a future restructuring, which means the UAW lived to fight another day.

The Chrysler bankruptcy produced winners and losers. It had wide-ranging distributional effects. Yet bankruptcy's procedural tools for liberating encumbered assets and productively redeploying them arguably prevented the assets from going to waste and avoided spillover effects throughout the automotive industry and the economy as a whole. Chrysler had significant assets—such as its Auburn Hills headquarters complex and specialized factory machinery—that could not easily be redeployed for other productive uses. Likewise, its labor force could not easily be redeployed to new market rate employment without tremendous collateral costs relating to relocation and interrupted employment. Thus, as bankruptcies go, Chrysler is a success story.

Problem Set 1

Which of the following enterprises do you think have going-concern value that significantly exceeds liquidation value?

(1) Best Buy, an electronics retailer: assets include leases on stores and warehouses, inventory, trademarks, employment contracts, customer list, accounts receivable, goodwill, and cash.

(2) Weil, Gotshal & Manges, LLP, a large international law firm: assets include leases on office space, leases on office equipment, an art collection, accounts receivable, at-will employment contracts, goodwill, and cash.

(3) Facebook: assets include office space, equipment, at-will employment contracts with engineers, accounts receivable, IP (copyrights, trademarks, and patents), customer list and database, goodwill, and cash.

(4) United Airlines Corporation: assets include airplane leases, equipment (gate/ramp and maintenance), employment contracts (pilots, machinists, flight attendants, executives), FAA gate rights, FAA licenses, accounts receivable, trademarks, customer list, goodwill, and cash.

(5) General Motors Corporation: assets include real estate (headquarters, plants, etc.), equipment, employment contracts, IP (trademarks, copyrights, patents), dealership franchisor rights, inventory, accounts receivable, customer list, goodwill, and cash.

CHAPTER 2

PRIORITY I

After graduating law school you struck out on your own as a solo practitioner. You've just won your first case, an employment discrimination suit. The jury awarded your client a $1 million judgment. As your client is congratulating you, a terrible thought enters your head: How do you go about collecting the judgment? This isn't just an academic question—you took the case on contingency, and your fee depends on being able to collect.

After your client releases you from a bear hug of relief, you walk over to opposing counsel and tell them that you'll be contacting them with payment information. Opposing counsel laughs and says, "Fat chance a check's coming. My client's never gonna to pay." "But the jury just awarded a $1 million judgment against you!" you object. "You've got a lot to learn, kid," the grizzled lawyer says. "You sure've got a lot to learn. Good luck."

Law school is very good at teaching students whether McGee is liable to Hawkins for a hairy hand, whether Putney is liable to Vosberg for a broken eggshell knee, whether Walker-Thomas Furniture can recover from Ora Lee Williams on its attempt to replevy her household goods, etc. Most of the courses in law school deal with determining whether a party has liability to someone else. And this is an important part of what lawyers do. But liability is not self-executing. Not all debts are repaid voluntarily.

This, then, is the creditor's dilemma: How to ensure repayment? Some creditors are in a better situation than others: Some creditors are voluntary creditors—they have chosen to extend credit—and thus have some ability to negotiate the terms on which they extend credit. Other creditors are involuntary creditors—tort victims, taxing authorities. They do not choose to whom credit is extended or the terms of that credit.

Often creditors seek voluntary repayment. Debtors will repay because they feel legally, morally, or reputationally bound to do so or because they hope to get further credit from the creditor. But not all debtors repay voluntarily. Some are unable or unwilling to pay all their creditors. How does a creditor ensure that *she* is the one who will be repaid, especially when there are limited assets?

This chapter and the following one consider the process of collecting on a debt and explore seven ways that a contractual creditor can improve its chances of repayment: temporal priority, setoff rights, security interests, negative pledge clauses, contractual subordination, guaranties, and structural priority. All of these methods aim to improve either the priority of a creditor's claim against a limited pool of assets or expand the pool of assets from which recovery is available. None of these contractual tools are available to involuntary creditors.

I. TEMPORAL PRIORITY AND ACCELERATION

All else being equal, then, a shorter-term debt is less risky than a longer-term debt. The debt with the shorter term means that the creditor is exposed to risk for a shorter period of time: a lot more could go wrong for a debtor that would affect its ability to repay over a ten-year period than over 90 days.

When there is both a short-term and a longer-term debt outstanding, which one is likely to get paid first? The shorter-term debt, because it is due first. Thus, perhaps the easiest way for a creditor to ensure that it is repaid first is to have its debt come due first. If a debtor simply pays its obligations in the order they come due and payable, those whose debts are due first have priority over those whose debts are due later. If the debtor runs out of money down the line, it is the later-due creditors' problem. Thus, a short-term debt inherently has a type of temporal priority over a long-term debt in the ordinary course of business.

If a debtor (as opposed to some of the debtor's assets) is liquidated, all temporal priorities collapse to equal priority because all debts, due or not, are accelerated and become owing in a liquidation proceeding. Outside of a liquidation, however, creditors may have the ability to alter their temporal priority. It may seem obvious, but creditors are entitled to collect only on debts that are actually owed, meaning not only that there is indebtedness, but that the indebtedness has come due and payable. A creditor normally has no right to collect on a debt that is due in the future.

For contractual obligations, the question of the exact amount of the indebtedness and the question of whether it has come due and payable are not always straightforward. In a complicated loan agreement, there can be disputes about the applicability of various fees and interest rates. There can also be disputes about whether a debt is due and payable.

Some loans are **demand loans,** meaning that they are repayable whenever the lender demands repayment. But many loans are **term loans,** with a definite maturity date. Such term loans are often **installment loans**—loans where the borrower makes periodic payments—rather than a single payment at maturity.[1] In an installment loan, a missed periodic payment does not, by itself, entitle the creditor to collect the full outstanding balance on the loan. Instead, the creditor can collect only the missed periodic payment, as that is all that is due and owing.

---

1. Whether an installment loan is **amortized**, meaning that the periodic payment includes repayment of principal not merely payments of interest, is a separate issue. An installment loan can be fully amortized (with the principal paid off by maturity), partially amortized (paying down some principal during with a **balloon** or **bullet** payment of remaining principal at maturity), or non-amortized (interest only payments followed by a balloon payment of the entire principal). Amortization can occur over a different term than the maturity of the loan; if an amortization period is longer than the term of the loan, the loan will necessarily have a balloon payment at maturity.

Loan documentation will typically give a creditor the right to **accelerate** a debt in certain conditions. **Acceleration** means that the entire debt, not just past-due installments, becomes immediately due and payable, meaning that the debt can be "called." Absent acceleration, the most a creditor is entitled to collect is past-due installments. Acceleration is the gateway for a creditor to pursue remedies on a term loan, including installment loans. Acceleration, then, allows a creditor to improve its temporal priority, as it does not have to wait to seek repayment.

Acceleration is a contractually defined right. Acceleration generally requires a material breach of the loan contract by the debtor. The contract may, however, provide for an alternative standard, such as when the creditor "deems itself insecure" or a defined material event of default, such as a missed periodic payment or an unremedied covenant default. (A **covenant** is just a Biblical-sounding term meaning a promise to do something or not do something. A **covenant default** is a default unrelated to payment, in contrast to a **payment default**.) What is required to exercise acceleration varies by loan agreement, but usually it requires nothing more than notice from the lender to the borrower, and sometimes not even notice.

Exercising acceleration is potentially perilous for a creditor. Acceleration must be exercised only in good faith. UCC § 1-309. No such requirement exists for demand notes, which by definition cannot be accelerated. UCC § 1-309, Cmt. 1. A demand note can be called at will; continued extension of credit is not required. *Kham and Nate's Shoes No. 2, Inc. v. First Bank of Whiting*, 908 F.2d 1351 (7th Cir. 1990). *But see K.M.C., Inc. v. Irving Trust Co.*, 757 F.2d 752 (6th Cir. 1986) (holding refusal to advance additional funds must be made in good faith). Whether a borrower violated a particular loan covenant is sometimes a matter of debate, as is the question of whether the breach was "material," thus entitling the creditor to call the loan. If a creditor is too aggressive, it may find itself calling a debt improperly, which can result in a host of consequential damages for the borrower, and potentially liability for the creditor. Moreover, a creditor that calls a loan for non-payment default may find itself subject to a claim that it has breached its implied covenant of good faith and fair dealing.

The following case illustrates the dangers in calling a loan prematurely, even if there is an undisputed technical default. A lender cannot generally call a loan for a non-material breach. Moreover, whether a lender behaved in good faith depends, in part, on whether a default is material, which tees up a pair of factual questions that are difficult to resolve without going to trial, a situation lenders are usually keen to avoid because of concerns about juries favoring sympathetic debtors.

Sahadi v. Continental Illinois National Bank & Trust Co.

706 F.2d 193 (7th Cir. 1983)

WOOD, Circuit Judge.

This is an appeal from the district court's order granting partial summary judgment in favor of the defendant-appellee Continental Illinois Bank (the Bank) in an action alleging that the Bank breached its agreement with the plaintiff-appellant's business, Great Lakes and European Lines, Inc. (GLE), by calling a $7 million loan when GLE tendered interest payments less than one day after they were due. On appeal, the plaintiffs argue that the district court erred in granting summary judgment because there existed an array of genuine and material disputed factual issues concerning, inter alia, whether GLE's day-late tender of payment was a "material" breach of the underlying agreement warranting the Bank's calling of the loan, whether the Bank's conduct in accepting late interest payments under the predecessor loan agreement with GLE resulted in a waiver of its right to call the loan for the delayed tender without notice, and whether the Bank's calling of the loan without notice violated its duty of "good faith" under the Uniform Commercial Code and the common law. Because there existed a genuine factual dispute at least as to the question of whether there was a "material" breach of the agreement, we find that the district court's award of summary judgment to defendant on the question of breach was inappropriate, and we remand for a trial.

I.

Viewing the facts in the light most favorable to the plaintiffs, as we must, there emerges a story of financial brinkmanship and opaque dealing in which neither side emerges wholly blameless. GLE, an international shipping line, began its relationship with the Bank in 1976 with a $3 million loan, personally guaranteed by the Sahadis. The Bank increased its loan commitment to $11 million in 1977, a commitment upon which GLE relied in expanding its business, but which was repudiated by the Bank, to the detriment of GLE, when personal and institutional friction developed between the parties. The parties quickly reached a stalemate, with GLE threatening to sue the Bank for breach of its loan commitment and the Bank threatening to call the loans already extended. Meanwhile, GLE successfully interested another lender which conditioned its backing on GLE's settlement of it differences with the Bank.

Negotiations ensued in which, the evidence indicated, the Bank primarily sought to obtain release from the Sahadis and GLE of their claims stemming from the Bank's purported breach of its loan commitment, and to obtain further collateral from the Sahadis to secure their guarantee of the outstanding loan. The Bank also sought to have GLE's outstanding interest payments, which had been withheld during the several months of the dispute, brought up to date.

The negotiations resulted in two agreements executed on October 25, 1977. One agreement ran between the Sahadis and the Bank, completely releasing the Bank from any claims stemming from its failure to fulfill the loan commitment; it also extensively collateralized the Sahadis' guarantee of the Bank's outstanding loan to GLE. The other agreement, cross-referenced to the first and running between GLE and the Bank, provided in turn for the payment of interest and for the Bank's forbearance from demanding payment of the entire outstanding loan and accrued interest:

> 1. [The Bank] hereby agrees to forbear from demanding payment of the Liabilities during the period ending December 31, 1977, except for payment of current interest thereon as more fully set forth in clause (i) of paragraph 3 below.

The agreement went on to state:

> 3. Notwithstanding the foregoing, [the Bank] may demand payment in full of the Liabilities prior to December 31, 1977 if . . . (i) [GLE] shall fail to make payment of

interest accrued on the Liabilities through September 30, 1977 on or before November 15, 1977.

This latter paragraph, as initially drafted, provided for October 7, 1977 as the deadline for the payment of accrued interest. This date was changed to November 15, 1977 at Sahadi's request with no objection by the Bank; moreover, there was no evidence that the precise date on which accrued interest was to be paid was ever a point of contention in the negotiations.

Despite the seeming air of reconciliation surrounding these agreements and despite the fact that the Bank had routinely accepted late interest payments from GLE under the underlying loan which the agreement modified, plaintiff's evidence established that after October 25, the Bank furtively prepared to take advantage of GLE's propensity for late payment to call the loan under the technical letter of the new agreement. Although the Bank sent a billing to GLE headquarters on November 9, 1977 reminding GLE of the interest due on November 15 and referring to the October 25, 1977 agreement, the letter made no mention of the Bank's intent to call the loan if payment did not arrive on the precise contractually specified date. In speaking with top GLE representatives on November 14 and 15, the Bank made no mention of its intent to call the loan.

Sahadi was reminded by a subordinate on November 14 of the November 15 interest payment date, but Sahadi responded that the payment should be delayed so that GLE monies in Chicago would be available to satisfy other immediate liabilities. As Sahadi noted in his affidavit, "There was no great significance attached to the payment of interest in this covenant; it did not occur to us that the bank would treat the interest payment date any differently than it had treated previous payment dates." On the morning of November 16, a GLE representative was queried by the Bank as to whether the interest payments had been made; when the GLE representative responded negatively but indicated that the payment would be made by the end of the week, the Bank representative responded that the matter could be discussed later that day. At that later meeting, the Bank presented the surprised GLE representative with notification that the loan was called. The GLE representative immediately offered to tender payment for the due interest from the company's account with the Bank, but the Bank refused. The calling of the loan destroyed GLE and subjected the Sahadis to liability on the personal guarantee.

The Sahadis, indirectly as assignees of GLE, thereafter filed this action against the Bank, seeking release from their personal guarantee agreement and damages for the destruction of GLE. Chiefly, they contended that GLE's brief delay in tender of the November 15 interest payment did not amount to a "material" breach of the October 25 agreements justifying the Bank's cessation of forbearance, and that the Bank's conduct was in any case unjustified under principles of waiver and "good faith."

In granting partial summary judgment to the Bank, the district court rejected the Sahadis' waiver argument, but did not directly address their "material" breach or "good faith" contentions, either of which, the Sahadis argued, required a trial to assess the confliction evidence. Instead, the district court chose the alternative analytical framework of "ambiguity" and held that, since the November 15 date was not "ambiguous," there was no room for factual difference as to whether a brief delay in payment was permitted. After the district court denied the Sahadis' motion for reconsideration, this appeal followed.

II.

The limitations upon the use of summary judgment are stringent, and we may not affirm the district court's order unless the record reveals the absence of any genuine issue of material fact. Fed. R. Civ. P. 56(c). We cannot agree with the district court that under Illinois law, expressly made applicable in the agreements here, this record presents no issues of material fact requiring a full trial. While outstanding issues of material fact may well exist also in relation to the Sahadis' waiver and breach of "good faith" claims, we need not reach those questions here and so confine our analysis for the purposes of this appeal to the issues of "material" breach.

It is black letter law in Illinois and elsewhere that only a "material" breach of a contract provision by one party will justify non-performance by the other party. Moreover, the determination of "materiality" is a complicated question of fact, involving an inquiry into such matters as whether the breach worked to defeat the bargained-for objective of the parties or caused disproportionate prejudice to the nonbreaching party, whether custom and usage considers such a breach to be material, and whether the allowance of reciprocal non-performance by the non-breaching party will result in his accrual of an unreasonable or unfair advantage. All of these issues must be resolved with reference to the intent of the parties as evidenced in large part by the full circumstances of the transaction, thus making these issues especially unsuited to resolution by summary judgment.

The need for a complete factual inquiry into the underlying circumstances and commercial custom is especially acute where, as here, the purportedly breaching party claims that time was not of the essence of the contract. Even where the contract contains a provision, not present here, explicitly stipulating that "time is of the essence," the Illinois courts will inquire into the situation of the parties and the underlying equities to determine whether a delay in performance resulted in a "material" breach.

The record in the case at bar discloses evidence that would permit a trier of fact to find that payment of the interest due precisely on November 15 was not "of the essence" of the agreement from the Bank's point of view. For example, Sahadi himself was allowed unilaterally to choose the payment date, and there was no contention in negotiations over the fixing of that date; the prejudice to the Bank's rights stemming from a payment delay of several hours was de minimis in view of the Bank's retention of the enhanced collateralization, its retention of the complete release of legal claims stemming from the reneged-upon loan commitment, and the Bank's clear knowledge that GLE had on hand in the Bank, and tendered, funds sufficient to satisfy the interest requirement; the Bank had previously accepted late payments in its course of dealings with GLE; and there was evidence that calling a loan for such a brief delay was without precedent in the banking community.

Significantly, even the Bank conceded at oral argument on appeal, "The important thing . . . is not the date of the fifteenth in that sense; it's the fact of the promise." Whether or not these facts would be sufficient to prove non-materiality in light of all the other evidence adduced at trial, they at least raise a genuine issue as to whether the "promise" was in any important way defeated by the hours of delay in tender of payment. Indeed, it would be difficult to posit a set of alleged facts making summary resolution of the issue of "materiality" in favor of the defendant less appropriate.

. . .

CONCLUSION

Although we need not reach the question of whether summary judgment may properly be applied to plaintiffs' assertion of waiver and "good faith," we hold that such a procedure was an inappropriate short-cut in resolving the necessarily fact-bound, complex question of "material" breach. The "materiality" issue cannot be avoided. The holding that the deadline date for interest payments in the contract was "unambiguous" does not resolve the matter. The plaintiffs concede the existence of an unambiguous, contractually specified date, but this is merely the beginning, not the end, of the required fact-finding analysis. REVERSED AND REMANDED.

II. SETOFF RIGHTS

A second way a creditor can obtain priority is through **setoff.** Setoff is an equitable right to offset a debt one owes against a debt owed to one. The precise requirements for engaging in setoff vary by state, but typically setoff requires there to be mutually owing obligations; that is, A must owe B and B must owe A. If A owes B, but B owes C (an affiliate of A), there is likely not mutuality. Moreover, some states require that the obligations be matured—that is due and owing—as part of mutuality. *See In re Patterson*, 967 F.2d 505, 510 (11th Cir. 1992) (Alabama law requires both obligations to be matured for mutuality). Setoff is similar to but doctrinally distinct from **recoupment,** which involves offsetting reciprocal obligations from one single, integrated transaction.

To see how setoff functions as a priority, consider the following. Abel owes Cain $100, and Cain owes Abel $25. In net, Abel owes Cain $75. If Abel paid Cain the full $100, Abel would still have to seek to recover the $25 from Cain. That would require Abel to go through the regular judicial collection process if Cain were unwilling or unable to pay. It's much simpler for Abel to simply withhold $25 from the payment and pay Cain only $75 in satisfaction of both debts. By engaging in setoff, Abel is able to jump ahead of all of Cain's other creditors for the $25. Setoff means that a creditor does not have to go through judicial collection or even comply with whatever procedures are required for self-help repossession and sale of collateral.

III. SECURITY INTERESTS

A third way a creditor can obtain priority is to obtain priority in a particular asset or set of assets through a **lien,** which is a type of property interest contingent upon the nonpayment of a specified debt. Debts secured by liens are critical to finance, and are best understood in contrast to debts that are not secured by liens.

Debt obligations can be created by both state and federal law. State law creates contract, tort, and various statutory obligations, while federal law creates statutory obligations (e.g., federal tax liabilities) and federal torts (e.g., section 1983 actions). As a result, the rights of creditors can vary significantly based on the type of debt obligation and the state in which it was created. Nonetheless, there are basic features of debt obligations that apply uniformly. At core there are two types of debt, **secured** and **unsecured**, and two types of creditors, secured and unsecured.

A. Unsecured Creditors

Secured and unsecured creditors have substantially different rights. Unsecured creditors have a hard and unhappy life. If an unsecured creditor wishes to collect on a debt, the unsecured creditor must first go to court, prove the debt and that it is due, and obtain a judgment. There is no right to self-help for unsecured creditors; an unsecured creditor cannot seize a debtor's assets absent a court judgment, and even then there are procedures that must be followed.

Just obtaining a judgment is a slow and expensive process, especially if the judgment is contested. In federal court it takes a minimum of 21 days to get an uncontested judgment under the Federal Rules of Civil Procedure. A party has 21 days to answer a complaint. FED. R. CIV. PROC. 12(a)(1). If there is no answer, then the plaintiff may move for a default judgment. FED. R. CIV. PROC. 55. A contested judgment can easily take a year or longer to achieve with motion practice, discovery, and court calendars; some litigation can drag on for over a decade.

Once the unsecured creditor has gotten a judgment, the unsecured creditor becomes a **judgment creditor**. This is the first step toward collection, but a judgment creditor cannot collect immediately on the judgment. Instead, it must wait for the debtor to have a chance to appeal. In federal court this means a minimum of ten days' wait after a final judgment before proceeding to collection while the debtor can determine whether to appeal, and a longer time if judgment is stayed pending resolution of the appeal, as it often is.

After exhaustion of all appeals, a judgment creditor can try to collect the court judgment either by garnishing the debtor's funds or by levying or executing on the debtor's property under a writ of execution. **Garnishment** involves obtaining a court order directing a third party that owes money to a debtor, such as a bank or an employer, to pay the money to the garnishing judgment creditor instead of to the debtor. To **levy** or **execute** on the debtor's property means having a law enforcement officer (typically a sheriff or U.S. Marshal) seize and sell the debtor's property pursuant to a writ of execution, with the sale proceeds going to the levying creditor. (The specific procedures and their names vary locally, but do not concern us here.) Once the sheriff or marshal has seized a debtor's property, but before the property is sold, the unsecured creditor becomes a **judgment lien creditor**, which gives the creditor enhanced rights in that particular property—the creditor has a lien on the seized (but not yet sold) property to secure its judgment. This process of obtaining a judgment and then collecting through garnishment or execution is known as **judicial collection**.

Collection for unsecured creditors is a costly and time-consuming procedure, and it can often be frustrated by the debtor. For natural person debtors, some property is **exempt** by statute from levy or garnishment,[2] and the debtor can conceal or move or encumber non-exempt property, making it difficult to find enough property to satisfy the judgment. Corporate debtors can also frustrate collections in various ways, including moving assets overseas or encumbering it with liens from friendly creditors.

Even if a debtor is not recalcitrant in paying on a judgment, that is no guarantee of repayment, as the unsecured creditor may be competing with other creditors for repayment from the debtor's limited assets.

If there are multiple competing creditors, who gets paid first? This is a question of **priority**. Priority means the right to be repaid before others. One can conceive of priority in a debtor's assets as equivalent to the situation of people standing in line for a slice of a pie. If there's enough pie for everyone, it doesn't particularly matter where one stands in line. But if there isn't enough pie to serve everyone, then one's place in line matters tremendously, as it will determine whether one gets a slice of pie or goes hungry.

As among unsecured creditors, there is no inherent priority. Instead, it is first come, first served. If the debtor does not have sufficient assets to satisfy all of its creditors, those who collect quickly will get paid and those who move slowly will not. This creates what is known as the **race to the courthouse**, as unsecured creditors compete for limited assets. The unsecured creditors are racing to get a judgment and execute on it before other unsecured creditors do the same. Who wins such a race? Presumably the diligent, the sophisticated, and the insiders, who might get a head start in the race. Of course, a problem unsecured creditors face is that they may not even know that they are in a race to the courthouse. They may not know of the existence (much less the identity) of other creditors, or of the actions those creditors have taken in furtherance of collection.

One way creditors deal with the problem of temporal priority and the risk that other creditors will get a jump on them in the race to the courthouse is through *cross-default clauses*. A cross-default clause is a provision in a loan that makes a default on another obligation a default on the loan. Thus, a loan might provide that a default (or at least a payment default) on any of the debtor's other financial obligations (defined in the loan) would constitute an event of default under the loan, *even if the debtor is otherwise in good standing on the loan*. A cross-default clause can provide a trigger for acceleration, enabling a creditor to pursue its remedies without having to wait for a default on its obligation. Of course, the effectiveness of a cross-default clause is dependent upon the creditor actually learning of the default on the other obligation (and being sure it is in fact a default).

While a cross-default clause makes sense for creditors individually, they may be suboptimal collectively. A default on a single obligation can produce a cascade of

---

2. Every state has an **exemption statute** that protects some property from creditors' collection. Exemptions can range from meager amounts of clothing and personal items to unlimited protection of homes. Only individuals, not firms, can invoke exemption statutes. Federal bankruptcy law provides its own set of exemptions. 11 U.S.C. § 522. A debtor in bankruptcy is permitted to pick between the federal and applicable state exemptions.

defaults and accelerations, leaving the debtor in an acute liquidity crisis as all of its obligations simultaneously come due. Instead of having to deal with one defaulted loan, the debtor now has to juggle multiple defaulted obligations, raising the problem of how to coordinate attempts to negotiate with multiple creditors, all of whom can pursue their remedies at will.

B. Secured Creditors

The world looks very different for secured creditors. Unlike an unsecured creditor, a secured creditor has a **lien** on particular property of the debtor. The property that is subject to the lien is called **collateral**. A lien is a contingent property right: It is the right to have an obligation satisfied from the proceeds of a forced sale of the collateral property *if* the debtor does not repay the obligation secured by the lien. The lien secures the debt, but the lien is a property right separate and distinct from the debt.

A lien gives the secured creditor special rights *only as to the collateral*, not as to the rest of the debtor's assets. (Some liens do cover all or virtually all of a debtor's assets, however. These are known as "blanket liens" because they cover everything.) Having a lien on a piece of property means the creditor has "dibs" on the liquidation proceeds of a particular piece of property, but not priority in the debtor's other assets. Relative to the other assets, the secured creditor is in exactly the same position as an unsecured creditor.

A secured creditor can always proceed with judicial collection just like an unsecured creditor, but it also has a right of **self-help repossession** of the collateral. Upon default and without a court order, the secured creditor may seize its collateral as long as it does not **breach the peace**.[3] The secured creditor must then either sell the collateral in any commercially reasonable manner or, if the debtor does not object, the secured creditor may keep the property in satisfaction of the debt. This sale is called a **foreclosure sale**. The sale forecloses (eliminates) the debtor's equitable **right to redeem** the collateral by paying off the loan balance.[4]

A secured creditor whose collateral is worth more than the debt it secures is called **oversecured**; if the collateral is worth less than the debt it secures, the secured creditor is **undersecured** (which is different from **unsecured**!). For example, suppose Robert Morris (the Founding Father who declared bankruptcy) loaned John Hancock $1 million, secured by Hancock's saucy sloop *Liberty*. If the *Liberty* is worth $1.2 million, Morris is oversecured. If the *Liberty* is worth exactly $1 million, Morris is **fully secured**. And if the *Liberty* is worth $800,000, then Morris is undersecured.

There can be multiple liens on the same property. Every lien has a priority relative to other liens on the same collateral. Priority of liens is equivalent to having "first dibs," "second dibs," "third dibs," and so on, on the liquidation proceeds of the collateral. Thus, there might be a first lien, a second lien, etc. Lien priority can

---

3. The process is different for real estate collateral, as discussed below.
4. Some states have a post-sale statutory right of redemption for real property. This is distinct from the pre-sale equitable right of redemption.

be **senior, junior,** or ***pari passu*** (equal among two or more creditors, with liquidation proceeds divvied up pro rata). Liens can also have one priority up to a certain amount and then a different priority beyond that amount.

Now suppose that Morris loaned Hancock $2 million, secured by Hancock's inventory of Madeira wine, which is worth $2.7 million. Morris is oversecured by $700,000. Now suppose that Haym Salomon also loaned Hancock $1 million, also secured by Hancock's inventory of Madeira wine. If Morris's loan is secured by a first lien, and Salomon's loan is secured by a second lien, then Morris is still oversecured by $700,000, while Salomon is undersecured by $300,000.

Now suppose that Alexander Hamilton also loaned Hancock $1 million, and took a third lien in the inventory of Madeira wine. Hamilton would have collateral for his loan, meaning that he is secured, but he would be entirely undersecured. If the collateral were subsequently to rise in value by $600,000, to $3.3 million, Morris would then be oversecured by $1.3 million, Salomon would be oversecured by $300,000, and Hamilton would be undersecured by $700,000. We're going to be using this terminology of oversecured, undersecured, and unsecured quite a bit, so make sure you master it!

C. Foreclosure Sales

Foreclosure sales work slightly differently for personal property (personalty) and real property (realty). For personalty, there is a self-help right of repossession. UCC § 9-609(a). Following repossession, the secured creditor may put the collateral up for sale. For sales of personalty, the only standard is that the sale must be "commercially reasonable," UCC § 9-610(b). That means the pre-sale notice and advertising procedures and the manner in which the sale itself is conducted are left to the discretion of the creditor bringing the sale.

For real property there is no self-help right of repossession; instead there is a special foreclosure sale process that varies by state and by contract. In some states the sale process goes through the courts (judicial foreclosure); in other states it is a private sale (non-judicial foreclosure), but in all cases there is advance notice of the sale, and the debtor cannot be evicted until the sale is completed because until that point it is still the debtor's property. Some states go further and specify particular bidding procedures, and a few states even allow a period for post-sale rights of redemption, meaning that the debtor can recover the property by paying off the debt and thereby divesting the foreclosure sale purchaser of the property.

Any secured creditor, regardless of lien priority, can bring a foreclosure sale upon default, and a default with one creditor is not necessarily a default with other creditors. A foreclosure sale, however, does not affect the rights of any lien senior to that of the one of the foreclosing creditor. Liens senior to the foreclosing one stay attached to the property (as do some statutory tax liens, even if junior). The obligation to pay the debt associated with the lien, however, does not transfer with the property. This means that a purchaser at a foreclosure sale might purchase property subject to a lien that secures a debt owed by the debtor, not the purchaser. The debtor will have little incentive to pay the debt after the foreclosure, so there will be a default on the debt, entitling the lienholder to foreclose on the property in the hands of the purchaser. As a result, foreclosure sale purchasers will typically discount their purchase price by the amount of any liens senior to that of the foreclosing lender and use those funds to pay off the senior liens.

A foreclosure sale does affect the rights of junior liens. The sale proceeds go to pay the foreclosing creditor first, then, if there is any **surplus**, to any junior secured creditors *with liens on that collateral*, in order of priority, and then, if there is still a surplus, to the debtor. If there are not sufficient funds to pay off junior secured creditors, their lien is discharged. They are still owed the debt, but they are now just unsecured creditors.

Similarly, if the foreclosure sale does not bring in sufficient funds to pay off the foreclosing creditor's debt (meaning that the creditor was undersecured), the foreclosing creditor will be an unsecured creditor for the **deficiency**. Not all states permit deficiencies, especially when it is a private sale; sometimes the secured creditor is able to recover only the sale price of the collateral and no more. To collect on the deficiency the creditor must obtain a judgment and proceed from there, just as with any other unsecured debt. This means that it may be difficult to collect a deficiency judgment.

Even if state law allows for a deficiency, deficiency judgments are not possible for all loans. Loans may be either **recourse** or **non-recourse**. Recourse refers to a secured creditor's ability to look to the debtor's assets other than specific collateral for recovery. Deficiencies are not possible on non-recourse loans, which limit the creditor's recovery to the value of the collateral. Given that collateral values can fluctuate and are not necessarily equal to the amount of the debt (including sale expenses), recourse status can matter a great deal.

While bidding procedures at foreclosure sales vary by jurisdiction, virtually all jurisdictions allow for **credit bidding**. Credit bidding means that a secured creditor bids by offering to pay the debt it is owed, rather than cash. Thus, if a secured creditor is owed $1 million, it can bid in that $1 million in debt, instead of having to come up with the cash. The reasoning for this is that if the secured creditor bid in cash and won, it would just be paying itself the cash. Credit bidding is not limited to the foreclosing creditor; junior lienholders can credit bid, provided that they first cash bid an amount sufficient to satisfy all senior liens. Thus, if there were a $2 million first lien that brought the foreclosure action and a $1 million second lien, the first lien creditor could put in a credit bid of up to $2 million. Any additional bid would have to be in cash. The second lien creditor could credit bid up to $1 million, but would have had to first cash bid $2 million. Any bid beyond $3 million by the second lien creditor would again have to be in cash.

Finally, perhaps the most fundamental rule of foreclosure sales bears emphasis: Only property on which the secured creditor has a lien may be forcibly sold; the debtor's other property is not affected by the sale. Thus, there is an inherent alignment between the creditor's lien and the property being sold in a foreclosure sale. It is this alignment that makes credit bidding possible. The importance of this point will become clearer when we learn about assets sales in bankruptcy, because credit bidding works somewhat differently in bankruptcy.

We can sum up the rules governing payment of the proceeds of foreclosure sales as follows:

1. Sale expenses are paid off the top. (If the gravedigger isn't paid, no one will dig graves.)
2. The liens of creditors senior to foreclosing party are unaffected by the sale and remain attached to the property in the hands of the new owner. The debt obligation remains with the original debtor.
3. Payment goes first to the foreclosing creditor.
4. If any funds remain, they are distributed to junior lienholders in order of the priority of their liens.
5. The lien of the creditor bringing the foreclosure sale is cancelled upon closure of the sale.
6. Junior liens to the foreclosing creditors are discharged by the foreclosure sale to the extent they are not satisfied.
7. Any deficiencies in the amount owed to the foreclosing or junior lienholders become unsecured debt, but only if the original debt was recourse and state law allows.
8. There is no distribution to unsecured creditors.
9. There is no distribution to creditors with security interests solely in other collateral, irrespective of whether a default has occurred on their debt.
10. Any surplus goes back to debtor. Creditors are welcome to try to capture this through the normal collections process.

These rules are more intuitive than they might seem. Problem Set 2.1 goes through a series of foreclosure sales to see how they play out. See if you can figure out who gets what in the foreclosure sale distribution. Mastering this exercise is essential for understanding much of what happens in bankruptcy, which is largely built on a foreclosure sale paradigm.

Problem Set 2.1

(1) Property is being sold by the sheriff in a foreclosure sale. How should the foreclosure sale proceeds be divvied up in the following scenarios? Assume that the sale costs are a meager $100, and that deficiency judgments are possible.

- Sale 1: $1,000 is owed in first lien debt on the collateral. The first lien creditor brings the foreclosure action. The collateral sells for $1,000.
- Sale 2: $1,000 is owed in first lien debt on the collateral. The first lien creditor brings the foreclosure action. The collateral sells for $500.
- Sale 3: $1,000 is owed in first lien debt on the collateral. The first lien creditor brings the foreclosure action. The collateral sells for $2,000.
- Sale 4: $1,000 is owed in first lien debt on the collateral. Another $1,000 is owed in debt secured by a lien on another asset. The first lien creditor brings the foreclosure action. The collateral sells for $2,000.

- Sale 5: $1,000 is owed in first lien debt on the collateral. Another $1,000 is owed in unsecured debt. The first lien creditor brings the foreclosure action. The collateral sells for $2,000.
- Sale 6: $1,000 is owed in first lien debt on the collateral and another $1,000 in second lien debt on the collateral. The first lien creditor brings the foreclosure action. The collateral sells for $700.
- Sale 7: $1,000 is owed to both first and second lien creditors in the collateral. The first lien creditor brings the foreclosure action. The collateral sells for $1,500.
- Sale 8: $1,000 is owed to both first and second lien creditors in the collateral. There is also $1,000 in unsecured debt owed. The first lien creditor brings the foreclosure action. The collateral sells for $2,500.
- Sale 9: $1,000 is owed to both first and second lien creditors in the collateral. Another $1,000 is owed in unsecured debt. The *second* lien creditor brings the foreclosure sale. The collateral sells for $1,500.
- Sale 10: $1,000 is owed to each of first, second, and third lien creditors in the collateral. The second lien creditor brings the foreclosure sale. The collateral sells for $1,500.
- Sale 11: $1,000 is owed to each of first, second, third, and fourth lien creditors in the collateral. The first lien creditor brings the foreclosure action. The collateral sells for $2,500.
- Sale 12: $1,000 is owed to each of first, second, third, and fourth lien creditors in the collateral. The third lien creditor brings the foreclosure action. The collateral sells for $2,500.
- Sale 13: $1,000 is owed to each of first, second, and fourth lien creditors in the collateral. Two other creditors each have a *pari passu* third lien in the collateral. One is owed $750 and the other $250. The second lien creditor brings the foreclosure action. The collateral sells for $1,500.

(2) You are advising a foreclosure sale bidder regarding how much to bid.
- In Sale 11, if the bidder believes the collateral is worth $2,500, what is the most the bidder should be willing to pay? How about if the bidder values the collateral at only $1,500?
- In Sale 12, if the bidder believes the collateral is worth $2,500, what is the most the bidder should be willing to pay? What if the bidder values the collateral at only $1,500?

(3) Which of the creditors with a deficiency in Sale 13 has priority over the other ones? How could that change?

Foreclosure sales operate as a matter of state law. That means that it is not always possible to foreclose in a single sale on assets in multiple states. Likewise, because there are different rules for the foreclosure of real property and personalty, it is difficult, if not impossible to conduct a single foreclosure sale for a combined package of real estate and personalty. Instead, multiple sales must be conducted. This means that state law foreclosure sales are an effective tool for creditors to foreclose on particular assets of the debtor, but not for a general liquidation of the debtor. Such a general liquidation can be conducted through a bulk sale of the debtor's assets, but some states have bulk sale laws requiring that certain notices be provided and for escrow of funds. *See, e.g.,* CAL. COMM. CODE §§ 6101-6111.

D. Security Interest Operation and Terminology

The terminology of liens can be confusing, but some fluency with the terms below is important for being able to speak the language of financial restructuring law.

Liens go under a variety of names, depending on the type of property and how the lien was created. There are voluntary and involuntary liens. Voluntary liens are usually called **mortgages** when they apply to realty and **security interests** when they apply to other types of property. A frequent point of confusion is that colloquially the term "mortgage" is used to refer not just to the lien, but also to the loan associated with the lien. Thus, we say that "there is a mortgage on my home," meaning that the home is *collateral* for a loan, but we can also say that "I'm having trouble paying my mortgage," meaning that the *loan* payments on a debt secured by the home are onerous.

Security interests in personalty are governed primarily by Article 9 of the Uniform Commercial Code; realty mortgages are governed by non-uniform state law; other types of liens exist by state and federal statute, or are created when a judgment creditor levies on property. The document (instrument) creating the security interest is called the **security agreement** for personalty or the **mortgage** or **deed of trust** for realty. The security instrument is distinct from the loan agreement (the **note**), but can be combined into a single document. The security agreement must describe the collateral.

A security agreement/mortgage/deed of trust gives a secured creditor self-help repossession rights against the debtor as soon as it is signed, sufficient value has been exchanged to uphold a simple contract, and the debtor has rights to the collateral. This enforceability is called **attachment**. It does not create priority against other creditors, secured or unsecured, unless it is properly filed in the relevant recording system (a complex and technical topic) or the secured party has possession (a pledge) or control of the collateral (control being for bank accounts primarily).

An entire law school course—secured transactions—covers the highly technical details of how security interests operate. It is impossible to do justice to this complex topic in a couple of pages, but the following section covers the basic ideas; be aware that there are many exceptions not discussed.

A security agreement is filed by submitting a **financing statement** in the proper filing system (usually the secretary of state's office in the relevant state). The financing statement must contain a description of the collateral (which may be broader than in the security agreement, and may cover multiple items of collateral) and some information about the debtor and secured creditor, but nothing about the loan. The debtor must authorize the filing of the financing statement. For mortgages, the mortgage itself is **recorded** in the proper county land office. The various filing systems are searchable, and are presumed to provide constructive notice of consensual liens to other potential creditors. If a financing statement or mortgage is improperly filed such that it doesn't show up in a proper search of the system, the security interest or mortgage is not perfected.

For security interests in personalty, a filing can be done before attachment, and often is, but it must be authorized. (A security agreement authenticated by the debtor is itself authorization for filing the agreement in the recording office. UCC § 9-509(b).) A filing by itself does not create any legal rights. When a security agreement/mortgage has attached and is filed/recorded (or the secured creditor has possession/control), it is **perfected**. **Perfection** requires attachment. For most types of collateral, attachment does not result in perfection, which requires a separate step to be taken.

Generally speaking, priority of a security interest dates from the earlier of filing or perfection. (Mortgage priority dates from recording.) Thus, if a financing statement were filed before attachment, priority would relate back to the date of the financing statement's filing, not the date of attachment. Alternatively, if perfection were achieved prior to a filing by physical possession of the collateral by the creditor, then priority would **relate back** to the date of physical possession. Among perfected security interests and mortgages in the same collateral, priority is generally determined by a **first-in-time, first-in-right** principle. **Unperfected** security interests have lower priority than any perfected security interest.

Involuntary liens are simply called liens, regardless of the type of property to which they apply. Involuntary liens include a wide variety of liens created by statute (such as tax liens and landlords' liens and mechanics' liens), those created by court order (**judicial liens**), and those created when an unsecured creditor levies on a debtor's property (**judgment lien**). Once an involuntary lien is created, it is treated essentially like a voluntary lien.

The priority of involuntary liens among themselves dates from the time of their creation under a first-in-time, first-in-right principle, although state laws may vary regarding exactly what date is to be used in this calculation. The first-in-time, first-in-right principle running from time of creation is also generally true about the relationship between involuntary liens and real estate mortgages. For security interests in personalty, however, which are governed by the UCC, the situation is more complex.

As between consensual security interests in personalty, priority ranks based on the earlier of filing of a financing statement (which can predate the creation of the lien) *or* perfection. UCC § 9-322(a)(1). As between a consensual security interest in personalty and an involuntary lien, however, priority is based on a first-in-time principle using the date of the perfection, rather than the creation or filing, of the security interest. UCC § 9-317(a)(2). This means that a judgment lien has priority over a subsequently perfected security interest.

Security interests cover not only the collateral described in the security agreement, but also any **proceeds** of that collateral, and the proceeds of the proceeds, etc. Proceeds are defined by the UCC as: "whatever is acquired upon the sale, lease, license, exchange or other disposition of collateral" and "whatever is collected on, or distributed on account of, collateral" as well as rights arising out of the collateral, and litigation and insurance claims arising from damage or defect or loss of the collateral. UCC § 9-102(a)(64). For example, a firm holds widgets as inventory. The firm sells the widgets on credit, with payment to follow in 90 days. Thus, the widgets have been exchanged for accounts receivable. The accounts receivable are the proceeds of the widgets. When the accounts receivable are collected, the cash is the proceeds of the accounts receivable. Likewise, if the widgets were destroyed in a fire, but were insured, the insurance claim would be proceeds of the widgets, and the payment on the insurance claim would be proceeds of the insurance claim and hence also of the widgets. All proceeds are automatically perfected for 21 days. Afterwards, perfection may lapse depending on the type of property the proceed is. (This stuff gets quite technical.)

A security interest may also cover collateral acquired after the time it was created (**after-acquired property**). For example, I can grant you a security interest in my Lamborghini and authorize you to file a financing statement against it. There's just one catch: I don't *yet* own a Lamborghini. (*Yet!*) When I do get a Lamborghini, then the security interest will attach and will also be perfected, if you filed properly.

Likewise, if the security interest covers "all vehicles, now owned or hereafter acquired," it will cover not only my current Honda Odyssey minivan, but also the Lamborghini I will buy next week. Thus, additional collateral that meets the collateral description in a security agreement is also after-acquired property. Whether the phrase "now owned or hereafter acquired," or the equivalent is required for a security interest to extend to after acquired property is not settled. The Official Commentary to the UCC punts on the issue:

> Much litigation has arisen over whether a description in a security agreement is sufficient to include after-acquired property if the agreement does not explicitly so provide. The question is one of contract interpretation and is not susceptible to a statutory rule (other than a rule to the effect that it is a question of contract interpretation). Accordingly, this section contains no reference to descriptions of after-acquired property.

UCC § 9-108, Cmt. 3. Thus, context will determine whether after-acquired property is covered by a security interest, but a safe way to ensure that it does is to include the phrase "now owned or hereafter acquired" or the like in the description of the collateral in the security interest.

Similarly, if there is a security interest in the inventory of a firm, the actual goods that make up that inventory are likely to change from day to day. A security interest with an after-acquired property clause will cover the inventory regardless of the changes in its make-up. Collateral can be both proceeds of collateral and after-acquired property; the two are not exclusive categories. For example, using the example from the previous paragraph, if I swap out my Honda Odyssey for a Honda Accord, that Accord is also covered by the security interest as after-acquired property, but it is also covered as proceeds of the Odyssey because it is what I received upon disposition of the Odyssey.

A security interest stays with a property upon disposition unless the disposition was authorized by the secured creditor or in the ordinary course of the debtor's business. UCC § 9-320(a). Perfection of a security interest (but not a real property mortgage) can lapse; security interests must be renewed every five years, but can only be renewed within the six-month renewal window before lapse. UCC § 9-515(a), (d). Once a security interest lapses, there is no way to cure the lapse; the creditor will need to obtain a new security interest, which requires the debtor's consent. *See* UCC § 9-510(c). Mortgages never lapse; they remain on the property until released.

Problem Set 2.2

(1) Manhattan Motors, a manufacturer of high-end sports cars, owes $60 million in 1-year unsecured notes. Manhattan Motors also owes $100 million on a 5-year unsecured balloon loan from Biddle Bros. Bank.

    a. Why should Biddle Bros. be concerned about this situation?

    b. What could Biddle Bros. have done to protect itself?

(2) John Hancock Fine Teas, Inc. is an upscale grocery chain. Hancock funds its operations primarily through a loan from Commonwealth Bancorp. The loan consists of both a $12 million term loan and a $3 million revolving line of credit and is secured by Hancock's inventory. Commonwealth estimates that the inventory is currently worth perhaps $10 million. A recent economic downturn has severely hurt Hancock's sales, and Hancock has told Commonwealth Bancorp that it may not be able to make the interest payment coming due on the loan at the end of next month. Commonwealth estimates that between now and the end of next month, the inventory's value will decline by $4 million through sales and spoilage. Hancock would normally use the revenue from sales (supplemented by a draw on the line of credit if sales are poor) to replenish its inventory.

Hancock has given Commonwealth the contractually required two-weeks advance notice for a draw on the line of credit and is seeking to draw down the whole line. You're advising the loan officer at Commonwealth Bancorp. She's convinced that Hancock is going to fail and wants to do whatever is necessary to limit losses. What do you advise?

(3) Alexander Hamilton & Co., a rum distiller, owes $5 million on a loan from First Federal Bank. The loan is secured by Hamilton's inventory of rum. The inventory would sell for at least $8 million in an arms-length transaction. There is also a $1 million second lien on the inventory that secured a loan from Commonwealth Bancorp. Hamilton has defaulted on the First Federal loan, and First Federal has brought a foreclosure action. You are counsel for First Federal and have been asked for your advice regarding a sale strategy.

    a. How vigorously should First Federal market the sale?

    b. Many of the likely buyers at a sale are liquor distributors. Only the largest distributors are likely to bid on more than a $500,000 lot of rum. Should the inventory be sold in a single sale in bulk or piecemeal in separate sales?

    c. Should First Federal bid at the sale?

(4) Marv's on Addison is a casual dining restaurant. Marv's had a $400,000 unsecured line of credit from Lakeshore Community Bank, but when Marv's business turned down, Lakeshore Community Bank asked Marv's for a security interest. Marv's agreed on the condition that Lakeshore not actually file the security interest with the Secretary of State's office unless Marv's defaulted on the loan. "It's a valid security interest, so if I default, you'll be able to collect without going to court. But as long as the security interest isn't filed, I can take the interest payments as a tax deduction, which will help ensure that I am able to repay the loan in the first place," explained Marv's owner, Marvin Zingerman, to the loan officer at Lakeshore over a complimentary lunch at Marv's.

The loan officer agreed to the deal, and Zingerman executed a security agreement with Lakeshore that pledged the restaurant's equipment and fixtures as collateral to secure the line of credit. Lakeshore failed to file the security interest until after Marv's defaulted to the line of credit. When it did, it discovered that two days after Zingerman had signed the security agreement, he had also taken out a $500,000 loan from Pulaski Savings Bank. The Pulaski loan was also secured by the restaurant's equipment and fixtures, and it had been immediately filed with the Secretary of State's office. What will likely happen if Lakeshore tries to foreclose on the equipment and fixtures, which are worth around $300,000?

(5) Long Shot Finance loaned Julia Dimitriadis $25,000 to purchase Ambulance Chaser, a promising, purebred racing greyhound. The financing statement filed with the Secretary of State described the collateral for the loan as "purebred racing greyhounds, now owned or hereafter acquired." What is the status of Long Shot Finance's collateral if:

    a. Ambulance Chaser wins $10,000 at the next sweeps? UCC § 9-102(a)(64)(B).

    b. Julia uses the $10,000 of winnings to purchase a Vespa 946 scooter? UCC § 9-102(a)(64)(A).

    c. Ambulance Chaser is injured and has to be put down. Julia purchases Jackleg, another purebred racing greyhound?

    d. Julia trades Jackleg for Illegal Beagle, a very successful racing beagle that competes with greyhounds in unsanctioned competitions. UCC § 9-102(a)(64)(A).

    e. Julia buys Pettifogger, a retired purebred racing greyhound, to keep as a pet.

CHAPTER 3

PRIORITY II

I. COVENANTS AND NEGATIVE PLEDGES

Another mode of ensuring priority is to contract against competition for the debtor's assets. Additional debt relative to the same asset base results in diluting the ratio of assets to claims, and thus the dilution of a creditor's claim. The same problem can occur if the asset base is diminished relative to the amount of claims against it. Thus, asset withdrawal is the flip side of claim dilution.[1] Claim dilution involves a growth in the denominator of the asset-to-claim ratio, whereas asset withdrawal results in a reduction of the numerator in the ratio. The impact on a creditor is the same. A simple mechanism for preventing claim dilution and asset withdrawal are contractual covenants that restrict the debtor's ability to incur more debt and remove assets.

A. Debt Limitation Covenants

Debt limitation covenants restrict the debtor's ability to incur additional debt, or to incur additional debt beyond a specified threshold, whether as an absolute amount or, more commonly, as a ratio of net tangible assets to total debt and of earnings to debt service requirements. The following covenant, for example, has a financial debt ("Borrowed Money") to earnings ("EBITDA") ratio requirement:

> **Section 5.03** _Financial Covenant_. The Borrower will maintain, from and after the Closing Date, as of the last day of each fiscal quarter, commencing with the first fiscal quarter ending following the Closing Date, a ratio of Consolidated Debt for Borrowed Money to Consolidated EBITDA [earnings before income, taxes, depreciation, and amortization] of the Borrower and its Subsidiaries for the four quarters then ended of not more than 3.0 to 1.

AT&T Credit Agreement, dated as of Mar. 31, 2011, § 5.03.[2] This sort of debt limitation covenant relates only to voluntary debts—for "Borrowed Money." But involuntary obligations are just as much of a concern. Thus, related to such debt limitation

---

1. A separate, if related concern, is asset substitution, wherein the value of assets does not necessarily change, but the risks entailed by the assets might.
2. The full agreement is available at: http://bit.ly/2Gt5RJ7.

covenants are covenants requiring timely payment of taxes, as unpaid taxes can result in a creation of a tax lien. Likewise, the incurrence of final, non-appealable judgments beyond a specified amount could constitute an event of default.

Note that violation of a debt limitation covenant by itself is only an event of default. Thus, from the same credit agreement:

> **Section 6.01.** *Events of Default.* If any of the following events ("Events of Default") shall occur and be continuing:
>
> . . .
>
> (c) . . . The Borrower shall fail to perform or observe any term, covenant or agreement contained in Section 5.01(d), (e) or (h), 5.02 or 5.03. . . .

AT&T Credit Agreement, dated as of Mar. 31, 2011, § 6.01. That might, in turn, enable acceleration and pursuit of remedies, but it does not avoid the debt incurred in violation of the covenant. In other words, debt limitation covenants do not actually prevent claim dilution, but instead ensure that claim dilution will trigger the creditor's right to pursue its collection remedies.

B. Merger and Dissolution Restriction Covenants

Claim dilution can also occur through a merger. A merger can alter the asset to claim ratio by combining the assets and claim of two (or more entities). Consider, for example, two firms: one with assets of 100 and claims against it of 75, and the other with assets of 100 and claims against it of 25. When combined, they have assets of 200 and claims of 100. The creditors of the first firm benefit from an improved asset-to-claim ratio, but those of the second firm face a diluted ratio. As a result, lenders will often require covenants that restrict the debtor's ability to merge with affiliates or unrelated parties or to dissolve its corporate existence (thereby merging with its parent entity). For example, consider the following anti-dissolution and anti-merger provisions:

> **Section 5.01.** *Affirmative Covenants.* So long as any Advance shall remain unpaid or any Lender shall have any Commitment hereunder, the Borrower will:
>
> . . .
>
> (d) Preservation of Corporate Existence, Etc. Preserve and maintain, and cause each of its Subsidiaries to preserve and maintain, its corporate existence and its material rights (charter and statutory) and franchises. . . .

AT&T Credit Agreement, dated as of Mar. 31, 2011, § 5.01.[3]

> **Section 5.02.** *Negative Covenants.* So long as any Advance shall remain unpaid or any Lender shall have any Commitment hereunder, the Borrower will not:
>
> . . .

---

3. *Id.*

(b) Mergers, Etc. Merge or consolidate with or into, or, directly or indirectly, convey, transfer, lease or otherwise dispose of (whether in one transaction or in a series of transactions) all or substantially all of its assets (whether now owned or hereafter acquired) to, any Person.

AT&T Credit Agreement, dated as of Mar. 31, 2011, § 5.02.[4] Again, a violation of a merger or dissolution restriction covenant will constitute nothing more than an event of default; it does not avoid the merger or dissolution, although a creditor is always entitled to try to seek specific enforcement of the covenant.

C. Dividend, Repurchase, Redemption, and Asset Sale Restriction Covenants

The flip side of claim dilution is asset withdrawal.[5] Claim dilution involves a growth in the denominator of the asset to claim ratio, whereas asset withdrawal results in a reduction of the numerator in the ratio. The impact on a creditor is the same.

Asset withdrawal can occur in several ways. First, assets can be dividended up from a subsidiary to a parent. Second, assets can be used to repurchase equity-holders' equity, which functions much like a dividend. Third, assets can be used to redeem debts. While such redemption reduces both the numerator and denominator in the asset-to-claim ratio, it will reduce it at a 1:1 ratio for the redeemed debt, potentially resulting a lower ratio for the remaining debts. Fourth, assets can simply be sold for less than their value.

Lenders will typically address asset withdrawal risk through covenants that restrict asset sales, dividends, redemptions, and repurchases. For example:

SECTION 4.04. Limitation on Restricted Payments.

(a) The Issuer shall not, and shall not permit any of its Restricted Subsidiaries to, directly or indirectly:

(i) declare or pay any dividend or make any distribution on account of the Issuer's or any of its Restricted Subsidiaries' Equity Interests, including any payment made in connection with any merger, amalgamation or consolidation involving the Issuer . . . ;

(ii) purchase or otherwise acquire or retire for value any Equity Interests of the Issuer or any direct or indirect parent of the Issuer;

(iii) make any principal payment on, or redeem, repurchase, defease or otherwise acquire or retire for value, in each case prior to any scheduled repayment or scheduled maturity, any Subordinated Indebtedness or Long-Term Retained Notes of the Issuer or any of its Restricted Subsidiaries. . . .

Harrah's Operating Company, Inc., Indenture dated as of Dec. 24, 2008, ¶ 4.40.[6]

---

4. *Id.*

5. A separate, if related concern, is asset substitution, wherein the value of assets does not necessarily change, but the risks entailed by the assets might.

6. The full agreement is available at: http://bit.ly/2FV1B7m.

SECTION 4.06. <u>Asset Sales</u>.

(a) The Issuer shall not, and shall not permit any of its Restricted Subsidiaries to, cause or make an Asset Sale, unless . . . the Issuer or any of its Restricted Subsidiaries, as the case may be, receives consideration at the time of such Asset Sale at least equal to the Fair Market Value (as determined in good faith by the Issuer) of the assets sold or otherwise disposed of. . . .

Harrah's Operating Company, Inc., Indenture dated as of Dec. 24, 2008, ¶ 4.40.[7]

D. Negative Pledge Clauses

When a debtor grants a creditor a security interest, the debtor is essentially allowing that creditor to jump ahead in the collection line as to the specified collateral. Not every debtor wants to give out a security interest. The next best thing to being able to jump ahead of others is to make sure that no other creditor can jump ahead of you. As it turns out, this is easier said than done.

The device for preventing other creditors from getting priority is called a **negative pledge**. A negative pledge is a promise not to grant a security interest to someone else. The effect of a negative pledge clause is to forbid anyone else from jumping ahead in line for recovery by obtaining collateral. By itself, a negative pledge clause does not make a creditor first; it only keeps the creditor from becoming second by requiring that the creditor's obligation be "equally and ratably secured." Often negative pledge clauses will be drafted to provide tag-along rights that require the debtor to provide equal priority security to the negative pledge beneficiary in the event that the debtor gives security to another party or is otherwise saddled with a lien:

SECTION 4.12. <u>Liens</u>. (a) The Issuer shall not, and shall not permit any of its Restricted Subsidiaries to, directly or indirectly, create, Incur or suffer to exist (i) any Lien on any asset or property of the Issuer or such Restricted Subsidiary securing Indebtedness unless the Notes are equally and ratably secured with (or on a senior basis to, in the case of obligations subordinated in right of payment to the Notes) the obligations so secured until such time as such obligations are no longer secured by a Lien. . . .

Harrah's Operating Company, Inc., Indenture dated as of Dec. 24, 2008, ¶ 4.12.[8] Note that a negative pledge clause can be drafted to exclude pledges of certain collateral, but allow pledges of other collateral.

The problem with a negative pledge clause is in the remedy for violation. It is simply a contract covenant—just a promise not to do something. A breach of the covenant is nothing more than a breach of contract, which entitles the recipient of the negative pledge to exercise its contract remedies. Absent security, this means suing and proceeding with judicial collection. It does not void the grant of security to another party. Thus, UCC Article 9 provides that "[a]n agreement between the debtor and secured party which prohibits a transfer of the debtor's rights in

---

7. *Id.*
8. *Id.*

collateral or makes the transfer a default does not prevent the transfer from taking effect." UCC § 9-401(b).[9] Likewise, the affirmative promise of tag-along rights does little good if it cannot be specifically enforced. If the debtor files for bankruptcy, all the beneficiary of the negative pledge clause has is a general unsecured claim.

At best, a creditor whose negative pledge clause has been violated can plead for an equitable lien or the equitable subordination of the secured party. An equitable lien is a lien granted by the court on equitable grounds, while equitable subordination would be the demotion in priority of another party on equitable grounds. No court, however, has granted an equitable lien for a violation of a negative pledge clause since the early twentieth century, and there is only one reported case on the issue since. *Hechinger Liquidation Trust v. BankBoston Retail Finance, Inc.*, 2004 U.S. Dist. LEXIS 5537 (D. Del. Mar. 28, 2004), *aff'd*, 147 Fed. Appx. 248 (3d Cir. 2005) (denying equitable lien). The lack of negative pledge clause litigation does not mean that these clauses are ineffective. Indeed, they are quite common in lending documents. They appear to generally be honored, but the lack of recent case law should make creditors pause before relying exclusively on a negative pledge clause to ensure their priority.

II. CONTRACTUAL SUBORDINATION BETWEEN CREDITORS

A. The Legal Status of Subordination Agreements

Yet another way a creditor can obtain priority is by contracting for it with other creditors via **subordination agreements.** These agreements may be direct bilateral agreements between creditors, or may be indirectly achieved through separate, interlocking agreements between different creditors and the debtor. At state law, absent a security interest or other agreement, the priority rule for creditors is essentially the law of the jungle: Whoever wins the race to the courthouse has priority. No state law dictates the order in which a debtor must pay its creditors voluntarily. Fraudulent transfer statutes (discussed in Chapter 8) place some limitations on debtors' transference of assets when insolvent or to frustrate collection attempts, but this is not a priority rule, but rather an anti-priority rule that forces creditors back to the race to the courthouse.

Creditors can, and often will, contract to change priority rules. This is a matter of bargaining among the parties (and few parties would agree to be subordinated absent receiving some sort of tangible value), and is not controlled by anything other than general principles of contract law. Subordination agreements are honored by both UCC Article 9 and the Bankruptcy Code. UCC § 1-310 provides that:

> An obligation may be issued as subordinated to performance of another obligation of the person obligated, or a creditor may subordinate its right to performance of an

---

9. To be sure, this provision only applies to a negative pledge made to a *secured* party, but the same rationale would apply to a negative pledge made to an unsecured party.

obligation by agreement with either the person obligated or another creditor of the person obligated.

Thus, subordination may be established by either the initial terms of a debt or by subsequent contract.[10] Thus, subordination agreements are simply a matter of private contract law.

Obviously, subordination agreements are not possible for involuntary creditors. As Official Comment 2 to UCC § 9-339 notes, however, "[o]nly the person entitled to priority may make such an agreement: a person's rights cannot be adversely affected by an agreement to which the person is not a party." Instead, the only method for a debtor to effectively subordinate involuntary creditors is through the granting of security interests to other creditors. *See* UCC § 9-317(a).

B. Subordination of Payment vs. Subordination of Lien

Although liens help ensure repayment, a lien is not the same thing as a payment. Likewise, priority of liens is not the same as either priority of payment or priority of recoveries. A debtor can choose to pay a junior lienholder before paying a senior lienholder. UCC Article 9, which deals with security interests in personalty, provides that "[t]his article does not preclude subordination by agreement by a person entitled to priority." UCC § 9-339. Moreover, relative maturity dates can also effectively create priority of payment—loans maturing earlier will be paid off before those maturing later, irrespective of lien priority.

All that priority of liens indicates are rights upon the foreclosure of the collateral. Prior to foreclosure, a lien does not create a legal right to payment. Similarly, recoveries can come from things other than voluntary payments by the debtor or foreclosures (e.g., setoff or payments by guarantors). Priority of recoveries is not necessarily the same as priority of voluntary payments or of liens.

Subordination agreements can exist for liens or for payments (or less frequently, recoveries). For example, the Fannie Mae/Freddie Mac Uniform Multistate Subordination Agreement provides for a subordination of a senior mortgage lien to a junior one. It does not provide that the junior mortgagee will be paid before the senior mortgagee, only that it will have a senior lien:

> Subordinating Lender is the owner and holder of the Junior Mortgage and obligations secured by the Junior Mortgage; the Junior Mortgage is a lien on the title to the Property or an interest in that title.

> For value received and to induce the Senior Lender to modify the Original Mortgage, Subordinating Lender unconditionally subordinates its lien on, and all other rights and interests in, the title to the Property resulting from the Junior Mortgage to the lien on, and all other rights and interests in, the title to the Property resulting from the Modified Mortgage. Subordinating Lender agrees that its lien on, and all other

---

10. As we will see in a later chapter, federal bankruptcy law recognizes subordination agreements to the extent they are enforceable under nonbankruptcy law. 11 U.S.C. § 510(a).

rights and interests in, the title to the Property resulting from the Junior Mortgage will remain subordinate to the lien on, and all other rights and interests in, the title to the Property resulting from the Modified Mortgage regardless of any renewal, extension or further modification of the Modified Mortgage.

This Subordination Agreement shall be binding upon the successors and assigns of the Subordinating Lender.

Consider why the priority of liens alone might not suffice for a mortgage lender with a recourse mortgage. What if the collateral home were destroyed by a hurricane and was not insured? (Let's suppose that the casualty insurer claims that the damage was caused by flood, which is excluded from coverage under the insurance policy.) The liens are worthless, as there is nothing to foreclose on. Yet the debt is still owed by the homeowner.

At this point, it is a race to the courthouse. If the senior lender wins, it has no obligation to hand over any of the funds it obtains to the junior, as it had only subordinated its lien, not its right to payment. Yet in spite of this problem, lien subordination will frequently occur without payment subordination. For example, the American Bar Association's Model Intercreditor Agreement,[11] a document designed to be a template for law firms to use, provides as follows:

1.2 No Payment Subordination

The subordination of Liens securing the Second Lien Obligations to Liens securing First Lien Obligations set forth in the preceding section 1.1 affects only the relative priority of those Liens, and does not subordinate the Second Lien Obligations in right of payment to the First Lien Obligations. Nothing in this Agreement will affect the entitlement of any Second Lien Claimholder to receive and retain required payments of interest, principal, and other amounts in respect of a Second Lien Obligation unless the receipt is expressly prohibited by, or results from the Second Lien Claimholder's breach of, this Agreement.

The effect of this clause is that should the liens turn out to be undersecured (or unsecured), then the second lienholders are looking to recover pro rata with the first lienholders in bankruptcy. In other words, there is subordination, but only as long as the basic assumption of security exists.

For an unsecured debt, a subordination of payment will typically suffice. Although it will not prevent the subordinated party from obtaining a senior lien, that lien will be of limited value if the right to payment that it protects is subordinated. Below is an example of a subordination of payment claims.

Subordination of Obligation. The Lender irrevocably agrees that the obligations of the Borrower under the Agreement with respect to the payment of principal and interest are and shall be fully and irrevocably subordinate in right of payment and subject to the prior payment or provision for payment in full of all claims of all other present and future creditors of the Borrower whose claims are not similarly subordinated (claims hereunder shall rank pari passu with claims similarly subordinated)

---

11. Report of the Model First Lien/Second Lien Intercreditor Agreement Task Force, 65 Bus. Law. 809, 820 (2010).

and to claims which are now or hereafter expressly stated in the instruments creating such claims to be senior in right of payment to the claims of the class of this claim arising out of any matter occurring prior to the date on which the Borrower's obligation to make such payment matures consistent with the provisions hereof. In the event of the appointment of a receiver or trustee for the Borrower or in the event of its bankruptcy, insolvency, assignment for the benefit of creditors, reorganization whether or not pursuant to bankruptcy laws, or any other marshaling of the assets and liabilities of the Borrower, the holder hereof shall not be entitled to participate or share, ratably or otherwise, in the distribution of the assets of the Borrower until all claims of all other present and future creditors of the Borrower, whose claims are senior hereto, have been fully satisfied, or adequate provision has been made therefor.

Because subordination agreements are a matter of private law, they can be crafted however the parties want. Subordination can be for only some types of rights and not others, or it can be triggered only upon the occurrence of certain events. For example, a subordination clause might be triggered by the debtor's bankruptcy.[12]

Subordination agreements do not necessarily have to be between creditors, however. They can also be implemented through the debtor. Security interests are perhaps the clearest example of this—by giving security to one creditor, a debtor is necessarily subordinating the claims of other creditors. But this sort of indirect subordination can also occur for unsecured debt, and frequently does for bonds. A bond indenture might provide that the right of payment under the bond is subordinated to the prior payment in full of "all Senior Indebtedness of the Company." The Senior Indebtedness may be defined as including existing obligations *or future* obligations (possibly up to a cap). The effect of this is that there can be "junior debt" without there being any "senior debt" in existence. Similarly, a bond indenture could include covenants prohibiting the debtor from issuing any debt that does not rank *pari passu* with the bonds or that is not subordinated to the bonds. This does not necessarily mean that any such debt will ever be issued. Thus, there can be "senior debt" without there being any "junior debt" in existence. The mere labeling of debt as "senior" or "junior" does not in and of itself indicate that there are any corresponding junior or senior obligations.

The consequences of a poorly drafted subordination agreement can be catastrophic. The result is an inevitable combination of windfalls and forfeitures: Payments can be rerouted to parties that have not bargained for them, thereby depriving other parties of the benefit of their economic bargain.

Subordination agreements are usually interpreted under the **Rule of Explicitness.** This rule means that courts will enforce the subordination agreement only when it is clear and express; ambiguity is to be resolved against subordination. *See, e.g., Chemical Bank v. First Trust, N.A. (In re Southeast Banking Corp.)*, 93 N.Y.2d 178 (N.Y. 1999); *U.S. Bank, N.A. v. T.D. Bank, N.A.*, 569 B.R. 12 (S.D.N.Y. 2017).

What exactly is required for a court to determine that a subordination agreement is sufficiently express? Explicitness is in the eye of the beholder.

---

12. Such an *ipso facto* subordination clause would be enforced in bankruptcy because it does not prejudice the bankruptcy estate.

III. STRUCTURAL PRIORITY

A final way that a creditor can obtain priority is through **structural priority**. Most debtors are not single stand-alone entities. Instead, most firms are structured to involve numerous entities. Assets are partitioned into various units either for the purpose of shielding them from liabilities or for regulatory purposes (some entities may not be permitted to undertake certain activities, for example). In most cases, a firm is part of a corporate family that will at the very least have a parent holding company and a network of subsidiaries.

The basic idea of **structural subordination** is something fundamental to corporate finance: In a liquidation, creditors get paid off before equity. That is to say, creditors of a firm have priority over the firm's shareholders for receiving liquidation proceeds. Outside of a liquidation, priorities are looser. (Indeed, for entities such as sovereign states, which cannot be liquidated, it is not clear what priority really means.) If its debt is not due, the creditor has little ability to prevent a payment to shareholders, such as a dividend, with one important exception: State law universally prohibits insolvent corporations from paying dividends to shareholders. Note, however, that in many states once a dividend is declared (but before it is paid), the shareholders are considered *creditors* for the amount of that dividend.

Consider, then, the application of structural priority to a corporate family. Let's start with a simple two-entity firm consisting of a parent and a subsidiary. The parent holds the equity of the subsidiary, meaning that the parent is the shareholder of the subsidiary. Therefore, in a liquidation of the subsidiary, the parent is junior vis-à-vis the subsidiary's creditors as to the assets of the subsidiary.

The parent itself may have creditors. Their claim on the assets of the subsidiary is only through their claim on the equity of the parent—if the parent is insolvent. If the parent is solvent, its creditors have no generic claim on the assets of the subsidiary. Thus, the creditors of the subsidiary have priority in the assets of the subsidiary over the creditors of the parent.

What if the situation is flipped around? What is the priority of the creditors of the subsidiary in the assets of the parent? None. Because of limited liability, absent unusual circumstances when corporate separateness will be dishonored, the creditors of a subsidiary have no claim on the assets of the parent corporation.

Thus, in Figure 3.1, below, Creditor A is owed $100 by the parent (which has $50 in assets other than its stock in the subsidiary) and Creditor B is owed $100 by the subsidiary (which has $125 in assets). Creditor A will recover $50 from the parent and will have a claim on the parent's equity value in the subsidiary. What is that equity value worth? $25, namely the value of the subsidiary's assets after Creditor B is paid.

Alternatively, in Figure 3.2, below, the parent has assets (other than the subsidiary's stock) worth $125, while the subsidiary has only $50 in assets. Creditor A will recover its full $100 from the parent's assets. Creditor B, however, will recover only $50 from the assets of the subsidiary. Creditor B will have no claim on the parent's assets, even though Creditor B has not been paid in full and the parent has assets remaining. This is the effect of limited liability.

60

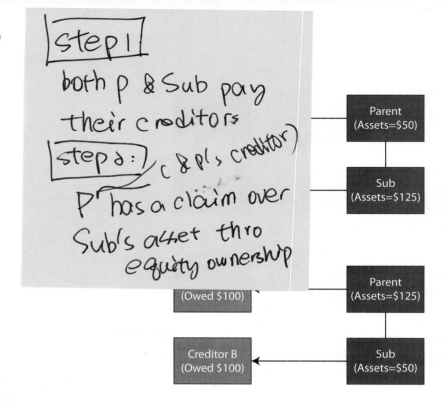

(Owed $100)

Creditor B
(Owed $100)

Parent
(Assets=$50)

Sub
(Assets=$125)

Parent
(Assets=$125)

Sub
(Assets=$50)

Handwritten note:
step 1
both P & Sub pay
their creditors
step 2: (c & P's creditor)
P has a claim over
Sub's asset thro
equity ownership

Just for completeness, let's suppose that the parent is itself the subsidiary of another corporation, so we have grandparent, parent, and child. What's the priority of the creditors of each entity for each entity's assets?

Grandparent: Grandparent's creditors only.
Parent: Parent's creditors first, then Grandparent (and its creditors).
Child: Child's creditors first, then Parent (and its creditors), and then ultimately Grandparent (and its creditors).[13]

Now let's suppose that the parent entity acquires another subsidiary, so that there is now a parent and two sister subsidiaries, X and Y. What is the priority of the creditors of the various entities vis-à-vis the assets of X? X's creditors come first, then the parent and its creditors. Y's creditors have no claim on the assets of X or vice-versa. The parent's creditors have a claim on the assets of both X and Y, but it is junior to that of the direct creditors of X and Y.

We can, then, summarize structural priority in three rules. First, creditors have priority over equityholders in a liquidation. That is why the creditors of a subsidiary have priority over the creditors of the parent in the assets of the subsidiary, because the creditors of the parent can only access the assets of the subsidiary through the

---

13. This situation is a bit trickier, however. If the Parent is sufficiently solvent, then the Grandparent may be able to force the assets of the Child to be dividended up to the Parent and then to it and made available for its creditors without the Parent's creditors being paid first. Thus, the Grandparent's creditors may in fact be able to come before the Parent's in some cases.

Figure 3.3

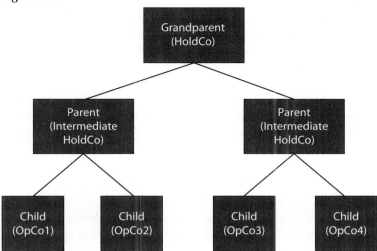

parent company's equity interest in the subsidiary. Second, the creditors of a firm will have no claim against the other assets of the firm's owner. This is the limited liability principle (and there are exceptions that do not concern us here). And third, the creditors of a firm have no claim on the assets of a firm's affiliated corporate sisters.

To see the importance of structural priority, consider the collapse of the insurance company American International Group (AIG) in 2009. AIG, one of the world's largest insurance companies, had entered into lots of swaps in which it assumed the credit risk on debt securities. The swaps were an obligation of AIG, the parent holding company, but most of AIG's assets were not held at the parent holding company level. Instead, they were held by numerous subsidiary insurance companies, which were subject to different state regulation. The parent holding company's main assets were the stock of the subsidiary insurance companies. As the shareholder of the subsidiary insurance companies, the AIG holding company stood in line behind the creditors of those subsidiary insurance companies for their assets. The major creditors of those subsidiary insurance companies were the insurance policyholders. While most policies were not due and owing, state insurance regulators refused to permit the subsidiary insurance companies to upstream cash and other assets to bail out the holding company, as they feared that the subsidiaries would be left insolvent and unable to pay out on their policies. AIG provides an important lesson in what is termed "structural subordination." Lending at the holding company level when the assets are locked up in subsidiaries risks being subordinated to the creditors of the subsidiaries.

Structural priority can obviously be undermined if assets are transferred within the affiliated group, whether by sale or dividend, or if affiliated entities are merged. Thus covenants restricting asset transfers or mergers function to ensure that structural priorities are respected.

IV. GUARANTIES

We've seen that it isn't so easy for an unsecured creditor to get repaid. Debt collection can be slow, costly, and unsuccessful. A determined debtor can often frustrate collection. Collateral might help—it might provide a source for recovery or the threat of repossession might induce voluntary repayment. But what if the collateral is worthless? What if the collateral was a portrait supposedly by Picasso that turns out to be a forgery? What if the collateral has been destroyed? Suppose the collateral was millions of dollars of wine in a cellar that was flooded during a hurricane? Or the collateral was stored in a bank vault at the World Trade Center in September 2001? Collateral can be lost in lots of ways. The basic problem, then, is that even a compliant debtor might not repay a debt, simply because it lacks the assets to do so. Blood can't be squeezed from a stone. So what's a creditor to do?

One solution to the problem of the potentially insolvent debtor is to obtain a guaranty from another entity. The guaranty substitutes the credit of the guarantor for that of the guarantee, or more precisely, adds the creditworthiness of the guarantor to that of the guarantee. Thus, instead of being able to recover solely from the debtor, the creditor can also look to the guarantor for repayment. The whole idea is to have some deeper pockets obligated on the loan. Guaranties, either from third-parties or from affiliates of the debtor, are a seventh way that a creditor can obtain priority. When guaranties are made by affiliates of the debtor, they serve to loosen or supplement structural priority.

Guaranties are common in commercial finance, but there's a good chance that you yourself have been involved in a guaranty transaction at some point in your life. Prior to 2010, the federal government guaranteed repayment of many student loans which were made by private lenders. (Since 2010, the federal government has simply made the loans directly, as it was assuming the credit risk in either case.) There may also have been a "co-signor" on the loan—your parent(s) might have co-signed the loan, making your parent(s) jointly liable on the obligation with you.

Why would a student lender want a co-signor? In some cases it might be because the student cannot be held liable for the debt due to minority. Seventeen-year old college matriculates might only be able to enter into voidable contracts. But more typically, the problem is that a student has few, if any, assets and has limited earning ability, at least for a while. The lender wants a more creditworthy source of repayment. Hence the co-signor.

Notice that there is a subtle, but important distinction between a co-signor and a guarantor. It is the difference between joint liability and secondary liability.[14] If parties are jointly liable, the creditor may pursue either one for repayment of the entire amount, while if there is a primary and secondary liability structure, the

---

14. You might also remember the terms "several liability" and "joint and several liability." With several liability, multiple parties are liable, but only for their appropriate share of the total liability. With joint and several liability, the creditor may recover from any of the parties the entire extent of the liability, leaving the liable parties to sort out between themselves the appropriate shares of the liability.

creditor must first unsuccessfully pursue the party that is primarily liable before pursuing the party that is secondarily liable. This means that the party that is secondarily liable has contingent liability, as it is contingent on the primarily liable party not repaying. The primary versus secondary liability distinction is captured by the concept of **guaranties of payment** and **guaranties of collection.** A guaranty of payment does not require the creditor to first attempt to recover from the obligor; a guaranty of collection requires the creditor to first attempt to recover from the obligor unless such attempt would be futile. Unless specified, a guaranty is usually treated as a guaranty of payment, not of collection. *See* UCC § 3-419(d).

You might have noticed that a guaranty looks an awful lot like insurance. Economically they are indistinguishable—a guarantee is a type of credit insurance. Critically, however, only some types of insurance and some insurers are regulated. Firms that issue guaranties as their business, such as "monoline" bond insurers like ACA, Ambac, FGIC, MBIA, and Syncora, or mortgage insurers, such as Genworth, MGIC, Radian, and United Guaranty (a subsidiary of AIG), are all regulated entities. Likewise, the federal government–sponsored entities Fannie Mae and Freddie Mac, which guarantee mortgage bonds they have issued, are regulated. But if IBM wants to issue a guaranty for one of its subsidiaries, it will not fall within state insurance regulation because IBM is not in the business of insurance.

So what's a guaranty worth? The value of a guaranty really depends on the creditworthiness of the guarantor. A guaranty substitutes the credit of the guarantor for that of the guarantee, or more precisely, adds the creditworthiness of the guarantor to that of the guarantee. But if the guarantor is insolvent, the guaranty isn't worth very much. Put another way, a guaranty does not eliminate credit risk. This was a lesson brought home very clearly during the financial crisis in the fall of 2008. Monoline bond insurers had guaranteed large amounts of mortgage-backed securities (MBS), essentially bonds backed by payments from pools of mortgages. These firms also guaranteed many municipal bonds. As losses mounted on MBS, the monoline insurers teetered or became insolvent. The result was to render their guaranties of municipal bonds of little value, which in turn reduced the value of those municipal bonds.

A. Standby Letters of Credit

Guaranties can be either from unrelated third parties or from affiliates of a debtor. A particular type of third-party guaranty is the standby **letter of credit.** There are two types of letters of credit: commercial (or documentary) and standby. Both types of letters of credit are payment obligations issued to beneficiaries by banks on behalf of third parties, known as applicants or account parties. **Commercial (or documentary) letters of credit** are used as payment mechanisms, primarily in international transactions, where they are used somewhat like cashier's checks, so that the payee is assuming the payment risk of a domestic bank rather than of a foreign purchaser.

A standby letter of credit, as its name implies, is also a payment mechanism, but it is a secondary, rather than primary, payment mechanism. A standby letter of credit makes the issuing bank the functional absolute guarantor of the applicant's *contingent .*

payment obligation. If the applicant itself fails to pay the beneficiary, then the beneficiary can draw down the letter of credit from the bank. The bank is then subrogated to the rights of the beneficiary and can seek indemnification from the applicant. Typically, the bank takes a security interest in the property of the applicant to protect its contingent creditor status. If the beneficiary draws on the letter of credit, then the bank becomes a secured creditor of the applicant. (The paperwork necessary to create the security interest can be pre-filed.)

Standby letters of credit are commonly used as security deposits for leases, as collateral for commercial mortgage debt, and as earnest money deposits for real estate purchase transactions. They are also often provided to municipalities as security for bonding obligations for municipal contracts. Domestic standby letters of credit are governed by Article 5 of the Uniform Commercial Code. International standby letter of credit practice is summarized by the International Chamber of Commerce's International Standby Practices (ISP98).

A critical feature of standby letters of credit is their legal treatment. The standby letter of credit consists of three legal relationships: (1) between the applicant and the issuing bank, (2) between the issuing bank and the beneficiary, and (3) between the applicant and the beneficiary. Part of what makes standby letters of credit popular is that these three relationships are treated as entirely separate and independent under what is called the "doctrine of independence." This doctrine puts forth a useful legal fiction, namely that each relationship is a separate contract, and while they support each other, each is an independent transaction. The purpose of this is to allow the beneficiary to draw the funds without having to obtain a judgment, which allows the standby letter of credit to function as a fast and certain payment device. Thus, if an applicant has various claims or defenses against a beneficiary, the applicant cannot use those claims or defenses to prevent the issuing bank from paying the beneficiary, provided that the beneficiary has satisfied the issuing bank's requirements for payment. Similarly, as we shall see, if the applicant were to file for bankruptcy, that will not prevent the issuing bank from paying the beneficiary.

Of course, a standby letter of credit is only as valuable as the creditworthiness of the issuing bank. If the issuing bank fails, the beneficiary of the standby letter of credit has a claim in the bank's receivership, but it is an unsecured claim that is subrogated to the claims of insured depositors, and unlikely to result in a full recovery.

B. Guaranties Within the Corporate Family

A guaranty can be from an unrelated third party, as with a standby letter of credit or a credit default swap (discussed in Chapter 6). But they can also be provided by affiliates of the debtor. Affiliate guaranties provide a way for firms to selectively alter structural priority. Guaranties can run upstream, downstream, or cross-stream. That is, a subsidiary can guaranty a parent, a parent can guaranty a subsidiary, or affiliates can guaranty each other. An **upstream guaranty** is one made from a subsidiary of an obligation of its parent company, while a **downstream guaranty** is made by a parent or owner of the obligor. A guaranty between affiliates is called a **cross-stream guaranty**. Thus, a subsidiary's guaranty of a particular debt of the parent makes that creditor of the parent a direct creditor also of the subsidiary, which it would not otherwise be. The effect is to make the creditor of the parent of equal priority to the creditors of the subsidiary.

Consider the effect on our structural subordination example. In Figure 3.1, above, Creditor A recovered $50 from the parent and then the parent's $25 of equity in the subsidiary for a maximum total of $75. With an upstream guaranty (Figure 3.4, below), Creditor A not only has first dibs on the parent's assets ($50 plus the $25 equity value of the sub), but also has equal rights to the assets of the sub ($125) as Creditor B. Thus, Creditor A could conceivably recover in full with the upstream guaranty.

Likewise, in Figure 3.2, above, Creditor A recovered in full from the assets of the parent, while Creditor B's recovery was capped at the $50 of the subsidiary's assets, even though the parent still had assets. Limited liability protected the parent's assets from Creditor B. With a downstream guaranty (Figure 3.5, below), Creditor B not only has first dibs on the subsidiary's assets, but also has equal rights in the parent's assets to Creditor A. Thus, Creditor B could conceivably recover in full with the downstream guaranty.

What makes structural subordination tricky in practice is that there are frequently intercompany guaranties within a corporate structure. These guaranties level the priority playing field, but only as to the particular creditors who have received the guaranties. Thus, imagine a firm X, that has two subsidiaries, Y and Z. Z has two creditors, #1 and #2. Y has guarantied Z's debt to #1. In this situation, creditor #1 has a claim on Z's assets. It also has a claim in Y's assets, along with Y's other creditors. Creditor #1 has no claim on X's assets. Creditor #2 has no claim on

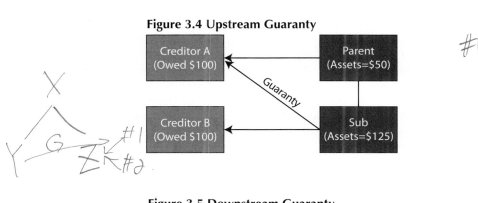

Figure 3.4 Upstream Guaranty

Figure 3.5 Downstream Guaranty

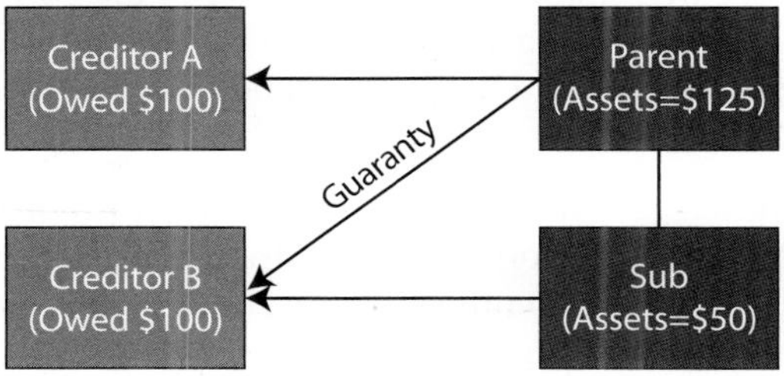

the assets of *Y*, however, or of *X*. Creditor #1's claim on the assets of both *Y* and *Z* and Creditor #2's claim on the assets of *Z* are both senior to that of the parent, *X*, and its creditors.

Different types of debt are typically incurred at different levels of the corporate structure. Financial debt, such as loans and bonds, is usually incurred at the parent holding company level and guaranteed by key (or all) subsidiaries. Trade and tort debt, however, is usually incurred at the subsidiary level. This means that financial creditors usually have a direct claim on all or almost all of the entities in the corporate family, while trade and tort creditors have a claim against only a single entity. Public equity is usually only at the holding company level; the rest of the equity is held within the firm. Further complicating the picture is the reality that there are often intra-firm debts. One entity might own the real estate, while another performs the operations. The OpCo will rent from the RealtyCo, creating a credit-debtor relationship *within* the firm. In short order, the financial relationships in the firm can get quite complicated.

While guaranties can be used to selectively alter priority, they are also used to make entire corporate families effectively the borrowers for certain loans. Typically the guaranties are not simply unsecured obligations, but are instead secured by the assets of the guarantor. The result is that all or virtually all of the assets of a corporate family can be locked up as collateral securing a loan made to one member of the corporate family. As Professor William Widen explains:

> [I]n many cases, the real "debtor" is not a single legal entity but instead is a "borrowing group" consisting of multiple legal entities that are members of a consolidated family of companies. . . .
>
> The concept of a "borrowing group" is important to understand. A paradigmatic corporate structure starts with a top-tier holding company owned by multiple investors. In turn, this top-tier holding company owns 100% of a second holding company. This second holding company owns multiple subsidiaries. The lending syndicate makes loans to the second holding company as the "primary debtor." The top tier holding company provides a downstream guarantee of the loans. The subsidiaries provide upstream guarantees of the loans. The primary debtor borrows money from the [lender] and transfers the loan proceeds to those members of the consolidated group that need funds. Typically, the primary debtor transfers funds to other legal entities in the group by making inter-company advances or loans, though sometimes transfers may be made as capital contributions. This system of guarantees and advances breaks down the boundaries of limited liability created by the myriad legal entities in a consolidated group of companies and creates a single economic unit. In a secured financing, each member of the borrowing group (other than the borrower) grants a security interest in its assets to secure repayment of its guarantee. The borrower grants a security interest in its assets to secure directly repayment of the loans.
>
> In substance, the lend[er] sees itself as making loans to the borrowing group rather than to individual legal entities. Ideally, this synthetically created "group borrower" is co-extensive with all the legal entities whose results are reported in the consolidated financial statements of the top tier holding company.

Guaranties are a central part of commercial lending that work hand-in-glove with security interests to expand lenders' prospects of repayment. Such guaranties are only as valuable as they are enforceable. As we will see, there are circumstances in which creditors with valid guaranties will nonetheless be enjoined from pursuing guarantors.

Affiliate guaranties work with corporate family webs to effectuate selective asset partitioning. Asset partitioning can have important tax and liability limitation consequences: While limited liability limits an equityholder's potential liability to creditors, asset partitioning by placing separate assets into separate corporate entities limits the assets that are available to each entity's creditors. The creditors can only look to recover from the assets of a debtor, not from the debtor's parents or affiliates. Affiliate guaranties create exceptions to asset partitioning through corporate structures. This enables contractual creditors to potentially have a greater pool for recovery than involuntary creditors.

What we have seen in this chapter is that creditors have a very strong incentive to get some sort of enhanced repayment rights relative to other creditors because of the simple problem that a debtor might not have enough assets to repay all of its creditors. Sometimes this is as simple as ensuring that one's debt comes due before that of other creditors. Even this may not be enough, however, because unsecured creditors face a slow and costly race to the courthouse with uncertain prospects of collection. Accordingly, creditors use structural priority and affiliate guaranties to attempt to gain priority over other creditors. Secured creditors obtain enhanced repayment rights vis-à-vis the debtor, while guaranteed creditors obtain enhanced repayment rights vis-à-vis third-party guarantors. And creditors with negative pledge and subordination clauses attempt to ensure that no one else gets enhanced rights vis-à-vis them, while creditors use debt and merger covenants to limit the extent of competition and sale and dividend restrictions to limit the ability of their debtors to reduce the pool of assets available for repaying them and to frustrate structural priority.

These different methods of obtaining priority operate along different dimensions and do not all interlock. A creditor might have contractual liquidation priority, but be temporally subordinated, or it might be structurally subordinated, but be protected by a negative pledge clause against asset-based claims. These different types of priority also operate differently in different contexts. In a liquidation, for example, temporal priority and covenant-based priorities are meaningless, but in the ordinary course of business, they are quite powerful. As we will see in subsequent chapters, this difference is significant in bankruptcy because bankruptcy is largely based on a liquidation paradigm.

Problem Set 3

(1) Aaron Burr contracted to sell Thomas Jefferson an antique statue for $200,000. It turns out that the statue Burr delivered is not in fact antique, but merely made to look so. Jefferson sued Burr for breach of contract and fraud and wins a $200,000 judgment.

getting judgment ≠ getting paid

Burr has refused to pay the judgment. How can Jefferson collect? What sort of information would Jefferson want to know to facilitate his collection efforts?

(2) Robert Morris purchased a new car for $35,000. Morris borrowed $30,000 of the money from Hancock Auto Finance Corp. and pledged the car as security for the loan. If Morris fails to make his monthly payments on the loan, how may Hancock Auto Finance Corp. collect?

(3) George Washington loves his home at Mt. Vernon, but when his neighbor's parcel, Mt. Alban, comes on the market, Washington cannot resist the opportunity to expand his estate. Washington does not have enough ready cash, so he borrows $4 million from his open-pocketed friend Alexander Hamilton on a non-recourse basis, and pledges Mt. Alban as collateral for the loan. Mt. Vernon is worth $10 million, and Mt. Alban is worth only $2 million to anyone else but Washington. Washington's other assets are worth $5 million. When Washington defaults on the loan, how may Hamilton collect?

(4) Continental Enterprises borrowed $100 million from Franklin Financial. The loan is evidenced by an unsecured note. The note includes the following clause:

> *Negative Pledge.* Continental will not create or permit to subsist any Encumbrance on the whole or any part of its present or future Assets without effectively providing that the Note shall be secured equally and ratably with (or prior to) such secured indebtedness, so long as such secured indebtedness shall be so secured.

Capitalized terms are all defined elsewhere in the note, with "Assets" defined as virtually all of Continental's assets. Continental subsequently borrows $75 million on a secured basis from Banque Rochambeau, secured by Continental's equipment and accounts receivable. What are Franklin Financial's rights?

(5) John Adams is a wealthy real estate developer whose firm, Upp & Adams LLC, is building the Custom House Hotel in Washington, D.C. The hotel, when completed, will probably be worth around $300 million. Upp & Adams wants to borrow $250 million for the construction of the Custom House Hotel from First Federal Loan & Trust. The project looks like a good one—if it is completed. Until the hotel is finished, its value will be much less than $300 million. How can First Federalist protect itself until the hotel is completed?

(6) Franklin Financial and Southern State Bank have each loaned $100 million to Delaware Design. Both loans are secured by substantially all of Delaware Design's assets. Franklin Financial has a first lien, and Southern State Bank has a second lien. Last month, Delaware Design paid off the Southern State Bank loan in full, but failed to pay First Franklin its monthly payment.

   a. What are Franklin Financial's rights vis-à-vis Southern State Bank?
   b. What are Franklin Financial's rights vis-à-vis Delaware Design?

(7) Franklin Financial and Susquehanna State Bank have each loaned $100 million to Mystic Machine Tools. Both loans are secured by substantially all of Mystic's assets. Franklin Financial has a first lien, and Susquehanna State Bank has a second lien. Susquehanna State Bank has also agreed to subordinate its right to payment of principal to Franklin Financial until Franklin Financial has been paid in full. Last month, Mystic paid Susquehanna State Bank $40 million, but paid Franklin Financial nothing. At the time, there was still $30 million owing on the Franklin Financial loan.

> **a.** What are Franklin Financial's rights vis-à-vis Susquehanna State Bank?
> **b.** What are Franklin Financial's rights vis-à-vis Mystic?

(8) Samuel Adams & Sons Inc. (SAS) is the parent company of Malting, Inc. (a malt maker), Brewing, Inc. (a brewery), and Samuel Adams Editions, LLC) (a publishing house). Malting's assets are worth $60 million, Brewing's assets are worth $90 million, and Edition's assets are worth $20 million. SAS's assets consist of $10 million in cash and the stock of the subsidiaries.

Knox Bank has loaned $50 million to SAS on an unsecured basis. Revere Frères has loaned $70 million to Brewing, Inc., secured by a first lien on all of the brewery's assets. Joseph Warren & Co. has loaned $25 million to Brewing, Inc., secured by a second lien on all of the brewery's assets. Brewing, Inc. owes a $5 million tort judgment to John Parker, who was seriously poisoned by a bad case of Brewing Inc.'s swill. Parker has not yet executed on the judgment. Thomas Hutchinson has a $10 million tort judgment against Samuel Adams Editions for defamation. Hutchinson has executed on the judgment and obtained a judgment lien, but no sale has yet been conducted.

> **a.** When Hutchinson's execution sale is conducted, what is the distribution of the sale proceeds?
> **b.** If Brewing, Inc. were to liquidate, what would be the distribution of funds?
> **c.** Suppose that Joseph Warren & Co.'s loan is guaranteed by the SAS. Does that change your answers to question (b)?
> **d.** If SAS liquidated, what will be the distribution of funds?
> **e.** Suppose that Joseph Warren & Co.'s loan to Brewing is guaranteed by SAS and is secured not only by a second lien on Brewing, Inc.'s assets, but also by a first lien on SAS's assets. Does that change your answers to question (d)?

(9) Clarion Entertainment, Inc., is the holding company for a firm that owns radio stations across the Untied States. Clarion is negotiating a $1 billion loan from your client, Banque Lafayette. Clarion has insisted that the loan be guaranteed by only some, but not all of its subsidiaries. What concerns does this structure raise for you and what provisions do you want in the loan to address them?

• priority of payment vs collection.

CHAPTER 4

EQUITY AND BONDS

Before diving into the depths of financial restructuring, it is necessary to have an understanding of the cast of characters that appear in modern commercial finance, both in terms of institutions and instruments. Firms have a variety of stakeholders. Some of them are undoubtedly familiar, others, perhaps less so. This chapter provides an overview of the cast of characters that we'll see, but it focuses on bonds, which are one of the chief financing structures for larger firms. The following two chapters cover syndicated loans and securitizations and derivatives, which are some of the other common financing techniques for large businesses.

I. EQUITY

All firms have some sort of equityholder. The precise name of these equityholders depends on the form of corporate organization: shareholders (corporations), partners (partnerships), members (limited liability companies or LLCs), or (rarely) proprietors (sole proprietorships). Some firms have only one type of equityholder. Others may have multiple classes of equity with different rights.

The easiest way to understand equity is in comparison to debt. Debt is a fixed claim against a firm—if a firm owes $100 of debt, the amount owed does not change depending on the firm's performance. This means that a creditor has limited upside and limited downside exposure to the debtor firm's performance. If the debtor firm does well, it increases the likelihood that the creditor will be repaid, but the creditor will never be repaid more than the fixed amount for which it has contracted. Likewise, if the debtor firm does poorly, it decreases the likelihood of repayment, but the amount of the obligation does not change. Because the amount of debt obligations are not affected by the marginal performance of the debtor firm, creditors do not have any inherent governance rights; absent contractual agreement, creditors have no authority for telling a debtor firm how to operate. Voluntary creditors will sometimes contract for governance rights to limit the riskiness of the debtor's business so as to increase the likelihood of repayment, but such governance rights are not an essential feature of debt.

In contrast to debt, equity is not a fixed claim on a firm, but a claim on the residual value of the firm after debts have been paid. This means that the value of equity is closely tied to a firm's performance. If a firm is more likely to be able to pay off its obligations, that means that it is more likely to have value left over for equityholders, and vice-versa. Most businesses operate as limited liability entities, meaning that by law equityholders have no liability for the business's debts beyond whatever they paid to acquire their equity interests. This means that equityholders have limited downside exposure to a firm's performance, but unlimited upside benefits. Because equityholders have the residual interest in the firm, they are the ones vested with governance rights—they are the ones most immediately affected by the riskiness of the firm's business strategy. These governance rights can be limited by contract, however. For a corporation, these rights are exercised indirectly: The equityholders elect the corporation's board of directors, and the directors appoint the corporation's officers.

Not all equityholders necessarily have governance rights (or the same governance rights). Some firms with multiple classes of equity have non-voting equity; that is, equity with dividend payment or liquidation rights, but not governance rights. For example, a firm might have both common and preferred stock, with the preferred stock having some sort of priority rights relative to the common stock in the case of dividends or liquidation. While preferred stock can have some debt-like characteristics, equity interests of any sort do not have an absolute right to payment; they cannot obtain a judgment and force payment from a firm simply because they have not been paid.[1]

Firms don't run themselves. Someone must make decisions and govern a firm. At state law, firm governance structure is clear enough. In a corporation, the shareholders elect the directors, and the directors appoint the officers. Typically, the officers handle the day-to-day affairs of the firm, while the directors provide directional supervision and attend to major transactions.

At state law, the directors and officers both normally owe fiduciary duties—a duty of undivided loyalty and a duty of care—to the shareholders, and controlling shareholders owe duties to minority shareholders and the firm. *See, e.g., Ivanhoe Partners v. Newmont Mining Corp.*, 535 A.2d 1334 (Del. 1987); *Citron v. Fairchild Camera & Instrument Corp.*, 569 A.2d 53 (Del. 1989); *Kahn v. Lynch Communication Sys., Inc.*, 638 A.2d 1110 (Del. 1994); *Gantler v. Stephens*, 965 A.2d 695, 708-709 & n.37 (Del. 2009) (extending duties to officers). Under Delaware corporate law—the state law governing many of the largest public corporations—when a firm is in financial difficulty, directors may, but are not required to, consider the interests of creditors in their decision-making. *Credit Lyonnais Nederland, N.V. v. Pathe Communications Corp.*, 1991 WL 277613 (Del. Ch. 1991).

---

1. Once a dividend has been declared, state law is likely to treat the right to the declared but unpaid dividend as a debt. Such a declared but unpaid dividend debt is a separate right from the rights that go with the equity.

Directors do not, however, owe fiduciary duties to creditors, even if the firm is insolvent and creditors will end up with the residual value of the firm. *North American Catholic Educational Programming Foundation, Inc. v. Gheewalla*, 930 A.2d 92 (Del. 2006). Like shareholders, however, creditors may bring derivative suits—that is, suits brought on behalf of the corporation rather than directly—against directors for failing to fulfill their fiduciary duties to the corporation. *Id.* A derivative suit has procedural requirements that do not exist for direct suits.

This rule applies only to corporations under Delaware law. It does not apply to LLCs, where creditors have no right to bring a derivative action. *CML V, LLC v. Bax*, 2011 Del. LEXIS 480 (Del. Sept. 2, 2011). Presumably, creditors of a partnership are also prohibited from bringing derivative suits given similar language in the Delaware partnership statute to the LLC statute at issue in *CML V, LLC*. It is not clear whether *Credit Lyonnais* flexibility applies for partnerships or LLCs.

The key takeaway here is that at state law a firm's management owes fiduciary duties to the firm's shareholders, not to creditors. The firm is not managed for its creditors, which means that the firm's management is supposed to pursue strategies that benefit equityholders, even if unfavorable to creditors.

Let's consider what this all means by imagining three firms with different balance sheets. All three firms, *A*, *B*, and *C*, have assets of $100. Firm *A* has no debt, so its equity value is $100. Firm *B* has $50 in debt, so its equity value is $50. And Firm *C* has $90 in debt, so its equity value is $10.

If the value of the firms' assets increases to $120, then the value of the equity in Firm *A* has increased by 20 percent, while the value of the equity in Firms *B* and *C* has increased by 40 percent and 200 percent respectively.

In contrast, if the value of the firms' assets decreases to $80, Firm *A* is still solvent on a balance sheet basis, as its assets are greater than its liabilities, and its equity value has declined to $80, a 20 percent decline. Firm *B* is also still solvent, but its equity value is now $30, a decline of 40 percent. Firm *C*, however, is insolvent, as its liabilities exceed its assets. But because of limited liability, the equityholders of Firm *C* have only lost $10. Thus, we see that equityholders face asymmetric upside and downside risk from a firm's exposure.

What this all means is that creditors and equityholders have different incentives in terms of the governance of firms. Creditors generally want firms to pursue less risky business strategies, because they have no upside, but have potential downside, while equityholders want firms to take on more risk because they have unlimited upside and limited downside exposure. Given that governance rights rest with equityholders in the first instance and that management owes fiduciary duties to equityholders, not creditors, how can creditors control risk?

Creditors have several tools, namely pricing, covenants (such as we saw in the previous chapter), and express governance rights, such as veto power over certain transactions. State law also enables creditors to unwind certain transactions undertaken by debtors. But a creditor's ultimate protection is in having priority in terms of being able to collect if the debtor will not willingly pay.

II. NON-FINANCIAL CREDITORS

Firms have a variety of creditors. Some are financial creditors who have loaned firms money. Others are non-financial creditors who extend other forms of value to firms. There are several major types of non-financial creditors: employees, vendors, landlords and lessors, bailees and consignors, tax authorities, and tort creditors.

Employees are not usually paid in advance. Instead, they typically provide services to the firm and then are paid on a weekly, biweekly, or monthly basis. Employees are virtually always unsecured creditors.

Firms also rely on vendors to supply goods and services. These can range from the suppliers of raw materials and parts, to providers of utilities, to providers of information technology services, to the janitorial and landscaping services, to outside legal counsel, accountants, and financial advisors. Vendors may also include affiliates of a firm: A subsidiary may supply parts to a parent, for example.

Vendors do not typically contract on a cash-only basis, although there are exceptions, such as law firms that work on advances or retainer. Generally, vendors extend **trade credit** to the firm by providing goods and services on a deferred payment basis. For example, vendors may expect payment on "net 30" or "net 60" terms, meaning the total amount of an invoice is due 30 or 60 days after receipt of invoice. Some vendors, such as suppliers of raw materials and parts, recognize that their buyers are converting their goods into finished products to be sold and that they are likely to be repaid from the proceeds of the buyer's sales. In these cases, longer trade credit terms, such as 90, 120, or 180 days, may prevail. In virtually all cases, these vendors are supplying unsecured credit, although they may be able to obtain statutory liens in certain situations. Moreover, an unpaid vendor can obtain a judgment and then get a judgment lien after executing on the debtor's property.

A particularly important group of vendors are landlords and lessors. Landlords and lessors are usually not formally secured creditors, but functionally they are: If they are not paid, they can evict the debtor or reclaim the leased property. Commercial lessees lack the myriad statutory protections available to residential lessees. As with other types of vendors, landlords and lessors may be affiliated with the lessee.

Some firms hold goods for others as bailees or consignees. A bailee—such as a parking valet or a shipping company—holds goods for another and has a responsibility to care for those goods and return those specific goods. Title to the bailment remains with the bailor, and a bailor has a right to demand the return of its specific bailment. If the bailee has lost the bailment, however, the bailor is just a regular unsecured tort creditor.

A consignee holds the goods of another for sale. While consignment stores probably come to mind, a great deal of the food sold at supermarkets is actually sold on consignment—the supermarket is basically renting shelf space. Title to consigned goods remains with the consignor until the goods are sold or used. A consignment functions much like a security interest—if the consignor has not taken the necessary steps, its interest in the consigned goods could be junior to that of various lienholders, such as those with liens covering the seller's inventory, or a bankruptcy trustee.

Firms also often have involuntary creditors: tax authorities and tort creditors. Whereas other creditors can to various degrees bargain over the terms under which they extend credit, tax authorities and tort creditors have no choice in extending credit or in the terms on which it is extended. These creditors are typically unsecured, but can obtain liens on a debtor's assets.

We'll see all these different types of non-financial creditors throughout this book. Their prominence will vary from case to case, and we'll consider their incentives when dealing with a defaulted firm more closely in later chapters.

III. FINANCIAL CREDITORS

Most firms have **financial creditors** who have extended debt financing to the firm. This financing comes in four main forms: loans (traditional, syndicated, and participated); bonds; securitization; and derivatives. A goal of this chapter is to familiarize you with these financing methods.

A. Simple Bank Loans

Perhaps the simplest type of financing is a traditional bank loan: The borrower borrows money from a bank. For example, John Hancock might borrow $10 million from Franklin State Bank. This loan is a direct, bilateral contract. It might be a **term loan** with a stated maturity date, or it might be a **revolving line of credit** that is repeatedly drawn down and repaid, like a credit card. The loan is likely collateralized, but it need not be. The particular terms of the loan—its pricing and the various representations, warranties, and covenants that protect the lender's ability to be repaid—are determined by a direct bilateral negotiation between the borrower and the lender.

Such simple bank loans still exist, but they are not the norm for larger enterprises. Instead, larger financings tend to involve debt securities, loan syndications and participations, securitization, and/or repos and derivatives. This chapter focuses on debt securities, which we will generally refer to as bonds. The next chapter covers loan syndications and participations, and the following one covers securitization, repos, and derivatives.

B. Debt Securities

Another common way of financing is through the issuance of debt securities. These debt securities go under various names—notes, debentures, or bonds—but the names have no particular legal significance.[2] All these debt securities are at

---

2. The terminology of bonds and debentures is not standardized. *See* Note, *Debenture Bond*, 24 Harv. L. Rev. 389 n.1 (1911). In American usage, the term "bond" is often used for *all* publicly issued debt securities, with "debenture" (pronounced either de-BEN-chur or DE-ben-chur) referring to unsecured debt securities and "bond" referring to secured debt securities. Most publicly issued debt securities are unsecured. Be aware that the terminology is often reversed in UK and Canadian usage.

core is a promise to repay money under specified terms. The securities are then sold, either through a private placement or offered to the public at large. The sale is typically not conducted directly by the issuer, but instead by investment banks that act as **underwriters** that help market the sale and often act as the initial purchasers of the securities, which they immediately resell as part of the offering.

The major distinction between debt securities and a simple bank loan is that debt securities enable financing to come from multiple investors, rather than from a single investor. Thus, if a firm issues $100 million in bonds, the bonds could be bought by 100 different investors; no single investor has to buy the entire $100 million issue. With a traditional single-lender bank loan, one bank would make the entire loan. We will see presently that a bank loan can in fact be funded by multiple investors, through what are known as syndications and participations, which end up looking very similar to debt securities. Multi-investor funding is the norm for larger bank loans, but those are more complex transactions than the plain vanilla bank loan.

Because debt securities are not funded by a single investor, but instead are sold into the market, the terms of debt securities are not typically negotiated between the issuer and the investors. Instead, the terms—the pricing and the representations, warranties, and covenants that protect the investors' ability to be repaid—are determined by the issuer (borrower) of the securities based on market conditions and what the issuer's financial advisors and underwriters think is necessary to make the security saleable at the desired price. Essentially a debt security is a unilateral offer, given on a first-come, first-served basis, rather than a bilaterally negotiated contract. This is a major distinction between a debt security and a traditional bank loan, in which the terms are the product of negotiation between the lender and the borrower.

For a debt security, the rights of all the investors (let's call them bondholders for simplicity) are determined by a single contract commonly called an **indenture**.[3] Because the indenture is a single contract that governs the rights of multiple bondholders, any modification of the indenture affects the holders of all outstanding bonds identically. Often a single indenture is used for issuance of multiple series of securities.

Depending on the specifics of the debt security, all of the investors may have identical, pro rata rights, or their rights may be **structured** by the indenture so that some have priority over others in regards to receiving certain payments or otherwise. Securities in which the rights are structured are called "**structured securities**," although the term is often used imprecisely. The different groupings of bondholders in a structured security are variously known as classes, series, or tranches.

The presence of multiple investors in a debt securities issuance can complicate efforts to restructure the security because of intercreditor coordination problems. This problem is somewhat ameliorated by the presence of a trustee who represents

---

3. The name derives from the medieval practice of writing two copies of a contract on a single piece of parchment and then cutting a tooth-like zig-zag between them so as to make it clear that they are a matched set of counterparts.

the bondholders and can take action to enforce the indenture independent of the bondholders. Because any recoveries under the indenture would be shared ratably among the bondholders, there is a free-riding problem that discourages individual bondholders from taking action to enforce the indenture. The use of a common agent charged with acting in the interests of the bondholders is the solution to this free-riding problem. The agent is called an **indenture trustee,** and is virtually always a bank, named in the indenture.[4] While the investors in the debt securities may direct the indenture trustee in certain circumstances, the trustee is also authorized and, in some cases, required to take action on its own to protect the interests of the investors. In many circumstances the indenture trustee is the only party with standing to bring suit or to take action to enforce the provisions of the indenture.

Do not let the term "trustee" confuse you here. There is not an actual trust involved—there is no corpus of assets held in trust for anyone in the context of a debt security. Not surprisingly, an indenture trustee is a very different creature than a trustee for a donative trust, and its duties differ, as the following case illustrates.[5]

Elliott Assoc. v. J. Henry Schroder Bank & Trust Co.

838 F.2d 66 (2d Cir. 1988)

ALTIMARI, Circuit Judge:

This appeal involves an examination of the obligations and duties of a trustee during the performance of its pre-default duties under a trust indenture. . . . The instant action was brought by a debenture holder who sought to represent a class of all debenture holders under the trust indenture. The debenture holder alleged in its complaint that the trustee waived a 50-day notice period prior to the redemption of the debentures and did not consider the impact of the waiver on the financial interests of the debenture holders. The debenture holder alleged further that, had the trustee not waived the full 50-day notice period, the debenture holders would have been entitled to receive an additional $1.2 million in interest from the issuer of the debentures. The debenture holder therefore concludes that the trustee's waiver was improper and constituted a breach of the trustee's duties owed to the debenture holders under the indenture, the Act and state law.

The district court dismissed the debenture holder's action after conducting a bench trial and entered judgment in favor of the defendants. The district court held that the trustee's waiver did not constitute a breach of any duty owed to the debenture holders—under the indenture or otherwise—because, as the court found, a trustee's pre-default duties are limited to those duties expressly provided in the indenture. *See* 655 F. Supp. 1281, 1288-89 (S.D.N.Y. 1987). We agree with the district court that no breach

---

4. The indenture trustee is the first of three different types of trustees that we will encounter in this book, the other two being the United States Trustee and the trustee in bankruptcy. Do not confuse them.

5. The following case excerpt omits discussion of the federal law governing indenture trustees. That law is addressed in a subsequent chapter.

of duty was stated here. Accordingly, we affirm the district court's decision dismissing the action.

FACTS AND BACKGROUND

Appellant Elliott Associates ("Elliott") was the holder of $525,000 principal amount of 10% Convertible Subordinated Debentures due June 1, 1990 (the "debentures") which were issued by Centronics Data Computer Corporation ("Centronics") pursuant to an indenture between Centronics and J. Henry Schroder Bank and Trust Company ("Schroder"), as trustee. Elliott's debentures were part of an aggregate debenture offering by Centronics of $40,000,000 under the indenture. . . .

The indenture and debentures provided, inter alia, that Centronics had the right to redeem the debentures "at any time" at a specified price, plus accrued interest, but the indenture also provided that, during the first two years following the issuance of the debentures, Centronics' right to redeem was subject to certain conditions involving the market price of Centronics' common stock. To facilitate its right to redeem the debentures, Centronics was required to provide written notice of a proposed redemption to the trustee and to the debenture holders. Section 3.01 of the indenture required that Centronics give the trustee 50-day notice of its intention to call its debentures for redemption, "unless a shorter notice shall be satisfactory to the trustee." Section 3.03 of the indenture required Centronics to provide the debenture holders with "at least 15 days but not more than 60 days" notice of a proposed redemption.

At the option of the debenture holders, the debentures were convertible into shares of Centronics' common stock. In the event Centronics called the debentures for redemption, debenture holders could convert their debentures "at any time before the close of business on the last Business Day prior to the redemption date." Subject to certain adjustments, the conversion price was $3.25 per share. The number of shares issuable upon conversion could be determined by dividing the principal amount converted by the conversion price. Upon conversion, however, the debentures provided that "no adjustment for interest or dividends [would] be made."

Debenture holders were to receive interest payments from Centronics semi-annually on June 1 and December 1 of each year. Describing the method of interest payment, each debenture provided that

> the Company will pay interest on the Debentures (except defaulted interest) to the persons who are registered Holders of Debentures at the close of business on the November 15 or May 15 next preceding the interest payment date. Holders must surrender Debentures to a Paying Agent to collect principal payments.

To insure the primacy of the debenture holders' right to receive interest, the indenture provided that "notwithstanding any other provision of this Indenture, the right of the Holder of a Security to receive payment of . . . interest on the Security . . . shall not be impaired."

On March 20, 1986, Centronics' Board of Directors met and approved a complete redemption of all of its outstanding debentures and designated May 16, 1986 as the redemption date. On April 4, 1986—42 days prior to the redemption—Centronics'

President, Robert Stein, wrote Schroder and informed the trustee that "pursuant to the terms of the Indenture, notice is hereby given that the Company will redeem all of its outstanding 10% Convertible Subordinated Debentures due June 1, 1990, on May 16, 1986."

On May 1, 1986 . . . pursuant to section 3.03 of the indenture, Centronics gave formal notice of the May 16, 1986 redemption to the debenture holders. In a letter accompanying the Notice of Redemption, Centronics' President explained that . . . accrued interest was not payable upon conversion:

> *No adjustments for Interest or Dividends upon Conversion*. No payment or adjustment will be made by or on behalf of the Company (i) on account of any interest accrued on any Debentures surrendered for conversion or (ii) on account of dividends, if any, on shares of Common Stock issued upon such conversion. Holders converting Debentures will not be entitled to receive the interest thereon from December 1, 1985 to May 16, 1986, the date of redemption. (emphasis in original).

On May 15, 1986, the last day available for conversion prior to the May 16, 1986 redemption, Centronics' common stock traded at $6 5/8 per share. At that price, each $1,000 principal amount of debentures was convertible into Centronics' common stock worth approximately $2,038. Thus, it was clear that conversion at $2,038 was economically more profitable than redemption at $1,146.11. Debenture holders apparently recognized this fact because all the debenture holders converted their debentures into Centronics' common stock prior to the May 16, 1986 redemption.

Elliott filed the instant action on May 12, 1986 and sought an order from the district court enjoining the May 16, 1986 redemption. Elliott alleged in its complaint that Schroder and Centronics conspired to time the redemption in such a manner so as to avoid Centronics' obligation to pay interest on the next interest payment date, i.e., June 1, 1986. This conspiracy allegedly was accomplished by forcing debenture holders to convert prior to the close of business on May 15, 1986. Elliott contended that, as part of this conspiracy, Schroder improperly waived the 50-day notice in section 3.01 of the indenture and thus allowed Centronics to proceed with the redemption as planned. Elliott claimed that Schroder waived the 50-day notice without considering the impact of that waiver on the financial interests of the debenture holders and that the trustee's action in this regard constituted, inter alia, a breach of the trustee's fiduciary duties. Finally, Elliott alleged that, had it not been for the trustee's improper waiver, debenture holders would have been entitled to an additional payment of $1.2 million in interest from Centronics.

After filing the instant action, Elliott filed a motion pursuant to Fed. R. Civ. P. 23 to have itself certified as representative of a class comprised of "all persons who held, as of May 1, 1986, the 10% convertible subordinated debentures due June 1, 1990 of Centronics Data Computer Corp." Schroder and Centronics filed motions to dismiss the action, or, in the alternative, for summary judgment, on the ground that Elliott's complaint failed to state a claim. . . .

The district court . . . denied Elliott's motion for class certification and granted Schroder and Centronics' motions to dismiss. . . .

DISCUSSION

The central issue on this appeal is whether the district court properly held that the trustee was not obligated to weigh the financial interests of the debenture holders when it decided on March 12, 1986 to waive Centronics' compliance with section 3.01's 50-day notice requirement. We agree with the district court's conclusion that the trustee was under no such duty. *See* 655 F. Supp. at 1288-89.

At the outset, it is important to sort out those matters not at issue here. First, Elliott does not dispute that Centronics complied in all respects with the indenture's requirement to provide notice of redemption to the debenture holders. Elliott's claim only challenges the sufficiency of the notice to the trustee and the manner in which the trustee decided to waive that notice. Moreover, Elliott does not dispute that Schroder's actions were expressly authorized by section 3.01, which specifically allows the trustee discretion to accept shorter notice of redemption from Centronics if that notice was deemed satisfactory. Finally, except for bald assertions of conflict of interest, Elliott presents no serious claim that Schroder personally benefitted in any way from the waiver, or that, by waiving the notice period, it was taking a position that would harm the interests of the debenture holders and correspondingly inure to the trustee's benefit. Rather, Elliott's claim essentially is that the trustee was under a duty—implied from the indenture, [federal law] or state law—to secure greater benefits for debenture holders over and above the duties and obligations it undertook in the indenture.

. . .

It is . . . well-established under state common law that the duties of an indenture trustee are strictly defined and limited to the terms of the indenture, *see, e.g., Green v. Title Guarantee & Trust Co.*, 223 A.D. 12 (1st Dep't), *aff'd*, 248 N.Y. 627 (1928); *Hazzard v. Chase National Bank*, 159 Misc. 57, 287 N.Y.S. 541 (Sup. Ct. N.Y. County 1936), *aff'd*, 257 A.D. 950, 14 N.Y.S.2d 147 (1st Dep't), *aff'd*, 282 N.Y. 652, *cert. denied*, 311 U.S. 708 (1940), although the trustee must nevertheless refrain from engaging in conflicts of interest. *See United States Trust Co. v. First National City Bank*, 57 A.D.2d 285 (1st Dep't 1977), *aff'd*, 45 N.Y.2d 869 (1978).

In view of the foregoing, it is no surprise that we have consistently rejected the imposition of additional duties on the trustee in light of the special relationship that the trustee already has with both the issuer and the debenture holders under the indenture. *See Meckel v. Continental Resources Co.*, 758 F.2d 811, 816 (2d Cir. 1985); *In Re W.T. Grant Co.*, 699 F.2d 599, 612 (2d Cir.), *cert. denied*, 464 U.S. 822 (1983); *Browning Debenture Holders' Comm. v. DASA Corp.*, 560 F.2d 1078, 1083 (2d Cir. 1977). As we recognized in *Meckel*,

> an indenture trustee is not subject to the ordinary trustee's duty of undivided loyalty. Unlike the ordinary trustee, who has historic common-law duties imposed beyond those in the trust agreement, *an indenture trustee is more like a stakeholder whose duties and obligations are exclusively defined by the terms of the indenture agreement.*

758 F.2d at 816 (citing *Hazzard v. Chase National Bank, supra*) (emphasis added). We therefore conclude that, so long as the trustee fulfills its obligations under the express terms of the indenture, it owes the debenture holders no additional, implicit pre-default duties or obligations except to avoid conflicts of interest.

Our analysis here is therefore limited to determining whether the trustee fulfilled its duties under the indenture. As set forth above, section 3.01 requires that, when the company intends to call its debentures for redemption, it must provide the trustee with 50-day notice of the redemption, "unless a shorter notice shall be satisfactory to the trustee." Section 3.02 of the indenture sets forth the manner in which the trustee selects which debentures are to be redeemed when the company calls for a partial redemption. The American Bar Foundation's *Commentaries on Model Debenture Indenture Provisions* (1971) (the "Commentaries") explains that "notice of the Company's election to redeem *all* the debentures need not be given to the Trustee since such a redemption may be effected by the Company without any action on the part of the Trustee. . . ." *Id.* at § 11-3, p. 493. Thus, it appears that section 3.01's notice requirement is intended for the trustee's benefit to allow it sufficient time to perform the various administrative tasks in preparation for redemption. While compliance with a full notice period may be necessary in the event of partial redemption, the full notice may not be required in the event of a complete redemption. We find that, although the trustee may reasonably insist on the full 50-day notice in the event of a complete redemption, it nevertheless has the discretion to accept shorter notice when it deems such shorter notice satisfactory.

. . . [I]t is clear that Schroder complied with the letter and spirit of the indenture when it waived compliance with the full 50-day notice. Schroder was given the discretion to waive full notice under appropriate circumstances, and we find that it reasonably exercised that discretion.

To support its argument that Schroder was obligated to consider the impact of the waiver on the interests of the debenture holders, Elliott relies on our decision in *Dabney v. Chase National Bank*, 196 F.2d 668 (2d Cir. 1952), *as suppl'd*, 201 F.2d 635 (2d Cir.), *cert. dismissed per stipulation*, 346 U.S. 863 (1953). *Dabney* provided that

> the duty of a trustee, not to profit at the possible expense of his beneficiary, is the most fundamental of the duties which he accepts when he becomes a trustee. It is a part of his obligation to give his beneficiary his undivided loyalty, free from any conflicting personal interest; an obligation that has been nowhere more jealously and rigidly enforced than in New York where these indentures were executed. "The most fundamental duty owed by the trustee to the beneficiaries of the trust is the duty of loyalty * * * In some relations the fiduciary element is more intense than in others; it is peculiarly intense in the case of a trust." We should be even disposed to say that without this duty there could be no trust at all.

196 F.2d at 670. *Dabney* arose, however, in an entirely different factual context than the instant case.

The *Dabney* court examined the conduct of a trustee who knew or should have known that the company for whose bonds it served as trustee was insolvent. While possessing knowledge of the company's insolvency, the trustee proceeded to collect loan obligations from the company. The court held that the trustee's conduct in this regard constituted a breach of its obligation not to take an action which might disadvantage the debenture holders while providing itself with a financial advantage, i.e., the trustee engaged in a conflict of interest. *See* 196 F.2d at 673. Thus, while *Dabney* stands for the proposition that a trustee must refrain from engaging in conflicts of interest, it simply does not support the broader proposition that an implied fiduciary duty is imposed on a trustee to advance the financial interests of the debenture holders during the period prior to default. Because no evidence was offered in the instant case to suggest that Schroder benefitted, directly or indirectly, from its decision to waive the 50-day notice, and thus did not engage in a conflict of interest, it is clear that *Dabney* is inapposite to the instant appeal.

Schroder also contends that, even if we were to find that the trustee owed the debenture holders a duty to consider the impact of the waiver, we would nevertheless be compelled to dismiss this action because the debenture holders were not entitled to payment of accrued interest upon conversion. However, since we agree with the district court that the trustee had no duty to consider the impact of the waiver, we do not decide this question.

CONCLUSION

In view of the foregoing, we affirm the judgment of the district court which dismissed Elliott's action. . . .

Affirmed.

What exactly, then, is the precise role of an indenture trustee? The following discussion regarding the role of the indenture trustee references particular paragraphs from the Sunstone Hotel Partnership Indenture, which is excerpted at length below.

The indenture trustee is an agent of the bondholders, with duties set forth by contract, common law, and state and federal statutes. Absent a specified event of default on the bonds, however, the trustee usually plays a purely ministerial role and benefits from broad exculpation. *See* Indenture §§ 601(1), 603. The indenture trustee may or may not also be the payment agent for the bonds, meaning the party that actually collects the payments on the bonds from the issuer and distributes them to the bondholders.

Upon an event of default, an indenture trustee's duties change. *See* Indenture § 601(2). The trustee is charged with acting as a prudent person would in the circumstances. Among other things, the trustee is authorized to take action to accelerate the principal outstanding on the bonds following an uncured event of default and to bring suit to collect following the acceleration. *See* Indenture §§ 502, 503.

Trustees are selected and paid by the issuers, which would seem to raise some concerns about conflicts of interest. Moreover, to the extent that the trustee is able to recover funds, the trustee's own fees and costs are paid first, before any of the bondholders. *See* Indenture § 506. Trustees, however, face potential liability to the bondholders to the extent they fail to act to the required standard of care, particularly following an event of default. Moreover, while an indenture trustee is permitted to have potentially conflicting economic interests prior to an event of default, *see* Indenture § 605, federal securities law requires the trustee to either eliminate the conflicts within 90 days or resign the trusteeship upon an event of default. 15 U.S.C. § 77jjj(b). Moreover, for corporate bonds, different series will have separate trustees, thus eliminating the possibility of a trustee conflicted between series. This is not always the case for structured securities, like mortgage-backed securities, which can have thorny inter-series conflicts, sometimes called "tranche warfare."

While indenture trustees are required to act as a prudent person following an event of default, trustees still may not always enforce indentures to the liking of investors. Accordingly, investors in the debt securities are authorized to direct the trustee's actions in certain circumstances. *See* Indenture § 512. Such direction typically requires a majority vote of the bondholders.

Bondholders are often able to force other actions through lesser pluralities. For example, often bondholders of 25% of the outstanding principal in a series can give notice of events of default caused by breaches of covenant or warranties—that is, non-payment events of default. *See* Indenture § 501. Thus, if the trustee has not given the issuer notice of an event of default (sometimes referred to as "declaring an event of default"), the bondholders still can. This is important because the trustee is heavily exculpated for inaction prior to an event of default, and has no incentive to notice non-payment events of default. (The trustee cannot easily claim to have missed a payment event of default, so bondholder action isn't required for payment events of default.) Likewise, bondholders of 25% of the principal in a series can accelerate the debt following an event of default. *See* Indenture § 502. Such an acceleration can be rescinded by a majority of bondholders provided certain conditions are met. *See* Indenture § 502. Likewise, events of default—other than payment defaults—can be waived by the majority of bondholders. *See* Indenture § 513.

Bondholders' ultimate ability to bring suit themselves to enforce the indenture against the obligor is limited by what are known as **"no-action clauses."** *See* Indenture § 507. The typical no-action clause prohibits any individual bondholder from bringing suit unless it qualifies for one of two contractual exceptions. The first exception requires a formal demand on the trustee to take action from bondholders holding a sufficient percentage of the bonds (typically 25 percent) as well as provision of suitable indemnity to the trustee. If the trustee does not take action on an event of default within a specified time period following a direction and indemnity (typically 60 days), the individual bondholders are free to bring suit themselves.

The second exception comes from what is called a **"non-impairment clause."** *See* Indenture § 508. Non-impairment clauses permit investors to bring suit for non-payment, which, as we will see, is required by federal law. Thus, no-action clauses limit bondholder suits for covenant defaults, but not for payment defaults. *Great Plains Trust Co. v. Union Pac. R.R. Co.*, 492 F.3d 986, 991 (8th Cir. 2007). Of course, the two can potentially be linked, as a covenant default can result in an acceleration of the debt.

Balanced together, no-action clauses and non-impairment clauses prevent suits for breach of covenants by individual bondholders unless the direction and indemnity requirements are met. But individual bondholders can always sue for payment defaults, but the non-impairment clause does not allow an individual bondholder to accelerate the debt; that is a right reserved for the trustee or the holders of 25 percent of the outstanding bonds by amount. *See* Sunstone Indenture, § 502. If an investor is successful on an individual suit, the "ratable recovery" clause provides that it must share the proceeds on a pro rata basis with the other investors. *See* Indenture § 507. In other words, no investor can get a leg up on the others by bringing litigation itself. The mandatory sharing of course reduces the incentive for an investor to bring litigation itself, as it will bear all of the costs, but share the recoveries.

No-action clauses are generally interpreted narrowly, based on the specific contractual language. Thus, in *Quadrant Structured Products Co., Ltd. v. Vincent Vertin*, 23 N.Y.3d 549 (N.Y. 2014), the New York Court of Appeals (the state's highest court) held that under New York law, a no-action clause that referred to pursuit of a remedy "upon or under or with respect to this Indenture" but omitted the words "or the Securities" only served to bar contract suits on the indenture, and did not bar investors' other common law or statutory claims. The implication, however, is that a well-drafted no-action clause with the phrase "on the Indenture or the Securities" is generally enforceable to prevent "lone ranger" suits on state law causes of action. Thus, language in a no-action clause that noteholders "may not pursue any remedy with respect to this Indenture or the Securities" has been held to prevent state law fraudulent transfer actions, as they are actions taken "with respect to" the Indenture or Securities," even though it is not enforcing either. *See Akanthos Capital Mgmt., LLC v. CompuCredit Holdings Corp.*, 677 F.3d 1286, 1293-95 (11th Cir. 2012).

Courts have, however, refused to enforce no-action clauses if a trustee is conflicted or is unjustified in its unwillingness to undertake action, *see, e.g., CFIP Master Fund, Ltd. v. Citibank, N.A.*, 738 F. Supp. 2d 450, 477 (S.D.N.Y. 2010), or if the no-action clause would conflict with unwaiveable rights under public laws. For example, in *McMahan & Co. v. Wherehouse Entm't Inc.*, 65 F.3d 1044 (2d Cir. 1995), the Second Circuit held that a no-action clause did not bar individual investors from bringing claims under the Securities Act of 1933 and the Securities Exchange Act of 1934, which contain explicit anti-waiver provisions. *See* 15 U.S.C. §§ 77n, 78cc. Federal law trumped the contractual provisions of the indenture because a no-action clause "can operate to bar a minority plaintiff class from exercising its substantive rights under federal securities law upon the vote of a majority of the debentureholders. Further, a plaintiff's inability to indemnify the Trustee, as required by the no-action clause here, would bar that plaintiff from commencing a securities law claim." *Id.* at 1051. In the same litigation, however, the plaintiffs' state law tort claims were held to be barred by the no-action clause. *McMahan & Co. v. Wherehouse Entm't Inc.*, 859 F. Supp. 743 (S.D.N.Y. 1994). Similarly, no-action clauses have been held not to bar suits under the Trust Indenture Act, *MeehanCombs Global Credit Opportunities Funds, LP v. Caesars Entertainment Corp.*, 2015 U.S. Dist. Lexis 5111 (S.D.N.Y. Jan. 15, 2015).

The various collective action thresholds in indentures are actually more daunting than they might appear. First, trustees are given the discretion to withhold notice of non-payment events of default from bondholders as a whole if the trustee believes in good faith that the notice would not be in the interest of the bondholders. *See* Indenture § 602. Thus, the trustee might decide that notifying the bondholders could undermine attempts at a settlement with the issuer over the non-payment default and thus not provide the notice. Without such notice, it will be difficult for bondholders to take action, however. Second, even with knowledge of a non-payment event of default, bondholders must coordinate. That means identifying and communicating with each other. This is more challenging than you might expect. Bondholders do not generally know each other's identities, and they have no general right to learn them. The indenture trustee maintains a list of the bondholders. Federal securities law provides that the trustee need only make the list available upon joint request of at least three bondholders, all of whom must have held the bonds for at least six months. 15 U.S.C. § 77lll(b). Even if this coordination problem can be surmounted, the trustee's list is unlikely to identify individual bondholders, only brokerages, because most bonds are held in "street name," meaning that they are held in the name of a brokerage for its customers; the indenture trustee may not know the identity of the ultimate beneficial interest holders. All of this makes it difficult for individual bondholders to communicate with other bondholders and form coalitions to force trustee action or bypass the trustee. Despite these problems, bondholders are often successful at organizing and taking action, but the ability to do so is much greater for large, institutional investors than for individual retail investors.

SUNSTONE HOTEL PARTNERSHIP, LLC,[6]

Issuer,

SUNSTONE HOTEL INVESTORS, INC.,

Parent Guarantor,

CERTAIN SUBSIDIARIES OF SUNSTONE HOTEL INVESTORS, INC.,

Subsidiary Guarantors,

and

WELLS FARGO BANK, NATIONAL ASSOCIATION,

Trustee

————

INDENTURE

Dated as of June 18, 2007

DEBT SECURITIES

. . .

------

6. If you wish to view the entire indenture, it is available at https://bit.ly/2MNRsJz.

Section 501. Events of Default.

"Event of Default" means, wherever used herein with respect to any particular series of Securities, any one of the following events and such other events as may be established with respect to the Securities of such series:

(1) default in the payment of any installment of interest upon any Security of that series when it becomes due and payable, and continuance of such default for a period of 30 days; or

(2) default in the payment of the principal of . . . any Security of that series at its Maturity . . . ; or

. . .

(4) default in the performance of, or breach of, any covenant or warranty of the Issuer or any of the Guarantors in respect of any Security of that series contained in this Indenture or in such Securities . . . and continuance of such default or breach for a period of 60 days after there has been given, by registered or certified mail, to the Issuer or the Parent Guarantor by the Trustee for the Securities of such series or to the Issuer, the Parent Guarantor and such Trustee by the Holders of at least 25% in principal amount of the Outstanding Securities of that series a written notice specifying such default or breach and requiring it to be remedied and stating that such notice is a "Notice of Default" hereunder. . . .

Section 502. Acceleration of Maturity; Rescission and Annulment.

If an Event of Default with respect to any particular series of Securities occurs and is continuing . . . then and in every such case either the Trustee for the Securities of such series or the Holders of not less than 25% in principal amount of the Outstanding Securities of that series may declare the entire principal amount . . . and accrued and unpaid interest . . . of all the Securities of that series, to be due and payable immediately, by a notice in writing to the Issuer and the Parent Guarantor (and to such Trustee if given by Holders), and upon any such declaration of acceleration such principal or such lesser amount, as the case may be, together with accrued interest and all other amounts owing hereunder, shall become immediately due and payable, without presentment, demand, protest or notice of any kind, all of which are hereby expressly waived.

. . .

At any time after such a declaration of acceleration has been made and before a judgment or decree for payment of the money due has been obtained by the Trustee for the Securities of any series as hereinafter provided in this Article Five, the Holders of a majority in principal amount of the Outstanding Securities of that series, by written notice to the Issuer, the Parent Guarantor and such Trustee, may rescind and annul such declaration and its consequences if:

(1) the Issuer or any of the Guarantors has paid or deposited with such Trustee a sum sufficient to pay in the currency or currency unit in which the Securities of such series are payable . . . :

> **(a)** all overdue interest on all Securities of that series;
>
> **(b)** the principal of . . . any Securities of that series which have become due otherwise than by such declaration of acceleration . . . and interest thereon from the date such principal became due at a rate per annum equal to the rate borne by the Securities of such series . . . , to the extent that the payment of such interest shall be legally enforceable;
>
> **(c)** to the extent that payment of such interest is lawful, interest upon overdue interest at a rate per annum equal to the rate borne by the Securities of such series . . . ; and
>
> **(d)** all sums paid or advanced by such Trustee hereunder and the reasonable compensation, expenses, disbursements and advances of such Trustee, its agents and counsel and all other amounts due to such Trustee . . . ;

and

(2) all Events of Default with respect to the Securities of such series, other than the nonpayment of the principal of the Securities of that series which has become due solely by such acceleration, have been cured or waived as provided in Section 513. No such rescission shall affect any subsequent default or impair any right consequent thereon.

Section 503. Collection of Indebtedness and Suits for Enforcement by Trustee.

The Issuer and the Guarantors covenant that if:

> **(1)** default is made in the payment of any interest upon any Security of any series when such interest becomes due and payable and such default continues for a period of 30 days; or
>
> **(2)** default is made in the payment of the principal of (or premium, if any, on) any Security of any series at its Maturity;

the Issuer and the Guarantors shall, upon demand of the Trustee for the Securities of such series, pay to the Trustee, for the benefit of the Holders of such Securities, the whole amount then due and payable on such Securities for principal . . . and interest, if any, with interest upon the overdue principal . . . and, to the extent that payment of such interest shall be legally enforceable, upon any overdue installments of interest at a rate per annum equal to the rate borne by such Securities . . . ; and, in addition thereto, such further amount as shall be sufficient to cover the costs and expenses of collection, including the reasonable compensation, expenses, disbursements and advances of such Trustee, its agents and counsel and all other amounts due to such Trustee. . . .

If the Issuer or the Guarantors fail to pay such amounts forthwith upon such demand, such Trustee, in its own name and as trustee of an express trust, may institute a judicial proceeding against the Issuer or any of the Guarantors for the collection of the sums so due and unpaid, and may prosecute such proceedings to judgment or final decree, and may enforce the same against the Issuer or any of the Guarantors or any other obligor upon the Securities of such series and collect the moneys adjudged or decreed to be payable in the manner provided by law out of the property of the Issuer or any of the Guarantors or any other obligor upon the Securities of such series, wherever situated.

If an Event of Default with respect to Securities of any particular series occurs and is continuing, the Trustee for the Securities of such series may in its discretion proceed to protect and enforce its rights and the rights of the Holders of Securities of that series by such appropriate judicial proceedings as such Trustee shall deem most effectual to protect and enforce any such rights, whether for the specific enforcement of any covenant or agreement in this Indenture or in aid of the exercise of any power granted herein, or to enforce any other proper remedy. . . .

Section 506. Application of Money Collected.

Any money collected by the Trustee for the Securities of any series pursuant to this Article Five with respect to the Securities of such series shall be applied in the following order, at the date or dates fixed by such Trustee and, in case of the distribution of such money on account of principal (or premium, if any) or interest, if any, upon presentation of the Securities of such series, or both, as the case may be, and the notation thereon of the payment if only partially paid and upon surrender thereof if fully paid:

FIRST: To the payment of all amounts due such Trustee under Section 607;

SECOND: To the payment of the amounts then due and unpaid upon the Securities of such series for principal of (and premium, if any) and interest, if any, on such Securities in respect of which or for the benefit of which such money has been collected, ratably, without preference or priority of any kind, according to the amounts due and payable on such Securities for principal (and premium, if any) and interest, if any, respectively; and

THIRD: The balance, if any, to the Issuer.

Section 507. Limitation on Suits.

No Holder of any Security of any particular series shall have any right to institute any proceeding, judicial or otherwise, with respect to this Indenture, or for the appointment of a receiver or trustee, or for any other remedy hereunder, unless:

(1) an Event of Default with respect to that series shall have occurred and be continuing and such Holder shall have previously given written notice to the Trustee for the Securities of such series of such default and the continuance thereof;

(2) the Holders of not less than 25% in principal amount of the Outstanding Securities of that series shall have made written request to the Trustee for the Securities of such series to institute proceedings in respect of such Event of Default in its own name as Trustee hereunder;

(3) such Holder or Holders have offered to such Trustee indemnity reasonably satisfactory to the Trustee against the costs, expenses and liabilities to be incurred in compliance with such request;

(4) such Trustee for 60 days after its receipt of such notice, request and offer of indemnity has failed to institute any such proceeding; and

(5) no direction inconsistent with such written request has been given to such Trustee during such 60-day period by the Holders of a majority in principal amount of the Outstanding Securities of that series;

it being understood and intended that no one or more Holders of Securities of that series shall have any right in any manner whatsoever by virtue of, or by availing of, any provision of this Indenture to affect, disturb or prejudice the rights of any other Holders of Securities of that series, or to enforce any right under this Indenture, except in the manner herein provided and for the equal and ratable benefit of all the Holders of Securities of that series.

Section 508. Unconditional Right of Holders to Receive Principal . . . and Interest, if any.

Notwithstanding any other provision in this Indenture, the Holder of any Security shall have the right which is absolute and unconditional to receive payment of the principal and interest on the notes at the respective due dates for payment and delivery upon exchange of cash and shares of common stock of the Parent Guarantor . . . and . . . interest, if any, on such Security on the respective Stated Maturities expressed in such Security . . . and to institute suit for the enforcement of any such payment, and such right shall not be impaired without the consent of such Holder. . . .

Section 512. Control by Holders.

The Holders of a majority in principal amount of the Outstanding Securities of any particular series shall have the right to direct the time, method and place of conducting any proceeding for any remedy available to the Trustee for the Securities of such series with respect to the Securities of that series or exercising any trust or power conferred on such Trustee with respect to such Securities, provided that:

(1) such direction shall not be in conflict with any rule of law or with this Indenture;

(2) such Trustee may take any other action deemed proper by such Trustee which is not inconsistent with such direction; and

(3) such Trustee need not take any action which might expose it to personal liability, without the prior receipt of reasonable indemnity (as determined by the Trustee in its reasonable discretion) from Holders requesting such action, or be unduly prejudicial to the Holders of Securities of such series not joining therein.

Section 513. Waiver of Past Defaults.

Subject to Section 502, the Holders of not less than a majority in principal amount of the Outstanding Securities of any particular series may on behalf of the Holders of all the Securities of that series waive any past default hereunder with respect to that series and its consequences, except:
    (1) a default in the payment of the principal of (or premium, if any) or interest, if any, on any Security of that series; or
    (2) a default with respect to a covenant or provision hereof which under Section 902 cannot be modified or amended without the consent of the Holder of each Outstanding Security of that series affected.
Upon any such waiver, such default shall cease to exist, and any Event of Default arising therefrom shall be deemed to have been cured, for every purpose of this Indenture; but no such waiver shall extend to any subsequent or other default or impair any right consequent thereon.
. . .

Section 601. Certain Duties and Responsibilities.

(1) Except during the continuance of an Event of Default with respect to the Securities of any series for which the Trustee is serving as such,
    (a) such Trustee undertakes to perform such duties and only such duties as are specifically set forth in this Indenture, and no implied covenants or obligations shall be read into this Indenture against such Trustee and permissive rights of the Trustee hereunder shall not constitute performance duties; and
    (b) in the absence of gross negligence, bad faith or willful misconduct on its part, such Trustee may conclusively rely, as to the truth of the statements and the correctness of the opinions expressed therein, upon certificates or opinions furnished to such Trustee and conforming to the requirements of this Indenture; but in the case of any such certificates or opinions which by any provisions hereof are specifically required to be furnished to such Trustee, such Trustee shall be under a duty to examine the same to determine whether or not they conform to the requirements of this Indenture (but need not confirm or investigate the accuracy of any mathematical calculations or other facts stated therein).

(2) In case an Event of Default with respect to a series of Securities has occurred and is continuing, the Trustee for the Securities of such series shall exercise such of the rights and powers vested in it by this Indenture, and use the same degree of care and skill in their exercise, as a prudent man would exercise or use under the circumstances in the conduct of his own affairs.

(3) No provision of this Indenture shall be construed to relieve the Trustee for Securities of any series from liability for its own negligent action, its own negligent failure to act, or its own willful misconduct, except that:

    (a) this Subsection shall not be construed to limit the effect of Subsection (1) of this Section 601;

    (b) such Trustee shall not be liable for any error of judgment made in good faith by a Responsible Officer, unless it shall be proved that the Trustee was negligent in ascertaining the pertinent facts;

    (c) such Trustee shall not be liable with respect to any action taken, suffered or omitted to be taken by it in good faith in accordance with the direction of the Holders of a majority in principal amount of the Outstanding Securities of any particular series . . . relating to the time, method and place of conducting any proceeding for any remedy available to such Trustee, or exercising any trust or power conferred upon such Trustee, under this Indenture with respect to the Securities of that series; and

    (d) no provision of this Indenture shall require the Trustee for any series of Securities to expend or risk its own funds or otherwise incur any financial liability in the performance of any of its duties hereunder or in the exercise of any of its rights or powers, if it shall have reasonable grounds for believing that repayment of such funds or adequate indemnity against such risk or liability is not reasonably assured to it.

(4) Whether or not therein expressly so provided, every provision of this Indenture relating to the conduct or affecting the liability of or affording protection to the Trustee for any series of Securities shall be subject to the provisions of this Section 601.

(5) The Trustee shall not be liable for interest on any money received by it, except as the Trustee may agree in writing with the Issuer or the Parent Guarantor.

Section 602. Notice of Defaults.

Within 90 days after the occurrence of any default hereunder with respect to Securities of any particular series, the Trustee for the Securities of such series shall give to Holders of Securities of that series . . . notice of such default known to such Trustee, unless such default shall have been cured or waived; provided, however, that, except in the case of a default in the payment of the principal of or interest, if any, on any Security of that series . . . such Trustee shall be protected in withholding such notice if and so long as the Responsible Officers of such Trustee in good faith determine that the withholding of such notice is in the interest of the Holders of Securities of that series. For the purpose of this

Section 602, the term "default" means any event which is, or after notice or lapse of time or both would become, an Event of Default with respect to Securities of that series.

Section 603. Certain Rights of Trustee.

Except as otherwise provided in Section 601:

(1) the Trustee for any series of Security may conclusively rely and shall be protected in acting or refraining from acting upon any resolution, certificate, statement, instrument, opinion, report, notice, request, discretion, consent, order, bond, debenture or other paper or document (whether in original or facsimile form) believed by it to be genuine and to have been signed or presented by the proper party or parties;

. . .

(3) whenever in the administration of this Indenture the Trustee shall deem it desirable that a matter be proved or established prior to taking, suffering or omitting any action hereunder, such Trustee (unless other evidence be herein specifically prescribed) may request and, in the absence of bad faith on its part, rely upon an Officers' Certificate or an Opinion of Counsel;

(4) the Trustee may consult with counsel of its selection and the advice of such counsel or any Opinion of Counsel shall be full and complete authorization and protection in respect of any action taken, suffered or omitted by it hereunder in good faith and in reliance thereon;

(5) the Trustee shall be under no obligation to exercise any of the rights or powers vested in it by this Indenture at the request or direction of any of the Holders of Securities of any series pursuant to this Indenture for which it is acting as Trustee, unless such Holders shall have offered to such Trustee security or indemnity reasonably satisfactory to the Trustee against the costs, expenses and liabilities which might be incurred by it in compliance with such request or direction;

(6) the Trustee shall not be bound to make any investigation into the facts or matters stated in any resolution, certificate, statement, instrument, opinion, report, notice, request, discretion, consent, order, bond, debenture or other paper or document, but such Trustee, in its discretion, may make such further inquiry or investigation into such facts or matters as it may see fit, and, if such Trustee shall determine to make such further inquiry or investigation, it shall be entitled to examine the books, records and premises of the Issuer or the Guarantors, personally or by agent or attorney at the sole cost of the Issuer and the Guarantors and shall incur no liability of any kind by reason of such inquiry or investigation;

(7) the Trustee may employ or retain such counsel, accountants, appraisers or other experts or advisers as it may reasonably require for the purpose of determining and discharging its rights and duties hereunder and shall not be responsible for any misconduct on the part of any of them;

(8) the Trustee shall not be liable for any action taken, suffered, or omitted to be taken by it in good faith and reasonably believed by it to be authorized or within the discretion or rights or powers conferred upon it by this Indenture;

(9) the Trustee shall not be deemed to have notice of any default or Event of Default unless a Responsible Officer of the Trustee has actual knowledge thereof or unless written notice of any event which is in fact such a default is received by the Trustee at the Corporate Trust Office of the Trustee, and such notice references the Securities and this Indenture;

(10) the rights, privileges, protections, immunities and benefits given to the Trustee, including, without limitation, its right to be indemnified, are extended to, and shall be enforceable by, the Trustee in each of its capacities hereunder, and each agent, custodian and other Person employed to act hereunder;

. . .

(12) the Trustee shall not be responsible or liable for special, indirect, or consequential loss or damage of any kind whatsoever (including, but not limited to, loss or profit) irrespective of whether the Trustee has been advised of the likelihood of such loss or damage and regardless of the form of action;

(13) the Trustee shall not be responsible or liable for any failure or delay in the performance of its obligations under this Indenture arising out of or caused, directly or indirectly, by circumstances beyond its reasonable control, including without limitation, acts of God, earthquakes, fire, flood, terrorism, wars and other military disturbances, sabotage, epidemics, riots, interruptions, loss or malfunction of utilities, computer (hardware or software) or communication services, labor disputes, acts of civil or military authorities and governmental actions; and

(14) the permissive rights of the Trustee enumerated herein shall not be construed as duties.

. . .

Section 605. May Hold Securities.

The Trustee for any series of Securities . . . in its individual or any other capacity, may become the owner or pledgee of Securities and . . . may otherwise deal with the Issuer and the Guarantors with the same rights it would have if it were not such Trustee. . . .

Section 901. Supplemental Indentures Without Consent of Holders.

Without the consent of any Holders of Securities, the Issuer and the Guarantors, when authorized by a Board Resolution, at any time and from time to time, may enter into one or more indentures supplemental hereto, in form satisfactory to the Trustee, for any of the following purposes:

(1) to evidence the succession of another Person to the Issuer or any of the Guarantors and the assumption by any such successor of the covenants of the Issuer or such Guarantor, as the case may be, herein and in the Securities; or

(2) to add to the covenants of the Issuer or any of the Guarantors for the benefit of the Holders of all or any particular series of Securities (and if such covenants are to be for the benefit of less than all series of Securities, stating that such covenants are expressly being included solely for the benefit of such series), or to surrender any right or power herein conferred upon the Issuer or any of the Guarantors; or

(3) to add any additional Events of Default with respect to any or all series of Securities (and, if any such Event of Default applies to fewer than all series of Securities, stating each series to which such Event of Default applies); provided, however, that in respect of any such additional Events of Default, such supplemental indenture may provide for a particular period of grace after default (which period may be shorter or longer than that allowed in the case of other defaults) or may limit the remedies available to the Trustee upon such default or may limit the right of Holders of a majority in aggregate principal amount of any such series of Securities to which such additional Events of Default apply to waive such default; or

(4) to change or eliminate any of the provisions of this Indenture, provided, however, that any such change or elimination shall become effective only when there is no Security Outstanding of any series created prior to the execution of such supplemental indenture which is entitled to the benefit of such provision; or

(5) to pledge property to the Trustee as security or the Securities or to add guarantees with respect to the Securities; or

(6) to evidence and provide for the acceptance of appointment hereunder of a Trustee other than Wells Fargo Bank, National Association as Trustee for a series of Securities and to add to or change any of the provisions of this Indenture as shall be necessary to provide for or facilitate the administration of the trusts hereunder by more than one Trustee, pursuant to the requirements of Section 609; or

(7) to evidence and provide for the acceptance of appointment hereunder by a successor Trustee with respect to the Securities of one or more series and to add to or change any of the provisions of this Indenture as shall be necessary to provide for or facilitate the administration of the trusts hereunder by more than one Trustee, pursuant to the requirements of Section 611(2); or

(8) to establish the form or terms of Securities of any series as permitted by Sections 201 and 301; or

(9) to cure any ambiguity, to correct or supplement any provision herein which may be defective or inconsistent with any other provision herein, or to make any other provisions with respect to matters or questions arising under this Indenture which shall not be inconsistent with the provisions of this Indenture, provided that such cures may not adversely affect the interests of the Holders in any material respect; or

(10) to supplement any of the provisions of this Indenture to such extent as shall be necessary to permit or facilitate the defeasance and discharge of any series of Securities pursuant to Sections 401, 402 and 403; provided, however, that any such action shall not adversely affect the interests of the Holders of Securities of such series or any other series of Securities in any material respect; or

(11) to add to or change or eliminate any provisions of this Indenture as shall be necessary or desirable in accordance with any amendments to the Trust Indenture Act or to maintain the qualification of this Indenture under the Trust Indenture Act; or

(12) subject to Section 301, to provide for the issuance of any additional Securities of a series, which shall have terms substantially identical in all material respects to the Securities of that series (in each case, other than with respect to the date of issuance, issue price and amount of interest payable on the first Interest Payment Date applicable thereto), as the case may be, and which shall be treated together with any Outstanding Securities and any previously issued additional Securities of that series, as a single issue of Securities.

Any supplemental indenture authorized by the provisions of this Section 901 may be executed by the Issuer and the Trustee without the consent of the Holders of any of the Securities at the time Outstanding, notwithstanding any of the provisions of Section 902.

Section 902. Supplemental Indentures With Consent of Holders.

The Issuer and the Guarantors, when authorized by a Board Resolution, may enter into an indenture or indentures supplemental hereto for the purpose of adding any provisions to or changing in any manner or eliminating any of the provisions of this Indenture or of modifying in any manner the rights of the Holders of such Securities under this Indenture, but only (i) as provided in Section 901 or (ii) with the consent of the Holders of more than 50% in aggregate principal amount of the Outstanding Securities of each series of Securities then Outstanding affected thereby, in each case by Act of said Holders of Securities of each such series delivered to the Issuer and the Trustee for Securities of each such series; provided, however, that no such supplemental indenture shall, without the consent of the Holder of each Outstanding Security affected thereby:

(1) change the Stated Maturity of the principal of, or any installment of principal of or interest on, any Security, or reduce the principal amount thereof or the rate of interest thereon, if any . . . , or any premium payable upon the redemption thereof . . . ; or

(2) change the currency or currency unit in which any Security or the principal or interest thereon is payable, or impair the right to institute suit for the enforcement of any such payment on or after the Stated Maturity thereof . . . ; or

(3) reduce or alter the method of computation of any amount payable upon redemption, repayment or purchase of any Securities by the Issuer or the Guarantors (or the time when such redemption, repayment or purchase may be made); or

(4) reduce the percentage in principal amount of the Outstanding Securities of any particular series, the consent of whose Holders is required for any such supplemental indenture, or the consent of whose Holders is required for any waiver (of compliance with certain provisions of this Indenture or certain defaults hereunder and their consequences) provided for in this Indenture . . . ; or

(5) modify or effect in any manner adverse to the Holders the terms and conditions of the obligations of any of the Guarantors in respect of the due and punctual payments of principal of (or premium, if any), or interest, if any, on, or any sinking fund requirements or additional amounts . . . ; or

(6) modify any of the provisions of this Section 902 or Section 513 [dealing with waiver of Events of Default], except to increase any such percentage or to provide that certain other provisions of this Indenture cannot be modified or waived without the consent of the Holder of each Security affected thereby. . . .

A supplemental indenture which changes or eliminates any covenant or other provision of this Indenture which has expressly been included solely for the benefit of one or more particular series of Securities, or which modifies the rights of the Holders of Securities of such series with respect to such covenant or other provision, shall be deemed not to affect the rights under this Indenture of the Holders of Securities of any other series.

. . .

Problem Set 4

(1) Juno Natural Products hasn't paid its common shareholders a dividend for years, but has instead been retaining its significant earnings. Argie Peacock, one of Juno's common shareholders, thinks it's time Juno started to pay dividends. Is there anything Argie can do?

(2) Ceres Bioextracts sells organic wheatberry extracts to Juno Natural Products, which Juno uses in its proprietary anti-aging skin-cream formula. Ceres deals with Juno on "net 30" terms. Juno hasn't paid Ceres since taking its last shipment two weeks ago. Is there anything Ceres Bioextracts can do?

(3) Juno Natural Products rents office equipment—photocopiers and 3-D printers—from Diana Supply Co. Juno has missed two monthly rental payments in a row. Is there anything Diana can do?

(4) Juno Natural Products took out a bank loan from Proserpina State Bank. The loan is secured by Juno's inventory and accounts receivable. If Juno defaults on the loan, what can Proserpina State Bank do?

(5) Juno Natural Products issued $200 million of unsecured senior notes under an indenture. The indentures provisions are identical to those of the Sunstone Indenture in this chapter. Aventine Pension Fund owns $10 million of the Juno notes. Based on front-page reporting in the New York Times and the Wall Street Journal about an accounting scandal at Juno, Aventine believes that Juno breached some of the notes' representations and warranties about its financial condition. Aventine's general counsel, Ty Gracchus, can't understand why the trustee, Laverna National Bank & Trust, hasn't declared an event of default and accelerated the notes. "While we're sitting around on our duffs, Juno's other creditors are going to grab all the assets," Ty fumes. "I sent copies of the newspaper articles to Laverna last month and demanded that it do something, but nothing's happened." What, if anything, can Aventine do about this problem? *See* Sunstone Indenture §§ 501, 601, 602, 603.

(6) After curing its default on the covenant default, Juno Natural Products failed to make its semi-annual interest payment on the unsecured senior notes, and the 30-day cure period has expired, creating an unambiguous Event of Default under the indenture.

    a. What can Laverna National Bank & Trust, as trustee for the unsecured senior notes, do? Sunstone Indenture §§ 501, 502, 503.

    b. If Laverna does not undertake any actions, what can Capitoline Wealth Management, which owns $48.5 million of the notes, do? Sunstone Indenture §§ 502, 507, 508, 512.

    c. How might the situation change if Palatine Bank, which owns $105 million of Juno's unsecured senior notes, also owns $400 million of Juno's subordinated unsecured notes, on which Juno has remained current? Sunstone Indenture §§ 503, 513.

(7) Leviathan Corp.'s 10-year, 10 percent non-amortizing secured bonds were issued under an indenture containing the following provisions:

Limitation on Suits. A Securityholder may pursue a remedy with respect to this Indenture or the Securities only if:

(1) the Holder gives to the Trustee notice of a continuing Event of Default;
(2) the Holders of at least 25 percent in principal amount of the Securities make a request to the Trustee to pursue the remedy;
(3) such Holder or Holders offer to the Trustee indemnity satisfactory to the Trustee against any loss, liability or expense;
(4) the Trustee does not comply with the request within 60 days after receipt of the request and the offer of indemnity; and
(5) during such 60-day period, the Holders of a majority in principal amount of the Securities do not give the Trustee a direction inconsistent with the request.

A Securityholder may not use this Indenture to prejudice the rights of another Securityholder or to obtain a preference or priority over another Securityholder.

Rights of Holders to Receive Payment. Notwithstanding any other provision of this Indenture, the right of any Holder of a Security to receive payment of principal and interest on the Security, on or after the respective due dates expressed in the Security, or to bring suit for the enforcement of any such payment on or after such respective dates, shall not be impaired or affected without the consent of the Holder.

You have been engaged by Braswell Capital Management, an investor in the Leviathan bonds. Braswell believes that Leviathan violated a bond covenant last month. Braswell also believes that the trustee, Laverna National Bank & Trust has not honored its own contractual obligations under the indenture and that Laverna has conspired with Leviathan to overlook the covenant default. Braswell wants you to file suit as quickly as possible. Can you file suit for the following causes of action? How quickly? And what will you need to do in order to sue?

    a. A state law suit against Leviathan for breach of contract.

    b. A state law suit against Leviathan for fraud.

    c. A state law suit against Leviathan for fraudulent transfer.

    d. A state law suit against Laverna for breach of contract.

    e. A federal securities suit against Leviathan under the Securities Act of 1933 for misstatements in the bonds' offering documents.

    f. Would the answer to any of these preceding questions be different under the Sunstone Indenture?

(8) Laverna National Bank & Trust is the indenture trustee for a $500 million issue of non-recourse secured notes of Leviathan Power Corporation, a public utility holding company. The indenture's terms are, except as described below, identical to the Sunstone Indenture.

The notes are secured by pledge to and deposit with Laverna, as trustee, of the common stock of Leviathan's subsidiary Gotham Generating Corp., which owns power plants throughout the New York metropolitan area. The indenture for the notes permits substitution by Leviathan of other securities if the prior year's dividends on the securities remaining on deposit with the trustee after the substitution are at least twice the annual interest payments on the notes. Two years ago, Laverna agreed to allow Leviathan to substitute the Gotham Generating Corp. common stock with the common stock of xRG Corp., a battery technology company also owned by Leviathan. The xRG stock deposited in substitution had paid dividends in the prior year that more than twice exceeded the interest payments due on the secured notes. The Executive Vice President of Laverna who signed off on the substitution, Patricia Morehead, also serves as a director of xRG.

Four months ago, xRG filed for bankruptcy, apparently hopelessly insolvent, and shortly thereafter Leviathan defaulted on the secured notes. You represent Gupta Investment Partners, an investor in the secured notes. Gupta wants to know whether it has any recourse against Leviathan or Laverna. What's your analysis? Sunstone Indenture §§ 507, 508. *Elliott Assoc. v. J. Henry Schroder Bank & Trust Co.*, 838 F.2d 66 (2d Cir. 1988).

CHAPTER 5

SYNDICATED LOANS

Historically, larger financings have been done through capital markets—bonds and stock offerings. This is because of the limitation on the ability of individual banks to make large loans. Single banks have limited funds available. Particularly in the days before inter-state banking, when banks were much smaller in terms of asset size, there was a practical limit on how much any single bank could fund. Moreover, individual lenders do not want the concentrated risk of a large loan. Indeed, banks are subject to regulatory lending limits to single borrowers. Capital markets enabled larger-scale financing by aggregating smaller financing contributions from numerous lenders.

While bonds and stocks still provide large-scale financing, multi-billion-dollar secured loans are also quite common now. The key driver in this change is a change in how loans are funded. Loans are now funded as team efforts involving multiple lenders. This approach has been able to produce loans as large as $75 billion to a single borrower (funding AB InBev's 2015 takeover bid for SABMiller). As with debt securities, the involvement of multiple parties in a loan can raise intercreditor coordination problems that can complicate the restructuring of the loan.

The solution to the limits on individual banks' ability to fund was to use funding consortiums. Two main forms evolved, the **syndication** and the **participation**. The differences between loan syndications and participations are discussed below, but the fundamental distinction is whether all of the lenders in the consortium have contractual privity with the borrower or just a lead lender. In a loan syndication, there is privity for all lenders, while a participation involves privity only for the lead lender. We're going to do a bit of a deep dive into syndications and participations because an understanding of how these structures function is very helpful in understanding the dynamics in current bankruptcy cases.

While participations and syndications have been around for over a century, they took off in the late 1980s with the rise of the leverage buyout financing and came into their own in the 2000s with the development of a deep secondary market in syndicated loans. Syndication forms and documentation became standardized and credit ratings agencies began to rate syndicated loans (which are assigned CUSIPs—standard identification numbers for clearing purposes) just as they do corporate debt securities. Not surprisingly, syndication pieces began to trade much like securities. Just as debt securities are divided into investment and speculative (junk) grades, so too are syndicated loans, with higher-cost, speculative loans referred to as "leveraged loans." Notably, however, trading in syndicated loans is not regulated under federal securities loans, as they are not considered securities despite the functional convergence of the syndicated loan and securities markets.

With the development of a secondary market in syndicated loans, secured loans funding capability has equaled and in fact surpassed that of bonds, although both are funded by capital market investors (including banks). In 2016, there were 3,630 syndicated loans originated in the United States for a total amount of $2.09 trillion. Thomson Reuters, Global Syndicated Loans Review (Full Year 2016). By contrast, U.S. corporate bond issuance in 2016 was $1.52 trillion for some 1,388 deals. SIFMA, US Fact Book (2017). For corporate borrowers, syndicated loans have surpassed bonds as the preferred method of financing. (For comparison, there were 891 equity issuances in 2016, totaling only $197.5 billion—of which only 119 deals, for $20.8 billion, were initial public offerings. *Id.*)

While single bank funding limitations explain some of the use of syndication and participation, there are other reasons that may apply as well.

William Widen
Lord of the Liens: Toward Greater Efficiency in Secured Lending
25 Cardozo L. Rev. 101, 106-107 (2004)

A common explanation for the syndication process is that, when sums get large, individual lenders lack the funds necessary to supply all the credit needs of a borrower or do not want to supply those funds because of a desire to diversify investments. The lenders, thus, must band together so that collectively the sums required by the borrower may be advanced. Another explanation for the syndication process relates to efficiencies created by agent signaling. If an agent holds a significant portion of the syndicated loan, other potential syndicate members view the large retained position in the loan as a signal that the credit represents a good loan investment. Based on this signal, syndicate members participate in the loan after conducting more limited due diligence than they would conduct in the absence of the signal. In effect, the participants join syndicates based on the brand name of the agent, thus saving them costs. These explanations tell only part of the story.

Syndication is also a technique for minimizing the direct transaction costs associated with the contracting process. Instead of a borrower separately negotiating with multiple lenders for the funds needed in its specific operations, multiple negotiations at the borrower level are replaced by a single negotiation for the benefit of the borrower, with the agent acting for the syndicate.

Participations are additionally appealing to banks because they allow the lead lender to keep the relationship with the borrower all to itself without having to commit to the entire funding itself, even while collecting origination and servicing fees. Participations may also allow lenders with expertise in managing particular types of loans, such as those related to oil and gas extraction or construction, to sell their expertise as loan managers to other lenders. And lenders with an abundance of funds, a shortage of customers, or lack of administrative capacity or expertise in a particular type of lending may want to purchase participations, either as a place to park their funds or as a way of developing expertise in an area of lending.

A. Syndications vs. Participations: Definitional Issues

The fundamental difference between a syndication and a participation is whether there is contractual privity between the debtor and all of the lenders or just between the borrower and the agent bank. In a syndication, all of the lenders have contractual privity with the borrower, while in a participation, only the lead bank has contractual privity.

Several implications follow from privity. A borrower may not be aware that a loan has been participated, but it will necessarily know if the loan has been syndicated and thus that it is dealing with multiple lenders. In a syndicate, the lenders have direct rights against the borrower. While these rights may be waived by the syndication agreement, in theory, at least, each syndicate member could pursue remedies on its own. Relatedly, in a syndication, the direct relationship between each lender and the borrower enables syndicate members to exercise setoff, which requires mutually owing debts. In a participation, the borrower's obligation runs only to the lead bank, so only the lead can exercise setoff. Likewise, in a syndication, lenders are not responsible for each other's funding commitments—if one lender is unable to meet its commitment, the other members are not responsible for the funding. In contrast, in a participation, the lead is responsible for the funding and is on the hook if the participants fail to fund. Finally, in a syndication, it is theoretically possible to change the agent because the agent is not the lender (although it often is also a member of the syndicate). In a participation, it is not possible to change the lead without selling or refinancing the loan.

It is important not to place too much emphasis on the differences between syndication and participation, however. The exact nature of the relationship between the various lenders and the borrower and among the various lenders is a function of contract. Syndication and participation agreements are methods for addressing the collective action problems that arise when there are multiple lenders for one loan or credit facility.

Thus, even if there isn't privity, a participation can grant participants contractual rights to enforce their shares in a loan in the event that the lead bank is insolvent. Conversely, even with privity, lenders may (and typically do) agree to give up their individual rights and subject themselves to collective decision making or the discretion of an agent. Moreover, syndicated interests can be participated and participations can be syndicated. Furthermore, syndication interest and participation interests can be pooled and reparticipated or securitized into collateralized loan obligations (CLOs).

B. Syndications

In a syndication, all of the lenders have contractual privity with the borrower, but the loan is documented through a common negotiated agreement that designates one or more agents for the lenders. The syndicates' recoveries are shared on a pro-rata basis among syndicate members. The syndication agreement sets forth the rights, duties, and compensation of the agents and provides a coordination mechanism. Syndications typically require lender votes with majorities determined (by dollar amount loaned or committed) for major decisions such as calling the loan, waivers, amendments, releases, collection actions, and disposing of collateral. The level of majority required varies by deal and sometimes by action within the deal: Sometimes a simple majority is required, sometimes a supermajority, and sometimes unanimity. This arrangement means that smaller lenders risk losing control over the management of the loan to larger lenders, who may have different interests.

A central feature of syndication is that the lenders surrender contractually their individual rights to enforce the loan by suit. This feature is so fundamental that courts have even implied it when express contractual language of surrender is absent. *Bank of Tokyo-Mitsubishi Ltd. v. Enron Corp.* (*In re Enron*), 2005 WL 356985 (S.D.N.Y. Feb. 15, 2005). Related to this surrender of litigation rights, syndication agreements also typically involve the relinquishment of non-judicial enforcement rights. While there is contractual privity on the loan itself, normally the security interest is granted to the syndicate's agent for the benefit of the syndicate lenders.[6]

The excerpted provisions from the Colt Term Loan Agreement below illustrate the pro-rated recoveries (§ 2.4(b)(i)), the appointment of an agent (§ 15.1), the secession of individual lenders' right to sue (§ 15.12(a)), the several, rather than joint nature of the lenders' obligations (§ 15.18), and the majority rule mechanism (Schedule 1.1).

TERM LOAN AGREEMENT

by and among

COLT DEFENSE LLC,
COLT FINANCE CORP.,

---

6. UCC Article 9 is accommodating to this structure. UCC § 9-102(a)(73)(E) defines "secured party" to include a "trustee, indenture trustee, agent, collateral agent or other representative in whose favor a security interest . . . is created." Comment 2.b to § 9-102 further states that "[t]he definition of 'secured party' clarifies the status of various types of representatives. Consider for example, a multi-bank facility under which Bank A, Bank B and Bank C are lenders and Bank A serves as collateral agent. If the security interest is granted to Bank A as collateral agent, then Bank A is the secured party." Likewise, UCC § 9-502(a)(2) requires a financing statement to provide "the name of the secured party *or a representative of the secured party*." (Emphasis added.) And UCC § 9-503(d) notes that a financing statement is not ineffective solely because of "[f]ailure to indicate the representative capacity of a secured party or representative of a secured party." Thus, even though each member of a syndicate is in contractual privity with the borrower, there will typically be only one financing statement filed for the entire syndicate, and it will be filed by the agent bank. The agent bank may also be named as the secured party in the security agreement.

NEW COLT HOLDING CORP.,
COLT'S MANUFACTURING COMPANY, LLC AND
COLT CANADA CORPORATION,

as Borrowers,

THE SUBSIDIARIES OF COLT DEFENSE LLC
NAMED AS GUARANTORS HEREIN,

as Guarantors,

THE LENDERS THAT ARE PARTIES HERETO,

as the Lenders,

and

WILMINGTON SAVINGS FUND SOCIETY, FSB,

as Agent

Dated as of November 17, 2014

. . .

2.4 Payments; Reductions of Commitments; Prepayments.

. . .
(b) Apportionment and Application.
(i) So long as no [Event of Default] has occurred and is continuing and except as otherwise provided herein . . . all principal and interest payments received by Agent shall be apportioned ratably among the Lenders (according to the unpaid principal balance of the Obligations to which such payments relate held by each Lender) entitled to such payments and all payments of fees and expenses received by Agent (other than fees or expenses that are for Agent's separate account) shall be apportioned ratably among the Lenders having a Pro Rata Share of the type of Obligation to which a particular fee or expense relates. All payments to be made hereunder by Borrowers shall be remitted to Agent and all such payments, and all proceeds of Collateral received by Agent, shall be applied, so long as no [Event of Default] has occurred and is continuing, to repay the remaining Term Loan (which payments shall be applied against the Term Loan in the inverse order of maturity), and, thereafter, to Borrowers (to be wired to the Designated Account) or such other Person entitled thereto under applicable law. . . .

13. Assignments and Participations; Successors.

13.1 Assignments and Participations.

. . .

(e) Any Lender may at any time sell to one or more commercial banks, financial institutions, or other Persons (a "Participant") participating interests in all or any portion of its Obligations, its Commitment, and the other rights and interests of that Lender (the "Originating Lender") hereunder and under the other Loan Documents; provided, however, that (i) the Originating Lender shall remain a "Lender" for all purposes of this Agreement and the other Loan Documents and the Participant receiving the participating interest in the Obligations, and the other rights and interests of the Originating Lender hereunder shall not constitute a "Lender" hereunder or under the other Loan Documents and the Originating Lender's obligations under this Agreement shall remain unchanged, (ii) the Originating Lender shall remain solely responsible for the performance of such obligations, (iii) Borrowers, Agent, and the Lenders shall continue to deal solely and directly with the Originating Lender in connection with the Originating Lender's rights and obligations under this Agreement and the other Loan Documents, (iv) no Lender shall transfer or grant any participating interest under which the Participant has the right to approve any amendment to, or any consent or waiver with respect to, this Agreement or any other Loan Document, except to the extent such amendment to, or consent or waiver with respect to this Agreement or of any other Loan Document would (A) extend the final maturity date of the Obligations hereunder in which such Participant is participating, (B) reduce the interest rate applicable to the Obligations hereunder in which such Participant is participating, (C) release all or substantially all of the Collateral or guaranties (except to the extent expressly provided herein or in any of the Loan Documents) supporting the Obligations hereunder in which such Participant is participating, (D) postpone the payment of, or reduce the amount of, the interest or fees payable to such Participant through such Lender (other than a waiver of default interest), or (E) decreases the amount or postpones the due dates of scheduled principal repayments or prepayments or premiums payable to such Participant through such Lender, and (v) all amounts payable . . . by Borrowers hereunder shall be determined as if such Lender had not sold such participation, except that, if amounts outstanding under this Agreement are due and unpaid, or shall have been declared or shall have become due and payable upon the occurrence of an Event of Default, each Participant shall be deemed to have the right of set off in respect of its participating interest in amounts owing under this Agreement to the same extent as if the amount of its participating interest were owing directly to it as a Lender under this Agreement. The rights of any Participant only shall be derivative through the Originating Lender with whom such Participant participates and no Participant shall have any rights under this Agreement or the other Loan

Documents or any direct rights as to the other Lenders, Agent, Loan Parties, the Collections of Loan Parties, the Collateral, or otherwise in respect of the Obligations. . . . No Participant shall have the right to participate directly in the making of decisions by the Lenders among themselves.

***

15. Agent; the Lender Group.

15.1 Appointment and Authorization of Agent. Each Lender hereby designates and appoints Wilmington Savings Fund Society, FSB as its agent under this Agreement . . . and each Lender hereby irrevocably authorizes Agent to execute and deliver each of the other Loan Documents . . . on its behalf and to take such other action on its behalf under the provisions of this Agreement and each other Loan Document . . . and to exercise such powers and perform such duties as are expressly delegated to Agent by the terms of this Agreement or any other Loan Document . . . , together with such powers as are reasonably incidental thereto. Agent agrees to act as agent for and on behalf of the Lenders on the conditions contained in this Section 15. Any provision to the contrary contained elsewhere in this Agreement or in any other Loan Document notwithstanding, Agent shall not have any duties or responsibilities, except those expressly set forth herein or in the other Loan Documents, nor shall Agent have or be deemed to have any fiduciary relationship with any Lender, and no implied covenants, functions, responsibilities, duties, obligations or liabilities shall be read into this Agreement or any other Loan Document or otherwise exist against Agent. Without limiting the generality of the foregoing, the use of the term "agent" in this Agreement or the other Loan Documents with reference to Agent is not intended to connote any fiduciary or other implied (or express) obligations arising under agency doctrine of any applicable law. Instead, such term is used merely as a matter of market custom, and is intended to create or reflect only a representative relationship between independent contracting parties.

Each Lender hereby further authorizes Agent to act as the secured party under each of the Loan Documents that create a Lien on any item of Collateral. Except as expressly otherwise provided in this Agreement, Agent shall have and may use its sole discretion with respect to exercising or refraining from exercising any discretionary rights or taking or refraining from taking any actions that Agent expressly is entitled to take or assert under or pursuant to this Agreement and the other Loan Documents. Without limiting the generality of the foregoing, or of any other provision of the Loan Documents that provides rights or powers to Agent, Lenders agree that Agent shall have the right to exercise the following powers as long as this Agreement remains in effect: . . . (b) execute or file any and all financing or similar statements or notices, amendments, renewals, supplements, documents, instruments, proofs of claim, notices and other written agreements with respect to the Loan Documents, (c) exclusively receive, apply, and distribute [all payments from the Borrowers] as provided in the Loan Documents, . . . (e) perform, exercise, and enforce any and all other rights and remedies of the Lender Group with respect to Parent or its Subsidiaries, the Obligations, the Collateral, the Collections of Parent and its Subsidiaries, or otherwise related to any of same as provided in the Loan Documents, and (f) incur and pay such Lender Group Expenses as Agent may deem necessary or appropriate for the performance and fulfillment of its functions and powers pursuant to the Loan Documents.

. . .

15.12 Restrictions on Actions by Lenders; Sharing of Payments.

(a) Each of the Lenders agrees that it shall not, without the express written consent of the Required Lenders, and that it shall, to the extent it is lawfully entitled to do so, upon the written request of the Required Lenders, set off against the Obligations, any amounts owing by such Lender to Parent or its Subsidiaries or any deposit accounts of Parent or its Subsidiaries now or hereafter maintained with such Lender. Each of the Lenders further agrees that it shall not, unless specifically requested to do so in writing by the Required Lenders, take or cause to be taken any action, including, the commencement of any legal or equitable proceedings to enforce any Loan Document against any Borrower or any Guarantor or to foreclose any Lien on, or otherwise enforce any security interest in, any of the Collateral.

. . .

15.18 Several Obligations; No Liability. Notwithstanding that certain of the Loan Documents now or hereafter may have been or will be executed only by or in favor of Agent in its capacity as such, and not by or in favor of the Lenders, any and all obligations on the part of Agent (if any) to make any credit available hereunder, shall constitute the several (and not joint) obligations of the respective Lenders on a ratable basis in accordance with such Lender's percentage of the Term Loan outstanding. Nothing contained herein shall confer upon any Lender any interest in, or subject any Lender to any liability for, or in respect of, the business, assets, profits, losses, or liabilities of any other Lender. Each Lender shall be solely responsible for notifying its Participants of any matters relating to the Loan Documents to the extent any such notice may be required, and no Lender shall have any obligation, duty, or liability to any Participant of any other Lender. Except as provided in Section 15.7, no member of the Lender Group shall have any liability for the acts of any other member of the Lender Group. No Lender shall be responsible to Borrower or any other Person for any failure by any other Lender to fulfill its obligations to make credit available hereunder, nor to advance for such Lender or on its behalf, nor to take any other action on behalf of such Lender hereunder or in connection with the financing contemplated herein.

Schedule 1.1 [Definitions]

. . .

"Pro Rata Share" means, as of any date of determination: with respect to a Lender's obligation to make all or a portion of the Term Loan and right to receive payments of principal, interest, fees, costs, and expenses with respect thereto, the percentage obtained by dividing (a) the outstanding principal amount of the Term Loan owed to such Lender, by (b) the aggregate outstanding principal amount of the Term Loan.

. . .

"Required Lenders" means, at any time, Lenders whose aggregate Pro Rata Shares exceed 50.0%.

. . .

As the secured party, the agent bank is the only party entitled to exercise the syndicate's rights against the debtor, but the agent bank will typically be acting on instructions from the requisite majority of syndicate members or pursuant to enforcement discretion granted to it in the syndication agreement.

Although a syndicated loan is made by a consortium of lenders, typically a single bank was the debtor's original point of contact, and that bank undertakes to syndicate the loan, a process not unlike the underwriting of a bond. (Because of this, syndications—and participations as well—will usually have recitals that the investors have each made their own independent credit analysis and not relied on information provided by the lead.)

One effect of this is that there can actually be numerous entities involved with a syndicated loan with fancy-sounding titles. While for our purposes we will refer simply to an "agent" or "lead" bank in a syndication, a variety of titles get used to indicate different roles vis-à-vis the loan. Some of them are quite meaningless, as the Standard & Poor's credit rating agency explains.

Standard & Poor's A Guide to the Loan Market (Sept. 2011)

In the formative days of the syndicated loan market (the late 1980s), there was usually one agent that syndicated each loan. "Lead manager" and "manager" titles were doled out in exchange for large commitments. As league tables [industry rankings] gained influence as a marketing tool, "co-agent" titles were often used in attracting large commitments or in cases where these institutions truly had a role in underwriting and syndicating the loan.

During the 1990s, the use of league tables and, consequently, title inflation exploded. Indeed, the co-agent title has become largely ceremonial today, routinely awarded for what amounts to no more than large retail commitments. In most syndications, there is one lead arranger. This institution is considered to be on the "left" (a reference to its position in an old-time tombstone ad). There are also likely to be other banks in the arranger group, which may also have a hand in underwriting and syndicating a credit. These institutions are said to be on the "right."

The different titles used by significant participants in the syndications process are administrative agent, syndication agent, documentation agent, agent, co-agent or managing agent, and lead arranger or book runner:

- *The administrative agent* is the bank that handles all interest and principal payments and monitors the loan.
- *The syndication agent* is the bank that handles, in purest form, the syndication of the loan. Often, however, the syndication agent has a less specific role.
- *The documentation agent* is the bank that handles the documents and chooses the law firm.
- *The agent* title is used to indicate the lead bank when there is no other conclusive title available, as is often the case for smaller loans.
- *The co-agent* or *managing agent* is largely a meaningless title used mostly as an award for large commitments.
- *The lead arranger* or *book runner* title is a league table designation used to indicate the "top dog" in a syndication.

––––––––––––––––––––

Typical duties of an agent bank are transmitting repaid funds from the borrower to the syndicate members; filings financing statements, continuation statements, and amendments; distributing notices, documents, and information to syndicate members; delivering all requests, demands, approvals, and consents from banks to the borrower and notices to the banks; ensuring that conditions precedent to the borrower's drawdown of funds are met; determining the applicable interest rate for borrowings (an issue with floating rate loans and multi-facility loans); ensuring compliance with facility limits and sub-limits; following instructions from the syndicate, when applicable, particularly regarding amendments and waivers; and enforcing remedies against the borrower, including foreclosures and filings claims in bankruptcy.

Sometimes the agent bank is charged with monitoring covenants and collateral, but agent banks are frequently exculpated from a range of actions and omissions, including notice of defaults absent actual knowledge. The agent bank is also indemnified by the syndicate for its expenses as long as they do not result from gross negligence or willful malfeasance. In essence, the agent bank is meant to perform ministerial tasks, rather than exercise discretion outside of a narrow range of activities. The agent bank is not intended to be a fiduciary for the syndicate and is usually allowed to conduct other business with the borrower, even if that other business would create a conflict of interest with the other members of a syndicate. The following decision indicates the extent to which the lead bank is truly an "agent" with concomitant liability to its "principals."

UniCredito Italiano SPA v. JPMorgan Chase Bank

288 F. Supp. 2d 485 (S.D.N.Y. 2003)

SWAIN, District Judge.

This action concerns loans, made by Plaintiffs [UCI and Pekao] to or for the benefit of the Enron Corporation, that were administered by [Defendants] JP Morgan Chase Bank and Citibank. Plaintiffs contend that Defendants defrauded them in connection with the formation of certain syndicated credit facilities and payments under those facilities. . . . Defendants now move . . . for an order dismissing the Second Amended Complaint. . . . For the following reasons, Defendants' motions are granted. . . .

THE CREDIT FACILITIES

The bulk of Plaintiffs' damages claims in this action arise from losses sustained on investments in credit facilities for Enron for which the Defendant banks served as Administrative and/or Paying Agents . . . and which were marketed by the Defendant securities subsidiaries. Defendants JP Morgan Chase Bank (through its predecessor in interest, The Chase Manhattan Bank) and Citibank were the Co–Administrative Agents for three Enron credit facilities in which Plaintiffs participated: 1) a $1.25 billion medium-term credit facility entered into on May 18, 2000 (the "2000 Credit Facility"), 2) a $1.75 billion short-term facility entered into on May 14, 2001 (the "2001 Credit Facility"), and 3) a $500 million letter of credit facility . . . (collectively, the "Syndicated Facilities"). Citibank was also the Paying Agent for the 2000 and 2001 Credit Facilities. . . .

The agreements establishing each of the Syndicated Facilities contained disclaimer, covenant, and acknowledgment provisions identical in all relevant respects to the following provisions of the 2000 Credit Facility:

Section 7.02 Paying Agent's Reliance, Etc.
[T]he Paying Agent shall not have, by reason of this Agreement or any other Loan Document a fiduciary relationship in respect of any Bank or the holder of any Note; and nothing in this Agreement or any other Loan Document, expressed or implied, is intended or shall be so construed as to impose upon the Paying Agent any obligations in respect of this Agreement or any other Loan Document except as expressly set forth herein. Without limitation of the generality of the foregoing, the Paying Agent . . . (iii) makes no warranty or representation to any Bank for any statements, warranties or representations (whether written or oral) made in or in connection with any Loan Document or any other instrument or document furnished pursuant hereto or in connection herewith; (iv) shall not have any duty to ascertain or to inquire as to the performance or observance of any of the terms, covenants or conditions of any Loan Document or any other instrument or document furnished pursuant hereto or in connection herewith on the part of the Borrower or to inspect the property (including the books and records) of the Borrower[.]

Section 7.03 Paying Agent and Its Affiliates
With respect to its Commitment, the Advances made by it and the Note issued to it, each Bank which is also the Paying Agent shall have the same rights and powers under the

Loan Documents as any other Bank and may exercise the same as though it were not the Paying Agent; the term "Bank" or "Banks" shall, unless otherwise expressly indicated, include any Bank serving as the Paying Agent in its individual capacity. Any Bank serving as the Paying Agent and its affiliates may accept deposits from, lend money to, act as trustee under indentures of, accept investment banking engagements from and generally engage in any kind of business with, the Borrower, any of the Subsidiaries and any Person who may do business with or own securities of the Borrower or any Subsidiary, all as if such Bank were not the Paying Agent and without any duty to account therefor to the Banks.

Section 7.04 Bank Credit Decision
Each Bank acknowledges that it has, independently and without reliance upon the Paying Agent or any other Bank and based on the financial statements referred to in Section 4.01(d) and such other documents and information as it has deemed appropriate, made its own credit analysis and decision to enter into this Agreement. Each Bank also acknowledges that it will, independently and without reliance upon the Paying Agent or any other Bank and based on such documents and information as it shall deem appropriate at the time, continue to make its own credit decisions in taking or not taking action under this Agreement and the other Loan Documents. The Paying Agent shall not have any duty or responsibility, either initially or on a continuing basis, to provide any Bank or the holder of any Note with any credit or other information with respect thereto, whether coming into its possession before the making of the Advances or at any time or times thereafter.
. . .

In each of the agreements for the Syndicated Facilities, Enron (which was referred to in the agreements as the "Borrower") entered into certain covenants concerning the participating banks' due diligence rights. . . .

Defendants [Citibank] and J.P. Morgan Securities [a JPMorgan subsidiary] (the "Securities Subsidiaries") were co-lead arrangers of the Syndicated Facilities. They distributed to participant banks offering memoranda and invitations to offer in connection with the Syndicated Facilities. . . .

Plaintiff UCI contributed $10,416,667.67 under the 2000 Credit Facility, $11,666,666.67 under the 2001 Credit Facility. . . . Plaintiff Pekao purchased a participating interest in the 2000 Credit Facility in the amount of $6.25 million.

In determining whether to extend credit under the Facilities, Plaintiffs conducted credit assessments that included, *inter alia*, a review of Enron's financial statements, including its 10-K and 10-Q Forms filed with the SEC.

If Plaintiffs had known the true facts of Enron's financial condition, especially its actual amount of debt and its actual debt-to-capitalization ratio, and the extent of the improper transactions conducted by Enron with Defendants and others, Plaintiffs would not have participated in the Facilities.

Defendants withheld information from Plaintiffs concerning Enron's debt, its inflated revenues, and Defendants' role in [unrelated] improper transactions that allowed Enron to fraudulently manipulate its publicly reported financial condition.

Under the agreements for the Syndicated Credit Facilities, Enron represented that it was in compliance with applicable laws, that there had been no adverse change in its financial condition since the end of its prior fiscal year, and that it had and would maintain a ratio of total senior debt to total capitalization of no more than 65%. Defendants knew that Enron's debt-to-capitalization ratio was higher than reported. A 1999 internal Citibank document revealed that Citibank was aware that Enron had a debt-to-capitalization ratio of over 65%. Defendants also knew that Enron was in violation of securities and commodities laws.

The Defendant banks and securities subsidiaries through, *inter alia*, the offering memoranda and invitations to offer, directed Plaintiffs to public information regarding Enron's financial information that they knew to be materially false.

THE OCTOBER 25, 2001 BORROWING REQUESTS

Under the credit agreements governing the 2000 and 2001 Credit Facilities, Enron had to satisfy certain conditions before it could receive loan funds, including compliance with all laws and the maintenance of a 65% debt-to-capitalization ratio. On October 25, 2001, Plaintiff UCI received borrowing demands at 11:48 A.M. and 12 noon, conveyed through Citibank, for immediate payment of its shares of the 2000 and 2001 Credit Facilities, and Plaintiff Pekao received a demand at 12 noon, conveyed through Citibank, to fund immediately its share of the 2000 Credit Facility.

At 2:45 P.M., the Managing Director of JP Morgan Chase Securities, Claire O'Connor, notified UCI that Enron would explain its need for cash to redeem its commercial paper at a conference call at 3:00 P.M. The Defendant banks helped manage Enron's commercial paper program, but O'Connor did not mention their role. O'Connor falsely stated that Enron was drawing down the funds to reestablish market confidence. At the 3:00 P.M. conference call, Enron's CFO explained that Enron needed the full amounts of the 2000 and 2001 Credit Facilities so that Enron could redeem its commercial paper. The Defendant banks participated in the conference call, but said nothing about Enron's defaults under the credit agreements, defaults of which they were aware.

At 4:06 P.M., UCI received a facsimile from Citibank conveying Enron's certification that its representations and warranties, including those in the credit agreements, continued to be correct, and that there was no default or event of default under the credit agreements. UCI and Pekao subsequently forwarded their respective contributions under the credit facilities to Citibank, to be conveyed to Enron.

Pursuant to section 6.01 of the credit agreements governing the 2000 and 2001 Credit Facilities, if a majority of the participating banks had determined that a default or event of default had occurred that relieved them of their obligations under the agreements, the banks could have instructed Citibank to declare the termination of each bank's obligation to make advances. Defendants knew that Enron's debt-to-capitalization ratio put it in breach of the credit agreements, and their concealment of that breach prevented Plaintiffs from exercising their rights under section 6.01.

The Defendant banks, who were also participants in the 2000 and 2001 Credit Facilities, contributed their shares of the October 25, 2001 funding. The credit facilities enabled the banks to reduce their aggregate exposure and take a "smaller hit" with respect to Enron.

On November 1, 2001, the Defendant banks announced that they were negotiating to extend $1 billion in secured loans to Enron. Citibank conditioned its participation in that secured loan on Enron's payment of an earlier $250 million unsecured Citibank loan.

. . .

PLAINTIFFS' CAUSES OF ACTION

Plaintiffs UCI and Pekao assert common law claims against all Defendants for fraudulent concealment (Count I), fraudulent inducement (Count II), . . . [and] negligent misrepresentation (Count IV). . . . Plaintiffs assert a claim against JP Morgan Chase Bank and Citibank for breach of an implied duty of good faith in connection with the Syndicated Facilities (Count VI).

PLAINTIFFS' FRAUD AND NEGLIGENT MISREPRESENTATION CLAIMS

. . .

Plaintiffs' fraud and misrepresentation claims must be dismissed because the contracts pursuant to which they made their Enron loan investments preclude them from establishing essential elements of those claims, namely, that the Defendant banks had a duty to disclose information regarding or gained from their business dealings with Enron, and that any reliance by Plaintiffs on misrepresentations by the Defendants was reasonable.

Sections 7.02 and 8.02 of the 2000 Credit Facility and parallel provisions of the other operative documents provided specifically that the Defendant banks, in their capacities as Paying or Co–Administrative Agents, would have no obligations other than those expressly specified in the relevant agreements and that they had no duty "to ascertain or to inquire as to the performance or observance of any of the terms, covenants or conditions of any Loan Document or any other [relevant] instrument or document . . . on the part of Borrower." Sections 7.03 and 8.03 of that agreement and the parallel provisions of the other relevant operative documents permitted the Defendant banks, in their capacities as Paying or Co–Administrative Agent . . . and their affiliates to engage in banking and other business transactions with Enron and its affiliates, "without any duty to account therefor to the [lending] Banks." Under section 7.04 and 8.04, the lenders agreed that the bank Defendants, in their capacities as Paying or Co–Administrative Agent, would "not have any duty or responsibility, either initially or on a continuing basis, to provide any [lending] Bank or the holder of any Note with any credit or other information with respect thereto, whether coming into [their] possession before the making of the [loan] Advances or at any time or times thereafter."

Plaintiffs' fraudulent concealment and negligent misrepresentation claims as against Defendant banks thus must fail because, even if the bank Defendants had the knowledge the Complaint attributes to them, the banks had no duty to disclose it to Plaintiffs. Sophisticated parties such as Plaintiffs are held to the terms of their contracts.

The operative documents also, on their face, preclude Plaintiffs from claiming that they relied reasonably on any alleged representations by the Defendants. In addition to the above-quoted provisions disclaiming any duties on the banks' part to monitor

Enron's compliance with its obligations in connection with the loan facilities and permitting the banks and their affiliates to carry on business transactions with Enron and its affiliates without accounting to the other lenders for that activity, the lenders specifically agreed that they had, and would continue to, make their own credit decisions and would not rely on the Defendant banks, either in entering into the facilities or in making decisions in the course of the performance of the relevant agreements. Having failed to bargain for the right to rely on the banks as monitors of Enron's compliance with its disclosure, financial condition and other covenants, or for the right to benefit from any knowledge gained by the Defendant banks or their affiliates in connection with their own business dealings with Enron and its affiliates, Plaintiffs cannot, as a matter of law, be held reasonably to have relied on any misrepresentations or omissions by the Defendants concerning those matters.

Counts I, II and IV of the Complaint will therefore be dismissed for failure to state a claim.

. . .

PLAINTIFFS' CLAIM FOR BREACH OF THE IMPLIED DUTY OF GOOD FAITH AND UCI'S CLAIM FOR DECLARATORY RELIEF

The express disclaimers in the credit agreements preclude Plaintiffs' claim for breach of the implied duty of good faith in those agreements to the extent that claim is premised on the allegedly fraudulent conduct addressed above. Plaintiffs allege that the failure of Defendant banks to disclose Enron's true financial condition in connection with the credit transactions prevented Plaintiffs from taking advantage of their various rights under the credit agreements. Although New York law implies a duty of good faith and fair dealing in every contract, "no obligation can be implied that would be inconsistent with other terms of the contractual relationship." *Dalton v. Educational Testing Service*, 87 N.Y.2d 384, 639 (N.Y. 1995). Here, as explained above, the operative contracts specifically absolve the Defendant banks from any duty to disclose financial information regarding Enron and contain Plaintiffs' undertakings to rely on their own credit analyses in making the relevant decisions. Implication of a duty, notwithstanding these provisions, of the banks to make disclosures regarding Enron's financial conditions would clearly be inconsistent with the governing contracts.

. . .

C. Participations

A loan participation is a sale of an undivided interest in a loan. The legal relationship in a participation is not always completely clear, however. While it can be understood as a "sale of an undivided interest in the loan" or "a sale of an undivided interest in the loan, the collateral, and the documents," it can also be understood as a secured loan from the participants to the lead bank, with the loan from the lead bank to the borrower as the collateral. If so reconceptualized, then the participant interests would be unperfected secured loans (absent a financing statement). A participation can also be a disguised guarantee. For example, a participation might be structured so that it is not required to be funded until the borrower has defaulted on its payment obligations. Thus, if the borrower does not pay, the lead bank can still be made whole when the participants fund their interest. *See CCP Limited Partnership v. First Source Financial Inc.*, 368 Ill. App. 3d 476 (Ill. Ct. of App. 2006).

The critical feature of a participation is that there is no direct contractual relationship between the participants and the borrower. This means that the lead bank's business relationship with the borrower remains undisturbed. The loan documents may not contain any reference to the participants. There may be one participant or many, and the lead bank may have sold all of its interest and may act solely as the administrative agent, servicing the loan, for which it is paid a servicing fee by the participants. The servicing fee is often in the form of an interest differential. To wit, if the borrower pays 6.25% on the loan, the lead bank might keep 0.25% as a servicing fee and remit interest payments equal to 6.00% of the principal to the participants. Participants usually share pro rata after the lead's fees are deducted.

The participation structure often means that the lead bank has more discretion than in a syndication. Participants may have the ability to veto certain matters such as changes in principal, interest, fees, maturity and amortization, and collateral releases, but the lead will usually have discretion regarding whether to declare a default, and will usually have its liability to participants limited to acts taken or omitted out of gross negligence, willful misconduct, and bad faith. Both the promissory note and security interest will always be in the name of the lead, but the lead need not maintain any actual interest in the loan in a participation; to the extent that the loan is participated, the lead may be able to derecognize the loan for accounting purposes.

The lead-participant relationship is usually memorialized in either a "participation agreement" or a "participation certificate." The former is generally a more detailed document, while the latter is a statement that the participant has a specific percentage interest in the loan and contains a summary of the rights and obligations of the lead and participants.

Section 13 in the Colt Term Loan Agreement, excerpted above, addresses the possibility of syndicate members participating their portion of the loan. Note both the limitations on the powers of the participants, and that participation agreements are allowed to give participants a voice regarding certain loan restructuring decisions.

D. Modern Syndicated Commercial Loan Structures

Further complicating restructurings is that many modern bank loans are not just a straightforward syndication of a single term loan. Instead, modern bank loans typically involve a "deal"—a term referring to the overall financing arrangement—that consists of multiple "facilities." A facility is an individual commitment under a deal with unique terms, such as amount, maturity date, borrowing structure, and price. Within a deal, there may be different lenders for different facilities; each facility may be syndicated (or participated) separately. A common structure is the one illustrated in Figure 3.1, below, in which the deal is documented by a single credit agreement, and that credit agreement creates three facilities: a Revolver, a Term Loan A, and a Term Loan B facility.

The **Revolver** is a revolving line of credit. Term Loans A and B are facilities for different amounts of funding, and may have different maturity dates and thus different pricing. Typically, Term Loan A facilities are shorter maturity than Term Loan B (or C or D) facilities and have regular repayment/amortization schedules and lower pricing. Term Loan A facilities are usually funded by bank investors. Term Loan B facilities have longer maturities, less regular repayment schedules, higher pricing, and are usually funded by institutional investors—pension plans, insurance companies, investment funds. The Revolver and the Term Loan A and B facilities all have the same priority, however, and there is only one security agreement for the entire deal. Term Loan facilities trade much more robustly in secondary markets than revolvers as they are much more like bonds in that they have fixed repayment obligations, whereas repayments under a revolver is dependent upon the borrower's usage.

In addition to these major facilities, modern loans will also often have sub-facilities for letters of credit, etc. Figure 3.1 includes "sub-limits" under the Revolver.

Figure 5.1 Sample Multi-Facility Deal Structure

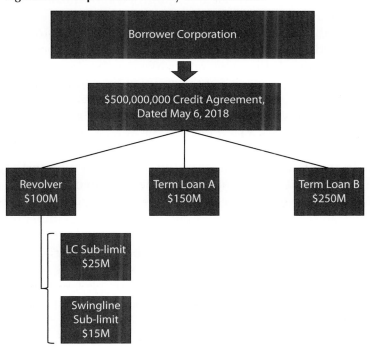

A sub-limit is a maximum amount under a facility that can be used for a specific purpose. Sub-limits are typically found as part of revolvers. Usually they include "swingline" facilities, letters of credit, foreign currency, multiple borrowers, and competitive bid sub-limits. A swingline is a sub-limit of a revolver that is available for same-day borrowing. The swingline thus lets the borrower have immediate liquidity to cover unexpected needs, whereas the revolver in general will typically require more advance notice prior to a draw. This convenience and flexibility comes at a price, of course.

For a syndicated loan, the funding for a swingline facility does not come from the consortium of lenders because of the immediate funding of a swingline facility. Instead, the swingline bank—usually the agent bank—will front the money for the entire syndicate in the revolver. The swingline lender will, however, participate the risk in the swingline. Typically this is done by a provision that allows the swingline lender to "put" the amount outstanding on the swingline to the other banks in the revolver syndicate at any time. When that happens, the swingline loan converts into a regular loan under the revolver that is to be funded pro rata by the syndicate.

Multi-currency sub-limits allow borrowing in other currencies per exchange rates and dates indicated in the credit agreement. Competitive bid sub-limits are priced based on lenders' competitive bidding to make the loan. The reason all revolvers are not entirely competitive bid is that an additional commitment fee is usually required. Finally, most deals will include a letter of credit sub-limit. This limit can cover both standby letters of credit and commercial letters of credit. A standby letter of credit is an unfunded, contingent commitment used to guarantee payment by the borrower to a particular counterparty. Standby letters of credit are only drawn upon if the borrower fails to pay its counterparty. In contrast, a commercial letter of credit is a device used for the payment of the borrower's (generally overseas) counterparties. It functions rather like a cashier's check, as the counterparty is assuming the payment risk of the issuer of the commercial letter of credit, not that of the borrower.

Figure 5.2, below, illustrates a variation in which the deal consists of two separate credit agreements. One is a First Lien Credit Agreement, which consists of two facilities, while the other is a Second Lien Credit Agreement with only one facility. There might be an intercreditor agreement in addition, setting forth the rights of lenders under each credit agreement vis-à-vis the other in more detail.

Other deals will have a senior/subordinate structure within a single credit agreement. Such an agreement might specify that borrowings under the Term Loan B facility are subordinate to those under the Term Loan A facility. This is called an A/B structure. Within facilities there might also be "tranching" or senior/subordinate structures that provide that lenders in a senior tranche are repaid before those in a junior tranche. Tranching can become quite complex, as subordination may only exist for funds repaid up to a certain level and in a certain time period.

Figure 5.2 Sample First Lien/Second Lien Deal Structure

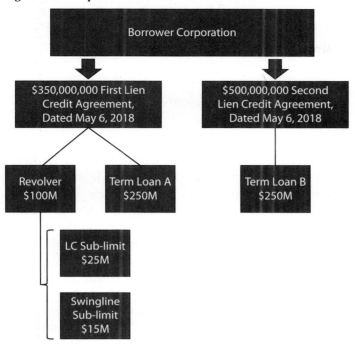

E. Second Lien Loans and Intercreditor Agreements

Modern capital structures frequently include more than one level of priority of financial debt. There are several forms of junior debt available: junior secured loans (second liens or third liens, etc.), mezzanine debt (debt of the parent company secured by the equity of the operating subsidiaries, but structurally subordinate to the creditors of the subsidiaries), and simple unsecured subordinated debt. Historically, most junior debt was mezzanine and unsecured debt, but beginning in the 2000s, there was an explosion of second lien lending.

Two basic forms of second lien loans exist. Sometimes, a second lien loan is documented as an entirely separate loan from the first lien loan. In such a situation, the second lien loan will have a separate security agreement, distinct covenants, and a separate agent bank. Such a second lien loan may be either an entirely separate transaction from the first lien loan or coordinated with the first lien loan through an **intercreditor agreement**.

Other times, however, a second lien loan will be structured as a separate, subordinated class within the same credit facility as a first lien loan. Having one credit agreement with internal tranching reduces documentation costs, avoids the need for a separate intercreditor agreement, and requires only one agent bank with one set of loan covenants to monitor.

Irrespective of how a second lien loan is structured, it implicates a variety of intercreditor conflicts. Loan agreements and intercreditor agreements aim to smooth over these problems and are highly negotiated, but unexpected contractual gaps and ambiguities can arise. We will turn to these issues in a later chapter.

Problem Set 5

Juno Natural Products took out a $500 million bank loan from a syndicate led by Mercury National Bank. The loan included a $200 million Term Loan A facility, a $100 million Term Loan B facility, and a $200 million Revolver. All three facilities were secured by liens on Juno's equipment and real estate. The loan also includes a cross-default clause that references Juno Natural Products' other financial debt. The facilities have a maturity of seven years. Mercury National retained only $10 million on the Juno National Products loan, all in the Term Loan A facility. The rest was sold to investors, including Vestal Capital, a hedge fund that purchased a $25 million piece of the Revolver.

A year before the syndication of the Juno Natural Products loan, Mercury National Bank had itself purchased $100 million in unsecured 10-year notes from Juno. Mercury discovered that Juno has been inflating its sales figures for several quarters and threatened to declare a default on the unsecured notes unless Juno repurchased the notes at a premium above current market prices. Juno agreed to do so, but lacked the ready cash to do so. Accordingly, Juno drew down on the Revolver, using the funds to redeem the unsecured notes from Mercury. Several months later, Juno ended up filing for bankruptcy.

(1) As the details of Juno's transactions emerge, is there anything Vestal can do? *See UniCredito Italiano SPA v. JPMorgan Chase Bank.*

(2) Would the answer to question 1 be different if the loan had been participated instead of syndicated?

(3) Would the answer to question 1 change if the loan had been first syndicated and then Vestal had purchased a participated interest in a syndication piece?

CHAPTER 6

SECURITIZATION AND DERIVATIVES

I. SECURITIZATION

Securitization is a financing technique that involves the issuance of securities payable from a pool of cash flow-producing assets, typically loans, which have been segregated from the other assets and liabilities of a firm. Thus, what a securitization does is take a loan or loans and turn them into securities. Because these securities are backed by a pool of assets that have been legally segregated from the firm's other assets and liabilities, investors in the securities are assuming solely the risks inherent in the assets, and not the general risks of an operating firm.

Securitization provides the funding for a sizeable part of the U.S. economy, especially mortgages and consumer credit, but also for syndicated loans. Securitizations constitute over a quarter of the U.S. bond market, and at peak have constituted over a third of the market.

A securitization is somewhat like a participation in which the lead bank has no other assets or liabilities than the participated loan.[1] Recall that a typical participation involves the sale of undivided interests in a single loan. But it is also possible to participate a pool of loans (or of any other type of cash flows). The participants in a loan assume the credit risk of the lead bank; if the lead bank fails to pass along payments to the participants, the participants lack contractual privity with the borrower and usually cannot pursue remedies against the borrower themselves.

Given that the lead bank has many other assets and liabilities beside the participated loan, the participants are effectively assuming the risk of the totality of the lead bank's operations, such as agency risk—the risk the firm's managers will make bad and possibly self-interested decisions regarding the firm's assets and liabilities—and asset substitution risk—the risk the firm will substitute lower value or riskier assets for its current assets. The risk profile of the lead bank is, of course, dynamic. The lead bank's assets and liabilities may change over time, and with it, the risk assumed by the participants in the loan. Many investors do not want to take on this sort of risk, or, if they did, they would simply invest in the lead bank in other forms of investment.

---

1. Securitization and participation are not formally defined terms, so some transactions styled as "participations" might in fact fit the description of a securitization above and vice-versa.

It is possible, however, to isolate the risks involved in the participated loan from the risks of the lead bank. By segregating selected cash flows (such as a loan or pool of loans) from the other assets and liabilities of a firm, it is possible for investors to invest solely in the selected cash flows. The segregation of the assets is accomplished by transferring them to a legally separate entity that will have virtually no other assets or liabilities. The separate entity will then issue debt, which is to be repaid from the segregated cash flows. The transfer of cash flow-producing assets from the other assets and liabilities of a firm to a non-operating entity enables investment based solely on the risks inherent in the segregated assets, rather than in the total package of the firm's assets and liabilities. This is securitization.[2]

Securitizations take two basic forms. Some securitizations, particularly those used for mortgage securitization, involve the issuance of pass-through certificates that evidence a beneficial interest in the underlying pool of financial assets. Such pass-through certificates are typically treated as equity securities, not debt, even if they have certain debt-like characteristics. *See Retirement Bd. of the Policemen's Annuity & Benefit Fund of Chi. v. Bank of N.Y. Mellon*, 775 F.3d 154, 164-165 (2d Cir. 2014). Other securitizations involve the issuance of debt securities secured by a security interest in the underlying pool of financial assets (with the residual interest assigned to an equity security).

Securitization is often advantageous for both investors and borrowers. Investors can invest in a more targeted, bespoke package of risks than if they were investing in an operating firm, and securitization borrowers may be able to raise capital at a lower cost than if they borrowed directly. For example, a firm with high-quality cash flows but significant liabilities can raise funds at costs set solely on the quality of the cash flows. Thus, a petroleum company with excellent cash flows but major environmental liabilities might itself be able to borrow at the market rate for a BBB-rated credit, but it could raise funds through securitization at the market rate for a superior AAA-rated credit.

The transactional goals of securitizations can vary considerably. Some securitization transactions are designed to arbitrage the difference in credit ratings between a firm and the issuance entity it creates for the securitization. Other securitization transactions are designed to enable the firm to arbitrage the spread between short-term and long-term interest rates. And still other securitization transactions are designed to arbitrage regulatory requirements.

Securitization is sometimes used as a risk-transfer device and sometimes as little more than secured financing on steroids. Some securitizations, such as mortgage securitizations, meaningfully transfer the risk of the securitized assets performance to investors. If there are losses on the assets, the securitizing firm will not cover them. Other securitizations formally transfer such risks, but functionally do not, as the securitizing firm is expected (but not formally obligated) to cover the losses as long as it is itself solvent. Credit card securitizations and many auto loan securitizations fit this profile. In these cases, the securitization is simply a way for a firm to borrow against

---

2. Again, some transactions styled as "participations" also have these features.

the strength of specific pools of its loan receivables without the investors assuming the general credit risk of the firm. *See* Adam J. Levitin, *Skin-in-the-Game: Risk Retention Lessons from Credit Card Securitization*, 81 Geo. Wash. L. Rev. 813 (2013).

A. The Securitization Transaction

The details of securitization transactions vary depending on the asset class involved and even within asset classes, but generally securitizations follow a particular form. The cash-flow producing assets, typically loans or debt securities, are pooled together by an entity known as the **sponsor**. These assets may have been generated ("originated") or purchased by the sponsor from other parties. The sponsor then transfers the selected assets to a newly created securitization entity (known variously as a **special purpose entity** or SPE, or as a **special purpose vehicle** or SPV). The SPE then will have no assets other than the transferred assets. The reason for the use of the SPE is to legally isolate the assets from those of the sponsor and thus shield them from the claims of or against the sponsor.[3]

In exchange for the assets, the SPE issues securities, which will be secured by the SPE's assets. These securities are generically known as **asset-backed securities** (ABS), unless the underlying assets are mortgages, in which case they are known as **mortgage-backed securities** (MBS).[4] The securities are typically rated by credit rating agencies, which play an important role in deal design, as they will indicate to sponsors the deal features that they require to award particular ratings levels. Thus, the cash flow-producing assets are effectively formed into securities.

The sponsor through its investment bank underwriters will then sell the securities into the market. The cash flows from the SPE's assets are used to pay the periodic payments on the securities, as well as the SPE's management costs. To the extent that the cash flows from the SPE's assets are insufficient to make the periodic payments on the securities, the investors do not have recourse against the sponsor absent specific contractual arrangement.

The particular corporate form of the SPE will vary by transaction class. Mortgage-related securitizations will typically use a common law or statutory trust, while other asset classes will often employ a limited liability company or corporation as the SPE. The difference of corporate form is significant, as some corporate forms (limited liability company or corporation) potentially allow the sponsor to retain substantial control over the securitized assets, while other forms (common law and statutory trusts) effectively transfer the assets beyond the control of the sponsor. Thus, the difference in corporate forms often reflects differences in transactional purposes of securitizations.

---

3. Frequently, securitization transactions involve an additional intermediate step. The sponsor will first sell the loans to a special-purpose subsidiary (the "**depositor**"), which has no other assets or liabilities. This is done to segregate the loans from the sponsor's assets and liabilities.

4. Securitization convention treats securitizations of home equity lines of credit as ABS, rather than MBS.

The precise legal structure used for the SPE, the nature of the securities issued, and the bankruptcy concerns involved vary by transaction type. Two basic forms are used, although hybrids appear in resecuritization transactions, one for mortgage securitizations, the other for securitizations of other assets.

For residential and commercial mortgage securitization, the SPE is usually a common law trust. A common law trust is not a legal entity in and of itself. Instead, a common law trust consists of a corpus of trust assets, legal title to which is held by a trustee, in trust for the trust's beneficiaries. In exchange for the securitized assets, the trust issues certificates of beneficial interest in the assets to the sponsor. The sponsor then sells all or a portion of the certificates to investors. The certificates are considered equity for state law and securities law purposes, but they may be treated as debt securities for federal income tax purposes (other than one class of residual certificates with little or no economic value) if a federal tax election is made to treat the underlying mortgage loans as a Real Estate Mortgage Investment Conduit (REMIC). 26 U.S.C §§ 860A-860G.

Significantly, for our purposes, a common law trust that is not a "business trust" is not eligible to be a debtor in bankruptcy. Moreover, as long as the trustee is a legally separate entity from the sponsor, the assets in the trust should be immune to the sponsor's bankruptcy. Thus, the investors will be assuming only the credit risk on the assets, not on the sponsor's business as a whole.

Other securitizations, such as those for automobile lease loans, credit card receivables, equipment leases and loans, student loans, and home equity lines of credit, will often use corporations, LLCs, or Delaware statutory trusts (a separate legal entity under Delaware law) as the SPE. The sponsor or an affiliate will often hold the equity interest in the SPE and thus control the SPE; in contrast, the sponsor will not legally control the common law trust's trustee (although it may have significant relational leverage over the trustee). As with the common law trustee, these SPEs pay for the securitized assets by issuing securities. The securities issued by these SPEs, however, are debt securities not just for federal taxation purposes, but also for securities law and state law purposes.

Unlike common law trusts, the SPEs in these securitizations are potentially eligible to be debtors in bankruptcy. They are, however, often set up so that a bankruptcy filing is unlikely to be authorized. Moreover, they are often designed so that the securitized assets will be legally "remote" from the bankruptcy risk of the sponsor. **Bankruptcy remoteness** requires both a **"true sale"** of the assets to the SPE, and for the SPE to be structured so that it cannot be substantively consolidated with the sponsor. These issues are covered in more depth in the penultimate chapter of the book.

Irrespective of whether a common law trust or some other form of SPE is used, however, the legal separation of the SPE from the sponsor (and depositor) is crucial to securitization because it enables favorable bankruptcy and tax treatment.[5] If done

---

5. Prior to 2010, such separation was also necessary for favorable accounting treatment, namely non-consolidation of the SPE with the sponsor for accounting purposes. This is particularly important for banks because accounting for bank regulatory capital purposes is based on generally accepted accounting

properly, the assets of the SPE are unaffected by the sponsor's bankruptcy, as they are like any other assets that have been sold in an arm's length transaction for fair market value. This means that investors in the ABS or MBS do not need to worry about the financial condition of the sponsor, only the quality of the securitized assets. (As it turns out, the division is not so neat. The sponsor always gives representations and warranties about the securitized assets, and the value of those representations and warranties depends on the financial condition of the sponsor. But this is something many investors recognized only in the aftermath of the 2008 financial crisis, as some of the largest sponsors ended up insolvent.) Legal separation is also necessary for pass-through tax status. The investors in the ABS or MBS are subject to only one level of taxation (their own), rather than to both corporate tax and their own taxation, which would occur if the securitized assets were still with the sponsor. Such double taxation would destroy the economics of the transaction.

Figure 6.1 illustrates the basic securitization transaction structure for a commercial mortgage securitization using a corporation as the SPE. Figure 6.2 illustrates the basic securitization transaction structure for a private-label (non-government-sponsored) residential mortgage securitization involving a common law trust as the SPE.

Figure 6.1 Commercial Mortgage Securitization Structure

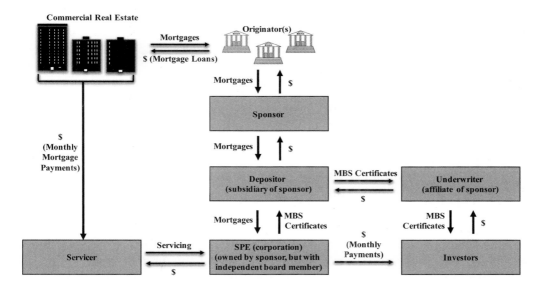

---

practices, and consolidation can increase the amount of capital required for a bank. Since 2010, however, consolidation is generally required if the sponsor both controls the assets (e.g., services the assets) and has either the upside residual interest in their performance or formal downside exposure to their performance. Statement of Financial Accounting Standards 167.

Figure 6.2 Private-Label Residential Mortgage Securitization Structure

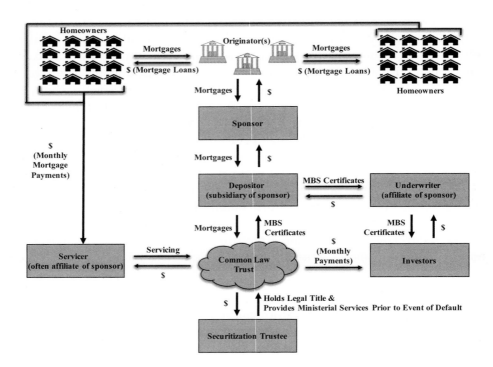

B. Management of Securitized Assets

What happens to the assets once they are securitized? Securitized assets need to be managed. If the assets are loans, someone needs to collect the loan payments and manage the loans if they default, produce payoff statements, etc. The securitization sponsor often wants to manage the loans so as to retain its relationship with the borrowers (who may not even know that their loan has been securitized). Yet the sponsor also wants to transfer the risk on the loan's performance to investors, or at least have the appearance of doing so in order to obtain the bankruptcy, accounting, and tax benefits (namely lower costs of credit) from doing so.

The solution to this problem is to split the legal ownership of the securitized assets from their day-to-day management. The way this is done depends on the SPE's corporate form. If the SPE is a trust, there will be a trustee that holds legal title to the trust corpus. The day-to-day management of the SPE will typically be handled by a separate entity, known as a **servicer**, which is engaged through a contract with the trustee and the investors to manage or "service" the securitized assets. If the SPE is an LLC or corporation, there might or might not be a separate servicer or management company that handles day-to-day management of the securitized assets. The servicer or management company is often an affiliate of the sponsor, but is not required to be. (The servicing may be subsequently subcontracted.)

One of the appeals of securitization to investors is that it allows them to invest in very narrowly tailored risks—they do not want to be assuming the operational risk of the sponsor or any other entity, only the performance risk on the assets. It is not possible, however, to entirely separate out the performance of the assets from the operations of the servicer or legal title holder (either a securitization trustee or SPE). But investors want this operational risk minimized. They do not want the risk of poor asset management (agency costs), asset substitution (the sale and replacement of securitized assets), or the creation of competing, non-contractual (tort) liability for the securitization trust's or SPE's income. As a result, securitization trustees or SPEs operate more or less robotically, following a nearly completely pre-programmed set of instructions in their deal documents. These deal documents generally aim to cabin the discretion of a servicer and trustee or SPE to a narrow set of circumstances: dealing with defaulted loans and dealing with a default by a servicer or trustee. Even then, in both cases, discretion is still limited by contractual provisions requiring or forbidding particular actions.[6]

C. Risks Involved in Securitizations

All securitizations involve the allocation of a range of risks relating to the securitized assets, and virtually all transactions will result in the retention of some risks on the assets by the sponsor, if only because of the representations and warranties made by the sponsor regarding the securitized assets. These risks include credit risk, liquidity risk, interest rate risk, and market value risk.

Credit risk is the risk that, if the securitized assets are debt obligations such as loans or debt securities, the debt obligations will not be collected. In other words, credit risk is the risk of realized losses *on the underlying assets*. This is distinct from the risk of non-payment on the ABS themselves. The initial non-payment risk on the ABS comes from realized losses on the underlying assets. But to the extent that the party which is supposed to absorb the realized losses is itself insolvent, illiquid, or unwilling to pay, there is the risk of non-payment on the ABS. Unlike credit risk, non-payment risk is not allocated in securitization transactions, and transactions are generally designed to minimize non-payment risk.

Most securitizations contain some form of **credit enhancement**, meaning a deal feature that reduces the credit risk for investors. Common credit enhancements include various forms of guaranties and insurance, such as sponsor-guaranties against credit losses, pool or bond insurance,[7] credit default or total return swaps,

---

6. As with agent banks and syndicate members, the incentives of securitization trustees and servicers may not be aligned with investors. Securitization trustees' and servicers' compensation is not based on the performance of the loans. The trustees are paid a minimal fee based on the balance of the outstanding loans. Servicers receive a more substantial fee based on the balance of the loans, as well as the ability to keep some fees charged to borrowers and some "float" income on payments received by borrowers that is briefly invested before turning it over to the investors. The compensation of both the trustee and servicer is senior to that of the investors, further complicating the incentives.

7. Pool-level insurance either covers losses or provides cash-flow maintenance up to specified levels for the entire pool owned by the SPE. Pool-level insurance is typically provided by private mortgage-insurance

and asset-level credit insurance.[8] Other common credit enhancements include pool-level overcollateralization,[9] excess spread,[10] shifting interest,[11] and reserve accounts.[12] Standby letters of credit and total return swaps with third parties are also sometimes used.

The best known form of credit enhancement, however, is the use of a senior-subordinate structure known as "**tranching**" (*tranche* is the French word for slice). Some securitizations are straight "**pass-throughs**" in which investors have a pro rata interest in the securitized assets. But many securitizations involve a "tranching" or senior-subordinate structuring of risks. Tranching means that risks are concentrated on certain subordinated investors (who receive higher rates of return in compensation), rather than spread out equally. Thus, for credit risk tranching, losses are borne first by those in the lowest tranche and only once their position has been wiped out—meaning that losses exceed the principal allocated to that tranche—does the next most junior tranche begin to absorb losses. Different types of risks, such as credit risks and prepayment risk, for example, can be tranched separately, meaning that the senior-subordinate structure for application of credit losses is not the same as for application of prepayments. Tranching can be quite complex; six or more tranches are common in securitizations.[13]

Liquidity risk is the risk that the SPE will not be able to pay its obligations under the ABS as they come due, even if the SPE is solvent. If the SPE's own collections are delayed, it may not be able to pay on the ABS on time. Many investors

---

companies. Bond-level insurance involves a monoline bond insurer guaranteeing the timely payment of principal and interest on a tranche of bonds.

8. Examples of this are loan-level private mortgage insurance, FHA loan insurance, VA loan guaranties, and SBA loan guaranties.

9. Pool-level overcollateralization means that the initial principal balance of the securitized assets is greater than the principal balance on the securities. Pool-level overcollateralization is distinct from asset-level overcollateralization, which is when the asset is a secured loan with a loan-to-value ratio of under 100 percent.

10. Excess spread is the difference between the income of the SPE in a given period and its payment obligations on the ABS in that period—essentially the SPE's periodic profit. Excess spread is accumulated to supplement future shortfalls in the SPE's cash flow but is periodically released to the residual tranche holder. Excess spread generally cannot be released if certain triggers are tripped, such as a decline in the amount of excess spread trapped during a specified period.

11. Shifting interest involves the reallocation of subordinate tranches' share of prepayments (both voluntary prepayments and the proceeds of involuntary liquidations) to senior tranches. Shifting-interest arrangements are often stepped down over time, with a decreasing percentage of prepayments shifted. The effect is to make senior tranches' share of a securitization larger at the beginning of the deal and smaller thereafter.

12. A reserve account is a segregated trust account, typically invested in highly liquid, investment-grade investments (for example, commercial paper). It provides a cushion for losses caused by defaults on the securitized assets. Reserve accounts come in two types: prefunded cash reserves and excess spread. Prefunded reserve accounts are funded in full at the closing of the deal; the arranger of the deal typically funds the account with a share of the deal proceeds. The reserve account thus is a holdback or discount on the SPE's purchase price of the assets. This type of prefunded reserve account is known as a cash collateral account. Reserve accounts either are required to be maintained at a specified level regardless of losses or are permitted to be drained in accordance with losses. In the former case, the credit enhancement of the reserve account actually *increases* as the principal and interest due on the securities decreases.

13. Tranching does not always mean that the senior tranche gets paid in full before the junior tranche(s) receive anything. Instead, in most securitizations, the tranching is applied on a monthly basis. Thus, in month one, there might be enough funds to pay the senior in full and also something to the junior, while in month two, there might not be enough to even pay the senior in full. In such a situation, the senior cannot recover the payment made to the junior in month one. Each payment period is a separate application of the tranching.

in fixed-income securities need reliable, timely payment because of their own payment obligations. For example, a pension fund that invests in ABS is relying on receiving revenues on time in order to make payments to the pensioners. Liquidity risk is a particular concern for asset-backed commercial paper transactions because of the short-term nature of commercial paper.

Securitizations will often involve liquidity enhancements, often combined with credit enhancements. Some liquidity enhancements are built into deals, such as a cash collateral or reserve account (pre-funded or funded from retained excess spread) that provides a liquidity buffer for the SPE. Alternatively, a third-party guarantor might guarantee not only the payment of principal and interest on the ABS, but also the *timely* payment of principal and interest. This is the typical arrangement in mortgage securitizations guaranteed by Fannie Mae, Freddie Mac, Ginnie Mae, and monoline bond insurers. Asset-backed commercial paper conduits are more likely to have dedicated liquidity facilities, such as a swingline repo facility, liquidity put, or swap line that enable the SPE to sell its illiquid assets for immediate cash.

Interest rate risk is the risk that interest rates will move in a way that reduces the value of the securitized assets. This can happen in one of two ways. First, if the assets are fixed-rate debt obligations, then if market interest rates rise, the value of the fixed-rate debt obligations will decline. For example, if the securitized assets are a pool of loans with an annual 5% interest rate and market rates rise to 8%, the securitized loan pool will have below-market rates, and will have tied up investors' capital that could be reinvested at a higher interest rate. Second, if the assets are callable fixed-rate debt obligations and market interest rates fall, then the fixed-rate debt obligations might be refinanced, thereby depriving investors of an above-market rate asset and forcing reinvestment in a lower interest rate environment. This second type of interest rate risk is sometimes referred to as "negative convexity" risk.[14]

Market value risk is the risk that the market value—that is the immediate sale value—of the securitized assets will decline, separate and apart from realized losses or interest rate movements. Thus, market value risk would include anticipated, but unrealized credit losses, as well as market uncertainty about future interest rates or credit quality, and the risk of a market freeze for unrelated reasons. Market value risk on the securitized assets is distinct from market value risk on the ABS. Investors in ABS always assume market value risk on the ABS.

To the extent that a securitization transaction holds assets to maturity, market value risk is of little consequence, but if the assets are held for sale, then market

---

14. "Convexity" refers to the shape of the curve of the relationship between a security's yield and its price. Callable securities have negative convexity, meaning that price decreases on the securities will be *greater* than price increases for equally large changes in yield. Non-callable securities have positive convexity, meaning that price decreases will be *less* than price increases for equally large changes in yield. Negative convexity is a particular feature of RMBS because most U.S. mortgages are callable by the borrower—that is they are prepayable. Thus, when rates fall, borrowers refinance and prepay, which deprives the MBS investors of an above-market-yielding asset. Negative convexity is generally an undesirable characteristic of an investment because it means that the investor is not able to capture the full increase in value that comes from holding an asset with an above-market yield when interest rates decline.

value risk is a concern. The SPEs in most securitizations have little or no ability to sell the securitized assets, so market value risk is not a concern in these transactions.[15]

D. Structured Financing

Securitization not only allows targeted investment in the risks inherent in only a select group of assets, but it also allows the risks inherent in those assets to be unbundled and separately assigned. Thus, one party could hold the credit risk, while another holds the interest rate and market value risk.

Each type of risk can itself be further unbundled. For example, credit risk need not be allocated pro rata among ABS investors. Instead, credit risk can be (and commonly is) divided in a senior-subordinate tranching, with realized losses allocated first to the junior most tranche, then to the next most junior tranche, and so on.

Similarly, payments of principal and interest can be unbundled, with principal payments credited in one order of priority and interest payments credited in a different one. Likewise, prepayments can be allocated separately from regularly scheduled payments, with one tranche receiving prepayments first, but being junior for regularly scheduled payments.

This unbundling of risks is what is known as **structured financing.** It can be done separately from securitization, but it is most effective when paired with asset segregation. The nature and part of the economic appeal of securitization is the ability to customize transactions to maximize on market demand. Securitization allows for bespoke tailoring that off-the-rack fixed-income products such as generic corporate bonds lack. There is a cost to this bespokeness, however, in that a security issued in a $1 billion securitization is likely less liquid than a $1 billion corporate bond, all else being equal, because the corporate bond produces a single security, whereas the securitization is likely to produce several nonfungible securities, each of which exists in a market of less than $1 billion.

E. Resecuritization and CLOs

A securitization interest can itself be resecuritized, either by itself or after being pooled with other rights to cash flows. A resecuritization is typically called a "collateralized debt obligation" or CDO. (In the UK, the term "collateralized loan obligation" or CLO is often used.) CDO interests can themselves be resecuritized, resulting in a CDO^2 and so on.

Securitization has affected the shape of the syndicated loan market and corporate restructurings. Pieces of syndicated loans are frequently pooled and securitized

---

15. For asset-backed commercial paper, however, market value risk is a major concern, particularly for asset-backed commercial paper conduits that lack 100 percent standby liquidity support. Some asset-backed commercial paper conduits are "extendible," meaning that the issuer has the option of extending the term of the commercial paper in certain situations, but requiring the issuer to then liquidate the underlying assets to pay off the extended obligations.

into what in the United States are known as CLOs. CLOs provide an important class of investor in syndicated loans. While a bank will typically serve as the agent for a syndicated loan because of its borrower relationship and administrative capacities, the real "skin in the game" and thus voting power in the syndicate may come from non-bank institutional investors, including CLOs. What this means is that the real lending relationship is heavily intermediated. For example, a consumer might have a defined-benefit pension plan. That pension plan might invest in a mutual fund. The mutual fund will invest in a CLO. The CLO will in turn invest in a syndicated loan. Thus, the funds flow very indirectly from the end-investors to the end-borrowers.

A CLO can be thought of as an actively managed, closed-end investment fund, meaning that there is no new investment in the CLO after the initial investment. The typical CLO initially invests in around 150 syndicated loans. To the extent that the CLO's income exceeds its required payouts to investors, the CLO managers are permitted to reinvest excess proceeds in more loans during a specified reinvestment period. The reinvestment period is typically six years, during which time the CLO manager can buy and sell assets at his discretion.

CLOs' ability to reinvest in new loans is performance dependent. CLOs are designed with checks to limit losses to investors. Most notable are interest coverage (I/C) and overcollateralization (O/C) tests. The I/C test evaluates the interest payments received by the CLO relative to the interest payments it must make to the CLO investors. The O/C test evaluates the par value of the CLO's assets relative to the CLO's liabilities to investors. The I/C and O/C tests will have different triggers for different tranches of investors. If the trigger is hit for any tranche, then the CLO must divert funds from junior tranches (including the CLO manager's subordinated tranche) to pay down the senior tranches whose triggers have been hit. The result is to delever the CLO and thereby raise its I/C and O/C levels. Once the I/C or O/C levels are back under their triggers, the CLO continues making payments according to its cash flow waterfall, including to the subordinated tranches. Thus, CLOs have some ability to self-correct.

F. The Effect of Securitization on Investors

When a CLO or any other securitization invests in a loan, the securitization vehicle becomes the legal creditor on the loan. The investors in the securitization vehicle are economically the creditors on the loan, but legally they do not own the loan, any more than a company's creditors and shareholders own the company's assets. The same is true for loan participations.

For loan syndications and bonds, there is formal contractual privity between the debtor and the syndicate member or bondholder, but the syndication agreement or indenture typically assigns the ability to exercise key legal rights in the agent bank or indenture trustee. In a securitization, these rights are allocated to a servicer (or sometimes to a trustee or collateral manager) via contract, producing much the same result. Just as no-action clauses limit the ability of investors in syndicated loans and bonds to pursue remedies themselves directly against obligors (and any recoveries must be shared pro rata with other investors), so too are securitization investors limited in their ability to pursue remedies individually. Instead, they rely on the servicer and trustee to protect their interests. As with syndicated loans and bonds, however, these agents' interests do not always align with those of the investors.

II. DERIVATIVES

Financial derivatives provide an additional method of financing. "Derivatives" are a range of financial products that are so named because their value derives from an underlying contract rather than from their own inherent value. Derivatives are often complex, and certain aspects of derivatives are subject to extensive regulatory regimes, but our interest in them is limited to their being another class of contracts allocating risks between the contracting parties (or in financial contract parlance, between the **counterparties**). Included among derivatives (writ largely) are forward contracts, future contracts, repurchase agreements or repos, swaps, credit-linked notes, and master netting agreements. Each of these types of derivatives contracts is reviewed in turn below.

A. Forward Contracts and Futures Contracts

A **forward contract** is an agreement to sell an asset with delivery in the future. For example, Apollo Investments agrees to sell 100 barrels of oil to Bacchus Bank for $10/barrel in one year. Importantly, the seller need not own the asset at the time of the sale. The forward contract is a way for parties to lock in prices to deal with future uncertainty or to speculate on future commodity prices—Apollo is betting that the oil will be worth less than $10/barrel and Bacchus is speculating that the oil will be worth more than $10/barrel.

Forward contracts, however, can also be used to mimic the economic structure of a loan. Consider what would happen if we had two forward contracts between Apollo and Bacchus. In the first contract, Apollo agrees to sell 100 barrels of oil to Bacchus for $10/barrel in one month. In the second contract, Bacchus agrees to sell 100 barrels of oil to Apollo for $11/barrel in 13 months. Economically, it is as if Bacchus loaned $1,000 to Apollo at 10% annual interest with the oil as collateral.

A particular subspecies of a forward contract is a **futures contract**. Futures contracts are a regulated medium for speculating on commodity prices, such as orange juice, soybeans, gold, or porkbellies. Futures contracts differ from forward contracts in a few key ways.

Futures contracts are a trading instrument—the contract is itself expected to be bought and sold in a secondary market. Futures contracts are financial market instruments, rather than bespoke arrangements that allocate risk between two parties. While forward contracts can be assigned, they are not meant to be trading instruments, and when they are assigned, it is in an over-the-counter market; there is no standing secondary market for forward contracts.

Futures contracts, in contrast, are an exchange-traded market. This is possible in part because futures contracts are usually settled for cash, rather than via physical delivery. Buying porkbelly futures does not normally mean that one is going to end up with a freezer full of bacon. In contrast, forward contracts typically involve physical delivery.

The robust secondary market in futures contracts exists because futures contracts trade on exchanges and are cleared through clearinghouses. In order to trade on exchanges (or boards of trade), it is necessary that futures contracts be standardized, as standardization is key to liquidity, so that buyers and sellers need to do diligence on the particular porkbelly or soybean future that is the subject of their transaction. To this end, it is necessary that there be cash settlement because cash is standardized and does not raise issues about whether goods conform to the contract.

A secondary market for futures contracts also exists because they clear (meaning are paid) through clearinghouses. The contracts to buy and sell futures are made on the exchange, which matches buyers and sellers, who are unlikely to know each other's identities. Clearinghouses are payment guarantee mechanisms designed to reduce counterparty risk. If Apollo buys a pork belly future from Bacchus, Bacchus assumes the risk that Apollo will not pay on the settlement date. This is a credit risk that Bacchus probably does not want; Bacchus wants to assume only the risk on the price movement on porkbellies.

The solution is to have a guarantor of the payment. The clearinghouse fills this role by stepping into the shoes of each of the counterparties to the futures contract sale. Apollo pays the clearinghouse and the clearinghouse pays Bacchus, which delivers the futures contract to the clearinghouse, which delivers the futures contract to Apollo. Technically, this is done by having the clearinghouse enter into matched contracts with Apollo and Bacchus.

Thus, the futures contract is not between the buyer and seller, but actually two matched contracts, one between the buyer and the clearinghouse (acting as seller) and one between the seller and the clearinghouse (acting as buyer). What this means is that for settlement, just as for entering into the contract, buyer and seller need not actually know the identity of each other. It also means that a party to a futures contract can "close out" its position and eliminate its exposure on the contract by buying an offsetting position. Thus, if I have a contract to buy 100 porkbellies in one year, I can eliminate my obligation by purchasing a contract to sell 100 porkbellies in one year. Because both contracts are effectively contracts with the clearinghouse, they simply cancel each other out. This is not possible with a forward contract because there is not a commonality of counterparties nor is there a liquid market to purchase offsetting positions.

B. Repos

A "repo" is a sale-and-repurchase agreement. For example, Apollo Investments sells a security to Bacchus Bank for $100 with an obligation to repurchase the security a year later for $110. Economically, a repo transaction mirrors a recourse loan of $100 from Bacchus to Apollo secured by the security and with $10 of interest. Thus, repo markets are really recourse-secured lending markets, typically using securities as collateral, and frequently with very short (such as overnight) terms. (A repo can be structured to be equivalent to a non-recourse secured loan, but most are not.)

Some repos are conducted on a bilateral basis, while others are tri-party repos that use a clearing bank as an intermediary. The clearing bank technically contracts with each of the repo counterparties, creating a matched set of novated repo agreements. The result is that each repo counterparty assumes the credit risk of the clearing bank, rather than of its counterparty.

Repo provides the major form of financing for many financial institutions. Broker-dealers finance themselves primarily through repo, often on an overnight basis. Similarly, hedge funds lever up their equity with term repo credit from their prime brokers. Repo is used not only by Wall Street, but also by Main Street financial institutions. Repo need not use securities as collateral. The Bankruptcy Code's definition of repo includes mortgages as collateral, as mortgage banks obtain much of their financing through repo lines of credit.

C. Swaps

A **swap** is simply a trade of one asset for another. Swaps are frequently used financial instruments. The major types of swaps are interest rate, currency, credit (credit default or total return), commodity, and equity.

To illustrate an interest rate swap, let's have Apollo Investments agree to pay Bacchus Bank a fixed rate of interest on a notional amount, while Bacchus agrees to pay Apollo a variable rate of interest on the same notional amount. Apollo is gambling that the variable rate will be above the fixed rate, while Bacchus is betting on the inverse. Apollo might do this to hedge its interest rate risk on an asset of the notional amount that pays a fixed rate and Bacchus vice-versa. The same idea holds for currency swaps, such as a swap of dollars for euros. Each party is betting on the change in the relative values of the currencies.

A particularly important type of swap for bankruptcy purposes is the **credit default swap** or **CDS**. A credit default swap is a wager between two parties about whether a defined "**credit event**" will occur on the "**reference obligation**," of a "**reference entity**" or in plain English, it is a bet about whether a loan will default. The reference obligation need not be an actual obligation, however. It could be a single real obligation or it could be an index or a portfolio of obligations.

Credit default swaps are essentially a form of credit insurance. Let's imagine an insurance or guarantee arrangement in which a third-party insurer or guarantor guarantees payment of a borrower's debt to a lender in exchange for a fee. Figure 6.3, above, illustrates. This is exactly what monoline bond insurers do, providing third-party insurance on financial contracts. Private mortgage insurers do the same for home mortgage loans. Importantly, if the guarantor or insurer pays out on its guarantee, it is subrogated to the rights of the lender, meaning that the guarantor or insurer can pursue the borrower for repayment of the defaulted loan.

The insurance or guarantee contract could be structured as a swap, however, instead of as a guarantee. Bacchus Bank and Saturn Special Situations Fund, a hedge fund, enter into a CDS that references a corporate loan or bond or pool of

Figure 6.3 Guarantee Arrangement

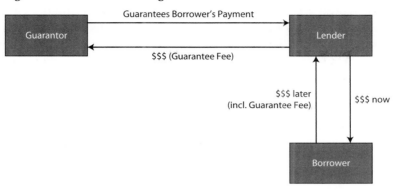

loans or bonds (the "reference obligation(s)"). Under the deal, Bacchus pays Saturn fixed payments (like insurance premia) throughout the duration of the swap. In exchange, Saturn agrees that if there is a defined credit event on the reference obligation, however defined, then Saturn makes a payment to Bacchus. Bacchus is the **"protection buyer"** (short on the reference obligation, meaning expecting the value of the reference obligation—which is an asset to the obligee—to fall), while Saturn is the **"protection seller"** (long on the reference obligation, meaning expecting the value of the reference obligation to rise).

If the deal is a "cash settled" CDS, then upon a credit event Saturn pays Bacchus the difference between the value of the reference obligation without the default and its present value. If the deal is for a physically settled CDS, then Saturn would pay Bacchus the non-defaulted value of the obligation and Bacchus tenders Saturn the obligation. Figure 6.4, below, illustrates a credit default swap.

Figure 6.4 Credit Default Swap (Covered)

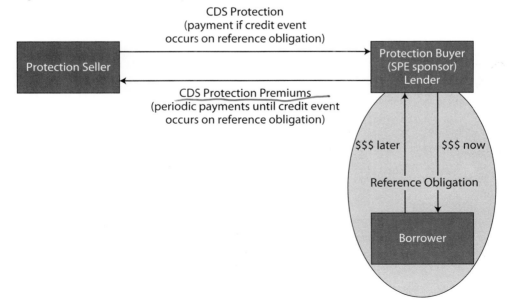

Significantly, Bacchus may or may not own the reference loan or bond. If it does, it is called a "**covered CDS**," while if it does not, the deal is called a "**naked CDS**" and physical settlement is potentially a problem if Bacchus does not own the reference obligation. Figures 6.5 and 6.6, below, illustrate naked credit default swaps involving a single reference obligation and a pool of reference obligations, respectively. Buying CDS protection of either sort is a way to go "short."

Figure 6.5 Credit Default Swap (Naked, Single Reference Obligation)

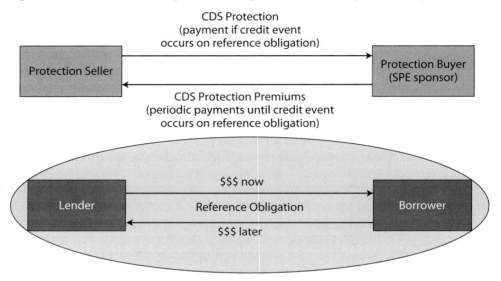

Figure 6.6 Credit Default Swap (Naked, Multiple Reference Obligations)

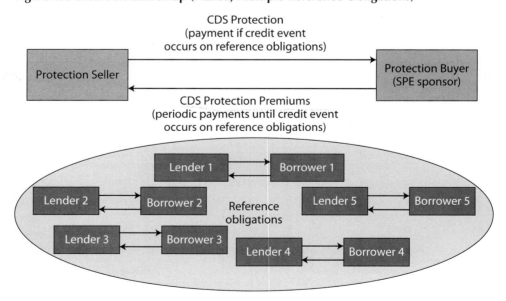

The result of the CDS is that Saturn has assumed the credit risk on the reference obligation, while Bacchus has assumed the credit risk on Saturn. Because of this risk shift, some CDS require the protection seller to post collateral to guarantee its payment. Covered CDS provide a means of hedging credit risk for the protection buyer, while naked CDS provide a way of expressing a short position on an obligation that might be insufficiently liquid to sell short.

Covered CDS provide a means for a creditor to hedge its credit risk. If Bacchus has a $100 million loan out to Rhea Industries, it may wish to lay off some of the credit risk. Thus, Bacchus might purchase $40 million of CDS protection on the loan from Saturn. Saturn now bears up to $40 million in credit risk on the Rhea Industries loan, while Bacchus still holds $60 million in credit risk. Bacchus now has up to $40 million in credit risk exposure to Saturn; if there is a credit event on the Rhea Industries loan, Bacchus may look to Saturn to pay up on the CDS.

This does not mean that Saturn will necessarily pay $40 million—or anything—however. Suppose the loan is priced in the auction at $90 million, meaning that there are losses of $10 million (assuming that the loan's coupon is such that it would otherwise trade at par). Who bears that $10 million loss? It depends on how the CDS was written. That $40 million of CDS protection might be protection on the *first* $40 million in losses, but it might alternatively be protection on losses between $15 million and $55 million or between $30 million and $70 million. Only if it covered the first $40 million of losses would there be any payout, and because the loan's value has fallen to $90 million, the payout on the CDS would be limited to $10 million.

The actual payout may be determined in one of two ways. Either Saturn may take physical delivery of the reference asset in exchange for payment at par, or it may simply make a cash payment that represents the difference between an auction price for the reference asset and the par value of the reference asset. In other words, the payment on a CDS is not simply a matter of credit losses, but will also reflect interest rate risk and market conditions.

There is a twist, however. The auction pricing is not necessarily of the reference asset itself. Instead, it is of the cheapest-to-deliver loan or security that qualifies under the auction protocol. This is important because if there is a particular loan or bond that is trading well below par—such as because of a below-market coupon—that particular loan would be the cheapest-to-deliver and would set the auction price, thereby magnifying the payout on the CDS.

Exactly what qualifies depends on whether it is the protection buyer or the protection seller who declares that the swap has been triggered. If it is the protection buyer who declares that the swap is triggered, then the auction pricing is based on the cheapest-to-deliver option in relation not just to the reference loan itself, but to any loan with a similar maturity date to the reference loan. If the protection seller declares that the swap is triggered, however, then the auction is based on the cheapest-to-deliver pricing for any loan outstanding from the reference entity, no matter the maturity date. This difference is based on the theory that because the seller forced the settlement, something unusual must be going on and the buyer should therefore be able to deliver obligations across the maturity curve.

It is important to recognize that Bacchus has not eliminated its credit risk with the CDS. Instead, it has diversified it, and, to the extent that Saturn is a better risk than Rhea Industries, it has reduced the risk. Bacchus has paid a price for diversifying and reducing its risk in the form of the premiums it will pay to Saturn.

Note that Rhea Industries never needs to know about the CDS, which is one reason that the transaction is attractive to Bacchus. Bacchus Bank can maintain the client relationship with Rhea Industries and keep any up-front fees on the loan without holding all of the risk on the loan. At the same time, Saturn, which lacks the ability to get a direct client relationship with Rhea, is able to still assume the credit risk on a loan to Rhea.

Buying CDS protection provides a mechanism for parties to short markets that cannot be shorted directly. For example, real estate cannot be shorted. Selling an asset short means selling the asset presently for future delivery without owning the asset at present. The short seller is hoping that between the time of the sale and the time of delivery, the asset's price will fall, enabling the short seller to go and buy the asset in the open market at a lower price than the sale price and thus meet its delivery obligation while pocketing the spread between the sale price and the (lower) purchase price. Shorting is only possible in liquid markets because a short seller cannot count on being able to meet its delivery obligation in an illiquid market.

To illustrate, if I sell the Parthenon short, I will need to be able to go and purchase the Parthenon before I need to deliver it to my buyer. If the Parthenon is not for sale, I won't be able to meet my delivery obligation. Knowing that markets like real estate are illiquid because of non-standardized assets, if I want to express my belief that the market is currently overpriced, I will need to find another way to do so. Buying CDS protection provides one such mechanism. If real estate prices fall, there are likely to be defaults on mortgage loans (particularly on non-recourse loans). Thus, if I buy CDS protection on those loans, I am able to be benefit from prices falling, just as I would if I had sold short.

For protection sellers, CDS also present a way of arbitraging "long" positions in real (non-derivative) markets, but without the costs of having to actually own the real assets. Thus, instead of buying real estate itself, I could simply sell CDS protection on mortgage loans if I thought real estate was underpriced.

D. Credit-Linked Notes

Credit default swaps can be used to construct a type of **synthetic debt** instrument known as a **credit-linked note** (CLN) that effectuates the sale of CDS protection by the CLN investors to a protection buyer. The CLN transaction structure enables CDS to be underwritten by unaffiliated groups of capital market investors rather than by single operating firms. It does so by securitizing the protection seller's position in CDS.

The CLN transaction structure involves three transactions all going through a special purpose entity (SPE) created by the protection buyer. The SPE sells CDS protection to the protection buyer. This means that the SPE is receiving regular CDS premiums as long as the reference obligation for the CDS is performing. The SPE is thus "long" on the reference obligation and the protection buyer is "short" on the reference obligation. At this point, the SPE has no funds to pay the protection buyer if the reference obligation defaults. To obtain funds, the SPE issues credit-linked notes to investors in exchange for cash, which the SPE will invest in safe securities such as Treasuries. These securities will serve as the source of payment should there be a default on the reference obligation. Thus, the SPE has effectively transferred the risk of its "long" position on the reference obligation to investors, as the only funds available to repay the CLNs are the protection premiums the SPE receives on the credit default swap and the (small) yield on the Treasuries.

Figure 6.7 Credit-Linked Note Transaction (Simplified)

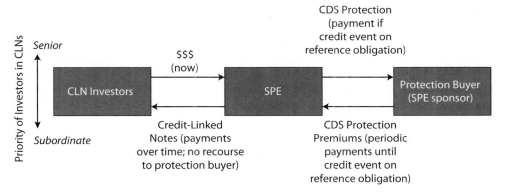

This transaction structure using an intermediate SPE in what is economically a credit default swap between the CLN investors and the protection buyer enables the "long" risk to be shared among multiple CLN investors, thereby expanding the CLN protection-selling market. Figure 6.7, below, illustrates the basic risk pass-through of the CLN transaction.

The CLN transaction also enables the "long" risk to be tranched in a senior-subordinate structure, thereby enabling investors to assume much more targeted (and concentrated) risks. Figure 6.8, below, illustrates the CLN transaction in more detail. In particular, it shows the SPE's investment and the use of an independent trustee to hold a security interest in the SPE's assets to secure repayment of the CLNs for the CLN investors against any possible involuntary creditors of the SPE.

At the same time, the protection buyer has obtained a segregated cash pool that guarantees payment on the credit default swap should there be a default on the reference obligation. Because the SPE has no other assets or creditors and does not engage in other business, the protection buyer need not worry about its priority or about asset substitution. Thus, the asset partitioning effectuated by use of the intermediate SPE structure between the ultimate protection sellers (the CLN investors) and the protection buyer reduces the counterparty risk for the protection buyer.

The CLN structure has some other appeals. Like CDS, it enables a transfer of credit risk without a transfer of assets or a change in the servicing of the assets or of the client relationship. It also avoids upfront taxation because there is no sale, and can often be used to enable regulatory capital arbitrage for banks and insurance companies.

Figure 6.8 Credit-Linked Note Transaction (Expanded)

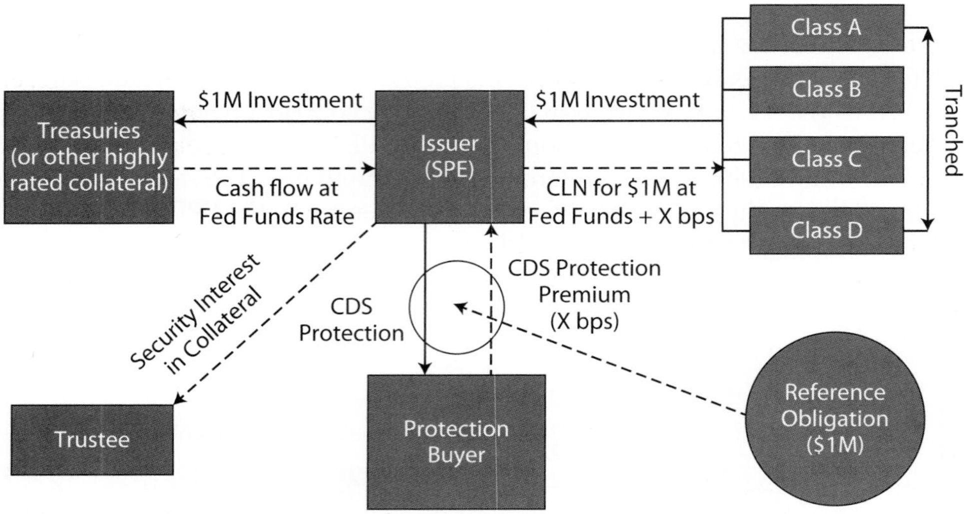

E. Master Netting Agreements

Firms frequently have multiple financial contracts with each other. Thus, Bacchus might owe Saturn money on some of its contracts, while Saturn might owe Bacchus money on some of its contracts. A **master netting agreement** permits all of the cross-obligations to be netted out and a single payment made. Not only is this administratively easier, but it reduces the counterparties' exposure to each other.

Absent a master netting agreement, if Saturn failed to pay Bacchus on the financial contracts where it had a payment obligation, Bacchus would still be obligated to pay Saturn on the financial contracts where it had a payment obligation. A breach of one contract does not excuse a breach of a separate contract. Let's imagine that Saturn owes Bacchus 100 and Bacchus owes Saturn 80. Bacchus would pay Saturn 80 and be trying to collect 100. Instead of being up 20, Bacchus is now down 80 and is chasing 100. Now imagine that Saturn turns out to be insolvent and Bacchus cannot recover. If Bacchus has paid Saturn, Bacchus is not up by 20, or even down by 20, but down by 80. Good money is chasing bad. A master netting agreement gets Bacchus out of this problem by creating a limited right of setoff for the financial contracts covered by the agreement. Bacchus may still owe Saturn money in the end, but its potential exposure is reduced.

F. International Swaps and Derivatives Association Documentation

Financial contracts of all stripes can be documented however the parties desire, but many financial contracts are documented using standardized documentation developed by the International Swaps and Derivatives Association (ISDA), a private trade association, which also provides dispute resolution services regarding certain questions of interpretation of the documentation.

ISDA documentation is a set of modular contract documentation built around the **ISDA Master Agreement**, a standardized central document, which is then customized through various elections, schedules, and supporting documents. There are three iterations of the ISDA Master Agreement: 1987, 1992, and 2002. The 1992 version is still sometimes used despite being supplanted by the 2002 version.

The ISDA Master Agreement sets forth the **events of default** and **termination events**. The Master Agreement specifies what constitutes an event of default and what entitles the counterparties to terminate the contract. Various counterparty bankruptcy-related events are included among events of default. If there is a counterparty event of default, the non-defaulting counterparty may elect to declare an early termination event, resulting in the parties being required to settle the contract. Claims of events of default are determined by an **ISDA Determinations Committee** comprised of fifteen voting members: ten sell-side firms and five buy-side firms, with four observing members. Determinations Committees apply the terms of the ISDA Agreement to specific cases and make factual determinations on whether a Credit Event has occurred based on information provided to market participants. Determination Committees also determine whether an auction should be held following a Credit Event.

The ISDA Master Agreement also contains the provisions on close-out of positions, netting, and settlement. Significantly, the Master Agreement contains an election for the counterparties regarding settlement. The counterparties may choose whether a settlement payment may be made only to the non-defaulting counterparty or to both counterparties. This is important because there might be payment obligations going both ways, particularly if there are multiple, non-netted contracts. If only the non-defaulting counterparty may be paid, then the amount owed by the non-defaulting counterparty to the defaulting counterparty is deemed to be zero.

The calculation of damages varies between the 1992 and 2002 ISDA Master Agreements. The 1992 Master Agreement permits the counterparties to choose between two methods of calculating damages: the Market Quotations method or the Loss method. The Market Quotations method looks to quotations in the relevant market to calculate the damages, whereas the Loss method looks to the non-defaulting counterparty's actual loss, including its costs of unwinding hedges and related transactions. The 1992 Master Agreement also permitted the non-defaulting party to "walk away" if it was out of the money and not pay the defaulting party. The 2002 ISDA Master Agreement uses a single "Close-out Amount" that the non-defaulting party must determine in good faith and through commercially reasonable procedures to determine its losses. There is no "walk away" option in the 2002 ISDA Master Agreement.

Further customization of derivatives contracts is done through a number of supporting documents that accompany the ISDA Master Agreement, the most important of which are a set of **Definitions**, a **Credit Support Annex**, **Schedules** (to the Master Agreement and to the Credit Support Annex), and a **Confirmation**.

Every type of derivative transaction—credit derivatives, equity derivatives, currency derivatives, interest rate derivatives, etc.—has its own ISDA definitions booklet. These definitions are separate from the Master Agreement. They are not negotiated, but in some instances provide for default definitions, which the parties can vary via the Confirmation. For example, there is substantial flexibility in defining a credit event for a credit default swap; the parties can decide whether an event of default will be limited to a specific reference obligation or also cover other obligations of a reference entity, and which ones.

The ISDA Credit Support Annex is where the counterparties will specify whether collateral (known as "**margin**") must be posted to reduce counterparty risk on the transaction. Margin can take numerous forms and requirements may change over the course of the contract to account for changes in the market value of the parties' exposure to each other. If parties have posted margin, the non-breaching party may liquidate the margin upon termination of the transaction, with the margin being applied to the balance owed.

The Schedules to the Master Agreement are where parties indicate any elections made under the Master Agreement (as opposed to under the definitions), and any amendments or additions they wish to make to the Master Agreement. A common provision in the Schedule will relate to setoff rights between the contract and other contracts between the counterparties and/or their affiliates. Additional Schedules may be used for the Credit Support Annex.

Finally, one of the counterparties will send the other a transaction Confirmation at some point after the contract is agreed upon. The Confirmation will recite the basic terms such as dates, amounts, and rates, indicate whether the transaction is a financial or physical transaction, meaning whether settlement is to be in cash or via physical delivery, and specify any variation from the default terms provided in the Definitions.

III. CASE STUDY: HOVNANIAN ENTERPRISES

Our story begins in late 2017. Hovnanian Enterprises was a homebuilder based in New Jersey. Hovnanian had substantial debt obligations, including some debt maturing in 2019. Hovnanian's financial situation was dicey, and there were substantial CDS outstanding on its debt, including a very large short position held by GSO Capital Partners, a hedge fund embedded within the Blackstone Group, a major asset manager. GSO has purchased some $330 million in CDS protection on Hovnanian debt from Solus Alternative Asset Management, another hedge fund. Solus both sold CDS protection on Hovnanian and also held a position in Hovnanian bonds, apparently long in both synthetic and cash markets.

As Hovnanian looked to refinance the debt maturing in 2019, it had offers from some banks and a hedge fund. But it also got an offer that was too good to refuse from GSO. GSO offered Hovnanian a substantially below-market rate on a new loan, but it came with a catch. GSO wanted Hovnanian to default on some of its other debts by skipping an interest payment. To make sure that no creditors would be harmed by the maneuver, GSO had Hovnanian covenant to issue a small amount of new debt to a Hovnanian subsidiary—that would be the debt on which Hovnanian would default, by paying itself a few days late, despite having the liquidity to pay on time. The amount of the default would be too small to trigger the cross-default clauses on Hovnanian's other obligations, but it would be a credit event that would trigger the CDS GSO held with Solus. And, in order to magnify the recovery on the CDS, GSO ensured that Hovnanian would issue the new debt with a coupon substantially below market, so that it would be the cheapest-to-deliver option for the pricing of the bonds that would determine the CDS payout.

Not surprisingly, Solus brought suit against GSO and Hovnanian, alleging securities fraud and tortious interference with prospective economic advantage. Complaint, *Solus Alternative Asset Mgmt. LP v. GSO Capital Partners LP*, No. 1:18-cv-00232 (S.D.N.Y. Jan. 11, 2018). Solus's motion for a preliminary injunction was denied because the court found that it would be readily protected by monetary damages if it were to ultimately prevail on its suit. *Solus Alt. Asset Mgmt. LP v. GSO Capital Partners L.P.*, 2018 U.S. Dist. Lexis 13961 (S.D.N.Y. Jan. 29, 2018). Solus, however, would have to first pay out the money on the CDS or risk being in default on the CDS itself. After Solus threatened to buy the Hovnanian bonds in order to boost their price and thus reduce the payout on the CDS, Solus and GSO ultimately settled on confidential terms.

Problem Set 6

(1) Zeus Capital LLP has entered into a non-recourse repo financing agreement with First Bank of Delphi in which Zeus will initially sell Delphi 10,000 shares of the common stock of Aegis, Inc. for $100/share. The parties have agreed that Zeus will repurchase the shares in a month for $102/share. If the value of the Aegis stock rises above $102/share in a month, what will Zeus do? What if the value of the stock in a month has fallen to below $100/share? And what if the stock is worth $101/share in a month?

(2) Minotaur Industries engages in natural gas extraction through hydraulic fracturing, a process that raises significant environmental concerns. Minotaur is looking to expand its operations and needs capital to do so. The lenders it has approached have expressed reluctance to lend on anything close to reasonable terms because of the environmental risks. The lenders are concerned that they will end up owning a Superfund site. How might Minotaur be able to get funding?

(3) Heracles Investments is considering investing in a residential mortgage securitization. The securitization is sponsored by Augeus Bancorp. It is the 200th such securitization that Augeus has done in the last two years. The servicer for the securitization is Augeus Mortgage Servicing, an affiliate of Augeus Bancorp. The trustee is Laverna National Bank & Trust, one of the largest trustees in the business. Laverna is trustee on all of the Augeus Bancorp securitizations. Heracles CIO, Megara Singh, knows that the mortgages in the deal aren't the best, but she figures that if Heracles buys a senior tranche, it shouldn't matter. "There'd have to be pervasive problems on the underwriting before we'd take losses," she says. "And there are a bunch of reps and warrants that guarantee that the underwriting is up to snuff." Is there anything Singh should be worried about?

(4) Argonaut Partners, L.P., purchased the senior tranche in a commercial mortgage securitization called Golden Fleece CMBS XVII backed by the mortgages on several shopping malls owned and managed by Jason & Co. Argonaut Partners purchased the tranche at a substantial discount from face. Jason & Co. has defaulted on its mortgages and filed for bankruptcy. The servicer for the Golden Fleece CMBS XVII deal, Medea Loan Servicing, has indicated that it will vote to approve Jason & Co.'s plan of reorganization, which would restructure the mortgages by extending their term and reducing their interest rate. In Medea's judgment, the restructuring will substantially increase the total return to Golden Fleece CMBS XVII.

   a. Is Argonaut Partners likely to prefer a restructuring or a foreclosure? Why?

   b. Is there anything Argonaut Partners can do to force its preferred outcome?

(5) Athena Capital entered into a one-year interest rate swap with Ares Investments. Athena promised to pay Ares a 5% fixed rate on a notional principal of $100 million, while Ares promised to pay Athena a variable rate of LIBOR + 400 basis points on the notional principal. Both sides promised to post periodic "margin" to collateralize the deal, with margin requirements to be recalculated weekly. The deal is documented with the 2002 ISDA Master Agreement. Seven months into the deal, however, Ares Investments filed for bankruptcy, having exhausted its capital in a takeover war. What actions may Athena take?

(6) Athena Capital entered into a one-year total return swap with Poseidon CLO XIII in which Athena promised to pay Poseidon $50 million in exchange for whatever revenue Poseidon received from its $100 million secured loan to Arachne Textiles, Inc.

   a. If Arachne makes its annual $1 million interest payments on time for the next year and does not otherwise default, what are the payments on the swap agreement?

   b. If Arachne files for bankruptcy a month after the swap agreement commences and promptly liquidates within the year, resulting in a $100 million payout to Poseidon, what are the payments on the swap agreement? What if the liquidation payout was not made until 14 months after the commencement of the swap?

   c. Arachne has requested an extra $10 million loan from Poseidon in order to help it stave off bankruptcy. Should Poseidon make the loan?

   d. Athena has the opportunity to take a controlling stake in Arachne's major supplier, for $10 million. If Athena thinks the stock is overpriced by $1 million, should it buy?

(7) Athena Capital entered into a one-year credit default swap with Hades Special Situations Fund III. For a monthly fixed rate payment of $100,000 Athena sold Hades $30 milllion in protection on Hades's $40 million loan to the Persephone Pomegranate Syndicate, which controls a large part of the California pomegranate market. The swap contains the following provisions (which are from the 2003 ISDA Credit Derivatives Definitions):

Section 4.1. Credit Event. "Credit Event" means, with respect to a Credit Derivative Transaction, one or more of Bankruptcy, Failure to Pay, Obligation Acceleration,

Obligation Default, Repudiation/Moratorirum or Restructuring, as specified in the related Confirmation. . . .

Section 4.3 Obligation Acceleration. "Obligation Acceleration" means one or more Obligations in an aggregate amount of not less than the Default Requirement have become due and payable before they would otherwise have become due and payable as a result of, or on the basis of, the occurrence of a default, event of default or similar condition or event (however described), other than a failure to make any required payment, in respect of a Reference Entity under one or more Obligations.

Section 4.4 Obligation Default. "Obligation Default" means one or more Obligations in an aggregate amount of not less than the Default Requirement have become due and payable before they would otherwise have become due and payable as a result of, or on the basis of, the occurrence of a default, event of default or similar condition or event (however described), other than a failure to make any required payment, in respect of a Reference Entity under one or more Obligations.

Section 4.5 Failure to Pay. "Failure to Pay" means . . . the failure by a Reference Entity to make, when and where due, any payments in an aggregate amount of not less than the Payment Requirement under one or more Obligations, in accordance with the terms of such Obligations at the time of such failure.

The swap's Confirmation provides that "Obligations" includes all "any obligation (whether present or future, contingent or otherwise) for the payment and repayment of money" other than the $30 million Loan from Hades, which is defined as the "Reference Obligation." The Confirmation also specifies that the Default Requirement is $10 million.

    a. If Persephone breaches a covenant on a separate $15 million unsecured note 32 days after the swap commences, who pays whom what? Would your answer change if the $15 million unsecured note was owed to an affiliate of Hades Special Situation Fund III?

    b. If Persphone defaults on the $40 million loan from Hades 13 months after the commencement of the swap, who pays whom what?

(8) Hermes National Bank has multiple derivative contracts with Cronos Bank. On some of them Hermes owes Cronos money, while on others Cronos owes Hermes money. One Friday afternoon, Hermes sent Cronos a wire transfer of $50 million in payment for all of the contracts on which it owed Cronos money. Hermes was expecting Cronos to simultaneously send it a wire transfer of $80 million for the contracts on which Cronos owed Hermes money, but instead Hermes learned that the FDIC had put Cronos into receivership, and that Cronos was not making payments on any of its contracts. "We should be Cronos's creditor for only $30 million, but instead, we're trying to collect $80 million from them," grouses Hermes's CEO Cad Talaria. "Isn't there something you lawyers can do to prevent this problem in the future?" What do you tell him?

PART *II*

FINANCIAL RESTRUCTURING OUTSIDE OF BANKRUPTCY

CHAPTER 7

OBSTACLES TO OUT-OF-COURT RESTRUCTURING AND LIQUIDATION

I. RESTRUCTURING OUTSIDE OF BANKRUPTCY

What happens when a firm isn't able to repay its debts as they come due? The answer may depend on the firm's creditors. Let's imagine that you're the CEO of Leviathan Industries, a mid-sized widget manufacturer. Business is down, and it's uncertain whether Leviathan will be able to make its annual interest payment on a bank loan. The loan is a $100 million, unsecured loan at 10% annual simple interest with ten years left on its maturity. The loan is structured as a non-amortizing balloon, meaning that for the term of the loan, the borrower pays only periodic interest with the principal due as a lump sum on maturity. If you're not sure that Leviathan will be able to make the loan payment, what can you do?

You could do nothing and hope that things pick up before the loan payment is due. You could try making operational and management changes, but even if that would help, it's unlikely that you'll be able to turn things around fast enough. You could try to refinance the loan, that is, get a new loan from a new lender and use the proceeds to pay off the current loan. But what lender would have you? Even if you could find a lender on short notice, it's hard to believe that it would be at a more favorable rate than the current loan, so your annual payment obligation is likely to go up.

What about working with your current lender? Maybe you should call the bank and see if there's a deal to be cut. You've got some leverage—if the bank doesn't cut you some slack, your whole business will fall apart, and there isn't a lot of resale value to your firm's assets. You've got some inventory, some raw materials, some leases and licenses, and some customized widget-making equipment. Given the widget industry's problems, there really isn't much of a market for the licenses or equipment. Good luck to the bank in its collections. If the bank can lower your annual payments, you think you can last long enough for the business to turn the corner. Maybe they'll listen.

Now let's switch hats. Imagine that you are the new loan officer at a bank that has made the loan to Leviathan Industries. (What was the old loan officer thinking?) Leviathan's CEO has contacted you to discuss the loan. He tells you that business is down. Leviathan Industries is still generating revenue, but not enough to pay the interest of $10 million/year. He claims that Leviathan can only afford to pay $8 million in annual payments. What are your options?

You could always do nothing. Suppose you don't believe that business actually is down—Leviathan is just scamming you, hoping to get a reduction in loan payments. Perhaps Leviathan can actually pay $10 million or even if it can't, it could still manage $9 million. Doing nothing makes it a game of "chicken." Will Leviathan Industries default? You cannot exercise any of your rights under the loan agreement until there is a default, so you don't lose anything by waiting. Who knows? Leviathan may cough up the money. In other words, mistrust (a type of information problem) or simply disparate expectations about the performance of Leviathan Industries' business may prevent the debt from being restructured. *See* Mark J. Roe, *The Voting Prohibition in Bond Workouts*, 97 YALE L.J. 232 (1987).

On the other hand, maybe Leviathan isn't bluffing. If it isn't, you'll know soon enough, as the next payment won't be made or won't be made in full.

Let's suppose that Leviathan isn't bluffing and defaults on the loan. Now you've got three options. You could do nothing. A creditor can always forbear. There may be factors, such as bank capital regulations, that disincentivize forbearance. *See* Sarah Pei Woo, *Regulatory Bankruptcy: How Bank Regulation Causes Fire Sales,* 99 GEO. L.J. 1615 (2011). Nonetheless, if you forbear, maybe Leviathan's fortunes will change, and Leviathan will cure the default. There's a danger, however, that forbearing will be deemed a waiver of rights or a de facto modification of the debtor's obligation. But a non-fiduciary creditor is never required to take action.

A second option is to proceed with collection activity. The missed payment will constitute a default under the loan agreement, which will allow you to accelerate the loan and proceed with trying to collect judicially. You'll have to go to court, get a judgment, and then attempt to execute on the judgment. If you had gotten a security interest, you could have commenced a foreclosure on your collateral. But without it, you'll have to spend some time—and money—in the courts. If Leviathan is solvent and you proceed with collection, you'll be OK. There will be sufficient assets to pay off your debt.

But if Leviathan is insolvent or if Leviathan lacks enough unpledged assets to satisfy your debt, you've got a problem. Collection actions won't get you a return of 100 cents on the dollar, and your collection actions might trigger actions by Leviathan's other creditors, resulting in competition for a limited pool of assets. Who knows? They might be faster and smarter at collecting than you. They may have collection shortcuts, such as "confessions of judgment" in their contracts that allow them to proceed immediately to a judgment and then collection. Even worse, some may have security interests, allowing them to avoid the judicial collection process entirely while you're stuck in court.

Even if you're able to recover 100 cents on the dollar from Leviathan, it might still be less than optimal. You won't receive any future interest payments from Leviathan. You could loan the money out again, but suppose that your best reinvestment possibility today would pay only 8%. If so, even if you could recover in full—and certainly if you can't—it might not be the best course of action to declare a default and proceed with collection. Instead, you might consider negotiating a loan **restructuring** with Leviathan that would leave you with an asset generating a better return than your best alternative investment and is affordable to Leviathan. Another term for this kind of restructuring of distressed debt is a **workout**, as the creditor(s) and debtor work out their problems.

There's no need to wait until a default to do the restructuring; indeed, it might be better not to wait, because a default on your loan could trigger problems with Leviathan's other creditors. If you don't wait for a default, you still have to be concerned whether Leviathan is bluffing you, but some diligence should protect you there (if Leviathan is willing to cooperate), and the costs can be put to Leviathan.

What will this loan restructuring look like? Anything you and Leviathan agree upon. There are no particular legal restrictions on the terms of the loan restructuring, beyond generally applicable contract law. A typical restructuring might involve the bank lowering the interest rate and extending the term of the loan. It might also involve the pledge of additional collateral or guarantees from corporate affiliates or owners. You might also think about getting a security interest in some of Leviathan's property, so that if Leviathan runs into subsequent problems you'll be better positioned for the collection race.

For example, the bank might agree to lower the rate to say 8%, but it would also charge an upfront fee of $1.25 million for agreeing to the restructuring. Because the firm cannot pay that fee currently, the bank might allow it to be added to the principal balance. Thus, the principal balance would increase to $11.25 million. At 8% interest, the annual payments would be $900,000, which is the same as a 9% interest rate on a $10 million principal balance—exactly what the firm can afford. And critically, the term of the loan would be extended by five years. This means that the firm is paying more years of interest, but has to be combined with the increase in the principal balance, so that the net present value of the loan does not decline because of the delay of the balloon payment. Depending on the discount value assumptions used, this restructuring should result in a loan with a greater net present value to the bank, but also be more affordable to the debtor, at least for now. In other words, it looks like it's win-win.

But there's a catch. (There's always a catch.) What if you made the wrong decision? You could have conceded too little . . . or too much, and knowing the right amount is an informational problem. Suppose you agreed, as part of a workout, to reduce the interest rate on the debt and to forgive some of the principal. But those concessions turn out not to be enough for the debtor, which subsequently defaults. At that point, your legal rights are not the original terms of the debt, but the restructured terms. Suppose that to enable the debtor to obtain more credit, you agreed to release a security interest. Now you're an unsecured creditor, and someone else is secured, and if there isn't enough to pay everyone, you're probably not in a good position. Making inadequate concessions may both worsen a creditor's legal rights and increase the possibility of a default, leading to the worst of all worlds.

Conceding too much, however, can also be a problem. What if you decided to restructure the loan, when in fact Leviathan could have made the payments? That's your loss, although perhaps you could make the concessions contingent upon

Leviathan's future poor performance with some sort of clawback upon good performance. For example, perhaps you take warrants (call options) on Leviathan's stock that will be valuable only if Leviathan performs beyond a certain level.

The problem, however, is not simply the transfer of future upside performance to Leviathan. It's that that value may be transferred to other creditors. If you took warrants, for example, the equity interests into which those warrants could convert would come after Leviathan's other creditors. Even worse, your concession might have enabled Leviathan to make payments in full to other creditors. In other words, there is a free-riding problem in restructuring. And if you're worried that you'll be the chump on whom other creditors will free-ride, you're going to be more hesitant to make concessions.[1] After all, why should you be making concessions, not them?

In a world in which your debt's priority is clear vis-à-vis other creditors' debts, this sort of free-riding problem appears addressable: Losses should fall on junior priority creditors first, before senior creditors incur any losses, because that was the deal they cut. Stylized law-and-economics-101 thinking imagines a world in which there are such crystalline priorities. In the real world, however, priorities are often less-than-clear.

First, there are simple questions about which obligations are enforceable and to what extent. Enforceability is the *sine qua non* of priority, and there may be disputes about who even is a creditor and to what extent. For example, a party might claim that it is a creditor because of an alleged tort. Whether there is in fact liability and the extent of the liability may be unknown and in dispute. Or a party might claim that the debtor owes it money on a contract, but the debtor might claim that it has a defense to the enforcement of the contract.

Second, priorities may be disputed among creditors. For example, there may be a dispute between two creditors as to exactly what is covered by their subordination agreement. The agreement might explicitly provide for subordination of certain types of payment rights, but be silent about others. The parties might disagree as to whether those other types of payment rights are subject to the agreement.

Third, priorities may be unclear because of the existence of several overlapping priority systems. Security interests, for example, create priority in particular assets, but not a priority for repayment in general. Liquidation priority is just that . . . priority in a liquidation, and not for payment outside of liquidation. Outside of a liquidation, payment due dates function as a type of temporal priority that can be altered via acceleration. Structural priority and guaranties further muddy the waters. And then there is the problem of involuntary creditors who did not bargain for any priority at all, but who might feel that they have a strong moral case for repayment based on having been harmed by the debtor or by virtue of being tax authorities.

If parties cannot agree on their debts' extent and priorities, it becomes much harder for them to reach a deal regarding a restructuring, as they all may believe

---

1. Note that there could also be free-riding off of your diligence efforts. If other creditors see that you've been willing to make concessions after doing diligence, it conveys important information to them about the state of the debtor's finances.

that they are entitled to more than is being offered. Restructuring is not Garrison Keillor's Lake Wobegon, however, and not all creditors can be above average.

Modern financial instruments add a further twist. Some creditors may in fact be net "short" on the debtor because of offsetting derivative positions or interests in competitors. These creditors are motivated to frustrate a restructuring, whether by action or inaction. The mere possibility of such creditors creates the possibility of mistrust that can complicate coordination, and it can also mean that a creditor cannot expect other creditors to make parallel concessions.

What can we take away from the Leviathan Industries problem? There are several critical points to see:

1. The Restructuring Baseline Is Likely Not Performance Under the Original Loan Terms

The baseline for analyzing the possible restructuring is not necessarily performance under the original loan. Instead, it is the probability-weighted sum of performance under the original terms of the loan (the value of doing nothing) and reinvestment value upon default including any losses on the loan (the value of accelerating, collecting, and reinvesting). To be sure, you would also want to account for the possibility that Leviathan Industries would default on the restructured loan as well, but we don't need to work through the entire calculation. Instead, the point is that your comparison is neither performance under the original terms of the loan nor reinvestment opportunity, but the probability-weighted sum thereof.[2]

2. Transaction Costs of Restructuring Are Low for Bilateral Negotiations, but Information Problems May Persist

There are relatively low transaction costs to the restructuring negotiation. Coordination between a single bank and a single firm is not particularly onerous, especially in relationship to the size of the loan. As long as a restructuring remains a bilateral matter, negotiations should not be too burdensome. The one major catch is that informational problems may frustrate bilateral restructurings. Limited information breeds mistrust and discourages concessions.

3. Transaction Costs of Restructuring Are Likely to Rise with Multilateral Negotiations

The situation is likely to change, however, when restructuring becomes a multilateral matter. When there are multiple parties involved in a restructuring—multiple

---

2. In the real world, however, things might be trickier. Because of the term extension, the bank is now assuming the firm's risk for another five years. The interest rate is supposed to compensate for that risk . . . but the interest rate has been lowered despite the risk increasing, and because part of the risk premium has been shifted into a higher principal, to be paid at maturity in a balloon, the bank is assuming even more risk. If the firm were to default in year 11, the bank would be in a worse spot, and if Leviathan Industries is having trouble coming up with the annual interest payments, how is it going to come up with the balloon of principal? Of course, that's not your problem. You'll be retired or at another bank in a decade. It's a problem for some future loan officer to worry about.

creditors, but also multiple co-debtor entities and guarantors, a host of coordination problems may arise. The parties may have trouble identifying each other, may disagree about their respective rights and priorities, may not wish to coordinate with each other, may try to free-ride off each others' efforts and concessions, and may not ultimately trust each others' motives. We take up coordination problems in the following two chapters.

4. Creditors Cannot Be Compelled to Compromise Their Legal Rights Outside of Bankruptcy

In a bilateral contract situation, no creditor can be forced to accept impairment of its legal rights without its consent. A creditor can always say "no." Saying "no," however, does not mean that a creditor gets paid, only that it has not compromised its right to seek payment in full. The basic rule of restructuring outside of bankruptcy, then, is a "property rule," in which a debtor cannot divest a creditor of its rights absent the creditor's consent.[3] This means that the terms of a debt cannot be changed without the creditor's consent. It also means that property which is subject to a lien cannot (outside of the ordinary course of business) be sold free-and-clear of the lien without the lienholder's consent or the redemption of the property from the lien, which means paying off the obligation to the lienholder in full. It means that a debtor cannot provide a lien of higher priority to an existing lien without the lienholder's consent. And it means that lessors, landlords, and contract counterparties cannot generally be compelled to accept assignments of leases or contracts without their consent.

5. There Are No Generic Legal Limitations on Restructuring Bilateral Debts, Except When Third Parties Are Affected

The flip side of the previous point is that with any bilateral creditor-debtor relationship, there are no special legal restrictions on debt restructuring beyond normal contract law, *except to the extent third parties are affected*.[4] General principles of contract and tort of course apply to restructuring transactions. Thus, if a lender fails to keep its promises, makes misrepresentations, or fails to act in accordance

---

3. *See* Guido Calabresi & A. Douglas Melamed, *Property Rules, Liability Rules, and Inalienability: One View of the Cathedral*, 85 HARV. L. REV. 1089 (1972). As you will see, bankruptcy substitutes a liability rule for the non-bankruptcy property rule, enabling a debtor to divest a creditor of its rights if a minimum statutory "price" is paid, but this comes with the problem of judicial "assessment costs," wherein the court may assess the incorrect price. *See* A. Mitchell Polinsky, *On the Choice Between Property Rules and Liability Rules*, 18 ECON. INQUIRY 233 (1980); James E. Krier & Steward J. Schwab, *Property Rules and Liability Rules: The Cathedral in Another Light*, 70 NYU L. REV. 440, 453-454 (1995).

4. The same is not true regarding the multilateral creditor-debtor relationships in certain bonds and notes issued under indentures, as discussed below. The presence of multiple debtors (or, more precisely, sureties), also places some potential limitations on restructuring because of the possibility of so-called "suretyship defenses" that can arise if a debtor takes actions that would prejudice the rights of its surety. Suretyship defenses are waivable and are, in fact, frequently waived in guaranty agreements.

with the implied covenant of good faith and fair dealing, it may face liability to the borrower. This sort of lender liability is an issue we will return to in the bankruptcy context.

Thus, as long as third parties are not affected, the restructuring can take whatever form the debtor and creditor agree upon. The problem, however, is that there are almost always third parties. Single-creditor firms are rare. While many firms may have only a single *financial* creditor, they almost always have other types of creditors: suppliers, employees, tax authorities, landlords, and tort creditors. Remember: Any contract that is not paid immediately upon receipt of goods or services creates a debtor-creditor relationship.

6. Third-Party Relationships Limit Restructurings

Third-party relationships may restrict restructurings in four ways. First, specific contractual provisions in third-party relationships may restrict how another debt is restructured. For example, another creditor may have contracted with Leviathan Industries with a covenant that Leviathan Industries will not grant a lien on certain assets or will not have monthly debt service obligations above a certain limit. Such contractual limitations will restrict Leviathan Industries' debt restructuring—or necessitate that it also involve the third party in the restructuring, which raises coordination problems. Contractual limitations are important, but they are bespoke and cannot be generalized.

Second, if third-party relationships are contractual, they will include an implied covenant of good faith and fair dealing. Actions in a restructuring that affect that third-party relationship may violate the debtor's duty under the implied covenant of good faith and fair dealing that automatically attaches to all contracts by operation of law. The implied covenant of good faith and fair dealing requires the contracting parties "to refrain from arbitrary or unreasonable conduct which has the effect of preventing the other party to the contract from receiving the fruits of the bargain." *Dunlap v. State Farm Fire & Cas. Co.*, 878 A.2d 434, 442 (Del. 2005). The nature of the implied covenant of good faith and fair dealing is that it is a type of equitable catch-all standard; there is no bright line test. We will see a particular application of the implied covenant of good faith and fair dealing in Chapter 10, when we consider coercive exchange offers.

Third, the presence of third-party relationships alters a creditor's calculus when dealing with the debtor because of questions about how the creditor's debt will stack up against the third-party's interests. This is where all of the various coordination problems covered under point 3 above appear.

The fourth way third-party relationships restrict restructurings is through fraudulent transfer law. Every state has a fraudulent transfers statute, as does the federal government for when the government is a creditor, 28 U.S.C. § 3304. Additionally, the federal bankruptcy law contains a general purpose fraudulent transfer statute that can be used when a firm has filed for bankruptcy. We take up fraudulent transfer law in the next chapter.

II. LIQUIDATION OUTSIDE OF BANKRUPTCY

So far, this chapter and the preceding have one considered the legal and institutional constraints on restructuring debts. But sometimes creditors—or debtors—decide that a restructuring isn't possible. When that happens, one possibility is bankruptcy. Bankruptcy provides a framework for the orderly liquidation of a firm. But firms can also liquidate outside of bankruptcy. There are several mechanisms for doing so: foreclosure sales, receiverships, and assignments for the benefit of creditors.

A. Foreclosure

Foreclosure is a type of liquidation option, at least for single-asset entities. While most firms are not single-asset entities, real estate assets are often held in single-asset entities, and a foreclosure of that real estate functionally liquidates the entity. Although there is still a corporate entity remaining after a foreclosure sale of the property of a single-asset entity, it is just an empty shell. Foreclosure, however, is not limited to real estate or to single-asset entities. In multiple-asset entities, a foreclosure still effectuates a partial liquidation.

Foreclosure has some benefits and drawbacks as a liquidation process. From a foreclosing creditor's standpoint, one of the benefits of foreclosure is that it is a process initiated by and controlled by that creditor. That may, however, be exactly what other creditors dislike about foreclosure as a liquidation process.

Another benefit of foreclosure sales is that they pass clear title to the property by extinguishing junior liens and other interests, such as those of tenants (at least to the extent that they have received notice of the sale). While ability to pass clean title increases sale prices, it may be offset by limitations on sale advertisement and limitations on bidders' ability to inspect the property pre-sale, as the property remains the debtor's until the conclusion of the sale (and a subsequent eviction action may be necessary).

Foreclosure sales have other limitations as liquidation options. They can sometimes be quite slow. Foreclosure speed can vary significantly by jurisdiction. Depending on the state, the foreclosure sale may take months or even a few years (as in New York); much depends on whether the foreclosure must be conducted through a judicial action or merely through a private right of sale.

Foreclosures are also not always able to address multiple assets in multiple jurisdictions. Article 9 of the Uniform Commercial Code creates a private right of sale foreclosure for personalty, with few limitations on sale procedures beyond a general requirement of "commercial reasonableness." UCC § 9-610. In theory, a creditor could foreclose on multiple personalty assets located in multiple states in one single sale. Real estate foreclosure, however, is a judicial procedure in roughly half the states, and bidding procedures vary greatly. This means that real estate foreclosure sales can only be done for single properties in single states.

An additional limitation on foreclosure as a liquidation option is that foreclosures do not address anything other than the claims of the secured creditor bringing the sale and those junior to the foreclosing creditor. The claims of senior secured creditors as well as those of unsecured creditors and injunctive claimants are unaddressed. Similarly, all types of foreclosures can leave issues of deficiency judgments and guarantor liability (and subrogation rights) unresolved. Likewise, foreclosure sales only dispose of property that is subject to a lien; the debtor's other assets—whether valuable or cumbersome, such as environmentally polluted property—must be addressed through other procedures.

Critically, all types of foreclosures can be stopped by a bankruptcy filing by the debtor, essentially giving the debtor a "veto" over the foreclosure as a liquidation process. As a result, a foreclosure is an effective way of liquidating a debtor with a single asset and nothing other than secured debt—such as a debtor that owns a single piece of mortgaged commercial real estate—but foreclosures are not effective for liquidating debtors with more complicated assets and liabilities.

B. Receivership

A second non-bankruptcy liquidation option is use of a receivership. Receivership is a traditional equitable remedy in which a court will appoint a neutral third party (the "receiver") to take possession of property and preserve it for a beneficiary. Today, receiverships exist both under statute and as a common law right or equitable remedy. There are a wide range of federal and state statutory receiverships: Federal bank and securities regulators can initiate receiverships for their regulated entities, and states allow receiverships in insurance insolvencies, divorces, criminal proceedings, and corporate insolvencies.

Federal Rule of Civil Procedure 66 authorizes federal equity receiverships. There is little statutory law governing federal equity receivers (as opposed to statutory receivers for banks), but there are a couple of key provisions: First, a federal receiver's jurisdiction covers the debtor's property irrespective of the jurisdiction in which it is located. 28 U.S.C. § 754. This means that a single federal receiver can administer the property of a debtor nationwide. Second, if the receiver brings suit against other parties, it benefits from nationwide service of process and personal jurisdiction without regard to minimum jurisdictional contacts. 28 U.S.C. § 1692.

Some states have detailed general business receivership statutes for insolvent firms. *See, e.g.,* 8 Del. Code Ann. § 291; N.J. Stat. Ann. § 14A:14-2; N.Y. Bus. Corp. Law §§ 1201 *et seq.*; Md. Corps. & Ass'ns Code, § 3-418; Ohio Rev. Code. Ann. § 2735.01; 9 Pa. Cons. Stat. §§ 1 *et seq.*; 3 Tex. Civ. Prac. Code §§ 64.001 *et seq.* Other states have common law or equitable rights to a receiver. State receivership jurisdiction is limited to in-state assets, but unlike a foreclosure sale, it is not necessarily limited to specific assets of the debtor.

The main attractions of receiverships are their flexibility, protection of assets, and relatively low cost. There are few mandatory rules governing the powers of a receiver once appointed. The duties and powers of a federal equity receiver are primarily determined by the receivership order. Even for receivers appointed under state statutory receiverships for insolvent firms, there are few detailed rules. Consider the Texas receivership statute, which provides:

Subject to the control of the court, a receiver may:

(1) take charge and keep possession of the property;

(2) receive rents;

(3) collect and compromise demands;

(4) make transfers; and

(5) perform other acts in regard to the property as authorized by the court.

3 Tex. Civ. Prac. Code § 64.031. Within these boundaries, the receiver has a great deal of discretion. The basic idea is clear, however: The receiver is to take control of the debtor's property, manage it (including possibly selling it), and to use the revenues from the debtor's property to pay claims made by creditors to the extent that the receiver believes the claims are valid.

For a receiver to be appointed, a creditor must show that it has a right to a receiver. Only a single creditor need petition for a receiver. Usually showing a right to a receiver involves showing that the creditor has an interest in the property, such as a lien, and that the receiver is necessary because there is danger to the property being diminished in value. For state statutory receiverships, a showing of insolvency may be enough for a receiver to be appointed, but this requires a showing of insolvency (however defined by statute). For federal and state equity receiverships, insolvency is not typically required, nor is it necessarily sufficient for the appointment of a receiver. In some states, such as New York, a mere default on a loan is sufficient ground for appointment of a receiver. While a debtor will sometimes gladly acquiesce to a receivership, the appointment of a receiver can be litigated. Some states (again, including New York) permit debtors to contractually waive notice of the motion to appoint a receiver.

Typically, a receiver is a neutral third party with fiduciary duties to all creditors, not just the one that petitioned for a receiver. The particular receiver might be proposed by a lender, but courts are not bound to choose the candidate. Receivers are generally authorized to collect the rents and revenues from the property and undertake the managerial steps necessary to maximize the value of the property. A secured creditor might prefer this to a foreclosure because until a foreclosure sale is complete, the debtor retains control of the collateral, which can depreciate through neglect and mismanagement. A receiver gives a secured creditor some confidence that its collateral will be protected by a neutral fiduciary and relieves the secured creditor of assuming liability for the management of the property. Thus, a common use of receiverships under state statutes is by commercial real estate mortgagees, who want to ensure the collection of rents prior to foreclosure.

Receivers often sell receivership properties, but may need specific court authorization to do so. *First Southern Properties, Inc. v. Vallone*, 533 S.W.2d 339 (Tex. 1976). If a receiver sells a property, the receiver can do so in a private sale without having to go through the procedures required by state foreclosure law. This can result in a much faster sale. Moreover, federal and state receivers are often allowed to sell property "free and clear" of existing liens, much like in a foreclosure sale; the lienholders can look only to the proceeds of the sale for payment. This helps receivers maximize property values by eliminating junior lienholders' ability to block a sale.

Receivers can also bring suit on behalf of the receivership estate to recover the estate's assets and, in some situations, to unwind pre-receivership transactions as fraudulent transfers or preferences. (We'll learn about these concepts in later chapters.) The precise power of a receiver to do so depends on whether a receivership is federal or state, and on which state.

Because receiverships are generally informal affairs, their costs may be lower than a court-intensive process like bankruptcy. The receiver's own costs are paid out of the proceeds of the receivership assets, but otherwise there are no costs paid by the receivership estate. In a bankruptcy, in contrast, there may be additional expenses.

A receivership is a potentially flexible framework for an orderly out-of-court liquidation of a debtor's assets. Yet there are drawbacks to receiverships. State receiverships have jurisdictional limitations, and receiverships in general do not stay individual creditors' collection actions. Whereas the filing of a bankruptcy petition automatically enjoins most collection actions; there is no "automatic stay" for receiverships, although courts may be petitioned to stay individual collection actions. *See S.E.C. v. Wencke*, 622 F.2d 1363 (9th Cir. 1980). This means that creditors that do not wish to be bound by the receivership may attempt to "jump ahead in line" by levying on assets. Similarly, receiverships offer no protection against so-called *ipso facto* clauses in contracts that are triggered by the receivership. *Ipso facto* clauses could include forfeitures, penalty provisions, or enhanced creditor rights that inure to the benefit of one creditor over others. As a result, a creditor might be able to leapfrog in priority or substantially inflate the size of its claim in a receivership, thereby shifting the distribution of the debtor's assets. In contrast, the enforcement of *ipso facto* clauses is highly circumscribed in bankruptcy.

While receiverships are flexible, the flip side is that there is uncertainty about how they will function. States with receivership statutes often have rules about the priority of distributions from a receivership. *See, e.g.,* 3 Tex. Civ. Prac. Code § 64.051. But there are no such rules for federal equity receiverships (and presumably also for state equity receiverships). *See SEC v. Wealth Mgmt. LLC*, 628 F.3d 323 (7th Cir. 2010). Moreover, receiverships do not generally have restrictions on claim allowance. Finally, a receivership does not discharge the debtor from liability for unpaid debts or actually liquidate the debtor as an entity. To the extent that debts remain unpaid by the receiver, the debtor is still liable. A receivership is merely a way of protecting the debtor's assets from mismanagement prior to their liquidation.

C. Assignments for the Benefit of Creditors

A third possibility for an out-of-court liquidation is an "assignment for the benefit of creditors" or ABC. In an ABC, the debtor assigns its assets to a third-party fiduciary to manage and liquidate for the benefit of the debtor's creditors. ABCs exist only as a matter of state law. Some states, such as California, Delaware, and Wisconsin, have ABC statutes. *See* CAL. CODE CIV. PROC. §§ 493.010-493.060, 1800-1802;

10 DEL. CODE §§ 7381 *et seq.*; WIS. STAT. ch. 128.001 *et seq.* Other states, such as Illinois, permit ABCs as common law devices. ABCs often function similarly to receiverships, but with a key difference: An ABC is initiated by the debtor, who chooses the assignee, while a receivership is initiated by creditors, with the receiver appointed by a court.

Like a receivership, an ABC does not automatically stay actions against the debtor (although some states will stay actions against the property held by the assignee). Like a receivership, an ABC also does not discharge debts owed by the debtor to the extent that they remain unpaid. Like receiverships, ABCs do not always have clear priority schemes for allocation of liquidation proceeds, although some states do have detailed priority statutes. A federal statute, however, specifies that when an insolvent party makes a voluntary assignment, a "claim of the United States Government shall be paid first." 31 U.S.C. § 3713(a)(1). Moreover, any person (such as an assignee) who pays that insolvent person's debt prior to paying Uncle Sam's claim, is liable to the extent of the payment for the government's unpaid claims. 31 U.S.C. § 3713(b).

Some ABC statutes allow the assignee to avoid certain liens and other transfers prior to the assignment, although the avoidance rights may be preempted by federal bankruptcy law. *See Sherwood v. Lycos*, 394 F.3d 1198 (9th Cir. 2005) (right of assignee under California ABC statute to avoid preferential transfers is preempted by Bankruptcy Code). And, like a receivership, an ABC can always be end-run with a bankruptcy filing by the debtor or an involuntary bankruptcy filing by creditors.

Foreclosure sales, receiverships, and ABCs are all methods for liquidating a debtor's assets (including selling the debtor as a going concern). Yet these procedures all have significant jurisdictional and substantive limitations as methods of orderly liquidation of a debtor's assets because they are not capable of binding all of the debtor's assets and all of the debtor's creditors into one distributional procedure. Foreclosure sales are creditor-by-creditor, jurisdiction by jurisdiction, and not necessarily coordinated. It is not possible to conduct a single foreclosure sale for real property in multiple jurisdictions. Similarly, ABCs and state law receiverships are single-state affairs, making them poorly suited for enterprises doing business nationally, but a better fit for enterprises that might own a single asset (such as an office building or apartment building) in one state. ABCs are also subject to the federal priority rule of Uncle Sam first, which makes them unattractive to many creditors. Federal equity receiverships are not subject to jurisdictional limitations or to the Uncle Sam first rule, but like all the other procedures, they lack the ability to force the sale of property free and clear of liens, to force landlords and contract counterparties to accept assignment of leases and contracts, and to prevent the effect of so-called *ipso facto* clauses—penalty clauses that are triggered by insolvency proceedings of any type. Depending on the particular situation faced by a firm, then, a foreclosure sale, receivership, or ABC might be a viable method for liquidation—or it might not. The point here is that these particular methods all have their limitations as liquidation procedures.

Problem Set 7

(1) You've just started working as a default specialist at Texas Beneficial Bank. The first file on your desk is for Lone Star Petroleum, an oil-and-gas drilling company. A year ago, Lone Star and its subsidiaries borrowed $400 million from your bank on a five-year balloon loan, secured by its drilling rights (oil and gas leases) and equipment. The collateral is spread around Texas, Oklahoma, Louisiana, North Dakota, Ohio, Pennsylvania, and the Outer Continental Shelf (federal government mineral leases). The drilling rights and the equipment are held by separate subsidiaries in each jurisdiction. Applicable law differs by jurisdiction on whether oil and gas leases are considered fee simple interests in real property or contract rights. The drilling rights were originally appraised at $500 million, but a downturn in oil and gas prices means that the rights are now worth somewhere between $100 million and $120 million. Lone Star's equipment is currently worth perhaps $30-35 million. Lone Star's other assets (primarily at the parent level) are worth perhaps $10-$20 million. All cash management, IT, and human resources management are done at the parent level. Lone Star has contacted you to tell you that it is not going to be able to make next month's payment on the loan. Lone Star would like to discuss workout possibilities.

  a. What are your options for what to do next? How will you choose between them? What information would want to know to assist your choice? How will you find it out?
  b. Suppose you decide to foreclose on the drilling rights and equipment. What will you have to do to foreclose? Will this be an expensive process? Who will bear the costs?
  c. Would things be different if Texas Beneficial had taken a security interest in the stock of the subsidiaries?
  d. Suppose you decide to negotiate a workout with Lone Star. What are some potential structures?

(2) Wager Weasel Fantasy Sports Corporation is in serious financial distress. It borrowed heavily to build a state-of-the-art daily fantasy sports gaming platform, only to find its revenue projections wildly off base due to legal interpretations in several states that daily fantasy sports constitutes illegal gambling. Accordingly, Wager Weasel has stopped operating in those states. Wager Weasel is able to operate profitably in other states, but with its diminished revenue it is unable to service its debt. Wager Weasel has reached out to its main creditors, Gadarian Bank and Roth Financial, and proposed a very reasonable restructuring of its debt. To Wager Weasel's surprise, Gadarian Bank has declined the offer and is insisting on repayment in full according to the original maturity schedule. "We never restructure loans," Gadarian Bank tells Wager Weasel. "That's not how we roll." Roth Financial is willing to undertake a restructuring, but insists that it will not make any concessions unless Gadarian Bank makes them. "Otherwise, we'd just be paying Gadarian," Roth says. Is there anything Wager Weasel can do?

(3) You are general counsel of Harper Nephrotics Corp., a wholesaler of diabetes testing equipment. The company president has been relating to you a conversation she had at breakfast with her old friend Ritu Bala. Both your firm and Ritu's are wholesale

suppliers for Oka Medical Supply Co., a major retailer of home medical equipment. Ritu mentions to you that Oka has been losing market share to on-line competitors and hasn't paid her firm in months, and that she hears it may well be insolvent if it loses a tort suit against it for selling a defective product. The company president says, "I told Ritu how funny that was, given that Oka has been late on some of our bills too." What do you tell the company president?

(4) Your client, Bedford Capital Partners, is a small hedge fund that made a loan to Potomac Realty Corporation. Potomac has indicated that it is likely to default on the loan as well as on other obligations.

    a. Bedford Capital Partners wants more information about Potomac's financial condition in order to evaluate its response. Can Bedford Capital Partners get this information? If so, can it rely on it?

    b. Hyde Park Financial claims that Potomac is liable on a guaranty of collection on a loan it made to a Potomac affiliate. Potomac contends that the guaranty has not been triggered. If Potomac is liable, the liability will materially change Potomac's liabilities. How does the possibility of the liability affect Bedford Capital Partners' ability to negotiate a restructuring of its loan to Potomac?

    c. Bedford's loan is secured by a security interest in Potomac's accounts receivable. Potomac also has a loan outstanding from Silver Spring Bank, which has a security interest in Potomac's deposit accounts. How is this situation likely to affect Potomac's ability to restructure its obligations with Bedford and Silver Spring Bank?

    d. Bedford Capital Partners is worried that a default by Potomac will result in a race to the courthouse that will end badly for it. Bedford would like to coordinate with Potomac's other creditors in order to avoid such a race. Is this possible?

(5) Reeling from a massive tort judgment, Granados Construction is deeply insolvent. Granados still has some liquidity, however, and is continuing to operate in an attempt to earn its way back to solvency. Your client, Cantitoe Sheet Rock, is a supplier to Granados Construction. Granados is 120 days late on its bill. Douglas Ramsey, the president of Cantitoe, just called you fuming that he heard that Granados paid another of its suppliers, Tompkins Steel, in full for the steel Tompkins had supplied. "It's not fair. It's only because Oscar Granados, the CEO of Granados, is golf partners with the CEO of Tompkins," he complains.

    a. Is there anything you can do about this situation? What information would you need to know? How can you learn it?

    b. What could Cantitoe have done to prevent this situation?

(6) It's worse than you realized with Granados Construction (from the previous problem). It turns out that not only has the insolvent Granados Construction paid Tompkins Steel in full while not paying Cantitoe anything, but Granados has granted a security interest in all of its assets to Bethesda Bank & Trust, NA, at which it had a previously unsecured $20 million line of credit. Bethesda was threatening to call the line unless it received security.

    a. Why is this situation a problem for Cantitoe?

    b. Is there anything Cantitoe can do about this situation now?

    c. What could Cantitoe have done to prevent this situation?

(7) Colossus Corporation is developing the gargantuan Croesus Casino in Atlantic City, New Jersey. The Croesus project, which constitutes substantially all of Colossus's assets, is already suffering from serious cost overruns, and a sharp downturn in the Atlantic City gaming business has put the ultimate profitability of the unfinished project in doubt. Colossus's lending syndicate, which is secured by a first-lien loan on substantially all of Colossus's assets, has declared the loan in default and announced that it will not advance any further funds for the project. There is currently $2 billion outstanding on the first-lien loan.

In its unfinished state, the Croesus project is worth perhaps $300 million. If finished, it would be worth between $1.6 and $1.8 billion, but to complete the project will require an additional $1 billion in financing.

    a. What difficulties will Colossus have in obtaining additional funding from new lenders?

    b. Colossus wants to sell the Croesus project in order to pay off the lenders. If the first-lien lenders do not consent to the sale, will Colossus be able to sell the Croesus project?

    c. Colossus's vendors have been providing goods and services on 90- or 120-day terms. Now that the lenders have announced that they will not be making further advances, what terms are the vendors likely to demand? How will that affect Colossus's ability to complete the Croesus project?

(8) Auld Block & Chain (AB&C), a blockchain technology startup, is a privately held corporation. AB&C has received a number of rounds of investment, but given disappointing recent product tests, the investors have decided not to provide further funding for AB&C. AB&C will run out of cash in a couple of months at most, and financial institutions are not willing to lend to it, as the little readily sellable collateral is already pledged. AB&C's list of accounts payable is growing and graying, and some vendors have begun to demand repayment. Among AB&C's valuable assets is a below-market lease of a specialty nitrogen-cooled cloud storage space at a high-security computing facility. There are four years remaining on the lease, which prohibits subleasing or assignment. AB&C's board of directors is hopeful that a sale of the business may be possible; a potential buyer has indicated that it is likely to present a term sheet soon. Will it be possible for AB&C to sell the business?

CHAPTER *8*

FRAUDULENT TRANSFERS

Fraudulent transfer law is one of the most powerful protections available for creditors and one of the most significant limitations on out-of-court restructurings. Every state has a "fraudulent transfer" or "fraudulent conveyance" statute, most of which are uniform law, but of several vintages. Nine states have adopted the Uniform Voidable Transfer Act (UVTA), which was promulgated by the Uniform Law Commission in 2014. Thirty-four states, the District of Columbia, and the Virgin Islands still use its predecessor, the 1984 Uniform Fraudulent Transfer Act or UFTA (which is not always perfectly uniform among adoptions). Maryland and New York still use UFTA's predecessor, the 1918 Uniform Fraudulent Conveyance Act or UFCA. Another five states (Alaska, Kentucky, Louisiana, South Carolina, and Virginia) and Puerto Rico have their own non-uniform statutes. This chapter will mainly address the UFTA; the differences between the UFTA and the UVTA are not material for our purposes.

Whatever the statute, fraudulent transfer laws allow creditors to bring suit to avoid certain transfers of property made by debtors. By avoiding the transfers, the creditors are able to restore assets to the debtor, thereby making the assets available to the creditors.

Fraudulent transfers come in two varieties. A transfer may be avoided as either an **actual fraudulent transfer** or as a **constructive fraudulent transfer**.

I. ACTUAL FRAUDULENT TRANSFERS

An actual fraudulent transfer is a transfer undertaken for the purpose of frustrating one's creditors. The intent behind such a transfer may be proven circumstantially by showing the existence of so-called badges of fraud—acts that are consistent with intent to frustrate one's creditors.

The Uniform Fraudulent Transfer Act defines an actual fraudulent transfer as any transfer of an asset or incurrence of an obligation "with actual intent" "to hinder, delay or defraud" creditors. UFTA § 4(a)(1).

For the UFTA, the intent in question is the transferor's not the transferee's. The UFCA's language is arguably vaguer, and courts are split regarding whether the transferee's intent must be proven as well as the transferor's. *See Picard v. Merkin* (*In re Bernard L. Madoff Inv. Sec. LLC*), 440 B.R. 243, 257 (Bankr. S.D.N.Y. 2010) (discussing cases). Section 4(b) of the UFTA enumerates several potential badges of fraud that can be used to circumstantially determine actual intent.

Actual fraudulent transfers are conceptually distinct from common law. An actual fraudulent transfer does not have to involve a misrepresentation or omission of a material fact that induces reliance, etc. Merely intending to "hinder" or "delay" a creditor will suffice. Indeed, there need be nothing "fraudulent" about a fraudulent transfer. That said, some jurisdictions, such as New York, require a heightened pleading standard for fraudulent transfer actions alleging actual intent to defraud. (Presumably the fraud-based heightened pleading standard does not apply to actual intent to merely hinder or delay.) Because of the difference between common law fraud and fraudulent transfers, fraudulent transfer law might better be thought of as "voidable transfer" law, as the UVTA's title makes clear.

A fraudulent transfer need not actually involve the transfer of an asset. First, the statutes cover not just "transfers" but the "incurrence of obligations." Second, "transfer" is defined to include the granting of a lien, among other things. The UFTA defines "transfer" as "every mode, direct or indirect, absolute or conditional, voluntary or involuntary, of disposing of or parting with an asset or an interest in an asset, and includes payment of money, release, lease, and creation of a lien or other encumbrance." UFTA § 1(12).

Fraudulent transfer statutes apply not just to businesses, but to individuals as well. Take note of the complex definition of "insider" and the associated definitions of "affiliate," "person," and "relative" in section 1 of the UFTA. Transfers between affiliated companies may well be transfers to "insiders" and thus a factor to consider under UFTA section 4(b).

II. CONSTRUCTIVE FRAUDULENT TRANSFERS

The second type of fraudulent transfer is a "constructive fraudulent transfer." A constructive fraudulent transfer merely requires a transferor that is insolvent, rendered insolvent, or insufficiently capitalized and that failed to receive "reasonably equivalent value" (UFTA). The transferor's (and transferee's) intent is irrelevant for a constructive fraudulent transfer.

The UFTA has three provisions regarding constructive fraudulent transfers. First section 4(a)(2) provides that a transfer or obligation incurred is fraudulent if it was made without receiving reasonably equivalent value (REV) *and* the debtor was insufficiently capitalized or intended to or believed or should have reasonably believed that it would incur debts beyond its ability pay as they came due. Section 4(a)(2) claims can be brought by both parties that were creditors at the time of the transaction *and* parties that subsequently became creditors. In other words, even if a debtor has no creditors, a transfer can still be subsequently challenged (within the applicable statute of limitations) when it gets creditors.

Second, section 5(a) allows creditors to avoid a transfer or obligation incurred if there was no REV *and* the debtor was insolvent or was rendered insolvent as a result of the transaction.

Third, section 5(b) allows creditors to avoid transfers by a debtor if the transfer was made to an insider for an antecedent debt while the debtor was insolvent and the insider had reason to believe the debtor was insolvent. Remember that the definition of insider under section 1 of the UFTA is quite broad and incorporates definitions of "affiliate," "person," and "relative."

Unlike UFTA section 4(a)(2), UFTA section 5(a) and section 5(b) actions are available only to creditors that exist at the time of the transaction.

Two valuation concepts are key for applying UFTA sections 4(a)(2), 5(a), and 5(b). The first valuation concept is what constitutes "reasonably equivalent value." The UFTA does not define "reasonably equivalent value." What is "reasonably equivalent" is deliberately vague. But the UFTA does define "value." If something is not "value," then it cannot count toward "reasonably equivalent value."

UFTA section 3 defines value as either a transfer of property, the satisfaction of an antecedent debt, or the grant of security for an antecedent debt. Excluded from the definition of value is an unperformed promise outside of the ordinary course of business to help the debtor or another person. In other words, value under the UFTA is not the same as "consideration" under a contract.

A particular issue that has bedeviled the courts is whether forbearance constitutes value. For example, Leviathan Industries has a $10 million unsecured loan from the Minotaur Leveraged Opportunity Fund. Leviathan has defaulted on the loan. Minotaur demands a security interest in Leviathan's inventory and receivables in exchange for forbearing on its rights under the loan and not seeking judgment. Is this forbearance value? And, if so, is it "reasonably equivalent value" to the security interest? How does one even start to value forbearance? Generally, courts have not treated forbearance as value, but they are not uniform on the matter. *See, e.g., Official Comm. of Unsecured Creditors v. Credit Suisse First Boston (In re Exide Techs., Inc.)*, 299 B.R. 732, 748 (Bankr. D. Del. 2003) (forbearance can constitute value, but reasonable equivalency must be shown).

So what, then, is "reasonably equivalent value"? Again, there is no bright line test. Historically, some courts have used a 70% rule of thumb, *Durrett v. Washington Nat'l Ins. Co.*, 621 F.2d 201, 203 (5th Cir. 1980), but that precedent has been effectively overruled by the Supreme Court. *BFP v. Resolution Trust Corp.*, 511 U.S. 531, 545 (1994). Today, courts employ a totality of the circumstances analysis. This analysis focuses on the disparity in the value of the property transferred and what the debtor received, whether the transaction was at arm's length, and in some cases, whether the parties were acting in good faith. *Asarco LLC v. Ams. Mining Corp.*, 396 B.R. 278, 338 (S.D. Tex. 2008). This insertion of good-faith analysis in the "reasonably equivalent value" inquiry is a holdover from the UFCA, which included "good faith" in its definition of "fair consideration," and is not universally considered. Even with a totality of the circumstances analysis, courts are unlikely to find a lack of reasonably equivalent value when the value given to the debtor is significantly above 70%.

The second valuation concept that is critical for UFTA sections 4(a)(2), 5(a), and 5(b) is the question of solvency. If a debtor is not insolvent or rendered insolvent, then UFTA sections 5(a) and 5(b) do not apply. And if a debtor is able to pay its debts as they come due and are sufficiently capitalized, then UFTA section 4(a)(2) and UFCA sections 5 and 6 do not apply.

The UFTA defines insolvency in section 2 of the respective acts. The UFTA's definition is a balance sheet test ("balance sheet insolvency"), but the UFTA also has a rebuttable presumption that a firm that is generally not paying its obligations as they come due ("equity insolvency") is balance sheet insolvent. UFTA § 2(a)-(b). What "generally" means is not explained by the statute. Does it refer to the number of debts, their amount, their importance, their nature, or how late they are paid? Importantly, secured debts are excluded from the calculation of the debtor's obligations, UFTA § 2(e), and assets that serve as collateral are excluded from the definition of a debtor's assets, UFTA § 1(2).

Leibowitz v. Parkway Bank & Trust Co. (*In re* Image Worldwide)

139 F.3d 574 (7th Cir. 1997)

ESCHBACH, Circuit Judge.

Image Worldwide, Ltd. guaranteed loans paid to an affiliate corporation, Image Marketing, Ltd. Both corporations were owned by the same person, but only Image Marketing received funds from the loan. The Image Worldwide's bankruptcy trustee filed suit to avoid the guarantees as a fraudulent transfer, alleging that the guarantees made Image Worldwide insolvent, and that Image Worldwide did not receive reasonably equivalent value in exchange for its guarantees. . . .

Richard Steinberg was the sole shareholder, sole officer, and sole director of Image Marketing, Ltd. (IM), an Illinois corporation incorporated in June 1991. IM was in the commercial printing business, primarily dealing in wholesale sales of music and sports merchandise. IM leased space from FCL Graphics, a printing company that did all of the printing for IM.

In 1992, IM obtained a line of credit from Parkway Bank secured by a first lien against substantially all of IM's assets (IM loan). The line of credit allowed IM to borrow against up to 70% of its eligible accounts receivable, and required IM to reduce its indebtedness to 70% of its accounts receivable in the event that its eligible accounts receivable declined. By June 1993, IM had borrowed $300,000 on its line of credit.

At the end of 1993, IM was several hundred thousand dollars in debt to trade creditors. So in December 1993, Steinberg incorporated a new Illinois corporation, Image Worldwide, Ltd. (IW). Steinberg was the sole shareholder, officer, and director of IW as well. IW leased the same space from FCL as IM, used the same suppliers, and had many of the same customers. In early 1994, Steinberg liquidated IM. Parkway knew of and cooperated in the liquidation of IM. Instead of demanding that IM pay off its loan under the terms of the agreement, however, Parkway allowed Steinberg to use the money obtained from the liquidation of IM to pay down IM's trade debts. Parkway never required IM to pay off its loan, even when its accounts receivable declined to zero in 1994.

Instead, Parkway demanded that IW guarantee IM's $300,000 debt. IW executed the guarantee on May 27, 1994. The guarantee was secured by a first lien on substantially all of IW's assets. IW never borrowed any money from Parkway on its own. Parkway's consideration for the guarantee was its allowing IW to stay in business. Between May 27, 1994 and when IW was forced into bankruptcy, IW paid principal and interest on the loan as it became due.

Even after IM was wound down, IM still owed $200,000 to FCL Graphics. Parkway lent $200,000 to Steinberg to pay this debt (Steinberg loan). The bank paid the proceeds from this loan directly to FCL. The loan was secured by all of IW's accounts receivable. As of the date of its bankruptcy, IW had paid down $72,076.49 in principal and $26,863.45 in interest on the loan.

IW was no more successful than IM. At trial, Parkway stipulated that the guarantees made IW insolvent. In August 1995, FCL stopped doing work for IW, and filed an involuntary Chapter 7 petition for bankruptcy against IW. [A trustee was appointed to represent the interests of IW's creditors. Parkway subsequently] collected IW's accounts receivable to pay down the debts guaranteed by IW. All told, Parkway collected $444,507.55 from IW, including the amounts paid prior to the bankruptcy.

The trustee instituted this . . . proceeding in July 1996 to recover the amounts transferred to Parkway. . . . [T]he trustee charged that the transfers to Parkway were fraudulent transfers in violation of the Uniform Fraudulent Transfer Act (UFTA), 740 ILCS 160/5, because IW never received reasonably equivalent value for its guarantees to Parkway. . . .

Because Parkway has stipulated that the transaction rendered IW insolvent, the key issue in this case is whether IW, as guarantor, received reasonably equivalent value for its guarantee when the direct benefits of the transaction were received by a third party, IM. Parkway argues that its allowing IW to stay in business constituted reasonably equivalent value for IW's guarantee of IM's debt. Parkway also attempts to argue that IM and IW were the same entity.

Because the UFTA is a state law, we must predict how the Illinois courts would handle Parkway's claims. The Illinois courts have not yet elaborated on what "reasonably equivalent value" is for purposes of § 160/5. . . . Thus, we can look to interpretations of "reasonably equivalent value" from . . . cases from courts interpreting other states' versions of the UFTA for assistance in predicting what an Illinois court would do.

The bankruptcy court determined as a matter of law that "a conveyance by a corporation for the benefit of an affiliate is not regarded as given [sic] fair consideration to the creditors of the conveying corporations," citing *Rubin v. Manufacturers Hanover Trust Co.*, 661 F.2d 979 (2d Cir. 1981). This determination is an overly narrow statement of law, and misreads the holding of *Rubin*. Nevertheless, under the appropriate law, the bankruptcy court did not clearly err in ruling that the guarantees were fraudulent transfers.

The transactions in question are known in corporate law lingo as an "intercorporate guarantee." These fall into three types: "upstream," "downstream," and "cross-stream." An upstream guarantee is when a subsidiary guarantees the debt of its parent; a downstream guarantee is when a parent corporation guarantees a debt of its subsidiary; a cross-stream guarantee is when a corporation guarantees the debt of an affiliate. IW's guarantees in this case were cross-stream guarantees.

Intercorporate guarantees are a routine business practice, and their potential void-ability creates a risk for unwary lenders. Intercorporate guarantees are common because they benefit both the creditor and debtor in a loan transaction. Within a corporate group, some units will often have better credit ratings than others. The units which are perceived as credit risks by lenders will be either unable to obtain loans, or able to obtain a loan only at a higher interest rate. However, when the corporate group exploits the units with good credit ratings by having them guarantee the debt of the weaker unit, the weaker unit will benefit from either obtaining the loan, or getting the loan at a better rate. The creditor benefits from greater security in repayment. So between creditor and debtor, the guarantee is a win-win situation.

However, the creditors of the guarantor making a cross-stream guarantee can some-times lose out in the transaction, because the guaranteeing corporation may not receive a direct economic benefit from the guarantee. Should the guarantee push the guaran-tor into insolvency, these transactions will be scrutinized under a fraudulent transfer analysis. Fraudulent transfer law seeks to preserve assets of the estate for creditors. Some courts applying traditional fraudulent transfer rules to intercorporate guarantees therefore found that the guarantor had not received reasonably equivalent value for the guarantee, because from the standpoint of the unsecured creditor, the guarantor had received no consideration for the guarantee.

However, requiring a direct flow of capital to a cross-guarantor to avoid a finding of a fraudulent transfer "is inhibitory of contemporary financing practices, which rec-ognize that cross-guarantees are often needed because of the unequal abilities of inter-related corporate entities to collateralize loans." *TeleFest, Inc. v. Vu-TV Inc.*, 591 F. Supp. 1368, 1379 (D.N.J. 1984). Often, these guarantees are legitimate business transactions, and not made to frustrate creditors. In recognition of this economic reality, courts have loosened the old rule that transfers primarily for the benefit of a third party invariably give no consideration to the transferor. Thus, even when there has been no direct eco-nomic benefit to a guarantor, courts performing a fraudulent transfer analysis have been increasingly willing to look at whether a guarantor received indirect benefits from the guarantee if there has been an indirect benefit. "One theme permeates the authori-ties upholding guaranty obligations: that the guaranty at issue was the result of arm's length negotiations at a time when the common enterprise was commercially viable." Williams, *Fallacies*, 15 CARDOZO L. REV. at 1438.

Generally, a court will not recognize an indirect benefit unless it is "fairly concrete." *See Heritage Bank Tinley Park v. Steinberg (In re Grabill Corp.)*, 121 B.R. 983, 995 (N.D. Ill. 1990). The most straightforward indirect benefit is when the guarantor receives from the debtor some of the consideration paid to it. But courts have found other economic benefits to qualify as indirect benefits. For example, in *Mellon Bank, N.A. v. Metro Communications, Inc.*, 945 F.2d 635, 646-48 (3d Cir. 1991), the court found reasonably equivalent value for a debtor corporation's guarantee of an affiliate's debt when the loan strengthened the corporate group as a whole, so that the guarantor corporation would benefit from "synergy" within the corporate group. The *Mellon* court stated that indi-rect benefits included intangibles such as goodwill, and an increased ability to borrow working capital. *TeleFest* indicated that indirect benefits to a guarantor exist when "the transaction of which the guaranty is a part may safeguard an important source of supply, or an important customer for the guarantor. Or substantial indirect benefits may result from the general relationship" between affiliates. 591 F. Supp. at 1380-81. In *Xonics*, we recognized the ability of a smaller company to use the distribution system of a larger affiliate as an indirect benefit as well. *See Xonics*, 841 F.2d at 202. . . .

The Steinberg loan presents a much closer case, because IW may have received an indirect benefit from this guarantee. FCL Graphics was IW's printer, and thus its most important supplier. FCL also allowed IM and IW to operate their business on FCL's premises. At trial, Steinberg testified as follows about the benefits to IW from the Steinberg loan:

> Q: What, if any, benefit was there to Image Worldwide for you to pay FCL Graphics $200,000? . . .
> A: It was allowed to continue doing business remaining on FCL's premises and having FCL as a supplier.
> Q: Is it your testimony that if you hadn't paid FCL the $200,000, it would have put Image Worldwide out of business?
> A: Yes.
> Q: It would have moved Image Worldwide off the premises?
> A: Yes.
> Q: It would not have supplied product to Image Worldwide?
> A: Yes.

If the Steinberg loan had not been made to pay off IM's debt to FCL, FCL Graphics clearly posed a substantial threat to IW because of its ability to evict IW and discontinue providing services to IW. TeleFest states that:

> [Some courts have] rationalized upholding various transfers against fraudulent conveyance challenges by finding that sufficient consideration passed to the transferor because an opportunity had been given to it to avoid bankruptcy through the strengthening of an affiliated corporation that received the benefit of the transfer. Such an approach seems indisputably proper when a weak but still solvent entity is rendered insolvent only because of the inclusion of the guaranty on the liability side of the balance sheet. This permits the analysis to focus upon economic reality in the appropriate factual context without rewarding legal laxity or inflexibly ignoring real benefits merely because they have no place on the company's balance sheet.

TeleFest, 591 F. Supp. at 1379. Under the broad reading of the indirect benefit doctrine laid down in cases like *TeleFest*, IW received an indirect benefit from the payment of the Steinberg loan because the loan kept FCL Graphics from kicking Steinberg and his companies off of FCL's property, and from refusing to do business with Steinberg. True, the balance sheet showed that IW was insolvent after taking on the IM loan and the Steinberg loan, but IW was not finished as a going concern, as IW was able to remain in business for 17 months after guaranteeing the Steinberg loan.

On the other hand, the circumstances of this case do not fit the circumstances when indirect benefits from a guarantee are found to constitute reasonably equivalent value. As indicated above, courts that uphold cross-stream guarantees generally do so when the transaction strengthens the viability of the corporate group. In this case, though, there were not two functioning corporations that benefitted mutually from the loan. By the time IW guaranteed the Steinberg loan, IM had been wound down. Even though it was not officially dissolved, the company had been liquidated and was inactive. IW became insolvent to pay an inactive affiliate's debts. Indeed, while IW was able to timely pay the bank pursuant to the loans for a time after guaranteeing the loans, IW eventually fell behind in payments to trade creditors just like IM had. In effect, by paying off IM's debts, IW kept IM out of bankruptcy by bankrupting itself. This shift of risk from the creditors of the debtor to the creditors of the guarantor is exactly the situation that fraudulent transfer law seeks to avoid when applied to guarantees. Thus, while IW received an indirect benefit from the transaction, it did not receive reasonably equivalent value. . . .

We therefore hold that indirect benefits to a guarantor may be considered when determining whether a corporation receives reasonably equivalent value for a guarantee. However, we do not believe that the bankruptcy court clearly erred when it found that IW did not receive reasonably equivalent value for its guarantees. Thus, the judgment of the district court is AFFIRMED.

III. LIABILITY FOR AND DEFENSES TO FRAUDULENT TRANSFERS

So far we've learned that there are two types of fraudulent transfers and the elements thereof. But what is the effect of a court ruling that a transfer was fraudulent? Let's go back to Leviathan Industries. Leviathan had defaulted on a $10 million unsecured loan from the Minotaur Leveraged Opportunity Fund. Minotaur demanded that it be granted a security interest in Leviathan's inventory and receivables in exchange for forbearing on the default. Leviathan complied. Now let's say that the Pegasus Strategic Investments Fund, a creditor of Leviathan's, successfully challenges the grant of security as a fraudulent transfer. What is the consequence? Section 7 of the UFTA spells out creditors' remedies. The key remedy is that a creditor like Pegasus may avoid the transfer, meaning that the Minotaur Leveraged Opportunity Fund loses the lien. (Injunctive relief would also be possible to stop a future fraudulent transfer.)

Section 8(b) of the UFTA further explains how this remedy works. A creditor can recover judgment for the value of the transferred asset from either the initial transferee of the asset or from subsequent transferees, subject to certain other limitations in section 8 of the UFTA. Thus, if the Minotaur Leveraged Opportunity Fund had sold its loan (now including the lien on the inventory and receivables) to Gorgon Strategic Investments, LLP, Pegasus may seek to recover from *either* Minotaur or Gorgon. Subsequent transferees become jointly liable with the initial transferee; the initial transferee's liability does not disappear upon transfer. If it were so, there'd be a strong incentive to "launder" fraudulent transfers by retransferring them, in a "hot potato" game.

It might seem intuitive in the example above that Minotaur should be required to disgorge a fraudulent transfer, but why should Gorgon, the subsequent transferee? What if Gorgon was unaware of the circumstances by which Minotaur acquired the lien?

Likewise, suppose that when Leviathan Industries was desperate for cash, it sold its art collection to luxury goods buyer Johnny Midas. The sale was for far less than Leviathan could have obtained if it had the art collection auctioned off by an auction house. Does Midas have any defense? Why should Midas lose out just because he got too good a deal to be true?

Section 8 of the UFTA provides for certain defenses for transferees. Section 8(a) provides a good faith defense—but only against actual fraudulent transfer actions under section 4(a)(1). Notice that "good faith" is not defined in the UFTA. What exactly is good faith? Is it an equitable "smell test"? Does it merely require "honesty in fact" or also "reasonable standards of commercial fair dealing," UCC § 1-201(20), or something more? The UFTA doesn't say, although state law decisions may explicate the matter.

The section 8(a) good faith defense also requires that the transferee paid reasonably equivalent value. Thus, a good faith recipient of a gift cannot avail himself of section 8(a)'s defense. Accordingly, Gorgon might not be able to avail itself of the section 8(a) defense because of lack of good faith, while Midas might not be able to use the defense because of lack of "reasonably equivalent value."

The section 8(a) good faith defense underscores that it is the transferor's intent, not the transferee's, that matters for an actual fraudulent transfer. It also indicates that there can be an actual fraudulent transfer *even if reasonably equivalent value is paid*. How might this work? Consider a debtor who enters into a sale and repurchase arrangement with a friend in order to shield an asset that has idiosyncratic value to the debtor, such as an asset that is much more valuable in the debtor's business than for anyone else. There might be reasonably equivalent value paid, insofar as market value goes, but the arrangement would still not be in good faith if the friend knew the purpose of the transaction.

A close reading of section 8(a)(1) would also indicate that subsequent transferees can shelter in it only if the initial transferee could itself do so. That is, if the initial transferee did not take in good faith and for reasonably equivalent value, it will not matter for section 8(a)(1) purposes if a subsequent transferee did so. Were it otherwise, section 8(a)(1) would allow initial transferees to launder fraudulently transferred assets. As it happens, however, there are other defenses available for subsequent transferees.

Section 8(a) is not the only good faith defense to a fraudulent transfer. Section 8(b)(2) provides a good faith defense from all types of fraudulent transfers, actual and constructive, but only for subsequent transferees who took for value or who themselves took from a subsequent transferee. Thus, a secondary transferee must take in good faith and for value, but a tertiary or a quaternary transferee need only take in good faith. Notice that section 8(b)(2) does not require reasonably equivalent value, unlike section 8(a). Thus, suppose that Midas had resold the art (at a substantial markup) to Sally Apollo, who gave the art as birthday presents to her friends. Apollo should be protected under section 8(b)(2), as well as her friends, assuming that they took in good faith.

Section 8(d) provides any party against whom a fraudulent transfer judgment is entered with a right of setoff or lien on the recovered asset to the extent that the value was given to the debtor. One would presume that this right of setoff is limited to value given by the transferee, but the UFTA's wording is not so precise. Thus, Apollo might be able to offset a fraudulent transfer judgment to the extent that Midas paid Leviathan Industries for the art.

Table 8.1 below summarizes who is liable for different types of fraudulent transfer actions. Despite the subtle distinctions between taking in good faith, taking in good faith for value, and taking in good faith for reasonably equivalent value, the basic effect of section 8 is to limit liability to initial transferees and those in cahoots with them or those subsequent transferees who do not give value.

Table 8.1 Liability for Fraudulent Transfer Actions

	Liability for Actual Fraudulent Transfer Unless:	Liable for Constructive Fraudulent Transfer Unless:
Initial Transferee	• Took in good faith and for REV. UFTA § 8(a)(1).	• Took in good faith, to extent gave value. UFTA § 8(d).
Secondary Transferee	• Took in good faith and for value. UFTA § 8(b)(2). • Or *initial transferee* took in good faith and for REV. UFTA § 8(a).	• Took in good faith and for value. UFTA § 8(b)(2).
Tertiary Transferee	• Took in good faith and for value. UFTA § 8(b)(2). • Or *initial transferee* took in good faith and for REV. UFTA § 8(a).	• Took in good faith. UFTA § 8(b)(2).
Quaternary Transferee, etc.	• Took in good faith. UFTA § 8(b)(2). • Or *initial transferee* took in good faith and for REV. UFTA § 8(a).	• Took in good faith. UFTA § 8(b)(2).

In addition to the statutory defenses provided to fraudulent transfers, general equitable doctrines, such as estoppel or ratification, may serve as bars to fraudulent transfer actions. Thus, even though UFTA section 4 applies to both present and future creditors, future creditors who extended credit with knowledge of the transfer and the financial situation of the debtor may be deemed to have ratified the transaction. Likewise, creditors who were complicit in a fraudulent transfer—such as by providing the financing for the transfer—may be estopped from avoiding the transfer.

A final consideration. Statutes of limitation matter a lot for fraudulent transfer law. Once a statute of limitation has lapsed, a fraudulent transfer is not avoidable. The UFTA has a four-year statute of limitations, but some states have adopted non-uniform versions of the UFTA and have three-, five- or six-year statutes of limitations. Significantly for financial transactions, the New York version of the UFCA has a six-year statute of limitations. And a special federal statute allows the Internal Revenue Service to bring a fraudulent transfer action up to ten years after tax liability has been assessed (with assessment running from various times). 26 U.S.C. § 6502(a)(1).

It's easy to get lost in the weeds of fraudulent transfer law. While it is important that you learn to navigate the UFTA—a powerful tool for creditors—it is also important to keep sight of the big picture. Fraudulent transfer law provides two types of limits on restructurings. First, it places a firm limit on restructurings by allowing the avoidance of transfers for less than reasonably equivalent value from an insolvent (or rendered insolvent) firm. This keeps insolvent debtors from favoring individual creditors over their other creditors. Second, it provides a type of equitable catch-all, by allowing the avoidance of transfers intended to hinder, delay, or defraud creditors. Beyond these limitations, however, fraudulent transfer law does not dictate the particular terms that are permitted or required in a restructuring.

Problem Set 8

(1) BHB, Inc. is a leading custom home builder. BHB's CEO, Wild Bill Bratton, is famous for speeding around town in an expensive, cherry red Lamborghini Countach with vanity plates. The car is owned by BHB, but Wild Bill's the only one who ever gets to drive it. A downturn in the housing market has placed BHB in tough times and the company has defaulted on some of its obligations. In fact, some of BHB's creditors have obtained judgments against it and directed the sheriff to levy on BHB's assets.

   a. When the sheriff shows up to levy on the Lamborghini, Wild Bill takes out the registration and shows it to the sheriff. It appears that the car is now registered in the name of Wild Bill's nephew Rex. "The company decided to give Rex the car as a birthday present for his third birthday," explains Wild Bill, with a smile on his face. "Rex has asked that I continue to keep the car in my garage. He's also very nice about letting me drive it." Is there anything BHB's creditors can do? UFTA § 4.

   b. Would your answer change if the Lamborghini served as collateral for a $1 million secured loan to BHB from National Capitol Bancorp? UFTA § 1(2). The car is insured for $300,000.

(2) You just found the deal of a lifetime! You were shopping at Eileen's Basement and found an amazing Kiera Tang designer wedding dress on sale for a fraction of its usual retail price. Normally this dress would run $10,000, but you got it for $500. No wonder people are saying that Eileen's is about to go bankrupt.

You inspected the dress carefully and are sure there are no defects and that it is a genuine Kiera Tang product. The timing couldn't be better, as your wedding is just months away. Is there anything you should be concerned about? UFTA § 5(a).

(3) You are working as in-house counsel at Finjan Partners, a private equity firm. The oil and gas industry is currently in the midst of a serious downturn, and many oil and gas companies are selling off wellhead assets at favorable prices in order to stay afloat. You'd like to snatch up some of the bargains out there because you believe you can hold on to them until their market value rebounds, but you are worried that the oil and gas companies' creditors might bring fraudulent transfer actions against you. What can you do to protect yourself? What are the consequences if you're wrong?

(4) Skinny-Oren, Inc. has announced that it plans to forgive a $5 million intercompany debt owed to its parent company Youngjae Shipping, Inc. Skinny-Oren is currently running two months late on its utility bills, but was paying its employees on time. Last month Skinny-Oren was also 29 days late on one payment of its secured notes, late enough to trigger a default, but within the contractual grace period for a cure before the secured noteholders were allowed to take legal action. Skinny-Oren has been sued for wrongful discharge by its former chief technology officer. The CTO has asked the court to enjoin the debt forgiveness. Should the CTO prevail? UFTA §§ 1(1), 1(7), 2, 4(a)(2), 5(a), 5(b).

(5) The law firm of Barrow, Monet & DeWalt LLP is on the verge of collapse. Key partners have been defecting, and the firm's revenue is simply insufficient to support the remaining partners, associates, and staff. BMD missed its rental and malpractice insurance payments last month, and its lender Continental Express Bank has declared a default on BMD's $20 million secured line of credit. Desperate to maintain access to its operating cash lifeline, BMD agreed to sell its art collection to Continental Express in exchange for Continental Express agreeing to forbear on the default for 60 days. The art collection was appraised at and insured for $10 million, but Continental Express purchased it for $8 million and the promise of 60 days' forbearance. One of BMD's former partners is owed $3 million under a guaranteed compensation agreement. The former partner has challenged the sale of the art collection as a fraudulent transfer. Is he likely to succeed? UFTA §§ 4(a)(2), 5(a).

(6) Energy firm Helios sold its drilling rights on the North Slope of the Brooks Range in Alaska to Ajax Exploration for $40 million one month before filing for bankruptcy. The drilling rights had been appraised at $75 million just months before the sale, and increased oil prices make them even more valuable. With weeks, Ajax had sold the drilling rights to Bellerophon for $60 million. Several months later, Bellerophon sold the drilling rights to Calliope for $80 million. Helios's creditors have successfully challenged the sale to Ajax as a fraudulent transfer. What remedy is available to them? UFTA § 8.

CHAPTER 9

THE TRUST INDENTURE ACT

In the previous chapter we sketched out some possibilities for restructuring a firm's debt. We saw that there were information problems but few general legal restrictions. The situation sketched out in section I of the previous chapter regarding Leviathan Industries does not hold true for every type of creditor. Some creditors have specific legal restrictions on their ability to renegotiate debts. Others face coordination problems. And others may lack an incentive to renegotiate. This chapter deals with trade, labor, tax, tort, and lease debt, but mainly focuses on bonds, which are subject to particular statutory and contractual limitations on restructuring. The following two chapters address, respectively, further issues with bonds and issues with syndicated loans, which have contractual, but not statutory limitations on restructuring.

I. COORDINATION AND LEGAL PROBLEMS BY TYPE OF DEBT

A. Trade Creditors

Trade creditors—the vendors who supply a firm with raw materials and services—are probably the most willing to restructure debts. Trade creditors frequently hope to do continued business with a firm. Trade creditors are often willing to forgive or forbear on old debts in order to ensure that the customer remains around to provide new business. No formal legal restrictions or generic coordination problems exist for trade debt.

B. Employees

Employees are also often quite willing to restructure debts. Employees are in a similar position to trade creditors, but unlike trade creditors, employees are unlikely to have a diversified customer base. Most employees have a single employer. This means that employees are particularly exposed to the financial situation of an employer. The lack of diversification gives employers particular leverage vis-à-vis employee creditors. As with trade creditors, no formal legal restrictions or generic coordination problems exist for employees. In both cases, however, a critical supplier or employee (or group of employees) can command tremendous leverage over a firm, as we saw in the Chrysler case study in Chapter 1, where the value of the firm was highly dependent upon its having a labor deal with the UAW.

C. Tax Authorities

Firms often owe tax debt, and restructuring that debt can present complications. There are no coordination problems when dealing with a tax authority, but there may be some legal restrictions. While taxing authorities tend to have broad ability to enter into settlements for tax liabilities, they may have their own guidelines that constrain what they can or will do. Tax authorities also have little incentive to restructure unless they are firmly convinced that doing so will increase collections; they are not looking to assume the risk of a business's future performance.

D. Tort Debt

The ability to restructure tort debt depends on whether the tort is a one-off, unique tort or a mass tort. There is never a legal restriction on how tort debt can be restructured, irrespective of whether there is a judgment for the debt or not. Coordination problems are another story.

If a tort is a one-off, unique event—say a single employment discrimination suit—there's no coordination problem. But with a mass tort—thousands of consumers have been injured by a firm's product—then coordination issues are harder. It does not do a firm a lot of good to reach a deal with one tort claimant, but not the others. This means that there's a problem coordinating the deals in order to avoid ratcheting problems. Things can be further complicated if not all tort claimants are similarly situated—some might have currently manifested injuries, while some might have still latent harms. Class actions can help with coordination when there has not yet been liability established, but litigation is a slow process, and once there is a judgment, the class action mechanism doesn't help with restructuring. As a result, there is limited ability to restructure mass tort debt outside of bankruptcy.

E. Leases

Leases are generally a relatively easy type of debt to restructure. Most leases are made by a single lessor, so there are not coordination problems among creditors. (When leases are securitized, the situation can be more complicated, however.) Lessors are in a position similar to secured lenders; if they aren't paid, they can come and get their stuff, be it leased equipment or real property. There are no legal restrictions or special coordination problems in dealing with lessors. Instead, the main question is whether they prefer restructuring to reinvestment. If a lessor replevies its goods or reclaims its premises, the lessor will need to find another productive use for the assets. Can the lessor find another lessee that will pay as much (on a risk-adjusted basis)? And what will be the transaction costs of reclaiming and releasing the property? Much depends on market conditions. If the lease is above market, the lessor may be quite incentivized to cut a deal with a lessee and ease the terms of a loan in order to maintain active use of the leased asset. Alternatively, if the lease is below market, the lessor will be highly incentivized to get out of the lease and relet the property.

II. BOND DEBT AND THE TRUST INDENTURE ACT OF 1939

Publicly held debt securities present unique challenges for restructuring because of the difficulties in coordinating among bondholders. Publicly held debt has both legal restrictions and coordination problems for restructuring. The Trust Indenture Act of 1939 (TIA), part of the federal securities laws, governs the terms of most publicly offered debt securities not issued by a governmental entity. The TIA recognizes that bondholders have coordination problems because they are dispersed geographically, lack sufficiently large interests to make litigation over the bonds cost-effective, and face a free-rider problem, in that individual bondholders would have to finance litigation that would benefit all bondholders. Accordingly, the regulatory structure of the TIA is designed to protect bondholders from being coerced into modifications of rights. It requires that certain bonds be issued under an indenture with certain mandatory terms and that the bondholders be represented by a sufficiently qualified trustee who is to act on their behalf.

- - -

Trust Indenture Act of 1939 § 302 (15 U.S.C. § 77bbb)

Necessity for Regulation

(a) Practices adversely affecting public

Upon the basis of facts disclosed by the reports of the Securities and Exchange Commission made to the Congress . . . and otherwise disclosed and ascertained, it is hereby declared that the national public interest and the interest of investors in notes, bonds, debentures, evidences of indebtedness, and certificates of interest or participation therein, which are offered to the public, are adversely affected—

> **(1)** when the obligor fails to provide a trustee to protect and enforce the rights and to represent the interests of such investors, notwithstanding the fact that
>
>> **(A)** individual action by such investors for the purpose of protecting and enforcing their rights is rendered impracticable by reason of the disproportionate expense of taking such action, and
>>
>> **(B)** concerted action by such investors in their common interest through representatives of their own selection is impeded by reason of the wide dispersion of such investors through many States, and by reason of the fact that information as to the names and addresses of such investors generally is not available to such investors;
>
> **(2)** when the trustee does not have adequate rights and powers, or adequate duties and responsibilities, in connection with matters relating to the protection and enforcement of the rights of such investors; when, notwithstanding the obstacles to concerted action by such investors, and the general and reasonable assumption by such investors that the trustee is under an affirmative duty to take action for the protection and enforcement of their rights, trust indentures

(A) generally provide that the trustee shall be under no duty to take any such action, even in the event of default, unless it receives notice of default, demand for action, and indemnity, from the holders of substantial percentages of the securities outstanding thereunder, and

(B) generally relieve the trustee from liability even for its own negligent action or failure to act;

(3) when the trustee does not have resources commensurate with its responsibilities, or has any relationship to or connection with the obligor or any underwriter of any securities of the obligor, or holds, beneficially or otherwise, any interest in the obligor or any such underwriter, which relationship, connection, or interest involves a material conflict with the interests of such investors. . . .

The TIA does not apply to all bonds. Instead, the TIA's coverage is limited to only certain types of publicly offered debt securities. Thus, the TIA does not apply to private placements of debt securities or most other securities exempted from registration with the Securities and Exchange Commission under section 4 of the Securities Act of 1933, such as Rule 144A offerings made to qualified institutional buyers or Reg S offerings made to foreign investors.[1] 15 U.S.C. §§ 77d, 77ddd(b). Similarly, the TIA does not apply to offerings of municipal bonds, sovereign bonds, bonds issued or guarantied by banks, or commercial paper (debt securities with a maturity of no more than nine months). 15 U.S.C. §§ 77c(a), 77ddd(a). A private placement involves either the direct sale of the debt securities by an issuer to the buyers or the sale through a placement agent. The debt securities issued in a private placement are often called **notes**, but this terminology has no legal significance.

The TIA creates an extensive merit-based regulation system for publicly offered debt securities. For a debt security that is subject to registration with the SEC to be offered to the public, it must be issued under an indenture that has been "qualified" with the SEC. The TIA provides certain default terms, some mandatory and some not, for qualified indentures. Some of these terms affect the ability to restructure the debt security, particularly limitations on the modification of the terms of the indenture and on the debt security holder's right to sue for non-payment.

The TIA also places limitations on the conflicts of interest a trustee may have—prior to an event of default under the indenture, the trustee may have certain conflicts of interest. For example, the trustee may itself make a loan to the issuer. Following an event of default on the bonds, however, the trustee must either end its trusteeship or the conflict. 15 U.S.C. § 77jjj(b). Thus, the investors in the debt securities are guaranteed representation by an unconflicted agent once their securities are

---

1. At the time of the TIA's enactment, there were no registration exemptions for offerings made only to qualified institutional buyers or foreign investors. As a result, the TIA covered virtually all of the non-municipal, non-sovereign debt securities market. This meant that there was essentially a two-track restructuring regulation system, one for bi-lateral contracts like corporate loans and another for debt securities. Outside of bankruptcy, changes in payment terms could not be forced on any party absent its consent.

in default. Notice, however, that this protection requires an event of default, and to the extent that a trustee must declare such an event of default, the trustee may be disincentivized to do so.

The critical provision in the TIA for our purposes is section 316, 15 U.S.C. § 77ppp. Section 316 places limitations on the amendment of an indenture. There are two key limitations. First, section 316(b) provides that a bondholder's right to institute suit for nonpayment on the security may not be "impaired or affected" without that individual holder's consent. 15 U.S.C. § 77ppp(b). Thus, if there is a payment default, the bondholder may always bring suit for payment. The bondholder does not have to rely on the trustee to bring suit on its behalf or comply with other contractual procedural hurdles before bringing suit for nonpayment. Notably, this provision only protects the right to sue for nonpayment. It does not protect the right to sue for defaults unrelated to payments, although acceleration provisions in the security may mean that a covenant default triggers a right to payment. Section 316(b) is why no-action clauses in bond indentures are always limited by non-impairment clauses that allow for individual bondholder suits in the event of a payment default (but such bondholders may not be able to accelerate the debt individually, limiting the value of the right).

Section 316(b) contains a pair of exceptions to the protection of the right to institute suit: The indenture itself may limit or deny the right to sue if a suit or judgment would result in impairment of any lien that secures the indenture, and the right to sue does not apply to an interest payment that has been postponed (for up to three years) with the consent of the holders of 75 percent of the principal amount of the outstanding securities.

The second key limitation is in the same section 316(b), and is a prohibition on the impairment of any bondholder's right of payment, absent consent of that individual bondholder. 15 U.S.C. § 77ppp(b). In other words, no bondholder can be compelled by other bondholders (or the issuer) to accept a reduction in principal, interest, or an unfavorable change in payment timing or amortization. This provision gives bondholders a powerful right to hold out against restructurings; we'll explore the dynamics of holding out presently.

The sole exception to section 316(b)'s protection of the right of payment is section 316(a)(2), 15 U.S.C. § 77ppp(a)(2), which allows the holders of 75% of the principal amount of the securities to consent to the postponement of interest payments for up to three years. Such a postponement would not forgive the interest payments, and it would all be due in a balloon at the end of the postponement.

Critically, section 316(b) only protects the right to payment. It does *not* protect the myriad bond covenants that might protect the right to payment indirectly, such as debt or lien limitations. The TIA is silent on the matter, but other provisions may generally be amended by consent of a majority of bondholders (in terms of dollar amount), unless the indenture provides for a different amendment threshold.

Lastly, section 316(a)(1) creates a non-mandatory default provision in indentures that allows a majority of bondholders to direct the trustee as to when and how to pursue particular remedies or to waive past (but not prospective) defaults. 15 U.S.C. § 77ppp(a)(1). In other words, a majority of bondholders can direct the trustee to temporarily forbear or even forgive non-payment defaults. Section 316(b)'s protection of the right to payment limits section 316(a)(1) forbearance and forgiveness to non-payment defaults.

Trust Indenture Act of 1939 § 303 (15 U.S.C. § 77ccc)

Definitions

When used in this subchapter, unless the context otherwise requires—

. . .

(7) The term "indenture" means any mortgage, deed of trust, trust or other indenture, or similar instrument or agreement (including any supplement or amendment to any of the foregoing), under which securities are outstanding or are to be issued, whether or not any property, real or personal, is, or is to be, pledged, mortgaged, assigned, or conveyed thereunder.

. . .

(9) The term "indenture to be qualified" means
  (A) the indenture under which there has been or is to be issued a security in respect of which a particular registration statement has been filed, or
  (B) the indenture in respect of which a particular application has been filed.

. . .

(12) The term "obligor", when used with respect to any such indenture security, means every person (including a guarantor) who is liable thereon, and, if such security is a certificate of interest or participation, such term means also every person (including a guarantor) who is liable upon the security or securities in which such certificate evidences an interest or participation; but such term shall not include the trustee under an indenture under which certificates of interest or participation, equipment trust certificates, or like securities are outstanding.

Trust Indenture Act of 1939 § 316 (15 U.S.C. § 77ppp)

Directions and Waivers by Bondholders; Prohibition of Impairment of Holder's Right to Payment; Record Date

(a) Directions and waivers by bondholders
  The indenture to be qualified—
  (1) shall automatically be deemed (unless it is expressly provided therein that any such provision is excluded) to contain provisions authorizing the holders

of not less than a majority in principal amount of the indenture securities or if expressly specified in such indenture, of any series of securities at the time outstanding

> (A) to direct the time, method, and place of conducting any proceeding for any remedy available to such trustee, or exercising any trust or power conferred upon such trustee, under such indenture, or
>
> (B) on behalf of the holders of all such indenture securities, to consent to the waiver of any past default and its consequences; or

(2) may contain provisions authorizing the holders of not less than 75 per centum in principal amount of the indenture securities or if expressly specified in such indenture, of any series of securities at the time outstanding to consent on behalf of the holders of all such indenture securities to the postponement of any interest payment for a period not exceeding three years from its due date.

For the purposes of this subsection . . . in determining whether the holders of the required principal amount of indenture securities have concurred in any such direction or consent, indenture securities owned by any obligor upon the indenture securities, or by any person directly or indirectly controlling or controlled by or under direct or indirect common control with any such obligor, shall be disregarded, except that for the purposes of determining whether the indenture trustee shall be protected in relying on any such direction or consent, only indenture securities which such trustee knows are so owned shall be so disregarded.

(b) Prohibition of impairment of holder's right to payment

> Notwithstanding any other provision of the indenture to be qualified, the right of any holder of any indenture security to receive payment of the principal of and interest on such indenture security, on or after the respective due dates expressed in such indenture security, or to institute suit for the enforcement of any such payment on or after such respective dates, shall not be impaired or affected without the consent of such holder, except as to a postponement of an interest payment consented to as provided in paragraph (2) of subsection (a) of this section, and except that such indenture may contain provisions limiting or denying the right of any such holder to institute any such suit, if and to the extent that the institution or prosecution thereof or the entry of judgment therein would, under applicable law, result in the surrender, impairment, waiver, or loss of the lien of such indenture upon any property subject to such lien.

. . .

Many of the provisions of the TIA are incorporated in bond indentures themselves, including indentures that are not formally subject to the TIA. An example of this may be found in section 902 of the Sunstone Hotel Partnership Indenture that you encountered in Chapter 4.

Trust Indenture Act litigation is relatively rare. The following cases represent the most recent (and controversial) interpretations of the Trust Indenture Act. Notice how the TIA is interpreted along with a claim for breach of the implied covenant of good faith and fair dealing. Could the courts have arrived at the same outcome without the TIA?

Marblegate Asset Mgmt., LLC v. Educ. Mgmt. Fin. Corp.

846 F.3d 1 (2d Cir. 2016)

LOHIER, *Circuit Judge*:

Defendant-appellant Education Management Corporation ("EDMC") and its subsidiaries appeal from a judgment following a bench trial before the United States District Court for the Southern District of New York (Failla, J.). The District Court held that a series of transactions meant to restructure EDMC's debt over the objections of certain noteholders violated Section 316(b) of the Trust Indenture Act of 1939, 15 U.S.C. § 77ppp(b). The transactions at issue, the District Court determined, stripped the non-consenting noteholders, plaintiffs-appellees Marblegate Asset Management, LLC and Marblegate Special Opportunity Master Fund, L.P. (together, "Marblegate"), of their practical ability to collect payment on notes purchased from EDMC's subsidiaries. As a result, the District Court ordered EDMC to continue to guarantee Marblegate's notes and pay them in full.

On appeal, EDMC argues that it complied with Section 316(b) because the transactions did not formally amend the payment terms of the indenture that governed the notes. We agree with EDMC and conclude that Section 316(b) prohibits only non-consensual amendments to an indenture's core payment terms. We therefore VACATE the judgment and REMAND to the District Court for further proceedings consistent with this opinion.

BACKGROUND

1. Facts

EDMC is a for-profit higher education company that relies heavily on federal funding through Title IV of the Higher Education Act of 1965, 20 U.S.C. §§ 1070-1099. EDMC is the parent company of defendants-appellants Education Management, LLC and Education Management Finance Corporation (together, the "EDM Issuer").

In 2014 EDMC found itself in severe financial distress. Its enterprise value had fallen well below its $1.5 billion in outstanding debt. But restructuring its debt by resorting to bankruptcy court was not a realistic option for EDMC, which, the parties agree, would lose its eligibility for Title IV funds if it filed for bankruptcy and discontinued as an ongoing concern. See 20 U.S.C. § 1002(a)(4)(A).[1] EDMC therefore had to cooperate with its

---

1. Section 1002(a)(4)(A) states, in relevant part: "An institution shall not be considered to meet the definition of an institution of higher education in paragraph (1) if—(A) the institution, or an affiliate of the institution that has the power, by contract or ownership interest, to direct or cause the direction of the management or policies of the institution, has filed for bankruptcy. . . ."

creditors outside of the bankruptcy process if it hoped to restructure its debt and persist as a viable entity.

EDMC's outstanding debt consisted of both secured debt (roughly $1.3 billion) and unsecured debt ($217 million). The secured debt was governed by a 2010 credit agreement between the EDM Issuer and secured creditors (the "2010 Credit Agreement"). The 2010 Credit Agreement gave EDMC's secured creditors the right, upon default, to deal with the collateral securing the loans "fully and completely" as the "absolute owner" for "all purposes." The collateral securing the debt consisted of virtually all of EDMC's assets.

The unsecured debt, to which we will refer as the "Notes," was also issued by the EDM Issuer and governed by an indenture executed in March 2013 and qualified under the Trust Indenture Act of 1939 (the "Indenture"). The Notes were guaranteed by EDMC as the parent company of the EDM Issuer (we refer to this guarantee as the "Notes Parent Guarantee") and carried a high effective interest rate—nearly 20 percent per year—to compensate for the riskier nature of the unsecured debt. Both the Indenture and the offering circular relating to the Notes informed lenders who had purchased them (the "Noteholders") about their rights and obligations as junior, unsecured creditors. For example, the offering circular explained that the Notes Parent Guarantee was issued solely to satisfy EDMC's reporting obligations, that it could be released solely by operation of the release of any later guarantee EDMC issued to secured creditors, and that Noteholders should therefore not assign any value to the Notes Parent Guarantee. Marblegate holds Notes with a face value of $14 million but never held any secured debt.

As EDMC's financial position deteriorated, its debt burden became unsustainable. After negotiating with EDMC, a majority of secured creditors agreed in September 2014 to relieve the EDM Issuer of certain imminent payment obligations and covenants under the 2010 Credit Agreement. The resulting agreement was a new amended credit agreement entered in the fall of 2014 (the "2014 Credit Agreement"). As consideration for these changes, EDMC agreed to guarantee the secured loans (the "Secured Parent Guarantee").

Around the same time, a group of creditors formed an Ad Hoc Committee of Term Loan Lenders (the "Ad Hoc Committee") and established a Steering Committee, which is an intervenor-appellant in this appeal, to negotiate with EDMC.[2] The Steering Committee and EDMC eventually devised two potential avenues to relieve EDMC of its debt obligations.

The first option, which obtained only if creditors unanimously consented, was designed to result in (1) most of EDMC's outstanding secured debt being exchanged for $400 million in new secured term loans and new stock convertible into roughly 77 percent of EDMC's common stock, and (2) the Notes being exchanged for equity worth roughly 19 percent of EDMC's common stock. EDMC estimated that this first option would amount to roughly a 45 percent reduction in value for secured lenders and a 67 percent reduction in value for Noteholders.

---

2. The Ad Hoc Committee held 80.6 percent of the secured debt and 80.7 percent of the Notes. Of that total, the Steering Committee of the Ad Hoc Committee held 35.8 percent of secured debt and 73.1 percent of the Notes.

The second option would arise only if one or more creditors refused to consent. Under that circumstance, a number of events would occur that together constituted the "Intercompany Sale." Secured creditors consenting to the Intercompany Sale would first exercise their preexisting rights under the 2014 Credit Agreement and Article 9 of the Uniform Commercial Code (UCC) to foreclose on EDMC's assets. In addition, the secured creditors would release EDMC from the Secured Parent Guarantee. That release in turn would effect a release of the Notes Parent Guarantee under the Indenture. With the consent of the secured creditors (but without needing the consent of the unsecured creditors), the collateral agent would then sell the foreclosed assets to a subsidiary of EDMC newly constituted for purposes of the Intercompany Sale. Finally, the new EDMC subsidiary would distribute debt and equity only to consenting creditors and continue the business.

The Intercompany Sale was structured to incentivize creditors to consent. While non-consenting secured creditors would still receive debt in the new EDMC subsidiary, that debt would be junior to the debt of consenting secured creditors. Non-consenting Noteholders would not receive anything from the new company: though not a single term of the Indenture was altered and Noteholders therefore retained a contractual right to collect payments due under the Notes, the foreclosure would transform the EDM Issuer into an empty shell. In offering to exchange the Notes for equity in the new EDMC subsidiary, therefore, EDMC and the Ad Hoc Committee explicitly warned Noteholders that they would not receive payment if they did not consent to the Intercompany Sale.

Except for Marblegate, all of EDMC's creditors (representing 98 percent of its debt) eventually consented to the Intercompany Sale.

2. Procedural History

Marblegate, the sole holdout, sued to enjoin the Intercompany Sale on the ground that it violated Section 316(b) of the Trust Indenture Act of 1939 (the "TIA"), 15 U.S.C. § 77ppp(b). *Marblegate Asset Mgmt. v. Educ. Mgmt. Corp.*, 75 F. Supp. 3d 592 (S.D.N.Y. 2014) ("*Marblegate I*"). Section 316(b) of the TIA, entitled "Prohibition of impairment of holder's right to payment," provides as follows:

> Notwithstanding any other provision of the indenture to be qualified, *the right of any holder of any indenture security to receive payment of the principal of and interest on such indenture security, on or after the respective due dates expressed in such indenture security, or to institute suit for the enforcement of any such payment on or after such respective dates, shall not be impaired or affected without the consent of such holder,* except as to a postponement of an interest payment consented to as provided in paragraph (2) of subsection (a) of this section, and except that such indenture may contain provisions limiting or denying the right of any such holder to institute any such suit, if and to the extent that the institution or prosecution thereof or the entry of judgment therein would, under applicable law, result in the surrender, impairment, waiver, or loss of the lien of such indenture upon any property subject to such lien.

15 U.S.C. § 77ppp(b) (emphasis added).

Before the District Court, EDMC argued that "the right . . . to receive payment" is necessarily defined by the payment terms in the Indenture itself, such that Section 316(b) prohibits only non-consensual amendments to an indenture's core payment terms. Therefore, EDMC asserted, the Intercompany Sale complied with Section 316(b) because it did not amend any Indenture term and because Marblegate's right to initiate suit against the EDM Issuer to collect payment remained intact.

In response, Marblegate contended that although the contractual terms governing Marblegate's Notes had not changed, its practical ability to receive payment would be completely eliminated by virtue of the Intercompany Sale, to which it did not consent. Section 316(b), Marblegate warned, would be rendered meaningless if issuers and secured creditors could collaborate to restructure debt without formally amending any payment terms.

The District Court initially declined to grant a preliminary injunction but believed that Marblegate was likely to succeed on the merits of its TIA claim. *Marblegate I*, 75 F. Supp. 3d at 615-17. After reviewing the text and legislative history of Section 316(b), the District Court concluded that the TIA "protects the *ability*" of the Noteholders "to receive payment in some circumstances." *Id.* at 612-15. Even where the payment terms of an indenture are not explicitly modified by a transaction, the District Court held, Section 316(b) is violated whenever a transaction "effect[s] an involuntary debt restructuring." *Id.* at 614.

The Intercompany Sale occurred in January 2015. The foreclosure sale took place, the secured creditors released the Secured Parent Guarantee, the new EDMC subsidiary was capitalized with the EDM Issuer's old assets, and consenting bondholders participated in the debt-for-equity exchange. But Marblegate continued to hold out. And in light of the District Court's decision, EDMC and the Steering Committee refrained from releasing the Notes Parent Guarantee. Instead, they filed a counterclaim against Marblegate, seeking a declaration that the Notes Parent Guarantee could be released without violating the TIA.

Since the bulk of the Intercompany Sale was already completed, the subsequent bench trial focused on whether the District Court should permanently enjoin release of the Notes Parent Guarantee and thereby force EDMC to continue its guaranteed payment on Marblegate's Notes. On that question, the District Court ultimately sided with Marblegate by reiterating that the release of the Notes Parent Guarantee would violate Section 316(b). *Marblegate Asset Mgmt., LLC v. Educ. Mgmt. Corp.*, 111 F. Supp. 3d 542, 556-57 (S.D.N.Y. 2015) ("*Marblegate II*").

This appeal followed. At present, because EDMC was able to reduce its debt burden through the very transaction to which Marblegate objected, it currently has the assets to pay on Marblegate's Notes. Marblegate, as the owner of Notes that had been poised to receive only limited additional payments because of EDMC's pending insolvency, is now the only creditor receiving full payouts according to the original face value of its Notes.

DISCUSSION

EDMC appeals the judgment on the ground that the District Court misinterpreted Section 316(b) of the TIA. We review the District Court's conclusions of law *de novo*.

. . .

1. Text

The core disagreement in this case is whether the phrase "right . . . to receive payment" forecloses more than formal amendments to payment terms that eliminate the right to sue for payment. 15 U.S.C. § 77ppp(b). We agree with the District Court that the text of Section 316(b) is ambiguous insofar as it "lends itself to multiple interpretations" that arguably favor either side on that issue. *Marblegate I*, 75 F. Supp. 3d at 611; *see also Marblegate II*, 111 F. Supp. 3d at 547. Likewise, Marblegate conceded at oral argument that the interpretation it advances is not supported by reference to the plain text alone.

On the one hand, Congress's use of the term "right" to describe what it sought to protect from non-consensual amendment suggests a concern with the legally enforceable obligation to pay that is contained in the Indenture, not with a creditor's *practical* ability to collect on payments. On the other hand, adding that such a right cannot be "impaired or affected" arguably suggests that it cannot be diminished, relaxed, or otherwise affected in an injurious manner.

To be sure, Marblegate's broad reading of the term "right" as including the practical ability to collect payment leads to both improbable results and interpretive problems. Among other things, interpreting "impaired or affected" to mean any *possible* effect would transform a single provision of the TIA into a broad prohibition on any conduct that could influence the value of a note or a bondholder's practical ability to collect payment. 15 U.S.C. § 77ppp(b). Furthermore, if the "right . . . to receive payment" means a bondholder's practical ability to collect payment, then protecting the "right . . . to institute suit for the enforcement of any such payment" would be superfluous, because limiting the right to file a lawsuit for payment constitutes one of the most obvious impairments of the creditor's practical ability to collect payment. *Id.* The "right . . . to receive payment" is not, in other words, so broad as to encompass the "right . . . to institute suit." *Id.*

If for no other reason than the general rule that different statutory phrases can indicate that different meanings were intended, these two rights are best viewed as distinct from one another. The former right, it seems to us, prohibits non-consensual amendments of core payment terms (that is, the amount of principal and interest owed, and the date of maturity). It bars, for example, so-called "collective-action clauses" —indenture provisions that authorize a majority of bondholders to approve changes to payment terms and force those changes on all bondholders. *See NML Capital, Ltd. v. Republic of Argentina*, 699 F.3d 246, 253 (2d Cir. 2012). The latter right (to sue) ensures that individual bondholders can freely sue to collect payments owed under the indenture. So construed, the right to sue clearly bars so-called "no-action clauses," which preclude individual bondholders from suing the issuer for breaches of the indenture, leaving the indenture trustee as the sole initiator of suit. *See Cruden v. Bank of New York*, 957 F.2d 961, 967-68 (2d Cir. 1992). An indenture that contains only a collective-action clause violates the "payment" right, not the "suit" right; an indenture that contains only a no-action clause violates the "suit" right, not the "payment" right. Regardless, we agree with the District Court that the plain text of Section 316(b) is ultimately ambiguous and fails to resolve the principal question before us.

Nor does any party seriously contend that the structure of the TIA provides a clear answer to that question, as the dissenting opinion suggests. At best, we have observed that "[n]othing in Section 316(b), or the TIA in general, requires that bondholders be afforded 'absolute and unconditional' rights to payment." *Bank of New York v. First Millennium, Inc.*, 607 F.3d 905, 917 (2d Cir. 2010). So, for example, Section 316(a)(1) permits bondholder majorities to both waive past defaults and control the manner in which the indenture trustee pursues remedies. *See* 15 U.S.C. § 77ppp(a).

Our statement in *First Millennium* seems at odds with the broad protection of dissenting bondholders seeking to collect payment that Marblegate urges. But it does not really help us determine whether Congress intended Section 316(b) to protect a broad right to actual payment or merely a right to sue for payment under fixed indenture terms. Notably, though, no other provision in the TIA purports to regulate an issuer's business transactions, which would be a likely result of Marblegate's broad reading of Section 316(b).

2. Legislative History

Because the text of Section 316(b) is ambiguous and the TIA's structure fails to remove the ambiguity, we turn to legislative history.

. . . The District Court concluded that the legislative history compels [an interpretation of Congressional intent to prohibit an out-of-court debt restructuring that has the purpose and effect of eliminating *any* possibility of receiving payment under their notes] because at the time that Section 316(b) was drafted Congress did not contemplate the use of foreclosures as a method of reorganization. This reading also reflects the District Court's understandable concern that "a sufficiently clever issuer [would] gut the Act's protections" by using a foreclosure action instead of amending the indenture or filing for bankruptcy. *Marblegate I*, 75 F. Supp. 3d at 613; *see also Marblegate II*, 111 F. Supp. 3d at 555-56. The District Court thought the TIA's drafters "did not anticipate precisely the mechanisms through which such a [nonconsensual majoritarian] restructuring might occur," but rather only "understood involuntary reorganizations to operate in a rather straightforward fashion: a majority of the bondholders would simply vote to amend the payment or interest provisions of the indenture." *Marblegate II*, 111 F. Supp. 3d at 554-55; *id.* at 555-56 (stating that "there is no reason to think that the [TIA] was targeted only at a particular method of restructuring").

Based on our review of the legislative history of Section 316(b), we conclude that Congress did not intend the broad reading that Marblegate urges and the District Court embraced. Starting in 1936, the Securities and Exchange Commission (SEC) published a comprehensive eight-part report examining the role of protective committees in reorganizations. Part VI of that report, published in 1936 and entitled "Trustees Under Indentures" (the "1936 SEC Report"), led to enactment of the TIA. *See* 15 U.S.C. § 77bbb(a) (citing "reports of the [SEC]" as "the basis of facts" for promulgating the TIA). Subsequent congressional reports, testimony, and other contemporaneous statements by SEC officials relating to earlier bills also shaped the final legislation enacted in 1939.

Among other things, the drafters of the TIA appear to have been well aware of the range of possible forms of reorganization available to issuers, up to and including foreclosures like the one that occurred in this case but that the District Court concluded violated Section 316(b). Indeed, foreclosure-based reorganizations were widely used at the time the TIA was drafted. [T]he history of the TIA, and of Section 316(b) in particular [detailed discussion of which is omitted here], shows that it does not prohibit foreclosures even when they affect a bondholder's ability to receive full payment. Rather, the relevant portions of the TIA's legislative history exclusively addressed *formal* amendments and indenture provisions like collective-action and no-action clauses.

. . . Our review of the testimony and reports leading up to and immediately following the enactment of Section 316(b) convinces us, in sum, that Congress sought to prohibit formal modifications to indentures without the consent of all bondholders, but did not intend to go further by banning other well known forms of reorganization like foreclosures.

. . .

3. Workability and Dissenting Bondholder Remedies

Finally, we highlight an additional difficulty with Marblegate's interpretation of Section 316(b) and address a potential concern with our holding.

Marblegate's interpretation of Section 316(b) requires that courts determine in each case whether a challenged transaction constitutes an "out-of-court debt restructuring . . . designed to eliminate a non-consenting holder's ability to receive payment." Appellee Br. 21. The interpretation thus turns on the subjective intent of the issuer or majority bondholders, not the transactional techniques used. But we have expressed a particular distaste for interpreting boilerplate indenture provisions based on the "relationship of particular borrowers and lenders" or the "particularized intentions of the parties to an indenture," both of which undermine "uniformity in interpretation." *See Sharon Steel Corp. v. Chase Manhattan Bank, N.A.*, 691 F.2d 1039, 1048 (2d Cir. 1982).[17] Marblegate similarly argues that the right to receive payment is impaired "when the source of assets for that payment is deliberately placed beyond the reach of non-consenting noteholders."[18] Appellee Br. 25. But this description could apply to every foreclosure in which the value of the collateral is insufficient to pay creditors in full.

Marblegate and the District Court respond that Section 316(b) permits "genuinely adversarial" foreclosures but prohibits the type of foreclosure that occurred here. *Marblegate I*, 75 F. Supp. 3d at 615-16. But neither the text nor the legislative history

---

17. *Compare Sharon Steel*, 691 F.2d at 1048 ("Just such uncertainties would be created if interpretation of boilerplate provisions were submitted to juries sitting in every judicial district in the nation."), *with BOKF, N.A. v. Caesars Entm't Corp.*, 144 F. Supp. 3d 459, 474-75 & n.86 (S.D.N.Y. 2015) (adopting Marblegate's interpretation of Section 316(b), but sending to the factfinder the question of whether the "overall *effect*" of the transactions at issue was "a debt restructuring or a series of routine corporate transactions").

18. The dissent similarly objects that Marblegate's "legal claim was surely impaired by actions that intentionally made the company unable to pay any judgment awarded against it." But the Intercompany Sale to which Marblegate is objecting allowed EDMC to reduce its debt burden and maintain federal funding such that it has the assets to pay legal claims. Without that transaction, EDMC would be unable to meet these legal claims that the dissent seeks to protect.

of Section 316(b) supports a distinction between adversarial and "friendly" foreclosures.[19] Nor do we agree with the District Court's description of the negotiations. To the contrary, our reading of the record convinces us that the negotiations were clearly adversarial before the parties agreed on a course to preserve the value of the assets. The negotiations leading to the creation and release of the Secured Parent Guarantee were, in our view, also adversarial.

Limiting Section 316(b) to formal indenture amendments to core payment rights will not leave dissenting bondholders at the mercy of bondholder majorities. Our holding leaves Marblegate with some recourse. By preserving the legal right to receive payment, we permit creditors to pursue available State and federal law remedies. (And of course, sophisticated creditors, like Marblegate, can insist on credit agreements that forbid transactions like the Intercompany Sale.) Having foregone the protection of bankruptcy in this case, the secured creditors and EDMC have also shed the protection of the Bankruptcy Code, including a discharge order. The foreclosure in this case therefore may be challenged by other creditors under State law. Moreover, where creditors foreclose on a debtor's collateral and sell the collateral to a new entity meant to carry on the business, the debtor's other creditors may be able to sue the new entity under State law theories of successor liability or fraudulent conveyance. . . .

CONCLUSION

To summarize, we hold that Section 316(b) of the TIA does not prohibit the Intercompany Sale in this case. The transaction did not amend any terms of the Indenture. Nor did it prevent any dissenting bondholders from initiating suit to collect payments due on the dates specified by the Indenture. Marblegate retains its legal right to obtain payment by suing the EDM Issuer, among others. Absent changes to the Indenture's core payment terms, however, Marblegate cannot invoke Section 316(b) to retain an "absolute and unconditional" right to payment of its notes. For the foregoing reasons, the judgment is VACATED and the case is REMANDED to the District Court for further proceedings consistent with this opinion.

STRAUB, *Circuit Judge*, dissenting:

The question before this Court is whether Section 316(b) of the Trust Indenture Act (the "TIA") prohibits Defendant-appellant Education Management Corporation ("EDMC") from engaging in an out-of-court restructuring that is collusively engineered to ensure that certain minority bondholders receive no payment on their notes, despite the fact that the terms of the indenture governing those notes remain unchanged. Because the plain text of the statute compels the conclusion that it does, I would answer that question in the affirmative and uphold the judgment of the District Court. I therefore respectfully dissent.

---

19. Marblegate also fails to explain why Section 316(b) would permit a purely adversarial foreclosure that eliminates any recovery for unsecured creditors but prohibit a friendly foreclosure designed to maximize the going-concern value of the assets and provide unsecured creditors the only possibility of recovery. We note that the UCC appears to contemplate this type of cooperation. *Cf.* N.Y. UCC §§ 9-601(a), 9-609(c).

I begin my analysis with the language of Section 316(b) of the TIA . . . Here, the plain language of Section 316(b) requires the conclusion that the Intercompany Sale as envisioned in the Restructuring Support Agreement violates the TIA.

. . .

As delineated by the District court, "[t]he text poses two questions: what does the 'right . . . to receive payment' consist of, and when is it 'impaired or affected' without consent?" *Marblegate Asset Mgmt., LLC v. Educ. Mgmt. Corp.*, 111 F. Supp. 3d 542, 546 (S.D.N.Y. 2015) ("*Marblegate II*"). EDMC and the Steering Committee (together, "Appellants") read the text narrowly, with EDMC arguing that "[o]n its face, the statutory text is unambiguous in protecting only the 'right' of a noteholder to receive payment when due and to sue for enforcement of such payment." EDMC App. Br. 19. By contrast, Marblegate reads the text broadly, arguing that "the right to receive payment is 'impaired' or 'affected' when the ability to receive payment under the bond is stripped away—not only through formal amendment of a bond's payment terms, but also by other means." Marblegate App. Br. 24. I am persuaded by Marblegate's reading of the statute.

The terms "right," "impair," and "affect" are undefined in the TIA, so we must look to their ordinary meaning. A "right" is typically defined as "[s]omething that is due to a person by just claim, legal guarantee, or moral principle," or "[a] legally enforceable claim that another will do or will not do a given act." Black's Law Dictionary (10th ed. 2014). On the basis of this definition, Appellants argue that actions only violate Section 316(b) if those actions affect the "legal entitlement" to payment — i.e. by altering the terms of the bond so that a bondholder can no longer legally *claim* the right to receive payment under their original terms. Nothing in Section 316(b), Appellants urge, entitles bondholders to *actual* payment on their notes.

This argument, however, nearly eliminates the import of the terms "impair" and "affect" and imposes qualifications in Section 316(b) that simply do not exist. The term "impair" means "to diminish the value of." *Id*. The term "affect" means "to produce an effect on; to influence in some way." Black's Law Dictionary (10th ed. 2014). Even defined as a "legal entitlement" or "claim," it is unquestionable that the "right" to receive payment can be "diminished" or "affected" without actual modification of the payment terms of the indenture. By making it impossible for a company to pay the amount due on its notes, for example, the "right" to receive payment is "diminished" because it literally has been made worthless. Surely, a bondholder's right or "legal entitlement" to receive payment is impaired when actions are taken to ensure that the bondholder either consents to a change in his payment terms or receives *no* payment on his notes at all.[3] *See* Black's Law Dictionary (10th ed. 2014) (explaining that the term

---

3. Of course, there are a number of actions that could be said to impair the right of noteholders to receive payment, ranging from poor business decisions at one end to deliberate attempts to devalue the business at the other. But whereas noteholders clearly give their implied consent for ordinary course business transactions and decisions to be carried out, and are compensated for the risk that the business will be run unsuccessfully by the interest that they receive on the notes, the same cannot be said of a deliberate act to render their right to receive payment worthless. In that latter circumstance, Section 316(b) requires the noteholder's explicit consent.

"impair" is "commonly used in reference to diminishing the value of a contractual obligation to the point that the contract becomes invalid *or a party loses the benefit of the contract*" (emphasis added)).

Had Congress intended merely to protect against modification of an indenture's payment terms, it could have so stated. Nothing in the language of Section 316(b), however, cabins the prohibition on impairing or affecting the "right . . . to receive payment" to mere *amendment* of the indenture. In fact, that Congress used the broad phrase "impaired or affected" implies that it did not intend Section 316(b) to be limited in its scope to mere amendments. Because we are compelled to give every term in a statute effect, our reading of the statute must account for rather than ignore this phraseology. Further, Section 316(b) is written in the passive voice; its prohibition is nowhere limited to actions taken by a noteholder majority. Despite Appellants' arguments to the contrary, nothing in the text of the statute requires the narrow reading that Section 316(b) merely prohibits modification of an indenture's core payment terms (amount and due date) by noteholder majority action without consent of the individual noteholder.

Although not determinative to my analysis, it is worth considering the structural argument that Appellants make in further support of their textual interpretation. This argument, however, is also unconvincing. Section 316(a) of the TIA relates to collective action clauses—i.e., clauses permitting a certain percentage of holders to consent to changes to the indenture terms.

Unlike Section 316(b), which is mandatory, Section 316(a) is permissive. It states, for example, that an indenture *may* contain provisions permitting the majority of noteholders to consent on behalf of all noteholders "to the waiver of any past default and its consequences." 15 U.S.C. § 77ppp(a). It also permits indentures to contain provisions whereby 75% of noteholders can consent on behalf of all noteholders "to the postponement of any interest payment for a period not exceeding three years from its due date." *Id.*

Appellants argue that Section 316(b) should thus be read as an "exception" to 316(a); while 316(a) states what collective action clauses are permitted, 316(b) simply states what collective action clauses are *not* permitted. But nothing in either of the two provisions in Section 316 indicates that 316(b) is meant to be an exception to 316(a). Moreover, as Marblegate urges, it is perhaps more reasonable to view 316(a)(2)—which permits a 75% vote to defer interest for three years—as an exception to 316(b). *See* 15 U.S.C. § 77ppp(b) (prohibiting modification of right to receive payment without noteholder's consent "except . . . as provided in paragraph (2) of subsection (a) of this section.").

At a minimum, the language of Section 316(b) covers the actions taken by EDMC and the Steering Committee here. The Restructuring Support Agreement presented Marblegate with what the District Court rightfully deemed a Hobson's choice—to accept a modification of the payment terms of its notes, or to receive no payment at all. The Intercompany Sale, which stripped the issuers of their assets and removed the parent guarantee, ensured that no future payments of principal or interest would be made on the notes. This scheme did not simply "impair" or "affect" Marblegate's right to receive payment—it annihilated it.[5]

The methodology used to accomplish that annihilation is of little interest when the end result is squarely at odds with the plain intent of Section 316(b). We therefore need look no further than the plain text of Section 316(b) to hold that the Intercompany Sale, as envisioned by the Restructuring Support Agreement, violates the TIA. Based on the plain terms of Section 316(b), I would hold that an out-of-court debt restructuring "impairs" or "affects" a non-consenting noteholder's "right to receive payment" when it is designed to eliminate a non-consenting noteholder's ability to receive payment, and when it leaves bondholders no choice but to accept a modification of the terms of their bonds.

I am cognizant of the parade of horrors that Appellants predict will result from interpreting the TIA in the manner above. However, threatening dire commercial consequences from the refusal to read a statute in a manner inconsistent with its plain language is not a sufficient basis to override the correct interpretation of the law. We must not forget the long-standing imperative that *making* law is the job of the legislature and not of the courts. Where, as here, the statute's language is plain and unambiguous, the "sole function of the courts is to enforce it according to its terms." *Ron Pair Enters., Inc.*, 489 U.S. at 241. Certain undesirable consequences might well arise from the fact that Section 316(b) prohibits actions such as those taken by EDMC in this case. But "[r]esolution of the pros and cons of whether a statute should sweep broadly or narrowly is for Congress." *United States v. Rodgers*, 466 U.S. 475, 484 (1984).[6]

---

5. Appellants argue that Marblegate's right to receive payment was not annihilated, or even impaired or affected, by their actions because Marblegate still maintains a legal claim for payment and it may sue, perhaps in state court, for enforcement of that payment. But this argument misses the point. Even if Marblegate maintains a "legal claim" for payment upon which it can sue, that legal claim was surely impaired by actions that intentionally made the company unable to pay any judgment awarded against it. The effect of the Intercompany Sale was to transfer all or substantially all of EDMC's assets to a new, wholly owned subsidiary of EDMC, and EDMC explicitly warned that this meant its assets "would not be available to satisfy the claims of [dissenting] Holders." App'x 52. The Intercompany Sale thus deliberately placed EDMC's assets beyond the reach of non-consenting noteholders, while the effect of the release of the parent guarantee would be to eliminate noteholders' ability to seek payment from EDMC's guarantor. We have held that a company's complete inability to pay a monetary judgment constitutes a risk of irreparable harm when a company is nearly insolvent in the context of preliminary injunctions. *See Brenntag Int'l Chems., Inc. v. Bank of India*, 175 F.3d 245, 249-50 (2d Cir. 1999). Surely, then, a bondholder's right to receive payment on its bond by the bringing of a lawsuit has been impaired or harmed when the company has rendered itself unable to satisfy any monetary judgment. While the right to sue remains intact, the ability to recover anything as a result of that suit has vanished, rendering the suit meaningless.

6. Significantly, Congress recently abandoned two proposals to amend § 316(b), first through a 2015 highway bill rider and then through an omnibus appropriations legislation rider. The proposals would have narrowed the definitions of impairment of the right to payment and the right to institute suit for nonpayment. In response to the latter proposal, 18 law professors [led by the author of this book] sent a letter to members of Congress urging them to reject the proposed amendment, which would have been undertaken without legislative hearings or public comment, because the amendment "could have broad negative unintended consequences in the securities market." Letter sponsored by Georgetown University Law Center to Members of Congress (Dec. 8, 2015). Several major asset managers also sent a letter expressing their disapproval for amendment without the opportunity for hearings and public comment, as "the adverse consequences to the economy and to capital markets could be significant." Letter from BlackRock, Inc, DoubleLine Group LP, Oaktree Cap. Mgmt., L.P., Pac. Inv. Mgmt. Co, T. Rowe Price Assocs., & Western Asset Mgmt. Co. to Members of Congress (Dec. 14, 2015). This past March, the Chamber of Commerce sent a letter "encourag[ing] Congress to clarify the rules of the road on this important subject." Letter from R. Bruce Josten, U.S. Chamber of Commerce, to Members of Congress (Mar. 31, 2016). That Congress has to date declined the invitation to take up this issue does not provide this Court with a directive to override and narrow the clear language of § 316(b).

The bond market has surely undergone significant alterations since the enactment of the TIA, including that the main players are now sophisticated corporate entities on both sides. But it is not for this Court to alter the TIA on its own accord, and "none of this establishes why the plaintiffs should be barred from vindicating their rights under the [TIA]" as it currently stands. *NML Capital, Ltd. v. Republic of Argentina*, 727 F.3d 230, 248 (2d Cir. 2013). "Our role is not to craft a resolution that will solve all the problems that might arise in hypothetical future litigation involving other bonds and other [parties]," *id.*, but it is instead to interpret the TIA in as fastidious a manner as we are able. In so doing I would hold that Section 316(b) of the TIA bars the actions at issue in this case.

CONCLUSION

Because the Intercompany Sale as proposed under the Restructuring Support Agreement would have the effect of imposing on Marblegate a choice between a modification of their core payment terms or receiving no payment at all—thereby clearly impairing Marblegate's right to receive payment under the original terms of the indenture—I would hold that it violates the plain text of Section 316(b) of the Trust Indenture Act and affirm the judgment of the District Court. Our system of governance is organized such that Congress is tasked with writing the law and the federal courts are tasked with applying, not rewriting, it. If Congress and the parties affected by the TIA are unsatisfied with the law's consequences, it is for Congress rather than this Court to amend it. I therefore respectfully dissent.

MeehanCombs Global Credit Opportunities Funds, LP v. Caesars Entertainment Corp.

80 F. Supp. 3d 511 (S.D.N.Y. 2015)

SHIRA A. SCHEINDLIN, United States District Judge.

release of Guaranty

I. INTRODUCTION

The plaintiffs in these related actions are holders of Notes issued by Caesars Entertainment Operating Company, Inc. ("CEOC") pursuant to indentures, and—until the issuance of supplemental indentures in August 2014 (the "August 2014 Transaction" or the "Amendments")—guaranteed by Caesars Entertainment Corporation ("CEC"; together with CEOC, "Caesars"). Plaintiffs allege that the August 2014 Transaction violated the Trust Indenture Act of 1939 ("TIA") and breached the governing Indentures as well as the implied covenant of good faith and fair dealing.

Plaintiffs contend that the August 2014 Transaction removed the Guarantees given by the asset-rich parent company, CEC, leaving plaintiffs and the other bondholders with a worthless right to collect principal and interest from the issuer, CEOC, a company divesting itself of assets and holding approximately $17 billion of senior secured debt. The crux of plaintiffs' allegations is that the release of the Guarantees effected a non-consensual change to plaintiffs' payment rights and affected plaintiffs' practical ability to recover payment in violation of section 316 of the TIA and the governing Indentures.

Both defendants moved to dismiss the Complaint for failure to state a claim upon which relief can be granted pursuant to Rule 12(b)(6) of the Federal Rules of Civil Procedure. On January 13, 2015, holders of Second Lien Notes issued by CEOC filed an involuntary Chapter 11 petition against CEOC in the United States Bankruptcy Court for the District of Delaware. As a result, this action is stayed as to CEOC pursuant to section 362(a) of the Bankruptcy Code. However, this action is not stayed as to non-debtor defendant CEC, and for the following reasons CEC's motion to dismiss the Danner Complaint is DENIED in its entirety, and its motion to dismiss the MeehanCombs Complaint is GRANTED in part and DENIED in part.

II. FACTS

A. The Notes and Indentures

CEC, formerly known as Harrah's Entertainment, Inc., owns, manages, and operates dozens of casinos throughout the United States. CEOC is a direct operating subsidiary of CEC.

Pursuant to Indentures dated September 28, 2005 and June 9, 2006, CEOC issued $750 million of 2017 Notes and $750 million of 2016 Notes. MeehanCombs is the beneficial holder of approximately $15,318,000 of the 2016 Notes and $5,632,000 of the 2017 Notes. Danner is the beneficial holder of 2016 Notes. Holders of the 2016 Notes are entitled to receive interest payments each year on June 1 and December 1; holders of the 2017 Notes are entitled to receive interest payments on April 1 and October 1 annually. The vast majority of outstanding Notes—approximately $137 million—are held by individual investors.

When issued, the 2017 and 2016 Notes were investment grade. The governing Indentures each included unconditional Guarantees by CEC and provisions prohibiting CEOC from divesting its assets.

B. The August 2014 Transaction

In January 2008, Caesars was acquired in a leveraged buyout by two private equity funds, Apollo Global Management, Inc. and TPG Capital, LP. Caesars subsequently entered into a series of transactions aimed at transferring assets away from CEOC to affiliates, and leaving it (CEOC) holding company debt.

CEC's ultimate plan is to push CEOC into bankruptcy while protecting Apollo and TPG from CEOC's creditors. The Amendments effectively left CEC free to transfer CEOC's assets without any obligation to back CEOC's debts. Furthermore, the purchase price paid for the Notes of the noteholders who approved the August 2014 Transaction (the "Favored Noteholders")—par plus accrued interest and transactional fees and costs—represented an extraordinary one hundred percent premium over market. In exchange for receiving all amounts owed under their Notes, the Favored Noteholders promised to: (1) support any future restructuring proposed by Caesars; (2) consent to "the removal and acknowledgment of the termination of the CEC guarantee of the Securities"; and (iii) consent to the "modif[ication of] the covenant restricting disposition of 'substantially all' of CEOC's assets to measure future asset sales based on CEOC's assets as of the date of the amendment."

. . .

IV. APPLICABLE LAW

A. The Trust Indenture Act

The TIA provides that instruments to which it applies must be issued under an indenture that has been qualified by the Securities and Exchange Commission ("SEC"). The requirements of such indentures are "designed to vindicate a federal policy of protecting investors."

Section 316 of the TIA relates to collective action clauses. For example, it is permissible for a majority of noteholders to direct the trustee to exercise its powers under the indenture or for not less than seventy-five percent of noteholders "to consent on behalf of the holders of all such indenture securities to the postponement of any interest payment for a period not exceeding three years from its due date." Section 316(a)'s terms are permissive—meaning an indenture can expressly exclude such majority action.

However, section 316(b) is mandatory. It states that:

> Notwithstanding any other provision of the indenture to be qualified, the right of any holder of any indenture security to receive payment of the principal of and interest on such indenture security, on or after the respective due dates expressed in such indenture security, or to institute suit for the enforcement of any such payment on or after such respective dates, shall not be impaired or affected without the consent of such holder, except as to a postponement of an interest payment consented to as provided in paragraph (2) of subsection (a) of this section, and except that such indenture may contain provisions limiting or denying the right of any such holder to institute any such suit, if and to the extent that the institution or prosecution thereof or the entry of judgment therein would, under applicable law, result in the surrender, impairment, waiver, or loss of the lien of such indenture upon any property subject to such lien.

15 U.S.C. § 77ppp(b). Thus, section 316(b) acts to protect a bondholder's right to receive payment of both principal and interest.

Section 316(b) addressed prior practice whereby majority bondholders—often controlled by insiders—used collective or majority action clauses to change the terms of an indenture, to the detriment of minority bondholders. As result of section 316(b), a company cannot—outside of bankruptcy—alter its obligation to pay bonds without the consent of each bondholder. In this way, section "316(b) was designed to provide judicial scrutiny of debt readjustment plans to ensure their equity."

. . .

C. Breach of Contract and the Implied Covenant of Good Faith and Fair Dealing

To state a breach of contract claim under New York law, a plaintiff must allege: (1) a valid contract; (2) plaintiff's performance; (3) defendant's failure to perform; and (4) damages resulting from the breach.

"Under New York law, the implied covenant of good faith and fair dealing inheres in every contract." However, breach of this implied covenant is "merely a breach of the underlying contract," not a separate cause of action. "'[I]f the allegations do not go beyond the statement of a mere contract breach and, relying on the same alleged acts, simply seek the same damages or other relief already claimed in a companion contract cause of action, they may be disregarded as superfluous as no additional claim is actually stated.'"

V. DISCUSSION

A. Plaintiffs' Claims Under TIA Section 316

1. Plaintiffs State a Claim Under TIA Section 316(b)

CEC argues that the Complaint fails to allege impairment of the legal right to payment under the Notes because CEOC is not in default of its obligation to make payments. According to CEC, "the statute does not guarantee that the issuer will be able to meet its obligations. Rather, it protects only a noteholder's *legal* right to receive payment when due."

> "[T]he starting point in any case of [statutory] interpretation must always be the language itself, giving effect to the plain meaning thereof." Under section 316(b), a noteholder's right "to receive payment of the principal of and interest on [the] indenture security, on or after the respective due dates expressed in such indenture security, or to institute suit for the enforcement of any such payment on or after such respective dates, shall not be impaired or affected without the consent of such holder[.]"

CEC's narrow reading is not mandated by the statutory text; it is possible for a right to receive payment to be impaired prior to the time payment is due. Nor does CEC's narrow reading follow from the legislative history and purposes of the TIA. Although there is scant case law on point, I find the reasoning of two decisions from this District persuasive, particularly in light of the conduct alleged in the Complaint. Specifically, "the Court finds [ ] unsatisfying the notion that Section 316(b) protects only against formal, explicit modification of the legal right to receive payment, and allows a sufficiently clever issuer to gut the Act's protections through a transaction such as the one at issue here." As explained in *Federated Strategic Income Fund*:

> By defendant's elimination of the guarantors and the simultaneous disposition of all meaningful assets, defendant will effectively eliminate plaintiffs' ability to recover and will remove a holder's "safety net" of a guarantor, which was obviously an investment consideration from the outset. Taken together, these proposed amendments could materially impair or affect a holder's right to sue. A holder who chooses to sue for payment at the date of maturity will no longer, as a practical matter, be able to seek recourse from either the assetless defendant or from the discharged guarantors. It is beyond peradventure that when a company takes steps to preclude any recovery by noteholders for payment of principal coupled with the elimination of the guarantors for its debt, that such action . . . constitute[s] an "impairment" . . . [of] the right to sue for payment.

Likewise, I find that the Complaint's plausible allegations that the August 2014 Transaction stripped plaintiffs of the valuable CEC Guarantees leaving them with an empty right to assert a payment default from an insolvent issuer are sufficient to state a claim under section 316(b).

. . . Had the CEC Guarantees not been improperly removed, CEOC's filing would have had no impact on CEC's liability under the Guarantees. Thus, as alleged in the Complaint, removal of the Guarantees through the August 2014 Transaction is an impermissible out-of-court debt restructuring achieved through collective action. This is exactly what TIA section 316(b) is designed to prevent.

2. MeehanCombs Failed to Adequately Allege Ownership or Control Under Section 316(a)

Section 316(a) permits the holders of a majority of the principal amount of any series of notes governed by the statute to direct the trustee to exercise any power conferred on the trustee by the indenture. However, the statute provides that in determining whether a majority of holders of the securities "have concurred in any such direction or consent," securities held by the issuer "or by any person directly or indirectly controlling or controlled by or under direct or indirect common control" of the issuer shall be disregarded.

MeehanCombs alleges that Caesars either controlled the Favored Noteholders or owned the Favored Noteholders' notes and therefore those notes should not have been counted toward the required majority needed for approval of the August 2014 Transaction. Accordingly, MeehanCombs alleges that the Amendments are invalid.

Because the August 2014 Transaction was structured so that the Favored Noteholders' consents were given *before* the notes were sold to Caesars, MeehanCombs does not allege *ownership*. In addition, the *control* allegations, as pled, are insufficient. The MeehanCombs Complaint "does not allege that the Participating Noteholders were anything other than unaffiliated, independent third parties that entered into an arm's length transaction to provide their consents." Accordingly, MeehanCombs' claim under TIA section 316(a) is dismissed without prejudice.

. . .

C. The Complaint Adequately Alleges Breach of the Indentures

Each of the enumerated breach of contract claims, along with the claim for breach of the implied covenant of good faith and fair dealing, are ultimately derivative of the claim that section 508 of the 2016 Indenture and section 6.8 of the 2017 Indenture were breached. The Court therefore treats these claims as a single claim for purposes of this motion.

Based on the foregoing, the Complaint adequately alleges a breach in connection with these provisions. The Complaint plausibly alleges that the actions taken by CEC impaired plaintiffs' right to payment under the Notes and therefore plaintiffs' consent to the supplemental indentures was required.

VI. CONCLUSION

For the foregoing reasons, CEC's motion to dismiss the Danner Complaint is DENIED in its entirety, and CEC's motion to dismiss the MeehanCombs Complaint is GRANTED with respect to the section 316(a) claim, without prejudice, and DENIED in all other respects. MeehanCombs shall have until January 29, 2015 to file an amended complaint.

Problem Set 9

(1) Leviathan Corp. has $200 million in 10-year, 10% non-amortizing secured bonds outstanding. The bonds are guaranteed by Leviathan's parent company, Primeval Enterprises, Inc. The other terms are identical to those in the Sunstone Indenture. Leviathan Corp. would like to restructure the bonds in order to free up cash flow to enable the acquisition of Basilisk Enterprises.

Consider the following possible changes to the indenture for the Leviathan bonds. What percentage of the bondholders would need to consent for the changes to be binding? 51 percent? 75 percent? 99 percent? Unanimous consent? 15 U.S.C. § 77ppp(a)-(b); Sunstone Indenture §§ 901, 902.

    a. Reduction of the principal amount owed on the bonds.
    b. Extension of the maturity date on the bonds.
    c. Reduction in the interest rate on the bonds.
    d. Forbearance of interest payments for two years.
    e. Forbearance of interest payments for five years.
    f. Waiving a default on a late interest payment.
    g. Forgiving a missed interest payment.
    h. Changes in the collateral securing the bonds.
    i. A change to an indenture covenant limiting the total debt Leviathan can issue.
    j. A change to a covenant limiting Leviathan's ability to pledge certain assets as collateral.

(2) Leonidas Capital purchased $40 million of the $300 million unsecured notes issued by Argus Amphora, Inc., a manufacturer of ceramic containers. The notes were issued under a qualified indenture (which is substantially similar to the Sunstone Indenture), and were guarantied by Argus Container Corporation, Ltd., the parent corporation of Argus Amphora, Inc. The guaranty expressly provided that it would be automatically released if the Argus Container Corporation, Ltd.'s guaranty of a separate $250 million term loan to Argus Amphora, Inc. was released.

Following concerns about the lead content in its ceramics, Argus Amphora has been in financial difficulty. Its assets are worth only around $120 million, and are fully pledged to the term lenders. Argus Container Corporation, Ltd., is readily solvent.

Last month, the term lenders released the parent guaranty on the term loan as part of a workout of the loan. In exchange for the release of the parent guaranty on the term loan, the term lenders received $90 million from Argus Container Corporation, Ltd.

Is there any reason for Leonidas Capital to be concerned? And if so, is there anything Leonidas Capital can do? *Marblegate Asset Mgmt. LLC v. Educ. Mgmt. Fin. Co.*; 15 U.S.C. § 77ppp(b).

(3) Jugarex S.A., is a Spanish gaming corporation that runs casino and slot machines in Spain and across Latin America. A downturn in the global economy has left Jugarex with depressed revenues that are insufficient to service its bond debt, the terms of

which are identical to [the Sunstone Indenture. A restructure under Spanish law is not
possible for Jugarex: Jugarex would have declared bankruptcy, which would result in
the forfeiture of its gaming license and all other licenses.

Jugarex would like to restructure its bonds using an English "Scheme of Arrangement,"
a procedure wherein a court may alter the restructuring of certain obligations. Critically,
a Scheme of Arrangement is permitted under English law. Jugarex
filed a petition for a Scheme of Arrangement with an English court, but the court was
skeptical that it had jurisdiction and concerned that Jugarex was merely forum
shopping. In order to strengthen its case for English jurisdiction, Jugarex has proposed
to amend its bonds in three ways:

[handwritten: — notes always unsecured (?)]

[handwritten: — how to reconcile the 2 cases ?]

- Adding a co-issuer to the bonds. The co-issuer will be a newly created English
  subsidiary of Jugarex.
- Changing the governing law for the bonds. The bonds are currently governed by
  New York law. Jugarex is proposing changing the bonds to English law.
- Changing the venue consent provision in the bonds. The bonds currently contain
  a provision in which the issuer and trustee consent to venue in the courts of New
  York. Jugarex is proposing either changing the consent to either New York or
  London, or simply to a London venue.

The English court has indicated that if these changes are made, it will view the jurisdiction question more favorably, but the English court wants to be sure that Jugarex
can legally make these changes. Jugarex has come to you, a noted Trust Indenture Act
expert, for an opinion letter that it can present to the English court regarding the proposed changes.

Can you tell the English court that each of these proposed changes is permitted under
the Trust Indenture Act and the indenture? 15 U.S.C. § 77ppp(b); Sunstone Indenture
§§ 901, 902. What level of consent would be required?

(4) Jugarex is back with two additional proposed changes, this time in an attempt
to restructure a different bond (with an identical indenture) out of court. Jugarex is this
time proposing the following:

- Changing the definition of "Events of Default" under section 501 to define a
  missed payment as an Event of Default only if it is one year late.
- Changing section 502, which provides for acceleration of the principal upon an
  Event of Default, to allow for acceleration only three years and one day after an
  Event of Default.
- Changing the percentage of outstanding securities required to approve a waiver
  of an Event of Default under section 513. *[handwritten: no]*

What level of consent would be required for each of these changes? 15 U.S.C.
§ 77ppp(b); Sunstone Indenture §§ 901, 902.

CHAPTER 10

EXCHANGE OFFERS AND EXIT CONSENTS

There are two ways a debtor can change the terms of its bond debt. First, it can seek to get the bondholders to agree to an amendment of the bond indenture. Alternatively, it can refinance that bond debt, substituting new debt or equity for the old debt.

The mandatory terms of the Trust Indenture Act (TIA), particularly the prohibition of impairment of the right to payment, make amendment difficult. The only way to amend the terms of a bond issuance is to get unanimous consent of the bondholders. A simple or even supermajority will not suffice. Each bondholder can bind himself, and only himself, to an impairment of the right to payment. Bondholders are unlikely to agree individually to amendment of their bonds because of the free-riding problem: any bondholder that accepts less favorable terms buoys up the non-amending bondholders.

At the same time, however, refinancing is also difficult. Bondholders cannot generally be forced to accept new bonds or equity in exchange for their current bonds. The process for such a refinancing is called an **exchange offer**, and it is governed by the securities laws. They are only likely to take an offer of exchanging their current bonds for new bonds or equity if the new bonds or equity are more valuable than the current bonds, and the nature of the debtor's financial distress makes it difficult to offer more attractive terms on new bonds or equity. Perhaps the debtor can offer to pay more over a longer period of time, but that comes with two risks. First, it creates temporal priority for any bonds that are not exchanged, and second, it imposes the operational risks of the debtor on the bondholders who take the exchange for a longer period of time.

Imagine that Leviathan Industries, our mid-sized widget manufacturer, has a 10-year, 10% bond outstanding. Leviathan wants to reduce the interest rate on the bonds to 8%; if it can't get the payments down below 8.5%, it will default, resulting in serious losses for all of the bondholders. There are 100 bondholders, each with a bond worth $1 million. Leviathan makes these bondholders an offer, namely that it will give them new, 5-year, 8% bonds in exchange for their 10-year, 10% bonds. This is the exchange offer. The mechanics are identical to a tender offer for equity securities: an offer will be made to all or a subset of bondholders to tender their bonds in exchange for new securities. The offer will often be contingent upon a minimum percentage of bondholders agreeing to the exchange.

Let's say that 80 of Leviathan's 100 bondholders agree to the exchange. Leviathan still has $100 million in bond liability, and $80 million of it is now due in 5 years, rather than in 10 years, but Leviathan's annual interest payments have declined from $10 million to $8.4 million (= .08 × $80M + .10 × $20M). Let's imagine that this is enough of a payment reduction for Leviathan Industries—for now, at least, it can make the payments on both the new 8% bonds and the remaining 10% bonds.

Notice what this means. Who benefitted from the exchange of the old 10% bonds for the new 8% bonds? The twenty holders of the 10% bonds who did not exchange their bonds. They still have their original bonds, which are now more likely to get paid, thanks to the sacrifice of the exchanging bondholders. Put another way, the exchanging bondholders are the suckers, and the holdouts are the winners.

Let's now suppose that the bondholders all know how this game works before the exchange is offered to them. What happens then? The result is a prisoner's dilemma, as illustrated by Figure 10.1, below.[1] If no one (or not enough bondholders) exchanges, everyone loses a lot (lower-right quadrant). If everyone exchanges, everyone loses a little (upper-left quadrant), and if only some exchange (upper-right and lower-left quadrants), then the exchangers lose a little, and the holdouts lose nothing.

Figure 10.1 Bond Exchange Game

		Bondholder 1	
		Exchange	Holdout
Bondholder 2	Exchange	(−2, −2)	(−2, 0)
	Holdout	(0, −2)	(−4, −4)

There are almost always some holdouts, if only because an exchange requires affirmative action. Some bondholders are strategic in holding out, while others hold out simply by virtue of not opening their mail. Is there any way to get out of the prisoner's dilemma?

The answer is perhaps, at least to the extent that the holdouts are strategic. One possibility is the use of **exit consents**, described below. The other, as we shall see, is bankruptcy, where the restrictions of the TIA do not apply.

Recall that *non-payment terms* on an entire issue of bonds can be changed with the consent of a sufficient majority of bondholders. The threshold for modification of other terms of the indenture is simply whatever is required by the indenture, but typically 50 percent + 1 or a two-thirds majority is needed. If the requisite majority accepts, the change of terms is imposed upon the non-consenting minority of

---

1. Figure 10.1 is a common way for presenting game theory outcomes. You should read the numbers in each set of parentheses as showing the outcomes for the x-axis and then the outcome for the y-axis, or, in this case, the outcome for Bondholder 1, followed by the outcome for Bondholder 2. Thus, the upper right quadrant, which reads "(−2, 0)," should be read as "Bondholder 1 gets −2, and Bondholder 2 gets 0."

bondholders. The process for requesting approval of amendments by bondholders is known as a **consent solicitation**, and it is governed by the securities laws.

The ability to amend non-payment terms of bonds on a simple majority basis (or even supermajority basis) provides debtors with a powerful lever for restructuring by combining an amendment of bond terms with an offer to exchange the bonds for new bonds or equity. This process is called an **exit consent**: the bondholders are given an exchange offer that can be accepted only if a bondholder first agrees to a solicitation of consent to amend the current bonds' terms by stripping out covenants. Stripping of covenants makes the current bonds less valuable, which in turn makes the bonds offered in the exchange relatively more valuable, and makes the exchange more attractive for the bondholders. Because the vote on the consent solicitation goes into effect immediately prior to the exchange, the exchanging bondholders are voting on an amendment of terms to the current bonds that will not affect them (because they are exchanging into the new bonds), only the holdouts.

The key to understanding exit consents is to recognize that the value of a bond is not determined simply by its payment terms. Instead, the value also depends on the various covenants that accompany the bond, most importantly those relating to repayment source, debt levels, and repayment priority.[1] The repayment source for a bond can be changed, such that it could be a repayment from the revenue stream of one of the issuer's subsidiaries, instead of another.[2] If the bond is guaranteed by certain affiliates of the issuer, those guarantees could possibly be changed or eliminated.

If the bonds' covenants provide that the issuer limit its total debt or that it meet certain financial targets, those covenants could be changed or eliminated, enabling the issuer to engage in riskier behavior and thereby reducing the value of the bonds, even as the payment terms stay the same.

A bond may be secured or unsecured. A consent solicitation could change the collateral securing a bond, making it much less secure, without violating the TIA. Similarly, an unsecured bond might have a covenant known as a negative pledge clause that limits the granting of collateral to other creditors. Such a negative pledge clause could be removed through a consent solicitation. The effect of either of these changes would be to change the repayment priority of the bond, but would enable other creditors to have first dibs on valuable assets.

Bonds can be general unsecured debt or they can be contractually senior or subordinate to other debt. For example, one issue of bonds can be contractually subordinated to another by the indenture. So, an exit consent could include a consent solicitation to either subordinate a bond or permit the future issuance of debt that is senior to the bond. Indeed, the newly issued exchange bonds could themselves have priority over the unexchanged bonds.

---

1. The value of a bond also depends on its liquidity. Any successful exchange offer necessarily has a detrimental effect on the liquidity of the unexchanged bonds—there are fewer of them around and hence a small and less liquid market exists for them. Thus, any exchange offer, even without exit consents, has some negative impact on the value of the unexchanged bonds.

2. This would only be for a bond that is non-recourse, like a "revenue bond," such as those issued by many municipalities, for example, a bond whose repayment is secured by the revenues from a particular tax.

Exit consents can thus put in all sorts of changes that significantly affect the value of a bond in terms of what it will sell for on the market without ever affecting the right to payment. An exchange offer with exit consents, then, is an invitation for bondholders to set their old ship on fire in order to force all of the passengers to jump into the lifeboat that is offered. If enough bondholders exchange for the exit consents to go through, holding out is less profitable than it would be otherwise.

The exit consent process is far from failsafe, however. It still requires getting enough bondholders to vote for the amendment, but here there is a game theory problem that helps the debtor: bondholders do not want to be stuck with the current bonds if the amendment goes through. Therefore, the risk-averse bondholder will be tempted to vote for the amendment and take the exchange. The debtor can further encourage this by setting a minimum percentage of acceptance necessary for the exchange to be effective, setting a time limit for the exchange, and paying more for early consents in order to make it more difficult for bondholders to organize opposition to the exchange. Figure 10.2 shows how exit consents change the calculus in the restructuring game from Figure 10.1, making it more likely for risk-averse holdouts to accept the exchange offer.

Figure 10.2 Bond Exchange Game with Exit Consents

		Bondholder 1	
		Exchange	Holdout
Bondholder 2	Exchange	(−2, −2)	(−2, −1)
	Holdout	(−1, −2)	(−4, −4)

The TIA itself does not generally regulate exit consents, except insofar as they impair or affect the right to payment or the right to institute suit for nonpayment. But the TIA does, however, provide that when calculating whether a sufficient majority of bondholders have voted to direct the trustee to take action or to consent to a waiver of a default, that bonds controlled directly or indirectly by the obligor are to be disregarded. 15 U.S.C. § 77ppp(a) (hanging paragraph). The TIA does not specify what constitutes "control." Are bondholders who have voted for an exit consent as part of an exchange offer "indirectly controlled" by the obligor? Arguably these bondholders have parted with any real economic interest in the old bonds and their vote is being cast in the interest of the obligor, not their own economic interests (indeed, they would never vote for the consents if they were not exchanging). Even if such an argument were to be credited, however, it would apply only to consents of waivers of defaults, rather than to exit consents more broadly.

Bondholders do not take kindly to coercive exit consents, but precisely because of their coercive nature, consent solicitations often succeed. Notice, however, that a successful consent solicitation only restructures the bond debt of a firm; other types of liabilities need to be addressed through other mechanisms, and not all of them are readily addressable out-of-court.

↑ Control*

Only bond debt

There is little case law on exit consents; the following two cases—indeed the leading two cases—present different approaches to exit consents that have emerged on different sides of the Atlantic. Can they be reconciled?

Moise Katz v. Oak Industries, Inc.

508 A.2d 873 (Del. Ch. 1986)

ALLEN, Chancellor.

A commonly used word—seemingly specific and concrete when used in every-day speech—may mask troubling ambiguities that upon close examination are seen to derive not simply from casual use but from more fundamental epistemological problems. Few words more perfectly illustrate the deceptive dependability of language than the term "coercion" which is at the heart of the theory advanced by plaintiff as entitling him to a preliminary injunction in this case.

Plaintiff is the owner of long-term debt securities issued by Oak Industries, Inc. ("Oak"), a Delaware corporation; in this class action he seeks to enjoin the consummation of an exchange offer and consent solicitation made by Oak to holders of various classes of its long-term debt. As detailed below that offer is an integral part of a series of transactions that together would effect a major reorganization and recapitalization of Oak. The claim asserted is in essence, that the exchange offer is a coercive device and, in the circumstances, constitutes a breach of contract. This is the Court's opinion on plaintiff's pending application for a preliminary injunction.

I.

. . . Through its domestic and foreign subsidiaries and affiliated entities, Oak manufactures and markets component equipments used in consumer, industrial and military products (the "Components Segment"); produces communications equipment for use in cable television systems and satellite television systems (the "Communications Segment") and manufactures and markets laminates and other materials used in printed circuit board applications (the "Materials Segment"). . . .

Even a casual review of Oak's financial results over the last several years shows it unmistakably to be a company in deep trouble. During the period from January 1, 1982 through September 30, 1985, the Company has experienced unremitting losses from operations; on net sales of approximately $1.26 billion during that period it has lost over $335 million. As a result its total stockholders' equity has first shriveled (from $260 million on 12/31/81 to $85 million on 12/31/83) and then disappeared completely (as of 9/30/85 there was a $62 million deficit in its stockholders' equity accounts). Financial markets, of course, reflected this gloomy history.[2]

---

2. The price of the company's common stock has fallen from over $30 per share on December 31, 1981 to approximately $2 per share recently. The debt securities that are the subject of the exchange offer here involved . . . have traded at substantial discounts.

Unless Oak can be made profitable within some reasonably short time it will not continue as an operating company. Oak's board of directors, comprised almost entirely of outside directors, has authorized steps to buy the company time. In February, 1985, in order to reduce a burdensome annual cash interest obligation on its $230 million of then outstanding debentures, the Company offered to exchange such debentures for a combination of notes, common stock and warrants. As a result, approximately $180 million principal amount of the then outstanding debentures were exchanged. Since interest on certain of the notes issued in that exchange offer is payable in common stock, the effect of the 1985 exchange offer was to reduce to some extent the cash drain on the Company caused by its significant debt.

About the same time that the 1985 exchange offer was made, the Company announced its intention to discontinue certain of its operations and sell certain of its properties. Taking these steps, while effective to stave off a default and to reduce to some extent the immediate cash drain, did not address Oak's longer-range problems. Therefore, also during 1985 representatives of the Company held informal discussions with several interested parties exploring the possibility of an investment from, combination with or acquisition by another company. As a result of these discussions, the Company and Allied-Signal, Inc. entered into . . . the Stock Purchase Agreement, [which] provides for the purchase by Allied-Signal for $15 million cash of 10 million shares of the Company's common stock together with warrants to purchase additional common stock.

The Stock Purchase Agreement provides as a condition to Allied-Signal's obligation that at least 85% of the aggregate principal amount of all of the Company's debt securities shall have tendered and accepted the exchange offers that are the subject of this lawsuit. Oak has six classes of such long term debt. If less than 85% of the aggregate principal amount of such debt accepts the offer, Allied-Signal has an option, but no obligation, to purchase the common stock and warrants contemplated by the Stock Purchase Agreement. An additional condition for the closing of the Stock Purchase Agreement is that the sale of the Company's Materials Segment contemplated by the Acquisition Agreement shall have been concluded.

Thus, as part of the restructuring and recapitalization contemplated by the Acquisition Agreement and the Stock Purchase Agreement, the Company has extended an exchange offer to each of the holders of the six classes of its long-term debt securities. These pending exchange offers include a Common Stock Exchange Offer (available only to holders of the $9\frac{5}{8}$% convertible notes) and the Payment Certificate Exchange Offers (available to holders of all six classes of Oak's long-term debt securities). The Common Stock Exchange Offer currently provides for the payment to each tendering note holder of 407 shares of the Company's common stock in exchange for each $1,000 $9\frac{5}{8}$% note accepted. . . .

The Payment Certificate Exchange Offer is an any and all offer. Under its terms, a payment certificate, payable in cash five days after the closing of the sale of the Materials Segment to Allied-Signal, is offered in exchange for debt securities. The cash value of the Payment Certificate will vary depending upon the particular security tendered. In each instance, however, that payment will be less than the face amount of the obligation. The cash payments range in amount, per $1,000 of principal, from $918 to $655. These cash values however appear to represent a premium over the market prices for the Company's debentures as of the time the terms of the transaction were set.

The Payment Certificate Exchange Offer is subject to certain important conditions before Oak has an obligation to accept tenders under it. First, it is necessary that a minimum amount ($38.6 million principal amount out of $83.9 total outstanding principal amount) of the $9\frac{5}{8}\%$ notes be tendered pursuant to the Common Stock Exchange Offer. Secondly, it is necessary that certain minimum amounts of each class of debt securities be tendered, together with consents to amendments to the underlying indentures.[4] Indeed, under the offer one may not tender securities *unless at the same time one consents to the proposed amendments to the relevant indentures.*

The condition of the offer that tendering security holders must consent to amendments in the indentures governing the securities gives rise to plaintiff's claim of breach of contract in this case. *Those amendments would, if implemented, have the effect of removing significant negotiated protections to holders of the Company's long-term debt including the deletion of all financial covenants. Such modification may have adverse consequences to debt holders who elect not to tender pursuant to either exchange offer.*

Allied-Signal apparently was unwilling to commit to the $15 million cash infusion contemplated by the Stock Purchase Agreement, unless Oak's long-term debt is reduced by 85% (at least that is a condition of their obligation to close on that contract). . . . But existing indenture covenants . . . prohibit the Company, so long as any of its long-term notes are outstanding, from [buying] any of the debentures. . . . Thus, in this respect, amendment to the indentures is required in order to close the Stock Purchase Agreement as presently structured.

Restrictive covenants in the indentures would appear to interfere with effectuation of the recapitalization in another way. Section 4.07 of the 13.50% Indenture provides that the Company may not "acquire" for value any of the $9\frac{5}{8}\%$ Notes or $11\frac{5}{8}\%$ Notes unless it concurrently "redeems" a proportionate amount of the 13.50% Notes. This covenant, if unamended, would prohibit the disproportionate acquisition of the $9\frac{5}{8}\%$ Notes that may well occur as a result of the Exchange Offers; in addition, it would appear to require the payment of the "redemption" price for the 13.50% Notes rather than the lower, market price offered in the exchange offer.

In sum, the failure to obtain the requisite consents to the proposed amendments would permit Allied-Signal to decline to consummate both the Acquisition Agreement and the Stock Purchase Agreement.

. . .

The Exchange Offers are dated Feb. 14, 1986. This suit seeking to enjoin consummation of those offers was filed on Feb. 27. Argument on the current application was held on March 7.

---

4. The holders of more than 50% of the principal amount of each of the 13.5% notes, the 9-5/8% notes and the $11\frac{5}{8}\%$ notes and at least $66\frac{2}{3}\%$ of the principal amount of the 13.65% debentures, $10\frac{1}{2}\%$ debentures, and $11\frac{7}{8}\%$ debentures, must validly tender such securities and consent to certain proposed amendments to the indentures governing those securities.

II.

Plaintiff's claim that the Exchange Offers and Consent Solicitation constitutes a threatened wrong to him and other holders of Oak's debt securities[6] appear to be summarized in paragraph 16 of his Complaint:

> The purpose and effect of the Exchange Offers is [1] to benefit Oak's common stockholders at the expense of the Holders of its debt securities, [2] to force the exchange of its debt instruments at unfair price and at less than face value of the debt instruments [3] pursuant to a rigged vote in which debt Holders who exchange, and who therefore have no interest in the vote, *must* consent to the elimination of protective covenants for debt Holders who do not wish to exchange.

. . . [P]laintiff's claim is that no free choice is provided to bondholders by the exchange offer and consent solicitation. Under its terms, a rational bondholder is "forced" to tender and consent. Failure to do so would face a bondholder *with the risk of owning a security stripped of all financial covenant protections and for which it is likely that there would be no ready market.* A reasonable bondholder, it is suggested, cannot possibly accept those risks and thus such a bondholder is coerced to tender and thus to consent to the proposed indenture amendments.

It is urged this linking of the offer and the consent solicitation constitutes a breach of a contractual obligation that Oak owes to its bondholders to act in good faith. Specifically, plaintiff points to three contractual provisions from which it can be seen that the structuring of the current offer constitutes a breach of good faith. Those provisions (1) establish a requirement that no modification in the term of the various indentures may be effectuated without the consent of a stated percentage of bondholders; (2) restrict Oak from exercising the power to grant such consent with respect to any securities it may hold in its treasury. . . .

III.

. . . This case does not involve the measurement of corporate or directorial conduct against that high standard of fidelity required of fiduciaries when they act with respect to the interests of the beneficiaries of their trust. Under our law—and the law generally—the relationship between a corporation and the holders of its debt securities, even convertible debt securities, is contractual in nature. . . . Arrangements among a corporation, the underwriters of its debt, trustees under its indentures and sometimes ultimate investors are typically thoroughly negotiated and massively documented. The rights and obligations of the various parties are or should be spelled out in that documentation.

---

6. It is worthy of note that a very high percentage of the principal value of Oak's debt securities are owned in substantial amounts by a handful of large financial institutions. Almost 85% of the value of the 13.50% Notes is owned by four such institutions (one investment banker owns 55% of that issue); 69.1% of the $9^5/_8$% Notes are owned by four financial institutions (the same investment banker owning 25% of that issue) and 85% of the $11^5/_8$% Notes are owned by five such institutions. Of the debentures, 89% of the 13.65% debentures are owned by four large banks; and approximately 45% of the two remaining issues is owned by two banks.

The terms of the contractual relationship agreed to and not broad concepts such as fairness define the corporation's obligation to its bondholders.[7]

Thus, the first aspect of the pending Exchange Offers about which plaintiff complains—that "the purpose and effect of the Exchange Offers is to benefit Oak's common stockholders at the expense of the Holders of its debt"—does not itself appear to allege a cognizable legal wrong. It is the obligation of directors to attempt, within the law, to maximize the long-run interests of the corporation's stockholders; that they may sometimes do so "at the expense" of others (even assuming that a transaction which one may refuse to enter into can meaningfully be said to be at his expense) does not for that reason constitute a breach of duty. It seems likely that corporate restructurings designed to maximize shareholder values may in some instances have the effect of requiring bondholders to bear greater risk of loss and thus in effect transfer economic value from bondholders to stockholders. . . . But if courts are to provide protection against such enhanced risk, they will require either legislative direction to do so or the negotiation of indenture provisions designed to afford such protection.

The second preliminary point concerns the limited analytical utility, at least in this context, of the word "coercive" which is central to plaintiff's own articulation of his theory of recovery. If, *pro arguendo*, we are to extend the meaning of the word coercion beyond its core meaning—dealing with the utilization of physical force to overcome the will of another—to reach instances in which the claimed coercion arises from an act designed to affect the will of another party by offering inducements to the act sought to be encouraged or by arranging unpleasant consequences for an alternative sought to be discouraged, then . . . further refinement is essential. Clearly some "coercion" of this kind is legally unproblematic. Parents may "coerce" a child to study with the threat of withholding an allowance; employers may "coerce" regular attendance at work by either docking wages for time absent or by rewarding with a bonus such regular attendance. Other "coercion" so defined clearly would be legally relevant (to encourage regular attendance by corporal punishment, for example). Thus, for purposes of legal analysis, the term "coercion" itself—covering a multitude of situations—is not very meaningful. For the word to have much meaning for purposes of legal analysis, it is necessary in each case that a normative judgment be attached to the concept ("inappropriately coercive" or "wrongfully coercive," etc.). But, it is then readily seen that what is legally relevant is not the conclusory term "coercion" itself but rather the norm that leads to the adjectives modifying it.

In this instance, assuming that the Exchange Offers and Consent Solicitation can meaningfully be regarded as "coercive" (in the sense that Oak has structured it in a way designed—and I assume effectively so—to "force" rational bondholders to tender), *the relevant legal norm that will support the judgment whether such "coercion" is wrongful or not will, for the reasons mentioned above, be derived from the law of contracts.* I turn then to that subject to determine the appropriate legal test or rule.

---

7. To say that the broad duty of loyalty that a director owes to his corporation and ultimately its shareholders is not implicated in this case is not to say, as the discussion below reflects, that as a matter of contract law a corporation owes no duty to bondholders of good faith and fair dealing. *See, Restatement of Law, Contracts 2d,* § 205 (1979). Such a duty, however, is quite different from the congeries of duties that are assumed by a fiduciary. *See generally,* Bratton, *The Economics and Jurisprudence of Convertible Bonds,* 1984 WIS. L. REV. 667.

Modern contract law has generally recognized an implied covenant to the effect that each party to a contract will act with good faith towards the other with respect to the subject matter of the contract. *See, Restatement of Law, Contracts 2d*, § 205 (1981) . . . . The contractual theory for this implied obligation is well stated in a leading treatise:

> If the purpose of contract law is to enforce the reasonable expectations of parties induced by promises, then at some point it becomes necessary for courts to look to the substance rather than to the form of the agreement, and to hold that substance controls over form. What courts are doing here, whether calling the process "implication" of promises, or interpreting the requirements of "good faith," as the current fashion may be, is but a recognition that the parties occasionally have understandings or expectations that were so fundamental that they did not need to negotiate about those expectations. When the court "implies a promise" or holds that "good faith" requires a party not to violate those expectations, it is recognizing that sometimes silence says more than words, and it is understanding its duty to the spirit of the bargain is higher than its duty to the technicalities of the language.

Corbin on Contracts (Kaufman Supp. 1984), § 570.

It is this obligation to act in good faith and to deal fairly that plaintiff claims is breached by the structure of Oak's coercive exchange offer. Because it is an implied *contractual* obligation that is asserted as the basis for the relief sought, the appropriate legal test is not difficult to deduce. It is this: *is it clear from what was expressly agreed upon that the parties who negotiated the express terms of the contract would have agreed to proscribe the act later complained of as a breach of the implied covenant of good faith—had they thought to negotiate with respect to that matter[?]* If the answer to this question is yes, then, in my opinion, a court is justified in concluding that such act constitutes a breach of the implied covenant of good faith. . . .

With this test in mind, I turn now to a review of the specific provisions of the various indentures from which one may be best able to infer whether it is apparent that the contracting parties—*had they negotiated with the exchange offer and consent solicitation in mind*—would have expressly agreed to prohibit contractually the linking of the giving of consent with the purchase and sale of the security.

IV.

Applying the foregoing standard to the exchange offer and consent solicitation, I find first that there is nothing in the indenture provisions granting bondholders power to veto proposed modifications in the relevant indenture that implies that Oak may not offer an inducement to bondholders to consent to such amendments. Such an implication, at least where, as here, the inducement is offered on the same terms to each holder of an affected security, would be wholly inconsistent with the strictly commercial nature of the relationship.

Nor does the second pertinent contractual provision supply a ground to conclude that defendant's conduct violates the reasonable expectations of those who negotiated the indentures on behalf of the bondholders. Under that provision Oak may not vote debt securities held in its treasury. Plaintiff urges that Oak's conditioning of its offer to purchase debt on the giving of consents has the effect of subverting the purpose of that provision; it permits Oak to "dictate" the vote on securities which it could not itself vote.

The evident purpose of the restriction on the voting of treasury securities is to afford protection against the issuer voting as a bondholder in favor of modifications that would benefit it as issuer, even though such changes would be detrimental to bondholders. But the linking of the exchange offer and the consent solicitation does not involve the risk that bondholder interests will be affected by a vote involving anyone with a financial interest in the subject of the vote other than a bondholder's interest. *That the consent is to be given concurrently with the transfer of the bond to the issuer does not in any sense create the kind of conflict of interest that the indenture's prohibition on voting treasury securities contemplates.* Not only will the proposed consents be granted or withheld only by those with a financial interest to maximize the return on their investment in Oak's bonds, but the incentive to consent is equally available to all members of each class of bondholders. Thus the "vote" implied by the consent solicitation is not affected in any sense by those with a financial conflict of interest.

In these circumstances, while it is clear that Oak has fashioned the exchange offer and consent solicitation in a way designed to encourage consents, I cannot conclude that the offer violates the intendment of any of the express contractual provisions considered or, applying the test set out above, that its structure and timing breaches an implied obligation of good faith and fair dealing.

. . .

Accordingly, I conclude that plaintiff has failed to demonstrate a probability of ultimate success on the theory of liability asserted.

V.

An independent ground for the decision to deny the pending motion is supplied by the requirement that a court of equity will not issue the extraordinary remedy of preliminary injunction where to do so threatens the party sought to be enjoined with irreparable injury that, in the circumstances, seems greater than the injury that plaintiff seeks to avoid. . . . That principal has application here.

Oak is in a weak state financially. Its board, comprised of persons of experience and, in some instances, distinction, have approved the complex and interrelated transactions outlined above. It is not unreasonable to accord weight to the claims of Oak that the reorganization and recapitalization of which the exchange offer is a part may present the last good chance to regain vitality for this enterprise. I have not discussed plaintiff's claim of irreparable injury, although I have considered it. I am satisfied simply to note my conclusion that it is far outweighed by the harm that an improvidently granted injunction would threaten to Oak.

For the foregoing reasons plaintiff's application for a preliminary injunction shall be denied.

Assénagon Asset Management SA v. Irish Bank Resolution Corporation Ltd. (formerly Anglo Irish Bank Corp. Ltd.)

[2012] EWHC 2090 (British High Court of Justice, Chancery Division, July 27, 2012)

BRIGGS, J:

INTRODUCTION

[1] This [case] test[s], for the first time, the legality under English law of a technique used by the issuers of corporate bonds which has acquired the label "exit consent."

The technique may be summarised thus. The issuer wishes to persuade all the holders of a particular bond issue to accept an exchange of their bonds for replacement bonds on different terms. The holders are all invited to offer their bonds for exchange, but . . . are required to commit themselves irrevocably to vote at a bondholders' meeting for a resolution amending the terms of the existing bonds so as seriously to damage or, as in the present case substantially destroy, the value of the rights arising from those existing bonds. The resolution is what has become labelled the exit consent.

[2] The exit consent has no adverse effect in itself upon a holder who both offers his bonds for exchange and votes for the resolution. That is either because the issuer nonetheless fails to attract the majority needed to pass the resolution (in which case both the resolution and the proposed exchange do not happen) or simply because, if the requisite majority is obtained, his bonds are exchanged for new bonds and cancelled by the issuer. By contrast, a holder who fails to offer his bonds for exchange and either votes against the resolution or abstains takes the risk, if the resolution is passed, that his bonds will be either devalued by the resolution or, as in this case, destroyed by being redeemed for a nominal consideration. This is in part because the efficacy of the technique depends upon the deadline for exchange being set before the bondholders' meeting so that, if the resolution is then passed, the dissenting holder gets no *locus poenitentiae* during which to exchange his bonds on the terms offered, and accepted in time, by the majority.

[3] It is readily apparent, and not seriously in dispute, that the purpose of the attachment of the exit consent to the exchange proposal is to impose a dissuasive constraint upon bondholders from opposing the exchange, even if they take the view that the proffered new bonds are (ignoring the exit consent) less attractive than the existing bonds. The constraint arises from the risk facing any individual bondholder that a sufficient majority of his fellow holders will participate in the exchange and therefore (as required to do) vote for the resolution. The constraint is variously described in textbooks on both sides of the Atlantic as encouraging, inducing, coercing or even forcing the bondholders to accept the exchange.

[4] The technique depends for its persuasive effect upon the difficulties faced by bondholders in organising themselves within the time allowed by the issuer in such a way as to find out before the deadline for accepting the exchange whether there is a sufficient number (usually more than 25% by value) determined to prevent the exchange going ahead by voting against the resolution. They were described in argument as facing a variant of the well-known prisoner's dilemma.

[5] Exit consents of this type (but falling short of expropriation) have survived judicial scrutiny in the USA, in the face of challenge by minority bondholders. In *Katz v. Oak Industries, Inc.*, 508 A.2d 873 (1986), the attachment of an exit consent designed to devalue the existing bonds in the hands of dissenting holders who declined an associated exchange offer was challenged in the Delaware Chancery Court as amounting to a breach of the contractual obligation of good faith by the issuer, as against the bondholders. It was not suggested that the participation in the process by the majority bondholders (by committing themselves to vote for the proposed amendment devaluing the existing bonds) constituted an abuse by them of their rights under the terms of the bond issue to bind the minority to a variation of those terms. Chancellor Allen

concluded that the particular exit consent in that case, (which included the removal of significant negotiated protections to the bondholders, and the deletion of all financial covenants), did not despite its coercive effect amount to a breach of the contractual obligation of good faith between issuer and bondholders in what he evidently regarded as an ordinary commercial arms-length contract.

[6] By contrast, the challenge made in the present case to the exit consent technique is mainly based upon an alleged abuse by the majority bondholders of their power to bind the minority, albeit at the invitation of the issuer. The challenge is based upon the well recognised constraint upon the exercise of that power by a majority, namely that it must be exercised *bona fide* in the best interests of the class of bondholders as a whole, and not in a manner which is oppressive or otherwise unfair to the minority sought to be bound. Such limited published professional comment as there is upon the use of this technique within an English law context appears to assume that, provided the exchange offer and associated exit consent proposal is made and fairly disclosed to all relevant bondholders, no question of oppression or unfairness can arise. I was told (although it is impossible for the court to know for sure) that this technique has been put into significant, if not yet widespread, use within the context of bonds structured under English law, in particular in connection with the affairs of banks and other lending institutions requiring to be re-structured as a result of the 2008 credit crunch, so that a decision on this point of principle may be of much wider consequence than merely the amount at issue between the parties to this claim, which relates to subordinated notes in the company then known as Anglo Irish Bank Corporation Ltd ("the Bank") acquired by the Claimant Assenagon Asset Management SA in tranches between September 2009 and April 2010, for an aggregate of just over €17m.

THE FACTS

. . .

[9] The bond issue to which this dispute relates consists of the Bank's subordinated floating rate notes due 2017 ("the 2017 Notes") issued by the Bank on 15 June 2007 pursuant to the terms of a trust deed . . . between the Bank and Deutsche Bank Trustee Co. Limited ("the Trustee"). . . . I shall refer to the re-stated form of the trust deed applicable to the 2017 Notes as "the Trust Deed." Terms particular to the 2017 Notes are also contained in written Final Terms dated 15 June 2007 ("the Final Terms"). The commercial terms of the 2017 Notes may be summarised as follows:

i) They were to mature in 2017, for redemption at par, unless redeemed earlier at the Bank's election (also at par) on any interest payment date after 19 June 2012.

ii) In the meantime they carried a floating rate of interest at 0.25% above three months Euribor until 2012 and 0.75% above three months Euribor thereafter.

iii) The Notes were subordinated, so as to be prioritised for payment in an insolvency after all secured and unsecured creditors (including the Bank's depositors) and ahead only of equity shareholders. They were wholly unsecured.

[10] . . . The nominal amount of the 2017 Notes was €750m. I am invited to assume that, for the most part, holders of the 2017 Notes were, at the time of the exchange offer, sophisticated professional investors.

. . .

[16] Paragraph 13 of Sch 3 contained provision as to who might attend or speak at Noteholders' meetings, but continued:

> Neither the Issuer nor any Subsidiary shall be entitled to vote at any meeting in respect of Notes beneficially held by it or for its account.

[17] Paragraph 18 of Sch 3 set out in detail the powers capable of being exercised by a majority of Noteholders by Extraordinary Resolution. They included:

> **(a)**   Power to sanction any compromise or arrangement proposed to be made between the Issuer and the Noteholders. . . .
> **(c)**   Power to assent to any modification of the provisions contained in these presents which shall be proposed by the Issuer or the Trustee.

[18] Paragraph 20 provided that an Extraordinary Resolution required a three-fourths majority of persons voting. Paragraph 19 provided that a resolution duly passed at a Noteholders' meeting would be binding upon all Noteholders whether present or absent, voting or abstaining.

[19] By September 2008 the Bank had become the third largest bank in the Irish domestic market with €101 billion of gross assets on its balance-sheet, representing about 50% of Irish GDP. It had a particular focus on commercial property lending, and as a result of the 2008 financial crisis, with a linked rapid decline in commercial property values, the Bank faced a liquidity crisis which, unless it was rescued by the Irish Government, would have forced it into insolvent liquidation. Nonetheless, being regarded as of systemic importance to the maintenance of the stability of the Irish financial system, it was indeed rescued by the Irish government by a series of steps, which I shall briefly summarise. The first consisted of a guarantee by the Irish government of certain liabilities of Irish financial institutions, including the 2017 Notes, for the period from 30 September 2008 to 29 September 2010 pursuant to the Credit Institutions (Financial Support) Scheme 2008. The Scheme prohibited any call on that guarantee after 29 September 2010.

[20] Secondly, in December 2009 the Irish government guaranteed certain eligible liabilities of participating institutions, including the Bank, pursuant to the Credit Institutions (Eligible Liabilities Guarantee) Scheme 2009. Those liabilities did not include the 2017 Notes, because they were subordinated.

[21] On 21 January 2009 the Bank was nationalised, because of its systemic importance to the maintenance of the stability of the Irish financial system, pursuant to the Anglo Irish Bank Corporation Act 2009.

[22] On 7 April 2009 the Minister for Finance announced the creation of the National Asset Management Agency ("NAMA") formed to purchase certain distressed loans from banks carrying on in business in Ireland. This had no direct effect upon the 2017 Notes.

[23] On 29 May 2009, in view of the continued deterioration in the Bank's financial position following nationalisation, the Irish government announced its intention to make urgent provision of up to €4 billion of capital to the Bank through the purchase of new ordinary shares. This support (but not the earlier nationalisation) required approval from the European Commission[,] which was granted on 26 June 2009. The Commission required to be satisfied that financial support by a member state to a domestic bank was provided on terms that minimised the amount of state aid to that necessary to protect the wider financial system in Ireland and, to that end, the Bank proposed to increase its Core Tier 1 capital by engaging in a "Liability Management Exercise" under which it intended to buy back subordinated loans, at a premium above the prevailing market rates no higher than "necessary only to ensure a participation rate sufficient to make the Liability Management Exercise worthwhile."

[24] By December 2009 the Bank had incurred an aggregate loss of some €12.7 billion. In March, May and August 2010 the Irish government increased its support to the Bank by amounts of €8.3 billion, €2 billion and €8.58 billion respectively.

[25] On 8 September 2010, just before the expiry of the October 2008 guarantee, the Minister of Finance made an announcement about the proposed re-structuring of the Bank, which contemplated its being split into a depositors' bank and an asset management entity. In the event this did not proceed. By 30 September, the day after expiry of the October 2008 guarantee, the Irish government had provided a total of €22.88 billion of capital to the Bank by way of share subscription and promissory notes, and NAMA had purchased €6.5 billion worth of distressed loans.

[26] It was during the staged rescue of the Bank which I have summarised, and the currency of the October 2008 guarantee of (inter alia) the 2017 Notes, that the Claimant acquired its holding of 2017 Notes in the market, at prices ranging between 0.418 and 0.420 per nominal Euro, between 23 September 2009 and 1 April 2010. The substantial discount at which the Notes were trading in the market no doubt reflected a perception that the 2008 guarantee was unlikely to be extended indefinitely, and that holders of subordinated debt could not expect to be treated with the same sympathy as the Bank's retail customers. The Claimant acquired its holding as manager of two Luxembourg funds. It may safely be inferred that it did so on behalf of sophisticated investors.

[27] On 30 September 2010 (immediately after the expiry of the 2008 guarantee) the Minister of Finance made a statement on the banking system in Ireland[,] which, while stating an intention to respect all senior debt obligations in the Bank, continued:

> The principle of appropriate burden sharing by holders of subordinated debt, however, is one with which I agree. As can be seen from the figures outlined above, the losses in the bank are substantial and it is right that the holders of Anglo's subordinated debt should share the costs[,] which have arisen.

> . . .

> I expect the subordinated debt holders to make a significant contribution towards meeting the costs of Anglo.

[28] This announcement contemplated a . . . voluntary re-structuring of subordinated debt, if possible, by agreement with Noteholders (or a qualifying majority of them). . . . The exchange proposal to the 2017 Notes was part of the first of those two stages.

THE 2010 EXCHANGE OFFER

[29] On 21 October 2010 the Bank announced exchange offers in respect of certain series of its Notes, including the 2017 Notes. . . .

[30] The Announcement . . . propos[ed] to Noteholders an exchange of . . . the 2017 Notes for new Notes ("the New Notes") in the exchange ratio 0.20, *i.e.*, an offer of a holding of 20 cents New Notes for every one Euro of 2017 Notes. The New Notes were not to be subordinated. They were to carry a coupon of three month Euribor* plus 3.75%, to be guaranteed by the Irish government and to mature in December 2011. The Announcement continued as follows:

> In connection with the Exchange Offers, the Bank is also convening (at the times specified in the . . . Memorandum) separate meetings inviting the Holders of each Series of Existing Notes (a definition which included the 2017 Notes) to approve, by separate Extraordinary Resolution in respect of each Series, proposed amendments to the terms and conditions of each Series including giving the Bank the right to redeem all, but not some only, of the Existing Notes of each Series at an amount equal to €0.01 per €1000 in principal amount of Existing Notes at any time after the relevant Settlement Date. . . .

> . . .

[32] . . . By contrast with the exchange ratio of 0.20 in the Exchange Offer this amounted to a payment ratio of 0.00001.

[33] [The Bank also noted:]

> By offering to exchange its Existing Notes, a holder will be deemed to have given instructions for the appointment of the exchange and tabulation agent (or its agent) as its proxy to vote in favour of the relevant Extraordinary Resolution in respect of all Existing Notes of the relevant series offered for exchange by such holder and which are accepted by the Bank at the . . . 2017 Notes Meeting. . . .

> It will not be possible for Holders . . . to validly offer to exchange Existing Notes pursuant to the Exchange Offer without at the same time appointing the Exchange Tabulation Agent (or its agent) as their proxy to vote in favour of the Extraordinary Resolution in respect of the relevant Series as described above. . . .

[34] Under the heading Risk Factors and Other Considerations, the Memorandum provided (inter alia) as follows:

> If an Extraordinary Resolution is passed in respect of any Series of Existing Notes and the approved amendments are implemented . . . the amendments shall be binding on all Holders of Existing Notes . . . , whether or not those Holders attended or were otherwise represented at the relevant Meeting and/or voted in favour of the relevant Proposal.

> If the Bank chooses to exercise such call right (which the Bank currently intends to do . . .), the redemption amounts payable to a Holder of Existing Notes (being €0.01 per €1000 in principle amount of Existing Notes) will be significantly less than the principal amount of the New Notes such Holder would have received had such Existing Notes been exchanged pursuant to the relevant Exchange Offer. [Emphasis original.]

> . . .

---

* This is a standard reference interest rate for floating-rate, Euro-denominated debt.—ED.

[36] The exchange ratio of 0.20 in the Exchange Offer broadly reflected the price at which the 2017 Notes were then trading in the market, although there is some dispute, which I need not resolve, about the then liquidity of that market. No premium over the then market price for the 2017 Notes was added as an incentive, but the combined effect of the exchange offer and the disincentive to rejecting it constituted by the linked resolution to permit the Bank to redeem the 2017 Notes (if not exchanged) for 0.00001 of their face value was sufficient to ensure that 92.03% of the 2017 Noteholders by value offered their notes for exchange and conditionally bound themselves to vote in favour of the Resolution. . . .

[37] The Bank notified acceptance of all notes offered for exchange on 22 November and the Resolution was therefore duly passed by at least the same majority at the 2017 Noteholders' meeting held on the following day. Settlement of the exchange of Existing Notes for New Notes duly then occurred in accordance with the advertised timetable and, on 30 November 2010, the Bank exercised its newly acquired right to redeem the remaining 2017 Notes at the nominal price of €0.01 per €1000 face value pursuant to which the Claimant received €170 for its €17 million face value of 2017 Notes.
. . .

THE CLAIMANT'S CASE

[39] In their skeleton argument and in oral submissions, [Claimant's counsel] put the Claimant's case for a declaration that the resolution purportedly passed at the 2017 Noteholders' meeting on 24 November 2010 was invalid [because] . . . :
. . .

(2) At the time of the Noteholders' meeting on 23 November, all those noteholders whose votes were counted in support of the Resolution held their Notes beneficially, or for the account of, the Bank. Accordingly, all those votes are to be disregarded pursuant to paragraph 13 of Schedule 3 to the Trust Deed.

(3) . . . the Resolution constituted an abuse of the power of the voting majority because:

   (i) It conferred no conceivable benefit or advantage upon the 2017 Noteholders as a class; and,

   (ii) It affected, and could by then only have affected, the Notes of that minority which had not coupled an offer of their Notes for exchange with a commitment to vote in favour of the resolution. Accordingly it was both oppressive and unfair as against that minority.

. . .

[49] [S]tatute may also intervene. There is in England and Wales the statutory remedy for unfairly prejudicial conduct now to be found in Pt 30 of the Companies Act 2006. In the USA, the US Trust Indenture Act of 1939 provides at § 316(b) a general prohibition against the modification of payment terms without the unanimous consent of all the holders of securities issued and registered with the SEC under the US Securities Act of 1933. There are however no statutory safeguards against abuse of power by a majority of the 2017 Noteholders in the present context.

. . .

DISENFRANCHISEMENT UNDER PARA 13 OF SCH 3

[56] It was, as I have said, common ground that the purpose of the disentitlement to vote in respect of Notes beneficially held by the Bank or for its account was to prevent a vote designed to serve the interests of the Noteholders from being undermined by the exercise of votes cast in the interests of the Bank. Specifically, the prohibition was designed to prevent a Noteholder from succumbing to a conflict between the interests of the Noteholders and the interests of the Bank. It was also common ground that, although the language of the prohibition speaks in terms of the Issuer or its Subsidiary being disentitled to vote, it applies equally to any other person who or which holds his or its Notes for the benefit or for the account of the Bank.

. . .

[61] [Counsel for the Bank] gained considerable support from the analysis of a similar point by Chancellor Allen in the *Oak Industries* case (*supra*) at p 881. The terms of the bonds in that case prohibited the Issuer (Oak) from voting debt securities held in its treasury, and it was submitted that by linking its exchange offer with the giving by the bondholders of consent to the amendment to the terms of the bonds, Oak had been permitted to "dictate" the vote on securities which it could not itself vote. He continued:

> The evident purpose of the restriction on the voting of treasury securities is to afford protection against the issuer voting as a bondholder in favour of modifications that would benefit it as an issuer, even though such changes would be detrimental to bondholders. But the linking of the exchange offer and the consent solicitation does not involve the risk that bondholder interests will be affected by a vote involving anyone with a financial interest in the subject of the vote other than a bondholder's interest. That the consent is to be given concurrently with the transfer of the bond to the issuer does not in any sense create the kind of conflict of interest that the indenture's prohibition on voting treasury securities contemplates. Not only will the proposed consents be granted or withheld only by those with a financial interest to maximize the return on their investment in Oak's bond, but the incentive to consent is equally available to all members of each class of bondholders. Thus the "vote" implied by the consent solicitation is not affected in any sense by those with a financial conflict of interest.

. . .

[64] I have nonetheless concluded that [the claimant's counsel's view] that . . . Notes . . . offered and accepted for exchange were held for the benefit of the Bank by the time of the meeting, is correct. All those Notes were by that time held under contracts for sale between the relevant majority Noteholders and the Bank. . . .

. . .

ABUSE OF POWER

. . .

[84] . . . I have concluded that [claimant's counsel] arrived eventually at the correct question, which is whether it can be lawful for the majority to lend its aid to the coercion of a minority by voting for a resolution which expropriates the minority's rights under their bonds for a nominal consideration. In my judgment the correct answer to it is in the negative. My reasons derive essentially from my understanding of the purpose of the exit consent technique, as described at the beginning of this judgment. It is not that the issuer positively wishes to obtain securities by expropriation, rather than by the contractual exchange for value which it invites the bondholders to agree. On the contrary, the higher percentage of those accepting, generally the happier the issuer will be. Furthermore, the operation of the exit consent (here the Bank's new right to redeem for a nominal consideration) is not the method by which the issuer seeks to achieve the reconstruction constituted by the replacement of existing securities with new. The exit consent is, quite simply, a coercive threat which the issuer invites the majority to levy against the minority, nothing more or less. Its only function is the intimidation of a potential minority, based upon the fear of any individual member of the class that, by rejecting the exchange and voting against the resolution, he (or it) will be left out in the cold.

[85] This form of coercion is in my judgment entirely at variance with the purposes for which majorities in a class are given power to bind minorities, and it is no answer for them to say that it is the issuer which has required or invited them to do so. True it is that, at the moment when any individual member of the class is required (by the imposition of the pre-meeting deadline) to make up his mind, there is at that point in time no defined minority against which the exit consent is aimed. But it is inevitable that there will be a defined (if any) minority by the time when the exit consent is implemented by being voted upon, and its only purpose is to prey upon the apprehension of each member of the class (aggravated by his relative inability to find out the views of his fellow class members in advance) that he will, if he decides to vote against, be part of that expropriated minority if the scheme goes ahead.

[86] Putting it as succinctly as I can, oppression of a minority is of the essence of exit consents of this kind, and it is precisely that at which the principles restraining the abusive exercise of powers to bind minorities are aimed.

CONCLUSIONS

[87] The Claimant therefore . . . succeeds. . . .

Problem Set 10

(1) You are counsel to a firm planning on issuing high-yield (junk) bonds. You know there is a reasonable chance that the bonds will need to be restructured prior to maturity or refinancing. Does it matter whether Delaware or English law applies to the bonds in the deal documents? Do you think there is likely to be any effect on the demand for the bonds and hence the cost of the financing?

(2) W. Herschel Astronomics, a manufacturer of precision telescopic lenses, has come to your law firm for advice on restructuring their high-yield debt. Herschel needs to be able to do a bond exchange or it will have to file for bankruptcy. The outstanding bonds have a 10% annual coupon and a 10-year maturity. The covenants include a negative pledge clause (promising that no other lenders will be given collateral), leverage limitations, asset and merger limitations, and prepayment limitations. The bonds are

guaranteed by all of Herschel's subsidiaries. Herschel wishes to exchange the bonds for ones with a lower coupon and a 15-year balloon payment structure. William Herschel, the firm's CEO, says, "I really want to put the screws to the bondholders. This exchange had better work. We need to get 90 percent of bondholders exchanging and within a month, and this can't get held up in litigation." What provisions do you propose putting into the exit consents? Will these provisions stand up if challenged as unduly coercive and not in good faith?

(3) Real estate developer and celebrity playboy David Dennison has engaged your firm to help him restructure the debt of his decadent Atlantic City casino, Nero's Palace. The casino's parent company, DD Holdings, has guaranteed the casino's publicly held senior notes. Dennison wants to free DD Holdings of the guarantee, in part because he knows that the casino is likely to default on its obligations under the notes unless the gaming climate picks up considerably. Not surprisingly, the notes are currently trading at 45 cents on the dollar, even with the parent guarantee.

Dennison has identified several key noteholders, who collectively own 52 percent of the senior notes. Dennison is proposing offering these senior noteholders 100 cents on the dollar for their notes, conditioned on their first voting to strip the notes of the parent guarantee. Dennison does not intend to offer anything to the other senior noteholders. The notes' indenture requires a simple majority of noteholders (by dollar amount) to approve amendments to the indenture. What do you tell Dennison? Would it make any difference if Dennison purchased the notes and instead of retiring them instead voted them himself for amendment of the indenture? Would it matter if the notes were privately placed?

CHAPTER 11

RESTRUCTURING LOAN SYNDICATIONS AND PARTICIPATIONS

I. RESTRUCTURING LOAN SYNDICATIONS AND PARTICIPATIONS

Syndicated and participated loans and privately placed notes can involve restructuring challenges that are similar to those with bonds. These challenges arise from contract, through, rather than federal law. Several issues arise. First, there is the question of the authority of the agent or lead bank to act on behalf of the syndicate or participation or noteholders. Second, there is the related question of whether individual lenders are bound by the decisions made by the collective or by the lead. Third, there is the problem of holdouts blocking a restructuring deal. While many features of syndications will seem familiar to you from the bond indenture in Chapter 4, notice that the syndication anticipates more in the way of loan restructuring than the indenture.

A. Authority of the Agent Bank

What proposals the agent or lead bank can accept in a restructuring depends on the specifics of the syndication or participation agreement. The terms of these agreements are not standardized, but typically a majority vote is required for some restructuring actions and unanimous consent for other restructuring actions. Thus, a syndication might provide that half or two-thirds of the voting power (based on dollars loaned) must approve the waiver of a covenant default, whereas unanimous consent is required for changes to the payment schedule of the loan or the release of any collateral. Consider the following provisions from a syndication agreement for firearms manufacturer Colt Defense LLC, particularly the definition of "Required Lenders" and section 14.1(a).

TERM LOAN AGREEMENT

by and among

COLT DEFENSE LLC,
COLT FINANCE CORP.,
NEW COLT HOLDING CORP.,
COLT'S MANUFACTURING COMPANY, LLC AND
COLT CANADA CORPORATION,

as Borrowers,

THE SUBSIDIARIES OF COLT DEFENSE LLC
NAMED AS GUARANTORS HEREIN,

as Guarantors,

THE LENDERS THAT ARE PARTIES HERETO,

as the Lenders,

and

WILMINGTON SAVINGS FUND SOCIETY, FSB,

as Agent

Dated as of November 17, 2014

. . .

"Agent-Related Persons" means Agent, together with its Affiliates, officers, directors, employees, attorneys, and agents.

. . .

"Loan Documents" means the Agreement, . . . each Guaranty, the Intercompany Subordination Agreement, any Mortgage, . . . the Security Agreement, . . . any other Security Document, any UCC Filing Authorization Letter or similar authorization, any Agent Fee Letter or similar document, any note or notes executed by Borrower in connection with the Agreement and payable to any member of the Lender Group, any letter of credit application entered into by any Borrower in connection with the Agreement, and any other agreement entered into or certificate issued, now or in the future, by Parent or any of its Subsidiaries in connection with the Agreement. "Loan Party" means Borrower or any Guarantor.

. . .

"Lender Group Expenses" means all . . . reasonable and documented out-of-pocket fees or charges paid or incurred by Agent and each Lender in connection with the Lender Group's transactions with Parent or its Subsidiaries under any of the Loan Documents, . . . reasonable out-of-pocket costs and expenses paid or incurred by the Lender Group to correct any default or enforce any provision of the Loan Documents, or during the continuance of an Event of Default, in gaining possession of, maintaining, handling, preserving, storing, shipping, selling, preparing for sale, or advertising to sell the Collateral, or any portion thereof, irrespective of whether a sale is consummated, . . . [and] Agent's and each Lender's reasonable and documented costs and expenses (including reasonable attorneys, accountants, consultants, financial advisors, and other advisors fees and expenses) incurred in terminating, enforcing (including attorneys, accountants, consultants, and other advisors fees and expenses incurred in connection with a "workout," a "restructuring," or an Insolvency Proceeding concerning Parent or any of its Subsidiaries or in exercising rights or remedies under the Loan Documents). . . .

"Pro Rata Share" means, as of any date of determination: with respect to a Lender's obligation to make all or a portion of the Term Loan and right to receive payments of principal, interest, fees, costs, and expenses with respect thereto, the percentage obtained by dividing (a) the outstanding principal amount of the Term Loan owed to such Lender, by (b) the aggregate outstanding principal amount of the Term Loan. . . .

"Required Lenders" means, at any time, Lenders whose aggregate Pro Rata Shares exceed 50.0%.
. . .

---

9. RIGHTS AND REMEDIES.

9.1 Rights and Remedies. Upon the occurrence and during the continuation of an Event of Default, Agent, upon the written instruction of the Required Lenders, shall (in each case under clause (a) by written notice to . . . Borrower), in addition to any other rights or remedies provided for hereunder or under any other Loan Document or by applicable law, do any one or more of the following:

(a) declare the Obligations, whether evidenced by this Agreement or by any of the other Loan Documents to be immediately due and payable, whereupon the same shall become and be immediately due and payable and Borrowers shall be obligated to repay all of such Obligations in full, without presentment, demand, protest, or further notice or other requirements of any kind, all of which are hereby expressly waived by each Borrower;

. . . and

(c) exercise all other rights and remedies available to Agent or the Lenders under the Loan Documents or applicable law.

. . .

---

10. WAIVERS; INDEMNIFICATION.

. . .

10.3 Indemnification. Borrowers shall pay, indemnify, defend, and hold the Agent-Related Persons, the Lender-Related Persons (each, an "Indemnified Person") harmless (to the fullest extent permitted by law) from and against any and all claims, demands, suits, actions, investigations, proceedings, liabilities, fines, costs, penalties, and damages, and all reasonable fees and disbursements of attorneys (limited to one U.S. counsel to Agent-Related Persons and one U.S. counsel to Lender-Related Persons . . . and any local or regulatory counsel to Agent-Related Persons and Lender-Related Persons reasonably selected by Agent, one additional counsel for the Lenders (taken as a whole) if an Event of Default has occurred and is continuing and, if the interests of any Agent-Related Person or Lender-Related Person are distinctly and disproportionately affected, one additional counsel for such affected Person), experts, or consultants and all other costs and expenses actually incurred in connection therewith or in connection with the enforcement of this indemnification . . . at any time asserted against, imposed upon, or incurred by any of them (a) in connection with or as a result of or related to the execution and delivery incurred in advising, structuring, drafting, reviewing, administering or syndicating the Loan Documents), enforcement, performance, or administration (including any restructuring or workout with respect hereto) of this Agreement, any of the other Loan Documents, or the transactions contemplated hereby or thereby or the monitoring of Parent's and its Subsidiaries' compliance with the terms of the Loan Documents (provided, however, that the indemnification in this clause (a) shall not extend to (i) disputes solely between or among the Lenders or (ii) disputes solely between or among the Lenders and their respective Affiliates; it being understood and agreed that the indemnification in this clause (a) shall extend to Agent (but not the Lenders) relative to disputes between or among Agent (in its capacity as such) on the one hand, and one or more Lenders, or one or more of their Affiliates, on the other hand, (b) with respect to any investigation, litigation, or proceeding related to this Agreement, any other Loan Document, or the use of the proceeds of the credit provided hereunder (irrespective of whether any Indemnified Person is a party thereto), or any act, omission, event, or circumstance in any manner related thereto . . . (each and all of the foregoing, the "Indemnified Liabilities"). . . . The foregoing to the contrary notwithstanding, no Borrower shall have any obligation to any Indemnified Person under this Section 10.3 with respect to any Indemnified Liability that a court of competent jurisdiction finally determines to have resulted from the gross negligence, willful misconduct or bad faith of such Indemnified Person or its officers, directors, employees, attorneys, or agents. . . .

14. AMENDMENTS; WAIVERS.

14.1 Amendments and Waivers.

(a) No amendment, waiver or other modification of any provision of this Agreement or any other Loan Document, and no consent with respect to any departure by any Loan Party therefrom, shall be effective unless the same shall be in writing and signed by the Required Lenders (or by Agent at the written request of the Required Lenders) and the Loan Parties that are party thereto, and then any such waiver or consent shall be effective only in the specific instance and for the specific purpose for which given; provided, however, that no such waiver, amendment, or consent shall, unless in writing and signed by all of the Lenders directly affected thereby and all of the Loan Parties that are party thereto, do any of the following:

(i) increase the amount of or extend the expiration date of any Commitment of any Lender,

(ii) postpone or delay any date fixed by this Agreement or any other Loan Document for any payment of principal, interest, fees, or other amounts due hereunder or under any other Loan Document,

(iii) reduce the principal of, or the rate of interest on, any loan or other extension of credit hereunder, or reduce any fees or other amounts payable hereunder or under any other Loan Document (except (y) in connection with the waiver of applicability of [the default rate of interest] (which waiver shall be effective with the written consent of the Required Lenders), and (z) that any amendment or modification of defined terms used in the financial covenants in this Agreement shall not constitute a reduction in the rate of interest or a reduction of fees for purposes of this clause (iii)),

(iv) amend, modify, or eliminate this Section or any provision of this Agreement providing for consent or other action by all Lenders,

(v) amend, modify, or eliminate Section 15.11,

(vi) release Agent's Lien in and to any of the Collateral, except as permitted by Section 15.11,

(vii) amend, modify, or eliminate the definition of "Required Lenders" or "Pro Rata Share,"

(viii) contractually subordinate any of Agent's Liens, except as permitted by Section 15.11,

(ix) release any Borrower or any Guarantor from any obligation for the payment of money or consent to the assignment or transfer by any Borrower or any Guarantor of any of its rights or duties under this Agreement or the other Loan Documents, except in connection with a merger, wind up, liquidation, dissolution or sale of such Person expressly permitted by the terms hereof or the other Loan Documents,

. . .

(xi) amend, modify, or eliminate the definition of Term Loan Amount, or

. . .

(b) No amendment, waiver, modification, elimination, or consent shall amend, modify, or waive (i) any of the terms or provisions of Section 2.10 [regarding fees], without the written consent of the Required Lenders and Borrowers, and (ii) any provision of Section 15 pertaining to Agent, or any other rights or duties of Agent under this Agreement or the other Loan Documents, without the written consent of Agent, Borrowers and the Required Lenders. Notwithstanding anything to the contrary contained in this Agreement or the other Loan Documents, the consent of Loan Parties and Lenders shall not be required for the exercise by Agent of any of its rights under this Agreement in accordance with the terms of this Agreement.

. . .

15. AGENT; THE LENDER GROUP.

15.1 <u>Appointment and Authorization of Agent</u>. Each Lender hereby designates and appoints Wilmington Savings Fund Society, FSB as its agent under this Agreement . . . and each Lender hereby irrevocably authorizes Agent to execute and deliver each of the other Loan Documents . . . on its behalf and to take such other action on its behalf under the provisions of this Agreement and each other Loan Document . . . and to exercise such powers and perform such duties as are expressly delegated to Agent by the terms of this Agreement or any other Loan Document . . . , together with such powers as are reasonably incidental thereto. Agent agrees to act as agent for and on behalf of the Lenders on the conditions contained in this Section 15. Any provision to the contrary contained elsewhere in this Agreement or in any other Loan Document notwithstanding, Agent shall not have any duties or responsibilities, except those expressly set forth herein or in the other Loan Documents, nor shall Agent have or be deemed to have any fiduciary relationship with any Lender, and no implied covenants, functions, responsibilities, duties, obligations or liabilities shall be read into this Agreement or any other Loan Document or otherwise exist against Agent. Without limiting the generality of the foregoing, the use of the term "agent" in this Agreement or the other Loan Documents with reference to Agent is not intended to connote any fiduciary or other implied (or express) obligations arising under agency doctrine of any applicable law. Instead, such term is used merely as a matter of market custom, and is intended to create or reflect only a representative relationship between independent contracting parties.

Each Lender hereby further authorizes Agent to act as the secured party under each of the Loan Documents that create a Lien on any item of Collateral. Except as expressly otherwise provided in this Agreement, Agent shall have and may use its sole discretion with respect to exercising or refraining from exercising any discretionary rights or taking or refraining from taking any actions that Agent expressly is entitled to take or assert under or pursuant to this Agreement and the other Loan Documents. Without limiting the generality of the foregoing, or of any other provision of the Loan Documents that provides rights or powers to Agent, Lenders agree that Agent shall have the right to exercise the following powers as long as this Agreement remains in effect: . . . (b) execute or file any and all financing or similar statements or notices, amendments, renewals, supplements, documents, instruments, proofs of claim, notices and other written agreements with respect to the Loan Documents, (c) exclusively receive, apply, and distribute [all payments from the Borrowers] as provided in the Loan Documents, . . . (e) perform, exercise, and enforce any and all other rights and remedies of the Lender Group with respect to Parent or its Subsidiaries, the Obligations, the Collateral, the Collections of Parent and its Subsidiaries, or otherwise related to any of same as provided in the Loan Documents, and (f) incur and pay such Lender Group Expenses as Agent may deem necessary or appropriate for the performance and fulfillment of its functions and powers pursuant to the Loan Documents.
. . .

15.3 <u>Liability of Agent</u>. None of the Agent-Related Persons shall (a) be liable for any action taken or omitted to be taken by any of them under or in connection with this Agreement or any other Loan Document or the transactions contemplated hereby (except for its own gross negligence or willful misconduct), or (b) be responsible in any manner to any of the Lenders for any recital, statement, representation or warranty made by Parent or any of its Subsidiaries or Affiliates, or any officer or director thereof, contained in this Agreement or in any other Loan Document, or in any certificate, report, statement or other document referred to or provided for in, or received by Agent under or in connection with, this Agreement or any other Loan Document, or the validity, effectiveness, genuineness, enforceability or sufficiency of this Agreement or any other Loan Document, or for any failure of Parent or its Subsidiaries or any other party to any Loan Document to perform its obligations hereunder or thereunder. No Agent-Related Person shall be under any obligation to any Lenders to ascertain or to inquire as to the observance or performance of any of the agreements contained in, or conditions of, this Agreement or any other Loan Document, or to inspect the books and records or properties of Parent or its Subsidiaries. . . .

15.4 <u>Reliance by Agent</u>. Agent shall be entitled to rely, and shall be fully protected in relying, upon any writing, resolution, notice, consent, certificate, affidavit, letter, telegram, telefacsimile or other electronic method of transmission, telex or telephone message, statement or other document or conversation believed by it to be genuine and correct and to have been signed, sent, or made by the proper Person or Persons, and upon advice and statements of legal counsel (including counsel to Borrowers or counsel to any Lender), independent accountants and other experts selected by Agent. Agent shall be fully justified in failing or refusing to take any action under this Agreement or any other Loan Document unless Agent shall first receive such advice or concurrence of the Lenders as it deems appropriate and until such instructions are received, Agent shall act, or refrain from acting, as it deems advisable. If Agent so requests, it shall first be indemnified to its reasonable satisfaction by the Lenders against any and all liability and expense that may be incurred by it by reason of taking or continuing to take or refraining from taking any such action. Agent shall in all cases be fully protected in acting, or in refraining from acting, under this Agreement or any other Loan Document in accordance with a request or consent of the Required Lenders and such request and any action taken or failure to act pursuant thereto shall be binding upon all of the Lenders.

15.5 <u>Notice of Default or Event of Default</u>. Agent shall not be deemed to have knowledge or notice of the occurrence of any Default or Event of Default, except with respect to defaults in the payment of principal, interest, fees, and expenses required to be paid to Agent for the account of the Lenders and, except with respect to Events of Default of which Agent has actual knowledge, unless Agent shall have received written notice from a Lender or any Borrower referring to this Agreement, describing such Default or Event of Default, and stating that such notice is a "notice of default." Agent promptly will notify the Lenders of its receipt of any such notice or of any Event of Default of which Agent has actual knowledge. If any Lender obtains actual knowledge of any Event of Default, such Lender promptly shall notify the other Lenders and Agent of such Event of Default. Each Lender shall be solely responsible for giving any notices to its Participants, if any. Subject to Section 15.4, Agent shall take such action with respect to such Default or Event of Default as may be requested by the Required Lenders in accordance with Section 9; provided, however, that unless and until Agent has received any such request, Agent may (but shall not be obligated to) take such action, or refrain from taking such action, with respect to such Default or Event of Default as it shall deem advisable.

. . .

15.7 <u>Costs and Expenses; Indemnification</u>. Agent may incur and pay Lender Group Expenses to the extent Agent reasonably deems necessary or appropriate for the performance and fulfillment of its functions, powers, and obligations pursuant to the Loan Documents, including court costs, attorneys' fees and expenses, fees and expenses of financial accountants, advisors, consultants, and appraisers, costs of collection by outside collection agencies, auctioneer fees and expenses, and costs of security guards or insurance premiums paid to maintain the Collateral, whether or not Borrowers are obligated to reimburse Agent or Lenders for such expenses pursuant to this Agreement or otherwise. Agent is authorized and directed to deduct and retain sufficient amounts from the [payments from the Borrowers] received by Agent to reimburse Agent for such out-of-pocket costs and expenses prior to the distribution of any amounts to Lenders. In the event Agent is not reimbursed for such costs and expenses by [the Borrowers], each Lender hereby agrees that it is and shall be obligated to pay to Agent such Lender's ratable share thereof. Whether or not the transactions contemplated hereby are consummated, each of the Lenders, on a ratable basis, shall indemnify and defend the Agent-Related Persons (to the extent not reimbursed by or on behalf of Borrowers and without limiting the obligation of Borrowers to do so) from and against any and all Indemnified Liabilities; provided, that, no Lender shall be liable for the payment to any Agent-Related Person of any portion of such Indemnified Liabilities resulting solely from such Person's gross negligence or willful misconduct nor shall any Lender be liable for the obligations of any Defaulting Lender in failing to make an extension of credit hereunder. Without limitation of the foregoing, each Lender shall reimburse Agent upon demand for such Lender's ratable share of any costs or out-of-pocket expenses (including attorneys, accountants, advisors, and consultants fees and expenses) incurred by Agent in connection with the preparation, execution, delivery, administration, modification, amendment, or enforcement (whether through negotiations, legal proceedings or otherwise) of, or legal advice in respect of rights or responsibilities under, this Agreement or any other Loan Document to the extent that Agent is not reimbursed for such expenses by or on behalf of Borrowers. The undertaking in this Section shall survive the payment of all Obligations hereunder, the termination of this Agreement and the resignation or replacement of Agent.

15.8 <u>Agent in Individual Capacity</u>. Agent and its Affiliates may make loans to, issue letters of credit for the account of, accept deposits from, provide bank products to, acquire equity interests in, and generally engage in any kind of banking, trust, financial advisory, underwriting, or other business with Parent and its Subsidiaries and Affiliates and any other Person party to any Loan Document as though Agent were not Agent hereunder, and, in each case, without notice to or consent of the other members of the Lender Group. The other members of the Lender Group acknowledge that, pursuant to such activities, Agent or its Affiliates may receive information regarding Borrowers or their Affiliates or any other Person party to any Loan Documents that is subject to confidentiality obligations in favor of Borrowers or such other Person and that prohibit the disclosure of such information to the Lenders, and the Lenders acknowledge that, in such circumstances (and in the absence of a waiver of such confidentiality obligations, which waiver Agent will use its reasonable best efforts to obtain), Agent shall not be under any obligation to provide such information to them. The terms "Lender" and "Lenders" may include Agent in its individual capacity.

. . .

15.10 Lender in Individual Capacity. Any Lender and its respective Affiliates may make loans to, issue letters of credit for the account of, accept deposits from, provide bank products to, acquire equity interests in and generally engage in any kind of banking, trust, financial advisory, underwriting, or other business with Parent and its Subsidiaries and Affiliates and any other Person party to any Loan Documents as though such Lender were not a Lender hereunder without notice to or consent of the other members of the Lender Group. The other members of the Lender Group acknowledge that, pursuant to such activities, such Lender and its respective Affiliates may receive information regarding Parent or its Affiliates or any other Person party to any Loan Documents that is subject to confidentiality obligations in favor of Parent or such other Person and that prohibit the disclosure of such information to the Lenders, and the Lenders acknowledge that, in such circumstances (and in the absence of a waiver of such confidentiality obligations, which waiver such Lender will use its reasonable best efforts to obtain), such Lender shall not be under any obligation to provide such information to them.

15.11 Collateral Matters.
    (a) The Lenders hereby irrevocably authorize (and by entering into a Bank Product Agreement, each Bank Product Provider shall be deemed to authorize) Agent, at its option and in its discretion, to release, or subordinate, any Lien on any of the Collateral (i) upon satisfaction of all of the Obligations, or (ii) constituting property being sold or disposed of . . . , or (iii) constituting property in which any Loan Party did not own an interest at the time the security interest, mortgage or lien was granted or at any time thereafter, or (iv) having a value in the aggregate in any twelve (12) month period of less than $2,500,000, and to the extent Agent may release its Lien on any such Collateral pursuant to the sale or other disposition thereof, such sale or other disposition shall be deemed consented to by Lenders, or (v) if required or permitted under the terms of any of the other Loan Documents, including any intercreditor agreement, or (vi) constituting property leased to a Loan Party under a lease that has expired or is

terminated, or (vii) subject to <u>Section 14.1</u>, the Canadian Security Agreement and the Security Agreement, if the release is approved, authorized or ratified in writing by the Required Lenders. Nothing contained herein shall be construed to require the consent of any Bank Product Provider to any release or subordination of any Collateral or termination of security interests in any Collateral. Upon request by Agent or any Borrower at any time, the Lenders will (and if so requested, the Bank Product Providers will) confirm in writing Agent's authority to release or subordinate any such Liens on particular types or items of Collateral pursuant to this <u>Section 15.11</u>. . . .

(b) The Loan Parties and the Lenders hereby irrevocably authorize Agent, upon the written instruction of the Required Lenders, to (A) consent to, credit bid or purchase (either directly or through one or more acquisition vehicles) all or any portion of the Collateral at any sale thereof conducted under the provisions of the Bankruptcy Code or other bankruptcy laws, including under Section 363 of the Bankruptcy Code, (B) credit bid or purchase (either directly or through one or more acquisition vehicles) all or any portion of the Collateral at any sale or other disposition thereof conducted under the provisions of the Code . . . , including pursuant to Sections 9-610 or 9-620 of the Code, or (C) credit bid or purchase (either directly or through one or more acquisition vehicles) all or any portion of the Collateral at any other sale or foreclosure conducted by Agent (whether by judicial action or otherwise) in accordance with applicable law. In connection with any such credit bid or purchase, the Obligations owed to the Lenders shall be entitled to be, and shall be, credit bid on a ratable basis . . . and the Lenders whose Obligations are credit bid shall be entitled to receive interests (ratably based upon the proportion of their Obligations credit bid in relation to the aggregate amount of Obligations so credit bid) in the asset or assets so purchased (or in the Equity Interests of the acquisition vehicle or vehicles that are used to consummate such purchase).

(c) Agent shall have no obligation whatsoever to any of the Lenders to assure that the Collateral exists or is owned by a Loan Party or is cared for, protected, or insured or has been encumbered, or that Agent's Liens have been properly or sufficiently or lawfully created, perfected, protected, or enforced or are entitled to any particular priority . . . or to exercise at all or in any particular manner or under any duty of care, disclosure or fidelity, or to continue exercising, any of the rights, authorities and powers granted or available to Agent pursuant to any of the Loan Documents, it being understood and agreed that in respect of the Collateral, or any act, omission, or event related thereto, subject to the terms and conditions contained herein, Agent may act in any manner it may deem appropriate, in its sole discretion, regardless of whether Agent shall obtain its own interest in the Collateral in its capacity as one of the Lenders, and that Agent shall have no other duty or liability whatsoever to any Lender as to any of the foregoing, except as otherwise provided herein.

(d) In no event shall the Agent be responsible or liable for special, indirect, or consequential loss or damage of any kind whatsoever (including, but not limited to, loss of profit) irrespective of whether the Agent has been advised of the likelihood of such loss or damage and regardless of the form of action.

Notwithstanding any provision of this Agreement, the Agent shall not have any duties or responsibilities except those expressly set forth herein and the permissive provisions with respect to the Agent set forth herein shall not be deemed to be duties. Notwithstanding anything to the contrary contained herein, the Agent shall have no responsibility for the preparing, recording, filing, re-recording, or re-filing of any financing statement, continuation statement or other instrument in any public office. . . .

15.12 <u>Restrictions on Actions by Lenders; Sharing of Payments</u>.
(a) Each of the Lenders agrees that it shall not, without the express written consent of the Required Lenders, and that it shall, to the extent it is lawfully entitled to do so, upon the written request of the Required Lenders, set off against the Obligations, any amounts owing by such Lender to Parent or its Subsidiaries or any deposit accounts of Parent or its Subsidiaries now or hereafter maintained with such Lender. Each of the Lenders further agrees that it shall not, unless specifically requested to do so in writing by the Required Lenders, take or cause to be taken any action, including, the commencement of any legal or equitable proceedings to enforce any Loan Document against any Borrower or any Guarantor or to foreclose any Lien on, or otherwise enforce any security interest in, any of the Collateral.
(b) If, at any time or times any Lender shall receive (i) by payment, foreclosure, setoff, or otherwise, any proceeds of Collateral or any payments with respect to the Obligations, except for any such proceeds or payments received by such Lender from Agent pursuant to the terms of this Agreement, or (ii) payments from Agent in excess of such Lender's Pro Rata Share of all such distributions by Agent, such Lender promptly shall (A) turn the same over to Agent . . . for the account of all of the Lenders and for application to the Obligations in accordance with the applicable provisions of this Agreement, or (B) purchase, without recourse or warranty, an undivided interest and participation in the Obligations owed to the other Lenders so that such excess payment received shall be applied ratably as among the Lenders in accordance with their Pro Rata Shares. . . .

15.17 <u>Agent May File Proofs of Claim</u>.
(a) In case of the pendency of any receivership, insolvency, liquidation, bankruptcy, reorganization, arrangement, adjustment, composition or other judicial proceeding relative to any Loan Party, Agent . . . shall be entitled and empowered, upon the direction of the Required Lenders, by intervention in such proceeding or otherwise:
    (i) to file and prove a claim for [the amounts due the Lenders and Agent]; and
    (ii) to collect and receive any monies or other property payable or deliverable on any such claims and to distribute the same. . . .
(b) Nothing contained herein shall be deemed to authorize Agent to authorize or consent to or accept or adopt on behalf of any Lender any plan of reorganization, arrangement, adjustment or composition affecting the Obligations or the

rights of any Lender or to authorize Agent to vote in respect of the claim of any Lender in any such proceeding.

15.18 <u>Several Obligations; No Liability</u>. Notwithstanding that certain of the Loan Documents now or hereafter may have been or will be executed only by or in favor of Agent in its capacity as such, and not by or in favor of the Lenders, any and all obligations on the part of Agent (if any) to make any credit available hereunder, shall constitute the several (and not joint) obligations of the respective Lenders on a ratable basis in accordance with such Lender's percentage of the Term Loan outstanding. Nothing contained herein shall confer upon any Lender any interest in, or subject any Lender to any liability for, or in respect of, the business, assets, profits, losses, or liabilities of any other Lender. Each Lender shall be solely responsible for notifying its Participants of any matters relating to the Loan Documents to the extent any such notice may be required, and no Lender shall have any obligation, duty, or liability to any Participant of any other Lender. Except as provided in Section 15.7, no member of the Lender Group shall have any liability for the acts of any other member of the Lender Group. No Lender shall be responsible to Borrower or any other Person for any failure by any other Lender to fulfill its obligations to make credit available hereunder, nor to advance for such Lender or on its behalf, nor to take any other action on behalf of such Lender hereunder or in connection with the financing contemplated herein.

17. GENERAL PROVISIONS.

. . .

17.10 <u>Lender Group Expenses</u>. Borrowers agree to pay any and all Lender Group Expenses promptly upon demand therefor by Agent. Borrowers agree that their respective obligations contained in this Section 17.10 shall survive payment or satisfaction in full of all other Obligations and the termination of this Agreement. Similar provisions can be found in privately placed debt that is not subject to the TIA. For example, a private placement of notes might provide that

> no modification, amendment, waiver or consent shall, without the consent of the holders of all the outstanding Notes, (1) alter the fixed maturity of any Note, or reduce the rate or extend the time of payment of interest thereon, or reduce the principal amount thereof or modify any of the provisions of this Agreement with respect to the prepayment of the Notes (including, without limitation, provisions with respect to the premium payable upon any prepayment); (2) reduce the aforesaid aggregate principal amount of Notes the holders of which are required to consent to any such amendment; or (3) increase the aggregate principal amount of the Notes the holders of which may declare the Notes to be due and payable.

B. Individual Rights of Action

A second problem in syndicated and participated loans is the extent to which individual syndicate members or participants forfeit their individual rights and are subject to majority rule. In recent years, the question of whether an individual lender in a syndicated loan is bound by a decision made by the collective or by the lead has arisen in three contexts:

1. whether the individual lender has the right to sue unilaterally;
2. whether the individual lender is bound by the syndicate's decision on credit bidding in bankruptcy. *See In re Metaldyne Corp.*, 409 B.R. 671 (Bankr. S.D.N.Y. 2009) (syndication agent had right to credit bid on behalf of syndicate and to release collateral); and
3. whether the individual lender is bound by the syndicate's decision to consent to a sale of a bankruptcy firm's assets "free and clear" of the syndicate's liens under section 363(f) of the Bankruptcy Code.

The analysis in all these situations is fundamentally similar: It is a contract analysis. How clearly do sections 15.11 and 15.12 from the Colt Term Loan Agreement address these issues?

C. Holdouts

The previous section addressed whether an individual syndicate member forgoes its right to take action on its own in the face of collective opposition. Closely related is whether the collective can force an action on an individual holdout. While the TIA has no application to syndicated and participated loans or privately placed debt, contractual provisions requiring majority, supermajority, or unanimous consent present similar challenges for restructuring.

Contractual provisions may in fact be more problematic because the TIA requires that all bonds in an issuance be pro rata with their own trustee. Different issuances can have intercreditor agreements or subordination agreements, but each issuance has a separate indenture and hence a separate contractual relationship with the lender, such that an exchange offer would be done for a specific issuance. This means that there is a reasonable degree of common interest among the bondholders in an issuance (external positions aside). The same is not true for loans and privately placed notes, which can involve multiple tranches, series, or facilities. The lenders in different facilities, or with different lien priority or in different tranches, may have very different and even adverse incentives, particularly in regard to a restructuring. Other incentive splits might be because some lenders loaned the funds at par, while others bought into the syndicate at a discount in the secondary market. Moreover, unanimous consent and supermajority voting provisions potentially enable holdout behavior by lenders seeking to extract extra value for themselves in exchange for their approval of a restructuring.

That said, syndications typically involve a fairly discrete number of lenders who have a coordination mechanism through the lead or agent bank. Although lenders in syndicated loans explicitly disavow any duties to each other, they might still have certain unwaiveable duties, such as duties of good faith and fair dealing. *See Redwood Master Fund Ltd and others v. TD Bank Europe Ltd and others*, [2002] EWHC 2703 (Ch). There is no modern American law on this, but 19th century cases consistently held that while majorities could bind minorities, creditors under the same instrument owed each other a duty of good faith and fair dealing and were prohibited from colluding with the debtor. *See, e.g., Jackson v. Ludeling*, 88 U.S. 616 (1874); *Shaw v. Railroad Co.*, 100 U.S. 605, 612 (1879); *Hackettstown National Bank v. D.G. Yuengling Brewing Co.*, 74 F. 110, 112 (2d Cir. 1896). The enactment of the Trust Indenture Act appears to have largely supplanted this line of jurisprudence as a protection for minority creditors, even if the case law, while forgotten, remains good law. *See* William W. Bratton, Jr. & Adam J. Levitin, *The New Bond Workouts*, 166 U. Pa. L. Rev. 1 (2018).

Holdout problems can exist for syndicated or participated loans or privately placed notes, just as for publicly traded bonds. While privately placed notes are amenable to coercive exit consents, there is no such possibility of a coercive exit consent mechanism for a syndicated or participated loan. While a majority of lenders can typically strip out covenants, there is no ability for individual lenders to exchange their syndication or participation interest for that in a new loan, as individual lenders cannot be paid off without sharing with the entire syndicate. Thus, if a majority of lenders strip out covenants, they are stuck with the devalued loan themselves. At the same time, however, holdout problems are because of "sharing clauses"—any payment one lender receives must be shared with the other lenders. At best, then, one lender can hold out for an additional payment from the other lenders.

D. Securitization and CLOs

Securitization raises its own set of complications for loan restructuring in two ways. First, sometimes whole loans are securitized. This is frequently the case for commercial mortgage loans; it is less common for entire corporate loans to be securitized. The restructuring decisions for a securitized loan are made by the loan's servicer. The servicer's incentives may not track those of investors. Moreover, the servicer may be subject to contractual restrictions on loan restructuring. While these are more pervasive problems for residential mortgage securitization than for commercial mortgages (where the servicer of a defaulted loan is compensated with a 1% share of the loan, thereby incentivizing value maximization), the fact that the servicer is not the same as the investors can raise complications.

Second, syndicated pieces of corporate loans are often securitized via CLOs. The involvement of CLOs in syndicated loans raises potential complications for restructuring troubled loans in three contexts.

First, the CLO manager may not be able to accept restructuring terms that fail to match the maturity schedule of the CLO's own obligations. If a CLO has to pay out its investors in five years, the CLO will not want to accept (and may perhaps be contractually forbidden from accepting) loan restructuring terms that provide it a 10-year income stream.

Second, to the extent a restructuring involves the commitment of new funds, the CLO may not have the funds to pony up because it is a closed-ended fund. This is particularly a problem if the CLO is past its reinvestment period or if its interest coverage and overcollateralization triggers have been tripped, thus requiring the CLO to divert funds to redeeming the interests of its investors.

And third, CLOs may not be able to raise the funds for cash bidding in a fore-closure sale. A CLO is unlikely to have significant cash on hand other than loan payments it has not yet disbursed. Therefore, the ability to credit bid is critical to CLOs (and any other liquidity-constrained entity). The presence of CLOs in lending syndicates presents a potential complication for loan restructurings. We will return to this issue in a later chapter when considering attempts to limit credit bidding in bankruptcy.

E. Second Lien Loans and Intercreditor Agreements

As noted in Chapter 3, the presence of second lien debt can make attempts to restructure the first lien debt more difficult. Can the second lien lenders get paid when the first lien lenders have not been? Can the second lien lenders take actions to collect before the first lien lenders have been paid? And can the second lien lenders object or otherwise try to impede the first lien lenders' collection efforts in order to extract value for themselves?

Anticipating these sorts of problems, intercreditor agreements between first and second lien lenders are common. Intercreditor agreements typically contain two key provisions. The first is a subordination clause that will subordinate the second lien debt in right of payment to the first lien debt. Second lien loans are subordinate in their liens as to common collateral, but not in their right to payment. A subordination clause will make the second lien debt junior in right to payment as well as in lien priority. Such subordination will typically prohibit prepayment of the second lien debt.

Second, intercreditor agreements will typically provide for a "**standstill**" period following an event of default during which the second lien lenders will forbear from exercising any remedies. Obviously a standstill agreement only lasts until it expires, thus placing pressure on the first lien lenders to reach a solution before the expiry of the standstill. Some intercreditor agreements also contain an "**x clause**" that will require the second lien lenders to notify the first lien lenders in advance of exercising their remedies even after the standstill period expires.

Additionally, intercreditor agreements will often restrict amendment of the first and second lien debt's terms and provide that the parties will cooperate (or at least not interfere) with each other; will not contest each others' liens; will provide the first lien lenders with power of attorney to execute documents for the second lien lenders so that the second lien lenders cannot frustrate restructurings by footdragging; and will enable the first lien lenders to commit the second lien lenders to release their liens under certain conditions in the context of a restructuring. Intercreditor agreements will also frequently provide for bankruptcy-specific rights. Because intercreditor agreements are often also subordination agreements, they are frequently read narrowly along the lines of the Rule of Explicitness discussed in Chapter 3.

II. THE SHADOW OF BANKRUPTCY

When we view the limitations on bond and loan restructuring covered in the previous chapters, what do we see? First, we see that there are lots of possibilities of dealing with distressed debt outside of bankruptcy. Debt can be refinanced or it can be restructured. For many types of creditors—bank loans, leases, trade debt, tax debt, and tort debt—there are no legal restrictions on how the debt can be restructured, and putting aside mass torts, there are no unusual coordination problems. It is simply a matter of the parties finding an economic deal they like. These deals will be evaluated in the shadow of bankruptcy—how does the non-bankruptcy alternative compare with the outcome in bankruptcy? Indeed, the possibility of bankruptcy may be like the hanging that sharpens creditors' (and debtors') minds.

Thus, even for firms that never end up filing for bankruptcy, an understanding of bankruptcy law can be critically important for both creditors and debtors as it presents the backdrop against which all negotiations occur. By the same token, the difficulties sovereigns and sub-sovereigns (such as U.S. states and some U.S. municipalities) have in dealing with their own debts is in some measure due to the lack of a bankruptcy option. For bankruptcy-ineligible sovereigns, there is no way of coercing creditors or debtors into cutting deals.

There can be coordination problems, however, and, in the case of bond debt, legal restrictions on restructuring. The existence of multiple creditors may raise coordination problems. Most debtors have a limited number of major creditors, and once a deal is struck among them, the remaining creditors are not an issue. Mass torts, however, present a scenario in which there may be major liability, but spread out over numerous parties that are poorly positioned to negotiate with the debtor. Bonds can present a similar problem. Syndicated or participated loans can present similar issues, although on a smaller scale. If coordination problems are too great, then bankruptcy presents a solution, as it forces all the parties into a single forum and provides a mechanism for encouraging, or if need be, forcing coordination, as we shall see.

Only publicly traded bond debt has unavoidable legal limitations on its restructuring because of the Trust Indenture Act. Consent solicitations and exchange offers, especially coupled with exit consents, can get around some of the limitations of the TIA, but they are not guaranteed to work, and *Assénagon* suggests that they may not always be kosher. The only guaranteed way of bringing bondholders to the negotiating table is through bankruptcy. Like other creditors, bondholders make their own decisions regarding exchange offers in the shadow of bankruptcy. A similar dilemma confronts creditors in a syndicated loan.

Bankruptcy, however, is not just a specter. Instead, for firms with mass tort or bond debt, bankruptcy is often necessary for financial restructuring. When firms only have bank, lease, trade, and tax debt, they are frequently able to restructure outside of court. A bankruptcy filing might still be used in these situations to deal with a "squeaky wheel" or to enable a "clean" asset sale with judicial blessing—basically a comfort order for buyers. But a great deal of debt restructuring occurs outside of court and is solely in the realm of contract negotiation.

Problem Set 11

You've just joined the in-house legal department at Midas Bank (known for its golden touch) and have been assigned to handle all issues arising with Midas's loan to the Phaeton Corporation, a major power utility support firm. The Phaeton Corporation received a $1 billion secured loan from a syndicate of lenders led by Midas Bank. The loan consists of a $200 million revolver, a $300 million Term Loan A facility, and a $500 million Term Loan B facility. Midas Bank only has a $10 million interest in the syndicate in the Term Loan A facility. The entire loan is secured by "all of the debtor's accounts, deposit accounts, equipment, inventory, general intangibles, goods, now owned or hereafter acquired, including all fixtures and accessions thereto." The financing statement was duly filed by the Midas Bank and covers "all assets." The syndicate is governed by the sample syndication agreement above.

(1) One syndicate member, the Helios Funds CLO, has claimed that the Phaeton Corporation is in default for having incurred debt beyond the limits allowed by the loan covenants. Ares Fraser, one of the bank's hard-charging loan officers for Midas Bank, wants your advice on the situation. He tells you that Midas Bank has no knowledge of the alleged default beyond that claimed by the Helios Funds. He wants to know what, if anything, the Midas Bank has to do, particularly as he expects the Phaeton Corporation to draw down on its revolver in the next couple of days. He also wants to know who will be footing the bill, especially if Midas Bank has to engage outside counsel. *See* Colt Syndicated Loan Agreement §§ 9.1, 10.3, 15.4, 15.5, 15.7, 15.8, 17.10. *See also UniCredito Italiano SPA v. JPMorgan Chase Bank* (in Chapter 5).

(2) If there is a default, Fraser wants to know whether Midas Bank can foreclose on its own initiative? "I'm eager to test out the new forklift," Fraser squeals in anticipatory delight. *See* Colt Syndicated Loan Agreement § 15.12(a).

(3) After you contact the Phaeton Corporation, they suggest that you enter into a tolling or forbearance agreement to create the space for negotiations. Can Midas Bank unilaterally decide to forbear? *See* Colt Syndicated Loan Agreement § 14.1.

(4) Fraser just got a call from the CFO of the Phaeton Corporation, who is proposing an exchange of the $1 billion obligation for a new, longer-term, non-amortized $1.2 billion obligation at a lower interest rate. Can Fraser accept? *See* Colt Syndicated Loan Agreement § 14.1.

(5) The Phaeton Corporation maintains its bank accounts at Aphrodite Trust Co., one of the banks in the Midas Bank syndicate. Aphrodite's outstanding share of the syndicated loan is $50 million. At the time the Phaeton Corporation defaulted on the syndicated loan, it had $20 million on deposit with the Aphrodite Trust Co. Can the Aphrodite Trust Co. grab the funds the Phaeton Corporation has on deposit with it? If so,

will it have to share the funds with the other syndicate members? *See* Colt Syndicated Loan Agreement § 15.12.

(6) Ares Fraser is back. He tells you that he's just learned that the Midas Bank failed to file a timely continuation statement for the Phaeton Corporation loan and that the Phaeton Corporation was just hit with a $2 billion mass tort class action judgment, and that class counsel has obtained a judgment lien on virtually all of the Phaeton Corporation's assets. Fraser wants to know the consequences. *See* Colt Syndicated Loan Agreement § 15.3, 15.11(c)-(d).

(7) Fraser is back once again. He tells you that the Phaeton Corporation would like to enter into a series of interest rate swaps with the Midas Bank. These swaps will potentially make the Midas Bank a creditor of the Phaeton Corporation. He also tells you that the Midas Bank has already purchased $100 million in credit default swap insurance on the Phaeton Corporation loan from Odysseus LP, a notorious hedge fund. Fraser is curious if either of these transactions need to be disclosed to the members of the syndicate or if they are permitted. *See* Colt Syndicated Loan Agreement § 15.8.

(8) The revolver on the Phaeton Corporation loan is syndicated to 10 banks. One of the banks, the Argos State Bank, has just been taken into receivership by the FDIC and has failed to fund its latest portion of the Phaeton Corporation's latest draw on the loans. Does the Midas Bank have to step up to fund the Argos State Bank's portion of the draw? Do the other banks in the revolver syndicate? The entire syndicate? *See* Colt Syndicated Loan Agreement § 15.18. What is the risk posed by an incorrect answer?

(9) The Phaeton Corporation filed for bankruptcy, and is proposing to sell some of its assets. All but one of the lenders in the syndicate has directed Midas Bank to place a credit bid for the assets. That sole lender, the Eris Funds LP, does not want to credit bid its $40 million interest. Can Midas Bank make a credit bid? Can that credit bid include the $40 million owed to the Eris Funds LP? If so, what value, if any, will the Eris Funds LP receive on account of its claims if the credit bid is successful? Conversely, what if the Eris Funds wanted to credit bid, but the rest of the syndicate was opposed? Colt Syndicated Loan Agreement, Definition of "Required Lenders" §§ 15.11(b), 15.12.

PART III

RESTRUCTURING IN BANKRUPTCY

CHAPTER 12

BANKRUPTCY IN A NUTSHELL

All bankruptcies, irrespective of whether they are under Chapter 7 or Chapter 11 of the Bankruptcy code, start the same way: with the filing of a **bankruptcy petition.** The filing of a petition creates a legal entity called the **bankruptcy estate,** which accedes to title and control of the debtor's property, wherever located.

The filing of a bankruptcy petition also triggers an injunction against most collection activities. The injunction is called the **automatic stay,** and it is one of the key features of bankruptcy law. The automatic stay has the effect of channeling all claims against the debtor and its property into a single forum, the bankruptcy court, which enables an orderly adjudication of those claims. The stay thus works to prevent the race-to-the-courthouse problem of nonbankruptcy restructuring. And, if the debtor is restructuring, rather than liquidating, the stay also gives the debtor financial breathing room while undertaking operational changes.

Creditors can seek to have the automatic stay lifted. One of the critical issues regarding motions to lift the automatic stay deals with the valuation of the debtor's property and whether a creditor's interest in the property is **adequately protected**. Valuation issues are not limited to lift stay motions; instead, valuation questions permeate bankruptcy. Bankruptcy courts frequently have to engage in valuation of assets and firms in order to determine parties' rights. While there is scant law on valuation, there is a set of commonly used valuation methodologies.

After a bankruptcy petition is filed, there is a time window for creditors to file **claims** with the bankruptcy court for obligations that they believe they are owed by the debtor. Whether or not an obligation constitutes a claim is critical because bankruptcy only affects creditors' claims. To the extent that a party does not have a claim, its rights are (at least formally) unaffected by the bankruptcy, and it can subsequently pursue those rights against a reorganized debtor.

Not all claims are allowed in a bankruptcy. Some claims are disallowed, meaning that the debtor need not pay those obligations. Bankruptcy disallows claims based on obligations that are not enforceable outside of bankruptcy, but it also disallows some claims that are based on otherwise enforceable obligations. Even if a claim is allowed, however, it does not mean that the claim gets paid, only that it is theoretically eligible to receive a distribution in the bankruptcy.

The treatment of an allowed claim in bankruptcy depends, in the first instance, on whether the claim is secured or not. Secured claims are treated substantially better than unsecured claims. In particular, secured claims can accrue post-bankruptcy interest, which is usually unavailable for other claims. Bankruptcy also generally respects lien and payment priority (but not temporal priority) from applicable non-bankruptcy law, and it also generally allows liens to attach to proceeds, although it does cut off liens on after-acquired property.

Bankruptcy is a legal process, and it presents many opportunities for litigation. Litigation in bankruptcy comes in two flavors procedurally: contested matters and adversary proceedings. A **contested matter** is simply a contested request for relief in the context of the main bankruptcy proceeding. For example, if a creditor moves to lift the automatic stay and the debtor opposes the motion, that is a contested matter. If the motion is unopposed, it is not a contested matter. Contested matters are commenced by the filing of a motion, FED. R. BANKR. PROC. 9014, rather than the filing of a complaint. Filings in contested matters are part of the electronic docket of the bankruptcy case itself.

In contrast, an **adversary proceeding** is a litigation involving one of a set of matters set forth in the Federal Rules of Bankruptcy Procedure. The ones that we will examine are avoidance actions to recover money or property for the estate; suits to determine the validity, priority or extent of a lien; suits to subordinate allowed claims; objections to discharges; and requests for injunctions or other equitable relief. FED. R. BANKR. PROC. 7001. Adversary proceedings are commenced by the filing of a complaint, FED. R. BANKR. PROC. 7003, and are treated as separate legal actions with their own electronic docket; in an adversary proceeding, there is a plaintiff and a defendant, whereas a contested matter merely has a movant and some party opposing the motion. Procedure in adversary proceedings is largely similar to regular federal civil procedure, whereas contested matters have a more streamlined procedure.

Chapter 7 Bankruptcy

What happens next depends on whether a bankruptcy is a Chapter 7 or a Chapter 11 proceeding. Chapter 7 is a liquidation-only process. In a Chapter 7 bankruptcy, the estate is controlled by an independent trustee, but other parties play an important role in the governance of the estate.

The Chapter 7 trustee is responsible for liquidating the assets of the estate and overseeing the distribution of the assets to creditors. The liquidation is generally done through asset sales, with cash distributed to creditors, but the trustee may also distribute non-cash assets. Significantly, bankruptcy law provides a federal sales power that overrides state law limitations on foreclosure sales and the ability of lienholders to effectively veto asset sales on underwater properties. The bankruptcy sale power thus overcomes important impediments to out-of-court restructurings. Moreover, the Chapter 7 trustee is incentivized to maximize sale values in a way that a secured creditor conducting a foreclosure sale is not; the secured creditor recovers only to the extent of its debt, whereas the trustee is trying to maximize recovery for all creditors. There is no particular timeline for a Chapter 7 bankruptcy, but because there is usually little involved beyond liquidating the assets and distributing the liquidation proceeds, it can generally be done fairly expeditiously—in a matter of months in most cases.

Among a debtor's valuable assets may be various unperformed contracts and unexpired leases. The trustee is not allowed to perform certain contracts and leases, but for others, the trustee may decide which to perform and which to breach. Whereas the standard contract law damages rule should make a party in as good a position with performance as with breach, bankruptcy law allows the debtor to pay pennies on the dollar for breached contracts. This lets the trustee cherry-pick which contracts and leases to honor, which is quite valuable for the bankruptcy estate.

In addition to liquidating the debtor's existing assets, the trustee is able to claw certain assets, which the debtor transferred before the bankruptcy filing, back into the bankruptcy estate. The ability to unwind pre-bankruptcy asset transfers is essential to ensuring a fairness of distribution in bankruptcy; without it, debtors could transfer assets to favored creditors on the eve of bankruptcy and bypass the bankruptcy distribution rules. Suits brought by the trustee to claw back assets or avoid certain pre-bankruptcy transfers are sometimes called "avoidance actions."

Avoidance actions are litigation claims and potentially valuable assets of the estate. Unlike many other types of assets, however, their value is often not immediately realizable. Instead, it takes prosecution of litigation, which can take years. Rather than hold up a Chapter 7 distribution while waiting for the resolution of such litigation, a common solution is to place the litigation claims in a trust and distribute shares of the beneficial interest in the trust to creditors in the Chapter 7 liquidation.

Once all of the debtor's assets have been liquidated, they are distributed to creditors according to a statutory priority system. High up in the priority system are the administrative costs of the bankruptcy estate, including attorneys and financial advisors. These costs are the "gravedigger's fee" or "Charon's obol." The statutory prioritization of the administrative costs of the bankruptcy effectively places them on the lower priority creditors, but in so doing, eliminates disputes about who will pay for the costs of the restructuring.

In order to follow a statutory priority system, the allowance and priority of all claims must first be determined. Bankruptcy thus addresses the informational problems of uncertain claims and uncertain priorities that can frustrate out-of-court restructuring. While the priority ladder in Chapter 7 is dictated by statute, courts have certain equitable powers to re-rank claims.

Once the debtor's estate has been fully administered, a Chapter 7 bankruptcy is over. For natural person debtors, a **discharge injunction** prevents creditors from trying to collect on claims that have not been paid in full. The discharge, however, is available only for individuals. For corporate entities, there is no discharge in Chapter 7 (there is in Chapter 11). This means that claims which have not been paid in full are collectible after the bankruptcy. State law limited liability, however, means that there is nothing to collect—all of the debtor's assets have been distributed, and creditors cannot look to the debtor's owners for recourse (absent a guaranty or veil piercing). Notably, although a corporate debtor will have no assets (or at least none of value) after a Chapter 7, it will still exist as a corporate entity. Dissolution of the entity must be done through state law procedures. Figure 12.1, below, shows the timeline of a Chapter 7 bankruptcy.

Figure 12.1 Timeline of a Chapter 7 Bankruptcy

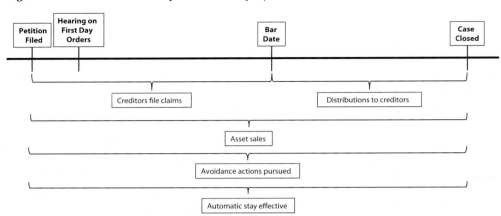

Chapter 11 Bankruptcy

In a Chapter 11 bankruptcy, many things operate just as in Chapter 7 bankruptcy: the filing of a petition, the automatic stay, valuation, claim allowance, secured status, avoidance actions, and equitable changes to priority do not generally change. There are, however, five fundamental differences between Chapter 7 and Chapter 11 bankruptcy.

The first fundamental difference is that whereas an independent trustee always controls the debtor's assets and manages the distribution in Chapter 7, the default arrangement in Chapter 11 is that the existing management remains in place as the **debtor in possession,** with virtually the same rights and duties as a trustee. It is possible for a trustee to be appointed in Chapter 11, but that is an exceptional arrangement. Other parties, particularly **official creditors' committees**, also play an important role in governance in Chapter 11. An official creditors' committee is a device designed to solve a collective action problem for unsecured creditors. Because unsecured creditors are paid on a pro-rated basis, they have limited incentive to be active in a bankruptcy, as the benefits of such activities are shared with other creditors. An official committee is a fiduciary to the creditors whom it represents, and is funded by the estate as an administrative expense, so it forces cost-sharing on unsecured creditors.

The second fundamental difference between Chapter 7 and Chapter 11 is that the distribution to creditors in Chapter 11 is much more flexible than in Chapter 7, although it must meet the baseline distribution of a hypothetical Chapter 7 distribution. As with a Chapter 7 bankruptcy, the ultimate goal of the Chapter 11 process is a distribution to creditors. It is crucial, however, to understand that the distribution need not be of the debtor's actual current assets (cash, etc.). A distribution of all of the debtor's assets—effectively a liquidation—is possible in Chapter 11, but often the distribution is of new debt obligations and/or the equity of the restructured debtor or some combination thereof. Thus, Chapter 11 can be used to restructure the debtor's finances by effectuating an exchange of old debt and old equity for new debt and new equity.

Whereas the Chapter 7 distribution is done according to a detailed statutory priority system, the Chapter 11 distribution is done according to a document known as a **plan**. The plan may either be a plan of liquidation or a plan of reorganization. If the latter, the plan will not propose merely a distribution of the debtor's assets, but a distribution of both assets and claims in the reorganized debtor's capital structure—prepetition creditors and equityholders may be given new notes or equity or warrants (call options) to purchase equity.

The plan is usually proposed by the debtor in possession, which has an exclusive right to propose a plan for a limited time period, but may also be proposed by other parties if the exclusive period has lapsed. There is no time frame required, however, for proposing a plan. The plan typically provides not just for a distribution to creditors, but also other terms relating to the restructuring of the debtor and its operations and the details of how the plan will be implemented—asset sales, litigation settlements and releases, changes to the debtor's corporate charter and bylaws, mergers, etc.

The culmination of the Chapter 11 bankruptcy process is confirmation of the plan by the bankruptcy court. As with plan proposal, there is no time frame required for confirming a plan, and it is not uncommon for multiple plan iterations to be proposed before one is confirmed. Confirmation results in a court order for putting the plan's various provisions into effect, resulting in the lifting of the automatic stay, and the effectiveness of the Chapter 11 discharge injunction (discussed below). The timeline for a standard Chapter 11 plan is shown below in Figure 12.2.

Confirmation of a Chapter 11 plan first requires disclosure of the plan to creditors and equityholders. The disclosure process is regulated in bankruptcy. Bankruptcy

Figure 12.2 Chapter 11 Timeline

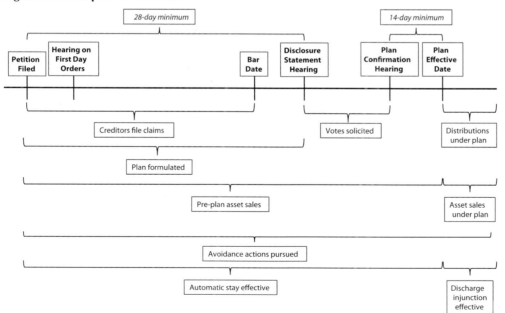

law also regulates the substantive terms of the plan. In order to be confirmed, the court must make numerous findings about the proposed plan. Among the basic plan confirmation requirements is a cross-check against a hypothetical Chapter 7 liquidation baseline. This is why it is necessary to learn Chapter 7 bankruptcy first.

The first plan confirmation requirement is that "the plan complies with the applicable provisions" of the Bankruptcy Code. 11 U.S.C. § 1129(a)(1). This means, among other things, that the plan must comply with certain rules about what must and what may be in a plan. Foremost among these rules is the requirement that a plan place creditors' claims into classes and specify the treatment of each class. The classification rules are important because plan confirmation requires an affirmative creditor vote. The vote is done by class, and standard "consensual" plan confirmation requires an affirmative vote in every class of "impaired" creditors. Classification and impairment rules determine the plan proponent's ability to shape the creditor electorate and gerrymander the vote in its favor.

Generally, voting on a plan occurs only after a **disclosure statement** about the plan has been approved by the court. The Chapter 11 disclosure regime is an antidote to the informational problems that can frustrate out-of-court restructurings, and it is essential for ensuring a vote that actually expresses creditors' real preferences. It is possible, however, to conduct the voting on a plan before the bankruptcy, with the plan and votes both presented to the court for confirmation. In this situation, the bankruptcy disclosure rules do not apply, although other disclosure laws, such as federal and state securities laws, may apply. This procedure employing pre-bankruptcy voting on a plan is called a "prepackaged" bankruptcy. A timeline for a "prepackaged" plan is shown below in Figure 12.3.

Figure 12.3 Prepackaged Chapter 11 Timeline

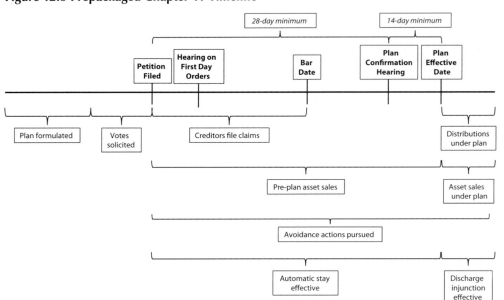

If a plan complies with all of the statutory requirements but does not achieve the requisite creditor majority for every class, it may still be confirmed through an alternative process known as "**cramdown.**" Cramdown confirmation substitutes three additional substantive plan requirements for creditor consent as indicated by a majority vote in every impaired class. Cramdown turns the "property rule" of out-of-court restructuring, under which a creditor can always say "no," to a liability rule, under which a creditor can be forced to accept a restructuring if a minimum "price" (compliance with the cramdown rules) is paid.

The third fundamental difference between Chapter 11 and Chapter 7 is that the debtor firm will continue operating in Chapter 11; in Chapter 7, firms will typically cease operations or go into wind down. While the debtor is operating, it can sell or use its property, including contracts and leases, just as in Chapter 7. Critically, however, asset sales can function as ersatz restructuring of the debtor's assets. All of the desirable assets of a firm can be transferred to a buyer that will continue to operate those assets as a going concern. The consideration paid for those assets and the undesirable assets can then be liquidated, either in Chapter 11 or in Chapter 7.

Once the desirable assets have been sold, plan confirmation is substantially easier because the debtor can credibly threaten a cramdown plan because the equity in the debtor firm, now that it has been denuded of the desirable assets, has only notional option value, and there is unlikely to be a serious contest over control of the "reorganized" rump firm. Thus, the sale functions as the real reorganization, but it is not subject to the plan confirmation requirements. What's more, sales sometimes involve a selective assumption of liabilities, which in turn impacts distributional priority, as the assumed liabilities get paid in full by the buyer rather than treated under a Chapter 11 plan. Thus, while Chapter 11 was designed around a negotiated reorganization plan process, contemporary Chapter 11s frequently follow a different paradigm of reorganization through asset sale coupled with a subsequent liquidating plan.

Continued operations in Chapter 11 (or Chapter 7) necessitate liquidity for the debtor. Financing the debtor while in bankruptcy is a topic covered in Chapter 32 of this textbook, along with so-called **first day orders**—a battery of motions filed at the beginning of a Chapter 11 seeking court authorization of all the various activities necessary to keep the debtor operating: paying the electric company to keep the lights on, continuing using existing cash management systems, continuing customer loyalty programs, etc. Additionally, ongoing operations may necessitate renegotiation of collective bargaining agreements and retiree benefits.

The fourth fundamental difference between Chapter 11 and Chapter 7 is that there is a vibrant market in Chapter 11 bankruptcy claims. It is possible for bankruptcy claims to trade irrespective of chapter, but there is more value to trading in Chapter 11 because the greater uncertainty involved regarding the distribution given the flexibility in terms of the amount and kind of assets distributed and the timing of the distribution, and the ability of creditors to affect plan confirmation through their vote. The presence of a claims trading market facilitates a variety of distressed debt trading strategies and means that the identity of creditors may change throughout the course of a case, which can complicate attempts to assemble stable majorities to support plans. A common response to this problem is the use of restructuring support agreements that bind claimholders and their assigns to supporting a plan that has certain characteristics.

The final fundamental difference between Chapter 11 and Chapter 7 is that there is a discharge available to corporate entities in Chapter 11 (only consumers can get a Chapter 7 discharge, but there are no assets left with the debtor from which creditors can recover after a Chapter 7 case). The discharge injunction goes into effect after plan confirmation and enjoins attempts to collect any pre-confirmation debts except as provided for by the plan. Sometimes Chapter 11 plans include non-debtor releases; this is a controversial issue. Plans can be appealed or modified, but both are difficult procedures.

Bankruptcy is a potentially costly procedure, and more importantly, it is one that cannot be controlled by contract. Accordingly, parties often seek to contract *around* bankruptcy, although not always successfully. The possibilities for restructuring outside of bankruptcy are quite different, however, when there is no possibility of a bankruptcy filing as an alternative.

COMMENCING A
BANKRUPTCY

CHAPTER 13

FILING FOR BANKRUPTCY

I. FILING FOR BANKRUPTCY

Not much is required to start a bankruptcy case. A bankruptcy case is commenced by the filing of a petition with the clerk of the bankruptcy court. FED. R. BANKR. PROC. 1002(a), 9001(3). The bankruptcy court is deemed "always open," for the purpose of filing a petition or any pleading, and petitions can be filed electronically. FED. R. BANKR. PROC. 5001(a). Ironically, the petition must be accompanied by a filing fee—$335 for a Chapter 7 filing, and $1,717 for a Chapter 11 filing. FED. R. BANKR. PROC. 1006; 28 U.S.C. § 1930(a). In other words, you could be too broke to file for bankruptcy! Local court rules determine the form of payment accepted, but credit cards are not always accepted.

The petition may be filed voluntarily by the debtor under section 301 of the Bankruptcy Code, or involuntarily by creditors under section 303. All petitions must be either verified (sworn under oath) by the filer or contain an unsworn declaration that comports with certain legal requirements. FED. R. BANKR. PROC. 1008. The petition must also be signed by the debtor's attorney of record, if there is one. FED. R. BANKR. PROC. 9011(a).

A. Voluntary Bankruptcy Filings

The overwhelming majority of bankruptcy petitions are voluntary. There are no contemporary statistics on the percentage of bankruptcy filings that are voluntary, but anecdotally, nearly all bankruptcy filings are voluntary. With a voluntary petition, no court order is needed to make the petition effective, although it may be later dismissed.

A voluntary petition is a bare-bones three-page form providing only the most minimal information about the debtor.[1] The debtor is required to file with the court a list of creditors and (absent a court order to the contrary) various schedules of assets, liabilities, current income and expenditures, etc. 11 U.S.C. § 521. These schedules do not need to be filed with the petition, and for business entities, however,

---

1. *See* U.S. Courts, Official Form B1, *available at* http://www.uscourts.gov/uscourts/rulesandpolicies/rules/BK_Forms_Official_2010/B_001_0410.pdf.

there is no statutory deadline for filing these schedules. Indeed, for a large multi-national business, assembling the schedules can take a surprising amount of time. This means that at the time a bankruptcy case is filed, there may be very limited information about the debtor's financial condition. It also means that creditors may not receive affirmative notice about the bankruptcy filing for some time—if at all.

All voluntary filings must be authorized by the debtor. *Price v. Gurney*, 324 U.S. 100, 107 (1945). This means that if the debtor is a corporate entity, there must be authorization in accordance with the appropriate state's corporation, partnership, or company law.[3] *Id.* Thus, for a corporation, a bankruptcy filing would require approval by the corporation's board of directors. A filing that has not been authorized might be ratified subsequently, however.

In a voluntary petition, a business debtor chooses whether it wants to seek relief under Chapter 7 or Chapter 11 of the Bankruptcy Code. (Some very small businesses are eligible for Chapter 13.) As we will see later in this book, there are significant differences associated with this choice. A case can be converted from one chapter to another, but for now it is necessary to understand only that Chapter 7 is a liquidation process, whereas Chapter 11 can be either a liquidation process or a reorganization.

B. Involuntary Bankruptcy Filings

Involuntary bankruptcy petitions are filed by a debtor's creditors. The creditors may choose which chapter of the Bankruptcy Code to file the petition under. An involuntary petition is an even more bare-bones two-page form that contains even less information about the debtor, although it does contain some information about the petitioning creditors.[4]

Unlike a voluntary petition, an involuntary petition is not immediately and automatically effective, and only becomes effective when a court enters an order for relief. Instead, the debtor has an opportunity to challenge the involuntary petition, although if it is not timely challenged, then the petition is granted, much like a default judgment. 11 U.S.C. § 303(h). Until the petition is granted, the debtor can go about its business normally. 11 U.S.C. § 303(f).

An involuntary petition must meet two requirements. The first is that it must be filed by a requisite number of creditors holding at least $15,775[5] in noncontingent, undisputed, unsecured claims. 11 U.S.C. § 303(b). Why restrict involuntary petitions just to unsecured creditors? The answer will become more apparent to you as you learn more about the bankruptcy process, but secured creditors are protected in and out of bankruptcy by their liens. They are not harmed if the debtor is wasting or dissipating its other assets, such as through preferential transfers to favored

---

3. Federal Rule of Bankruptcy Procedure 1004 can be interpreted to require that all general partners of a partnership authorize a bankruptcy filing.
4. See U.S. Courts, Official Form B5, *available at* https://bit.ly/2NqUQev.
5. This figure is periodically adjusted for inflation.

creditors. Unsecured creditors, on the other hand, are vulnerable to dissipation and waste, which reduces the assets available for their repayment. (Of course, a secured creditor whose collateral value is declining may have similar concerns, as it is fast becoming an unsecured creditor, at least for part of what it is owed. Such creditors might be able to avail themselves of a receivership, however.)

An involuntary petition requires at least three qualified unsecured creditors on the petition unless there are fewer than 12 such creditors in total, in which case only one creditor is required for a petition. How, though, can creditors determine the number of creditors with at least $15,775 in noncontingent, undisputed, unsecured claims? That information resides generally with the debtor. Thus, unless creditors are very confident that there are only a handful of qualified creditors, they will want to have three creditors on the petition. That itself creates problems. How is a creditor to know who the other qualified creditors are? Again, that information resides with the debtor. There can be significant coordination problems for creditors considering an involuntary bankruptcy petition.

On the other hand, creditors have some potential ability to manipulate the numerosity requirements of section 303(b)(1). A creditor could sell part of a claim to an affiliate, thus increasing the number of creditors. Thus, in a noted case that predates the current Bankruptcy Code, a creditor sold a claim to a wholly owned subsidiary substantially before the filing of the involuntary petition. The Second Circuit held that because the parties had observed the formalities of corporate separateness, they could be counted as separate creditors. *In re Gibraltor Amusements*, 291 F.2d 22 (2d Cir. 1961). Whether this analysis would hold under the current Code and with a transfer on the eve of the petition is uncertain. A more recent case, *In re Iowa Coal Mining Co.*, 242 B.R. 661 (Bankr. S.D. Iowa 1999), treated three separate bonding company creditors as one creditor because their claims were tied together with subrogation and joint obligations.

The minimum dollar threshold of section 303(b)(1) means that debtors cannot be forced into bankruptcy for de minimis obligations. But it also means that creditors owed small amounts of money cannot force the use of the bankruptcy process. (While $15,775 may be a relatively small debt from most businesses' perspective, it is not from the perspective of a consumer or a small business. Consider that median U.S. household income is only around $59,000 as of 2016. Consumers and small businesses are unlikely to incur the costs of filing an involuntary petition with representation of counsel, however, so they may not be meaningfully harmed by the dollar threshold.)

The second requirement for ordering relief on an involuntary bankruptcy petition is that the debtor is "generally not paying [its] debts as such debts become due," unless the debts are the subject of a bona fide dispute. 11 U.S.C. § 303(h)(1). This is what is known as an "equity" insolvency test. But what does it mean to be "generally" not paying debts? Is that determined by reference to the number of debts unpaid, the amount of debts unpaid, the type of the debts unpaid, or some combination thereof? And what is a "bona fide dispute"? It would seem that debtors could frustrate involuntary petitions to some degree by controverting debts. Section 303 is full of questions for which courts have not produced definitive answers.

The lack of clarity about section 303 is particularly troublesome for creditors because there are risks to filing an unsuccessful involuntary petition. If the petition is dismissed other than by unanimous consent, the court may enter a judgment for the debtor against the petitioning creditors for the debtor's costs and, if the creditors acted in bad faith, for proximately caused damages and punitive damages. The court may also require petitioning creditors to post a bond for such possible damages. 11 U.S.C. § 303(f). This means that creditors who have not been paid must come up with money in order to attempt to collect through the bankruptcy process. Section 303's lack of clarity combined with information and coordination problems and the risks it imposes on creditors explains why involuntary petitions are so rare.

II. ELIGIBILITY TO FILE FOR BANKRUPTCY

While anyone may file a bankruptcy petition, not just anyone can obtain more than temporary relief from a bankruptcy court. The Bankruptcy Code restricts who may be a debtor, and the petitions of ineligible debtors may be dismissed. 11 U.S.C. § 109. Excluded from bankruptcy relief are regulated entities with their own insolvency regimes, such as depositaries and insurance companies. Sovereigns are also excluded from bankruptcy. This includes U.S. states, the District of Columbia, and the Commonwealth of Puerto Rico, but does not exclude municipalities or other local government units, although their ability to file must be authorized by state law.

Additionally, to be eligible for bankruptcy, a filer must be a "person," as defined by the Bankruptcy Code. 11 U.S.C. § 101(41). For flesh-and-blood people and for many legal entities, such as corporations, partnerships, and limited liability companies, this is not an issue, but it is for certain types of trusts, an issue explored later in Chapter 43, regarding contracting around bankruptcy. U.S. domicile is not required for bankruptcy eligibility—at least not formally. Instead, there must be either domicile or a place of business or property in the United States *at the time of the bankruptcy filing* for eligibility.

The property alternative opens the door of United States courts to foreign debtors. Thus Yukos, a Russian petroleum company, filed for bankruptcy in the Southern District of Texas in 2004 based on a $480 million bank deposit in an account held by a newly created U.S. subsidiary and its American CFO's Houston home, which had been used as the CFO's office for the previous ten days. Yukos's filing was an attempt to avoid a $27.5 billion Russian tax judgment that came as part of a Russian-government campaign to nationalize the company and silence Yukos's politically outspoken principal owner, Mikhail Khodorkovsky, who had challenged Russian President Vladimir Putin. While the filing was upheld as allowed under section 109, it was nevertheless dismissed under the court's broad discretionary "for cause" dismissal power. 11 U.S.C. § 1112(b). *See In re Yukos Oil Co.*, 321 B.R. 396 (Bankr. S.D. Tex. 2005).

Similarly, a Singapore-based debtor that had issued bonds under a New York law governed indenture, which named a New York bank as indenture trustee and consented to jurisdiction in New York courts, was eligible to file for bankruptcy in the United States because the intangible property rights that existed under the indenture, which was subject to New York law, were situated in New York. *In re Berau Cap. Res. Pte Ltd.*, 540 B.R. 80 (Bankr. S.D.N.Y. 2015) (noting the irony that would result if there was no bankruptcy eligibility, as the creditors could sue on the indenture in New York, but not restructure the debt there). Thus, as long as the debtor is a "person," the domicile, place of business, or property requirement is not likely to be much of an obstacle.

III. GOOD FAITH

While the Bankruptcy Code itself does not impose many requirements for filing, a federal common law of bankruptcy has developed that has grafted on additional non-statutory requirements to the Bankruptcy Code. As we will see repeatedly, the status of these uncodified provisions of bankruptcy law is sometimes in question, but non-Code law is still an important part of bankruptcy law and practice.

In re SGL Carbon Corp.
200 F.3d 154 (3d Cir. 1999)

SCIRICA, Circuit Judge.

The issue on appeal is whether, on the facts of this case, a Chapter 11 bankruptcy petition filed by a financially healthy company in the face of potentially significant civil antitrust liability complies with the requirements of the Bankruptcy Code. In this case, the Official Committee of Unsecured Creditors of SGL Carbon Corporation appeals the District Court's order denying its motion to dismiss SGL Carbon's Chapter 11 bankruptcy petition on bad faith grounds.

This case also presents the threshold issue whether we will adopt a "good faith" requirement for Chapter 11 petitions. We will. After undertaking the fact intensive analysis inherent in the good faith determination, we conclude that SGL Carbon's Chapter 11 petition lacks a valid reorganizational purpose and, therefore, lacks the requisite good faith. We will reverse.

SGL Carbon is a Delaware corporation that manufactures and sells graphite electrodes used in steel production. In 1997, the United States Department of Justice commenced an investigation of alleged price-fixing by graphite electrode manufacturers, including the SGL Carbon Group. Soon thereafter, various steel producers filed class action antitrust lawsuits in the United States District Court for the Eastern District of Pennsylvania against SGL Carbon and other graphite electrode manufacturers.

In June 1998, SGL Carbon's German parent SGL AG recorded a charge in Deutschmarks of approximately $240 million as its "best estimate" of the SGL Carbon Group's potential liability in the criminal and civil antitrust litigation.

On December 16, 1998, at the direction of SGL AG, SGL Carbon filed a voluntary Chapter 11 bankruptcy petition in the United States District Court for Delaware. In

SGL Carbon's Disclosure Statement, in a section addressing "Factors Leading to [the] Chapter 11 Filing," SGL Carbon only discussed the antitrust litigation. The bankruptcy filing contained a proposed reorganization plan under which only one type of creditor would be required to accept less than full cash payment for its account, namely the antitrust plaintiffs who obtained judgments against SGL Carbon. Under the plan, potential antitrust judgment creditors would receive credits against future purchases of SGL Carbon's product valid for 30 months following the plan's confirmation. The proposed plan also bars any claimant from bringing an action against SGL Carbon's affiliates, including its parent SGL AG, "based on, relating to, arising out of, or in any way connected with" their claims against SGL Carbon.

The next day, on December 17, in a press release, SGL Carbon explained it had filed for bankruptcy "to protect itself against excessive demands made by plaintiffs in civil antitrust litigation and in order to achieve an expeditious resolution of the claims against it." The press release also stated:

> SGL CARBON Corporation believes that in its case Chapter 11 protection provides the most effective and efficient means for resolving the civil antitrust claims. . . .

> "SGL CARBON Corporation is financially healthy," said Wayne T. Burgess, SGL CARBON Corporation's president. "If we did not face [antitrust] claims for such excessive amounts, we would not have had to file for Chapter 11. We expect to continue our normal business operations." . . .

However, because certain plaintiffs continue to make excessive and unreasonable demands, SGL CARBON Corporation believes the prospects of ever reaching a commercially practicable settlement with them are remote. After much consideration, SGL CARBON Corporation determined that the most appropriate course of action to address the situation without harming its business was to voluntarily file for Chapter 11 protection. . . .

Contemporaneous with the press release, SGL AG Chairman Robert Koehler conducted a telephone conference call with securities analysts, stating that SGL Carbon was "financially healthier" than before and denying the antitrust litigation was "starting to have a material impact on [SGL Carbon's] ongoing operations in the sense that . . . [it was] starting to lose market share." He also stated that SGL Carbon's Chapter 11 petition was "fairly innovative [and] creative" because "usually Chapter 11 is used as protection against serious insolvency or credit problems, which is not the case [with SGL Carbon's petition]."

[The court first followed a number of prior decisions in holding that a Chapter 11 case is subject to dismissal if not filed in good faith.]

[T]he District Court found SGL Carbon's Chapter 11 petition was filed in good faith for two reasons: first, because the distractions caused by the antitrust litigation "posed a

---

11. Although we conclude these findings were clearly erroneous, we do not hold that under the proper circumstances managerial distraction and other litigation harms may not constitute factors contributing to good faith.

serious threat to [SGL Carbon's] continued successful operations," and second, because the litigation might result in a judgment that could cause the company "financial and operational ruin," SGL was required to file when it did. *SGL Carbon,* 233 B.R. at 291. Although mindful of the careful consideration given by the able District Court, we believe each of these findings of fact was clearly erroneous.[11]

Although there is some evidence that defending against the antitrust litigation occupied some officers' time, there is no evidence this "distraction" posed a "serious threat" to the company's operational well being.

We also find clearly erroneous that SGL Carbon's Chapter 11 petition was filed at the appropriate time to avoid the possibility of a significant judgment that "could very well force [SGL Carbon] out of business." There is no evidence that the possible antitrust judgments might force SGL Carbon out of business. To the contrary, the record is replete with evidence of SGL Carbon's economic strength. At the time of filing, SGL Carbon's assets had a stipulated book value of $400 million, only $100,000 of which was encumbered. On the date of the petition, SGL Carbon had $276 million in fixed and non-disputed liabilities. Of those liabilities, only $26 million were held by outsiders as the remaining liabilities were either owed to or guaranteed by SGL AG. Although SGL Carbon's parent, SGL AG, recorded a $240 million charge on its books as "its best estimate of the potential liability and expenses of the SGL Carbon Group in connection with all civil and criminal antitrust matters," SGL Carbon is only one part of the SGL Carbon Group covered by the reserve. Furthermore, at the time SGL Carbon filed its petition, that is, before SGL AG paid its $135 million criminal fine, the $240 million reserve was untouched. In documents accompanying its petition, SGL Carbon estimated the liquidation value of the antitrust claims at $54 million. In contrast, no evidence was presented with respect to the amount sought by the antitrust plaintiffs beyond SGL Carbon's repeated characterization of their being "unreasonable."

Whether or not SGL Carbon faces a potentially crippling antitrust judgment, it is incorrect to conclude it had to file when it did. As noted, SGL Carbon faces no immediate financial difficulty.

The District Court was correct in noting that the Bankruptcy Code encourages early filing. It is well established that a debtor need not be insolvent before filing for bankruptcy protection. It also is clear that the drafters of the Bankruptcy Code understood the need for early access to bankruptcy relief to allow a debtor to rehabilitate its business before it is faced with a hopeless situation. Such encouragement, however, does not open the door to premature filing, nor does it allow for the filing of a bankruptcy petition that lacks a valid reorganizational purpose.

SGL Carbon, therefore, is correct that the Bankruptcy Code does not require specific evidence of insolvency for a voluntary Chapter 11 filing. But SGL Carbon cites no case holding that petitions filed by financially healthy companies cannot be subject to dismissal for cause. At any rate, as we explain more fully, SGL Carbon's ability to meet its debts is but one of many factors compelling the conclusion it did not enter Chapter 11 with a valid reorganizational purpose.

We do not hold that a company cannot file a valid Chapter 11 petition until after a massive judgment has been entered against it. Courts have allowed companies to seek the protections of bankruptcy when faced with pending litigation that posed a serious threat to the companies' long term viability.

Although SGL Carbon may have to file for bankruptcy in the future, such an attenuated possibility standing alone is not sufficient to establish the good faith of its present petition.

We also consider whether other evidence establishes the good faith of SGL Carbon's petition, that is, whether the totality of facts and circumstances support a finding of good faith. Courts have not been unanimous about what constitutes "good faith" in the Chapter 11 filing context.

Courts, therefore, have consistently dismissed Chapter 11 petitions filed by financially healthy companies with no need to reorganize under the protection of Chapter 11.

The absence of a valid reorganizational purpose and the consequent lack of good faith by SGL Carbon is evident here. SGL Carbon's financial disclosure documents give no indication the company needed to reorganize under Chapter 11 protection. Prior to filing, SGL Carbon had assets of $400 million and liabilities of only $276 million, or a net worth of $124 million. In addition, there is no evidence that SGL Carbon had difficulty meeting its debts as they came due, that it had any overdue debts, or that it had defaulted on any debts. Nor is there any evidence that SGL had any difficulty raising or borrowing money, or otherwise had impaired access to the capital markets.

Statements by SGL Carbon and its officials confirm the company did not need to reorganize under Chapter 11.

We are not convinced by SGL Carbon's claim that a Chapter 11 filing was necessary because we see no evidence the antitrust litigation was significantly harming its business relationships with the antitrust plaintiffs. For example, none of SGL Carbon's officers stated that any customer terminated its purchases from the company because of the litigation. As noted, SGL AG Chairman Koehler denied the litigation was having a material impact on SGL Carbon's customer relationships.

Based on the facts and circumstances of this case, we conclude SGL Carbon's Chapter 11 petition lacks a valid reorganizational purpose and consequently lacks good faith making it subject to dismissal "for cause" under 11 U.S.C. § 1112(b).

In reaching our conclusion, we are cognizant that it is growing increasingly difficult to settle large scale litigation. We recognize that companies that face massive potential liability and litigation costs continue to seek ways to rapidly conclude litigation to enable a continuation of their business and to maintain access to the capital markets. As evidenced by SGL Carbon's actions in this case, the Bankruptcy Code presents an inviting safe harbor for such companies. But this lure creates the possibility of abuse which must be guarded against to protect the integrity of the bankruptcy system and the rights of all involved in such proceedings. Allowing SGL Carbon's bankruptcy under these circumstances seems to us a significant departure from the use of Chapter 11 to validly reorganize financially troubled businesses.

For the reasons stated, we will reverse the judgment of the District Court and remand to the District Court so that it may dismiss SGL Carbon's Chapter 11 petition.

Study Notes and Questions

1. In a subsequent case, *Solow v. PPI Enterprises (U.S.), Inc.* (*In re PPI Enterprises (U.S.), Inc.*), 324 F.3d 197 (3d Cir. 2002), the Third Circuit held that a bankruptcy plan filed for the primary purpose of capping a landlord's allowed claim against the debtor under section 502(b)(6) was not filed in bad faith. The Third Circuit noted that this was not an unintended use of section 502(b)(6), but rather exactly the intended purpose of the cap on landlord's claims. Can *Solow* be reconciled with *SGL Carbon*?

2. The Bankruptcy Code does not currently contain a statutory good faith filing requirement for Chapters 7 or 11, but it does for Chapter 13, a chapter authorizing consumer debtor repayment plans. For a Chapter 13 plan to be confirmed, the court must find that "the action of the debtor in filing the petition was in good faith." 11 U.S.C. § 1325(a)(7). Does the inclusion of this provision in Chapter 13 indicate that Congress did not intend a good faith filing requirement for other chapters of the Bankruptcy Code?

3. Good faith filing doctrine appears to apply to involuntary petitions as well as voluntary petitions. The Bankruptcy Code allows damages to be assessed against a party that filed an involuntary petition in bad faith *if the petition is dismissed,* 11 U.S.C. § 303(i)(2), but that suggests that bad faith is not grounds itself for the dismissal. Yet in *In re Forever Green Athletic Fields, Inc.,* 804 F.3d 328 (3d Cir. 2015), the court held that an involuntary petition may be dismissed as filed in bad faith if it was filed as "a litigation tactic or to collect a debt ahead of other creditors, contrary to bankruptcy's collective action spirit, or for retribution might constitute bad faith. Here, the creditor's effort to prevent the arbitration, collect his own claim and prevent other creditors from being paid through a potential arbitration award against the creditor constituted bad faith and justified dismissal." How is this likely to affect parties' calculus about filing involuntary petitions?

IV. VENUE

Do you recall from Chapter 1 where Chrysler filed for bankruptcy? In the Southern District of New York. Does that strike you as strange? Isn't Chrysler a "Detroit" firm? What's its connection to the Southern District of New York? (Hint: It doesn't have anything to do with the Chrysler Building.) How about General Motors, which also filed for bankruptcy in the Southern District of New York?

The bankruptcy venue statute, 28 U.S.C. § 1413, gives debtors a great deal of flexibility regarding where they file. A debtor may file in the district where for the longest part of the previous 180 days it had its "domicile, residence, principal place of business in the United States, or principal assets in the United States." 28 U.S.C. § 1413(1). Additionally, however, a debtor may file in the district "in which there is pending a case under title 11 concerning the person's affiliate, general partner, or partnership." 28 U.S.C. § 1413(2). This second clause allows the debtor to "bootstrap" itself into venue via the filing of an affiliate. Thus, Eastern Airlines, which was Miami-based, first filed the petition of Ionosphere Clubs, its frequent-flier club affiliate that was based in the Southern District of New York. Eastern filed its own petition six minutes later, with venue appropriate in the Southern District under section 1413(2). Likewise, Enron, a Houston-based energy company filed in the Southern District of New York based on a small affiliate that was incorporated in Delaware but with its principal place of business in New York. The affiliate employed in New York only 63 employees of Enron's 25,000-person workforce. *In re Enron Corp.*, 274 B.R. 327 (Bankr. S.D.N.Y. 2002) (denying venue transfer motion). And General Motors first filed its wholly-owned dealer subsidiary, Chevrolet-Saturn of Harlem, in order to bootstrap itself into venue in the Southern District of New York.

Other debtors have ignored the statute entirely. Thus, Borders bookstore filed in the Southern District of New York without any affiliate domiciled, residing, or having principal assets or principal place of business in Manhattan. No one objected, and improper venue does not deprive a court of jurisdiction. Federal Rule of Bankruptcy Procedure 1014 provides for a situation of improper venue, but it is not a mandatory provision.

Federal Rule of Bankruptcy Procedure 1014

Dismissal and Change of Venue

If a petition is filed in an improper district, the court, on the timely motion of a party in interest or on its own motion . . . may dismiss the case or transfer it to any other district if the court determines that transfer is in the interest of justice or for the convenience of the parties.

Why might no one object to improper venue? Let's leave aside the question of the court raising the issue *sua sponte* or the United States Trustee objecting. Some creditors might well like the venue. Others might not, but if they are smaller and less sophisticated they might not notice the venue flaw or have the resources to challenge it. But even if a sophisticated, well-heeled creditor notices the venue problem, it might not be worthwhile to raise a challenge. Consider this scenario. Let's say that a venue challenge would cost $100,000. No creditor will bring such a challenge unless it knows it will get at least $100,001 worth of benefit. This means there could be lots of creditors who would get $99,999 worth of benefit, but none would bring the motion. Added up, this could be a lot of money. Given that there is a litigation risk involved, the benefit of winning the motion would actually have to be substantially more than the cost involved, and benefits are often uncertain. Thus, very legitimate objections to venue might not be brought because they aren't worth the candle.

There are numerous reasons why a firm might want to file in a particular district. Some are perfectly reasonable, while others are more problematic. Consider the non-exclusive possibilities:

- There might be favorable law for the debtor in that district. For example, a debtor with labor issues might want to avoid the Third Circuit.
- There might be a mass of judicial expertise in a particular district; the Southern District of New York and the District of Delaware have significant experience in handling large, complex cases.

- Judges in some districts are known for being incredibly flexible in scheduling hearings, including holding telephonic hearings from home in the middle of the night if necessary.
- The debtor might want to end up with a particular judge (possible by filing in certain offices in certain districts, e.g., a filing in Reno, Nevada will end up with a particular judge).
- The debtor might not want hearings to be convenient for disgruntled employees. (There are no auto plants in Manhattan.)
- There might be convenience factors for the debtor and its professionals—the debtor's attorneys and financial advisers might not want to shlep around the country (the costs of which would be borne by creditors).
- There might also be convenience factors for creditors and their attorneys.
- Attorneys' fees might play a role. Some courts might be more willing to approve higher attorneys' fees than others. A New York court is less likely to balk at a $1,000/hr rate than one in Montana.

Professor Lynn LoPucki has controversially suggested that the ability of debtors to choose venue has led to a type of destructive competition between bankruptcy courts trying to attract "business" either for judges' personal prestige or to bring in revenue for the local bar, and that this competition is corrupting the outcomes of bankruptcy cases. LYNN M. LOPUCKI, COURTING FAILURE: HOW COMPETITION FOR BIG CASES IS CORRUPTING THE BANKRUPTCY COURTS (2006).

In more recent years, however, both the Southern District of New York and the District of Delaware have shown a willingness to dismiss venue when venue is inappropriate. *See In re Patriot Coal Corp.*, 482 B.R. 718 (Bankr. S.D.N.Y. 2012) (transferring venue of coal company debtor); *In re Qualteq, Inc.*, 2012 Bankr. Lexis 503 (Bankr. D. Del. Feb. 16, 2012) (order venue transfer because of debtors' obvious attempt to "escape" the forum best suited for administration of its case).

An important corollary to the debtor's substantial ability to pick the venue of the case is that bankruptcy law provides for nationwide service of process. FED. R. BANKR. PROC. 7004(d).

Federal Rule of Bankruptcy Procedure 7004

. . .

(d) Nationwide Service of Process. The summons and complaint and all other process except a subpoena may be served anywhere in the United States.

(f) Personal Jurisdiction. If the exercise of jurisdiction is consistent with the Constitution and laws of the United States, serving a summons or filing a waiver of service in accordance with this rule . . . is effective to establish personal jurisdiction over the person of any defendant with respect to a case under the Code or a civil proceeding arising under the Code, or arising in or related to a case under the Code.

Rule 7004 means that creditors can be forced to litigate bankruptcy-related litigation ("proceeding[s] arising under title 11 or arising in or related to a case under title 11") in a jurisdiction with which they have no connection. 28 U.S.C. § 1409. Normal rules of personal jurisdiction simply do not apply. *See* Jeffery T. Ferriell, *The Perils of Nationwide Service of Process in a Bankruptcy Context*, 48 Wash. & Lee L. Rev. 1199 (1991). For example, a California-based creditor might have done business with a California-based, California-incorporated company that is located in the same city as the creditor. The California debtor firm, however, is affiliated with a Delaware entity. The Delaware entity files for bankruptcy first and bootstraps the California affiliate into Delaware venue. Despite having no connections to Delaware and no basis for personal jurisdiction in Delaware, the California creditor will be forced to litigate in the Delaware bankruptcy court absent extraordinary facts. The same would be true not just for the California creditor, but also for a Taiwanese creditor firm. The idea behind nationwide service of process is to marshal all claims against the debtor into a single forum for adjudication, just as bankruptcy marshals all of the debtor's assets into the court's jurisdiction, as addressed in the next chapter.

Problem Set 13

(1) It's 10 P.M., and you're checking your e-mail before you go to sleep. You see an urgent message from the general counsel of your firm's marquee client, Pentucky Oil, asking you to call her at home. You know that a $10 billion judgment was recently entered against Pentucky in a state trial court, but you were sure it would be overturned on appeal. When you call the general counsel, she tells you that Pentucky was prepared to file its appeal when it learned that it must post a bond for the entire judgment amount. The appellate deadline is at midnight. There's no way that Pentucky will be able to assemble the cash for a bond before the deadline, but a bankruptcy filing might buy it some space. How fast can you get the petition filed? What will you need to do? What will Pentucky need to do? Are you worried about your law license if something is inaccurate in the petition? Are you concerned that the courts are closed at this hour? Fed. R. Bankr. Proc. 1002(a), 1006, 5001(a), 9011(a)-(b).

(2) You are advising Fireshield Asbestos Corporation, which has just been sued for tortious interference with contract by Texoil Corporation after it swooped in and purchased Petty Fibreboard Corporation, shortly after Petty announced that it would be merging with Texoil. You're pretty sure that Fireshield Asbestos will lose the tortious interference suit and may face billions in damages. Other than the Texoil suit, Fireshield is a profitable enterprise. Rick Bettan, the CEO of Fireshield Asbestos wonders if there's some trick for getting rid of the Texoil suit. "Perhaps we could 'reorganize' in bankruptcy, with a plan that pays all creditors in full other than Texoil." Bettan tells you, "We'd have to do some messaging, of course, to let our suppliers know that they have nothing to worry about, but I'm sure our communications office can handle that." Do you see any issues with this plan? Would your advice change after Texoil obtains a judgment? *In re SGL Carbon Corp.; Solow v. PPI Enterprises.*

(3) You are outside counsel to Aperture, a national chain of clothing stores that is thinking of filing for bankruptcy. Aperture's holding company is a Colorado corporation, but Aperture is headquartered in Portland, Oregon, and has corporate subsidiaries incorporated in Arizona, Delaware, and Maine. All of the subsidiaries are headquartered in Portland. Aperture has two large unionized factories. One is in Delaware and the other in Oregon. Aperture expects to try to renegotiate its collective bargaining agreement with its union while in bankruptcy. Aperture has lined up financing to operate in bankruptcy from the New York branch of the Fiduciary Fidelity Bank, an august London institution. FFB also happens to be Aperture's largest pre-petition creditor. You have a good relationship with the case manager at FFB, whose office is just across the street from yours. When he asks you where you are planning on filing the bankruptcy, what do you say? 28 U.S.C. § 1413.

(4) Phizzy, Inc., a beverage manufacturer, is a Delaware corporation, with its principal place of business in Florida, but with a small Alaska-based subsidiary. Colada, Inc., is a Delaware corporation with its principal place of business in the U.S. Virgin Islands. Bubalah, Inc. is a supplier to Phizzy, Inc. The only jurisdictions in which Colada, Inc. does business are Florida and the U.S. Virgin Islands.

    a. Outside of bankruptcy, if Phizzy wished to sue Bubalah, Inc. for breach of contract, where could it bring suit with proper venue? 28 U.S.C. § 1391.

    b. Phizzy, Inc. filed for Chapter 11 in the District of Alaska. Prior to filing, Phizzy, Inc. had made a payment to Bubalah, Inc. Where is proper venue for Phizzy, Inc., acting as a debtor-in-possession (essentially a trustee) to bring suit against Bubalah, Inc. to recover the payment as a voidable preference? Fed. R. Bankr. Proc. 7004(d), (f).

(5) Admiral Properties, Inc. is the holding company for a vast empire of over 200 shopping malls in 44 states. Admiral controls a variety of subsidiary entities, each of which in turn directly owns a separately incorporated "project-level" mall property. Admiral takes a nationwide, integrated approach to the development, operation, and management of its properties, offering centralized leasing, marketing, management, cash management, property maintenance, and construction management. Most of Admiral's debt is mortgage debt at the project-level entities. The individual project-level obligations are also guarantied by the holding company. Most of the mortgages have cross-default clauses such that a default of the holding company guarantor is a default on the project-level obligation.

Most of the Admiral entities are current on their obligations, but a pair of Admiral entities defaulted, and their defaults triggered cross-defaults on certain other Admiral entities. Admiral's efforts to restructure the debts were unsuccessful in large part because the defaults occured at a time when capital markets were largely frozen due to a financial crisis triggered by an impasse over the U.S. government debt ceiling. The crisis both pushed down property valuations and made it difficult to find financing of any sort. Faced with these uncured defaults, Admiral and its entire corporate family filed for bankruptcy protection.

A mortgagee on one of the non-defaulted, project-level mortgages has moved to dismiss the bankruptcy filing of its project-level debtors on the basis that the project-level debtor's filing was not in good faith. You represent Admiral Properties. What is your response?

(6) Kenji Takeuchi, the general counsel at Hyde Park Associates LP, a mid-sized hedge fund, is on the phone. Your firm has done legal work for Hyde Park before, and Kenji is hoping you can help him out again. "Here's the problem," he says. "We made a $5 million installment loan to Lakeside Ventures, a real estate development firm that concentrates on 'revitalizing' impoverished neighborhoods. Since the housing market downturn this year, Lakeside hasn't made a payment on their loan. They're three months in arrears, and we're prepared to accelerate the balance. I've heard that Lakeside has been selling off its properties at firesale prices, but I don't know where the money is going. I'm also worried that Lakeside might be paying dividends or other creditors. In particular, I know Lakeside has a $30 million loan from its parent Shoreline Capital." Kenji is worried that Lakeside will dissipate its assets long before Hyde Park is able to obtain a judgment. "By the time we go to execute, there'll be nothing left to recover," wails Kenji. What do you advise? 11 U.S.C. § 303; receivership statutes (see Chapter 7).

(7) You were recently invited to join a World Bank advisory committee on debtor-creditor laws. At the first meeting of the committee, you found yourself talking with an attorney from South Africa. She tells you that she was surprised to learn that the United States does not require insolvency as a precondition of bankruptcy relief. She's curious why. What do you tell her? 11 U.S.C. §§ 109, 303.

CHAPTER 14

PROPERTY OF THE ESTATE

I. THE BANKRUPTCY ESTATE

The filing of a bankruptcy petition automatically creates a new federal juridical entity, known as the **bankruptcy estate**, that accedes to most of the debtor's property interests. 11 U.S.C. § 541. The geographic location or physical control of the property is immaterial, and property held by other parties must be surrendered. 11 U.S.C. §§ 542, 543. The bankruptcy estate also accedes to the debtor's legal rights, such as the ability to raise those defenses the debtor could raise. 11 U.S.C. § 558. For individual debtors, certain property is exempted from the estate, but not so for firms. 11 U.S.C. § 522.

The bankruptcy estate is the corpus of a trust held for the benefit of creditors and shareholders (holders of "interests" in bankruptcy parlance). While the Bankruptcy Code does not refer to the estate as a trust corpus, it is managed by a "trustee" or a party that assumes the rights and duties of a trustee. 11 U.S.C. §§ 701-704, 1104-1108.

The importance here is not the metaphysics of the bankruptcy estate, but to recognize that it is a separate legal entity from the pre-petition debtor. The juridical separateness of the bankruptcy estate has a number of important implications that we shall see.

Most importantly, because of the deemed transfer of the debtor's property to the bankruptcy estate, the property of the estate is not the debtor's property to manage as he or she wishes. Instead, the property of the estate is held in trust by the trustee for the benefit of creditors and interest holders. This means that the estate's corporate governance must be in the interests of the creditors and interest holders. More generally, as we shall see, the separateness of the bankruptcy estate implicates the ability of the debtor to bind the estate via pre-petition actions; the debtor cannot waive the estate's rights, which are determined by federal law. (The trustee can waive the estate's rights, but that is a separate issue.)

Section 541 creates an incredibly broad definition of the bankruptcy estate. It covers "all legal or equitable interest of the debtor in property as of the commencement of the case" "wherever located and by whomever held." 11 U.S.C. § 541(a)(1). It includes proceeds or rents from the property, and any interest in property the estate acquires after the bankruptcy filing. 11 U.S.C. § 541(a)(6)-(7). The estate's interest in the property, however, is limited to the debtor's interest; thus, if the debtor only held legal title to property, but not the beneficial interest in the property, only the legal title, not the beneficial interest, would be property of the estate. 11 U.S.C. § 541(d). The regular property law rule of *nemo dat*—that one can only give what one has— still applies to the deemed transfer to the estate.

Section 541 explicitly excludes certain property interests from the estate. Most are not relevant for our purposes, other than the exclusion of funds designated for contribution to retirement and health insurance plans. 11 U.S.C. § 541(b)(7).

Finally, section 541(c)(1) provides that non-bankruptcy law or contractual provisions that purport to restrict or prevent the deemed transfer of the debtor's property to the estate are ineffective. An exception exists that respects otherwise enforceable terms restricting the alienability of beneficial trust interests. 11 U.S.C. § 541(c)(2). This exception covers what are known as "spendthrift" trusts, which restrict the alienability of the beneficial trust interests. These sorts of trusts are commonly set up by parents for prodigal sons to ensure that their patrimony will not be bartered away, but also include other trusts such as ERISA-qualified pension trusts. *See* 26 U.S.C. § 401(a)(13). Notice that such a restriction only covers the transfer of the beneficial interest in the trust itself. Any funds paid out by the trust would be freely alienable. By analogy, a spendthrift trust prevents the sale of the right to milk the cow, but not the actual sale of the milk.

Sections 542 and 543 go hand in glove with section 541. Whereas section 541 sets forth the property of the estate, sections 542 (for non-custodians of property) and 543 (for custodians of property) provide that anyone who is holding estate property must turn it over to the trustee managing the estate. This includes parties who were holding the debtor's property without the consent of the debtor.

Sections 541 through 543 form one of the two main procedural pillars of bankruptcy law, namely the marshaling of all of the debtor's assets into the estate. In the next chapter we shall see the other pillar, which marshals all of the claims against the debtor into a single forum. Together, these provisions are designed to lay the groundwork for a single, orderly process of distributing the debtor's assets among creditors.

The following cases illustrate the breadth of the concept of "property of the estate" under section 541.

United States v. Whiting Pools, Inc.

462 U.S. 198 (1983)

Justice BLACKMUN delivered the opinion of the Court.

Promptly after the Internal Revenue Service (IRS or Service) seized respondent's property to satisfy a tax lien, respondent filed a petition for reorganization under the Bankruptcy [Code]. The issue before us is whether § 542(a) of that Code authorized the Bankruptcy Court to subject the IRS to a turnover order with respect to the seized property.

I.

A.

Respondent Whiting Pools, Inc., a corporation, sells, installs, and services swimming pools and related equipment and supplies. As of January 1981, Whiting owed approximately $92,000 in Federal Insurance Contribution Act taxes and federal taxes withheld from its employees, but had failed to respond to assessments and demands for payment by the IRS. As a consequence, a tax lien in that amount attached to all of Whiting's property.

On January 14, 1981, the Service seized Whiting's tangible personal property—equipment, vehicles, inventory, and office supplies—pursuant to the levy and distraint provision of the Internal Revenue Code of 1954. According to uncontroverted findings, the estimated liquidation value of the property seized was, at most, $35,000, but its estimated going-concern value in Whiting's hands was $162,876. The very next day, January 15, Whiting filed a petition for reorganization, under the Bankruptcy Code's Chapter 11 in the United States Bankruptcy Court for the Western District of New York. Whiting was continued as debtor-in-possession.

The United States, intending to proceed with a tax sale of the property,[4] moved in the Bankruptcy Court for a declaration that the automatic stay provision of the Bankruptcy Code, § 362(a), is inapplicable to the IRS or, in the alternative, for relief from the stay. Whiting counterclaimed for an order requiring the Service to turn the seized property over to the bankruptcy estate pursuant to § 542(a) of the Bankruptcy Code.[5]

Whiting intended to use the property in its reorganized business.

B.

The Bankruptcy Court determined that the IRS was bound by the automatic stay provision. *In re Whiting Pools, Inc.*, 10 B.R. 755 (1981). Because it found that the seized property was essential to Whiting's reorganization effort, it refused to lift the stay. . . . [T]he court directed the IRS to turn the property over to Whiting on the condition that Whiting provide the Service with specified protection for its interests.[7]

---

4. Section 6335, as amended, of the 1954 Code, 26 U.S.C. § 6335, provides for the sale of seized property after notice. The taxpayer is entitled to any surplus of the proceeds of the sale. § 6342(b).

5. Section 542(a) provides in relevant part:

[An] entity, other than a custodian, in possession, custody, or control, during the case, of property that the trustee may use, sell, or lease under section 363 of this title, or that the debtor may exempt under section 522 of this title, shall deliver to the trustee, and account for, such property or the value of such property, unless such property is of inconsequential value or benefit to the estate.

7. Section 363(e) of the Bankruptcy Code provides:

Notwithstanding any other provision of this section, at any time, on request of an entity that has an interest in property used, sold, or leased, or proposed to be used, sold, or leased, by the trustee, the court shall prohibit or condition such use, sale, or lease as is necessary to provide adequate protection of such interest. In any hearing under this section, the trustee has the burden of proof on the issue of adequate protection.

Pursuant to this section, the Bankruptcy Court set the following conditions to protect the tax lien: Whiting was to pay the Service $20,000 before the turnover occurred; Whiting also was to pay $1,000 a month until the taxes were satisfied; the IRS was to retain its lien during this period; and if Whiting failed to make the payments, the stay was to be lifted.

The United States District Court reversed, holding that a turnover order against the Service was not authorized by § 542(a). The United States Court of Appeals for the Second Circuit, in turn, reversed the District Court. It held that a turnover order could issue against the Service under § 542(a), and it remanded the case for reconsideration of the adequacy of the Bankruptcy Court's protection conditions.

II.

By virtue of its tax lien, the Service holds a secured interest in Whiting's property. We first examine whether § 542(a) of the Bankruptcy Code generally authorizes the turnover of a debtor's property seized by a secured creditor prior to the commencement of reorganization proceedings. Section 542(a) requires an entity in possession of "property that the trustee may use, sell, or lease under section 363" to deliver that property to the trustee. Subsections (b) and (c) of § 363 authorize the trustee to use, sell, or lease any "property of the estate," subject to certain conditions for the protection of creditors with an interest in the property. Section 541(a)(1) defines the "estate" as "comprised of all the following property, wherever located: . . . all legal or equitable interests of the debtor in property as of the commencement of the case." Although these statutes could be read to limit the estate to those "interests of the debtor in property" at the time of the filing of the petition, we view them as a definition of what is included in the estate, rather than as a limitation.

A.

In proceedings under the reorganization provisions of the Bankruptcy Code, a troubled enterprise may be restructured to enable it to operate successfully in the future. Until the business can be reorganized pursuant to a plan [of reorganization], the trustee or debtor-in-possession is authorized to manage the property of the estate and to continue the operation of the business. See § 1108. By permitting reorganization, Congress anticipated that the business would continue to provide jobs, to satisfy creditors' claims, and to produce a return for its owners. [Citations to the legislative history of the Bankruptcy Code omitted.] Congress presumed that the assets of the debtor would be more valuable if used in a rehabilitated business than if "sold for scrap." The reorganization effort would have small chance of success, however, if property essential to running the business were excluded from the estate. Thus, to facilitate the rehabilitation of the debtor's business, all the debtor's property must be included in the reorganization estate.

This authorization extends even to property of the estate in which a creditor has a secured interest. Although Congress might have safeguarded the interests of secured creditors outright by excluding from the estate any property subject to a secured interest, it chose instead to include such property in the estate and to provide secured creditors with "adequate protection" for their interests. At the secured creditor's insistence, the bankruptcy court must place such limits or conditions on the trustee's power to sell, use, or lease property as are necessary to protect the creditor. The creditor with a secured interest in property included in the estate must look to this provision for protection, rather than to the nonbankruptcy remedy of possession.

Both the congressional goal of encouraging reorganizations and Congress' choice of methods to protect secured creditors suggest that Congress intended a broad range of property to be included in the estate.

B.

The statutory language reflects this view of the scope of the estate. As noted above, § 541(a)(1) provides that the "estate is comprised of all the following property, wherever located: . . . all legal or equitable interests of the debtor in property as of the commencement of the case." 11 U.S.C. § 541(a)(1). The House and Senate Reports on the Bankruptcy Code indicate that § 541(a)(1)'s scope is broad. Most important, in the context of this case, § 541(a)(1) is intended to include in the estate any property made available to the estate by other provisions of the Bankruptcy Code. Several of these provisions bring into the estate property in which the debtor did not have a possessory interest at the time the bankruptcy proceedings commenced.

Section 542(a) is such a provision. It requires an entity (other than a custodian) holding any property of the debtor that the trustee can use under § 363 to turn that property over to the trustee. Given the broad scope of the reorganization estate, property of the debtor repossessed by a secured creditor falls within this rule, and therefore may be drawn into the estate. While there are explicit limitations on the reach of § 542(a),[12] none requires that the debtor hold a possessory interest in the property at the commencement of the reorganization proceedings.

As does all bankruptcy law, § 542(a) modifies the procedural rights available to creditors to protect and satisfy their liens.[14] In effect, § 542(a) grants to the estate a possessory interest in certain property of the debtor that was not held by the debtor at the commencement of reorganization proceedings. The Bankruptcy Code provides secured creditors various rights, including the right to adequate protection, and these rights replace the protection afforded by possession.

. . .

We conclude that the reorganization estate includes property of the debtor that has been seized by a creditor prior to the filing of a petition for reorganization.

III.

A.

We see no reason why a different result should obtain when the IRS is the creditor. The Service is bound by § 542(a) to the same extent as any other secured creditor.

---

12. Section 542 provides that the property be usable under § 363, and that turnover is not required in three situations: when the property is of inconsequential value or benefit to the estate, § 542(a), when the holder of the property has transferred it in good faith without knowledge of the petition, § 542(c), or when the transfer of the property is automatic to pay a life insurance premium, § 542(d).

14. One of the procedural rights the law of secured transactions grants a secured creditor to enforce its lien is the right to take possession of the secured property upon the debtor's default. Uniform Commercial Code § 9-503 (1981). A creditor's possessory interest resulting from the exercise of this right is subject to certain restrictions on the creditor's use of the property. See U.C.C. § 9-504. Here, we address the abrogation of the Service's possessory interest obtained pursuant to its tax lien, a secured interest.

The Bankruptcy Code expressly states that the term "entity," used in § 542(a), includes a governmental unit. § 101(14). Moreover, Congress carefully considered the effect of the new Bankruptcy Code on tax collection, and decided to provide protection to tax collectors, such as the IRS, through grants of enhanced priorities for unsecured tax claims, § 507(a)(6), and by the nondischarge of tax liabilities, § 523(a)(1). Tax collectors also enjoy the generally applicable right under § 363(e) to adequate protection for property subject to their liens. Nothing in the Bankruptcy Code or its legislative history indicates that Congress intended a special exception for the tax collector in the form of an exclusion from the estate of property seized to satisfy a tax lien.

B.

Of course, if a tax levy or seizure transfers to the IRS ownership of the property seized, § 542(a) may not apply. The enforcement provisions of the Internal Revenue Code of 1954, 26 U.S.C. §§ 6321-6326, do grant to the Service powers to enforce its tax liens that are greater than those possessed by private secured creditors under state law. But those provisions do not transfer ownership of the property to the IRS.

The Service's interest in seized property is its lien on that property. The Internal Revenue Code's levy and seizure provisions, 26 U.S.C. §§ 6331 and 6332, are special procedural devices available to the IRS to protect and satisfy its liens and are analogous to the remedies available to private secured creditors. They are provisional remedies that do not determine the Service's rights to the seized property, but merely bring the property into the Service's legal custody. At no point does the Service's interest in the property exceed the value of the lien. The IRS is obligated to return to the debtor any surplus from a sale. Ownership of the property is transferred only when the property is sold to a bona fide purchaser at a tax sale. In fact, the tax sale provision itself refers to the debtor as the owner of the property after the seizure but prior to the sale. Until such a sale takes place, the property remains the debtor's and thus is subject to the turnover requirement of § 542(a).

IV.

When property seized prior to the filing of a petition is drawn into the Chapter 11 reorganization estate, the Service's tax lien is not dissolved; nor is its status as a secured creditor destroyed. The IRS, under § 363(e), remains entitled to adequate protection for its interests, to other rights enjoyed by secured creditors, and to the specific privileges accorded tax collectors. Section 542(a) simply requires the Service to seek protection of its interest according to the congressionally established bankruptcy procedures, rather than by withholding the seized property from the debtor's efforts to reorganize.

The judgment of the Court of Appeals is affirmed.

Study Questions

1. What is going-concern value? How does it differ from liquidation value?
2. What is the IRS requesting? What is the debtor requesting?

3. What is the policy behind the Supreme Court's ruling? Whom does it help?
4. Would the outcome be different if the IRS had sold the property?

The following case considers whether a more unusual type of property—a brothel license—is property of the estate. (Prostitution is legal in most Nevada counties.)

In re David Burgess

234 B.R. 793 (D. Nev. 1999)

EDWARD C. REED, JR., U.S. Dist. J.

BACKGROUND

Since 1983, the debtor has operated a legal brothel (or "house of ill fame") in Storey County, Nevada. On July 30, 1997, the debtor filed a voluntary petition for bankruptcy under Chapter 11 of the Bankruptcy Code. On June 2, 1998, the Storey County Commission and the Sheriff of Storey County held a hearing to express their displeasure with the debtor's continuing association with the Hell's Angels motorcycle "club" (or, in the County's terminology, "outlaw motorcycle gang"). At the hearing, the Commissioners revoked the debtor's brothel license.

[The bankruptcy court denied the debtor's request to undo the County's attempt to revoke his license, and the debtor appealed to the district court. Under section 362 of the Code, whether the debtor was entitled to a reversal of the revocation of his license and damages depended on whether the license was property of the estate.] In denying relief to the debtor, the bankruptcy court held that the brothel license was not "property," but rather a "personal privilege." The County now argues that the question of whether the license is property is completely irrelevant to this appeal, and did not, in fact, brief the issue. On the contrary, however, the question is quite important, as we explain below.

DISCUSSION

When a bankruptcy petition is filed, an "estate" is created, consisting of all of the debtor's interests, both legal and equitable, in all property, both tangible and intangible. 11 U.S.C. § 541(a). Although "property" is not defined in the Code, it has been interpreted liberally in order to further the policies underlying the bankruptcy laws. *See United States v. Whiting Pools, Inc.*, 462 U.S. 198, 202-04 (1983). "The congressional goal of encouraging reorganizations . . . suggest[s] that Congress intended a broad range of property to be included in the estate." *Id.* at 204.

. . . As noted above, the County did not provide any insight into the "property" issue. Likewise, we have not been overwhelmed with citations to cases involving the issue of whether a license to operate a legal brothel is "property" or not. The County cites to cases from the Nevada Supreme Court and this Court which indicate that Nevada law views prostitution as an activity that can be heavily regulated or forbidden altogether. From this, the bankruptcy court reasoned that the license was not property, but merely "a personal privilege granted to certain counties"—a "state matter . . . subject to discretionary control of the county."

Unfortunately, this analysis is incorrect. The fact that Nevada law may not consider brothel licenses to be property is not dispositive. The fact that the right/privilege to operate a brothel is defined by state law does not matter—most property rights are defined by state law. That does not mean that those rights receive no protection from federal law, bankruptcy and otherwise. In fact, state-created "rights" expressly denominated by the state as "privileges" have often been treated as "property" for purposes of the bankruptcy laws. While state law creates the right, federal law determines whether it is "property" for purposes of the federal bankruptcy laws, tax laws, etc. *In re Nejberger*, 934 F.2d at 1301-02 ("While state law creates legal interests and defines their incidents, the ultimate question whether an interest thus created and defined falls within a category stated by a Federal statute, requires an interpretation of that statute which is a Federal question."); *In re Terwilliger's Catering*, 911 F.2d at 1171-72 ("While the nature and extent of the debtor's interest are determined by state law once that determination is made, federal bankruptcy law dictates to what extent that interest is property of the estate.").

While we have found no published bankruptcy decisions regarding brothel licenses, numerous cases have held that similar licenses issued by state agencies are property for bankruptcy purposes. Most of these cases involve liquor licenses, rather than brothel licenses, but the principal is the same. Most states or local governments require businesses that wish to sell alcoholic beverages to be licensed, and regardless of how the issuing state characterizes such licenses, most courts have held that they are property under the bankruptcy laws. Courts have also held that a license to operate a racetrack or a casino is property of the estate. *In re National Cattle Congress, Inc.*, 179 B.R. 588, 593 (Bankr. N.D. Iowa 1995) (racetrack), *remanded on other grounds*, 91 F.3d 1113 (8th Cir. 1996); *Elsinore Shore Assocs. v. Casino Control Comm'n (In re Elsinore Shore Assocs.)*, 66 B.R. 723, 734 (Bankr. D.N.J. 1986) (casino license). In addition, many other cases have held similar licenses and certifications to be property. *E.g., Ramsay v. Dowden (In re Central Arkansas Broadcasting Co.)*, 68 F.3d 213, 214-15 (8th Cir. 1995) (FCC license); *Federal Aviation Admin. v. Gull Air, Inc. (In re Gull Air, Inc.)*, 890 F.2d 1255, 1260 (1st Cir. 1989) (airport landing slots); *Shimer v. Fugazy (In re Fugazy Express, Inc.)*, 124 B.R. 426, 430 (S.D.N.Y. 1991) (FCC license), *appeal dismissed*, 982 F.2d 769 (2d Cir. 1992); *Nu-Process Brake Engineers, Inc. v. Benton (In re Nu-Process Brake Engineers, Inc.)*, 119 B.R. 700, 701 (Bankr. E.D. Mo. 1990) (right to pursue reinstatement of a sales tax license); *Brizendine v. Humboldt Express, Inc. (In re Brown Transport Truckload, Inc.)*, 118 B.R. 889, 893 (Bankr. N.D. Ga. 1990) (trucking certificate); *In re Draughon Training Inst., Inc.*, 119 B.R. 927, 930-31 (Bankr. W.D. La. 1990) (state and federal certifications of eligibility to receive educational funding); *Beker Indus. Corp. v. Florida Land & Water Adjudicatory Comm'n (In re Beker Indus. Corp.)*, 57 B.R. 611, 621-22 (Bankr. S.D.N.Y. 1986) (permission to truck phosphate ore); *American Cent. Airlines, Inc. v. O'Hare Reg'l Carrier Scheduling Comm. (In re American Cent. Airlines, Inc.)*, 52 B.R. 567, 571 (Bankr. N.D. Iowa 1985) (airport landing slots); *Coben v. Lebrun (In re Golden Plan of California, Inc.)*, 37 B.R. 167, 170 (Bankr. E.D. Cal. 1984) (corporate name).

Of course, some courts have gone the other way. In *In re Gammo*, for instance, the court held that a state-issued license to sell lottery tickets was not property. *In re Gammo, Inc.*, 180 B.R. 485, 487 (Bankr. E.D. Mich. 1995); *see also Pension Benefit Guaranty Corp. v. Braniff Airways, Inc. (In re Braniff Airways, Inc.)*, 700 F.2d 935, 942 (5th Cir. 1983) (holding that airport landing slots are not property); *Geiger v. Pennsylvania (In re Geiger)*, 143 B.R. 30, 35-36 (E.D. Pa. 1992) (holding that a "driver's license is a privilege and not property"), *aff'd*, 993 F.2d 224 (3d Cir. 1993). Clearly, though, the majority of cases examining the issue have held that liquor and similar licenses are property for bankruptcy purposes. The case that most concerns us, however, is *Wade v. State Bar of Arizona (In re Wade)*, 115 B.R. 222 (B.A.P. 9th Cir. 1990), *aff'd*, 948 F.2d 1122 (9th Cir. 1991). In *In re Wade*, the Bankruptcy Appellate Panel of the Ninth Circuit held that an attorney's license to practice law was not property. *In re Wade*, 115 B.R. at 228. While the B.A.P.'s decision was affirmed by the Ninth Circuit, that court did not address the property question at all. The only question before the Circuit was whether the state bar was a government agency for purposes of the government exception. *In re Wade*, 948 F.2d 1122, 1123-25 (9th Cir. 1991). Thus the Ninth Circuit's decision is not particularly strong authority for the proposition that a license to practice law is not property. Nonetheless, we are convinced (although we suspect there may be some who would argue to the contrary) that a brothel license is more like a liquor license than a license to practice law.

Beyond the bankruptcy context, the Ninth Circuit has held that, for instance, a property right exists in license tags required for coin-operated "crane" games. *Wedges/Ledges of California, Inc. v. City of Phoenix*, 24 F.3d 56, 63-64 (9th Cir. 1994). Further, we note that the very license at issue here has recently been held by Judge Hagen, in the debtor's civil rights case, to constitute a property right for purposes of procedural due process analysis. . . . Thus, we hold that the brothel license at issue here is "property," at least for the purposes of 11 U.S.C. § 362(a)(3). The license has enormous value to the estate—in fact, without the license to operate as a brothel, there would essentially be no business left to reorganize. To hold that the license is not property would be to contravene the broad definition of property meant to further "the congressional goal of encouraging reorganizations." *United States v. Whiting Pools, Inc.*, 462 U.S. 198, 204 (1983).

II. "TRUE SALES" AND THE BANKRUPTCY ESTATE

It would seem axiomatic that an asset sold by the debtor prior to the filing of the bankruptcy petition could not be part of the bankruptcy estate. We will see in later chapters that there are bankruptcy "clawback" provisions that allow for the avoidance of certain pre-petition transfers. Putting these clawback provisions aside, there is still the question of what exactly constitutes a sale.

At what point does a transaction actually suffice to transfer assets from the debtor such that there is no "legal or equitable interest" remaining that would be part of the bankruptcy estate under section 541? If the seller retains some risk, say through a warranty, hasn't the seller also retained some interest in the transferred property? What if the seller maintains control over the transferred asset, such as operating it? What if the seller retains some of the upside on the transferred asset's performance?

Whether a transaction is a "true sale" is a critical issue not just for bankruptcy purposes, but also for accounting, bank regulation, secured credit, and tax purposes. All of these areas use similar tests, although with slightly different linguistic formulations. Ultimately, however, there is no bright line rule guiding the "true sale" question. Whether a transaction is a "true sale" is a matter of facts and circumstances.

Determining what is and what isn't a "true sale" is particularly important for asset securitization. You may recall from Chapter 6 that securitization is a financing technique centered around the segregation of cash flow–producing financial assets (such as loans or leases) from the other assets and liabilities of a firm in order to enable a very targeted investment in those assets that does not involve the operational risks of the firm as a whole. The segregation of financial assets typically involves the transfer of selected financial assets of a firm to a separate (and usually newly created) legal entity with no other assets or liabilities. This separate entity pays for the financial assets by issuing securities. The securities are backed by the cash flow from those assets (and, for debt securities, secured by them). The idea is that the value of the securities will be determined solely by the quality of the assets transferred to the separate entity, thereby enabling investment solely in the discrete risks of those financial assets, rather than in all of the risks involved in an operating firm. In other words, securitization is supposed to separate the risk on certain financial assets of a firm from the risk on the firm as a whole.

The economics of securitization transactions depend heavily on whether for legal purposes the transaction is considered a sale or not (which would likely make the transaction a secured financing), because the difference determines the nature of the non-payment risk assumed by securitization investors. If the transaction is a sale, then the securitization sponsor will have no claim on the securitized assets. Therefore, if the sponsor were to file for bankruptcy or be placed in receivership, the sponsor's bankruptcy or receivership estate would have no claim on the securitized assets. The securitized assets would be "**bankruptcy remote**," in the sense of being remote from the sponsor's potential bankruptcy.

If, on the other hand, the securitization were considered merely a secured financing or something other than a sale, the securitized assets would be property of the sponsor's bankruptcy or receivership estate. Accordingly, the securitization investors (or technically, the trustee for the securitization) would be creditors in the bankruptcy.

If the securitization transaction were not a sale, but a financing, there would be a question about whether the securitization investors had a perfected security interest and exactly what that security interest covered. The securitization investors would be unsecured creditors unless a proper security interest had been timely filed. For this reason, securitizations will generally file a prophylactic security interest in the securitized assets. Even if a security interest were filed, there would still be a question about whether it was perfected because unperfected security interests are avoidable in bankruptcy. Security interest filings require technical precision, and the law is unforgiving of even technical mistakes, which can result in a creditor being deemed partially or fully unsecured. Thus, if the transaction were a financing, the securitization investors would be assuming a risk that they were unsecured and therefore competing with the other assorted creditors of the sponsor for a limited pool of assets.

If the transaction were deemed a financing, and a proper security interest had been timely filed, the securitization investors would be secured creditors in the sponsor's bankruptcy. But this is still a less than perfect situation for the securitization investors, as they would cease receiving any payment of principal and interest until a bankruptcy or receivership plan became effective (which could take years), or a liquidation were effectuated, or the automatic stay were lifted for them. At the very least, then, there would be disruption and uncertainty for the securitization investors, and there would also be the very real risk that their security interest could be primed or their collateral could be used by the debtor sponsor.

For these reasons, securitization investors are particularly concerned that the securitized assets be bankruptcy remote. The securitization investors want to invest in the risks attendant to the securitization vehicle, not the risks attendant to the sponsor's operations.

Despite the enormous size of securitization markets and the centrality of sale treatment to securitization's economics, there is little formal law on what constitutes a sale versus a secured financing (or lease), and none of it is definitive. The difficulty of determining what is in fact a sale stems from the mismatch between the binary legal question of whether a transaction was a sale and the real life nature of transactions as transferring some, but not all of the rights associated with an asset. Property rights can be understood as a bundle of rights. BENJAMIN CARDOZO, THE PARADOXES OF LEGAL SCIENCE 129 (1928). These rights can be transferred in a bundle or can be unbundled and transferred individually or severally. A securitization might transfer some, but not all of the bundle of rights. It might involve the sponsor's retention of part of the risks and benefits attendant to the transferred assets. For example, every securitization involves the seller making to the buyer various representations and warranties about the quality of the securitized assets, and thus retaining some risk on the assets. The true sale inquiry, then, is: A what point has enough of the rights attendant to the assets—risk, reward, and control—been transferred such that it is a sale? It is by nature a fact-specific inquiry.

The market solution to the uncertainty about what is a sale is to rely on "true sale" opinion letters issued by law firms. True sale opinion letters are issued as part of the credit rating process. Credit rating is a critical part of securitization. Many institutional investors are restricted to purchasing only investment-grade securities. Securitization transactions often seek to arbitrage the credit ratings of the sponsor and the SPE: The SPE can be designed to have a superior credit profile to the sponsor's and hence a lower cost of funding.

In order to achieve such a credit ratings arbitrage, it is imperative that a securitization obtain the desired credit ratings. The credit rating agencies all have rating methodologies for securitizations that include various legal requirements that must be fulfilled prior to rating. Among these legal requirements are "true sale" opinion letters from law firms addressed to the rating agencies. These "true sale" opinion letters are required by rating agencies to give them comfort about rating the SPE's credit profile separately from that of the sponsor. As Standard & Poor's Rating Services explains, it "generally requests true sale opinions in structured finance transactions to enable us, in our analysis, to isolate the creditworthiness of an issuer's assets from the creditworthiness of the transferor." Standard & Poor's Rating Services, *Methodology for "Springing" True Sale Opinions in U.S. RMBS Transactions*, Feb. 12, 2009.

A "true sale" legal opinion letters (signed by the law firm, not by an individual partner) reflects a law firm's position on whether the transferred assets would be treated as "bankruptcy remote," meaning that the transferred assets would not be part of the transferor's bankruptcy or receivership estate. True sale opinion letters involve a totality of the circumstances analysis that typically looks at several factors, to the extent they are relevant:

1. Whether the creditors of the securitization vehicle have effective recourse to the sponsor.
2. Whether the sponsor has retained rights in the transferred assets.
3. Whether the sponsor has retained the administration of the transferred assets.
4. Whether the transfer is irrevocable and whether the transferee can freely alienate the assets by an additional sale or pledge.
5. Whether the pricing mechanism for the transfer is based on a fixed cost or either floats on a market rate or is adjustable by the transferor and securitization vehicle.
6. Whether the sponsor is obligated to pay the operating costs of the securitization vehicle.
7. Whether the language of transaction documentation is the language of sale.
8. Whether the parties' indicated that they intended a sale.
9. Whether the transaction allows the securitization vehicle to cease purchasing assets from the sponsor based on the sponsor's financial condition.

No particular factor in this list carries decisive weight. Instead, true sale opinions consider the totality of these factors in an attempt to determine whether the sponsor truly parted with the future economic risks and benefits of ownership and control and whether the securitization vehicle assumed those risks, benefits, and control. That is, legal isolation is dependent on an analysis of the economic realities of a transaction. Yet mere transfer or retention of risk is not alone dispositive. Were it otherwise, hedging or insurance of a position without a transfer of control would be considered a sale, when it clearly is not. Thus, control-factors are also an integral part of the true sale analysis.

A true sale opinion letter has no formal legal effect. It does not determine whether a transaction is in fact a true sale. What it does is give securitization investors potential recourse to the law firm's malpractice insurance policy if the opinion is incorrect. This is likely to be of little comfort ex post if the policy coverage is less than the investors' losses or if there are multiple problematic opinion letters all under the same malpractice insurance policy. Nonetheless, the willingness of the law firm to put its malpractice policy on the line is an indicator of the law firm's confidence in the transaction, and that provides investors with comfort ex ante.

The following case shows the property of the estate issue in the context of a securitization. The debtor securitized assets through a transfer to a special purpose entity called "Sales Finance" that then issued debt securities. The transferor filed for bankruptcy, but the special purpose entity did not file for bankruptcy. Are the transferred assets property of the debtor's estate or of the separate special purpose entity? That is, are the assets "bankruptcy remote" in the sense that they are remote from the transferor's bankruptcy estate?

In re LTV Steel Company, Inc.

274 B.R. 278 (Bankr. N.D. Ohio 2001)

BODOH, U.S. Bankr. J.

. . . Debtor is one of the largest manufacturers of wholly-integrated steel products in the United States. Debtor mainly produces flat rolled steel products, hot and cold rolled sheet metal, mechanical and structural tubular products, and bimetallic wire. Debtor currently employs approximately 17,500 people in various capacities, and Debtor is also responsible for providing medical coverage and other benefits to approximately 100,000 retirees and their dependents. Debtor and 48 of its subsidiaries filed voluntary petitions for relief under Chapter 11 of Title 11, United States Code, on December 29, 2000. These cases are jointly administered.

. . . [T]he current controversy stems from a series of financial transactions that Debtor executed after its previous reorganization. The transactions in question are known as asset-backed securitization or structured financing ("ABS"), and are generally designed to permit a debtor to borrow funds at a reduced cost in exchange for a lender securing the loan with assets that are transferred from the borrower to another entity. By structuring the transactions in this manner, the lender hopes to ensure that its collateral will be excluded from the borrower's bankruptcy estate in the event that the borrower files a bankruptcy petition.

Abbey National is a large financial institution located in the United Kingdom. Debtor and Abbey National entered into an ABS transaction in October 1994. To effectuate this agreement, Debtor created a wholly-owned subsidiary known as LTV Sales Finance Co. ("Sales Finance"). Debtor then entered into an agreement with Sales Finance[,] which purports to sell all of Debtor's right and interest in its accounts receivables ("receivables") to Sales Finance on a continuing basis. Abbey National then agreed to loan Two Hundred Seventy Million Dollars ($270,000,000.00) to Sales Finance in exchange for Sales Finance granting Abbey National a security interest in the receivables. . . .

. . . Sales Finance [is not] . . . a debtor in this proceeding. Nevertheless, Debtor filed a motion with the Court on December 29, 2000 seeking an interim order permitting it to use cash collateral. This cash collateral consisted of the receivables . . . ostensibly owned by Sales Finance [and inventory ostensibly owned by another special purpose subsidiary]. Debtors stated to the Court that it would be forced to shut it doors and cease operations if it did not receive authorization to use this cash collateral. A hearing was held on Debtor's cash collateral motion on December 29, 2000 as part of the first day hearings. [Interim authorization was granted, with Abbey National to receive newly generated inventory and receivables as substitute collateral.]

. . .

Abbey National argues that the interim cash collateral order should be modified because . . . there is no basis for the Court to determine that the receivables which are Abbey National's collateral are property of Debtor's estate. . . .

Section 541(a) of the Bankruptcy Code provides that upon the filing of a bankruptcy petition an estate is created consisting of "all legal or equitable interests of the debtor in property as of the commencement of the case." 11 U.S.C. § 541(a)(1). The estate created by the filing of a Chapter 11 petition is very broad, and property may be included in Debtor's estate even if Debtor does not have a possessory interest in that property. *United States v. Whiting Pools, Inc.,* 462 U.S. 198, 204 (1983).

Abbey National contends that the interim order is flawed because, on its face, the transaction between Debtor and Sales Finance is characterized as a true sale. Therefore, Abbey National argues, since Debtor sold its interests in the receivables to Sales Finance, Debtor no longer has an interest in the receivables and they are not property of the estate.

. . .

[T]here seems to be an element of sophistry to suggest that Debtor does not retain at least an equitable interest in the property that is subject to the interim order. Debtor's business requires it to purchase, melt, mold and cast various metal products. To suggest that Debtor lacks some ownership interest in products that it creates with its own labor, as well as the proceeds to be derived from that labor, is difficult to accept. Accordingly, the Court concludes that Debtor has at least some equitable interest in the inventory and receivables, and that this interest is property of the Debtor's estate. This equitable interest is sufficient to support the entry of the interim cash collateral order.

Finally, it is readily apparent that granting Abbey National relief from the interim cash collateral order would be highly inequitable. The Court is satisfied that the entry of the interim order was necessary to enable Debtor to keep its doors open and continue to meet its obligations to its employees, retirees, customers and creditors. Allowing Abbey National to modify the order would allow Abbey National to enforce its state law rights as a secured lender to look to the collateral in satisfaction of this debt. This circumstance would put an immediate end to Debtor's business, would put thousands of people out of work, would deprive 100,000 retirees of needed medical benefits, and would have more far reaching economic effects on the geographic areas where Debtor does business. However, maintaining the current status quo permits Debtor to remain in business while it searches for substitute financing, and adequately protects and preserves Abbey National's rights. The equities of this situation highly favor Debtor. As a result, the Court declines to exercise its discretion to modify the interim order. . . .

. . .

The bankruptcy estate exists as a juridical entity throughout the duration of the bankruptcy. The estate terminates at different times depending under which Chapter in the Bankruptcy Code a case is filed. In Chapter 7 bankruptcies, all of the property of the estate is distributed in the liquidation with any residual property going to the debtor, at which point there ceases to be an estate, as there is no longer any property held in trust. 11 U.S.C. §§ 725, 726(a). In Chapter 11 bankruptcies, upon confirmation of a plan of reorganization, all of the property of the estate is revested in the debtor, which likewise ends the trust, as there is no remaining trust corpus. 11 U.S.C. § 1141(b).

Problem Set 14

Gemini International Corp., a renowned satellite manufacturer and operator, has filed for bankruptcy. Which of the following are property of the Gemini International bankruptcy estate?

a. Gemini's equipment.

b. Gemini's mortgaged headquarter's building.

c. Gemini's leased warehouse. The lease contains a provision providing for its automatic termination if Gemini files for bankruptcy. 11 U.S.C. § 541(c)(1)(B).

d. The stock of Gemini's subsidiaries.

e. Tax withholding from Gemini's employees' salaries and wages that has not yet been remitted to the IRS by Gemini.

f. Gemini's employee's pension funds. *See* 11 U.S.C. § 541(b)(7), 29 U.S.C. § 1103(a).

g. Gemini's contract with the National Geospatial-Intelligence Agency (NG-IA) to design and construct a spy satellite.

h. Gemini's FCC satellite spectrum license for its Bellatrix I satellite. *See In re Burgess.*

i. Gemini's security clearance for creation of the NG-IA satellite.

j. Gemini's patent for a critical component of the NG-IA satellite.

k. Gemini's currently unprosecuted claim against Scorpio Inc. for patent infringement.

l. Gemini's Betelgeuse II satellite, being shipped on a Liberian-flagged vessel somewhere in the North Atlantic. Gemini has a bill of lading for the satellite.

m. Gemini's Betelgeuse I satellite, currently in space in a geosynchronous orbit, but controlled from Houston, Texas.

n. Gemini's Rigel-12 satellite, sold six months ago to Ursa Major, Inc., on arms' length terms, but under warranty by Gemini.

o. Gemini's securitized receivables generated by its Procyon-3 telecommunications satellite for the next seven years. The expected lifetime of the satellite is eight years. The receivables are generated from royalties paid by telecommunications companies or government agencies for use of the satellite and were transferred in the securitization to a trust that issued securities. The trust has no recourse against Gemini for shortfalls on the receivables, but the securitization was made with a number of representations and warranties about the contracts Gemini already had in place for use of the satellite. To the extent that there is a shortfall on the receivables in any given month relative to the payment owed on the securities, any surplus receivables collected in future months will be applied to the past shortfall. Gemini services the receivables on behalf of the trust, meaning that it handles all billing and collections. The securitization was accompanied by a true sale opinion from the eminent law firm of Olde, Whyte, & Hsu, which states that if a court were to consider the transaction it "would" treat the transaction as a sale. *See In re LTV Steel Company, Inc.*

CHAPTER 15

THE AUTOMATIC STAY

I. THE AUTOMATIC STAY

The automatic stay is one of the most important features of bankruptcy law. The filing of a bankruptcy petition triggers an automatic injunction against a wide array of acts to collect from the debtor or the debtor's property. 11 U.S.C. § 362(a). The stay prevents both judicial and non-judicial debt collection, as well as attempts to create liens against the property of the debtor or the estate. Thus, all lawsuits based on pre-petition claims are stayed, 11 U.S.C. § 362(1), as are attempts to collect on pre-petition debts. 11 U.S.C. § 362(a)(2), (a)(5)-(8). Lawsuits arising from post-petition claims are not stayed, but their collection is stayed. 11 U.S.C. § 362(a)(3)-(4). The stay also covers setoffs of a pre-petition debt owed to the debtor against a pre-petition claim against the debtor by the same party.[1] 11 U.S.C. § 362(a)(7). The stay, which may be supplemented by injunctions issued under section 105(a), gives the debtor breathing time to take stock of its assets and liabilities and figure out how to restructure both its operations and its financial structure.

The stay works in accord with sections 541, 542, and 543 regarding property of the estate. Section 541 creates and defines the bankruptcy estate. The turnover provisions of sections 542 and 543 then marshal together the assets of estate that are not in the control of the debtor. Section 362 simultaneously stays collection actions against the estate outside of the bankruptcy process. These provisions combine with the venue provision of Federal Rule of Bankruptcy Procedure 7004 to bring all claims against the debtor and the debtor's bankruptcy-related claims against other parties together in one court. Giving one court oversight of both the debtor's assets and all claims against the debtor enables a much more orderly process of either liquidation or reorganization. Absent these provisions, the bankruptcy process simply would not work.

---

1. The stay does not extend to recoupment, which is the netting out of reciprocal obligations arising from the same transaction.

II. SCOPE OF THE AUTOMATIC STAY

Often there is little question about whether an action would or would not be covered by the stay, but there are some situations that are more complex. For example, is a criminal prosecution for failure to pay a debt (such as child support) or for writing a bad check really a debt collection action? What if the prosecution would be dropped upon payment? The following section considers the extent to which the stay protects not only debtors, but co-defendants, insurers, guarantors, and letters of credit.

A. Co-Defendants

A.H. Robins Company, Inc. v. Piccinin
788 F.2d 994 (4th Cir. 1986)

RUSSELL, Circuit Judge:

Confronted, if not overwhelmed, with an avalanche of actions filed in various state and federal courts throughout the United States by citizens of this country as well as of foreign countries seeking damages for injuries allegedly sustained by the use of an intrauterine contraceptive device known as a Dalkon Shield, the manufacturer of the device, A.H. Robins Company, Incorporated (Robins) filed its petition under Chapter 11 of the Bankruptcy Code, 11 U.S.C. §§ 101 *et seq.*, in August, 1985.

BACKGROUND

The device, which is the subject of these suits, had been developed in the 1960's by Dr. Hugh Davis at the Johns Hopkins Hospital in Baltimore, Maryland. In mid-1970 Robins acquired all patent and marketing rights to the Dalkon Shield and engaged in the manufacture and marketing of the device from early 1971 until 1974, when it discontinued manufacture and sale of the device because of complaints and suits charging injuries arising allegedly out of the use of the device. The institution of Dalkon Shield suits did not, however, moderate with the discontinuance of manufacture of the device, since Robins did not actually recall the device until 1984.[3] By the middle of 1985, when the Chapter 11 petition was filed the number of such suits arising out of the continued sale and use of the Dalkon Shield device earlier put into the stream of commerce by Robins had grown to 5,000. More than half of these pending cases named Robins as the sole defendant; a co-defendant or co-defendants were named in the others. Prior to the filing, a number of suits had been tried and, while Robins had prevailed in some of the actions, judgments in large and burdensome amounts had been recovered in

---

3. In response to that recall, 4,500 women had removed the shield as of August 1985, at a cost of $1,600,000.

others. Many more had been settled.[4] Moreover, the costs of defending these suits both to Robins and to its insurance carrier had risen into the millions. [There was a limitation on coverage under the product liability insurance policy, which covered A.H. Robins as well as Robins' officers, directors, and Dr. Davis and another individual, Dr. Clark.] A large amount of the time and energies of Robins' officers and executives was also being absorbed in preparing material for trial and in attending and testifying at depositions and trials. The problems arising out of this mounting tide of claims and suits precipitated this Chapter 11 proceeding.

The filing of the Chapter 11 petition automatically stayed all suits against Robins itself under section 362(a) of the Bankruptcy Code, even though no formal order of stay was immediately entered. But a number of plaintiffs in suits where there were defendants other than Robins, sought to sever their actions against Robins and to proceed with their claims against the co-defendant or co-defendants [who were also covered by the same Aetna product liability insurance policy as A.H. Robins]. Robins responded to the move by filing an adversary proceeding in which it named as defendants the plaintiffs in eight such suits pending in various state and federal courts. In that proceeding, the debtor sought (1) declaratory relief adjudging that the debtor's products liability policy with Aetna Casualty and Insurance Company (Aetna) was an asset of the estate in which all the Dalkon Shield plaintiffs and claimants had an interest and (2) injunctive relief restraining the prosecution of the actions against its co-defendants. Service of the summons and complaint in that adversary proceeding, a memorandum of law in support of the motion for a preliminary injunction therein, a notice of the debtor's intention to apply for a temporary restraining order, a copy of the proposed temporary restraining order and affidavits in support were duly mailed by first-class mail and by Federal Express to all the defendants and their attorneys at their addresses.

The debtor's application for a temporary restraining order and for the setting of a date for a hearing on the request for preliminary injunction in the adversary proceeding was heard *ex parte* by the district judge who had jurisdiction over the proceedings. The district judge granted at the time a temporary restraining order in the proceedings and set a hearing on the debtor's application for a preliminary injunction. On that same day, Robins mailed by first-class mail and by Federal Express to all the defendants and their attorneys at their addresses "Notice of Hearing on Plaintiff's Motion for Preliminary Injunction."

At the hearing on the motion for a preliminary injunction, a number of defendants as well as the Committee constituted by the court to represent Dalkon Shield Claimants appeared by counsel. At the commencement of the hearing the defendant Piccinin, a plaintiff in one of the Dalkon Shield actions which Robins sought to stay, filed through her attorney a written motion to dismiss as against her. No other defendant filed a motion in response to the motion for a preliminary injunction. After receiving certain

---

4. Of the approximately 7,500 Dalkon Shield cases settled from 1972 to February 1985, fewer than 40 went to a jury. A recent article in the Nat. L.J., p. 10, (March 17, 1986), states that by mid 1985, Robins, along with its insurer, Aetna Casualty & Surety Company, "had paid roughly $517 million for 25 trial judgments and 9,300 settlements since the first verdict in 1975."

testimony, admitting various records, and hearing arguments of parties, the district court granted Robins' request for a preliminary injunction.

In his order granting the preliminary injunction, the district judge found (1) that continuation of litigation in the civil actions threatened property of Robins' estate, burdened and impeded Robins' reorganization effort, contravened the public interest, and rendered any plan of reorganization futile; (2) that this burden on Robins' estate outweighed any burden on the Dalkon claimants caused by enjoining their civil actions; and (3) that all remaining insurance coverage in favor of the debtor under its liability policy issued by Aetna was property of the Robins' Chapter 11 estate. The district judge then held that all actions for damages that might be satisfied from proceeds of the Aetna insurance policy were subject to the stay pursuant to 11 U.S.C. § 362(a)(3) and enjoined further litigation in the eight civil actions, pursuant to 11 U.S.C. § 362(a)(1), (3) as supplemented by 11 U.S.C. § 105.

Only the defendants Piccinin, the Mosas, and Conrad filed timely notices of appeal from the grant of the preliminary injunction. Their appeals, questioning the propriety of that preliminary injunction as against suits by Robins' co-defendants is the first of the issues now before this Court. [Discussion of the second issue, relating to jurisdiction over related cases, is omitted.]

I.

The initial question in the appeal of the first issue relates to the court's jurisdiction to grant a stay or injunction of suits in other courts against co-defendants of the debtor or of third parties; none of the parties herein contest the jurisdiction of the bankruptcy court to stay actions against the debtor itself in any court. Jurisdiction over suits involving co-defendants or third parties may be bottomed on two statutory provisions of the Bankruptcy Act itself as well as on the general equitable powers of the court. The first of these statutory grants of jurisdiction is found in section 362, 11 U.S.C. The purpose of this section by its various subsections is to protect the debtor from an uncontrollable scramble for its assets in a number of uncoordinated proceedings in different courts, to preclude one creditor from pursuing a remedy to the disadvantage of other creditors, and to provide the debtor and its executives with a reasonable respite from protracted litigation, during which they may have an opportunity to formulate a plan of reorganization for the debtor. As the Court in *Fidelity Mortg. Investors v. Camelia Builders, Inc.*, 550 F.2d 47, 55 (2d Cir. 1976), *cert. denied*, 429 U.S. 1093, put it, "the stay insures that the debtor's affairs will be centralized, initially, in a single forum in order to prevent conflicting judgments from different courts and in order to harmonize all of the creditors' interests with one another."

Section 362 is broken down into several subsections, only two of which are relevant on this appeal. The first of such subsections is (a)(1), which imposes an automatic stay of any proceeding "commenced or [that] could have been commenced against the debtor" at the time of the filing of the Chapter 11 proceeding; the second is (a)(3), which provides similar relief against suits involving the possession or custody of property of the debtor, irrespective of whether the suits are against the debtor alone or others. We shall discuss the extent of jurisdiction given the bankruptcy court under these two subsections, beginning with (a)(1).

(a)

Subsection (a)(1) is generally said to be available only to the debtor, not third party defendants or co-defendants. As the Court in *Johns-Manville Sales Corp.*, 26 Bankr. 405, 410 (S.D.N.Y. 1983), remarked, "there are cases [under 362(a)(1)] where a bankruptcy court may properly stay the proceedings against non-bankrupt co-defendants" but, it adds, that in order for relief for such non-bankrupt defendants to be available under (a)(1), there must be "unusual circumstances" and certainly "'something more than the mere fact that one of the parties to the lawsuit has filed a Chapter 11 bankruptcy must be shown in order that proceedings be stayed against non-bankrupt parties.'" This "unusual situation," it would seem, arises when there is such identity between the debtor and the third-party defendant that the debtor may be said to be the real party defendant and that a judgment against the third-party defendant will in effect be a judgment or finding against the debtor. An illustration of such a situation would be a suit against a third party who is entitled to absolute indemnity by the debtor on account of any judgment that might result against them in the case. To refuse application of the statutory stay in that case would defeat the very purpose and intent of the statute.

(b)

But (a)(1), which stays actions against the debtor and arguably against those whose interests are so intimately intertwined with those of the debtor that the latter may be said to be the real party in interest, is not the only part of section 362 providing for an automatic stay of proceedings. Subsection (a)(3) directs stays of any action, *whether against the debtor or third parties*, to obtain possession or to exercise control over property of the debtor. A key phrase in the construction and application of this section is, of course, "property" as that term is used in the Act. Section 541(a)(1) of the Bankruptcy Act defines "property" in the bankruptcy context. It provides that the "estate is comprised of all the following property, wherever located . . . all legal or equitable interests of the debtor in property as of the commencement of the case." The Supreme Court in construing this language in *United States v. Whiting Pools, Inc.*, 462 U.S. 198, 205, n.9, quoted this language in the legislative history of the Section:

> The scope of this paragraph [541(a)(1)] is broad. It included all kinds of property including tangible or intangible property, causes of action (see Bankruptcy Act § 70a(6)), and all other forms of property currently specified in section 70a of the Bankruptcy Act.

Under the weight of authority, insurance contracts have been said to be embraced in this statutory definition of "property." For example, even the right to cancel an insurance policy issued to the debtor has uniformly been held to be stayed under section 362(a)(3). A products liability policy of the debtor is similarly within the principle: it is a valuable property of a debtor, particularly if the debtor is confronted with substantial liability claims within the coverage of the policy in which case the policy may well be, as one court has remarked in a case like the one under review, "the most important asset of [*i.e.*, the debtor's] estate," *In re Johns Manville Corp.*, 40 Bankr. 219, 229 (S.D.N.Y. 1984). Any action in which the judgment may diminish this "important asset" is unquestionably subject to a stay under this subsection. Accordingly actions "related to" the bankruptcy proceedings against the insurer or against officers or employees of the debtor who may be entitled to indemnification under such policy or who qualify as additional insureds under the policy are to be stayed under section 362(a)(3).

(c)

The statutory power of the bankruptcy court to stay actions involving the debtor or its property is not, however, limited to section 362(a)(1) and (a)(3). It has been repeatedly held that 11 U.S.C. § 105 which provides that the bankruptcy court "may issue any order, process, or judgment that is necessary or appropriate to carry out the provisions of this title," "empowers the bankruptcy court to enjoin parties other than the bankrupt" from commencing or continuing litigation. *In re Otero Mills, Inc.,* 25 Bankr. 1018, 1020 (D.N.M. 1982).

Accepting that section 105 confers on the bankruptcy court power . . . to enjoin suits against parties in other courts, whether state or federal, it is necessary to mark out the circumstances under which the power or jurisdiction may be exercised. In *Otero Mills, supra,* the Court approved a ruling that "to so enjoin a creditor's action against a third party, the court must find that failure to enjoin would effect [sic] the bankruptcy estate and would adversely or detrimentally influence and pressure the debtor through the third party." 25 Bankr. at 1020. In *Johns-Manville,* the Court phrased somewhat fuller the circumstances when section 105 may support a stay:

> In the exercise of its authority under § 105, the Bankruptcy Court may use its injunctive authority to "protect the integrity of a bankrupt's estate and the Bankruptcy Court's custody thereof and to preserve to that Court the ability to exercise the authority delegated to it by Congress" [citing authority]. Pursuant to the exercise of that authority the Court may issue or extend stays to enjoin a variety of proceedings [including discovery against the debtor or its officers and employees] which will have an adverse impact on the Debtor's ability to formulate a Chapter 11 plan. 40 Bankr. at 226.

(d)

Beyond these statutory powers under section 362 and section 105 to enjoin other actions whether against the debtor or third-parties and in whatsoever court, the bankruptcy court . . . has the "inherent power of courts under their general equity powers and in the efficient management of the dockets to grant relief" to grant a stay. In exercising such power the court, however, must weigh competing interests and maintain an even balance and must justify the stay by clear and convincing circumstances outweighing potential harm to the party against whom it is operative.

(e)

There are thus four grounds on which the bankruptcy court may enjoin suits against the bankrupt or its assets and property. In some instances only one of these grounds may be relevant; in an involved and complex case, several or even all of the grounds may require consideration. The present case is such an involved and complex case.

II.

The district court in this case applied the test for a grant of preliminary injunctive relief. It found that irreparable harm would be suffered by the debtor and by the defendants since any of these suits against these co-defendants if successful, would reduce and diminish the insurance fund or pool represented in Aetna's policy in favor of Robins and thereby affect the property of the debtor to the detriment of the debtor's creditors as a whole. The likelihood of success by the debtor under these circumstances appeared indisputable. The hardships which would be suffered irreparably by the debtor and by its creditors generally in permitting these plaintiffs to secure as it were a preference in the distribution of the insurance pool herein to which all creditors were entitled, together with the unquestioned public interest in promoting a viable reorganization of the debtor can be said to outweigh any contrary hardship to the plaintiffs. Such finding does not appear unreasonable here.

The appellants, however, suggest that the record is insufficient to support such findings by the district judge. We disagree. The record is not extensive but it includes every fact necessary for the decision. The rights of Dr. Davis, Dr. Clark and the two Robins to indemnity and their status as additional insureds under Robins' insurance policy are undisputed on the record. That there are thousands of Dalkon Shield actions and claims pending is a fact established in the record and the limited fund available under Robins' insurance policy is recognized in the record. It seems incontestable that, if the suits are permitted to continue and discovery allowed, any effort at reorganization of the debtor will be frustrated, if not permanently thwarted. It is obvious from the record that if suits are permitted to proceed against indemnitees on claims on which the indemnitees are entitled to indemnity by Robins, either a binding judgment against the debtor will result or inconsistent judgments will result, calling for the exercise of the court's equitable powers. In our opinion, the record was thus more than adequate to support the district court's grant of injunctive relief. Certainly, the district court did not commit an abuse of discretion in granting the injunction herein.

In summary, we have no difficulty in sustaining the grant of a preliminary injunction herein. We are sustained in this conclusion by the fact, recognized by the district judge on the record, that any Dalkon Shield plaintiff may at any time petition for the vacation of the stay as it affects his or her suit and he or she is entitled to a hearing on such petition. Actually, there is one such petition pending and the district judge has agreed to set a hearing on that petition.

. . .

In summary, we affirm the district court's order staying the suits of the plaintiffs against the debtor and all co-defendants but remand with directions the order fixing venue for all pending suits against the debtor and transferring the suits to the district court before which the bankruptcy proceedings were pending.

AFFIRMED IN PART and REMANDED WITH DIRECTIONS.

Study Questions and Note

1. Exactly what grounds does the *A.H. Robins* decision stand on? Which of the court's reasons do you think is the most solid?

2. What policy do you see as underlying the court's decision in *A.H. Robins*?

3. Would the decision in *A.H. Robins* have been different if the insurance coverage were unlimited?

4. Should the automatic stay protect the debtor's officers and directors from litigation in which they are personal defendants? Does it matter if the litigation is related to the debtor's business?

5. For a detailed (and often troubling) history of the A.H. Robins bankruptcy, *see* RICHARD B. SOBOL, BENDING THE LAW: THE STORY OF THE DALKON SHIELD BANKRUPTCY (1993).

B. Guarantors

Credit Alliance Corp. v. Williams

851 F.2d 119 (4th Cir. 1988)

WILKINSON, Circuit Judge:

Gary Williams, guarantor of a note executed by Penn Hook Coal Co. in favor of Credit Alliance Corp., appeals the decision of the district court that a default judgment against Williams on the note was not rendered void by virtue of Penn Hook's petition for bankruptcy. We agree with the district court that the automatic stay provision of the Bankruptcy Code, 11 U.S.C. § 362, stays proceedings against the debtor only, and that no such relief is available to the non-bankrupt guarantor. Because principles of res judicata preclude relitigation of issues which could have been litigated in the earlier proceeding, the default judgment entered in that proceeding is enforceable against the guarantor.

I.

On February 22, 1980, Penn Hook Coal Co. signed a three year conditional sales contract note with Croushorn Equipment Co. for the purchase of a John Deere wheel loader. Croushorn assigned Penn Hook's note to Credit Alliance Corp. and Gary Williams and Malcolm C. Williams executed a guaranty of Penn Hook's obligation in favor of Credit Alliance.

Penn Hook subsequently defaulted on its obligation. On January 14, 1981, Credit Alliance filed suit in the United States District Court for the Southern District of New York against Penn Hook and the guarantors, Gary and Malcolm Williams. Credit Alliance sought judgment in the amount of $54,018.07, the balance due on the note after crediting the proceeds realized from the sale of the collateral, plus attorneys' fees, interest, and costs. Defendants failed to respond to the summons and complaint, and on March

4, 1981, Penn Hook petitioned for bankruptcy under Chapter 11 of the Bankruptcy Code in the District Court for the Western District of Virginia. On April 15, 1981, the District Court for the Southern District of New York entered a default judgment in the amount of $62,866.70 against the three defendants.

On October 5, 1984, Credit Alliance instituted garnishment proceedings against Penn Hook and the guarantors in the Western District of Virginia. The matter was referred to the bankruptcy court which held that the automatic stay provision of the Bankruptcy Code, 11 U.S.C. § 362, rendered void the default judgment against the debtor and the non-debtor guarantors, entered after Penn Hook petitioned for bankruptcy. The district court reversed the decision of the bankruptcy court with respect to the guarantors, and held that Credit Alliance's claim against Gary Williams and Malcolm Williams was not stayed or void. Guarantor Gary Williams now appeals.

II.

Appellant seeks to invoke the automatic stay provision of 11 U.S.C. § 362 to invalidate the New York judgment entered against him in his capacity as guarantor of the now bankrupt debtor's note with Credit Alliance.

The plain language of § 362, however, provides only for the automatic stay of judicial proceedings and enforcement of judgments "against the debtor or the property of the estate." *See Williford v. Armstrong World Industries, Inc.,* 715 F.2d 124, 126-27 (4th Cir. 1983). The legislative history of the provision reveals that Congress enacted § 362 to provide protection for bankrupt debtors and to facilitate the orderly distribution of debtors' assets among their creditors. "The automatic stay is one of the fundamental protections provided by the bankruptcy laws. It gives the debtor a breathing spell from his creditors. . . . It permits the debtor to attempt a repayment or reorganization plan, or simply to be relieved of the financial pressures that drove him into bankruptcy." S. Rep. No. 989, 95th Cong., 2d Sess. 54-55 (1978); H. R. Rep. No. 595, 95th Cong., 2d Sess., 340 (1978).

Nothing in § 362 suggests that Congress intended that provision to strip from the creditors of a bankrupt debtor the protection they sought and received when they required a third party to guaranty the debt. Congress knew how to extend the automatic stay to non-bankrupt parties when it intended to do so. Chapter 13, for example, contains a narrowly drawn provision to stay proceedings against a limited category of individual cosigners of consumer debts. *See* 11 U.S.C. § 1301(a). No such protection is provided to the guarantors of Chapter 11 bankrupts by § 362(a). *See Williford,* 715 F.2d at 126-27.

Guarantors of debtors proceeding in bankruptcy under Chapter 11 are limited to claims for reimbursement or contribution to the extent allowed under 11 U.S.C. § 502(e) or subrogation to the rights of the creditor under 11 U.S.C. § 509. This scheme protects the assured creditor "to the extent that a surety or codebtor is not permitted to compete with the creditor he has assured until the assured party's claim has been paid in full." 124 Cong. Rec. H11089 (Sept. 28, 1978) (statement of Rep. Edwards). A reading of § 362 restricting a creditor's ability to proceed against its guarantor would eliminate the protection of assured creditors contemplated by the Bankruptcy Code.

A.H. Robins Co. v. Piccinin, 788 F.2d 994 (4th Cir.), *cert. denied*, 479 U.S. 876 (1986), is not to the contrary. We recognized in *Robins* that in "unusual circumstances" a court, pursuant to § 362, may properly stay proceedings against non-bankrupt code-fendants of the bankrupt debtor. Such unusual circumstances might arise where "there is such identity between the debtor and the third-party defendant that the debtor may be said to be the real party defendant and that a judgment against the third-party defendant will in effect be a judgment or finding against the debtor," *id.* at 999, or where proceedings against non-debtor codefendants would reduce or diminish "the property of the debtor [such as the debtor's insurance fund or pool] to the detriment of the debtor's creditors as a whole." *Id.* at 1008.

There is nothing "unusual" about this guaranty agreement that would permit the guarantor, Williams, to invoke the statutory protection of § 362 or that would permit us to stay the enforcement of the New York judgment against him on equitable grounds. *See A.H. Robins*, 788 F.2d at 1000. It is unnecessary to stay proceedings or void the judgment against the non-bankrupt guarantor to protect Penn Hook or to prevent the dissipation of its assets, since neither Penn Hook nor its estate is jeopardized by the judgment against Williams. "The very purpose of a guaranty is to assure the [creditor] that in the event the [debtor] defaults, the [creditor] will have someone to look to for reimbursement." *Rojas v. First Bank National Ass'n*, 613 F. Supp. 968, 971 (E.D.N.Y. 1985). The purpose of the guaranty would be frustrated by interpreting § 362 so as to stay Credit Alliance's action against the non-bankrupt guarantor when the defaulting debtor petitioned for bankruptcy.

. . .

We conclude that the judgment against Gary Williams is valid and enforceable. The judgment of the district court is therefore AFFIRMED.

Even if a guarantor is not normally sheltered by the automatic stay, the guarantor might still find protection under section 105(a). The following cases considers this issue with a sensitive discussion about the expectations of parties with guaranties.

Lyondell Chemical Co. v. Centerpoint Energy Gas Services (*In re* Lyondell Chemical Co.)

402 B.R. 571 (Bankr. S.D.N.Y. 2009)

ROBERT E. GERBER, U.S. Bankr. J.

. . .

1. Corporate Structure

The Debtors' corporate family is a complex one, but the corporate relationships relevant here can be more briefly stated. The Debtors, all but one of which do business in the United States, are indirect subsidiaries of a holding company, LBIAF. LBIAF is organized under the laws of Luxembourg, and has its principal place of business in the Netherlands. [LBIAF is not itself in bankruptcy.]

LBIAF has a single subsidiary, Basell Funding S.a.r.l. ("Basell Funding"), which has many direct and indirect subsidiaries, all or most of which are in Europe. Of those, only one of them . . . is a debtor in the Chapter 11 [bankruptcy] cases here. All of LBIAF's other subsidiaries, direct and non-direct, are nondebtors in this case, and so far as the record reflects, are not debtors anywhere else. There are no ongoing foreign insolvency proceedings in progress elsewhere in the world to which to grant comity or to consider doing so.

2. LBIAF's Obligations

a. The Guaranties

Various of the Debtors in this case . . . entered into commercial transactions with contract counterparties, and failed to pay the counterparties all that was due. Thus the unpaid counterparties have claims (for the most part, unsecured) against those Debtors in these Chapter 11 cases. Additionally, however—and critical to the issues here—those counterparties (the "Guaranty Creditors") sought and obtained, prior to the filing of the Debtors' Chapter 11 cases, guaranties of those Debtors' obligations by LBIAF.

. . . Collectively, the guaranty claims against LBIAF now total approximately $131 million, and may total $200 million.

b. The 2015 Notes

LBIAF is . . . the principal obligor on the 2015 Notes, though the Notes are guarantied by certain of LBIAF's subsidiaries (in both Europe and the United States), including a number of the Debtors. The 2015 Notes are secured by a pledge of the shares of Basell Funding (which, as noted above, is LBIAF's only direct subsidiary), and certain other collateral.

The Debtors' bankruptcy filings triggered an event of default under the indenture under which the 2015 Notes were issued (the "2015 Notes Indenture"). As a consequence, the 2015 Notes' indenture trustee (the "Indenture Trustee") or the holders of 25% in principal amount of the outstanding 2015 Notes may declare the 2015 Notes due. To date, there has been no such declaration. . . .

Many of the objecting parties in this adversary proceeding are holders of the 2015 Notes ("2015 Noteholders"). . . . [A]part from the covenant default under the 2015 Notes Indenture that resulted from the Debtors' Chapter 11 filings, there has now also been a payment default under the 2015 Notes Indenture, although it is potentially subject to cure. On February 17, 2009 . . . LBIAF failed to make the interest payment that was due on the 2015 Notes at that time.

. . . [I]n light of LBIAF's inability to pay the principal and interest that would be due under the 2015 Notes upon acceleration, the Indenture Trustee or 2015 Noteholders could attempt to commence involuntary insolvency proceedings against LBIAF in Luxembourg, the Netherlands, or (less likely) elsewhere.

3. LBIAF's Assets

[LBIAF's assets consisted primarily of (1) the stock in its sole direct subsidiary, which was pledged to secure the pre-petition senior secured and postpetition bridge loans,

(2) certain intercompany obligations, (3) and a small amount of cash on hand. The assets were collectively] "plainly insufficient to pay any significant portion of the Guaranty claims (much less the 2015 Note obligations). . . .

5. Prejudice and Injury to the Debtors

. . . I find that there would be serious and irreparable injury to the Debtors if some relief, for some period of time, weren't granted here. Satisfactory showings have been made to me that:

a. If the Guaranty Creditors were allowed to assert claims on the Guaranties, LBIAF could be forced into involuntary insolvency proceedings in Luxembourg, the Netherlands, or (though less likely) elsewhere;

b. A European involuntary insolvency proceeding would be unlikely to involve a process of reorganization or restructuring as in the United States, and could cause a fast liquidation of LBIAF;

c. That, in turn, could have the effect of triggering fiduciary (or other legal) obligations of directors of nondebtor affiliates of the Debtors and LBIAF located in Europe, which, in turn, could force all the European debtors into their own liquidation proceedings in as many as 8 countries;

d. It would not be possible to coordinate each of those disparate proceedings.

Additionally, a satisfactory showing has been made to me, and I so find, that each of the entities owned directly and indirectly by LBIAF (with the exception of certain legacy entities that have no ongoing operations) is an important part of the *integrated operations* of the Debtors and nondebtors. The Debtors and their nondebtor affiliates operate as an integrated enterprise through the worldwide coordination of their businesses and their operation as a vertically integrated group of companies. These entities' operations—and the Debtors' restructuring and reorganization efforts—benefit substantially from maintaining coordinated control and management over all of the worldwide operations. Operating together, the U.S. and European entities achieve substantial synergies (estimated at the time of the merger between Lyondell Chemical Company and Basell Polyolefins to increase [earnings] by approximately $420 million through 2010); benefit from access to credit (which is very important in the present economic environment); and by their coordinated operations receive other benefits, such as operational improvement. Because the Debtors and their European affiliates operate as an integrated global enterprise, the cessation of European operations would require the Debtors to expend substantial resources in order to replace the goods, services, and systems formerly provided by the European nondebtors.

I believe that a *voluntary*, properly planned and organized, *restructuring* of the affairs of LBIAF would not result in irreparable injury, or at least that an insufficient showing has been made to me that irreparable injury in that event would result. But I believe than an *involuntary* proceeding against any of the European nondebtor entities would be a disaster, and the resulting injury would indeed be irreparable. I'm satisfied that the synergies associated with the coordinated operations of the entities, in both the U.S. and Europe, that form the integrated whole in the worldwide enterprise are real.

And the recoveries of the creditors in the chapter 11 cases before me—particularly those in the unsecured creditor community, who are of course junior to secured debt, but whose needs and concerns I very much care about—depend upon maximizing the value of the Debtors here. It also is reasonable to assume, at least for now, that the interests of all creditors in this case, secured and unsecured, would be well served by finding as many ways as possible for the *secured* creditors in these chapter 11 cases to look to value to realize upon their claims—being mindful that a significant component of the secured creditors' collateral is in Europe, and that the value of this collateral could be materially impaired if financial affairs in Europe go into a freefall.

. . .

All of those matters, in my view, would constitute irreparable injury, to the extent a finding of such is required, and equally plainly are relevant to any balancing of relative hardships.

6. Prejudice and Injury to the Guaranty Creditors and 2015 Noteholders

. . . LBIAF does not have sufficient liquid assets to pay the 2015 Notes (approximately $1.3 billion), and the Guaranty Claims (approximately $130 million). Also, to the extent LBIAF has liquid assets, they are pledged to the prepetition senior secured and bridge lenders, and are therefore unavailable to pay more junior claims.

Thus the 2015 Noteholders and Guaranty Creditors could recover only after all of the creditors of LBIAF's subsidiaries were satisfied, including claims related to over $20 billion of debt owed to the Senior Secured Lenders. Allowing the 2015 Noteholders and Guaranty Creditors to proceed against LBIAF would as a practical matter get them very little, other than an opportunity to complicate the Debtors' affairs (and thus to exercise leverage) and perhaps get a possible leg up against other LBIAF junior creditors in the ultimate event of an LBIAF insolvency in which secured lenders have been paid in full.

To the extent Guaranty Creditors have valid claims against LBIAF . . . , they also have valid claims against one or another of the Debtors. Yet by bringing claims against LBIAF, they risk damaging the very Debtors against whom they have their claims and diminishing the value of their own claims as well as those of all of the other creditors of those entities.

Moreover, because LBIAF has virtually no liquid assets to satisfy the Guaranty Claims and its only meaningful assets are indirect equity interests in, and receivables from, European subsidiaries, Guaranty Creditors will recover only after all of the creditors of LBIAF's subsidiaries are satisfied, and are thus very unlikely to have their Guaranty Claims satisfied in any event.

The situation of the 2015 Noteholders is slightly different in detail, but ultimately with the same result. . . . Accordingly . . . accelerating and filing an involuntary bankruptcy case will not, in any reasonably foreseeable way, afford the 2015 Noteholders any meaningful recovery.

. . .

II. STANDARDS FOR ISSUANCE OF A SECTION 105(a) INJUNCTION

Section 105 of the Code provides that "the court may issue any order, process, or judgment that is necessary or appropriate to carry out the provisions of this title." No one considering this matter objectively disputes the power of a bankruptcy court, under section 105(a) of the Code, to enjoin acts against third parties when they impair a debtor's ability to reorganize in a chapter 11 case—even though such acts are not proscribed by the automatic stay of section 362 of the Code. The issue, once more, is the appropriate exercise of the court's power.

Thus I look to the standards for invocation of section 105(a) in instances where parties seek to protect their reorganizations by enjoining acts against nondebtor entities that are not entitled to section 362 protection.

The applicable law relating to the exercise of the 105(a) power . . . [consists of an] analysis using the following factors:

(1) whether there is a likelihood of successful reorganization;
(2) whether there is an imminent irreparable harm to the estate in the absence of an injunction;
(3) whether the balance of harms tips in favor of the moving party; and
(4) whether the public interest weighs in favor of an injunction.

I consider those in turn.

. . .

D. Public Interest

The request here places constraints on the enforcement of guaranties, raises a risk of theoretical unequal treatment of creditors, and impairs creditors from proceeding with their normal remedies, when the more traditional way by which that would be done would be by resort to court-supervised insolvency processes.

Most of the Guaranty Creditors have argued, and some have backed up their arguments with evidence, that guaranties are an important device in commercial transactions, and that as a matter of public policy their enforcement should not be limited. They further point out, persuasively, that of the various alternatives for giving vendors and other contract counterparties comfort that they'll get paid, parent guaranties are among the most cost-effective and beneficial to the primary obligors—more cost effective, by way of example, than letters of credit would be, or arrangements for payment COD or CBD. They further point out that the very purpose of guaranties is to protect the party that asked for the guaranty from the insolvency of the primary obligor, and that any regular practice permitting the enforcement of guaranties to be blocked or impaired when the primary obligor went into bankruptcy would frustrate the very purpose for which the guaranties were secured in the first place.

I agree that for those reasons, and perhaps others, guaranties should be respected and honored wherever possible, and believe that courts should be wary of placing limits on the enforcement of commercial guaranties except in cases of the most pressing need. But I do not believe that the law does or should require that the enforcement of guaranties can *never* be blocked. First, as a practical matter, as counsel for the Creditors' Committee observed, guaranties are hardly iron-clad assurances of payment. They are much less reliable than letters of credit. The Guaranties are only as good as the financial strength of the guarantor, and their enforcement may be delayed, or blocked, by senior claims or security interests tapping the assets of the guarantor; bankruptcy of the guarantor; failure of consideration; and fraudulent conveyance doctrine. . . . Here, for instance, where LBIAF has billions of dollars of secured debt ahead of unsecured claims, and the Guaranty Creditors' claims against their guarantor are structurally subordinated, it is not at all clear that the guaranties, notwithstanding their commercial importance, might yield anything anyway. Secondly, there will sometimes be a harm requiring judicial intervention where the needs and concerns of other creditors simply trump commercial predictability. That, in my view, is the case here. [The court went on to temporarily enjoin the enforcement of the Guaranties for 60 days, conditioned on tolling agreements and restrictions on LBIAF transferring or encumbering assets or making payments outside the ordinary course of business. LBIAF and the other guarantors used the injunction window to file for voluntary bankruptcy in various European jurisdictions.]

. . .

Study Question

If the 2015 Noteholders and Guaranty Creditors would receive little or nothing in a European involuntary bankruptcy, why would they want to commence such a case?

C. Standby Letters of Credit

As *Lyondell* discusses, contractual creditors use a variety of devices to enhance the likelihood that they will be repaid. We've seen the range of these devices in Chapter 3. One such device is a standby letter of credit.

Recall that a standby letter of credit makes the bank that issues the letter an absolute guarantor of the applicant's payment obligation. If the applicant fails to pay the beneficiary, the beneficiary can draw on the letter of credit and get paid by the bank. The bank is then subrogated to the rights of the beneficiary and may seek indemnification from the applicant. If the bank has taken a security interest in property of the applicant, the bank becomes a secured creditor of the applicant upon a draw on the letter of credit.

Standby letters of credit raise two potential automatic stay issues. First, is the drawing down on the letter of credit by the beneficiary a stay violation? And second, does the bank's secured right of subrogation create a stay violation?

Courts have generally held that the draw on a letter of credit by a beneficiary does not violate the stay, as the letter of credit is not property of the estate, and the beneficiary is not enforcing the lien against the estate. This position is founded on the **doctrine of independence**, a legal doctrine that treats each relationship in a standby letter of credit (debtor-creditor; debtor-issuer; issuer-creditor) as a separate and independent relationship, such that the debtor has no interest in the letter of credit itself.

The doctrine of independence is, of course, a legal fiction required for standby letters of credit to work. The relationships within a standby letter of credit are of course linked, particularly as a draw on the letter of credit subrogates the issuer to the rights of the creditor, enabling the issuer to pursue the debtor. The debtor's estate has essentially guaranteed the letter of credit, so the situation would seem no different than any other sort of indemnity given by the estate to a third party. Without the doctrine of independence, however, the entire guaranty structure of standby letters of credit would cease to work—the debtor would be recognized as having rights in the letter of credit, so the automatic stay would operate to prevent a draw by the creditor upon the debtor's bankruptcy. This would defeat the whole point of obtaining a standby letter of credit. The ability to create a guaranty that is immune to the debtor's bankruptcy is critical for the operation of the letter of credit.

Even if the draw on the letter of credit is not a stay violation, the bank's right of subrogation could raise stay issues, depending on when the attachment of the security interest occurs. If the security interest attached before bankruptcy, then there is no problem. But if it had not yet attached, then the bank would be unsecured and an attempt to create a lien would violate the stay. The question, then, is when attachment occurs. Typically, this should happen when the letter of credit is issued, as attachment requires that the debtor have rights in the collateral, that there is an authenticated security agreement, and that sufficient value to support a simple contract has been given. UCC § 9-203(b). Has value been given? Arguably, the bank's obligation to pay the letter of credit is giving value. Of course, that value is not given to the debtor, but to the beneficiary. Generally speaking, however, letters of credit are outside the scope of the automatic stay.

D. Setoff vs. Recoupment

The automatic stay applies to the exercise of setoff rights. 11 U.S.C. § 362(a)(7). It does not, however, extend to the similar, but distinct right of **recoupment**. Whereas setoff involves offsetting debts from separate and distinct transactions, recoupment involves reciprocal obligations from one single, integrated transaction. The distinction may seem minor, but setoff is covered by the automatic stay, whereas recoupment is not. Thus, in order to exercise a setoff right postpetition, a creditor must move to lift the stay under section 362(d)(1).

E. Account Freezes

For a setoff to exist, the debts must remain owing. This means that a debtor can defeat a creditor's setoff rights by ending the mutual indebtedness. For example, if the debtor has funds deposited at a creditor bank, the debtor can destroy the bank's setoff rights by withdrawing the funds. The following case considers what steps a bank may take to prevent such actions without running afoul of the automatic stay.

Citizens Bank v. Strumpf

516 U.S. 16 (1995)

Justice SCALIA delivered the opinion of the Court.

We must decide whether the creditor of a debtor in bankruptcy may, in order to protect its setoff rights, temporarily withhold payment of a debt that it owes to the debtor in bankruptcy without violating the automatic stay imposed by 11 U.S.C. § 362(a).

I

On January 25, 1991, when respondent filed for relief under Chapter 13 of the Bankruptcy Code, he had a checking account with petitioner, a bank conducting business in the State of Maryland. He also was in default on the remaining balance of a loan of $ 5,068.75 from the bank. Under 11 U.S.C. § 362(a), respondent's bankruptcy filing gave rise to an automatic stay of various types of activity by his creditors, including "the setoff of any debt owing to the debtor that arose before the commencement of the [bankruptcy case] against any claim against the debtor." § 362(a)(7).

On October 2, 1991, petitioner placed what it termed an "administrative hold" on so much of respondent's account as it claimed was subject to setoff—that is, the bank refused to pay withdrawals from the account that would reduce the balance below the sum that it claimed was due on respondent's loan. Five days later, petitioner filed in the Bankruptcy Court, under § 362(d), a "Motion for Relief from Automatic Stay and for Setoff." Respondent then filed a motion to hold petitioner in contempt, claiming that petitioner's administrative hold violated the automatic stay established by § 362(a).

The Bankruptcy Court ruled on respondent's contempt motion first. It concluded that petitioner's "administrative hold" constituted a "setoff" in violation of § 362(a)(7) and sanctioned petitioner. Several weeks later, the Bankruptcy Court granted petitioner's motion for relief from the stay and authorized petitioner to set off respondent's remaining checking account balance against the unpaid loan. By that time, however, respondent had reduced the checking account balance to zero, so there was nothing to set off.

The District Court reversed the judgment that petitioner had violated the automatic stay, concluding that the administrative hold was not a violation of § 362(a). The Court of Appeals reversed. "An administrative hold," it said, "is tantamount to the exercise of a right of setoff and thus violates the automatic stay of § 362(a)(7)." 37 F.3d 155, 158 (CA4 1994). We granted certiorari. 514 U.S. 1035 (1995).

II

The right of setoff (also called "offset") allows entities that owe each other money to apply their mutual debts against each other, thereby avoiding "the absurdity of making A pay B when B owes A." *Studley* v. *Boylston Nat. Bank,* 229 U.S. 523, 528 (1913). Although no federal right of setoff is created by the Bankruptcy Code, 11 U.S.C. § 553(a) provides that, with certain exceptions, whatever right of setoff otherwise exists is preserved in bankruptcy. Here it is undisputed that, prior to the bankruptcy filing, petitioner had the right under Maryland law to set off the defaulted loan against the balance in the checking account. It is also undisputed that under § 362(a) respondent's bankruptcy filing stayed any exercise of that right by petitioner. The principal question for decision is whether petitioner's refusal to pay its debt to respondent upon the latter's demand constituted an exercise of the setoff right and hence violated the stay.

In our view, petitioner's action was not a setoff within the meaning of § 362(a)(7). Petitioner refused to pay its debt, not permanently and absolutely, but only while it sought relief under § 362(d) from the automatic stay. Whether that temporary refusal was otherwise wrongful is a separate matter—we do not consider, for example, respondent's contention that the portion of the account subjected to the "administrative hold" exceeded the amount properly subject to setoff. All that concerns us here is whether the refusal *was a setoff*. We think it was not, because—as evidenced by petitioner's "Motion for Relief from Automatic Stay and for Setoff"—petitioner did not purport permanently to reduce respondent's account balance by the amount of the defaulted loan. A requirement of such an intent is implicit in the rule followed by a majority of jurisdictions addressing the question, that a setoff has not occurred until three steps have been taken: (i) a decision to effectuate a setoff, (ii) some action accomplishing the setoff, and (iii) a recording of the setoff. See, *e. g., Baker* v. *National City Bank of Cleveland*, 511 F.2d 1016, 1018 (CA6 1975) (Ohio law); *Normand Josef Enterprises, Inc.* v. *Connecticut Nat. Bank*, 230 Conn. 486, 504-505 (1994). But even if state law were different, the question whether a setoff *under § 362(a)(7)* has occurred is a matter of federal law, and other provisions of the Bankruptcy Code would lead us to embrace the same requirement of an intent permanently to settle accounts.

Section 542(b) of the Code, which concerns turnover of property to the estate, requires a bankrupt's debtors to "pay" to the trustee (or on his order) any "debt that is property of the estate and that is matured, payable on demand, or payable on order . . . *except to the extent that such debt may be offset under section 553 of this title against a claim against the debtor*." 11 U.S.C. § 542(b) (emphasis added). Section 553(a), in turn, sets forth a general rule, with certain exceptions, that any right of setoff that a creditor possessed prior to the debtor's filing for bankruptcy is not affected by the Bankruptcy Code. It would be an odd construction of § 362(a)(7) that required a creditor with a right of setoff to do immediately that which § 542(b) specifically excuses it from doing as a general matter: pay a claim to which a defense of setoff applies.

Nor is our assessment of these provisions changed by the fact that § 553(a), in generally providing that nothing in the Bankruptcy Code affects creditors' prebankruptcy setoff rights, qualifies this rule with the phrase "except as otherwise provided in this section and in sections 362 and 363." This undoubtedly refers to § 362(a)(7), but we think it is most naturally read as merely recognizing that provision's restriction upon *when* an *actual setoff* may be effected—which is to say, not during the automatic stay. When this perfectly reasonable reading is available, it would be foolish to take the § 553(a) "except" clause as indicating that § 362(a)(7) requires immediate payment of a debt subject to setoff. That would render § 553(a)'s general rule that the Bankruptcy Code does not affect the right of setoff meaningless, for by forcing the creditor to pay *its* debt immediately, it would divest the creditor of the very thing that supports the right of setoff. Furthermore, it would, as we have stated, eviscerate § 542(b)'s exception to the duty to pay debts.   It is an elementary rule of construction that "the act cannot be held to destroy itself." *Texas & Pacific R. Co.* v. *Abilene Cotton Oil Co.*, 204 U.S. 426, 446 (1907).

Finally, we are unpersuaded by respondent's additional contentions that the administrative hold violated §§ 362(a)(3) and 362(a)(6). Under these sections, a bankruptcy filing automatically stays "any act to obtain possession of property of the estate or of property from the estate or to exercise control over property of the estate," 11 U.S.C. § 362(a)(3), and "any act to collect, assess, or recover a claim against the debtor that arose before the commencement of the case under this title," § 362(a)(6). Respondent's reliance on these provisions rests on the false premise that petitioner's administrative hold took something from respondent, or exercised dominion over property that belonged to respondent. That view of things might be arguable if a bank account consisted of money belonging to the depositor and held by the bank. In fact, however, it consists of nothing more or less than a promise to pay, from the bank to the depositor, see *Bank of Marin* v. *England*, 385 U.S. 99, 101 (1966); *Keller* v. *Frederickstown Sav. Institution*, 193 Md. 292, 296 (1949); and petitioner's temporary refusal to pay was neither a taking of possession of respondent's property nor an exercising of control over it, but merely a refusal to perform its promise. In any event, we will not give § 362(a)(3) or § 362(a)(6) an interpretation that would proscribe what § 542(b)'s "exception" and § 553(a)'s general rule were plainly intended to permit: the temporary refusal of a creditor to pay a debt that is subject to setoff against a debt owed by the bankrupt.

The judgment of the Court of Appeals for the Fourth Circuit is reversed.

III. STAY EXEMPTIONS

While the stay is broad, there are also myriad exceptions to it. The exceptions are laid out in section 362(b) of the Bankruptcy Code. They include exceptions for regulatory enforcement actions (other than money judgments), criminal actions, tax audits, and eviction actions for commercial real estate if the lease has already expired. The stay normally remains in place for the duration of the bankruptcy. 11 U.S.C. § 362(c). Violation of the stay can result in sanctions, but there are procedures for having the stay lifted, discussed later in this chapter. 11 U.S.C. § 362(d). Below is an excerpt of *some* of the stay exceptions. Be aware that there are other stay exceptions (not provided below) that are specific to certain industries, such as shipping and higher education.

There are good reasons for many of the stay exceptions, such as policies that override bankruptcy policy concerns. Thus, section 362(b)(1) provides that the automatic stay does not prevent criminal prosecutions against the debtor. Nor does the stay prevent regulatory enforcements other than money judgments, or tax audits and assessments (not actual collection). 11 U.S.C. §§ 362(b)(4), (b)(9). Thus, the stay does not prevent enforcement of an injunction against the debtor or loss of a license or excuse the debtor from filing tax returns. Likewise, the stay does not prevent securities self-regulatory organizations—such as FINRA or stock exchanges—from taking actions against their members, other than enforcing monetary sanctions. 11 U.S.C. § 362(b)(25). Nor does the stay prevent commercial landlords from evicting the debtor from property on which a lease terminated pre-bankruptcy. 11 U.S.C. § 362(b)(10).

The stay also does not prevent the *presentment* of negotiable instruments. A negotiable instrument is a particular type of payment or credit instrument that meets a statutory definition under Article 3 of the UCC. UCC § 3-104(a). Checks are the most common type of negotiable instrument. Presentment refers to presenting the instrument to a financial institution for payment. Thus, if the debtor wrote a check, the payee could deposit the check at his bank and his bank could present the check for payment at the debtor's bank. The payee's bank would not violate the automatic stay for presentment, and indeed, the debtor's bank could even honor the check and pay the payee's bank, but the debtor's bank would not be entitled to withdraw funds from the debtor's account. Presentation of a non-negotiable payment order, such as an automatic clearing house (ACH) item (including a check that has been converted into an ACH item) is not covered by section 362(b)(11), and would be stayed.

The automatic stay also has an important carveout for the perfection of purchase money security interests (PMSI). 11 U.S.C. § 362(b)(3). A PMSI is a security interest taken to secure a loan to purchase something. Recall that a lien is enforceable against the debtor when it has "attached," but only gives the creditor priority in the collateral vis-à-vis third parties when it has been "perfected." The requirements of attachment and perfection vary by collateral type, but for personalty, attachment requires an authenticated security agreement, value to have been given, and the debtor to have rights in the collateral. UCC § 9-203(b). Perfection, then generally requires a financing statement to be properly filed with the appropriate governmental office. UCC § 9-310(a). The financing statement can be filed before or after attachment, but perfection will normally date from the latter of filing or attachment. In the case of PMSIs, however, perfection will relate back to the date of attachment if a financing statement is filed within 20 days of attachment. UCC § 9-317. This relation back is essentially a grace period for purchase money lenders designed to encourage purchase money financing. Section 362(b)(3) allows the post-petition filing of a financing statement in order to achieve the relation back (which is allowed under section 546(b)), and thereby preserves the grace period. Curiously, the time permitted under section 362(b)(3) is not 20 days, but 30 days, per section 547(e), and a financing statement filed between days 20 and 30 will not violate the automatic stay, but may render the security interest vulnerable to avoidance by the trustee or debtor in possession.

Section 362(b)(3) also permits the filing of "continuation statements" for pre-existing security interests. Financing statements for security interests in personalty are effective for only five years. UCC § 9-515. To extend a security interest beyond five years, a "continuation statement" must be filed. Section 362(b)(3) means that the filing of a continuation statement to "maintain or continue" an existing security interest is not a violation of the automatic stay.

One of the most important set of exceptions from the automatic stay is for financial contracts. The Bankruptcy Code gives very favorable treatment to financial contracts in several ways: they are not subject to the automatic stay; they are not subject to cherry-picking by the debtor; and they are generally exempted from clawback actions.

Section 362(b) includes a number of stay exemptions for the exercise of "any contractual right . . . under any security agreement or arrangement or other credit enhancement forming part of or related to any" commodity contract, forward contract, securities contract,[1] repurchase agreement, swap agreement, or master netting agreement, as well as the right to offset or net out any such financial contracts. 11 U.S.C. §§ 362(b)(6), (7), (17), (27). "Contractual right" is elsewhere defined as including

> a right set forth in a rule or bylaw of a derivatives clearing organization . . . , a multilateral clearing organization . . . , a national securities exchange, a national securities association, a securities clearing agency, a contract market designated under the Commodity Exchange Act, a derivatives transaction execution facility registered under the Commodity Exchange Act, or a board of trade . . . , or in a resolution of the governing board thereof, and a right, whether or not in writing, arising under common law, under law merchant, or by reason of normal business practice.

11 U.S.C. §§ 555, 556, 559, 560, 561(c). Sections 555, 556, and 559-561 further provide that the exercise of a contractual right of most counterparties on financial contracts "to cause the liquidation, termination, or acceleration" of the contract "because of a condition of the kind specified in section 365(e)(1)" is not stayed. Section 365(e)(1) lists what are known as *"ipso facto* clauses"—clauses triggered by the debtor's financial condition or bankruptcy. Recall from the previous chapter that section 541(c) provides that *ipso facto* clauses are ineffective at preventing property from becoming property of the estate. Section 362(b) does not change this result. Financial contracts, and any collateral the debtor has posted to back those contracts, are property of the estate, but section 362(b) allows the debtor's counterparties to seize and sell collateral as if there were no automatic stay.

Thus, if a financial contract contains an *ipso facto* clause—which virtually all do—the counterparty will have the right to liquidate, terminate, or accelerate the contract, and will not be prevented from doing so by the automatic stay. This means that when the counterparty is out of the money, the counterparty can terminate the contract and exercise its right to simply walk away without payment, while when the counterparty is in the money, the counterparty can terminate the contract and liquidate the collateral (margin) the debtor has posted to cover its position. Of course, if the debtor has not posted sufficient collateral to cover its position, the

---

1. The stay exemptions cover not only the derivatives discussed in Chapter 4, but also "securities contracts." What is a securities contract? The term is defined in section 741 of the Code in a manner that is broader than one might expect. A "securities contract" is defined to include not just a contract for a sale and purchase of a debt or equity security, but also option contracts and contracts for CDs, mortgage loans, loan participations, margin loans, and repos, among other things. Thus, even repos that do not meet the statutory definition of repos might still be covered as securities contracts. *Calyon New York Branch v. Am. Home Mortgage Corp.,* 379 B.R. 503 (Bankr. D. Del. 2008).

counterparty simply has an unsecured claim for the deficiency, and any attempt to collect on that will be covered by the automatic stay.

To see what the stay exception means in practice, let's imagine that Apollo Investments was in an interest rate swap contract with Bacchus Bank. Apollo promised to pay Bacchus a fixed 5% on a notional $100 million over a year, and in exchange Bacchus promised to pay Apollo the Federal Funds rate plus 300 basis points on the notional $100 million. Let's suppose that Apollo Investments filed for bankruptcy when four months were left to run on the swap, and that under the terms of the swap either counterparty was entitled to terminate the swap upon the bankruptcy of the other. Let's also suppose that there was a margin provision for the swap: Both parties were required to post collateral in the form of AAA-rated securities to cover their obligations to each other as the swap was marked to market on a daily basis. If on a particular day the Federal Funds rate was such that Apollo would owe Bacchus $10 million at the end of the swap (if the Federal Funds rate held steady), then Apollo would have to post $10 million on collateral to guarantee that it would be money good at the end of the swap. The collateral would, of course, still be Apollo's property, not Bacchus's.

When Apollo files for bankruptcy, it will constitute an event of default under the ISDA Master Agreement and will entitle Bacchus to declare an early termination event. In other words, Bacchus has the option of terminating the swap. Bacchus will do so if the swap position is favorable based on the damages calculation. If the parties elected that a settlement payment would only need to be made to the non-defaulting party, it would not matter if Bacchus's position was currently favorable: Bacchus would either be able to walk away from any liability it would have on the swap or Bacchus would be able to itself collect damages based on the damages calculation method elected under the ISDA Master Agreement.

Let's assume that Bacchus's position is favorable and that the parties opted for the Market Quotation method of damages calculation. Let's also assume that the calculation results in damages of $9.75 million, and that there's currently $10 million in margin posted by Apollo. Bacchus could then upon termination take the collateral in lieu of a cash payment from Apollo. Given that Apollo isn't going to make a cash payment any time soon, Bacchus will grab enough of the collateral to satisfy its $9.75 million in damages. The right to take the collateral is the "security agreement . . . related to" the swap agreement. Bacchus is a swap participant exercising this contractual right, and the automatic stay will not prevent Bacchus from seizing Apollo's property.

Given that one factor that might push Apollo into bankruptcy is if its financial contract positions turn against it and its margin demands exceed its ability to post margin, the likelihood that financial contract creditors will be able to grab collateral upon the bankruptcy filing is high. Note that the financial creditors are able to take their collateral without having to show lack of adequate protection or other cause and irrespective of whether the debtor has equity in the collateral or the collateral is necessary for an effective reorganization. The anti-forfeiture principle and the general policy of favoring reorganization are not limitations on financial contract creditors.

The importance of the stay exceptions for financial creditors has increased in recent years, not least as creditors began adapting their lending practices to ensure that they fell within exceptions to the automatic stay. While priority is good, not being subject to bankruptcy is even better, went the thinking. A stay exception is essentially the ultra super-priority. While the policy behind the financial contract exceptions to the stay is to maintain liquidity in financial markets, it also had clear distributional politics. Sophisticated creditors could tailor their deals to take advantage of stay exceptions. Most critically, avoiding the stay means that creditors with executory contracts—typically defined as contracts where material performance is still due from both parties—would not be subject to debtor's cherry-picking of profitable contracts for assumption under section 365 (discussed in depth in a later chapter).

The stay exceptions for financial contracts are some of the most controversial provisions in the Bankruptcy Code. Originally, these provisions were designed to enhance the stability of financial markets. The logic was that bankruptcy created uncertainty and illiquidity for a bankrupt firm's broker-dealer counterparties, which could spill over into financial markets more generally. The stay exceptions, however, are defined to protect far more than broker-dealers. Moreover, some of the exceptions are now redundant given the post-2010 Dodd-Frank Wall Street Reform and Consumer Protection Act requirement that certain financial contracts clear through clearinghouses, which mutualize risk among clearinghouse members. *See* Adam J. Levitin, *Clearinghouses and the Redundancy of Financial Contract Safe Harbors in Bankruptcy*, 10 Brook. J. of Corp., Fin. & Comm. Law 129 (2016).

The financial contract stay exceptions prevent bankrupt firms from cherry-picking which contracts to pay in full and which to pay in "bankruptcy dollars", but the flip side, as discussed to above, is that the stay exceptions allow the non-bankrupt counterparty to cherry-pick the contracts. The non-bankruptcy counterparty chooses which contracts to terminate resulting in payment based on current market values under the 2002 ISDA documentation and which to see out to maturity. Thus, the financial contract exceptions to the stay can also be understood as the fruits of rent-seeking by particular industries.

While the stay exceptions were originally designed to enhance the stability of financial markets, they have been heavily criticized post-2008 for actually contributing to financial instability. The bankruptcy stay exceptions encourage greater (and perhaps excessive) financing relative to traditional loan products because the stay exceptions create a perception of lower credit risk. Many of these financial contracts, such as repo, are often very short-term financing, so firms that finance themselves through derivatives need to regularly refinance their debts. This means these firms are vulnerable to market disruptions that make refinancing costly or impossible. The variable margining of many financial derivatives can also exacerbate the stress on a debtor—as its financial condition deteriorates, the debtor may be required to post more margin, thereby reducing its ability to gain fresh financing. And the liquidation of collateral en masse following contract terminations upon bankruptcy resulted in markets being flooded with often similar collateral, which pushed down collateral values and hence recoveries for creditors.

repo

All three criticisms reflect in part the Lehman Brothers' 2008 bankruptcy. Lehman financed itself heavily through repo; if Lehman had been financed through traditional secured loans, it would presumably have had less credit in the first place. Lehman also found itself pressured to come up with more margin to cover its derivative and repo positions—JPMorgan Chase, Lehman's clearing bank in the tri-party repo market, demanded $8 billion of additional margin shortly before the bankruptcy, straining Lehman's liquidity. Finally, because Lehman's financial contract counterparties were not subject to the stay, they terminated their contracts and grabbed their collateral (generally, securities). The stampede of creditors grabbing and liquidating similar collateral simultaneously resulted in fire sale conditions, as the market was flooded with similar assets. Stay exemptions merely return creditors to a grab race, which is not necessarily beneficial for a creditor if there are multiple other creditors able to utilize stay exemptions. As a result, market values of the collateral plummeted, greatly reducing creditors' recoveries. The value of the stay exceptions thus turned out to be not as great as some creditors anticipated.

Problem Set 15

(1) Which of the following are stayed? Which of the following require property to be turned over to the bankruptcy estate? 11 U.S.C. §§ 362(a)-(b), 542.

a. Creditor files suit against the debtor for breach of contract in state court the day after the bankruptcy petition was filed.

b. The day after bankruptcy, creditor moves for summary judgment against the debtor for breach of contract in state court in a suit that was filed two years prior.

c. Creditor conducts a non-judicial foreclosure sale of the debtor's real property after the bankruptcy petition has been filed. Creditor is unaware of the bankruptcy filing.

d. Creditor files a financing statement against the debtor's accounts, equipment, and inventory in the state UCC filing system a day after the bankruptcy filing.

e. Creditor repossesses debtor's equipment three days before bankruptcy with the foreclosure sale scheduled in a month. *U.S. v. Whiting Pools.*

f. Creditor sends a billing statement to the debtor three weeks after the bankruptcy filing.

g. The day after the bankruptcy, the creditor tells the debtor that it won't deal with the debtor any more because the debtor is a "deadbeat."

h. The day after the bankruptcy, the creditor tells the debtor that it won't provide future services unless paid in full for debts already owed.

i. Debtor has sold credit default swap protection. After debtor files for bankruptcy, protection buyer accelerates and terminates the swap and liquidates the margin the debtor has posted. 11 U.S.C. § 560.

j. Debtor has sold credit default swap protection. After debtor files for bankruptcy, protection buyer demands that debtor post additional margin

stayed

for the swap as assurance that debtor will perform the contract. 11 U.S.C. §§ 362(b)(6), 560.

⊗ stayed

k. Debtor has an interest rate swap with counterparty. After debtor files for bankruptcy, creditor accelerates and terminates the swap and liquidates $10 million in margin to satisfy the swap balance. 11 U.S.C. §§ 362(b)(6), 560.

⊗ stayed

l. A week after the bankruptcy, creditor sues the parent company of the debtor, which had <u>guaranteed</u> the debtor's obligation to the creditor. The parent company is not in bankruptcy. The parent company provides corporate treasury services, IP licensing, and IT support to the debtor.

⊗ stayed

m. Post-petition, the state environmental protection agency orders the debtor to engage in a cleanup of a toxic waste spill. 11 U.S.C. § 362(b)(4).

(2) When Delaware Industries filed for Chapter 11, it had $2 million in its account with Laverna National Bank & Trust. Delaware owed Laverna $10 million on a revolving line of credit.

a. Can Laverna freeze the account so Delaware Industries cannot withdraw the funds?

b. Can Laverna engage in setoff if last month Laverna required Delaware to maintain at least $1.5 million on deposit? 11 U.S.C. §§ 362(a)(7), 553(a)-(b).

CHAPTER 16

LIFTING THE AUTOMATIC STAY

I. LIFTING THE AUTOMATIC STAY AND ADEQUATE PROTECTION

The automatic stay remains in place until a case is confirmed or dismissed, unless it is lifted by court order. 11 U.S.C. § 362(c). The stay is lifted or modified only upon motion.

Section 362(d) provides four methods for lifting the stay. Two apply to all cases: lifting the stay under section 362(d)(1) for cause, including "lack of adequate protection of an interest in property," and lifting the stay under section 362(d)(2) if the debtor lacks equity in property and the property is "not necessary to an effective reorganization."

What does it mean to lift the stay "for cause"? The term is capacious. In the business bankruptcy context, it could mean, among other things, a decline in the value of a creditor's collateral because of use or obsolence or because the debtor has failed to pay insurance premiums or taxes on collateral property. "For cause" could also mean that the debtor engaged in some sort of bad faith activity (including the bankruptcy filing). Or "for cause" could mean that the debtor is engaged in some sort of behavior that is damaging property in which another party, be it a creditor or co-owner or guarantor, has an interest.

The automatic stay is not an all-or-nothing matter. The court is authorized to "terminate, annul, modify, or condition" the stay. Thus, the court can continue the stay subject to conditions or lift it for limited purposes. Accordingly, "for cause" could also mean that there's a more appropriate forum for resolving a creditor's claim: Ordinary civil suits that have already gone to trial might be permitted to continue for reasons of judicial economy, although collection will not be allowed outside of the bankruptcy process. Similarly, a court might lift the stay to allow a judgment to be entered against a debtor for the purpose of allowing the creditor to recover from the debtor's insurance policy. Likewise, a court might lift a stay to allow a creditor to commence a foreclosure action, but not to actually complete the foreclosure sale. It may take some time between commencing the foreclosure action and getting to the sale, so allowing the creditor to do everything but have the sale means that the creditor will not be prejudiced by delay if the stay is later lifted.

Generally, however, "for cause" under section 362(d)(1) relates to concerns of secured creditors and lessors. In particular, it often relates to a "lack of adequate protection of an interest in property" as cause for lifting the stay. "Adequate protection" is a term defined in section 361. It requires an interest in specific property of the debtor's; only secured parties or lessors can get adequate protection. Unsecured creditors (other than lessors) cannot receive adequate protection, even though they can otherwise petition for the stay to be lifted "for cause."

So what is "adequate protection"? Adequate protection refers to the protection of a creditor's collateral or leased property against depreciation, whether by the wear and tear of regular use, becoming outmoded, or catastrophic loss. The idea is that the automatic stay prevents a secured creditor from foreclosing on its property (and a lessor from replevining its property), but that secured creditors and lessors should not be prejudiced by the delay imposed by the automatic stay. Critically, as we shall see in a later chapter, adequate protection does not cover the lost time value of the use of property.

Adequate protection typically takes the form of cash payments (lump sum or, more typically, periodic) that offset the property's depreciation. 11 U.S.C. § 361(1). Such payments can put a strain on a debtor's liquidity; if a debtor is not able to provide adequate protection, the stay will be lifted, and the debtor may be forced to liquidate. Thus, a motion for adequate protection can also function as a motion to lift the automatic stay.

Adequate protection can also consist of the granting of additional liens on other property of the debtor's. 11 U.S.C. § 361(2). The value of the additional collateral is to offset the original collateral's depreciation. This is only possible if the debtor has sufficient equity in other property.

Additionally, adequate protection can consist of the granting of other relief that will result in the realization of the "indubitable equivalent" of the creditor's interest in the property. What is "indubitable equivalence"? The phrase comes from Judge Learned Hand's opinion in *In re Murel Holding Corp.*, 75 F.2d 941 (2d Cir. 1935), relating to a proposal to provide the creditor with tangible non-cash property as additional security. In theory, a debtor could provide adequate protection payments in the form of the stock of its subsidiaries or cattle or widgets rather than cash, but that property would have to be valued so as to ensure that the creditor would receive a full recovery of the value of its interest in the collateral at the time from which adequate protection ran.

Often the indubitable equivalence standard is satisfied without any sort of transfer of value to the creditor. Instead, it is simply satisfied by the creditor's equity cushion in collateral. For example, if a creditor has an $8 million claim and is secured by a first lien on a $20 million property, the equity cushion alone should assure that the creditor will recover the indubitable equivalence of its $8 million interest in the property. How much of an equity cushion is sufficient to meet the indubitable equivalence standard? There's no clear answer, but much smaller cushions than the one in the example have sufficed. Obviously, an equity cushion can provide adequate protection only for an oversecured creditor.

Finally, adequate protection might mean the maintenance of insurance on a creditor's collateral or leased property or even the provision of security guards to protect against loss. While periodic or lump sum payments, replacement liens, an equity cushion will protect a debtor against regular depreciation or the obsolence of its collateral, they will not protect against catastrophic loss. Thus, a creditor can typically ensure that its collateral is insured by moving for adequate protection.

The second method of lifting the automatic stay relates only to the lifting of the stay against specific assets of the debtor. Section 362(d)(2) requires the creditor seeking to lift the stay to show that the debtor does not have any equity in the property at issue and that the property is not necessary to an effective reorganization. Thus, if there is either equity in the property or it is necessary to an effective reorganization, the stay cannot be lifted under section 362(d)(2). Neither factor has any bearing, however, on a "for cause" lift stay motion under section 362(d)(1).

Notice what is involved in a section 362(d)(2) determination. First, there are a pair of valuation questions: What is the property worth, and what is the value of the interest of the parties other than the debtor in the property? Unless the parties concur on valuation, a valuation hearing will be necessary. Second, the court will need to determine if the property is necessary for an "effective reorganization." How is the court supposed to know this, especially at the beginning of a case? What is an effective reorganization anyhow? Aren't there multiple possible reorganizations, some of which might involve parting with much of the debtor's pre-petition property? (If the debtor is in Chapter 7 and liquidating, the effective reorganization analysis will be obvious.) Section 362 provides no guidance.

The burden of proof for all motions under section 362(d) is specified in section 362(g). The party seeking relief from the stay has the burden of proof on the question of the debtor's equity in the property under section 362(d)(2), but otherwise the burden of proof is on the debtor. Thus, the burden of proof on the question of an effective reorganization being possible is on the debtor. How exactly does one prove this, especially at the outset of a case? The following case illustrates the application of sections 362(d)(1) and (d)(2), and also addresses an important question: namely, from what point in time does adequate protection, if granted, run?

Lincoln National Life Insurance Co. v. Craddock-Terry Shoe Corp.

98 B.R. 250 (Bankr. W.D. Va. 1988)

WILLIAM E. ANDERSON, U.S. Bankr. J.

The plaintiffs, Lincoln National Life Insurance Company ("Lincoln") and Westinghouse Credit Corporation ("Westinghouse"), have moved the Court to lift the automatic stay imposed by section 362(a) of the Bankruptcy Code, 11 U.S.C. § 362(a), or in the alternative, to provide Lincoln and Westinghouse adequate protection for certain collateral in which they have a security interest. The collateral at issue is the customer mailing lists, catalogues, and certain trademarks of Hill Brothers, a division of Craddock-Terry Shoe Corporation ("Craddock-Terry"), the debtor.

BACKGROUND FACTS

On April 30, 1986, the plaintiffs, Lincoln and Westinghouse, loaned the debtor, Craddock-Terry, $9,000,000. As security for that loan, Lincoln and Westinghouse obtained a security interest in the mailing list, customer list, catalogues and four trademarks ("the collateral") of Hill Brothers, a mail-order division of Craddock-Terry. Debtor's Chapter 11 petition was filed on October 21, 1987. Craddock-Terry has shut down all its operations, except for Hill Brothers.

As of the petition date, debtor owed Lincoln and Westinghouse $9,587,812.50. The debtor does not dispute that Lincoln and Westinghouse have a valid and perfected lien on the mailing list, customer list, catalogues and trademarks of Hill Brothers. The collateral is worth less than the amount owed Lincoln and Westinghouse. In fact, the debtor had on the petition date, and still has, no equity in the collateral.

On January 5, 1988 Lincoln and Westinghouse obtained a court order authorizing a Bankruptcy Rule 2004 examination of the debtor. The examination and document production was conducted during January. Concerned that the value of their collateral appeared to be seriously declining, Lincoln and Westinghouse filed their motion for relief from stay on March 22, 1988.

The evidence introduced at the hearing indicates that, during the Chapter 11 case, Hill Brothers has experienced a serious cash flow problem which has reduced the number of orders which can be filled (the fill rate), cut in half the number of spring catalogues planned to be mailed, and reduced the rate at which new names are added to the Hill Brothers mailing list. In addition, returns of merchandise have increased. These factors have resulted in a serious decline in the value of the collateral.

The plaintiffs presented evidence that on the date debtor's petition was filed, before the adverse impact of the cash flow problems and the list management problems, the value of the mailing list in place and in use at Hill Brothers, was $8.7 million, but that its value on April 30, 1988 was $5.7 million. Their expert at trial had used the same valuation method as that used by an accounting firm whose earlier appraisal the debtor had used to obtain the loans. He testified that he had used a method appropriate for valuing a mailing list in use by a company, known as the discounted cash flow method. The resulting value is the value to the business which is using the list. A mailing list is carefully built up over the years, by adding names each year, and developing an active list of persons who like and buy the particular product of the company. Its value in place to the company using it is necessarily much greater than to an outside buyer or renter.

The debtor presented its own expert testimony from an individual heavily involved in the direct marketing industry. The debtor's expert stated that the fair market value of the list, if sold to other companies, was $700,000 on the petition date and $330,000 as of the hearing date. He utilized a model containing twelve factors from which he calculated the value of the list. These factors included expected revenues and expenses, customer attrition, rental income, comparison to outside lists, and customer affinity for the debtor's product.

DISCUSSION

Bankruptcy Code section 362(d) provides relief from the stay imposed by section 362(a) in either of two circumstances. The stay will be lifted "for cause, including the lack of adequate protection of an interest in property of [a] party in interest." 11 U.S.C. § 362(d)(1). The stay will also be lifted "with respect to a stay of an act against property under subsection (a) of this section, if—(A) the debtor does not have an equity in such property; and (B) such property is not necessary to an effective reorganization." 11 U.S.C. § 362(d)(2). Lincoln and Westinghouse have asserted that they are entitled to relief under either part of section 362(d). The debtor claims to the contrary that its mailing list is vital to its reorganization and that it has offered adequate protection for any decline in the collateral's value. The court will consider sections 362(d)(1) and 362(d)(2) in reverse order.

I. SECTION 362(d)(2)

Neither party disputes that Craddock-Terry has no equity in the collateral. The debt secured by the collateral is greater than $9,000,000, and although the parties have widely divergent views of the value of the collateral for purposes of this motion, each places a lower value on it than the amount of the debt. "Equity" is defined as the amount by which the value of the collateral exceeds the debt it secures. Thus the debtor has no equity in the collateral and the first requirement of section 362(d)(2) is met.

Each party also agrees that if the debtor can possibly reorganize, this collateral is essential to its survival. Lincoln and Westinghouse claim, however, that even if the debtor retains and uses the collateral, no *effective* reorganization is possible. In short, Lincoln and Westinghouse have no faith in the debtor's proposed plan for reorganization or its proposed business plan. They point to reduced catalog mailings and the reduced fill rate for customers' orders since the initiation of bankruptcy proceedings, both of which have caused the decline in value of the mailing list and, therefore, of the business itself.

The debtor, on the other hand, while admitting that its fill rate and catalog mailings have decreased, introduced evidence that the intrinsic value of the mailing list has not been irreparably harmed. The debtor's expert testified that an infusion of capital appropriately applied to the mailing list could revive the list's value, and that he had in fact seen this occur in a similar situation. The debtor's own representative testified that approximately $4,000,000.00 would be available to the debtor from the recent sale of the bulk of the company's assets to The Old Time Gospel Hour and to T/W Properties. He further testified that $900,000.00 of this influx of cash was designated for revitalization of the mailing list, and thereby, the company.

Since the filing of the debtor's petition the general theme of this reorganization has been to sell most of the company's assets and use the proceeds to reorganize the company's Hill Brothers division into a viable entity. The debtor has finally reached the point where it will have capital with which to effect those plans. The law is clear that a court "should not precipitously sound the death knell for a debtor by prematurely determining that the debtor's prospects for economic revival are poor." *In re Shockley Forest Indus., Inc.* The evidence before the court as yet gives no basis for a conclusion that this reorganization is no longer in prospect, and therefore the court finds that the collateral at issue here is necessary to an effective reorganization. Consequently, the automatic stay will not be lifted pursuant to section 362(d)(2).

II. SECTION 362(d)(1)

Lincoln and Westinghouse are entitled to relief from the stay, however, if the debtor cannot satisfy section 362(d)(1) by providing adequate protection for the interest of Lincoln and Westinghouse in the collateral. The debtor has offered replacement liens in all its assets, which it claims will provide adequate protection either from the date of the motion or, if necessary, from the date of the petition. The parties agree that the value of the collateral has declined since the date the petition was filed and also since the date the motion was filed. They disagree as to the amount of decline in value and as to the date from which adequate protection is necessary.

The major focus of the parties during the hearing on this motion and in their final arguments was on the proper value to assign to the collateral at the various stages herein. The Bankruptcy Code provides no specific guidance as to the standard to be used to value property for purposes of providing creditors adequate protection with respect to section 362(d). Section 361 establishes three non-exclusive methods of providing adequate protection of a creditor's interest in property, but specifies no means for valuing that interest. Section 506(a) states that the value of a creditor's interest in the estate's interest in property "shall be determined in light of the purpose of the valuation and of the proposed disposition or use of such property, and in conjunction with any hearing on such disposition or use or on a plan affecting such creditor's interest," 11 U.S.C. § 506(a), but gives no other insight into how such value should be determined.

Consequently courts have looked to the legislative history behind these two sections to find reasonable and proper methods of valuation. The legislative history of section 506(a) establishes that valuation methods should not be rigid:

> "value" does not necessarily contemplate forced sale or liquidation value of collateral; nor does it always imply a full going concern value. Courts will have to determine value on a case-by-case basis, taking into account the facts of each case and the competing interests in the case.

H.R. Rep. No. 95-595, 95th Cong., 1st Sess. 356 (1977). The legislative history of section 361 presents the same idea:

> The section does not specify how value is to be determined, nor does it specify when it is to be determined. These matters are left to case-by-case interpretation and development. . . . This flexibility is important to permit the courts to adapt to varying circumstances and changing modes of financing.

> Neither is it expected that the courts will construe the term value to mean, in every case, forced sale liquidation value or full going concern value. There is wide latitude between those two extremes although forced sale liquidation value will be a minimum.

> In any particular case, especially a reorganization case, the determination of which entity should be entitled to the difference between the going concern value and the liquidation value must be based on equitable considerations arising from the facts of the case.

S. Rep. No. 95-989, 95th Cong., 2d Sess. 54 (1978). Courts have applied this flexibility by attempting to determine "the most commercially reasonable disposition practicable in the circumstances."

In order to determine the most commercially reasonable disposition practicable, the court must follow the directive of section 506 and consider the purpose of the valuation. The purpose of adequate protection "as stated in the legislative history [of section 361] . . . is to insure that the secured creditor receives in value essentially what he bargained for." *In re Ram Mfg., Inc.* Therefore "adequate protection for a secured creditor means that the creditor must receive the same *measure* of protection in bankruptcy that he could have had outside of bankruptcy although the *type* of protection may differ from the bargain initially struck between the parties." *Id.* In other words, the value of the interest of Lincoln and Westinghouse in the collateral is equivalent to what they could have recovered through foreclosure, had the debtor defaulted but not filed its petition for Chapter 11 relief. The benefit initially bargained for, and to be protected under sections 361 and 362, was the value obtainable from the most commercially reasonable disposition of the collateral within the context of foreclosure proceedings.

Each side put on evidence as to the value of the collateral. Lincoln and Westinghouse presented evidence as to the value the collateral would contribute to the price of the business if the business were sold as a going concern, and referred to this as "going concern" value. Their experts used a discounted cash flow analysis[,] which essentially amounted to determining the net of projected revenues and expenses associated with the collateral in the future, and reducing the result to a present value. This capitalization represented the value of the collateral to its owner, the debtor. The plaintiffs' witness testified that in his opinion the value of the collateral to the debtor was approximately $8.7 million prior to bankruptcy, but that it had declined to approximately $5.7 million on April 30, 1988, four days before the hearing.

This type of analysis, however, is inappropriate for the purposes of this motion. Had the debtor defaulted prior to the initiation of bankruptcy proceedings, Lincoln and Westinghouse would not have had the right to force a sale by Craddock-Terry of the entire Hill Brothers division in order to enforce their right of foreclosure. Thus this evidence is irrelevant.

Much of the case law does advocate using "going concern" value if a debtor is reorganizing, usually when the collateral is of a type the debtor itself might be expected to sell, such as inventory or old equipment. In these cases, including the cases cited by Lincoln and Westinghouse, however, "going concern" value generally signifies fair market value based on an arms'-length transaction between a willing buyer and a willing seller, not the value added by the collateral to a sale of the entire business were the business to be sold as a going concern.

[A technical valuation discussion is omitted. The court concludes that the collateral was worth $700,000 as of the filing of the bankruptcy petition.]

Since there is no dispute that the debtor has no equity in the collateral or that its value has declined during these proceedings, the debtor must provide adequate protection to Lincoln and Westinghouse. The final question presented in this case is the date from which adequate protection is required. Lincoln and Westinghouse argue that they should be protected from the decrease in value of the property resulting from the stay in its entirety, and therefore from the date of the petition. The debtor contends that relief should only cover the period of decline following the date these creditors filed their motion for relief.

The debtor contends that to allow a creditor adequate protection from the commencement of the case, even though the creditor does not formally request such protection until some months later, would place an undue burden on the debtor by forcing it to make back payments for an arrearage which the debtor didn't know was accruing. The debtor also claims that such a rule would encourage secured creditors to "sit on their rights" rather than acting to preserve their security. These arguments are not persuasive.

To the contrary, to adopt the rule which the debtor suggests would be even more harmful to the purposes of bankruptcy law. Such a requirement would force creditors to rush to the courthouse as soon as they learn of a debtor's petition in order to ensure that they obtain adequate protection from as early a date as possible. The resulting litigation would likely be prodigious, and certainly would interrupt the expected "breathing space" which debtors normally enjoy after a petition is filed. Surely a debtor in possession will do all it can to preserve the value of all property of the estate whether encumbered or not. Such a requirement, even absent a formal motion by a secured creditor, and even from the commencement of the case, is consonant with bankruptcy policies.

To the extent that the reasoning in *Greives* [cited by the debtor] is attractive, that case is also distinguishable from the case at bar. The collateral in that case was equipment[,] which, unlike a mailing list, was certainly depreciating over a predetermined lifetime. The creditor had already repossessed the collateral, and on the debtor's motion for emergency hearing for turnover, the court ordered the debtor to make a $1000 payment to the creditor as interim adequate protection, and also required written proof of insurance covering the collateral. The creditor itself also had delayed the hearing on the matter.

Moreover, case law has overwhelmingly established that what is protected is the decrease (in value) attributable to the stay, and therefore since the filing of the petition.

CONCLUSION

The Court finds that Lincoln and Westinghouse are entitled to adequate protection for all decline in the value of the collateral since the petition date. The value of the collateral on that date, for the purposes of this motion, was $700,000. The debtor has offered replacement liens in all its remaining assets, which its representative testified are worth in excess of $2,000,000 (not including $7,000,000 in accounts receivable). Therefore the automatic stay imposed by 11 U.S.C. § 362(a) will remain in effect, and this court will enter an order directing the debtor to execute a security agreement, all necessary financing statements, and any other supporting documents necessary to perfect a valid security interest in remaining assets in which the estate has an aggregate equity of no less than $700,000, in favor of Lincoln and Westinghouse, to secure the same indebtedness secured by the collateral at issue here.

ORDER

For the reasons expressed in the accompanying Memorandum Opinion . . . , it is hereby ORDERED AND ADJUDGED that the automatic stay . . . shall remain in effect with respect to the collateral at issue herein, and it is further ORDERED AND ADJUDGED that the debtor, Craddock-Terry Shoe Corporation, be and is hereby DIRECTED to execute a security agreement, all financing statements, and any other supporting documents necessary to perfect a valid security interest, in assets in which it has an aggregate equity of not less than $700,000, in favor of the plaintiffs herein, Lincoln National Life Insurance Company and Westinghouse Credit Corporation, to secure the same debt as that secured by the collateral at issue herein.

Study Questions

1. How much does the debtor owe Lincoln and Westinghouse?

2. What is the collateral that secures the debt?

3. What is the value of Lincoln and Westinghouse's collateral? Why are the creditors Lincoln and Westinghouse upset?

4. What are the possible methods of valuation of the collateral considered in this case? Why does it matter?

5. Why couldn't the automatic stay be lifted under section 362(d)(2)? Who bears the burden of proof under section 362(d)(2) regarding the possibility of an effective reorganization? 11 U.S.C. § 362(g). Who bore the burden of proof on this issue in *Craddock-Terry Shoe*?

6. Why couldn't the automatic stay be lifted under section 362(d)(1)?

7. What is the relevant date for calculating the value of collateral for adequate protection purposes? What is the alternative date argued by the debtor? What is the problem the court identifies with the debtor's proposed rule? What does the statutory language of section 362(d)(1) suggest is the proper date? What is the impact of the court's ruling on debtors' ability to reorganize? Does it make it easier or harder? It is important to recognize that courts are divided on the question of the relevant date for adequate protection.

II. SINGLE-ASSET REAL ESTATE CASES

The Bankruptcy Code provides an additional method of lifting the stay in so-called "single-asset real estate" cases. 11 U.S.C. § 362(d)(3). These are cases in which the debtor's assets consist primarily of a single real estate venture. A major concern creditors have with the automatic stay is that it lets the debtor—whose management was appointed by and might be coextensive with its equityholders—"gamble on resurrection" with creditors' money.

Let's imagine that a firm currently has assets of 100 and liabilities of 105. The firm is currently insolvent. The firm's assets—drilling rights for oil wells in the Arctic—have volatile values. If the price of oil goes up, the value of the firm's assets goes up too. Let's say there's a 20% chance that six months hence oil prices will have risen sufficiently to increase the assets of the firm to 110. If so, the firm would then be solvent. There's also a 20% chance that oil prices in six months will have fallen such that the assets of the firm are worth only 90. The firm's equityholders would like to sit pat for six months. If oil prices rise, they win. If they fall, the creditors lose, as the equityholders are already "out of the money." The equityholders are playing with creditors' money if they can sit in bankruptcy, shielded from collection by means of the automatic stay. If the debtor is willing and able to make adequate protection payments, the stay cannot be lifted under 11 U.S.C. § 362(d)(1)-(2) because the drilling rights are the firm's only asset and necessarily required for an effective reorganization. The adequate protection payments, then, are what the equityholders have to pay to effectively have an option on the firm six months hence. And there's nothing the creditors can do about it.

This situation became a common occurrence with real estate entities in the 1980s. When the real estate market turned down, these entities filed for bankruptcy in order to avoid foreclosure (and tax liabilities), while waiting for a market reversal. Real estate is often held for limited liability purposes in single-purpose entities. These entities' sole asset will be a single property. They are known as single-asset real estate (SARE) debtors. Typically the largest creditor of a SARE is a mortgagee that loaned the SARE entity the money to purchase the real estate.

In 1994, Congress responded to the perceived abuse of the bankruptcy system by SARE debtors by defining SARE debtors in section 101(51)(B) and enacting section 362(d)(3), which enables the automatic stay to be lifted against a SARE debtor that fails to file a viable plan of reorganization within a limited time window and fails to make interest payments on the mortgage loan at the contractual non-default rate. Originally, SARE debtors were also defined as having secured debt of less than $4 million, but in 2005 Congress amended the definition to remove the size cap. Single-asset real estate is now defined as "real property constituting a single property or project, other than residential real property with fewer than 4 residential units, which generates substantially all of the gross income of a debtor who is not a family farmer and on which no substantial business is being conducted by a debtor other than the business of operating the real property and activities incidental thereto." 11 U.S.C. § 101(51)(B).

Despite this definition, what is a "single-asset real estate" debtor is not as obvious as it might appear. In particular, the terms "single property or project" and "substantial business" are not defined. Could a single project consist of several properties? Could it consist of holding the stock of several entities, each of which owned an interconnected property? That is, must there be direct holding of the real estate? Case law has not explored this question in much detail, but some of the rulings are instructional. In *In re Scotia Development, LLC*, the bankruptcy court concluded that the debtor's 200,000 acres of real property used for timber harvesting were not a "single property or project" because they were "spread out across a diverse landscape and [] timber rights are not appurtenant to the land and are not real estate under either the Bankruptcy Code or California" law. 375 B.R. 764 (Bankr.

S.D. Tex. 2007), *aff'd, Ad Hoc Group of Timber Noteholders v. Pac. Lumber Co. (In re Scotia Pac. Co. LLC),* 508 F.3d 214 (5th Cir. 2007). Moreover, the debtor's revenue was not simply from passive ownership (rents), but from "active entrepreneurial labor" and the debtor "operate[d] a substantial commercial business on the property" other than managing the real property. On the other hand, in *In re Light Foot Group LLC,* 2011 Bankr. Lexis 4399 (Bankr. D. Md. Nov. 9, 2011), the bankruptcy court held that 17 residential units on 5 tracts of land were a "single property or project." All told, it appears that the application of the SARE definition is highly fact-specific.

III. CONTRACTUAL WAIVER OF THE AUTOMATIC STAY

Can the automatic stay be waived in advance? While courts generally agree that contracts not to file for bankruptcy are unenforceable as against public policy, *see, e.g., In re Citadel Properties, Inc.,* 86 B.R. 275 (Bankr. M.D. Fla. 1988), there is little agreement among courts on this issue. Workout agreements frequently include waivers of the automatic stay, but whether such waivers are enforceable is another matter. Some courts have enforced stay waivers on grounds that there is no prohibition on such waivers in the Bankruptcy Code, freedom of contract is to be encouraged, and because waivers are thought to facilitate workouts. *See, e.g., In re Club Tower L.P.,* 138 B.R. 307 (Bankr. N.D. Ga. 1991); *In re McBride Estates, Ltd.,* 154 B.R. 339 (Bankr. N.D. Fla. 1993); *In re Cheeks,* 167 B.R. 817 (Bankr. D.S.C. 1994).

Some courts have taken stay waivers as a factor to be considered in terms of lifting the stay "for cause" or adopted a case-by-case approach. *See, e.g., In re Powers,* 170 B.R. 480 (Bankr. D. Mass. 1994); *In re Darrell Creek Assocs., L.P.,* 187 B.R. 908 (Bankr. D.S.C. 1995); *In re Bryan Road, LLC,* 382 B.R. 844 (Bankr. S.D. Fla. 2008).

The other courts, however, have held that stay waivers are *per se* unenforceable both because the debtor has no power to waive a right of the bankruptcy estate, which is a distinct legal entity, and because the stay waiver affects not just the debtor but also other creditors. *See, e.g, In re Sky Group Int'l, Inc.,* 108 B.R. 86 (Bankr. W.D. Pa. 1989); *Farm Credit of Central Florida, ACA v. Polk,* 160 B.R. 870 (M.D. Fla. 1993); *Matter of Pease,* 195 B.R. 431 (Bankr. D. Neb. 1996). Indeed, if debtors could waive the stay, they might be able to do so selectively. If they could, it would allow the debtor to give preferential treatment to insiders, favored creditors, etc., and substantially undermine the bankruptcy fairness norm "equity is equality."

IV. TERMINATION OF BUSINESS WITH DEBTOR AS ATTEMPT TO COLLECT

Some attempts to collect can be more subtle than others. Going to court to seek a judgment or attempting to seize collateral is clearly covered by the automatic stay. But what about refusing to continue business dealings with the debtor? If continued business is conditioned on repayment, it is likely a stay violation. But what about simply terminating relations with the debtor without any explicit conditions?

There is no obligation for anyone to continue doing business with a bankrupt entity, although normal breach of contract rules apply. Although there is no obligation to do business with a bankrupt or a formerly bankrupt entity, governmental units—federal, state, and local—are prohibited from discriminating in terms of licensing, chartering, and employment against firms and individuals *solely* because of bankruptcy. 11 U.S.C. § 525(a). Specifically, section 525(a) prohibits discrimination because of the bankruptcy filing, because of insolvency, or because of non-payment of a debt that is dischargeable. Thus, the fact that someone owes the government money, such as back taxes, does not allow the government to deny a license, permit, charter, grant, etc.

The purpose of section 525(a) is to prevent the government from coercing payment in order to avoid the loss of licenses, charters, or employment that might be necessary for the debtor's reorganization. The operation of section 525(a) is illustrated by *FCC v. Nextwave Personal Communications, Inc.*, 537 U.S. 293 (2003). In *Nextwave*, the debtor had won at auction FCC licenses for billions of dollars of broadband wireless spectrum, but had not paid for the licenses beyond a small down payment before it defaulted on its installment payment plan and filed for bankruptcy. The FCC then revoked the licenses. The debtor's ability to meaningfully reorganize depended on ownership of the licenses—without the licenses, the debtor had little in the way of assets. The Supreme Court held that the FCC violated section 525(a) because it had revoked the licenses solely because the debtor had failed to pay a dischargeable debt. By the plain meaning of section 525(a), the FCC's revocation of the licenses was invalid. Nextwave was therefore able to keep—and then sell—the licenses, which had appreciated significantly during the duration of the case.

The section 525(a) prohibition does not extend to the government's financial transactions. Thus, it does not cover government loan guarantees or direct loans. Accordingly, the government is allowed to consider a loan applicant's history of bankruptcy, insolvency, and non-payment of debts when deciding whether to make a loan.

Notably, the prohibition in section 525(a) applies solely to the government, not to private parties. Why would there be this distinction? The answer lies in the nature of the government activities covered in section 525(a): licenses, permits, charters, and franchises. These are rights that can be obtained only by the government; the government has an effective "monopoly" on granting of certain types of licenses, etc. Absent section 525(a), the government could leverage its monopoly power to extract payment for pre-petition debts. Private parties do not always have that leverage, although there are certainly situations in which they do, such as suppliers of customized goods. How bankruptcy law deals with the negotiating leverage of these private parties, known as "critical vendors," is addressed in Chapter 40.

V. POST-PETITION UTILITY SERVICE

Section 525 applies to all governmental units, including public utilities. A separate section of the Bankruptcy Code includes additional limitations on utilities dealings with debtors. To continue operating after filing for bankruptcy, it's necessary to keep the lights on, the water running, and the phones ringing. Many utility providers, however, will cut off service if bills remain unpaid. This is a particular problem for debtors because many utilities have monopolies on services. When faced with a monopoly utility that refuses to deal with a debtor on the basis of non-payment of past debts, the debtor has no alternative provider of services.

Section 366 of the Bankruptcy Code addresses this problem by limiting when utilities can cut off service in bankruptcy. Whereas most creditors can decline to do business post-petition with a debtor, utilities are generally forbidden from doing so: A utility may not "alter, refuse, or discontinue service to, or discriminate against, the trustee or the debtor solely on the basis of the commencement of a case under this title or that a debt owed by the debtor to such utility for service rendered before the order for relief was not paid when due." 11 U.S.C. § 366(a). The Bankruptcy Code does, however, allow utilities to alter, refuse, or discontinue service if the trustee or debtor has not furnished "adequate assurance of payment" for *future* service within twenty days. 11 U.S.C. § 366(b). What this means is that the utility has to continue providing service to the debtor for 20 days post-petition irrespective of whether the debtor can and will pay. Moreover, even though the utility need not provide services beyond 20 days absent adequate assurances, the utility cannot discriminate in future terms of service based on the debtor's bankruptcy filing or non-payment of pre-petition obligations.

The general prohibition against cut-offs or discriminatory treatment applies in Chapter 11 cases, but with special limitations. First, the applicable deadline for Chapter 11 cases is apparently 30 days, not 20.[1] 11 U.S.C. § 366(c)(2). Second, the adequate assurance of payment in Chapter 11, which is required to avoid a utility cut-off, is determined based on what is "satisfactory *to the utility*." 11 U.S.C. § 366(c)(2) (emphasis added). In other words, under section 366(c), adequate assurance is determined in the first instance by the utility, not the court. This utility's determination of what is satisfactory adequate assurance of payment can be challenged, but in determining what is adequate, the court is prohibited from considering the absence of security for payment prepetition, debtor's past timely payment history (untimely payment can be considered), and the possibility of paying the utility as an administrative expense of the bankruptcy estate, which would prioritize the utility's claim. 11 U.S.C. § 363(c)(3). Moreover, adequate assurance in Chapter 11 is restricted to specific forms, such as cash deposits, letters of credit, surety bonds, or prepayments. 11 U.S.C. § 363(c)(1). None of this prevents a utility from agreeing to continue providing services in exchange for administrative priority for its post-petition services claim. Finally, in Chapter 11, utilities are permitted to engage in setoff of pre-petition security deposits without regard to section 362(a)(7)'s stay of the exercise of setoff rights. 11 U.S.C. § 366(c)(4).

The utility service provision in the Bankruptcy Code is designed to deal with the problem of utilities exercising monopoly power to compel payment from the debtor on past debts as a condition of future service. Section 366, however, is both overbroad and too narrow for addressing this problem. The Code does not define

---

1. The Code does not explain how the 30-day period in section 366(c) fits with the 20-day period in section 366(b), but presumably, a 30-day period controls for Chapter 11 cases.

"utility," but not all entities we think of as utilities have monopoly power. There might be only one water company, but there might be several competing telecom options. In other words, the monopoly problem might exist for some utilities, but not for others. The Bankruptcy Code, however, was written in an age when there was less competition in all utility sectors.

At the same time, though, not all entities that have monopoly power are utilities. For example, in manufacturing, many parts are "single-sourced," meaning that they are purchased from a single supplier. It may well be that there are other firms that can supply equivalent parts for a debtor manufacturer, but they are not prepared to do so immediately. Switching suppliers will necessitate a delay in supplies: It takes time to contract, to retool the supplier's production line to meet the debtor's specifications, and to test the product to ensure that it meets the required standards. Suppose that takes six to eighteen months. For a bankrupt firm, that's an eternity, which it cannot afford. While waiting for the parts from the new supplier, the debtor's production is shut down, which means that the debtor will not have any cash flow. The debtor's fixed costs, however, are still present. How will the debtor be able to make payroll and keep the lights on if it doesn't have revenue for six to eighteen months? The debtor will almost assuredly have to liquidate. The supplier knows this and while it might be loathe to lose a customer, it might be willing to play a game of chicken with the debtor, claiming that it will not deal unless it is paid for its past shipments. While section 366 is an attempt to balance out the monopoly power of utilities, there are many other suppliers that can have situational monopoly power vis-à-vis the debtor, even if they lack monopoly power in an antitrust sense. The "critical vendor" doctrine, discussed in Chapter 40, takes up this issue.

Problem Set 16

1) Thoth Publishing LLC filed for Chapter 11 bankruptcy. Among Thoth's creditors is Horus Finance Corp. Thoth owes Horus $30 million, secured by a first lien loan on Thoth's printing presses. Thoth believes that the presses are worth approximately $40 million and are only marginally depreciating. Horus argues that they are worth only $32 million and rapidly becoming obsolete. Thoth has another $10 million in unencumbered assets and free cash flow of around $500,000 per month. Horus has moved for adequate protection or, in the alternative, for the stay to be lifted under section 362(d)(1).

    a. What happens if the court accepts Thoth's valuation?

    b. What if the court accepts Horus's valuation?

2) Osiris Factors is also a creditor of Thoth Publishing (from the previous problem). Osiris has loaned Thoth $20 million, secured by Thoth's intellectual property (the copyrights on some of its publications and trademarks) and Thoth's inventory. Osiris has moved to lift the stay under section 362(d)(2).

    a. What sort of evidence should Osiris present to support its motion? 11 U.S.C. § 362(d)(2).

    b. Who has the burden of proof on the motion? 11 U.S.C. § 362(g).

(3) Isis Papyrus Co. supplies Thoth with paper. Isis's supply contract with Thoth included a confession of judgment clause in which Thoth appoints Isis as its attorney-in-fact (agent) with authority to "confess" judgment of liability to Isis to a clerk of the court. The clerk may then enter the confession in the court records, which will function as a judicial judgment. In another clause in the contract, Thoth irrevocably waived the automatic stay. After Thoth filed for bankruptcy and defaulted on its obligations to Isis, Isis confessed a judgment for $5 million and on that basis obtained a writ of execution and directed the sheriff to levy on Thoth's unused paper supplies and vehicles. Can Thoth stop the execution?

(4) Ra-Atum Shipping, Ltd. has filed for bankruptcy. Its assets include a fleet of tramp freighters that traverse the high seas to take on cargo wherever there is an excess of demand. The ships are each secured by a ship mortgage from a different lender. Sobek Maritime Corp. holds a non-recourse mortgage on the *Khufu I*. Ra-Atum had allowed the contractually required insurance policy on the ship to lapse shortly before bankruptcy, and a week after the bankruptcy filing the ship hit an unmarked reef and foundered, although all hands were rescued. Sobek Maritime had not yet made an appearance in the bankruptcy case.

    a. Does Sobek Maritime Corp. have any recourse? 11 U.S.C. § 362(d)(1); *Craddock-Terry Shoe.*

    b. Would your answer be different if the *Khufu I* had not sunk, but was just damaged, and Ra-Atum wished to keep operating the ship?

(5) Swashbuckling plaintiff's attorney James Sturdevant has taken the case of a lifetime to trial. The case is a multi-billion dollar tort suit against one of the largest pharmaceutical companies in the world. Just after Sturdevant has conducted a devastating cross-examination of the defendant's chief witness, the defendant files for bankruptcy. "Well, this stinks," fumes Sturdevant. "There were just a couple of days of trial left. Now I've got to go through the whole bankruptcy process and retry the case, and that's really not fair—I've had to show all my cards." Is there anything Sturdevant can do? 11 U.S.C. § 362(d)(1).

(6) The Lynx Mountain Golf Club and Ski Resort has filed for bankruptcy. The Lynx Mountain firm is structured as a parent corporation, Lynx Mountain, Inc. with five subsidiaries: LynxLinks, LLP, which owns the real estate for the golf course; SnowLynx LLP, which owns the real estate for the ski course, including the ski lifts; LynxDen LLP, which owns the real estate for the resort facilities; LynxTreat LLP, which provides the luxury catering for the resort; and ServiceLynx, which provides the management and other service for the operation.

Lynx Mountain, Inc. and all of its subsidiaries filed for bankruptcy last year after the economy turned down and resort bookings and club membership declined and left Lynx Mountain, Inc. unable to service its debt, which is guaranteed by all of its subsidiaries. Can any of the following creditors get the stay lifted? 11 U.S.C. § 362(d)(1)-(3).

    a. Fidelity Fiduciary Bank, Ltd., the indenture trustee for Lynx Mountain, Inc.'s unsecured bond debt.

    b. Goliath National Bank, the agent bank for a syndicate of lenders with a first lien security interest in all assets of Lynx Mountain, Inc.

c. Bailey Building & Loan, which holds a first lien mortgage on the ski course from SnowLynx, LLP. The mortgage is for $25 million; the property is worth $27 million.

d. Chaste Manhattan Bank, which holds a $10 million second lien mortgage on the ski course.

e. C. Montgomery Burns & Co., N.A., which holds a first lien security interest in all of the assets of LynxTreat LLP. LynxTreat has assets of $1 million, which secure a $2 million loan.

(7) Hammerhead Bar & Grill filed for bankruptcy last spring. Hammerhead's liquor license needs to be renewed this month; without a liquor license, Hammerhead is not a viable business. Hammerhead owes the county $1 million in back taxes. The county is refusing to renew the liquor license until all taxes are paid, citing a county regulation that requires all debts to the county to be paid prior to the issuance of a liquor license. What do you advise Hammerhead? 11 U.S.C. §§ 362(b)(2)(D), 362(b)(4), 525(a).

(8) Hammerhead Bar & Grill depends on Bronfman Distributors for its supply of alcoholic beverages. In the past Bronfman sold to Hammerhead on 90 days' credit. This meant that when Hammerhead filed for bankruptcy, it had actually four months of unpaid deliveries. Bronfman is refusing to sell any more alcohol to Hammerhead unless Hammerhead pays it back for the four months of unpaid deliveries. What do you advise Hammerhead? 11 U.S.C. §§ 362(a)(6), 525(a).

(9) Cryostash Inc. provides long-term cold storage for sperm, eggs, and embryos. The cold-storage uses massive amounts of electricity. Cryostash was recently found liable for a large tort judgment related to its mixing up of clients' materials and filed for Chapter 11 yesterday. Energetica, the local power company, is threatening to turn off the juice in 30 days unless Cryostash provides a deposit equal to its past year's utility usage. Cryostash is strapped for cash and cannot provide such a large deposit. At most, it can scrape together two months, worth of electricity. What's going to happen to all the gametes and zygotes in Cryostash's freezers? 11 U.S.C. § 366.

CHAPTER 17

VALUATION

I. VALUATION ISSUES IN BANKRUPTCY

Valuation is the heart of bankruptcy. Valuation decisions are the crux of any reorganization. They determine whether a debtor will be able to retain its hypothecated assets (those pledged as collateral) and have a chance to reorganize. They determine how creditors' claims are treated in terms of being secured or unsecured. Valuation, then, is part of the process of clarifying creditors' relative claims and priorities, and it provides the input for numerous Bankruptcy Code provisions that entitle creditors to *value*.

Despite the importance of valuation, the process remains unfamiliar to most attorneys because it is not a legal analysis, but a financial one. Attorneys, however, need to understand what rides on valuation decisions. They also need to be able to prepare, examine, and cross-examine experts at valuation hearings. Understanding the basics of valuation—and the risks and uncertainty involved—is therefore an important skill for bankruptcy attorneys as well as for anyone engaged in the financial restructuring process.

Sometimes valuation is of an individual asset; sometimes it is of the debtor as a firm. When determining whether a creditor is secured and to what extent, as well as whether the creditor may lift the automatic stay, the valuation is of an asset or group of assets. Similarly, when determining the value of property given to creditors on account of their claims, valuation is of that particular property. When determining whether an unsecured creditor or equityholder is "in the money" or "out of the money" for purposes such as whether to appoint additional official creditor or equityholder committees or whether a plan of reorganization is in creditors' "best interests," valuation of the entire firm is necessary. You have already had a small taste of valuation with the lift-stay motion in *Craddock-Terry Shoe*. The ruling there depended on how much equity the court believed the debtor to have in the collateral and whether that equity value was falling.

The Bankruptcy Code provides precious little instruction about valuation. Section 506, regarding the determination of a creditor's secured status, provides that "[s]uch value shall be determined in light of the purpose of the valuation and of the proposed disposition or use of such property. . . ." 11 U.S.C. § 506(a)(1). This language does little to explain *how* valuations are to be undertaken, only that *what* is to be valued—the proposed disposition or use of the property as well as the reason the valuation is being undertaken—affects the valuation.

The Supreme Court has provided some further guidance on the *what* question in the context of a Chapter 13 consumer case called *Associates Commercial Corp. v. Rash*, 520 U.S. 953 (1997). *Rash*'s applicability to other circumstances is not clear, however. The *how* question is more vexing. There are several standard methodologies deployed, although the parties frequently disagree on which is the appropriate one and on the inputs to use for the valuation analysis.

Valuation rulings are typically made following evidentiary hearings at which the concerned parties present (expensive) expert witnesses who opine on valuation. The experts will have prepared reports on the valuation and then testify regarding their findings. Because judges are not themselves valuation experts, the court is essentially being asked to find which expert's estimate is more convincing. The court, of course, need not accept any of the experts' estimates. The court can appoint its own expert or can choose a valuation that it believes is correct based on, but not following, the experts' testimony. Sometimes this can be as crude as taking the midpoint of the experts' valuations.

The adversarial system of valuation is not required nor is it the only possible one. Nothing in the Bankruptcy Code prescribes the type of evidence that a bankruptcy court must hear regarding valuation, and bankruptcy judges have the leeway to appoint special masters to assist them in providing neutral valuation advice.

Historically, this sort of neutral valuation was provided under the Chandler Act of 1938 by the SEC. The SEC was required to provide advisory opinions to the court that included a valuation of the debtor in a Chapter 10 bankruptcy. This requirement was eliminated with the enactment of the Bankruptcy Code in 1978.

The idea behind having the SEC provide valuation opinions was to have a neutral party advising the court. The SEC's action was often lugubriously slow, which imposed costs on parties in Chapter 10 bankruptcies and, what's more, it was not always accurate. In the infamous case of Atlas Pipeline, an oil company, the SEC provided a June 1941 advisory opinion that included a low valuation for the company. *In re Atlas Pipeline Corp., Debtor*, SEC Advisory Opinion, under the Corporate Reorganization Act, June 7, 1941, 9 S.E.C. 416 (1941). Yet within the year oil prices had skyrocketed because of the United States' December 1941 entry into World War II. It's easy to criticize the *Atlas Pipeline* valuation opinion with hindsight, but could or should the SEC have foreseen the rise in oil prices? Perhaps. The possibility of an increase in oil prices because of U.S. rearmament was certainly an issue discussed in the opinion. If the United States was rearming, surely the United States' involvement in the already raging World War might have been contemplable.

The accuracy of bankruptcy valuations has not been studied, but one recent study suggests that the current valuation system might be systematically biased toward the valuations proposed by management and/or senior secured creditors. (Remember that management is often working hand in glove with senior secured creditors.) The study compares the valuations of debtors emerging from bankruptcy with the valuations of similar publicly traded firms. It concludes that "debtors' enterprise and equity valuations are systematically undervalued by 10% and 20%, respectively, relative to their peers." Such widespread discount, the study suggests, may be evidence of management and senior creditors using lowball valuations in order to capture value that would otherwise flow to junior creditors. *See* Michael T.

Roberts, *The Bankruptcy Discount: Profiting at the Expense of Others in Chapter 11,* AM. BANKR. INST. L. REV. 157 (2013).

Critically, valuation decisions by bankruptcy courts are incredibly difficult to appeal. Valuation decisions are findings of fact, not findings of law, and they receive deferential review for clear error. More practically, there are few district or circuit court judges who have the fortitude to wade into the details of valuation decisions. On top of this, valuation decisions may not be able to receive timely appellate review because they may not be "final" decisions. If they are not final, they will have to wait until the end of the bankruptcy case, by which point they might well be equitably moot. Thus, what are often the most important decisions in bankruptcy cases effectively evade any sort of appellate review. It is not surprising, then, that there is precious little law regarding valuation, as critical as the topic is.

II. WHAT IS BEING VALUED?

The following case provides the most definitive statement regarding what a valuation should be measuring, but it leaves open many questions, including its applicability to Chapters 7 and 11.

Associates Commercial Corp. v. Rash
520 U.S. 953 (1997)

Justice GINSBURG delivered the opinion of the Court.

We resolve in this case a dispute concerning the proper application of § 506(a) of the Bankruptcy Code when a bankrupt debtor has exercised the "cram down" option for which Code § 1325(a)(5)(B) provides. Specifically, when a debtor, over a secured creditor's objection, seeks to retain and use the creditor's collateral in a Chapter 13 plan, is the value of the collateral to be determined by (1) what the secured creditor could obtain through foreclosure sale of the property (the "foreclosure-value" standard); (2) what the debtor would have to pay for comparable property (the "replacement-value" standard); or (3) the midpoint between these two measurements? We hold that § 506(a) directs application of the replacement-value standard.

I.

In 1989, respondent Elray Rash purchased for $73,700 a Kenworth tractor truck for use in his freight-hauling business. Rash made a down payment on the truck, agreed to pay the seller the remainder in 60 monthly installments, and pledged the truck as collateral on the unpaid balance. The seller assigned the loan, and its lien on the truck, to petitioner Associates Commercial Corporation (ACC).

In March 1992, Elray and Jean Rash filed a joint petition and a repayment plan under Chapter 13 of the Bankruptcy Code (Code). At the time of the bankruptcy filing, the balance owed to ACC on the truck loan was $41,171. Because it held a valid lien on the truck, ACC was listed in the bankruptcy petition as a creditor holding a secured claim.

Under the Code, ACC's claim for the balance owed on the truck was secured only to the extent of the value of the collateral; its claim over and above the value of the truck was unsecured. *See* 11 U.S.C. § 506(a).

[The Rashes contended that ACC's claim was undersecured and therefore proposed a plan that invoked the Chapter 13 "cram down" power that requires a non-consenting secured credit or to retain its lien and receive over the life of the plan payments that total the present value of its allowed secured claim. 11 U.S.C. § 1325(a)(5)(B).]

[Specifically, the Rashes proposed to] retain the truck for use in the freight-hauling business and pay ACC, over 58 months, an amount equal to the present value of the truck [which would be ACC's allowed secured claim]. That value, the Rashes' petition alleged, was $28,500. ACC objected to the plan and asked the Bankruptcy Court to lift the automatic stay so ACC could repossess the truck. [ACC also contended that] its claim was fully secured in the amount of $41,171 [meaning that the truck's value was equal to or greater than the amount of the debt]. . . .

The Bankruptcy Court held an evidentiary hearing to resolve the dispute over the truck's value. At the hearing, ACC and the Rashes urged different valuation benchmarks. ACC maintained that the proper valuation was the price the Rashes would have to pay to purchase a like vehicle, an amount ACC's expert estimated to be $41,000. The Rashes, however, maintained that the proper valuation was the net amount ACC would realize upon foreclosure and sale of the collateral, an amount their expert estimated to be $31,875. The Bankruptcy Court agreed with the Rashes and fixed the amount of ACC's secured claim at $31,875; that sum, the court found, was the net amount ACC would realize if it exercised its right to repossess and sell the truck.

. . .

Courts of Appeals have adopted three different standards for valuing a security interest in a bankruptcy proceeding when the debtor invokes the cram down power to retain the collateral over the creditor's objection. *See, e.g., In re Taffi,* 96 F.3d 1190 (9th Cir. 1996) (en banc).[2] In contrast to the Fifth Circuit's foreclosure-value standard, a number of Circuits have followed a replacement-value approach. Other courts have settled on the midpoint between foreclosure value and replacement value. We granted certiorari to resolve this conflict among the Courts of Appeals, and we now reverse the Fifth Circuit's judgment [which had upheld the bankruptcy court's valuation ruling].

II.

The Bankruptcy Code provision central to the resolution of this case is § 506(a), which states:

---

2. In *In re Taffi,* the Ninth Circuit contrasted replacement value with fair-market value and adopted the latter standard, apparently viewing the two standards as incompatible. By using the term "replacement value," we do not suggest that a creditor is entitled to recover what it would cost the debtor to purchase the collateral brand new. Rather, our use of the term replacement value is consistent with the Ninth Circuit's understanding of the meaning of fair-market value; by replacement value, we mean the price a willing buyer in the debtor's trade, business, or situation would pay a willing seller to obtain property of like age and condition.

An allowed claim of a creditor secured by a lien on property in which the estate has an interest . . . is a secured claim to the extent of the value of such creditor's interest in the estate's interest in such property, . . . and is an unsecured claim to the extent that the value of such creditor's interest . . . is less than the amount of such allowed claim. Such value shall be determined in light of the purpose of the valuation and of the proposed disposition or use of such property. . . .

11 U.S.C. § 506(a).

Over ACC's objection, the Rashes' repayment plan proposed, pursuant to § 1325(a)(5)(B), continued use of the property in question, *i.e.*, the truck, in the debtor's trade or business. In such a "cram down" case, we hold, the value of the property (and thus the amount of the secured claim under § 506(a)) is the price a willing buyer in the debtor's trade, business, or situation would pay to obtain like property from a willing seller.

Rejecting this replacement-value standard, and selecting instead the typically lower foreclosure-value standard, the Fifth Circuit trained its attention on the first sentence of § 506(a). In particular, the Fifth Circuit relied on these first sentence words: a claim is secured "to the extent of the value of such *creditor's interest* in the estate's interest in such property." *See* 90 F.3d at 1044 (citing § 506(a)) (emphasis added). The Fifth Circuit read this phrase to instruct that the "starting point for the valuation [is] what the creditor could realize if it sold the estate's interest in the property according to the security agreement," namely, through "repossessing and selling the collateral." 90 F.3d at 1044.

We do not find in the § 506(a) first sentence words—"the creditor's interest in the estate's interest in such property"—the foreclosure-value meaning advanced by the Fifth Circuit. Even read in isolation, the phrase imparts no valuation standard: A direction simply to consider the "value of such creditor's interest" does not expressly reveal *how* that interest is to be valued.

Reading the first sentence of § 506(a) as a whole, we are satisfied that the phrase the Fifth Circuit considered key is not an instruction to equate a "creditor's interest" with the net value a creditor could realize through a foreclosure sale. The first sentence, in its entirety, tells us that a secured creditor's claim is to be divided into secured and unsecured portions, with the secured portion of the claim limited to the value of the collateral. To separate the secured from the unsecured portion of a claim, a court must compare the creditor's claim to the value of "such property," *i.e.*, the collateral. That comparison is sometimes complicated. A debtor may own only a part interest in the property pledged as collateral, in which case the court will be required to ascertain the "estate's interest" in the collateral. Or, a creditor may hold a junior or subordinate lien, which would require the court to ascertain the creditor's interest in the collateral. The § 506(a) phrase referring to the "creditor's interest in the estate's interest in such property" thus recognizes that a court may encounter, and in such instances must evaluate, limited or partial interests in collateral. The full first sentence of § 506(a), in short, tells a court what it must evaluate, but it does not say more; it is not enlightening on how to value collateral.

The second sentence of § 506(a) does speak to the *how* question. "Such value," that sentence provides, "shall be determined in light of the purpose of the valuation and of the proposed disposition or use of such property." § 506(a). By deriving a foreclosure-value standard from § 506(a)'s first sentence, the Fifth Circuit rendered inconsequential the sentence that expressly addresses how "value shall be determined."

As we comprehend § 506(a), the "proposed disposition or use" of the collateral is of paramount importance to the valuation question. If a secured creditor does not accept a debtor's Chapter 13 plan, the debtor has two options for handling allowed secured claims: surrender the collateral to the creditor, see § 1325(a)(5)(C); or, under the cram down option, keep the collateral over the creditor's objection and provide the creditor, over the life of the plan, with the equivalent of the present value of the collateral, see § 1325(a)(5)(B). The "disposition or use" of the collateral thus turns on the alternative the debtor chooses—in one case the collateral will be surrendered to the creditor, and in the other, the collateral will be retained and used by the debtor. Applying a foreclosure-value standard when the cram down option is invoked attributes no significance to the different consequences of the debtor's choice to surrender the property or retain it. A replacement-value standard, on the other hand, distinguishes retention from surrender and renders meaningful the key words "disposition or use."

Tying valuation to the actual "disposition or use" of the property points away from a foreclosure-value standard when a Chapter 13 debtor, invoking cram down power, retains and uses the property. Under that option, foreclosure is averted by the debtor's choice and over the creditor's objection. From the creditor's perspective as well as the debtor's, surrender and retention are not equivalent acts.

When a debtor surrenders the property, a creditor obtains it immediately, and is free to sell it and reinvest the proceeds. We recall here that ACC sought that very advantage. If a debtor keeps the property and continues to use it, the creditor obtains at once neither the property nor its value and is exposed to double risks: The debtor may again default and the property may deteriorate from extended use. Adjustments in the interest rate and secured creditor demands for more "adequate protection," 11 U.S.C. § 361, do not fully offset these risks. *See* 90 F.3d at 1066 (Smith, J., dissenting) ("vast majority of reorganizations fail . . . leaving creditors with only a fraction of the compensation due them"; where, as here, "collateral depreciates rapidly, the secured creditor may receive far less in a failed reorganization than in a prompt foreclosure").

Of prime significance, the replacement-value standard accurately gauges the debtor's "use" of the property. It values "the creditor's interest in the collateral in light of the proposed [repayment plan] reality: no foreclosure sale and economic benefit for the debtor derived from the collateral equal to . . . its [replacement] value." *In re Winthrop Old Farm Nurseries,* 50 F.3d at 75. The debtor in this case elected to use the collateral to generate an income stream. That actual use, rather than a foreclosure sale that will not take place, is the proper guide under a prescription hinged to the property's "disposition or use." *See ibid.*

The Fifth Circuit considered the replacement-value standard disrespectful of state law, which permits the secured creditor to sell the collateral, thereby obtaining its net foreclosure value "and nothing more." *See* 90 F.3d at 1044. In allowing Chapter 13 debtors to retain and use collateral over the objection of secured creditors, however, the Bankruptcy Code has reshaped debtor and creditor rights in marked departure from state law. *See, e.g.,* UCC §§ 9-504, 9-505 (1992). The Code's cram down option displaces a secured creditor's state-law right to obtain immediate foreclosure upon a debtor's default. That change, ordered by federal law, is attended by a direction that courts look to the "proposed disposition or use" of the collateral in determining its value. It no more disrupts state law to make "disposition or use" the guide for valuation than to authorize the rearrangement of rights the cram down power entails.

Nor are we persuaded that the split-the-difference approach adopted by the Seventh Circuit provides the appropriate solution. *See In re Hoskins,* 102 F.3d at 316. Whatever the attractiveness of a standard that picks the midpoint between foreclosure and replacement values, there is no warrant for it in the Code. Section 506(a) calls for the value the property possesses in light of the "disposition or use" in fact "proposed," not the various dispositions or uses that might have been proposed. The Seventh Circuit rested on the "economics of the situation," *In re Hoskins,* 102 F.3d at 316, only after concluding that the statute suggests no particular valuation method. We agree with the Seventh Circuit that "a simple rule of valuation is needed" to serve the interests of predictability and uniformity. *Id.,* at 314. We conclude, however, that § 506(a) supplies a governing instruction less complex than the Seventh Circuit's "make two valuations, then split the difference" formulation.

In sum, under § 506(a), the value of property retained because the debtor has exercised the § 1325(a)(5)(B) "cram down" option is the cost the debtor would incur to obtain a like asset for the same "proposed . . . use."[6] [Reversed and remanded.]

[Justice Stevens's dissent is omitted.]

III. VALUATION METHODOLOGIES

While *Rash* provides some insight regarding what is to be valued, at least for the purposes of a Chapter 13 cramdown, it does not explain how that value should be computed. There are several well-established methodologies for computing values, as Judge Sontchi explains in the article excerpted below. They do not necessarily produce the same valuation. Even when parties can agree on the appropriate methodology, it hardly guarantees agreement on valuation, as the outputs are heavily dependent upon the inputs used. In short, despite its mathematical carapace, valuation is as much an art as a science.

---

6. Our recognition that the replacement-value standard, not the foreclosure-value standard, governs in cram down cases leaves to bankruptcy courts, as triers of fact, identification of the best way of ascertaining replacement value on the basis of the evidence presented. Whether replacement value is the equivalent of retail value, wholesale value, or some other value will depend on the type of debtor and the nature of the property. We note, however, that replacement value, in this context, should not include certain items. For example, where the proper measure of the replacement value of a vehicle is its retail value, an adjustment to that value may be necessary: A creditor should not receive portions of the retail price, if any, that reflect the value of items the debtor does not receive when he retains his vehicle, items such as warranties, inventory storage, and reconditioning. *Cf.* 90 F.3d at 1051-1052. Nor should the creditor gain from modifications to the property—*e.g.,* the addition of accessories to a vehicle—to which a creditor's lien would not extend under state law.

Christopher S. Sontchi*
Valuation Methodologies: A Judge's View
20 Am. Bankr. Inst. L. Rev. 1 (2012)

At heart, Chapter 11 is a simple exercise. In bankruptcy parlance, it is to gather the property of the estate, determine the amount and nature of the claims and confirm a plan of reorganization that distributes the property of the estate to the creditors in accordance with the requirements of the Bankruptcy Code. Inherent in this process is determining the *value* of the property of the estate and the claims. Understanding the methodologies used to determine value is critical for any attorney or judge in this field. The goal of this article is to provide the reader with a basic understanding of the methodologies used to value an asset.

What is the value of an asset or a firm? The standard definition is that the value of an asset is its material or monetary worth, i.e., "the amount of money, goods, etc., for which a thing can be exchanged or traded." Of course, the easiest and most accurate way to determine the amount of money for which an asset can be exchanged is to do just that—exchange the asset for money or, put more plainly, sell it. When one does not wish to sell the asset or simply cannot do so it becomes more difficult to determine the asset's value. Nonetheless, in determining an asset's value the ultimate goal remains the same—to determine as accurately as possible what the sale price would be.

The most obvious method for estimating an asset's potential sale price is to consult the current market price for that asset. Of course, not all assets can be readily bought and sold in a market. For example, while there is a ready market for trading in bushels of wheat there is no such market for wheat farms (if for no other reason that each farm is unique) such that one could consult a market price to determine the farm's value. Even when there is a market it may not fairly estimate the potential sale price of an asset if the market is inefficient, disrupted or dysfunctional.

Financial academics and professionals have established a variety of methodologies to determine the value of assets that are not readily valued by reference to a market. Broadly speaking, a firm, its assets and/or its equity can be valued in one of four ways: (i) asset-based valuation where one estimates the value of a firm by determining the current value of its assets, (ii) discounted cash flow or "DCF" valuation where one discounts cash flows to arrive at a value of the firm or its equity, (iii) relative valuation approaches, which include the "comparable company analysis" and the "comparable transaction analysis" that base value on how comparable assets are priced, and (iv) option pricing that uses contingent claim valuation. Other than option pricing, all of these valuation methodologies, either individually or in various combinations, are routinely presented to bankruptcy courts in valuation hearings. No matter which methodology is used, however, the purpose remains the same—to determine as accurately as possible what the sale price would be, which is referred to as "price discovery."

---

* U.S. Bankruptcy Judge, District of Delaware—Ed.

I. ASSET-BASED VALUATION

An asset-based valuation is where one calculates the value of individual assets owned by a firm and aggregates them to arrive at a firm value. There are two primary asset-based valuation models. The first is liquidation value, which is obtained by aggregating the estimated sale proceeds of the assets owned by the firm. The second is replacement cost, where one estimates what it would cost to replace all of the assets that a firm owns today.

Asset-based valuations are different from DCF valuations and of much more limited utility. In liquidation valuation, for example, one looks only at the assets in place and estimates their value based on how similar assets are currently priced in the market. In a DCF valuation, which is discussed more fully below, one considers all the firm's assets *and their expected growth potential* to arrive at value. Only in the instance where (i) a firm does not have any growth assets and (ii) the market accurately reflects expected cash flows in its pricing of the firm's assets will an asset-based valuation result in a similar conclusion as a DCF valuation.

Nonetheless, asset-based valuations are commonly used in Chapter 11. For example, under section 1129(a)(7)(A) of the Bankruptcy Code, in order for a debtor to confirm a plan of reorganization it must establish that *each holder* of a claim or interest in an impaired class has either voted for the plan or will receive or retain under the plan on account of such claim or interest in property of the value, as of the effective date of the plan, that is not less than the amount that such holder would so receive or retain if the debtor were liquidated under Chapter 7 of this title on such date.

As a case under Chapter 7 of the Bankruptcy Code involves the liquidation of the debtor's assets, a debtor seeking to satisfy section 1129(a)(7)(A) will often present expert testimony as to the liquidation value of the debtor's assets.

A liquidation analysis simply lists the various items of assets owned by the debtors, lists a value for each of these assets (usually book value), determines an appropriate recovery percentage based on the difficulty of liquidating the asset, and multiplies the appropriate recovery percentage by the asset's value. Of course, nothing in life is free. This includes liquidating assets. Thus, the analysis must include an estimate of the amount of money required to liquidate the assets.

II. DISCOUNTED CASH FLOW (DCF) VALUATION

The discounted cash flow or DCF valuation has its foundation in the present value rule under which the value of any asset is the present value of expected future cash flows from it. . . .

C. The Elements of a Discounted Cash Flow Valuation

. . . Basically, a discounted cash flow valuation consists of an estimate of the firm's future cash flows discounted to present value. The complicating factors include determining by what metric one determines the firm's future cash flows, from what source one draws the future cash flows, and how one calculates the appropriate discount rate.

Indeed, these issues are so sufficiently complex as to almost certainly require that the valuation be performed by an expert in the field.

. . .

D. Using a DCF to Value the Firm

. . . [B]y far the most commonly used [type of DCF analysis] before bankruptcy courts is that of valuing the firm by discounting expected cash flows to the firm at the weighted average cost of capital or WACC. The expected cash flows to the firm used in this valuation are generally referred to as the "free cash flow to the firm" or "FCFF." A number of metrics are used to calculate the FCFF. These include the "un-levered cash flow," which is the firm's earnings before interest and taxes, net of taxes and reinvestment needs. Another measure of FCFF that is widely used in valuation is the firm's earnings before interest, taxes, depreciation, and amortization ("EBITDA"). Other measures are earnings before interest and taxes ("EBIT"); net operating profit or loss after taxes ("NOPLAT"); or the net operating income ("NOI").

The cash flows themselves usually come from management's estimates of the firm's future performance. As such, they are necessarily subject to uncertainty relating to matters specific to the firm as well as to broader issues such as the general state of the economy, advances in technology, effectiveness of management, labor issues, actions of competitors, price of raw materials, etc. Given the inherent uncertainty in predicting the future, one generally only uses three to five years of projections in performing a DCF analysis. The final year is used to calculate a "terminal value," which is the value of the firm as of the date of the last estimate. For example, were one to use management projections for the next five years to perform a DCF, the estimate of the firm's performance in that fifth year would be used to calculate the value of the firm as of that fifth year, i.e. its terminal value. Generally, that is performed by assuming that the cash flows of the firm at that fifth year will grow at a constant rate forever beyond that time. One simply calculates the present value of that perpetual growth as of the fifth year and then calculates the present value as of the date of the valuation of that conclusion.

. . .

III. RELATIVE VALUATION

In relative valuation, the value of an asset is derived from the pricing of comparable assets, standardized using a common variable such as earnings, cash flows, book value, or revenues. Unlike discounted cash flow valuation, which is a search for intrinsic value, relative valuation relies more on the market. In other words, one assumes that the market is correct in the way it prices assets and firms on average, but that it makes errors on the pricing of individual assets and firms.

Finding similar and comparable assets and/or firms is the challenge of a relative valuation. Frequently one has to accept firms that are different from the firm being valued in one dimension or the other. In such a case, one has to either explicitly or implicitly control for the differences. In practice, controlling for these variables can range from the simple—such as using industry averages—to the very sophisticated—such as multivariant regression models.

. . .

The two most common relative valuation methodologies used in Chapter 11 cases are the comparable companies analysis and the comparable transactions analysis. Under both methods, one determines a metric by which to value the company such as EBITDA. One then looks to either comparable publicly-traded companies or control transactions involving comparable companies to determine the appropriate multiple to apply to the selected metric to reach a conclusion of the subject firm's value. For example, one may conclude that the firm is worth 8.5 times its trailing 12 month EBITDA. . . .

A. COMPARABLE COMPANIES ANALYSIS

Under the comparable companies analysis, value is calculated by examining the trading ranges of comparable publicly-traded companies. Public companies are used because they are the only ones for which economic data (stock value, revenue, EBITDA, EBIT, etc.) is readily available. Trading ranges are viewed as a multiple of a performance metric, generally revenues, EBITDA, or EBIT. The multiples are then applied to the same metric of the company being evaluated in order to determine its value. The more similar the guideline or comparable companies are, the more supportable is the use of the comparable companies method. Use of companies that are clearly not comparable will lead to unsupportable conclusions.

Now for a simple illustration. Assume you are performing a comparable companies analysis on a glass manufacturing company in bankruptcy. The metric you chose as a determinant of value is the company's EBITDA for the last 12 months (LTM EBITDA), which is $40 million.

You determine that the following companies are comparable:

Company	Stock Price	Number of Shares	Market Capitalization (Stock Price x No. of Shares)	LTM EBITDA	Multiple [ratio] of Market Capitalization to LTM EBITDA
Acme Glass Co.	$10.00	75MM	$750MM	$50MM	15.0
Bird Glass Co.	$12.50	100MM	$1.25B	$80MM	15.6
Campbell Glass Co.	$5.00	100MM	$500MM	$65MM	7.7
Delta Glass Inc.	$20.00	150MM	$3B	$150MM	20.0
Mean					14.6
Median					15.3

Applying the mean multiple [that is, ratio] of the comparable companies, which is 14.6, to the debtor's LTM EBITDA of $40 million results in a value of $584 million. Applying the median multiple of the comparable companies, which is 15.3, to the debtor's LTM EBITDA of $40 million results in a value of $612 million. Thus, the value of the debtor under the comparable companies analysis is between $584 million and $612 million.

B. COMPARABLE TRANSACTIONS ANALYSIS

Under the comparable transactions analysis, value is determined by examining the consideration paid to acquire a comparable entity through a publicly reported merger or acquisition. Like the comparable companies analysis, the purchase price is viewed as a multiple of an appropriate earning measure (revenue, EBITDA, or EBIT). Value is calculated by applying the resulting multiple to the same metric of the company being evaluated. Like the comparable companies analysis, the more similar the target company is to the firm being valued, the more confidence one can place in the valuation.

Now for a simple illustration. Assume you are performing a comparable transactions analysis on the glass manufacturing company discussed above. The metric you chose as a determinant of value is again the company's EBITDA for the last 12 months (LTM EBITDA), which is $40 million.

You determine that the following transactions are comparable:

Purchaser	Target Company	Purchase Price	LTM EBITDA	Multiple of Purchase Price, i.e., value, to LTM EBITDA
Johnson Conglomerate, Inc.	Zeta Glass Corp.	$200MM	$20MM	10.0
Omni Corp.	Yellow Mountain Glass, Inc.	$600MM	$80MM	7.5
Mega-Company, Inc.	X-Ray Glass	$400MM	$80MM	5.0
Monopoly, Inc.	Veri-Glass Corp.	$1.2B	$100MM	12.0
Mean				8.6
Median				8.75

Applying the mean multiple of the comparable transactions, which is 8.6, to the debtor's LTM EBITDA of $40 million results in a value of $344 million. Applying the median multiple of the comparable companies, which is 8.75, to the debtor's LTM EBITDA of $40 million results in a value of $350 million. Thus, the value of the debtor as determined by the comparable transactions analysis is between $344 million and $350 million.

. . .

Valuations are typically done by "hired gun" experts, and courts frequently face dueling expert valuation testimony. While the experts will utilize the same basic valuation methods, they will often arrive at very different valuations based on the assumptions and inputs they use. This means that traditional valuation methods are all subject to manipulation to achieve desired valuation outcomes.

IV. VALUATION FIGHT: *IN RE CHEMTURA CORP.*

Up to this point, our discussion of valuation has been fairly abstract. The materials from the Chemtura Corp. bankruptcy illustrate a valuation dispute in action. The decision is often technical, but the resolution of the bankruptcy, and who would own the reorganized company, turns on the valuation question.

Financial Advisor Retention Application, *In re* Chemtura Corp.

No. 09-11233 (Bankr. S.D.N.Y. June 16, 2010)

APPLICATION FOR ENTRY OF AN ORDER . . . AUTHORIZING THE EMPLOYMENT AND RETENTION OF UBS SECURITIES LLC AS FINANCIAL ADVISOR TO THE OFFICIAL COMMITTEE OF EQUITY SECURITY HOLDERS . . .

The Official Committee of Equity Security Holders (the "Equity Committee") appointed in the above-captioned jointly administered Chapter 11 cases . . . submits this Application . . . for entry of an order . . . , authorizing the employment and retention of UBS Securities LLC ("UBS") as financial advisor to the Equity Committee. . . . In support of the Application . . . the Equity Committee respectfully represents as follows:
. . .

TERMS OF RETENTION

20. The Equity Committee's retention of UBS for the Chapter 11 Cases is governed by an engagement letter agreement dated May 11, 2010 (the "Engagement Agreement"). . . .

21. Subject to the Court's approval, UBS will be entitled to be compensated in accordance with the structure set forth below for its services pursuant to, and as further explained by, the Engagement Agreement.

22. For UBS's services rendered hereunder to and on behalf of the Equity Committee, the Debtors shall pay to UBS the following fees in cash:

(a) The aggregate of:

(i) a nonrefundable monthly cash advisory fee (each, a "Monthly Advisory Fee") of $150,000 per month, in advance on the first business day of each month, beginning on January 7, 2010, provided, however, that (x) following the payment of the first six Monthly Advisory Fees, all additional Monthly Advisory Fee payments shall be credited against the "Transaction Fee" (as defined below); and (y) the Monthly Advisory Fee shall be prorated for the month of January 2010; provided, further, that UBS shall not be required to rebate any portion of the creditable Monthly Advisory Fees paid in excess of the Transaction Fee; and

(ii) a transaction fee (the "Transaction Fee"), payable on the date a Transaction is consummated that results in any Common Equity Security Recovery, determined according to the following schedule:

(x) If the Common Equity Security Recovery is greater than $225,000,000 but less than $450,000,000, UBS shall be entitled to a Transaction Fee equal to 1.25% of the amount by which the Common Equity Security Recovery exceeds $225,000,000 (determined as set forth below), payable on the date a Transaction is consummated.

(y) If the Common Equity Security Recovery is greater than $450,000,000, UBS shall be entitled to a Transaction Fee equal to

   (A) 1.25% of the amount by which the Common Equity Security Recovery exceeds $225,000,000 up to a maximum Common Equity Security Recovery of $450,000,000 (determined as set forth below), plus

   (B) 2.00% of the amount by which the Common Equity Security Recovery exceeds $450,000,000 (determined as set forth below), payable on the date a Transaction is consummated.

(b) The Transaction Fee shall be calculated as follows:

(i) "Common Equity Securities" means the issued and outstanding common stock, par value $0.01 per share, of Chemtura as of the date Chemtura filed the Chapter 11 Cases with the Bankruptcy Court (the "Common Stock"), including without limitation, any exchange, conversion, repurchase, repayment or distribution (including any repayment in liquidation using proceeds from the sale of the Debtors' assets) of or on account of any such common stock.

(ii) "Common Equity Security Recovery" means all consideration received, distributed or otherwise provided in the aggregate on account of any and all Common Equity Securities, including, without limitation, cash (whether immediately payable or payable in installments), securities (debt or equity), property or other interests in property, instruments, contract rights, contingent payments or obligations, or any other form of consideration, and including, without limitation, the Common Equity Securities if unimpaired or otherwise retained or distributed. The value of any equity security (including any Common Equity Securities) shall be equal to the price implied by the plan value determined by the Court or, if no such determination is made, then the value shall equal the value proffered by the Chapter 11 plan proponent, except that the value of any equity security listed, quoted, or traded on any securities exchange shall be equal to the greater of the price implied by such plan value and the mean of the prices at the close of business on each of the five business days following the consummation of a Transaction.

In re Chemtura Corp.

439 B.R. 561 (Bankr. S.D.N.Y. 2010)

ROBERT E. GERBER, United States Bankruptcy Judge.

In this contested matter in the Chapter 11 cases of specialty chemicals company Chemtura Corporation ("Chemtura") and its affiliates (collectively, the "Debtors"), the Debtors seek confirmation of their Chapter 11 plan (the "Plan"). Confirmation is supported by the Official Committee of Unsecured Creditors (the "Creditors' Committee") and an *ad hoc* committee of Chemtura bondholders (the "Bondholders Committee,"[2] and together with the Debtors and the Creditors' Committee, the "Plan Supporters"). But confirmation is opposed by the Official Committee of Equity Security Holders ("the Equity Committee"), and two other entities that are equity holders or act on equity holders' behalf.

The Equity Committee expresses several objections to confirmation. But the most serious of them is that the Plan—which as described below, effects its distributions to bondholders and most other creditors by means of a combination of cash and stock—undervalues the Debtors, and that a global settlement of several constituencies' entitlements (the "Settlement"), upon which the Plan is based, does likewise. While the Plan proposes a distribution to equity, the Equity Committee contends that the Plan doesn't deliver enough—and, as relevant to the Code's requirements for confirmation, that each of the Settlement and the Plan provide for payment to creditors more than in full, violating section 1129(b)'s "fair and equitable" requirement.

After an evidentiary hearing focusing nearly entirely on the disputed issues of valuation, I find that the Debtors' total enterprise value ("TEV") is no higher than the valuation upon which the Settlement was based. Under those circumstances, I find that the creditors in this case will not be overpaid, or, more to the point, will not be paid more than in full. . . .

FINDINGS OF FACT

1. Background

On March 18, 2009 (the "Filing Date"), Chemtura, a publicly-traded company, and 27 of its affiliates filed Chapter 11 petitions in this Court. The Debtors produce specialty chemicals, polymer products, crop protection chemicals, and pool and spa chemicals. . . .

[Chemtura's debts and liabilities], combined with sharp declines in demand and restricted access to credit resulting from the global recession, forced the Debtors into reorganization in March 2009.

4. Post-Petition

After the Filing Date, the Debtors continued to operate their businesses as debtors in possession and improved their financial condition, particularly as a consequence of settling and otherwise reducing claims. . . . Though they disagree as to the extent, all constituencies in this case now agree that, due in substantial part to the resolution of these liabilities, the Debtors are once again solvent.

. . .

5. The Plan

On June 17, 2010, the Debtors filed the Plan and disclosure statement (the "Disclosure Statement"). The foundation for the Plan was the Settlement, which was negotiated

---

2. Members of the Bondholders Committee hold approximately 68% of the Debtors' bonds.

between the Debtors, the Creditors' Committee, the Bondholders' Committee, and the Pension Benefit Guarantee Corporation ("PBGC"). In this settlement, the parties resolved a number of key issues:

> a. *Debtors' total enterprise value for Plan and distribution purposes*: In accordance with a June 4 valuation of the Debtors' TEV prepared by Lazard (the "Lazard June Report"), the Plan would be based on a value of Chemtura of $2.05 billion. . . .

6. Marketing of the Company

After the Debtors issued the Plan and Disclosure Statement, but before the time for voting on the Plan, the Equity Committee, in the hope of having a fully-funded alternative plan, marketed Chemtura to try to secure investors willing to purchase equity in it. Although the Debtors had plan exclusivity, and on July 21, 2010 defeated an Equity Committee motion to end exclusivity, they cooperated in the Equity Committee's marketing efforts, in a manner that I find to be in good faith and fully satisfactory.

A total of 19 parties were contacted, and the Debtors signed non-disclosure agreements with 7 investors, including certain members of the Equity Committee themselves. The presentations made to these potential investors relied on valuation reports prepared by UBS in June 2010 (the "Paulson Presentation"), which estimated the TEV of Chemtura to be between $2.2 and $2.7 billion. The Equity Committee's attempts to solicit investments at that value, or any other, were ultimately unsuccessful. That fact, along with others, informs my finding, discussed below, that the Debtors' TEV is not as high as the Equity Committee contends.

7. Valuation

A. The Experts' Analyses

Before the valuation hearing (and in the Debtors' case, before the Settlement was reached), the Debtors and Equity Committee each secured expert opinions as to the Debtors' TEV, reflected first in expert reports and then in testimony before me. The Debtors' analysis, dated August 29, 2010 and also prepared by Lazard (the "Lazard Expert Report") estimated the Debtors' TEV to be in a range of $1.9 billion to $2.2 billion, with a midpoint at $2.05 billion. The Equity Committee's analysis, expressed in a report prepared by UBS on August 29, 2010 (the "UBS Expert Report"), estimated the Debtors' TEV to be in a range of $2.3 billion to $2.6 billion, with a midpoint of $2.45 billion.

Both the Lazard and UBS analyses employed three standard valuation methodologies:

(i) discounted cash flow ("DCF");

(ii) comparable companies ("Comparable Companies"); and

(iii) precedent comparable transactions ("Precedent Transactions").

Lazard prepared a chart, colloquially referred to as the "football field," upon which the valuation ranges that resulted from each methodology appeared, and which showed a range near the middle where the individual methodology results, for the most part, overlapped. This area of overlap correlated to Lazard's conclusion of that valuation range of $1.9 billion to $2.2 billion. The UBS Report, under UBS policy, did not include a football field.

The Creditors' Committee also obtained expert analysis as to TEV. It secured an expert opinion from its financial advisor, Houlihan, Lokey, Howard & Zukin, confirmed in a report dated August 29, 2010 (the "Houlihan Expert Report"), and thereafter, live testimony.

The Houlihan analyses did not provide a valuation of Chemtura, but instead critiqued the analyses of Lazard and, particularly, UBS. Houlihan made a number of observations, many of which I ultimately came to agree with, the most significant of which were that:

(a) Chemtura had historically traded at a discount relative to its peers prior to the bankruptcy, and that any valuation would require a discount as a consequence; and

(b) the Debtors' admittedly aggressive projections in the LRP were overly aggressive, because they were based on assumptions of near-term economic growth that were not supported by recent evidence, and that any valuation of Chemtura that assumed that the Debtors would exceed their 2010 EBITDA forecast or meet their projections for 2011-2014 would, without appropriate risk adjustments, overstate the value of the Debtors.

B. The Experts' Methodologies

Though Lazard and UBS implemented their methodologies in different ways (and seemingly modest differences in assumptions, comparables, and means of implementation resulted in substantial differences in valuation), their basic methodologies were largely similar. Each, as noted, gave at least some attention to DCF, Comparable Companies, and Precedent Transactions. And they applied those valuation techniques in largely similar ways—though UBS did not compute actual valuations based on the latter two means, and instead used them only as a check on its DCF conclusion.

i. Discounted Cash Flow

The DCF valuation methodology estimates the net present value of a company by:

(i) projecting unlevered free cash flows over a given fixed forecast period, then discounting those cash flows back to the present using an estimated discount rate based upon the company's weighted average cost of capital ("WACC") and

(ii) deriving the value of all unlevered free cash flows beyond the explicit forecast period—the "terminal value"—and then discounting that terminal value back to the present by applying the estimated discount rate.

The enterprise value is determined by adding the numbers derived from (i) and (ii).

Translating that technical jargon into more easily understood terms and applying it here, the two DCF analyses computed TEV by adding the present value of two assumed future cash flow streams:

(1) the cash flow projected for each of years during which the LRP made a specific projection, and

(2) the cash flow projected for the period thereafter, as derived from a figure—the terminal value—that was used as a basis to capture those later cash flows.

With respect to the years for which there was a specific forecast, Lazard and UBS, for the most part, used the annual future cash flows from 2010 to 2014 that had been projected in the LRP. The two also used similar discount rate rates.[35] In their terminal value calculations, however, the two reports differed, most significantly, in the EBITDA value to which the multiples were applied.

To calculate terminal value, UBS applied its multiples to the EBITDA for the *last year* of the forecast period (2014), or $528 million, taken from the Debtors' LRP. Discount rates between 11.6% and 13.6% were applied. Using this method, UBS calculated a DCF range for TEV between $2.47 billion and $2.927 billion.

Lazard calculated terminal value by applying multiples of a higher 6.5x to 7.5x based on an analysis of enterprise values and 5-year and 3-year average EBITDA for the peer group to a *mid-cycle or normalized* EBITDAR of $404 million. The mid-cycle EBITDAR was based on the *average* of 2009 through 2014 EBITDAR, which included both actual results and forecasted EBITDAR from the LRP. Lazard applied discount rates between 11.75% and 13.75% and calculated the Debtor's TEV range to be between $2.175 billion and $2.570 billion.

Lazard's witness explained that a multiple of mid-cycle EBITDAR was used to account for the cyclical nature of the Debtors' earnings and cash flows after the projection period. But UBS and Lazard debated the extent of the Debtors' cyclicality, which could affect the appropriate terminal value calculation. UBS contended that Lazard's use of a normalized EBITDAR inappropriately drove the present worth of the terminal value down. Conversely, Lazard contended that UBS's use of the EBITDAR for the final year, at a level never before achieved in Chemtura's history, caused the UBS DCF analysis to significantly overstate value.

ii. Comparable Companies

The comparable company analysis estimates the value of a firm by taking the value of comparable peer firms and using their values as an indicator of the subject company. Values are standardized using one or more common variables such as revenue, earnings, or cash flow, with the expert then applying a multiple of the financial metric or metrics that yields the market's valuation of these comparable companies. A key element in this analysis is the choice of the "comparables"—the selection of companies that are most comparable to the subject firm or its specific businesses. Each of the Lazard and UBS expert reports gave at least some attention to both consolidated and sum-of-the-parts comparable company analyses. While the consolidated approach looks at comparables for the entire company as a whole, a "Sum-of-the-Parts" analysis uses similar techniques for individual lines of the Debtors' businesses and then aggregates those results to estimate overall TEV.

---

35. *See* Lazard Expert Report at 16 (applying discount rates between 11.75% and 13.75%); UBS Expert Report at 8 (applying discount rates between 11.6% and 13.6%).

For the consolidated analysis, UBS examined 4 categories of multiples (LTM, and 2010, 2011 and 2012 Estimated EBITDAR) for each of 11 *domestic* companies in its peer group and calculated the mean multiple for each category. Again, UBS did not actually calculate a TEV range from these mean multiples; it back-calculated multiples from its overall Chemtura TEV range of $2.3 million to $2.6 million using LTM and actual and projected EBITDAR to demonstrate the reasonableness of its estimated DCF TEV. The UBS Report did provide an implied valuation range from its Sum-of-the-Parts analysis, which was $2.394 billion to $2.789 billion.

Lazard's trading peer group contained 15 companies—10 domestic and 5 *foreign*. Lazard analyzed 5 categories of multiples on a full-company basis: multiples based on 2010 and 2011 Estimated EBITDAR, 2010 and 2011 Estimated EBITDAR less capital expenditures, and 2010 Estimated EBITDAR, taking also into account underfunded pension and OPEB obligations, which Lazard referred to as "EBITDARP." Lazard also performed a Sum-of-the-Parts analysis.

In its various EBITDAR computations, Lazard, like UBS, used "6+6" figures—actual results for the first 6 months of 2010 and the LRP projections for the last 6 months—for the three 2010 analyses. Lazard applied the derived range of multiples to "6+6" figures for the three 2010 analyses, and to LRP projections for the 2011 analyses.

Three differences in those analyses are worthy of note. First, while UBS used foreign comparables in its Sum-of-the-Parts analysis but only domestic comparables in its consolidated company analysis, Lazard *included foreign comparables in both*. UBS contended that the foreign companies were, on the whole, inappropriate comparables for Chemtura, and noted that Lazard's inclusion of foreign companies (which all had EBITDA lower than any of the domestic companies) drove down the mean multiples and reduced the derived TEV for Chemtura by $198 million to $237 million. However, Lazard and Houlihan contended that any analysis could not exclude foreign companies that were otherwise comparable. And they noted that in the period 2005 to 2008, Chemtura on average traded below its full peer group—including Lazard's foreign and domestic comparables.

Second, UBS's list of comparables included DuPont and PPG Industries, but not Solutia, while the Lazard comparables contained the opposite. Lazard and the Creditors' Committee argued that the inclusion of DuPont and PPG, which are much larger than Chemtura and not specialty chemical companies, inappropriately inflated the multiples that UBS derived from the analysis, and that the failure to include Solutia, an assertedly very similar company, did likewise.

Third, the Lazard and UBS analyses differed with respect to the year chosen for their Sum-of-the-Parts analysis. Lazard derived multiple ranges from select comparable companies' business units, then valued unallocated corporate overhead using a weighted average multiple calculated on the basis of each business unit's contribution to total to *2010* 6+6 EBIDTAR. Its estimated TEV range from this analysis was $1.88 billion to $2.23 billion. By contrast, UBS pegged its valuations of the Debtors' component businesses on multiples of *2011* EBITDAR. UBS found Lazard's reliance on 2010 actual and projected numbers to be flawed, contending that generally by Q3, market valuations would be driven by projections for the following year, and that 2010 was a transition year for the Debtors, with uniquely depressed EBITDAR numbers.

iii. Precedent Transactions

Precedent Transaction methodology applies multiples derived from the purchase prices of comparable companies in *past M&A transactions* to the subject firm's LTM earnings, cash flow, or EBITDA to determine a range of TEV. This method requires qualitative judgments in light of the unique circumstances of each precedent transaction and inherent differences between the precedent acquired companies and the subject company. In considering the circumstances as to the various precedent transactions, the parties debated the extent to which a Precedent Transactions analysis would appropriately take into account the financial environment at the present time.

The Lazard Expert Report analyzed 14 transactions between 2004 and 2010, all between $1 billion and $10 billion in value. But over this time, there were dramatic changes in the global economy and capital markets, as evidenced most dramatically by the economic and financial environments after the reversals suffered by Bear Stearns and Lehman Brothers. Considering these changes to be highly material, Lazard "reviewed many transactions and presented transactions from before the Lehman Brothers bankruptcy in [its] Report, but [] ultimately relied upon" the transactions that occurred after September 15, 2008, the day Lehman Brothers filed for Chapter 11. Three transactions fell into this category. . . .

The mean EBITDA multiple for these three transactions was 6.2x. Using that mean as a midpoint, Lazard determined the appropriate multiple range for Chemtura to be 5.75x to 6.75x LTM estimated EBITDAR. After applying this multiple range to LTM EBITDAR as of September 30, 2010, or $342 million, Lazard estimated the Debtors' TEV to be between $1.970 billion and $2.315 billion.

The UBS Expert Report considered 19 transactions between 2005 and 2009, which had a range of values between $290 million and $18.666 billion and a mean EBITDAR multiple of 9.7x. But UBS did not actually calculate a TEV range from these mean multiples. Instead, as a way to demonstrate the reasonableness of its TEV range, it took its estimated TEV range for the Debtors of $2.3 million to $2.6 million, and, using an LTM EBITDAR of $331 million, back-calculated EBITDAR multiples of 6.9x to 7.9x. That back-calculated multiple range of 6.9x to 7.9x was lower than the Precedent Transaction analysis mean of 9.7x LTM EBITDAR, which caused UBS to believe that its TEV did not exceed the actual value of Chemtura.

With respect to their consideration of precedent transactions, the two reports differed materially in their lists of transactions considered. Most notably, UBS included many transactions pre-dating the Lehman bankruptcy and the change in the financial climate, while Lazard did not. . . .

However, Lazard and Houlihan contended that the heavy reliance by UBS on pre-Lehman transactions, entered into before the financial markets crashed, was a serious flaw.

. . .

C. Valuation Conclusions

If I were required to find a specific valuation for the Chemtura Debtors here, I think that, based on the foregoing and the additional factual analysis discussed below, any valuation would be at the low end of the Lazard range. But for the purposes of this controversy, I don't need to find an exact valuation. To determine that the Plan does not violate section 1129(b)'s "fair and equitable" requirement by paying creditors more than in full, I need only find that the Debtors' TEV doesn't exceed the TEV underlying the Settlement.

For the reasons set forth below, I so find. I do so for the following reasons.

i. Methodology

As previously indicated, Lazard's valuation presented a TEV in the range of from $1.9 to $2.2 billion, with a midpoint of $2.05 billion. The Settlement was based on that midpoint valuation. Lazard's valuation conclusion was reached after consideration of three traditional methods—value implied by consideration of: (1) discounted cash flow[;] (2) comparable companies; and (3) prices in precedent comparable transactions.

The UBS valuation, by contrast, presented a TEV in the range of from $2.3 to $2.6 billion, with a midpoint at $2.45 billion, approximately 20% higher than the Lazard valuation. But the UBS valuation was reached by computation only of DCF, which, as discussed below, is subject to projections under an aggressive LRP in an uncertain economic environment. In such an environment, I think that Precedent Transactions (if in that same environment and if the sample size wasn't too small) and, especially, Comparable Companies, would provide a more persuasive indicator of value, and I was surprised that these latter two techniques did not play a greater role in the UBS analysis. . . .

Although in holding valuation hearings before, I've seen experts come to valuation conclusions using several different methodologies, and then come to various weighted averages for the final valuation, that was not done here. Instead, Lazard prepared the "football field" chart, described above and pictured below, reflecting the general overlap in valuation ranges derived from its various methodologies, and then submitted an essentially subjective valuation consistent, for the most part, with the overlap.

While Lazard developed a valuation range using individual valuations derived from several different methodologies, UBS did not do so. UBS computed valuations like Lazard's only by DCF. The Creditors' Committee noted this in its briefing on this motion. Though I wouldn't express the thought in quite the way that the Creditors' Committee did [namely claiming that UBS worked backwards from the valuation number it wanted], I agree with the Creditors' Committee's underlying point: the difference in technique makes the Lazard analysis superior.

ii. DCF Analysis

As previously mentioned, the DCF valuations by each of Lazard and UBS were for the most part predicated on the cash flows anticipated in management's LRP, which was unchallenged by UBS or the Equity Committee. The LRP assumed that a general macroeconomic recovery to pre-recessionary levels would occur in 2011, which would result in further earnings improvements through 2014. It projected EBITDAR of $528 million in 2014, after five years of increasing EBITDA, without any drops, or even flatness, each year.

The Debtors' CFO, whom I found competent and credible, described the Long Range Plan as "aggressive," and I so find. The Long Range Plan called for levels of performance, for years after 2011, that had never before been achieved at Chemtura. And it was prepared in the context of an economy that, while certainly improved since 2008 (when the U.S. nearly faced a depression), is improving only slowly. The Equity Committee's expert conceded that UBS has lowered its GDP forecasts for 2010 and 2011. I don't have any greater ability than the political and economic pundits to predict how quickly the economy will improve, and I don't think that I should do so. But I can and do find that since the Debtors' Long Range Plan is already aggressive, and since the speed (and in the views of some, the fact) of the economic recovery is uncertain, it is inappropriate to be as confident as the Equity Committee is as to future growth in the American economy and increasing Chemtura EBITDA growth.

The Lazard and UBS DCF analyses both assume continuously increasing growth, but the effect of that assumption is magnified in the UBS analysis, which uses the $528 million EBITDAR in the last year, 2014, as the basis for determining terminal value. I take it as true, as the Equity Committee and UBS contended, that, for the terminal value calculations, using the cash flows in the last projected year is not just common, but the more traditional approach (at least before considering the cyclicality of the company's business). But that reality underscores the importance of the projections that get us the $528 million in expected EBITDAR for that last year. The extent to which that $528 million is an appropriate benchmark for gauging future performance (and hence terminal value) depends upon both the confidence that one has in expectations as to the Debtors' future economic growth as well as the extent to which the expectations would be subject to cyclical variations.

I've previously noted that the Debtors' projections are aggressive, and that I have uncertainty as to the country's—apart from Chemtura's—economic prospects over the next five years. This uncertainty cuts materially in favor of the Lazard view, which doesn't place as much reliance on the unprecedented EBITDA for 2014.

. . .

Lazard considered it appropriate to regard the Debtors as cyclical, requiring their actual and projected cash flows—which went down from 2007 to 2009 and then were projected to go up to 2014, with a graph resembling a hockey stick—to be normalized to account for the business cycle. Lazard did that by computing 3-year and 5-year averages for EBITDA, which at least seemingly were not necessarily for complete business cycles. But the Equity Committee contended that Chemtura, a specialty (as contrasted to commodity) chemicals company, is not that cyclical, and that Lazard thus erred by failing to compute Terminal Value based on the final year's cash flows[89] and/or by failing to capture an entire business cycle. In the hearing, the extent of Chemtura's cyclicality was a matter of sharp debate.

---

89. As noted in n.88, the shape of the hockey stick was such that projected EBITDAR reached its peak in the final year, 2014. Using an average from the middle would result in use of a lower EBITDAR in computing the Terminal Value, and result in a lower TEV. Conversely, use of the EBITDAR at the time of the 2014 high point would result a higher Terminal Value, and result in a higher TEV.

I find that Chemtura, as a specialty chemicals company that in several significant respects can differentiate its products from others, is not as cyclical as other chemical companies, particularly those that are wholly or largely commodity chemical companies. But I find that its business still is cyclical in material respects, in no small part because many of its customers are. Thus I think that normalizing for cyclicality was not inappropriate.

But with that said, I believe that to engage in normalization best, one would need to capture an entire business cycle, and I don't believe that Lazard necessarily did so. Also, the Equity Committee established by cross-examination that in Lazard's valuations of several other Chapter 11 debtors (at least some of which would seemingly be as cyclical as Chemtura), Lazard nevertheless used the final year's cash flows in its computation of Terminal Value, and did not use the normalization technique it used here. One may legitimately wonder, then, why the normalization technique was appropriate here but was not appropriate there—or vice versa.

While Lazard was not necessarily wrong to take cyclicality into account, its failure to do so over a complete business cycle, and its doing so here but not in other cases, undercut the persuasiveness of its cyclicality normalization techniques.

Looking back, then, at the Lazard and UBS DCF analyses, I find flaws in each. But in my mind, the flaws in the UBS analysis are more pronounced. In this economic environment, relying on the very high terminal value in the last year of an admittedly aggressive string of growth projections is in my mind too aggressive. In a more stable economic environment, I'd likely consider use of the last year's cash flows for determining terminal value to be perfectly ordinary, if not also preferred. But I don't think that the present economic uncertainties permit an analysis that is so subject to assumptions that are so optimistic. Also, though I find flaws in Lazard's efforts to capture cyclicality, I'm troubled that UBS made no effort to address cyclicality at all.

As I indicated, I have problems with Lazard's implementation of its efforts to address cyclicality. But on balance, I believe its DCF analysis is somewhat superior because it is less subject to the economic uncertainty that I find to be of material concern.

iii. Comparable Companies Analysis

As noted above, Lazard engaged in an extensive Comparable Companies analysis, examining the values suggested by comparable companies by six means. (Of the value ranges derived from that Comparable Companies analysis, one was wholly below Lazard's overall TEV range (and presumably disregarded by Lazard, in a decision that the Equity Committee would presumably welcome), and two others would support valuations only at the lower end of Lazard's range.) But for the most part UBS did not engage in Comparable Companies to provide an independent indicator of value, instead using it merely as a means of confirming the reasonableness of its DCF analysis.

That's disappointing, as I consider Comparable Companies analysis to be somewhat more meaningful here than either DCF or Comparable Transactions analysis, because it's less susceptible to uncertainties in projections (in the case of DCF) or extraneous factors such as control premiums, synergies, or bidding wars (in the case of Precedent

Transactions). . . . I note that for these reasons, I give Comparable Companies analysis relatively greater weight.

. . .

I also think that Lazard was right to include European companies as part of its Comparable Companies analysis, and that UBS was wrong to leave them out—especially since UBS considered them at other times and for other purposes. I accept Lazard's testimony that the European companies that Lazard included in its comparables analysis operate in many of the same markets as Chemtura, make similar products, and are subject to similar tax and regulatory environments. And half of Chemtura's revenue comes from outside the U.S., where Chemtura would have to compete with those foreign companies. It also is puzzling that UBS included several European companies in its Precedent Transactions Analysis, and in its Sum-of-the-Parts Comparable Companies analysis, but left them out here—a fact that further undercuts UBS criticisms in this regard.

Thus I find Lazard's reasoning to be sound in its Comparable Companies analysis, which I find, in turn, to be one of the most important indicia of value here. Especially since UBS didn't put forward an alternate valuation on this basis, I give Lazard's conclusions here substantial weight.

iv. Precedent Transactions Analysis

Here too, I note that Lazard derived a valuation range based on Precedent Transactions Analysis and that UBS didn't do so. Instead, UBS used this methodology merely as a means of verifying its DCF conclusions. I think that Precedent Transactions analysis has to be used with some care to normalize for extraneous factors that may be present in individual cases and increase the prices in those transactions—like control premiums, a willingness to pay more to obtain operational synergies, and hostile transactions. And I'm a little concerned about the post-Lehman bankruptcy sample size. But I think that Precedent Transactions methodology still is helpful, and that it tends to support a valuation lower than the valuation for which the Equity Committee argues. Additionally, I believe that UBS's criticism of Lazard's Precedent Transactions was materially flawed itself.

As noted above, a significant difference between the Lazard and UBS approaches was the heavy reliance by UBS on transactions that predated the recent financial collapse, as measured by the date of filing of the Lehman bankruptcy case. Lazard noted that the global economy fell into a tailspin after the Lehman bankruptcy, and that the financial system froze and global stock markets collapsed, causing the worst recession since the Great Depression. Credit necessary to finance acquisitions is far less available today. I accept Lazard's testimony that advanced economies are fundamentally different today, and that relying on multiples from a time period before the crash is inappropriate.

. . .

Of course, the small number of transactions in the post-Lehman environment makes for a small sample size. That's a cause for some concern, and a reason for not giving this methodology as much weight as I otherwise would. But with two comparables coming in at 6.2x EBITDA in the post-Lehman bankruptcy era, I feel relatively comfortable in still giving some weight to this methodology. The upper end of Lazard's Precedent Transactions range ($2.315 billion) is somewhat higher than the upper end of Lazard's final valuation range ($2.2 billion). But the transactions on which Lazard relies had synergistic and control characteristics, which would result in a higher implied valuation, and we know that Chemtura has historically traded lower than its peers. Lazard's Precedent Transactions upper end is of course well below the upper end of UBS's valuation (based solely on DCF and the aggressive projections) of $2.6 billion, and suggests that UBS's valuation is too high.

v. Marketing Efforts

Another matter that informs my finding that the Debtors' TEV doesn't exceed $2.05 billion is the lack of buyers or investors for the Debtors at higher values or values within the Equity Committee's range—a species of "market" information that informs, though it does not solely support, my conclusion that the Debtors have met their burden as to value here.[106]

As I've discussed before, the Debtors cooperated with Equity Committee efforts to market the company, which led to contacts with 19 potential investors, of whom 7 signed confidentiality agreements. UBS made presentations to potential investors valuing the company at $2.2 to $2.7 billion, a valuation which would have the same midpoint (of $2.45 billion) as the present UBS valuation. But there were no takers, or offers, at that price or at any price that might ultimately lead to that price. Nor were any members of the Equity Committee itself, though several were hedge funds, prepared to put their own money into the Debtors at those (or even lower) prices—a fact that I also find meaningful. Though I hardly expect that investors would have simply accepted offers to invest at the prices that the presentations were putting forward, the lack of any interest in proposals at those values lends further support to my conclusion that a $2.45 billion midpoint would be too high.

vi. Creditors' Preferences for Cash

I take note of another kind of "market" type information—the fact that the Plan gave most creditors and all bondholders the right to elect, within limits, to take stock or cash as the currency by which they'd get their distributions. The overwhelming majority of them elected to take the maximum recovery in cash, rather than stock. A very major

---

106. Many observers believe that behavior in the marketplace is the best indicator of enterprise value. *See, e.g., Bank of America Nat. Trust and Sav. Ass'n v. 203 North La Salle Partnership,* 526 U.S. 434 (1999) (acknowledging that "the best way to determine value is exposure to a market"). *See also In re Granite Broad. Corp.,* 369 B.R. 120, 140-43 (Bankr. S.D.N.Y. 2007) (Gropper, J.) ("*Granite Broadcasting*") (noting that what a willing purchaser is willing to pay "'typically trumps all other[ ]' indications of value"). I don't believe that always to be the case, since as I saw in the *Global Crossing* and *Adelphia* cases on my watch, financial accounting techniques (such as capitalizing expenses without writing them down to realizable value) or fraud can give the marketplace a distorted impression of a company's worth. But as a general matter, where, as here, there isn't a suggestion that the company's financials or projections are inflated or misleading, I think the marketplace is often as good or better an indication of a company's value than expert testimony alone would be. *See VFB LLC v. Campbell Soup Co.,* 482 F.3d 624, 633 (3d Cir. 2007) ("Absent some reason to distrust it, the market price is a more reliable measure of the stock's value than the subjective estimates of one or two expert witnesses.").

proportion of the Debtors' non-Diacetyl[-caused "popcorn lung" disease tort] and environmental creditors (including all or substantially all of the Bondholders' Committee,
which held about 68% of the bonds) were hedge funds and other distressed debt
investors, sophisticated in financial analysis and having the ability to efficiently dispose
of stock if it were received as an alternative currency. Yet approximately 78% of the
electing bondholders indicated a preference for cash—even though they'd make an
immediate return of 20 or 25% by taking stock if it were worth as much as the Equity
Committee contends.

I agree with the point made by several Plan supporters that if those creditors thought
the New Common Stock was undervalued at the price at which it was offered—the
natural consequence of the Equity Committee's position—they would have snapped
it up. And if they thought Chemtura was worth what UBS says it's worth, they would
really have snapped it up. Their failure to do so, and their preference for cash under the
Plan, suggests to me that they don't think that the stock is worth more than the cash,
and, more fundamentally, the higher amount that the Equity Committee contends.

vii. Credibility

While, over the years, very few of the cases before me have involved witness credibility to any material degree, this case was an exception. The opinions of all four experts
were subject to at least some question by reason of their prior activities, the circumstances under which they testified, inconsistencies between their trial and deposition
testimony, or some combination of those factors. With respect to the Equity Committee's
two experts, these issues—causing reason to question their judgment, their credibility,
or both—were particularly pronounced.

UBS's first witness (a UBS Chemicals Industry expert) repeatedly seemed unwilling to
give straight answers to questions on cross-examination, even questions that were quite
preliminary and not at all argumentative. Much more troublesome, however, were the
many times he was impeached by inconsistent statements in his deposition testimony.

UBS's second witness (the more senior of the Equity Committee's two experts, who
pitched the engagement and who signed the Equity Committee-UBS retention letter)
was likewise impeached on many occasions by inconsistent deposition testimony. In
addition, he showed unusually strong indications of bias. In making the pitch to the
Equity Committee [to] secure the engagement for UBS in the first place, he told the
Equity Committee that he would "try to be aggressive in valuation," and in depositions
acknowledged acting "with the outlook of what would achieve the maximum value for
the equity."

Also undermining the credibility of the two experts for the Equity Committee—
and similarly, albeit to a lesser degree, the experts for the Debtors and the Creditors'
Committee—were the terms of their engagement agreements. The UBS retention agreement provided that in addition to getting the customary monthly fee, UBS would get a
"transaction fee" of 1.25% of amounts distributed to Equity between $225 million and
$450 million, and 2.0% of amounts over $450 million. (At the Lazard $2.05 billion valu-
ation, UBS would not get a transaction fee.) The distribution to Equity would of course
turn on the ultimate TEV, upon which the UBS experts would later testify.

The Lazard retention agreement provided for an additional $7 million fee payable upon consummation of a reorganization plan, and the Houlihan agreement provided for a "deferred fee" of $3 million on the confirmation of a plan that was supported by the Creditors' Committee. It was foreseeable that Lazard would have to offer trial testimony—which, of course, is exactly what happened here. Likewise, although Houlihan could (and ultimately did) rely in substantial part on Lazard, it too would financially gain if a plan were confirmed based on its testimony generally supporting Lazard.

In my experience, provisions like those in the Lazard and Houlihan agreements are common, and provisions like those in the UBS agreement are, if not also common, at least not uncommon. I approved each of them when authorizing the retentions of the three firms, and in my view there is nothing inherently wrong with them. They're unobjectionable as a means of incentivizing investment bankers to find buyers or investors, or to make deals, if they're regarded by stakeholders as necessary or desirable to achieve those ends. But such provisions can't be ignored when investment bankers testify. Especially in the case of the UBS agreement—and, to a lesser degree, also in the case of Lazard's and Houlihan's—they materially and adversely affect witness credibility.

The usual stated rationale for including such provisions in retention agreements for investment bankers is to incentivize them. But UBS had no material role in soliciting buyers or investors or capital for the enterprise; the Debtors had plan exclusivity, and the solicitation of investors to meet the Equity Committee's needs was principally engaged in by hedge fund members of the Equity Committee, rather than by UBS. If the purpose of the transaction fee for UBS was indeed to incentivize it (as contrasted to simply paying UBS more), the transaction fee had a heavy effect on its credibility. Likewise, if the purposes of the different contingent compensation provisions for Lazard and Houlihan were in fact to incentivize them, as contrasted to simply paying them more, their contingent fees—dependent on confirmation, which would turn on Lazard's testimony supporting the underlying TEV and Houlihan's testimony generally supporting Lazard—bore adversely on the credibility of their expert testimony as well.

The rather obvious adverse effect of incentive compensation on witness credibility has been recognized in the caselaw, in this district and elsewhere, including in several Chapter 11 valuation decisions.[125] While it's been suggested in the commentary that an expert's contingent fee should generally result in the expert's disqualification as a witness,[126] I think it's sufficient—since we bankruptcy judges conduct non-jury trials and

---

125. See *Granite Broadcasting*, 369 B.R. at 142 (an expert's testimony "was seriously undermined by the fact that his compensation from the Preferred Holders is contingent on the total consideration to be received by the Preferred Holders under a confirmed plan"); *In re Oneida Ltd.*, 351 B.R. 79, 92 (Bankr. S.D.N.Y. 2006) (Gropper, J.) (a valuation expert's retention with a contingency fee "seriously undermine[d]" the expert's credibility); *In re Tousa, Inc.*, 422 B.R. 783, 839-40 (Bankr. S.D. Fla. 2009) (taking into account fact that expert was to receive a $2 million contingency fee and where expert, after only 5 days, announced that it would have a favorable opinion).

126. See Bernstein, Seabury & Williams, *The Empowerment of Bankruptcy Courts in Addressing Financial Expert Testimony*, 80 Am. Bankr. L.J. 377, 432 (Summer 2006) ("[T]he existence of a contingency in the retention of an expert should generally result in the disqualification of the expert. An expert who has a 'financial dog in the fight' cannot be objective; his opinion will be swayed by his financial stake and, thus, be inherently unreliable.").

are used to provisions of this character—that we merely take contingent fees or incentive compensation into account as adversely affecting credibility, and ultimately take such opinions with a grain of salt.

Finally, failures by UBS and Lazard to change the midpoints of their valuations after the passage of time, and in the face of seemingly different circumstances, tend to undercut the persuasiveness of each. In June 2010, UBS valued Chemtura within the range of $2.2 billion to $2.7 billion, with a midpoint of $2.45 billion. On August 29, UBS issued the valuation opinion it offered at trial—within the narrower range of $2.3 billion to $2.6 billion, but with the exact same midpoint.

On June 4, Lazard valued Chemtura within the range of $1.9 billion to $2.2 billion, with a midpoint of $2.05 billion. On August 29, Lazard issued the updated report that it offered at trial. But Lazard's range and midpoint (the latter being the valuation upon which the Settlement was based) were exactly the same, despite a variety of events that would at least seemingly have affected the Debtors' ultimate TEV, American trading markets, or both—such as the Debtors' beating EBITDA projections for Q2 by $30 million and failing to make the projections in August, reduced uncertainty in the European trading markets, and progress in controlling the oil spill in the Gulf.

That these similarities were mere coincidence is of course possible, but I find such coincidence improbable in each case. They tend to cause me to be more proactive in making my own valuation judgment, rather than to accept either of the proffered ones.

D. Conclusions re: Valuation

The facts found above underlie my ultimate factual finding, set forth above and again now, that the Debtors' TEV is no higher than the $2.05 billion TEV underlying the Settlement. The evidence to the contrary is unpersuasive. In fact, the Creditors' Committee makes some persuasive points—that the projections in the LRP are aggressive; that in the face of an economy that, while getting better, is getting better slowly, projections will be difficult to achieve; that the Debtors may not retain the above-forecast EBITDA generated in the first half of 2010; and that Lazard failed to impose a valuation discount for the Debtors' historic rank below the majority of their peers. But I don't need to rule on the Creditors' Committee's points in that regard. By each of the traditional valuation techniques and by the evidence of behavior in the "marketplace," the Debtors have shown, by a preponderance of the evidence, that the actual TEV of Chemtura is no higher than the level upon which the Settlement is based.

Given the limitations of expert valuation opinions, some courts have started to look for independent market measures of valuation, such as credit spreads and bond pricing as a substitute for expert testimony. *See VFB LLC v. Campbell Soup Co.,* 482 F.3d 624 (3d Cir. 2007); *In re Iridium Capital Corp. v. Motorola, Inc. (In re Iridium Operating),* 373 B.R. 283 (Bankr. S.D.N.Y. 2007). Market data, however, is often not available for many types of valuation determinations, and even when it is, one must still ask whether the market in question is in fact an efficient market.

V. THE COST OF VALUATION MISTAKES

Eastern Airlines' 1989 bankruptcy is often the poster child for valuation decisions gone awry—the bankruptcy judge permitted Eastern's equityholders to keep calling the shots on the assumption that Eastern was solvent, and the equityholders gambled on resurrection on the creditors' dime, and lost. The result was much smaller recoveries for creditors than if Eastern had liquidated immediately rather than years into the bankruptcy. *See* AARON BERNSTEIN, GROUNDED: FRANK LORENZO AND THE DESTRUCTION OF EASTERN AIRLINES 15 (1990); DAVID LEE RUSSELL, EASTERN AIRLINES: A HISTORY, 1926-1991 (2013); Lawrence A. Weiss & Karen H. Wruck, *Information Problems, Conflicts of Interest and Asset Stripping: Chapter 11's Failure in the Case of Eastern Airlines*, 48 J. FIN. ECON. 55 (1998).

Eastern Airlines, however, is hardly the only notable valuation goof. A more recent case is *In re Exide Technologies*, 303 B.R. 48 (Bankr. D. Del. 2003). In *Exide*, the debtor's financial advisor valued the company at between $950 million and $1.05 billion. The unsecured creditors' committee's advisor valued the company at between $1.478 billion and $1.711 billion. Both sides employed the same methodologies: comparable company analysis, comparable transaction analysis, and discounted cash flow analysis. In addition, however, the debtor's financial advisor had also solicited bids from potential buyers. The court determined the valuation to be between $1.4 billion and $1.6 billion.

In May 2004, Exide emerged from bankruptcy. Its market capitalization (equity value) was $544 million, and its enterprise value (equity value plus debt minus cash and cash equivalents) was $1.03 billion. By November of 2005, however, Exide's market capitalization had dropped to $109 million, and its enterprise value was $788 million.

It would appear that the court massively overvalued Exide. As a result, the unsecured creditors were able to receive a distribution in the case, including the equity in the reorganized company, that they otherwise would not have received.

Valuation is key to determining the distribution of value in bankruptcy, but it remains a highly subjective matter and with little appellate review. As a result, valuation remains perhaps the most critical, and most problematic, issue in bankruptcy.

Problem Set 17

(1) Swanky Realty, a privately held real estate company that owns and operates several South Florida ultra-premium luxury hotels, has filed for bankruptcy at the beginning of December. An incredibly hot summer and a devastating summer-fall hurricane

season as well as a tragic oil spill in the Gulf of Mexico drove down tourism, but increased the operating costs of the hotels. Swanky is hoping to use bankruptcy to slough off some of its debt so it can borrow afresh to spruce up its properties.

Among Swanky's properties is the famous SWAG Hotel in Miami. The mortgagee of the SWAG has moved to lift the stay on the grounds that it is not adequately protected. The mortgagee is owed $40 million, and it claims that the SWAG is only worth $39 million and that its value is rapidly declining because Swanky has not updated the décor or addressed a cockroach problem. According to the mortgagee's motion, the Swanky's signature ballroom, the Rhumba-Rhumba Room, "is so last year."

The lift stay motion bases its valuation of the hotel on a discounted cash flow analysis. The analysis is based on an annualized last six-month EBITDA projected out to seven years, and uses a discount rate of 900 basis points over the Federal Funds Rate. What might Swanky Realty argue to contest the lift stay motion? 11 U.S.C. § 362(d)(1).

(2) United Airlines has filed for bankruptcy (again). Your firm is representing United. You know that there will be a series of valuation issues in the case and are working with United's financial advisor to come up with valuations of the company and key assets.

You've been asked to value United's gate slots at its main hub, Chicago O'Hare International Airport. United licenses the gate slots from the FAA; without a license, United cannot land at O'Hare. O'Hare is one of the busiest airports in the world and is well-served by many airlines, including United's Star Alliance partners. Most of United's gate slots are in the main and recently updated United Terminal, but a few are in an older terminal that cannot handle larger airplanes.

Which of the following would be relevant to your valuation?

a. The sale price of gate slots from six months ago at the large but dated Washington (D.C.) Dulles International Airport.

b. The rental price of gate slots at Washington (D.C.) Dulles International currently.

c. The sale price of gate slots two years ago at a modern terminal at Houston George Bush Intercontinental Airport.

d. The sale price of gate slots a year ago at Ithaca Tompkins Regional Airport.

e. Last week's sale price of gate slots at Chicago Midway International Airport, which is located on the other side of Chicago from O'Hare. While the Midway terminal is modern, Midway has shorter runways than O'Hare, and the Midway runways cannot be expanded. Thus, it is impossible for Midway to handle larger planes, such as 747s and 767s.

(3) You are doing a comparable company valuation analysis of United.

a. Which firms would you look at? American? Delta? British Airways? Lufthansa? Southwest? Spirit Air?

b. Suppose that a 20% stake in Jet Blue recently sold for $800 million. Jet Blue's last 12-month EBITDA was $750 million. What purchase price multiple does this imply for Jet Blue? Would your answer change if the sale price were for only a one percent stake in Jet Blue?

c. Suppose that the mean and median multiples for the companies you believe are appropriate comparables is 5.0. If United Airline's 12-month trailing EBITDAR was $3.5 billion, what valuation does this indicate for United?

(4) A year and a half ago, Gemini Interterrestrial, a publicly traded company, decided to spin off its struggling Betelgeuse telecommunications satellite division, which had been weighing down the returns of the rest of the business. After the spin-off, both Gemeni Interterrestrial and Betelgeuse were publicly traded. The spin-off resulted in a 10% increase in Gemini's stock price, which traded up at a market valuation of $1.25 billion, even though its book value was $1.5 billion. While a couple of analysts thought Gemini's stock was massively overpriced, they were generally ignored by the market. Gemini's stock prices were fairly steady until last month, when Gemini filed for bankruptcy after federal intelligence agencies—one of Gemini's major customers—suddenly cancelled their contracts with Gemini for unspecified reasons. Betelgeuse—an independent company, now unaffiliated with Gemini—is not in bankruptcy. Gemini's Official Committee of Unsecured Creditors has alleged that the Betelgeuse spin-off was a fraudulent transfer because the company was insolvent at the time and did not receive reasonably equivalent compensation in return.

   a. Could Gemini have had a positive equity value while still being balance sheet insolvent?
   b. Gemini's bonds were trading at 45 cents on the dollar at the time of the spin-off. Is this evidence of insolvency?
   c. After Gemini's bankruptcy, evidence of an accounting fraud at Gemini has emerged. Does that affect the Official Committee's valuation evidence?

(5) Cascadia Generating, a hydroelectric power producer in the Pacific Northwest, has filed for bankruptcy. Cascadia has proposed to sell its Willamette River hydroelectric plant. The plant is subject to a $150 million first lien security interest and a $250 million second lien security interest. To that end, Cascadia has held an auction for the plant, with the winning bid subject to court approval. Thirty firms bid for the plant. The high bid at the auction was $135 million. Hydra Funding Corp., which holds a second lien on the plant, has objected to the sale arguing that the price is inadequate. Hydra claims that the market has not anticipated future regulatory changes (namely, a crackdown on coal-fired electric plants) that will vastly increase the value of the plant, which it believes is worth almost $500 million. Hydra is proposing to present Professor Jan Pisher, a valuation expert who has appeared in over 366 cases in the past year, who it claims will use a discounted cash flow analysis to demonstrate that the plant is worth between $380 million and $420 million. What should the bankruptcy judge do?

(6) Senator Prudence Dogood (D-Mass.) was previously a crack bankruptcy practitioner. From her experience, she knows just what a bramble bankruptcy valuation can be. "It's so easy to get it wrong, there's so much hindsight bias, the consequences are so major, and there's no effective appellate review," she says. The Senator is wondering if there might be a better way to do valuations. She's curious for your thoughts on four ideas:

   a. Appointment by the court of an independent master for valuation issues, compensated by the estate.

b. Requirement that the SEC submit an advisory valuation opinion to the court regarding the value of the firm as a whole and its secured assets.

c. A requirement that courts look to market valuations whenever possible, and when market and expert valuations conflict, to adopt market valuations absent clear and convincing evidence that they are less reliable than expert valuations.

d. Adoption of a baseball salary arbitration-type system: The court will be limited to selecting one party's valuation or the other, but will not be allowed to adopt its own valuation.

What are the benefits and pitfalls of these approaches? Are they better than the current system?

OPERATING
THE FIRM IN
BANKRUPTCY

CHAPTER 18

GOVERNANCE IN BANKRUPTCY I

Bankruptcy changes the state law ordering of governance rights. Outside of bankruptcy, the firm is managed for the benefit of its shareholders. Governance rights are vested with the shareholders who have the ability to vote on certain major transactions themselves, and who select the firm's directors (who in turn select the firm's officers), both of whom owe fiduciary duties to the shareholders.

In bankruptcy, however, creditors obtain some governance rights. In both Chapter 7 and Chapter 11, creditors have a right to object and be heard on any transaction outside of the ordinary course of business. In Chapter 7, creditors have a right to elect a trustee, while in Chapter 11, creditors have the right to propose new management (a trustee, although not of their choosing) and, if they are impaired, to vote on plans of reorganization—a major transaction (or really set of transactions) for the firm. In Chapter 11, creditors may also be entitled to obtain certain information about the debtor's business that will enable them to evaluate the possible courses of restructuring.

I. THE DEBTOR-IN-POSSESSION

When a firm files for bankruptcy, all of its assets are transferred by function of law to a new juridical entity, the bankruptcy estate. Who governs the bankruptcy estate?

In a Chapter 7 bankruptcy, a trustee is always appointed. 11 U.S.C. §§ 701-703. The Chapter 7 trustee is in charge of liquidating the debtor. 11 U.S.C. § 704. The trustee owes fiduciary duties to the estate. *Commodity Futures Trading Comm'n v. Weintraub*, 471 U.S. 343 (1985). These duties are, essentially, maximizing the value of the debtor's assets (including collecting debts owed to the debtor), objecting to improper claims filed against the debtor, and distributing the debtor's assets.

It is important not to confuse the Chapter 7 trustee, known as a **trustee in bankruptcy (TIB)** with other trustees in the bankruptcy ecosystem: the **United States Trustee (UST)** or an **indenture trustee**. The United States Trustee is a Department of Justice official in charge of ensuring the integrity of the bankruptcy process. The UST does not manage debtors. An **indenture trustee** is a representative of creditors whose debt obligation—a bond or debenture—also includes a contract with the trustee called a trust indenture. The indenture trustee has statutory duties under the Trust Indenture Act. It is less clear whether the indenture trustee has fiduciary duties otherwise, as no property is necessarily held in trust by the indenture trustee. Indenture trustees will often claim that they do not have non-contractual duties, but certain fiduciary duties may be unwaiveable. The indenture trustee represents the interests of the bondholders in the bankruptcy, but (like the UST) does not manage the debtor's affairs.

In Chapter 11, the default mode is for existing management to remain in place and to operate the debtor as a "debtor-in-possession" (DIP). For almost all purposes, the DIP has the same powers as the TIB. 11 U.S.C. § 1107. The Bankruptcy Code refers almost exclusively to a "trustee," but that term should generally be read as "debtor in possession." 11 U.S.C. § 1101. Chapter 11 never explicitly states that a DIP is the default arrangement. Instead, it states that the trustee (read trustee or DIP) may operate the debtor's business, 11 U.S.C. § 1108, and does not require the appointment of a trustee (read trustee). Therefore, unless a trustee is appointed, the DIP may operate the debtor's business, subject to the restrictions of the Bankruptcy Code.

If there is a debtor-in-possession, the DIP is directed by the debtor's *board of directors* (or an LLC's members or partnership's partners), not the officers of the debtor. The officers are employed under contract with the debtor firm. The DIP can choose to honor those contracts or replace the officers just like it could outside of bankruptcy. Alternatively, the DIP may have to offer the officers special incentives to remain at a bankrupt company. Such retention incentives are regulated when paid to insiders, as discussed in the next chapter.

So the directors choose the officers. But who chooses the directors? A fundamental piece of shareholders' rights outside of bankruptcy is to hold a meeting for the purpose of electing directors. Delaware law, for example, allows shareholders to petition for such a meeting if one has not been held in the past 13 months, and such petitions are usually granted absent unusual circumstances. Del. Code Ann. § 211(c). Nothing in the Bankruptcy Code directly addresses the question of whether shareholder meetings may occur in bankruptcy or whether shareholders may replace the existing board of directors. Courts have generally permitted shareholder meetings to occur when a corporation is in bankruptcy, unless holding such a meeting would be a "clear abuse" and cause "irreparable harm" to the debtor. *Manville Corp. v. Equity Sec. Holders Comm.*, 801 F.2d 60, 68 (2d Cir. 1986).

Yet herein lies a puzzle. At state law, the directors of a solvent corporation owe fiduciary duties to the shareholders—and to no one else. But in bankruptcy, the debtor-in-possession—and hence its board of directors—owes "the same fiduciary obligation to creditors and shareholders as would the trustee for a debtor out of possession." *Commodity Futures Trading Comm'n v. Weintraub*, 471 U.S. 343, 355 (1985). So if the directors owe fiduciary duties to all of the creditors and shareholders, why are only the shareholders (or perhaps only a subset of the shareholders) selecting the directors during bankruptcy?

The answer might be that the alternatives are little better. Creditors do not bargain to have the right to choose directors, and it is not clear how a vote would be weighted if anyone other than shareholders with voting shares had a vote. Moreover, if there were no possibility of replacing directors, bad management could remain entrenched during a bankruptcy, which is precisely when it should be removed. And if the court could order replacement, then the whole concept of a DIP would make little sense, as the replacement directors would basically be trustees. Beyond this, the harm of having shareholders choose directors in bankruptcy is less clear. If the directors act solely in the interest of the shareholders, they could face litigation by creditors. Of course, the possibility of litigation is no guarantee of good behavior because of the difficulties in successfully prosecuting litigation.

The puzzle about the status of shareholder governance rights in bankruptcy reflects a general confusion about the interaction between state and federal law in bankruptcy. Bankruptcy law is, of course, federal law, but it incorporates state law inputs, such as the definition of property rights, and authorizes the estate to file suit under state law. 11 U.S.C. §§ 502, 541, 544(b). The confusion is particularly acute when it comes to corporate governance.

Corporate governance has traditionally been the province of state law, but this is because most corporate entities are state-law entities; there are relatively few federally chartered corporations, and federal corporate law is poorly developed. The bankruptcy estate is a new juridical entity created by the filing of the bankruptcy petition. 11 U.S.C. § 541. The bankruptcy estate is a creation of federal law. Accordingly, it would seem to follow that federal law, rather than state law, applies to the governance of the bankruptcy estate. The Bankruptcy Code allows the DIP to serve as the trustee and thus allows the directors chosen by a state law process to run the DIP. But these directors are no longer serving simply as directors of a state law entity.

Bankruptcy courts generally defer to state corporate law, but this makes little sense. Instead, the governance of the bankruptcy estate is properly determined by an ill-defined federal common law of business organizations. This means that the filing of a bankruptcy petition can result in a shift of the corporate law applicable to a debtor's directors and officers, and duties that might not exist at state law might apply under federal common law. *In re Houston Regional Sports Network, L.P.*, 2014 Bankr. Lexis 572 (Feb. 12, 2014). It might also affect the proper venue for bringing suits against the directors and officers for breach of fiduciary duty—these suits would be federal questions, not state law issues, and thus enable a federal court venue.

II. APPOINTMENT OF A TRUSTEE

In many countries outside the United States, a trustee is the default setting for all insolvencies. A trustee was also mandatory under Chapter X of the old Bankruptcy Act for all cases involving public security holders. Why would the Bankruptcy Code have a DIP rather than a trustee as the default setting for Chapter 11, but make a trustee mandatory in Chapter 7? Is the board of directors likely to have real expertise in the debtor's business? Or does that expertise more likely lie with the managers? Isn't the board implicated in the fact that the debtor is in bankruptcy? If so, can it be relied upon to correct the affairs of the debtor firm?

If a TIB is appointed, the TIB assumes the powers of the debtor's board of directors, and can hire or fire officers and otherwise run the firm's business. 11 U.S.C. § 1108. The TIB also assumes any attorney-client privilege owed to the firm. This may be a particular source of concern for former officers and directors who are concerned about shareholder suits against them.

Section 1104 of the Bankruptcy Code sets forth the conditions under which a trustee may be appointed. It includes a broad "for cause" provision, with cause including "fraud, dishonesty, incompetence, or gross mismanagement of the affairs of the debtor by current management." 11 U.S.C. § 1104. Is the fact that a firm is in bankruptcy a sign of "gross mismanagement"? Not necessarily. Sometimes a firm files for bankruptcy in order to use bankruptcy's procedural tools to deal with a holdout creditor or to sell an asset free and clear of liens. Other times, a firm files for bankruptcy because of liabilities that could not have been avoided by better management, such as in cases of mass toxic torts. And other times, a bankruptcy might be filed for because a firm was not able to refinance due to market-wide conditions, rather than management. This is hardly an exhaustive list, but bankruptcy is not synonymous with mismanagement, gross or otherwise.

Section 1104(a)(1) applies not just to pre-bankruptcy behavior, but also to post-bankruptcy behavior; a DIP can be replaced by a TIB in the middle of a case. The *Sharon Steel* case below illustrates circumstances that might trigger a motion for a trustee.

Section 1104(a)(2) creates a second standard for appointment of a trustee: if it is "in the interests of creditors, any equity security holders, and other interests of the estate." This is a broader catchall than section 1104(a)(1). While it may appear to be a less onerous threshold than section 1104(a)(1), section 1104(a)(2) requires the appointment of a trustee to be in the interest of both creditors and equityholders. If equityholders support current management, appointment of a trustee under section 1104(a)(2) will be difficult. There are few situations that would seem to meet the section 1104(a)(2) standard that would not also qualify under section 1104(a)(1). One potential situation, however, is when there is an intractable divide among the debtor's directors or partners. In such a case, appointment of a trustee may be in the interests of everyone in order to break the logjam.

Finally, the United States Trustee is directed to move for appointment of a trustee if there is reason to suspect fraud, dishonesty, or criminal conduct in the debtor's management. 11 U.S.C. § 1104(e). This does not mean that a trustee will be appointed, only that the United States Trustee is directed to make a motion in such circumstances. When the motion must be made is left up to the discretion of the United States Trustee, seemingly reducing some of the force of the requirement. Some courts will also appoint a trustee *sua sponte*, but most hesitate to do so. *See, e.g., In re Bibo, Inc.*, 76 F.3d 256 (9th Cir. 1996).

While the decision of whether to appoint a trustee is the court's, the selection of the trustee is outside of the court process. Instead, if any party in interest so moves, the United States Trustee must hold an election for the trustee. 11 U.S.C. § 1104(e). If there is no motion or in the interim, the United States Trustee may appoint a trustee. 11 U.S.C. § 1104(d). Only a "disinterested person" is eligible for election as trustee, meaning that no creditor or equityholder, insider, recent employee or director, or adverse party may be elected. 11 U.S.C. § 101(14). A trustee need not be a natural person, as the Code's definition of person includes corporate entities, but a natural person is almost always appointed. Only unsecured creditors vote in the election of a trustee. 11 U.S.C. §§ 1104(b), 702. To be elected, a candidate must get at least half of the votes cast and 20% of the eligible votes. *Id.*

An important point to note is that the possibility of a trustee being appointed gives creditors leverage when dealing with the debtor. A creditor that can credibly threaten a motion to appoint a trustee may be able to wring concessions from a debtor's management. Of course, the threat may be a bit of a suicide pact—the creditor would get rid of existing management, but would then be stuck with a trustee who might not run the company as well as existing management and also might not be inclined to make concessions to the creditor.

In re Sharon Steel Corp.

871 F.2d 1217 (3d Cir. 1989)

GIBBONS, Chief Judge:

Sharon Steel Corporation manufactures steel in a facility located near Sharon, Pennsylvania. The Sharon facility includes two blast furnaces. By April, 1987, only one of these—number 3—was operational. Sharon's most efficient blast furnace, number 2 [nicknamed "Judy"], was shut down pending $18 million in repairs. Furthermore, furnace number 3, which was three years overdue for relining, faced imminent shutdown. On April 17, 1987, confronted with $742 million in liabilities, only $478 million in assets, and pressing creditors, Sharon filed a voluntary petition for reorganization under Chapter 11 of the Bankruptcy Code.

Sharon management remained in control of the corporation's operations as debtor-in-possession. At all times relevant to this case, appellant Victor Posner served as Sharon's chairman, president, and chief executive officer. Appellant DWG, under common control with Sharon, provided financial management services to Sharon and other Posner-controlled companies. It operated out of a Miami office building owned by Posner and provided 13,000 square feet of office space to Sharon to house its executive offices, charging Sharon $24 per square foot.

Some five months after Sharon filed for reorganization, the committee, dissatisfied with the progress—or lack thereof—made by Sharon's management, petitioned the bankruptcy court for appointment of a trustee pursuant to 11 U.S.C. § 1104.

The bankruptcy court's Opinion on Appointment of a Trustee, dated May 2, 1988, sets forth its reasons for granting the motion for appointment of a trustee. . . . It cited numerous prepetition transfers of Sharon assets that amounted at best to voidable preferences and at worst to fraudulent conveyances, none of which had been questioned by the debtor-in-possession.[9]

Not only had Sharon failed to sue for recovery of these transfers, but the bankruptcy court questioned the current management's ability to fulfill its fiduciary duty to pursue these claims since Sharon shares common management with the recipients of the transfers, who also owe conflicting fiduciary duties to the recipients. Disclosure of the transfers did not cure the preferential or fraudulent transfers.

The bankruptcy court also faulted Sharon's day-to-day management of the estate. Sharon, which continued to rely on DWG for financial services, had not yet closed out its books for the period preceding reorganization. Thus, not only was the debtor continuing to hemorrhage money at an estimated $2 million per month at a time when steel prices were rising, but the debtor could not even measure the precise size of these losses since it had no postpetition profit and loss statements.

Similarly, the court also criticized Sharon's failure to renegotiate its $30 million working capital loan from the 28% to 30% interest rate originally agreed to to a reasonable 14% to 15%—an action that would save Sharon $4 million a year. It also impugned the wisdom (and the propriety) of Sharon's repayment during 1985 and 1986 of $294 million in secured bank loans "in order to facilitate new loans from those banks to other Posner companies." Given Sharon's blast furnace crisis and the fact that the payments left Sharon so cash-poor that it was forced to enter into the $30 million, high-interest working capital loan, it concluded such actions amounted to gross mismanagement.

---

9. These either preferential transfers or fraudulent conveyances include a $3.7 million wire transfer made by Sharon to DWG on April 16, 1986 apparently in payment of a $3.58 million annual charge including $122,433.21 rent for the chairman's office, $74,465.53 for use of a yacht that Sharon owned, $170,483.26 for airplane usage (although the plane also was owned by Sharon), $230,422.28 for use of the guest apartments in Miami, and $100,833.21 for accommodations in the Waldorf-Astoria; a December 1986 transfer by Sharon to NPC Leasing Company, under common control with Sharon, of title to a yacht and airplane, each minimally valued at $750,000; a March 16, 1987 transfer of 141,000 common shares in Chesapeake Financial Corporation, valued by the trustee at $24 million, to Insurance and Risk Management, also connected to Sharon by interlocking directors, in satisfaction of an antecedent debt of $1,512,493.75; and approximately $16 million in compensation paid to Victor Posner between 1983 and September 1987, including $4.4 million paid by Sharon for his defense in a criminal action for individual tax evasion and conspiracy, and approximately $1.8 in compensation paid to Stephen Posner.

In its conclusions of law, the bankruptcy court held the transfers of the $3.7 million to DWG, the yacht and plane to NPC Leasing, and the 141,000 shares of Chesapeake Financial Corporation to Insurance and Risk Management constituted prima facie voidable preferences. It also held that the 1985 through March 1987 transfers of $9.8 million to Victor Posner and $940,000 to Stephen Posner "were not shown to be for an adequate consideration, and prima facia [sic] constitute fraudulent conveyances." App. 2124. The bankruptcy court also credited expert testimony that valued the Miami office space at $12.50 per square foot and noted that DWG charged Sharon $24.

The trustee has instituted several actions to recover various of these assets for the estate. He has sued Posner in United States district court for reimbursement of the criminal defense costs, excessive compensation paid to him, and damages caused by his mismanagement of the debtor. The trustee also has brought two actions in the bankruptcy court: on August 19, 1988, to obtain books, records and financial information from DWG, Posner, and others; and on March 11, 1988, to recover the 141,000 shares of Chesapeake Financial Corp. stock from Insurance and Risk Management. The trustee also filed suit against Posner in the bankruptcy court on June 3, 1988 for the return of 14 original Norman Rockwell oil paintings that belonged to Sharon. In October 1988, the bankruptcy court approved without prejudice a stipulation requiring Posner to return the paintings.

Last, the bankruptcy court raised an even more fundamental issue when it questioned the $279,872.50 in attorneys' fees expended during the last quarter of 1987 to fight the appointment of the trustee:

> While the equity owners are entitled to representation and to assert their rights, one must speculate whether the expenditure of such resources was appropriate, and whether Sharon's counsel in doing so was fulfilling its fiduciary duty to the debtor's estate, or was defending the private position of the equity owners. The funds expended come from the estate, and in view of the admitted insolvency, will likely be borne chiefly by creditors.

The bankruptcy court determined that the sum of the above behavior amounted to cause under section 1104(a)(1). It also demonstrated the necessity of new management just to keep Sharon operating, therefore implicating the interests of the creditors and equity holders alike specified for appointment of a trustee under subsection (b). . . .

It is settled that appointment of a trustee should be the exception, rather than the rule. H.R. Rep. No. 595, 95th Cong., 1st Sess. 233 (1977), *reprinted in* 1978 U.S. Code Cong. & Admin. News 5963, 6192 ("Very often the creditors will be benefited by continuation of the debtor-in-possession, both because the expense of a trustee will not be required, and the debtor, who is familiar with his business, will be better able to operate it during the reorganization case."). While 11 U.S.C. § 1104(a) mandates appointment of a trustee when the bankruptcy court finds cause—seemingly requiring plenary review, "a determination of cause . . . is within the discretion of the court." . . .

Subsection (a)(2) also creates a flexible standard, instructing the court to appoint a trustee when doing so addresses "the interests of the creditors, equity security holders, and other interests of the estate." 11 U.S.C. § 1104(a)(2).

Because subsection (a)(2) envisions a flexible standard, an abuse of discretion standard offers the most appropriate type of review for this subsection as well.

The bankruptcy court opinion conveys the image of a titanic industrial vessel foundering on the shoals of bankruptcy, steered there by at best careless management practices. These practices include payment of $294 million to secured creditors and $9.8 million and $970,000 without consideration to Victor and Stephen Posner respectively during a period when Sharon was so cash-poor that it could not afford to reline the vital number 2 blast furnace—so cash-poor that to continue operations on a daily basis it borrowed $30 million at 28% to 30% interest.

Other questionable management actions cited by the court include the petition-eve payment of $3.7 million to DWG, transfer of Sharon's yacht and plane to NPC, and transfer of the 141,000 shares of Chesapeake Financial Corporation stock to Insurance and Risk Management. At no time did Sharon's postpetition management try to recover any part of these transfers (or any part of the sums paid to Victor and Stephen Posner).

DWG and Posner claim that the court's November 1988 authorization for the committee to sue for recovery of these transfers cures its failure and eliminates any management conflicts of interest, rendering the court's determination erroneous. In fact, they claim that all of the alleged prepetition incidents of gross mismanagement have been corrected, forcing the court to rely on postpetition mismanagement, which they claim falls short of providing clear and convincing proof that a trustee is required. Specifically, they point to the appointment of Walter Sieckman as chief operating officer, and the court-acknowledged management improvements he had wrought since coming aboard. They also claim that Sharon's by-laws, in compliance with Pennsylvania law, authorized payment of Posner's $4.4 million in legal fees. According to Posner and DWG, these factors make the court's reliance upon the prepetition management problems improper.

For support, they rely on three cases that they contend stand for the proposition that appointment of a trustee is inappropriate where prepetition gross mismanagement has been corrected and no postpetition gross mismanagement has occurred: . . .

These cases present very different scenarios than does the case at hand. [M]anagement here is extremely sophisticated. This sophistication colors interpretation of their actions. While DWG and Posner cite other case law holding that business dealings between a debtor and its subsidiaries or related entities does not per se create a conflict of interests, they ignore the presence of "something more" in this case.

Unlike *General Oil,* Sharon's management appears to have engaged on the eve of bankruptcy in a systematic syphoning of Sharon's assets to other companies under common control. Despite DWG and Posner's contention to the contrary, such behavior raises grave questions about current management's ability to fulfill its fiduciary duty as debtor-in-possession to Sharon's creditors. Judicial intervention enabling the committee to sue for recovery of per se voidable preferences and fraudulent conveyances may have solved that isolated management problem, but it has not cleared up the question about current management's fitness to continue running Sharon Steel and its commitment to see it through to a successful reorganization. *See In re Concord Coal Corp.,* 11 Bankr. 552 (Bankr. S.D. W. Va. 1981) (trustee appointed under 11 U.S.C. § 1104(a)(2) on grounds that debtor's many competing business interests rendered questionable his commitment to rehabilitation and that debtor could not secure and maintain lenders' and creditors' trust). . . .

Believing that they had cleared the prepetition gross mismanagement determinations, Posner and DWG hoped to sail past the trustee appointment by arguing that the court's remaining determinations of postpetition gross mismanagement do not satisfy the heavy burden of proof imposed on the movants. The court concluded that current management's failure to negotiate a reduction in the interest rate on the $30 million operating loan, to obtain up-to-date, comprehensive postpetition financial statements from DWG, and to cut or eliminate the estimated $2 million lost monthly despite the protection of the bankruptcy laws satisfied both subsections of section 11 U.S.C. § 1104(a). Furthermore, it held "the ongoing problem of fair allocation of costs of the Miami offices among Sharon and other Posner-owned businesses is exacerbated by the conflicts of interest, and only an independent trustee can make a proper investigation and determination of the best interests of Sharon."

Once again, we cannot say that the bankruptcy court abused its discretion. Under the discretionary determination of cause required by 11 U.S.C. § 1104(a)(1) and the flexible standard embodied in (a)(2), the court acted within its discretion in concluding that the totality of the circumstances signaled the need for a trustee. Despite improvements instituted by Walter Sieckman, too many major problems remained—problems symptomatic of potential bankruptcy despite the calm harbor provided by Chapter 11. Failure to force closure of the prepetition books and production of current financial statements nine months after filing, combined with continued losses exacerbated by the failure to cut a major expense like the approximately $4 million in added interest on the operating loan, signaled the court that as captain, the debtor-in-possession had continued to steer Sharon toward bankruptcy rather than to turn her about toward solvency. Corrective measures that are too few too late cannot defeat a change in command. The bankruptcy court's opinion clearly indicates it felt appointment necessary to save Sharon from bankruptcy. We agree.

III. APPOINTMENT OF AN EXAMINER

Instead of a trustee, a bankruptcy court may appoint an examiner, another type of estate fiduciary whose expenses are paid by the estate as administrative expenses with priority over general unsecured creditors. 11 U.S.C. §§ 330(1), 503(b)(2), 507(a)(2). Unlike a trustee, an examiner does not manage the assets of the debtor. The Bankruptcy Code allows the appointment of an examiner to "conduct such an investigation of the debtor as is appropriate." This includes "an investigation of any allegations of fraud, dishonesty, incompetence, misconduct, mismanagement, or irregularity in the management of the affairs of the debtor of or by current or former management of the debtor." 11 U.S.C. § 1104(c). Like the trustee, the examiner is usually a person (often an attorney) of stature appointed in large part because of a reputation for integrity and expertise with bankruptcy matters.

The precise functions of an examiner differ between cases. As Professor Daniel Bussel has observed:

> In some chapter 11 cases they serve as mediators breaking negotiating impasses. In others they take on the role of quasi or limited purpose trustee because the court lacks confidence in the debtor in possession to perform certain of the functions of a trustee that are usually performed by the debtor in possession, but is unwilling to remove the debtor in possession altogether. . . . Most examiner appointments occur in only the largest cases, they are rare there too, and the typical mandate remains an investigation into causes of action or claims held by the estate, the traditional role of the examiner, and the only one expressly set out in the Bankruptcy Code.

> . . . Investigations in reorganization cases are commonly conducted by trustees and official creditors' committees. Such investigations may be conducted outside the context of a pending adversary proceeding or contested matter. Trustees and committees, like examiners, are estate fiduciaries that employ professionals at estate expense to discharge these duties. But unlike examiners, neither trustees nor committees are neutrals charged with finding truth. They occupy adversarial roles and are charged with advancing the interests of particular constituencies. Trustees of insolvent estates typically represented general creditor interests, and their fiduciary obligation is to maximize the value of the estate. They are not neutrals as to any claims or defenses that affect the estate. Indeed, trustees' personal economic interests are directly aligned with the goal of estate maximization. They're compensated on the basis of a

percentage of distributions. Similarly, committees are composed of members of particular interested constituencies and serve the interests of those constituencies . . . in the hands of a committee, investigations are plan negotiations by other means. It is unsurprising that their investigations quickly and naturally fall into the adversarial model.

Daniel J. Bussel, *A Third Way: Examiners as Inquisitors*, 90 AM. BANKR. L.J. 59, 62-63 (2015). The traditional model of examiner involves the examiner either "determin[ing] the legal sufficiency of a disputed claim, but not opining on the merits of the claim or undertaking to resolve factual disputes . . . [or] abjur[ing] an investigate rule to mediate resolution of a disputed claim, or of the bankruptcy as a whole." *Id.* at 67.

More recently, though, examiners have engaged in direct fact-finding and have drawn explicit legal conclusions from the facts they found, acting somewhat like "[o]utside counsel engaged by a corporation to conduct an independent investigation under the direction of the board of directors or an independent committee of directors." *Id.* at 122. When examiners undertake investigations, they typically file a report with the court. The report has no formal legal binding—it is hearsay—but it is likely to be quite influential because of the examiner's neutrality in the matter.

The precise scope of the examiner's role is defined by the order appointing the examiner: What issues may the examiner examine? What powers will the examiner have? For example, may the examiner issue subpoenas and administer oaths? May the debtor invoke privileges against the examiner? Employ experts? Will the examiner have immunity from suits?

While examiners can potentially have broad discovery powers, it is important to recognize that they cannot bring suit on behalf of the estate, absent special authorization, and given that the examiner's expenses are borne by the estate, why would a creditor want an examiner to be appointed? In what circumstances would the expense of the examiner be outweighed by the benefits?

The court is required to appoint an examiner only if the appointment is in the interests of creditors, equity security holders, or other interest of the estate or if the debtor's unsecured, liquidated financial debt is over $5 million. 11 U.S.C. § 1104(c). Creditors have considerable leverage if they can credibly threaten to move for the appointment of an examiner.

The appointment of a trustee or examiner does not affect the fact that a case is still in Chapter 11. A party in interest may, however, alternatively move to convert the case to Chapter 7 or for the case to be dismissed entirely. 11 U.S.C. § 1112. Conversion to Chapter 7 will result in the appointment of a trustee, of course, but will also preclude a reorganization. Dismissal will void any discharge and restore any avoided transfers. 11 U.S.C. § 349. Section 1112 of the Code sets forth the grounds for conversion or dismissal. It is a "for cause" standard. Section 1112(b)(4) contains a non-exclusive list of potential grounds for conversion or dismissal. Many deal with non-compliance with various legal requirements—payment of fees, compliance with court orders, or unauthorized use of cash collateral. But others deal with mismanagement of the estate, diminution in value of the estate, or the inability to effectuate a confirmed plan. Notably, inability to confirm a plan is not itself on the list, although the list is non-exclusive.

Section 1112 also prohibits conversion or dismissal if the court finds that it would not be in the best interests of creditors and the estate and there is a reasonable likelihood that a plan will be confirmed in the near future. 11 U.S.C. § 1112(b)(2). The court may, however, always decide instead to appoint a trustee or examiner in Chapter 11 instead of converting or dismissing the case. 11 U.S.C. § 1112(b)(1).

IV. COMMITTEES

Creditors and equityholders of a bankrupt firm face a collective action problem in a bankruptcy. To the extent that any individual creditor or equityholder undertakes an action that benefits the estate, it only recovers its pro rata share of the benefit (if that), while it would bear the full cost of the action itself.[1] This free-riding problem disincentivizes unsecured creditor and equity participation in a bankruptcy. Why do the work when others will benefit? Why not let them do the work and free-ride off them?

This is exactly the same problem we saw confronting bondholders in Chapter 9. Bondholders' solution, as we saw, is the indenture trustee, a common agent for all the bondholders. The indenture trustee owes fiduciary duties to the bondholders—at least after an event of default—and its right to compensation is senior to the claims of the bondholders.

Bankruptcy has a similar institutional device for dealing with this problem: the official committee. Bankruptcy authorizes the formation of committees to represent unsecured creditors and equityholders. 11 U.S.C. § 1102(a)(1). The committees owe fiduciary duties to the creditors or equityholders they represent, and are entitled to receive substantial information from the debtor and to hire their own counsel and advisors. The costs of counsel and professionals, of individual committee members performing committee duties, and of the committee as a whole if it makes a "substantial contribution" to the case are paid by the estate as section 503(b) expenses, with section 507(a)(2) priority, which entitles them to payment in full in cash on the effective date of a confirmed plan. 11 U.S.C. §§ 330(a); 503(b)(2), 503(b)(3)(D); 503(b)(3)(F); 507(a)(2); 1103; 1129(a)(9). Thus, the committee will get its expenses paid before the general unsecured creditors or equityholders.

Despite the committee's expenses being borne by the estate, it is not always easy to recruit committee members. Why would one want to serve on a committee? The individual creditor's benefit from a committee's actions is often small. Accordingly, section 1102(b) states that a committee shall ordinarily consist of the seven largest claims holders. 11 U.S.C. § 1102(b). Still, in many cases even large claims holders will decline to serve on a committee. Why? Being a committee member has downsides. It involves time and effort that are not typically reimbursed. Committee members are fiduciaries of the claims or interests they represent. This means that they cannot use the information they gain while serving on a committee for their own individual

---

1. Potentially, the entrepreneurial creditor could seek a recovery for its expenses as an administrative claim under section 503(b)(3)(D) of the Code for making a "substantial contribution" to the case, but it could not rely on such treatment.

benefit. Accordingly, committee members are restricted from trading in claims on the debtor, except with other committee members. Failure to adhere to confidentiality or to trade on the restricted information can result in sanctions from the bankruptcy court and may violate federal and state securities laws. *See In the Matter of Van D. Greenfield and Blue River Capital LLC*, 2005 SEC Lexis 2892 (Nov. 7, 2005).

The committees appointed under section 1102 are called "**Official Committees.**" This is to distinguish them from so-called ***ad hoc* committees** that are not appointed by the United States Trustee and are not entitled to reimbursement of expenses from the estate. Such *ad hoc* committees are addressed in the next chapter. Counsel for Official Committees is heard or at least consulted by the court on most matters. Even if unsecured creditors are not very powerful in terms of leverage over a debtor, their opinions are frequently requested in court.

Official Committees always have a "seat at the table" at hearings, along with the debtor, and they frequently play a critical role in cases, serving as a vehicle that provides voice to unsecured creditors. Official Committees are also sometimes permitted to pursue litigation derivatively on behalf of the estate if the debtor-in-possession is seen as conflicted. *The Official Committee of Unsecured Creditors of Cybergenics Corp. on Behalf of Cybergenics Corp., Debtor in Possession v. Chinery*, 330 F.3d 548 (3d Cir. 2003).

The default rule in Chapter 11 cases is that the United States Trustee appoints a single committee of unsecured creditors. 11 U.S.C. § 1102(a)(1). The United States Trustee is given discretion regarding appointment of additional committees. *Id.* The court may, on motion, direct appointment of additional committees "if necessary to assure adequate representation." 11 U.S.C. § 1102(a)(2). Types of creditors or equity interests that are "out of the money" will not get committees appointed because they are playing with estate money despite having no real interest in the estate. Making a determination of whether a type of creditor or equityholder is in the money is not always easy, however, and may require a valuation.

How many committees should be appointed is sometimes a source of friction, as different types of unsecured creditors may have very different interests. For example, retirees or tort plaintiffs may have different interest than unsecured bondholders. Whether the differences in their interests merit separate committees is a question for which there is not a definitive answer, as illustrated by the *Hills Stores* case below.

Likewise, in multiple-debtor cases, does there need to be a separate committee for every entity within a corporate family? The creditors of a parent firm have different interests than the creditors of a subsidiary. But it hardly seems practical to have a separate committee for every entity, especially when corporate families can have hundreds of members. In many cases, the administrative claims from multiple committees' expenses would leave nothing for the creditors represented by the committees. One committee remains the norm, even in complex cases, but multiple committees are sometimes employed. The Bankruptcy Code is simply not designed to deal with multi-entity debtors because such firms were rare among likely bankruptcy filers in 1978.

In re Hills Stores Co.

137 B.R. 4 (Bankr. S.D.N.Y. 1992)

TINA L. BROZMAN, Bankruptcy Judge.

Almost a year ago, the United States Trustee appointed a single committee of unsecured creditors (the Committee) in this Chapter 11 reorganization for a very large retailer. No challenge to the U.S. Trustee's action has been voiced, let alone mounted, until now. Four subordinated bondholders ask for the appointment of either an official subordinated bondholders' subcommittee of the Committee or, in the alternative, for their own committee.

The motion was submitted for my consideration on affidavits. Most of the salient facts were undisputed and, through stipulations placed on the record today, those factual disputes which did exist have now been resolved. All parties have waived the right to present live testimony.

I.

This case was commenced on February 4, 1991 when Hills Stores Co. and the other related debtors (collectively, Hills or the Debtor) filed voluntary Chapter 11 petitions. All were continued in the management of their businesses as debtors in possession pursuant to Sections 1107 and 1108 of the Bankruptcy Code, 11 U.S.C. §§ 1107 and 1108. At the time of its bankruptcy, Hills operated 154 department stores in twelve states. Sales at the end of its last fiscal year, ending February 3, 1991, were $2.1 billion.

Eleven days after Hills sought refuge in Chapter 11, the U.S. Trustee appointed a 15 member committee pursuant to Section 1102(a) of the Code. Its membership consisted of three banks, two holders of senior notes, five trade creditors, one factor and four representatives of the four separate tranches of subordinated debt, each tranche with different priorities from the other.

Given that the Committee is large, to aid in its smooth operation its constituencies formed three subcommittees all of which have subordinated bondholder representation. The Orders Subcommittee makes decisions on matters between $50,000 and $2 million that are not deemed policy issues and recommendations on matter in excess of $2 million or on questions of policy. Throughout the course of this case the decision and/or recommendation of the Orders Subcommittee almost always has been unanimously approved by the full Committee. The Plan Subcommittee was formed to discuss preliminary plan of reorganization proposals with the Debtor and report back to the full Committee. The Finance Subcommittee was formed to work closely with the accountants and investment advisors.

The Subordinated Bondholders urge today that similarly situated creditors are not adequately represented by the Committee. This is so they say because:

(i) they have economic interests that diverge dramatically from the senior and trade creditors who dominate the committee;

(ii) the Committee has failed to investigate possible preference claims and lender liability actions against senior creditors on the Committee;

(iii) the various subordinated bondholders are numerically underrepresented in relation to the size of their aggregate unsecured claim vis-à-vis other types of creditors;

(iv) the structure of a plan of reorganization will likely follow that in other retail cases, a structure which they find unpalatable;

(v) the Committee has not acceded to their several requests to ask the U.S. Trustee to change the composition of the Committee; and

(vi) the Committee was underhanded in its selection almost a year ago of professionals.

The Debtor and the Committee oppose the motion, contending that the subordinated bondholders' arguments are factually unfounded and based on speculation; the conflicts advanced are not unusual; the timing of the motion so late into the case will jeopardize the anticipated emergence of the Debtor from bankruptcy this spring or summer at unnecessary additional cost; and, finally, the Court lacks jurisdiction to direct the existing Committee to form a subcommittee.

II.

Section 1102(a)(2) of the Bankruptcy Code provides that "on request of a party in interest, the court may order the appointment of additional committees of creditors or equity holders if necessary to assure adequate representation of creditors or of equity security holders." Thus, the Committee must provide adequate representation for unsecured creditors, including the subordinated bondholders. As the statute affords no "bright-line" test for adequate representation, the court is armed with the discretion after examining the facts to determine if additional committees are warranted. Considerations such as the ability of the committee to function, the nature of the case and the standing and desires of the various constituencies assume significance. While bankruptcy courts have generally been reluctant to appoint separate committees of unsecured creditors notwithstanding the diverse and sometimes conflicting interests of creditors, a case which is sufficiently large and complex may strongly indicate the need for additional committees representing different interests. The potential added cost is not sufficient in itself to deprive the creditors of the formation of an additional committee if one is otherwise appropriate.

Turning to the different economic interests argument, the subordinated bondholders posit that they will potentially support a business plan and plan of reorganization that will maximize the company's long term equity value while the senior and trade creditors are likely to press for an early payout at the expense of the company's operations and enterprise value. The subordinated bondholders claim that as a result of a wave of major retail bankruptcies, a consistent pattern (which, ironically, they have described in two different fashions) has emerged in which the senior debt is reinstated with an adjusted maturity, principal balance and interest rate; the trade debt is paid with cash and possibly new equity; and the bulk of the new equity and new subordinated debt is given to the subordinated bondholders. The subordinated bondholders then baldly advance that this preordains the future if their motion is not granted. Not only is this rank speculation but it is at odds with the facts. Hills has proposed terms for a plan which are materially different from what the subordinated bondholders project.

Contrary to the bondholders' assertion, the presence of potential conflict may not always require separate committees in order for representation to be adequate. Indeed, creditors' committees often contain creditors having a variety of viewpoints. Conflicts are not unusual in reorganization and in most cases can be expected among creditors who are acting to protect their separate business interests. What the subordinated bondholders have painted is a picture reflecting no darker image than the ordinary fears, concerns, and conflicts that are inherent in the reorganization process. Were this a case where the creditors of separate debtors had vastly conflicting aims and entitlement and had shown themselves unable to function on a single committee, I might be more inclined to the subordinated bondholders' view, but here there is only one operating debtor engaged in a single business. Albeit that Hills has a complicated capital structure, these cases are not nearly so complex as those multi-debtor, multi-business cases where more than one committee may be appointed.

The contention that the Committee has failed to investigate possible preference claims and lender liability actions against senior creditors on the Committee borders on bad faith, for the Debtor is undertaking a preference analysis, as is its obligation, and until this motion was made the subordinated bondholders never gave voice to their theory that there may be a lender liability claim available to the creditors. Moreover, Hills has agreed to investigate this theory as well and that function is more properly its than any committee's, in the first instance at least. The bondholders are correct in asserting that a committee's failure to investigate lender liability claims could under certain circumstances constitute a breach of fiduciary duty if proven. However, it certainly hasn't been proven here and a far better remedy for such an alleged dereliction would be the appointment of an independent examiner. This Committee has functioned admirably well in passing upon the various motions and requests made by the Debtor. To monkey with the Committee because one group of creditors has just raised the specter of possible lender liability makes little sense.

I turn now to the subordinated bondholders' claim that they are numerically underrepresented in relation to the size of their unsecured claim. Nowhere does the Code mandate a committee must faithfully reproduce the exact complexion of the creditor body. What is required is adequate representation of various creditor types. The disparity between the bondholders' claims, which constitute 35% of the debtor's total liabilities, and their Committee representation, which is approximately 27%, does not establish such inadequate representation as to warrant the formation of a separate committee. Under any scenario the bondholders will never comprise a majority of a single committee representing all unsecured creditors. More importantly, the bondholders have put forth no tangible evidence whatsoever which would tend to substantiate their claim that, as a result of their alleged underrepresentation the Committee will be unable to negotiate successfully with the Debtor. Despite the fact that the bondholders do not have a majority voice on the Committee, there is not one group which by itself can control the decisions of the Committee without the aid of another. Moreover, the subordinated bondholders have neglected to mention a most salient fact in their papers—that they have one-third of the seats on all three of the Committee's subcommittees, and to a large extent it is those subcommittees which exercise the initial decision-making authority of the Committee. To make an argument respecting numerical representation without mentioning the subcommittee membership evidences a surprising lack of candor to the Court.

This motion confuses adequate representation on a Committee with the right to charge a debtor's estate for separate professionals. What the Code requires is that conflicting groups of creditors have a voice through adequate representation on a Committee. That voice exists here. The subordinated bondholders' argument that they are effectively rendered impotent to protect their interests without a majority voice in the Committee ignores the role of the Committee as a catalyst for negotiation and compromise between the parties in the reorganization process. The fact that the Bondholders may not be able to protect all their interests and achieve *all* their goals is not paramount, as the ultimate aim is to strike a proper balance between the parties such that an effective and viable reorganization of the debtor may be accomplished. As in most Chapter 11 cases, there will be common interests among various groups of unsecured creditors. The inclusion of such groups within one committee may facilitate the consensual resolution of the conflicting priorities among the holders of unsecured claims and thereby facilitate the negotiation of a consensual plan. The bondholders have not demonstrated that there exists conflict among the unsecured creditors which is so profound as to impede the Committee's ability to function. Their claim of a pattern of discrimination by the senior and trade creditors against them is devoid of factual support.

The argument respecting the appointment of the Committee's professionals is also wholly frivolous. Nothing in this record suggests that one of the four subordinated bondholders was deliberately excluded from the meeting of the Committee at which counsel was selected nor does anything bear out the claim that the Committee intended to select an investment banker who gave the lowest initial estimate of the value of the Debtor's assets. Indeed, whereas the investment advisor selected may have valued the assets originally somewhat lower than other candidates, it has revised its estimate substantially upward, putting to rest any suggestion of improper or base motive.

It is late in the day for the subordinated bondholders' motion. The proceedings have advanced to a point where the detailed business plan has been critiqued and plan negotiations are about to commence. The Debtor has represented that the plan in these cases can be confirmed during the spring or summer of this year. The subordinated bondholders could have moved for the requested relief six or more months ago when the complained of action or inaction of the Committee was alleged to have occurred, instead of at a time when the appointment of an additional committee or subcommittee would no doubt delay the confirmation process, result in additional expense for the estate and possibly cause the proliferation of other committees. Nevertheless, if I believed the delay and expense were justified by facts instead of speculation, I would not hesitate to order the appointment of an additional committee to assure adequate representation.

What the subordinated bondholders seek is the appointment of a new committee which may retain professionals or the appointment of a subcommittee which may retain professionals. As the composition, function and rights of each as proposed are the same, aside from the jurisdictional issue raised by the Committee, this is a distinction without a difference. While I may order the appointment of additional *committees* under § 1102(a)(2) of the Code, the statute no longer permits the addition or deletion of *members* of committees by the court except in circumstances not relevant here. Section 1102(c) was amended in 1986 as part of a nearly nationwide expansion of the

U.S. Trustee program, not only to revise § 1102(a) by vesting the appointment power in U.S. Trustees, but also to delete former § 1102(c) which expressly enabled the court to add and subtract creditors from creditors committees. For this reason, and because the reasons advanced for the appointment of a subcommittee, which are identical to those for appointment of a separate Committee, are without merit, I will not add a subcommittee to the committee.

Finally, as the Debtor points out, if the subordinated bondholders believe that the cases would be advanced by their taking a more active role, they are not precluded from forming an unofficial committee, retaining counsel and a financial advisor and seeking reimbursement of their expenses to the extent that they make a substantial contribution to the case, as permitted and even envisioned by § 503(b) of the Code. In fact, it emerged in oral argument this morning that the subordinated bondholders have had counsel for one year. This is not then a dispute about adequate representation, but about adequate assurance of alternative compensation.

The motion by the subordinated bondholders for the appointment of a subordinated bondholders' subcommittee of the Official Committee of Unsecured Creditors or, in the alternative, an official committee of subordinated bondholders is denied.

Problem Set 18

(1) Your client, Freya Cosmetics, a Delaware corporation, is in Chapter 11. Freya is considering selling its hair products division. The hair products division has struggled in recent years, but has a promising new product line. The sale transaction is urged by its creditors, but opposed by its equityholders. How should Freya decide whether to sell?

(2) Valhalla Airlines, Inc., has always been known for generous management compensation packages and free-spending ways. The lavishness of its board meetings was only matched by the lavishness of its first-class compartments. But rumors have been circulating that Valhalla's Chairman-CEO was secretly diverting funds from the company for personal use. In particular, a story has been making the rounds about the firm paying for a diamond-encrusted bidet for the Chairman-CEO's home. There are also tales of scandalous half-clothed goings-on on a party jet owned by the firm. Valhalla has been in Chapter 11 for about 10 months. No plan has yet been proposed, but conventional wisdom is that Valhalla is preparing to propose a plan that will pay something, but not very much, to the second lien and unsecured debt, while splitting the equity in the reorganized firm between the first lien debt and old equity. Many of the second lien and unsecured creditors seem resigned to such an outcome. Thor Capital holds some of Valhalla's second lien notes. Valhalla's obligations include $300 million in first lien debt, $200 million in second lien debt, $40 million in trade debt, $3 million in back taxes, and unresolved tort claims that could total tens of millions. Is there anything Thor Capital might do? 11 U.S.C. §§ 1104, 1112.

(3) Valhalla Airlines, Inc., is a mid-sized domestic airline that specializes in serving regional airports, rather than major markets. Valhalla filed for Chapter 11 after a recent surge in fuel prices forced it to raise ticket prices and a tragic crash resulted in decreased demand for flights. Valhalla has long contracted with Mead & Co. to supply food and

beverages for its flights. Valhalla also contracts with Valkyrie LLC for the provision of flight attendants. Both the Mead and Valkyrie contracts are on very generous terms to the vendors. Valhalla moved to assume both contracts on the first day of the case, and the assumption went unchallenged at the time.

Your client, Loki Investments LLP, holds some of Valhalla's second lien notes. Loki has just learned that Mead & Co. is wholly owned by the boyfriend of Valhalla's Chairman-CEO and that a majority stake in Valkyrie is controlled by the Chairman-CEO's daughter from her former marriage (who goes by a different last name). Loki does not believe other creditors are aware of this . . . yet. What might Loki do with this information? 11 U.S.C. §§ 1104, 1112, 1122.

(4) The Odin Fund holds 4% of the equity in Asgard Corp., a Delaware corporation, which is in Chapter 11 bankruptcy. The Odin Fund thinks that the current management of Asgard has completely the wrong vision for how to restructure the company. It has been 16 months since Asgard has last held a shareholders meeting. Asgard used to be listed on the New York Stock Exchange, but it was delisted shortly before filing for bankruptcy, and the stock is only thinly traded now. Is there anything the Odin Fund can do? 11 U.S.C. § 1103.

(5) You are representing Andvari Bancorp, which is a member of the Official Committee of Unsecured Creditors in the Chapter 11 bankruptcy of Valhalla Airlines, Inc. Loki Investments LLP, a hedge fund, has approached Andvari about buying Andvari's claim in the bankruptcy. Loki is offering a good price. Andvari has asked you to draft the sale documents. Is there anything that concerns you?

(6) Tyr Industries is one of the largest unsecured creditors of Valhalla Airlines, Inc. Tyr is one of the major part suppliers for Valhalla. The United States Trustee has requested that Tyr serve on the Official Committee of Unsecured Creditors. What should Tyr consider before responding to the request?

CHAPTER 19

GOVERNANCE IN BANKRUPTCY: ADVANCED TOPICS

I. *AD HOC* COMMITTEES

In addition to Official Committees, groups of creditors will sometimes organize themselves as *"ad hoc* committees." An *ad hoc* committee need be nothing more than two creditors that have agreed to move jointly on some matter and call themselves an *ad hoc* committee, which makes them seem perhaps more impressive and broadly representative than just random hedge funds *A* and *B*. *Ad hoc* committees are often formed by activist distressed debt investors, who are often reluctant to reveal information about their investment positions or the real nature of their economic interest in the debtor. Unlike Official Committee members, *ad hoc* committee members are not fiduciaries to holders of similar claims, and indeed, their ultimate interests do not necessarily align with the type of claims they purport to represent. For example, if two creditors band together to call themselves "The *Ad Hoc* Committee of Second Lien Noteholders," those two creditors do not in fact represent anyone but themselves, and their interests may in fact be adverse to those of other second lien noteholders.

Federal Rule of Bankruptcy Procedure 2019 provides the only regulation of these *ad hoc* committees. Rule 2019 is a disclosure rule, requiring parties moving collectively to disclose their "disclosable economic interest" in the debtor. The idea is that this disclosure will prevent any confusion about whose interests an *ad hoc* committee represents. "Disclosable economic interest" is defined broadly to include not just any claim, but also any option, derivative, or "other right or derivative right granting the holder an economic interest that is affected by the value, acquisition or disposition of a claim or interest." FED. R. BANKR. PROC. 2019(a)(1). Thus, if an *ad hoc* committee member held a total return swap on the debtor or a position in a competitor of the debtor, that swap or position would have to be disclosed. The Rule 2019 disclosure requirement also requires the disclosure of the date of acquisition of the interest by quarter and year, which provides a rough proxy for the price at which the interest was acquired. FED. R. BANKR. PROC. 2019(c)(2). Rule 2019 disclosures must be updated when there is a material change. Critically, the disclosure requirement in Rule 2019 applies not just to the *ad hoc* committee's members, but to their attorneys, FED. R. BANKR. PROC. 2019(a)(2), which helps guaranty better compliance with the rule.

II. OFFICERS

When a firm is in financial trouble, prior to bankruptcy, the board, at the insistence of senior creditors, often brings in new **turnaround management**. Turnaround managers are generally not looking for continued employment with restructured companies; they are management paratroopers whose skill-set lies in crisis management, not quotidian management or industry-specific expertise.

Sometimes turnaround managers recognize that a bankruptcy is inevitable and perhaps the best way to fix the firm's business. Turnaround managers are experienced in dealing with bankruptcy and understand the operational and financial constraints bankruptcy places on a firm. They also have long-standing relationships with other members of the restructuring community—lawyers and bankers.

The reputational discipline from these relationships helps the use of turnaround managers address the agency problems that can exist in a bankruptcy, in which management might be incentivized to manage a firm for its own benefit, as during a bankruptcy, shareholders lack the ability to dislodge ineffectual or disloyal managers. A turnaround manager's effectiveness largely depends on his ability to tap into new sources of funding, which depends, in turn, on the manager's reputation in the creditor community. As repeat players in the bankruptcy business, turnaround managers derive significant reputational value from the results of a bankruptcy, which affects their ability to get future business and the fees they can command prospectively. Accordingly, turnaround managers desire outcomes the market considers a success, which should be equivalent to maximizing the debtor's value. *See* Adam J. Levitin, *The Problematic Case for Incentive Compensation in Bankruptcy*, 156 U. PA. L. REV. PENNUMBRA 88, 96 (2007).

Once firms file for bankruptcy, the creditors providing the financing for the firm to continue operating in bankruptcy will frequently insist on choosing or having veto rights over a **Chief Restructuring Officer (CRO)** who reports directly to the debtor-in-possession's board, rather than to the CEO. Frequently, the CRO will be the turnaround manager who was working with the firm (and the senior creditors providing the financing) prior to the bankruptcy filing.

The Bankruptcy Code is silent regarding officers of the debtor other than the use of **key employee retention plans** or KERPs. It can be difficult for a bankrupt firm to retain its human capital. Working at a bankrupt firm means uncertainty and hassle. Employees are often tempted to look for alternative employment. A debtor might, therefore, find it necessary to pay employees more to stay to compensate them for the uncertainty.

The Bankruptcy Code does little to help debtors retain their human capital. Section 503(c)(1) regulates retention payments. Section 503(c) requires that before a post-petition retention incentive can be paid to an insider (defined by section 101(31)), the recipient must be essential to the survival of the business, have an equally good or better competing job offer, and that the payment is either no more than 10 times the compensation of nonmanagement employees in the same year, or if no such payments were made, 25% of what was paid to an insider in the previous year. 11 U.S.C. § 503(c).

The concern in section 503(c)(1) was to prevent the debtor's officers from getting handsome retention packages, while ordinary workers saw their compensation and benefits slashed. Still, consider what the restriction on KERPs means. In order to pay a retention bonus to a key employee, that employee must go out and obtain a bona fide job offer from another business at the same or greater rate of compensation. Once an employee has searched for and obtained an equivalent or better job offer, is that employee likely to stay at a bankrupt firm? Does it make sense for the Bankruptcy Code to encourage the debtor's employees to look for other work?

Section 503(c)(2) similarly regulates severance payments to insiders. Section 503(c)(2) prohibits golden parachutes for the executives of bankrupt firms. (Golden parachutes triggered, but not paid prior to filing would normally be general unsecured claims.) Moreover, any payment that is outside of the ordinary course of business—such as a retention or severance payment—that is "not justified by the facts and circumstances of the case"—can be disallowed, irrespective of whether it is made to an insider or non-insider. 11 U.S.C. § 503(c)(3).

Local bankruptcy practice in some districts provides further informal regulation of managerial compensation in bankruptcy. For example, the unofficial policy of the United States Trustee for the Second Region is to object to any retention agreement that does not comply with its "Jay Alix Protocol," a protocol developed as part of a settlement agreement that requires disclosure of conflicts of interest; limits turnaround companies from serving in multiple capacities to the debtor (the "one hat" policy); limits indemnification of turnaround managers to the terms provided to regular officers and directors; prohibits the turnaround company's affiliates from investing in the reorganized debtor for three years after the case's conclusion; and requires court approval of success fees and other back-end fees on a reasonableness standard at the end of the case. Protocol for Engagement of Jay Alix & Associates and Affiliates (Nov. 3, 2004), *available at* https://bit.ly/2NrDzBY. The Jay Alix Protocol is not binding, but it has in many courts become a de facto shibboleth for management compensation in bankruptcy.

III. PROFESSIONALS

What would a bankruptcy be without the lawyers? Or the bankers? The Bankruptcy Code provides that the debtor may retain attorneys, accountants, and various other professionals (such as financial advisors), so long as they are "disinterested persons." 11 U.S.C. § 327. A disinterested person may not be a creditor, equityholder, insider, or recent (or current) director, officer, or employee of the debtor, or hold a materially adverse interest to the estate. 11 U.S.C. § 101(14). Pre-petition representation alone does not disqualify a party. 11 U.S.C. § 1107. This means that a law firm or financial advisor that wishes to be retained by the estate must not have a pre-petition claim on the estate. In other words, pre-petition law firms and financial advisors need to be paid before the bankruptcy petition is filed. The filing itself is apparently complimentary.

This is not to say that a law firm or financial advisor that represented a debtor pre-petition is a disinterested person. The problem of disinterestedness is most acute when major assets of the estate include avoidance action claims that seek to unwind pre-petition transactions in which a law firm or financial advisor was involved. These firms can hardly provide neutral advice about the avoidance actions. Professionals retained by any official committee must also meet the disinterestedness requirement.

transfer of property

In re Project Orange Associates, LLC

431 B.R. 363 (Bankr. S.D.N.Y. 2010)

MARTIN GLENN, U.S. Bankr. J.

This opinion addresses an important issue whether the use of conflicts counsel to deal with the debtor's largest unsecured creditor and essential supplier is sufficient to permit court approval under section 327(a) of the Bankruptcy Code of a debtor's choice for general bankruptcy counsel that also represents that creditor in unrelated matters. Project Orange Associates, LLC ("Project Orange" or "Debtor") seeks to retain DLA Piper LLP (US) ("DLA Piper") as general bankruptcy counsel pursuant to section 327(a) of the Bankruptcy Code. The United States Trustee ("U.S. Trustee") objects, arguing that DLA Piper's representation of certain General Electric ("GE") entities, as well as inadequate disclosure about DLA Piper's relationship with other creditors, requires the Court to deny DLA Piper's employment application. GE is the Debtor's largest unsecured creditor. Perhaps more importantly, the Debtor has acknowledged that resolving all past and future issues with GE—the supplier of gas turbines to Debtor's operations—is essential to the Debtor's successful reorganization. DLA Piper argues that it does not have a disqualifying conflict with GE, and that, in any event, the Debtor's use of conflicts counsel to deal with certain aspects of the Debtor's relationship with GE, is sufficient to avoid DLA Piper's conflict and to permit its retention as general bankruptcy counsel. For the following reasons, the Court agrees with the U.S. Trustee and denies DLA Piper's employment application.

I. BACKGROUND

. . .

The Debtor has retained ownership and continues to operate a steam and electricity cogeneration facility in Syracuse, New York. The Debtor earns money by, *inter alia*, [selling electricity]. . . . The Debtor states that it is not generating sufficient income because of maintenance issues with its [two] GE gas turbines[, which power its electric turbines (the "Turbines")].

[Prior to bankruptcy the debtor withheld payment to GE because of a dispute over maintenance of the turbines. GE won a $4.1 million arbitration award.] GE filed a motion to have the arbitration award confirmed in New York State Supreme Court. Briefing in that matter is stayed as a result of the automatic bankruptcy stay. GE also filed a motion requesting relief from the automatic stay to permit the state court to confirm the arbitration award.

Despite these issues, the Debtor now maintains that "all major litigation with GE has been substantially resolved." Indeed, the Debtor has presented a settlement stipulation (the "Stipulation") between itself and GE to the Court for approval. The Stipulation recites that GE asserts that, at a minimum, [$1.23 million] of the Arbitration award represents amounts invoiced for services in repairing one of the Turbines and is secured by a possessory artisan's lien on the Turbine and spare parts. The terms of the Stipulation call for certain payments to GE, funded by the Debtor's various insurers, to satisfy this lien and pay for the installation of certain Turbine components, a gas generator and accompanying spare parts. These payments, however, do not eliminate GE's entire claim against Project Orange, only the secured portion. After receipt of these amounts, GE would deliver the gas generator and the spare parts to the Debtor. GE would then install these components after the completion of repairs and installation of another key Turbine component, the power turbine.

B. DLA Piper's Relationship with GE and Other Potential Parties in Interest

The Debtor's application to employ DLA Piper is supported with three declarations from Timothy W. Walsh ("Walsh"), a partner and Vice Chair of DLA Piper's Restructuring Practice Group. The first Walsh Declaration (the "Initial Walsh Declaration") reveals that Walsh and his partners represent certain GE affiliates in matters unrelated to this bankruptcy. Walsh maintains that the "vast majority" of work DLA Piper completes for GE entities is for General Electric Healthcare ("GEHC"). The Initial Walsh Declaration also discloses that the GE affiliate which is a creditor in this case, General Electric International, Inc. ("GEII"), is not, and never has been, a client of DLA Piper, but instead is a client of DLA Piper International, LLP ("DLA Piper International"), a separate affiliate of DLA Piper.

Walsh's second declaration (the "Supplemental Walsh Declaration") further explains the relationship between DLA Piper and DLA Piper International. DLA Piper and DLA Piper International are the two components of DLA Piper Global, a Swiss verein entity. The Supplemental Walsh Declaration claims that GEII is technically a client of Advokafirma DLA Piper Norway DA, which is a limited partner in DLA Piper International. Walsh argues that as a result DLA Piper receives no financial benefit from the work DLA Piper International and its components complete for GEII.

The Walsh Declarations also state that DLA Piper has represented, and may currently represent, numerous other potential parties in interest including Syracuse University, AECOM, National Grid, JP Morgan Chase, U.S. Bank, City of Syracuse, Chartis National Union Fire Insurance Company of Pittsburgh, PA., and BP Energy Company (together with GEII, the "Conflict Parties"). Walsh's Supplemental Declaration clarifies that DLA Piper may be adverse to Syracuse University. Walsh further reveals that the Conflict Parties, with the exception of GE, represent less than 1% of the revenues generated by DLA Piper in 2008, 2009, and to date in 2010. Walsh also notes, however, that DLA

Piper's work for GE entities constituted .92% of revenue in 2008, 1.6% of revenue in 2009, and has accounted for .90% of revenues to date in 2010.

Walsh's third declaration (the "Second Supplemental Walsh Declaration"), filed after the June 7, 2010 hearing on this motion, clarifies that DLA Piper would not sue certain Conflict Parties, specifically AECOM, Chartis National Union Fire Insurance Company of Pittsburgh, PA., BP Energy Company, and GEII.

The DLA Employment Application acknowledges that DLA Piper's relationship with GE gives rise to a conflict. At the June 7, 2010 hearing on the DLA Employment Application, DLA Piper affirmed its conflict with GE. ("The Court: . . . Don't you agree you have a conflict [with GE]? Mr. Walsh: I do.").) Following the June 7, 2010 hearing, however, DLA Piper retreated from its position, and now argues that it has no conflict of interest in representing the Debtor. Notably, DLA Piper does not maintain that it doesn't have a conflict with GE. In fact, the Debtor has retained Golenbock Eisenman Assor Bell & Peskoe LLP ("Golenbock") to handle all matters for which DLA Piper cannot adequately represent the Debtor, including issues regarding GEII.

Despite DLA Piper's current position, its relationship with GE caused it sufficient concern that it obtained a conflict waiver from GE to shield it from allegations of ethical wrongdoing (the "Conflict Waiver"). . . . The Conflict Waiver is contained in a letter from DLA Piper, not DLA Piper International, and is addressed to GEII, care of senior general counsel for GE. The Conflict Waiver states that DLA Piper "will not bring any litigation or threaten any litigation for the recovery of monetary damages from GE or its affiliates or for any equitable relief against GE or any of its affiliates." The Conflict Waiver, however, would permit DLA Piper to

> (a) negotiate with GE on all matters, and (b) review loan, lease or other documents relating to the prepetition credit facilities or lease; provided, however that [the Debtor] has engaged special counsel of its own choosing . . . with respect to the potential of bringing or prosecuting any such adversary proceeding or contested matter against GE. . . . Lastly, the Conflict Waiver indicates that DLA Piper may take positions regarding relief from the automatic stay, use of cash collateral, DIP financing, or confirmation of a plan that differ from that of GE "except to the extent that any such position taken by [the Debtor] may not be more inconsistent with any provision of any intercreditor agreement."

DLA Piper claims that no such intercreditor agreement exists.

II. DISCUSSION

A. Retention of Professionals Under Section 327(a) of the Bankruptcy Code

Section 327(a) of the Bankruptcy Code permits a debtor in possession to employ professionals to represent the estate during bankruptcy with court approval. The statute reads:

> Except as otherwise provided in this section, the trustee, with the court's approval, may employ one or more attorneys, accountants, appraisers, auctioneers, or other professional persons, that do not hold or represent an interest adverse to the estate, and that are disinterested persons, to represent or assist the trustee in carrying out the trustee's duties under this title.

11 U.S.C. § 327(a). Professionals must be both disinterested and not hold or represent any interest adverse to the estate to be employed under section 327(a).

The structure of the Bankruptcy Code distills these dual requirements into a single test for analysis of a conflict of interest. Bankruptcy Code § 101(14) defines a "disinterested person." Under section 101(14)(C) a disinterested person is one who "does not have an interest materially adverse to the interest of the estate or of any class of creditors" for any reason. 11 U.S.C. § 101(14)(C). This definition overlaps with the adverse interest requirement of section 327(a), creating a single test for courts to employ when examining conflicts of interest. A professional must not "hold or represent an interest adverse to the estate." See In re AroChem Corp., 176 F.3d 610, 622-23 (2d Cir. 1999).

The Second Circuit has defined "hold or represent an adverse interest" as

> (1) to possess or assert any economic interest that would tend to lessen the value of the bankruptcy estate or that would create either an actual or potential dispute in which the estate is a rival claimant; or (2) to possess a predisposition under circumstances that render such a bias against the estate.

Id. at 623. The prohibition on adverse interests includes "economic and personal interests of an attorney." The test is not retrospective; courts only examine present interests when determining whether a party has an adverse interest. Generally stated, the adverse interest test is objective and excludes "any interest or relationship, however slight, that would even faintly color the independence and impartial attitude required by the Code and Bankruptcy Rules."

Courts determine whether an adverse interest exists on a case-by-case basis, examining the specific facts in a case. Bankruptcy courts may consider the interests of the estate and the debtor's creditors, accounting for the expeditious resolution of a case when analyzing a retention order. Courts, however, must take the requirements of section 327 seriously, as they ensure that a professional fulfills his duties in accordance with his fiduciary duties to the estate. Moreover, courts lack the power to authorize the "employment of a professional who has a conflict of interest."

Congress has explicitly stated that a professional's representation of a creditor in another case does not automatically disqualify it from being retained under section 327. See 11 U.S.C. § 327(c) ("a person is not disqualified for employment under this section solely because of such person's employment or representation of a creditor"). The statute, however, requires disqualification of a professional following an objection from the U.S. Trustee or a creditor where there is an actual conflict of interest. Id. ("the court shall disapprove such employment if there is an actual conflict of interest"). Section 327(c) acknowledges the difficulties debtors have in large Chapter 11 bankruptcies to retain competent attorneys with the resources to handle the scope of the cases. See 3 COLLIER ON BANKRUPTCY ¶327.04[7][b] (15th ed. rev. 2010). The statute "prevents disqualification based solely on the professional's prior representation of or employment by a creditor" but does not obviate the essential requirement that a professional not have an interest adverse to the estate. In re Arochem, 176 F.3d at 621. Thus, even where section 327(c) is applicable, if a court determines that there is an actual conflict of interest following an objection from the U.S. Trustee or a creditor the court must disapprove the employment.

B. DLA Piper's Relationship with GE Precludes It from Being Employed by the Debtor Under § 327(a)

DLA Piper attempts to distance itself from GE, maintaining that the creditor in this case, GEII, is not even a client of DLA Piper, but rather a client of DLA Piper International. But the Conflict Waiver severely undermines DLA Piper's effort to segregate its relationship to GEII. Specifically, the Conflict Waiver was sent by DLA Piper, not DLA Piper International. Moreover, it is addressed to GEII "care of" an attorney at GE itself. Lastly, the Conflict Waiver combines GEII and GE into a single entity, GE, when requesting a waiver. Thus, the Court does not accept DLA Piper's effort to draw artificial lines in an attempt to isolate itself from GEII. As DLA Piper's Conflict Waiver conflates GE and GEII as a single entity, this Court too will treat them as one and the same for purposes of this motion.[3]

Using this approach the U.S. Trustee argues that DLA Piper's ongoing relationship with GE precludes it from being retained as general bankruptcy counsel in this matter. Indeed, the Debtor and DLA Piper agree that DLA Piper cannot represent the Debtor in many matters regarding GE. Specifically, the DLA Employment Application admits that DLA Piper is conflicted from taking certain actions in the bankruptcy due to its representation of GE affiliates. And, during the hearing on the retention application, counsel for DLA Piper confirmed the presence of a conflict with GE. DLA Piper's Supplemental Brief also confirms the presence of conflict between the DLA Piper and GE. ("[N]o conflict will exist between DLA Piper and GE going forward after a settlement is finalized regarding the turbine").

Despite this acknowledged conflict, DLA Piper argues that it "does not have a conflict of interest in representing the Debtor." It is only barred from acting in "litigation directly adverse to GE" and it has "no conflict with representing the Debtor opposite GE in developing and negotiating a plan of reorganization." In support of this position, DLA Piper argues that the Court should focus "on the actions DLA Piper proposes to take as to [Project Orange] in this bankruptcy case" and eschew DLA Piper's other relationships. LA Piper apparently believes that the Stipulation with GE—which would provide for the eventual return of Turbine components to the Debtor, but not resolve GE's unsecured claim against the estate—combined with the Conflict Waiver and its use of conflicts counsel somehow permits DLA Piper to represent the Debtor as general bankruptcy counsel despite its close relationship and acknowledged conflict with GE. The Court disagrees with DLA Piper's assessment of the law.

---

3. Since DLA Piper dealt with itself and its affiliates as one entity in negotiating a conflict waiver with GE entities (likewise treated as one entity), the Court does not need to consider whether different conflicts rules might apply in some circumstances where international law firms share a relationship through a Swiss verein. DLA Piper's website proclaims that "DLA Piper became one of the largest legal service providers in the world in 2005 through a merger of unprecedented scope in the legal sector. While large in scale, the merger strategy was simple—to create an international legal practice capable of taking care of the most important legal needs of clients wherever they do business. . . . DLA Piper today has 3,500 lawyers in offices throughout Asia, Europe, the Middle East and the United States. We represent more clients in a broader range of geographies and practice disciplines than virtually any other law firm in the world." *See* http://www.dlapiper.com/global/about/overview/ (last visited June 23, 2010). DLA Piper holds itself out to the world as one firm, although it now tries to separate itself into separate firms for conflicts purposes. Followed to its logical conclusion, this would lead to the anomalous result that DLA Piper, on behalf of one client, could be adverse to DLA Piper International, on behalf of one of its clients, without violating ethical standards.

1. The Debtor's Execution of the Stipulation Did Not Resolve DLA Piper's Conflict with GE

DLA Piper argues in its Supplemental Brief—filed after the Debtor entered into the Stipulation with GE—that the Debtor's signing of the Stipulation resolved all conflicts between itself and GE. DLA Piper is severely mistaken. The Stipulation, by its own terms, is not effective until this Court reviews the Stipulation in accordance with Federal Rule of Bankruptcy Procedure 9019 and approves the settlement. Until then, no settlement exists and GE remains directly adverse to Project Orange. Notably, even if the Court approves the Stipulation, adversity would still remain. Under the terms of the settlement, GE must complete repairing a Turbine component before it can install the Turbine in accordance with other Stipulation provisions. Repairs on the component are anticipated to be completed by July 10, 2010, but the Stipulation states that this date is subject to change. If repairs are more difficult than anticipated, the return of the Debtor's Turbines to operation is not assured. Moreover, there would likely be contentious litigation over the installation of the Turbines. As summer is the Debtor's busiest months, any delay on GE's part would almost necessitate the Debtor to threaten a lawsuit to expedite the repair and installation process. Indeed, until the repair and installation of the Turbines is complete, GE and Project Orange remain wholly adverse.

Moreover, Project Orange is locked in highly contentious—but currently stayed—litigation in state court with its landlord, Syracuse University, regarding the validity of their lease. The University maintains that the lease was terminated prepetition as a result of several Project Orange defaults. Under the terms of the Debtor's lease with the University, arguments exist that termination of the lease would result in the entire Facility reverting to the University: Section 27.02(b)(ii) of the lease specifically allows the University to repossess both the leased property as well as the Facility on termination of the lease. As defined in other agreements between the two parties, the Facility includes the Turbines. Thus, even if the Stipulation and settlement become effective, if Syracuse University is successful in establishing that the lease terminated prepetition, Project Orange will have no assets to liquidate to pay its largest unsecured creditor.

DLA Piper, however, ignores these clear conflicts, suggesting that the Stipulation resolved all adversity in this case. DLA Piper cites to cases that distinguish between present and potential conflicts, arguing that because only the *potential* for adversity with GE exists, it may be retained in this case. But other bankruptcy judges in this district have refused to distinguish between actual and potential conflicts. These judges instead focus on the facts of each case to determine whether an attorney has an adverse interest without limiting labels.

. . .

2. DLA Piper's Conflict Waiver Does Not Permit DLA Piper's Employment Under 327(a)

The Conflict Waiver does not save DLA Piper's application from these infirmities. Both commentators and courts conclude that disabling adverse interests may exist where the professional to be retained also represents creditors of the debtor. *In re American Printers & Lithographers, Inc.*, 148 B.R. 862, 865-66 (Bankr. N.D. Ill. 1992) (finding adverse interest between debtor's proposed law firm and the debtor's secured creditor based on law firm's continuing representation of secured creditor in unrelated matters). Indeed, in *American Printers*, the court concluded that a conflict existed because debtor's proposed counsel, who represented a secured creditor of the debtor in unrelated matters, could not negotiate with the secured creditor on the debtor's behalf. Thus, the proposed attorney was disqualified. *See In re American Printers*, 148 B.R. at 865-66. Here, DLA Piper contemplates engaging in the *exact conduct* the *American Printers* court determined created a disabling conflict between proposed counsel and the debtor's secured creditor—"developing and negotiating a plan of reorganization."

DLA Piper argues that because GE has contractually permitted DLA Piper to represent the Debtor on some matters adverse to GE that it cures *all* conflicts for purposes of section 327(a). But an agreement between DLA Piper and GE, *i.e.*, the Conflicts Waiver, cannot trump the requirements of section 327(a). Even if GE agreed that DLA Piper could act against GE on all issues, through litigation, negotiation or otherwise, DLA Piper must still satisfy the statutory requirements of section 327(a) to be retained as general bankruptcy counsel. *See, e.g., In re Granite Partners, L.P.*, 219 B.R. at 34 (observing that while clients may, in some instances, waive conflicts, "the mandatory provisions of section 327(a) do not allow for waiver"); *In re Perry*, 194 B.R. 875, 880 (E.D. Cal. 1996) (stating that "section 327(a) has a strict requirement of disinterestedness and absence of representation of an adverse interest which trumps the rules of professional conduct").

Moreover, the Conflict Waiver severely limits DLA Piper's ability to act in the best interests of the Debtor with regards to GE. Under the terms of the Conflict Waiver, DLA Piper is barred from both bringing suit and threatening to bring suit against GE or its affiliates for monetary damages or equitable relief. While the Conflict Waiver purportedly allows DLA Piper to negotiate with GE "on all matters" and review loan or lease documents relating to the Debtor's prepetition credit facilities and lease, the Court does not believe that DLA Piper can negotiate with full efficacy without at least being able to hint at the possibility of litigation.

This is particularly true with regards to the Stipulation. The Debtor's ongoing relationship with GE is a core issue for a successful reorganization of the Debtor. Specifically, return of the Turbines to operation is central to the Debtor's profitability. ("Mr. Victor: Nobody's going to get paid unless we can run [both Turbines] and let . . . us see how we can maximize [them].") Yet, as indicated above, under the Stipulation there is a possibility that the installation date of the Turbines may slip. If this occurs, Project Orange will be forced to quickly and vigorously negotiate the installation schedule to take advantage of the summer electricity season. Valid negotiation strategies may include threatening lawsuits or withholding payments to be made under the Stipulation. It is unclear whether the Conflict Waiver would permit DLA Piper to take either course of action.

3. The Debtor's Use of Conflicts Counsel Does Not Warrant DLA Piper's Employment Under 327(a)

In many cases, the employment of conflicts counsel to handle issues where general bankruptcy counsel has an adverse interest solves most questions regarding the retention of general bankruptcy counsel. . . . DLA Piper has not provided the Court with any case law indicating that the use of conflicts counsel warrants retention under section 327(a) where the proposed general bankruptcy counsel has a conflict of interest with a creditor that is central to the debtor's reorganization. The Court determines that this is such a case where the use of conflicts counsel does not allow the retention of the Debtor's chosen counsel under section 327(a).

Even if Golenbock performed *all* work related to GE in this case, the fig leaf of conflicts counsel does not convince the Court that retention of DLA Piper as general bankruptcy counsel is appropriate in these circumstances. As previously indicated, GE is central to this case. It is the Debtor's largest unsecured creditor. The return and installation of the Turbines, which are central to the Debtor's ability to reorganize, is currently subject to a Stipulation which may or may not be entered by the Court. Moreover, even if the Court approves the Stipulation, there is considerable uncertainty regarding the timeline for installation of the Turbines. Any disagreement on installation would likely give rise to highly contentious proceedings. In fact, GE has shown its willingness to vigorously defend itself in this forum by making multiple filings. GE has moved the Court to lift the automatic stay to confirm its $4.1 million arbitration award. GE has also objected to the Debtor's request to pay prepetition wages, salaries, and taxes. GE has further filed a motion to lift the automatic stay with regards to two checks issued by AIG to both the Debtor and GE. Given GE's strong interests and active stance in this case, it is clear that addressing issues with GE will take considerable time and skill on a range of matters. Indeed, the Debtor essentially acknowledged that Golenbock would need to take numerous actions in this case by seeking to retain the firm pursuant to section 327(a) of the Bankruptcy Code and not the more limited "special purpose" contemplated by section 327(e). Thus, even assuming DLA Piper does not complete *any* work regarding GE, the Court does not believe DLA Piper's employment is permissible.

. . .

On the facts of this case, as DLA Piper's conflict is with the Debtor's largest unsecured creditor that is central to the issues in this case, the Court concludes that it is inappropriate to approve the retention application. It is not a sufficient answer, as DLA Piper posits, that the firm has had a long-standing relationship with the Debtor. Conflicts rules do not apply only when application of the rules will not inconvenience the party seeking to retain conflicted counsel.

CONCLUSION

DLA Piper's representation of GE creates a conflict of interest with the Debtor. GE is the largest creditor in this case, has been highly active in the proceedings, and is certain to play a key role in any plan negotiations or confirmation hearing. Here, given DLA Piper's admitted conflict of interest with GE and GE's central role in this case, the Court does not believe that the use of conflicts counsel warrants DLA Piper's retention in this matter. Thus, the DLA Employment Application is DENIED.

Conflicts issues can arise not only when a firm represents a debtor and a creditor, but also when a firm has done pre-petition work for the debtor. What if the firm committed malpractice? Wouldn't the debtor have a claim against its own counsel? Who would prosecute that? Does this suggest that debtor-side bankruptcy practices really need to be stand-alone boutiques that do not handle non-bankruptcy transactional or litigation work for clients? Or does it suggest that firms should only represent debtors that they did not represent outside of bankruptcy? Section 1107(b) provides that there is no automatic disqualification because of pre-petition work, but is there any way to avoid the potential conflict? On the other hand, as a practical matter, is it realistic to demand a debtor obtain fresh counsel when it files for bankruptcy? Wouldn't a company want to have its regular counsel representing it in a major corporate moment like bankruptcy? Wouldn't it want counsel that already knew its operations well to be representing it?

Likewise, conflicts problems can also arise when a firm represents two or more related debtors, as there might be intercompany claims that need to be addressed. Conflicts counsel is often used in such situations, but who selects conflicts counsel? The conflicted law firm may well have a say in the selection.

Perhaps the most unusual feature of the regulation of professionals in bankruptcy is that their fees must be approved by the court and are public. In other words, the bankruptcy court regulates (some) attorneys' fees. The only other situation similar to this is approval of attorneys' fees in class actions. Estate and official committee professionals' fees are allowed only if they are "reasonable compensation for actual, necessary services rendered." 11 U.S.C. § 330. Section 330 sets forth criteria for evaluating fees, including that they be reasonable in light of the skill and experience of the professional, and prohibits fees for activities that were not necessary for the administration of the case or reasonably likely to benefit the estate or were unnecessarily duplicative. Thus, bringing a busload of first-year associates to observe a hearing is unlikely to be billable by debtor's counsel.

The court approval requirement is because the professionals of the estate and official committees are paid by the estate as administrative priority expenses under sections 503(b) and 507(a)(2), so they must be paid in full in cash for plan confirmation under section 1129(a)(9). Interim compensation is allowed to professionals, however, under section 331, so professionals' bills do not continue to accrue during the case. No waiting in line to be paid for the lawyers and bankers!

The professionals retained by the trustee/DIP or official committee(s) must submit detailed time records to the court (if billing on an hourly basis) as part of their period fee applications. These applications (and the billing rates) are public and can be challenged by parties in interest, the U.S. Trustee, or the court *sua sponte*.

Multi-debtor representations can present complications for billing by a debtor's professionals. How is billing supposed to be allocated among the debtor entities? On some pro rated formula? That makes sense for work developing a debtor-wide strategy for the bankruptcy? But what if the work only benefits certain entities within the debtor's corporate group? Or do the affiliated debtor entities generate various intangible synergies (such as bulk buying power) that they all necessarily benefit from legal work done for another member of the corporate group? There are no clear answers, but a firm that does not have a plan for how to allocate billing prior to the commencement of a representation is going to have a very unpleasant time trying to figure out how to allocate billable hours after the fact.

Problem Set 19

(1) Bifrost LLC designs and manufactures cutting edge lasers. Bifrost has recently filed for Chapter 11. Several of Bifrost's top research scientists, including Bifrost's Chief Science Officer, have indicated that they will leave for other employers unless they are paid substantial retention bonuses. "We're not sure this company's going to come out of bankruptcy," they say, "and we don't want to be left holding the bag." Bifrost's management desperately wants to keep these scientists, as their research is critical for developing Bifrost's next generation of lasers, which Bifrost hopes to bring into production in three years. Can Bifrost pay retention bonuses? 11 U.S.C. §§ 101(31), 503(c). If so, how much can Bifrost offer? Bifrost paid an average of $65,000 to its non-management employees last year.

(2) Two of Bifrost LLC's secured noteholders, Fenrir Capital, LLP and Ouroboros Partners, LLP, file a joint motion for the lifting of the automatic stay. Do Fenrir and Ouroboros have to file any disclosures with their motion? FED. R. BANKR. PROC. 2019. What if Fenrir and Ouroboros created a new special-purpose entity, Jotenheimer LLC, to which they transferred their notes in exchange for the LLC interests. Would Jotenheimer LLC be required to file any disclosures if it filed a lift-stay motion?

(3) In the run-up to its Chapter 11 bankruptcy, Valhalla Airlines, Inc. engaged in a number of transactions with its non-bankrupt affiliates. In some of these cases, Valhalla transferred assets to the affiliates, while in others, it contracted for its affiliates to provide it with services. Valhalla is now debtor-in-possession. Valhalla's Official Committee of Unsecured Creditors has alleged that the asset transfers were for less than reasonably equivalent value and that the service contracts were at substantially above-market rates. The Committee thinks that the transfers and contracts might be avoidable under various bankruptcy law provisions, but Valhalla has refused to move on them.

   a. If the Committee moved for the appointment of a trustee, would the motion be granted? 11 U.S.C. § 1104(a).

   b. Valhalla's current management team has been in place for several years and has significant industry experience and good relations with the unions representing most of Valhalla's well-compensated work force: pilots, flight attendants, mechanics, and ramp personnel. What options does the Committee have for dealing with these transfers and contracts?

(4) Two years ago, the Almaty office of the international law firm Steele & Meikoff, LLP, advised energy firm Gazoz about an acquisition in Kazakhstan. Things went badly after the acquisition, and Gazoz was sued. The litigation is still pending.

One year ago, Steele & Meikoff itself added a crack bankruptcy practice group (or as they call it, "Business Finance Deal" group) headed by the famed bankruptcy maven Radcliffe H. Miller ("Rad"). Rad is often said to have represented someone important in nearly every bankruptcy case of note. The Business Finance Deal group had previously been at the old white shoe firm of Barrow, Lotts & de Walt, LLP. Gazoz regularly employed Barrow, Lotts for its creditor-side bankruptcy work, but Barrow, Lotts recently imploded (shortly after the defection of Rad and the Business Finance Deal group) and is currently in receivership. The receiver has been attempting to collect a disputed bill from Gazoz.

Gazoz itself has run into financial difficulties and has turned to Rad and the Business Finance Deal group to represent it in its proposed Chapter 11.

a. Can Rad take the representation? 11 U.S.C. §§ 101(14), 327, 1107.

b. Would it matter if Steele & Meikoff got a conflict waiver from Gazoz?

(5) Steele & Meikoff, LLP's crack bankruptcy practice, still led by the indomitable Radcliffe H. Miller, is now representing household product manufacturer Spick & Span in its Chapter 11. Spick & Span has determined that it has a litigation claim against one of its lenders, the ever-proper Chaste Manhattan Bank. Chaste is an important client of Steele & Meikoff. What should Rad do? 11 U.S.C. §§ 101(14), 327, 1107.

CHAPTER 20

FIRST-DAY ORDERS AND FINANCING IN BANKRUPTCY

I. FINANCING IN BANKRUPTCY

Cash is the lifeblood of a firm. Firms require liquidity to operate. There are bills that must be paid to keep the lights on, the machines running, and employees on the job. Much of this cannot be done on a deferred payment basis. Bankrupt companies are no exception. Bankrupt businesses require funds to reorganize, and reorganizations are expensive. A company cannot reorganize without funds to pay its operating expenses and reorganization-specific expenses. It is impossible to rehabilitate a bankrupt company without adequate cash on hand or an unfettered cash flow.

Almost by definition, though, bankrupt companies lack sufficient cash. The underlying problems of bankrupt businesses vary tremendously, but the proximate cause of most bankruptcy filings is a liquidity crunch; most companies will avoid filing for bankruptcy filing until they lack sufficient cash on hand to cover their debts as they come due. Until that point, companies keep hoping that they will somehow turn the corner; bankruptcy is usually seen as a last resort, not least because of the potential loss of control that can occur in bankruptcy.

Because bankrupt companies typically lack the cash on hand or access to receivables to finance a reorganization, a first order of business for a bankrupt company that seeks to reorganize is to obtain financing.

There are several ways a firm can finance itself in bankruptcy. Some firms have enough unrestricted cash flow—that is, revenue that is not subject to a security interest—to operate. Other firms obtain "trade credit" from their vendors. This means that the vendors will ship on deferred payment terms. For example, a vendor might ship widgets to the bankrupt company with payment required in 90 days. That gives the debtor time to use and sell the widgets before payment to the vendor is due. If trade credit is done in the ordinary course of business, it does not require court approval. Query whether an increase in the amount of trade credit, say going from 90-day to 120-day payment terms, would be in the ordinary course of business. Would the analysis likely track that in *Roth American* (in Chapter 21)? Would a court look to the ordinary course of the debtor's industry (the "horizontal" test), at the expectations of a hypothetical creditor (the "vertical" test), or at the ordinary course of the debtor's actual business? *See* Benjamin Weintraub & Alan N. Resnick, *The Meaning of "Ordinary Course of Business" Under the Bankruptcy Code—Vertical and Horizontal Analysis*, 19 UCC L.J. 364 (1987). If the financing is not in the ordinary course of business, then court approval is required under section 364 of the Bankruptcy Code.

Other firms rely on **"cash collateral"**—the use of cash and cash-like proceeds of collateral for security interests or security-like interests (such as rights of setoff) to finance ongoing operations. An example of this would be a debtor with liens on its inventory. When the debtor sells the inventory, it becomes cash (sometimes first having been an account receivable). That cash (and account receivable) is the proceeds of the inventory. As such, it is subject to the lien that was on the inventory. UCC §§ 9-203(f), 9-315. (If the sale is in the ordinary course of business, then the security interest ceases to exist on the goods in the hands of the purchaser. UCC § 9-320.) Use of cash collateral requires either the consent or adequate protection of the secured creditor. 11 U.S.C. §§ 361, 363(c).

Finally, a debtor might seek to obtain new loans or lines of credit, known as **"debtor-in-possession financing"** or **"DIP financing."** Pre-bankruptcy financing agreements are not assumable by the trustee/DIP under section 365(c)(2), so any new financing outside of the ordinary course of business must be approved by the court pursuant to section 364.

Financing arrangements are often proposed on the first day of a bankruptcy case as part of a bevy of motions called "first-day motions" or "first-day orders." The timing of these motions is important to consider, as it affects the likelihood of their approval. Thus, this chapter starts with a consideration of first-day motions and then proceeds to examine cash collateral and DIP financing agreements, which are two of the most important type of first-day motions. Note throughout how much control these agreements may provide the financier over the entire bankruptcy. Because of the circumstances under which DIP financing is sought, the financier is often able to dictate terms that provide it with extraordinary protections and a great deal of substantive control over the restructuring.

II. FIRST-DAY ORDERS

The first day of a bankruptcy typically sees a flurry of court filings by the debtor seeking court approval for both administrative and operational matters and major substantive transactions. Preparing such motions is a major part of the work for debtor's counsel leading up to the filing of a case. The administrative and most operational first-day motions are unlikely to be opposed; the substantive ones are another matter. First-day motion practice is in response to the intersection of particular Bankruptcy Code provisions with the economic realities of running a firm, but is nowhere to be found in the Bankruptcy Code. The following section summarizes the major types of first-day motions commonly filed. Not all motions are filed in every case, although many are filed in virtually all cases.

First-day administrative motions include the following:

Joint Administration Motion

This motion seeks joint administration of the cases of multiple affiliated debtors for administrative convenience. Such a motion does not merge the assets and the liabilities of these entities. Federal Rule of Bankruptcy Procedure 1015 contemplates joint administration of the estates of affiliated entities, and Federal Rule of Bankruptcy Procedure 2009 allows for a single trustee or DIP for the jointly administered estates.

Notice and Case Management Motion

This motion seeks approval of a form of service list for the case. It may also request that certain parties in interest, such as employees or customers, need to be served with routine motions. It may also request regular case hearings.

Extensions of Time Motions

These motions seek extensions of time to file required schedules and statements of financial affairs. Sometimes these motions are more substantive, seeking extensions of the timetable for assumption and rejection of unexpired leases and executory contracts and plan exclusivity.

Bar Date Motion

This motion seeks to set a deadline for the timely filing of proofs of claim.

Employment of Professionals and Fee Procedures

These motions seek to get court approval for the debtor's employment of professionals (including counsel) and for the way their fees are to be paid. Fees and expenses are typically paid on a monthly basis under section 331, but the United States Trustee will sometimes contest this motion if there is not a sufficient "holdback"—a percentage of the fee (not expenses) that will only be paid at the conclusion of the case. 20% is a standard holdback amount.

Committee Information Access Protocols

This motion seeks to maintain confidentiality of information shared with creditors committees, which are required to provide access to their constituencies under section 1102(b)(3) and to solicit input from their constituencies.

Filing of Documents Under Seal

This motion seeks to keep certain commercially sensitive documents under seal.
Debtors also need court approval for continuing various parts of their operations. Hence another battery of first-day motions:

Cash Management Motion

This motion requests that the debtor be allowed to continue using its existing cash management system without complying with guidelines created by the United States

Trustee that generally require the debtor to close existing bank accounts and establish new ones indicating that it is a debtor-in-possession. Moreover, many large firms will sweep cash from various corporate affiliates into a central treasury account. Ensuring that all the funds can flow as need be back to the various corporate affiliates (including those outside of the United States) is critical for ensuring uninterrupted operations. As an operational matter, this motion is critical because absent access to cash management systems, liquidity cannot be accessed and the debtor cannot operate.

Investment Guidelines Motion

Trustees and DIPs are subject to investment restrictions on estate money under section 345. This motion seeks a permission waiver or leniency in the application of section 345, often to allow the debtor to follow its pre-petition practices.

GOB Sale Motion

Some states regulate going-out-of-business (GOB) sales. There is split authority regarding whether these regulations apply to debtors in bankruptcy, but these motions are intended to provide protection for the debtor from these regulations. Often the motion will prohibit activities like the sale of gift cards prior to the GOB sale (as the cards will not be redeemable in the future) or augmenting inventory or raising prices before the GOB sale.

Reclamation Procedures Motion

In certain circumstances, creditors who shipped to the debtor within 45 days pre-petition may reclaim their goods. 11 U.S.C. § 546(c). This motion seeks to establish procedures for reclamation, including deadlines for exercising the right, which is important because a creditor with a reclamation right may in some cases have a right to instead receive an administrative priority claim, and the debtor needs to know the extent of its administrative priority claims in order to know if it can confirm a plan.

Utilities Motion

This motion requests the court to prohibit utilities from altering, refusing, or discontinuing services to the debtor on account of pre-petition debts. It also requests approval of any adequate assurance payments required for post-petition utility services under section 366. (See Chapter 16 for a fuller discussion of section 366.) Simply put, this motion is necessary to keep the lights on and the phones ringing. This motion is sometimes contested by utilities, which in Chapter 11 are entitled to "satisfactory" adequate assurances and may disconnect within 30 days if adequate assurances are not given. 11 U.S.C. § 366(c).

Equity Trading Motion

This motion seeks to require notice and hearing procedures prior to certain transfers of the debtor's equity securities being deemed effective. The concern is that certain transfers could result in the loss of valuable tax attributes, such as net operating losses that can otherwise be carried forward to future years. A change in control may cause these tax attributes to be lost.

Some of the operational motions do in fact involve significant deviations from the Bankruptcy Code's priority system, as they would authorize certain pre-petition (and usually unsecured) creditors to be paid outside of a plan.

Critical Vendor Motion

This motion requests permission to pay the pre-petition claims of certain "critical" vendors in full, prior to a plan, in order to induce future cooperation from the vendors.

Employee Benefits Motion

This motion requests permission to pay pre-petition claims of necessary employees for wages, benefits, and out-of-pocket business expenses in full, prior to a plan, in order to induce future cooperation from the employees.

Sales and Use Tax Motion

This motion seeks permission to pay pre-petition sales, use, franchise, and business taxes in full, prior to a plan, in order to avoid tangles with local taxing authorities, especially when there is personal liability for officers and directors for taxes collected and held in trust for the taxing authority. Note that such a motion transfers value from the estate to the officers and directors by relieving them of personal liability.

Customer Programs Motion

This motion seeks to continue pre-petition customer-service programs such as gift certificates, gift cards, layaways, deposits, warranty service, and refund policies. The theory behind the motion is that the cost of these programs is more than compensated for by customer goodwill maintained.

Shippers, Freight Handlers, and Warehousers Motion

This motion requests permission to pay pre-petition claims of shippers, freight handlers, and warehousers in full, prior to a plan. These entities often have a state law statutory lien on property in their custody, and its perfection is not covered by the automatic stay. 11 U.S.C. § 362(b)(3). *See also* 11 U.S.C. § 546(i) (prohibiting trustee/DIP from avoiding such liens under section 545(2)-(3)). Because these are secured creditors, they would likely be paid in full under a plan (the value of the goods in their possession is almost assuredly greater than the amount of their claim), and paying them ensures smooth logistics for the debtor.

Some first-day motions are substantive. These motions are more likely to result in objections, and include the following:

Abandonment Motions

An abandonment motion seeks authority to abandon property that is burdensome or of inconsequential value to the estate. This might be a property on which there is an environmental liability that outweighs its value or a property completely encumbered by liens. Abandonment motions might be opposed by environmental protection agencies or by creditors that do not want to actually take back their collateral. Few banks want to become the proud owners of a 100-ton machine lathe in Sandusky, Ohio or of 40-year old industrial dyeing equipment in Vernon, Connecticut. These entities would rather see the debtor hang on to the property and keep paying.

Assumption/Rejection Motions

The debtor may seek to assume or reject certain executory contracts or unexpired leases at the outset of the case. How this works and what it means is explored in the following chapter, but contract and lease counterparties may not want their contracts and leases assumed or rejected, or assigned if assumed. They may also argue that assumption requires cure and adequate assurance of future performance or that rejection does not affect certain of their rights. If the debtor does not assume or reject a contract, it must continue performing its obligations thereunder, so delay can be costly.

KERP Motion

This motion seeks to authorize payments and incentive plans (key employee retention plans or KERPs) to retain key employees. Section 503(c) of the Bankruptcy Code places major limitations on KERPs, as discussed in the previous chapter.

Emergency Sale Motions

Sometimes a debtor will seek permission on the first day of bankruptcy to enter into an expedited section 363 sale, arguing that the asset is a "melting ice cube" that must be sold immediately or else its value will be lost. Creditors are sometimes wary of these motions, as they have not had the time to evaluate the asset's value, the sale procedures, and how the sale would affect the value of the debtor's remaining assets.

Cash Collateral Motions

Discussed below.

DIP Financing Motions

Discussed below.

First-day motions can result in work overload that makes it impossible for a court to adequately and fairly address them all. Chrysler, for example, filed 21 first-day motions in its bankruptcy. The paperwork attached to these motions ran into the thousands of pages. It included not only the motions, but supporting documentation, such as affidavits, and proposed orders for the court to sign. (It is common practice in bankruptcy for movants to draft court orders, with the court either simply adding its signature or else sometimes indicating changes by hand on the document and then signing. It is the language of the order, rather than the motion, that governs once approved, so the precise order language can be critical.)

It is unrealistic to expect any judge to be able to adequately process all of the details of the case within a short time period and rule on the motions. Recall that the judge likely has numerous *other* cases that she is trying to handle at the same time, all with their own set of first-day motions or other pressing matters.

Moreover, consider who is likely to make an objection to a first-day motion. Creditors may not even have notice that the debtor has filed for bankruptcy, much less have counsel retained. No official committees yet exist. (Indeed, the United States Trustee may not even have sufficient information to form a committee. A Chapter 11 petition is required to include a list of the debtor's 20 largest unsecured creditors per Federal Rule of Bankruptcy Procedure 1007(d), but a petition without such a schedule is unlikely to be immediately dismissed.) The United States Trustee might make an objection, but the Trustee has no information to go on other than that provided by the debtor in its motions and supporting affidavits and the Trustee's sense of what are prevailing market norms. This means that the United States Trustee has little ammunition to push back against first-day motions that are overreaching. If a first-day motion is too outlandish, the Trustee may be able to defeat it, but if the motion only overreaches slightly, it will be harder for the Trustee to notice—and to defeat. This sets up a situation in which there can be gradual creep of acceptable first-day motions, with small accretions left unchallenged in each case and then past cases used as precedent to justify further expansion of the relief requested in first-day motions.

All told, there may not be a party with an actual economic interest in the case that is in a position to oppose a first-day motion. Instead, what normally results with first-day motions is a dialogue between the debtor, the court, and the United States Trustee, sometimes with the senior secured lender lurking in the shadows (as we shall see), but saying little.

It is possible to subsequently move to have some motions reconsidered or amended, but the burden of persuasion shifts and there may be equitable factors weighing against amendments to orders on which the debtor has relied. But certain first-day transactions, once approved, cannot be reversed even if approval is overturned on appeal. (So why bother appealing unless the transaction is stayed pending appeal?) Section 363(m) protects sales from reversal, while section 364(e) protects financing arrangements from reversal. Thus, the stakes of getting it right the first time in the bankruptcy court are huge. There is no second bite at the apple on sales and financing.

One solution to the lack of creditor participation with first-day motions is for certain critical motions, like debtor-in-possession financing motions, to receive only interim approval as first-day motions, with a subsequent hearing on final approval required. 11 U.S.C. § 363(c)(3). Federal Rule of Bankruptcy Procedure 4001 provides that a hearing on final approval of use of cash collateral or of a financing arrangement may not take place until 14 days after service of the motion. FED. R. BANKR.

PROC. 4001(b)(2), (c)(2). Cash collateral and financing motions must also include concise highlights of major material terms, including any terms covered by an extensive listing in Rule 4001. The idea behind Rule 4001 is to make it easy for the court and creditors to identify and evaluate potentially controversial terms of financings, as DIP financing agreements can run to hundreds of pages of dense legal text. Rule 4001 is designed to deal with problems of insufficient notice and information overload. But notice and information alone may not matter unless there are viable alternatives to the financing offered.

(trade financing)

III. FINANCING THROUGH USE OF CASH COLLATERAL

§363

Perhaps the single most critical first-day motion is the motion to obtain financing for the debtor's operations in bankruptcy. This might be a cash collateral motion, or a debtor-in-possession financing motion, or both. In practice, a consensual cash collateral financing arrangement can resemble a DIP loan agreement, but statutorily, cash collateral is treated differently from DIP financing.

if biz authorized to operate

Section 363(c)(1) of the Bankruptcy Code provides that the debtor may enter into transactions using the property of the estate in the ordinary course of business without court approval. Section 363(c)(2), however, contains an exception for the use of cash collateral from this permission unless the secured creditor has consented. Absent consent, there must be notice and a hearing and court approval, which may require that the debtor provide adequate protection under section 363(e). (Recall, however, that under section 102(1), "after notice and a hearing" does not necessarily require either notice or a hearing, only such "as is appropriate in the particular circumstances." 11 U.S.C. § 102(1).) The trustee or DIP is also required to segregate any cash collateral from other cash, because commingling can erode a security interest. See UCC §§ 9-315(d), 9-336.

A secured creditor might object to the use of its cash collateral—it knows that the value of cash held in a bank account is unlikely to sharply depreciate, but if the cash is used to fund new ventures, those new ventures may not be successful. For example, imagine that the debtor wishes to use the cash proceeds from inventory to make a new product. Perhaps a down-on-its-luck motorcycle manufacturer now wishes to make a line of high-end leather furniture or an impecunious pajama manufacturer decides to get into the bubble gum business. If the new product is a hit, the upside is captured by the estate, and not the secured creditor if it is oversecured and only partially if it is undersecured as the unsecured deficiency portion of its claim would get a pro rata share of the upside. If the new product is a flop, the secured creditor's collateral may have dropped in value.

eg. new venture

?

Accordingly, there is little benefit to a secured creditor in agreeing to use of cash collateral unless it can get something in exchange. As a result, cash collateral agreements are often negotiated between trustees/DIPs and secured creditors. These agreements might give the secured creditor administrative priority for its entire claim or adequate protection in the form of additional collateral or replacement liens. The replacement liens are court approved and necessarily valid and replace liens that might otherwise be challenged by the debtor. The secured creditor might also receive some control over the debtor, such as requiring the cash collateral to be used for limited purposes or for the debtor to remain on a budget. Conversely, if the debtor is unable to offer adequate protection, the debtor will not be able to use cash collateral absent creditor consent.

In theory, cash collateral can be used either with the consent of the secured creditor or non-consensually, if the debtor can provide adequate protection. Historically, many debtors financed their bankruptcies through non-consensual use of cash collateral. Non-consensual cash collateral use is rare in contemporary practice because few debtors are able to provide adequate protection. Most debtors enter bankruptcy with "blanket liens" covering all of their assets; if the original credit agreements had "Mother Hubbard" clauses covering all assets as collateral (when other creditors looked in the cupboard, the cupboard was bare . . .), then the remaining unencumbered assets were pledged to obtain financing or obtain forbearance while trying to stave off bankruptcy. The debtors lack the free cash flows to make adequate protection payments and do not have sufficient unencumbered assets or equity value in their encumbered assets to provide adequate protection to creditors secured in inventory and receivables. As a result, most cash collateral arrangements are highly negotiated documents that bear a strong resemblance to debtor-in-possession financing agreements.

§364

IV. DEBTOR-IN-POSSESSION FINANCING AGREEMENTS

Free cash flow, trade credit, and cash collateral may provide sufficient financing for some debtors. Others, however, need additional financing. The Bankruptcy Code allows debtors to obtain new financing pursuant to section 364.

Who would ever lend new money to a bankrupt company? It seems like an obviously bad idea, good money chasing bad. Actually, lending to a bankrupt company, known as DIP financing or DIP lending, is an incredibly safe and profitable endeavor. Indeed, DIP financing appears to be the market chimera in which high returns are coupled with low risks.

DIP financing arrangements can play a critical role in shaping a bankruptcy, as DIP lenders frequently gain significant control over both the routine governance of the debtor and the terms of a plan. This is a power that can be used offensively to further loan-to-own strategies or defensively to protect recoveries on pre-petition debt. A DIP loan often means that there is functionally a "creditor in possession." Indeed, the DIP lending agreement is probably the single most important document in most bankruptcies prior to the plan.

Most of the critical features of DIP financing agreements are simply contractual. This means that they are heavily negotiated prior to the bankruptcy filing. It also means that they are subject to interpretation by the court. DIP financing is mainly shaped by contract because the Bankruptcy Code imposes few restrictions on DIP financing. Instead, it is simply a question of what the court will approve. Section 365(c) prohibits the assumption (or assignment) of executory pre-petition financing agreements. Therefore, a debtor cannot simply arrange for financing before filing for bankruptcy and assume the agreement under the standards of section 365.

Instead, the debtor must get court approval under section 364 if the post-petition financing is other than in the ordinary course of business. The fact that the Code does not require approval of post-petition financing in the ordinary course of business enables post-petition trade financing.

The debtor is authorized to obtain unsecured financing as a regular administrative priority expense under section 503(b). 11 U.S.C. § 364(b). If the debtor cannot obtain post-petition financing on an unsecured administrative priority basis, then the debtor is also authorized to obtain financing either with a super-administrative priority claim under section 364(c)(1) or by granting liens on unencumbered assets or junior liens on encumbered assets under section 364(c)(2)-(3). A claim with section 364(c)(1) priority is paid ahead of all other administrative priority claims, including those for inadequate protection under section 507(b). New money is accorded more protection than old. Section 364(b) and (c) mean that pre-petition contractual prohibitions on liens, such as negative pledge clauses (prohibiting liens), or other contractual restrictions on indebtedness are necessarily violated, rendering those claims impaired, even if they are paid in full under a plan, if the liens (or debt) exist after the effective date on the plan.

Finally, section 364(d) permits the debtor to grant senior liens on encumbered property. These senior liens are known as "priming liens." They may only be granted if credit cannot be otherwise obtained and there is adequate protection for the pre-petition liens that are primed. The burden of proof of adequate protection is on the trustee or DIP. 11 U.S.C. § 364(d)(2). Any financing authorized by the bankruptcy court under section 364 is treated as valid, irrespective of the outcome of an appeal. 11 U.S.C. § 364(e). Thus, a hugely important event in a bankruptcy is once again, as we have seen with sales and valuations, effectively immune from judicial review.

A. Low Risk and High Reward

DIP loans combine the normally antithetical features of low risk and high reward. The high reward comes in the form of interest rates and fees. DIP loans are historically priced at 200-400 basis points above a risk-free rate such as LIBOR (the London Inter-Bank Overnight Rate—the rate that London banks paid to borrow funds from each other overnight). During the 2008-2009 credit crisis, rates went substantially higher, to 600-1,000 basis points above LIBOR with some loans even topping 1,200 basis points above LIBOR. In addition, there are significant fees on DIP loans, both up-front fees and exit fees often amounting to 2%-4% of the loan, as well as arranging, underwriting, and syndication fees charged by the initial arranger(s) of the loan facility. On top of these, there are often forbearance fees for waiving covenant defaults during the bankruptcy.

Lyondell Chemical, for example, received a one-year $8 billion DIP financing in early 2009 (as of July 2018, the third largest ever after GM's $33 billion loan and Energy Future Holdings's $11.8 billion loan) at a 13% interest rate and with fees equivalent to another 7% of the loan. Thus, Lyondell's DIP lenders might have received a 20% annual return at a time when 12-month LIBOR was 1.9%.

Historically, DIP loans were usually revolving lines of credit, although term loans were not uncommon, and many DIP facilities had both. (The pricing is usually separate for the revolver and the term facility, making DIP loan pricing comparisons problematic.) Changes in bank capital rules, however, have made funded term loans more common, and these are more expensive for borrowers because they are actually borrowing the funds, rather than paying a smaller availability fee for the line of credit and only paying interest to the extent drawn down. The shift from revolvers to term loans has raised the cost of DIP loans for borrowers. The high costs do not dissuade borrowers; a DIP loan is in some ways a classic duress situation.

What's more, even if the borrower does not need the DIP loan to fund operations, it may need the DIP loan as a signal to its employees and vendors and customers that it is a viable firm. The DIP loan may be used as a way of signaling the market that a firm is viable by indicating lenders' confidence in the firm. If large, sophisticated financial institutions are staking their money on the debtor, shouldn't that put to rest any concerns about the firm? (Never mind that they are staking their money at a high cost and with senior priority and numerous protections.)

DIP loans are also incredibly low risk. Out of nearly one thousand major bankruptcy cases since 1980, most of which have involved DIP financing, there have only been two DIP loans that were not repaid in full per their original terms: Marvel Entertainment Group and Winstar Communications. Moody's Corporate Finance, *Moody's Comments on Debtor-in-Possession Lending*, Oct. 2008. The Marvel DIP loan was ultimately repaid in full, just not on its original schedule.

The low risk of DIP loans comes from several features. First, DIP loans have short maturities. Historically, they have been around two years, but in the last few years they have often been for maturities of one year or less. The short maturity limits the universe of risks the lender assumes.

Second, DIP loans usually come with priming liens and super-senior 364(c)(1) priority. In most cases, the DIP loan will be made by the pre-petition senior secured lender(s). Such a loan is known as a "defensive" DIP loan. There are variations on this, to be sure. Sometimes senior secureds split with only a subgroup making the loan; sometimes pre-petition junior lenders will make the loan; sometimes, in a closely held firm, an individual equityholder will make the loan; and for private-equity portfolio companies, the private equity sponsor may make the loan. And sometimes there will even be a new money ("offensive") DIP lender, often as part of a takeover strategy. But the most common arrangement is for the senior secured lender to make the loan. The reason for this is section 364(d).

Few parties are willing to make a DIP loan except with seniormost priority. That is, lending to a bankrupt entity is good business, but only if you're senior. Otherwise it truly is risky. If the lender's assets are all tied up with pre-petition liens, then the only way to become senior is through the priming lien provision of section 364(d). Such a "priming lien" requires that all of the subordinate lienholders receive adequate protection of their interests. As a practical matter, providing adequate protection may not be possible. There may not be enough unencumbered value to give them sufficient replacement liens, and the cost of making cash adequate protection payments (or likely a lump sum payment) would be prohibitive.

Moreover, in order to provide adequate protection, there would have to be a valuation. That valuation would have to be done *before* the priming lien could be approved. It may simply not be possible to perform the valuation right at the beginning of the case, and in the interim, the debtor will not have financing. Moreover, having a fight over a priming lien at the beginning of a case is a high-risk strategy. If the priming lien is denied, then the debtor is left without financing and will likely have to liquidate immediately, possibly with a conversion to Chapter 7. (If there is a fallback financing, it would make the debtor's section 364(d) financing appear to be in bad faith because financing under section 364(d) is authorized "only if . . . the trustee is unable to obtain such credit otherwise." 11 U.S.C. § 364(d)(1)(A).)

In theory, it might be possible to prepare valuations, etc. prior to the filing of a case, but most debtors are spending their time prior to filing attempting to avoid bankruptcy. They don't have time to be humoring prospective post-petition lenders' diligence requests, and their pre-petition secured lenders are unlikely to view attempts to cut them out of the DIP lending business kindly. Moreover, other pre-petition creditors are poorly positioned to make DIP loans. Bondholders and trade creditors cannot easily coordinate to assemble a lending syndicate, so unless a single creditor is willing to make a loan, these types of creditors are unlikely to provide DIP financing. Second lien bank loan lenders or unusual lending entities (think of the U.S. government in the Chrysler case) are the main alternative, but they face the priming lien problem.[1] Finally, there is speculation of a "gentlemen's agreement" between the major banks not to poach each other's DIP lending business, but instead to farm out the DIP loans in syndications, with fees going to the bank that originated the business lead by arranging the pre-petition loan. As a result, contested DIP loans are a rarity. Instead, they are usually the prerogative of the senior pre-petition secured lender.

The fact that DIP loans are typically made by the senior pre-petition secured lender is hugely important to the course of bankruptcy cases. DIP financing agreements, as we shall see, provide the DIP lender with enormous influence over the course of the bankruptcy. In many cases, it is the DIP lender, rather than the DIP itself, that is in the driver's seat. The DIP becomes the puppet of the DIP lender. And because most firms want to file with a DIP lender already lined up, the senior pre-petition secured lender often has a major role in deciding when and where a filing occurs. Thus, venue choices may reflect the DIP lender's concerns as much as the DIP's.

The growth of loan syndications has complicated DIP lending. Frequently the senior pre-petition secured lender is a syndicated loan, and often it has an inter-creditor agreement with a syndicated second lien loan. The members of the first lien syndicate may not all want or be able to make a DIP loan, which involves a new

---

1. Even within the senior secured syndicate there may be difficulties financing a DIP loan, as some of the senior lenders may be collateralized loan obligations, which may not have the liquidity and the investment authority to make DIP loans. Additional, outside members might be brought into a syndicate in such cases or unrestricted syndicate members might be able to buy out the restricted members' right to participate in a DIP loan.

*collateralized
loan obligation* [handwritten annotation]

extension of credit. This is a similar problem to the one we saw earlier regarding credit bidding in bankruptcy, where CLOs, as close-ended funds, lack the ability to raise cash to make a cash bid. A well-drafted syndication agreement will contemplate the possibility of a defensive DIP lending opportunity and will have a procedure to allocate rights accordingly. Nonetheless, it is common for defensive DIP loans to be made by a subset of syndicate members, with the DIP loan itself separately syndicated. There is a much smaller market for syndicated DIP loans than for leveraged loans in general—most CLOs and mutual funds do not purchase DIP loans, or have only a small part of their capital allocated for that purpose. The smaller secondary market for DIP loans may be a factor that raises DIP loan pricing.

Junior liens also pose challenges for DIP lending. Section 364(d)(1)(B) requires adequate protection not just of the senior lien, but of all liens. This gives junior lienholders some leverage to impede DIP financing arrangements. As a result, intercreditor agreements frequently provide for the second lien lenders to give advance consent to the use of cash collateral or to a priming DIP loan from the first lien lenders.

Intercreditor agreements will also include provisions stating that the first and second lien lenders agree that their liens are distinct and that they must be separately classified. Such a provision is not binding upon the DIP, even if the debtor was a party to the intercreditor agreement. Yet because of the influence of the senior secured lender on the DIP and hence on the plan, a provision that binds the senior secured lender has much the same effect as binding the DIP.

B. Priming and Cross-Collateralization

Despite DIP lending typically being done by the pre-petition senior secured lender, it will usually be done under sections 364(d) and 364(c)(1). That is, the DIP loan is secured by priming liens and given super-senior administrative expense status to the extent it is not fully secured.[2] What this means is that the pre-petition senior secured lenders are *priming themselves*. Why would they want to prime themselves? What's the point of such a maneuver?

The answer is that the liens granted under 364(d) are perfected pursuant to court order. They cannot be challenged as unperfected and thus avoidable under the trustee's "strong arm" power. 11 U.S.C. § 544(a). Thus, if the lenders had any concerns about the perfection of their liens, the priming liens start to take care of the problem. The priming liens, however, only secure the *new* extension of credit. The *old* pre-petition extensions are still secured by the pre-petition liens. But there's a solution for that. It's called "cross-collateralization." The new liens are made to secure *both* the new and old extensions of credit. Court have not been well disposed toward cross-collateralization, not least because cross-collateralization allows undersecured pre-petition loans to be linked to new post-petition collateral, thus

---

2. To the extent that the DIP loans are undersecured, they will still get administrative expense priority, so they must be paid in full in cash on the effective date of the plan for a plan to be confirmable. 11 U.S.C. § 1129(a)(9)(A).

*Same collateral secures
multiple loans* [handwritten annotation]

enabling a creditor that should have had an undersecured pre-petition claim (and hence an unsecured deficiency) and a secured post-petition claim to instead have a secured pre-petition and post-petition claim and no deficiency.

To wit, imagine that Continental Express Bank, N.A., (ConEx) loaned Cheatham & Meikoff, Inc., $100 million pre-petition, secured by assets that are at the time of the bankruptcy filing worth only $75 million. ConEx then makes a post-petition loan for $25 million, secured by other assets worth $50 million. If there is cross-collateralization, then ConEx has collateral of $125 million that can be applied to both loans. Thus, ConEx would have a $125 million secured claim. Without cross-collateralization, ConEx has secured claims of $75 million (the pre-petition debt) and $25 million (the post-petition loan) and a $25 million unsecured claim (the deficiency on the pre-petition loan). The effect of cross-collateralization is to raise the priority of ConEx's pre-petition loan. This only works, however, if the pre-petition loan is secured by a subset of assets. If it is a blanket lien, then cross-collateralization does nothing for ConEx in terms of priority, although it may still matter in terms of loan perfection. The *Saybrook* case that follows is the paradigmatic discussion of cross-collateralization.

lien on all assets collateralized

Shapiro v. Saybrook Manufacturing Company, Inc.
(In the Matter of Saybrook Manufacturing Company, Inc.)
963 F.2d 1490 (11th Cir. 1992)

Cox, Circuit Judge:

Seymour and Jeffrey Shapiro, unsecured creditors, objected to the bankruptcy court's authorization for the Chapter 11 debtors to "cross-collateralize" their pre-petition debt with unencumbered property from the bankruptcy estate. . . .

I. FACTS AND PROCEDURAL HISTORY

Saybrook Manufacturing Co., Inc., and related companies (the "debtors"), initiated proceedings seeking relief under Chapter 11 of the Bankruptcy Code on December 22, 1988. On December 23, 1988, the debtors filed a motion for the use of cash collateral and for authorization to incur secured debt. The bankruptcy court entered an emergency financing order that same day. At the time the bankruptcy petition was filed, the debtors owed Manufacturers Hanover approximately $34 million. The value of the collateral for this debt, however, was less than $10 million. Pursuant to the order, Manufacturers Hanover agreed to lend the debtors an additional $3 million to facilitate their reorganization. In exchange, Manufacturers Hanover received a security interest in all of the debtors' property—both property owned prior to filing the bankruptcy petition and that which was acquired subsequently. This security interest not only protected the $3 million of post-petition credit but also secured Manufacturers Hanover's $34 million pre-petition debt.

This arrangement enhanced Manufacturers Hanover's position vis-à-vis other unsecured creditors, such as the Shapiros, in the event of liquidation. Because Manufacturers Hanover's pre-petition debt was undersecured by approximately $24 million, it originally would have shared in a pro rata distribution of the debtors' unencumbered assets along with the other unsecured creditors. Under the financing order, however, Manufacturers Hanover's pre-petition debt became fully secured by all of the debtors' assets. If the bankruptcy estate were liquidated, Manufacturers Hanover's entire debt—$34 million pre-petition and $3 million post-petition—would have to be paid in full before any funds could be distributed to the remaining unsecured creditors.

Securing pre-petition debt with pre- and post-petition collateral as part of a post-petition financing arrangement is known as cross-collateralization. The Second Circuit aptly defined cross-collateralization as follows:

> In return for making new loans to a debtor in possession under Chapter XI, a financing institution obtains a security interest on all assets of the debtor, both those existing at the date of the order and those created in the course of the Chapter XI proceeding, not only for the new loans, the propriety of which is not contested, but [also] for existing indebtedness to it.

Otte v. Manufacturers Hanover Commercial Corp. (*In re Texlon Corp.*), 596 F.2d 1092, 1094 (2d Cir. 1979).

Because the Second Circuit was the first appellate court to describe this practice in *In re Texlon*, it is sometimes referred to as *Texlon*-type cross-collateralization. Another form of cross-collateralization involves securing post-petition debt with pre-petition collateral. This form of non-*Texlon*-type cross-collateralization is not at issue in this appeal. The Shapiros challenge only the cross-collateralization of the lenders' pre-petition debt, not the propriety of collateralizing the post-petition debt.

. . .

III. CONTENTIONS OF THE PARTIES

The lenders argue that . . . [c]ross-collateralization is a legitimate means for debtors to obtain necessary financing and is not prohibited by the Bankruptcy Code.

The Shapiros contend that . . . [p]ermitting cross-collateralization would undermine the entire structure of the Bankruptcy Code by allowing one unsecured creditor to gain priority over all other unsecured creditors simply by extending additional credit to a debtor.

. . .

V. DISCUSSION

B. Cross-Collateralization and Section 364

Cross-collateralization is an extremely controversial form of Chapter 11 financing. Nevertheless, the practice has been approved by several bankruptcy courts. *See, e.g., In re Vanguard Diversified, Inc.*, 31 Bankr. 364 (Bankr. E.D.N.Y. 1983) [other citations omitted]. Even the courts that have allowed cross-collateralization, however, were generally reluctant to do so.

In *In re Vanguard,* for example, the bankruptcy court noted that cross-collateralization is "a disfavored means of financing" that should only be used as a last resort. *In re Vanguard*, 31 Bankr. at 366. In order to obtain a financing order including cross-collateralization, the court required the debtor to demonstrate (1) that its business operations would fail absent the proposed financing, (2) that it is unable to obtain alternative financing on acceptable terms, (3) that the proposed lender will not accept less preferential terms, and (4) that the proposed financing is in the general creditor body's best interest. *Id.* This four-part test has since been adopted by other bankruptcy courts which permit cross-collateralization.

The issue of whether the Bankruptcy Code authorizes cross-collateralization is a question of first impression in this court. Indeed, it is essentially a question of first impression before any court of appeals. Neither the lenders' brief nor our own research has produced a single appellate decision which either authorizes or prohibits the practice.

We . . . decline to rule whether cross-collateralization is appropriate in this case, or whether as a matter of law it is ever permissible.

The Second Circuit expressed criticism of cross-collateralization in *In re Texlon.* The court, however, stopped short of prohibiting the practice altogether. At issue was the bankruptcy court's ex parte financing order granting the lender a security interest in the debtor's property to secure both pre-petition and post-petition debt. The court, in an exercise of judicial restraint, concluded that:

> In order to decide this case we are not obliged, however, to say that under no conceivable circumstances could "cross-collateralization" be authorized. Here it suffices to hold that . . . a financing scheme so contrary to the spirit of the Bankruptcy Act should not have been granted by an ex parte order, where the bankruptcy court relies solely on representations by a debtor in possession that credit essential to the maintenance of operations is not otherwise obtainable.

In re Texlon, 596 F.2d at 1098. Although *In re Texlon* was decided under the earlier Bankruptcy Act, the court also considered whether cross-collateralization was authorized under the Bankruptcy Code. . . .

Cross-collateralization is not specifically mentioned in the Bankruptcy Code. We conclude that cross-collateralization is inconsistent with bankruptcy law for two reasons. First, cross-collateralization is not authorized as a method of post-petition financing under section 364. Second, cross-collateralization is beyond the scope of the bankruptcy court's inherent equitable power because it is directly contrary to the fundamental priority scheme of the Bankruptcy Code.

Section 364 authorizes Chapter 11 debtors to obtain secured credit and incur secured debt as part of their reorganization. . . . By their express terms, sections 364(c) & (d) apply only to future—i.e., post-petition—extensions of credit. They do not authorize the granting of liens to secure pre-petition loans.

. . .

Given that cross-collateralization is not authorized by section 364, we now turn to the lenders' argument that bankruptcy courts may permit the practice under their general equitable power. Bankruptcy courts are indeed courts of equity, *see, e.g., Young v. Higbee Co.*, 324 U.S. 204; 11 U.S.C. § 105(a), and they have the power to adjust claims to avoid injustice or unfairness. *Pepper v. Litton*, 308 U.S. 295 (1939). This equitable power, however, is not unlimited.

> The bankruptcy court has the ability to deviate from the rules of priority and distribution set forth in the Code in the interest of justice and equity. The Court cannot use this flexibility, however, merely to establish a ranking of priorities within priorities. Furthermore, absent the existence of some type of inequitable conduct on the part of the claimant, which results in injury to the creditors of the bankrupt or an unfair advantage to the claimant, the court cannot subordinate a claim to claims within the same class.

In re FCX, Inc., 60 Bankr. 405, 409 (E.D.N.C. 1986).

Section 507 of the Bankruptcy Code fixes the priority order of claims and expenses against the bankruptcy estate. 11 U.S.C. § 507. Creditors within a given class are to be treated equally, and bankruptcy courts may not create their own rules of superpriority within a single class. Cross-collateralization, however, does exactly that. As a result of this practice, post-petition lenders' unsecured pre-petition claims are given priority over all other unsecured pre-petition claims. The Ninth Circuit recognized that "there is no . . . applicable provision in the Bankruptcy Code authorizing the debtor to pay certain pre-petition unsecured claims in full while others remain unpaid. To do so would impermissibly violate the priority scheme of the Bankruptcy Code." *In re Sun Runner*, 945 F.2d at 1094.

The Second Circuit has noted that, if cross-collateralization were initiated by the bankrupt while insolvent and shortly before filing a petition, the arrangement "would have constituted a voidable preference." *In re Texlon*, 596 F.2d 1092, 1097 (2d Cir. 1979) (Friendly, J.). The fundamental nature of this practice is not changed by the fact that it is sanctioned by the bankruptcy court. We disagree with the district court's conclusion that, while cross-collateralization may violate some policies of bankruptcy law, it is consistent with the general purpose of Chapter 11 to help businesses reorganize and become profitable. Rehabilitation is certainly the primary purpose of Chapter 11. This end, however, does not justify the use of any means. Cross-collateralization is directly inconsistent with the priority scheme of the Bankruptcy Code. Accordingly, the practice may not be approved by the bankruptcy court under its equitable authority.

VI. CONCLUSION

Cross-collateralization is not authorized by section 364. . . . Because *Texlon*-type cross-collateralization is not explicitly authorized by the Bankruptcy Code and is contrary to the basic priority structure of the Code, we hold that it is an impermissible means of obtaining post-petition financing. The judgment of the district court is REVERSED and the case is REMANDED for proceedings not inconsistent with this opinion.

C. Roll-Ups

While cross-collateralization is now rarely approved, it may not matter because blanket liens are much more common in today's lending environment than in the early 1990s. Instead of cross-collateralization, a new device has emerged, known as the "roll-up." In a roll-up financing, the proceeds of the DIP loan are applied to pay off the pre-petition secured debt. Thus, if Cheatham & Meikoff, Inc., had a $100 million pre-petition loan from Continental Express Bank, N.A., (ConEx), and ConEx provided the DIP financing via a roll-up, it would provide a $125 million loan, rather than the $25 million loan in the cross-collateralization example above. $100 million of the loan's proceeds would be used to pay off the pre-petition debt. There would be only $25 million in new funding, in addition to $100 million of debt as before. All of the new funding would be fully secured by court-issued liens. And there would be no cross-collateralization. Instead, there would simply be a pre-plan payment that was approved by court order as a condition of the DIP loan.

The arrangement illustrated here is for a dollar-for-dollar roll-up. Some roll-ups are at lower ratios. But they all achieve arguably a more problematic result than cross-collateralization, as they not only raise the priority of the pre-petition loan, but they raise it to the highest possible level: paid in full. If the pre-petition liens in the prior example were invalid, the cross-collateralization would not have saved ConEx, as its post-petition collateral was only $50 million, which would not have covered both the DIP loan and the entire pre-petition loan. Roll-up financing removes that risk. While roll-ups are a common enough arrangement in large bankruptcy cases in the Southern District of New York and the District of Delaware, no circuit court of appeals has opined on them under the Bankruptcy Code.

In re Eastman Kodak Co.

No. 12-10202 (Bankr. S.D.N.Y.), Final Order (I) Authorizing the Debtors (A) to
Obtain Postpetition Financing . . . (Feb. 16, 2012)

12. *Refinancing of the Pre-Petition First Lien Debt.* Following the entry of this Interim Order and as part of the initial borrowing under the Financing, the Debtors shall use a portion of the proceeds from the Financing in accordance with the DIP Documents and this Interim Order to (a) refinance in full (other than the Continuing Pre-Petition First Lien Obligations) the Pre-Petition First Lien Debt then outstanding, upon which repayment, the existing liens on the Pre-Petition First Lien Collateral shall be released and terminated, and (b) deposit cash collateral, issue back-to-back letters of credit or make other arrangements satisfactory to the holders or issuers of the Non-Assumed Pre-Petition First Lien Obligations, in each case in accordance with the terms and conditions set forth in this Interim Order. The Assumed Pre-Petition First Lien Obligations shall be deemed to be issued pursuant to, and secured under, the DIP Credit Agreement or designated as "Obligations" under the DIP Credit Agreement and secured by the DIP Collateral, as the case may be.

D. Collateral Charge Waivers

The estate is normally allowed to reduce a secured lenders' claim by any amounts the estate spends to care for or maintain the creditor's collateral, including payment of property taxes and expenses in selling the collateral. 11 U.S.C. § 506(c). DIP lenders also protect the priority of their loan by having the DIP financing order waive charges against the loan under section 506(c). The trustee/DIP may recover the costs of caring for a creditor's collateral per section 506(c). The theory is that the trustee/DIP provided a benefit to the creditor that creates something like a bankruptcy law equivalent of a construction lien. In other words, a section 506(c) charge from the estate is senior to the first lien creditor's claim.

DIP financing orders routinely waive the section 506(c) charge, meaning that the cost of caring for and potentially selling the DIP lender's collateral—a benefit for the DIP lender—is borne by the estate, rather than by the DIP lender. The section 506(c) waiver effectively raises the cost of the DIP loan to the estate, but in a nontransparent manner.

E. Carve-Outs

The DIP lender's liens are usually subject to a "**carve-out**." A carve-out provides that if there is a DIP default, then the professionals of debtor (and often of committee) get paid before the DIP. In effect, it is a subordination agreement between the DIP and the debtor's professionals. The amount of the carve-out varies and is highly negotiated, but usually covers all pre-default work and a specified sum for post-default work.

Sometimes a carve-out will provide line-by-line allowances for specific professionals. What do you think the effect is for the debtor's counsel and all committee counsels to be on an allowance from the DIP lender, which might also be the senior secured pre-petition creditor? On the one hand, the carve-out functions as a ceiling of how much work the debtor's counsel and committee counsel will do—they risk going unpaid for additional work. On the other hand, it also guarantees that they will get paid up to that amount—there's a pool of money that is set aside for them and only them. Does this seem like a conflict of interest?

Carve-outs also frequently cap how much of the work may be undertaken to investigate the DIP lender(s)' pre-petition dealings with the debtor or to challenge the DIP lender's claims or liens. The DIP lender is not going to agree to fund a challenge of its own claims, including its pre-petition claims, or to fund any other subsequent DIP lender that could have priority over it. The carve-out thus functions to neuter both debtor's counsel and committee counsel, at least in regard to the DIP lender. Does this seem consistent with the system envisioned in bankruptcy? Or does the urgent need for immediate and reliable liquidity upon filing for Chapter 11 override the Code's other provisions?

There is a flip side to this question. If DIP lenders are so powerful, why would they agree to a carve-out at all? It's the price of doing business. The debtor's and committees' professionals are the groups that can make life difficult for a DIP lender. By buying them off and restraining them through the carve-out, the DIP lender assures itself that there will not be a powerful opposition group to its dominance.[3]

F. Stay Relief

Another key piece of DIP lenders' protection is the definition of events of default. Events of default typically include the appointment of a trustee or examiner, conversion from Chapter 11 to Chapter 7, loss of plan exclusivity, case dismissal, or filing of a plan that doesn't pay the DIP lender in full in cash on confirmation. In the event of a default, the DIP lender can not only cut off revolving lines of credit, but often can proceed against collateral without getting the stay lifted, as many DIP loans include waiver of stay provisions.

G. Appointment of Chief Restructuring Officer

DIP loans also provide the DIP lenders with enormous control over the bankruptcy case. The loan agreement might require the debtor to appoint a chief restructuring officer (CRO) acceptable to the lenders (with an attached schedule listing the lenders' sole acceptable CRO). The CRO is a direct report to the debtor's board, rather than to the CEO, and is effectively the lender's replacement CEO. Consider this provision from Patriot Coal Corporation's 2012 DIP financing agreement.

In re Patriot Coal Corp.

No. 12-12900 (Bankr. S.D.N.Y.), [Proposed] Interim Order (I) Authorizing Debtors (A) to Obtain
Post-Petition Financing . . . July 10, 2012, Exhibit B (Superpriority Secured
Debtor-in-Possession Credit Agreement, Dated as of July 9, 2012)

Section 6.23. *Financial Restructuring Officer and Advisor.* The Borrower shall retain a restructuring advisor reasonably acceptable to the Arrangers to provide restructuring advice and assistance during the pendency of the Cases (it being understood and agreed that AlixPartners LLP is acceptable to the Arrangers). The Borrower shall appoint a Chief Restructuring Officer satisfactory to the Arrangers (it being understood and agreed that Ted Stenger is acceptable to the Arrangers) and file a motion for such appointment as soon as is practicable after the Petition Date but in any event on or before the Final Order Entry Date. The Chief Restructuring Officer shall report to the Chairman of the board of directors of the Borrower.

The right to appoint a chief restructuring officer is a striking measure of DIP lender power. DIP lenders are creditors, but they frequently obtain the right to pick the firm's

---

3. Query whether a carve-out negotiation creates some fiduciary duty issues for a debtor's professionals. On the one hand, they are looking out for their own interests, not the debtor's per se. On the other hand, they will only work if paid, so they are acting in the debtor's interests. And they are not taking funds away from the debtor, but merely reallocating funds from the DIP lender to themselves. (This assumes that the DIP lender doesn't simply charge more to make up for the carve-out.)

managers, a quintessential right of equityholders, rather than creditors. DIP lending is not just profitable, but can result in considerable control over a firm.

H. Milestones

DIP loan agreements will frequently include provisions requiring various case "milestones" to be met by various dates. These milestones might include sales of particular assets or a percentage of assets of a certain type, or a requirement of the closing of a certain number of stores or the filing of disclosure statements and plans or plan confirmation. An asset sale milestone covenant might be used to force the sale of an asset that can be used to pay down the DIP loan. Plan confirmation milestones are meant to ensure a quick case—and quick return of the DIP lenders' funds. (If the lenders can relend in a similar interest rate environment, they will be able to get fees from the DIP loan *and* fees from a subsequent loan without sacrificing interest income.) All in all, the effect of milestones is to limit the debtor's options in terms of conducting the case, which means that the approval of the DIP financing agreement is essentially the approval of a roadmap for the case that gives the DIP lender substantial control over how the debtor will restructure.

The following excerpt from DIP financing agreement for Aéropostale, Inc. provides a sense of just how detailed milestones can be. The milestones were incorporated into the DIP financing agreement and the court order approving it as covenants to the loan.

In re Aéropostale, Inc.

No. 16-11275 (Bankr. S.D.N.Y.), Debtor-in-Possession Financing Order (June 13, 2016).

MILESTONES

. . .

(iv)

(a) No later than 60 days after the Petition Date the Borrower shall have filed the Plan of Reorganization (as defined in the DIP Credit Agreement) in form and substance reasonably satisfactory to the DIP Agent and the Required Lenders (it being understood and agreed that such Plan of Reorganization shall either repay all outstanding obligations under the DIP Facility in cash on the effective date or provide alternative treatment satisfactory to the DIP Agent and the DIP Lenders in their sole and absolute discretion) and Disclosure Statement (as defined in the DIP Credit Agreement) in form and substance satisfactory to the DIP Agent and the Required Lenders;

(b) the Court shall have entered an order approving the Disclosure Statement on or prior to 95 days after the Petition Date;

(c) the DIP Loan Parties shall have commenced solicitation on the Plan of Reorganization no later than 100 days after the Petition Date;

(d) the Court shall have commenced the hearing to consider confirmation of the Plan of Reorganization on or prior to 130 days after the Petition Date;

(e) the Court shall have entered an order confirming the Plan of Reorganization on or prior to 140 days after the Petition Date; and

(f) the Plan of Reorganization shall have been consummated on or prior to 145 days after the Petition Date.

(v) Simultaneously with the plan process outlined in clause (iv) above, the Borrower shall pursue a sale process under Section 363 of the Bankruptcy Code, in accordance with the following timeline:

(a) No later than 75 days after the Petition Date, the Borrower shall file a motion with the Court to approve bid procedures and establish the date of an auction (the "Auction") to sell all or substantially all of the assets of the Borrower and the Guarantors (the "Bid Procedures Motion"), which shall include a form of a stalking horse sale and purchase agreement ("Stalking Horse SPA"), which shall be in form and substance acceptable to the DIP Agent and the Required Lenders in their reasonable discretion;

(b) No later than 75 days after the Petition Date, the Borrower shall forward the so-called "bid packages" to any potential bidders, including, without limitation, alternative bid packages to liquidation firms;

(c) No later than 105 days after the Petition Date, the Court shall have entered an order approving the Stalking Horse SPA and Bid Procedures Motion, which shall be in form and substance acceptable to the DIP Agent and the Required Lenders in their sole and absolute discretion;

(d) No later than 141 days after the Petition Date, the Borrower shall conduct the Auction;

(e) No later than 143 days after the Petition Date, the Court shall enter an order approving the sale of the Borrower's assets to the party determined to have made the highest or otherwise best bid for all or substantially all of the assets of the Borrower and the Guarantors (the "Sale Order"), which shall be in form and substance acceptable to the DIP Agent and the Required Lenders in their sole and absolute discretion; and

(f) No later than 145 days after the Petition Date, the Borrower shall have consummated the sale to the party determined to have made the highest or otherwise best bid for all or substantially all of the assets of the Borrower and the Guarantors in accordance with the Sale Order pursuant to the Stalking Horse SPA or other sale and purchase agreement, which shall be in form and substance acceptable to the DIP Agent and the Required Lenders in their sole and absolute discretion.

It is understood and agreed that the Borrower may choose to abandon the plan process outlined in clause (iv) above at any time. The Borrower may not abandon the sale process outlined in clause (v) above without the prior written consent of the DIP Agent and Required Lenders.

I. Other Common DIP Loan Provisions

DIP loan covenants will look somewhat different from regular bond or loan covenants. Some of the covenants are bankruptcy-specific, but the most significant will usually be a minimum EBITDAR covenant, rather than leverage or interest coverage covenants. DIP loans will also often have a detailed line-item budget for the debtor, and extensive indemnity provisions for the DIP lender(s).

Some DIP loan agreements will even require that the lender pre-approve any plan or that a plan contain particular features. In short, there is such a high level of creditor control in some DIP lending agreements that they start to function as a sub rosa plan, with the debtor being little more than a puppet for the senior secured lender. In such circumstances, how much protection does the absolute priority rule provide for junior creditors? The absolute priority rule protects against gifting arrangements, but if the senior secured creditor(s) can push through a low-ball valuation, they will be able to keep the equity in the reorganized company without having to share it with anyone.

Federal Rule of Bankruptcy Procedure 4001(c) requires disclosure in summary form of certain key features of DIP financing agreements (as well as disclosure of the loan agreement itself). The disclosure of these terms seems to have had little effect on their prevalence; absent a viable financing alternative, judges and United States Trustees have little ability to push back against DIP financing agreements. When they do, they are playing "chicken" with the proposed DIP lender, which threatens to take its money and go home unless it gets its way. If a firm is not able to obtain financing while in bankruptcy, it will liquidate. Thus, a motion opposing a DIP financing is in some ways a motion to liquidate the firm. Few judges or United States Trustees want to take on that sort of gamble on the first day of a case (and recall the forum shopping problem looming in the background). To be sure, most motions in opposition to a proposed DIP financing are objecting to a particular term of the financing, not to the financing in general, but DIP lenders often adopt a "take it or leave it" posture, which makes an objection to a provision an objection to the financing in general. The typical result is that a DIP financing agreement might have a few of the most aggressive terms whittled down, but overall, DIP financing agreements tend to result in a high-return/low-risk product because of pre-petition senior lenders' ability to lock up the assets of the debtor and if challenged to threaten a priming fight on the first day or simply not to fund.

Further enhancing DIP lenders' leverage is the bankruptcy forum-shopping problem. If even a single judge in a district were to refuse to sign off on significant terms in DIP loans, what do you think would be the effect on future filings? DIP lenders would likely insist that the case be filed in another, more accommodating district. Even if judges are completely immune to the considerations of getting interesting and prestigious cases and generating business for the local bankruptcy bar, the jurisdictional arbitrage problem would still exist because the filings would simply migrate to less restrictive districts if a district cracked down too much on DIP lending agreements. All in all, we see that DIP lending is governed by the Golden Rule: He Who Has the Gold Makes the Rules.

Problem Set 20

(1) You're preparing Golden Fleece Fashionware's Chapter 11 bankruptcy filing. Golden Fleece designs, manufactures, and retails high-end couture. Each part of its operation is run through separate subsidiaries, each of which in turn has its own subsidiaries. In particular, each retail outlet is run by a separate subsidiary of the retail subsidiary, and the manufacturing is done through separate subsidiaries in each country in which Golden Fleece produces its wares: Bangladesh, China, Mexico, Vietnam, and the United States. Golden Fleece operates a centralized corporate treasury in the United States, sweeping all cash from the subsidiaries into the corporate treasury's account for overnight investment before distributing it daily for operational needs. You anticipate needing to file petitions for most, if not all, of the Golden Fleece subsidiaries. What do you need to do to make sure that Golden Fleece can be open for business without any interruption the day after the filing?

(2) Jason Chemicals and its 200 subsidiaries recently filed for Chapter 11 bankruptcy. Jason owes $50 million to a syndicate led by Medea Commercial Capital. The loan is guaranteed by all of the subsidiaries and is secured by a first lien security interest in Jason's inventory, which is currently worth perhaps $80 million. Jason has $15 million in its bank accounts, including $7 million that recently came in from a post-petition sale.

   a. Jason wishes to make its monthly $10 million purchase of various materials from several suppliers. Does Jason need court approval of this transaction? 11 U.S.C. §§ 363(a), (c), (e); 552; UCC § 9-315.

   b. On the first day of its bankruptcy, Jason Chemicals, as debtor-in-possession, moved for approval of a $250 million post-petition financing agreement with a syndicate led by Glauce National Bank. The financing agreement would give Glauce a section 364(c)(1) priority claim and a first priority lien over all of Jason's assets as well as the assets of Jason's subsidiaries, which would guarantee the loan. Jason argued in its motion that the fresh cash from Glauce is essential for Jason to be able to continue operations, to undertake needed operational reforms, and to signal its viability to vendors. What must Jason show to get this loan approved? 11 U.S.C. §§ 364(c)-(d).

(3) The very day Minos Casinos ("Home of the Golden Touch") filed for Chapter 11 bankruptcy it moved for authorization of a $450 million DIP financing agreement with a syndicate led by its pre-petition senior lender Daedalus Bank & Trust Co. The proposed DIP agreement would require Minos to sell all of its Atlantic City and Mississippi riverboat casinos within 90 days, leaving Minos with its Las Vegas and Reno properties. The proposed DIP agreement also gives the DIP lenders a first priority replacement lien on all of Minos's assets, including all recoveries from avoidance actions; waives all section 506(c) charges; and waives any claims that Minos might have against Daedalus and other members of its syndicate. The DIP agreement also has a carve-out of $15

million for the expenses of the Official Creditors Committee, but the carve-out may not be applied to litigation against Daedalus and its syndicate.

    a. You represent the Service Employees International Union Local 703, which represents many of the workers at Minos's Atlantic City casinos. You are very concerned that a quickie sale will result in the purchase of the casinos by the Minotaur Group, which is led by celebrity playboy and real estate developer David Dennison, who has been very hostile to organized labor at his casinos. You're confident that the Atlantic City casinos can be run profitably by Minos, if Minos could simply reduce its cost of debt service. How might you try to prevent the sale of Minos's Atlantic City casinos?

    b. The bankruptcy court was not receptive to your objections to the DIP financing agreement in parts (a) and (b) of this question, but you think you've got a decent chance on these issues on appeal to the district court or the circuit court of appeals. Will an appeal help you? 11 U.S.C. § 364(e).

    c. Minos agreed to certain concessions regarding the sale procedures for the Atlantic City casinos to settle the SEIU's objection to the DIP financing agreement, namely that the sale will be subject to the buyer's assumption of the SEIU's collective bargaining agreement. With the SEIU's objection out of the way, explain which of the following parties is likely to object to the DIP financing agreement. _Yes._

      i. Minos's management? _Yes._
      ii. Minos's shareholders?
      iii. Minos's pre-petition second lien lender? _Yes._
      iv. Minos's other individual unsecured creditors (basically vendors)?
      v. The Official Committee of Unsecured Creditors?
      vi. The United States Trustee?
      vii. The bankruptcy judge?

(4) U.S. Representative Rachel Jackson is chairing the House Judiciary Committee's Subcommittee on Administrative Law and the Courts. Jackson is concerned that Chapter 11 bankruptcies are too frequently resulting in asset sales and de facto liquidations rather than reorganizations. She has reached out to you for insight.

    a. Rep. Jackson wants to know if you think DIP lending agreements might be contributing to the asset sale phenomenon. Would a DIP lender have any reason to favor a quick asset sale over a reorganization?

    b. Rep. Jackson wants your evaluation of a proposal to introduce greater competition into the DIP lending market by requiring the right to make a DIP loan be auctioned off. What would be necessary to make a DIP loan auction market work? What obstacles do you foresee?

CHAPTER *21*

USE AND SALE OF ESTATE PROPERTY

I. USE, SALE, AND LEASE OF ESTATE PROPERTY

The Bankruptcy Code permits the use, sale, or lease of property of the estate in both Chapter 7 and Chapter 11 bankruptcies. Section 363(c) permits the use, sale, or lease of the property of the estate in the ordinary course of business without any notice or hearing, excluding the sale of property that constitutes "cash collateral." If the use, sale, or lease of property is not in the ordinary course of business, the transaction requires court approval following notice and a hearing. 11 U.S.C. § 363(b). Exactly what is ordinary course of business is not always apparent, as the following case illustrates.

II. WHAT IS AN ORDINARY COURSE TRANSACTION?

In re Roth American, Inc.
975 F.2d 949 (3d Cir. 1992)

SLOVITER, Chief Judge.

Before us is an appeal by the International Brotherhood of Teamsters Local 401 (the Union) from a district court order that affirmed a bankruptcy court order . . . rejecting the Union's claim for unearned wages for breach of a post-petition agreement to maintain operations for two years. . . .

I. FACTS AND PROCEDURAL HISTORY

Roth American, Inc., was a manufacturer of toys and gym sets in Wilkes-Barre, Pennsylvania, employing over 200 persons who were represented by Teamsters Local 401. In 1985, the company and the Union entered into a collective bargaining agreement* covering the period from November 1, 1985 until June 30, 1988.

---

* A collective bargaining agreement is a group contract negotiated by a union for the members of the union.—ED.

On February 2, 1988, Roth American filed a voluntary petition for reorganization under Chapter 11 of the Bankruptcy Code. In the meantime, Roth American had negotiated with the Union to obtain a modification of the collective bargaining agreement that was embodied in a separate memorandum of agreement. The 1988 memorandum of agreement, which became effective on February 4, 1988,[1] extended the existing collective bargaining agreement until January 1, 1989 and provided for a reduction in wages of seventy cents per hour across the board. Of particular importance to this appeal, it also provided:

> The Employer will maintain the operations covered by the current Collective Bargaining Agreement in the Wilkes-Barre area for a minimum of two (2) years, commencing upon the effective date of this Memorandum of Agreement. This commitment also includes the representation that equipment necessary to the operations of those facilities will not be moved from the Wilkes-Barre area.

Neither party sought approval of the new agreement from the bankruptcy court, nor was there any hearing before the bankruptcy court at which creditors could object to the new agreement.

Despite the seventy-cent wage concession provided in the 1988 memorandum agreement, the employer only paid the lower wage for a two-week period. It resumed paying the preexisting higher wage when it could no longer provide the health insurance coverage mandated by the memorandum agreement.

Roth American continued its operations for several months following the bankruptcy petition. In April 1988, the company entered into a contract, approved by the bankruptcy court, whereby the Michael Fox Company would solicit bids for the company initially in its entirety and, if that were unsuccessful, in its various parts. On June 5, 1988, Roth American ceased all manufacturing activity and laid off all its employees. On August 17, 1988, the bankruptcy court approved, over the Union's objection, the piecemeal sale of Roth American pursuant to the best bids that were received.

The Union filed [a proof] of claim in the bankruptcy proceeding on behalf of the Roth American employees it represented. One claim sought damages of approximately $6.5 million in future wages and benefits for breach of the provision in the February 1988 memorandum agreement to maintain operations in Wilkes-Barre for at least two years.

The bankruptcy court granted the Union's claim for damages for breach of contract only to the extent of the reduction in wages the employees were paid during the two-week period following the new agreement. The bankruptcy court reasoned that because the 1988 memorandum agreement "was not accepted or rejected under the terms of the United States Bankruptcy Code," it was not "a valid post-petition Collective Bargaining Agreement."

. . .

[On appeal the] district court agreed with the bankruptcy court that the 1988 memorandum agreement was not valid. . . .

---

1. The union concedes that the 1988 memorandum agreement did not become effective until after Roth American filed its bankruptcy petition.

On this appeal, the Union argues that the 1988 memorandum agreement was a transaction in the "ordinary course of business" within the meaning of 11 U.S.C. § 363(c) and that therefore a hearing before the bankruptcy court was not required for the agreement to be fully enforceable. . . .

II. DISCUSSION

A. Union's Claim for Breach of 1988 Memorandum Agreement

The validity of the Union's claim for breach of the 1988 memorandum agreement turns on whether notice to creditors and a hearing before the bankruptcy court was required for the 1988 memorandum agreement to be enforceable. Only if the agreement is enforceable, would we need to answer the extent to which the Union is entitled to damages for its breach.

Section 363(c)(1) of the Bankruptcy Code provides:

> If the business of the debtor is authorized to be operated under section . . . 1108 . . . of this title and unless the court orders otherwise, the trustee may enter into transactions . . . *in the ordinary course of business*, without notice or a hearing, and may use property of the estate in the ordinary course of business without notice or a hearing.

11 U.S.C. § 363(c)(1) (1988) (emphasis added). In contrast, a notice and hearing are required before the trustee (or debtor-in-possession) may use property of the estate other than in the ordinary course of business. 11 U.S.C. § 363(b)(1).[3]

The framework of section 363 is designed to allow a trustee (or debtor-in-possession) the flexibility to engage in ordinary transactions without unnecessary creditor and bankruptcy court oversight, while protecting creditors by giving them an opportunity to be heard when transactions are not ordinary. *See United States ex rel. Harrison v. Estate of Deutscher (In re H & S Transp. Co.)*, 115 Bankr. 592, 599 (M.D. Tenn. 1990) ("Section 363 is designed to strike [a] balance, allowing a business to continue its daily operations without excessive court or creditor oversight and protecting secured creditors and others from dissipation of the estate's assets."). Creditors are not given the right to notice and a hearing when transactions are in the ordinary course of business "because their objections to such transactions are likely to relate to the bankrupt's chapter 11 status, not the particular transactions themselves." *In re James A. Phillips, Inc.*, 29 Bankr. 391, 394 (S.D.N.Y. 1983).

Neither the Bankruptcy Code nor its legislative history provides a framework for analyzing whether particular transactions are in the ordinary course of a debtor's business for the purpose of section 363. In prior cases, the courts have engaged in a two-step inquiry for determining whether a transaction is in "the ordinary course of business": a "horizontal dimension" test and a "vertical dimension" test. See Benjamin Weintraub & Alan N. Resnick, *The Meaning of "Ordinary Course of Business" Under the Bankruptcy*

---

3. In the event that a transaction is undertaken that is not in the ordinary course of business without notice and a hearing, it may be avoided in bankruptcy. *See* 11 U.S.C. § 549(a)(2)(B).

Code—Vertical and Horizontal Analysis, 19 UCC L.J. 364 (1987) [hereinafter Weintraub & Resnick].[4]

The inquiry deemed horizontal is whether, from an industry-wide perspective, the transaction is of the sort commonly undertaken by companies in that industry. *Id.* at 367. For example, "raising a crop would not be in the ordinary course of business for a widget manufacturer because that is not a widget manufacturer's ordinary business." *In re Waterfront Cos.*, 56 Bankr. 31, 35 (Bankr. D. Minn. 1985).

The inquiry deemed vertical (more appropriately characterized as the creditor's expectation test) analyzes the transactions "from the vantage point of a hypothetical creditor and [the inquiry is] whether the transaction subjects a creditor to economic risk of a nature different from those he accepted when he decided to extend credit." Weintraub & Resnick, 19 UCC L.J. at 365. Under this test, "the touchstone of 'ordinariness' is . . . the interested parties' reasonable expectations of what transactions the debtor in possession is likely to enter in the course of its business." James A. Phillips, 29 Bankr. at 394. The primary focus thus is on the debtor's pre-petition business practices and conduct, although a court must also "consider the changing circumstances inherent in the hypothetical creditor's expectations." Weintraub & Resnick, 19 UCC L.J. at 366.

In this case, satisfaction of the horizontal test is readily apparent—many manufacturing companies have routinely entered into extensions of collective bargaining agreements in order to secure the continued benefits of a unionized workforce. Accordingly, several courts have ruled that post-petition collective bargaining agreements were in the ordinary course of business. *See In re DeLuca Distributing Co.*, 38 Bankr. 588, 594 (Bankr. N.D. Ohio 1984) (new collective bargaining agreement in ordinary course of business because employees were covered by agreement prior to bankruptcy); *see also In re Illinois-California Express, Inc.*, 72 Bankr. 987, 991 (D. Colo. 1987) (post-petition renegotiation of labor agreement without prior court approval was valid because it was transaction in the ordinary course of business); *In re IML Freight, Inc.*, 37 Bankr. 556, 559 (Bankr. D. Utah 1984) (decision to enter into a post-petition collective bargaining agreement falls within debtor-in-possession's discretion to make decisions in the ordinary course of business). The National Labor Relations Board** has also noted that a debtor may enter into valid collective bargaining agreements in the ordinary course of business. *See Sealift Maritime, Inc.*, 265 N.L.R.B. 1219 (1982) (petition of rival union seeking to represent employees of Chapter 11 debtor denied because modification and extension of preexisting collective bargaining agreement with different union was valid without bankruptcy court approval as transaction in the ordinary course of business).

---

4. This framework has been routinely applied by many courts. *See, e.g., In re Dant & Russell, Inc.*, 853 F.2d 700, 704-06 (9th Cir. 1988) (applying vertical and horizontal framework to conclude debtor-in-possession's post-petition execution of leases was in ordinary course of business); *Habinger, Inc. v. Metro. Cosmetic & Reconstructive Surgical Clinic*, 124 Bankr. 784, 786 (D. Minn. 1990) (applying framework to debtor's post-petition payments for furniture and equipment); *United States ex rel. Harrison*, 115 Bankr. at 598-99 (applying framework to conclude trustee's use of funds to repair boats, institute maintenance program, and reinstate insurance was in ordinary course of business); *In re Glosser Bros.*, 124 Bankr. 664, 667-68 (Bankr. W.D. Pa. 1991) (applying framework to execution of licensing agreement to operate department in debtor's stores).

** The NLRB is the independent federal government administrative agency charged with supervising the negotiation and enforcement of collective bargaining agreements.—ED.

The particular provisions of post-petition collective bargaining agreements must also be examined with reference to the reasonable expectations of creditors. Roth American argues that even if post-petition collective bargaining agreements may be "ordinary course of business" transactions, the nature of the particular agreement here was extraordinary inasmuch as it purported to bind the debtor to maintain its existing operations in the Wilkes-Barre area for two years.

We find Roth American's argument persuasive. The 1988 memorandum agreement is fundamentally different from the previous collective bargaining agreements entered into between Roth American and the Teamsters insofar as it contains the provision purporting to bind Roth American to maintain its operations. As has been stated by the Supreme Court:

> Collective bargaining between employer and the representatives of a unit . . . results in an accord as to terms which will govern hiring and work and pay in that unit. The result is not, however, a contract of employment except in rare cases; no one has a job by reason of it and *no obligation to any individual ordinarily comes into existence from it alone.*

J.I. Case Co. v. NLRB, 321 U.S. 332, 334-35 (1944) (emphasis added); *see also In re Continental Airlines Corp.*, 901 F.2d 1259, 1264 (5th Cir. 1990) ("ordinarily a collective bargaining agreement . . . neither obligates any employee to perform work *nor requires the employer to provide work*") (emphasis added).

In contrast, the 1988 memorandum agreement here sought to bind the hands of a Chapter 11 debtor to maintain its then existing operations for two years in the Wilkes-Barre area. Thus, while "changes between prepetition and postpetition business activity alone are not per se evidence of extraordinariness," *In re Johns-Manville Corp.*, 60 Bankr. at 612, 617 (Bankr. S.D.N.Y. 1986), we conclude that the nature of the agreement here ventures beyond the domain of transactions that a hypothetical creditor would reasonably expect to be undertaken in the circumstances. *See In re Century Brass Prods.*, 107 Bankr. 8 (Bankr. D. Conn. 1989) (large post-petition severance pay agreements entered into between debtor and debtor's officer not in ordinary course of business because no comparable severance pay agreement had ever been entered into between the debtor and its officers in past); *cf. In re Waterfront Cos.*, 56 Bankr. at 35 ("Some transactions either by their size, nature or both are not within the day-to-day operations of a business and are therefore extraordinary."). Accordingly, we hold that the 1988 memorandum agreement was not a transaction in the ordinary course of business. It follows that the district court did not err in holding that notice and a hearing in the bankruptcy court on that agreement was required for it to be enforceable.[5]

III. CONCLUSION

We have concluded that the 1988 memorandum agreement entered into between Roth American and the Teamsters was not a transaction in the ordinary course of

---

5. In light of our disposition, we need not reach the alternative argument raised by Roth American that the 1988 memorandum agreement does not constitute a guarantee of employment and therefore cannot give rise to a claim for future wages.

business within the meaning of section 363(c). Therefore, the Union's claim for breach of contract could be granted only for the two week period in which the wages paid to the employees were below the amount required by the 1985 collective bargaining agreement. . . . Therefore, we will affirm the order of the district court affirming the judgment of the bankruptcy court.

Study Questions

1. Why wasn't section 363(m) invoked to uphold the 1988 memorandum agreement? Section 363(m) provides that the reversal on appeal of the authorization of a sale or lease of property of the estate under section 363 "does not affect the validity of a sale or lease to an entity that purchased or leased such property in good faith. . . ."

2. Did Roth American and the union know the memorandum agreement was not in the ordinary course of business? Consider the dates of the bankruptcy filing and the effective date of the collective bargaining agreement. Does this put good faith in question?

3. Which test did the court adopt, "vertical" or "horizontal"? Does the court rule on both?

4. If the memorandum agreement were to be upheld, what constraints would that place on Roth American's ability to liquidate? To reorganize? Would the agreement function like a plan?

III. SALE PROCEDURES

Section 363 and the Federal Rules of Bankruptcy Procedure contain provisions governing how sales are to be conducted. First, section 363(d) provides that the sale must be in accordance with applicable non-bankruptcy law. Thus, to the extent that any non-bankruptcy law would apply to the sale, it might also apply in bankruptcy. For example, some states have laws regulating going-out-of-business (GOB) sales, which could potentially affect sales of substantially all assets of a firm. Likewise, regulatory requirements might apply to certain sales. Thus, a federal prohibition on the sale of certain technologies to hostile countries would apply to a section 363 sale. Similarly, Clayton Act antitrust notices must be filed if normally required. 11 U.S.C. § 363(b)(2).

Second, section 363(e) requires the estate to provide adequate protection of any interest in the property that is being sold. Section 363(p) puts the burden of proving the interest on the party asserting the interest, but the burden of proof on adequate protection is on the trustee or DIP.

Third, if the assets sold would violate a disclosed company policy regarding personally identifiable information about consumers, the sale must either be consistent with the policy or a consumer privacy ombudsman must be appointed to advocate for appropriate privacy protections. 11 U.S.C. § 363(b)(1). For companies with privacy policies stating that information will not be shared with unaffiliated third parties, this provision can be an issue if assets such as customer lists or databases are sold.

Fourth, Federal Rule of Bankruptcy Procedure 6004(a) requires sales to be undertaken in accordance with Federal Rule of Bankruptcy Procedure 2002(a)(2), which in turn requires 21-days' notice before the court may grant the motion, although the timeframe may be reduced for cause.

Finally, sections 363(m) and 363(n) address the finality of bankruptcy sales. Section 363(m) provides that once a sale has closed—meaning the assets have been transferred in exchange for the purchase price—the sale cannot be reversed on appeal in most circumstances. Thus, if a sale is not stayed, an appeal will likely be moot. The one exception to this is section 363(n), which allows the avoidance of sales with collusive bids (known as "kippers"). Federal Rule of Bankruptcy Procedure 6004(h) requires a 14-day stay of effectiveness of the sale after approval, but that stay may be shortened for cause.

Section 363 is perhaps most notable for what it does not say in regard to sales procedures. It provides no guidance regarding the standard for approving a transaction or for the procedures for conducting sales or leases. In this regard, it is similar to UCC Article 9's requirement that a foreclosure sale need only be "commercially reasonable," but it is a sharp contrast to state real estate foreclosure law, where sales procedures are often prescribed (and litigated) in minute detail regarding how sales are to be advertised, how bidding is to work, when sales are to be conducted, and how payment is to occur.

The *Philadelphia Newspapers* case provides a glimpse of common sale procedures that the court must approve for section 363(b) transactions. Bear in mind, however, that because of the lack of requirements in section 363, sales procedures can be highly customized, including limitations on who can bid, the form of bids, etc. The customization can come both from the terms approved by the court in the particular case or, in some cases, from local court rules that apply to all cases.

In re Philadelphia Newspapers, LLC

2009 Bankr. Lexis 3167 (Bankr. E.D. Pa. 2009)

Stephen Raslavich, Chief U.S. Bankr. J.

[Philadelphia Newspapers was the holding company for the Philadelphia Inquirer and other newspapers. It filed for Chapter 11 bankruptcy in 2009, and proposed a plan of reorganization that included a sale of substantially all the debtors' assets.]

Before the Court is the above Debtors' Motion for an Order: (A) Approving Procedures for the Sale of Certain of the Debtors' Assets; (B) Scheduling an Auction; (C) Approving Assumption and Assignment Procedures; (D) Approving Form of Notice; and (E) Granting Related Relief (hereinafter referred to as the "Bid Procedures Motion" or "the Motion"). The Bid Procedures Motion is opposed to one degree or another by the Office of the United States Trustee (UST) and every represented creditor constituency in these jointly administered cases. In addition to the UST, opponents include

1) the Official Committee of Unsecured Creditors (the "Committee"), 2) the Steering Group of Prepetition Secured Lenders and Citizens Bank of Pennsylvania as Agent for the Prepetition Secured Lenders (collectively "the Lenders"), and 3) certain Plaintiffs in prepetition tort suits against the Debtors ("the Plaintiffs"). Those opposed to the relief sought by the Debtors are sometimes hereinafter collectively referred to as "the Objectors."

Via the Bid Procedures Motion the Debtors seek Court approval of procedures to govern a public auction sale of substantially all of the Debtors' businesses and assets. To this end the Debtors have entered into an Asset Purchase Agreement dated August 20, 2009, with an entity known as Philly Papers, LLC, a Delaware Limited Liability Company ("The Stalking Horse Bidder").

The Debtors also filed a Disclosure Statement and Plan of Reorganization on August 20, 2009 (collectively "the Plan"). The Plan contemplates that the purchase offer of the Stalking Horse Bidder will be marketed and made subject to higher and better offers in accordance with the bid procedures for which approval is presently sought. Subsequent to an auction the Plan contemplates consummation of the transaction with the party determined to have submitted the highest and best bid. . . .

The bid procedures have been extensively negotiated, along with many other issues in these cases. [These parties cannot agree, however, about] the entitlement of the Stalking Horse Bidder to be reimbursed its expenses (up to $500,000) and to receive a $1 million "break-up" fee if it is not determined to be the winning bidder after the auction.

. . . [T]he Court finds the Debtors' position . . . to be unsustainable. Accordingly, [the break-up fee provision will not be] approved as part of the bid procedures. . . .

. . . The Bid Procedures could easily dictate the outcome of the case. It is clear, moreover, that there is an "insider" relationship between the Debtors and the Stalking Horse Bidder. The Stalking Horse Agreement of Sale was signed on August 20, 2009 by Brian Tierney, the Debtors' CEO, on behalf of the Debtors, and by Bruce Toll, as Chairman of the Stalking Horse Bidder. Mr. Toll is also Chairman of Philadelphia Media Holding, LLC ("PMH"). PMH is the holding company which owns or controls the various Debtor entities. Until just recently, Mr. Toll held 20% of the equity in PMH. The Carpenters Pension Fund, which is another entity having a significant ownership interest in PMH, also holds an ownership interest in the Stalking Horse Bidder. The foregoing facts unquestionably render the proposed sale to the Stalking Horse Bidder an insider transaction. As such, it warrants close scrutiny. . . .

As noted, the Bid Procedures Motion seeks authority 1) to reimburse the Stalking Horse Bidder its out-of-pocket expenses up to a limit of $500,000, and 2) pay a $1 million fee to the Stalking Horse Bidder, in the event it is not the successful bidder at the auction (collectively, the "Break-Up Fee").

The Debtors' rationale is that:

> [t]he Stalking Horse Bid for the Debtors' assets provides considerable value to these estates because it guarantees a floor price for the Debtors' assets that will enable the Debtors to provide some recovery to unsecured creditors and affords the Debtors sufficient time to test its floor bid in a competitive bid process.

The Objectors oppose this request on various grounds, these include the insider nature of the relationship between the Debtors and the Stalking Horse Bidder, and the allegedly false premises 1) that guarantee of the Break-Up Fee was necessary to induce the Stalking Horse Bidder to tender an "opening bid," and 2) that the Stalking Horse Bid is necessary to induce competitive bidding.

The Debtors dismiss all objections to the proposed Break-Up Fee as baseless, but clearly they are not, and under applicable controlling authority the Break-Up Fee cannot be approved.

All parties agree that controlling authority on the allowance of break-up fees is found in the Court of Appeals decision in *Calpine Corp. v. O'Brien Environmental Energy, Inc. (In re O'Brien Environmental Energy, Inc.)*, 181 F.3d 527 (3d Cir. 1999).

In determining the permissibility of a break-up fee, the Third Circuit has held that the party requesting the break-up fee must show that the fees were actually necessary to preserve the value of the estate. In this respect the Circuit Court elaborated that such value might be found to exist if 1) the guarantee of a break-up fee led to more competitive bidding, 2) the bid of the bidder served as a "catalyst" to higher bids and 3) the promise of a break-up fee enticed a bidder to conduct diligence on the Debtor's value and then proceeded to convert that value to a dollar amount on which other bidders could rely.

Of significance, the *O'Brien* Court held that a request for a break-up fee should not be treated any differently than any other request for the allowance of administrative expense claims under 11 U.S.C. § 503(b). As such, the Court held that the "business judgment rule" discussed, *supra*, should not be applied in this context.

On a similar note, and of equal significance, the Objectors all emphasize case law which takes the matter further by stressing that transactions involving insiders should be subjected to a heightened level of scrutiny.

Measured against the foregoing standards, it is clear that the requested break-up fee cannot be justified.

In the first place, it bears reiterating that this is manifestly an insider transaction. Even the Debtors concede that fact. As a consequence, the proposed break-up fee must be carefully scrutinized.

As the Lenders point out, there is a well-established record in this case of the existing equity holders attempting to retain control of the Debtors. Indeed, despite maintaining that they are extensively marketing their assets to potential bidders throughout the country, the Debtors have made no secret whatsoever of their preference for the success of the Stalking Horse Bidder and the perpetuation of "local ownership" of the Debtors. It simply is not credible against this backdrop to contend that the Stalking Horse Bidder required a financial inducement to submit its opening bid.

Further, it is likewise not credible to maintain that the Stalking Horse Bid was necessary to serve as a catalyst for other bids. The Lenders have been contesting the Debtors' retention of exclusivity for months specifically so that they could submit their own liquidating plan of reorganization. At present they have made abundantly clear their desire to submit a competing (albeit credit) bid for the Debtors' assets. Moreover, even where subsequent bids higher than the Stalking Horse Bid are received, the *O'Brien* Court has specifically held that the mere showing that subsequent bids were higher than the Stalking Horse Bid is not sufficient to prove that the Stalking Horse Bid was a catalyst for higher bids.

Finally, it once again cannot credibly be argued that the Break-Up Fee is warranted to compensate the Stalking Horse Bidder for the time and expense it has invested in formulating and submitting its bid. As all of the Objectors emphasize, the Stalking Horse Bidder is comprised of insider individuals and entities which have had "free" and unfettered access to all information concerning the Debtors, financial and otherwise, since the inception of these Chapter 11 cases and long before that. Such pre-existing knowledge wholly undercuts any claimed entitlement predicated on expensive due diligence and arms length negotiation.

In sum, it makes no difference that break-up fees are still sometimes allowed, or that if this particular break-up fee were to be allowed it would fall within a range not otherwise out of line with fees allowed for transactions of a similar size. Nor is it controlling that the Stalking Horse Bidder has asserted that it was unwilling to go forward without a guarantee of the instant Break-Up Fee. The bar for allowance of a break-up fee has been raised considerably in the wake of the *O'Brien* decision. The Debtors have not met criteria which it is their burden to do. The Bid Procedures Motion in this respect will therefore be denied.

Study Questions and Notes

1. What's a stalking horse bidder? Why would a company want one? Why would someone agree to be a stalking horse?

2. What's a break-up fee? Is it possible to have a stalking horse without one?

3. In addition to break-up fees, another common fee is a "topping fee," which requires the stalking horse to be paid a percentage of the amount by which a third party tops its bid (the "overbid"). Thus, if an overbid was $1 million and the topping fee was 20%, the estate would have to pay $200,000 to the stalking horse.

4. Most sales will have "overbid procedures" that determine what is considered a "qualified bid." Note that a qualified bid is distinct from a qualified bidder. Such overbid procedures often include minimum bidding increments (usually including any break-up fee or expense reimbursement for the stalking horse), provision of financial statements showing the bidder's ability to pay; provision of adequate assurances of future performance of any contracts/leases sold, cash deposits, confidentiality agreements relating to due diligence, requiring bids to conform to the stalking horse's asset purchase agreement; and prohibitions on contingencies or conditions on the bid.

5. Some stalking horse agreements will have a "window-shop" clause in which the estate undertakes not to solicit offers other than the stalking horse's bid, but to consider unsolicited offers.

IV. PRIVACY PROTECTIONS IN SALES

Businesses often possess personally identifiable information about their customers. Sometimes, this information can be quite sensitive from a consumer privacy standpoint, because it reveals information about the customers' identity, transaction habits, interests, or even medical conditions. For example, a pharmacy will have records of its customers' prescriptions. These records might indicate whether consumers are sexually active, whether they have a sexually transmitted disease, or whether they are suffering from depression, all of which may be private matters to the consumer. Such sensitive personal information is hardly limited to medical records. It can extend to all sorts of purchases, and even to informational inquiries. It can even extend to concerns over control of payment card and bank account information. The fact that a consumer has chosen to share personally identifiable information with the debtor does not necessarily mean that the consumer has consented to a broader disclosure of that information such as might occur if the information were sold in a bankruptcy.

The Bankruptcy Code recognizes the consumer privacy concerns involved in sales of estate property and has some protections for consumers. The Code provides that if the debtor has disclosed a privacy policy that prohibits the transfer of personally identifiable information to unaffiliated parties and that policy is still in effect when the case commences, then the court may not approve the sale or lease of such personally identifiable information by the debtor except in two circumstances. 11 U.S.C. § 363(b)(1). The first circumstance under which the sale may be approved is if the debtor complies with its own privacy policy.

The second circumstance in which a sale or lease may be approved if it does not comply with the debtor's privacy policy is after a hearing under 363(b)(1). At least seven days before the hearing, the court must appoint a disinterested person as a "consumer privacy ombudsman" under section 332. The consumer privacy ombudsman has a right to be heard at the hearing, and functions somewhat like a special master, advising the court on the "facts, circumstances, and conditions of the proposed sale or lease of personally identifiable information," including what the privacy policy actually is, the costs and benefits to consumers and their privacy from the proposed transaction, and ways to mitigate the costs. 11 U.S.C. § 332. Following the hearing, the court may approve a sale or lease of personally identifiable information only upon the finding that "no showing was made that such sale or lease would not violate applicable nonbankruptcy law," and that there is appropriate consideration of the facts, circumstances, and conditions of the sale.

There is little caselaw explicating section 363(b)(1)'s privacy provisions. The statute's drafting raises several questions. First, exactly what is meant by "applicable nonbankruptcy law"? Presumably, it excludes private contracts and only covers public law. But what public law? Only statutes specifically addressing privacy policies? Or how about general state and federal unfair and deceptive acts and practices (UDAP) statutes, like section 5 of the Federal Trade Commission Act, 15 U.S.C. § 45? Second, what is the relationship between section 363(b)(1)(A) and 363(b)(1)(B)? For example, what if nonbankruptcy law requires compliance with the privacy policy? In that case, isn't compliance with the policy the only way to sell the assets, making section 363(b)(1)(B) a nullity? Or is the importance of section 363(b)(1)(B) that it extends beyond section 363(b)(1)(A), because section 363(b)(1)(A) requires compliance with a privacy policy only if it is in effect at the commencement of the case? An applicable nonbankruptcy law could require compliance with a policy that is not currently in effect, but was when the information was given to the debtor. Third, what is the purpose of the "due consideration" of the "facts, circumstances, and conditions" of the sale? What exactly has to be considered? What does the court have to find? Finally, what is meant by a finding that "no showing was made" that the sale would not violate applicable law? A "showing" usually refers to a finding of fact, rather than a conclusion of law, but this is a legal question. Is the "showing" here a colorable allegation, or is it something else? The standard of proof is not clear.

Still we may summarize the rules regarding a sale or lease of personally identifiable information as follows. The sale or lease may be approved if:

(1) the debtor does not have a privacy policy in effect at the commencement of the case;

(2) if the sale or lease complies with the debtor's privacy policy; or

(3) if the sale or lease does not comply the debtor's privacy policy, but an ombudsman is appointed, the sale does not violate public law, and the court finds, following a hearing, that the facts, circumstances, and conditions of the sale are appropriate.

Beyond the protections for consumer privacy in transactions under section 363, another Code provision, section 351, provides for the disposal of patient records from debtor health care firms (defined in 11 U.S.C. § 101(27A)) if the debtor does not have sufficient funds to store the records in the manner required by law. Thus, if a hospital, clinic, nursing home, or dental practice were to go out of business, it would have to continue caring appropriately for patient records or dispose of them under section 351. (The Code also has a provision for appointment of a patient care ombudsman, 11 U.S.C. § 333, but that is not particularly a privacy issue.)

V. CREDIT BIDDING

Generally, secured creditors have a right to credit bid if their collateral is sold under section 363. This right is important because it means that a secured creditor can bid on its collateral without having to raise cash (as it would just be paying itself if it were to win the auction). For certain types of creditors, this freedom from a liquidity constraint is key to enabling bidding. At the same time, however, the ability to credit bid is key for secured creditors to be able to use the bankruptcy process to capture value: A secured creditor's ability to credit bid may chill bidding from outside parties and make it easier for the secured creditor to obtain the debtor's assets through the section 363 process, which it might control if it is the DIP lender.

The term "credit bid" is never used in the Bankruptcy Code. Instead, section 363(k) provides for a right of setoff for the holder of an allowed secured claim when the property that secured such claim is sold under section 363(b). The distinction is important, but often overlooked. Section 363(k) is not preserving the state law right to credit bid. It is a distinct federal right.

The right to credit bid at a state law foreclosure sale is an equitable practice, not ensconced in statute in most jurisdictions. At state law, a secured creditor can credit bid the entire debt that is owed to it, not just the value of the collateral. Thus, an undersecured creditor can credit bid the full debt, not just the secured portion of the debt. The reasoning for the state law right to credit bid is straightforward: The sale is solely of the secured creditor's collateral, and if the secured creditor were to win the sale, the secured creditor would just be paying itself. Therefore, there's no reason to require the secured creditor to go through the hassle of paying out actual cash to itself, when it can all be done notionally.

The bankruptcy situation is different. A 363 sale might be of a single item of collateral, like a state law foreclosure sale. But it might also be a sale of multiple assets, only some of which are subject to a secured creditor's lien. How much should a secured creditor be allowed to credit in such a situation? Should the bid be for the full amount of the debt or limited to the value of the collateral?

The language of section 363(k) would indicate that the bid should be limited to the secured claim, not to the amount of the debt. Section 363(k) refers to a sale "of property that is subject to a lien that secures an allowed claim" and says that the holder of the claim "may offset such claim against the purchase price of such property." That reference is to a lien that "secures an allowed claim," which would seem to refer to a secured claim, not to the debt.

Moreover, if the secured creditor is undersecured and is allowed to credit bid the full amount of the debt, it is effectively being given a lien on more than its collateral and getting an unfair advantage over cash bidders. It would seem that the secured creditor's credit bid would have to be capped at the amount of its secured claim, not the total amount of the debt. To do so, however, requires a judicial valuation of the claim prior to the sale.[1]

The results of allowing the credit bid to be for the full amount of the debt get even more absurd when there are multiple secured creditors, as Professor Edward Janger has explained:

> [I]magine a debtor that owns three adjoining pieces of real estate, purchased with the intention to join them together to build a large shopping mall. Each plot of land was purchased separately with a distinct lender and a separate mortgage. Further, imagine that the values are as follows. Parcel A would sell at foreclosure for $25,000 as a stand-alone piece of property. It is encumbered by a mortgage debt of $200,000. Parcel B would similarly sell for $30,000, and is encumbered by a mortgage of $150,000.

---

1. The sale price itself cannot be used as evidence of the value. Not only is that tautological, but it also conflicts with the *Rash* valuation standard, which is looking to an arm's-length sales price, which would be a cash sales price, not a credit bid price.

Parcel C would sell for $50,000, and is unencumbered. Assume further that the three properties, if sold as an assemblage, could be sold for $135,000. In other words, the three properties are worth more when sold together than separately. $135,000 is more than $105,000. The value of the assemblage is also considerably more than what any of the three creditors would stand to receive if they were to liquidate their collateral under state or separately under bankruptcy law. However, there is no practical way to allow the creditors to bid the full amount of their debt against the assemblage. The property being sold is not all their collateral. If Creditor A is allowed to bid $200,000, it would be able to purchase all three properties when it contributed assets worth less than twenty percent of the true value.

Edward J. Janger, *The Logic and Limits of Liens*, 2015 U. ILL. L. REV. 603-604. The problem here arises because at state law the foreclosure would be asset-by-asset; the additional value created by the assemblage is not something that any of the creditors could capture in a state law foreclosure. Instead, it is value created by the bankruptcy process. The only sensible approach here is to cap the credit bid at the amount of the secured claim, rather than the amount of the debt. That means undertaking a judicial valuation of the collateral, rather than relying on the sale price as evidence of the collateral's value.

Now let's circle back to the situation in which the only item being sold is the secured creditor's collateral. Should the same rule apply? It might seem silly to undertake a judicial valuation when there is about to be a market valuation, but it's hard to see why a different credit bid should be allowed. While this reading is not generally followed by courts, *see Cohen v. KB Mezzanine Fund II, LP (In re SubMicron Sys. Corp.)*, 432 F.3d 448 (3d Cir. 2006), it nevertheless is the reading that most closely comports with the text of section 363(k), which would seem to allow setoff only of the secured claim, rather than the total debt, and with the observation that a 363 sale is fundamentally different from a state law foreclosure sale because it may include more than the secured creditor's collateral.

The right to credit bid under the Bankruptcy Code is not absolute. Section 363(k) allows the credit bidding right of setoff to be restricted for cause, and 363(k), by its own terms, would seem to allow credit bidding only for property that is actually subject to a lien. Creditors virtually never have liens on *all* of a debtor's assets. UCC Article 9 allows for financing statements covering "all assets," UCC § 9-504(2), thus enabling so-called blanket liens that appear to "cover everything," but in practice it is difficult for a creditor to obtain a lien on all of a debtor's assets. First, UCC Article 9 does not cover all types of collateral—real property being the most important exclusion, but also certain types of intellectual property, aircraft, and vessels, among other things. Second, legal and contractual restrictions may result in some collateral being excluded from a blanket lien. Third, foreign subsidiaries' assets require separate foreign security interests, and tax considerations often prevent security interests in foreign subsidiaries' equity. Finally, it is burdensome to take security interests in some types of collateral (motor vehicles), while other types of collateral are eschewed for liability and reputational reasons (*e.g.*, deposit accounts used for payroll). Thus, it is rare that a creditor actually has a lien on all of a debtor's assets. The following case addresses both the incomplete or moth-eaten "blanket lien" issues.

In re **Free Lance-Star Publishing Co.**
512 B.R. 798 (Bankr. E.D. Va. 2014)

KEVIN R. HUENNEKENS, United States Bankruptcy Judge.

The Free Lance-Star Publishing Company of Fredericksburg, VA ("The Free Lance-Star") and William Douglas Properties, LLC ("William Douglas" and, together with The Free Lance-Star, the "Debtors") filed voluntary petitions for relief under Chapter 11 [bankruptcy]. . . . The Debtors are continuing to operate their business as Debtors-in-Possession ("DIP") under §§ 1107 and 1108 of the Bankruptcy Code.

The Debtors filed on the Petition Date a Motion to Sell Business Assets and a Motion to Sell Tower Assets[1] (collectively, the "Sale Motions") seeking approval of bidding procedures for an auction of substantially all of the Debtors' assets. On March 10, 2014, the Court entered orders approving the bidding procedures set out in each of the Sale Motions, including the right of DSP Acquisition, LLC ("DSP") to credit bid its claim against the Debtors' assets on which it had valid liens or security interests, as either (i) agreed to by the Debtors, DSP, and the Official Committee of Unsecured Creditors (the "Committee") or (ii) as determined by the Court at a hearing to be held on March 24, 2014.

Also on March 10, 2014, DSP filed a Complaint (the "Complaint") initiating [an] Adversary Proceeding [that is, a lawsuit between two parties that is related to a bankruptcy case]. The Complaint seeks a declaration that DSP has valid and perfected liens on substantially all of the Debtors' assets including the Tower Assets. DSP has also filed a motion seeking summary judgment . . . on all counts set forth in its Complaint (the "Plaintiff's Motion for Summary Judgment"). . . . The Debtors, who are the named defendants in the Complaint, filed their own motion for summary judgment against DSP. . . .

. . .

Section 363(b)(1) of the Bankruptcy Code provides that a trustee, "after notice and a hearing, may use, sell, or lease, other than in the ordinary course of business, property of the estate." 11 U.S.C. § 363(b)(1). DSP argues that, as the holder of a secured claim, the Bankruptcy Code gives it the right to credit bid its claim at such a sale. *See* 11 U.S.C. § 363(k). The Debtors submit that "cause" exists in this case to limit the credit bid amount. *See id.* DSP, as the entity asserting an interest in property of the estate, has the burden of proof on the issue of the validity, priority, or extent of its liens. 11 U.S.C. § 363(p)(2). . . .

---

1. The Debtors own and operate four radio stations in addition to its printing and newspaper businesses. The Tower Assets are employed in broadcasting activities associated with the Debtors' operation of its radio business. . . . The Sale Motions included a procedure for a separate sale of the Debtors' Tower Assets, as the Debtors assert that no entity has a lien on or security interest in the Tower Assets.

FACTS

The Free Lance-Star is a family-owned publishing, newspaper, radio, and communications company located in Fredericksburg, Virginia (the "Company"). William Douglas is a related entity that owns a portion of the land on which The Free Lance-Star operates its business. The Free Lance-Star owns the Tower Assets, which include three parcels of real estate (the "Tower Parcels"). The Tower Assets are the primary focus of the Sale Motions and the Cross Motions for Summary Judgment. The Tower Assets are used predominately in The Free Lance-Star's radio broadcasting operations. . . .

In 2006, the Debtors developed a plan to expand their commercial printing business. To undertake this expansion, the Debtors borrowed funds from Branch Banking and Trust ("BB&T") in the approximate amount of $50.8 million (the "Loan"). To secure this Loan the Debtors granted liens on, and security interests in, certain of the Debtors' real and personal property. The Debtors did not agree to grant any liens on or security interests in the Tower Assets, nor did BB&T record deeds of trust covering the Tower Parcels. BB&T did not obtain or record any assignment of leases or rents concerning the Tower Parcels. The Credit Agreement makes no reference to granting liens on the Tower Assets, nor does the Security Agreement specifically reference the Tower Assets. It appears that during the time that BB&T held the Loan, BB&T did not record any financing statements perfecting a security interest in any of the Tower Assets.

With the Loan, the Debtors built a state-of-the-art printing facility that began operation in 2009. Construction of the facility coincided with the severe recession that began in December 2007 and ended in June 2009. In early 2009 the Company fell out of compliance with certain of the Loan covenants contained in its Loan agreement with BB&T. In December of 2011, the Company signed a forbearance agreement with BB&T. The Company continued to make timely payments to BB&T even as its revenue declined. Prevailing economic conditions prevented the Company from restructuring its business and becoming compliant with its Loan covenants. The Company was unsuccessful in its attempts to obtain replacement refinancing. Finally, in late June of 2013, BB&T sold its Loan to Sandton Capital Partners ("Sandton").[5]

On July 3, 2013, Sandton informed the Debtors that it wanted the Company to file a Chapter 11 bankruptcy case and sell substantially all of the Debtors' assets pursuant to 11 U.S.C. § 363. Sandton indicated that it intended to be the entity that purchased the Debtors' assets at the bankruptcy sale. Sandton advised that it would continue to operate the business and that it intended to keep the Debtors' management in place. Thereafter, the Debtors agreed to work on implementing a plan that would involve the Debtors filing a Chapter 11 bankruptcy case and selling all of their assets to DSP pursuant to 11 U.S.C. § 363, so long as it was done in the best interests of the estate, and was within the fiduciary duties of the Debtors' officers and directors.

---

5. Counsel for DSP suggested at the Hearing that DSP is an affiliated entity operated by Sandton Capital Partners and that DSP is now the holder of the Draw Commercial Note dated September 11, 2007, made by the Debtors payable to the order of BB&T in the original principal amount of $45,842,400.00.

On or about July 25, 2013, the Debtors received, on behalf of DSP, a request that the Debtors execute three deeds of trust to encumber the Tower Parcels.[6] On or about August 8, 2013, counsel for DSP provided a "Restructuring Timetable" that contained an expectation for the timely recordation of the executed deeds of trust and the commencement of the bankruptcy case in September of 2013. Over the next several days, email correspondence concerning the "Restructuring Timetable" was exchanged between counsel for the Debtors and DSP. Communication between the parties stopped abruptly in mid-August. Unbeknownst to the Debtors, during the several weeks of ensuing silence, DSP unilaterally filed UCC Fixture Financing Statements. . . . DSP was the first entity since the Loan's inception to attempt to perfect a security interest in the Debtors' Tower Assets.[7]

On September 24, 2013, DSP resumed negotiations by providing the Debtors with a revised Forbearance Agreement that did not require that the Debtors execute the deeds of trust. The revised Forbearance Agreement included instead a provision for a blanket release of all claims held by the Debtors against DSP. The Debtors' attempts to limit the blanket release provision to apply only to all known claims were soundly rejected by DSP. DSP explained that the new Forbearance Agreement did not include the additional mortgages and liens on the Tower Assets as DSP expected to pick up that collateral in a DIP post-petition financing order.

Ninety days after DSP had recorded its UCC Fixture Filings, DSP renewed its pressure on the Company for a speedy bankruptcy filing. The Debtors requested a meeting with DSP and its counsel at which a coordinated, global, planned approach for a bankruptcy case could be developed. On December 3, 2013, the Debtors held a phone conference with representatives of DSP. During this meeting, DSP indicated, among other things, that there was no reason to market the Debtors' assets. DSP insisted that the timeframe for conducting a bankruptcy sale of its business, with a credit bid, should be no more than six weeks from petition date to closing. DSP strongly objected to the Debtors' engagement of Protiviti as the Debtors' financial consultant. When Protiviti insisted upon distributing marketing materials in connection with the bankruptcy sales process, DSP required that the marketing materials contain on the front page, in bold font, a statement that DSP had a right to a $39 million credit bid.

The Debtors continued to express a willingness, consistent with their fiduciary responsibilities, to work with their secured lender in order to develop a fair process to market the Company's assets in a manner designed to maximize value for the benefit of the estate as a whole. When Protiviti developed cash flow projections for the Company, which cash flow projections indicated that the Company could survive in bankruptcy without a post-petition DIP loan facility, the relationship between the Debtors and the secured lender turned sour. Counsel for DSP challenged Protiviti's projections as too optimistic. DSP insisted that the Company had to have a new post-petition loan facility made by DSP. Otherwise, DSP would not be able to get the liens it coveted on the

---

6. These Deeds of Trust sought to expand the scope of the initial Security Agreement entered into between BB&T and the Debtors by granting consensual liens on the Debtors' Tower Parcels and the improvement thereon.

7. The financing statements purported to perfect a security interest in, among other things, "all machinery, equipment, fixtures, and other property of every kind and nature whatsoever owned by the Debtor . . . located upon the [Tower Parcels]."

Tower Assets. The Debtors refused the new loan and all negotiations between the Debtors and DSP ceased at that point.

On January 11, 2014, DSP contacted counsel for the Debtors and informed them that DSP no longer supported a bankruptcy filing under the terms proposed by the Debtors. DSP advised that it would be suspending all work in connection with the bankruptcy filing. The next week, DSP recorded additional financing statements in various jurisdictions without giving any notice to the Debtors. The Debtors commenced the bankruptcy case without the support of their secured lender.

Following the Petition Date, DSP objected to the Debtors' use of cash collateral. At a contested hearing conducted on January 24, 2014, DSP asked the Court to give DSP new liens on the Tower Assets as additional adequate protection to supplement the post-petition replacement liens and adequate protection payments offered by the Debtors. DSP did not disclose to the Court or the Debtors that it had already recorded financing statements against the Tower Assets in August of 2013 and again in January of 2014. The Court denied DSP's request for the supplemental liens, finding that DSP's interest in cash collateral was adequately protected.

[The Debtor alleged that DSP engaged in inequitable behavior by filing unauthorized financing statements, which it argued was cause for denying DSP the right to credit bid.] DSP failed to provide any witness at the [evidentiary] Hearing to refute the Debtors' allegations that DSP's conduct was inequitable. DSP provided no evidence concerning its acquisition of the BB&T loan. In fact, there is no evidence that DSP is the holder of the Draw Commercial Note dated September 11, 2007, made by the Debtors payable to the order of BB&T in the original principal amount of $45,842,400 (the "Note"). The Court invited DSP to supplement the record with this information and with information about the amount paid for the Loan, but DSP made the calculated decision not to do so. The only witness DSP did provide at the Hearing was found to be not credible. The declaration filed by DSP in support of its Complaint was found to be both false and misleading.

ANALYSIS

A secured creditor should be entitled to credit bid the full amount of its claim at any sale of its collateral outside the ordinary course of the debtor's business. *In re SubMicron Sys. Corp.*, 432 F.3d 448, 459-60 (3d Cir. 2006) (collecting cases and holding that the district court did not err in allowing secured creditors to credit bid the full face value of their claims when the plan administrator sought to limit the secured creditors' credit bids to the economic value of their claims). *See also Suncruz Casinos*, 298 B.R. 833, 838-39 (S.D. Fla. 2003) (stating that a secured creditor may credit bid the full amount of its claim, including any deficiency claim). The right to credit bid is codified in § 363(k) of the Bankruptcy Code which provides:

> At a sale under subsection (b) of this section of property that is subject to a lien that secures an allowed claim, unless the court for cause orders otherwise, the holder of such claim may bid at such sale, and, if the holder of such claim purchases such property, such holder may offset such claim against the purchase price of such property.

11 U.S.C. § 363(k).

The right to credit bid under § 363(k) of the Bankruptcy Code is an important safeguard that insures against the undervaluation of the secured claim at an asset sale. Credit bidding "allows the secured creditor to bid for its collateral using the debt it is owed to offset the purchase price[,]" which "ensures that, if the bidding at the sale is less than the amount of the claim the collateral secures, the secured creditor can, if it chooses, bid up the price to as high as the amount of its claim." *Quality Props. Asset Mgmt. Co. v. Trump Va. Acquisitions, LLC,* No. 3:11-CV-00053, 2012 U.S. Dist. Lexis 115225, 2012 WL 3542527, at *7 n.13 (W.D. Va. Aug. 16, 2012); *RadLax Gateway Hotel, LLC v. Amalgamated Bank*, 132 S. Ct. 2065, 2070 n.2 (2012) ("The ability to credit-bid helps to protect a creditor against the risk that its collateral will be sold at a depressed price [ ]" by enabling the secured "creditor to purchase the collateral for what it considers the fair market price (up to the amount of its security interest) without committing additional cash to protect the loan.").

Credit bidding, however, is not an absolute right. *See In re Antaeus Tech. Servs., Inc.,* 345 B.R. 556, 565 (Bankr. W.D. Va. 2005). The Bankruptcy Court in Delaware recently admonished that while "[i]t is beyond peradventure that a secured creditor is entitled to credit bid its allowed claim . . . [t]he law is equally clear, as § 363(k) provides, that the Court may 'for cause order otherwise.'" 11 U.S.C. § 363(k). *See, e.g., In re Fisker Auto. Holdings, Inc.,* Case No. 13-13087-KG, 510 B.R. 55, 2014 Bankr. Lexis 230 at *15-17 (Bankr. D. Del. Jan. 17, 2014). . . . Generally, "a court may deny a lender the right to credit bid in the interest of any policy advanced by the Code, such as to ensure the success of the reorganization or to foster a competitive bidding environment." *Philadelphia Newspapers,* 599 F.3d, at 316, n. 14. . . .

The court in *In re Antaeus Tech. Servs., Inc.* denied the right of a secured creditor to credit bid in order to facilitate a fully competitive auction. *In re Antaeus,* 345 B.R. at 565. The court in *In re Fisker* found "cause" existed under § 363(k) of the Bankruptcy Code where the secured lender had chilled the bidding process by inequitably pushing the debtor into bankruptcy so that it could short-circuit the bankruptcy process. *In re Fisker,* 2014 Bankr. Lexis 230 at *15-17.

The Debtors in the case at bar urge the Court to find cause exists to limit DSP's credit bid rights. The Debtors advance three reasons for doing so. First, DSP does not have a lien on all of the Company's assets. The Debtors argue that it is axiomatic that a creditor cannot credit bid the economic value of its claim against assets in which it holds no security interest. Second, the Debtors maintain that DSP has engaged in inequitable conduct that has damped interest in the auction and depressed the potential sales price the Debtors otherwise might have realized from the sale of the business. Finally, limiting the amount of the credit bid in this case will restore enthusiasm for the sale and foster a robust bidding process. Maximizing the value debtors might be able to realize from the sale of their assets is an important policy advanced by the Bankruptcy Code.

The Court has addressed separately the validity and extent of DSP's liens. The Court has held that DSP does not have a valid perfected security interest in all of the assets upon which it asserts it does. DSP does not have valid, properly perfected liens on, or security interests in, the Debtors' Tower Assets, the Debtors' motor vehicles, the Debtors' FCC licenses, the Debtors' insurance policies, or the Debtors' bank account deposits. DSP's lien on general intangibles does not give it a lien on the proceeds the

Debtors will generate from the bankruptcy sale. The Court has denied Plaintiff's Motion for Summary Judgment and has granted partial judgment on Defendants' Motion for Summary Judgment. DSP does not have a right to assert a credit bid on assets that do not secure DSP's allowed claim.

From the moment it bought the loan from BB&T, DSP pressed the Debtor "to walk hand in hand" with it through an expedited bankruptcy sales process. It was a classic loan-to-own scenario. DSP made no secret of the fact that it acquired the Loan in order to purchase the Company. It planned from the beginning to effect a quick sale under § 363 of the Bankruptcy Code at which it would be the successful bidder for all the Debtors' assets utilizing a credit bid.

The bump in the road occurred in July of 2013, when DSP learned that it did not have a lien on the Debtors' Tower Assets. DSP made the unilateral decision to expand the scope of its security interest when DSP's overt requests for the Debtors to grant such liens on the Tower Assets failed. DSP's protestations to the contrary notwithstanding, DSP knew it did not have a valid lien on the Tower Assets when it filed the Financing Statements. The Court is troubled by DSP's recordation of the UCC Fixture Financing Statements . . . in August of 2013 and again in January of 2014. The Court is disappointed that DSP neglected to disclose the Fixture Filings at the January 24, 2014, contested cash collateral hearing during which DSP requested the Court to grant it liens on those very assets. DSP pressured the Debtors to shorten the Debtors' marketing period for the sale of its business and to put language in the marketing materials conspicuously advertising DSP's credit bid rights. The Court is equally troubled by DSP's efforts to frustrate the competitive bidding process.

The Court finds that DSP did engage in inequitable conduct. The credit bid mechanism that normally works to protect secured lenders against the undervaluation of collateral sold at a bankruptcy sale does not always function properly when a party has bought the secured debt in a loan-to-own strategy in order to acquire the target company. In such a situation, the secured party may attempt to depress rather than to enhance market value. Credit bidding can be employed to chill bidding prior to or during an auction, or to keep prospective bidders from participating in the sales process. DSP's motivation to own the Debtors' business rather than to have the Loan repaid has interfered with the sales process. DSP has tried to depress the sales price of the Debtors' assets, not to maximize the value of those assets. A depressed value would benefit only DSP, and it would do so at the expense of the estate's other creditors. The deployment of DSP's loan-to-own strategy has depressed enthusiasm for the bankruptcy sale in the marketplace.

The only testimony provided at the Hearing regarding the proposed bidding procedures and auction process was from the Debtors' expert witness, Suzanne Roski ("Roski") from the firm of Protiviti, Inc ("Protiviti"). Roski presented evidence at the Hearing that many interested parties have executed nondisclosure agreements. Many of those same parties have visited the data room, which is populated with confidential financial information concerning the Debtors' business, in order to conduct preliminary inquiry in connection with the sale. To date, however, only one party has made a site visit. Numerous parties are awaiting resolution of the credit bid issue before launching advanced due diligence. There is genuine confusion among potentially interested parties over on what assets DSP has a lien and on how the auction process may unfold.

Potential bidders are now less likely to participate in the sale process. Roski testified that under the unique circumstances of this case, limiting DSP's credit bid would help restore a competitive bidding environment and engender enthusiasm for the sale. DSP chose not to present any evidence to refute or otherwise contradict this testimony. The Court can only conclude from the uncontroverted evidence presented that it is necessary to limit DSP from bidding the full amount of its claim against all of the Debtors' assets in order to foster a fair and robust sale.

. . .

CONCLUSION

The confluence of (i) DSP's less than fully-secured lien status; (ii) DSP's overly zealous loan-to-own strategy; and (iii) the negative impact DSP's misconduct has had on the auction process has created the perfect storm, requiring curtailment of DSP's credit bid rights. First, the Debtors' business operation necessarily includes unencumbered assets upon which DSP has no lien. The credit bid amount must be configured to prevent DSP from credit bidding its claim against assets such as the FCC licenses that are not within the scope of its collateral pool. Second, DSP's loan-to-own strategy has depressed enthusiasm for the sale in the marketplace. Potential bidders now perceive the sale of the business to DSP as a *fait accompli*. Those parties are not inclined to participate in an auction process. Third, limiting DSP's credit bid will attract renewed interest in the bidding process and will serve to increase the value realized for the assets.

Although DSP has engaged in inequitable conduct, the Court will not extinguish DSP's right to credit bid entirely. But sufficient cause exists for the Court to limit that credit bid amount in order to foster a robust and competitive bidding environment. Accordingly, the Court will sustain the Debtors' objection. DSP's right to credit bid under § 363(k) of the Bankruptcy Code will be limited to $1,200,000 for assets related to the Debtors' radio business on which DSP has a valid, properly perfected lien and $12,700,000 for assets related to the Debtors' newspaper and printing business on which DSP has a valid, properly perfected lien.[14]

Problem Set 21

(1) Voltage, a hip teen clothing retailer, is in Chapter 11 bankruptcy. Voltage's newest line of retro-polyester teen wear was a bust, and Voltage is not able to service its debt at its current level of sales. Voltage wants to continue operating in Chapter 11. Which of the following does it need the court's approval for?

    a. Paying its salaried employees.

    b. Paying its top sales staff their traditional annual bonuses (based on sales figures).

---

14. For purposes of this decision, the Court has presumed that DSP is the holder of the Note. In order to take advantage of any credit bid, DSP must first provide proof that the Debtors and the Committee agree is sufficient, or if there is a disagreement as to the sufficiency of the proof, proof the Court concludes is sufficient, that it is indeed the lender who holds the Note that gives rise to a credit bid pursuant to 11 U.S.C. § 363(k).

    c. Hiring new sales staff, as it does every month. (There is high turnover in retail employment.)

    d. Hiring a new CFO. *depends*

    e. Continuing to sell its retro-polyester teen wear line.

    f. Selling its retro-polyester teen wear line at a 40% off sale.

    g. Placing orders with vendors for its new fall product line.

    h. Acquiring a new IT system.

    i. Selling the leases to its unprofitable storefronts.

    j. Ceasing to operate its unprofitable stores.

    k. Buying BKLYN, an even hipper teen retailer.

11 U.S.C. §§ 363(b)-(c).

    (2) Storied undergarment manufacturer Tighty-Whitey is in Chapter 11. Tighty-Whitey, as DIP, proposes to sell all of its assets to Gaines Corp. for shares of Gaines Corp.'s common stock, valued by Tighty-Whitey's valuation expert at $40 million. Gaines has already conducted extensive diligence on Tighty-Whitey's assets. At the sale hearing an unassuming man in a hoodie stands up and announces that he is the famed Internet bazillionaire Narcissus ("Narc") Smuckerberg. Narc announces that he would like to bid on some of the firm's assets. Specifically, Narc offers to pay $27 million in cash, "And I mean cash—it's all sitting in suitcases in an armored car double-parked outside the courthouse," he says, for Tighty-Whitey's signature product line of men's briefs, which is run out of a separately incorporated subsidiary of Tighty-Whitey. Narc has no interest in the rest of Tighty-Whitey's assets. Narc is offering to purchase without conducting any diligence. "I've been wearing this stuff my whole life," say Narc, "It's hard to get any closer to the product. I'm even sporting it now. What more diligence do I possibly need? I know this is a quality product." The Official Unsecured Creditors Committee likes Narc's offer, but the DIP wants to proceed with the originally planned sale and argues that it will have difficulty selling the remaining assets, and that the equity of Gaines is better value than Narc's cash.

    a. What should the court do? Whose decision is the sale?

    b. If the court approves the sale to Narc, what happens to Gaines?

    c. The next time Gaines Corp. considers entering into this sort of transaction, what should it negotiate for as protection?

    (3) Mercury Motorcycles, a high-end custom motorcycle manufacturer, is in Chapter 11. Mercury owes Jupiter Ventures $30 million on a line of credit secured by first priority liens on Mercury's equipment, inventory, receivables, and the stock in Mercury's subsidiaries. Juno Bancorp has a first mortgage on Mercury's headquarters, warehouse, and factory buildings. These mortgages collectively secure a $20 million term loan. Mercury has other unencumbered assets, including its intellectual property, insurance policies, tort claims, and some free cash.

    a. If Mercury were to sell all of its assets in a section 363 sale, can Jupiter or Juno credit bid? If so, how much? 11 U.S.C. § 363(k).

    b. Suppose that Mercury were to sell just its headquarters building, which is valued at $5 million. Its other real estate assets are worth $12 million. Would Jupiter or Juno be able to credit bid? If so, how much? 11 U.S.C. § 363(k).

No — depends on which method

Juno. 17

   c. Jupiter Ventures has long coveted Mercury's headquarters building. Jupiter believes that the building is worth perhaps $4.5 million, but the bankruptcy court has valued it at $5 million. Is it possible for Jupiter to win the auction if Juno credit bids? 11 U.S.C. § 363(k).

(4) Ares Ballistics is in Chapter 7 as the result of tort liability from its firearm product. The trustee is selling Ares's substantial inventory of large-caliber Grim Reaper hollow-point ammunition. "One of these rounds could bring down an elephant," the trustee marvels. The trustee had expected the ammunition—in high demand among firearm enthusiasts for its lethal force, yet available for consumer sale because of a technicality in Bureau of Alcohol, Tobacco, and Firearms regulations—to bring in $40 million. Yet at the sale only one bidder, Phobos, Inc., placed a bid. The trustee later discovered that Phobos had worked with two other prospective purchasers, Deimos LLC and Eris, Inc., to avoid a bidding war. Instead of filing competing (and escalating) bids, Phobos alone bid, and then later divvied up the inventory with Deimos and Eris. "It's a kipper!" the trustee exclaims when he hears of the collusive bid. When the trustee moves to have the sale avoided, what is the result, assuming that the trustee is able to prove the collusion? 11 U.S.C. §§ 363(m), (n).

(5) The Rhonda Jeremy Agency is an on-line dating service and social network-ing service marketed at married individuals. Founded by famed pornographic actress Rhonda Jeremy, the Rhonda Jeremy Agency's marketing slogan is "Life is too short. Have an affair." The Rhonda Jeremy Agency was hacked last spring. The hackers threat-ened to release the identity of the Rhonda Jeremy Agency's customers unless they were paid a ransom. The Rhonda Jeremy Agency refused, and the hackers revealed the identity of several thousand Rhonda Jeremy customers. Following the hacking, most of Rhonda Jeremy Agency's remaining customers cancelled their subscriptions, resulting in a sharp decline in revenue, which triggered a covenant default from Jeremy Agency's bank lender, Chaste Manhattan Bank. The Rhonda Jeremy Agency filed for Chapter 11 bankruptcy last August. The Rhonda Jeremy Agency is proposing selling its chief assets: its proprietary customer matching formula and customer list. The customer list contains subscribers' names, billing address, and email addresses, and how many "connections" the user has made through the Rhonda Jeremy Agency website and the gender of the "connection."

The Rhonda Jeremy Agency has a "privacy policy" posted on its website. The policy states, "We strive to maintain the necessary safeguards to protect your personal infor-mation. We guaranty the use of our best efforts to ensure that your secrets remain confidential. We cannot, however, ensure the security or privacy during transmission of information you provide through the Internet or your email messages. We do not warrant that any information you provide or we collect will not be disclosed to third parties."

   a. Can the Rhonda Jeremy Agency sell the customer lists in bankruptcy? If so, what steps are required? 11 U.S.C. §§ 101(41A); 363(b)(1).

   b. What if the Rhonda Jeremy Agency had also posted on its website (separate from the privacy policy) that "At Rhonda Jeremy, we respect your privacy. We do not sell our customer list." 11 U.S.C. §§ 101(41A); 363(b)(1).

   c. Separately the Rhonda Jeremy Agency is proposing selling the following:

- subscribers' account user names and passwords;
- subscribers' credit card account numbers and expiry dates (without corresponding accountholder names);
- the IP addresses for all computers used by the subscriber to log on to the Rhonda Jeremy Agency's website and all data on the associated user's browsing habits harvested from the cookies placed by the Rhonda Jeremy Agency's website in the consumer's web browser.

Can the Rhonda Jeremy Agency sell this data? If so, what steps are required? 11 U.S.C. §§ 101(41A); 363(b)(1).

    d. You represent Chaste Manhattan Bank. After the issues you've encountered with the Rhonda Jeremy Agency, is there anything you might consider requiring in future loan agreements? 11 U.S.C. §§ 101(41A); 363(b)(1) .

    e. Suppose that the Rhonda Jeremy Agency customer lists were collateral for the loan from Chaste Manhattan Bank. If the automatic stay were lifted, could Chaste Manhattan foreclose on the customer lists? UCC § 9-408.

  (6) 600 New Jersey Partners entered Chapter 11 bankruptcy two months ago, having defaulted on the $40 million mortgage loan from Hotung Imperial Corp. on the Partners' real estate assets. 600 New Jersey Partners also owes $10 million in unsecured trade obligations and $10 million in unsecured tort debt. The debtor has proposed a plan of reorganization that contemplates

- the cure and reinstatement of the mortgage loan;
- payment of $4 million in cash to a class of trade creditors;
- payment of a $5 million, 5-year floating rate note at the judgment rate for tort debt;
- no distribution to the old partners "on account of" their old equity shares;
- recapitalization of the partnership through the sale of the equity of the reorganized partnership for at least $15 million.

The plan contemplates that the equity in the reorganized partnership will be auctioned off with the sale's closing contingent upon plan confirmation. The bidding procedures for the auction of the equity in the reorganized partnership provide for a seven-day due diligence window, after which there will be open bids placed. The old partners have agreed to serve as the stalking horse bidder, with an opening bid of $15 million, so competing bids will have to be "higher and better" than that of the old partners. Bids must be in cash and in $1 million increments. Any topping bid will also have to cover the old partners' stalking horse break-up fee of five percent of the stalking horse's highest bid plus the stalking horse's legal fees. The class of trade creditors is likely to support the plan.

    a. Hotung Imperial Corp. wants to credit bid its debt. Can it? 11 U.S.C. §§ 102, 363(k); 1123(a)(5)(D), 1123(a)(5)(J); 1129(b)(2)(A).

    b. McDonough Properties wants to bid at the sale, and is willing to bid up to $30 million, but is only willing to pay with its securities rather than cash. Can it bid?

    c. Is the plan confirmable given these bidding procedures? 11 U.S.C. §§ 363; 1123(a)(5)(D), 1123(a)(5)(J); 1129(a)(1), 1129(a)(3), 1129(a)(4), 1129(b)(2)(B)(ii).

    d. McDonough Properties is really primarily interested in just one of 600 New Jersey Partners' assets, a building at 600 New Jersey Ave., NW, in Washington, D.C. Is there any way that McDonough Properties could bid just on that building? 11 U.S.C. § 1121(d).

CHAPTER 22

FREE AND CLEAR SALES & SUCCESSOR LIABILITY

I. FREE AND CLEAR SALES

Section 363 is one of the most powerful tools offered by the Bankruptcy Code, because it can override non-bankruptcy law restrictions on sale or use of estate assets, thereby unlocking value for the bankruptcy estate that is otherwise not available under state law sale procedures. It does so in three significant ways.

A. *Ipso Facto* Clauses

First, contractual or non-bankruptcy transfer prohibitions based on the solvency of the debtor ("*ipso facto* clauses") are made ineffective by section 363(l). Thus, a lease provision restricting the debtor from subletting the property if insolvent would not be enforceable in bankruptcy. Similarly, a provision giving a mortgagee a right to approve any sale in bankruptcy would not be enforceable.

B. Free and Clear Sales

Under section 363(f) estate property can be sold "free and clear" of interests in the property, meaning that the buyer takes the property without being subject to the interests in the property, giving the buyer clean title. This means that a section 363 sale power can create tremendous value for the bankruptcy estate by eliminating various types of liability that relate to the transferred assets. A sale under section 363(f) must still comply with the relevant provisions of section 363(b) or (c), such as the section 363(b)(1) privacy provisions, as section 363(f) is a special power used under those provisions.

The "free and clear" sale power is not unique to bankruptcy. The free and clear sale power exists at state law. A state law foreclosure sale accomplishes a free and clear sale, *in regard to junior liens.* State foreclosure sales do not affect senior liens to the foreclosing lien, but it is rare for a junior lienholder to bring a sale. To the extent that various interest holders in a property, including lessees, were not notified about the foreclosure, a separate action (known as "strict foreclosure") may be necessary to divest these parties of their rights.

Moreover, both state and federal receivers are often authorized to sell property free and clear of liens without going through foreclosure sale procedures. *See, e.g., AgStar Fin. Servs., PCA v. Eastwood Dairy, LLC*, 2012 U.S. Dist. LEXIS 51052 (S.D. Ohio 2012) (federal receivership); *Park Nat'l Bank v. Cattani, Inc.*, 187 Ohio App. 3d 186 (Ohio Ct. App. 12th Dist. 2010) (state receivership). Some state receivership statutes have express authorization for free and clear sales, and individual receivership orders may contain such authorization or a receiver can petition a court for such authorization. But both state and federal receiverships have limitations that constrain the value of their free and clear sales authority.

State receiverships are not able to exercise control over property in multiple states. Thus, if a debtor has assets in multiple states, a single state receiver will be unable to effectuate a sale of assets other than in the state of the receivership. Federal receivers are not so limited in their jurisdiction; like the bankruptcy estate, federal receivers have jurisdiction over the property of the debtor irrespective of where it is located. 28 U.S.C. § 754.

Yet federal receiverships are straddled with a statutory restriction on sales: Either the sale must be a public sale or there must be three independent appraisals of the property being sold, and the sale must be for at least two-thirds of the appraised value. 28 U.S.C. §§ 2001, 2004. Moreover, public sales must be advertised for at least four weeks in general circulation newspapers, and private sales must be advertised in a general circulation newspaper for at least ten days prior to the sale. 28 U.S.C. §§ 2001, 2002. This puts a floor on the minimum time for a sale. Furthermore, any bid in a private sale can be topped by a bona fide offer of at least 10% more than the sale price that complies with the sale conditions. 28 U.S.C. § 2001(b). And, the receivership sale can always be stopped if the debtor files for bankruptcy, with the receiver—federal or state—then being required to turn over to the estate any property of the debtor it possesses. 11 U.S.C. § 543.

The bankruptcy free and clear sale power is a "cleaner" free and clear power than the federal receivership free and clear power. Like the federal receivership power, it has nationwide reach, but is not subject to federal receivership's statutory requirements on sale procedures. 28 U.S.C. § 2001(c).

The interests from which a section 363(f) sale is free and clear can include liens and other types of property interests, such as easements, sale veto rights, or transfer restrictions unrelated to the debtor's solvency. They can also include various flavors of successor liability, be it under "mere continuity" doctrine, "substantial continuity" doctrine, "de facto merger" doctrine, or "successor liability" doctrine. (Successor liability is *in personam* liability based on the purchaser having essentially subsumed the seller, as might be the case in a sale of all assets. This is distinct from the *in rem* liability of a lien that travels with an asset not sold in the ordinary course of business.) Eliminating successor liability concerns for purchasers increases the value of the assets sold under section 363.

Likewise, a section 363(f) sale can be done without regard to transfer taxes or state bulk sale laws that require certain procedural notifications. And a section 363(f) sale need not comply with corporate charter provisions requiring shareholder approval of a sale of substantially all corporate assets.

Section 363(f) means that the bankruptcy estate can transfer clear title of its assets to buyers, even if title to those assets is in dispute. The ability to transfer clear title has the effect of increasing the value of the estate's assets. Consider, for example, if a debtor owned a tract of property and there was a bona fide dispute as to the validity of liens on the property. The property could be sold now before the dispute about the liens was resolved and the buyer could obtain clear title. Similarly, if the property was environmentally contaminated, a section 363(f) sale might enable the buyer to avoid environmental clean-up liability.

If, on the other hand, the debtor had entered into a consumer protection settlement with the Federal Trade Commission in which it agreed to certain undertakings about a product it sold, the obligations relating to that settlement might still transfer with the asset, depending on whether they would transfer with the asset under applicable non-bankruptcy law (including the settlement agreement itself) and if the FTC could not be compelled to take money damages for breach of the settlement.

Free and clear sales do not completely deprive the holders of interests in property of their rights. Section 363(e) requires that there be adequate protection of the interests, notwithstanding section 363(f). Typically this means that the party with the interest in the property will receive a lien on the sale proceeds. Indeed, section 552(b) provides that the non-bankruptcy rules regarding proceeds will generally apply, so if the interest in the property is a lien, it will attach to the proceeds of the sale. (Were it otherwise, there might be a Fifth Amendment takings problem, but as long as a lien attaches to the proceeds of the sale, it is constitutionally sufficient. *Van Huffel v. Harkelrode*, 284 U.S. 225 (1931).)

There are five potential ways for a trustee or DIP to satisfy the requirements for a free and clear sale. The first two alternatives are relatively straightforward. The estate can sell property free and clear if it could do so under non-bankruptcy law or if the entity with an interest in the property consents. 11 U.S.C. §§ 363(f)(1)-(2). Remember that a sale under non-bankruptcy law arguably includes a foreclosure sale, which may transfer property free and clear of any liens junior to the creditor bringing the sale.

The third alternative is often the most important. It allows the estate to sell property free and clear of a lien if the sale price is "greater than the aggregate value of all liens on such property." 11 U.S.C. § 363(f)(3). Courts are split on how to interpret this provision. Some courts read section 363(f)(3) as requiring the sale price to be greater than the amount of the debt secured by the liens and some merely require that the sale price be for the economic value of the liens, which is the value of the collateral, which is, in turn, the sale price.

To wit, if a secured creditor is owed $2 million, secured by a lien on collateral worth $1.5 million, the estate could sell the collateral free and clear under the former reading only if the sale price were above $2 million. Thus, the former reading makes

[handwritten margin note: Sale price > value of collateral]

section 363(f)(3) useable only if the estate has equity in the property; if the creditor is undersecured, its collateral cannot be sold free and clear. Under the latter reading, however, the collateral could be sold free and clear of the lien as long as the sale price was at least $1.5 million. The latter, and more widely adopted, reading makes section 363(f)(3) a viable method for selling virtually any property subject to a lien.

[handwritten margin note: ②]

[handwritten margin note: w/o consent →]

Under either reading, there is an important implication: A secured creditor cannot veto the sale of its collateral in bankruptcy. As long as the sale price is sufficient to satisfy the statute, the sale can proceed.

While a secured creditor cannot veto the free and clear sale, a secured creditor is still adequately protected because it automatically has a perfected security interest in the proceeds of the sale under UCC § 9-315 and 11 U.S.C. § 552(b), so it is not deprived of security. Given that most courts allow the secured creditor to credit bid its entire *debt*, not just the secured portion of its debt against the collateral, *Cohen v. KB Mezzanine Fund II, LP (In re SubMicron Sys. Corp.)*, 432 F.3d 448 (3d Cir. 2006), a secured creditor can also protect itself against low-ball bids that would satisfy the economic value interpretation of section 363(f)(3) by their very existence.

In re Boston Generating, LLC

440 B.R. 302 (Bankr. S.D.N.Y. 2010)

SHELLEY C. CHAPMAN, United States Bankruptcy Judge.

. . .

The Second Lien Agent argues that the Sale Transaction cannot satisfy the requirements of section 363(f)(3) with respect to the liens of the Second Lien Lenders. In support of its position, the Second Lien Agent primarily relies on *Clear Channel Outdoor, Inc. v. Knupfer (In re PW, LLC)*, 391 B.R. 25 (9th Cir. B.A.P. 2008) ("*Clear Channel*"). *Clear Channel* interpreted the term "value," as used in section 363(f)(3), to refer to the face amount of the lien. Accordingly, the Second Lien Agent argues that, in order to satisfy section 363(f)(3), the proceeds of the Sale Transaction must exceed the aggregate amount of the First Lien Debt and the Second Lien Debt, which amounts to approximately $1.45 billion.

[handwritten margin note: approach }]

I decline to follow *Clear Channel*; rather, on the whole, the Court finds cases such as *In re Beker Industries Corp.*, 63 B.R. 474 (Bankr. S.D.N.Y. 1986) to be more persuasive than *Clear Channel* in their interpretations of a less than perfect statutory provision. As this Court held in *Beker Industries*, section 363(f)(3) should be interpreted to mean that "the price must be equal to or greater than the aggregate *value* of the liens asserted against it, not their *amount*." *Id.* at 476 (emphasis added).

The "value" of a lien is to be determined by reference to section 506(a)—that is, it is the amount by which the lienholder's claim is actually secured. *See Beker*, 63 B.R. at 475; *see also United Sav. Ass'n of Texas v. Timbers of Inwood Forest Associates, Ltd.*, 484 U.S. 365, 372 (1988) ("The phrase 'value of such creditor's interest' in § 506(a) means 'the value of the collateral.'" (citations omitted)). As this Court previously held, the best evidence of the value of the Debtors' assets is the $1.1 billion Constellation bid. Based on Mr. Hunter's testimony, the proceeds of the Sale Transaction may be insufficient to pay the First Lien Debt in full; if that is the case, then the Second Lien Lenders' claims are not secured. Under *Beker* and the many decisions of other Bankruptcy Courts following its reasoning, I find that section 363(f)(3) is satisfied. To hold otherwise would effectively mean that most section 363 sales of encumbered assets could no longer occur either (a) absent consent of all lienholders (including those demonstrably out of the money) or (b) unless the proceeds of the proposed sale were sufficient to pay the face amount of all secured claims in full. If section 363(f)(3) and (as discussed below) section 363(f)(5) are read in the manner suggested by the Second Lien Lenders, it seems unlikely that a Court, under any circumstance, could approve a non-consensual section 363 sale. As both a practical matter and a matter of statutory construction, that cannot be the case. It is hard to imagine that Congress intended to so limit a debtor's power to dispose of encumbered assets, particularly where such disposition otherwise satisfies the requirements of section 363(b).

The fourth alternative under section 363(f) requires a bona fide dispute about the interest in the property. 11 U.S.C. § 363(f)(4). This is not a question of whether there is an interest in the property, so much as who has the interest. Imagine that the property is real estate and two different adjacent landowners each claim an exclusive easement. The property can be sold before the dispute between the quarreling adjacent landowners has been resolved, with the funds held for whoever prevails in the dispute, much like an interpleader.

[handwritten: ④ sale first then resolve dispute]

Finally, section 363(f)(5) provides that the property can be sold free and clear if the party with an interest in the property could be compelled to accept monetary satisfaction of the interest. Thus, if a lienholder that could *theoretically* be forced to accept a monetary satisfaction of its lien, for example, through the foreclosure of a *hypothetical* senior lien, such as a priming tax lien or even a priming lien in bankruptcy, then the lienholder would not be able to stop a free and clear sale under section 363(f)(5). Some courts have even held that if a party could be forced to accept a monetary satisfaction of its interests through a hypothetical cramdown plan, then a free and clear sale would be allowed. While this would cover liens, it would not extend to interests such as co-ownership of a property or *in rem* interests that run with the land. In theory, virtually all property interests could be reduced to a monetary satisfaction through an eminent domain proceeding, although that reading would seem to make section 363(f)(5) the exception that swallows the rule. *See* Basil R. Mattingly, *Sale of Property of the Estate Free and Clear of Restrictions and Covenants in Bankruptcy*, 4 AM. BANKR. INST. L. REV. 431 (1996). Not surprisingly, then, no court has adopted such a position.

[handwritten: ⑤]

II. SUCCESSOR LIABILITY

Liens and other types of *in rem* property interests are clearly cut off by section 363(f) sales. But what about personal liabilities of the debtor that are not specific to certain assets? Normally the answer would depend on whether the debtor's property was transferred by merger or by acquisition. If the debtor merged with another firm, the merged firm would accede to the debtor's pre-existing liabilities. If the assets were transferred via sale, however, the purchaser does not accede to the seller's liabilities. There are exceptions to this rule, however, that fall under the rubric of "successor liability."

Every state in the Union recognizes the doctrine of successor liability, in which an asset purchaser can accede to a seller's liabilities. All states follow a set of five basic principles of successor liability:

1. Where the purchaser expressly or impliedly agrees to assume the seller's liabilities.
2. Where the sale amounts to a consolidation or a de facto merger of the firms.
3. Where there is a substantial identity between purchaser and seller, such that the buyer is a mere continuation of the seller.
4. Where the transaction is a sham to avoid liability or is intended to hinder, delay, or defraud creditors.
5. Where the seller gave inadequate consideration for the sale. (Note this is not an examination of consideration to determine whether the contract is valid, but instead to see if there was implied consideration of assumption of liabilities.)

Some states recognize successor liability in additional circumstances:

1. Where the acquirer acquires all or substantially all of the manufacturing assets of the seller and continues essentially the same manufacturing operation (the "product line" exception). In such cases, the purchaser is strictly liable for injuries caused by the product line, even if they were made and distributed by the seller.
2. Where the acquirer is a mere continuation of the seller in terms of operations (the "continuity of enterprise" exception), the acquirer may be held liable for injuries caused by the seller's products. The change in ownership is irrelevant to this exception.

Because successor liability is a common law doctrine that arises in several different contexts, it is difficult to succinctly summarize the state of law on the doctrine. For our purposes, however, it is sufficient to recognize its existence as a set of exceptions to the traditional rule that sales are only of assets, not of liabilities.

The following cases underscore that the extent to which section 363(f) cuts off successor liability is not as clear as purchasers might always wish.

In re TWA

322 F.3d 283 (3d Cir. 2003)

FUENTES, Circuit Judge:

The issues in this bankruptcy appeal involve the doctrine of successor liability and arise out of the Bankruptcy Court's order approving the sale of the assets of Trans World Airlines ("TWA") to American Airlines ("American"). The primary question is whether the District Court erred in affirming the Bankruptcy Court's order, which had the effect of extinguishing the liability of American, as successor to TWA, for (1) employment discrimination claims against TWA and (2) for the Travel Voucher Program awarded to TWA's flight attendants in settlement of a sex discrimination class action. Because

EEOC

section 363(f) of the Bankruptcy Code permits a sale of property "free and clear" of an "interest in such property[,]" and because the claims against TWA here were connected to or arise from the assets sold, we affirm the Bankruptcy Court's order approving the sale "free and clear" of successor liability.

On January 10, 2002, TWA filed a Chapter 11 bankruptcy petition. Although it was the nation's eighth largest airline at the time, it had not earned a profit in over a decade. Months earlier, in the Spring of 2000, TWA determined that it could not continue to operate as an independent airline and that it needed to enter into a strategic transaction, such as a merger with, or sale of, TWA as a going concern to another airline. Throughout 2000, TWA held intermittent discussions with American concerning the possibility of a strategic partnership. On January 3, 2001, American contacted TWA with a proposal to purchase substantially all of TWA's assets. On January 9, 2001, American agreed to a purchase plan subject to an auction and Bankruptcy Court approval.

Though TWA's assets were being sold under a court-approved bidding process, as of February 28, 2001, the deadline for the submission of bids, TWA had not received any alternate proposals other than American's that conformed with the bidding procedures. Accordingly, TWA's Board of Directors voted to accept American's proposal to purchase TWA's assets for $742 million.

. . . The EEOC [for the employment discrimination claims] and the [sex discrimination suit] class objected to the sale to American. After conducting an evidentiary hearing, the Bankruptcy Court approved the sale to American over the objections of the EEOC and the [sex discrimination suit] plaintiffs. In approving the Sale Order, the Bankruptcy Court determined that there was no basis for successor liability on the part of American and that the flight attendants' claims could be treated as unsecured claims. In keeping with the Bankruptcy Court's conclusions, the Sale Order extinguished successor liability on the part of American for the Travel Voucher Program and any discrimination charges pending before the EEOC. Specifically, the Order provided that, in accordance with § 363(f) of the Bankruptcy Code:

> the free and clear delivery of the Assets shall include, but not be limited to, all asserted or unasserted, known or unknown, employment related claims, payroll taxes, employee contracts, employee seniority accrued while employed with any of the Sellers and successorship liability accrued up to the date of closing of such sale.

The Sale Order also enjoined all persons from seeking to enforce successor liability claims against American. The Court's order provided that:

> Pursuant to sections 105(a) and 363 of the Bankruptcy Code, all Persons are enjoined from taking any action against Purchaser or Purchaser's Affiliates including, without limitation, TWA Airlines LLC, to recover any claim which such Person had solely against Sellers or Sellers' Affiliates.

Immediately after the Sale Order was entered, the EEOC filed a Notice of Appeal. On October 11, 2001, the District Court affirmed the Bankruptcy Court's decision, finding that TWA's assets were properly transferred free and clear of (1) the Travel Voucher Program and (2) the charges of employer misconduct filed with the EEOC. The District Court affirmed the Bankruptcy Court's holding that the claims against the debtor (TWA) were "interests in property" within the meaning of 11 U.S.C. § 363(f), and therefore, the debtor's assets could be transferred free and clear of those claims. The District Court determined that the Bankruptcy Court's findings of fact were not clearly erroneous and that the Bankruptcy Court's legal conclusions were supported by the factual record. The District Court further noted that:

> there is record evidence supporting the bankruptcy court's conclusions that: (a) pursuant to a court-approved bidding procedure, debtors determined that American's offer was the highest and best offer for the purchase of substantially all of debtor's assets; (b) it was unlikely that debtors and American would have consummated the sale if appellants' claims were not extinguished; (c) if the sale did not go forward, it was highly likely that debtors would have been liquidated with resulting material harm to creditors, employees and the St. Louis, Missouri region, as well as rendering debtors unable to satisfy its [sic] obligations under the Travel Voucher Program; and (d) the travel vouchers may be reduced to a monetary satisfaction.

On November 13, 2001, the [sex discrimination suit] class filed a Notice of Appeal. On December 7, 2001, the EEOC also appealed the District Court's order. The appeals have been consolidated.

. . .

The parties' dispute in this case concerns the meaning of the phrase "interest in such property" (hereafter "interest in property") as that phrase is used in § 363(f) of the Bankruptcy Code. This section "permits sale of property free and clear of any interest in the property of an entity other than the estate." S. Rep. No. 95-989, at 56 (1978). Appellants assert that the Travel Voucher Program and the pending EEOC charges are not interests in property within the meaning of this section and that, therefore, these claims were improperly extinguished by the Sale Order. They assert that interests in property are limited to "liens, mortgages, money judgments, writs of garnishment and attachment, and the like, and cannot encompass successor liability claims arising under federal antidiscrimination statutes and judicial decrees implementing those statutes." Appellants also assert that their claims are outside the scope of § 363(f), and therefore cannot be extinguished, because they could not "be compelled, in a legal or equitable proceeding, to accept a money satisfaction of [their] interest[s]." 11 U.S.C. § 363(f)(5). The Airlines, on the other hand, argue that, while Congress did not expressly define "interest in property," the phrase should be broadly read to authorize a bankruptcy court to bar any interest that could potentially travel with the property being sold, even if the asserted interest is unsecured. They also assert that appellants' claims lie within the scope of § 363(f)(5), and therefore, can be extinguished because appellants can be compelled to accept a money satisfaction of their claims. We agree with the Airlines.

The contentions of the parties require us to consider whether the claims in this case constitute an interest in property as understood within the meaning of § 363(f). . . . Some courts have narrowly interpreted interests in property to mean *in rem* interests in property, such as liens. *See, e.g., In re White Motor Credit Corp.*, 75 B.R. 944, 948 (Bankr. N.D. Ohio 1987) ("General unsecured claimants including tort claimants, have no specific interest in a debtor's property. Therefore, section 363 is inapplicable for sales free and clear of such claims."). However, the trend seems to be toward a more expansive reading of "interests in property" which "encompasses other obligations that may flow from ownership of the property." 3 COLLIER ON BANKRUPTCY ¶363.06[1].

[Here] . . . the assets of the debtor . . . gave rise to the claims. Had TWA not invested in airline assets, which required the employment of the EEOC claimants, those successor liability claims would not have arisen. Furthermore, TWA's investment in commercial aviation is inextricably linked to its employment of the [sex discrimination suit] claimants as flight attendants, and its ability to distribute travel vouchers as part of the settlement agreement. While the interests of the EEOC and the [sex discrimination suit] class in the assets of TWA's bankruptcy estate are not interests in property in the sense that they are not *in rem* interests . . . they are interests in property within the meaning of section 363(f) in the sense that they arise from the property being sold.

Indeed, to equate interests in property with only *in rem* interests such as liens would be inconsistent with section 363(f)(3), which contemplates that a lien is but one type of interest. . . .

. . . We recognize that the claims of the EEOC and the [sex discrimination suit] class of plaintiffs are based on congressional enactments addressing employment discrimination and are, therefore, not to be extinguished absent a compelling justification. At the same time, in the context of a bankruptcy, these claims are, by their nature, general unsecured claims and, as such, are accorded low priority. To allow the claimants to assert successor liability claims against American while limiting other creditors' recourse to the proceeds of the asset sale would be inconsistent with the Bankruptcy Code's priority scheme.

Moreover, the sale of TWA's assets to American at a time when TWA was in financial distress was likely facilitated by American obtaining title to the assets free and clear of these civil rights claims. Absent entry of the Bankruptcy Court's order providing for a sale of TWA's assets free and clear of the successor liability claims at issue, American may have offered a discounted bid. This is particularly likely given that the EEOC has been unable to estimate the number of claims it would pursue or the magnitude of the damages it would seek. The arguments advanced by appellants do not seem to account adequately for the fact that American was the only entity that came forward with an offer that complied with the court-approved bidding procedures for TWA's assets and provided jobs for TWA's employees.

The Bankruptcy Court found that, in the absence of a sale of TWA's assets to American, "the EEOC will be relegated to holding an unsecured claim in what will very likely be a piece-meal liquidation of TWA. In that context, such claims are likely to have little if any value." The same is true for claims asserted pursuant to the Travel Voucher Program, as they would be reduced to a dollar amount and would receive the same treatment as the unsecured claims of the EEOC. Given the strong likelihood of a liquidation absent the asset sale to American, a fact which appellants do not dispute, we agree with the Bankruptcy Court that a sale of the assets of TWA at the expense of preserving successor liability claims was necessary in order to preserve some 20,000 jobs, including those of [the sex discrimination suit class members] and the EEOC claimants still employed by TWA, and to provide funding for employee-related liabilities, including retirement benefits.

After carefully considering the arguments discussed above and all other arguments advanced by appellants, we join the District Court in affirming the Bankruptcy Court's authorization of the sale of TWA's assets to American free and clear of the claims of the EEOC and the [sex discrimination suit] class.

Morgan Olson, LLC v. Frederico (*In re* Grumman Olson Industries, Inc.)

445 B.R. 243 (Bankr. S.D.N.Y. 2011)

STUART M. BERNSTEIN, U.S. Bankr. J.

This case concerns the extent of *in personam* relief that a court can grant to a buyer under Bankruptcy Code § 363(f). Morgan Olson LLC ("Morgan") purchased the debtor's assets at a bankruptcy sale free and clear of liens, claims and interests. The sale order also exonerated Morgan from certain successor liability claims. John and Denise Frederico (the "Fredericos") subsequently sued Morgan as the debtor's successor, contending that they were injured after the bankruptcy sale by a product manufactured and sold by the debtor before the bankruptcy. In response, Morgan commenced this adversary proceeding for declaratory and injunctive relief barring the Fredericos from proceeding against Morgan in state court, and each side moved for summary judgment. For the reasons that follow, the Fredericos' motion is granted, Morgan's motion is denied, and the complaint is dismissed.

BACKGROUND

Except as noted, the material facts are not disputed. At all relevant times, Grumman Olson Industries, Inc. ("Grumman" or the "Debtor") designed, manufactured and sold products for the truck body industry that were mounted on chassis sold by Ford Motor Company and General Motors Corporation ("GM"). On December 9, 2002, Grumman filed a chapter 11 petition in this Court.

The Sale

On July 1, 2003, this Court entered an Order approving the sale of certain of the Debtor's assets (the "Lot 2 Assets") to MS Truck Body Corp., a predecessor of Morgan (collectively, "Morgan") pursuant to Bankruptcy Code §§ 363 and 365. The Sale Order included certain provisions that bear on the present controversy, and in particular, on Morgan's potential liability for tort claims arising after the sale from allegedly defective products manufactured and sold by Grumman prior to the sale. First, the Sale Order granted in rem relief; the Lot 2 Assets were transferred free and clear of any claims against the estate. In other words, a creditor could not seek to collect its claim against the estate from the assets sold to Morgan:

> The sale . . . of the assets to be purchased under the Lot 2 APA (the "Lot 2 Assets") shall be free and clear of all . . . claims . . . and other interests . . . and all debts arising in any way in connection with any acts of the Debtor, claims (including but not limited to "claims" as that term is defined in the Bankruptcy Code) . . . and matters of any kind and nature, whether arising prior to or subsequent to the commencement of this Chapter 11 case . . . (the foregoing collectively referred to as "Claims") . . . and holders thereof shall be permanently enjoined from asserting such against the Lot 2 Assets and the [sic] shall look solely to the proceeds of the sale.

Second, the Sale Order released Morgan from *in personam* liability for certain claims:

[T]he Purchaser shall have no liability or responsibility for *any liability or other obligation of the Debtor* arising under or related to the Lot 2 Assets other than for the purchase price payable under the Lot 2 APA. Without limiting the effect of the foregoing, the transfer of the Lot 2 Assets . . . will not subject the Purchaser to any liability for claims against the Debtor or the Lot 2 Assets, including, but not limited to, claims for successor or vicarious liability, by reason of such transfer under the laws of the United States, any state, territory or possession thereof or the District of Columbia applicable to such transactions. The Purchaser shall not be deemed, as a result of the consummation of the transaction contemplated by the Lot 2 APA to: (a) be the successor of the Debtor; (b) have, de facto or otherwise, merged with or into the Debtor; (c) be a mere continuation or substantial continuation of the Debtor or the enterprise of the Debtor; or (d) be responsible for *any liability of the Debtor* or for payment of any benefit accruing to the Debtor, except as specifically provided for in the Lot 2 APA.

The Court retained jurisdiction, *inter alia*, "to interpret, implement and enforce the provisions of this Order." By order dated October 31, 2005, the Debtor and the Official Committee of Unsecured Creditors confirmed a joint liquidating plan. The Court signed the Final Order and Decree and thereafter reopened the case "for the limited purpose of determining the effect of the [Sale Order] issued by the Court on the parties to the Frederico Action."

This Adversary Proceeding

On October 8, 2009, the Fredericos, defendants in this adversary proceeding, commenced a personal injury action against Morgan and others in the Superior Court of New Jersey. According to their Amended Complaint, Ms. Frederico, a FedEx employee, sustained serious injuries on October 15, 2008 when the FedEx truck she was driving hit a telephone pole. The Fredericos alleged, *inter alia*, that the FedEx truck involved in the accident was manufactured, designed and/or sold by Grumman in 1994, and was defective for several reasons. The Amended Complaint asserted that Morgan continued Grumman's product line, and was, therefore, liable to the Fredericos as a successor to Grumman under New Jersey law.

On March 24, 2010, Morgan commenced this adversary proceeding for declaratory and injunctive relief. Morgan alleged that the Sale Order and the accompanying Asset Purchase Agreement exonerated it from any liability arising from products manufactured and sold prior to the sale, including liability under state successor liability laws. According to the Complaint, the truck involved in the accident was manufactured and sold by Grumman prior to the bankruptcy sale, hence, the Court should declare that §§ 363 and 365 and the Sale Order freed Morgan from successor liability and direct the Fredericos to dismiss Morgan from the state court action.

[B]oth sides moved for summary judgment. . . . [T]he motions present a straightforward, threshold legal question: does the Sale Order exonerate Morgan from liability to the Fredericos?

. . .

The Scope and Effect of the Sale Order

Section 363(f) of the Bankruptcy Code authorizes the trustee in certain circumstances to sell the estate's interest in property "free and clear of any interest in such property of an entity other than the estate." "Interests in property" as used in section 363(f) include "claims" that arise from the assets being sold. . . . By its terms, § 363(f) cleanses the transferred assets of any attendant liabilities, and allows the buyer to acquire them without fear that an estate creditor can enforce its claim against those assets.

In addition, § 363(f) has been interpreted to authorize the bankruptcy court to grant *in personam* relief, similar to the discharge under Bankruptcy Code § 1141(d), that exonerates the buyer from successor liability, including liability for tort claims. Extending the "free and clear" provisions in this manner serves two important bankruptcy policies. First, it preserves the priority scheme of the Bankruptcy Code and the principle of equality of distribution by preventing a plaintiff from asserting *in personam* successor liability against the buyer while leaving other creditors to satisfy their claims from the proceeds of the asset sale. Second, it maximizes the value of the assets that are sold.

The *in rem* relief granted under the Sale Order is immaterial to the current dispute. The Fredericos are not attempting to collect their claim by liquidating the Lot 2 Assets; they are seeking *in personam* relief against Morgan. Nevertheless, the Sale Order also includes several provisions, quoted above, that limit Morgan's *in personam* successor liability. The Sale Order freed Morgan from successor liability for claims against the Debtor "arising prior to or as a result of the purchase and sale of the Lot 2 Assets." It provided that transfer of the Lot 2 Assets did not subject Morgan to any liability for claims against the Debtor "arising under or related to the Lot 2 Assets," including claims for successor liability under non-bankruptcy law, "by reason of such transfer." Finally, Morgan would not be deemed to be a successor of the Debtor or be responsible for "any liability of the Debtor" as a result of the consummation of the sale. (*Id.*)

Certain of these limitations on Morgan's successor liability clearly do not apply. The Fredericos' claims do not arise from or relate to the Lot 2 Assets. As Morgan concedes, the truck involved in the accident was not included as part of the sale. Furthermore, the Fredericos are not basing their claims on the transfer of the Lot 2 Assets or the consummation of the sale transaction. If Morgan had immediately resold the Lot 2 Assets to a third party, the Fredericos would not be suing Morgan in state court.

Instead, the Fredericos are basing their claims on what Morgan did *after* the sale. According to their state court Amended Complaint, Morgan is liable as a successor under New Jersey law because it "continued the product line since the purchase," "traded upon and benefited from the goodwill of the product line," "held itself out to potential customers as continuing to manufacture the same product line of Grumman trucks" and "has continued to market the instant product line of trucks to Federal Express." The Sale Order did not give Morgan a free pass on future conduct, and the suggestion that it could is doubtful. . . . Section 363(f) authorizes the Court to absolve the buyer of *in personam* liability for *pre-confirmation* claims in a chapter 11 case. The rule does not extend to potential future tort claims of the type now asserted by the Fredericos. . . .

The Fredericos' cross-motion for summary judgment is granted and Morgan's motion for summary judgment is denied. The Clerk of the Court is directed to enter a judgment dismissing the Complaint.

Study Questions and Notes

1. Are *TWA* and *Grumman Olson* consistent decisions?

2. What was the basis for the successor liability claim in each case? What type of law did it arise under? Do you find it puzzling that there is no discussion of the source of the alleged successor liability claim in *TWA*?

3. *TWA* appears to involve a sort of enterprise continuity claim of successor liability. As the Third Circuit notes, the liability springs from American having purchased TWA's assets, so therefore it involves an "interest in property." But is the interest actually in any of the property? Isn't this more akin to the liability a new partner assumes when joining an existing partnership?

4. Does it matter that the liability in *TWA* existed at the time of the sale, whereas the liability in *Grumman Olson* was latent, but arose post-sale based on the conduct of the purchaser?

5. In *TWA*, does the Third Circuit seem to think it matters whether or not the EEOC and sex discrimination suit class would have a valid successor liability claim but for section 363(f) and the sale order? Or does section 363(f) trump any successor liability claim, even if valid?

Problem Set 22

purchase price > lien (approach σ)

(f)(5)

1) Leviatown is a massive commuter development planned for the Illinois prairie, about 100 minutes southwest of Chicago. "Build it, and they will come," was the exuberant exurban exclamation of Leviatown Development Co. LLC's CEO. He was wrong. The real estate market tanked, and Leviatown Development Co. is in Chapter 11. The 1,000 acres of soybean fields that were to become Leviatown are subject to a $1 billion mortgage from a syndicate led by Behemoth Bank, N.A. Lincoln County, Illinois would like to purchase 300 acres of the Leviatown land to develop into a bison preserve. Behemoth Bank refuses to release the lien on any of the property unless it is paid in full. Is there any way for the County to purchase the land for the bison preserve without having to pay off the entire $1 billion loan? Would it matter if the County had a $10 million tax lien on the property, which under state law primes the mortgage? 11 U.S.C. § 363(f).

price

2) Sousa Brass Instruments is in Chapter 11. Sousa's inventory of Sousaphones, Saxophones, Sarrousophones, Saxoboes, Saxhorns, and Serpentines (all musical instruments) would bring in perhaps $5 million at auction.

    a. If the inventory is subject to a $4 million lien from Invercargill Finance, can the property be sold over Invercargill's objection? 11 U.S.C. § 363(f). — *Yes*

    b. What if the Invercargill lien is for $6 million? 11 U.S.C. § 363(f).

depends on which approach?

"mere continuation"

("product line" exception)

(3) Demeter Farm Products, a manufacturer of quality agricultural equipment that is sold under the brand name Cornucopia, is proposing to sell substantially all of its assets to Ceres Industries pursuant to section 363(f). Some of Demeter's tort creditors have objected to the sale; they want the sale order to make clear that Ceres is also assuming liabilities caused by the farm equipment lines that caused their injuries.

a. Is Ceres able to purchase the assets free of the existing tort creditors' liabilities?
b. Is Ceres able to purchase the assets free of future tort claims by the users of Demeter products?   *no ?*

(4) Textile manufacturer Lausaunne, Inc. is one of the last remaining American textile firms. Lausaunne is a textile "converter" that designs fabrics, but outsources the production to mills and dyers. Lausaunne has survived by focusing on high-end textiles, but to produce these textiles, Lausaunne requires very sophisticated mills and dyers. Lausaunne has depended heavily on Amerbelle for its dyeing, but Lausaunne's business alone is not enough to support Amerbelle's cost structure. Amerbelle has had great difficulty attracting enough capital because of its enormous potential environmental and personal injury tort liability due to the toxicity of the chemicals in various dyes.

Amerbelle's dyeing process involves large volumes of water pumped from the Providence River. Following the dyeing process, the water is cleaned and returned to the river, but Amerbelle's cleaning process leaves something to be desired. Amerbelle borrowed heavily to improve its dyeing process so as to eliminate new environmental contamination, but the borrowing costs were too much for its cash flow.

When Amerbelle filed for Chapter 7, Lausaunne bid on Amerbelle's assets and purchased them in a sale under section 363(b). Lausaunne was keen to maintain the expertise of an important supplier, and Lausaunne's management believed that it might also be able to turn around Amerbelle and continued to operate the firm under the Amerbelle name. Amerbelle continued to supply Lausaunne and other firms with dyeing.

A year after the purchase, the Environmental Protection Agency (EPA) brought suit against Lausaunne, contending that Lausaunne was responsible for cleaning up the environmental contamination of the Providence River caused by Amerbelle's pre-sale operations. An attorney representing former Amerbelle employees and retirees has also filed a putative class action against Lausaunne for personal injuries deriving from the employees' exposure to toxic chemicals. Doug Ramsey, the CEO of Lausaunne, is beside himself. "I thought we were buying just the assets," he moans. "How are we possibly stuck with the liabilities?" What do you tell Doug? And what do you advise him to do next time? 11 U.S.C. § 363(b), (f).

---

product line ?

CHAPTER 23

EXECUTORY CONTRACTS AND UNEXPIRED LEASES

I. BREACHING CONTRACTS IN BANKRUPTCY

The baseline rule of contract law is that a non-breaching party to a contract receives expectancy damages following a breach. For example, imagine a forward contract to sell winter wheat in six months for $10/bushel. Suppose that there's a drought, and the market price of wheat soars to $15/bushel. The seller will be tempted to breach the contract and sell at the higher market price and capture the favorable swing in the price for itself.

Contract law doesn't let the seller get away with this. If the seller engages in such a breach, the seller is liable for expectancy damages, namely the difference between the market price at the time the buyer learned of the breach and the contract price, plus any incidental and consequential damage (but less expenses saved in consequence of the breach). UCC § 2-713. Expectancy damages mean that the seller is not able to keep the increase in market price. This is a reasonable outcome: The whole point of the forward contract was to allocate the risk of changes in the market price between the buyer and the seller, so letting the seller keep the gain in market prices undermines the basis of the contract.

Bankruptcy law changes this balance in some situations. When a debtor breaches a contract before bankruptcy, the counterparty's claim for breach of contract damages is just a regular pre-petition claim, and, absent a lien, is a general unsecured claim. But what happens when a debtor breaches a contract post-petition? The answer depends on whether the contract is an "executory contract" or "unexpired lease," or is something else. (What constitutes an executory contract is discussed in the next section.)

If the contract is an executory contract or unexpired lease, then the debtor must choose whether it wishes to "assume" or "reject" the contract. If the debtor assumes an executory contract or unexpired lease, that contract or lease becomes a post-petition obligation of the bankruptcy estate and therefore is entitled to payment as an administrative priority claim, under sections 507(a)(2) and 503(b), which must be paid in full in cash on the effective date of a plan per section 1129(a)(9), unless it would otherwise be paid outside of a plan in the ordinary course of business under section 363(c).

If the debtor rejects an executory contract or unexpired lease, then the contract or lease is treated as if it had been breached immediately before the bankruptcy filing. This means that the claim for contract or lease damages is a pre-petition claim, and therefore likely an unsecured claim under section 502. Limitations on claims allowance, such as those for landlords' claims and employment termination claims, still apply. 11 U.S.C. § 502(b)(6)-(7). Thus, rejection of an unexpired lease does not result in a claim for damages for the entire amount of rent remaining on the lease, but in a claim for the rent for the greater of one year or 15 percent of the remaining rent (but no more than three years), as well as any past due pre-petition rent and other charges for repairs and maintenance.

Thus, an assumed contract gets paid in full in most cases, whereas a rejected contract gets paid as an unsecured creditor in "bankruptcy dollars" (if at all). This situation is a remarkable departure from the traditional contract performance option, in which the choice is to perform the contract or pay damages (usually for the expectancy value).

Consider, then, Oliver Wendell Holmes, Jr.'s famous dictum: "The duty to keep a contract at common law means a prediction that you must pay damages if you do not keep it—and nothing else." *The Path of the Law*, 10 HARV. L. REV. 457 (1897). In 1897, Holmes's statement correctly described the law. Starting a year later, however, with the Bankruptcy Act of 1898, Holmes's statement requires qualification: "The duty to keep a contract means a prediction that you must pay damages if you do not keep it—*or file for bankruptcy and pay those damages in little tiny bankruptcy dollars.*" Thus, the calculus underlying the traditional contract performance option is altered. With expectancy damages as the norm, performance and breach are frequently equally costly. But when damages for breaches have to be paid in bankruptcy dollars, breach becomes cheaper, and therefore more attractive if contract performance would result in little or no benefit to the debtor.

What's more, bankruptcy gives the debtor some time in which to decide whether to exercise the breach option. This allows the debtor to "play the market" and see if a contract would be "in the money" or "out of the money" before breaching. Suppose a debtor has contracted to purchase a shipment of 100 boxes of widgets in 100 days for $10/box. Now let's imagine that the market price of widgets at the time performance is due is only $8/box. The debtor should reject the contract and pay the damages in bankruptcy dollars. The savings of $200 will augment the estate. While there will be additional unsecured claims of $1,000 from the rejection of the widget contract, that $1,000 will only have (at best) a pro rata share of the $200 savings. If, on the other hand, the price of widgets goes up and is $12/box at the time performance is due, the debtor will want to assume the contract. The debtor can thus "cherry-pick" only winning contracts to assume and reject the others at low cost. The ability to cherry-pick contracts is one of bankruptcy law's most distinctive and powerful tools for maximizing the value of the bankruptcy estate.

What happens when the contract is not an "executory contract" or unexpired lease? In such a situation, the debtor cannot assume or reject the contract. The Bankruptcy Code does not say, however, what happens to the contract. Generally, the debtor may continue to either perform the contract or breach it, just as it would outside of bankruptcy; bankruptcy does not impose any duty on the debtor to perform the non-executory contract, although if performance is outside of the ordinary course of business, then court approval is required under section 363(c). Thus, if the debtor performs the contract, the counterparty gets paid per the contract terms. But if the debtor breaches, the legal treatment gets murky.

Post-petition breaches of nonexecutory pre-petition contract claims are known as "straddle claims," and their legal treatment is unsettled. Some courts treat straddle claims as administrative expenses under section 503(b). Is a breach of contract claim truly an "actual and necessary cost[] and expense[] of preserving the estate" as section 503(b) requires? Arguably yes, because the alternative to a breach would be performance and the debtor would only breach if it was economically more advantageous than performance. Thus, if the choice is only between breach and performance, breach is an expense of preserving the estate. Yet both breach and performance are simply costs to the estate—they don't actually preserve the estate in any way. Accordingly, some courts treat straddle claims simply as dischargeable pre-petition claims on the theory that they arise from breaches of pre-petition contracts.[1] Table 23.1 summarizes the treatment of different breach of contract claims against the debtor.

Table 23.1 Treatment of Contract Breach Claims Against the Debtor in Bankruptcy

Timing and Nature of Breach	Treatment of Counterparty's Claim
Pre-petition breach of any pre-petition contract.	Regular pre-petition claim under 11 U.S.C. §§ 502 and 506.
Post-petition rejection of pre-petition executory contract or lease.	Deemed pre-petition breach claim under 11 U.S.C. §§ 365(g), 502(g).
Post-petition breach of nonexecutory pre-petition contract ("straddle claims").	Treatment unsettled. Possibly administrative expense under 11 U.S.C. § 503(b) or dischargeable pre-petition claim or potentially nondischargeable post-petition claim.
Post-petition breach of assumed pre-petition executory contract or lease.	Administrative expense claim. 11 U.S.C. §§ 365(g), 502(g).

The discussion here so far has focused solely on breaches of contract *by the debtor*. The non-debtor counterparty may always breach its contract with the debtor, just as if normal contract law applies. The debtor will then have a regular breach of contract claim—that will be paid in *real* dollars (unless a right of setoff applies). Executory contracts and leases are a one-way street. That is why certain executory contracts are carved out from the protection of the automatic stay under section 362(d)—swaps, futures contracts, forward contracts, repurchase agreements, and master netting agreements. The stay exemption permits counterparties to these

---

1. Some courts have also treated post-petition breaches of nonexecutory contracts simply as post-petition claims on the debtor, which are not dischargeable in Chapter 7, but given that corporate entities are not eligible for a discharge in Chapter 7, this is of little import. The Chapter 11 discharge covers post-petition claims that arise before plan confirmation. 11 U.S.C. § 1141(d)(1)(A).

contracts to terminate the contract (if termination is favorable) and thereby avoid "cherry-picking" by the debtor.

II. WHAT IS AN EXECUTORY CONTRACT?

The Bankruptcy Code's provisions on contract assumption and rejection are keyed to "executory contracts" and "unexpired leases." There is little controversy as to what constitutes an "unexpired lease." But what is an "executory contract"? The Bankruptcy Code does not contain a definition, and there is no Supreme Court case adopting one. The most commonly used definition is the "Countryman test," named after Professor Vern Countryman.[1] The Countryman test, sometimes also known as the "material breach test," provides that an executory contract is one "under which the obligation of both the bankrupt and the other party to the contract are so far unperformed that the failure of either to complete performance would constitute a material breach excusing the performance of the other." Vern Countryman, *Executory Contracts in Bankruptcy*, Pt. 1, 7 MINN. L. REV. 439, 460 (1973). The basic idea behind this test is that executory contracts and unexpired leases simultaneously involve both assets and liabilities of the estate—the estate has both obligations as well as some value owed to it on these contracts and leases.

While the Countryman test is widely used as the rule of thumb for determining what is an executory contract, there are some situations that it does not comfortably address, as the following case illustrates, and courts have added extensions to the Countryman test to account for these situations.

In re Riodizio, Inc., Debtor

204 B.R. 417 (Bankr. S.D.N.Y. 1997)

STUART M. BERNSTEIN, U.S. Bankruptcy Judge.

Riodizio, Inc. (the "debtor") seeks, *inter alia*, to reject a stock option agreement . . . entered into in June, 1995. Riodizio Company, LLC ("LLC"), the optionee . . . , opposes the motion. The motion thrusts us into the "psychedelic" world of executory contracts, Jay Lawrence Westbrook, *A Functional Analysis of Executory Contracts*, 74 MINN. L. REV. 227, 228 (1989) ("Westbrook"), and reinforces the prophecy that the time that litigants and the courts spend searching for "executoriness" can be put to better use analyzing the benefits and burdens of the contract itself.

---

1. Countryman was nearly famous for the case of *Griswold v. Connecticut*, 381 U.S. 479 (1965), which was almost *Countryman v. Connecticut*. As an Associate Professor at Yale Law School, Countryman originally set out to be the plaintiff in that famous case, which established a "right to privacy" in the course of invalidating a Connecticut law prohibiting the use of contraceptives. Professor Countryman reportedly set out to purchase the contraceptives and did so from a New Haven Walgreen's only to discover that the store from which he purchased was a local franchise of a national chain, and for the litigation to be tee'd up well required a more substantial defendant. Gerald K. Smith, *Vern Countryman*, NORTON BANKR. ADVISER, JUNE 1999 at 2, 5. *Griswold* was, of course, authored by Countryman's mentor, Justice William O. Douglas, for whom he had clerked.

For the reasons discussed below, the Court concludes that the stock option is an executory contract, and grants the debtor's motion to reject it. . . .

FACTS

The debtor commenced this Chapter 11 case on August 19, 1996. It owns and operates a Brazilian grill restaurant (called a "Riodizio" in Brazil) at 417 Lafayette Street in New York, New York. Prior to commencing business, the debtor and its two shareholders, Alan Berfas and Frank Ferraro, entered into numerous agreements with LLC to secure financing and equipment for the restaurant. These included a Loan and Lease Agreement, dated June 1, 1995 (the "Loan and Lease") . . . and an undated stock option (the "Warrant") that the debtor granted to the LLC.

1. The Loan and Lease

Under the Loan and Lease, LLC advanced $200,000.00 to the debtor to operate the business. The terms of the loan, as evidenced by a promissory note, called for 15% interest, with principal and interest payable in 42 monthly installments. As security for the advances, the debtor gave LLC a priority security interest in all office equipment including, without limitation, computer equipment, kitchen equipment, fixtures, mailing lists, bank accounts, Transmedia agreements and proceeds, and accounts receivable. Berfas and Ferraro also provided a limited guaranty by depositing into escrow, in favor of LLC, their respective shares in the debtor, general stock powers, and their resignations as officers, directors and employees.

The Loan and Lease also provided that LLC would purchase and then lease kitchen and other equipment valued at $150,000.00 to the debtor. Previously, however, the Court denied the debtor's motion to reject this equipment lease. First, the equipment lease was not a true lease, but rather, a security financing arrangement involving a self-amortizing loan under which the debtor paid the entire purchase price, including interest, in forty-two monthly installments of $4,612.36 each. Second, the equipment lease was part of the single Loan and Lease agreement, and the debtor could not "cherry pick" and reject unfavorable provisions contained in an integrated agreement.

2. The Warrant and Shareholders Agreement

As part of the underlying transaction, the debtor also executed the Warrant.[1] It states, in its entirety, as follows:

Riodizio, Inc. (the "Corporation") hereby grants to the holder of this warrant the right to purchase all or part of an aggregate of 93 common shares of the Corporation for the consideration of one dollar ($1.00) per share.

This warrant may be exercised for a period of twenty five [sic] years.

The Warrant was signed on behalf of the debtor by Berfas and Ferraro, each of whom own 33 shares of the debtor's common stock. If LLC exercises its warrant (and the debtor

---

1. Although the Warrant and Shareholders Agreement were executed in connection with the lending transaction, both parties treat them as separate, independent agreements for purposes of section 365.

delivers the shares), LLC will own approximately 60% of the debtor's outstanding shares based upon an additional investment of only $93.00.

. . .

DISCUSSION

1. Introduction

Section 365(a) states that "the trustee, subject to the court's approval, may assume or reject any executory contract or unexpired lease of the debtor." 11 U.S.C. § 365(a). The Bankruptcy Code does not define the term "executory contract." The legislative history regarding this section states that "though there is no precise definition of what contracts are executory, it generally includes contracts on which performance remains due to some extent on both sides." [Citations omitted.] Finding this definition too broad and sweeping, . . . most courts have adopted Professor Countryman's definition of an executory contract as

> a contract under which the obligation of both the bankrupt and the other party to the contract are so far unperformed that the failure of either to complete performance would constitute a material breach excusing performance of the other.

Vern Countryman, *Executory Contracts in Bankruptcy: Part 1*, 57 MINN. L. REV. 439, 460 (1973).

Under Countryman's "material breach" test, a prepetition contract is executory when both sides are still obligated to render substantial performance. Where such performance remains due on only one side, the contract is non-executory, and hence, neither assumable nor rejectable. The materiality of the breach is a question of state law. Thus, if applicable non-bankruptcy law permits either party to sue for breach because of the other party's failure to perform, the contract is executory.

Ordinarily, executoriness is determined as of the petition date. Sometimes, however, postpetition events alter the executoriness of a contract, as when a contract expires postpetition. In those circumstances, a court will look to the date the motion to assume or reject is made or heard rather than the petition date. [Citations omitted.]

Some have found the Countryman "material breach" test too constraining and static. In *Chattanooga Mem'l Park v. Still (In re Jolly)*, 574 F.2d 349 (6th Cir.) (1978), a pre-Code case, the Court observed:

> [The Countryman] definition[] [is] helpful, but do[es] not resolve the problem. The key, it seems, to deciphering the meaning of the executory contract rejection provisions, is to work backward, proceeding from an examination of the purposes rejection is expected to accomplish. If those objectives have already been accomplished, or if they can't be accomplished through rejection, then the contract is not executory within the meaning of the Bankruptcy Act.

574 F.2d at 351.

In this same vein, some advocate a functional analysis which eliminates the requirement of executoriness. *See Westbrook, supra*, 74 MINN. L. REV. 227; *see also* Michael T. Andrew, *Executory Contracts in Bankruptcy: Understanding Rejection*, 59 U. COLO.

L. REV. 845 (1988) ("Andrew I"); Michael T. Andrew, *Executory Contracts Revisited: A Reply to Professor Westbrook*, 62 U. COLO. L. REV. 1 (1991) ("Andrew II"). Under the functional approach, "the question of whether a contract is executory is determined by the benefits that assumption or rejection would produce for the estate." *Sipes v. Atlantic Gulf Communities Corp. (In re General Dev. Corp.)*, 84 F.3d 1364, 1375 (11th Cir. 1996); *accord Drexel*, 138 Bankr. at 696 (synthesizing the Westbrook and Andrew articles, and concluding that a threshold requirement of executoriness is misplaced; rather, the proper analysis is whether rejection will produce a benefit to the estate).

The functional approach does not repudiate the Countryman rule; it merely recognizes its limitations. It also conserves the time and effort that the parties and the court otherwise spend resolving the question of executoriness. But it has its critics. To be subject to assumption or rejection, the statute expressly requires that the contract be executory. Ignoring executoriness rewrites the statute in a fundamental way. *See In re Child World, Inc.*, 147 Bankr. at 851 ("Manifestly, the functional approach ignores the statutory requirement that the contract to be assumed or rejected must be 'executory.'").

2. The Warrant

Options agreements, such as the Warrant, demonstrate the shortcomings of the Countryman definition. "An option contract is essentially an enforceable promise not to revoke an offer." *In re III Enterprises, Inc. V*, 163 Bankr. 453, 460-61 (Bankr. E.D. Pa.), *aff'd*, 169 Bankr. 551 (E.D. Pa. 1994). It is a unilateral contract until exercised; upon exercise, it becomes a bilateral contract.

An option contemplates performance by both parties but requires it from only one. The optionor must keep the offer open. The optionee may but need not exercise the option; if he does, each party must perform its obligations under the resulting bilateral contract. The optionee's failure to exercise the option constitutes a failure of condition rather than a breach of duty. The failure to perform a condition which is not also a legal duty cannot give rise to a material breach, and hence, an option contract is not executory under the Countryman definition.

Most courts, however, consider an option contract to be executory although they reach their conclusions through different routes. In *In re Waldron*, 36 Bankr. 633 (Bankr. S.D. Fla. 1984), the debtors granted a real estate option to the Shell Oil Company. The debtors subsequently filed a joint Chapter 13 petition in order to reject the contract since the value of the property exceeded the option price.

The *Waldron* court held that the option was executory, but relied on the "some performance due" standard cited in the legislative history rather than the more rigorous Countryman test. Initially, the court noted that "performance continues to remain due on the part of the Debtors" because they had to keep their offer open. *In re Waldron*, 36 Bankr. at 637. In addition, some performance also remained due from Shell. The court assumed, in light of the value of the real estate, that Shell would exercise the option. To do so, Shell had to tender its acceptance in accordance with the terms of the option contract, and this "is the performance that foreseeably remains due by Shell or its assignees." *Id.* Further, once Shell exercised the option, "the option contract will immediately transform into an executory contract for the sale of real property." *Id.*

The court reached the same conclusion by an alternative route. Quoting a lengthy passage from *In re Booth*, 19 Bankr. 53 (Bankr. D. Utah 1982), the court tacitly acknowledged the limitations of the Countryman test and presaged the functional analysis discussed above. It observed that executory contracts are not measured by the mutuality of commitments but the nature of the parties and the goals of reorganization. Thus, the benefit to the estate rather than the form of the contract controls. *In re Waldron*, 36 Bankr. at 637.

The option cases that came after *Waldron*, but adopted the Countryman definition, faced a dilemma. The optionor's obligation—to keep the option open—was substantial, but the optionee did not owe any substantial obligation that could result in a material breach. Andrew II, *supra*, 62 U. COLO. L. REV. at 32. To fit the option contract within the "material breach" test, they conflated the option contract with the contingent bilateral contract, finding the optionee's duty of substantial performance in the contingent obligation to perform under the bilateral contract created by the exercise of the option.

The case law confirms that executoriness lies in the eyes of the beholder. Despite the contrary case law discussed above, the Warrant, an option contract, is not an executory contract under Countryman's "material breach" test. The debtor granted the option to LLC as additional consideration for the loan. LLC fully performed any legal obligation in connection with the Warrant when it funded the loan. While the exercise of the Warrant is a condition to the debtor's obligation to deliver the shares to LLC, LLC is not legally obligated to exercise the Warrant or do anything (or refrain from doing anything).

If the "some performance due" test in the legislative history is overly inclusive, the Countryman test excludes too much. It imposes a "material breach" requirement, raising the threshold of executoriness above what Congress seemed to intend. In the case of options, it excludes contracts under which the debtor has benefits and burdens, each party must still perform as a condition to the other party's performance, and assumption or rejection may confer a net benefit on the estate. Under the circumstances, we should question the test rather than condemn the contract to a "legal limbo" in which it can be neither assumed nor rejected. *See* Westbrook, *supra*, 74 MINN. L. REV. at 239.

A test less exclusive than Countryman's that takes into account the mutual performance requirement embodied in the legislative history should be substituted. Under this test, a contract is executory if each side must render performance, on account of an existing legal duty or to fulfill a condition, to obtain the benefit of the other party's performance. Weighing the relative benefits and burdens to the debtor is the essence of the decision to assume or reject; if each party must still give something to get something, the contract is executory, and the debtor must demonstrate whether assumption or rejection confers a net benefit on the estate. If the debtor has done everything it needs to do to obtain the benefit of its bargain, assumption serves no purpose, and the debtor may simply sue to enforce its rights. Similarly, if the other party has done everything necessary to require the debtor to perform, the debtor's performance adds nothing to the estate, the debtor will not assume the contract, and the other party can file a prepetition claim.[6] Here, the Warrant is executory; each party must perform under the Warrant in order to obtain the benefits under the contingent bilateral contract of sale. To sell the shares and

---

6. The postpetition breach of a prepetition contract gives rise only to a prepetition claim.

receive payment, the debtor must keep the offer open. To make payment and acquire the shares, LLC must first exercise the option granted under the Warrant.[7]

Having concluded that the Warrant is executory, the Court must determine whether its rejection will benefit the estate. While a court will ordinarily defer to the business judgment of the debtor's management, *In re Minges*, 602 F.2d at 43, Berfas and Ferraro have an interest in preventing LLC from exercising the option and diluting their personal stakes in and control over the debtor. Consequently, the debtor cannot rely on the presumptions of business judgment rule to support its decision.

The Court's independent review nevertheless confirms that rejection benefits the estate without any significant downside. Proper business reasons for rejecting a contract include the following: (1) the contract is uneconomical to complete according to its terms; (2) the contract is financially burdensome to the estate; (3) rejection will make the debtor more attractive to a prospective purchaser or investor; (4) rejection will result in a large claim against the estate; and (5) in the case of a stock option contract, the debtor can market the shares and receive a higher or better price than the option offers.[9]

The Warrant provides a *de minimis* benefit to the debtor, granting it the right to receive $93.00 if LLC exercises its option. On the other hand, it deprives the debtor of the possibility that it can sell the same shares for more money to another investor during the next twenty-three years of its remaining life. It does not matter whether this hypothetical investor exists; a $93.00 payment is so *de minimis* that the mere possibility outweighs any benefit in performing the Warrant.

Breaching the Warrant through rejection produces a minimal, adverse effect on the estate. Rejection constitutes a breach of contract immediately prior to the petition date. 11 U.S.C. § 365(g)(1). At the outset, the Warrant does not create any property interest in LLC's favor that would survive rejection. A breach leaves LLC with a claim for damages equal to the difference between the option price and the market value of the shares at the time of the breach. If LLC suffered any damage, this goes far to proving the wisdom of rejection; the debtor can sell the shares (to LLC or a third party) for more than the per share price of $1.00, and pay LLC's claim in tiny bankruptcy dollars.[10] . . .

CONCLUSION

The Court grants the debtor's motion to reject the Warrant, and directs the parties to contact chambers to schedule an evidentiary hearing. The hearing will concern whether rejection of the Shareholders Agreement benefits the estate.

---

7. If the Warrant is not executory, the debtor's effort to reject it is a superfluous act. Thus, if LLC has fully performed under the Warrant, it is in no different position than the trade vendor who sold onions to the debtor prepetition, and never received payment; the seller has a damage claim, but must await a *pro rata* payment with the other unsecured creditors.

9. Some courts refer to a balancing of equities, suggesting that rejection should be refused if it will cause disproportionate harm to the non-debtor party. The right to assume or reject an executory contract is designed to permit the debtor to shed its obligations under burdensome and uneconomical contracts. Section 365 does not require any balancing of the equities.

10. This assumes that the shares are at least as valuable today or in the future as they were on the petition date. But even if they are not, the option price is so low as to confer no meaningful benefit on the estate.

III. STATUTORY RESTRICTIONS ON ASSUMPTION

Not all executory contracts and unexpired leases may be assumed. The Bankruptcy Code prohibits the assumption of certain types of executory contracts and unexpired leases and place conditions on the assumption of other contracts and leases.

A. Cure Requirements

In order to assume a contract, the trustee/DIP must, in most cases, cure defaults prior to assumption and provide adequate assurances of future performance. 11 U.S.C. § 365(b). There are some exceptions to this rule, however, and they dwell in one of the most abstrusely drafted provisions in the Bankruptcy Code, section 365(b)(1)(A). You are welcome to take the time puzzling through the language, but as far as anyone can tell, it is best thought of as a rule with an exception and an exception to the first exception plus a manqué exception to the first exception.

The rule is that a trustee/DIP is required to cure any default on an executory contract or unexpired lease prior to assumption. The exception is for defaults on nonmonetary obligations on real property leases. These breaches need not be cured, not least because they often cannot be cured.

Examples of such breaches would be violation of a lease provision requiring continuous operation or hours of operation (a "going dark" clause), maintenance of insurance or a security system, restrictions on the use of property, or key person provisions requiring continued employment of a named individual. None of these provisions can be cured without a time machine. If a store were closed for a day in breach of a lease, there is no way to effectuate a cure for the breach, and section 365(b)(1) does not require that it be cured for lease assumption.

The first exception to the exception for nonmonetary obligations on real property leases pertains to commercial real estate leases only. If the lease is of commercial real estate, then the trustee/DIP must provide monetary compensation for non-pecuniary harms.

The second, would-be exception, is for penalty provisions. On its own, section 365(b)(1)(A) would seem to carve out penalty provisions, and require that they be complied with for cure, but section 365(b)(2)(D) makes clear that penalty provisions need not be cured in any case. Therefore, it is likely that section 365(b)(1)(A)'s penalty provision language is simply a poorly drafted attempt to clarify that penalty provisions need never be cured. The language in question was part of the 2005 Bankruptcy Abuse Prevention and Consumer Protection Act, which contains numerous drafting errors, such as sentences with missing words, etc.

So, putting it all together, the trustee/DIP is required to cure any defaults in order to assume an executory contract or unexpired lease *unless* the default is of a nonmonetary obligation on a real property lease, *but if* the default is on a commercial lease, then monetary compensation must be provided for non-pecuniary harms. Cure always required compensation for pecuniary harms, 11 U.S.C. § 365(b)(1)(B), but penalty provisions need not be cured. 11 U.S.C. § 365(b)(2)(D). Therefore, it is necessary to cure *any* default on an executory contract or lease of personalty prior to assumption, but it is not necessary to provide monetary cure for nonmonetary defaults on residential property leases. Table 23.2 summarizes what sorts of cures are required to assume various types of leases.

Table 23.2 Assumption Requirements for Leases

	Monetary Default	Nonmonetary Default	Default Penalty
Personalty	Cure required.	No cure required.	No payment required.
Residential Real Estate	Cure required.	No cure required.	No payment required.
Commercial Real Estate	Cure required.	Monetary compensation required.	No payment required.

The cure requirement of section 365(b) requires pre-plan (or pre-liquidation) payment on a pre-petition debt. Regardless of the ultimate solvency of the debtor, the counterparty will be paid 100 cents on the dollar on the pre-petition breach amount. Thus section 365(b) functions as a de facto priority rule.

B. Categorically Unassumable Types of Contracts

Section 365(c) provides that three categories of contracts cannot be assumed or assigned. In reverse order, section 365(c)(3) provides that commercial real estate leases that were terminated prior to bankruptcy cannot be assumed. Bankruptcy cannot unwind a lease termination that occurred prior to bankruptcy.

Second, section 365(c)(2) provides that contracts for financing or securities underwriting are not assumable. Instead, any sort of post-petition financing agreement must comply with the requirements of section 364, as we saw in the previous chapter. If financing contracts could be assumed under section 365, then the protections of section 364 would have little meaning.

Third, section 365(c)(1) prohibits assumption or assignment of a contract or unexpired lease if the counterparty would be excused under applicable non-bankruptcy law from accepting performance from a party other than the debtor or debtor-in-possession, and the counterparty has not assented to the assumption or assignment.

The simplest situation this encompasses are contracts based on an expectation of personal performance by the debtor. Thus, if I have a contract with debtor Picasso to paint my portrait, the trustee—even if his name is Warhol—cannot assume the contract, nor can he assign it to Monet. This sort of concern has little applicability, however, in business cases. Instead, where the issue is joined in business cases is when a contract contains an anti-assignment clause or where federal IP law places restrictions on assignability.

Courts have split in their approach. Some courts have adopted what is known as the "hypothetical" test, meaning that an executory contract or unexpired lease cannot be assumed if it could not hypothetically be assigned, even if the estate has no intention of assigning the contract. Other courts, however, have adopted an "actual" test, meaning that an executory contract or unexpired lease can be assumed, if the estate does not intend to assign it. The following case considers this problem. To understand what's at stake, it is about whether the debtor can continue using valuable intellectual property licenses or not. If the contract cannot be assumed, there will be automatic rejection, which will let the non-debtor counterparty out of the contract. While rejection might result in a less favorable bankruptcy claim, that may be less important to the non-debtor counterparty than getting out of the contract, particularly if the contract is intellectual property that can be profitably relicensed (and maybe even on better terms than with the rejected contract).

Perlman v. Catapult Entertainment (*In re* Catapult Entertainment)

165 F.3d 747 (9th Cir. 1998)

FLETCHER, Circuit Judge:

Appellant Stephen Perlman ("Perlman") licensed certain patents to appellee Catapult Entertainment, Inc. ("Catapult"). He now seeks to bar Catapult, which has since become a Chapter 11 debtor in possession, from assuming the patent licenses as part of its reorganization plan. Notwithstanding Perlman's objections, the bankruptcy court approved the assumption of the licenses and confirmed the reorganization plan. The district court affirmed the bankruptcy court on intermediate appeal. Perlman appeals that decision. We are called upon to determine whether, in light of § 365(c)(1) of the Bankruptcy Code, a Chapter 11 debtor in possession may assume certain nonexclusive patent licenses over a licensor's objection. We conclude that the bankruptcy court erred in permitting the debtor in possession to assume the patent licenses in question.

I.

Catapult, a California corporation, was formed in 1994 to create an online gaming network for 16-bit console videogames. That same year, Catapult entered into two license agreements with Perlman, wherein Perlman granted to Catapult the right to exploit certain relevant technologies, including patents and patent applications.

In October 1996, Catapult filed for reorganization under Chapter 11 of the Bankruptcy Code. Shortly before the filing of the bankruptcy petition, Catapult entered into a merger agreement with Mpath Interactive, Inc. ("Mpath"). This agreement contemplated the filing of the bankruptcy petition, followed by a reorganization via a "reverse triangular merger" involving Mpath, MPCAT Acquisition Corporation ("MPCAT"), and Catapult. Under the terms of the merger agreement, MPCAT (a wholly-owned subsidiary of Mpath created for this transaction) would merge into Catapult, leaving Catapult as the surviving entity. When the dust cleared, Catapult's creditors and equity holders would have received approximately $14 million in cash, notes, and securities; Catapult, in turn, would have become a wholly-owned subsidiary of Mpath. The relevant third party creditors and equity holders accepted Catapult's reorganization plan by the majorities required by the Bankruptcy Code.

On October 24, 1996, as part of the reorganization plan, Catapult filed a motion with the bankruptcy court seeking to assume some 140 executory contracts and leases, including the Perlman licenses. Over Perlman's objection, the bankruptcy court granted Catapult's motion and approved the reorganization plan. The district court subsequently affirmed the bankruptcy court. This appeal followed. . . .

II.

Section 365 of the Bankruptcy Code gives a trustee in bankruptcy (or, in a Chapter 11 case, the debtor in possession) the authority to assume, assign, or reject the executory contracts and unexpired leases of the debtor, notwithstanding any contrary provisions appearing in such contracts or leases. See 11 U.S.C. § 365(a) & (f). This extraordinary authority, however, is not absolute. Section 365(c)(1) provides that, notwithstanding the general policy set out in § 365(a):

> (c) The trustee may not assume or assign any executory contract or unexpired lease of the debtor, whether or not such contract or lease prohibits or restricts assignment of rights or delegation of duties, if
>
> > (1)
> >
> > > (A) applicable law excuses a party, other than the debtor, to such contract or lease from accepting performance from or rendering performance to an entity other than the debtor or the debtor in possession, whether or not such contract or lease prohibits or restricts assignment of rights or delegation of duties; and
> > >
> > > (B) such party does not consent to such assumption or assignment. . . .

11 U.S.C. § 365(c). Our task, simply put, is to apply this statutory language to the facts at hand and determine whether it prohibits Catapult, as the debtor in possession, from assuming the Perlman licenses without Perlman's consent.

While simply put, our task is not so easily resolved; the proper interpretation of § 365(c)(1) has been the subject of considerable disagreement among courts and commentators. On one side are those who adhere to the plain statutory language, which establishes a so-called "hypothetical test" to govern the assumption of executory contracts. See In re James Cable Partners, 27 F.3d 534, 537 (11th Cir. 1994) (characterizing § 365(c)(1)(A) as posing "a hypothetical question"); In re West Elec., Inc., 852 F.2d 79, 83 (3d Cir. 1988) (same); In re Catron, 158 B.R. 629, 633-38 (E.D. Va. 1993) (same), aff'd without op., 25 F.3d 1038 (4th Cir. 1994). On the other side are those that forsake the statutory language in favor of an "actual test" that, in their view, better accomplishes the intent of Congress. See Institut Pasteur v. Cambridge Biotech Corp., 104 F.3d 489, 493 (1st Cir.) (rejecting the hypothetical test in favor of the actual test), cert. denied, 521 U.S. 1120 (1997). . . . [T]oday we hold that we are bound by the plain terms of the statute and join the Third and Eleventh Circuits in adopting the "hypothetical test."

III.

We begin, as we must, with the statutory language. The plain language of § 365(c)(1) "links nonassignability under 'applicable law' together with a prohibition on assumption in bankruptcy." 1 David G. Epstein, Steve H. Nickles & James J. White, BANKRUPTCY § 5-15 at 474 (1992). In other words, the statute by its terms bars a debtor in possession from *assuming* an executory contract without the nondebtor's consent where applicable law precludes *assignment* of the contract to a third party. The literal language of § 365(c)(1) is thus said to establish a "hypothetical test": a debtor in possession may not assume an executory contract over the nondebtor's objection if applicable law would bar assignment to a hypothetical third party, even where the debtor in possession has no intention of assigning the contract in question to any such third party.

Before applying the statutory language to the case at hand, we first resolve a number of preliminary issues that are either not disputed by the parties, or are so clearly established as to deserve no more than passing reference. First, we follow the lead of the parties in assuming that the Perlman licenses are executory agreements within the meaning of § 365. Second, it is well-established that § 365(c)'s use of the term "trustee" includes Chapter 11 debtors in possession. *See Institut Pasteur*, 104 F.3d at 492 n.7. Third, our precedents make it clear that federal patent law constitutes "applicable law" within the meaning of § 365(c), and that nonexclusive patent licenses are "personal and assignable only with the consent of the licensor." When we have cleared away these preliminary matters, application of the statute to the facts of this case becomes relatively straightforward:

> **(c)** *Catapult* may not assume . . . *the Perlman licenses,* . . . if
>
> **(1)**
>
>> **(A)** *federal patent law* excuses *Perlman* from accepting performance from or rendering performance to an entity other than *Catapult* . . . ; and
>>
>> **(B)** *Perlman* does not consent to such assumption. . . .

11 U.S.C. § 365(c) (substitutions in italics). Since federal patent law makes nonexclusive patent licenses personal and nondelegable, § 365(c)(1)(A) is satisfied. Perlman has withheld his consent, thus satisfying § 365(c)(1)(B). Accordingly, the plain language of § 365(c)(1) bars Catapult from assuming the Perlman licenses.

IV.

Catapult urges us to abandon the literal language of § 365(c)(1) in favor of an alternative approach, reasoning that Congress did not intend to bar debtors in possession from assuming their own contracts where no assignment is contemplated. In Catapult's view, § 365(c)(1) should be interpreted as embodying an "actual test": the statute bars assumption by the debtor in possession only where the reorganization in question results in the nondebtor actually having to accept performance from a third party. Under this reading of § 365(c), the debtor in possession would be permitted to assume any executory contract, so long as no assignment was contemplated. Put another way, Catapult suggests that, as to a debtor in possession, § 365(c)(1) should be read to prohibit assumption and assignment, rather than assumption *or* assignment.

Catapult has marshalled considerable authority to support this reading. The arguments supporting Catapult's position can be divided into three categories: (1) the literal reading creates inconsistencies within § 365; (2) the literal reading is incompatible with the legislative history; and (3) the literal reading flies in the face of sound bankruptcy policy. Nonetheless, we find that none of these considerations justifies departing from the plain language of § 365(c)(1).

A.

Catapult first argues that a literal reading of § 365(c)(1) sets the statute at war with itself and its neighboring provisions. Deviation from the plain language, contends Catapult, is necessary if internal consistency is to be achieved. We agree with Catapult that a court should interpret a statute, if possible, so as to minimize discord among related provisions. However, the dire inconsistencies cited by Catapult turn out, on closer analysis, to be no such thing.

Catapult, for example, singles out the interaction between § 365(c)(1) and § 365(f)(1) as a statutory trouble spot. Subsection (f)(1) provides that executory contracts, once assumed, may be assigned notwithstanding any contrary provisions contained in the contract *or applicable law*:

> (f)(1) Except as provided in subsection (c) of this section, notwithstanding a provision in an executory contract or unexpired lease of the debtor, *or in applicable law*, that prohibits, restricts, or conditions the assignment of such contract or lease, the trustee may assign such contract or lease under paragraph (2) of this subsection.

11 U.S.C. § 365(f)(1) (emphasis added).

The potential conflict between subsections (c)(1) and (f)(1) arises from their respective treatments of "applicable law." The plain language of subsection (c)(1) bars assumption (absent consent) whenever "applicable law" would bar assignment. Subsection (f)(1) states that, *contrary provisions in applicable law notwithstanding*, executory contracts may be assigned. Since assumption is a necessary prerequisite to assignment under § 365, *see* 11 U.S.C. § 365(f)(2)(A), a literal reading of subsection (c)(1) appears to render subsection (f)(1) superfluous. In the words of the Sixth Circuit, "Section 365(c), the recognized exception to 365(f), appears at first to resuscitate in full the very anti-assignment 'applicable law' which 365(f) nullifies." *In re Magness*, 972 F.2d 689, 695 (6th Cir. 1992) (Guy, J., concurring). Faced with this dilemma, one district court reluctantly concluded that the "conflict between subsections (c) and (f) of § 365 is inescapable." *See In re Catron*, 158 B.R. at 636.

Subsequent authority, however, suggests that this conclusion may have been unduly pessimistic. The Sixth Circuit has credibly reconciled the warring provisions by noting that "each subsection recognizes an 'applicable law' of markedly different scope." *In re Magness*, 972 F.2d at 695. Subsection (f)(1) states the broad rule—a law that, as a general matter, "prohibits, restricts, or conditions the assignment" of executory contracts is trumped by the provisions of subsection (f)(1). Subsection (c)(1), however, states a carefully crafted exception to the broad rule—where applicable law does not merely recite a general ban on assignment, but instead more specifically "excuses a party . . . from accepting performance from or rendering performance to an entity" different from the one with which the party originally contracted, the applicable law prevails over subsection (f)(1). *See id.* In other words, in determining whether an "applicable law" stands or falls under § 365(f)(1), a court must ask *why* the "applicable law" prohibits assignment. Only if the law prohibits assignment on the rationale that the identity of the contracting party is material to the agreement will subsection (c)(1) rescue it. *See id.* We agree with the Sixth and Eleventh Circuits that a literal reading of subsection (c)(1) does not inevitably set it at odds with subsection (f)(1).

Catapult next focuses on the internal structure of § 365(c)(1) itself. According to Catapult, the literal approach to subsection (c)(1) renders the phrase "or the debtor in possession" contained in § 365(c)(1)(A) superfluous. In the words of one bankruptcy court, "if the directive of Section 365(c)(1) is to prohibit assumption whenever applicable law excuses performance relative to any entity other than the debtor, why add the words 'or debtor in possession?' The [hypothetical] test renders this phrase surplusage."

A close reading of § 365(c)(1), however, dispels this notion. By its terms, subsection (c)(1) addresses two conceptually distinct events: assumption and assignment. The plain language of the provision makes it clear that each of these events is contingent on the nondebtor's separate consent. Consequently, where a nondebtor consents to the *assumption* of an executory contract, subsection (c)(1) will have to be applied a second time if the debtor in possession wishes to *assign* the contract in question. On that second application, the relevant question would be whether "applicable law excuses a party from accepting performance from or rendering performance to an entity other than . . . *the debtor in possession.*" 11 U.S.C. § 365(c)(1)(A) (emphasis added). Consequently, the phrase "debtor in possession," far from being rendered superfluous by a literal reading of subsection (c)(1), dovetails neatly with the disjunctive language that opens subsection (c)(1): "The trustee may not assume *or* assign. . . ." 11 U.S.C. § 365(c) (emphasis added).

A third potential inconsistency identified by Catapult relates to § 365(c)(2). According to Catapult, a literal reading of subsection (c)(1) renders subsection (c)(2) a dead letter. Subsection (c)(2) provides:

> **(c)** The trustee may not assume or assign any executory contract or unexpired lease of the debtor, whether or not such contract or lease prohibits or restricts assignment of rights or delegation of duties, if
>
> . . .
>
>> **(2)** such contract is a contract to make a loan, or extend other debt financing or financial accommodations, to or for the benefit of the debtor, or to issue a security of the debtor. . . .

11 U.S.C. § 365(c)(2). According to Catapult, the contracts encompassed by subsection (c)(2) are all nonassignable as a matter of applicable state law. As a result, a literal reading of subsection (c)(1) would seem to snare and dispose of every executory contract within subsection (c)(2)'s scope. Perlman, however, persuasively rebuts this argument, noting that even if the state law governing the assignability of loan agreements and financing contracts is relatively uniform today, Congress by enacting subsection (c)(2) cemented nationwide uniformity in the bankruptcy context, effectively ensuring creditors that these particular contracts would not be assumable in bankruptcy. Put another way, it is the national uniformity of applicable state law that has rendered subsection (c)(2) superfluous, not the terms of subsection (c)(1).

In any event, subsection (c)(1) does not completely swallow up subsection (c)(2). Subsection (c)(1) by its terms permits assumption and assignment of executory loan agreements *so long as the nondebtor consents. See* 11 U.S.C. § 365(c)(1)(B). Subsection (c)(2), in contrast, bans assumption and assignment of such agreements, *consent of the nondebtor notwithstanding.* Accordingly, contrary to Catapult's assertion, subsection (c)(1) does not necessarily catch upriver all the fish that would otherwise be netted by subsection (c)(2). Once again, the "inconsistency" identified by Catapult proves evanescent under close scrutiny. We see no reason why these two provisions cannot happily coexist.

We conclude that the claimed inconsistencies are not actual and that the plain language of § 365(c)(1) compels the result Perlman urges: Catapult may not assume the Perlman licenses over Perlman's objection. Catapult has not demonstrated that, in according the words of subsection (c)(1) their plain meaning, we do violence to subsection (c)(1) or the provisions that accompany it.

. . .

V.

hypothetical test

Because the statute speaks clearly, and its plain language does not produce a patently absurd result or contravene any clear legislative history, we must "hold Congress to its words." Accordingly, we hold that, where applicable nonbankruptcy law makes an executory contract nonassignable because the identity of the nondebtor party is material, a debtor in possession may not assume the contract absent consent of the nondebtor party. A straightforward application of § 365(c)(1) to the circumstances of this case precludes Catapult from assuming the Perlman licenses over Perlman's objection. Consequently, the bankruptcy court erred when it approved Catapult's motion to assume the Perlman licenses, and the district court erred in affirming the bankruptcy court.

REVERSED.

As *Catapult* notes, circuit courts of appeals disagree about whether "or" in section 365(c)(1) is disjunctive (the "actual" test) or conjunctive (the "hypothetical" test). Does section 102(5) answer the debate? Section 102(5) provides that in Title 11 "or" is "not exclusive." In other words, section 102(5) would lend support to the hypothetical test, even if as a policy matter, the actual test would seem more appealing. Curiously, this obscure Code provision appears in neither case's discussion.

The "actual" and "hypothetical" tests do not represent the only approaches to section 365(c)(1). Another approach is to focus on whether the term "trustee" in section 365(c)(1) is meant to refer solely to a trustee, or also encompass a DIP. *In re Footstar, Inc.*, 323 B.R. 566, 571 (Bankr. S.D.N.Y. 2005). While this approach runs contrary to the language of section 1107, which provides that the DIP has all of the rights and powers of a trustee, it does get at the reasonable policy distinction between performance by a trustee and performance by the original counterparty. Of course, all of this might prove too much. A trustee represents a change in management of the debtor, but it is still the same essential firm. The real concern expressed in section 365(c)(1) would seem to be about performance of services personally by the trustee instead of by an individual debtor, rather than about business entities at all.

C. *Ipso Facto* Clauses

The Bankruptcy Code provides that so-called *ipso facto* clauses—provisions in executory contracts or unexpired leases or non-bankruptcy law that are triggered post-petition by the debtor's bankruptcy or financial condition—are unenforceable. 11 U.S.C. § 365(e). *See also* 11 U.S.C. § 365(b)(2) (*ipso facto* clause breaches need not be cured for assumption). A provision that goes into effect *prior* to bankruptcy, however, such as one triggered on a default on a loan, is enforceable so long as it was enforced prior to the bankruptcy. There is an exception for clauses that would prohibit or restrict assignment or delegation of personal services or financing agreements, as such provisions are effectively honored by section 365(c).

D. Timing of Assumption

The Bankruptcy Code places limitations on when the trustee or DIP may assume or reject an executory contract or unexpired lease. The Bankruptcy Code does not specify when an executory contract or unexpired lease must be assumed or rejected other than in specific instances. Instead, the general rule is that assumption or rejection must occur in an unspecified, but reasonable time period, which may extend up until plan confirmation: "[I]t is clear policy of the Bankruptcy Code to provide the debtor with breathing space following the filing of a bankruptcy petition, continuing until confirmation of the plan, in which to assume or reject an executory contract." *In re Dana Corp.*, 350 B.R. 144, 147 (Bankr. S.D.N.Y. 2006). Some courts have permitted assumption or rejection even *after* plan confirmation, although for this to happen, the plan must expressly provide for it, as otherwise the property interest in the contract or lease ceases to belong to the trustee/DIP and instead belongs to the reorganized debtor. 11 U.S.C. § 1141(b).

There are several situations for which the Code mandates specific time frames for assumption or rejection. In Chapter 7, an executory contract or unexpired lease (other than a commercial property lease) is deemed rejected if it is not assumed or rejected within 60 days of the bankruptcy filing. 11 U.S.C. § 365(d)(1). The 60-day period may be extended by the court for cause. *Id.* In Chapter 11, a counterparty to an executory contract or unexpired lease of residential property may move for assumption or rejection to be done prior to the confirmation. 11 U.S.C. § 365(d)(2).

Perhaps most importantly, commercial leases in a Chapter 11 case must be assumed or rejected within 120 days (or confirmation if earlier). 11 U.S.C. § 365(d)(4)(A). Prior to 2005, there was a 60-day limit for assumption of nonresidential leases, but it was extendable indefinitely "for cause," which was routinely granted. The 2005 Bankruptcy Abuse Prevention and Consumer Protection Act (BAPCPA) imposed the 120-day deadline. The 120 days may be extended by another 90 days for cause, but extensions beyond 210 days require the written assent of the landlord. 11 U.S.C. § 365(d)(4)(B).

The 210-day deadline for assuming or rejecting commercial leases absent consent of the landlord has particular significance for retailers in bankruptcy, as most retailers lease their store spaces. These retailers need to be able to decide which leases to assume and which to reject; such decisions are often a critical part of a plan of reorganization, and creditors are unlikely to support a plan that they believe saddles the reorganized debtor with too many bad leases.

In many cases, the landlord will be happy to assent to an extension beyond 210 days and to other concessions regarding cure requirements. There may not be another viable tenant immediately on hand, and landlords would rather deal with a debtor than have an empty storefront, which may mean not only the loss of rent from that lease, but if in a mall, might also affect the traffic to other stores and thus endanger other lease revenues. Even if there is another possible tenant, the landlord may not want to lose rent in a transition period.

But if the landlord would rather have a different tenant, then the debtor will have to decide whether to assume the lease within the 210-day window. This provision places important constraints on reorganizing retailers. Historically, retailers would evaluate their stores for at least one commercial cycle, including a holiday season. The flexible time schedule from pre-BAPCPA gave retailers sufficient time, including at least one holiday business season, to analyze the value of each individual store lease prior to deciding whether to assume or reject. The BAPCPA's 210-day window means that this is no longer always possible; a retailer that files at the wrong time of the year will not be able to enjoy the holiday sales boom and will not have the sales data from that period available when evaluating its leases.

A further complication from the 210-day window is that it has resulted in DIP lenders putting retail debtors on very tight leashes, requiring them to determine reorganization plans within 60-90 days or liquidate. For a debtor that cannot even figure out which leases to assume and which to reject, this short time frame may make a reorganization impossible.

The reason DIP lenders require retail debtors to have a plan proposed (or confirmed) within 90 days is because it usually takes around 90 days (or 12 weeks) to conduct a well-run going-out-of-business (GOB) sale. A debtor's own premises are the most commercially advantageous location for a GOB sale. This means that lenders want to be sure that debtors will have sufficient time to conduct a GOB sale prior to lease rejection due to the expiry of the 210-day window. A cautious lender will want an extra month's cushion. That leaves just 90 days before the lender will want the assumption/rejection decision to be made.

Nibbling away at the other end, the final approval of the DIP financing agreement itself may not come until a month into the case. Thus, there may only be 60-90 days for the debtor to evaluate which leases it wants to assume or reject, so the chance it will overlap with the holiday season is lower than the 210-day window would suggest. Pre-BAPCPA, the flexible assumption/rejection timetable gave lenders the assurance that there would be time to conduct an on-premises GOB sale if necessary. The 210-day deadline leaves little room for retailers to reorganize.

Lawrence C. Gottlieb, Michael Klein & Ronald R. Sussman
BAPCPA's Effects on Retail Chapter 11s Are Profound

J. Corp. Renewal, Feb. 19, 2009

. . . [P]ost-BAPCPA Chapter 11 retail cases have almost uniformly been postured at the outset as either full-chain liquidations or a truncated sale process, followed by liquidation if going concern bids are not sufficient to pay off secured lenders. This pattern has been remarkably consistent, appearing in cases that occurred both before and after the credit crunch began to affect banks' ability to lend and the bursting of real estate bubble caused property values to decline.

The path on which a particular retail bankruptcy will proceed depends on the timing of the debtor's filing of petition. . . . Chapter 11 retailers that file for bankruptcy in the early or middle part of the calendar year are provided with the opportunity to quickly market their assets as going concerns, provided that these efforts do not interfere with the lenders' ability to conduct GOB sales.

On the other hand, retailers that file later in the year are given virtually no opportunity to conduct a going concern sale process, as lenders insist that GOB sales commence during the critical holiday shopping season to maximize the value of their collateral. In the latter scenario, lenders aware of the low likelihood of a successful reorganization are simply unwilling to risk conducting GOB sales after the holiday season.

For example, Boscov's Department Stores and its affiliates commenced a Chapter 11 proceeding in Delaware on August 4[, 2008]. After much negotiation among the debtors, the creditors' committee, and the post-petition lenders, the debtors were able to obtain sufficient DIP financing to conduct a robust sales process in the three-month period immediately prior to the shopping holiday season. As a result, on November 21[, 2008] the Bankruptcy Court approved the sale of the debtors as a going concern to former owners of the company.

Similarly, retailers Mervyn's and Linens 'n Things each filed bankruptcy petitions in the middle of 2008 and were afforded the opportunity to seek out going concern buyers prior to conducting liquidations of their respective chains.

In contrast, when The Bombay Company, Inc., filed for bankruptcy in late September 2007, its lenders were unwilling to finance a full marketing process, insisting that the retailer begin liquidating its stores soon after the filing. Notably, financial advisors for both the debtors and the creditors' committee acknowledged that Bombay's fate would have been far different had it filed for bankruptcy protection earlier in the year. Other retailers, such as KB Toys and Value City, both of which filed [late in 2008], suffered similar fates.

For commercial leases, the trustee or DIP must continue to perform its obligations under the contract or lease (other than *ipso facto* obligations), prior to assumption or rejection. 11 U.S.C. § 365(d)(3). For leases of personalty, the trustee or DIP must only perform obligations arising 60 days post-default. 11 U.S.C. § 365(d)(5). The trustee/DIP will still need to cure most defaults arising in the 60 days post-default to assume per section 365(b). Table 23.3 summarizes the section 365 assumption/rejection deadlines in somewhat simplified form.

Table 23.3. Assumption or Rejection Deadlines (Simplified)

	Executory Contract	**Residential Lease**	**Commercial Lease**
Chapter 7	60 days	60 days	Conclusion of case
Chapter 11	Reasonable time up to confirmation	Reasonable time up to confirmation	Earlier of 120 days or confirmation. 120 days' limit is extendable for another 90 for cause and further with the lessor's consent.

E. Real Property Tenant and IP Licensee Protections in Rejection

The Bankruptcy Code imposes some limitations on the effect of rejection when the debtor is a lessor of real property. The rejection does not simply terminate the lease and allow the debtor to evict its tenant. Instead, the tenant is given an option of treating the lease as terminated or retaining its rights under the lease. 11 U.S.C. § 365(h)(1)(A). In other words, the lessee receives a performance option upon rejection. Thus, the debtor has the first option—whether to assume the lease—but the lease may only be terminated if both parties agree to the termination. To protect this right, the debtor landlord cannot infringe on the lessee's quiet enjoyment of the property or change the terms of the rent, etc. The lessee may also offset against future rental payments any damages caused by prior nonperformance by the debtor lessor. 11 U.S.C. § 365(h)(1)(B).

The Bankruptcy Code also includes similar protections for licensees of intellectual property excluding trademarks. See 11 U.S.C. § 101(35A). If the debtor rejects an IP license that is an executory contract, the licensee receives a similar option to either treat the license as terminated or to retain its rights under the license for the duration of the contract. 11 U.S.C. § 365(n)(1). IP licensees that retain their rights, however, waive any setoff rights and claims to administrative priority for the contract.

IV. EXECUTORY CONTRACTS: ASSIGNMENT LIMITATIONS

If the debtor assumes an executory contract or unexpired lease, the debtor may also assign the contract or lease. This permits the debtor to realize value, even if it is unable to perform the contract or lease itself. Section 365(f)(1) provides that the trustee or DIP may assign an executory contract or unexpired lease irrespective of contract or lease provisions or other law to the contrary. In order to assign, the trustee must cure any defaults, as provided in section 365(b), and provide adequate assurances of the assignee's performance. 11 U.S.C. § 365(f)(2)(B). Moreover, assignment is subject to the same limitations on assumption in section 365(c)—to the extent that applicable non-bankruptcy law excuses the counterparty from accepting performance from anyone other than the debtor or debtor in possession, the contract cannot be assigned (even if assumed) absent the counterparty's consent.

Under section 365, the trustee must assume a contract prior to assigning it. 11 U.S.C. § 365(f)(2)(A). But section 363 permits use, sale, or lease of estate property without assumption being specifically required. Thus, an unresolved issue is whether a contract or lease must be assumed prior to assignment. *See Precision Industries, Inc. v. Qualitech Steel SBQ, LLC (In re Qualitech Steel Corp.)*, 327 F.3d 537 (7th Cir. 2003) (permitting section 363(f) sale without assumption).

Problem Set 23

(1) Lincoln Railsplitting Corp. is in Chapter 11. One year ago, Lincoln entered into a contract with the Transcontinental Railroad to provide wooden ties for 1,000 miles of track. Can Lincoln assume the contract under the following scenarios?

    a. Transcontinental has not yet paid Lincoln, but Lincoln has provided all of the ties.

    b. Transcontinental has paid Lincoln in full, but Lincoln has not yet begun performance.

    c. Transcontinental has not yet paid Lincoln, and Lincoln has begun production of the ties but not delivered any to Transcontinental.

(2) Garrison Publishing filed for Chapter 11 bankruptcy yesterday. Garrison had rented a warehouse space from Douglas Enterprises. There is still one year left on the lease, at $2 million per year.

    a. If Garrison Publishing rejects the lease, what is the status of Douglas Enterprises' claim? 11 U.S.C. §§ 365(g), 502(g).

    b. If Garrison Publishing assumes the lease, what is the status of Douglas Enterprise's claim? 11 U.S.C. § 503(b).

    c. Garrison has reduced the scope of its operations and no longer needs the Douglas warehouse space. The warehouse space is readily reconfigurable, and at current market rates would rent for perhaps $3 million/year. What should Garrison do? 11 U.S.C. § 365(f).

(3) Mary Todd Fabrics filed for Chapter 11 bankruptcy last month. Mary Todd has an unperformed contract to sell Barton Bandages $5 million of sterile cotton cloth for military grade bandages. Mary Todd Fabrics' cost to perform the contract depends on the price of cotton. When Mary Todd entered into the contract, cotton prices were low, and Mary Todd believed it would cost $4.5 million to perform the contract. Cotton prices have since increased substantially. When Mary Todd filed for bankruptcy, it would have cost $8 million to perform. Cotton prices have kept rising, and as of today it would cost Mary Todd $12 million to perform the contract. The market price of the bandages today would be $12 million.

    a. If Mary Todd Fabrics had not filed for bankruptcy and breached the contract today, what would Barton Bandages' remedy be at state law? UCC § 2-713.

    b. If Mary Todd Fabrics assumes the contract today, what is Barton Bandages' claim and how will it be paid? 11 U.S.C. §§ 503(b), 1129(a)(9).

8+7
=15

executory
K?

c. If Mary Todd Fabrics rejects the contract today, what is Barton Bandages' claim? 11 U.S.C. §§ 365(g), 502(g); UCC §§ 2-711(1), 2-712, 2-713.[2]

(4) Van Buren Drayage is in Chapter 11 bankruptcy. Van Buren leases a warehouse from Old Hickory Properties. The warehouse is encumbered with a mortgage from Burr Finance Corp. Van Buren has moved to reject the lease on the warehouse.

    a. Burr has filed an objection to the rejection of the lease, as Burr's mortgage is a non-recourse obligation secured by the property and the rents under the lease. What result and why? 11 U.S.C. § 365(a).

    b. Burr has, in the alternative, requested adequate protection for its interest in the warehouse. How is the court likely to rule? 11 U.S.C. § 361.

(5) Thomas Jefferson Properties is a real estate investment trust that owns several strip mall shopping centers, including the Monticello. One of Jefferson's tenants in the mall is Adams Federalist Furniture. Adams is in Chapter 11. Adams wishes to assign its lease to Pickney Produce, an organic green grocer.

Why assignable (?)

    a. Adams's lease contains a clause that requires Jefferson's prior written assent to any sale or assignment of the lease. Can Adams assign the lease to Pickney if Jefferson refuses to give its assent? 11 U.S.C. §§ 365(c), 365(f).

    b. Can Adams assign the lease if it instead contained a clause requiring that any sale or assignment of the lease be solely to another furniture store? 11 U.S.C. §§ 365(b)(3)(D), 365(c), 365(f).

(6) Coolidge Fashion Discounter operates several hundred leased retail locations selling overstocked and "seconds" of designer brands. Coolidge filed for Chapter 11 bankruptcy on August 15. Coolidge knows that some of its stores are profitable and some are not, but Coolidge is in the midst of a major operational overhaul that it believes will turn around the profitability of at least some of its stores.

no.
7 month.

    a. Coolidge would like to be able to go through the holiday season (through January) before determining which leases to reject and which to assume. Is this possible? 11 U.S.C. § 365(d)(4).

commercial lease

    b. Until Coolidge assumes or rejects its leases, is it required to make its monthly rental payments? 11 U.S.C. § 365(d)(3).

    c. Coolidge is in default on some of its leases. It has missed some rental payments, failed to maintain insurance coverage, and violated "going dark" clauses in its leases that require its stores to be open during certain hours. Is Coolidge able to assume these leases? 11 U.S.C. § 365(b).

(7) Polk Properties is a real estate investment company that owns several commercial office buildings, including one, 5440 Fyte Street, which happens to be where your law firm has its offices. Your firm has a very favorable long-term lease at 5440 Fyte; your firm would pay perhaps double per square foot at current market rates. The lease

---

    2. UCC § 2-711(1) gives an aggrieved seller a choice between covering on the market and recovering damages for the cost of cover plus incidental and consequential damages under UCC § 2-712 or suing for damages under UCC § 2-713. UCC § 2-713, entitled *Buyer's Damages for Non-delivery or Repudiation*, provides that ". . . the measure of damages for non-delivery or repudiation by the seller is the difference between the market price at the time when the buyer learned of the breach and the contract price together with any incidental and consequential damages provided in this Article, but less expenses saved in consequence of the seller's breach."

out of 4

contains a clause stating that it terminates upon either party successfully petitioning for bankruptcy relief. Polk Properties has filed for Chapter 11. Which of the following may Polk Properties do:

    a. Reject the lease? 11 U.S.C. § 365(a).

    b. Evict your law firm? 11 U.S.C. § 365(h)(1)(A).

    c. Stop providing heat to the building? 11 U.S.C. § 365(h)(1)(B).

(8) McKinley Technologies holds numerous industrial patents, including the patent for a high-speed tube microswager (sort of a pencil sharpener for metal). Several years ago McKinley Industries entered into an exclusive license agreement with Oyster Bay Engineering for the microswager patent. At the time, the patent did not seem particularly valuable, and the license calls for payments of $200,000 per year. Microswaging turns out to be essential in the construction of microchips, and the patent license is easily worth $40 million annually. McKinley Technologies has filed for Chapter 11. Which of the following may McKinley Technologies do:

    a. Reject the license? 11 U.S.C. § 365(n)(1).

    b. Increase the royalties? 11 U.S.C. § 365(n)(1)(B).

    c. License out the microswager patent to another firm? 11 U.S.C. § 365(n)(3)(B).

(9) Famed actor Grover Cleveland signed a contract to appear in a commercial for biodegradable diapers manufactured by the Gilded Age Baby Products Company. Cleveland agreed to appear in the commercial at far less than his usual rate in part as a favor to his old college friend, Ruth B. Hayes, who is the CEO of Gilded Age. Cleveland is very picky about with whom he works and insisted that the contract contain a "key man" provision that requires Ruth B. Hayes to be CEO of Gilded Age during shooting and production of the commercial. Following a tainted baby food scandal, Gilded Age filed for Chapter 11 bankruptcy, and an early motion for appointment of a trustee was successful. The filing and appointment of the trustee happened before the production of the commercial was completed or Cleveland was paid. May the trustee assume the contract? 11 U.S.C. §§ 365(c), 365(e).

(10) Jackson Payments Processing provides credit and debit card processing services to Van Buren Creameries, a maker of ice cream and other dairy products. Under its contract with Van Buren, Jackson advances Van Buren 94% of all credit and debit card receivables and retains all of the receivables that it then collects from the consumers' banks. (The consumers' banks in turn seek to collect from the consumers.) Jackson also has the right to "charge back" to Van Buren all advances for transactions that the consumer did not in fact authorize or subsequent to a data security breach that occurred because of Van Buren's negligence or willful malfeasance. The processing agreement also provides that it is void in the event of a bankruptcy filing by either party. Van Buren filed for Chapter 11 after several consumers died from listeria poisoning contracted from its Dutch Chocolate ice cream. Can Van Buren continue accepting credit and debt card payments on its existing contract with Jackson? 11 U.S.C. §§ 364, 365(c)(2), 365(e)(2)(B).

(11) Footwear company W.G. Harding & Co. has filed for Chapter 11 bankruptcy. W.G. Harding operated two lines of business: an unprofitable "Atalanta" line of stand-alone athletic shoe stores, and a profitable "Meleager" line of discount and family shoe departments in several large national department store chains. For each department store chain, W.G. Harding operates the footwear departments under a separate master agreement with the department store chain. W.G. Harding has sold off most of the Atalanta assets in Chapter 11, but its reorganization depends on its ability to assume the master agreements for its Meleager line. All of the master agreements contain a clause prohibiting the assignment of the contract. Will W.G. Harding & Co. be able to reorganize? 11 U.S.C. § 365(c)(1).

CHAPTER 24

LABOR AND RETIREE BENEFIT ISSUES

I. LABOR CONTRACTS AND RETIREE BENEFIT OBLIGATIONS

A. Collective Bargaining Agreements

Most employees negotiate their own term of employment, but unionized employees do not. Instead, unionized employees are employed pursuant to the terms of a **collective bargaining agreement** ("CBA") that is negotiated between union representatives and the employer. CBAs are required to set forth terms of employment such as wages, overtime, bonuses, benefits, grievance procedures, safety and work practices, seniority, and procedures for layoffs, and discipline. CBAs may also set forth additional employee rights and require the employer to maintain a certain level of employment or operate certain facilities. Relatively few American workers are unionized today. Only 6.4 percent of the private workforce belongs to a union, but certain industries—utilities, transportation, telecommunications, and construction, for example—are heavily unionized.

While CBAs are a type of a contract, they are treated differently than other contracts in bankruptcy. In 1984, the Supreme Court held that a debtor could reject a CBA under section 365 without first engaging in collective bargaining, and that such a rejection would not be a unilateral alteration of the CBA as prohibited by the National Labor Relations Act. *NLRB v. Bildisco & Bildisco*, 465 U.S. 513 (1984). Congress responded to the decision with incredible rapidity, passing legislation without any hearings or legislative reports. The result was section 1113 of the Bankruptcy Code, which imposes a duty on DIPs or trustees to engage in extensive good faith collective bargaining prior to rejection of a collective bargaining agreement.[1]

---

1. Note that Sections 1113 and 1114 do not apply in Chapter 9 municipal bankruptcies. Most of the provisions of Chapter 11 are made applicable in Chapter 9. 11 U.S.C. § 901. Sections 1113 and 1114 are not. This means that all executory contracts—including collective bargaining agreements—continue to be governed by section 365 and *Bildisco*, so a municipality in Chapter 9 does not need to go through the negotiation process of section 1113 prior to rejecting its collective bargaining agreements. Similarly, public sector pensions are not insured by the Pension Benefit Guarantee Corporation or subject to ERISA protections.

Section 1113 basically imports into bankruptcy law the standard labor law approach to dispute resolution—mandating good faith negotiations and then more good faith negotiations if agreement is not reached. Labor law represents a compromise that limits the circumstances in which workers are allowed to strike, but also forcing management to engage in good faith negotiations with workers. In other words, U.S. labor law policy is to dissuade both labor and management from taking unilateral actions.

Section 1113 echoes this approach by requiring a trustee or DIP that seeks to reject a CBA with a union to make a proposal to the union for a modification of the existing CBA.[2] 11 U.S.C. § 1113(b)(1). The trustee/DIP must provide the union with sufficient information for evaluating the proposal. 11 U.S.C. § 1113(b)(1). At that point, the trustee/DIP and the union are supposed to negotiate.

One of two outcomes may ensue. First, the trustee/DIP and the union may reach a deal. Alternatively, if no deal can be reached, then the court may approve a rejection of the CBA. In order to approve a rejection of a CBA, the court must find that the trustee has followed the necessary procedural steps; that the proposed modifications are "necessary to permit the reorganization of the debtor and assure[] that all creditors, the debtor and all affected parties are treated fairly and equitably"; that the union has refused to accept the modification proposal "without good cause"; and that "the balance of the equities clearly favors rejection of such agreement." 11 U.S.C. §§ 1113(b)-(c). A "financial distress" provision also exists permitting interim modification of a CBA "if essential to the continuation of the debtor's business, or in order to avoid irreparable damage to the estate." 11 U.S.C. § 1113(e).

Courts have split in their interpretation of the section 1113 modification standard, in particular what it means for a modification to be "necessary to permit the reorganization of the debtor" and to assure fair and equitable treatment for all affected parties. The following opinion discusses different approaches taken by the courts.

Truck Drivers Local 807, etc. v. Carey Transp., Inc.

816 F.2d 82 (2d Cir. 1987)

ALTIMARI, CIRCUIT JUDGE:

This appeal involves the showing a debtor-employer must make in order to obtain Bankruptcy Court approval of the employer's application to reject a collective bargaining agreement in accordance with 11 U.S.C. § 1113. . . .

FACTS AND PROCEEDINGS BELOW

Carey, a wholly owned subsidiary of Schiavone Carrier Corporation, commenced this litigation by filing a voluntary reorganization petition under Chapter 11 of the

---

2. If there is no CBA in place, the issue becomes more complex. *See Allied Pilots Ass'n v. AMR Corp. (In re AMR Corp.)*, 471 B.R. 51 (Bankr. S.D.N.Y. 2012) (finding that CBA could be rejected under section 1113 because it had not expired, but merely become "amendable" under the Railway Labor Act).

Bankruptcy Code in April 1985. Carey, both prior to and since that filing, has been engaged in the business of providing commuter bus service between New York City and Kennedy and LaGuardia Airports.

Local 807 has been the exclusive bargaining representative of Carey's bus drivers and station employees. Local 807 and Carey entered into collective bargaining agreements covering these two groups of employees on August 20, 1982, thereby settling a sixty-four day strike by union members. These two agreements were scheduled to expire on February 28, 1986.

Carey officials have blamed the strike for a subsequent 30% drop in ridership and the yearly revenue losses that preceded its filing for reorganization. Carey has operated at a loss since at least December 31, 1981, reporting annual losses of $750,000 for fiscal year 1983, $1,500,000 for fiscal year 1984, and $2,500,000 for fiscal year 1985.

In September 1983, Carey terminated fifty [members of the Truck Drivers] Local 807 [the "union"] employed as station workers, although an arbitrator later directed that ten of them be rehired with backpay. The net result of these forty layoffs, according to Carey officials, has been an annual cost savings of approximately $1 million.

In 1984 and 1985, Carey sought and obtained concessions from a union representing Carey's mechanics and repair-shop workers. Those concessions led to layoffs of approximately eight workers and annual cost savings estimated at $144,000.

In June 1984, Carey proposed several modifications in its agreements with Local 807. After negotiations, Local 807 and Carey agreed on certain supplemental provisions applicable only to drivers hired after July 1, 1984. These "second-tier" drivers would not get any paid sick days, and they would receive significantly reduced wages, overtime pay, and benefits. These changes, according to Carey, yielded savings of only $100,000 prior to Carey's filing for bankruptcy. The reason given for the relatively small savings was that seasonal variations in industry business resulted in few drivers being hired after the effective date of the Supplement.

On January 31, 1985, counsel for Carey wrote to Local 807 representatives, requesting additional modifications of the two agreements. A series of meetings took place during February and March of 1985, with Carey warning that a failure to reach agreement could force the company to file a Chapter 11 petition and, most likely, apply for permission to reject the existing agreements. Near the end of these sessions, union negotiators agreed to present to union members a set of modifications affecting lunch periods, booking and check-out time, driver rotation rules, holidays, vacation days, sick days, fringe benefit contributions, supplemental unemployment compensation, and supplemental disability insurance. Those concessions, if approved and implemented, would have yielded approximately $750,000 in yearly savings.

On March 27th, however, management added to this proposed modification several additional terms, and described the resultant package as its final offer. In essence, this last set of modifications would have extended the expiration date of the contract for an additional two years, with wages and fringe benefits frozen at the proposed levels until April 1, 1987. At that time, a "reopener" provision would permit the union to bargain for increased wages and benefits during the final year of the extended contract. The union requested that there be binding arbitration if reopener negotiations proved unsuccessful, but management rejected this demand.

This final offer was submitted to the bargaining unit employees on March 29, 1985 and rejected by an 82-7 vote. According to Local 807's business agent, the union members were particularly adamant about not accepting the two-year contract extension and the freeze on wages and benefits.

Carey filed its Chapter 11 petition with the Bankruptcy Court on April 4, 1985, and one day later, delivered to Local 807 a proposal to modify its collective bargaining agreements pursuant to 11 U.S.C. § 1113(b)(1)(A). This post-petition proposal was designed to achieve annual savings of $1.8 million for each of the next three fiscal years.

Carey planned to achieve savings of this magnitude by (1) freezing all wages for second-tier drivers and reducing wages for first-tier drivers (those on the payroll prior to July 1, 1984) by $1.00 per hour; (2) reducing health and pension benefit contributions by approximately $1.50 per hour; (3) replacing daily overtime with weekly overtime; (4) eliminating all sick days and reducing the number of paid holidays; (5) eliminating supplemental workers' compensation and supplemental disability payments; (6) eliminating premium payments and reducing commissions paid to charter drivers; and (7) changing numerous scheduling and assignment rules. All terms were to be frozen for three years under this post-petition proposal.

When Carey presented this proposal to Local 807, company officers were projecting fiscal year 1986 losses of approximately $950,000. (Carey revised this estimate shortly thereafter, projecting losses of $746,000. In a cover letter accompanying this proposal, Carey asserted that it needed to slash costs by considerably more than its projected losses in order to improve its long-term financial health by updating and expanding its bus fleet, operations, and maintenance facilities. Without savings of this magnitude, Carey explained, it would be unable to propose a feasible reorganization plan to creditors and resolve its indebtedness to them. Carey requested a meeting with Local 807 representatives "to discuss the proposals and to attempt to reach mutually satisfactory modifications of the agreement[s]."

Shortly after the Company submitted its post-petition proposal, dissension within Local 807 became obvious; in fact, virtually all union members formed a "Drivers Committee" and hired an attorney to represent them separately from Local 807 officials. The Drivers Committee then refused to participate in most post-petition negotiations, despite union officials' pleas that they reconsider that decision to "stonewall" these sessions.

In the meantime, Carey filed its section 1113 application to reject its bargaining agreements. The Bankruptcy Court scheduled and conducted five days of hearings on Carey's application, urging the parties to continue negotiations at the same time. After the third day of hearings, a Local 807 officer presented to Carey a counter-proposal designed to achieve annual cost savings of $776,000. The counter-proposal would have extended the expiration date of the existing agreements by fifteen months, and frozen wages and benefits except for a reopener, with binding arbitration. . . . Carey found the counter-proposal unacceptable, and the hearings continued. [The Bankruptcy Court ultimately approved Carey's application to reject the collective bargaining agreement.]

The central issues at the hearing, as on this appeal, were whether the post-petition proposal contained only necessary modifications of the existing agreements, *see* 11 U.S.C. § 1113(b)(1)(A), whether that proposal treated all parties fairly and equitably, *see id.*, whether Local 807 lacked good cause for rejecting that proposal, *see* § 1113(c)(2), and whether the balancing of the equities clearly favored rejection of the bargaining agreements. *See* § 1113(c)(3).

. . .

DISCUSSION

. . .

II. Merits of the Decision Below

. . .

Briefly stated, the statute permits the bankruptcy court to approve a rejection application only if the debtor, besides following the procedures set forth by Congress, makes three substantive showings. The first is that its post-petition proposal for modifications satisfies § 1113(b)(1), which in turn limits the debtor to proposing only "those necessary modifications in . . . benefits and protections that are necessary to permit the reorganization of the debtor," and obliges the debtor to assure the court that "all creditors, the debtor and all affected parties are treated fairly and equitably." Second, the debtor must show that the union has rejected this proposal without good cause. Bankr. Code § 1113(c)(2). Third, the debtor must prove that "the balance of the equities clearly favors rejection of [the bargaining] agreement." Code § 1113(c)(3). . . . We affirm the decision below because it substantially comports with our reading of the statute, and because Judge Lifland's factual findings are not clearly erroneous.

1. Compliance with § 1113(b)(1)

(a) Necessity of the modifications

[T]his provision "emphasizes the requirement of the debtor's good faith in seeking to modify its existing labor contract." Although all courts appear to agree on that basic principle, a judicial controversy has arisen over two additional, related questions raised by this provision: (1) how necessary must the proposed modifications be, and (2) to what goal must those alterations be necessary?

In answer to the first of these questions, the Third Circuit concluded that "necessary" as used in subsection (b)(1)(A) is synonymous with "essential" in subsection (e), which authorizes the court to approve certain non-negotiated interim changes while the rejection application is pending. Thus, the court held, necessity must "be construed strictly to signify only modifications that the trustee is constrained to accept." *Wheeling-Pittsburgh Steel*, 791 F.2d at 1088. As to the second question, the Third Circuit concluded that the statute requires the bankruptcy court to focus its attention on "the somewhat shorter term goal of preventing . . . liquidation . . . rather than the longer term issue of the debtor's ultimate future."

Local 807 asks us to adopt the Third Circuit's reasoning, arguing that the post-petition proposal must fail because it sought more than break-even cost reductions, because the proposed three year term was too long in relation to the eight months remaining under the existing agreement, and because it did not provide for wages and benefits to "snap-back" in the event that Carey's financial performance improved. We decline to do so.

First of all, the legislative history strongly suggests that "necessary" should not be equated with "essential" or bare minimum. Although the Third Circuit may be correct that the "necessary" language was viewed as a victory for organized labor because it approximated the "minimum modifications" language urged by Senator Packwood, Congress obviously did not adopt Senator Packwood's proposal. Instead, as the *Wheeling-Pittsburgh Steel* panel acknowledged, Congress settled on "a substitute for this clause." Congress' ultimate choice of this substitute clause suggests that it was uncomfortable with language suggesting that a debtor must prove that its initial post-petition proposal contained only bare-minimum changes.

Judge Lifland, in the decision below, properly pointed out a second reason for not reading "necessary" as the equivalent of "essential" or bare minimum. Because the statute requires the debtor to negotiate in good faith over the proposed modifications, an employer who initially proposed truly minimal changes would have no room for good faith negotiating, while one who agreed to any substantive changes would be unable to prove that its initial proposals were minimal. Thus, requiring the debtor to propose bare-minimum modifications at the outset would make it virtually impossible for the debtor to meet its other statutory obligations.

The Third Circuit's answer to the "necessary to what" question is also troubling. In our view, the *Wheeling-Pittsburgh* court did not adequately consider the significant differences between interim relief requests and post-petition modification proposals. Interim relief is available only until the hearing process is completed—normally within two months, *see* § 1113(d)(1), (2)—and only upon a showing that adherence to the agreement during that time could imperil "continuation of the debtor's business" or cause "irreparable damage to the estate." *Id.* § 1113(e). In the interim relief context, therefore, it is only proper that the court focus on the bare minimum requirements for short-term survival. In making the decision whether to permit the debtor to reject its bargaining agreement, however, the court must consider whether rejection would increase the likelihood of successful reorganization. A final reorganization plan, in turn, can be confirmed only if the court determines that neither liquidation nor a need for further reorganization is likely to follow. Thus, in virtually every case, it becomes impossible to weigh necessity as to reorganization without looking into the debtor's ultimate future and estimating what the debtor needs to attain financial health. As the *Royal Composing Room* court phrased it, "A debtor can live on water alone for a short time but over the long haul it needs food to sustain itself and retain its vigor."

Moreover, the length of Carey's proposal and the absence of a snap-back provision likewise did not require rejection of the proposal. While the Third Circuit relied on a similar argument in finding a proposed modification not "necessary" for purposes of section 1113, *Wheeling-Pittsburgh*, 791 F.2d at 1090-91, this argument was not raised in either court below and may not be raised in either court below and may not be raised here for the first time. The only exception to this rule, avoidance of manifest injustice, *id.*, is inapplicable here because Local 807 wholly failed to demonstrate that Carey's proposed three year term was unnecessary or exceeded either the prevailing industry practice or the parties' past experience.

In sum, we conclude that the necessity requirement places on the debtor the burden of proving that its proposal is made in good faith, and that it contains necessary, but not absolutely minimal, changes that will enable the debtor to complete the reorganization process successfully. . . . [W]e cannot conclude that the lower court either misread or misapplied the "necessary modifications" requirement as a matter of law.

Each of the findings pertinent to this inquiry, moreover, is supported by substantial evidence in the record. For instance, record evidence indicates that Carey was losing large sums of money, that its Local 807 labor costs (in contrast to other employees' salaries and benefits) were well above industry averages, and that Carey lacked sufficient assets to meet its current expenses. This well-documented testimony from Carey officials supports the court's finding that Carey had good faith reasons for seeking modifications in its Local 807 agreements. Moreover, record evidence also supports the view that Carey needed to upgrade its facilities and its vehicles in order to complete reorganization successfully. Therefore the bankruptcy court's conclusion that Carey needed to obtain modifications of the magnitude requested, and not merely break-even cost reductions as Local 807 argues, is not clearly erroneous.

The requirement that the debtor assure the court that "all creditors, the debtor and all affected parties are treated fairly and equitably." Code § 1113(b)(1)(A), is a relatively straightforward one. The purpose of this provision . . . "is to spread the burden of saving the company to every constituency while ensuring that all sacrifice to a similar degree." Local 807 argues that the bankruptcy court erred as a matter of both law and fact in assessing the burdens imposed on management, non-union employees, the parent company, and Carey's creditors. We disagree.

The debtor is not required to prove, in all instances, that managers and non-union employees will have their salaries and benefits cut to the same degree that union workers' benefits are to be reduced. To be sure, such a showing would assure the court that these affected parties are being asked to shoulder a proportionate share of the burden, but we decline to hold that this showing must be made in every case.

Rather, a debtor can rely on proof that managers and non-union employees are assuming increased responsibilities as a result of staff reductions without receiving commensurate salary increases; this is surely a sacrifice for these individuals. Particularly where, as here, the court finds that only the employees covered by the pertinent bargaining agreements are receiving pay and benefits above industry standards, it is not unfair or inequitable to exempt the other employees from pay and benefit reductions.

Local 807 has consistently argued that Carey's managers and supervisors are more than adequately compensated, that Local 807 members are not paid substantially more than their counterparts working for Carey's competitors, and that non-union staffing levels have increased rather than decreased since Schiavone purchased Carey. But substantial record evidence supports each of the bankruptcy court's contrary conclusions. For instance, the record contains unrebutted testimony that Carey drivers' hourly wages and benefits exceeded those paid by other private carriers by several dollars per hour, while managers' and supervisors' compensation packages were described as "barely competitive." Carey also offered evidence of pre-petition reductions in its managerial staff (from twenty-four to fifteen people) and its non-union supervisory staff (from fifteen to twelve), achieved by increasing the remaining officials' responsibilities. In light of this record evidence, we cannot disturb the bankruptcy court's findings on this score.

The lower court also correctly looked to pre-petition concessions obtained from the mechanics' union and two of Carey's principal creditors—the MTA and the Port Authority—as proof that these parties were contributing fairly and equitably to the effort to keep Carey afloat. Because a section 1113 application will almost always be filed before an overall reorganization plan can be prepared, the debtor cannot be expected to identify future alterations in its debt structure. Local 807 argues that the lower court overlooked Schiavone's status as a substantial creditor of its subsidiary and Carey's failure to show that Schiavone would write off part of this debt. We reject the suggestion that the statutory requirement that "all creditors" be treated fairly and equitably, see § 1113(b)(1)(A), means that a creditor who is also an owner of the debtor must ordinarily take a smaller percentage dividend than other creditors on its bona fide claims. The mere fact that there have been intercompany transactions between a debtor and its owner is not a source of unfairness to other creditors unless the transactions themselves were financially unfair to the debtor. Local 807 has not called to our attention, nor has our own review of the record disclosed, any evidence to indicate that Schiavone's claims against Carey arise from transactions that were financially unfair to Carey. And were there an indication of such unfair dealing, it would not necessarily support the Union's argument that Carey's rejection of its labor contracts should be disapproved. The more appropriate response would seem to be to seek the equitable subordination of claims by the owner, see 11 U.S.C. §§ 544, 548, 1104(a); these remedies would more fairly and equitably benefit all interested parties, not just the union members.

Finally, we note that even if a greater sacrifice is required of an owner-creditor than of other creditors, a write-off of outstanding debts is not the only way a creditor can assist its debtor. Here the record shows that Schiavone did not charge any interest on its loans to Carey, and that Schiavone otherwise subsidized Carey's day-to-day operations. By doing so, Schiavone made sacrifices that contributed significantly to Carey's survival.

In light of this evidence, we affirm the bankruptcy court's ruling that all parties were participating "fairly and equitably" in the attempt to save Carey from liquidation.

2. Good Cause

The debtor's obligation to prove that the union lacked good cause for refusing the post-petition proposal, like the necessity question, has been the subject of some debate among commentators and the courts. The Bankruptcy court here reasoned that because the proposed modifications were necessary, fair, and equitable, the union's refusal to accept them was without good cause. This reasoning, of course, suggests that the good cause provision adds nothing to the other substantive requirements of the statute.

We conclude, nonetheless, that this analysis is proper where, as here, the union has neither participated meaningfully in post-petition negotiations nor offered any reason for rejecting the proposal other than its view that the proposed modifications were excessive. At least one commentator has noted that the statute appears to authorize conduct similar to what the Drivers Committee did here: "stonewalling" post-petition negotiations and hoping that the courts will find that the proposal does not comply with subsection (b)(1). . . . This tactic is unacceptable and inconsistent with Congressional intent, as the *Royal Composing Room* opinion makes clear. This good cause requirement was "'intended to ensure that a continuing process of good faith negotiations will take place before court involvement.'".

Thus, even though the debtor retains the ultimate burden of persuading the court that the union lacked good cause for refusing proposed modifications, the union must come forward with evidence of "its reason for declining to accept the debtor's proposal in whole or in part. If prehearing, a union has assigned no reason for its refusal to accept a debtor's proposal, it has perforce refused to accept the proposal without good cause under Code § 1113(c)(2)." We agree with the bankruptcy court that because the union engaged in such prehearing stonewalling here, it now cannot claim that it had good cause for refusing the proposal.

Local 807 insists that because it later counter-proposed modifications that would have yielded significant cost savings, it had good cause for rejecting the debtor's proposal. We find, however, that ample record evidence supports the bankruptcy court's conclusion that this counter-proposal did not have the backing of union members. In fact, the counter-proposal was virtually identical to a pre-petition request that the union members had rejected overwhelmingly. A union's presentation of a counter-offer that its members do not support does not satisfy the good cause requirement. Moreover, we have already upheld the lower court's finding that greater than break-even cost savings were necessary. Therefore, this is not a situation where a union's counterproposal of an equally effective set of modifications might justify its refusal to accept management's proposal. The union's manifest failure to participate meaningfully in the post-petition negotiations confirms its lack of justification for rejecting Carey's proposed modifications.

3. Balancing the Equities

. . . [B]ankruptcy courts "must focus on the ultimate goal of Chapter 11 when considering these equities. The Bankruptcy Code does not authorize freewheeling consideration of every conceivable equity, but rather only how the equities relate to the success of the reorganization." 465 U.S. at 527.

. . . [W]e glean at least six permissible equitable considerations, many of which also factor into the other substantive requirements imposed by section 1113. Those are

(1) the likelihood and consequences of liquidation if rejection is not permitted; (2) the likely reduction in the value of creditors' claims if the bargaining agreement remains in force; (3) the likelihood and consequences of a strike if the bargaining agreement is voided; (4) the possibility and likely effect of any employee claims for breach of contract if rejection is approved; (5) the cost-spreading abilities of the various parties, taking into account the number of employees covered by the bargaining agreement and how various employees' wages and benefits compare to those of others in the industry; and (6) the good or bad faith of the parties in dealing with the debtor's financial dilemma. . . .

Substantial record evidence supports the lower court's other findings pertinent to this inquiry, despite the union's continued insistence that such support is lacking. For instance, documentary evidence in the record is consistent with the district court's findings that unionized labor costs were approximately 60% above the industry average, that 66% of Carey's employees are unionized, that managers, supervisors, and non-union workers were receiving less than average compensation while taking on increased workloads, and that Local 807, therefore, could fairly be expected to bear a substantial proportion of the needed cost-cutting measures. Record evidence also clearly shows that increasing losses in previous years, and continued but decreased projected losses in the then-current year, made liquidation a very real threat. The Union has not attempted to refute the evidence indicating that the company's low asset value, the secured creditors' existing claims, and the anticipated costs of administration and liquidation, would leave little or nothing for unsecured creditors and shareholders if the liquidation threat materialized. In view of this substantial and largely unrebutted evidence, we concur in the bankruptcy court's conclusion that the equities clearly favored rejection of the Local 807 agreements.

CONCLUSION

For these reasons, we affirm the judgment of the district court upholding the bankruptcy court's approval of Carey's section 1113 application to reject its bargaining agreements with Local 807.

Section 1113 is notable for imparting enormous discretion to the court with minimal guidance, and for not specifying what happens if a CBA is rejected. Once a CBA is rejected, what terms govern the continued employment of the unionized workers? Is rejection all or nothing, or is partial rejection possible? Does rejection entitle the trustee/DIP to impose a new CBA on whatever terms it wants or to implement the last offer it made? Can the court condition rejection upon implementation of new terms?

There is no language in section 1113 authorizing the court to implement permanent modified contract terms of any sort, including partial rejection; this is in contrast both to section 1113's authorization of interim modification and to language in the parallel section 1114 (discussed below) dealing with modification of retiree health benefits. *See Northwest Airlines Corp. v. Association of Flight Attendants—CWA,*

483 F.3d 160, 171 n.5 (2d Cir. 2007) ("Neither party appealed the bankruptcy court's implicit holding that it had the authority under § 1113 to impose new terms upon both carrier and union, . . . and we therefore assume without deciding that a bankruptcy court has such authority. We note simply that the text of § 1113 is not explicit on this score . . . and that the bankruptcy court must look elsewhere in the Bankruptcy Code to find such authority. . . ."). The Bankruptcy Code may not be the only source of law applicable following rejection of a CBA. Labor laws may also apply: The Bankruptcy Code deals with *rejection* of a CBA, but because of its silence regarding subsequent contract terms, it would stand to reason that regular labor laws would apply. This would mean that the debtor in possession or trustee would still be subject to labor law's duty of good faith bargaining. Under this approach, unilateral implementation of the last best offer made by the DIP or trustee would probably be acceptable, but not implementation of other terms.

The questions raised by section 1113 extend to the rights of the employees following rejection. What rights do the unionized employees have if they do not like the rejection? Can they strike? The Bankruptcy Code is silent on the issue, although to the extent a strike seeks recovery of pre-petition claims, it potentially violates the automatic stay.

A union's ability to strike in response to the rejection of a collective bargaining agreement may depend on which labor statute governs the industry. Labor relations in most industries are governed by the National Labor Relations Act. There are no cases directly holding that a rejection of a collective bargaining agreement gives rise to a right to strike under the NLRA. The Norris-LaGuardia Anti-Injunction Act, however, deprives courts of jurisdiction to enjoin even an illegal strike, and courts have held that this restriction is not superseded by the automatic stay. *In re Crowe & Assocs.*, 713 F.2d 211 (6th Cir. 1983); *In re Petrusch*, 667 F.2d 297 (2d Cir. 1981). Damages for a strike that violates the automatic stay might nonetheless be possible. *A.C.E. Elevator Co. v. Local No. 1 (In re A.C.E. Elevator Co.)*, 2009 Bankr. LEXIS 3089, 15-16 (Bankr. S.D.N.Y. Oct. 7, 2009). Thus, a union can probably strike (even if illegally) following the rejection of a collective bargaining agreement, but it might be liable for damages caused by violating the automatic stay if the strike sought recovery of pre-petition claims.

Labor relations for the airline and railways are governed by the Railway Labor Act. The Norris-LaGuardia Act does not prevent courts from enjoining violations of the Railway Labor Act, including unauthorized strikes. *Brotherhood of R.R. Trainmen v. Chicago River & Indiana R.R. Co.*, 353 U.S. 30 (1957); *Virginian Ry. Co. v. System Federation No. 40*, 300 U.S. 515 (1937). Moreover, the Railway Labor Act is generally more restrictive in its right to strike than the National Labor Relations Act, which governs labor relations in other industries, in part because strikes in the transportation industry are likely more disruptive to the economy as a whole. *See Chicago & N.W. Transp. Co. v. Railway Labor Executives' Ass'n*, 908 F.2d 144, 148 (7th Cir. 1990); *E.E.O.C. v. United Air Lines, Inc.*, 755 F.2d 94, 98 (7th Cir. 1985). Thus, one circuit court of appeals has ruled that under the Railway Labor Act, rejection of a collective bargaining agreement in bankruptcy does not give rise to a right to strike. *See Northwest Airlines Corp. v. Association of Flight Attendants—CWA*, 483 F.3d 160 (2d Cir. 2007).

If a CBA is rejected, do the unionized employees have a claim? If so, what sort? Is it a pre-petition or post-petition claim? Section 1113 is notably missing an analog to section 365(g), which provides that rejection of an executory contract is to be treated as a pre-petition breach. Similarly, section 502(g) addresses rejection claims under section 365, but not under section 1113. That would seem to imply that a rejected CBA is an administrative expense claim, but this is never how CBA rejections have been treated in the past.

If a CBA rejection is treated as a pre-petition claim, how are damages calculated? Presumably, they would be mitigated by any subsequent CBA and limited to the duration of the rejected CBA, but would there be any damages at all if the firm would have had to shut down operations and liquidate but for the rejection of the CBA? And on top of this, how does the section 502(b)(7) cap on employment contract termination claims apply, if at all? Are damages limited to one year? Or perhaps a rejected CBA does not give rise to a claim at all and that is why it is not addressed. Similar problems arise with an interim modification under section 1113(e). Is that a post-petition breach of a CBA? Are damages available in such a case?

Section 1113 raises many more questions than it answers. Case law is not sufficiently developed to offer definitive answers to any of the questions regarding section 1113. The lack of case law development is itself an indicator that section 1113 works as intended. It is a provision designed to induce compromise. In most cases, the stakes are too high for both workers and debtor firms to roll the dice on judicial decisions or even to wait for one. The lack of clarity about section 1113 might in fact be one of its virtues.

B. Retiree Benefits

Section 1113 addresses collective bargaining agreements, which deal with current labor contracts. But many firms also have substantial obligations to their retirees. Chrysler, for example, as we saw in Chapter 1, had significant legacy health care and pension costs. Simply rejecting a collective bargaining agreement would have had no effect on Chrysler's vested retiree obligations.

In 1986, LTV Steel filed for bankruptcy and terminated the benefits of some 78,000 retirees. In 1988, Congress responded by enacting a separate Bankruptcy Code provision, section 1114, that addresses for rejection of retiree health, disability, and death benefits of retirees whose gross income in the year prior to the bankruptcy was less than $250,000. 11 U.S.C. §§ 1114(a), (m). Unlike section 1113, there is a legislative history for section 1114, and the statute answers some of the questions for retiree benefits that are left unaddressed for collective bargaining agreements. The fact that these questions are addressed for section 1114 raises questions about how to interpret legislative silence in the context of section 1113.

Retiree benefits are typically not executory contracts; the retirees are unlikely to have material duties owing to the debtor. Precisely because retirees are not in executory contracts with the debtor, they are in a particularly vulnerable position. The retirees have given the debtor the benefit of their labor, with the expectation that some of the compensation would be paid in the form of deferred benefits. Retirees are also unlikely to have diversified their benefits because it is difficult for workers to diversify their employment. Thus, many retirees have all their eggs in one basket, yet they have little leverage over the debtor to ensure payment of the benefits.

Section 1114 is an attempt to balance out the need to protect vulnerable retirees with the recognition that in some cases, retiree benefits may be too onerous for a debtor seeking to reorganize. Thus, section 1114 requires the debtor to continue paying retiree benefits during the bankruptcy unless the court approves a modification of the benefits, which may only be done with the acceptance of the retirees (through a representative) or if the modification "is necessary the affected parties are treated fairly and equitably, and is clearly favored by the balance of the equities." 11 U.S.C. § 1114(g). Thus, the burden is on the DIP or trustee to show that the retiree benefits must be modified for a reorganization, and even then only the minimum modification necessary is approvable.

Section 1114 has five key protections for retirees. The first three are related to the payment of benefits, while the others deal with representation and the standard for modification of benefits. First, section 1114 requires that the DIP or trustee timely pay retiree benefits and prohibits modification of retiree benefits other than through its provisions. 11 U.S.C. § 1114(e). In other words, the debtor must keep making payments to its retirees until and unless a modification is approved by the court. If the DIP or trustee fails to make any post-petition payments, those payments are awarded administrative priority under section 503(b). 11 U.S.C. § 1114(e)(2). The timely payment requirement essentially elevates the priority of any post-petition retiree benefit claims. As with cure payments for assumption under section 365(b), section 1114(e)'s requirement of continuing payments is one of the Bankruptcy Code's few authorizations of pre-confirmation payments on pre-confirmation debts.

Second, section 1114 provides that all retiree benefit claims have administrative priority expense. Thus, any claims for failure to pay retiree benefits pre-petition are given administrative expense priority, putting them ahead of most creditors, including tax authorities. The clear administrative priority for retiree benefit claims is in contrast to section 1113's silence on the matter regarding CBAs. (If retiree benefits are modified, however, the diminution in benefits is a general unsecured claim. *In re Ionosphere Clubs, Inc.*, 134 B.R. 515, 526-527 (Bankr. S.D.N.Y. 1991).)

Third, section 1114 expressly provides that retiree benefit claims are not subject to the section 502(b)(7) cap on employment termination claims. 11 U.S.C. § 1114(j). This is also in contrast to section 1113's silence on the matter regarding CBAs.

Fourth, section 1114 provides for collective representation of retirees funded by the estate. Section 1114 requires that the retirees be collectively represented, either by a committee of retirees, or for benefits covered by a collective bargaining agreement, by the retirees' union, unless the union's interest is adverse to the retirees', as it often is, with retirees seeking to have their benefits preserved at the expense of current employees. 11 U.S.C. §§ 1114(b)-(d). The costs of retiree representatives are borne by the estate, as with other official committees. 11 U.S.C. § 1114(b)(2).

Finally, in order to modify retiree benefits, the trustee/DIP must present a proposal of any benefit modification to the retirees' representatives and provide them with enough information to evaluate it. 11 U.S.C. § 1114(f). The court may only approve the modification if the proposal has been made in the proper procedural manner; "the authorized representative of the retirees has refused to accept such proposal without good cause"; and "such modification is necessary to permit the reorganization of the debtor and assures that all creditors, the debtor, and all of the affected parties are treated fairly and equitably, and is clearly favored by the balance of the equities." 11 U.S.C. § 1114(g). An exception exists for emergency interim modifications of retiree benefits "if essential to the continuation of the debtor's business, or in order to avoid irreparable damage to the estate." 11 U.S.C. § 1114(h).

Section 1114 is not wholly protective of retirees. Their benefits can ultimately be modified, and most importantly, section 1114 only protects certain types of retiree benefits. Section 1114 applies only to "medical, surgical, or hospital care benefits, or benefits in the event of sickness, accident, disability, or death under any plan, fund, or program (through the purchase of insurance or otherwise)" for retired employees, their spouses, and their dependents. 11 U.S.C. § 1114(a). Thus, section 1114 does not cover pension benefits. Moreover, section 1114 excludes "top hat" employees—those earning over $250,000 (not inflation-adjusted) from the scope of its protections, on the theory that higher-earning employees can self-insure.

All in all, however, section 1114 is highly protective of retiree benefits, while recognizing that there are situations in which their modification is necessary in order to ensure that there is a viable firm capable of paying at least reduced benefits.

C. Pension Benefits

Employer pension obligations are not specifically covered by the Bankruptcy Code. Section 1114 covers only retiree health and medical benefits. It does not cover pension payments. 11 U.S.C. § 1114(a). While section 1113 covers future pension payments under current collective bargaining agreements, it does not cover pension obligations under past collective bargaining agreements or that are not part of collective bargaining agreements. The Bankruptcy Code has no provisions specifically on pension obligations, as these obligations are governed by a different statutory scheme, the Employee Retirement Income Security Act, or ERISA. ERISA is a comprehensive regulatory scheme for pension plans. It provides for vesting of pension benefits after a certain period of employment, and mandates the organization of pension plans as legally separate entities (trusts) with particular governance structures and duties.

Pension plans come in two flavors: defined benefit and defined contribution. Defined benefit plans promise a particular level of pension payments to the employee in the future. Under a defined benefit plan, the employer assumes the investment risk on the pension plan. If the plan's investments perform poorly, then the employer will have to make additional contributions to meet the plan's defined obligations. (In a defined benefit plan, the employee, of course, assumes the risk that the employer will be insolvent). In contrast, defined contribution plans, such as 401(k) and 403(b) plans, make no promise about the amount of payments that will be made to the employee. Instead, they promise a particular level of current payments into the pension plan. Thus, in a defined contribution plan, the employee, not the employer, assumes the investment risk on the pension plan.

Defined benefit plans can play an important role in bankruptcy. First, because employers bear the investment risk on the plans, the plans can themselves be a factor in bankruptcy filings. Second, employers will often fail to properly fund their plans. ERISA requires a certain minimum level of plan funding for defined benefit plans. When employers are unable to meet their pension funding obligations for defined benefit plans, ERISA also creates a system for the plans to be taken over by a federal agency, the Pension Benefit Guaranty Corporation (PBGC). The PBGC administers a pension insurance system for employees of defined benefit plans. The PBGC insurance fund is funded primarily by assessments on employers with defined benefit plans. It provides only limited insurance for defined benefit pensions: employees with higher benefit levels have less coverage by the PBGC. When the PBGC takes over a plan, it is subrogated to any claim for funding that the plan might have against the employer. Thus, the PBGC frequently appears as a creditor in bankruptcies, seeking to compel debtors to not only make missed contributions to defined benefit plans, but also to continue funding legacy plans.

Defined contribution plans play little role in bankruptcy. At most, employees have a claim for unpaid contributions. Such a claim either has priority under section 507(a)(5) or is a general unsecured claim. Claims for future contributions would only relate to current employees, and those would be administrative expenses of the estate. Funds that have been paid into a defined contribution plan are no longer under the control of the employer, so they do not present an issue in bankruptcy.

Problem Set 24

(1) Tippecanoe Water Craft, a leading domestic manufacturer of canoes, kayaks, and boogie boards, is facing vigorous foreign competition. Tippecanoe's foreign competitors have much lower labor costs than Tippecanoe with a unionized workforce represented by the International Brotherhood of Canoemakers and Kayakcrafters. Despite Tippecanoe's shrinking market share and uncertain financial future, the union has adamantly refused to renegotiate its current collective bargaining agreement, which expires in 10 years. That's not soon enough for Tippecanoe, argues the firm's CEO, John Tyler II. Tyler has engaged your firm for advice. He wants to know if Tippecanoe can force the union to accept less favorable terms in a bankruptcy, and what will be involved. Tyler is eager to use any means possible to force the union to accept lower wages, but he's very concerned that if he pushes too hard the union will go on strike. "A strike or a long, drawn out bankruptcy would both be terrible for us reputationally," he emphasizes. What do you tell him? 11 U.S.C. § 1113.

(2) Your feisty aunt Rhoda recently retired from Transamerica Motors, a manufacturer of buses and light trucks. Rhoda worked for over 35 years on the assembly line putting together "the best darn school buses in the world." Transamerica just filed for bankruptcy, and it has announced its intention of reducing retiree health

benefits. Transamerica's generous retiree health benefits were a major selling point when Transamerica recruited employees, but mean that Transamerica has much higher employee health care costs than its competitors.

    a. Aunt Rhoda is very worried about her health benefits. "I don't want to have to go on Obamacare," she says. "I just can't believe that Transamerica would be allowed not to keep its end of the bargain, after I worked there for so many years." What do you tell her? 11 U.S.C. § 1114.

    b. Aunt Rhoda is also worried about her pension. Transamerica offered a defined-benefit pension plan that pays Rhoda 70 percent of her peak salary until death, with Uncle Herb getting survivor benefits of 35 percent.

CLAIMS AND LIQUIDATION

CHAPTER 25

CLAIMS

I. WHO IS A CREDITOR? WHO HAS A CLAIM?

In bankruptcy parlance, creditors have "**claims**" against the debtor, while the holders of the debtor's equity securities have "interests" in the debtor. *See* 11 U.S.C. § 501(a). Who is a creditor, or more precisely, who has a claim? And who is an equity security holder with an interest in the debtor?

The Bankruptcy Code defines a "claim" as a "right to payment, whether or not such right is reduced to judgment, liquidated, unliquidated, fixed, contingent, matured, unmatured, disputed, undisputed, legal, equitable, secured, or unsecured" or a "right to an equitable remedy for breach of performance if such breach gives rise to a right to payment, whether or not such right to an equitable remedy is reduced to judgment, fixed, contingent, matured, unmatured, disputed, undisputed, secured, or unsecured." 11 U.S.C. § 101(5). Likewise, "equity security" is defined as including all types of corporate stock (in turn defined to include LLC membership interests) and limited partnership interests. 11 U.S.C. § 101(16).

It is usually relatively easy to identify who holds an interest in or claim against the debtor. Holders of preferred and common stock, partnership interests, and LLC memberships all have interests. Similarly, parties that loaned money to the debtor or that have not been paid on pre-petition contracts with the debtor have claims, and parties injured by the debtor pre-petition have claims.

Importantly, for a creditor to have a claim, there need not be a debt due and owing, much less reduced to judgment. The debt may be in dispute. The debt may be for an unliquidated amount. The debt may be contingent upon the occurrence (or nonoccurrence) of an event, such as the claim of a guarantor. And the debt need not even have matured. The maturity date of a debt may be years in the future, but it will still produce a claim in bankruptcy. Bankruptcy, then, telescopes all future maturity dates to the present, just like a liquidation, insofar as unmatured debts result in claims. The effect of claims not depending upon the maturity of debt obligations is to erase all temporal priorities that would otherwise hold outside of bankruptcy.

There are, however, potentially more complex situations: classification of injunctive beneficiaries, parties with potential *future* harms based on *past* conduct of the debtor, and financial relationships that have both debt and equity characteristics. This chapter addresses the first two of these situations. The question of whether a financial interest in the debtor is debt or equity is addressed in a later chapter.

The implications of whether a party holds a claim, an interest, or neither are significant for both that party and the debtor (and by implication other claimants and interest holders). Holders of claims and interests have both governance and distribution rights in a bankruptcy. Those who do not have claims or interests have neither.

Outside of bankruptcy, governance is primarily the province of equityholders. In bankruptcy, equity continues to have governance rights, but creditors—those with claims—also acquire certain governance rights, most critically, in Chapter 11, the right to vote on a plan of reorganization if their claims are impaired, meaning that their rights are changed by the plan (other than certain permitted exceptions). A party that is not a creditor (or an equityholder) does not have a right to vote on a plan of reorganization in Chapter 11. Likewise, various other Chapter 11 plan confirmation requirements create rights for claimants. If a party is not a claimant, it does not have those rights and thus cannot object to a Chapter 11 plan based on those rights.

Similarly, in both Chapters 7 and 11, the bankruptcy estate's assets are distributed solely to creditors and equityholders. A party that is not a creditor (or an equityholder) gets nothing in a liquidation or under a bankruptcy reorganization plan.[1]

Finally, the confirmation of a plan of reorganization discharges the debtor from pre-petition debts as well as from certain post-petition debts.[2] This discharge means that the enforcement of the debt against the debtor is permanently enjoined. Thus, a creditor is limited to recovering only what it receives in the bankruptcy distribution, which might be nothing. Creditors receive the possibility of being paid in a bankruptcy distribution, but lose the possibility of post-bankruptcy collection from the debtor. The discharge (discussed in more detail in a subsequent chapter) is one of the most important features of bankruptcy as it allows creditor's claims to be impaired in the bankruptcy—that is, not paid in full—without the creditor having recourse to the assets of the reorganized debtor after the bankruptcy. The discharge is what gives the reorganized debtor its fresh start.

If an entity does not have a claim and is thus not a creditor, it neither shares in the possibility of a distribution nor is bound by the discharge injunction. This means that a non-creditor can still enforce its remedies for pre-petition liabilities against the debtor post-petition in spite of the bankruptcy discharge.

Either outcome can affect other claimants and equityholders. To the extent a party has a claim, it increases the number of claims on the limited pool of assets that is the estate—a claimant is a competitor for limited resources. On the other hand, a non-claimant means that there may still be liability looming over the reorganized company, which could be a concern for any claimant who takes a distribution in a reorganized firm's new debt or equity.

---

1. 11 U.S.C. §§ 726 (distribution of property in a liquidation), 347 (unclaimed property escheat), 1123 (contents of plan of reorganization).

2. 11 U.S.C. §§ 1141 (discharge), 524 (discharge injunction).

II. INJUNCTIVE BENEFICIARIES

One complication in determining who has a claim relates to parties entitled to specific performance from the debtor, rather than monetary compensation. Section 101(10) of the Bankruptcy Code defines the term "creditor" as an "entity that has a claim against the debtor that arose at the time or before the order for relief concerning the debtor." Section 101(5)(A) defines "claim" as a "right to payment" irrespective of its nature. Section 101(5)(B) further defines "claim" to include a "right to an equitable remedy for breach of performance if such breach gives rise to a right to payment." In other words, a claim must be something that is capable of being reduced to a monetary obligation.

Questions can arise about which breaches of performance give rise to a right to payment, as opposed to a non-monetary obligation. If the non-monetary obligation is an absolute duty of performance, then the party to whom the performance is owed is not a creditor, and can neither partake in the bankruptcy distribution nor have its rights disturbed by the bankruptcy. The following two cases consider this issue.

Ohio v. Kovacs

469 U.S. 274 (1985)

Justice WHITE delivered the opinion of the Court.

Petitioner State of Ohio obtained an injunction ordering respondent William Kovacs to clean up a hazardous waste site. A receiver was subsequently appointed. Still later, Kovacs filed a petition for bankruptcy. The question before us is whether, in the circumstances present here, Kovacs' obligation under the injunction is a "debt" or "liability on a claim" subject to discharge under the Bankruptcy Code.

I.

Kovacs was the chief executive officer and stockholder of Chem-Dyne Corp., which with other business entities operated an industrial and hazardous waste disposal site in Hamilton, Ohio. In 1976, the State sued Kovacs and the business entities in state court for polluting public waters, maintaining a nuisance, and causing fish kills, all in violation of state environmental laws. In 1979, both in his individual capacity and on behalf of Chem-Dyne, Kovacs signed a stipulation and judgment entry settling the lawsuit. Among other things, the stipulation enjoined the defendants from causing further pollution of the air or public waters, forbade bringing additional industrial wastes onto the site, required the defendants to remove specified wastes from the property, and ordered the payment of $75,000 to compensate the State for injury to wildlife.

Kovacs and the other defendants failed to comply with their obligations under the injunction. The State then obtained the appointment in state court of a receiver, who was directed to take possession of all property and other assets of Kovacs and the corporate defendants and to implement the judgment entry by cleaning up the Chem-Dyne site. The receiver took possession of the site but had not completed his tasks when Kovacs filed a personal bankruptcy petition.

Seeking to develop a basis for requiring part of Kovacs' postbankruptcy income to be applied to the unfinished task of the receivership, the State then filed a motion in state court to discover Kovacs' current income and assets. Kovacs requested that the Bankruptcy Court stay those proceedings, which it did. The State also filed a complaint in the Bankruptcy Court seeking a declaration that Kovacs' obligation under the stipulation and judgment order to clean up the Chem-Dyne site was not dischargeable in bankruptcy because it was not a "debt," a liability on a "claim," within the meaning of the Bankruptcy Code. In addition, the complaint sought an injunction against the bankruptcy trustee to restrain him from pursuing any action to recover assets of Kovacs in the hands of the receiver. The Bankruptcy Court ruled against Ohio, as did the District Court. The Court of Appeals for the Sixth Circuit affirmed, holding that Ohio essentially sought from Kovacs only a monetary payment and that such a required payment was a liability on a claim that was dischargeable under the bankruptcy statute. We granted certiorari to determine the dischargeability of Kovacs' obligation under the affirmative injunction entered against him.

. . .

III.

Except for the nine kinds of debts saved from discharge by 11 U.S.C. § 523(a), a discharge in bankruptcy discharges the debtor from all debts that arose before bankruptcy. 11 U.S.C. § 727(b). It is not claimed here that Kovacs' obligation under the injunction fell within any of the categories of debts excepted from discharge by § 523. Rather, the State submits that the obligation to clean up the Chem-Dyne site is not a debt at all within the meaning of the bankruptcy law.

For bankruptcy purposes, a debt is a liability on a claim. [§ 101(12).] A claim is defined by § 101(5) as follows:

> **(5)** "claim" means—
>   **(A)** right to payment, whether or not such right is reduced to judgment, liquidated, unliquidated, fixed, contingent, matured, unmatured, disputed, undisputed, legal, equitable, secured, or unsecured; or
>   **(B)** right to an equitable remedy for breach of performance if such breach gives rise to a right to payment, whether or not such right to an equitable remedy is reduced to judgment, fixed, contingent, matured, unmatured, disputed, undisputed, secured, or unsecured.

The provision at issue here is [§ 101(5)(B)]. For the purposes of that section, there is little doubt that the State had the right to an equitable remedy under state law and that the right has been reduced to judgment in the form of an injunction ordering the cleanup. The State argues, however, that the injunction it has secured is not a claim against Kovacs for bankruptcy purposes because (1) Kovacs' default was a breach of the statute, not a breach of an ordinary commercial contract which concededly would give rise to a claim; and (2) Kovacs' breach of his obligation under the injunction did not give rise to a right to payment within the meaning of [§ 101(5)(B)]. We are not persuaded by either submission.

There is no indication in the language of the statute that the right to performance cannot be a claim unless it arises from a contractual arrangement. The State resorted to the courts to enforce its environmental laws against Kovacs and secured a negative order to cease polluting, an affirmative order to clean up the site, and an order to pay a sum of money to recompense the State for damage done to the fish population. Each order was one to remedy an alleged breach of Ohio law; and if Kovacs' obligation to pay $75,000 to the State is a debt dischargeable in bankruptcy, which the State freely concedes, it makes little sense to assert that because the cleanup order was entered to remedy a statutory violation, it cannot likewise constitute a claim for bankruptcy purposes. Furthermore, it is apparent [from the legislative history] that Congress desired a broad definition of a "claim" and knew how to limit the application of a provision to contracts when it desired to do so.[4] Other provisions cited by Ohio refute, rather than support, its strained interpretation.[5]

The courts below also found little substance in the submission that the cleanup obligation did not give rise to a right to payment that renders the order dischargeable under § 727. The definition of "claim" in [the House version of the legislation that became the Bankruptcy Code] as originally drafted would have deemed a right to an equitable remedy for breach of performance a claim even if it did not give rise to a right to payment. The initial Senate definition of claim was narrower, and a compromise version, [§ 101(5)], was finally adopted. In that version, the key phrases "equitable remedy," "breach of performance," and "right to payment" are not defined. See 11 U.S.C. § 101. Nor are the differences between the successive versions explained. The legislative history offers only a statement by the sponsors of the Bankruptcy Reform Act with respect to the scope of the provision:

> Section [101(5)(B)] . . . is intended to cause the liquidation or estimation of contingent rights of payment for which there may be an alternative equitable remedy with the result that the equitable remedy will be susceptible to being discharged in bankruptcy. For example, in some States, a judgment for specific performance may be satisfied by an alternative right to payment in the event performance is refused; in that event, the creditor entitled to specific performance would have a "claim" for purposes of a proceeding under title 11.

We think the rulings of the courts below were wholly consistent with the statute and its legislative history, sparse as it is. The Bankruptcy Court ruled as follows, *In re Kovacs*, 29 B.R., at 818:

> There is no suggestion by plaintiff that defendant can render performance under the affirmative obligation other than by the payment of money. We therefore conclude that plaintiff has a claim against defendant within the meaning of 11 U.S.C. [§ 101(5)], and that defendant owes plaintiff a debt within the meaning of 11 U.S.C. [§ 101(12)]. Furthermore, we have concluded that that debt is dischargeable.

---

4. See 11 U.S.C. § 365 (assumption or rejection of executory contracts and leases).

5. Congress created exemptions from discharge for claims involving penalties and forfeitures owed to a governmental unit, 11 U.S.C. § 523(a)(7), and for claims involving embezzlement and larceny. § 523(a)(4). If a bankruptcy debtor has committed larceny or embezzlement, giving rise to a remedy of either damages or equitable restitution under state law, the resulting liability for breach of an obligation created by law is clearly a claim which is nondischargeable in bankruptcy.

The District Court affirmed, primarily because it was bound by and saw no error in the Court of Appeals' prior opinion holding that the State was seeking no more than a money judgment as an alternative to requiring Kovacs personally to perform the obligations imposed by the injunction. To hold otherwise, the District Court explained, "would subvert Congress' clear intention to give debtors a fresh start." The Court of Appeals also affirmed, rejecting the State's insistence that it had no right to, and was not attempting to enforce, an alternative right to payment:

> Ohio does not suggest that Kovacs is capable of personally cleaning up the environmental damage he may have caused. Ohio claims there is no alternative right to payment, but when Kovacs failed to perform, state law gave a state receiver total control over all Kovacs' assets. Ohio later used state law to try and discover Kovacs' post-petition income and employment status in an apparent attempt to levy on his future earnings. In reality, the only type of performance in which Ohio is now interested is a money payment to effectuate the Chem-Dyne cleanup.

. . .

The impact of its attempt to realize upon Kovacs' income or property cannot be concealed by legerdemain or linguistic gymnastics. Kovacs cannot personally clean up the waste he wrongfully released into Ohio waters. He cannot perform the affirmative obligations properly imposed upon him by the State court except by paying money or transferring over his own financial resources. The State of Ohio has acknowledged this by its steadfast pursuit of payment as an alternative to personal performance.

As we understand it, the Court of Appeals held that, in the circumstances, the cleanup duty had been reduced to a monetary obligation.

We do not disturb this judgment. The injunction surely obliged Kovacs to clean up the site. But when he failed to do so, rather than prosecute Kovacs under the environmental laws or bring civil or criminal contempt proceedings, the State secured the appointment of a receiver, who was ordered to take possession of all of Kovacs' non-exempt assets as well as the assets of the corporate defendants and to comply with the injunction entered against Kovacs. As wise as this course may have been, it dispossessed Kovacs, removed his authority over the site, and divested him of assets that might have been used by him to clean up the property. Furthermore, when the bankruptcy trustee sought to recover Kovacs' assets from the receiver, the latter sought an injunction against such action. Although Kovacs had been ordered to "cooperate" with the receiver, he was disabled by the receivership from personally taking charge of and carrying out the removal of wastes from the property. What the receiver wanted from Kovacs after bankruptcy was the money to defray cleanup costs. At oral argument in this Court, the State's counsel conceded that after the receiver was appointed, the only performance sought from Kovacs was the payment of money. Had Kovacs furnished the necessary funds, either before or after bankruptcy, there seems little doubt that the receiver and the State would have been satisfied. On the facts before it, and with the receiver in control of the site, we cannot fault the Court of Appeals for concluding that the cleanup order had been converted into an obligation to pay money, an obligation that was dischargeable in bankruptcy.

IV.

It is well to emphasize what we have not decided. First, we do not suggest that Kovacs' discharge will shield him from prosecution for having violated the environmental laws of Ohio or for criminal contempt for not performing his obligations under the injunction prior to bankruptcy. Second, had a fine or monetary penalty for violation of state law been imposed on Kovacs prior to bankruptcy, § 523(a)(7) forecloses any suggestion that his obligation to pay the fine or penalty would be discharged in bankruptcy. . . . Fourth, we do not hold that the injunction against bringing further toxic wastes on the premises or against any conduct that will contribute to the pollution of the site or the State's waters is dischargeable in bankruptcy; we here address, as did the Court of Appeals, only the affirmative duty to clean up the site and the duty to pay money to that end. Finally, we do not question that anyone in possession of the site—whether it is Kovacs or another in the event the receivership is liquidated and the trustee abandons the property, or a vendee from the receiver or the bankruptcy trustee—must comply with the environmental laws of the State of Ohio. Plainly, that person or firm may not maintain a nuisance, pollute the waters of the State, or refuse to remove the source of such conditions. As the case comes to us, however, Kovacs has been dispossessed and the State seeks to enforce his cleanup obligation by a money judgment.

The judgment of the Court of Appeals is *affirmed*.

Justice O'CONNOR, concurring.

I join the Court's opinion and agree with its holding that the cleanup order has been reduced to a monetary obligation dischargeable as a "claim" under § 727 of the Bankruptcy Code. I write separately to address the petitioner's concern that the Court's action will impede States in enforcing their environmental laws.

To say that Kovacs' obligation in these circumstances is a claim dischargeable in bankruptcy does not wholly excuse the obligation or leave the State without any recourse against Kovacs' assets to enforce the order. Because "Congress has generally left the determination of property rights in the assets of a bankrupt's estate to state law," *Butner v. United States*, 440 U.S. 48, 54 (1979), the classification of Ohio's interest as either a lien on the property itself, a perfected security interest, or merely an unsecured claim depends on Ohio law. That classification—a question not before us—generally determines the priority of the State's claim to the assets of the estate relative to other creditors. *Cf.* 11 U.S.C. § 545 (trustee may avoid statutory liens only in specified circumstances). Thus, a State may protect its interest in the enforcement of its environmental laws by giving cleanup judgments the status of statutory liens or secured claims.

The Court's holding that the cleanup order was a "claim" within the meaning of [§ 101(5)] also avoids potentially adverse consequences for a State's enforcement of its order when the debtor is a corporation, rather than an individual. In a Chapter 7 proceeding under the Bankruptcy Code, a corporate debtor transfers its property to a trustee for distribution among the creditors who hold cognizable claims, and then generally dissolves under state law. Because the corporation usually ceases to exist, it has no postbankruptcy earnings that could be utilized by the State to fulfill the cleanup order. The State's only recourse in such a situation may well be its "claim" to the prebankruptcy assets.

For both these reasons, the Court's holding today cannot be viewed as hostile to state enforcement of environmental laws.

Study Questions

In *Kovacs*, Ohio first obtained an injunction for a cleanup and agreement to pay certain damages and then, upon Kovacs's default on that stipulation, appointed a receiver to clean up the polluted site, which involved taking possession of the polluted site, as well as Kovacs's other assets, which were to be used to finance the cleanup. Would the result have been different if Ohio had instead just obtained an injunction ordering Kovacs to clean up the site himself and enforced it through a contempt proceeding? If injunction and subsequent receivership resulted in a dischargeable claim, but a injunction enforced through contempt would not have resulted in a dischargeable claim, what do you think of the incentives it creates? Are the consequences for Kovacs more extreme in the latter case than the former? And which approach is more likely to result in remediation of the polluted site?

United States v. Apex Oil Company, Inc.

579 F.3d 734 (7th Cir. 2009)

POSNER, Circuit Judge.

Apex Oil Company appeals from the grant of an injunction, at the behest of the Environmental Protection Agency and on the authority of 42 U.S.C. § 6973 (a part of the Resource Conservation and Recovery Act [RCRA or "Rick-Rah"] of 1976, 42 U.S.C. §§ 6901 *et seq.*), that requires Apex to clean up a contaminated site in Hartford, Illinois. In a 178-page opinion following a 17-day bench trial, the district judge made findings that millions of gallons of oil, composing a "hydrocarbon plume" trapped not far underground, are contaminating groundwater and emitting fumes that rise to the surface and enter houses in Hartford and in both respects are creating hazards to health and the environment. The judge deemed it Apex's legal responsibility to abate this nuisance because the plume was created by an oil refinery owned by a corporate predecessor of Apex. Apex challenges these findings and conclusion, but the challenge has no possible merit.

The principal question presented by the appeal is unrelated to the district judge's findings and conclusions; it is whether the government's claim to an injunction was discharged in bankruptcy and therefore cannot be renewed in a subsequent lawsuit—this suit. The bankruptcy judge's confirmation (approval) of a claim in a Chapter 11 proceeding discharges the debtor from "any debt that arose before the date of" confirmation, 11 U.S.C. § 1141(d)(1)(A), with immaterial exceptions. "Debt" is defined as "liability on a claim," § 101(12), and "claim" as either a "right to payment," § 101(5)(A), or—the critical language in this case—a "right to an equitable remedy for breach of performance if such breach gives rise to a right to payment, whether or not such right to an equitable remedy is reduced to judgment, fixed, contingent, matured, unmatured, disputed, undisputed, secured, or unsecured." § 101(5)(B). The critical question is the meaning of "gives rise to a right to payment."

Because Apex no longer does refining and as a result has no in-house capability of cleaning up a contaminated site, it would have to hire another company to do the clean up in order to comply with the injunction. It estimates that it would have to pay such a company $150 million for the job, though it might be able to recover some of the expense from other contributors to the contamination.

The natural reading of the statutory provision that we quoted is that if the holder of an equitable claim can, in the event that the equitable remedy turns out to be unobtainable, obtain a money judgment instead, the claim is dischargeable. If for example you have a decree of specific performance (a type of injunction and therefore an equitable remedy) that you can't enforce because the property that the decree ordered the defendant to sell you was sold to someone else (from whom, for whatever reason, you cannot recover it), you are entitled to a money judgment for the value of the property . . . and your claim to that value is a claim to a right to receive payment and is dischargeable in the seller's bankruptcy.

In addition, some equitable remedies, such as backpay orders in employment cases . . . and orders of equitable restitution . . . are orders to pay, and so would be dischargeable were it not for specific exceptions in the Bankruptcy Code. That equitable remedies are always orders to act or not to act, rather than to pay, is a myth; equity often orders payment.

But the Resource Conservation and Recovery Act, which is the basis of the government's equitable claim, does not entitle a plaintiff to demand, in lieu of action by the defendant that may include the hiring of another firm to perform a clean up ordered by the court, payment of clean-up costs. It does not authorize any form of monetary relief. 42 U.S.C. § 6973(a). The Act's companion provision authorizing private suits, 42 U.S.C. § 6972(a)(2), has been held not to authorize monetary relief, *Meghrig v. KFC Western, Inc.*, 516 U.S. 479, 483-87 (1996), . . . and the relevant language of the two provisions is identical.

Thus the government's equitable claim, if well founded, as the district court ruled it to be, entitles the government only to require the defendant to clean up the contaminated site at the defendant's expense. Earlier cases . . . which allowed an award of clean-up costs on the basis of general equitable principles . . . are dead after *Meghrig*, if we are correct in thinking that the identical language in sections 6972(a)(2) and 6973(a) requires an identical conclusion with regard to a plaintiff's right to seek a money judgment.

That leaves Apex to argue that the cost of complying with an equitable decree should be deemed a money claim, and hence dischargeable. We [previously] rejected that proposition, which does not comport with the language of the Bankruptcy Code—the cost to Apex is not a "right [of the plaintiff] to payment." . . .

Almost every equitable decree imposes a cost on the defendant, whether the decree requires him to do something, as in this case, or, as is more common, to refrain from doing something. The logic of Apex's position is thus that every equitable claim is dischargeable in bankruptcy unless there is a specific exception in the Code. That is inconsistent with the Code's creation in 11 U.S.C. § 101(5)(B) of only a limited right to the discharge of equitable claims. And if "any order requiring the debtor to expend money creates a dischargeable claim, it is unlikely that the state could effectively enforce its laws: virtually all enforcement actions impose some cost on the violator."

It is true that in *Ohio v. Kovacs*, 469 U.S. 274 (1985), the Supreme Court allowed the discharge in bankruptcy of an equitable obligation to clean up a contaminated site owned by the debtor. An injunction ordering the clean up had been issued before the bankruptcy. The debtor had failed to comply with the injunction and a receiver had been appointed to take possession of his assets and obtain from them the money needed to pay for the clean up. The receiver thus was seeking money rather than an order that the debtor clean up the contaminated site. That was a claim to a "right to payment." The plaintiff in our case (the government) is not seeking a payment of money and the injunction that it has obtained does not entitle it to payment. [Citations omitted.]

. . . The distinctions that Apex suggests to limit the scope of a position that it realizes is untenable (that all equitable claims are dischargeable in bankruptcy in the absence of a specific exception in the Code)—between injunctions to do and injunctions not to do, between injunctions that require major expenditures and those that require minor ones, between injunctions that the defendant can comply with internally and injunctions that it has to hire an independent contractor in order to achieve compliance—are arbitrary.

The root arbitrariness of Apex's position is that whether a polluter can clean up his pollution himself or has to hire someone to do it has no relevance to the policy of either the Bankruptcy Code or the Resource Conservation and Recovery Act. If adopted by the courts, Apex's position would discourage polluters from developing an internal capability of cleaning up their pollution, even if hiring third parties to do it would be more expensive. Moreover, the cost of cleaning up pollution when the polluter does the cleaning up himself is as real a cost as the price paid to an outsider to clean it up. Why distinguish a check written to an employee from a check written to an independent contractor?

. . . [D]ischarge must indeed be limited to cases in which the claim gives rise to a right to payment because the equitable decree cannot be executed, rather than merely imposing a cost on the defendant, as virtually all equitable decrees do.

Apex argues that to deny discharge in a case such as this disserves the government's long-term interest in environmental quality by precluding, as a practical matter, reorganization in bankruptcy. . . . It says that had it known in 1986 when it declared bankruptcy that it might be liable for $150 million in clean-up costs, it would have had to liquidate—it could not have reorganized with such a huge debt overhanging it—and had it liquidated there would be no surviving or successor entity to conduct or pay for the clean up and so the full expense would fall on the government. But that is just to say that in some cases the government might benefit from the rule that Apex advocates; in others not and apparently the government believes . . . that it is better off on balance if the cost of clean up is not dischargeable.

. . . AFFIRMED.

Study Questions

1. How, if at all, can *Apex* be squared with *Kovacs*? Is it simply a matter of the interaction of different statutes with the Bankruptcy Code? If so, what should be made of the lack of discussion of the state statute at issue in *Kovacs*?

2. Would *Kovacs* have been decided differently had there not been a receiver in possession of the contaminated property and if the receiver was not seeking money from Kovacs to remediate the property, rather than trying to compel Kovacs to remediate the property himself? If so, does that suggest a major limitation on *Kovacs* as a precedent?

3. Judge Posner has little sympathy for Apex's argument that a remediation order is equivalent to a direction to spend money on a remediation, and thus equivalent to a monetary claim. He notes that "Apex's position would discourage polluters from developing an internal capability of cleaning up their pollution." Does this assertion ring true to you? What about its inverse: Is the *Apex* ruling likely to encourage polluters to develop an internal remediation capability? Do you think companies are likely to plan based on the bankruptcy treatment of injunctive remedies? What if the shareholders of those companies know that they are likely to have their stock cancelled in the bankruptcy? If *Apex* were to affect firm behavior, wouldn't it more likely encourage pollution prevention instead of remediation?

III. WHEN DOES A CLAIM ARISE?

Even when it is clear that a party has a claim, the question of when the claim arose is also important. Roughly speaking, the world of claims can be divided into two halves, temporally: pre-petition and post-petition. Only pre-petition claims are dischargeable in bankruptcy. Thus, a debtor may want a claim to be considered a pre-petition claim. Moreover, the treatment of claims depends in part on pre-petition or post-petition status. Certain pre-petition claims are entitled to priority treatment, meaning that they get paid ahead of general unsecured claims. At the same time, certain post-petition claims are treated as administrative expenses of the bankruptcy estate, which also are entitled to priority treatment. The following two cases consider aspects of when a claim arises.

Jensen v. California Department of Health Services
127 B.R. 27 (9th Cir. BAP 1991)

ASHLAND, U.S. Bankr. J.

The debtors Robert and Rosemary Jensen ("Jensens") appeal the bankruptcy court's grant of summary judgment in favor of the State of California Department of Health

Services ("DHS"), the California counterpart to the federal Environmental Protection Agency, upon the parties' cross-motions for summary judgment. We reverse.

INTRODUCTION AND FACTS

The Jensens individually wholly-owned Jensen Lumber Company ("JLC"), whose manufacturing process included dipping logs in fungicide tanks. DHS generally seeks indemnity for cleanup costs incurred related to the fungicide tanks, which remained on property (the "site") leased and later abandoned in bankruptcy by JLC. The California Regional Water Quality Control Board (the "Board") inspected the site on January 25, 1984 and issued a letter, received by the Jensens on February 2, stating a hazardous waste problem existed at the site. The Jensens thereafter individually filed bankruptcy under Chapter 7 on February 13, 1984. They did not list any claim for hazardous waste cleanup. The DHS later became involved in March, 1984 but did not expend funds for hazardous waste cleanup until substantially after that time.

Following the determination that no assets were available for distribution to creditors, the Jensens received a discharge on July 16, 1984. The Jensens filed an adversary proceeding on April 24, 1989, to determine that the DHS's claim for cleanup costs was discharged in the Jensen's individual bankruptcy, after the DHS had taken steps seeking recovery under the federal and state "Superfund" statutes, CERCLA[1] and HSA,[2] respectively. A more complete chronology of relevant events surrounding the Chapter 7 bankruptcies of JLC (converted from Chapter 11) and the Jensens as individuals appends this decision.

ISSUE PRESENTED

This case requires us to determine when claims arise for purposes of bankruptcy, specifically claims under CERCLA and HSA. As a preliminary matter, we note the DHS does not contend its claim is excepted from discharge. Rather, the DHS asserts its claim arose postpetition and is therefore not discharged. Thus, the sole issue as framed by the parties, and as addressed by the bankruptcy court, concerns when DHS's claim arose for purposes of bankruptcy. . . .

C. Three Points of Origination Find Authoritative Support

Authority generally supports three points of origination for claims, each of which is advocated by one or the other parties in the present case. The cases hold bankruptcy claims may arise: (1) with the right to payment; (2) upon the establishment of the relationship between the debtor and the creditor; or (3) based upon the debtor's conduct. Following the foregoing examination of each theory, we hold the DHS's claim arose for purposes of the Jensens' bankruptcy at the time of actual or threatened release of the hazardous waste, or based upon the debtors' conduct.

---

1. The Comprehensive Environmental Response, Compensation and Liability Act, 42 U.S.C. §§ 9601-9657.
2. The Hazardous Substance Account Act, CAL. HEALTH & SAFETY CODE §§ 25300 *et seq.*

1. The Claim Arises with the Right to Payment

DHS contends and the bankruptcy court held that DHS's claim did not arise until DHS incurred costs for hazardous waste cleanup. DHS argues and the bankruptcy court held that [§ 101(5)] specifically requires a "right to payment" before a claim cognizable in bankruptcy arises. The argument then proceeds that the right to payment under CERCLA or HSA does not arise until cleanup costs are incurred. DHS thus argues that until cleanup costs are incurred, no right to payment, and no cognizable claim, exists for bankruptcy purposes.

This theory has been adopted by at least one circuit court. In *In re Frenville*, 744 F.2d 332 (3d Cir. 1984), *cert. denied*, 469 U.S. 1160 (1985), a creditor appealed a district court order holding the creditor's indemnity action against the Chapter 7 debtor was barred by the automatic stay. While the debtor's acts underlying the indemnity occurred prepetition, the suit against the creditor was filed postpetition, prompting the indemnification action. In determining when the claim originated, the Third Circuit first noted the Bankruptcy Code does not clearly define when a "right to payment" arises, and therefore applied state law. *Id.* at 337. The relevant state law declared a right to payment on an indemnity arises upon payment of the judgment flowing from the act. The *Frenville* court then concluded the suit against the creditor had been filed postpetition, the creditor's claim therefore arose postpetition, and the automatic stay did not apply. *Id.* The court in *United States v. Union Scran Iron & Metal*, 123 Bankr. 831 (D. Minn. 1990), cited by the DHS, adopted the same reasoning, although without mention of *Frenville*.

However, *Frenville* has been roundly criticized by several courts.* As stated in *In re A.H. Robins Co.*, 63 Bankr. 986, 992 (Bankr. E.D. Va. 1986), the *Frenville* court confuses "a 'right to payment' for federal bankruptcy purposes with the accrual of a cause of action for state law purposes." Indeed, under *Frenville* and *Union Scran Iron* we can perceive no difference between claims inside or outside bankruptcy. Such an interpretation simply is unwarranted from a reading of [§ 101(5)], which includes contingent and unmatured rights to payment, as well as those having been reduced to judgments.

Further, holding that the cause of action, or in the present case, the statutory right to payment, triggers recognition of the bankruptcy claim contravenes the overriding goal of the Bankruptcy Code to provide a "fresh start" for the debtor. *Grogan v. Garner*, [498 U.S. 279] (1991). In a no-asset Chapter 7 case, like the one at hand, manipulation will surely result. The creditor, aware of a debtor's precarious financial situation, will delay expenditures in anticipation of the debtor's bankruptcy, thereby preventing discharge of the creditor's claims. Additionally, debtors having attentive creditors will be denied the benefit of bankruptcy's fresh start, although enjoyed by other debtors similarly situated but whose creditors are less well-informed. Such untenable results cannot be endorsed.

DHS offers cases [that] hold private causes of action under CERCLA do not arise until cleanup costs are incurred. See *Levin Metals Corp. v. Parr-Richmond Terminal Co.*, 799 F.2d 1312, 1316 (9th Cir. 1986); *Bulk Distribution Centers, Inc. v. Monsanto Co.*,

---

* *Frenville* has subsequently been rejected by the Third Circuit. *JELD-WEN, Inc. v. Van Brunt* (*In re Grossman's Inc.*), 607 F.3d 114 (3d Cir. 2010) (en banc) (adopting pre-petition relationship test); *In re Ruitenberg*, 745 F.3d 647 (3d Cir. 2014)—ED.

589 F. Supp. 1437, 1450-1452 (S.D. Fla. 1984). However, neither of these cases involved bankruptcy nor required determination of when a bankruptcy claim arises, but rather only determined that a private action under CERCLA could not be commenced prior to incurrence of cleanup costs. We conclude reliance on these cases is misplaced.

Other cases cited by DHS and the bankruptcy court appear equally inapposite. In *In re Hemingway Transport, Inc.*, 73 Bankr. 494 (Bankr. D. Ma. 1987), plaintiff in the adversary proceeding had purchased property from the bankruptcy trustee, property later determined to be contaminated with hazardous waste. The plaintiff was forced to clean up the waste and sought indemnification from the estate, specifically asserting administrative priority for its claim. While the court held plaintiff's claims were entitled to administrative expense priority, the court cited cases holding that negligence of a trustee or receiver gives rise to administrative priority claims. *Id.* at 504-505. The court relied heavily on equitable considerations, evidenced by the following statement:

> Not only is the Court moved by the concept of fairness emphasized by the Supreme Court and the First Circuit Court of Appeals, it is moved by its awareness that [other courts have] frowned on the notion of a debtor attempting to transfer its liability or potential for liability under state or federal environmental laws.

Id. at 505. *In re Wall Tube & Metal Products Co.*, 831 F.2d 118 (6th Cir. 1987), generally follows the same vein. While the DHS argues these decisions implicitly determined the claims at issue were postpetition, thus justifying administrative expense priority, neither case mentions [§ 101(5)] or addresses the subject of when bankruptcy claims arise. We conclude these cases are inapposite to the present appeal.

2. The Claim Arises upon the Establishment of the Relationship Between the Debtor and the Creditor

DHS alternatively asserts bankruptcy claims arise at the earliest point in the relationship between the debtor and the creditor. Adopting this theory would benefit DHS in that DHS did not become involved until after the filing of the Jensens' individual bankruptcy, causing DHS's claims to be postpetition.

Often cited in this respect is *In re Edge*, 60 Bankr. 690 (Bankr. M.D. Tenn. 1986). Edge involved prepetition negligence of two debtor dentists not discovered until postpetition. The plaintiff sought a declaration that her claim arose upon discovery of the injury and therefore was not subject to the automatic stay. After a thorough discussion, the court rejected the *Frenville* reasoning and held a claim resulting from debtor's prepetition misconduct arises at the earliest point in the relationship between the victim and the wrongdoer, in this case when the dentist performed the negligent act. *Id.* at 699. In so concluding, the court stated:

> These are individual Chapter 7 cases. A fresh start for these debtors is impossible if the victims of prebankruptcy negligence cannot be addressed in this case. Allowing those injured by the debtor's prepetition conduct to share in prepetition assets is consistent with the strong policy favoring compensation for injuries and is essential to the equitable distribution of these estates.

Id. at 699-700. Thus, the *Edge* court believed that recognition of prepetition negligence provided a fresh start to the debtor and compensated the victim from the estate. *Id.* at 699.

While we find *Edge* persuasive, we also believe the *Edge* reasoning to be consistent with the proposition, which we adopt below, that the creditor's claim arises based upon the debtor's conduct. *Edge* simply applies the proposition in the context of a tort committed while rendering services.

3. The Claim Arises Based upon the Debtor's Conduct

The final theory, that the bankruptcy claim arises based upon the debtor's conduct, we believe most closely reflects legislative intent and finds the most support in the case law. These cases have generally held the bankruptcy claim arises upon conduct by the debtor which would give rise to a cause of action, if other elements may later be satisfied. A brief review of frequently cited cases supporting this approach follows.

In *In re Johns-Manville Corp.*, 57 Bankr. 680 (Bankr. S.D.N.Y. 1986), creditors, not asbestos-related, seeking indemnity or contribution from debtor Johns-Manville, moved for relief from the stay to pursue their claims in state court. This necessitated interpreting [§ 101(5)] as to when bankruptcy claims arise. The bankruptcy court denied the relief from stay, noting ". . . the focus should be on the time when the acts giving rise to the alleged liability were performed. . . ." *Id.* at 690. The court found the operative time to be the sale of the defective goods by Johns-Manville to the creditors, which occurred prepetition. *Id.* Significantly, the *Johns-Manville* court was concerned with the policy of basing timing of claims on factors other than the debtor's conduct. "Procedural and extraneous factors such as the timing of the filing of a summons and complaint by a third party, which is not associated with the underlying nature of the cause of action . . . simply should not determine the existence or nonexistence of a 'claim.'" *Id.*

The bankruptcy court in *In re A.H. Robins Co.*, 63 Bankr. 986 (Bankr. E.D. Va. 1986), reached a similar conclusion. There, a Dalkon Shield claimant sought a declaration that her claim against the debtor manufacturer was postpetition and thus not subject to the automatic stay. The claimant had been inserted with the shield prepetition, but perceived no injury until postpetition. In analyzing when the bankruptcy claim arose, the *A.H. Robins* court rejected the reasoning in *Frenville* and found the definition of claim articulated in *Edge* broader than necessary to give effect to Bankruptcy Code goals. *Id.* at 993. The court then adopted the theory in *Johns-Manville*, that a "right to payment," and therefore a claim, arises at the time when the acts giving rise to the alleged liability were performed. *Id.* The *A.H. Robins* court held the right to payment arose at the time the shield was inserted. *Id.*

One bankruptcy court has applied the reasoning of *Johns-Manville* and *A.H. Robins* to environmental claims. In *In re Chateaugay Corp.* ("LTV"), 112 Bankr. 513 (Bankr. S.D.N.Y. 1990), the United States and New York State sought declaratory judgments regarding dischargeability of environmental claims in bankruptcy. The bankruptcy court examined the language of CERCLA, which requires as a predicate to liability "[a] 'release' or a 'threatened release' of a 'hazardous substance' . . . at the site." *Id.* at 518. The *LTV* court held so long as a prepetition triggering event has occurred, *i.e.*, the release or threatened release of hazardous waste, the claim is dischargeable, regardless of when the claim for relief may be in all respects ripe for adjudication. *Id.* at 522. As the *LTV* court states, very frequently only one part of a tort occurs prepetition, with the injury occurring postpetition, yet such claims should be considered dischargeable. *Id.*

We adopt the reasoning propounded in *Johns-Manville* and *A.H. Robins*, as applied in *LTV*. DHS attempts to distinguish *LTV* by noting an extensive relationship existed between the *LTV* parties prior to the bankruptcy filing. This argument is unpersuasive and overlooks the plain holding of *LTV* that a claim arises for purposes of discharge upon the actual or threatened release of hazardous waste by the debtor. *LTV* is directly analogous to the present case and we subscribe to its sound reasoning. This conclusion gives effect to the important bankruptcy goal of providing a fresh start to the debtor and discourages manipulation of the bankruptcy process.

D. Environmental Policy Considerations May Not Control the Bankruptcy Code in the Absence of Clear Legislative Intent

The bankruptcy court and DHS further contend that important public policy supporting environmental cleanup requires that environmental claims be treated differently from other claims. This argument ignores the only Ninth Circuit authority in this area, *In re Dant & Russell, Inc.*, 853 F.2d 700 (9th Cir. 1988). At issue there was whether private claims against the debtor under CERCLA could be accorded administrative expense priority. In holding the priority sought not merited, the Ninth Circuit sounded a strong policy against according preference to particular claims[:] "Although [the creditor] asserts that public policy considerations entitle its claims for cleanup costs to administrative expense priority, we acknowledge that Congress alone fixes priorities . . . (citation omitted). Courts are not free to formulate their own rules of super or sub-priorities within a specifically enumerated class." *Id.* at 709. While not addressed in determining the timing of a claim, the *Dant* court's language clearly discourages according preference to particular claims.

CONCLUSION

Based upon the Board letter dated February 2, 1984, threatened release of the hazardous waste involved here clearly occurred prior to filing of the Jensens' individual bankruptcy on February 13, 1984. Because we hold claims in bankruptcy arise based upon the debtor's conduct, we conclude that DHS's claim arose in this case prepetition, and was therefore discharged in the Jensens' bankruptcy. The decision of the bankruptcy court is reversed.

Study Questions

1. What is the difference between the right to payment test and the creditor-debtor relationship test (also known as the pre-petition relationship test)?

2. Is the debtor's conduct test applicable only to torts involving latent injuries? Does it have any bearing in a contractual relationship?

3. When would the claim have arisen under the right to payment test? The creditor-debtor relationship test? The debtor's conduct test? What effect would the application of different tests have had on the DHS claim?

4. On what basis does the Ninth Circuit Bankruptcy Appellate Panel choose between these tests? Do you think the decision was results-driven? Is there a principled way of choosing between these tests? Why shouldn't non-bankruptcy policy interests be taken into account?

5. Can *Jensen* be squared with *Apex Oil*? Does the difference in the outcomes depend on the fact that one involved the government's claim for damages under the Comprehensive Environmental Response, Compensation and Liability Act (CERCLA) while the other involved liability under the Resource Conservation and Recovery Act (RCRA)? CERCLA violations create liability for the costs of removal and remediation, which the government may perform, while RCRA violations result in a corrective action injunction. Should the bankruptcy treatment of environmental liability depend on whether the government does a remediation and sends the debtor a bill or whether the government orders a party to undertake a cleanup itself?

Epstein v. Official Committee of Unsecured Creditors of the Estate of Piper Aircraft Corp.

58 F.3d 1573 (11th Cir. 1995)

Black, Circuit Judge:

This is an appeal by David G. Epstein, as the Legal Representative for the Piper future claimants (Future Claimants), from the district court's order of June 6, 1994, affirming the order of the bankruptcy court entered on December 6, 1993. The sole issue on appeal is whether the class of Future Claimants, as defined by the bankruptcy court, holds claims against the estate of Piper Aircraft Corporation (Piper), within the meaning of § 101(5) of the Bankruptcy Code. After review of the relevant provisions, policies and goals of the Bankruptcy Code and the applicable case law, we hold that the Future Claimants do not have claims as defined by § 101(5) and thus affirm the opinion of the district court.

I. FACTUAL AND PROCEDURAL BACKGROUND

. . .

Piper has been manufacturing and distributing general aviation aircraft and spare parts throughout the United States and abroad since 1937. Approximately 50,000 to 60,000 Piper aircraft still are operational in the United States. Although Piper has been a named defendant in several lawsuits based on its manufacture, design, sale, distribution and support of its aircraft and parts, it has never acknowledged that its products are harmful or defective.

On July 1, 1991, Piper filed a voluntary petition under Chapter 11 of Bankruptcy Code in the United States Bankruptcy Court for the Southern District of Florida. Piper's plan of reorganization contemplated finding a purchaser of substantially all of its assets or obtaining investments from outside sources, with the proceeds of such transactions serving to fund distributions to creditors. On April 8, 1993, Piper and Pilatus Aircraft Limited signed a letter of intent pursuant to which Pilatus would purchase Piper's assets. The letter of intent required Piper to seek the appointment of a legal representative to represent the interests of future claimants by arranging a set-aside of monies generated by the sale to pay off future product liability claims.

On May 19, 1993, the bankruptcy court appointed Appellant Epstein as the legal representative for the Future Claimants. The Court defined the class of Future Claimants to include:

> All persons, whether known or unknown, born or unborn, who may, after the date of confirmation of Piper's Chapter 11 plan of reorganization, assert a claim or claims for personal injury, property damages, wrongful death, damages, contribution and/or indemnification, based in whole or in part upon events occurring or arising after the Confirmation Date, including claims based on the law of product liability, against Piper or its successor arising out of or relating to aircraft or parts manufactured and sold, designed, distributed or supported by Piper prior to the Confirmation Date.

See Order, May 19, 1993 (Mark, J.). This Order expressly stated that the court was making no finding on whether the Future Claimants could hold claims against Piper under § 101(5) of the Code.

On July 12, 1993, Epstein filed a proof of claim on behalf of the Future Claimants in the approximate amount of $100,000,000. The claim was based on statistical assumptions regarding the number of persons likely to suffer, after the confirmation of a reorganization plan, personal injury or property damage caused by Piper's pre-confirmation manufacture, sale, design, distribution or support of aircraft and spare parts. The Official Committee of Unsecured Creditors (Official Committee), and later Piper, objected to the claim on the ground that the Future Claimants do not hold § 101(5) claims against Piper.

After a hearing on the objection, the bankruptcy court agreed that the Future Claimants did not hold § 101(5) claims, and, on December 6, 1993, entered an Order Sustaining the Committee's Objection and Disallowing the Legal Representative's Proof of Claim. In a Memorandum Opinion dated January 14, 1994, that court entered final findings of fact and conclusions of law to support its December Order. Epstein, as Legal Representative, then appealed from the bankruptcy court's order. On June 6, 1994, the district court affirmed and accepted the decision of the bankruptcy court. Epstein now appeals from the district court's order, challenging in particular its use of the prepetition relationship test to define the scope of a claim under § 101(5).

II. DISCUSSION

The sole issue on appeal [is] whether any of the Future Claimants hold claims against Piper as defined in § 101(5) of the Bankruptcy Code. . . .

Since the enactment of § 101(5), courts have developed several tests to determine whether certain parties hold claims pursuant to that section: the accrued state law claim test*, the conduct test, and the prepetition relationship test. The bankruptcy court and district court adopted the prepetition relationship test in determining that the Future Claimants did not hold claims pursuant to § 101(5).

Epstein primarily challenges the district court's application of the prepetition relationship test. He argues that the conduct test, which some courts have adopted in mass tort cases, is more consistent with the text, history, and policies of the Code. Under the conduct test, a right to payment arises when the conduct giving rise to the alleged liability occurred. Epstein's position is that any right to payment arising out of the prepetition conduct of Piper, no matter how remote, should be deemed a claim and provided for, pursuant to § 101(5), in this case. He argues that the relevant conduct giving rise to the alleged liability was Piper's prepetition manufacture, design, sale and distribution of allegedly defective aircraft. Specifically, he contends that, because Piper performed these acts prepetition, the potential victims, although not yet identifiable, hold claims under § 101(5) of the Code.

The Official Committee and Piper dispute the breadth of the definition of claim asserted by Epstein, arguing that the scope of claim cannot extend so far as to include unidentified, and presently unidentifiable, individuals with no discernible prepetition relationship to Piper. Recognizing, as Appellees do, that the conduct test may define claim too broadly in certain circumstances, several courts have recognized "claims" only for those individuals with some type of prepetition relationship with the debtor. . . . The prepetition relationship test, as adopted by the bankruptcy court and district court, requires "some prepetition relationship, such as contact, exposure, impact, or privity, between the debtor's prepetition conduct and the claimant" in order for the claimant to hold a § 101(5) claim.

Upon examination of the various theories, we agree with Appellees that the district court utilized the proper test in deciding that the Future Claimants did not hold a claim under § 101(5). Epstein's interpretation of "claim" and application of the conduct test would enable anyone to hold a claim against Piper by virtue of their potential future exposure to any aircraft in the existing fleet. Even the conduct test cases, on which Epstein relies, do not compel the result he seeks. In fact, the conduct test cases recognize that focusing solely on prepetition conduct, as Epstein espouses, would stretch the scope of § 101(5). Accordingly, the courts applying the conduct test also presume some prepetition relationship between the debtor's conduct and the claimant.

While acknowledging that the district court's test is more consistent with the purposes of the Bankruptcy Code than is the conduct test supported by Epstein, we find that the test as set forth by the district court unnecessarily restricts the class of claimants to those who could be identified prior to the filing of the petition. Those claimants having contact with the debtor's product post-petition but prior to confirmation also could be identified, during the course of the bankruptcy proceeding, as potential victims, who might have claims arising out of debtor's prepetition conduct.

---

* This is the same test as the "right to payment" test in *Jensen*.—ED.

We therefore modify the test used by the district court and adopt what we will call the "Piper test" in determining the scope of the term claim under § 101(5): an individual has a § 101(5) claim against a debtor manufacturer if (i) events occurring before confirmation create a relationship, such as contact, exposure, impact, or privity, between the claimant and the debtor's product; and (ii) the basis for liability is the debtor's prepetition conduct in designing, manufacturing and selling the allegedly defective or dangerous product. The debtor's prepetition conduct gives rise to a claim to be administered in a case only if there is a relationship established before confirmation between an identifiable claimant or group of claimants and that prepetition conduct.

In the instant case, it is clear that the Future Claimants fail the minimum requirements of the Piper test. There is no preconfirmation exposure to a specific identifiable defective product or any other preconfirmation relationship between Piper and the broadly defined class of Future Claimants. As there is no preconfirmation connection established between Piper and the Future Claimants, the Future Claimants do not hold a § 101(5) claim arising out of Piper's prepetition design, manufacture, sale, and distribution of allegedly defective aircraft.

III. CONCLUSION

For the foregoing reasons, we hold that the Future Claimants do not meet the threshold requirements of the Piper test and, as a result, do not hold claims as defined in § 101(5) of the Bankruptcy Code.

AFFIRMED.

The number of different tests that courts use about when a claim arises can be confusing. Table 25.1 provides a summary of the four major tests. It indicates what sort of conduct is required for a claim to arise, whether the test also requires a relationship between the creditor and debtor to exist, and if so, by what point in time for the claim to be dischargeable in the bankruptcy.

Table 25.1. Tests for Claim Accrual

Test	Conduct Requirement	Relationship Requirement
Accrued State Law Claim Test	Harm to creditor	No relationship requirement
Prepetition Relationship Test	Wrongful conduct by debtor	Relationship before petition filed
Piper Test	Wrongful conduct by debtor	Relationship before plan confirmation
Debtor's Conduct Test (*Jensen*)	Wrongful conduct by debtor pre-petition	No relationship requirement

---

Problem Set 25

(1) Which of the following would qualify as future claimants under the *Piper* test:

    a. People who purchased defective Piper planes pre-petition and have suffered no injury to date, but may be injured at some future date?

    b. People who purchased defective Piper planes pre-petition and have suffered no injury to date, but will not fly the planes now that they know of the defect? (Assume that the defect is irremediable.)

    c. People who purchase defective Piper planes after the bankruptcy petition and are subsequently injured by the planes prior to the confirmation?

    d. People whose property or persons will be damaged when defective Piper planes crash on their houses post-petition, but pre-confirmation?

    e. People who purchased tickets pre-petition to fly (without specifying the type of airplane) and are then injured after the bankruptcy plan is confirmed as the result of being flown in a defective Piper plane?

    f. People who purchased tickets pre-petition to fly *in a Piper plane* and are then injured after the bankruptcy plan is confirmed as the result of being flown in a defective Piper plane?

(2) Would the results for question 1 be different if the debtor's conduct test from *Jensen* were applied?

(3) General Motors filed for bankruptcy in 2009. In its bankruptcy, GM sold its "good" assets, including the Chevy Cobalt product line and its name and associated trademarks to a "New GM," which promptly changed its name to "General Motors." The remaining assets of "Old GM" (renamed Motors Liquidation Company) were liquidated in bankruptcy.

Cosmo Kramer purchased a Chevy Cobalt (a GM product) in 2008. In 2011, when Kramer was driving on the Capital Beltway, the Cobalt's ignition suddenly turned off, resulting in an accident in which Kramer was seriously injured. Dozens of similar defective Cobalt ignitions have been subsequently reported, many allegedly causing injury and even death. Some GM employees were aware of problems with the ignition system since at least 2001, but did not initiate a recall or otherwise notify consumers of the defect. It is unclear if senior management was aware of the problem. GM did not specifically disclose anything about the defect and associated liability in its bankruptcy case.

George Costanza owns a Cobalt that has not yet experienced any problems. George would like to sell his car, however, but the market for Chevy Cobalts has significantly fallen since the ignition problems became public. George's attorney Jackie Chiles brought a class action suit against reorganized General Motors in Maryland state court seeking to recover economic losses for a class of Cobalt owners, with George as one of the named plaintiffs. Among the class's losses alleged in Jackie's suit are the depreciation of the value of the car, the cost of alternative transportation, and the loss of use, child care costs, and lost wages because of repair time. GM moved to have the suit removed to the bankruptcy court for the Southern District of New York, and asked the court for a declaratory judgment that the class action was enjoined by virtue of the court's asset sale order in the GM bankruptcy.

The bankruptcy court entered a Sale Order approving GM's Master Sale and Purchase Agreement. Section 2.3 of the Master Sale and Purchase Agreement enumerated the liabilities of Old GM that were to be assumed by New GM under the sale:

(a) The "Assumed Liabilities" shall consist only of the following Liabilities of Sellers:

. . .

(vii) (A) all Liabilities arising under express written warranties of Sellers [Old GM] that are specifically identified as warranties and delivered in connection with the sale of new, certified used or pre-owned vehicles or new or remanufactured motor vehicle parts and equipment (including service parts, accessories, engines and transmissions) manufactured or sold by Sellers or Purchaser [New GM] prior to or after the Closing [of the asset sale] . . .

. . .

(ix) all Liabilities to third parties for death, personal injury, or other injury to Persons or damage to property caused by motor vehicles designed for operation on public roadways or by the component parts of such motor vehicles and, in each case, manufactured, sold or delivered by Sellers (collectively, "Product Liabilities"), which arise directly out of accidents, incidents or other distinct and discreet occurrences that happen on or after the Closing Date and arise from such motor vehicles' operation or performance . . .

. . .

(b) Each Seller acknowledges and agrees that pursuant to the terms and provisions of this Agreement, Purchaser shall not assume, or become liable to pay, perform or discharge, any Liability of any Seller, whether occurring or accruing before, at or after the Closing, other than the Assumed Liabilities. In furtherance and not in limitation of the foregoing, and in all cases with the exception of the Assumed Liabilities, neither Purchaser nor any of its Affiliates shall assume, or be deemed to have assumed, any Indebtedness, Claim or other Liability of any Seller or any predecessor, Subsidiary or Affiliate of any Seller whatsoever, whether occurring or accruing before, at or after the Closing, including the following (collectively, the "Retained Liabilities"):

. . .

(ix) all Liabilities to third parties for death, personal injury, or other injury to Persons or damage to property caused by motor vehicles designed for operation on public roadways or by the component parts of such motor vehicles and, in each case, manufactured, sold, or delivered by Sellers (collectively, "Product Liabilities"), which arise directly out of accidents, incidents, or other distinct and discreet occurrences that happen on or after the Closing Date and arise from such motor vehicles' operation or performance. . . .

The Master Sale and Purchase Agreement that was approved by the court also contained the following definition:

"Liabilities" means any and all liabilities and obligations of every kind and description whatsoever, whether such liabilities or obligations are known or unknown, disclosed or undisclosed, matured or unmatured, accrued, fixed, absolute, contingent, determined or undeterminable, on or off-balance sheet or otherwise, or due or to become due, including Indebtedness and those arising under any Law, Claim, Order, Contract or otherwise.

The Sale Order was not timely appealed by any party with a Chevy Cobalt-related injury. Putting aside Fourteenth Amendment Due Process issues, there is clear precedent that to the extent there is a claim covered by the Sale Order, the Sale Order will be binding.

    a. Assuming there are no issues of contributory negligence, who, if anyone, is liable for the personal injury and wrongful death suits arising from the Chevy Cobalt problems?

    b. Based only on your knowledge of bankruptcy law and the sale order, who is liable for the costs of repairing the Cobalts that are still under warranty?

    c. Based only on your knowledge of bankruptcy law and the sale order, who is liable for the costs of repairing the Cobalts that are no longer under warranty?

    d. Who is liable for the economic loss suit brought by Jackie Chiles? Does it matter if GM management was aware of the problem with the Cobalt ignition prior to the asset sale or confirmation of Old GM's bankruptcy plan?

    e. What are the implications of the liability for any of these matters on Old GM (Motors Liquidation Company) or New GM (General Motors)? 11 U.S.C. §§ 101(5), 101(12), 727(a)(4), 1141(d)(1).

CHAPTER 26

CLAIM ALLOWANCE

Once it is clear that a party has a claim and is thus a creditor, the question then becomes one of the size and nature of the creditor's claim. How much is the claim for? The claim might be contingent or unliquidated. Moreover, the Bankruptcy Code caps certain claims. Is the creditor's claim secured or unsecured? And perhaps most critically, is the claim allowed or not? Determining which claims are allowed and which are not helps resolve an important informational problem that can impede out-of-court resolutions. By determining which claims are allowed and which are not, the court is determining who has a seat at the table in the restructuring, and what their baseline rights are vis-à-vis the debtor, and thus vis-à-vis other creditors. Absent such a determination, creditors might have trouble agreeing on resolutions because they might not be able to agree about the extent of their respective rights vis-à-vis the debtor.

While a party may be a creditor of the debtor, that does not in and of itself create a "claim." Instead, a claim is created in one of two ways. Either a creditor or its representative (including an indenture trustee or a creditor seeking to represent a class of creditors) may file a claim with the bankruptcy court or the debtor (or a trustee in bankruptcy) may file a proof of claim on behalf of the creditor based on the liabilities indicated in its books and records. 11 U.S.C. § 501(a), (c); FED. R. BANKR. PROC. 3003(c)(1). A proof of claim may also be filed by a co-debtor, such as a guarantor. 11 U.S.C. § 501(b). Proofs of claim are tracked in a "claims register" that is maintained by the clerk of the court. FED. R. BANKR. PROC. 5003(b). Often, however, in larger cases, a private claims register is maintained by a claims agent retained by the estate pursuant to court order.

The ability of the debtor to file a proof of claim is important for Chapter 7 bankruptcy because it ensures the possibility of an eventual discharge of the liability represented by the claim. To the extent that there is no proof of claim for a liability, the claim cannot be adjudicated, classified, and administered in Chapter 7 bankruptcy.

A different result obtains in Chapter 11, which specifically provides that the discharge covers all debts that arose before plan confirmation, "whether or not . . . a proof of claim based on such debt is filed or deemed filed under section 501 of this title." 11 U.S.C. § 1141(d). At the same time, however, section 1111(a) of the Code deems proofs of claim filed for any claim that appears in the schedules of liabilities filed by the debtor, unless a proof of claim is scheduled as disputed, contingent, or unliquidated.

The ability of co-debtors, such as guarantors, to file proofs of claim under section 501(b) is also important to enable co-debtors to preserve their rights: To the extent the creditor receives a distribution in the bankruptcy, the guarantor's liability will be reduced; if the creditor does not partake in the bankruptcy, it will not receive a distribution.

The filing of a claim with the court is quite simple. A single-page proof of claim form is submitted to the court along with any supporting documentation. For large business bankruptcies, processing claims are handled by a professional claims agent that has been retained by the debtor. These claims agents handle ministerial matters relating to claims for a debtor: aggregating proofs of claim, sending notices to claimants, and tabulating voting on claims. Claims agents also typically maintain a free electronic docket for the case that includes searchable lists of proofs of claim.

Once a claim is filed, it is deemed to be allowed, absent an objection. 11 U.S.C. § 502(a). If a claim is allowed, it means that the creditor can exercise the rights that come with being a claim holder: voting on and objecting to a plan of reorganization and partaking in the distribution of the assets of the bankruptcy estate. Critically, the mere fact that a claim is allowed does not mean that the creditor will be paid anything. Instead, allowance is an eligibility prerequisite for payment.

Not all claims are allowed. There are numerous grounds for a debtor or other "party in interest" to object to a claim. 11 U.S.C. §§ 502(b), (d)-(e). We will examine five of them later in this chapter: claims that are unenforceable outside of bankruptcy other than because they are "contingent or unmatured"; claims for "unmatured interest"; claims of insiders or attorneys; damages for termination of real property leases and employment contracts; and certain claims by guarantors and indemnitors. Note that a "party in interest" need not actually have an economic interest in the claim dispute and is not synonymous with Article III constitutional standing.

One other ground for claims objection bears mentioning: Tardily filed claims may be disallowed upon objection. The court will set a "bar date" for the timely filing of claims. In a Chapter 7 case, this bar date is 90 days after the first date set for a meeting of the creditors under section 341 (a "341 meeting"). FED. R. BANKR. PROC. 3002(c). In a Chapter 11 case, the bar date is committed to the court's discretion. FED. R. BANKR. PROC. 3003(c)(2).

In Chapter 7, claims not filed by the bar date are either disallowed or subordinated to timely filed claims. 11 U.S.C. §§ 502(b)(9), 726(a). Section 502(b)(9) contains a carve-out for claims that are allowed under section 726(a)(1)-(3) or the Federal Rules of Bankruptcy Procedure. Section 726(a) subordinates (but allows) late-filed claims, unless the creditor did not receive notice or have actual knowledge of the bar date. The claims of creditors who lack actual or constructive knowledge of the bar date are not subordinated and their claims are allowed to the extent practicable. Thus, the only claims actually disallowed under section 502(b)(9) are late-filed claims filed by a co-debtor or late-filed claims that are disputed, contingent, or unliquidated.

In Chapter 11, any claims that are either not scheduled by bar date or are scheduled as disputed, contingent, or unliquidated, and for which the creditor has not itself filed a proof of claim, are disallowed for purposes of voting and distribution.

FED. R. BANKR. PROC. 3003(c)(2).[1] In other words, as with Chapter 7, late-filed disputed, contingent, or unliquidated claims face disallowance. Otherwise, late claims are subordinated, just as in Chapter 7.

Thus, in both Chapter 7 and Chapter 11, the bar date functions like a statute of limitations on claims. For Chapter 7 cases, the bar date is inflexible. FED. R. BANKR. PROC. 3002(c). While Federal Rules of Bankruptcy Procedure generally allow extension of deadlines for "excuseable neglect," FED. R. BANKR. PROC. 9006 (b)(1), bar dates in Chapter 7 cases are excluded from this leniency principle. FED. R. BANKR. PROC. 9006(c); *Pioneer Services Co. v. Brunswick Associates Ltd. P'ship*, 507 U.S. 380 (1993). In contrast, Federal Rule of Bankruptcy Procedure 3003(c)(3) allow the court in Chapter 11 cases to extend the bar date "for cause," which may be done retroactively. This distinction reflects the different policy goals of Chapter 7 and Chapter 11. Chapter 7 aims at the prompt administration of the debtor's estate, whereas Chapter 11 is more flexible and seeks to avoid forfeitures by creditors based on failure to meet filing deadlines, but also elevates the goal of the debtor's rehabilitation by discharging debts irrespective of whether claims are ever filed.

Although claims are deemed allowed absent an objection, debtors will frequently file blunderbuss "omnibus claims objections" up to 100 claims scheduled. Omnibus claims objections are allowed only for objections based on certain ministerial grounds, such as late filings, duplicate claims, or other technical problems with the claim. FED. R. BANKR. PROC. 3007(d)-(e).

The filing of an objection to a claim does not mean that a claim is disallowed. Instead, it sets up an adjudication of the claim (or settlement negotiations). Still, the filing of an objection effectively shifts the burden of proof back to the creditor. This can be preclusive for small claims; the cost of litigating the claim must be discounted not only for the likelihood of success, but for the likely recovery in the bankruptcy. Claims of less than tens of thousands of dollars are effectively unenforceable if a debtor objects, even without good cause.

Section 502(b) sets forth several statutory grounds on which a claim may be disallowed in part or in full. The following section reviews the most important grounds. Chapter 32 discusses the possibility of non-statutory, equitable disallowance of claims, a doctrine of uncertain status given the codification of specific disallowance grounds in section 502(b).

I. UNENFORCEABLE CLAIMS

Section 502(b)(1) provides that claims that are unenforceable against the debtor or against the debtor's property are unenforceable under applicable non-bankruptcy

---

[1]. Disallowance for voting and distribution purposes is not the same as the debt being discharged, for if the case were to be dismissed, the debt would still exist and the creditor could pursue its non-bankruptcy remedies. To the extent that the Federal Rule of Bankruptcy Procedure 3003(c)(2) disallowance rule does not apply to a late claim, the subordination rules of section 726 still apply via sections 502(b)(9) and 1129(a)(7). *See In re Best Payphones, Inc.*, 523 B.R. 54, 75-76 (Bankr. S.D.N.Y. 2015).

law. Section 558 buttresses this provision by providing that the estate may raise any defense that would be available to the debtor, including statutes of limitations, statutes of fraud, and usury. The bankruptcy estate, then, is essentially subrogated to the rights of the debtor.

Accordingly, a claim for which a claimant lacks standing would be barred under section 502(b)(1). Similarly, a claim that would be barred by a statute of limitations or estoppel would be barred under section 502(b)(1), as these are defenses that the debtor could have raised itself per section 558. Note, however, that a bankruptcy filing tolls the statute of limitations for applicable non-bankruptcy law until the later of the expiration of that statute of limitations or 30 days after the lifting of the automatic stay. 11 U.S.C. § 108(c). Likewise, if the debtor could successfully raise defenses to a claim, such as usury, fraud, mutual mistake, unconscionability, contributory negligence, lack of consideration, or bad faith, the claim would not be allowed. Moreover, to the extent that a punitive damages or stipulated/liquidated damages claim would not be allowed under applicable non-bankruptcy law, it will not be allowed in bankruptcy. (And when allowed, punitive damages may be statutorily subordinated. 11 U.S.C. § 726(a)(4).) Section 558 also allows the estate to invoke setoff against creditors. The estate's right of setoff (unlike that of creditors, discussed in the next chapter) is not limited to offsetting pre-petition obligations against each other, but also allows the offset of pre-petition against post-petition obligations. *In re ADI Liquidation, Inc.,* 2015 Bankr. Lexis 1611, 2015 WL 4638605 (Bankr. D. Del. May 5, 2015); *In re Circuit City Stores, Inc.,* 2009 Bankr. Lexis 4011 (Bankr. E.D. Va. Dec. 3, 2009).

Some defenses, such as contributory negligence or usury, may operate to reduce a claim, rather than to make it wholly unenforceable. In such cases, section 502(b)(1) disallows only that part of the claim that could not be enforced under applicable non-bankruptcy law.

There is an important exception to 502(b)(1)'s disallowance rule: Claims that are unenforceable currently solely because they are contingent or unmatured may not be disallowed under section 502(b)(1). Thus, a contingent claim of a guarantor may not be disallowed under section 502(b)(1), and neither may a claim for a loan that is not yet due.

II. INTEREST

A. Unmatured Interest

Bankruptcy telescopes debts due in the future to the present, so principal balances due in future years are automatically accelerated and come due in a liquidation. This has the effect of significantly increasing the value of a claim for a debt with a long maturity relative to one for the same amount, but with a short maturity. To wit, a claim for $1 million in one year is treated identically to a claim for $1 million in 30 years, although $1 million in 30 years is worth considerably less than $1 million in one year. The natural way to account for this difference in time value would be to include interest on the claim for the maturity of the debt.

Bankruptcy law, however, expressly disallows such future interest. While principal balances are telescoped into the claim per section 101(5), contractual or statutory interest that would accrue over the remaining term of the debt, but which has not yet matured by the date of the bankruptcy filing ("unmatured interest") is disallowed under section 502(b)(2). The determination of unmatured interest disregards the effect of so-called *ipso facto* clauses triggered upon bankruptcy or insolvency. S. REP. NO. 95-989, 95th Cong., 2d Sess. 2 (1978).

Why does bankruptcy disallow such unmatured interest? The legislative history explains that

> [o]ne unarticulated reason for this is that the discounting factor for claims after the commencement of the case is equivalent to contractual interest rate on the claim. Thus, this paragraph does not cause disallowance of claims that have not been discounted to a present value because of the irrebuttable presumption that the discounting rate and the contractual interest rate (even a zero interest rate) are equivalent.

SEN. REP. NO. 95-989. If the triple negative in the final sentence of the Senate Report on the Bankruptcy Reform Act of 1978 confuses things, here it is in plain English: If we assume that the contract rate is the discount rate, then all section 502(b)(2) does is to limit claim allowance to the present value of all claims, which is defined as equal to the principal.

To wit, a claim for $1 million due in 30 years at 30% interest is deemed to have a present value of $1 million, just as a claim for a $1 million interest-free loan due in one year is deemed to have a present value of $1 million. The fact that these discount rates might be completely inconsistent is irrelevant. Instead, creditors are all assumed to have the proper discount rate on their loans. Accordingly, unmatured interest is disallowed under section 502(b)(2).

B. Original Issue Discount

Normally, determining what is unmatured interest is relatively easy. It is more complicated, however, in the case of securities (or loans) that were sold with an "original issue discount" or OID. OID is the difference between a bond's issuance price and its original face amount (par value). Thus, if a $10 million bond was issued for $9.5 million, there would be $0.5 million of OID. OID is only about the original issuance price; secondary market pricing is irrelevant for claim allowance.

When a bond or loan is issued at a discount, the discount is functionally interest. To wit, bonds have a "coupon"—a periodic interest payment amount (as opposed to a rate). For some bonds, this coupon is zero. These are known as "zero-coupon" bonds, meaning there is no periodic interest paid on the bonds. Instead, a zero-coupon bond involves simply a bullet payment of principal at maturity. Suppose a firm issues zero-coupon ten-year balloon bonds that at maturity will pay out a par value of $11 million. If the bonds are issued for $10 million, these bonds have $1 million in OID. The OID on these bonds is equivalent to 1% annual non-compounded interest rate: a $10 million balloon bond that accrued 1% annual non-compounded interest would pay $11 million ($10 million in principal plus $1 million in interest) at the end of ten years.

Why would a bond ever be issued for less than par value? In some cases it is because of the payment design of the bonds. For example, zero-coupon bonds pay interest only at maturity rather than periodically. This means that zero-coupon bonds are always sold at a discount from face value to account for time value. Thus, all zero-coupon bonds have built-in OID. Other bonds are not designed to have OID, but are issued at a discount because of an increase in market interest rates between the bonds' registration with the SEC and their actual sale date; issuance at a discount avoids the need to reregister the bonds.

Bankruptcy deals with OID by treating it as if it were interest amortized over the term of the debt security. The amortization allocates the OID throughout the maturity of the security, so that it is possible to determine as of any given date how much of the OID has accrued, and how much remains unaccrued. To the extent that OID has accrued as of the petition date, it is treated as matured interest, while OID that has not yet accrued is treated as unmatured interest. Accordingly, the method used to amortize OID can have a sizeable impact on a creditor's claim.

Most courts use the "constant interest" or "constant yield" or "yield to maturity" method of amortization, while a minority use straight-line amortization. (One would think that the correct approach to choosing an applicable amortization method would depend on the payment structure of the securities at issue, rather than be a generic rule. . . .) As explained by the Second Circuit, "[t]he constant interest method calculates OID amortization on the assumption that interest is compounded over time. Under the constant interest method, the amount of interest that accrues each day increases over time." *In re Chateaugay Corp. v. Valley Fidelity Bank & Trust Co.*, 961 F.2d 378 (2d Cir. 1992) (holding that there is no OID in a consensual debt-for-debt exchange).

The constant interest method thus assumes that the "yield to maturity"—the total rate of return on the security if it is held to maturity—is the same in all periods. Yield to maturity differs from a bond's "yield," which is simply the bond's coupon divided by the price of the bond. The key difference is the yield to maturity assumes a reinvestment of all coupon payments at the same yield to maturity. In other words, yield to maturity is a measure that accounts for compounded interest based on a constant interest rate throughout the life of the security. Because the constant interest method assumes compounded interest, the dollar amount of the OID is more heavily weighted to periods closer to the maturity date. This means that the imputed interest would accrue *later*, so there will be more unmatured interest than with a straight-line amortization method, which does not assume compounding. Instead, the straight-line amortization method simply takes the total amount of the OID and allocates it evenly over time. Straight-line amortization implies an interest rate that is declining over time, rather than staying constant. While straight-line amortization is easier to calculate, it may not always realistically reflect the structure of the security at issue.

To illustrate, Table 26.1 shows the two different amortization methods applied to our model debt security with an $11 million par value and 10% coupon, but a $10 million issuance price (and hence $1 million in OID). Under a straight-line amortization, the $1 million of OID is divided evenly among ten years, for $100,000 of

OID per year. This amortization implies a decreasing annual yield on the bond. If the firm filed for bankruptcy after four years, there would be $400,000 of OID accrued and treated as matured interest, while $600,000 would remain unaccrued and would be disallowed. The creditor's allowed claim would be for the $10 million in principal plus $400,000 in accrued interest.

In contrast, if the constant interest amortization method were used, we first need to calculate the implied yield to maturity (the internal rate of return for an investor) of the bond. The mathematics underlying this calculation are beyond the scope of this book, but the formula for calculating yield to maturity on zero-coupon bonds is: $YTM = \sqrt[n]{F/P} - 1$, where n=the number of years until maturity, F=the face amount of the bond, and P=the price of the bond.[2] For our bond, that gives us an implied yield of 0.958%, which must be compounded. Once we do so, we see that the annual accrual of OID varies and increases over time. If the firm had filed for bankruptcy after four years, then using the constant interest method, there would be a total of $388,601.18 of OID allocated to those four years using the constant interest method. Accordingly, the security holder's allowed claim would be $10,388,601.18 under the constant interest method, as opposed to $10.4 million under the straight-line method. The remaining $611,398.82 (constant interest) or $600,000 (straight-line) in OID would be disallowed as unmatured interest.

Table 26.1 OID Amortization Example

Year	Straight-line Amortization	Straight-line Implied Yield	Constant Interest Method	Constant Interest Implied Yield
1	$100,000.00	1.000%	$95,765.83	0.958%
2	$100,000.00	0.990%	$96,682.94	0.958%
3	$100,000.00	0.980%	$97,608.83	0.958%
4	$100,000.00	0.971%	$98,543.59	0.958%
5	$100,000.00	0.962%	$99,487.30	0.958%
6	$100,000.00	0.952%	$100,440.05	0.958%
7	$100,000.00	0.943%	$101,401.92	0.958%
8	$100,000.00	0.935%	$102,373.00	0.958%
9	$100,000.00	0.926%	$103,353.39	0.958%
10	$100,000.00	0.917%	$104,343.16	0.958%
Total	$1,000,000.00		$1,000,000.00	
Average Yield		0.958%		0.958%

---

2. Calculating the yield to maturity for a coupon-bearing bond is much more difficult. It's best to use an amortization calculator.

C. Post-Petition Interest vs. Unmatured Interest

Disallowance of *unmatured* interest does not mean that all *post-petition* interest is disallowed. First, post-petition interest is not synonymous with unmatured interest. A loan might have a maturity that is longer or shorter than the duration of a bankruptcy. Post-petition interest would apply only to the duration of a bankruptcy. Thus, if a bankruptcy lasted one year, post-petition interest on a loan with ten years remaining until maturity would cover one year, while unmatured interest would cover all ten years. Post-petition interest can overlap with unmatured interest. While all unmatured interest is disallowed, a claim may be permitted in some circumstances, as discussed below, to accrue post-petition interest, which would ultimately be added to the allowed claim.

Second, by *statute* under section 506(b) interest may accrue post-petition on a secured claim. For contractual creditors, post-petition interest will typically accrue on a secured claim at the contract rate. Non-contractual creditors are entitled to accrue post-petition interest too on secured claims. Typically, the applicable judgment rate will be used. The question of the applicable rate is distinct from the ability to accrue post-petition interest. Thus, even though contractual creditors are typically awarded interest at their contract rate, their right to post-petition interest derives from the Bankruptcy Code, and not from their contracts.

Significantly, a secured creditor's ability to accrue post-petition interest is capped by statutes. Interest only accrues on a secured claim until the amount of the initial claim plus any allowed post-petition fees and interest are equal to the value of the collateral at the date of plan confirmation or liquidation. 11 U.S.C. § 506(b). Once the debtor's equity in the collateral is exhausted, the secured creditor ceases to accrue interest. We will examine this issue in more depth in the following chapter.

Moreover, the right to post-petition interest is a right to accrual, not to periodic payment. Post-petition interest becomes part of a claim; there are no cash distributions of periodic interest payments during the bankruptcy. The debtor gets the liquidity benefit of accrual, while creditors find their liquidity stretched as a result.

Thus, section 502(b)(2) disallows unmatured interest for *all* creditors, while section 506(b) creates a limited *statutory* right to accrue post-petition interest for certain secured creditors. One section of the Code takes away from all, while another section gives back something similar (but not identical) to some creditors.

Third, in Chapter 7, creditors are allowed to recover post-petition interest "at the legal rate" to the extent that there are sufficient funds available. 11 U.S.C. § 726(a)(5). The entitlement to receive post-petition interest "at the legal rate" is an entitlement that is separate from a claim. While a creditor does not have a claim for such interest, the Bankruptcy Code separately mandates the payment of interest on all claims, *even if those claims do not bear interest* under applicable non-bankruptcy law. The right to receive post-petition interest is subordinated to payment of all claims, however. Therefore, interest is only paid on unsecured claims if the assets of the estate are sufficient to pay all allowed claims, meaning that there is a solvent bankruptcy estate. While solvent debtors are atypical, such cases do occur. Courts are split whether interest "at the legal rate" means at the federal judgment rate or at the contract (or even default) rate.

What, then, is the takeaway from all of this? Three major points:

1. Unmatured interest is disallowed under section 502(b)(2) and not telescoped into part of any allowed claim.
2. Secured creditors receive post-petition interest (but not necessarily all of their unmatured interest) on their claim at their contract rate until the debtor's equity in the collateral is exhausted. 11 U.S.C. § 506(b).
3. Unsecured creditors do not receive any sort of post-petition interest in bankruptcy unless the estate has sufficient assets to pay all of their claims for pre-petition debts in full. If it does, then unsecured creditors are paid post-petition interest at the "legal rate" before equityholders receive any distribution. 11 U.S.C. § 726(a)(5).

III. PREPAYMENT LIMITATIONS

Financing agreements frequently contain so-called "no-call" or "make-whole"or "yield maintenance" provisions (collectively, "prepayment limitations") that either prohibit prepayment of the obligation (no-call provisions) or that require payment of all unmatured interest on the contract in the event of prepayment (make-whole or yield maintenance provisions). These types of prepayment limitations are intended to ensure that the financier receives the interest rate it has bargained for for the term of the contract and that the loan is not refinanced when interest rates drop (a refinancing involves a prepayment of the old loan), leaving the financier to reinvest the prepaid funds in a lower interest rate environment.

To wit, if the loan were a ten-year loan at 8% interest, and in year three interest rates had declined (or the borrower became more creditworthy) and the borrower were to refinance the loan to one with a 5% interest rate, the original lender would get its principal returned, but would have to reinvest in a market paying 5%, not 8%. A make-whole provision would ensure that the lender would receive an accelerated payment of interest at the 8% rate. A no-call provision, in contrast, would simply prohibit the refinancing outright. (Presumably, if breached, the damages would be approximately the same as with a make-whole provision.)

Courts have split on how to handle these prepayment limitations. As an initial matter, there is the question of whether they are triggered by bankruptcy. Is a distribution in bankruptcy a prepayment for purposes of the financing agreement? The inquiry is highly dependent upon the particular drafting of the prepayment limitation. Sometimes contractual language requires voluntary redemption as a trigger, while sometimes any acceleration, including bankruptcy, which automatically accelerates the debt, will be the trigger. *See, e.g., U.S. Bank Trust Nat'l Ass'n v. AMR Corp. (In re AMR Corp.)*, 730 F.3d 88 (2d Cir. 2013) (under indenture language, default that resulted in acceleration of principal did not trigger the make-whole provision). If bankruptcy is not a trigger, then there is no allowable claim based solely on the prepayment limitation provision.

If bankruptcy does trigger the prepayment limitation, the next question is whether the prepayment limitation constitutes "unmatured interest" or whether it is a liquidated damage. If the former, the prepayment limitation is unenforceable under section 502(b)(2), while if the latter, it is enforceable if it would be under applicable non-bankruptcy law.

IV. SECURED TAX CLAIM

Section 502(b)(3) disallows tax claims that are assessed against a property to the extent that they exceed the value of the interest of the estate in property. For example, a municipal water district might have a claim for unpaid water bills, which are considered to be a tax. If the claim is for $1 million, but it is for a property in which the estate has equity of only $0.2 million, the claim will be capped at $0.2 million, with $0.8 million disallowed. This will be true even if the tax claim is secured by a lien on the property.

V. INSIDER AND ATTORNEY CLAIMS

Section 502(b)(4) limits the claims of insiders and of the debtor's attorneys to the reasonable value of services provided. "Insider" is a statutorily defined term. 11 U.S.C. § 101(31). It includes the debtor's officers, directors, and partners as well as certain of their relatives. It also includes the debtor's corporate affiliates. 11 U.S.C. § 101(31)(E). Section 502(b)(4) prevents overreaching by parties with influence over a debtor by giving the court authority to limit their claims. No inequitable conduct must be shown to disallow a claim under section 502(b)(4), only that a claim is by an insider or attorney of the debtor and that the claim is for an amount that exceeds the reasonable value of services rendered.

Section 502(b)(4) covers only *unpaid* claims at the time of filing; other Bankruptcy Code provisions enable unreasonable payments that have already been made pre-petition to be clawed back. 11 U.S.C. §§ 547-548. (An additional and independent Bankruptcy Code provision, section 329, deals with attorney compensation for the filing of the bankruptcy petition itself.)

VI. TERMINATED REAL ESTATE LEASES AND EMPLOYMENT CONTRACTS

Section 502(b)(6) and 502(b)(7) cap the allowed amount of claims based on real property leases and employment contract termination. Landlords' claims are capped at the unpaid pre-petition rent plus the rent for the greater of one year "or 15 percent, not to exceed three years, of the remaining term of [the] lease." 11 U.S.C. § 502(b)(6)(A).

The cap is not as simple as it looks. First, what is "rent"? It is determined in reference to local real property law, but be aware that it may include things such as real estate taxes, legal fees, and maintenance charges. Moreover, rent may not always be a definite liquidated amount, but may relate to sales. While the cap may cover more than just narrow "rent," it does not apply to fees unrelated to the termination of the lease, such as claims for repairs, maintenance, removal of property, or waste.

Second, what is the "15 percent" referring to in the cap? Is it 15 percent of the remaining time on the lease (the "time method")? Or is it 15 percent of the total rent remaining on the lease (the "rent method")? Courts are split on the interpretation, which can have a dramatic effect on the size of the claim if rental amounts are not fixed. Note the difficulty in applying either method if rental amounts vary by year and there is more than one year remaining. Which year's rent is to be used for the "one year" calculation or the "three year" calculation? The next year(s) or a hypothetical average year? Not surprisingly, landlords' claims can engender a lot of litigation.

Third, the cap is actually a secondary cap. It does not affect a landlord's duty to mitigate damages upon termination of a lease. If the landlord can relet the property, the landlord's claim will be reduced accordingly under section 502(b)(1) before the section 502(b)(6) cap is applied.

A similar caps exists for employees' employment termination claims, which are capped at one year of employment "compensation" plus any past due amounts. 11 U.S.C. § 502(b)(6)-(7). Similar questions exist for employment termination claims as for landlord claims, *e.g.*, are non-pecuniary benefits "compensation"?

Why do these caps exist? What would landlord and employment contract claims look like otherwise? Imagine a 99-year lease or a lifetime employment contract. How large would the damages be? On the other hand, how much work are the claims caps doing beyond the duty to mitigate? The following case illustrates section 502(b)(6) and the difficulties that can arise in determining post-mitigation damages.

Unsecured Creditors' Committee of Highland Superstores, Inc. v. Strobeck Real Estate, Inc. (*In re* Highland Superstores)

154 F.3d 573 (6th Cir. 1998)

R. Guy Cole, Jr., Circuit Judge.

Appellant Strobeck Real Estate, Inc. ("Strobeck") appeals the district court's order reversing a judgment of the bankruptcy court and determining that Strobeck suffered no actual damages resulting from Debtor Highland Superstores, Inc.'s rejection of its pre-petition lease (the "Highland Lease").

For the reasons set forth below, we REVERSE the decision of the district court.

I.

The relevant facts are not in dispute. Strobeck leased to Highland Superstores, Inc. ("Debtor") certain commercial real estate in a shopping center located in Hoffman Estates, Illinois. On August 24, 1992 (the "Petition Date"), the Debtor filed a petition for relief under Chapter 11 of the Bankruptcy Code, 11 U.S.C. §§ 101 *et seq.*

As of the Petition Date, the Debtor was in default under the Highland Lease with arrears of $190,632.35, and it had 14 years and 160 days remaining on the 20-year lease. Section 18.02 of the Highland Lease provided:

> In the event of any default specified in Section 18:01, Paragraph (i), (ii) and (iii) hereof, Landlord shall have the right to terminate this Lease or from time to time, without terminating this Lease, to relet the Demised Premises or any part thereof, upon such reasonable terms and conditions as Landlord shall deem advisable. The avails of such reletting shall be applied first to the payment of the reasonable cost of repossessing and reletting the Demised Premises; second, to the payment of the minimum rental and real estate taxes due hereunder and the residue, if any, shall be held by Landlord and applied in payment of future minimum rental and real estate taxes, as the same shall become due and payable hereunder. Should the avails of such reletting during any month be less than the minimum rental reserved hereunder, then Tenant shall, during each month, pay such deficiency to Landlord.

On the Petition Date, the Debtor publicly announced its intention to cease operating in Illinois; thereafter, it proceeded to close all its Illinois stores, including the store located in Hoffman Estates. Having failed to obtain a replacement tenant for the Highland Lease, the Debtor filed a motion to reject that lease. The bankruptcy court granted the Debtor's motion. Under 11 U.S.C. § 365(g), the Debtor's rejection of the unexpired Highland Lease constituted a breach of the lease that is deemed to have occurred immediately prior to the Petition Date.

Strobeck subsequently leased the subject space, as well as an additional 10,555 adjoining square feet, to Syms Corporation. The new lease (the "Syms Lease"), which commenced on September 2, 1993, provided for a term of ten years and five months, with two five-year-term renewal options. Although the initial term of the Syms Lease expires on January 31, 2004, which precedes the Highland Lease's expiration date of January 31, 2007, the bankruptcy court assumed in its claims analysis that payments under the Syms Lease would continue through January 31, 2007. That assumption was not challenged by the parties.

Strobeck filed a timely proof of claim in the amount of $839,871.46, arising out of the Debtor's rejection of the Highland Lease. Strobeck subsequently amended its claim to $923,446.98. The Unsecured Creditors' Committee (the "Committee") thereafter filed initial and supplemental objections to Strobeck's proof of claim.

The bankruptcy court held an evidentiary hearing in order to determine Strobeck's actual damages. Strobeck argued that its actual damages first must be determined based upon the language contained in the Highland Lease and applicable state law, in this case Illinois, with the actual damages then being limited by application of 11 U.S.C. § 502(b)(6).[1] Strobeck also argued that the court should apply Illinois' statutory rate of interest on judgments to compute the present value of the difference between the future streams of income under the Highland and Syms Leases.

---

1. Section 502(b)(6) of the Bankruptcy Code imposes a limit or cap on the damages a lessor may claim as a result of a debtor's lease rejection.

The Committee proposed a different method of calculating Strobeck's damages resulting from rejection of the Highland Lease. The Committee urged the bankruptcy court to determine the amount of Strobeck's claim by discounting to present value the stream of future payments that would have been received under both the Highland and Syms Leases, using discount rates that factor in the relative creditworthiness of the Debtor and Syms. The Committee conceded that the approach it advocated had not been adopted by any court of law. The Committee argued, however, that its approach was in harmony with general equitable bankruptcy principles. Had the bankruptcy court followed the approach espoused by the Committee, it would have been compelled to conclude that Strobeck suffered no damages from rejection of the Highland Lease inasmuch as Syms was a much more creditworthy replacement tenant and, thus, the present value of its future performance under the Syms Lease exceeded the present value of the Debtor's future performance under the Highland Lease. Relying on overwhelming case authority that a determination of lease rejection damages is computed in accordance with the terms of the debtor's lease and applicable state law, the bankruptcy court adopted Strobeck's approach and allowed its claim in the amount of $923,446.98, as limited by 11 U.S.C. § 502(b)(6).

On appeal, the district court, in apparent acknowledgment of the utter lack of precedential support for the approach advanced by the Committee, stated that "I am going to accept the argument of the Committee and see whether the law does develop in the direction toward which [the Committee is] pointing." The district court thus reversed the bankruptcy court and instead adopted the Committee's proposed methodology, effectively eliminating Strobeck's claim in its entirety.[4] Accordingly, the district court disallowed Strobeck's claim. This timely appeal followed.

. . .

III.

On appeal, we are asked to determine a single issue: what is the appropriate method by which to calculate a lessor's claim for damages arising out of the breach of a commercial lease; specifically, whether, for purposes of determining the present value of the future stream of payments under the respective leases, the bankruptcy court should have calculated and applied two different discount rates that account for the relative creditworthiness of each tenant.

---

4. The Committee's expert applied a different discount rate to each lease based on the Debtor's and Syms's credit ratings. He quantified the respective risk-based discount rates as 24% for the Debtor and 11.5% for Syms. The Committee's expert thus calculated Strobeck's actual damages as the sum of the following: (1) present value at a 24.0% discount rate of the rent due under the Highland Lease (yielding $1,402,627 after discount); (2) minus present value at 11.5% of the rent to be received from reletting the premises (yielding $1,880,746 after discount); (3) plus the cost of reletting ($190,000.55); (4) plus rent due from the Debtor as of the petition date ($190,632.35); and (5) minus post-petition rent paid by the Debtor. This approach, which was accepted by the district court, yielded negative actual damages of $176,305, thus precluding the application of the statutory limit of section 502(b)(6).

A.

In answering this question, we first turn to the applicable language of the statute. Section 502(b)(6) of the Bankruptcy Code provides:

> **(b)** Except as provided in subsections (e)(2), (f), (g), (h) and (i) of this section, if such objection to a claim is made, the court, after notice and a hearing, shall determine the amount of such claim in lawful currency of the United States as of the date of the filing of the petition, and shall allow such claim in such amount, except to the extent that—
>
> . . .
>
> **(6)** if such claim is the claim of a lessor for damages resulting from the termination of a lease of real property, such claim exceeds—
>> **(A)** the rent reserved by such lease, without acceleration, for the greater of one year, or 15 percent, not to exceed three years, of the remaining term of such lease, following the earlier of—
>>> **(i)** the date of the filing of the petition; and
>>> **(ii)** the date on which such lessor repossessed, or the lessee surrendered, the leased property; plus
>>
>> **(B)** any unpaid rent due under such lease, without acceleration, on the earlier of such dates. . . .

11 U.S.C. § 502(b)(6).

Section 502(b)(6) is aimed at compensating a lessor for his loss while not allowing a claim "so large (based on a long-term lease) as to prevent other general unsecured creditors from recovering a dividend from the estate. Thus, Congress intended to compensate landlords for their actual damages while placing a limit on large future, speculative damages which would displace other creditors' claims." *Vause v. Capital Poly Bag, Inc.*, 886 F.2d 794, 801-02 (6th Cir. 1989).

The courts that have applied section 502(b)(6)'s framework for determining the allowable amount of a lessor's total rejection damage claim generally employ a four-step process. First, the court calculates the total rents due under the lease from the earlier of the date of filing or the date on which the lessor repossessed or the lessee surrendered the leased property.[5] Second, the court determines whether 15% of that total is greater than the rent reserved for one year following the debtor's filing. Third, the 15% amount is compared to the rent reserved under the applicable lease for three years following the filing. Finally, the court, on the basis of the foregoing calculations, arrives at the total allowable amount of the landlord's rejection damages. *See, e.g., In re Financial News Network, Inc.*, 149 B.R. 348, 351 (Bankr. S.D.N.Y. 1993); *In re Atlantic Container Corp.*, 133 B.R. 980, 989 (Bankr. N.D. Ill. 1991).

The calculation of rejection damages as outlined above assumes the existence of a claim. Because a lessor has a duty to mitigate its damages, *see In re Bob's Sea Ray*

---

5. Although the statute is silent on this point, Strobeck and the Committee agree that the total future rents due under the Highland Lease must be discounted to present value. Because the parties are in agreement as to this issue, we need not decide whether section 502(b)(6) generally requires a discounting of total future rents due under the applicable lease.

Boats, Inc., 143 B.R. 229, 231 (Bankr. D.N.D. 1992), if the lessor has relet the premises at a higher rent, it generally will have no section 502(b)(6) claim. The Committee and Strobeck do not quarrel over the proper methodology for applying section 502(b)(6)'s limitation on rejection damages. Rather, it is the threshold question of whether Strobeck has a cognizable claim in the first instance on which the parties disagree.

. . .

The lower courts applying section 502(b)(6) . . . have not concluded that general equitable principles require a departure from state law in the calculation of rejection damage claims. They have uniformly held that a lessor's damages are computed in accordance with the terms of the debtor's lease and applicable state law, and then are limited by application of section 502(b)(6). . . .

We agree with the conclusion reached by these courts. Presumably, if Congress had intended to include in section 502(b)(6)'s claim calculus the element of risk arising from the debtor's creditworthiness—which would be a factor in nearly every bankruptcy proceeding because bankrupt debtors are almost invariably uncreditworthy—it would have expressly so provided in the statute. By enacting the rejection damages limitation contained in section 502(b)(6), Congress has established the appropriate safeguard to limit the risk that lessors will receive a windfall at the expense of other unsecured creditors. The Court need not embrace the Committee's draconian approach to achieve this end.

. . .

In sum, although the Committee has advanced an elegant and creative argument, at bottom, it is fatally flawed. Accordingly, we hold that the district court erred when it concluded as a matter of law that, for purposes of calculating the present value of Strobeck's claim, the bankruptcy court should have applied two different discount rates to the total future rental streams under the Highland and Syms Leases in order to account for the relative creditworthiness of the Debtor and Syms. In doing so, we adopt the widely accepted rule that a lessor's damages arising out of a debtor's lease rejection are determined in accordance with the terms of the debtor's lease and applicable state law, and then are limited by application of section 502(b)(6).

IV.

For the foregoing reasons, we REVERSE the judgment of the district court.

VII. GUARANTORS

The claims of guarantors, indemnitors, and other types of sureties are limited by sections 502(e) and 509. Depending on the specifics of the suretyship relationship, the surety may have a right of reimbursement, contribution, or subrogation. For example, if there is a guaranty of payment, not of collection, the guarantor might have to pay out in the first instance, and then try to recover from the creditor.

Bankruptcy law allows a surety to elect between making a claim for reimbursement or contribution under section 502 or for reimbursement, contribution, or subrogation under section 509. Sections 502 and 509 are exclusive alternatives. 11 U.S.C. §§ 502(e)(1)(C), 509(b)(1)(A).

The election between section 502 reimbursement and 509 subrogation matters if the rights of the creditor do not match the rights of the guarantor. For example, if the guarantor is secured, but the creditor is not, then the guarantor will want to file a claim under section 502 for reimbursement or contribution. This allows the guarantor to act as a secured creditor in its own right. Alternatively, if the creditor is secured, but the guarantor is not, then the guarantor will want to claim subrogation under section 509 and step into the shoes of the creditor and benefit from the creditor's lien. Of course, if the guarantor and creditor have the same type of rights, then the election is immaterial. The point of the election is to ensure that the guarantor can always get the secured claim.

Bankruptcy law places some restrictions on guarantor claims. If the claim for reimbursement or contribution remains contingent, it will be disallowed, 11 U.S.C. § 502(1)(B), while claims for subrogation are subordinated to those of the guarantied creditor until that creditor has been paid in full. 11 U.S.C. § 509(c). The bankruptcy of the obligor on the guarantied obligation will typically be sufficient to trigger the surety's liability, so contingency is not usually an issue. Critically, most courts hold that guarantors are not able to shelter in the claim limitations of section 502(b)(6) and (b)(7). The price for that protection is filing for bankruptcy.

VIII. ESTIMATION OF CONTINGENT AND UNLIQUIDATED CLAIMS

Some claims are either contingent or unliquidated, or both. For example, a debtor may have warranty obligations on its products. The warranty claims are contingent. They are also unliquidated, as the amount of the obligation is unknown. Yet, the warranty obligations are a very real obligation of the debtor.

Section 502(c) requires the bankruptcy court to estimate (yes, estimate!) the amount of the claim if waiting for the claim to become fixed or liquidated (including having a trial) "would unduly delay the administration of the case." 11 U.S.C. § 502(c). The bankruptcy court is also required to estimate what an equitable remedy for breach of performance is worth. That is, specific performance obligations become monetized as do some other injunctions.

Claims estimation is perhaps the most brutal feature of bankruptcy. In bankruptcy nearly everything gets monetized. There is a dollar figure put on almost everything, and there has to be for bankruptcy to work. It is necessary to convert all of the debtor's obligations into a common unit—dollars—in order to determine distributional rights.

An important exception exists, however. Bankruptcy courts may not estimate personal injury tort or wrongful death claims for the purposes of distribution; the right to a jury trial is preserved in such cases. 28 U.S.C. §§ 157(b), 1411. Bankruptcy courts are, however, permitted to estimate such claims for other purposes, namely the confirmation of a plan under Chapter 11, which means determination of voting rights and certain other plan confirmation requirements.

The Bankruptcy Code does not specify any particular method for estimation. Courts are free to use any methodology they want—reliance on expert testimony, deference to arbitration awards, etc.

Problem Set 26

(1) John Hancock Imports, Inc. filed for Chapter 11 bankruptcy. The court set a bar date of August 1, notice of which was published in several national newspapers. Caesar Rodney & Co. contends that Hancock violated its patent rights, but Caesar Rodney & Co. has not yet brought suit. Caesar Rodney & Co. files a proof of claim for $20 million. What is Caesar Rodney & Co.'s allowed claim in each of the following scenarios?

  a. John Hancock does not contest Caesar Rodney & Co.'s claim, but Franklin State Bank, another of Hancock's creditors, objects to the claim's allowance. 11 U.S.C. §§ 502(a), (c).

  b. Caesar Rodney & Co. never files its proof of claim, but Hancock schedules the claim as one of its liabilities. 11 U.S.C. §§ 501(c), 1111(a).

  c. Caesar Rodney & Co. filed its claim on August 15. 11 U.S.C. §§ 502(b)(9), 726(a), 1141(d); FED. R. BANKR. PROC. 3003(c).

  d. John Hancock does not contest liability to Caesar Rodney & Co., but disputes the amount of the liability, and it appears that it would take extensive discovery and a lengthy trial to resolve the issue. 11 U.S.C. § 502(c).

(2) George III Ventures has filed a $5 million proof of claim in Benedict Arnold, Ltd.'s bankruptcy.

  a. Assume that the claim is based on an oral contract for the sale of land near West Point, New York. What is George III Ventures' allowed claim? 11 U.S.C. § 502(b)(1).

  b. Assume that the claim is based on a written contract for the sale of land, but that the statute of limitations for a contract suit expired a month before the bankruptcy filing. 11 U.S.C. § 502(b)(1).

  c. Assume that the claim is based on a written contract for the sale of land, but that the statute of limitations for a contract suit expired a month after the bankruptcy filing. 11 U.S.C. §§ 108(c), 362(a), 502(b)(1).

(3) Washington & Custis Tobacco Corp. is in Chapter 11 bankruptcy. Among the proofs of claim is one filed by Artemus Ward. Ward has filed a $30 million proof of claim based on a pre-petition tort judgment he won. The judgment is still on appeal. The tort judgment is $5 million in actual damages and $25 million in punitive damages. Ward's home state limits punitive damages to twice actual damages. What is Ward's allowed claim? 11 U.S.C. § 502(a).

(4) Brandywine Industries has filed for Chapter 11. Shortly before filing, Brandywine Industries fired its CEO, Thomas Gage. Gage has filed a proof of claim for the compensation owed him for the five years remaining on his employment contract, of $2 million/year. What is Gage's allowed claim? 11 U.S.C. § 502(b)(7).

(5) JP Jones Shipping. Inc. has filed for Chapter 11 bankruptcy. At the time of the bankruptcy filing, Jones owed its CEO $5 million in back pay for the past year. At the time of the bankruptcy filing, Jones also owed its parent company, Bonhomme Richard, Inc., $3 million for "accounting and management services" under a management contract. Bonhomme Richard, Inc., has provided only *de minimis* accounting and management services to JP Jones Shipping, Inc.

   a. What is the CEO's allowed claim? 11 U.S.C. §§ 101(31)(B), 502(b)(4).
   b. What is Bonhomme Richard Inc.'s allowed claim? 11 U.S.C. §§ 101(2), 101(31)(E); 502(b)(4).

(6) TJ's, a mid-size clothing retail chain, is in Chapter 11 bankruptcy. TJ's leases one of its stores from Hamilton Properties. At the time of TJ's bankruptcy filing, there were ten years remaining on the Hamilton Properties' lease, with monthly lease payments of $100,000. TJ's was three months delinquent on the lease when it filed for bankruptcy.

   a. What is Hamilton Properties' allowed claim in TJ's bankruptcy? 11 U.S.C. § 506(b)(6).
   b. Would your answer change if TJ's was in fact solvent and capable of paying all of its creditors in full? *See Solow v. PPI Industries* (in Chapter 13).
   c. One year after the bankruptcy TJ's rejected (and hence terminated) the lease. Hamilton Properties managed to re-lease the property immediately, but for only $1.1 million per year rent. What is Hamilton Properties' allowed claim now? 11 U.S.C. §§ 502(b)(1), 502(b)(6).

(7) Your client Jimmy Madison has amassed significant commercial real estate holdings under his Montpellier Properties LLC holding company. Most of the properties are shopping malls. Jimmy's been burned by a number of recent tenant bankruptcy filings. "I keep finding my claim capped by the Bankruptcy Code," he complains to you. While Jimmy is sometimes able to find new tenants, he often struggles with vacant properties. What's worse, because of the synergies between mall properties, vacancies depress mall traffic and thus the rents his malls can command. Is there anything Jimmy can do to get around the Bankruptcy Code's cap on his claims? 11 U.S.C. §§ 506(b)(6), 506(e), 509.

(8) Samuel Adams Malting is in Chapter 7 bankruptcy. Three years before filing for bankruptcy, Adams Malting issued $50 million in unsecured 10-year balloon notes. The notes bear interest at a rate of 5% per annum with interest paid annually. The notes specify that interest shall not compound. At the time of the bankruptcy filing, Adams Malting had missed the last interest payment.

   a. Who files the proof of claim for the notes? 11 U.S.C. § 501.
   b. What is the allowed claim of the notes' indenture trustee? 11 U.S.C. § 502(b)(2).
   c. Suppose the $50 million in Adams Malting notes were issued for $48 million. What would be the allowed claim of the notes' indenture trustee?

CHAPTER *27*

SECURED STATUS

[handwritten annotation: a table with columns "pre", "post petition" and rows "secured", "unsecured"]

Just as all claims in bankruptcy are either pre-petition or post-petition and allowed or disallowed, so too are all claims either secured or unsecured. Disallowed claims have no rights in bankruptcy, irrespective of whether they are pre-petition or post-petition, secured or unsecured. The treatment of an allowed claim, however, depends on whether it is pre-petition or post-petition, and secured or unsecured.

An allowed claim can be any of the following: pre-petition secured, pre-petition unsecured, post-petition secured, or post-petition unsecured. In the previous chapter, we examined when a claim arises, which determines whether it is pre-petition or post-petition. The basic rule regarding secured and unsecured claims is that a claim is unsecured unless it qualifies as a "**secured claim**". 11 U.S.C. § 506(a)(1).

The Bankruptcy Code defines a secured claim as either a claim for which the creditor has a right of setoff or as a claim secured by a lien on property of the estate. 11 U.S.C. § 506(a)(1)(a). Each type of secured claim is discussed in turn.

I. SETOFF CLAIMS

Setoff is an equitable remedy allowing the offset of mutually owing debts. Section 506(a) provides an allowed claim that is subject to setoff under section 553 is a secured claim to the extent of the amount subject to setoff. Section 553, in turn, allows the exercise of any right to offset of mutual pre-petition debts between a creditor and a debtor. Section 553 does not itself create a right of setoff; that right must exist under applicable nonbankruptcy law. Thus, the first inquiry is whether there is a nonbankruptcy right to setoff. If so, it is then limited by section 553 to debts that are mutual between a creditor and a debtor. Mutuality is not defined by the Bankruptcy Code, but some states require as part of mutuality that the obligations both be due and owing, that is, matured. *See In re Patterson*, 967 F.2d 505, 510 (11th Cir. 1992) (Alabama law requires both obligations to be matured for mutuality).

The Bankruptcy Code also restricts any applicable nonbankruptcy right to setoff under section 553 to the setoff of pre-petition claims against pre-petition obligations to the debtor. (Note that this restriction does not exist when the *debtor* exercises setoff under section 558, as discussed in the previous chapter.) Finally, section 553 only covers setoff, not the similar doctrine of recoupment, which involves offsetting reciprocal obligations from one single, integrated transaction. Because the automatic stay does not apply to recoupment, only setoff, there is no need to include recoupment claims under sections 506 or 553.

Consider the impact of setoff rights with bankruptcy. Suppose that Abel owes Cain $100 (unsecured) from transaction #1, and Cain owes Abel $25 (unsecured) from transaction #2. Abel can offset the $25 Cain owes him and simply pay Cain $75. Absent setoff, Abel would have an obligation to pay Cain $100 and then would have to try to recover the $25 from Cain. This means that Abel could be out of pocket for another $25 while trying to collect. It might not be so easy to collect from Cain. And worse, what if Cain filed for bankruptcy?

If Cain filed for bankruptcy after Abel had paid the $100, Abel would have a general unsecured claim for $25 that would be paid in tiny little bankruptcy dollars. Let's assume that the bankruptcy dividend would be 10%. That would mean that Abel paid Cain $100 and only recovered $2.50. So instead of being down $75, Abel would be down by $97.50. If Abel could exercise setoff, however, Abel would not have to pay Cain $100 and then seek to recover $25, but would simply pay Cain $75.

If Abel could exercise setoff pre-petition, however, he would never have a bankruptcy claim in the first place. Because section 506(a) treats setoff rights as equivalent to security interests, even if Cain filed for bankruptcy, Abel would have a secured claim for $25. While Abel would still have to pay Cain $100, Abel would be guaranteed recovery for $25 under section.

Now suppose that Abel owed Cain $70, and Cain owed Abel $200. In that situation, should Cain file for bankruptcy, Abel would have a secured claim for $70—the extent of his setoff right. What about the other $130? That is a general unsecured claim because it exceeds the amount of the creditor's setoff interest. In other words, if the debtor owes the creditor more than the creditor owes the debtor, the creditor's setoff claim will be bifurcated into a secured claim for the amount of the setoff and an unsecured claim for the deficiency. This division of a creditor's claim into a secured and an unsecured component is called "bifurcation."

II. LIEN CLAIMS

The second type of claim that section 506(a) treats as a secured claim is one secured by a lien on the debtor's property. A lien is a contingent claim against specific collateral property that secures a payment obligation. 11 U.S.C. § 101(37). A lien might be created by contract, by statute, or by judicial order, and the law creating the lien might be state or federal or even foreign.

Under section 506(a), a creditor has a secured claim only to the extent of the value of its interest in the collateral. Thus, if the debtor owes the creditor $200, which is secured by property with a value of $80, the creditor has a secured claim for $80. The deficiency of $120 is treated as an unsecured claim under section 502. Although there is only a single creditor and a single contractual relationship, there are two separate claims, one secured and one unsecured. Thus, an undersecured creditor— one with collateral worth less than the amount of the debt—is given both a secured claim and an unsecured claim in bankruptcy. An oversecured or fully secured creditor, in contrast, has only a secured claim.

When determining the value of a secured creditor's interest in the collateral, it is necessary to first value the collateral and then to subtract from that value the amount of any prior liens on that collateral. To illustrate, let's imagine that there is collateral worth $10 million. It secures a first lien debt of $8 million, a second lien debt of $5 million, and a third lien debt of $4 million. In this case, the first lien creditor is oversecured and has a secured claim for $8 million. The second lien creditor is undersecured and its claim will be bifurcated into a secured claim for $2 million (the value if its interest in the collateral after the amount of the first lien has been accounted for) and an unsecured claim for $3 million. And the third lien creditor is wholly undersecured. After accounting for the interests of the prior lienholders in the collateral, the value of the third lien creditor's interest in the collateral is zero. Therefore, the third lien creditor's entire claim is treated as unsecured, even though there is a valid lien. Thus, the third lien creditor in this case will have only an unsecured claim for $4 million.

In a Chapter 7 liquidation, the secured claim is limited by the lower of the value of the *creditor's interest in the collateral* or the amount of the debt. In Chapter 11, determination of a secured claim is more complex. In Chapter 11, as in Chapter 7, the normal rule for an undersecured claim is that it is bifurcated into a secured claim for the value of the collateral, 11 U.S.C. § 506(a)(1), and an unsecured section 502 claim for the deficiency. An elective exception exists to this rule, however, and is addressed in Chapter 37.

III. CLAIM BIFURCATION VS. LIEN VALIDITY

It is important to differentiate claim bifurcation from lien validity. The former relates to the bankruptcy treatment of the claim, while the later is about the extent to which a debt is secured by collateral, which may have ramifications outside of bankruptcy. Chapter 11 bankruptcy functions to discharge a debtor's *in personam* liability for debts, but it does not eliminate *in rem* liability. 11 U.S.C. § 524(a)(2). (Only individual debtors receive a discharge in Chapter 7. Following a Chapter 7, a corporate debtor will have no assets, although it will continue to exist until it is dissolved under nonbankruptcy law.) Bankruptcy does not automatically eliminate liens, so even if the debtor is no longer personally liable for the debt after bankruptcy, a creditor with a lien can look to the collateral for satisfaction to the extent that there is a secured debt. All bankruptcy does is transform the debt into a non-recourse debt (if it were recourse to begin with).

Section 506(d) voids liens to the extent that they do not secure an "allowed secured claim." What this means may vary by Chapter of the Bankruptcy Code. In the Chapter 7 context, the Supreme Court has read the term "allowed secured claim" in section 506(d) to refer to a claim that is under section 502 and that has an associated lien, rather than as a creditor's section 506(a) claim. *See Dewsnup v. Timm*, 502 U.S. 410 (1987) (prohibiting Chapter 7 debtor from using 11 U.S.C. § 506(d) to void the undersecured portion of a lien on real property). In Chapter 11, however, courts generally read "allowed secured claim" to mean a section 506(a)(1) claim, rather than an allowed claim that has an associated lien. *See, e.g., In re Heritage Highgate, Inc.,* 679 F.3d 132 (3d Cir. 2012). These courts will therefore permit the lien to be stripped down to the extent that it is undersecured. Thus, in a Chapter 11, after the stay is lifted, the debtor may be able to keep some of the foreclosure sale value above judicial valuation in bankruptcy. (Some courts have also allowed the same in Chapter 7 for wholly undersecured loans.)

To illustrate, imagine a Chapter 7 debtor with real property securing a loan for $7 million. The bankruptcy court values the property at $5 million. This has the effect of limiting the creditor's secured claim in bankruptcy to $5 million. Because the creditor has an allowed claim, however, the lien may not be voided or "stripped down" to securing only $5 million under section 506(d). Instead, the lien continues to secure the full $7 million. In bankruptcy this does matter—the creditor still has a secured claim for $5 million and an unsecured claim for $2 million. But because the lien continues to secure the full $7 million debt, if the automatic stay were to be lifted and the creditor permitted to foreclose on the property, and the foreclosure sale subsequently brought in $6 million (indicating that the judicial valuation was wrong), the creditor could recover $6 million from the sale, rather than having its recovery capped at $5 million due to lien stripping. The debtor would get nothing from the sale.

If the same debtor were in Chapter 11, however, the lien could likely be stripped, so when the foreclosure sale brings in $6 million, the creditor's recovery would be limited to $5 million, and the debtor would get a surplus of $1 million. Lien stripping under section 506(d) places the risk of judicial undervaluation or subsequent appreciation of the collateral on the creditor.

IV. VALUING THE SECURED CREDITOR'S CLAIM

Section 506's criterion for determining whether a claim is secured immediately raises valuation questions because a claim is secured only to the extent that there is collateral. How and when is the value of the collateral to be determined?

Section 506(a)(1) provides that the value of the collateral "shall be determined in light of the purpose of the valuation and of the proposed disposition or use of such property." Thus, valuation might be different in a liquidation or a sale of the collateral than in a reorganization in which the debtor retains the property, as we saw in Chapter 16 in *Craddock-Terry Shoe.*

But to the extent that the collateral contributes to the going-concern value of the debtor, is that part of the value of the collateral or an externality that cannot be captured by the lienholder, as the only possible remedy for the lienholder would be through a forced sale? Section 506(a)(2) explains how valuation is to be done for a consumer debtor in Chapter 7 or 13. Does this imply a different methodology for business debtors in those Chapters or for any creditor in Chapter 11?

Beyond the question of how to value the collateral, there is also a question of when the valuation should occur. Collateral value can vary significantly during a bankruptcy. There is no single answer to the when question. Section 506(a)(2) provides that in consumer Chapter 7 and Chapter 13 cases, the "date of the filing of the petition" is to be used, but in the context of valuing a secured claim for Chapter 11 confirmation purposes, either the confirmation date of the plan or the effective date of the plan is usually used. *See In re Heritage Highgate, Inc.*, 679 F.3d 132 (3d Cir. 2012) (upholding bankruptcy court's use of the plan's confirmation date for valuation). But secured claims have to be valued at other times, such as for adequate protection motions.

Note that section 506 secured status does not depend on a lien being perfected, but as we will see in Chapter 29, an unperfected security interest may be avoided, resulting in the creditor simply having a general unsecured claim.

V. POST-PETITION CHANGES IN COLLATERAL

Because the amount of a secured claim depends on the extent of the creditor's collateral, it is important to delimit what collateral is properly attributable to the secured creditor. For example, if a creditor has a security interest in the debtor's "equipment," and the debtor acquires a new drill press—equipment in the debtor's hands—post-petition, is that drill press part of the creditor's collateral? Section 552 of the Bankruptcy Code sets forth a rule that addresses this question. Because the rule set forth in section 552 determines what collateral secures a claim, and thus what must be valued to determine the amount of the allowed secured claim, it is a rule that ultimately goes to the determination of the amount of an allowed secured claim, as well as to the question of what interest is entitled to adequate protection under section 361 when invoked by other Code sections.

The general rule is expressed in section 552(a), which provides that a secured creditor's collateral is limited to that which existed at the time of the bankruptcy filing. 11 U.S.C. § 552(a). Section 552(b) provides a pair of exceptions, and then an exception to those exceptions. Combined, the two basic exceptions create a rule that pre-petition security interests do not attach to property acquired post-petition *unless* such collateral is proceeds, products, offspring, profits, or hotel revenues. The exception to these exceptions is "based on the equities of the case." In other words, the court may, for cause, cut off the attachment of security interests to proceeds, etc.

The basic exceptions in section 552(b) are based on the distinction between **proceeds, products, offspring, profits, and hotel revenues** on the one hand, and **after-acquired** property on the other. Section 552(b)(1) provides that the section 552(a) limitation on pre-petition security interests does not apply to post-petition attachment to post-petition proceeds, products, offspring, and profits. In other words, if a security instrument would normally attach to proceeds, products, offspring, and profits acquired post-petition, then section 552(a) will not prevent such attachment absent countervailing equitable considerations. Section 552(b)(2) further specifies that a pre-petition security interest that would cover rents and other charges from use or occupancy of hotel rooms extends to the hotel room payments. The implication is that all other types of after-acquired property—collateral acquired post-petition—is subject to the section 552(a) limitation on attachment.

Critically, both of the section 552(b) exceptions permit the security interest to cover the proceeds, products, offspring, profits, or hotel revenues under applicable non-bankruptcy law. If a creditor's security interest would not cover these things under applicable non-bankruptcy law, section 552(b) has no effect. Section 552(b) does not create a substantive right, so much as exempt those rights from their curtailment under section 552(a). Thus, section 552(b) provides that a pre-petition security interest will cover all proceeds, products, offspring, and products to the extent provided for by the security agreement and applicable non-bankruptcy law.

What's the difference between proceeds, products, offspring, profits, and hotel revenues and after-acquired property? Unfortunately, the Bankruptcy Code does not define any of these terms. Some of these terms are defined in Article 9 of the Uniform Commercial Code, but Article 9 only covers security interests in personalty, not in realty.

A. Proceeds

For security interests in personalty, "proceeds" are defined by UCC Article 9 as whatever is acquired upon the "disposition" of collateral, whether that disposition is by sale, lease, exchange, casualty insurance payment, or tort or warranty claims for diminution in value. UCC § 9-102(a)(64). Security interests in personalty automatically attach to any proceeds. UCC §§ 9-203(f), 9-315(a)(2). Thus, if the collateral is a truck, and the truck is sold for cash, the cash is the proceeds of the truck, and subject to the original security interest without any action being required of the secured creditor. Similarly, if the truck were exchanged for another truck, the new truck would be proceeds of the old truck and subject to the creditor's security interest. If the debtor leased the truck, the rental payments on the lease would be proceeds, and if the truck were damaged, the insurance payments would be proceeds. Section 552(b)(1) provides that a pre-petition security interest will attach to such post-petition proceeds. Indeed, if the rule were otherwise, debtors would simply exchange all of their collateral upon filing for bankruptcy, leaving creditors unsecured.

Security interests in realty are more complicated. There is no generally adopted uniform state law (and indeed little state law whatsoever) regarding proceeds of realty. Instead, creditors ensure that their security interest includes proceeds by specifying so in the loan documentation and including "due on sale" clauses that accelerate the loans upon any sale.

A particular issue, however, arises with rents. States differ in whether a security interest in realty is considered to be a lien ("lien theory" states) or a transfer of legal title ("title theory" states) in a sale-and-repurchase transaction. In a lien theory state, the proceeds of a mortgage do not include rents from the mortgaged property, whereas in a title theory state, rents are proceeds from the mortgage. *See* R. Wilson Freyermuth, *Modernizing Security in Rents: The New Uniform Assignment of Rents Act*, 71 Mo. L. Rev. 1, 2 (2006). To be on the safe side, most commercial mortgages include a separate "assignment of rents" that gives the mortgagee a security interest in rents from the mortgaged property. (Under some states' law, the assignment of rents means that the rents are actually property of the lender, rather than collateral for the lender. *See In re Surma*, 504 B.R. 770 (Bankr. D.N.J. 2014).) Hotel revenues might not be considered "rent," but can be similarly separately assigned.

Proceeds of proceeds are also proceeds. Thus, if inventory is sold for a promise to repay (an "account receivable"), the account receivable is a proceed, and when the account receivable is collected for cash, that cash is a proceed of the account receivable, but also of the inventory.

B. Products, Offspring, and Profits

What about "products," "offspring," and "profits"? Products are something produced from collateral. Thus, the milk from a cow would be a "product" of the cow. So too is the manure (a potentially valuable fertilizer or fuel source).

Offspring are, well, offspring, such as a lamb from a ram or ewe. If a creditor has a security interest in Seabiscuit (the champion race horse), section 552(b) would allow that security interest to cover foals that Seabiscuit sires post-petition.

Profits does not mean the difference between revenue and expenses, but instead refers to products extracted from the earth, such as minerals, oil, mud, and possibly water.

What happens when collateral is combined with other items into a new product? Suppose the security interest were in flour, eggs, and sugar, and that collateral were used post-petition to make a cake. The security interest would attach only to the value of the cake attributable to the flour, eggs, and sugar, not to the other ingredients or to the labor. Similarly, if the collateral were steel and that steel were used to manufacture an engine block, the engine block would be collateral only to the extent that its value came from the steel and not from the electricity or intellectual property rights or labor involved in making the engine block. Obviously this rule poses thorny valuation issues, but the principle is that a secured creditor gets the value of its collateral through all of its transformations, but not anything more than that.

Significantly, whereas "proceeds" in personalty benefit from automatic attachment (enforceability under a security interest) at state law, UCC § 9-315, there is no such rule providing for the automatic attachment of security interests to products, offspring, and profits at state law. Instead, a security interest attaches to them only to the extent that the security agreement expressly so provides.

C. After-Acquired Property

Whereas proceeds, products, offspring, and profits all refer to some sort of value derived from the original collateral, after-acquired property refers to property acquired by a debtor after a security agreement has been authenticated. UCC § 9-204. A security agreement only attaches to collateral when the debtor has rights in the collateral, UCC § 9-203(b)(2), but a debtor can enter into a security agreement that provides that the creditor will have a security interest in the collateral if and when it is acquired by the debtor. Thus, in exchange for a loan of $100 due in five years, I can grant you a security interest in my Lamborghini, even though I don't currently own one. (One can always hope. . . .) But if I acquire a Lamborghini while the debt is still outstanding, then the security interest will attach to. (Whether the security interest is "perfected," giving it priority rights vis-à-vis other claimants, is another matter; if the security interest has attached, but is unperfected, it will be of little avail to the creditor in bankruptcy, as will be discussed in Chapter 29.)

For certain types of collateral—inventory and accounts receivable—after-acquired property is presumptively included in the security interest but for other types of collateral, an "after-acquired property clause" is necessary to make the after-acquired property subject to the security interest. Such a clause might simply be the insertion of the words "now owned or hereafter acquired" after a description of the collateral.

Making all of this even trickier is that products, offspring, and profits can also be after-acquired property. Thus, if the security agreement covers "Farmer Brown's ewes, now owned or hereafter acquired," and a ewe lamb is borne subsequently, that ewe lamb would after-acquired property, whereas a ram lamb would not be. Both lambs would also be offspring, but the ram lamb would not be covered by the security agreement. If the security agreement covered "Farmer Brown's ewes, now owned or hereafter acquired, and any offspring," then both the ewe lamb and the ram lamb would be covered as "offspring," and the ewe lamb also as after-acquired property. (All this assumes that the term "ewe" includes a "ewe lamb.")

The interaction between proceeds and after-acquired property can be messy because some after-acquired property might also be proceeds. This is particularly an issue when inventory or accounts receivable are collateral. For example, a security interest in "inventory" would cover all inventory owned by the debtor pre-petition. If the inventory were sold post-petition in exchange for an account receivable, the security interest would also cover the accounts receivable as proceeds of the inventory. And when the accounts receivable were collected for cash, the security interest would also cover the cash as the proceeds of proceeds. This cash is known as "cash collateral," and the debtor, as we saw in Chapter 20, would need court approval or creditor consent to use it. 11 U.S.C. § 363(c)(2).

Now let's imagine that the cash collateral were used to buy more inventory. That inventory would be proceeds of proceeds of proceeds and thus covered by the security interest. It would also be after-acquired property, but because it was proceeds, the creditor's pre-petition security interest would attach to it and its value would be accounted for in determining the allowed amount of the creditor's secured claim.

If, however, the new inventory were purchased post-petition not with cash collateral, but instead using funds that were not proceeds (even indirectly) of the original inventory, the security interest would not attach to the new inventory. The new inventory would be after-acquired property, but not proceeds, and attachment would be cut off by sections 362(a)(4) and 552(a).

Similarly, if the security interest were in "all the debtor's drill presses," and the debtor had three drill presses pre-petition, but purchased another post-petition, the security interest would only attach to the three drill presses owned pre-petition, not to the new one purchased post-petition, as it would be after-acquired property. Accordingly, the creditor's secured claim would be limited by the value of the three drill presses owned pre-petition, but not by the fourth.

If, however, one of the drill presses owned pre-petition were exchanged post-petition for a new drill press, that new drill press would be proceeds of the original drill press. Therefore, the secured creditor's claim would be limited by the value of the two remaining pre-petition drill presses and the drill press acquired post-petition in exchange for the pre-petition drill press.

D. Why the Distinction?

What is the policy for allowing a secured creditor to have post-petition proceeds, products, offspring, profits, and hotel revenue as part of its collateral, but not post-petition after-acquired property generally? Recall that the bankruptcy estate is a separate juridical entity than the pre-petition debtor. Any property acquired post-petition is the property of the bankruptcy estate. 11 U.S.C. § 541(a)(6)-(7). That means that property acquired post-petition is not the pre-petition debtor's to pledge as collateral. It can only be pledged by the bankruptcy estate. Hypothecation of such collateral generally requires a security agreement "authenticated" by the borrower. UCC § 9-203(b)(3). The bankruptcy estate, however, cannot pledge collateral for borrowing without court approval. 11 U.S.C. § 364. Thus, there is no way for the bankruptcy estate to authorize the pledge of collateral acquired post-petition to a pre-petition debt absent court approval. Moreover, section 362(a)(4) prohibits "any act to create, perfect, or enforce any lien against property of the estate."

The section 552(b) carve-outs are for new collateral that is attributable to the pre-petition collateral value—but only to the extent that the creditor would be entitled to such new collateral under applicable non-bankruptcy law. Thus, a creditor's claim is limited to the value at time of distribution of the collateral the creditor had *at the time of the bankruptcy filing*. To the extent that there is appreciation, be it through normal appreciation, the collateral's transformation, or the collateral's productive use, the creditor's secured claim may increase, but not from other post-petition increases in collateral.

E. Why Does It Matter?

The cutting off of security interests in after-acquired property by section 552 has two important functions. First, by limiting secured creditors' claims, it frees up value for unsecured creditors. In other words, section 552 is a provision that alters state law rights, and in so doing transfers value from secured to unsecured creditors. Second, by limiting secured creditors' claims, section 552 frees up assets for the debtor to use during bankruptcy. Specifically, to the extent that the debtor has free assets, it can use them as collateral for financing in bankruptcy or, if the assets are cash or readily convertible into cash, like accounts receivable and inventory, it can use the assets themselves to finance its operations in bankruptcy.

VI. POST-PETITION INTEREST

A. Allowance of Post-Petition Interest

A bankruptcy claim includes any interest on a debt that has accrued pre-petition. Section 502(b)(2), however, disallows claims for "unmatured interest," that is, for interest that has not yet accrued by the time of the bankruptcy filing. 11 U.S.C. § 502(b)(2). The Code, however, does contemplate the payment of post-petition interest on claims under section 726(a)(5)—but only if all other claims have been paid in full. In other words, post-petition interest is not included in an allowed claim, but is only awarded in the unusual circumstance of a solvent debtor.

Why would the Code curtail the post-petition payment of interest? Which creditors would that benefit? Those with lower or higher rates? How would it affect pro rata distributions among unsecured creditors? What incentives might it create for resolving bankruptcy cases? What if a creditor had an above market interest rate? A below market rate? What is the effect of not paying any interest?

Secured claims are treated differently. Section 506(b) provides that the secured claim of an *oversecured* creditor that has a security interest in the debtor's property includes contractually agreed upon or statutorily provided (as in judgment rate) post-petition interest, until such point as the creditor is fully secured.

To illustrate, imagine that at the time of the bankruptcy filing, the creditor is owed $6 million, secured by collateral with a value of $8 million. The creditor's secured claim could grow up to $8 million, as up to $2 million in post-petition interest could accrue as part of the secured claim.

Collateral cushion

Once the combined total of the pre-petition debt plus post-petition interest exceeds the value of the collateral, however, the creditor no longer gets to include post-petition interest as part of its claim (excluding the unusual situation of a solvent debtor). Thus, in our example, the creditor's secured claim is capped at $8 million. Additional interest ceases to accrue once the creditor's collateral cushion has been used up; it does not spill over into an unsecured claim.

Not all secured creditors are voluntary creditors. Statutory lien and judgment lien creditors are also secured creditors. Read section 506(b) carefully. Does it limit interest solely to situations where it is provided for by contract? The Supreme Court has read section 506(b) as creating an independent statutory right to post-petition interest for all oversecured creditors, irrespective of their rights under applicable non-bankruptcy law. Thus, a creditor with a non-contractual oversecured claim is entitled to post-petition interest. *United States v. Ron Pair Enterprises*, 489 U.S. 235 (1989). What this means for contractual creditors on loans that are interest-free by their own terms is unclear. Does bankruptcy override the contractual interest-free term of a loan?

Note that section 506(b) does not extend to all secured claims. It covers only secured claims that are "secured by property." What kind of secured claims are not secured by property? Secured claims based on setoff rights. Although setoff rights have been called "security of the most perfect kind," insofar as it can be exercised without any of the formalities required for perfecting a security interest, *Boston Ins.*

Co. v. Nogg (*In re Yale Express Sys., Inc.*), 362 F.2d 111, 114 (2d Cir. 1966), they are actually inferior in some ways. Whereas a security interest creates a right in a particular property, a setoff right does not. This means that a creditor with a setoff right cannot get adequate protection under section 361, cannot lift the automatic stay under section 362(d)(2), and cannot get interest on its claim under section 506(b), which is only for claims "secured by property."

Why do only oversecured creditors get post-petition interest? Consider what would happen if undersecured creditors were awarded such interest. Their claims would all inflate. If they all accrued interest at the same rate, there would be no effect on their pro rata distribution. If they all accrued interest at their contract rates, however, creditors with claims at higher interest rates (which are likely those who loaned money when the debtor was in distress) would see their claims inflated at the expense of creditors with claims at lower interest rates, such that there would be a value transfer from low-rate creditors to high-rate creditors. The effect would be to upset the equality principle for general unsecured creditors and to incentivize some general unsecured creditors to seek a longer bankruptcy not in order to maximize the value of the estate, but in order to maximize their share of the funds available for general unsecured creditors.

B. Rate of Post-Petition Interest

In *Ron Pair Enterprises*, the Supreme Court was silent on the question of what interest rate to apply under section 506(b). Most courts will apply the contract rate when there is a contract rate. If the obligation is a statutory one, courts will generally apply any statutory rate specified, and in the absence of that, apply either a state or federal judgment rate of interest. What if there is a contractual *default* rate, however, triggered by bankruptcy law? Several provisions in bankruptcy law express a strong policy against enforcement of so-called *ipso facto* clauses triggered by bankruptcy or insolvency. 11 U.S.C. §§ 365(b), 541(c)(1), 1124(2). Yet these provisions are limited to specific circumstances, rather than a general provision against *ipso facto* clauses. As such, most courts are willing to allow post-petition interest at the contract rate, even when the contract specifies a post-bankruptcy default rate.

C. Timing of Payment of Post-Petition Interest

Post-petition interest is included in an oversecured creditor's claim, but it is not paid until the conclusion of the case, meaning the distribution of the debtor's liquidated assets in Chapter 7 or as part of a Chapter 11 plan. This means there are no periodic payments of interest during a case. The absence of a periodic interest payment requirement means that there are lower cash flow demands for a debtor while in bankruptcy. It also means that the relevant time for valuing a secured creditor's claim for allowance of post-petition interest is at the time of the distribution (or plan confirmation), meaning at the end of the case, rather than at the beginning of the case.

The inclusion of post-petition interest in oversecured claims means that the longer a firm is in bankruptcy, the larger the secured claims can grow (to the extent that the debtor originally had equity in its assets). The effect is to shift value from unsecured creditors to secured creditors. The same dynamic affects secured creditors with junior liens. These junior creditors will also accrue interest to the extent they are oversecured, but the extent that they are oversecured diminishes with the accrual of interest on senior liens.

To illustrate, imagine that there is $10 million of collateral securing a $8 million first lien claim and a $1 million second lien claim at the time of the bankruptcy filing. Both the first and second lien claims are oversecured and can therefore accrue post-petition interest. If the bankruptcy concludes when $800,000 of post-petition interest has accrued on the first lien and $100,000 on the second lien claim, the first lien will get paid $8.8 million and the second lien $1.1 million, with $100,000 left for distribution to the unsecureds.

If the bankruptcy takes twice as long, however, $1.6 million of post-petition interest will accrue on the first lien claim. Thus, the first lien claim will be $9.6 million. There will only be $400,000 of collateral value for the second lien claim, which will be bifurcated into a secured claim for $400,000 and an unsecured claim for $600,000. No post-petition interest will be allowed on the claim. And of course there will be no value from the collateral left for distribution to the secured claims.

Because interest is paid only at the end of the case—and the right to receive interest is determined by a valuation at the end of the case—junior liens are not able to receive interest for the time period when they are still "in the money." Not surprisingly, the possibility of losing post-petition interest may incentivize junior lienholders to push for a quicker bankruptcy. (This incentive may be offset by the option value of delay if the junior lienholders' liens are underwater.)

D. Post-Petition Interest and Undersecured Creditors and Oversecured Creditors

The fact that post-petition interest (if allowed) is only paid at the conclusion of a case means that secured creditors may look to adequate protection as an alternative to interest. The following cases illustrate the tricky line between adequate protection payments and post-petition interest payments.

Orix Credit Alliance, Inc. v. Delta Resources, Inc. (*In re* Delta Resources, Inc.)

54 F.3d 722 (11th Cir. 1995)

PER CURIAM.

Delta Resources, Inc., ("Delta") appeals the district court's order requiring payment of postpetition interest as part of the adequate protection it was required to pay as debtor-in-possession to appellee, Orix Credit Alliance Inc. ("Orix"). We reverse.

I. FACTS AND PROCEDURAL BACKGROUND

[Appellant Delta filed for bankruptcy. A]ppellee Orix, claiming to be an oversecured creditor, moved for relief from the automatic stay, pursuant to 11 U.S.C. § 362, on the ground that, *inter alia,* its perfected security interest in the purchase money equipment was not adequately protected.

At the final hearing before the bankruptcy court the parties agreed that the then-value of the collateral, approximately 13 pieces of heavy equipment, was $643,500. The bankruptcy court concluded that the collateral was slightly depreciating but did not find whether Orix in fact was an oversecured creditor. Instead, the court merely assumed, as Orix had asserted, that Orix was an oversecured creditor.

The bankruptcy court determined that the equipment at issue was necessary to the effective reorganization of the debtor and thus, under 11 U.S.C. § 362(d)(2), Orix could not receive relief from the automatic stay. However, the bankruptcy court did not determine whether the creditor was entitled to postpetition interest reasoning that that issue should be dealt with at the time of confirmation of the debtor's Chapter 11 plan.

The bankruptcy court also determined that Orix's secured interest in its collateral would be adequately protected by periodic cash payments in accordance with 11 U.S.C. § 361(1). The bankruptcy court granted Orix adequate protection in the amount of $9,972.41 per month to cover accruing depreciation of the equipment, but rejected Orix's contention that as an oversecured creditor it was entitled to receive postpetition interest as part of adequate protection. Accordingly, the bankruptcy court denied Orix's motion for relief from stay.

. . . [Orix appealed from the order denying relief from the automatic stay and sought, alternatively, to compel payment.]

[T]he district court entered a "final order" reversing the bankruptcy court. Extending the holding of *United Sav. Ass'n v. Timbers of Inwood Forest Assocs., Ltd.,* 484 U.S. 365 (1988), the district court determined that an oversecured creditor is entitled to postpetition interest as part of adequate protection. The district court found that Delta should retroactively pay to Orix monthly adequate protection payments consisting of $9,972.41 for the monthly depreciation of its collateral, as well as an additional amount of $8,292.90 in postpetition interest to maintain its equity cushion. The district court remanded the case to the bankruptcy court directing that Delta pay that amount to Orix retroactive to . . . the date of the bankruptcy court's order from the bench denying relief from stay but ordering adequate protection. Delta [appealed the district court's reversal of the bankruptcy court's orders].

Thereafter, the equipment, which was the subject of the motion for relief from stay, was sold and Orix was paid the proceeds of the sale. [W]ith the approval of the bankruptcy court, the parties entered into a consent order on remand concerning the district court's order for adequate protection. The equipment at issue having "been sold and the proceeds of the equipment and the interplead adequate protection payments covering depreciation only," having been paid to Orix, the issue on appeal was limited to whether the postpetition interest payments ordered by the district court "are due to be paid now because it [Orix] is an unsecured creditor." *Id.* The parties also agreed that Orix would temporarily postpone its collection efforts for the adequate protection payments for postpetition interest and that, at that time, the bankruptcy court need not enforce the mandate of the district court.

. . .

II. ANALYSIS

. . .

C. Adequate Protection

The question before us is not whether an oversecured creditor whose collateral is worth more than the amount of its debt in a Chapter 11 bankruptcy case may obtain postpetition interest as part of its claim. Indeed, it seems beyond peradventure that a creditor's right to recover postpetition interest on its oversecured claim pursuant to 11 U.S.C. § 506(b) is virtually "unqualified." Rather, the narrow legal issue presented for decision is whether Orix, purportedly an oversecured creditor, was entitled to receive periodic cash payments for accruing postpetition interest as part of adequate protection, pursuant to 11 U.S.C. § 362(d)(1), in order to preserve the value of its equity cushion. Appellant Delta does not dispute that an oversecured creditor is entitled to postpetition interest on its claim, although, Delta does dispute whether Orix was, in fact, an oversecured creditor.

Here, the bankruptcy court did not make a factual finding as to Orix's status, but simply *assumed* that Orix was an oversecured creditor for purposes of determining the amount of adequate protection necessary to protect the creditor's interest. The district court, relying upon the Supreme Court's opinion in *Timbers*, reversed the bankruptcy court reasoning that

> as an oversecured creditor, Credit Alliance is entitled to post-petition interest under 11 U.S.C. § 506(b). This section states that "to the extent that an allowed secured claim is secured by property the value of which . . . is greater than the amount of such claim, there shall be allowed to the holder of such claim, interest on such claim, and any reasonable fees, costs, or charges provided for under the agreement under which the claim arose." As this interest accrues, it also becomes secured by the security interest held by the creditor in the property. Thus, the security cushion represented by the value of the property above the creditor's security interest in the property is depleted daily as the interest accrues. As used in the applicable bankruptcy provisions, the value of the creditor's interest means the value of the collateral. *The security or collateral cushion is an inherent part of the value of the collateral. Accordingly, the oversecured creditor has a valid property interest in this security cushion and has a right to adequate protection of this interest.*

United Savings Association v. Timbers of Inwood Forest Associates, Ltd., 484 U.S. 365 (1988) (emphasis added).

And, not surprisingly, on appeal both parties rely on the Supreme Court's opinion in *Timbers* as support for their position.

The Supreme Court has determined that "the phrase 'value of such creditor's interest' in § 506(a) means 'the value of the collateral.' . . . We think the phrase 'value of such entity's interest' in § 361(1) and (2), when applied to secured creditors, means the same." *Timbers*, 484 U.S. at 372. The enquiry before us turns on whether the "interest in property" to be protected by 11 U.S.C. § 362(d)(1) entitles an oversecured creditor to receive periodic postpetition interest payments to ensure against the diminution in value of its equity cushion as a part of adequate protection or whether it is designed only to protect against diminution in the value of the collateral, i.e.—depreciation.

Appellee Orix asserts that as interest accrues on its claim the interest by the terms of its contract also becomes secured by its security interest in Delta's assets. Therefore, Orix contends, an oversecured creditor's position erodes by the accrual of postpetition interest and ultimately the adequate protection becomes inadequate. That is, unless the interest is paid, Orix's debt becomes less and less oversecured and eventually becomes undersecured. While Orix is correct that the size of the equity cushion decreases as postpetition interest accrues, the increase in the size of its secured claim resulting from the accrual of that interest is entitled to adequate protection only to the extent that the value of the collateral at the time of filing exceeded the value of Orix's original secured claim.

To begin, "upon the filing of a bankruptcy petition, § 362 of the Code imposes an automatic stay on actions by creditors to collect their claims from a debtor." *Timbers*, 793 F.2d at 1387. Yet a creditor is not without recourse to protect its interests. "Under § 362(d), a creditor may obtain relief from the [automatic] stay (1) 'for cause, including the lack of adequate protection' of the creditor's interest in the collateral." *Id.* at 1387-88.

Ordinarily, creditors are not allowed a claim for interest accruing on their debts during bankruptcy proceedings. *Timbers*, 793 F.2d at 1385. Yet, *as an exception* to that rule, an oversecured creditor, but not an undersecured creditor having the same risk (indeed, it is possible for the undersecured creditor's risks to be much larger quantitatively), is entitled to receive postpetition interest as part of its claim at the time of confirmation of a plan or reorganization, that is, at or near the conclusion of the bankruptcy case. 11 U.S.C. § 506(b). Judge Randall of the Fifth Circuit explained the rationale for this exception.

> The interest provisions of the Code and its predecessors, as interpreted by the Supreme Court for almost a century, are premised on the equitable principle that the unencumbered assets of a debtor's estate will not be used to benefit one class of creditors at the expense of another. . . . [Thus,] allowing a claim for postpetition interest by an oversecured creditor, . . . is not inconsistent with that equitable principle, *because only assets encumbered by the creditor's lien will be used to fund the payment of postpetition accrued interest.*

Timbers, 793 F.2d at 1387 (emphasis added).

Nevertheless, the Supreme Court has indicated that an oversecured creditor's allowed secured claim for postpetition interest, which is determined near the conclusion of the bankruptcy case, must be denied to the extent that, together with the principal amount of the claim, it exceeds the value of the collateral. Or put another way, the oversecured creditor's allowed secured claim for postpetition interest is limited to the amount that a creditor was oversecured at the time of filing.

> Even more important for our purposes than § 506's use of terminology is its substantive effect of denying undersecured creditors postpetition interest on their claims—just as it

denies *oversecured* creditors postpetition interest to the extent that such interest, when added to the principal amount of the claim, will exceed the value of the collateral. Section 506(b) provides that *"to the extent that* an allowed secured claim is secured by property the value of which . . . is greater than the amount of such claim, there shall be allowed to the holder of such claim, interest on such claim." (Emphasis added.) Since this provision permits postpetition interest to be paid only out of the "security cushion," the undersecured creditor, who has no such cushion, falls within the general rule disallowing postpetition interest. See 11 U.S.C. § 502(b)(2). If the Code had meant to give the undersecured creditor, who is thus denied interest on his *claim*, interest on the value of his *collateral*, surely this is where that disposition would have been set forth, and not obscured within the "adequate protection" provision of § 362(d)(1). Instead of the intricate phraseology set forth above, § 506(b) would simply have said that the secured creditor is entitled to interest "on his allowed claim, or on the value of the property securing his allowed claim, whichever is lesser."

Timbers, 484 U.S. at 372-73.

The Supreme Court has recognized that an undersecured creditor may be entitled to adequate protection to ensure against the decline in the value of its collateral. However, an undersecured creditor is not entitled to receive postpetition "interest on its collateral *during the stay* to assure adequate protection under 11 U.S.C. § 362(d)(1)." *Timbers,* 484 U.S. at 382 (emphasis added).

Ordinarily, the matter of adequate protection is determined at or near the inception of a bankruptcy case. By contrast, the determination of a creditor's secured status, pursuant to 11 U.S.C. § 506, comes at or near the conclusion of a bankruptcy case.

Under [11 U.S.C.] § 506(c), the debtor may recover from property securing a creditor's allowed secured *claim* the reasonable and necessary costs and expenses of preserving or disposing of the property, to the extent of any benefit to the creditor. If, after reducing the amount of the allowed secured claim by the amount of that recovery, the creditor is oversecured, it is entitled to interest at the contract rate on its net allowed secured claim. § 506(b). *The timing of the payment of accrued interest to an oversecured creditor (at the conclusion of the proceeding) is doubtless based on the fact that it is not possible to compute the amount of the § 506(c) recovery (and, accordingly, the amount of the net allowed secured claim on which interest is computed) until the termination of the proceeding.*

Timbers, 793 F.2d at 1407 (emphasis added).

Similarly, we conclude that 11 U.S.C. § 506(b), providing for postpetition interest on oversecured claims, read *in pari materia* with 11 U.S.C. § 362(d)(1), concerning conditioning the automatic stay on adequate protection, and 11 U.S.C. § 502, regarding the allowance of claims, requires that the payment of accrued postpetition interest to an oversecured creditor await the completion of reorganization or confirmation of the bankruptcy case. The *ratio decidendi* enunciated by the Supreme Court in *Timbers* that an undersecured creditor is not entitled to receive postpetition interest on its collateral *during the stay* to assure adequate protection under 11 U.S.C. § 362(d)(1) applies equally well to an oversecured creditor. Such an interpretation of the Bankruptcy Code is consistent whether the secured creditor is undersecured or oversecured, otherwise "§ 506(b) would simply have said that the *secured* creditor [whether oversecured or undersecured] is entitled to interest 'on his allowed claim, or on the value of the property securing his allowed claim, whichever is lesser.'" *Timbers*, 484 U.S. at 372-73 (emphasis added). Accordingly, viewing the allowance of postpetition interest to oversecured creditors as a limited exception only, we hold that an oversecured creditor's interest in property which must be adequately protected encompasses the decline in the value of the collateral only, rather than perpetuating the ratio of the collateral to the debt. The bankruptcy court accomplished that by allowing adequate protection in the amount of accruing depreciation.

We think this rule results in the appropriate balance between the conflicting interests of the oversecured creditor on the one hand and the estate, as well as other creditors, secured and unsecured, on the other hand. As one commentator points out:

> there is certainly no reason intrinsic to the phenomenon of credit that entitles oversecured creditors to interest out of their collateral before junior creditors, whether secured [perhaps by the identical collateral] or unsecured, receive any of their principal.

Niall L. O'Toole, *Adequate Protection and Postpetition Interest in Chapter 11 Proceedings*, 56 Am. Bankr. L.J. 251, 253 (1982).

Here, even accepting the bankruptcy court's assumption that Orix was an oversecured creditor, although it never made such a factual finding, for the reasons stated above, Orix, as a matter of law, was not entitled to receive periodic payments for accruing postpetition interest as part of adequate protection for any period of time.

III. CONCLUSION

The district court's order awarding Orix monthly postpetition interest in the amount of $8,292.90 is REVERSED and this case REMANDED to the district court for further proceedings not inconsistent herewith.

Study Questions and Notes

1. Adequate protection shields a secured creditor from the depreciation of its collateral. The theory is that but for the automatic stay, the creditor could foreclose on its collateral and thus eliminate its exposure to depreciation. Adequate protection is meant to protect the secured creditor from the risk imposed by the automatic stay. But given the working of section 506, is depreciation the only risk a secured creditor faces because of the automatic stay? Isn't the possibility of losing its equity cushion (and potentially having its claim for post-petition interest capped) also a risk imposed by the stay? If so, does it make sense from a policy perspective to distinguish between compensation for these risks?

2. The Eleventh Circuit refers to both the "value of the equity cushion" and the "ratio of collateral to the debt." Are those the same thing?

VII. POST-PETITION ATTORNEYS' FEES

The Bankruptcy Code makes explicit allowance for the attorneys' fees of *over-secured* creditors. Just as with post-petition interest, section 506(b) provides that the secured claim of an oversecured creditor includes contractually agreed upon (or statutory) attorneys' fees incurred post-petition, until such point as it is fully secured. To illustrate, imagine that at the time of the bankruptcy filing, the creditor is owed $9 million, secured by collateral with a value of $10 million. The creditor's secured claim could grow up to $10 million, as up to $1 million in attorneys' fees and post-petition interest—if provided for by contract or statute—could accrue as part of the secured claim. Once the combined total of the pre-petition debt plus post-petition attorneys' fees and interest exceeds the value of the collateral, how-ever, the creditor no longer gets to include post-petition fees and interest as part of its *secured* claim (excluding the unusual situation of a solvent debtor).

Traditionally, it was assumed that the claims of unsecured creditors (and by extension undersecured creditors, including creditors whose claims exceeded the value of their collateral as the result of post-petition interest and/or attorneys' fees) did not include post-petition attorneys' fees. In 2007, the Supreme Court upset this long-settled understanding, holding in *Travelers Casualty & Surety Co. of Am. v. Pac. Gas & Elec. Co.*, 549 U.S. 443 (2007), that the Ninth Circuit's *Fobian* rule (from *In re Fobian*, 951 F.2d 1149 (9th Cir. 1991) that "attorney fees are not recoverable in bank-ruptcy for litigating issues 'peculiar to federal bankruptcy law,'" lacked any textual basis and thus did not provide grounds for disallowing a claim for post-petition attorneys' fees. *Travelers*, 549 U.S. at 451-452. The Supreme Court noted that "we gen-erally presume that claims enforceable under applicable state law will be allowed in bankruptcy unless they are expressly disallowed," *id.*, and that no reason was raised that changes that presumption. Significantly, however, the Supreme Court refused to consider the debtor's argument that such fees were not allowable under section 506(b) because that argument had not been raised in the lower courts. *Id.* at 454-455. The Supreme Court noted that "we express no opinion with regard to whether, following the demise of the *Fobian* rule, other principles of bankruptcy law might provide an independent basis for disallowing Travelers' claim for attorney's fees." *Id.* at 456. Thus, section 506(b) might still provide grounds for disallowing attorneys' fees for unsecured and undersecured creditors.[1]

Travelers is simply a restatement of the basic principle that creditors' rights are determined in the first instance by their non-bankruptcy rights. *Butner v. United States,* 440 U.S. 48 (1979). The implication is that if post-petition attorneys' fees would be permitted under applicable non-bankruptcy law, they are generally allowed in bankruptcy, unless another specific provision can be invoked to deny the fees. Conversely, if a creditor is not entitled to attorneys' fees by either contract or stat-ute, its claim for both pre-petition and post-petition attorneys' fees will be denied. *Travelers* has important distributional effects, as it favors contractual creditors over

---

1. Likewise, because setoff claims are not "secured by property," they would not automatically include attorneys' fees under section 506(b).

involuntary creditors and more powerful contractual creditors over those with less bargaining power. The effect of *Travelers*, is to confirm that bankruptcy law will not upset pre-existing relationships of market power.

While the *Travelers* decision left open the possibility that claims for post-petition attorneys' fees could be denied on other grounds, including section 506(b), subsequent lower court rulings have generally not found grounds to do so. The only two circuit courts of appeals to address the issue post-*Travelers* could not find any grounds for denying an unsecured creditor's claim for post-petition attorneys' fees, including section 502(b)'s requirement that a claim's amount be determined "as of the date of the filing of the petition," that *Timbers of Inwood Forest* disallows attorneys' fees claims, and public policy arguments. *SNTL Corp. v. Centre Ins. Co. (In re SNTL Corp.)*, 571 F.3d 826, 843-845 (9th Cir. 2009); *Ogle v. Fid. & Deposit Co.*, 586 F.3d 143 (2d Cir. 2009). While it may still be possible for post-petition attorneys' fees to be disallowed, the general presumption now is that they are allowed for all creditors when permitted by applicable non-bankruptcy law or contract.

Unresolved at present is how post-petition interest and attorneys' fees are to be applied to the debtor's equity cushion in the collateral. This matters because if interest is applied first to the equity cushion, attorneys' fees can spill over into part of an allowed unsecured claim, while if attorneys' fees are applied first, interest cannot spill over into part of an allowed unsecured claim because of the operation of sections 502(b)(2) and 506(b). Presumably, courts will devise some sort of allocation rule, but this problem underscores the difficulties posed by the *Travelers* decision.

VIII. CHARGES FOR CARE OF COLLATERAL

Section 506(c) provides that the bankruptcy estate may charge a secured creditor the costs of caring for or selling its collateral to the extent that such expenses benefit the creditor. The costs of caring for collateral include not only regular maintenance and storage expenses, but may also include maintenance of casualty insurance, as the insurance payments would be the proceeds of the collateral if the collateral were damaged or destroyed, and payment of value-based (*ad valorem*) property taxes on the property.

Section 506(c) attempts to ensure that a creditor's *secured* claim is not artificially inflated because of the expenses of the estate. Consider, for example, a loan secured by a race horse. If the debtor fails to feed the horse, its value will quickly dissipate. That would have the effect of reducing the creditor's *secured* claim. If the loan were recourse, it would not affect the creditor's total claim, only the portion of it entitled to secured treatment. If the debtor spends funds to feed the horse, the value of the collateral—and thus the size of the creditor's secured claim—will be maintained. The funds that the debtor has spent to maintain the collateral are funds that might otherwise be available to satisfy the claims of general unsecured creditors. Section 506(c) is meant to interact with section 361 (adequate protection) to lock in a creditor's secured claim other than as adjusted for post-petition interest and fees. Section 361 ensures that the creditor's secured claim is protected against depreciation losses.

Section 506(c) ensures that the creditor's secured claim is protected against offsetting appreciation (or more accurately, lack of depreciation) because of the estate's expenses.

Section 506(c) also permits the estate to charge the collateral for the costs of sale ("disposing of, such property"). Recall, however, that a section 506(c) charge is permitted only "to the extent of any benefit to the holder of such claim." When does a secured creditor benefit from an estate's payment of sale expenses?

The answer depends on whether the creditor is sufficiently oversecured. Virtually all secured loans will provide for the costs of a sale to be added to the debt. This means that in a foreclosure sale, an oversecured creditor can charge the costs of conducting the foreclosure sale to the amount of its secured debt and recover the entire amount from the sale proceeds. Therefore, such an oversecured creditor does not benefit from the estate's sale outlays because it would have just paid those expenses itself and added them to its secured claim. Thus, a creditor that is oversecured by more than the amount of the sale costs should not be charged under section 506(c) for sale costs. This does not necessarily hold true for creditors with non-consensual security interests, as they cannot necessarily recover sale costs outside of bankruptcy, and thus under *Travelers* such costs should not be part of their secured claim.

If, on the other hand, a creditor is undersecured or has a collateral cushion that is less than the sale expenses, then that creditor would not have otherwise been able to recover the sale costs from the costs of the collateral. Accordingly, such a creditor benefits from the estate's expenses in selling the collateral, and the creditor is liable for a section 506(c) charge against its collateral.

Note that the estate may contractually waive the right to section 506(c) charges (with court approval), and this is frequently done in the context of debtor-in-possession financing agreements.

IX. APPLICATION OF ADEQUATE PROTECTION PAYMENTS

Secured creditors may have received adequate protection payments during the course of the bankruptcy to compensate them for depreciation of their collateral. How are those payments to be credited against a creditor's claims?

If the creditor is oversecured, the answer is straightforward: The claim is reduced by the amount of the adequate protection payments. Thus, suppose that a secured creditor had a $80,000 claim, secured by $100,000 worth of collateral. If the collateral were depreciating at a rate of $1,000 per month, the secured creditor might be granted monthly adequate protection payments of $1,000. Over a year, these payments would total $12,000, and the collateral's value would have declined to $88,000. Let's assume that the secured creditor must be paid in full for its claim and that the payment happens after one year. If the secured creditor's claim remained $80,000, the secured creditor would receive a windfall, recovering $92,000 on an $80,000 claim. If the adequate protection payments were credited against the secured claim, however, the secured creditor would recover exactly $80,000—just what it should.

The secured credit, you will recall, is also accruing interest on its claim, whether by contract or under section 506(b). Let's assume that the interest is at a rate of 20%. Interest is increasing the claim at the same time that depreciation is reducing the value of the collateral and hence the maximum amount of interest that may accrue. The secured creditor is the bankruptcy equivalent of the Star Wars trash compactor.

Crediting adequate protection payments against the secured creditor's claim actually eases this problem for the secured creditor. The adequate protection payments are applied to the base claim, not post-petition interest. *Nantucket Investors II v. California Fed. Bank (In re Indian Palms Assocs.)*, 61 F.3d 197 (3d Cir. 1995). Adequate protection payments thus lower the principal amount on which interest accrues. To illustrate, let's simplify the math and apply the adequate protection not as monthly payments, but as a lump sum payment to the $80,000 base claim. The secured creditor now has a $68,000 claim on which interest accrues. At 20% interest annually that's an $81,600 secured claim, backed by $88,000 in collateral. The secured creditor thus recovers a total $93,600—$81,600 under the plan and $12,000 in pre-plan payments. The application of adequate protection to the principal of the claim potentially increases a secured creditor's recovery by increasing the amount of post-petition interest it can potentially recover.

What happens, however, if a secured creditor is undersecured? Are adequate protection payments credited to the secured claim or the unsecured claim? The case below considers this issue.

First Federal Bank v. Weinstein (*In re* Weinstein)

227 B.R. 284 (9th Cir. B.A.P. 1998)

D. RUSSELL, U.S. Bankr. J.:

Appellant First Federal Bank of California appeals an order by the bankruptcy court confirming appellees Norton and Joyce Weinstein's First Amended Plan of Reorganization. We AFFIRM.

In March 1991, appellant First Federal Bank of California (the "Bank") loaned appellees Norton and Joyce Weinstein ("Debtors") $1,000,000 with interest at a rate of 10.463 percent per annum. The loan was secured by a first deed of trust on Debtors' residence, an ocean front condominium located in Santa Monica, California (the "residential property") [that also served as the Debtor's office]. In February 1994, Debtors defaulted on their monthly loan payments. On July 29, 1994, Debtors filed a petition for relief under Chapter 11 of the Bankruptcy Code.

The Bank later filed a motion for relief from the automatic stay. Following a hearing on the motion, the bankruptcy court issued an order requiring Debtors to make "adequate protection" payments of $7,000 per month to the Bank commencing on April 1, 1995. These payments continued until the Debtors' plan of reorganization was confirmed in October 1996. Eventually, $98,000 in total payments were made.

The Bank's total claim for its loan is $1,012,700.71. On May 22, 1996, the bankruptcy court held an evidentiary hearing to determine the fair market value of the residential property. It concluded that the value of the property as of July 1994 was $850,000. . . .

$850,000 - 98,000$
$= 752,000$

The Debtors proposed their First Amended Plan of Reorganization (the "Plan") to creditors in July 1995 and the Bank filed various objections to the Plan. At the confirmation hearing, the bankruptcy court found that there had been no change in the value of the residential property between the date the petition was filed and the date the Plan was to be confirmed. Its value remained $850,000. The court also held that Debtors were entitled to credit the $98,000 in postpetition, preconfirmation payments to reduce the Bank's allowed secured claim of $850,000 to $752,000. . . . The Plan was confirmed on October 28, 1996 over the Bank's objections. . . . The Bank appeals the order confirming the Plan.

. . .

The Bank . . . argues that the bankruptcy court erred in crediting Debtors' $98,000 in "adequate protection" payments to reduce the secured portion, rather than the unsecured portion, of its claim. The bankruptcy court's credit of the $98,000 reduced the Bank's secured claim from $850,000 to $752,000 so that Debtors' Plan only had to provide the Bank with the present value of $752,000 [under section 1129(b)(2)(A)(1) in order to confirm the plan].

Section 361 of the Code, which addresses adequate protection payments, provides in relevant part:

> When adequate protection is required under section 362, 363, or 364 of this title of an interest of an entity in property, such adequate protection must be provided by—
>
> **(1)** requiring the trustee to make . . . periodic cash payments to such entity, to the extent that the stay under section 362 of this title . . . results in a decrease in the value of such entity's interest in such property. . . .

11 U.S.C. § 361(1). Adequate protection is provided to safeguard the creditor against depreciation in the value of its collateral during the reorganization process. If the value of the collateral decreases, the creditor is entitled to cash payments so that the value of its interest in the collateral remains constant. 11 U.S.C. §§ 362(d)(1) and 361(1). Thus, the amount by which the collateral depreciates is the amount of adequate protection to which the secured creditor is entitled. . . .

Characterizing the $98,000 in payments made in this case as being for adequate protection, as the Bank does, is inaccurate because there was no depreciation in the value of the Bank's collateral. Where there is no depreciation, there is no entitlement to adequate protection payments. The majority of courts have held that payments intended to provide adequate protection should be credited toward reducing the secured portion of the creditor's total claim where there is no depreciation in the value of the collateral.

Legal commentators considering the question have reached a similar conclusion. *See* 3 COLLIER ON BANKRUPTCY ¶361.03[2][a] (because adequate protection payments replace the lost value of collateral, "the better approach is to credit the payments against the secured claim rather than the unsecured claim"); David Gray Carlson, *Adequate Protection Payments and the Surrender of Cash Collateral in Chapter 11 Reorganization*, 15 CARDOZO L. REV. 1357, 1372 (1994) (adequate protection payments should reduce the secured claim and the total claim; the unsecured claim unaffected by adequate protection payments). We adopt the majority view and conclude that postpetition, preconfirmation payments made on nondepreciating collateral must be allocated to reduce the secured portion of the creditor's claim.

[T]he bankruptcy court properly credited the $98,000 in postpetition, preconfirmation payments to reduce the secured portion of the Bank's claim. . . . We thus AFFIRM the bankruptcy court. . . .

Study Questions and Note

1. Does *Weinstein* really answer the question of whether adequate protection payments must be applied to a secured claim, rather than an unsecured claim? Is it limited to a situation with non-depreciating collateral? Why would depreciating collateral affect the analysis?

2. Consider a situation in which a secured creditor is owed 70 at the time of filing, secured by collateral of 100. The collateral depreciates by 20 over the bankruptcy, while the secured creditor accrues post-petition interest and attorneys' fees of 5. The secured creditor would be paid 75 in this scenario without adequate protection. But if adequate protection were awarded as a dollar-for-dollar depreciation offset, the secured creditor would recover not only 75, but also 20 for a total recovery of 95, *even though the secured creditor's claim was only 75.* That result cannot be right. By reducing the secured creditor's claim by the amount of adequate protection paid, however, we get to the right recovery of 75. Therefore, it does not seem to follow that the rule in *Weinstein* should be limited to non-depreciating collateral.

3. Suppose the adequate protection payments were applied to the unsecured claim and that the payments exactly equaled the amount of the unsecured claim. What would be the recovery percentage for that unsecured claim? How does that seem if other unsecured claims are recovering 5%?

Problem Set 27

(1) Bacchus Wineries just filed for Chapter 7 bankruptcy. Bacchus's debts include $40 million outstanding on a loan from Jupiter Bankcorp. The loan was secured by Bacchus's inventory of Bacchus Gran Cru 2008, which has been aging for years.

   a. If the Bacchus Gran Cru 2008 turns out to be an extraordinary vintage, the inventory is worth $60 million. What is Jupiter's claim currently? 11 U.S.C. § 506(a).

   b. If the Bacchus Gran Cru 2008 is an unremarkable vintage, but suitable for sale as box wine, the inventory is worth $40 million. What is Jupiter's claim currently? 11 U.S.C. § 506(a).

   c. If the Bacchus Gran Cru 2008 is not even fit for use as vinegar, the inventory is worth $10 million. What is Jupiter's claim currently? 11 U.S.C. § 506(a).

(2) Ceres Natural Grains is in Chapter 7 bankruptcy. Ceres's debts at the time of filing include a $15 million loan from Jupiter Bankcorp. The loan is secured by Ceres's equipment, which has a liquidation value of $10 million, and by Ceres's real estate,

which has a liquidation value of $8 million. The loan accrues interest at a simple annual rate of 10%.

    a. What is Jupiter's claim at the time of filing? 11 U.S.C. § 506(a).

    b. What is Jupiter's claim one year after filing? 11 U.S.C. § 506(b).

    c. What is Jupiter's claim two years after filing? 11 U.S.C. § 506(b).

    d. What is Jupiter's claim three years after filing? 11 U.S.C. §§ 502, 506(a)-(b).

    e. Now suppose that the real estate was only worth $3 million. What is Jupiter's claim at the time of filing? 11 U.S.C. §§ 502, 506(a).

    f. If the real estate was only worth $3 million, what is Jupiter's claim one year after filing? 11 U.S.C. §§ 502, 506(a)-(b).

    g. How do your answers to questions (b)-(d) and (f) change if Jupiter has $1 million in post-petition attorneys' fees, provided for in its contract with Ceres? 11 U.S.C. §§ 502, 506(a)-(b).

(3) Neptune Canneries is in Chapter 11 bankruptcy. Neptune's debts at the time of filing include a $10 million balloon loan from Jupiter Bankcorp, secured by Neptune's equipment, which is worth $12 million as part of Neptune's operations, but with a resale value of only $3 million. The loan bears interest at a simple (non-compounded) annual rate of 12%. The loan was three months delinquent at the time of filing. 11 U.S.C. §§ 502, 506(b).

    a. What is Jupiter's claim at the time of filing when it moves to lift the stay under sections 362(d)(1) and (d)(2)? 11 U.S.C. §§ 362(d)(1)-(2), 506(b); *In re Craddock-Terry Shoe*.

    b. What is Jupiter's claim if the bankruptcy lasts one year before a plan of reorganization is confirmed? 11 U.S.C. § 506(b).

    c. What is Jupiter's claim if the bankruptcy lasts two years before a plan is confirmed? 11 U.S.C. §§ 502, 506(a)-(b).

    d. How do your answers to (b) and (c) change, if at all, if Jupiter has $1 million in post-petition attorneys' fees? 11 U.S.C. § 506(b).

    e. How does your answer to (d) change if Neptune spent $600,000 post-petition on maintaining the equipment? 11 U.S.C. § 506(c).

    f. How does your answer to (d) change if at the start of the bankruptcy Neptune made a lump sum $1 million adequate protection payment to Jupiter? 11 U.S.C. § 361; *In re Weinstein*, 227 B.R. 284 (9th Cir. B.A.P. 1998).

(4) Vulcan Foundries is in Chapter 7 bankruptcy. Vulcan's debts at the time of filing include a $10 million interest-free loan from Vulcan's controlling shareholder Aetna Investments. The loan is secured by Vulcan's two blast furnaces, which are worth $11 million. If Vulcan liquidates after a year in Chapter 7, what is Aetna's claim? 11 U.S.C. §§ 506(b), 726(a)(5); *United States v. Ron Pair Enterprises*, 489 U.S. 235 (1989).

(5) Mars Firearms is in Chapter 11 bankruptcy. Mars's debts at the time of filing include a $30 million wrongful death judgment secured by a judgment lien on Mars's inventory. Mars's inventory is worth $7 million to Mars as a going concern.

    a. What is the judgment lien creditor's claim at the time of filing? 11 U.S.C. § 506(b).

    b. What is the judgment lien creditor's claim after one year? 11 U.S.C. §§ 506(b), 726(a)(5).

c. Suppose the inventory is also subject to a senior lien that secures a $6 million loan with interest accruing at a simple annual rate of 6%. After one year, what are the respective claims of the senior lienholder and the judgment lien creditor? 11 U.S.C. §§ 502, 506(b).

d. After two years, what are the respective claims of the senior lienholder and judgment lien creditor? 11 U.S.C. §§ 502, 506(a)-(b).

(6) Vestal Properties owns and operates the immaculately clean Virgin Hotel in Florida, a lien theory state. Vestal has a $10 million line of credit (fully drawn) from Jupiter Bankcorp. The line of credit is secured by Vestal's accounts receivable and bank deposits. At the time of filing, Vestal had $500,000 in accounts receivable and $250,000 in bank deposits. $1 million of post-petition interest and $500,000 of post-petition attorneys' fees have accrued on the Jupiter line of credit.

Vestal also owes Pluto Special Situation Fund $25 million, secured by a first lien mortgage on the Virgin Hotel. Additionally, Vestal owes Minerva Capital $5 million secured by a second lien mortgage and assignment of rents and hotel revenues on the Virgin Hotel. The Virgin Hotel is worth only $22 million, but since filing for bankruptcy Virgin has generated $7.5 million in revenue from the Virgin Hotel, which it deposited in its bank accounts, including collections of its accounts receivable. $3 million in post-petition interest and $1 million in post-petition attorneys' fees have accrued on the Pluto mortgage, and $800,000 in post-petition interest and $200,000 in post-petition attorneys' fees have accrued on the Minerva mortgage.

a. What is Jupiter Bankcorp's claim? 11 U.S.C. §§ 552(a)-(b)(1).

b. What is Pluto Special Situation Fund's claim? 11 U.S.C. § 552(a).

c. What is Minerva Capital's claim? 11 U.S.C. § 552(b).

d. How much free cash does Vestal Properties have on hand?

(7) Diana Trail Outfitters is in Chapter 11 bankruptcy. Diana owes $20 million to Jupiter Bankcorp at 5% simple annual interest, secured by Diana's real estate. The real estate is currently worth $23 million and not depreciating. Jupiter has moved to have the automatic stay lifted for lack of adequate protection. Diana claims that Jupiter is adequately protected by its equity cushion. Jupiter claims that this is not enough, as its equity cushion will soon disappear.

a. Can Jupiter get the stay lifted? *Orix Credit Alliance v. Delta Resources.*

b. Suppose the value of the real estate were declining and Diana was ordered to pay Jupiter $125,000 in monthly adequate protection payments. What would Jupiter's claim be after one year? 11 U.S.C. § 361; *First Fed. Bank v. Weinstein.*

c. How would your answer to (b) change if the real estate was worth $17 million? *First Fed. Bank v. Weinstein.*

d. Suppose that the value of the real estate is in fact $23 million. What would Jupiter's claim be after one year if, in addition to the adequate protection payments in (b), Diana also incurred $2 million in maintenance costs and paid $2 million in property taxes on the real property? 11 U.S.C. § 506(c).

CHAPTER *28*

LIQUIDATION

In a Chapter 7 case, once the assets of the bankruptcy estate have been gathered up—a process that may include litigation to claw back certain assets—the trustee proceeds to liquidate them. Section 704 of the Bankruptcy Code provides that the trustee shall "collect and reduce to money the property of the estate for which such trustee serves, and close such estate as expeditiously as is compatible with the best interests of parties in interest." 11 U.S.C. § 704(a)(1). The trustee's actions in liquidating the assets are governed by the trustee's fiduciary duty to the bankruptcy estate, but as long as the trustee does not engage in self-dealing transactions, the liquidation is managed according to the trustee's business judgment.

The state law foreclosure sale provides our liquidation paradigm, but there are significant differences between the bankruptcy liquidation and the state law foreclosure sale. The state law foreclosure sale is a one-time event of a single sale, and a single distribution involves only a single asset or discrete pool of assets. It does not necessarily involve all of the debtor's assets. The bankruptcy liquidation may involve a series of sales and distributions encompassing all of the assets of the estate.

The fact that a bankruptcy liquidation may involve a series of sales is important. In a foreclosure sale, the only creditors that receive a distribution are ones with a lien on the collateral—a property right in the specific asset being sold. That means unsecured creditors never partake in the distribution from a foreclosure sale. It also means that a secured creditor never partakes in a foreclosure sale distribution unless *its collateral* is being sold. The sale of another creditor's collateral does not generate distribution rights for a creditor.

In bankruptcy, the assets being liquidated may include both assets encumbered by liens and unencumbered assets. The foreclosure sale principles of distribution apply to the bankruptcy liquidation of assets encumbered by liens. The priority of the liens is taken from applicable non-bankruptcy law, but with one twist: The bankruptcy estate, rather than the debtor, receives any surplus and is also potentially liable for any deficiency.

A different, if related, set of principles applies to the distribution of the unencumbered assets of the estate, including any surplus from the liquidation of the encumbered assets. The treatment of unencumbered assets is a function of bankruptcy law, and they are available to all unsecured claims.

Bankruptcy law provides that unsecured creditors share in these assets ratably, but also provides for certain statutory priorities among unsecured claims, such that these statutorily prioritized unsecured claims are paid first out of the unencumbered assets (with payment done ratably among each level of statutory priority) and only after all prioritized claims have been paid in full are general unsecured claims (those without priority) paid. After these general unsecured claims have been paid in full, certain statutorily subordinated claims are paid—if any assets remain. Thus, bankruptcy law, by statute, creates its own sort of absolute priority system for unsecured claims that interfaces with the non-bankruptcy law priority system for secured claims. So while bankruptcy law recreates something similar to the state law absolute priority system in foreclosures, it applies it not just to sales of discrete groups of assets, but to all of the assets of the estate, a process that might involve multiple asset sales.

Not only might there be multiple sales, but there might also be multiple distributions in a bankruptcy, unlike at state law. As we have already seen, some assets might be distributed before the final liquidation. Some assets might be abandoned, as discussed below. 11 U.S.C. § 554. Other assets are used to make adequate protection payments, as we have seen in Chapter 12. 11 U.S.C. §§ 361, 362(d)(1). Other assets are used to pay post-petition suppliers that will only take cash payments or that are paid periodically in the ordinary course of business. 11 U.S.C. § 363(c)(1). Yet other assets are used to make periodic payments to professionals employed by the estate—lawyers, accountants, financial advisors. 11 U.S.C. § 331.

The fact that there is not a single distribution in bankruptcy matters because parties that are paid first temporally effectively gain priority over parties paid later. To wit, imagine a debtor with two assets: a type A widget and a type B widget. The type A widget is liquidated first and yields $100. The type B widget is estimated to yield $200 when it is sold. If the $100 from the sale of the type A widget is distributed before the sale of the type B widget, parties that are not paid in the distribution assume the risk of the type B widget's sale price. Thus, imagine that we have two creditors, a senior and a junior, each owed $150. Let's say that when the type A widget was sold we paid the full $100 proceeds to the junior. If the type B widget only ends up selling for $125, what has happened? We would pay that $125 to the senior, but the senior would only have been paid $125 on the $150 it was owed, while the junior received $100 on the $150 it was owed. The result would be inconsistent with absolute priority—the idea that no one junior is paid anything until everyone senior has been paid in full—which is the animating logic of state law foreclosure sales. The senior still has priority over the junior, but because we paid the junior *earlier* than the senior, it had the effect of paying the junior *ahead of* the senior in terms of priority. Because bankruptcy allows certain distributions before the final liquidation, the effect is to potentially elevate the priority of parties who receive pre-liquidation distributions.

I. ABANDONMENT

Some assets are not worth liquidating and may be abandoned by the estate under section 554 of the Bankruptcy Code. Section 554 permits the trustee to abandon property that is "burdensome to the estate or that is of inconsequential value and benefit to the estate." Abandonment can take place at any time during a bankruptcy.

Sometimes the burdensome property might simply be an asset in which the debtor has no equity remaining and that is not necessary for reorganization, but that the secured creditor does not particularly want to take back. In such cases, abandonment essentially forces the same result as a lift stay motion under section 362(d) (lack of equity and not necessary to an effective reorganization).

Why wouldn't a creditor want to take back its collateral, though? The property that is burdensome to the estate may be burdensome to others as well—such as polluted land—which raises the question of whether non-statutory conditions may be placed on abandonment. The Supreme Court addressed this question in *Midlantic National Bank v. New Jersey Department of Environmental Protection*, 474 U.S. 494 (1986). The debtor had proposed abandoning a contaminated waste oil plant that was subject to mortgages that exceeded the property's value. State and local government objected, arguing that the abandonment would threaten the public's health and safety and violate state and federal environmental law. The Court held that section 554(a) did not pre-empt all state and local laws, so an abandonment may not be effectuated "in contravention of a state statute or regulation that is reasonably designed to protect the public health or safety from identified hazards." Instead, the abandonment can be conditioned on adequate protection of the public's health and safety.

If property is not abandoned by the estate or otherwise provided for under a plan of liquidation or reorganization, that property remains property of the bankruptcy estate. 11 U.S.C. § 554(d). The bankruptcy estate continues to exist until the estate has been "fully administered." 11 U.S.C. § 350.

This does not mean that a bankruptcy estate will continue indefinitely. In a Chapter 7 case, once 90 days run from the final distribution, any remaining funds escheat to the U.S. government. 11 U.S.C. § 347(a). In a Chapter 11 case, property that remains unclaimed at the expiration of the time allowed for claiming it under the plan becomes either property of the debtor or of an entity that acquired the assets of the debtor under the Chapter 11 plan. 11 U.S.C. § 347(b).

II. PROPERTY ENCUMBERED WITH LIENS

Just as burdensome property with no value to the estate will be abandoned, so too will the estate surrender property encumbered with liens in which the debtor has no equity. The trustee will hand over such property to the lienholder. Section 725 of the Bankruptcy Code provides that "before final distribution of property of the estate under section 726 . . . the trustee . . . shall dispose of any property in which any entity other than the estate has an interest, such as a lien, and that has not been disposed of under another section of this title." 11 U.S.C. § 725.

In the event that there are multiple liens, the trustee will typically sell the property and the lienholders will be compensated, according to their priority, from the proceeds of the sale, with unsecured claims for any deficiency. The Bankruptcy Code does not spell this out in detail, however.

If property of the estate is subject to a lien or liens, but there is still equity value for the estate, then the trustee will auction off the property and pay the lienholders from the proceeds. Notably, in all situations, the trustee may deduct from the secured creditor's claim "the reasonable necessary cost and expenses of preserving, or disposing of, such property to the extent of any benefit to the holder of such claim." 11 U.S.C. § 506(c). This means that the trustee can recover off the top of the sale proceeds of any encumbered assets the costs of the sale and any reasonable expenses the trustee incurred in caring for the property, such as maintaining casualty insurance on it, performing maintenance, or storage.

III. DISTRIBUTION OF REMAINING ASSETS

At this point, with the estate holding no encumbered assets, the trustee proceeds to distribute the property of the estate in the order specified by section 726. Under section 726, the assets of the estate are distributed first to creditors on account of various unsecured claims given statutory priority, then to creditors on account of general unsecured claims, then to creditors on account of certain types of statutorily subordinated claims, and then finally to the holders of the debtor's equity if there is any value left over.

Within each level of distribution priority, payment is made pro rata according to the amount of a creditor's claim. 11 U.S.C. § 726(b). The pro rata distribution with each class required by section 726 is a fundamental feature of U.S. bankruptcy law, and encapsulates the idea that likes should be treated alike or that "equity is equality."

One way to think of the priority system is that it creates a giant champagne glass pyramid, with glasses stacked on top of other glasses. The champagne is poured into the glass at the top of the pyramid. Only once that glass has been entirely filled does champagne overflow and start to fill up the glasses in the next level. And only when the second level is filled up completely does any champagne flow down to the third level. If the champagne runs out before all of the glasses are filled, the glasses at the bottom of the pyramid will be empty.

So too for creditors. Each glass can be thought of as a claim with each level of the pyramid representing a different priority level. (Do *not* think of each glass as a creditor, as a creditor can have multiple claims at different priority levels.) The champagne represents the liquidated assets of the estate—money. The assets of the estate are distributed first to the claims with the seniormost priority on a pro rata basis among those claims, and only once those claims have been paid in full are the estate's remaining assets then paid to the next most senior priority of claims, again on a pro rata basis. Claims cease to be paid once the funds are exhausted.

While the section 726 framework is itself reasonably straightforward, it is not the entirety of the Bankruptcy Code's priority scheme. Instead, it interfaces with several other statutory provisions. Stitching these provisions together into a complete priority structure is not a simple task, and its application is also difficult. The following provides an overview of how the different relevant sections of the Bankruptcy Code interface into a complete priority system.

First, property is distributed to claims with priority under section 507. Section 507 itself has nine different levels of priority. A number of them (such as domestic support obligations or claims relating to wrongful death from drunk driving) are not applicable to business bankruptcies.

A. Compensation for Inadequate Protection

Among the section 507 priorities, the first is payment to any creditor that was awarded adequate protection that turned out to be inadequate. 11 U.S.C. § 507(b). These creditors have the highest priority claim on the general (unencumbered) assets of the estate. The logic behind this is that such a creditor was denied the right to have the stay lifted and foreclose based on a court-ordered assurance that its collateral's value would be protected. This high level of priority is an acknowledgment that the bankruptcy system has failed such a creditor. The section 507(b) priority is a consolation prize that ensures that a creditor whose protection was inadequate is paid immediately after the secured creditors receive their collateral or its value.

B. Administrative Expenses of the Estate

1. "Actual, Necessary Costs of Preserving the Estate"

For business bankruptcy cases, the next level of priority is for the administrative expenses of the bankruptcy estate authorized by section 503(b). 11 U.S.C. § 507(a)(2). The administrative expenses of the estate include the "actual, necessary costs and expenses of preserving the estate." 11 U.S.C. § 503(b)(1)(A). Such actual and necessary expenses include almost all of the costs of operating the debtor post-petition, including contracts with vendors. Post-petition taxes are separately included as administrative expenses. 11 U.S.C. § 503(b)(1)(B).

Section 503(b)(1) is generally read with judicial glosses: Administrative priority will not ordinarily be granted to pre-petition transactions, but instead only to post-petition transactions that were induced by the post-petition debtor; and administrative priority requires either benefit to the estate or cognizable harm to the creditor. As the court in the Chrysler bankruptcy explained:

> Considering inducement by the debtor-in- possession to be a crucial element comports with the policy reason for allowing the priority, which is to encourage third parties to supply the debtor-in-possession with goods and services with the goal of achieving a reorganization to benefit all creditors. Thus, benefit to the debtor-in-possession alone, without its having induced the performance, is not sufficient to warrant entitlement to an administrative claim priority, as it would contradict this policy reason for allowing the priority.

Where a debtor-in-possession elects to continue to receive benefits from the other party to an executory contract pending a decision to assume or reject the contract, the debtor-in-possession is obligated to pay for the reasonable value of those services. Therefore, the claims of third parties who are induced to supply goods or services to a debtor-in-possession pursuant to a contract that has not been rejected are afforded administrative priority to the extent that the consideration supporting the claim was supplied during the reorganization. The claimant has the burden of establishing entitlement to the priority.

See In re Old Carco LLC, 424 B.R. 633 (Bankr. S.D.N.Y. 2010).

Also included under section 503(b) as administrative expenses are the post-petition compensation of employees of the estate as well as the expenses of the trustee and official committees of creditors and equityholders under section 330. 11 U.S.C. § 503(b)(2). The trustee and official committees are authorized by section 327 to retain professionals on behalf of the estate—accountants, financial advisors, and lawyers. Section 330(a)(1)(A) entitles the trustee to compensation for the fees of these professionals, but their fees must be approved by the bankruptcy court under section 330(a)(3).

Professionals' fees are thus expenses of the trustee and are compensable as administrative priority expenses, paid ahead of other unsecured creditors. Professionals don't like to wait until the end of a case to get paid, however, and the Bankruptcy Code permits interim disbursements to professionals, with the payments deducted from their final distribution. 11 U.S.C. § 331. This puts professionals in an even better position than other post-petition claimants with administrative expense priority.

Why would these administrative expenses have priority? Without this priority, it would be impossible to reorganize. The debtor wouldn't be able to find counsel if it couldn't make a credible promise of payment for legal services. Indeed, no one would be willing to represent a bankrupt entity absent priority for the post-petition expenses of the bankruptcy estate. This is particularly important if the debtor is being reorganized, but also matters in liquidations, which do not happen instantaneously. A bankruptcy estate may need several months or even years of time to liquidate its assets, and during this time the bankruptcy estate may need to continue transacting some business in order to preserve the value of the estate. Priority repayment for administrative expenses helps the estate avoid having to operate solely on a cash-on-the-barrelhead basis.

2. Reclamation Claims

Also included in section 507(a)(2) priority are so-called reclamation claims under section 503(b)(9) for goods received by the debtor within 20 days before the petition date that were sold to the debtor in the ordinary course of the debtor's business. What goods does a debtor purchase in the ordinary course of business? Presumably, regular orders of raw materials and inventory would qualify, but is new office furniture ordinary course? It might be something the debtor does periodically, but not routinely. The Code provides no guidance.

Section 503(b)(9) is a relatively new priority, added in 2005 as part of the Bankruptcy Abuse Prevention and Consumer Protection Act (BAPCPA). In theory, section 503(b)(9) priority encourages suppliers to ship to purchasers in financial difficulty, thereby perhaps helping them avoid bankruptcy.

One man's priority, however, is another's disadvantage in a zero-sum game. To the extent that priority for reclamation claims encourages suppliers to ship goods, it discourages the provision on the eve of bankruptcy of other components of production: labor, capital, and goods that do not qualify for reclamation. Moreover, as we shall see in Chapter 33, these reclamation claims must be paid in full to confirm a plan of reorganization, necessitating significant amounts of cash on hand for retailers attempting to reorganize.

The priority of reclamation claims is distinct from any rights a creditor might have to actually reclaim specific goods. Under state law, creditors may assert a right to physically reclaim specific goods shipped to an insolvent buyer. UCC § 2-702. Section 546(c) provides that a creditor's reclamation rights to goods shipped within 45 days of bankruptcy are, in some circumstances, superior to that of the estate. 11 U.S.C. § 546(c). Given that the UCC right of reclamation is inferior to a security interest, however, if a secured creditor has a blanket lien on the debtor's assets, then the right of reclamation cannot be feasibly exercised, because while the reclamation rights are superior to the estate's, they are inferior to the secured creditor. *See, e.g., In re Circuit City Stores, Inc.,* 441 B.R. 496 (Bankr. E.D. Va. 2010).

3. Prioritization of Chapter 7 "Burial Expenses"

Sometimes Chapter 7 liquidations occur following a conversion from a Chapter 11 case. If an attempt to reorganize is unsuccessful, the debtor or creditors may have the case converted to Chapter 7. 11 U.S.C. § 1112. Within section 503(b) claims, those incurred in a Chapter 7 case are paid prior to any incurred in a Chapter 11 case. 11 U.S.C. § 726(b). Because this is a priority within a priority, we might call it a "super-priority."

Section 726(b) expenses are subordinate to section 507(b) claims based on inadequate protection. Those inadequate protection claims are thus a "super-super-priority." Why do you think the Chapter 7 expenses, sometimes called "burial costs," would be prioritized above the Chapter 11 expenses? What effect do you think this might have on the debtor's counsel's advice about whether to convert a case from Chapter 11 to Chapter 7?

C. Employee Wage and Benefit Plan Claims

After the administrative claimants come certain pre-petition employee and employee benefit plan claims. 11 U.S.C. § 507(a)(4)-(5). These claims are capped at a dollar amount ($12,850 as of April 1, 2016) that is periodically inflation adjusted and also capped temporally—they must be for obligations incurred within 180 days before bankruptcy.

Why do you think these limits exist? Are employees likely to work for half a year without pay? More than half a year? Wage and salary and employee benefit claims beyond the cap are general unsecured claims without priority. Note that section 507(a)(4) priority applies only to wages and salaries, that is, to the claims of employees. An independent contractor performing the same services does not have a priority claim under section 507(a)(4).

Also included in employee wage and benefit claims are preclaims under the federal Worker Adjustment and Retraining Notification (WARN) Act or state "baby" WARN Acts based on pre-petition employment termination. *See* 29 U.S.C. §§ 2101-2109. The WARN Act requires certain employers (basically, those with 100 or more employees) to give employees 60-days' notice about potential termination if there is a "plant closing" or "mass layoff." A "plant closing" is the closing of a work site that results in the termination of 50 or more employees, while a "mass layoff" involves either the layoff of 50 or more employees who make up at least a third of the workforce or 500 or more employees at a single site.

Failure of an employer to give WARN Act notifications can result in subsequently terminated employees having a claim for 60 days of back pay and benefits. Because WARN Act claims are considered "earned" upon termination, they can result in sections 507(a)(4) and 507(a)(5) priority for employees who were terminated during the 180-day period prior to bankruptcy, *even if all regular wages and salaries have been paid*. WARN Act claims are still subject to the statutory dollar caps of sections 507(a)(4)-(5). Moreover, if the termination occurs post-petition, the WARN Act claim would have administrative priority status under sections 503(b) and 507(a)(2). *Henderson v. Powermate Holding Corp. (In re Powermate Holding Corp.)*, 394 B.R. 765 (Bankr. D. Del. 2008).

The WARN Act is of particular concern to failing businesses, as they are the ones most likely to have layoffs. There are exceptions to the WARN Act for faltering businesses (when advance notice of layoffs would preclude attempts to obtain new capital), unforeseeable business circumstances, and natural disasters. All of these exceptions can play a role in bankruptcy cases, but the application of these exceptions is beyond the scope of this text. You should be aware that states have their own "baby" WARN Acts that can have longer notice deadlines or somewhat different scopes. Failure to give timely WARN Act notices can greatly increase the priority claims on a debtor, and a well-planned bankruptcy filing will take care to file only after WARN Act notices have been filed and the notice deadline has run. Of course, the nature of bankruptcy is that well-planned filings are not always possible. Ultimately, the interaction of the WARN Act and the Bankruptcy Code can create priority claims for certain workers at larger employers, while similarly situated workers at smaller employers—even corporate affiliates of the larger employers—may be left with only general unsecured claims, as the WARN Act applies only to the immediate employer, and not to its corporate group.

D. Consumer Deposit Claims

The Bankruptcy Code gives priority to the claims of individual consumers for deposit of money in connection with the purchase, lease, or rental of property or the purchase of services for themselves or their household or family, that were not in fact provided or delivered. 11 U.S.C. § 507(a)(7). The deposit priority is capped at $2,850 (inflation adjusted periodically) per consumer. Thus, if a consumer prepaid $1,000 for a mattress and the mattress was never shipped, the consumer would have a $1,000 priority claim in the mattress company's bankruptcy. If a business fails and leaves numerous prepaid consumer orders unfilled, deposit claims can mount up.

E. Tax Claims

Next in line are certain pre-petition tax claims. 11 U.S.C. § 507(a)(8). Recall that post-petition tax claims are an administrative expense of the estate with section 507(a)(2) priority. Pre-petition tax claims are another matter. The calculation of which tax claims receive priority is somewhat complicated. An important initial point, however, is that the priority does not depend on the type of governmental unit assessing the taxes. Federal taxes are treated the same as state and local taxes. Some types of taxes, such as withholding obligations, are all priority claims under section 507(a)(8)(C). Other types, however, are priority only if incurred in a certain time window. Tax penalties that are in compensation of actual pecuniary losses are given priority to the extent that the related taxes themselves have priority.

Income tax claims have priority for those pre-petition tax years in which the tax return was last due within three years before the date of the bankruptcy. 11 U.S.C. § 507(a)(8)(A). (Property tax claims have only a one-year lookback period. 11 U.S.C. § 507(a)(8)(B).) Assume that tax returns (that is tax filings) for a particular calendar year are generally due on April 15 of the following calendar year. Thus, the tax return for 2018 is generally due on April 15, 2019.

Suppose a debtor files for bankruptcy on March 1, 2019. Which years' tax returns were due between March 1, 2016 and March 1, 2019? Those from 2015, 2016, and 2017. The 2018 tax return is not due until April 15, 2019. Therefore, there is administrative priority given to the taxes due from income earned in 2015-2017, but not for 2018. The 2018 taxes are a general unsecured claim, while the debtor's 2019 taxes have administrative priority under section 507(a)(2) because they are an expense of the bankruptcy estate, rather than a pre-petition expense. If the debtor filed for bank-ruptcy on May 1, 2019, however, then the tax returns that were due between May 1, 2015 and May 1, 2019 are those from the years 2016, 2017, and 2018. Thus, although the statute says "three years," there are four possible years of tax liabilities that can receive priority status, depending on when the debtor files. Only three of the four will actually receive priority under section 507(a)(8), however. (Section 507(a)(2) priority for the fourth year remains available if the bankruptcy filing was before April 15.)

Two final twists here aren't apparent from the Bankruptcy Code. First, if the debtor filed for an automatic extension of the tax return due date in 2016, then the due date would be automatically extended by four months. IRS Form 4868. This would mean that the 2015 tax year filing would not be due until August 15, 2016. Accordingly, if the debtor filed between April 15, 2019 and August 15, 2019, then the 2015 tax year would also get priority treatment, rather than being an unsecured claim. But this would have required the extension to have been requested more than three years before the bankruptcy filings.

Additionally, a debtor may declare a truncated or short tax year. 26 U.S.C. § 1398(d)(2). For example, our May filing debtor could declare a truncated 2019 tax year ending on May 1 or our March filer could declare a truncated 2019 tax year ending on March 1. In either case, the taxes due for the truncated portion of 2019 would be entitled to priority. For our March filer, however, the 2018 tax year would still not receive priority. But if a tax extension request was filed in 2013 and the bankruptcy filing occurred in May 2019 with a truncated tax year, then tax years 2015-2019 would all be given section 507(a)(8) priority. So when the Bankruptcy Code says "three," it turns out to possibly mean as many as "five."

F. Late Claims and Punitive Claims

Next come general unsecured pre-petition claims that have been timely filed, then tardily filed pre-petition unsecured claims, and then pre-petition claims that are for fines or penalties or punitive damages that are not compensatory for actual pecuniary losses.[1] 11 U.S.C. §§ 726(a)(3)-(4). Query whether statutory damage claims, like WARN Act claims, are punitive, rather than compensatory. Note that while section 726(a)(3) allows, but subordinates late claims, it applies only in Chapter 7. In Chapter 11, late claims are disallowed under Federal Rule of Bankruptcy Procedure 3003(c)(2).

G. Interest and Surplus to Equity

If there is still money left in the estate, interest "at the legal rate" is paid on these claims and if there is anything left over, it goes back to the debtor, meaning to the owners of the debtor's equity interests. (In bankruptcy jargon, equityholders have "interests" not "claims.") Note that section 726(a)(5) provides a statutory right to interest that does not depend on the terms of the debtor's contracts. Even if a contract does not provide for interest or provides for interest at a different rate, section 726(a)(5) is a right created by bankruptcy law over and above any contractual or statutory rights.

H. Super-Super-Super-Priority Under Section 364(c)(1)

Section 726, however, does not contain quite the entire priority scheme. In addition to secured creditors, addressed by section 725, another provision of the

---

1. Note that this statutory subordination applies only in Chapter 7. It does not apply to Chapter 11 except in terms of the calculation of the section 1129(a)(7) "best interest" test.

Bankruptcy Code, section 364(c)(1), authorizes the court to authorize the debtor to obtain new credit with priority above all administrative expenses in sections 507(b) and 503(b)(1). This section 364(c)(1) is a "super-super-super-priority" that comes ahead of the section 507(b) "super-super-priority" and the 507(a)(2) "super-priority." Creditors that are not subject to the stay, such as certain financial contract counterparties have, in many ways, the highest priority of all (super-duper-priority?), because they do not have to work within the bankruptcy distribution system due to their exemption from the automatic stay.

I. Subordination Agreements

The Bankruptcy Code's liquidation priority scheme is overlaid on top of non-bankruptcy law priorities. Secured status is determined, in the first instance, based on applicable non-bankruptcy law. (As we will see, bankruptcy law can, in some circumstances, change a creditor's secured status.) Similarly, bankruptcy law honors contractual subordination agreements to the extent they are enforceable under applicable nonbankruptcy law. 11 U.S.C. § 510(a).

Thus, imagine that there are three general unsecured creditors, Creditors *A*, *B*, and *C*, each owed $2 million by the debtor. Creditor *C* has agreed to be subordinated to Creditor *B*. Suppose that there is $3 million available for distribution to the general unsecured creditors. How would it be distributed? Absent the subordination agreement, the three creditors should each receive $1 million. With the subordination agreement, however, Creditor *A* should still receive $1 million, while Creditor *B* should receive $2 million, and Creditor *C* should receive nothing. If there were, instead, $4 million available for distribution to the general unsecured creditors, then Creditor *A* should receive $1.33 million, Creditor *B* should receive $2 million, and Creditor *C* should receive $0.67 million.

Note that if Creditor *C* agreed to be subordinated to Creditor *B* for payment priority, but not liquidation priority, that is all that would be honored in bankruptcy. The Rule of Explicitness (see Chapter 3) would apply to the subordination in bankruptcy just as it would at state law. Section 510(a) does not change non-bankruptcy priorities, but takes them as they are.

J. Priority Summary

Putting this all together is tricky, and applying it is even trickier. Thus, we can summarize the Chapter 7 priority scheme as follows:

1. Creditors not subject to the automatic stay can (but need not) seize their collateral. 11 U.S.C. § 362(b).
2. Secured creditors recover from their collateral. 11 U.S.C. § 725.
3. Post-petition financing with court-approved super-super-super-priority. 11 U.S.C. § 364(c)(1).
4. Inadequately protected creditors' super-super-priority. 11 U.S.C. §§ 726(a)(1), 507(b).

5. Administrative priority claims in Chapter 7 (super-priority). 11 U.S.C. §§ 726(a)(1), 726(b), 507(a)(2).
6. Administrative priority claims in Chapter 11. 11 U.S.C. §§ 726(a)(1), 726(b), 507(a)(2).
7. Employee wage claims and WARN Act wage claims up to cap. 11 U.S.C. §§ 726(a)(1), 507(a)(4). As of April 1, 2016, the cap was $12,850 per claim.
8. Employee benefit plan claims and WARN Act benefit claims up to cap. 11 U.S.C. §§ 726(a)(1), 507(a)(5). As of April 1, 2016, the cap was $12,850 per claim.
9. Consumer deposit claims, up to $2,850 per individual. 11 U.S.C. § 507(a)(7).
10. Tax claims entitled to priority, including penalties levied in compensation of pecuniary losses. 11 U.S.C. §§ 726(a)(1), 507(a)(8).
11. Timely general unsecured claims. 11 U.S.C. § 726(a)(2).
12. Tardily filed general unsecured claims. 11 U.S.C. § 726(a)(3).
13. Noncompensatory punitive claims. 11 U.S.C. § 726(a)(4).
14. Post-petition interest on claims numbered 5-12 above (unsecured claims) at the "legal rate" of interest. 11 U.S.C. § 726(a)(5).
15. Preferred Equity, to the extent of its liquidation preference. 11 U.S.C. §§ 510(a), 726(a)(6).
16. Common Equity. 11 U.S.C. § 726(a)(6).

IV. THE END OF A CHAPTER 7 BANKRUPTCY

A Chapter 7 bankruptcy continues until all of the property of the estate has been fully administered. 11 U.S.C. § 350. This requires the trustee to have made a final distribution of all of the estate's assets. At that point, the bankruptcy estate ceases to exist, but the debtor still exists as a corporate entity, albeit one with no or virtually no assets. Because business debtors do not have exempt assets, at the end of a Chapter 7 a business debtor should not have any remaining assets beyond those of de minimis value that the trustee abandoned to the debtor as burdensome. Absent unusual circumstances, these assets will be useless to the debtor. For example, a fully encumbered property might be abandoned to the debtor, but the debtor will only be able to retain the property until the creditor forecloses on it.

As a corporate entity, the debtor continues to exist after Chapter 7, but there is little reason to continue using the same corporate entity after a Chapter 7 for future business ventures. Unlike a consumer debtor, a Chapter 7 business debtor does not receive a "discharge" enjoining attempts to collect its unpaid debts. 11 U.S.C. § 727(a). Those debts still exist and are collectible, should the debtor somehow acquire assets in the future. (Chapter 11 is a different matter.) Therefore, Chapter 7 is typically followed by a corporate dissolution under state law. So while Chapter 7 disposes of a firm's assets, the final death blow to the firm is administered through a state law corporate dissolution process.

Problem Set 28

(1) Demeter Agricultural Supply is in Chapter 7 bankruptcy. Demeter has assets of $10 million and five general unsecured creditors, each owed $3 million. What is the dividend paid out to each creditor? 11 U.S.C. § 726(b).

(2) Vulcan Metallurgy is in Chapter 7. Vulcan has assets of $10 million and five general unsecured creditors. One creditor is owed $10 million, another $9 million, another $8 million, another $7 million, and another $6 million. What is the dividend paid out to each creditor? 11 U.S.C. § 726(b).

(3) Ares Ballistics is in Chapter 7. Ares has assets of $54 million including a $10 million headquarters building subject to a $4 million mortgage from Jupiter Bancorp. Ares also has general unsecured creditors owed $100 million, including Hermes Supply Co., which is owed $6 million.

    a. What is the distribution to Jupiter?

    b. What is the distribution to Hermes?

11 U.S.C. §§ 502, 506, 725, 726(b).

(4) Poseidon Canneries is in Chapter 7. Poseidon has assets of $44 million, including a $4 million headquarters building subject to a $14 million recourse mortgage held by the Hades Special Situation Fund II. Poseidon also has other general unsecured creditors owed $110 million, including Hermes Supply Co., which is owed $6 million.

    a. What is the distribution to Hades?

    b. What is the distribution to Hermes?

11 U.S.C. §§ 502, 506, 725, 726(b).

(5) Hestia Gas Fireplaces is in Chapter 7. Hestia has total assets of $58 million, including a $10 million factory building subject to a $6 million recourse first mortgage held by the Hades Special Situation Fund II, a $3 million recourse second mortgage held by Jupiter Bancorp, a $11 million recourse third mortgage held by Juno Capital Partners, and a $3 million fourth mortgage held by Cronos Capital. Gaia Advantage Funds additionally holds a $10 million lien on Hestia's inventory, which is worth $8 million. Hestia also has other general unsecured creditors owed $99 million, including Hermes Supply Co., which is owed $6 million.

    a. What is the distribution to Hades?

    b. What is the distribution to Jupiter?

    c. What is the distribution to Juno?

    d. What is the distribution to Cronos?

    e. What is the distribution to Gaia?

    f. What is the distribution to Hermes?

11 U.S.C. §§ 330(a), 502, 503(b)(1)(A)(i), 503(b)(2), 506, 507(a)(2), 725, 726(b).

(6) Bacchus Wineries is in Chapter 7. Bacchus has total assets of $20 million, including a $12 million vineyard, subject to a $15 million mortgage held by Juno Capital

Partners. Bacchus owes $1 million in post-petition attorneys' fees and $2 million to various post-petition vendors. Bacchus also owes $7 million to unsecured noteholders.

    a. What is the distribution to Juno Capital Partners?

    b. What is the distribution to the attorneys?

    c. What is the distribution to the post-petition vendors?

    d. What is the distribution to the general unsecured creditors?

    e. Suppose that Bacchus also had an additional $10 million in notes. What would be the effect on the distribution?

    f. Suppose that those $10 million in additional notes in part (e) were contractually subordinated to the other $7 million in unsecured notes. What is the effect on the distribution?

    g. How would the answer to (f) change if Bacchus's total assets were $30 million?

11 U.S.C. §§ 330(a), 502, 503(b)(1)(A)(i), 503(b)(2), 506, 507(a)(2), 510(a), 725, 726(b).

    (7) Apollo Records is in Chapter 7. Apollo has assets of $87 million, including a $9 million headquarters building, which is subject to a $12 million first lien recourse mortgage held by Delphic Bank. Apollo has various unsecured pre-petition claims of $324, including $2 million in pre-petition legal fees and $4 million in pre-petition property tax liabilities (half for the year before bankruptcy, half for the year prior to that). Additionally, while in Chapter 7, Apollo's attorneys and financial advisers billed $6 million. Apollo has also incurred post-petition income and property taxes of $5 million.

    a. What is the order in which the different claims will be paid?

    b. What is the distribution to Delphic Bank?

    c. What is the distribution to the tax authorities?

    d. What is the distribution to the attorneys?

    e. What is the distribution to general unsecured creditors?

    f. Suppose that Apollo's total assets were only $14.5 million, including the $9 million headquarters building. What would change in the distribution?

11 U.S.C. §§ 330(a), 502, 503(b)(1)(B), 503(b)(2), 506, 507(a)(2), 507(a)(8), 725, 726(b).

    (8) Washington & Custis Tobacco Corp. is in Chapter 11. Among the proofs of claim is one filed by Artemus Ward. Ward has filed a $30 million proof of claim based on a pre-petition tort judgment he won. The judgment is still on appeal. The tort judgment is $5 million in actual damages and $25 million in punitive damages. Ward's home state limits punitive damages to twice actual damages. What is Ward's allowed claim? (Hint: You answered this in problem 3 in Problem Set 26.) What is its priority? 11 U.S.C. §§ 502(a), 726(a)(4).

    (9) Professor Livingstone has entered into a retainer agreement with Dewey, DeWitt & Wright LLP to provide consulting expertise to their financial services practice at a rate of $30,000 per quarter, paid on net-30 terms. Either party was entitled to terminate the agreement at the end of the following quarter upon 30 days' notice. In mid-April, Dewey, DeWitt filed for bankruptcy. At the time of filing, it was current on the consulting contract. Dewey, DeWitt did not reject the contract with Professor Livingstone until mid-September. (Assume that rejection gives rise to a general unsecured claim for resulting damages.) At no point during the year did Professor Livingstone actually provide services to Dewey, DeWitt. What is Professor Livingstone's allowed claim against Dewey, DeWitt? 11 U.S.C. § 503(b)(1)(A); *In re Old Carco LLC.*

RESHAPING
THE BANKRUPTCY
ESTATE

CHAPTER 29

THE STRONG-ARM POWER AND STATUTORY LIENS

I. AVOIDANCE POWERS

The Bankruptcy Code includes a number of "avoidance powers" that allow the trustee/DIP to void pre-petition transfers. The statutory powers are the "strong arm" power (sections 544(a)), avoidance of certain statutory liens (section 545), avoidance of preferences (section 547), avoidance of certain setoff rights (section 553), and avoidance of fraudulent transfers (sections 544(b) and 548). These statutory provisions all interface with the common remedies and limitations sections (sections 546, 550, and 551).

This chapter addresses the strong-arm power and avoidance of certain statutory liens. The following two chapters take up voidable preferences, setoff limitations, and fraudulent transfers. The chapter thereafter addresses a number of equitable remedies available in bankruptcy that can function like avoidance powers.

The avoidance powers and equitable remedies (excluding voidable preferences) all have state law analogs: The strong-arm power explicitly incorporates state law, and fraudulent transfer law, equitable subordination, equitable disallowance, and recharacterization exist at state law as well as in the Bankruptcy Code. The avoidance powers are also one of the most ancient parts of bankruptcy law. These provisions emerged because of concerns about debtors hiding assets from creditors in connivance with friends and friendly creditors. The avoidance powers help ensure that the entirety of the debtor's assets are available for distribution to creditors and to ensure a basic level of fairness in the distribution process.

The avoidance actions maximize the size of the pie to be distributed to general unsecured creditors. The avoidance powers do not determine how the distribution works; the financial reorganization mechanics of Chapter 11 could be accomplished without the existence of the avoidance powers. Functionally, however, the avoidance powers give trustees/debtors significant leverage in dealing with certain creditors—the threat of an avoidance action may induce compromise, and the entire Chapter 11 process is, in part, one giant exercise in settlement.

Keep in mind that avoidance powers are not self-executing provisions. A pre-petition transfer or a creditor's priority stands as valid unless challenged. That is, unperfected liens, fraudulent transfers, and preferences are all voidable, not void.

II. THE STRONG-ARM POWER

The so-called strong-arm power lets the trustee/DIP avoid unperfected liens. Section 544(a) allows the trustee/DIP to avoid any transfer of the debtor's property that would not have priority at the time of the commencement of the case over the rights of three hypothetical actors: a judgment lien creditor, an unsatisfied execution creditor, and a bona fide purchaser of real estate. There is no requirement that any of these actual creditors exist.

Of these three hypothetical actors, the first is by far the most important because it gives the trustee priority over unperfected liens. An unperfected lien is enforceable at state law by the secured creditor against the debtor, but it is not enforceable against third-parties. If it were, then the entire system of secured credit would collapse, as no party could be sure of its priority when lending, and therefore no lender could price for its risk. But this only suggests that such unperfected liens be avoidable in bankruptcy if there was detrimental reliance by actual creditors.

Under UCC § 9-317(a)(2), a judgment lien has priority over an unperfected security interest. *See also* 28 U.S.C. § 3201(b) (federal government judgment lien priority for real property over "later perfected" liens); 28 U.S.C. § 3203(b) (federal government execution lien priority over "subsequent" liens). A lien (whether or not voluntary) is a transfer of the property of the estate—it is a contingent future interest in the property, 11 U.S.C. § 101(54). Therefore, the status of a hypothetical judicial lien creditor means that the trustee can generally avoid liens that are not perfected as of the filing of the bankruptcy. Accordingly, the trustee/DIP will generally examine all security interests in the debtor's property in order to determine if any may be avoided.

The other two hypothetical actors give the trustee more limited powers. In some states, an unsatisfied execution creates a legal presumption of insolvency and enables the trustee to pursue certain equitable remedies, such as marshaling, because of the presumption that legal remedies have been exhausted with the unsatisfied execution. The ability to invoke the status of a bona fide purchaser of real property enables the trustee to avoid unrecorded land transfers, as well as certain unperfected construction liens.

Why would the Bankruptcy Code give the trustee the power of various hypothetical creditors? The answer would appear to reflect concerns about detrimental reliance, administratibility, and fraud.

Liens are generally perfected either by a public filing or by possession. Either method of perfection provides constructive notice to third-parties of the possible existence of a lien, alerting them of the need for inquiry before extending credit. The affected parties are not only subsequent secured creditors, but also unsecured creditors that extended credit on the assumption that no lien existed. Obviously, a lien could be created subsequently—although it might violate various loan covenants.

Giving the trustee hypothetical powers makes the strong-arm power more administrable by dispensing with the need to inquire about the actual reliance of every creditor, no matter how small. Finally, without the strong-arm power, there would be a great temptation for debtors and friendly (insider) creditors to engage in fraud through the use of back-dated security interests. The requirement of perfection makes it harder to claim a back-dated security interest, as there will have to be evidence of the financing statement or possession pre-petition. (The security agreement itself could still be backdated, but that's a narrower problem.)

An important exception to the strong-arm judicial lien creditor power exists for purchase money security interests—security interests that secure the financing for the purchase of collateral. Section 546(b) subjects the trustee's avoiding powers to any generally applicable law that permits relation back of the date of perfection of a security interest. Such generally applicable law is UCC Article 9. Under Article 9, a purchase money security interest (PMSI) that is perfected within 20 days of the borrower receiving delivery of the collateral gets priority relating back to the time of attachment. UCC § 9-317(e). Therefore, if a PMSI is perfected post-petition, and the perfection occurred within 20 days of the delivery of the collateral to the borrower (which may be subsequent to the time of attachment), the trustee may not avoid the lien under section 544(a)(1). Post-petition perfection is possible because the automatic stay contains an exception allowing for perfection within 30-days after the debtor acquires rights in the collateral. 11 U.S.C. §§ 362(b)(3), 547(e)(2)-(3).[1] Section 546(b), thus protects many, but not all, PMSIs that are not perfected as of the filing date from the strong arm power.

The strong-arm power can be brutal because of the unforgiving nature of the UCC's perfection rules. In the General Motors bankruptcy, a syndicate led by JPMorgan Chase Bank lost the lien securing a $1.5 billion loan under section 544 because of an innocent filing mistake. A UCC filing terminating an unrelated set of synthetic leases accidentally included the UCC recording number for the lien securing the loan. The result was that JPMorgan's syndicate was unperfected and the lien was therefore avoidable. *Official Comm. of Unsecured Creditors of Motors Liquidation Co. v. JP Morgan Chase Bank, N.A. (In re Motors Liquidation Co.)*, 777 F.3d 100 (2d Cir. 2015). The following case illustrates just how important it is to properly dot one's i's and cross one's t's in UCC filings.

---

1. Note that whereas the 20 days of UCC § 9-317(e) run from delivery of the collateral to the debtor, the 30 days for the automatic stay run from the time the debtor has acquired rights in the property, which would presumably be at the date of purchase. Thus, if delivery is slow, the 30-day window could elapse so that the transferee could not benefit from the 20-day relation back because of the automatic stay.

Official Committee of Unsecured Creditors for Tyringham Holdings, Inc. v. Suna Brothers, Inc.

354 B.R. 363 (Bankr. E.D. Va. 2006)

DOUGLAS O. TICE, JR., U.S. Bankr. J.

Trial was held on November 13, 2006, on plaintiff's complaint to determine the validity, priority, or extent of a lien under a consignment held by defendant Suna Bros. Inc. The issue is whether Suna's financing statement was seriously misleading because it was not filed under the correct name of the debtor. For the reasons set forth below, the court finds that the financing statement is seriously misleading. Therefore, the defendant's lien is unperfected, and plaintiff may sell the collateral free and clear of any lien or interest of Suna.

FINDINGS OF FACT

Pursuant to a consignment agreement dated October 18, 2004, debtor Tyringham Holdings, Inc., held a number of pieces of jewelry inventory consigned to it by Suna. Suna held a security interest in the consigned inventory and attempted to perfect the security interest by filing a financing statement with the Virginia State Corporation Commission on June 10, 2005. The financing statement covered 65 pieces of jewelry totaling $310,925.00 worth of consigned inventory.

The financing statement was filed by Suna on June 10, 2005, and listed the debtor's name as "Tyringham Holdings." The debtor is a Virginia Corporation and is listed as "Tyringham Holdings, Inc." on the public records of the Virginia State Corporation Commission.

An official UCC search certified by the State Corporation Commission revealed a search conducted under the name "Tyringham Holdings, Inc.," which did not reveal the Suna financing statement.

DISCUSSION AND CONCLUSIONS OF LAW

Where a filed financing statement is required to perfect a security interest, it must substantially satisfy the requirements of a financing statement. Generally, the name of a corporate debtor, as indicated on the public record of the debtor's jurisdiction of organization, must be listed on the financing statement for it to be valid. VA. CODE ANN. § 8.9A-503(a)(1) (2006) [the Virginia version of the Uniform Commercial Code Article 9]. Where the requirements are substantially satisfied, a financing statement "is effective, even if it has minor errors or omissions, unless the errors or omissions make the financing statement seriously misleading." VA. CODE ANN. § 8.9A-506(a). By law, "[e]xcept as otherwise provided in subsection (c), a financing statement that fails sufficiently to provide the name of the debtor in accordance with § 8.9A-503(a) is seriously misleading." VA. CODE ANN. § 8.9A-506(b). There is no question in this case that the name of the debtor in the Suna financing statement, "Tyringham Holdings," was not the same corporate name as that on the public record for the state of Virginia, "Tyringham Holdings, Inc." Therefore, unless excepted by VA. CODE ANN. § 8.9A-506(c), the financing statement is seriously misleading and is ineffective to perfect Suna's security interest.

. . . Subsection (c) . . . provides a more concrete rule for determining if errors are seriously misleading, providing that:

> If a search of the *records of the filing office* under the *debtor's correct name*, using the *filing office's standard search logic*, if any, would disclose a financing statement that fails sufficiently to provide the name of the debtor in accordance with § 8.9A-503(a), the name provided does not make the financing statement seriously misleading.

VA. CODE ANN. § 8.9A-506(c) (emphasis added).

According to the statute, the appropriate standard by which to judge a search is the filing office's standard search logic for a search under the debtor's correct name, in the filing office's database. *See, e.g.,* VA. CODE ANN. § 8.9A-506 Official Comment 2 (stating that "a financing statement that is seriously misleading under this section is ineffective even if it is disclosed by (i) using a search logic other than that of the filing office to search the official records, or (ii) using the filing office's standard search logic to search a data base other than that of the filing office"). . . . [T]he filing office's standard search logic governs.

In the time period between filing of the financing statement and the trial in this Adversary Proceeding, a number of UCC searches were performed by private search companies such as Corporation Service Company, Access Information Services, Inc., and UCC Retrievals, Inc. Each of these searches disclosed the existence of the Suna financing statement. No evidence was presented as to the underlying methodology behind the Corporation Service Company or Access Information Services, Inc., searches. At trial, a witness for Suna testified that she had conducted the search by UCC Retrievals, Inc., under the name "Tyringham Holdings." Her search disclosed the existence of the Suna financing statement. Her rationale for searching under the name "Tyringham Holdings" rather than the correct "Tyringham Holdings, Inc.," was that she considered the term "Inc." to be a "noise word." Noise words for these purposes are words that are removed or ignored in the process of performing an electronic database search for financing statements. The witness classified "Inc." as a noise word because it is one of such words on a list promulgated by the International Association of Corporation Administrators (IACA). Other abbreviations on the IACA "noise word" list include "Corporation," "Corp," "Company," "Co," "Limited," and "Ltd."

Suna repeatedly emphasizes that these private searches used "standard search logic" to disclose the Suna financing statement. Suna would have this court read out the portion of the statute that specifies whose "standard search logic" is employed in the analysis. The relevant standard is clearly no longer the diligent searcher's standard search logic nor a private search organization's standard search logic, but it is instead the filing office's standard search logic.

The Virginia State Corporation Commission has promulgated filing rules in 5 VA. ADMIN. CODE 5-30-70(E) (2006) that describe the standard search logic employed by the commission when conducting a search. Search results are produced by the application of standardized search logic to the name presented to the filing officer, along with several additional requirements, including the following subsection 4:

> "Noise words" include, but are not limited to, "an," "and," "for," "of," and "the." The word "the" always will be disregarded and other noise words appearing anywhere except at the beginning of an organization name will be disregarded. Certain business words are modified to a standard abbreviation: company to "co," corporation to "corp," limited to "ltd," incorporated to "inc."

5 VA. ADMIN. CODE 5-30-70(E)(4). The State Corporation Commission has not adopted the full list of noise words promulgated by the IACA.

Plaintiff called as a witness an employee of the Virginia State Corporation Commission, who described the coding of the UCC search program utilized by the Corporation Commission in its official UCC searches. As explained by the witness, the search logic modifies a given entry by removing certain items from the name entered by a searcher, including punctuation, spaces, and the five noise words listed in the State Corporation Commission Rules. This creates a search key[,] which is then matched to names on filed financing statements, which have likewise been modified in accordance with the same standards.

No evidence was presented to show that the private searches were conducted in accordance with the *Virginia State Corporation Commission's* standard search logic on the *debtor's correct name*. The only private search supported by additional evidence at trial was the one conducted by UCC Retrievals, Inc. This search was conducted using the State Corporation Commission's website, but only after the witness truncated the name, "Tyringham Holdings, Inc." to "Tyringham Holdings," based solely on her own belief that "Inc." was a noise word in the state of Virginia. The searcher entered "Tyringham Holdings" into the search field and retrieved the Suna financing statement. No evidence was presented that the searcher ever entered "Tyringham Holdings, Inc.," into the search field and recovered the Suna financing statement.

Suna attempts to argue that the State Corporation Commission's search logic is faulty because it does not filter out "Inc." as a noise word, even though the IACA considers it as such. According to Plaintiff's witness, the State Corporation Commission is in the process of revising its list of noise words and changing the search logic to include terms such as "inc." However, the standard in place at all times relevant to this case did not include "Inc." as a noise word; at present, the underlying search engine code filters out only five articles as noise words. Suna makes much of the fact that noise words in the filing rules contained at 5 VA. ADMIN. CODE 5-30-70(E)(4) "include, but are not limited to" the five articles filtered out by the search engine. Suna essentially argues that the search engine improperly employs the search methodology prescribed by the statute, because it in fact filters out only the five articles and thus is "limited to" those words only. Regardless of whether this argument makes logical sense, the court cannot conclude on the basis of the statutory language that "Inc." should be considered a noise word. The third sentence of subsection 4 says that "Certain business words are modified to a standard abbreviation . . . ," the last of which is "incorporated" to "inc." 5 VA. ADMIN. CODE 5-30-70(E)(4). If "inc" is a standard abbreviation, it cannot simultaneously be a disregarded noise word according to the State Corporation Commission's standard search logic as embodied by this statute and the search engine code utilizing it. As a result, it is clear that "Inc." is not a noise word for purposes of a Virginia UCC search, and the State Corporation Commission's search logic is functioning as it was presently intended to function in this respect.

. . .

While application of the filing office's standard search logic may lead to situations where it appears that a relatively minor error in a financing statement leads to a security interest becoming unperfected, it is not that difficult to ensure that a financing statement is filed with the correct name of the debtor. Little more is asked of a creditor than to accurately record the debtor's name, and according to the statute, failure to perform this action clearly dooms the perfected status of a security interest.

The official search certified by the State Corporation Commission, under the correct name, "Tyringham Holdings, Inc.," fails to disclose the Suna financing statement. Thus, the only search which used the correct name under the standard search logic actually employed by the State Corporation Commission did not disclose the Suna financing statement. As a result, the court must conclude that the financing statement is seriously misleading and is insufficient to perfect Suna's security interest in the collateral. Therefore, Suna's security interest in the collateral is unperfected and the collateral may be sold free and clear of any lien held by Suna.

Accordingly, IT IS ORDERED that judgment is entered for plaintiff and the defendant's lien claim is denied.

Virginia has subsequently changed its UCC search logic, so the particular problem in *Tyringham* could not occur again, but the principle remains the same: If a lien would not be found using a proper UCC search, it will be avoidable by the trustee or DIP under the strong-arm power. Simple typos can be very costly.

III. STATUTORY LIENS

Some liens are created automatically by statute. Section 545 permits the trustee/DIP to avoid certain statutory liens triggered by insolvency (*ipso facto* clause triggers), that are not perfected as against a bona fide purchaser of the property at the time of the bankruptcy filing, or that are for rent or for distress for rent (*e.g.*, a landlord's lien on the debtor's property on the rented premises).

Section 545's lien avoidance powers are in addition to section 544 and allows avoidance of certain liens that would not be avoidable under section 544, such as certain liens that are automatically perfected and therefore would not be defeated by a subsequent judgment lien creditor, unsatisfied execution creditor, or bona fide purchaser of real estate.

One particular type of statutory lien, a warehousemen's lien (under UCC § 7-209) for the costs of storage or transportation, cannot be avoided under section 545 unless the lien is the result of an *ipso facto* clause. 11 U.S.C. § 546(i). UCC § 7-209 grants warehousemen a perfected, possessory lien on "all goods covered by a warehouse receipt or storage agreement or on the proceeds thereof in its possession for charges for storage or transportation, including demurrage and terminal charges, insurance, labor, or other charges, present or future, in relation to the goods, and for expenses necessary for preservation of the goods or reasonably incurred in their sale pursuant to law." UCC § 7-209(a). The lien lapses, however, with lapse of possession. UCC § 7-209(e). In other words, warehousemen have a perfected, possessory statutory lien on property in their possession irrespective of any *ipso facto* clause. Thus, warehousemen's UCC Article 7 lien is never avoidable under section 545 (other statutory liens created for warehousemen might be). Because avoided liens are preserved for the benefit of the estate, however, if the trustee avoids another lien on the same assets that has priority over the warehousemen's lien, the estate's claim will have priority over the warehousemen's.

What is the basis for the distinct treatment of warehousemen? Section 546(i) is one of several special interest provisions added to the Code by the 2005 Bankruptcy Abuse Prevention and Consumer Protection Act. Because of the carve-out for warehousemen's liens, first-day orders will often include a warehousemen's order allowing for payment of warehousemen.

IV. PRESERVATION OF AVOIDED LIENS: THE SWORD OF GRYFFINDOR

When the trustee successfully exercises its avoidance powers under sections 544, 545 (or under sections 547, 548, and 549, which are covered in the following chapters), the transfer is avoided, meaning that it is not effective between the debtor and the transferee, but the transfer is preserved for the estate under section 551. This means that the estate picks up all of the rights of transferee vis-à-vis other creditors. You might think of this as the bankruptcy equivalent to Harry Potter's magical Sword of Gryffindor, which picks up the powers of those things it defeats.

This provision is especially important in regard to lien avoidance. Avoidance of a lien does not avoid the underlying debt, only the lien. The debt remains owed, and its validity is not affected by lien avoidance. Without the lien, however, the debt becomes just general unsecured debt. Avoidance of the security interest does not destroy the security interest. Instead, it is automatically transferred to the bankruptcy estate under section 551. This means that the bankruptcy estate is subrogated to (stands in the shoes of) the transferee *as if the transfer had not been avoided*. In other words, the bankruptcy estate picks up the powers of the transferee. The estate does *not* pick up the debt, only the lien or other property transferred.

Section 551's preservation of avoided liens and transfers can be a powerful tool. If the transferred asset is monetizable, it is an asset that is then available for distribution to creditors. And if the transferred asset is a lien (the granting of a lien is a transfer), the bankruptcy estate becomes the lienor (on itself). If there were legitimate junior liens on a property on which the senior lien was avoided, they do not become senior by virtue of the avoidance of the senior lien.

Consider situation in which there are two mortgages on Blackacre. The first mortgage is for $1.4 million. The second mortgage is for $1 million. Blackacre is worth only $2.0 million. If the first mortgage is avoided by the DIP or trustee, what happens to the second mortgage? Does the last become first? No. The second mortgage remains the second mortgage. The avoided first mortgage is now property of the estate. What this means is that the estate gets the first $1.4 million worth of Blackacre, to distribute to the unsecured creditors (including the former first mortgagee) and potentially to equityholders, while the second mortgagee remains undersecured and will recover on $0.6 million from Blackacre. Thus, if the avoided transfer were not preserved for the benefit of the estate, the estate would have lost $0.4 million, as the second mortgagee would have become first and received $1.0 million from the sale of Blackacre, with the remaining $1.0 million going to the estate.

The preservation of transfers for the estate also lets the estate pick up any non-debtor warranties or guaranties and other rights. It can also help resolve a circularity of lien priority problem, such as that described in Chapter 2. Thus, imagine that lien A has priority over lien B, lien B over lien C, but lien C over lien A. Algebraically, this is $A>B$, $B>C$, and $C>A$. Now let's imagine that the trustee can avoid lien C because it is unperfected. As a result of section 551, lien C becomes property of the estate (C_T). This means that not only does the estate beat lienholder C, but the estate also beats lienholder A. Because $C>A$, so too is $C_T>A$. And because $A>B$, the trustee beats lienholder B. We end up with $C_T>A>B$. The trustee will only beat lienholder B, however, to the extent of the debts owed to C and A.

V. AVOIDANCE ACTION LIABILITY

The avoidance of a transfer avoids the transfer, but what does that actually mean? For a lien, the avoidance of a transfer is the end of the story: The creditor no longer has the lien, which is instead preserved for the benefit of the estate under section 551. But for other transfers, such as a setoff or unrecorded sale of real property or a voidable preference (which we will encounter in the next chapter), liability is more complex.

Section 550 of the Bankruptcy Code details the liability of transferees of avoided transfers other than statutory liens. There are two basic categories of transferees: initial and subsequent transferees (both immediate and mediate). Sections 550(a) and 550(d) provide for joint liability for initial transferees and subsequent transferees. The trustee or DIP can recover from either the initial or a subsequent transferee, but is limited to a single recovery. Liability under section 550 means that the transferee must either return the property transferred or its value (such as in a case where the transferee no longer possesses the transferred property).

Section 550(b) provides a limitation on liability only for certain subsequent transferees; the initial transferee is *always* liable under section 550. Section 550(b) provides that there is no liability under section 550(a) for subsequent transferees that take in good faith, for value, without knowledge of the voidability of the transfer. It also provides that the subsequent transferees of the first subsequent transferee are not liable as long as they took in good faith (i.e., there is no "for value" requirement).

Section 550(e) provides an additional protection for *all* good faith transferees, both initial and subsequent: Any good faith transferee is granted a lien on the recovered property to the extent that it improved the transferred property, including paying taxes on the property or paying off any senior liens on the property. The lien does *not* cover whatever value the transferee paid to acquire the property.

Finally, it is important to recognize that an action to avoid a transfer under sections 544, 547, 548, 549, or 553(b) is technically separate from an action to recover the avoided transfer under section 550. Section 550(f) creates a statute of limitations of one year from the avoidance ruling or the closing/dismissal of the case. This statute of limitations is on top of the two-year statute of limitations for avoidance actions themselves under section 546(a).

Avoidance of a transfer does not mean that the transferee gets nothing. Section 502(h) provides that if a transfer is avoided, the transferee has a claim for the liability, which is deemed to have arisen immediately before the bankruptcy filing.

Problem Set 29

(1) You just read in the newspaper that the Klimmek Corporation filed for bankruptcy. Two years ago you documented a $2 billion secured loan made to Klimmek. Anticipating that you might be asked to file a proof of claim in the bankruptcy, you ask your paralegal for the Klimmek file. As you open the file you see that it contains the executed security agreement and all of the associated paperwork necessary for filing with the secretary of state. Puzzled, you ask the paralegal, "You filed this security agreement, right?" He says, "Sure. Remember, you told me to 'take care of filing the security interest,' so I put it in the file cabinet under 'Klimmek.'" What do you do next? 11 U.S.C. § 544(a).

(2) A year ago you handled a large syndicated loan to Wheeling-Pittsburgh Steel Company, which just filed for bankruptcy. You were careful to make sure that the UCC-1 form was properly filed with the recording office, thereby perfecting the security interest. The syndicate's agent bank has asked you to double check that the security interest is perfected. You run a UCC debtor search and to your surprise the security interest does not show up. You pull up the copy of the UCC-1 from your files, complete with the recording office's time stamp indicating that it was filed. You notice that on the UCC-1 the debtor's name is listed as "Wheeling-Pittsburg Steel Co." What are you going to say to the agent bank? 11 U.S.C. § 544(a); *Official Comm. of Unsecured Creditors for Tyringham Holdings, Inc. v. Suna Bros., Inc.*

(3) 1465 Park Place LLP owns a commercial office building. The building is subject to a $10 million mortgage, held by Harper Bank Corp., and a subsequent $2 million tax lien owed to the IRS. The office building is worth $9 million in the present market. After 1465 Park Place LLP filed for bankruptcy, the trustee was able to avoid the mortgage using the strong-arm power. What is the status of the IRS's claim now? 11 U.S.C. § 551.

(4) Stanislawski Pirogi makes some of the tastiest pirogi you can find. They're easy to find because Stanislawski ships them all over the world through United Express Shipping. United Express also provides strategically located cold storage depots for the pirogi. Unfortunately, one batch of the pirogi was tainted with *E. coli*, and several wrongful deaths later, Stanislawski Pirogi has found itself in Chapter 11. At the time Stanislawski Pirogi filed for Chapter 11, it owed $500,000 to United Express for shipping and storage. State law provides that United Express automatically has a lien on all goods it holds for Stanislawski as long as it maintains possession. Can Stanislawski, as DIP, avoid the lien on the pirogi in United Express's possession? 11 U.S.C. §§ 545, 546(i).

X

CHAPTER *30*

VOIDABLE PREFERENCES AND SETOFFS

Imagine that you were insolvent and preparing to file for bankruptcy. You recognize that you do not have sufficient assets to pay all your creditors. But you do have some assets of value. You also know a fair amount about distributions in bankruptcy. You recognize that secured creditors get paid out of their collateral ahead of unsecured creditors, and that even better than being a secured creditor is not to be a creditor, meaning that the debt has been paid off. So what might you do?

Would you be tempted to pay back debts owed to family and friends? Or, if you couldn't liquidate your assets (because you still need them), would you grant your family and friends security interests in these assets? Maybe you wouldn't, but for centuries plenty of debtors have done exactly this, making payments and other transfers to preferred creditors on the eve of bankruptcy. The problem these preferential transfers create is manifest: To the extent that the preferential transfers are honored, it leaves fewer assets available to satisfy the claims of unpreferred creditors. Honoring preferential transfers allows a strategic debtor to completely change the distribution of the assets of the estate to the detriment of disfavored creditors, who are likely to include tax authorities and tort creditors.

Not surprisingly, perhaps, the Bankruptcy Code has a provision that addresses these preferential transfers. Section 547 of the Bankruptcy Code allows the trustee or DIP to avoid certain preferential transfers—transfers made to or for the benefit of a creditor by an insolvent on account of antecedent debts in a limited prepetition window that enable the creditor to do better than it would in a hypothetical liquidation.

The policy encapsulated in section 547 is that equity is equality: Similarly situated creditors should have similar recoveries, and a creditor's relationship with the debtor is not grounds to depart from this principle. A debtor should not be able to pick and choose which creditors it wants to distribute its assets to prior to filing for bankruptcy. Absent section 547, debtors might well pay off favored creditors—family, friends, various other insiders, or those from whom the debtor wishes to obtain future business—shortly before filing for bankruptcy. These favored creditors might receive 100 cents on the dollar (or more), while disfavored creditors would be left to share a diminished or vanished pool of assets. Section 547 allows the trustee or DIP to avoid those transfers that occur on the eve of bankruptcy that would actually affect bankruptcy distributions.

At the same time, voidable preference law helps discourage the race to the courthouse. A preferential transfer need not be a voluntary one. It can also include transfers made as the result of collection actions. To the extent that collections made on the eve of bankruptcy are avoidable, in bankruptcy it reduces the incentive for parties to "run" on the debtor and engage in a grab race for the debtor's assets.

Voidable preferences (along with fraudulent transfers, setoff restrictions, and equitable subordination and equitable disallowance) start to blur the line between the bankruptcy and pre-bankruptcy worlds. These types of avoidance actions allow for a reshaping of the debtor's assets and liabilities and the priority of creditors based on pre-bankruptcy activities. The estate is reconfigured based on actions that occurred before its creation, retroactively unwinding transactions that occurred at a time when the bankruptcy court had no jurisdiction.

A preference is simply a pre-bankruptcy transfer of property that enables a creditor to do better than it would have otherwise done in bankruptcy. Not all preferences are voidable, however, and even for those that are, they are merely voidable, not void. A preference stands unless somebody challenges it.

I. ELEMENTS OF A VOIDABLE PREFERENCE

Under section 547(b) of the Bankruptcy Code, a voidable preference has six basic elements:

1. There must be a transfer;
2. the transfer must be on account of an antecedent debt;
3. the transfer must be to or for the benefit of a creditor;
4. the transfer must be made while the debtor is insolvent (presumed for 90 days pre-petition);
5. the transfer must be made within the applicable preference period (90 days pre-petition generally, but one year for insiders); and
6. the transfer must enable the creditor to do better than the creditor would in a hypothetical Chapter 7 liquidation.

If a transfer is a preference, then the transferee (or, in some cases, its subsequent transferee, as discussed later in this chapter regarding section 550), must return the transferred asset to the estate. This does not mean that the transferee is left with nothing. Instead, it still has a claim against the estate. Thus, if a transfer were of $1 million, the transferee would return the $1 million, but would have a general unsecured claim of $1 million. What this means is that the transferee (or other liable party) is returning an asset in real dollars and getting a claim in bankruptcy dollars.

To illustrate, imagine that a debtor has $500 million in assets and owes $900 million. $400 million is owed to A, $200 million to B, and $100 million each to C, D, and E. All the creditors are unsecured. Suppose that the debtor pays A $300 million and then immediately files for bankruptcy. Would there be a voidable preference?

There would be a transfer to A on account of an antecedent debt made within 90 days of the bankruptcy filing when the debtor is presumed to be insolvent. Would

A do better in a hypothetical liquidation with the transfer than without it? This requires crunching some numbers.

Without the transfer, the liquidation dividend would be 55% (= $500 million in assets/$900 million in claims). 55% × $400 million = $222.2 million. Thus, without the transfer, *A* would receive $222.2 million in a hypothetical liquidation.

With the transfer, the liquidation dividend would be 33.3%, as there would be only $200 million in assets and $600 million in remaining claims to be paid out pro rata (33.3% = $200 million/$600 million). *A* would have a claim for $100 million rather than $400 million. That claim would be paid at the 33.3% dividend rate, meaning *A* would be paid $33.3 million. To this, however, we must add the $300 million transfer *A* received. Thus, with the transfer, *A* would get $333.33 million in a hypothetical liquidation, which is far better than the $222.2 million *A* would receive without the transfer. Accordingly the $300 million payment to *A* is a voidable preference.

Notice what happens if the transfer is to an oversecured creditor. Suppose that the debtor has $100 million in assets and owes $125 million. *A* is owed $55 million, secured by a first lien on all assets. The debtor pays *A* $5 million on January 1 and files for bankruptcy on March 1. We have a transfer to a creditor on account of an antecedent debt during the preference period when the debtor is presumed insolvent. But does the transfer enable *A* to do better in a hypothetical liquidation than otherwise? No. If the debtor liquidated without the transfer, *A* would recover $55 million from the debtor's assets. With the transfer, *A* would recover $50 million from the debtor's assets plus the $5 million payment for a total of $55 million, so there is no voidable preference. Thus we see two important rules of preference: First, a transfer to an oversecured creditor can never be a voidable preference. And second, a transfer to an undersecured credit will always be a voidable preference, unless a preference exception applies (or the debtor is solvent).

As a general rule, if a transfer is a preference, then the entire transfer may be avoided, not merely to the extent it improves the creditor's position. *Moore v. Bay,* 284 U.S. 4 (1931). Thus, if a $1 million transfer resulted in a creditor's position improving by 1¢, then the entire $1 million transfer would be avoided, meaning that the creditor would have to return the $1 million to the estate and would have instead a $1 million general unsecured claim. Some of the statutory exceptions to section 547(b), which we will examine below, provide for only partial avoidance. Also, note that a transfer may be both a preference and a fraudulent conveyance. For example, the granting of a security interest without consideration could be both a preference and a fraudulent transfer. Preferences and fraudulent transfers are not exclusive.

A. Has There Been a Transfer on Account of an Antecedent Debt?

A preference requires a transfer; absent a transfer, there is no preference. Section 101(54) of the Bankruptcy Code provides a broad definition of "transfer." Some of what is included is not intuitive; not all transfers are of cash or other tangible property. Instead, a preference may include things such as the granting of a security interest, granting additional collateral, perfection of a security interest, forgiveness of debt, granting of a guarantee, or even involuntary transfers such as executions of judgments and enforcement of liens. Critically, a change in market values is not itself a transfer. As the following case shows, the increase in the value of collateral because of its maturation or natural transformation is different from an increase in the value of collateral because of the addition of more collateral.

In re Nivens

22 B.R. 287 (Bankr. N.D. Tex. 1982)

BILL H. BRISTER, Bankruptcy Judge.

Arville Calvin Nivens and Danny Calvin Nivens, father and son, conducted a farming business as a partnership under the name of Nivens and Nivens. Each filed petition for order for relief under Chapter 7 of Title 11, United States Code, on March 18, 1982. The 1981 crop year was the last year in which they operated the farming partnership. As a result of the farming in the 1981 crop year they became entitled to receive "deficiency" payments totalling $36,648.70 and "low yield" or "disaster" payments totalling $912.05 from the Department of Agriculture under the 1981 support programs for upland cotton. The First State Bank of Abernathy ("Bank") . . . and the trustee are competing for those government support payments, represented by checks in the possession of the trustee.

[The Bank had a valid security interest in the crop, and thus on the checks, which were proceeds of the crop. The trustee] contends that the recognition of a lien on behalf of the bank . . . in the subsidy checks would result in an improvement of position by [the Bank] within ninety days of bankruptcy and, to the extent that the security interest has increased in value, there is an avoidable preference.

Pre-Code cases clearly indicated that a secured party maintained rights in after acquired inventory or receivables. [*See, e.g.,*] *DuBay v. Williams,* 9th Cir. 1969, 417 F.2d 1277. *DuBay* and its progeny was overruled in the Code by the provisions of § 547(c)(5), applicable to secured creditors claiming security interests in inventory and in accounts receivable, and § 553(b), applicable to any creditor who would otherwise have right of setoff under § 553(a). Crops are categorized as "inventory" by § 547(a)(1). Under § 547(c)(5) a preference will not result to the holder of a perfected security interest in inventory, including crops, unless and to the extent the holder improves his position during the ninety day period before bankruptcy. That is, the bank . . . can realize from the collateral only what they could have realized ninety days before the debtors filed their petition in bankruptcy.

. . .

The nature of a farm crop is unlike that of other types of inventory. For instance, the inventory of a grocery store might change in value from time to time, but the physical nature of the individual items comprising the inventory does not change. It is an easy matter to inventory a grocery store on separate dates and determine whether there has been an increase or decrease in inventory and in value. A lien does not exist until the property against which it is affixed comes into existence. Thus where there is an increase in the volume of the inventory of a grocery store within ninety days of bankruptcy the lien against that increase becomes fixed within the prohibited period and is avoidable. However, if there is only an increase in *value* of the inventory due to market fluctuations, without an accompanying increase in volume of inventory, there is no avoidable preference.

A crop as "inventory" is different from the grocery store inventory example. A crop is continuously undergoing change. Its existence commences as soon as the seed is planted and starts to germinate. It undergoes daily change until it finally matures and is ready for harvest. The lien which was initially fixed against the crops in its embryonic stages continues against the crop in all stages of development. It is the same lien and the same crop. Although the crop is increasing in value the crop was in existence at all relevant times. While there might be an increase in the value of the crop between the different stages of its development, the "inventory" itself is not increased. There is nothing added within the prohibited period which would mandate avoidance of lien against increase. [Therefore, the court ruled, there was no improvement in position and thus no voidable preference.]

B. Insolvency and the Preference Period

A voidable preference requires the debtor to be insolvent, but insolvency is presumed for 90 days prior to bankruptcy. 11 U.S.C. § 547(f). For preferences involving insiders, then, insolvency must be proven for transfers occurring more than 90 days pre-petition. Insider is a defined term, 11 U.S.C. § 101(31), and may include corporate affiliates, as well as parties that actually have no meaningful relationship with the debtor.

Why the 90 days/1 year limit? There's nothing magical about a quarter or a year; under the Bankruptcy Act, the preference period was 120 days for non-insiders. Instead, the preference period is meant to get at the period during which a bankruptcy filing would be readily in the contemplation of the parties. An insider should have more reason to know of a business going south than an outsider, hence the longer preference period.

While the goal of preference law is to prevent preferential transfers, the flip side of this is that it also prevents the race to the courthouse. Absent preference law, creditors could race to get judgments and execute before a bankruptcy filing. Preference law means that those judgments, executions, and foreclosures that happened on the eve of bankruptcy will be unwound. But does this really stop the race to the courthouse or just push it back by 90 days? Indeed, isn't the game with preferences simply to have the transfer take place 91 days pre-petition?

One result of the 90-day preference period is that it means out-of-court restructurings involving transfers, such as the granting of new security interests, are not really final until 90 days have passed. So, too, payments in settlement agreements. If you look back at the *Free Lance-Star* case in chapter 21, you'll see that during workout discussions the credit waits for 90 days after filing a financing statement for a security interest. Why? Presumably to avoid preference avoidance risk.

The bright line of 90 days/1 year opens the door to abusive prosecution of preferences through blunderbuss challenges to transfers. Debtors (or whoever holds the right to pursue avoidance actions) routinely send out demand letters to all parties that received payments within the preference period and bring preference actions against those who have not returned the transfer. While these mass preference actions are sometimes made upon a detailed review of the transfers, they are frequently filed just before the preference period expires without careful examination in order to preserve the estate's rights. The result is that the defendants must all engage counsel and litigate in the jurisdiction of the debtor's filing, while facing the very real possibility that their litigation costs will rapidly exceed the amount of the preference. All of this puts substantial pressure on preference defendants to settle. *See* Thomas D. Goldberg, *Curbing Abusive Preference Actions: Rethinking Claims on Behalf of Administratively Insolvent Estates*, AM. BANKR. INST. J. (May 2004).

C. Timing of a Transfer

The timing of a transfer is addressed in section 547(e). For most transfers, the timing is clear: The transfer is dated to when the rights of the transferee would trump other claimants at state law. 11 U.S.C. § 547(e)(1).

With a transfer of a security interest, however, the timing issue is more complicated because there are two separate steps that could occur in any sequence or simultaneously: the granting of a security interest and the acquisition of the collateral. A security interest can only "attach" to collateral when the debtor acquires rights in the collateral. That can happen before the granting of the security interest or afterward. The key question is whether the debtor owned the collateral before the granting of the security interest.

If the debtor acquired the collateral after the granting of the security interest, then the transfer is dated to when the debtor acquired rights in the collateral, which is when the security interest "attached," meaning that the security interest became enforceable *against the debtor*. 11 U.S.C. § 547(e)(3); UCC §§ 9-203(a)-(b). This is important for after-acquired property clauses—additional collateral attached under such a clause is a transfer on the date of the attachment. The effect is to override the general UCC priority rule that a security interest's priority dates from the *earlier* of filing of a financing statement covering the collateral or perfection. After-acquired property would be covered by a financing statement that had been previously filed, but perfection would only run from the date the after-acquired collateral was in fact acquired.

If the debtor owned the collateral before the security interest was granted, then the timing of the transfer depends on when perfection occurs. 11 U.S.C. § 547(e)(2). Section 547(e)(1) provides when perfection occurs. There is a general rule, section 547(e)(1)(B), and a special rule for real property (other than fixtures), section 547(e)(1)(A).

The general rule is that a security interest is perfected when it would have priority over a subsequent judicial lien. For real estate mortgages, the rule is that perfection occurs when the mortgage would have priority over the interest of a bona fide purchaser. Typically this will require the recordation of the mortgage.

If the debtor owned the collateral before the granting of the security interest and perfection occurred on or within 30 days of attachment, then the transfer date for section 547 relates back to the date of attachment. This may put the transfer outside of the preference period.[1]

If the debtor owned the collateral before the granting of the security interest and perfection occurred more than 30 days from attachment, then the transfer is timed for section 547 purposes as of the date of perfection. Table 30.1 below summarizes the timing rules.

Table 30.1 Timing of Transfer of Security Interests Under Section 547(e)

		Security Interest Perfected on or Within 30 Days of Attachment?	
		Yes	*No*
Collateral Acquired Before Security Interest Granted?	*Yes*	Date of attachment	Date of perfection
	No	Date of attachment (therefore after acquired property does not benefit from relation back of UCC § 9-322(a)(1))	Date of perfection

D. Has the Creditor's Position Improved as a Result of the Transfer?

Even if a transfer to a creditor on account of an antecedent debt has occurred and it has occurred during the preference period, there is still the question of whether the transfer improved the creditor's position. As noted above, this comparison is to a hypothetical Chapter 7 liquidation on the date of the bankruptcy filing, which means there would be no accrual of post-petition interest and fees. Were it otherwise, the hypothetical would simply be too difficult to calculate. Even so, there are obviously complications in determining a hypothetical liquidation when there may be disputed or contingent claims. Not surprisingly, preference cases rarely turn on such details.

---

1. Also, note that section 362(b)(3) permits perfection for 30 days post-transfer, including post-petition. Therefore, a security interest that is granted pre-petition may be perfected post-petition within a limited window and could, depending on the date of attachment, not be a preference. A lien that is perfected post-petition during the 30-day window is still liable to avoidance under section 544 because that section allows avoidance of liens based on the powers of hypothetical creditors "as of the commencement of the case." 11 U.S.C. § 544.

The comparison to a hypothetical liquidation has an important implication: It means that a creditor cannot receive a preference in regard to an oversecured claim. Only creditors with undersecured or unsecured claims can receive preferences.

II. PREFERENCE EXCEPTIONS

Even if a transfer meets the requirements of section 547(b), it may still not be voidable because it complies with section 547(c)'s statutory exceptions or a judicially created exception. Whereas the DIP or trustee has the burden of proof under section 547(b) in proving a preference, a party claiming shelter in one of the exceptions bears the burden of proof as to the exception. 11 U.S.C. § 547(g).

These statutory exceptions to preferences include:

- substantially contemporaneous exchanges, 11 U.S.C. § 547(c)(1);
- transfers in the ordinary course of business of both the debtor and transferee, 11 U.S.C. § 547(c)(2);
- creation of purchase money security interests (new value), 11 U.S.C. § 547(c)(3);
- transfers in exchange for the provision of new value by a creditor, 11 U.S.C. § 547(c)(4), with new value defined under section 547(a)(2);
- changes in the amount of inventory (defined in section 547(a)(1)) or receivables securing a lien within the 90 days prior to bankruptcy (calculated by determining the improvement in the creditor's position based on where it stood 90 days pre-petition and at the time of the bankruptcy filing), 11 U.S.C. § 547(c)(5);
- the fixing of statutory liens that are not avoidable under section 545, 11 U.S.C. § 547(c)(6); and
- a *de minimis* exception, 11 U.S.C. § 547(c)(9).

The first four of these exceptions are discussed below, as is a judicially created exception known as the "earmarking doctrine" that protects refinancings from preference avoidance.

A. Contemporaneous Exchanges

Section 547(c)(1) protects from preference avoidance roughly contemporaneous exchanges that might be considered credit transactions because the exchange between the debtor and its counterparty was not exactly contemporaneous. To wit, if I purchase a widget from you for $100 and you tender me the widget and a minute later I tender you the $100, you have technically been my creditor for that intermediate minute, but it is understood both objectively and subjectively to be a sale, rather than a credit transaction. So too with section 547(c)(1). The transaction must be both subjectively intended to be a roughly contemporaneous exchange, and it must objectively be one. What is roughly contemporaneous? That is less clear and may vary by context. No bright line rule exists.

B. Ordinary Course Transactions

Section 547(c)(2) creates an exemption from preference avoidance for ordinary course transactions. Section 547(c)(2) requires ordinary course both in the incurrence of the obligation and in the transfer. The incurrence of the obligation is defined subjectively in relation to both the debtor and the transferee. The ordinary course of the transfer, however, is to be determined either subjectively in relation to *both* the debtor and transferee, or objectively "according to ordinary business terms." What is left unresolved by the statute is the ordinary terms of *what* business. The following case addresses this issue.

In re Tolona Pizza Products Corp.

3 F.3d 1029 (7th Cir. 1993)

POSNER, Circuit Judge.

When, within 90 days before declaring bankruptcy, the debtor makes a payment to an unsecured creditor, the payment is a "preference," and the trustee in bankruptcy can recover it and thus make the creditor take pot luck with the rest of the debtor's unsecured creditors. 11 U.S.C. § 547. But there is an exception if the creditor can show that the debt had been incurred in the ordinary course of the business of both the debtor and the creditor, § 547(c)(2)(A); that the payment, too, had been made and received in the ordinary course of their businesses, § 547(c)(2)(B); and that the payment had been "made according to ordinary business terms." § 547(c)(2)(C). The first two requirements are easy to understand: of course to defeat the inference of preferential treatment the debt must have been incurred in the ordinary course of business of both debtor and creditor and the payment on account of the debt must have been in the ordinary course as well. But what does the third requirement—that the payment have been "made according to ordinary business terms"—add? And in particular does it refer to what is "ordinary" between this debtor and this creditor, or what is ordinary in the market or industry in which they operate? . . .

Tolona, a maker of pizza, issued eight checks to Rose, its sausage supplier, within 90 days before being thrown into bankruptcy by its creditors. The checks, which totaled a shade under $46,000, cleared and as a result Tolona's debts to Rose were paid in full. Tolona's other major trade creditors stand to receive only 13¢ on the dollar under the plan approved by the bankruptcy court, if the preferential treatment of Rose is allowed to stand. Tolona, as debtor in possession, brought an adversary proceeding against Rose to recover the eight payments as voidable preferences. The bankruptcy judge entered judgment for Tolona. The district judge reversed. He thought that Rose did not, in order to comply with section 547(c)(2)(C), have to prove that the terms on which it had extended credit to Tolona were standard terms in the industry, but that if this was wrong, the testimony of Rose's executive vice-president, Stiehl, did prove it. The parties agree that the other requirements of section 547(c)(2) were satisfied.

Rose's invoices recited "net 7 days," meaning that payment was due within seven days. For years preceding the preference period, however, Tolona rarely paid within seven days; nor did Rose's other customers. Most paid within 21 days, and if they paid later than 28 or 30 days Rose would usually withhold future shipments until payment was received. Tolona, however, as an old and valued customer (Rose had been selling to it for fifteen years), was permitted to make payments beyond the 21-day period and even beyond the 28-day or 30-day period. The eight payments at issue were made between 12 and 32 days after Rose had invoiced Tolona, for an average of 22 days; but this actually was an improvement. In the 34 months before the preference period, the average time for which Rose's invoices to Tolona were outstanding was 26 days and the longest time was 46 days. Rose consistently treated Tolona with a degree of leniency that made Tolona (Stiehl conceded on cross-examination) one of a "sort of exceptional group of customers of Rose . . . falling outside the common industry practice and standards."

It may seem odd that paying a debt late would ever be regarded as a preference to the creditor thus paid belatedly. But it is all relative. A debtor who has entered the preference period—who is therefore only 90 days, or fewer, away from plunging into bankruptcy—is typically unable to pay all his outstanding debts in full as they come due. If he pays one and not the others, as happened here, the payment though late is still a preference to that creditor, and is avoidable unless the conditions of section 547(c)(2) are met. One condition is that payment be in the ordinary course of both the debtor's and the creditor's business. A late payment normally will not be. It will therefore be an avoidable preference.

This is not a dryly syllogistic conclusion. The purpose of the preference statute is to prevent the debtor during his slide toward bankruptcy from trying to stave off the evil day by giving preferential treatment to his most importunate creditors, who may sometimes be those who have been waiting longest to be paid. Unless the favoring of particular creditors is outlawed, the mass of creditors of a shaky firm will be nervous, fearing that one or a few of their number are going to walk away with all the firm's assets; and this fear may precipitate debtors into bankruptcy earlier than is socially desirable.

From this standpoint, however, the most important thing is not that the dealings between the debtor and the allegedly favored creditor conform to some industry norm but that they conform to the norm established by the debtor and the creditor in the period before, preferably well before, the preference period. That condition is satisfied here—if anything, Rose treated Tolona more favorably (and hence Tolona treated Rose less preferentially) before the preference period than during it.

But if this is all that the third subsection of 547(c)(2) requires, it might seem to add nothing to the first two subsections, which require that both the debt and the payment be within the ordinary course of business of both the debtor and the creditor. For, provided these conditions are fulfilled, a "late" payment really isn't late if the parties have established a practice that deviates from the strict terms of their written contract. But we hesitate to conclude that the third subsection, requiring conformity to "ordinary business terms," has no function in the statute. We can think of two functions that it might have. One is evidentiary. If the debtor and creditor dealt on terms that the creditor testifies were normal for them but that are wholly unknown in the industry, this casts some doubt on his (self-serving) testimony. Preferences are disfavored, and subsection C makes them more difficult to prove. The second possible function of the subsection is to allay the concerns of creditors that one or more of their number may have worked out a special deal with the debtor, before the preference period, designed to put that creditor ahead of the others in the event of bankruptcy. It may seem odd that allowing late payments from a debtor would be a way for a creditor to make himself more rather than less assured of repayment. But such a creditor does have an advantage during the preference period, because he can receive late payments then and they will still be in the ordinary course of business for him and his debtor.

The functions that we have identified, combined with a natural reluctance to cut out and throw away one-third of an important provision of the Bankruptcy Code, persuade us that the creditor must show that the payment he received was made in accordance with the ordinary business terms in the industry. But this does not mean that the creditor must establish the existence of some single, uniform set of business terms, as Tolona argues. Not only is it difficult to identify the industry whose norm shall govern (is it, here, the sale of sausages to makers of pizza? The sale of sausages to anyone? The sale of anything to makers of pizza?), but there can be great variance in billing practices within an industry. Apparently there is in this industry, whatever exactly "this industry" is; for while it is plain that neither Rose nor its competitors enforce payment within seven days, it is unclear that there is a standard outer limit of forbearance. It seems that 21 days is a goal but that payment as late as 30 days is generally tolerated and that for good customers even longer delays are allowed. The average period between Rose's invoice and Tolona's payment during the preference period was only 22 days, which seems well within the industry norm, whatever exactly it is. The law should not push businessmen to agree upon a single set of billing practices; antitrust objections to one side, the relevant business and financial considerations vary widely among firms on both the buying and the selling side of the market.

We conclude that "ordinary business terms" refers to the range of terms that encompasses the practices in which firms similar in some general way to the creditor in question engage, and that only dealings so idiosyncratic as to fall outside that broad range should be deemed extraordinary and therefore outside the scope of subsection (C). Stiehl's testimony brought the case within the scope of "ordinary business terms" as just defined. Rose and its competitors pay little or no attention to the terms stated on their invoices, allow most customers to take up to 30 days to pay, and allow certain favored customers to take even more time. There is no single set of terms on which the members of the industry have coalesced; instead there is a broad range and the district judge plausibly situated the dealings between Rose and Tolona within it. These dealings are conceded to have been within the normal course of dealings between the two firms, a course established long before the preference period, and there is no hint either that the dealings were designed to put Rose ahead of other creditors of Tolona or that other creditors of Tolona would have been surprised to learn that Rose had been so forbearing in its dealings with Tolona.

Tolona might have argued that the district judge gave insufficient deference to the bankruptcy judge's contrary finding. The district judge, and we are required to accept the bankruptcy judge's findings on questions of fact as long as they are not clearly erroneous. FED. R. BANKR. P. 8013. But since Tolona did not argue that the district judge had applied an incorrect standard of review, we need not decide whether the district judge overstepped the bounds. Which is not to say that he did. While he did not intone the magic words "clear error," he may well have believed that the record as a whole left no doubt that Tolona's dealings with Rose were within the broad band of accepted practices in the industry. It is true that Stiehl testified that Tolona was one of an exceptional group of Rose's customers with whom Rose's dealings fell outside common industry practice. But the undisputed evidence concerning those dealings and the practices of the industry demonstrates that payment within 30 days is within the outer limits of normal industry practices, and the payments at issue in this case were made on average in a significantly shorter time.

The judgment reversing the bankruptcy judge and dismissing the adversary proceeding is AFFIRMED.

. . .

C. Purchase Money Security Interests

Section 547(c)(3) protects purchase money security interests (PMSIs) from avoidance as preference. A PMSI is a security interest granted to secure a loan for the purchase of an asset, as opposed to a loan to provide operating funds or to refinance an existing loan. A PMSI is often going to be on account of an antecedent unsecured debt, and is thus vulnerable to avoidance absent a safe harbor because the security interest might not be filed until after the purchase money loan has been funded. The policy rationale for protecting PMSIs is that the purchase money loan resulted in a corresponding increase in the assets of the estate: Lender A might have loaned the debtor $1 million to purchase an excavator, which would (at the time of purchase) have been worth roughly $1 million. The security interest transferred to the creditor in exchange for the purchase money loan would give the creditor "dibs" on the excavator, but the net position of the estate is essentially a wash, and to the extent that the new asset is used for revenue positive projects, it will actually increase the estate's assets. Accordingly, it makes sense to protect security interests that facilitate purchase money loans.

Section 547(c)(3) requires the PMSI to be perfected on or before 30 days after the debtor takes possession of the purchased property. 11 U.S.C. § 547(c)(3)(B). This provision aligns with the deemed timing of a transfer under section 547(e)(2)(A), which provides that a transfer that is perfected within 30 days is deemed to have taken place at the time of the transfer, rather than on the date of perfection.[2]

In contrast, UCC section 9-317(e) provides that a PMSI perfected within 20 days after the debtor receives possession will have priority relating back to the date of the attachment. *See also* UCC § 9-324(a). Otherwise, the PMSI's priority will date from the date of perfection. The difference between the 20-day UCC relation back

---

2. Prior to 2005, section 547(e)(2)(A) provided for a 10-day limit, which created a different set of complications than that discussed below.

window and the 30-day period under the Bankruptcy Code provisions means that a lien might not be avoidable as a preference under section 547, but it might still be avoidable under the strong-arm power.

Thus, suppose that the debtor granted a security interest on January 1 in exchange for a loan that it used to purchase the collateral that day and promptly took possession of the collateral. At that point we have a PMSI that has attached, but it has not yet been perfected. The debtor then files for bankruptcy on January 23, before the PMSI is perfected. On January 28, the creditor files a financing statement and thereby perfects the PMSI.

The post-petition filing of the financing statement is exempt from the automatic stay under section 362(b)(3) because it is within the 30-day window prescribed by section 547(e)(2)(A). Because perfection occurred within 30 days of the debtor taking possession of the purchased property, the transfer is deemed for purposes of section 547 as having occurred on January 1. Although this is within the 90-day preference window, the grant of the security interest is not avoidable as a preference under section 547(c)(3). The PMSI would, however, still be avoidable under the strong-arm power of section 544(a)(1), because a hypothetical judicial lien creditor whose lien was created at the time of the filing of the bankruptcy petition—Jan. 23—would have priority over the PMSI because the PMSI's priority under the UCC would run from the date of perfection—January 28. The section 547(c) exceptions to preference avoidance liability are not defenses to other avoidance actions.

D. New Value

Section 547(c)(4) provides that a transfer is not a voidable preference to the extent it is offset by *subsequent* extensions of new value by the creditor. The policy section 547(c)(4) appears to be furthering is to encourage creditors to continue extending new value to firms that are in financial distress; without such new value, these firms might well file for bankruptcy. By allowing the provision of new value to cover for past preferential transfers, section 547(c)(4) incentivizes the flow of credit and goods to struggling firms.

Note that the new value from the creditor can be used to cover both immediate and mediate *prior* transfers by the debtor, but not subsequent ones; transfers made after new value is provided are not protected by section 547(c)(4).

Thus, suppose that the debtor made a $2 million payment on an unsecured antecedent debt on January 1, and again on January 5. Then on January 10 and on January 15, the creditor gave the debtor $3 million of new value. On January 20, the debtor paid the creditor $3 million. On January 25, the creditor advanced $2 million of new value, and on January 30, the debtor paid the creditor $3 million. The debtor filed for Chapter 11 bankruptcy on February 1.

Section 547(c)(4) would allow the creditor to apply the $3 million in new value paid on January 10 to both the January 1 and January 5 payments. The new value from January 15 could also be applied to those payments. Although the new value advanced on January 10 and 15 totaled $6 million, the creditor cannot apply it to the debtor's January 20 or January 30 payments because they are subsequent transfers.

Thus, while the debtor transferred $10 million to the creditor and $8 million of new value was advanced, the creditor can only shelter in $6 million of new value because the sequence of payments allows for new value to be applied only to prior transfers by the debtor. Accordingly, there is a voidable preference of $4 million. This sequence is shown in Table 30.2.

Table 30.2. New Value and Preferences Example

Date	Paid by Debtor	New Value from Creditor	Preference as of date?
Jan. 1	$2 million		$2 million
Jan. 5	$2 million		$4 million
Jan. 10		$3 million	$1 million
Jan. 15		$3 million	$0
Jan. 20	$3 million		$3 million
Jan. 25		$2 million	$1 million
Jan. 30	$3 million		$4 million
Feb. 1	*Bankruptcy Filing*		

E. Floating Liens

Section 547(c)(5) creates an exception, or more precisely a different preferences rule, for so-called floating liens on inventory and receivables. These liens are often called "floating" liens because the value of the collateral will fluctuate on a frequent, often daily or hourly basis, bobbing up and down over time like something floating on the waves. Rather than attempting to calculate all of the daily (or hourly) changes and whether they are preferences, section 547(e)(5) imposes a simpler test looking at the difference in how much a creditor is undersecured at 90 days pre-petition and at the time of the bankruptcy filing. To the extent that the creditor is less undersecured at the time of the bankruptcy, that is a preference.

To apply section 547(e)(5), take a snapshot of the creditor's position at 90 days pre-petition. If the creditor is fully or oversecured at 90 days pre-petition, there is no preference because the creditor would not do better in a hypothetical liquidation. If the creditor is undersecured at 90 days pre-petition, then take another snapshot of the creditor's position at the time of bankruptcy. Has the creditor's position improved? If the creditor is now oversecured, fully secured, or just less undersecured, there is a preference to the extent that its position has improved.

For example, suppose that 90 days pre-petition the debtor owed the creditor $10 million, secured by inventory worth $8 million, and at the time of bankruptcy, the debtor owed the creditor $7 million, secured by inventory worth only $6.5 million. The creditor was undersecured by $2 million at 90 days pre-petition and was unsecured by $0.5 million at the time of bankruptcy. The creditor's position has improved by $1.5 million, which is the extent of the voidable preference. The creditor is therefore treated as having a security interest in only $5 million (= $6.5 million − $1.5 million) of the inventory. The remaining $1.5 million is unencumbered. (Well, technically, it is subject to a lien held by the estate under section 551.)

F. Refinancing and the Earmarking Doctrine

In addition to the statutory preference exceptions under section 547(c), there is a judicially created preference exception known as the "earmarking doctrine" that protects payments made in the context of refinancing existing debts. The statutory hook for this doctrine is section 547(b)'s requirement of the "transfer of an interest of the debtor in property." Economically, a refinancing transaction is a payment from the new lender, Lender B, to the old lender, Lender A, even if the payment might actually go from Lender B to the debtor to Lender A. The debtor is merely an intermediary or conduit between Lender B and Lender A. Economically, the transfer is of Lender B's property, not the debtor's. The logic behind this doctrine is that if Lender B refinances a debt that was owed to Lender A, there has been no change in the position of the estate or the other creditors—the same amount of debt is still owed, so there is no reason to avoid the payment to Lender A as a preference. For the earmarking doctrine to apply, the funds from Lender B must actually be "earmarked" for Lender A. The doctrine developed from the situation of a guarantor paying off an obligation of a debtor, but has been extended to non-guarantor situations.

There are two important negative implications from this doctrine. The first is that any improvement of the priority of the debt as a result of the refinancing is not protected because that change affects other creditors. Thus, if a refinancing also includes the grant of a security interest in additional or new collateral, the refinancing payment would be protected, but not the security interest given to the new lender. Second, to the extent that a refinancing is not dollar for dollar, it is not protected.

III. VOIDABLE SETOFFS

The Bankruptcy Code recognizes **setoff** rights for *mutual* pre-petition claims and pre-petition obligations owed to the debtor. Setoff rights exist as a matter of non-bankruptcy law. Section 553 of the Bankruptcy Code provides that they are generally honored, but limits setoff to mutually owed debts. Mutuality is not defined in the Bankruptcy Code, but by nonbankruptcy law, and in some states this requires that both obligations be matured; that is, due and owing. *See, e.g., In re Patterson*, 967 F.2d 505, 510 (11th Cir. 1992) (Alabama law requires both obligations to be matured for mutuality). Mutuality is limited to individual juridical entities—an obligation owed to an affiliate cannot be used for traditional setoff because there is no mutuality.

Parties can *contract* for "triangular setoff," meaning that they will consolidate debts owed to affiliates for setoff purposes. This sort of arrangement is common in swap contracts. For example, imagine that Castor Corp. owes Pollux Corp. $100 and Pollux Corp. owes $70 to Hercules Corp., a subsidiary of Castor. Castor, Pollux, and Hercules could contract to allow the setoff. While this triangular setoff is enforceable at state law as a matter of contract, because bankruptcy law requires mutuality for setoff, it will not honor such a contractual triangular setoff. *In re Lehman Brothers, Inc.*, 458 B.R. 134 (Bankr. S.D.N.Y. 2011).

Although the Bankruptcy Code honors setoff rights, it allows for the avoidance of preferential setoffs. Section 553(b) provides that if the right to setoff arose within 90 days before the filing of the bankruptcy petition, while the debtor was insolvent, with the purpose of creating a right to set off, then the setoff is not honored in bankruptcy. 11 U.S.C. § 553(a)(2)-(3). The debtor is presumed to have been insolvent for 90 days before the bankruptcy filing. 11 U.S.C. § 553(c). The trustee or DIP can recover the amount by which the creditor benefitted from the mandatory setoff that was created within the preference period. To the extent that there are other setoff rights, however, those are protected under 11 U.S.C. § 553(a); the rule of *Moore v. Bay* does not apply to setoff.

When would such a setoff preference arise? One possibility, contemplated by the statute, is that a party would purchase an obligation in order to create a setoff right. Just as a grant of security on account of a pre-existing debt in the preference window would be avoidable, so too is the artificially created setoff preference.

A more common setoff situation involves bank deposits. A bank deposit is a debt that the bank owes to the depositor. If the depositor also has a loan from the bank, the bank can set off the deposit against a balance owed to the bank. Sometimes, this takes the form of a "compensating balance" requirement: The bank will require a borrower to maintain a deposit account at the bank and to maintain a certain balance in the deposit account. Thus, the bank might loan $10 million, but require a ten percent compensating balance, so the borrower will have to keep $1 million at the bank.

Why would the bank bother to do this, rather than just loan $9 million? Consider how interest works with a compensating balance: The deposited funds are still on loan from the bank, so interest continues to accrue on them. Thus, the bank is earning interest on a $10 million loan, rather than a $9 million loan. The bank only has the risk of a $9 million loan. This can be favorable for both the bank and for the borrower if the borrower wishes to appear to be paying a lower rate of interest (say to obtain other credit).

Compensating balance requirements may also be imposed by a bank as a condition of continuing to extend credit. In such a situation, the compensating balance requirement functions as additional security for the bank. One particular situation in which compensating balance requirements are seen is with credit card processor "holdbacks." Here's the situation: A merchant sells a ticket to be used for future services, say an airline flight or a concert. The merchant accepts payment via credit card. When this happens, the merchant's account at its bank (the "acquirer bank") is credited with a payment from the consumer's card issuer. The consumer's card issuer then bills the consumer for the purchase. Thus, the merchant has been paid before the consumer is able to use the ticket.

What then happens if the merchant is unable to honor the ticket? For example, what if the airline ceases operations, or the concert artist is unable to perform? The cardholder will dispute the charge and exercise its right to withhold payment from the card issuer. 12 C.F.R. § 1026.12(c). The card issuer will then seek reimbursement from the acquirer bank, and credit card network rules entitle it to reimbursement (including via setoff). The acquirer bank, then, will be stuck trying to get the money back from the merchant. If the merchant has filed for bankruptcy, the acquirer bank will be an unsecured creditor. The acquirer bank's solution? Impose a compensating balance requirement or a "holdback." The holdback might limit the acquirer's losses in bankruptcy. But it also might make losses more likely, as the holdback will squeeze the merchant's liquidity.

Does the acquirer bank have a right of setoff? The bank owes the merchant money (the deposited funds). But does the merchant owe the bank money? Possibly, but often it is not clear how much money is actually owed, if any, at least prior to bankruptcy. The bank imposing a holdback may risk not only having its setoff voided under section 553, either because of lack of state law setoff rights or because the setoff rights were created on the eve of bankruptcy. The bank may also risk having its claim equitably subordinated or be subject to various affirmative causes of action if it wrongly exercised a holdback that resulted in the debtor's bankruptcy.

Notice the carve-outs for financial contracts through the statutory cross-references in sections 553(a)(2)(B)(ii), 553(a)(3)(C), and 553(b)(1). Setoffs for these financial contracts are not voidable, but this is only for mutually owing debts arising from separate transactions or circumstances.

Problem Set 30

(1) Frigg Medical Associates leased its office space from Wotan Properties. Wotan Properties required Frigg to maintain a security deposit equal to two months' rent. When Frigg Medical Associates files for bankruptcy, may Wotan Properties apply the security deposit against unpaid rent and damage to the property? 11 U.S.C. §§ 362(a)(7), 553(a).

(2) Valkyrie Airlines filed for Chapter 11 on February 10. At the time of the filing, it had $125 million in assets and owed $150 million in debt, including $100 million in outstanding principal on its 20% unsecured bond debt that was incurred to finance a leveraged buyout. The previous January 1, Valkyrie had triggered a penalty interest covenant, that increased the rate on the bonds by 1000 basis points, so Valkyrie had to make a quarterly interest payment of $7.5 million on the bonds instead of the regular $5 million interest payment. Can Valkyrie, as DIP, recover the interest payment? 11 U.S.C. §§ 547(b), (c)(2).

(3) Baldur Realty Partners owes Frida Development Corporation $10 million, secured by a first lien on the Valhalla Resort, which is worth $25 million. Baldur has been having some financial difficulties of late. Frida has demanded and received a payment of $1 million in exchange for forbearing on covenant defaults. Ten days after making the payment to Frida, Baldur filed for Chapter 11. Can Baldur Realty Partners, as DIP, recover the $1 million from Frida as a preference? 11 U.S.C. § 547(b).

(4) Midgard Mining Enterprises had borrowed $20 million on an unsecured basis from Uroboros Bank, N.A. As Midgard's financial condition deteriorated, Uroboros Bank requested that Midgard grant it security. Midgard complied by giving Uroboros a security interest in the stock of its main operating subsidiary Molnir Ignition. Molnir's stock is worth perhaps $25 million. A month later, Midgard filed for Chapter 11 bankruptcy. Can

Midgard, as DIP, avoid Uroboros Bank's security interest in the Molnir Ignition stock? 11 U.S.C. § 547(b).

(5) Low-Key Commercial Finance loaned $5 million to Andvari Jewelers, a manufacturer of gold and silver jewelry. Low-Key was secured by an enormous (and hideous) solid gold statue of a salmon that graced Andvari's lobby. The statue has little artistic value in most viewers' eyes; its value is primarily as gold. On June 1, the statue was worth $4.5 million. On that day, Andvari ceased all production. Andvari did not file for bankruptcy until August 29, when the value of the statue was $6.5 million, because gold prices had risen rapidly. Can Andvari, as DIP, avoid part or all of Low-Key's security interest? 11 U.S.C. §§ 547(a)(1), 547(b), 547(c)(5).

(6) Fenrir Associates obtained a judgment against Tyr Development Company on April 1. A month later, Fenrir Associates recorded a judgment lien against a strip mall owned by Tyr. Tyr filed for Chapter 11 on July 15. Can Tyr, as DIP, avoid Fenrir's lien? 11 U.S.C. §§ 101(54), 547(b).

(7) Bifrost Telecommunications settled a class action suit for a $270 million cash payment to the class and $30 million in attorneys' fees paid to your firm. Bifrost transferred the funds via wire transfer yesterday. Should your firm start paying out large bonuses to its associates? 11 U.S.C. § 547(b). If not, is there anything you might do differently?

(8) On October 26, Thor Electrical Enterprises borrowed $3 million from Low-Key Commercial Finance to fund its purchase of three new custom flux capacitors. That same day, Thor ordered the flux capacitors and gave Low-Key a separate security interest in each flux capacitor. Thor received delivery of the flux capacitors on November 2.

Low-Key did not record the first security interest until November 18, and neglected to record the second security interest until November 30 and the third security interest until December 4. Thor filed for Chapter 11 bankruptcy on the following January 28. Can Thor, as DIP, avoid Low-Key's security interest in any of the flux capacitors? 11 U.S.C. §§ 547(b), 547(c)(3), 547(e)(2); UCC §§ 9-203(a)-(b).

(9) On January 1, Sigmund Capital loaned Fafner Semiconductors $10 million, secured by a first lien on "all microetching machines now owned or hereafter acquired." At the time of the transaction, Fafner owned three XT-100 model microetchers. Their market value was $7 million. On May 1, Fafner acquired a new XT-200 microetcher, worth $4 million. On July 4, Fafner filed for Chapter 11 bankruptcy.

   a. Can Fafner, as DIP, avoid Sigmund's security interest? 11 U.S.C. §§ 547(b), 547(e)(2)-(3).

   b. Suppose that on June 1, Sigmund sold its loan (along with the security interest) to Brunhilde Equipment Finance Co. on arms's-length terms. Can Fafner, as DIP, avoid Brunhilde's security interest? 11 U.S.C. §§ 550(a)-(b).

   c. Now suppose that on July 1, Brunhilde Equipment Finance Co. dividended the loan (and security interest) to Wotan, Inc., its parent corporation. Can Fafner, as DIP, avoid Wotan's security interest? 11 U.S.C. §§ 550(a)-(b).

(10) Yggdrasil Lumber Company had a revolving line of credit with Norn National Bank. On January 1, Yggdrasil owed $20 million on the line. On January 10, Yggdrasil paid down the line by $8 million. On January 15, Yggdrasil paid down the line by another $4 million. On January 20, Yggdrasil drew $10 million on the line. On January

30, Yggdrasil paid back $6 million on the line and on February 15, Yggdrasil drew down $5 million. On March 1, Yggdrasil paid back $10 million on the line and on March 15, Yggdrasil drew down $7 million on the line, and on March 20, Yggdrasil repaid $3 million. On March 25, Yggdrasil filed for Chapter 11 bankruptcy. Can Yggdrasil, as DIP, avoid any of the repayments? 11 U.S.C. § 547(c)(4).

CHAPTER 31

LEVERAGED BUYOUTS AND FRAUDULENT TRANSFERS

I. FEDERAL FRAUDULENT TRANSFER LAW

In Chapter 8, we saw how state fraudulent transfer law was a limitation on out-of-court restructuring. In addition to state fraudulent transfer law, there is also federal fraudulent transfer law.[1] The Bankruptcy Code includes its own fraudulent transfer provision, section 548. The Bankruptcy Code permits the trustee or DIP to proceed under either the state statute or the federal statute. 11 U.S.C. § 544(b). Section 544(b) permits the trustee to avoid any transfer of an interest in property or obligation incurred by the debtor that could be avoided by an unsecured creditor under state law. Thus, the trustee or DIP has the option of proceeding under whichever statute is more favorable, which may depend on issues like statutes of limitations, defenses, and case law particulars.

Substantively, the Bankruptcy Code provision is quite similar to state law, having both actual and constructive fraudulent transfers. Section 548 does not contain an explicit list of badges of fraud like section 4(b) of the Uniform Fraudulent Transfer Act, and it combines the constructive fraudulent transfer provisions of sections 4(a)(2) and 5 of the UFTA into one single provision. Whereas the UFTA has different provisions for present and future creditors, section 548 only authorizes actions by the trustee (or DIP), not by creditors (except derivatively).

As with preference actions (or state law fraudulent transfer actions), the avoidance of a transfer results in the transferee (initial or subsequent) being liable for returning the property (or value thereof). 11 U.S.C. § 550(a). And, as with the UFTA, there are a number of limitations on the ability of the trustee to recover under section 548(a).

First, section 550(b), discussed in the previous chapter, applies to section 548, and thereby limits recovery from good faith secondary transferees for value and good faith tertiary transferees. As with preferences, there is no blanket good faith defense for the initial transferee. Second, section 550(e) allows good faith transferees (initial

---

1. There is also a separate fraudulent transfer statute available to the federal government as creditor. 28 U.S.C. §§ 3301-3308.

and subsequent) a lien on the recovered property to the extent that they improved the asset. And third, unlike for preferences, section 548(c) grants good faith transferees (initial and subsequent) a lien on the recovered property (or the right to retain the property) to the extent that they gave value to the debtor in exchange for the property or obligation. Thus, a good faith transferee has a defense to the extent it gave value.

To illustrate, let's suppose that the debtor sold an asset for $10 million, but the reasonably equivalent value was actually $30 million. The trustee could avoid the transfer under section 548(a)(1)(B) as a constructive fraudulent transfer. If the transferee took in good faith, the transferee would have a $10 million lien on the asset, and hence a $10 million secured claim on the estate. If the transferee did not take in good faith, the transferee would still have a $10 million claim, but unsecured.

II. LEVERAGED BUYOUTS AND FRAUDULENT TRANSFERS

A common application of fraudulent transfer law is to challenge transfers made in leveraged buyouts (LBOs). A leveraged buyout is a common type of corporate acquisition transaction. The basic idea of an LBO is that a firm is purchased by an acquirer using borrowed money. The borrowed money is to be repaid from the future earnings of the target firm, and repayment is to be secured by the assets of the target firm. Thus, in a 100% financed LBO (like in the *Bay Plastics* case below), the acquirer puts in no money itself. The acquirer therefore has a situation in which it gets 100% of the upside, but 0% of the downside. If the target firm performs well and pays off the loans, then the acquirer has purchased the target for free. If the target performs poorly and defaults, then the lenders take the target firm's assets, but the acquirer walks away without any losses.

The LBO structure enables firms to make acquisitions without committing a lot of their own capital or incurring liabilities themselves. Instead, the acquisition is done through borrowing that is essentially secured by a purchase money security interest in the target. This process helps expand the market for corporate control by funding potential acquirers that would not otherwise have access to sufficient capital to make the acquisition, but it also risks leveraging up the target firm with more debt than it can handle because of the limited liability of the acquirer firm.

The LBO structure is the favored acquisition mode for private equity funds. A private equity fund is a firm that purchases public companies ("portfolio companies"), taking them private (hence the "private" equity). The fund is typically a limited partnership with the general partner being the investment arm of the private equity firm that has organized the fund and serves as its investment advisor. By taking the company private, the private equity fund (or "sponsor") gains some breathing room to engage in a restructuring of the company's operations without pressure from shareholders for quarterly returns (and often without SEC reporting requirements). Having restructured the operations of the portfolio company to make it lean and mean, the sponsor then aims to exit by selling its equity interest in the portfolio company to the public in an initial public offering (IPO), perhaps five to seven years after the acquisition.

Ideally, the private equity fund reaps the benefits from the improvement in the portfolio company's value due to the operational restructuring while private. But things don't always work out so well. Recall that the sponsor purchased the portfolio company by borrowing all or a large portion of the acquisition funds. 100% financing is unusual, but private equity funds frequently finance 60-70% of the acquisition price. Figure 31.1, below, shows the average equity investment in LBOs over time, while Figure 31.2, which follows, shows a prototypical financing structure for an LBO, with the private equity LBO fund contributing the equity and the debt coming from a variety of institutional investor sources and purchasing a range of debt priorities.

Figure 31.1 Average LBO Equity Contribution

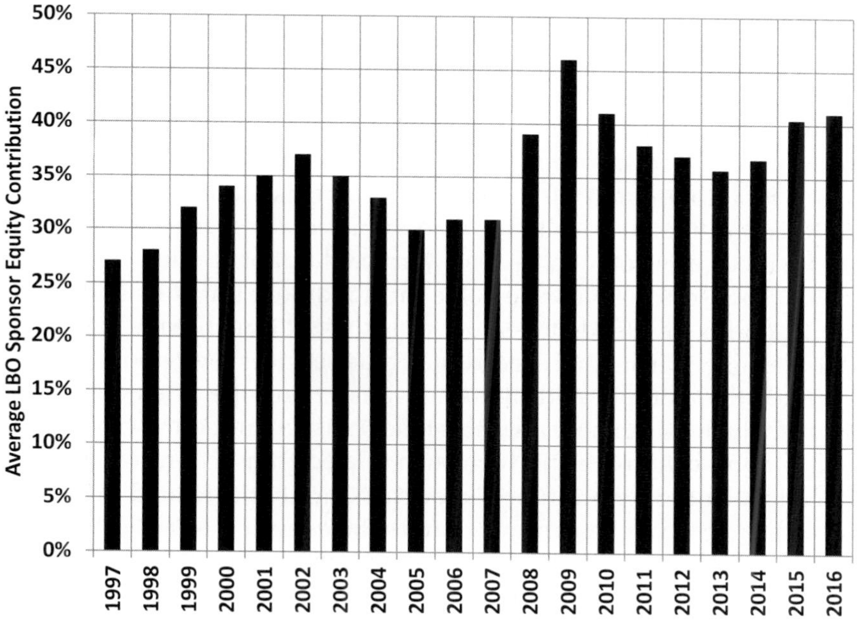

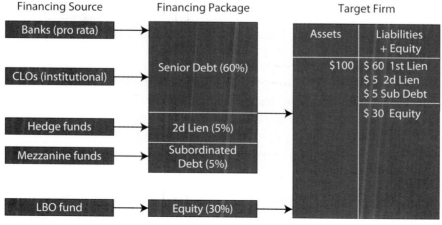

Figure 31.2 Prototypical LBO Financing Structure

The key for understanding LBOs is that it is the portfolio company that is liable for that debt, not the sponsor, even though the sponsor is the entity that benefits from the borrowing. The misalignment between benefits and burdens is precisely what makes LBOs problematic for fraudulent transfer law. If the portfolio company is able to pay its obligations, no one is likely to care, but often the only way the portfolio company can service the debt it assumed to finance its own acquisition is through extensive cost-cutting: layoffs, raiding of pension funds, etc. Such measures don't always work, and the portfolio company may simply be unable to service its debt. When that happens, the portfolio company will try to restructure its debts, but it may well end up in bankruptcy. When that happens, fraudulent transfer litigation is almost always on the horizon.

LBOs have been attacked both as actual fraudulent transfers—the idea being that the very concept of the LBO is an attempt to "hinder, delay, or defraud" creditors because of the heads-I-win, tails-you-lose nature of the gamble—and as constructive fraudulent transfers. There is usually little question that the target firm did not receive reasonably equivalent value—it has pledged its assets as collateral but not received the proceeds of the loan financing the transaction. If the target was therefore insolvent, rendered insolvent, or left with "unreasonably small capital," then the elements for a constructive fraudulent transfer exists, and the selling shareholders, the LBO sponsor (or at least its acquisition subsidiaries), the lender financing the LBO, and financial advisors whose fees were paid out of the deal all face potential liability. LBO sponsors may also be liable for fraudulent transfers and for state law causes of action for dividends taken out of insolvent target firms or advisory fees charged to the target firms that exceed the value services rendered.

LBOs (like other complicated financial transactions) are often done in multiple steps, each of which is arguably a stand-alone transaction. Courts have developed a common law approach to dealing with such related transactions called **step transaction doctrine**. Under step transaction doctrine, multiple, related transactions can be "collapsed" and treated as an integrated whole, even if substantially separated temporally. *See, e.g., U.S. v. Tabor Court Realty Corp.*, 803 F.2d 1288 (3d Cir. 1986). When applying step transaction doctrine, courts generally look to see if the defendant (1) had knowledge of all of the transactions, (2) if the transactions would have occurred without each other, and (3) whether the transactions were truly independent. Thus, transactional formalities may be disregarded when analyzing an LBO to get at the ultimate substance of the transaction.

The following case shows how an LBO works, and who is potentially harmed by the LBO.

Bay Plastics, Inc. v. BT Commercial Corp.

187 B.R. 315 (Bankr. C.D. Cal. 1995)

SAMUEL L. BUFFORD, U.S. Bankr. J.

I. INTRODUCTION

The debtor has brought this adversary proceeding against the selling shareholders of a leveraged buyout ("LBO") to recover the funds that they received in the buyout transaction. While the action was also brought against the bank that financed the transaction, the bank has settled. The Court grants summary judgment to the debtor on the undisputed facts.

The Court holds that the transaction may be avoided as a constructive fraudulent transfer under the California version of the Uniform Fraudulent Transfer Act ("UFTA"), on which the debtor relies pursuant to Bankruptcy Code § 544(b), and that in consequence the debtor is entitled to recover against the selling shareholders. The Court finds that the transaction rendered the debtor insolvent, and that the sellers did not act in good faith.

II. FACTS

The Court finds that the following facts are undisputed. Defendants Bob Younger, Abner Smith and Paul Dodson ("the selling shareholders") formed debtor Bay Plastics, Inc. ("Bay Plastics") in 1979 to manufacture polyvinyl chloride ("PVC") plastic pipe for water well casings and turf irrigation. Bay Plastics filed this bankruptcy case on January 25, 1990.

A. The Buyout

Because they were nearing retirement, on October 31, 1988 (fifteen months before this bankruptcy filing) the selling shareholders sold their Bay Plastics stock to Milhous Corporation ("Milhous") for $3.5 million in cash plus $1.8 million in deferred payments.[2] Milhous did not acquire the Bay Plastics stock directly. Instead, it caused its subsidiary Nicole Plastics to form its own subsidiary, BPI Acquisition Corp. ("BPI"), to take ownership of the Bay Plastics stock. Formally, the parties to the stock sale transaction were ultimately BPI and the selling shareholders.

The sale was unexceptional. The difficulty lay in the financing of the purchase. Milhous put no money of its own, or even any money that it borrowed, into this transaction. Instead, it caused Bay Plastics to borrow approximately $3.95 million from defendant BT Commercial Corp. ("BT") (a subsidiary of Bankers Trust), and then caused Bay Plastics to direct that $3.5 million of the loan be disbursed to BPI. BPI in turn directed that the $3.5 million be paid directly to the selling shareholders in substantial payment for their stock. Thus, at the closing, $3.5 million of the funds paid into escrow by BT went directly to the selling shareholders.

As security for its $3.95 million loan, BT received a first priority security interest in essentially all of the assets of Bay Plastics. In consequence, BT has received all of the proceeds of debtor's assets in this bankruptcy case, and nothing is left for unsecured or even for administrative creditors.

The financing also provided a revolving credit facility for working capital, in addition to the payment for the LBO, up to a total loan of $7 million. A total of just over $4 million was owing to BT at the time of the bankruptcy filing, according to the debtor's

---

2. Apparently the deferred payments have not been made. All but $100,000 of the deferred payments were designated as compensation for a non-competition agreement.

schedules. Thus most of the debt (all but approximately $500,000) owing to BT at the time of the filing resulted from the LBO.

The selling shareholders were not in the dark about the financing. On October 25, 1988 they and their attorney met with Milhous representatives in Los Angeles to finalize the deal. While the Milhous representatives provided rather little information about the Milhous finances, they did disclose the details of the BT secured loan to Bay Plastics to finance the stock purchase. In addition, the selling shareholders received a projected post-transaction balance sheet, which showed a balance of $250,000 in equity only because of the addition to the asset side of the ledger the sum of $2,259,270 in goodwill. Both the selling shareholders and their attorney were experienced in LBOs, and the selling shareholders discussed this feature of the transaction, and their exposure on a fraudulent transfer claim, with their attorney on that date. With this information in hand, Younger, Smith and Dodson approved the terms of the sale.

In contrast to the selling shareholders, the industry did not know about the LBO character of the transaction until a number of months later. Shintech Corp., a creditor at the time of the transaction (and continuously thereafter), did not learn of it until ten months later, in August 1989.

B. The Shintech Debt

Some three months before the LBO, on July 22, 1988, Bay Plastics entered into a requirements contract with Shintech to supply PVC resin. Shintech agreed under the contract to supply up to 2.6 million pounds of PVC resin per month on payment terms of 30 days after shipment. To induce Shintech to enter into this contract, Bay Plastics granted Shintech a security interest in all its assets, and the shareholders gave personal guaranties. This arrangement stood in the way of the BT transaction.

In consequence, the selling shareholders, their attorney, and Milhous representatives met with Shintech in late October, 1988 (after Milhous had disclosed to the selling shareholders the terms of the LBO), to arrange a new deal with Shintech. The parties to the LBO persuaded Shintech of Milhous' good credit, and induced Shintech to release both its security interest and the guaranties.[5] However, they did not disclose the LBO character of the transaction, and Shintech did not learn of this until ten months later.

The impact of this transaction on the balance sheet of Bay Plastics was dramatic. Immediately after the transaction, its balance sheet showed tangible assets of approximately $7 million, and liabilities of approximately $9 million. Only the addition of almost $2.26 million in goodwill, which had not appeared on prior balance sheets, and for which no explanation has been provided, permitted the balance sheet to show a modest shareholder equity of $250,000. But for the newly discovered goodwill, there would have been a net deficiency of some $2 million. In contrast, immediately before the transaction Bay Plastics had assets of $6.7 million and liabilities of $5.6 million, and a net equity of $1.1 million.

---

5. In consequence of giving up its security and its guaranties, Shintech now holds more than 99% of the unsecured debt in this case.

Bay Plastics was unable to service this overload of debt, and filed its bankruptcy petition fifteen months later. According to the debtor's schedules, at the time of filing its two principal creditors were BT and Shintech: it owed approximately $4 million in secured debt to BT, and $3.5 million in unsecured debt to Shintech. No other creditor was owed more than $20,000.

III. DISCUSSION

. . .

A. General

The basic structure of an LBO involves a transfer of corporate ownership financed primarily by the assets of the corporation itself.[11] Typically the corporation borrows the funds, secured by the assets of the corporation, and advances them to the purchasers, who use the funds to pay the purchase price to the selling shareholders. LBOs have two essential features:

First, the purchaser acquires the funds necessary for the acquisition through borrowings secured directly or indirectly by the assets of the company being acquired. Second, the lender who provides such funds is looking primarily to the future operating earnings of the acquired company and/or to the proceeds from future sales of assets of the company, rather than to any other assets of the purchasers, to repay the borrowings used to effect the acquisition.

LBO investors thus generally consider cash flow, the money available for working capital and debt service, as the most important factor in assessing a potential buyout candidate.

The application of fraudulent transfer law to LBOs has generated considerable debate among courts and commentators. LBOs were a popular form of consensual corporate takeover in the 1980's. They fell into disuse at the end of that decade for economic reasons. However, the use of the LBO as an acquisition device has recently become popular again.

The LBO dates back long before the 1980's. In earlier years, it was known as a "bootstrap acquisition." Some of these transactions were invalidated as fraudulent conveyances. . . .

We begin with the elements of the cause of action under the UFTA § 5, as adopted in California, for a constructive fraudulent transfer rendering the debtor insolvent. The elements of a cause of action under this statute are as follows: the debtor (1) made a transfer or incurred an obligation, (2) without receiving a reasonably equivalent value in exchange, (3) which rendered the debtor insolvent (or the debtor was already insolvent), and (4) which is attacked by a pre-transaction creditor.

---

11. While LBOs have frequently been used by management to buy out existing shareholders and take over the ownership of a business, management is not an essential party to an LBO. Indeed, in this case the purchaser was an outside third party.

1. Transfer or Obligation

The selling shareholders do not dispute that, in making the BT loan, the debtor made a transfer or incurred an obligation. In fact, the debtor did both. The debtor undertook the $3.95 million obligation to BT, it transferred a security interest in essentially all of its assets to BT, and it transferred $3.5 million ultimately to the selling shareholders. Thus the first element of the cause of action is satisfied.

2. Lack of Reasonably Equivalent Value

The selling shareholders likewise do not contest whether the debtor received reasonably equivalent value for the BT loan. However, this element is not apparent on its face.

Nominally, BT's transaction was only with Bay Plastics. It lent the $3.95 million *to the debtor*, the debtor promised to repay the loan, and the debtor gave a first priority security interest in essentially all of its assets to secure the repayment. If this were the transaction, creditors likely would have no grounds for complaint, and it would not be vulnerable to fraudulent transfer attack.

However, the foregoing structure obscures the reality of the transaction. The selling shareholders' transaction was formally with Milhous, and eventually with BPI, the new owner of Bay Plastics. BPI purchased their stock, and arranged for their payment with funds that Bay Plastics borrowed from BT. Before Bay Plastics received the funds, it directed that $3.5 million be transferred to its incoming parent, BPI, and BPI in turn directed that the funds be paid out for the stock purchase. Thus in substance $3.5 million of the funds that Bay Plastics borrowed from BT went to pay for the stock of the selling shareholders, rather than to Bay Plastics.

This raises the question whether the Court should collapse the various transactions in this case into one integrated transaction. . . . [T]his turns on whether, from the perspective of the selling shareholders, the transaction appeared to be a straight sale without an LBO. If, in contrast, there is evidence that the parties knew or should have known that the transaction would deplete the assets of the company, the Court should look beyond the formal structure. In *Kupetz* the Ninth Circuit found it improper to collapse the transactions where the selling shareholders had no knowledge of the LBO character of the transaction, and there were no pre-transaction creditors.

In this case, in contrast, the selling shareholders had full knowledge that this was an LBO. The Milhous representatives informed them of this at the October 25 meeting before the transaction was finalized, and it was disclosed in the financial projections provided at that time. In addition, the selling shareholders discussed this feature with their legal counsel on October 25, and specifically discussed their exposure to a fraudulent transfer claim. Both the selling shareholders and their legal counsel were familiar with leveraged buyouts, because they had done others previously, and they knew the fraudulent transfer risks.

In addition, because Shintech qualifies as a pre-transaction creditor, the Court does not need to reach the issue of the knowledge of the LBO feature of the transaction by the selling shareholders: this is material to whether the transaction's various parts should be collapsed only when challenged by post-transaction creditors.

Thus, in this case the Court finds it appropriate to collapse the various pieces of this transaction into one integral transaction, in which the funds went to the selling shareholders, not to Bay Plastics or to its new parent BPI. The loan obligation, in contrast, was undertaken by Bay Plastics, which also provided the security for the loan.

Bay Plastics received no reasonably equivalent value for the security interest in all of its assets that it gave to BT in exchange for BT's funding of the stock sale. Under California law, reasonable equivalence must be determined from the standpoint of creditors. . . . Payment of funds to a parent corporation prevents a transaction from satisfying the "reasonably equivalent value" requirement. A financially healthy entity may give away its assets as it pleases so long as there remains enough to pay its debts. A financially distressed donor, however, may not be so generous.

From the debtor's perspective, it is apparent that the $450,000 that Bay Plastics presumably received (the $3.95 million loan less the $3.5 million paid to the selling shareholders) is not reasonably equivalent to the $3.95 million obligation that it undertook. Cf. Shape, Inc. v. Midwest Engineering (In re Shape, Inc.), 176 Bankr. 1, 3 (Bankr. D. Me. 1994) (payment of $70,000 for stock worth more than $1.5 million lacks reasonably equivalent value). Thus Bay Plastics did not receive reasonably equivalent value for the loan obligation and security interest that it granted to BT.

3. Insolvency of the Debtor

The third element of the fraudulent transfer cause of action at issue in this litigation is that the transaction rendered the debtor insolvent, if it was not so already. In this case the Court finds the evidence undisputed that the LBO rendered the debtor insolvent.

Insolvency is defined in California Civil Code § 3439.02(a): "A debtor is insolvent if, at fair valuations, the sum of the debtor's debts is greater than all of the debtor's assets." UFTA § 2(a) is essentially the same. These statutes adopt the balance sheet test for insolvency: a debtor is insolvent if the liabilities exceed the assets. . . .

The valuation of assets for insolvency purposes is based on "a fair valuation." This differs from a balance sheet, where most assets apart from publicly traded stocks and bonds are carried at historic cost, rather than current market value. The values of assets must be updated in light of subsequent use and market conditions: in accounting parlance, they must be "marked to market."

In addition, a balance sheet may include intangible assets such as goodwill[24] that may have no liquidation or going concern value, and which thus must be deleted in evaluating the solvency of an entity. Goodwill cannot be sold to satisfy a creditor's claim. Thus, in a liquidation bankruptcy case it must be disregarded in determining solvency of the debtor at the time of an LBO.

---

24. Goodwill is generally understood to represent the value of intangible factors that are expected to translate into greater than normal earning power. In addition to the advantageous relationship that a business enjoys with its customers, goodwill also includes advantageous relationships with employees, suppliers, lenders and others.

Because goodwill has no independent market or liquidation value, generally accepted accounting principles require that goodwill be written off over a period of time. In acquisition accounting, going concern value in excess of asset value is treated as goodwill.

Goodwill frequently appears on a balance sheet after the sale of a business, where it represents the excess of the purchase price over the net value of the other assets purchased. It appears that this may be the explanation for the appearance of goodwill on the debtor's balance sheet in this case.

Nominally, Bay Plastic's corporate balance sheet showed the debtor to be solvent after the LBO. But this resulted only from the addition of $2.26 million of goodwill to the asset side of the balance sheet. Bay Plastics had not previously carried any goodwill on its balance sheets.

The parties to this litigation have accepted the debtor's balance sheet immediately after the LBO as a fair presentation of the debtor's financial status, with the exception of goodwill. Thus the Court is relieved of the burden of marking to market the debtor's assets. However, the trustee contends that the goodwill of $2.26 million that first appeared at that time must be deleted in determining the debtor's solvency.

The Court finds that the balance sheet must be adjusted by deleting the unamortized goodwill of $2.26 million. It was not carried on the balance sheet before the LBO, and in any case it could not be sold to satisfy a creditor's claim. This is a liquidation case, where goodwill has no other value. This downward adjustment left Bay Plastics with a negative net worth of approximately $2 million immediately after the LBO. For fraudulent transfer purposes, it was rendered insolvent by the transaction.

Indeed, this is exactly the type of transaction that poses the extreme risk of an LBO. No Milhous entity put any funds or assets at risk in the investment at all. In consequence of the structure of the transaction, all of the risks of the enterprise were placed on its creditors. Milhous retained only the right to reap the benefits if the business was sufficiently profitable to avoid bankruptcy.[25]

4. Attack by a Pre-Transaction Creditor

The final element of the cause of action for fraudulent transfer rendering a debtor insolvent is that the transaction must be attacked by a pre-transaction creditor. This element is satisfied in this case.

Shintech, the principal unsecured creditor in this case, which holds more than 99% of the unsecured debt, is the pre-existing creditor. It was secured until this transaction, and in addition it held guaranties from each of the selling shareholders. In this transaction the selling shareholders and Milhous induced it to relinquish its security and guaranties to permit the transaction to be consummated. Although knowing the LBO character of the transaction, both the selling shareholders and Milhous failed to disclose this feature to Shintech.

The selling shareholders make three arguments against considering Shintech a qualifying pre-transaction creditor. First, they argue that Shintech's account was current at the time of the LBO, and that in consequence all of its debt comes from a later date.

---

25. In such a transaction there is a danger that the selling shareholders will be paid more than their stock is worth. With nothing at risk if the business is not sufficiently profitable, the purchaser has less incentive to make sure that the price is not excessive. Absent fraudulent transfer law, there is nothing to deter the buyers, sellers and bank from imposing all of the risks of loss on the creditors, as they did in this case.

Second, they argue that Shintech had an opportunity at the pre-closing meeting, where it agreed to release its security interest and guaranties, to ask any questions that it wanted, and it declared that it was satisfied with the information provided to it. Third, they claim that Nicole Plastic's purchase of Shintech's claim in settlement of a lawsuit by Shintech against Nicole and other Milhous entities disqualifies this claim as a pre-transaction claim: in effect, the shareholders contend, the claim now belongs to the debtor itself. The Court finds all of these arguments unpersuasive.

a. Shintech as Creditor

First, the Court finds that Shintech is a pre-transaction creditor of Bay Plastics, even if the account was current at the time of the LBO. Just three months earlier Shintech had entered into a massive contract with Bay Plastics to provide all of its requirements of PVC, which were monumental—up to 2.6 million pounds (1,300 tons) per month. Under this contract Bay Plastics owed a duty to Shintech to buy its PVC from Shintech for the duration of the contract, whether or not the account was current on any particular day. The contract was in place on the day of the LBO, and remained in force until after the bankruptcy filing. . . .

Shintech's contract rights under its requirements contract to provide PVC were certainly not valueless, even if payments were current at the time of the LBO. If Bay Plastics had repudiated the contract on the day after the LBO, it would have owed massive damages to Shintech. [The court found this contract obligation to be sufficient to make Shintech a present creditor under the UFTA] immediately before the date of the filing of the petition. . . .

The Court holds that this made Shintech a creditor of Bay Plastics at that time, and that Shintech maintained this status until the bankruptcy case was filed. Thus this element of the cause of action is met.

b. Investigation of the Transaction

Second, the selling shareholders argue that Shintech, the largest supplier of PVC resin in the industry, had every opportunity to investigate the nature of the LBO transaction, and cannot now be heard to complain about it. The Court finds this is irrelevant to the cause of action for a fraudulent transfer that renders a debtor insolvent. . . .

Shintech did change its position at the time of the transaction, in giving up its security and its guaranties. It apparently could have prevented the transaction from going forward if it had refused to make these concessions. However, the LBO feature of the transaction was hidden from it. Thus it constituted a secret transaction as to both Shintech and the industry, of the sort that the Ninth Circuit in *Kupetz* declared to be within the scope of a fraudulent transfer claim, even if brought only on behalf of subsequent creditors.

c. Settlement

Third, the Court finds that [] Nicole Plastic's purchase of Shintech's claim in its settlement of Shintech's lawsuit against various Milhous entities does not moot Shintech's pre-LBO claim. Nicole Plastic's purchase of Shintech's claim does not eliminate the claim. While the selling shareholders contend that in effect Bay Plastics now owns this claim, this is not so. Nicole Plastics is a different entity, and not the debtor or the trustee. The claim is still pending against the Bay Plastic estate. It does not belong to the debtor, but to its parent corporation, which is a separate entity. Most important, the claim is clearly adverse to the selling shareholders. It thus continues to support the debtor's fraudulent transfer claim against the selling shareholders.

C. Application of Fraudulent Transfer Law to LBOs

The Court finds it appropriate to apply fraudulent transfer law to an LBO. An LBO is different, not just in degree, but in character from the ordinary business and investment transactions engaged in by a corporation's management. An LBO is not a routine business transaction that should normally be given deference by the courts. It is not a corporate investment in a new venture, new equipment or property. Indeed, an LBO normally does not affect the business of the corporation at all: it only changes the ownership and adds a large layer of secured debt. Rather, an LBO is an investment of corporate assets, by borrowing against them, for the *personal* benefit of both old and new equity owners. Thus, the application of fraudulent transfer law to LBOs does not limit corporate entrepreneurial decisions.

Since an LBO reduces the availability of unencumbered assets, the buyout depletes estate assets available to pay creditors' claims. As the Ninth Circuit has stated:

> Existing unsecured creditors are vulnerable in [an LBO]. From their perspective, a pledge of the company's assets as collateral to finance the purchase of the company reduces the assets to which they can look for repayment.

> An LBO is attractive to the sellers, the buyers and the lender because it shifts most of the risk of loss to other creditors of the corporation. The acquired corporation receives little or nothing in exchange for the debt that it incurs.

From a creditor's point of view, an LBO is indistinguishable from a distribution or a gift to shareholders. The harm is quite like the harm imposed on creditors by donative transfers to third parties, which is one of the most traditional kinds of fraudulent transfers. If the value of the security interest given by the corporation does not exceed the shareholders' equity as shown on the balance sheet (after suitable revisions to mark the assets to market and to eliminate intangible assets of dubious value), there is usually no substantial harm to creditors. Indeed, typical corporate distribution statutes permit the payment of dividends in such circumstances, to the extent of the balance sheet equity. If the price paid to selling shareholders is higher, however, there may be insufficient assets remaining to satisfy creditors.

The vice of an LBO lies in the fact that the selling shareholders are paid indirectly with assets from the corporation itself, rather than by the purchasers. In effect, in an LBO the shareholders are paid with a corporate dividend or distribution. An LBO enables the selling shareholders to liquidate their equity interests, which are otherwise subordinate to general unsecured claims, without first paying creditors, which a normal liquidation would require. The selling shareholders in the transaction in effect disregard the status of the corporation as a separate entity for their benefit, but insist on respect of the corporation's separate status when it comes to creditors' claims (apart from those of the lender providing the funds for the transaction).

The possible detriment to creditors is exacerbated if the corporation's cash flow is not sufficient to service the loan. The bank eventually proceeds to foreclose on the corporation's assets and sells them at foreclosure prices, and leaves nothing for other creditors. Such foreclosure is frequently interrupted by the filing of a bankruptcy case. So it happened in this case. . . .

Should all LBOs be exposed to fraudulent transfer challenge? Certainly not. Under this Court's analysis, two kinds of LBOs ordinarily escape fraudulent transfer attack. This includes many, if not most, LBOs.

First, in a legitimate LBO, in which the assets mortgaged by a corporation to support an LBO do not exceed the net equity of the business (after appropriate adjustments), the transaction will not make the corporation insolvent, at least according to the balance sheet test. If in addition it has sufficient projected cash flow to pay its debts as they come due, the cash flow solvency test is met, also. This leaves an LBO exposed to fraudulent transfer attack only if the margin of equity is too thin to support the corporation's business.

A second kind of LBO also escapes fraudulent transfer attack, even though it leaves the subject corporation insolvent. If the cash flow is sufficient to make the debt payments, the transaction also is unassailable. This ordinarily turns on two factors: the degree of risk of default undertaken in the first instance, and the degree to which projected economic developments impacting the business are not overly optimistic. These LBOs escape fraudulent transfer attack either because of good financial projections or because of good luck: either factor is sufficient.

The Court's view of the proper application of fraudulent transfer law to LBOs does not make the selling shareholders the guarantors of the success of the LBO. A legitimate LBO, as described supra, shifts the risk of failure off their shoulders. As to subsequent creditors, they should not be required to shoulder the risk if the failure is caused by outside forces not reasonably foreseeable at the time of the transaction.

However, an LBO that is leveraged beyond the net worth of the business is a gamble. A highly leveraged business is much less able to weather temporary financial storms, because debt demands are less flexible than equity interest. The risks of this gamble should rest on the shoulders of the shareholders (old and new), not those of the creditors: the shareholders enjoy the benefits if the gamble is successful, and they should bear the burdens if it is not. This, after all, is the role of equity owners of a corporation. The application of fraudulent transfer law to LBOs shifts the risks of an LBO transaction from the creditors, who are not parties to the transaction, back to the old and new shareholders who bring about such transactions. As Sherwin states:

> These parties, who are directly involved as the principal engineers and beneficiaries of the buyout, should bear the risk of negative consequences if the transaction does not in fact comply with the standards for creditor protection set out in the fraudulent conveyance statutes. . . . They should be accountable to creditors for the benefits diverted from the corporation if they knew or should have known . . . of facts the court determines to establish a constructive fraud against creditors.

[Emily L. Sherwin, *Creditors' Rights Against Participants in a Leveraged Buyout*, 72 MINN. L. REV. 449, 519 (1988).]

How long should selling shareholders be exposed to the risk that an LBO will go bad? There is a traditional answer to this question: until the statute of limitations runs. Perhaps there should be a shorter statute of limitations for LBOs than the four to seven years that is common under the UFTA. This is a decision for the legislature to make.

IV. CONCLUSION

Having found no triable issue of material fact, the Court concludes that the trustee is entitled to a summary judgment setting aside the constructive fraudulent transfer in this case to the selling shareholders.

Bay Plastics is a constructive fraudulent transfer case. It also pointedly says that not all LBOs should be vulnerable to attach as fraudulent transfers. But couldn't the LBO structure, by its very nature, be vulnerable to attach as an actual fraudulent transfer? *See Wieboldt Stores, Inc. v. Schottenstein*, 94 B.R. 488 (N.D. Ill. 1988).

In *Bay Plastics*, the suit was brought against the selling shareholders to recover the funds they received in the LBO. Do you think that such a suit would be likely to succeed if instead of there being only three shareholders, Bay Plastics had been a publicly traded firm with thousands of shareholders?

Selling shareholders are not the only possible defendant in fraudulent transfer litigation arising from an LBO. Other possible defendants include the lenders who financed the LBO and the financial advisors for the LBO. The lenders face potential liability because they received a lien from the target company (which also incurred an obligation), which did not receive reasonably equivalent value as the funds did not go to the target company but to the shareholders (directly or indirectly). Financial advisors are often paid with a percentage of deal proceeds, so they too have potential liability, much like the shareholders. Additionally, officers and directors of the target company who approved the transaction may face suits for breach of fiduciary duty if they knowingly caused the firm to part with assets for less than fair value.

What about the private equity sponsor, however? Don't they have some fraudulent transfer liability? The answer is "maybe." The initial problem is that there is generally no transfer of target firm assets to the private equity sponsor in the LBO. The private equity sponsor merely acquires the stock of the target firm (usually indirectly through an acquisition subsidiary, like in *Bay Plastics*). Yet UFTA § 8(b)(1) and 11 U.S.C. § 550(a)(1) both impose liability not just on the initial transferee, but also on any part "for whose benefit the transfer was made." That would seem to cover the private equity sponsor. Additionally, the private equity sponsor may face various state law claims, such as breach of fiduciary duty or aiding and abetting the fraudulent transfers (although not all states recognize such a cause of action). Moreover, to the extent that the sponsor has taken out management or advisory fees or the like from the target, those transfers may themselves be vulnerable to attack, particularly if the LBO is itself successfully avoided. As a result, LBO sponsors are frequently looking to obtain a release in Chapter 11, and a frequent bargain is for the sponsor to walk away from its investment and any claims it has against the estate in exchange for a release by the estate.

Fraudulent transfer litigation is usually long and complicated, and it rarely results in the actual avoidance of transfers. Instead, it often leads to settlement, and therefore the ability to credibly threaten fraudulent transfer liability can be very helpful for shaping a Chapter 11 plan, as the settlement can help fund the plan.

III. THE DOCTRINE OF *MOORE v. BAY*

An important doctrinal twist of fraudulent transfer law comes from a controversial Supreme Court decision, *Moore v. Bay*, which has come to stand for the principle that a transfer that is avoidable as to even a penny is avoidable in its entirety.

Moore v. Bay
284 U.S. 4 (1931)

Mr. Justice HOLMES delivered the opinion of the Court.

The bankrupt executed a mortgage of automobiles, furniture, show room and shop equipment that is admitted to be bad as against creditors who were such at the date of the mortgage and those who became such between the date of the mortgage and that on which it was recorded, there having been a failure to observe the requirements of the Civil Code of California, § 3440. The question raised is whether the mortgage is void also as against those who gave the bankrupt credit at a later date, after the mortgage was on record. The Circuit Court of Appeals affirmed an order of the District Judge giving the mortgage priority over the last creditors. Whether the Court was right must be decided by the Bankruptcy Act since it is superior to all state laws upon the subject.

The trustee in bankruptcy gets the title to all property which has been transferred by the bankrupt in fraud of creditors, or which prior to the petition he could by any means have transferred, or which might have been levied upon and sold under judicial process against him. Act of July 1, 1898, c. 541, § 70; U.S. Code, Title 11, § 110. By § 67, Code, Title 11, § 107(a), claims which for want of record or for other reasons would not have been valid liens as against the claims of the creditors of the bankrupt shall not be liens against his estate. The rights of the trustee by subrogation are to be enforced for the benefit of the estate. The Circuit Courts of Appeals seem generally to agree, as the language of the Bankruptcy Act appears to us to imply very plainly, that what thus is recovered for the benefit of the estate is to be distributed in "dividends of an equal percentum on all allowed claims, except such as have priority or are secured." Bankruptcy Act, § 65, Code, Title 11, § 105.

Decree reversed.

Moore v. Bay was one of Justice Oliver Wendell Holmes, Jr.'s last decisions, and surely one of his shortest. The opinion is enigmatic. The issue the Court faced was whether under the Bankruptcy Act of 1898 a trustee in bankruptcy could avoid a fraudulent transfer only to the extent that it could be avoided by actual creditors at state law, or whether it could be avoided in its entirety. At state law, the transfer at issue—a mortgage—was avoidable by those creditors who existed between the date of the mortgage and the date of its recording. But it was not avoidable at state law by creditors who gave credit after it was recorded, as they had notice of the transfer. The Supreme Court held that the entire transfer was avoidable. The trustee was subrogated to the rights of individual creditors, but these rights were to be enforced for the entire estate. Therefore, even if an actual creditor were able to avoid only one cent of a transfer under state law, the entire transfer could be avoided under bankruptcy law, even if the trustee were proceeding under state law per section 544(b) (or its predecessor). Section 544(b) (and its predecessor) allow the trustee to stand in the shoes of a single actual "golden" creditor to bring avoidance actions. *Moore v. Bay* creates a legal fiction that all creditors have the same powers and rights under state law as the actual "golden" creditor to unwind transactions.

The effect of *Moore v. Bay* is to make state law defenses to individual creditor's fraudulent transfer claims, such as estoppel or ratification, inapplicable to actions brought by the trustee. Thus, even if a creditor participated in the fraudulent transfer, such as providing financing for the transaction, its complicity would not prevent it from sharing in the estate's recovery in bankruptcy, even if it would have been precluded from bringing a fraudulent transfer suit at state law.

Moore v. Bay is a much-criticized opinion, but Congress nevertheless refused to reverse it when it enacted the Bankruptcy Code, perhaps out of a concern that the trustee would be saddled with the burden of proving which creditors could actually have avoided the transfer. Section 550 follows the rule of *Moore v. Bay*. By creating the legal fiction that the trustee, in bringing suit on behalf of the estate, can recover for all creditors as if they had the power of an actual "golden" creditor, *Moore v. Bay* and section 550 create a rule that is consistent with the strong-arm powers of section 544(a), which give the trustee the powers of a hypothetical creditor.

The doctrine of *Moore v. Bay* also opens the door to a substantial expansion of the statute of limitations for fraudulent transfer actions. Recall that under *Moore v. Bay* the trustee can leverage the power of a single "golden" actual creditor for the benefit of all creditors, even if those other creditors would not have had the power to avoid a transfer at state law. What if that creditor happens to be a super-powered creditor? Under the rule of *Moore v. Bay*, those super-powers transfer to the other creditors. Who is a super-powered creditor? The IRS. The IRS is empowered to collect a taxpayer's liability from transferees of the property of the taxpayer under state fraudulent transfer law. *See* 26 U.S.C. § 6901. The IRS, however, is not subject to state law statutes of limitations. Instead, the IRS is subject to a 10-year statute of limitations for collection, running from the time tax liability is assessed. 26 U.S.C. § 6502(a)(1). Assessment of liability runs, in turn, from varying points. 26 U.S.C. §§ 6501, 6901 (for the taxpayer, three years after the filing of a tax return, but only one year for the transferee after assessment of the taxpayer). What this means is that the IRS has at least 10 years to seek to recover a fraudulent transfer. Some courts have held that the trustee in bankruptcy can bootstrap section 544(b) claims to a 10-year statute of limitations, instead of the various state law one- to six-year statutes of limitations, if the IRS could have brought a fraudulent transfer claim. *In re Kaiser*, 525 B.R. 697 (Bankr. N.D. Ill. 2014). The doctrine of *Moore v. Bay* supercharges the trustee's power under sections 544(b) and 548, making the trustee more powerful than state law creditors.

IV. LIMITATIONS ON AVOIDANCE ACTIONS

Just as the Bankruptcy Code exempts financial contracts from the automatic stay (see Chapter 11 of this book), it also exempts them from being subject to certain avoidance actions. Because of the broad drafting of the financial contract exemptions, they also frustrate many fraudulent transfer actions, particularly involving LBOs.

A. Financial Contract Exemption from Section 548(a)(1)(B) Constructive Fraudulent Transfer Liability

Two sets of provisions protect financial contracts from avoidance actions. First, section 548(d) deems the counterparties in financial contracts—forward contracts, commodities, futures contracts, repos, securities contracts swaps, and master netting agreements—as having taken for value to the extent they receive a margin or settlement payment or other transfer. The effect of section 548(d) is to insulate these non-debtor counterparties from constructive fraudulent transfer liability under section 548(a)(1)(B).

B. "Settlement Payment" Defense: General Protection of Financial Contracts from Avoidance Actions

Second, sections 546(e)-(g), and 546(j) protect transfers made in repos, swaps, and master netting agreements, as well as "settlement payments" for commodities contracts, securities contracts, and forward contracts, from avoidance actions other than actions under section 548(a)(1) for actual fraudulent transfers. Sections 546(e)-(g) and (j) cover not only constructive fraudulent transfers under section 548(a)(1)(B), but also all fraudulent transfers (actual and constructive) brought by the trustee using state law via section 544(b), as well as all strong-arm actions, statutory lien avoidance, and preferences brought by the trustee.

Because sections 546(e)-(g) and (j) protect financial contracts from avoidance actions under section 544(b), state law actions for actual fraudulent transfers cannot be pursued, which means that the two-year federal statute of limitations is the only one applicable to actual fraudulent transfer actions regarding financial contracts. The six-year New York fraudulent conveyance statute of limitations, N.Y. C.P.L.R. § 213, is not a tool in the trustee's arsenal when a section 546 defense applies. *See In re Bernard L. Madoff Inv. Sec. LLC*, 773 F.3d 411 (2d Cir. 2014).

Section 546(e) contains two distinct safe harbors known collectively as the "settlement payment" defense. First, it protects transfers that are "margin payments" or "settlement payments." This is sometimes referred to as the "settlement payment safe harbor." Second, it protects transfers made by, or to, or for the benefit of a "commodity broker, forward contract merchant, stockbroker, financial institution, financial participant, or securities clearing agency, in connection with a securities contract, commodities contract, or forward contract." This is sometimes referred to as the "financial institution safe harbor." Thus, even if a payment is not a margin payment or settlement payment, it can still potentially be protected against avoidance actions under the financial institution safe harbor. Sections 546(f), (g), and (j) contain safe harbors for repos, swaps, and master netting agreements, respectively.

Enron Creditors Recovery Corp. v. Alfa, S.A.B. de C.V.

651 F.3d 329 (2d Cir. 2011)

JOHN M. WALKER, JR., Circuit Judge:

This appeal raises an issue of first impression in the courts of appeals: whether 11 U.S.C. § 546(e), which shields "settlement payments" from avoidance actions in bankruptcy, extends to an issuer's payments to redeem its commercial paper prior to maturity. Enron Creditors Recovery Corp. ("Enron") seeks to avoid and recover payments Enron made to redeem its commercial paper prior to maturity from Appellees Alfa, S.A.B. de C.V. ("Alfa"), ING VP Balanced Portfolio, Inc., and ING VP Bond Portfolio, Inc. (collectively, "ING"), whose notes were redeemed by Enron. Alfa and ING argue that § 546(e) protects these payments from avoidance.

. . .

I. Facts

Between October 25, 2001 and November 6, 2001, Enron drew down on its $3 billion revolving lines of credit and paid out more than $1.1 billion to retire certain of its unsecured and uncertificated commercial paper prior to the paper's maturity. Enron redeemed the commercial paper at the accrued par value, calculated as the price originally paid plus accrued interest. This price was considerably higher than the paper's market value.

The offering memoranda that accompanied the issuance of the commercial paper provided that the "Notes are not redeemable or subject to voluntary prepayment by the Company prior to maturity." This provision prohibited calls and puts: Enron could not force investors to surrender the notes and the investors could not require Enron to prepay them.

The Depository Trust Company (the "DTC"), a clearing agency, maintained bookkeeping entries that tracked ownership of Enron's commercial paper. This is the customary tracking method in the industry. Every issuer of commercial paper has an issuing and paying agent ("IPA") within the DTC to issue commercial paper and to pay at maturity or at an early redemption.

Three broker-dealers, J.P. Morgan, Goldman, Sachs & Co., and Lehman Brothers Commercial Paper, Inc., participated in Enron's redemption. They received the commercial paper from the individual noteholders and paid them the redemption price. The mechanics of these transfers were as follows. The DTC debited the redemption price from each broker-dealer's account and credited it to the noteholder's DTC account. The broker-dealers then transferred the notes to the DTC account of Enron's issuing and paying agent, Chase IPA, and received payment from Enron through the DTC. Immediately after the broker-dealer received payment, the commercial paper Enron redeemed was extinguished in the DTC system. Confirmations of these transactions referred to them as securities trades, termed them "purchases" from the holders, and referenced a "trade date" and "settlement date."

Prior to these transactions, ING and Alfa owned Enron commercial paper in the amount, respectively, of $48,200,000 and $5,667,255. They both agreed to transfer their commercial paper to broker-dealer J.P. Morgan in exchange for the redemption price.

The parties dispute the circumstances and motives surrounding Enron's redemption. Enron argues that it made the redemption payments under pressure from noteholders seeking to recover on their investments amidst rumors of Enron's imminent implosion. Alfa and ING argue that Enron redeemed its commercial paper to "calm the irrational markets" and leave a favorable impression that would allow it to reenter the commercial paper market once "bad publicity" about the company's stability "had blown over." They argue that the redemption was an economically rational move that allowed Enron to refinance its existing commercial paper debt with debt at a lower interest rate.

II. Procedural History

[On December 2, 2001, Enron petitioned for Chapter 11 bankruptcy. T]he reorganized entity brought adversary proceedings against approximately two hundred financial institutions, including appellees Alfa and ING, seeking to avoid and recover the redemption payments. It alleged that the payments were recoverable as (1) preferential transfers under 11 U.S.C. § 547(b), because they were made on account of an antecedent debt within ninety days prior to bankruptcy, and (2) constructively fraudulent transfers under 11 U.S.C. § 548(a)(1)(B), because the redemption price exceeded the commercial paper's fair market value.

In 2004, the defendants in the adversary proceedings moved to dismiss Enron's complaint for failure to state a claim. They argued that the redemption payments were "settlement payments" protected from avoidance under 11 U.S.C. § 546(e)'s safe harbor. Section 546(e) provides, in relevant part, that

> [n]otwithstanding sections . . . 547 [and] 548(a)(1)(B) . . . of this title, [which empower the trustee to avoid preferential and constructively fraudulent transfers,] the trustee may not avoid a transfer that is a . . . settlement payment, as defined in section . . . 741 of this title, made by or to (or for the benefit of) a . . . stockbroker, financial institution, financial participant, or securities clearing agency . . . that is made before the commencement of the case, except under section 548(a)(1)(A) of this title[, which empowers the trustee to avoid transfers made with actual intent to hinder, delay, or defraud creditors].

Section 741(8) of Title 11, in turn, defines a "settlement payment" as "a preliminary settlement payment, a partial settlement payment, an interim settlement payment, a settlement payment on account, a final settlement payment, or any other similar payment commonly used in the securities trade."

[The bankruptcy court denied the defendants' motion to dismiss, after which most of the defendants settled. Alfa and ING continued to litigate. The bankruptcy court denied them summary judgment on the basis that Alfa and ING had not demonstrated that Enron's payments were settlement payments as defined in section 741(8) because they had failed to establish that the payments were made to acquire title to the commercial paper rather than to retire debt. The bankruptcy court also emphasized the unusual nature of the transaction, including the above-market price and the insistence of the broker-dealers to act as intermediaries rather than principals.]

[On appeal the district court reversed.] The district court held (1) that § 741(8)'s definition of "settlement payment" is not limited to payments that are "commonly used," and, therefore, that the circumstances of a particular payment do not bear on whether that payment fits within the definition, (2) that a "settlement payment is any transfer that concludes or consummates a securities transaction," and (3) that Enron's redemption constitutes a securities transaction regardless of whether Enron acquired title to the commercial paper, because the redemption involved "the delivery and receipt of funds and securities." Enron appealed to this court.

DISCUSSION

. . . Enron argues that the bankruptcy court's decision was correct and that the district court erred by holding that settlement payments under § 741(8) are not limited to those that are commonly used in the securities trade and that involve the transfer of title to a security. . . . Here, we review only the issue the district court agreed to hear on appeal:

> whether the § 546(e) "safe harbor" . . . extends to transactions in which commercial paper is redeemed by the issuer prior to maturity, using the customary mechanism of the Depository Trust Company . . . for trading in commercial paper . . . , without regard to extrinsic facts about the nature of the [transactions], the motive behind the [transactions], or the circumstances under which the payments were made.

. . .

I. Judicial Interpretation of the Safe Harbor

Congress enacted § 546(e)'s safe harbor in 1982 as a means of "minimiz[ing] the displacement caused in the commodities and securities markets in the event of a major bankruptcy affecting those industries." *Kaiser Steel Corp. v. Charles Schwab & Co., Inc.*, 913 F.2d 846, 849 (10th Cir. 1990). If a firm is required to repay amounts received in settled securities transactions, it could have insufficient capital or liquidity to meet its current securities trading obligations, placing other market participants and the securities markets themselves at risk.

The safe harbor limits this risk by prohibiting the avoidance of "settlement payments" made by, to, or on behalf of a number of participants in the financial markets. By restricting a bankruptcy trustee's power to recover payments that are otherwise avoidable under the Bankruptcy Code, the safe harbor stands "at the intersection of two important national legislative policies on a collision course—the policies of bankruptcy and securities law." *In re Resorts Int'l, Inc.*, 181 F.3d 505, 515 (3d Cir. 1999).

Section 741(8), which § 546(e) incorporates, defines "settlement payment" rather circularly as "a preliminary settlement payment, a partial settlement payment, an interim settlement payment, a settlement payment on account, a final settlement payment, or any other similar payment commonly used in the securities trade." The parties, following our sister circuits, agree that courts should interpret the definition, "in the context of the securities industry," as "the transfer of cash or securities made to complete [a] securities transaction." *Contemporary Indus. Corp. v. Frost*, 564 F.3d 981, 985 (8th Cir. 2009).

Although our circuit has not yet addressed the scope of § 741(8)'s definition, other circuits have held it to be "extremely broad." Several circuits, for example, have rejected limitations on the definition that would exclude transactions in privately held securities or transactions that do not involve financial intermediaries that take title to the securities during the course of the transaction. *See, e.g., In re Plassein Int'l Corp.*, 590 F.3d 252, 258-59 (3d Cir. 2009); *In re QSI Holdings, Inc.*, 571 F.3d [545, 549-550 (6th Cir. 2009)]; *Contemporary Indus. Corp.*, 564 F.3d at 986. No circuit has yet addressed the safe harbor's application to an issuer's early redemption of commercial paper.

Alfa and ING argue that Enron's redemption payments are settlement payments within the meaning of § 741(8) because they completed a transaction involving the exchange of money for securities. . . .

Enron proposes three limitations on the definition of settlement payment in § 741(8), each of which, it argues, would exclude the redemption payments. First, it contends that the final phrase of § 741(8)—"commonly used in the securities trade"—excludes all payments that are not common in the securities industry, including, Enron argues, Enron's redemption. Second, Enron argues that the definition includes only transactions in which title to the securities changes hands. Because, Enron argues, the redemption payments here were made to retire debt and not to acquire title to the commercial paper, they are not settlement payments within the meaning of § 741(8). Finally, Enron argues that the redemption payments are not settlement payments because they did not involve a financial intermediary that took title to the transacted securities and thus did not implicate the risks that prompted Congress to enact the safe harbor.

Because we find nothing in the Bankruptcy Code or the relevant caselaw that supports Enron's proposed limitations on the definition of settlement payment in § 741(8), we reject them. We hold that Enron's redemption payments fall within the plain language of § 741(8) and are thus protected from avoidance under § 546(e).

II. "Commonly Used in the Securities Trade"

Section 741(8) defines "settlement payment" as "a preliminary settlement payment, a partial settlement payment, an interim settlement payment, a settlement payment on account, a final settlement payment, or any other similar payment commonly used in the securities trade." Enron argues that the phrase "commonly used in the securities trade" modifies all the preceding terms and thereby excludes from the definition all uncommon payments. We disagree.

First, as the district court held, the grammatical structure of the statute strongly suggests that the phrase "commonly used in the securities trade" modifies only the term immediately preceding it: "any other similar payment." Under the "rule of the last antecedent, . . . a limiting clause or phrase . . . should ordinarily be read as modifying only the noun or phrase that it immediately follows." *Barnhart v. Thomas*, 540 U.S. 20, 26 (2003).

Enron seizes on a corollary rule of construction under which "a modifier . . . set off from a series of antecedents by a comma . . . should be read to apply to each of those antecedents." For example, in the phrase "no person shall be deprived of life, liberty, or the pursuit of happiness, without due process of law," the phrase "without due process of law" modifies all three terms.

This rule, however, does not apply to the series in § 741(8) because the modifier is not set off from its antecedents by a comma. Because both the modifier and its immediate antecedent are set off from the preceding terms in the series, the last-antecedent rule applies. The phrase "commonly used in the securities industry" thus is properly read as modifying only the term "any other similar payment." The phrase is not a limitation on the definition of settlement payment, but rather, as our sister circuits have held, it is "a catchall phrase intended to underscore the breadth of the § 546(e) exemption." *In re QSI Holdings, Inc.*, 571 F.3d at 550.

Moreover, Enron's proposed reading would make application of the safe harbor in every case depend on a factual determination regarding the commonness of a given transaction. It is not clear whether that determination would depend on the economic rationality of the transaction, its frequency in the marketplace, signs of an intent to favor certain creditors—as suggested by the facts on which the bankruptcy court relied, such as the alleged coercion by Enron's commercial paper noteholders—or some other factor. This reading of the statute would result in commercial uncertainty and unpredictability at odds with the safe harbor's purpose and in an area of law where certainty and predictability are at a premium.

Accordingly, we hold that the phrase "commonly used in the securities industry" limits only the phrase immediately preceding it; it does not limit the other transactions that § 741(8) defines as settlement payments.

III. Redemption of Debt Securities

Enron next argues that the redemption payments are not settlement payments because they involved the retirement of debt, not the acquisition of title to the commercial paper. We find no basis in the Bankruptcy Code or the relevant caselaw to interpret § 741(8) as excluding the redemption of debt securities. Because Enron's redemption payments completed a transaction in securities, we hold that they are settlement payments within the meaning of § 741(8).

. . .

Nothing in the text of § 741(8) or in any other provision of the Bankruptcy Code supports a purchase or sale requirement. Enron argues that a "settlement payment" must involve a transaction in securities, which, in turn, must involve a purchase or sale. While we, like our sister circuits, agree that in the context of the securities industry a "'settlement' refers to 'the completion of a securities transaction,'" *Contemporary Indus. Corp.*, 564 F.3d at 985, we find little support for the contention that a securities transaction necessarily involves a purchase or sale. Several of the industry definitions of "settlement payment" on which other courts of appeals have relied define the term as an exchange of money or securities that completes a securities transaction; these definitions make no mention of a requirement that title to the securities changes hands. . . .

While . . . *Kaiser Steel Corp.* also cites industry definitions that reference a purchase or sale of securities, 913 F. 2d at 849, the range of definitions that the decision cites suggests that the securities industry does not universally consider a purchase or sale of securities to be a necessary element of a settlement payment.

. . .

Because we find no basis in the Bankruptcy Code or the caselaw for a purchase or sale requirement, and because we do not think such a requirement is necessary to exclude from the safe harbor repayment of ordinary loans, we decline to impose a purchase or sale requirement on § 741(8).

IV. Involvement of a Financial Intermediary

Enron also argues that the redemption of debt does not constitute a protected settlement payment because it did not involve a financial intermediary that took a beneficial interest in the securities during the course of the transaction. Enron argues that the redemption thus did not implicate the systemic risks that motivated Congress's enactment of the safe harbor. Although the role of the broker-dealers that participated in Enron's redemption is a disputed issue of fact, Enron is correct that the DTC acted as a conduit and recordkeeper rather than a clearing agency that takes title to the securities during the course of the transaction.*

Nevertheless, we do not think the absence of a financial intermediary that takes title to the transacted securities during the course of the transaction is a proper basis on which to deny safe-harbor protection. The Third, Sixth, and Eighth Circuits rejected similar arguments in affirming application of the safe harbor to leveraged buyouts of private companies that involved financial intermediaries who served only as conduits. *See In re Plassein Int'l Corp.*, 590 F.3d at 257-59; *In re QSI Holdings, Inc.*, 571 F.3d at 549-50; *Contemporary Indus. Corp.*, 564 F.3d at 986. In reasoning that provides an analog for us, these courts explained that undoing long-settled leveraged buyouts would have a substantial impact on the stability of the financial markets, even though only private securities were involved and no financial intermediary took a beneficial interest in the exchanged securities during the course of the transaction. *See In re Plassein Int'l Corp.*, 590 F.3d at 258; *In re QSI Holdings, Inc.*, 571 F.3d at 550; *Contemporary Indus. Corp.*, 564 F.3d at 987. We see no reason to think that undoing Enron's redemption payments, which involved over a billion dollars and approximately two hundred noteholders, would not also have a substantial and similarly negative effect on the financial markets.

Moreover, § 546(e) applies to settlement payments made "by or to (or for the benefit of)" a number of participants in the financial markets. It would appear inconsistent with this language for courts to limit the safe harbor circuitously by interpreting the definition of "settlement payment" to exclude payments that do not involve a financial intermediary that takes title to the securities during the course of the transaction.

In sum, we decline to adopt Enron's proposed exclusions from the definition of settlement payment and the safe harbor. The payments at issue were made to redeem commercial paper, which the Bankruptcy Code defines as a security. 11 U.S.C. § 101(49)(A)(i). They thus constitute the "transfer of cash . . . made to complete [a] securities transaction" and are settlement payments within the meaning of § 741(8). Because we reach this conclusion by looking to the statute's plain language, we decline to address Enron's arguments regarding legislative history, which, in any event, would not lead to a different result. . . .

CONCLUSION

For the foregoing reasons, we AFFIRM the district court's decision reversing the decision of the Bankruptcy Court and directing entry of summary judgment in favor of Alfa and ING.

[Judge Koeltl's dissent is omitted.]

As a practical matter, *Enron* means that, at least in the Second Circuit, virtually all transactions a firm makes in securities, commodities futures, forward contracts, repos, and swaps, or that are subject to a master netting agreement, are protected from avoidance actions by section 546. *Enron* makes clear that a "settlement payment" is a settlement payment is a settlement payment, no matter the lack of any policy justification for protecting the payment from avoidance. Instead, the safe harbor of section 546(e) (and presumably the analogous safe harbors of sections 546(f)-(g) and (j)) will be read literally and hence broadly. A settlement payment is just a payment on a contract, and as long as it is made "by or to" a "commodity broker, forward contract, merchant, stockbroker, financial institution, financial participant, or securities clearing agency," it is covered by the safe harbor.

Section 546(e) contains a second safe harbor, for "a transfer made by or to (or for the benefit of) a commodity broker, forward contract merchant, stockbroker, financial institution, financial participant, or securities clearing agency, in connection with a securities contract . . . commodity contract . . . or forward contract, that is made before the commencement of the case . . ." . This second safe harbor, known as the "financial institution safe harbor," shields the transfers made to financial institutions themselves in the context of a securities or commodities or forward contract. In 2018, the Supreme Court clarified that the financial institution safe harbor does not shield the ultimate recipient if it is not a financial institution. *Merit Mgmt. Grp., LP v. FTI Consulting, Inc.*, 138 S. Ct. 883 (2018). Thus, if a transfer in connection with a securities contract went from $A \to B \to C \to D$, in which B and C, but not D, were financial institutions, B and C could shelter in the financial institution safe harbor from avoidance actions, but *D* could not. In other words, the financial institution safe harbor protects financial intermediaries that act as conduits in the transaction from liability for constructive fraudulent transfers.

Merit Management Group left unresolved the extent to which the financial institution safe harbor protects *D*, the ultimate transferee, if *D* is a financial institution. Thus, does the financial institution safe harbor protect banks that provide the financing for an LBO or investment banks that provide advisory services for LBOs (and take their fees out of the financing)? These institutions are lending or providing services in connection with a securities contract (the buyout of the shares), but are in the position of *D*, the ultimate transferee, and the fact that they are financial institutions seems to be of no particular importance in that regard.

To see how far the "financial institution" safe harbor of section 546(e) might reach, consider *Krol v. Key Bank N.A.* (*In re MCK Millennium Ctr. Parking, LLC*), 2015 Bankr. LEXIS 1432 (Bankr. N.D. Ill. Apr. 24, 2015). In *Krol*, a Chapter 7 trustee sued to recover as fraudulent transfers some $2.2 million in payments the debtor had made on a commercial mortgage note owed by its affiliate, for which the debtor had received no consideration. The note had been securitized, and the intent to securitize was indicated on the note. The court held that the payments could not be avoided because the payments made to the national bank servicer of the securitization trust and then remitted to the trust by the servicer were "made by or to . . . a financial institution . . . in connection with a securities contract," namely the issuance of securities as part of the securitization. Presumably, further payments by the trustee (a financial institution) to the securitization investors (themselves primarily financial institutions) would also be covered by the safe harbor. This quite literal reading of the statute suggests that virtually all payments on securitized loans—whether business or consumer loans—cannot be avoided as fraudulent transfers or preferences. The financial institutions safe harbor clearly protects intermediary financial institution transferees and perhaps all financial institution transferees.

C. Why the Special Treatment?

Why the special treatment for financial contracts? One can tell two stories. One story is a noble one about the need to protect the financial system as a whole. The other story is a sordid tale of rent-seeking wearing a beard of systemic risk prevention. It is worthwhile drilling down into the systemic risk prevention story. The asserted policy basis for exemption of financial contracts from certain avoidance actions is somewhat different from the policy basis for exempting the termination, acceleration, liquidation, and setoff of these contracts from the automatic stay. The stay exemptions are justified as necessary to prevent the spillover effects in financial markets of a debtor's collapse were counterparties to find their positions illiquid and subject to cherry-picking by the debtor. (Never mind that the bankruptcy claims market is capable of providing significant liquidity and that instead of cherry-picking by debtors the current law permits not just cherry-picking by counterparties, but the ability to walk away from out-of-the-money contracts.)

Avoidance actions do not raise the same sort of market-wide liquidity disruptions as the automatic stay. Instead, they raise concerns about finality in financial contracts. If financial contracts were subject to avoidance actions, counterparties could not be certain of their gains until the statute of limitations had run on the avoidance actions; the contracts could have long since terminated, but there would be an extended subsequent period of uncertainty. There is a logic to the finality argument, but the proper scope of section 546(e) in particular remains controversial.

Problem Set 31

(1) Real estate developer Rail Seaone does not like fulfilling his obligations, and he goes to more trouble than most to avoid them. He broke a contract with Anna Sandor Design, leading a jury to award Sandor more than $2 million in damages. Before the jury could return its verdict, however, Seaone gave his 20-year old son, Rafael-Ilan, several valuable vacant lots he owned adjoining his home in Miami, Florida. The lots are worth several million dollars. Rafael-Ilan promptly recorded the deeds in the county land records. Seaone then filed for Chapter 7 bankruptcy, claiming that he had no non-exempt assets. Will the Chapter 7 trustee be able to recover anything? 11 U.S.C. §§ 544(b), 548(a)(1)(A)-(B).

(2) Mercury Computers maintains significant dollar deposits outside of the United States, which it cannot repatriate without paying large tax penalties. On May 1, a $275 million final judgment in an antitrust suit was entered against Mercury in federal court. Two days later, Mercury closed a financing deal in which it borrowed $150 million, secured by all of its domestic assets. Mercury promptly declared a dividend, which it paid using the $150 million. A year later, after an embarrassing string of security flaws resulted in a sharp decline in sales, Mercury filed for Chapter 11. Can Mercury, as DIP, avoid the dividend? 11 U.S.C. §§ 544(b), 548.

(3) The Vulcan Steel Corporation is a holding company with numerous operating subsidiaries. Vulcan utilizes a centralized cash management system. All receivables collected by Vulcan's operating subsidiaries are immediately dividended upstream to a central account controlled by the parent corporation. All of the subsidiaries' bills are paid by the parent from this central account. Thus, when the operating subsidiaries place orders with suppliers and vendors, the invoices are paid by the parent from the central account, while the goods and services are delivered to the subsidiaries. This centralized cash management system reduces its administrative costs, maximizes flexibility in allocating cash within the firm, and enables more efficient short-term investment of excess funds. When Vulcan files for Chapter 11, what arguments are the parent corporation's unsecured bondholders likely to make? What is the best response?

(4) DOM, Inc. is a large residential homebuilder. A year ago, DOM, Inc. had guaranteed a $675 million loan to a joint venture real estate finance company. The loan was not guaranteed by DOM, Inc.'s various subsidiaries, only by the parent. After the joint venture failed, the lenders (the "Old Lenders") sued DOM, Inc. on the guarantee. The suit presented a major threat to DOM's operations because a significant judgment against it would constitute a default on some of its other financial obligations. Those

other obligations were guaranteed by DOM's subsidiaries, which had pledged their assets as security for their guaranties. To avoid a cross-default problem, DOM agreed to settle the joint venture litigation with the Old Lenders for $400 million. To finance the settlement, DOM borrowed $400 million from a new group of lenders (the "New Lenders"). This loan was secured by substantially all of DOM's assets as well as its subsidiaries' assets. DOM filed for bankruptcy a few months ago as a recent housing market downturn has left DOM with a large inventory it cannot sell and expensive debt service. You are counsel to the Official Committee of Unsecured Creditors. Are there any transfers you might successfully challenge? 11 U.S.C. § 548.

(5) Nine months before filing for Chapter 11, Hercules Heavy Industries announced that it was exercising its right to redeem $100 million of its senior unsecured certificated debentures prior to the debentures' maturity. Hercules hoped to take advantage of lower interest rates with the redemption, although Hercules had to borrow $105 million on a secured basis to finance the redemption and the associated transaction fees. Hercules redeemed the debentures by directing its bank, Stygian Bank and Trust, to wire the redemption funds from Hercules' account at Stygian to the Repository Trust Corporation, which held legal title to the debenture certificates for their beneficial owners. (The beneficial owners have a "security entitlement" against the Repository Trust Corporation.) The wire transfer went through FedWire, the Federal Reserve's wire transfer system. Upon receipt of the wire transfer, the Repository Trust Corporation surrendered the certificates to Hercules, and transferred the payments via wire transfer (again via FedWire) to the Augean National Bank, the indenture trustee and paying agent for the debentures, which disbursed the funds to the debenture holders, again through FedWire. Can Hercules, as DIP, avoid any of these transactions? 11 U.S.C. §§ 101(22), 101(22A), 544(b), 546(e).

(6) The Clio Corp., a media conglomerate, owns several major newspapers, radio stations, a TV station, prime real estate, and a ne'er-do-well major league baseball team. Clio Corp. had $5.6 billion in debt at the holding company level, not guaranteed by its subsidiaries, which held its main assets. The print media business has been in serious decline for years, and Clio's major shareholders have been looking for a buyer to relieve them of their declining stock, but could not find a buyer until corporate raider Apollo Zellig decided to take a gamble on turning around the Clio Corp.

Zellig's acquisition of the Clio Corp. involved two transactions. First, the Clio Corp. repurchased (and retired) most of its shares through a tender offer. The tender offer was financed through an $8 billion loan that was guaranteed by all of Clio's subsidiaries. Part of the loan was also used to refinance $2.8 billion of Clio's previous debt.

Second, after the stock repurchase, Clio merged with an entity wholly owned by an entity owned by Zellig. The merger, which included the forced buyout of the remaining shareholders (whose shares were retired), was financed by an additional $2.7 billion in borrowing by Clio, guaranteed by its subsidiaries, as well as by $300 million contributed by Zellig. Zellig pushed hard to complete the acquisition in the face of concerns from some of the lenders that the Clio Corporation might be insolvent. The lenders, eager to attract future business from Zellig, ultimately agreed to accept various representations of Clio's solvency.

After the acquisition, Clio owed $13.5 billion in debt, $2.8 billion of which predated the stock repurchase/refinancing and acquisition transactions. As part of the stock repurchase/refinancing and acquisition transactions, Clio's $8.3 billion was paid out to outside shareholders, $150 million paid to various insiders, $2.8 billion repaid to some of Clio's old lenders, and $284 million paid to financial advisors and new lenders in fees.

Zellig was unable to turn around the Clio Corp., and just months after its acquisition the Clio Corp. recognized itself as worth only $7 billion. As the Clio Corp.'s advertising revenue plummeted with a recession, it was unable to service its debt and filed for Chapter 11. In the plan, the DIP assigned all fraudulent transfer actions to a litigation trust created to benefit the unsecured creditors of the Clio Corp. and its subsidiaries. From whom can the trust successfully recover what? 11 U.S.C. §§ 544(b), 546(e), 548(a)(1), 550(a)-(b).

CHAPTER 32

EQUITABLE REMEDIES

I. EQUITABLE DISALLOWANCE

Bankruptcy courts are often cited as having "equitable powers," particularly in regard to claim allowance and priority. As an initial matter, it is important to understand that bankruptcy courts are *not* and never have been "courts of equity," although this is a trope frequently repeated in cases. In England, bankruptcy proceedings were under the jurisdiction of the Chancellor, but were separate from pleadings in equity. In the United States, bankruptcy has only ever existed as a matter of statute. Federal courts never sat in equity when hearing bankruptcy cases, nor have they ever had unfettered jurisdiction to "do equity."

Nonetheless, the Bankruptcy Code itself entrusts courts with substantial discretion (consider all of the "for cause" and "good faith" provisions we have seen), and even at times directs such discretion to be undertaken consistent with "principles of equit[y]." Moreover, there is considerable precedent in both pre-Code law and under the Code for courts to exercise certain equitable powers regarding claims and the debtor, and section 105(a) of the Code is often cited as further authority for such actions.

Perhaps the most powerful equitable remedy exercised in bankruptcy is the equitable disallowance of claims. The foundations for such a remedy are found in a pair of New Deal Supreme Court decisions under the Bankruptcy Act, *Taylor v. Standard Gas & Electric Co.*, 306 U.S. 307 (1939) (known as "the Deep Rock case"), and *Pepper v. Litton*, 308 U.S. 295 (1939). Although decided under a previous statute, these cases continue to be routinely cited by litigants and courts and form part of the background against which equitable disallowance is still practiced and against which Congress drafted the equitable subordination provision of the Bankruptcy Code, section 510(c), which we shall take up in the next chapter.

Is equitable disallowance still viable after the enactment of the Bankruptcy Code? There is no provision expressly codifying equitable disallowance. In contrast, there is a provision, section 510(c), discussed in the next chapter, that codifies equitable subordination. Moreover, section 502(b) provides that a claim shall be allowed except to the extent that it fits into an enumerated exception, and a long line of Supreme Court cases hold that "whatever equitable powers remain in the bankruptcy courts must and can only be exercised within the confines of" the Bankruptcy Code. *Law v. Siegel*, 134 S. Ct. 1188, 1194-1195 (2014) (quoting *Norwest Bank Worthington v. Ahlers*, 485 U.S. 197, 206 (1988)).

On the other hand, "[t]he normal rule of statutory construction is that if Congress intends for legislation to change the interpretation of a judicially created concept, it makes that intent specific. . . . The Court has followed this rule with particular care in construing the scope of bankruptcy codifications." *Midlantic Nat'l Bank v. N.J. Dep't of Envtl. Prot.*, 474 U.S. 494, 501 (1986). And, section 502(b)(1) provides that a claim shall not be deemed allowed if "such claim is unenforceable against the debtor . . . under any . . . applicable law. . . ." 11 U.S.C. § 502(b)(1). Is equity an "applicable law"? The viability of equitable disallowance remains an open question, but some courts continue to approve of the doctrine.

In re Washington Mutual, Inc.

461 B.R. 200 (Bankr. D. Del. 2011)

MARY F. WALRATH, United States Bankruptcy Judge.

. . .

The Equity Committee has recently filed a motion for authority to prosecute an action to equitably . . . disallow the Settlement Noteholders' claims. The parties agreed to present evidence, brief and argue those issues in conjunction with confirmation of the Modified Plan.

In order for the Court to grant the Equity Committee's motion, the Court must find that it has stated a "colorable" claim, which the Debtors have unjustifiably refused to prosecute. *See Official Comm. of Unsecured Creditors of Cybergenics Corp. v. Chinery*, 330 F.3d 548, 566-67 (3d Cir. 2003). The party seeking standing bears the burden of proof.

The Court finds, through the Debtors' support of the Settlement Noteholders' opposition to the Equity Committee's motion, that the Debtors have refused to pursue the equitable . . . disallowance claim. Whether that was justified depends on whether the claim is colorable and the costs of pursuing that claim.

The threshold for stating a colorable claim is low and mirrors the standard applicable to a motion to dismiss for failure to state a claim.

. . .

2. CLAIM FOR EQUITABLE DISALLOWANCE

a. Availability of Remedy

The Equity Committee contends . . . that, because of the improper conduct of the Settlement Noteholders in trading on material non-public information, the equitable disallowance of their claims is warranted so that any distribution to which they would be entitled is redistributed to other creditors and ultimately to the shareholders.[44] *See,*

---

44. The Indenture Trustee for the [Trust Preferred Securities known as] PIERS contends that even if the Court equitably disallows the claims of the Settlement Noteholders, the Indenture Trustee as the holder of the claims is still entitled to payment of 100% of those claims. The Court disagrees. To the extent the Court disallows those claims, they are disallowed regardless of who holds them. *Cf. Enron Corp. v. Springfield Assocs., L.L.C. (In re Enron Corp.)*, 379 B.R. 425, 439-45 (S.D.N.Y. 2007) (concluding that transferee of a claim could be subject to equitable subordination and disallowance under section 502(d) for conduct of transferor if claim was assigned, though not if it was sold).

e.g., *Citicorp*, 160 F.3d at 991 & n.7 (3d Cir. 1998) (affirming equitable subordination of insider's claim to other creditors because of trading on insider information, but not precluding additional remedies such as equitable disallowance and an award of expenses, fees, and other costs caused by insider's conduct); *Adelphia Commc'ns Corp. v. Bank of Am., N.A. (In re Adelphia Commc'ns Corp.)*, 365 B.R. 24, 71-73 (Bankr. S.D.N.Y. 2007) (denying motion to dismiss because equitable disallowance of claims by bankruptcy court remains viable cause of action and equitable subordination is not the exclusive remedy for wrongdoing), *aff'd in relevant part*, 390 B.R. 64, 74-75 (S.D.N.Y. 2008).

The Equity Committee argues that equitable disallowance of the Settlement Noteholders' claims is warranted in this case because they traded on insider information obtained while they participated in settlement negotiations with the Debtor and JPMC. *See Pepper v. Litton*, 308 U.S. 295, 311 (1939) (holding that claim of insider who traded on inside information was properly subordinated on equitable principles).

The Equity Committee contends that the instant case is the "paradigm case of inequitable conduct by a fiduciary." *Citicorp*, 160 F.3d at 987. Like the creditor in *Citicorp*, the Equity Committee contends that the Settlement Noteholders purchased (and sold) the Debtors' securities with "the benefit of non-public information acquired as a fiduciary" for the "dual purpose of making a profit and influenc[ing] the reorganization in [their] own self-interest." *Id. See also Wolf v. Weinstein*, 372 U.S. 633, 642 (1962) ("Access to inside information or strategic position in a corporate reorganization renders the temptation to profit by trading in the Debtor's stock particularly pernicious.").

The Settlement Noteholders contend initially that equitable disallowance is not a valid remedy under the Bankruptcy Code, because it is not one of the specific exceptions to allowance of a claim articulated in section 502(b). *See, e.g., Travelers Casualty & Surety Co. of Am. v. Pac. Gas & Elec. Co.*, 549 U.S. 443, 449-50 (2007) (holding that Bankruptcy Code does not bar contractual claim for attorneys' fees incurred during bankruptcy case because it was not disallowable under one of the nine exceptions to disallowance under section 502(b)). *See also Mobile Steel*, 563 F.2d at 699 (concluding that "equitable considerations can justify only the subordination of claims, not their disallowance"). The Settlement Noteholders argue that the legislative history of the Code supports this argument, citing a version of the Senate bill that did not get included in the Bankruptcy Code, which would have provided that "the court may disallow, in part or in whole, any claim or interest in accordance with the equities of the case." S. 2266, 95th Cong. § 510(c)(3) (1977).

The Equity Committee responds that both arguments were rejected in the *Adelphia* case. 365 B.R. at 71, *aff'd in relevant part*, 390 B.R. at 74-75. The Bankruptcy Court in *Adelphia* noted that there is other legislative history that expressly states that section 510 "is intended to codify case law, such as *Pepper v. Litton* . . . and is not intended to limit the court's power in any way." 365 B.R. at 71. As a result, the District Court in *Adelphia* concluded that "the Court cannot give any weight to the omission of Section 510(c)(3) of S. 2266 from the Bankruptcy Code, Congress could have decided to do away with equitable disallowance, or it could have thought specific reference to it was superfluous." 390 B.R. at 76.

In addition, the District Court in *Adelphia* held that the *Travelers* decision did not overturn the *Pepper v. Litton* decision which "fairly read, certainly endorses the practice (in appropriate circumstances) of the equitable disallowance of claims, not on the basis of any statutory language, but as within the equitable powers of a bankruptcy court." *Id.*

Here, the Court agrees with the well-reasoned decisions of the Bankruptcy and District Courts in *Adelphia* and concludes that it does have the authority to disallow a claim on equitable grounds "in those extreme instances—perhaps very rare—where it is necessary as a remedy." *Adelphia*, 365 B.R. at 73. *See also, Citicorp*, 160 F.3d at 991 n.7 (disagreeing with district court's conclusion that equitable subordination was the exclusive remedy available for inequitable conduct and noting that *Pepper v. Litton* expressly upheld the bankruptcy court's power to disallow or subordinate a claim based on equitable grounds).

The cases cited by the Settlement Noteholders do not foreclose the equitable disallowance of claims albeit under a different analysis. *Cf. Travelers*, 549 U.S. at 449-50 (holding that "Section 502(b)(1) disallows any claim that is 'unenforceable against the debtor . . . under any agreement or applicable law' . . . [which is] most naturally understood to provide that, with limited exceptions, any defense to a claim that is available outside of the bankruptcy context is also available in bankruptcy."); *Mobile Steel*, 563 F.2d at 699 n.10 (concluding that equitable disallowance of claims is not available because it "would add nothing to the protection against unfairness already afforded the bankrupt and its creditors. . . . If the misconduct directed against the bankrupt is so extreme that disallowance might appear to be warranted, then surely the claim is either invalid or the bankrupt possesses a clear defense against it."). Because the Equity Committee seeks to disallow the claims of the Settlement Noteholders under facts that suggest they violated the securities laws, the Court believes that the Debtors would have a defense to those claims outside of the bankruptcy context as well.

b. Merits of Claim

In *Pepper v. Litton*, the Supreme Court upheld the equitable disallowance of the claim of an insider who traded on material inside information, concluding that:

> He who is in . . . a fiduciary position . . . cannot utilize his inside information and his strategic position for his own preferment. He cannot violate rules of fair play by doing indirectly through the corporation what he could not do directly. He cannot use his power for his personal advantage and to the detriment of the stockholders and creditors no matter how absolute in terms that power may be and no matter how meticulous he is to satisfy technical requirements.

308 U.S. at 311.

The TPS Group contends that, although the Court need not decide that the Settlement Noteholders have violated the securities laws, reference to insider trading cases illustrates the magnitude of the Settlement Noteholders' inequitable conduct. [The Court went on to find that the] Equity Committee and the TPS Group have stated a colorable claim that the Settlement Noteholders engaged in insider trading. . . .

The Settlement Noteholders warn that any finding of insider trading will chill the participation of creditors in settlement discussions in bankruptcy cases of public companies. The Court disagrees. There is an easy solution: creditors who want to participate in settlement discussions in which they receive material nonpublic information about the debtor must either restrict their trading or establish an ethical wall between traders and participants in the bankruptcy case. These types of restrictions are common in bankruptcy cases. Members of creditors' committees and equity committees are always subject to these restrictions. *See, e.g., Adelphia*, 368 B.R. at 152 n.11. The Court does not believe that a requirement to restrict trading or create an ethical wall in exchange for a seat at the negotiating table places an undue burden on creditors who wish to receive confidential information and give their input.

c. Burden on Estate

The Court is required, however, to balance the probability of success on the claim against the burden on the estate that would result from its prosecution. Judging from the vigor with which the Settlement Noteholders have opposed the Equity Committee's standing motion, the Court is concerned that the case will devolve into a litigation morass. In addition, the Court notes that as the case continues, the potential recoveries for all parties in the case dwindles. Regardless of which parties prevail, they may be disappointed to find their recovery significantly less than expected.

Therefore, before the Equity Committee proceeds with its claim any further, the Court will direct that the parties go to mediation on this issue. . . .

II. EQUITABLE SUBORDINATION

Bankruptcy courts are empowered to "equitably subordinate" claims and interests, meaning that the priority of the claim or interest may be demoted based on equitable principles. 11 U.S.C. § 510(c)(1). This power is relatively unique among the bankruptcy court's powers, as it is a standards-based power that looks to the conduct of a creditor or equityholder, rather than a rules-based power as exists for avoidance actions such as the strong-arm power, statutory lien avoidance, fraudulent transfers, preferences, and setoff. The only analogous provision is the "good faith" standard for claim designation (or perhaps the various "for cause" provisions in the Code).

There are a few things to note about section 510(c). First, it is an express codification of equity principles, but those principles are not spelled out, which leaves equitable subordination a potentially vague standard. Not surprisingly, as a standard, it is difficult to say exactly what will trigger or not trigger equitable subordination. (One might also wonder if the codification of equitable principles in section 510(c) suggests that bankruptcy courts do not otherwise have general equity powers, as is often claimed to justify non-Code practices.)

Second, section 510(c) places certain limits on these codified equity powers: Debt may be subordinated to debt and equity may be subordinated to equity, but debt may not be subordinated to equity. Thus, a senior debt may be subordinated to a junior debt or preferred stock may be subordinated to common stock. The limitation on subordinating debt to equity does not mean that debt cannot be recharacterized as equity (or vice-versa), but this is a matter of applicable non-bankruptcy law. Thus, if a debt were recharacterized as equity, it could be subordinated to other equity interests, but this would be a two-part process involving more than equitable subordination.

Third, equitable subordination is about priority. It is not about allowance. An equitably subordinated claim is still an allowed claim. It is just lower down on the priority ladder. If there are sufficient funds, it will still get paid in full. Thus, depending on the solvency of the estate, equitable subordination may not matter.

Fourth, equitable subordination is separate and distinct from whether a claim is secured. Section 510(c)(1) permits subordination of claims. A secured claim does not have general priority over an unsecured claim. Instead, the secured claim has a lien on a specific asset or assets, giving the secured claim special collection rights relating to that asset. In theory, it is possible to have a secured claim that is subordinated to an unsecured claim. Given that the secured claim still has its lien, however, its treatment would still be under section 725 rather than 726 in a liquidation and under section 1129(b)(2)(A) rather than 1129(b)(2)(B) in a cramdown plan. Unless the secured claim were undersecured (and no section 1111(b)(2) election were made), there would be no effect. Section 510(c)(2), however, permits the bankruptcy court to strip the lien from any subordinated claim, with the lien transferred to the estate, which can enable the estate to potentially defeat other liens under the strong-arm power beyond those that could be defeated by a hypothetical judgment lien creditor.

Finally, while section 510(c) is often grouped with avoidance actions, it does not involve an attempt to recover property for the estate (excluding lien stripping) from a creditor. Instead, it is about reordering priorities. Accordingly, sections 546 and 550, which place limitations on avoidance actions, do not apply to section 510(c).

The following cases illustrate how factually specific equitable subordination is, and how courts take very different views of exactly what behavior is or is not inequitable.

SI Restructuring, Inc. v. Faulkner (*In re* SI Restructuring, Inc.)

532 F.3d 355 (5th Cir. 2008)

W. EUGENE DAVIS, U.S. District Judge.*

. . .

This dispute arises from the loans made by John and Jeffrey Wooley ("the Wooleys") to Schlotzsky's, Inc. ("Schlotzsky's"). At the time of the events giving rise to this appeal, the Wooleys were officers and directors and the largest shareholders of Schlotzsky's. In order to relieve a critical cash crunch faced by Schlotzsky's, the Wooleys made two loans to the corporation: one in April 2003 for $1 million and another in November 2003 for $2.5 million.

---

* District Judge of the Eastern District of Texas, sitting by designation.

The Wooleys made the April loan after other financing options fell through. This loan was secured with the company's royalty streams from franchisees, the company's intellectual property rights, and other intangible property. Schlotzsky's and the Wooleys were represented by separate legal counsel for the April loan negotiations. The loan terms were approved by the audit committee and Schlotzsky's board of directors as a related-party transaction, and the transaction was disclosed in the company's filings with the SEC.

Throughout 2003, the company continued to experience severe cash flow problems, and the Wooleys continued their efforts to obtain financing. The board of directors was keenly aware of these efforts. In the fall of 2003, Schlotzsky's general counsel approached the International Bank of Commerce ("IBC") about a loan to the company. IBC declined to make the loan to the company but agreed to allow the Wooleys to borrow the funds directly from the bank so that the Wooleys could, in turn, lend the proceeds to Schlotzsky's. The need for this additional financing and the possibility of this loan by the Wooleys was discussed at an October 31, 2003 board meeting. The loan to the company was approved by the board and made on November 13, 2003.

In finding the Wooleys' conduct to be inequitable, the bankruptcy court focused on this second loan ("the November loan") and attached significance to the short notice given to the board for approval. IBC formally approved the loan to the Wooleys on November 10, 2003. The following day, the board was provided notice of a special meeting scheduled for November 13, 2003 to approve the Wooleys' loan to the company. Before the special meeting, the board members were provided with copies of the proposed promissory note and the security agreement along with e-mails from the company's assistant general counsel. As with the April loan, the November loan was secured with the company's rights to the royalty streams from franchisees, intellectual property rights, and, and general intangibles.

When the loan was made, the Wooleys had in place personal guarantees which guaranteed pre-existing Schlotzsky's debt in the amount of $4.3 million. As part of the November loan package, the Wooleys also secured this potential liability under the guarantees with the same collateral that secured the April and November loans.

At the November 13, 2003 board meeting, conducted via telephone conference call, the board was told that without the infusion of additional funds, payroll could not be met and that the company would default on a payment to a secured creditor. All of the non-interested directors in attendance approved the loan without objection. An independent audit committee also approved the loan, and the transaction was publicly disclosed in SEC filings.

In mid-2004, the Wooleys were removed as officers of the corporation and resigned their positions as directors. The financial condition of the company deteriorated further, and a Chapter 11 Bankruptcy proceeding was filed in August 2004. The Wooleys filed secured claims relating to the April and November loans. The committee of unsecured creditors brought an adversary proceeding against the Wooleys, challenging their right to be treated as secured creditors with respect to these claims.

The bankruptcy court found that John and Jeffrey Wooley, as fiduciaries, engaged in inequitable conduct in relation to the November transaction and that their conduct conferred an unfair advantage upon them. This inequitable conduct stemmed from a breach of fiduciary duties that the Wooleys owed to Schlotzsky's as officers and directors. According to the bankruptcy court, the Wooleys breached their fiduciary duties in part by the manner in which they presented the November loan transaction to the board. The court found that the transaction was presented as the only option available, at the eleventh hour, as a *fait accompli*. In other words, the board was given the option, "approve the loan or the company collapses tomorrow." Additionally, the judge questioned why the Wooleys required that the loan be secured if it was truly meant to be a temporary loan to secure permanent financing. By securing the loan with the income stream of the franchise company, the crown jewel of the Schlotzsky's complex, the bankruptcy court concluded that the Wooleys "grabbed for as much as they could get[,] and they got it all." The final straw to the bankruptcy court was the Wooleys' insistence on securing their pre-existing contingent liability on their personal guarantees with the revenue stream of the franchise company. The bankruptcy court found that securing the Wooleys' contingent liability effectively released them as guarantors on the debt at the expense of the corporation and its unsecured creditors. In the words of the bankruptcy court: "[t]hat's unfair advantage." The bankruptcy court, however, made no specific findings that the Wooleys' actions in securing either of the 2003 loans or their pre-existing contingent liability on the guarantees resulted in harm to the corporation or to the unsecured creditors.

The bankruptcy court ordered that the Wooleys' claims based on both the April and November loans be equitably subordinated and thus converted from secured to unsecured status. The district court agreed with the bankruptcy court and affirmed. The Wooleys then lodged this appeal.

. . .

Appellants argue that the bankruptcy court's application of the "extraordinary remedy" of equitable subordination is not warranted in this case. The Wooleys assert that none of the bankruptcy court's findings of inequitable conduct relate to the April transaction and that the court's findings do not support subordination of their claim based on this loan. They also argue that they did not act inequitably in structuring the loan to the corporation as they did and that the record does not support the finding that they breached their fiduciary obligations. They contend that their November loan to Schlotzsky's was an arms-length transaction with approval of the board, including disinterested directors and independent audit committee members. They point out that the company had its own in-house counsel and outside securities counsel who reviewed the transaction. The Wooleys assert that all members of the board of directors and audit committee knew of the precarious financial condition of the company, that they were not surprised about the urgent need for the loan, and that the bankruptcy court improperly faulted them for obtaining the board's quick approval of the transaction. They argue that the bankruptcy court improperly found that the transaction occurred at the "eleventh hour" or that the timing of the loan justified equitable subordination of the Wooleys' claims.

The Wooleys also assert that they did nothing improper in negotiating an agreement with the company to obtain security as a condition of making the loan. The Wooleys contend that no evidence was presented that the November transaction resulted in an unfair advantage to them. They contend that the bankruptcy court's conclusion amounts to a *per se* rule that an insider creditor cannot obtain security for a loan or for preexisting contingent liability from a solvent company. The Wooleys emphasize that the bankruptcy court found that the November loan was real money that was used by the company to pay off its debts, and it, therefore, benefitted the company's creditors. We now turn to a consideration of the law that applies to the issues these arguments raise.

. . .

The Bankruptcy Code does not . . . set forth the circumstances under which equitable subordination is appropriate; however, the case law has formulated a number of requirements to guide courts in their application of this remedy. This Court in *In re Mobile Steel Corp.* articulated the widely quoted three-prong test for equitable subordination: (1) the claimant must have engaged in inequitable conduct; (2) the misconduct must have resulted in injury to the creditors of the bankrupt or conferred an unfair advantage on the claimant; and (3) equitable subordination of the claim must not be inconsistent with the provisions of the Bankruptcy Code. *Benjamin v. Diamond (In re Mobile Steel Corp.)*, 563 F.2d 692, 700 (5th Cir. 1977). *In re Mobile Steel Corp.* adds an additional requirement, critical to the decision in this case: a claim should be subordinated only to the extent necessary to offset the harm which the debtor or its creditors have suffered as a result of the inequitable conduct. *Id.* at 701.

In *In re Mobile Steel Corp.*, the plaintiffs were insiders of the debtor steel corporation. Before the corporation filed for bankruptcy, it purchased commercial property for tax purposes and then sold the property. The commercial property was purchased from the insider plaintiffs in exchange for promissory notes; no cash changed hands. In a separate transaction, the plaintiffs loaned the corporation $250,000 in exchange for unsecured debentures in that amount, bearing 6% interest. The Trustee sought to have the plaintiffs' claims equitably subordinated, contending that the insider's sale of the commercial property to the debtor constituted over-reaching, mismanagement, and abuse of a fiduciary position and that the debentures should be treated as capital contributions and not entitled to debt treatment. The district court affirmed the bankruptcy court's order subordinating the plaintiffs' claims, finding that the plaintiffs failed to demonstrate that they had performed their fiduciary duties and acted in good faith in dealing with the corporation. We reversed, finding:

> [E]ven if it is assumed that the [A]ppellants acted unfairly in all of the ways suggested by the bankruptcy judge, equitable subordination of their claims to those advanced by the other unsecured creditors still could not be justified because the Trustee has made no factual showing that any of these purported improprieties injured either Mobile Steel or its creditors.

Id. at 706.

Thus, *In re Mobile Steel* teaches that equitable subordination is remedial, not penal, and in the absence of actual harm, equitable subordination is inappropriate. We have found no contrary authority, and none has been cited to us.

. . .

The bankruptcy court made no findings of inequitable conduct by the Wooleys with respect to the April loan. As to the November transactions, we assume, without deciding, that the record supports the finding of inequitable conduct and unfair advantage. However, the bankruptcy court made no finding of harm, and the record does not support a finding that either the debtor or the unsecured creditors were harmed by the November transaction.

Appellee argues that when the company secured the Wooleys' loan with the assets of Schlotzsky's Franchisor, L.L.C., this reduced the assets available to the unsecured creditors and injured them. This argument fails because neither the record nor the bankruptcy court's findings support a view that general unsecured creditors as a class were harmed. Indeed, the bankruptcy court found that the proceeds of the loan were used to pay the unsecured creditors and keep the company in operation . . . :

> I am not finding that the debtor didn't need the money. I'm not finding that the debtor didn't use the money. I'm not finding that the debtor didn't actually use the money to pay down debt. Of course, it did. Of course, it did.

Because the loan proceeds were used to pay current unsecured creditors, unsecured creditors, as a class, were not harmed when the Wooleys obtained security for the November loan. The general unsecured creditors who were paid from the proceeds of the November loan may have benefitted to the detriment of another group of unsecured creditors, but this does not mean that unsecured creditors were harmed when the Wooleys obtained security for their loan. Further, the unsecured creditors who remain unpaid have advanced no theory supporting a view that they were entitled to payment over the creditors who were paid from the proceeds of the April and November loans.

. . .

Appellee further argues that by taking securing their existing personal guarantees, the Wooleys were effectively released from liability for the guarantees, thus securing an unfair advantage. This argument could have merit if the company had defaulted on the underlying debt and the Wooleys' potential liability under the guarantees had been triggered. The record reveals, however, that the Wooleys' potential obligation on the guaranty agreements was never triggered because the company never defaulted on its principal obligation covered by the guarantees. Because no claim ever arose on these guarantees, no harm resulted.

The bankruptcy court made no finding that the Wooleys breached any obligations to the company or its creditors or that they engaged in inequitable conduct of any kind in connection with the April loan. With respect to the November loan, the bankruptcy court made no finding that Appellants' transactions with the debtor caused harm to either the debtor or the unsecured creditors. We have carefully considered the Trustee's damage theories and conclude that none are legally cognizable or supported by the record. Thus, neither claim should have been subordinated.

Section 550 and its good faith transferee defenses do not apply to equitable subordination under section 510(c). What protection, if any, does a transferee, such as a claims purchaser, have against equitable subordination, which might be for conduct unrelated to the claim?

III. RECHARACTERIZATION

Recharacterization of a claim is another means by which a bankruptcy court can equitably readjust voting and distributions. Recharacterization of a claim means that the court will hold what purports to be a debt claim to actually be an equity interest. The effect, of course, is to demote the claim within the capital structure, much as if the claim were subordinated.

The idea that a debt can be recharacterized as equity may seem counterintuitive. We tend to think of debt and equity as clearly distinct categories, and they often are, but two situations arise in which the nature of the relationship with the debtor may be less clear. First is when there is a debt owed to an equityholder. That alone is unlikely to be grounds for recharacterization, but if the equityholder controls the company and the debt is not on market terms, it may be seen as a disguised equity investment. Second, certain instruments are themselves hybrids, giving the debtor's counterparty both the upside of the debtor's financial performance and some guaranteed level of payment. In particular, various forms of preferred stock or convertible notes may blur the line between debt and equity.

A. Judicial Recharacterization

The Bankruptcy Code itself does not address judicial recharacterization. Instead, the power seems to either be inherent in the courts or to derive from state law. Different circuits have adopted different theories of the power's origin. The basic idea, however, is that the court is not actually changing the status of a creditor's claim so much as recognizing it for what it actually is, namely an equity interest.

As the following case explains, there is no bright line test for recharacterization. Some circuits have adopted 11- or 13-part tests for recharacterization, all of which try to get to the economic reality of the transaction, rather than its formal labeling. This is not an issue restricted to bankruptcy. There is a large tax jurisprudence on the issue, and it has accounting implications as well.

Cohen v. KB Mezzanine Fund II, LP (*In re* SubMicron Systems Corp.)

432 F.3d 448 (3d Cir. 2006)

AMBRO, Circuit Judge.

Appellant Howard S. Cohen ("Cohen"), as Plan Administrator for the bankruptcy estates of SubMicron Systems Corp. ("SubMicron") . . . challenges the sale to . . . Sunrise Capital Partners, LP ("Sunrise") of SubMicron's assets under 11 U.S.C. § 363(b), which authorizes court-approved sales of assets "other than in the ordinary course of business." Sunrise negotiated directly with several—but not all—of SubMicron's creditors before presenting its bid to the District Court. These creditors—The KB Mezzanine Fund II, LP ("KB"), Equinox Investment Partners, LLC ("Equinox"), and Celerity Silicon, LLC ("Celerity") (collectively, the "Lenders")—agreed to contribute toward the purchase of SubMicron's assets new capital along with all of their claims in bankruptcy against SubMicron in exchange for equity in the entity formed by Sunrise to acquire the assets—Akrion LLC ("Akrion"). Akrion in turn "credit bid" the full value of the Lenders' secured claims contributed to it as part of its bid for SubMicron's assets pursuant to 11 U.S.C. § 363(k). The District Court approved the sale.

Cohen, seeking as Plan Administrator of the SubMicron estates to aid unsecured creditors "cut out of the deal" by the Lenders and Sunrise, attacks the sale on several fronts. First, he argues that the purportedly secured debt investments made by the Lenders and contributed to Akrion should have been recharacterized by the District Court as equity investments. . . . For the reasons discussed below, we reject th[is] argument[] and affirm the judgment of the District Court.

I. FACTS AND PROCEDURAL POSTURE

A. SubMicron's Financing

Before its sale in bankruptcy, SubMicron designed, manufactured and marketed "wet benches" [automatic process tools used for cleaning and etching operations in semiconductor processing] for use in the semiconductor industry. By 1997, it was experiencing significant financial and operational difficulties. To sustain its operations in the late 1990s, SubMicron secured financing from several financial and/or investment institutions. On November 25, 1997, it entered into a $15 million working capital facility with Greyrock Business Credit ("Greyrock"), granting Greyrock first priority liens on all of its inventory, equipment, receivables and general intangibles. The next day, SubMicron raised another $20 million through the issuance of senior subordinated 12% notes (the "1997 Notes") to KB/Equinox (for $16 million) and Celerity (for $4 million) secured by liens behind Greyrock on substantially all of SubMicron's assets. SubMicron subsequently issued a third set of notes in 1997 (the "Junior 1997 Notes") for $13.7 million, comprising $8.7 million of 8% notes and a $5 million note to The BOC Group, Inc. The Junior 1997 Notes were secured but junior to the security for the 1997 Notes. Despite this capital influx, SubMicron incurred a net loss of $47.6 million for the 1997 fiscal year.

A steep downturn in the semiconductor industry made 1998 a similarly difficult year for SubMicron. By August of that year, it was paying substantially all of the interest due on the 1997 Notes as paid-in-kind senior subordinated notes. On December 2, 1998, SubMicron and Greyrock agreed to renew the Greyrock line of credit, reducing the maximum funds available from $15 to $10 million and including a $2 million overadvance conditioned on SubMicron's securing an additional $4 million in financing. To satisfy this condition, on December 3, SubMicron issued Series B 12% notes (the "1998 Notes") to KB/Equinox (for $3.2 million) and Celerity (for $800,000). The 1998 Notes ranked *pari passu* with the 1997 Notes and the interest was deferred until October 1, 1999. SubMicron incurred a net loss of $21.9 million for the 1998 fiscal year, and at year's end its liabilities exceeded its assets by $4.2 million.

SubMicron's financial health did not improve in 1999. By March of that year, its management determined that additional financing would be required to meet the company's immediate critical working capital needs. To this end, between March 10, 1999 and June 6, 1999, SubMicron issued a total of eighteen Series 1999 12% notes (the

"1999 Tranche One Notes") for a total of $7,035,154 (comprising nine notes to KB/Equinox totaling $5,888,123 and nine notes to Celerity totaling $1,147,031). The 1999 Tranche One Notes proved insufficient to keep SubMicron afloat. As a result, between July 8, 1999 and August 31, 1999, KB/Equinox and Celerity made periodic payments to SubMicron (the "1999 Tranche Two Funding") totaling $3,982,031 and $147,969, respectively. No notes were issued in exchange for the 1999 Tranche Two Funding. Between the 1999 Tranche One Notes and the 1999 Tranche Two Funding (collectively, the "1999 Fundings"), KB/Equinox and Celerity advanced SubMicron a total of $9,870,154 and $1,295,000, respectively. (The 1999 Fundings were recorded as secured debt on SubMicron's 10-Q filing with the Securities and Exchange Commission.) Despite the cash infusions, during the first half of 1999 SubMicron incurred a net loss of $9.9 million. On June 30, 1999, SubMicron's liabilities exceeded its assets by $3.1 million.

By January 1999, KB/Equinox had appointed three members to SubMicron's Board of Directors. All appointees were either principals or employees of KB/Equinox. By June 1999, following resignations of various SubMicron Board members, KB/Equinox employees Bonaparte Liu and Robert Wickey, and Celerity employee Mark Benham, represented three-quarters of the Board, with SubMicron CEO David Ferran the lone Board member not employed by KB/Equinox or Celerity.

. . .

III. RECHARACTERIZATION AS EQUITY

Cohen argues that the District Court erred by failing to recharacterize the infusion of the 1999 Fundings as an equity investment. To succeed with this argument, he must demonstrate that the District Court abused its discretionary authority or premised its determination on clearly erroneous findings of fact. Because he has failed to do so, we affirm the District Court's recharacterization holding.

A. Recharacterization/Equitable Subordination

At the outset, it is important to distinguish recharacterization from equitable subordination. Both remedies are grounded in bankruptcy courts' equitable authority to ensure "that substance will not give way to form, that technical considerations will not prevent substantial justice from being done." *Pepper v. Litton*, 308 U.S. 295, 305 (1939). Yet recharacterization and equitable subordination address distinct concerns. Equitable subordination is apt when equity demands that the payment priority of claims of an otherwise legitimate creditor be changed to fall behind those of other claimants. In contrast, the focus of the recharacterization inquiry is whether "a debt actually exists," or, put another way, we ask what is the proper characterization in the first instance of an investment.[7] For these reasons, we agree with those courts that have determined that

---

7. In this context, the label "recharacterization" is misleading. *See Citicorp Real Estate, Inc. v. PWA, Inc. (In re Georgetown Bldg. Assocs. Ltd. P'ship)*, 240 B.R. 124, 137 (Bankr. D.D.C. 1999) ("The debt-versus-equity inquiry is not an exercise in *recharacterizing* a claim, but of *characterizing* the advance's true character." (emphases in original)); *In re Cold Harbor Assocs., L.P.*, 204 B.R. 904, 915 (Bankr. E.D. Va. 1997) ("Rather than recharacterizing the exchange from debt to equity, or subordinating the claim for some reason, the question before this Court is whether the transaction created a debt or equity relationship from the outset.").

"the issues of recharacterization of debt as equity capital and equitable subordination should be treated separately."

Cohen advances both arguments. He argues that the infusion of the 1999 Fundings is most accurately characterized as an equity investment—a recharacterization argument—and, in the alternative, that if the infusion is deemed a debt investment, the Lenders' claims should be equitably subordinated. We turn first to the recharacterization argument, as "determining [an] equitable subordination issue prior to determining whether [an] advance is a loan or [an equity investment] is similar to taking the cart before the horse." If a "particular advance is a capital contribution, . . . then equitable subordination never comes into play."

B. Recharacterization Framework

In defining the recharacterization inquiry, courts have adopted a variety of multi-factor tests borrowed from non-bankruptcy caselaw. While these tests undoubtedly include pertinent factors, they devolve to an overarching inquiry: the characterization as debt or equity is a court's attempt to discern whether the parties called an instrument one thing when in fact they intended it as something else. That intent may be inferred from what the parties say in their contracts, from what they do through their actions, and from the economic reality of the surrounding circumstances. Answers lie in facts that confer context case-by-case.

No mechanistic scorecard suffices. And none should, for Kabuki outcomes elude difficult fact patterns. While some cases are easy (e.g., a document titled a "Note" calling for payments of sums certain at fixed intervals with market-rate interest and these obligations are secured and are partly performed, versus a document issued as a certificate indicating a proportional interest in the enterprise to which the certificate relates), others are hard (such as a "Note" with conventional repayment terms yet reflecting an amount proportional to prior equity interests and whose payment terms are ignored). Which course a court discerns is typically a commonsense conclusion that the party infusing funds does so as a banker (the party expects to be repaid with interest no matter the borrower's fortunes; therefore, the funds are debt) or as an investor (the funds infused are repaid based on the borrower's fortunes; hence, they are equity). Form is no doubt a factor, but in the end it is no more than an indicator of what the parties actually intended and acted on.

C. Review of the District Court's Recharacterization Holding

. . .

ii. The District Court's Determination Was Not Clearly Erroneous

The District Court's opinion includes ample findings of fact to support its recharacterization determination. Because these findings are not clearly erroneous and overwhelmingly support the Court's decision to characterize the 1999 Fundings as debt (under any framework or test), we affirm its factual determination.

The District Court set out numerous facts to support a debt characterization. Looking to the lending documents, it found "beyond dispute in the record that . . . the name given to the 1999 fundings was debt . . . and . . . the 1999 fundings had a fixed maturity date and interest rate." The Court also found evidence of the parties' intent to create a debt investment outside the lending documents. For example, it noted that "the 1999 notes were recorded as secured debt on SubMicron's 10-Q SEC filing and UCC-1 financing statements."

The District Court could not find, on the other hand, convincing evidence to support an equity investment characterization of the 1999 Fundings. It rejected Cohen's argument that the dire financial circumstances surrounding the infusion of the 1999 Fundings supported an equity characterization. Instead, it concluded, with reference to the conflicting testimony and relative credibility of witnesses presented by both parties, that Cohen "failed to prove that[,] under SubMicron's dire circumstances, [the Lenders'] transactions were improper or unusual [as debt investments]." Recognizing that "when a corporation is undercapitalized, a court is more skeptical of purported loans made to it because they may in reality be infusions of capital," the District Court also noted that "when existing lenders make loans to a distressed company, they are trying to protect their existing loans and traditional factors that lenders consider (such as capitalization, solvency, collateral, ability to pay cash interest and debt capacity ratios) do not apply as they would when lending to a financially healthy company[.]" Weighing these competing considerations, it did not find SubMicron's undercapitalization greatly supported an equity characterization.

Similarly, the Court found the Lenders' participation on the SubMicron Board did not, in and of itself, provide support for an equity characterization. Again relying on expert testimony, it emphasized that it is "not unusual for lenders to have designees on a company's board, particularly when the company [is] a distressed one." [R]eviewing conflicting evidence on the issue, the Court concluded that Cohen "[did] not prove[] that [Lenders] or their designees controlled or dominated SubMicron's Board in any way." Based on these factual determinations, the conclusion was inevitable that the Lenders' representation on SubMicron's Board did not necessarily support an equity characterization.

Lastly, the Court found unpersuasive Cohen's argument that SubMicron's failure to issue notes for the 1999 Tranche Two Funding should be understood as evidence of the parties' understanding that the 1999 Fundings were, in effect, equity investments. It noted that "the record is clear that SubMicron's accounting department made numerous mistakes and errors when generating notes," concluding that "the fact that notes were generated for some fundings and not others is not sufficient, in and of itself, to recharacterize the 1999 fundings as equity."

In short, the District Court found ample evidence to support a debt characterization and little evidence to support a characterization of equity infusion. On the basis of these findings, which comport with the record, it was hardly clear error for the Court to conclude that "[Cohen] had not proven by a preponderance of the evidence that the 1999 Fundings should be recharacterized as equity."

. . .

B. Statutory Recharacterization

In addition to judicial recharacterization, the Bankruptcy Code also provides for a statutory recharacterization of certain debt obligations—damages or rescissory rights—relating to securities contracts. Thus, if the debtor engaged in securities fraud prior to bankruptcy and a judgment was awarded to common equity investors, but remained unpaid, the judgment would be recharacterized for distribution purposes as equity, rather than as debt.

The policy embodied in section 510(b) is that a creditor with an equity interest should not be able to bootstrap that interest into a debt claim simply by alleging securities fraud of some sort. In particular, the concern over such bootstrapping is that it would harm other creditors who relied on the presence of an equity cushion when extending credit. Equity securities holders bargained for the risk of being equity, not of being debt. (Of course, one might point out that if defrauded, they by definition didn't bargain for the risk they assumed; the bargain for equity priority was not a separate and distinct bargain from the other terms of the investment.)

Section 510(b) is not limited to equity securities, however. It applies to all types of securities. The anti-bootstrapping logic applies to subordinated debt securities just as it would to equity securities: An investor in subordinated debt should not be able to end up with a general unsecured claim simply by virtue of being defrauded. The subordinated debt investor bargained for the risk of subordinated priority.

What, then, about unsubordinated debt securities? There the anti-bootstrapping rationale has no applicability. The legislative history is uninformative on this point. Indeed, both the House and Senate Reports on the bills that became the 1978 Bankruptcy Code refer to debt claims being subordinated only to claims that are senior to the underlying debt, and state that "[i]f the security is a debt instrument, the damages or rescission claim will be granted the status of a general unsecured claim." Yet when the House and Senate legislation went into conference committee, section 510(b) was changed to allow for subordination to claims with priority equal to the underlying security. One can only surmise at the rationale for this change, but it would appear to be based on concerns of dilution and double recovery.

Specifically, it is important to recognize that some defrauded investors will still hold the debt security, but some will not. These investors will likely have two claims: a claim on the debt security (most likely filed by an indenture trustee) and a claim for the fraud (filed by the investor individually). In theory there should only be one recovery on these two claims, but administratively there is a risk of confusion. Section 510(b) ensures that those defrauded investors who still hold the debt security will recover pro rata with other debt security holders of their class and not dilute the other holders' recovery with their fraud claims. For those defrauded debt security investors who no longer hold the debt securities, subordination will again prevent diluting the recovery of the remaining holders. This would seem to be rougher justice by subordinating a securities fraud claim to a securities claim. Given that Congress has subsequently amended section 510(b) without addressing the issue of debt securities, it would seem that no one is too exercised about the issue.

IV. SUBSTANTIVE CONSOLIDATION

The final equitable doctrine we will examine is substantive consolidation. While bankruptcy cases of multiple debtor entities are routinely jointly administered (also known as **administrative consolidation**), corporate separateness is normally honored in bankruptcy, as is structural priority. This can easily make things messy when some, but not all, entities in a corporate structure are in bankruptcy, as the bankruptcy may affect the non-debtors as well as the debtors on a variety of levels ranging from cash management systems and policies to liability on guarantees. Intercompany debt also raises fiduciary duty issues for managers and conflicts problems for attorneys. And intercompany debts are often recharacterizable as equity or otherwise contestable.

There is no one-size-fits-all solution that has emerged for these issues. Three approaches are of note, however. One is to have the separate corporate entities and their creditors simply duke it out. While this works reasonably well when there are only a couple debtor entities involved, it is generally avoided in more complex bankruptcies. A debtor can easily have upwards of a hundred affiliated debtor (and non-debtor) entities. They can be bound to each other by intercompany contracts, by guaranties, by joint liability, by corporate ownership, and by intercompany avoidance action claims. The complexity of figuring out exactly which entities owe which other entities what funds presents an accounting and legal nightmare. It also poses a daunting legal ethics problem: How is one bankruptcy counsel possibly supposed to represent hundreds of potentially adverse entities? If intercompany liabilities are taken seriously, reorganizations of complex firms become much more difficult.

Accordingly, a second solution to the intercompany liability problem is to have a global settlement of intercompany claims that is incorporated into a plan. This is the most common approach, particularly in bankruptcies involving complex, multiple entity debtors. Typically such a solution involves the subordination and/or waiver of all intercompany claims, so that these claims are functionally or formally ignored. The result will necessarily create winners and losers among creditors depending on how intercompany claims are treated, but creditors frequently lack the information to fully determine how such a functional consolidation affects them. We might call this approach, which has received surprisingly little attention, de facto or *selective* consolidation.

A third possibility is formal, de jure **substantive consolidation**, which means smooshing together all of the assets and liabilities of the different corporate entities and disregarding intercompany obligations.

Corporate structures can sometimes be collapsed under various state law doctrines, such as veil-piercing, alter-ego, and successor liability. Substantive consolidation is essentially bankruptcy's version of these veil-piercing and alter-ego doctrines, although a purist might dicker with the characterization. Be that as it may, formal substantive consolidation is a fairly rare and drastic step that is not distinctly authorized in the Bankruptcy Code; indeed, it is not clear that substantive consolidation is in fact *bankruptcy* law per se, rather than some version of state corporate law being applied in bankruptcy. All in all, it is generally quite difficult to disregard corporate structures and collapse entities within a corporate family absent unusual factual circumstances.

Substantive consolidation inherently produces winners and losers. To wit, imagine two separate firms with only general unsecured liabilities. Firm *A* has assets of 100 and liabilities of 150. Its creditors will get a 66.7% dividend. Firm *B* has assets of 100 and liabilities of 120. Its creditors will get an 83.3% dividend. If Firms *A* and *B* are consolidated, however, the consolidated firm will have assets of 200 and liabilities of 270. The creditors will get a 75% dividend. Obviously, consolidation benefits the creditors of Firm *A* and harms the creditors of Firm *B*. Because substantive consolidation necessarily produces winners and losers, it is an extraordinary remedy undertaken only when reliance on corporate separateness was inappropriate. The *Owens Corning* case below addresses "sub con."

In re Owens Corning

419 F.3d 195 (3d Cir. 2005)

THOMAS AMBRO, Circuit Judge.

We consider under what circumstances a court exercising bankruptcy powers may substantively consolidate affiliated entities. Appellant Credit Suisse First Boston ("CSFB") is the agent for a syndicate of banks (collectively, the "Banks")[1] that extended in 1997 a $2 billion unsecured loan to Owens Corning, a Delaware corporation ("OCD"), and certain of its subsidiaries. This credit was enhanced in part by guarantees made by other OCD subsidiaries. The District Court granted a motion to consolidate the assets and liabilities of the OCD borrowers[2] and guarantors in anticipation of a plan of reorganization.

The Banks appeal and argue that the Court erred by granting the motion, as it misunderstood the reasons for, and standards for considering, the extraordinary remedy of substantive consolidation, and in any event did not make factual determinations necessary even to consider its use. Though we reverse the ruling of the District Court, we do so aware that it acted on an issue with no opinion on point by our Court and differing rationales by other courts.

While this area of law is difficult and this case important, its outcome is easy with the facts before us. Among other problems, the consolidation sought is "deemed." Should we approve this non-consensual arrangement, the plan process would proceed as though assets and liabilities of separate entities were merged, but in fact they remain

---

1. Though CSFB is the named appellant, the real parties in interest are the Banks (which include CSFB). Thus, unless the context requires otherwise, CSFB and the Banks are referred to interchangeably in this opinion.

2. For ease of reference, we refer hereinafter solely to OCD as the borrower.

separate with the twist that the guarantees to the Banks are eliminated. From this we conclude that the proponents of substantive consolidation request it not to rectify the seldom-seen situations that call for this last-resort remedy but rather as a ploy to deprive one group of creditors of their rights while providing a windfall to other creditors.

I. FACTUAL BACKGROUND AND PROCEDURAL HISTORY

A. Owens Corning Group of Companies

OCD and its subsidiaries (which include corporations and limited liability companies) comprise a multinational corporate group. Different entities within the group have different purposes. Some, for example, exist to limit liability concerns (such as those related to asbestos), others to gain tax benefits, and others have regulatory reasons for their formation.

Each subsidiary was a separate legal entity that observed governance formalities. Each had a specific reason to exist separately, each maintained its own business records, and intercompany transactions were regularly documented. Although there may have been some "sloppy" bookkeeping, two of OCD's own officers testified that the financial statements of all the subsidiaries were accurate in all material respects. Further, through an examination of the subsidiaries' books, OCD's postpetition auditors (Ernst & Young) have eliminated most financial discrepancies, particularly with respect to the larger guarantor subsidiaries.

B. The 1997 Credit Agreement

In 1997 OCD sought a loan to acquire Fibreboard Corporation. At this time OCD faced growing asbestos liability and a poor credit rating that hindered its ability to obtain financing. When CSFB was invited to submit a bid, it included subsidiary guarantees in the terms of its proposal. The guarantees gave the Banks direct claims against the guarantors for payment defaults. They were a "credit enhancement" without which the Banks would not have made the loan to OCD. All draft loan term sheets included subsidiary guarantees.

A $2 billion loan from the Banks to OCD closed in June 1997. The loan terms were set out primarily in a Credit Agreement. Among those terms were the guarantee provisions and requirements for guarantors, who were defined as "present or future Domestic Subsidiaries . . . having assets with an aggregate book value in excess of $30,000,000." Section 10.07 of the Agreement provided that the guarantees were "absolute and unconditional" and each "constituted a guarantee of payment and not a guarantee of collection."[4] A "No Release of Guarantor" provision in § 10.8 stated that "the obligations of each guarantor . . . shall not be reduced, limited or terminated, nor shall such guarantor be discharged from any such obligations, for any reason whatsoever," except payment

---

4. This standard guarantee term means simply that, once the primary obligor (here OCD) defaults, the Banks can proceed against the guarantors directly and immediately without first obtaining a judgment against OCD and collecting against that judgment to determine if a shortfall from OCD exists.

and performance in full or through waiver or amendment of the Credit Agreement. Under § 13.05 of the Credit Agreement, a guarantor could be released only through (i) the unanimous consent of the Banks for the guarantees of Fibreboard subsidiaries or through the consent of Banks holding 51% of the debt for other subsidiaries, or (ii) a fair value sale of the guarantor if its cumulative assets totaled less than 10% of the book value of the aggregate OCD group of entities.

CSFB negotiated the Credit Agreement expressly to limit the ways in which OCD could deal with its subsidiaries. For example, it could not enter into transactions with a subsidiary that would result in losses to that subsidiary. Importantly, the Credit Agreement contained provisions designed to protect the separateness of OCD and its subsidiaries. The subsidiaries agreed explicitly to maintain themselves as separate entities. To further this agreement, they agreed to keep separate books and financial records in order to prepare separate financial statements. The Banks were given the right to visit each subsidiary and discuss business matters directly with that subsidiary's management. The subsidiaries also were prohibited from merging into OCD because both entities were required to survive a transaction under § 8.09(a)(ii)(A) of the Credit Agreement. This provision also prohibited guarantor subsidiaries from merging with other subsidiaries unless there would be no effect on the guarantees' value.

C. Procedural History

On October 5, 2000, facing mounting asbestos litigation, OCD and seventeen of its subsidiaries (collectively, the "Debtors") filed for reorganization under Chapter 11 of the Bankruptcy Code. Twenty-seven months later, the Debtors and certain unsecured creditor groups (collectively, the "Plan Proponents") proposed a reorganization plan (as amended, the "Plan") predicated on obtaining "substantive consolidation" of the Debtors along with three non-Debtor OCD subsidiaries. Typically this arrangement pools all assets and liabilities of the subsidiaries into their parent and treats all claims against the subsidiaries as transferred to the parent. In fact, however, the Plan Proponents sought a form of what is known as a "deemed consolidation," under which a consolidation is deemed to exist[7] for purposes of valuing and satisfying creditor claims, voting for or against the Plan, and making distributions for allowed claims under it. Plan § 6.1. Yet "the Plan would not result in the merger of or the transfer or commingling of any assets of any of the Debtors or Non-Debtor Subsidiaries, . . . [which] will continue to be owned by the respective Debtors or Non-Debtors." Plan § 6.1(a). Despite this, on the Plan's effective date "all guarantees of the Debtors of the obligations of any other Debtor will be deemed eliminated, so that any claim against any such Debtor and any guarantee thereof . . . will be deemed to be one obligation of the Debtors with respect to the consolidated estate." Plan § 6.1(b). Put another way, "the Plan eliminates the separate obligations of the Subsidiary Debtors arising from the guarantees of the 1997 Credit Agreement." Plan Disclosure Statement at A-9897.

---

7. "All assets and liabilities of each Subsidiary Debtor . . . *will be treated as though* they were merged into and with the assets and liabilities of OCD. . . ." Plan § 6.1(b) (emphasis added).

The Banks objected to the proposed consolidation. [District Judge John Fullam] . . . granted the consolidation motion[,] conclud[ing] that there existed "substantial identity between . . . OCD and its wholly-owned subsidiaries." He further determined that "there [was] simply no basis for a finding that, in extending credit, the Banks relied upon the separate credit of any of the subsidiary guarantors." In Judge Fullam's view, it was "also clear that substantive consolidation would greatly simplify and expedite the successful completion of this entire bankruptcy proceeding. More importantly, it would be exceedingly difficult to untangle the financial affairs of the various entities." As such, he held substantive consolidation should be permitted, as not only did it allow "obvious advantages . . . [, but was] a virtual necessity." In any event, Judge Fullam wrote, "the real issue is whether the Banks are entitled to participate, pari passu, with other unsecured creditors, or whether the Banks' claim is entitled to priority, in whole or in part, over the claims of other unsecured creditors." *Id.* But this issue, he stated, "cannot now be determined."

CSFB appeals on the Banks' behalf. . . .

III. SUBSTANTIVE CONSOLIDATION

Substantive consolidation, a construct of federal common law, emanates from equity. It "treats separate legal entities as if they were merged into a single survivor left with all the cumulative assets and liabilities (save for inter-entity liabilities, which are erased). The result is that claims of creditors against separate debtors morph to claims against the consolidated survivor." *Genesis Health Ventures, Inc. v. Stapleton (In re Genesis Health Ventures, Inc.)*, 402 F.3d 416, 423 (3d Cir. 2005). Consolidation restructures (and thus revalues) rights of creditors and for certain creditors this may result in significantly less recovery. . . .

A. History of Substantive Consolidation

The concept of substantively consolidating separate estates begins with a common-sense deduction. Corporate disregard as a fault may lead to corporate disregard as a remedy.

. . . It brings all the assets of a group of entities into a single survivor. Indeed, it merges liabilities as well. "The result," to repeat, "is that claims of creditors against separate debtors morph to claims against the consolidated survivor." *In re Genesis Health Ventures*, 402 F.3d at 423. The bad news for certain creditors is that, instead of looking to assets of the subsidiary with whom they dealt, they now must share those assets with all creditors of all consolidated entities, raising the specter for some of a significant distribution diminution.

. . .

B. Our View of Substantive Consolidation

Substantive consolidation exists as an equitable remedy. But when should it be available and by what test should its use be measured? . . .

In assessing whether to order substantive consolidation, courts consider many factors[, which aim to advance certain principles:] . . .

(1) Limiting the cross-creep of liability by respecting entity separateness is a "fundamental ground rule[]." As a result, the general expectation of state law and of the Bankruptcy Code, and thus of commercial markets, is that courts respect entity separateness absent compelling circumstances calling equity (and even then only possibly substantive consolidation) into play.

(2) The harms substantive consolidation addresses are nearly always those caused by *debtors* (and entities they control) who disregard separateness. Harms caused by creditors typically are remedied by provisions found in the Bankruptcy Code (*e.g.*, fraudulent transfers, §§ 548 and 544(b)(1), and equitable subordination, § 510(c)).

(3) Mere benefit to the administration of the case (for example, allowing a court to simplify a case by avoiding other issues or to make postpetition accounting more convenient) is hardly a harm calling substantive consolidation into play.

(4) Indeed, because substantive consolidation is extreme (it may affect profoundly creditors' rights and recoveries) and imprecise, this "rough justice" remedy should be rare and, in any event, one of last resort after considering and rejecting other remedies (for example, the possibility of more precise remedies conferred by the Bankruptcy Code).

(5) While substantive consolidation may be used defensively to remedy the identifiable harms caused by entangled affairs, it may not be used offensively (for example, having a primary purpose to disadvantage tactically a group of creditors in the plan process or to alter creditor rights).

The upshot is this. In our Court what must be proven (absent consent) concerning the entities for whom substantive consolidation is sought is that (i) prepetition they disregarded separateness so significantly their creditors relied on the breakdown of entity borders and treated them as one legal entity,[19] or (ii) postpetition their assets and liabilities are so scrambled that separating them is prohibitive and hurts all creditors.

Proponents of substantive consolidation have the burden of showing one or the other rationale for consolidation. The second rationale needs no explanation. The first, however, is more nuanced. A prima facie case for it typically exists when, based on the parties' prepetition dealings, a proponent proves corporate disregard creating contractual expectations of creditors that they were dealing with debtors as one indistinguishable entity. Proponents who are creditors must also show that, in their prepetition course of dealing, they actually and reasonably relied on debtors' supposed unity. Creditor opponents of consolidation can nonetheless defeat a prima facie showing under the first rationale if they can prove they are adversely affected and actually relied on debtors' separate existence.

---

19. This rationale is meant to protect in bankruptcy the prepetition expectations of those creditors. The usual scenario is that creditors have been misled by debtors' actions (regardless whether those actions were intentional or inadvertent) and thus perceived incorrectly (and relied on this perception) that multiple entities were one.

C. Application of Substantive Consolidation to Our Case

With the principles we perceive underlie use of substantive consolidation, the outcome of this appeal is apparent at the outset. Substantive consolidation fails to fit the facts of our case and, in any event, a "deemed" consolidation cuts against the grain of all the principles.

To begin, the Banks did the "deal world" equivalent of "Lending 101." They loaned $2 billion to OCD and enhanced the credit of that unsecured loan indirectly by subsidiary guarantees covering less than half the initial debt. What the Banks got in lending lingo was "structural seniority"—a direct claim against the guarantors (and thus against their assets levied on once a judgment is obtained) that other creditors of OCD did not have. This kind of lending occurs every business day. To undo this bargain is a demanding task.

1. No Prepetition Disregard of Corporate Separateness

Despite the Plan Proponents' pleas to the contrary, there is no evidence of the prepetition disregard of the OCD entities' separateness. To the contrary, OCD (no less than CSFB) negotiated the 1997 lending transaction premised on the separateness of all OCD affiliates. Even today no allegation exists of bad faith by anyone concerning the loan. In this context, OCD and the other Plan Proponents cannot now ignore, or have us ignore, the very ground rules OCD put in place. Playing by these rules means that obtaining the guarantees of separate entities, made separate by OCD's choice of how to structure the affairs of its affiliate group of companies, entitles a lender, in bankruptcy or out, to look to any (or all) guarantor(s) for payment when the time comes. As such, the District Court's conclusions of "substantial identity" of OCD and its subsidiaries, and the Banks' reliance thereon, are incorrect. For example, testimony presented by both the Banks and the Debtors makes plain the parties' intention to treat the entities separately. CSFB presented testimony from attorneys and bankers involved in negotiating the Credit Agreement that reflected their assessment of the value of the guarantees as partially derived from the separateness of the entities. As OCD concedes, these representatives "testified that the guarantees were . . . intended to provide 'structural seniority' to the banks," and were thus fundamentally premised on an assumption of separateness.

In the face of this testimony, Plan Proponents nonetheless argue that the Banks intended to ignore the separateness of the entities. In support of this contention, they assert, inter alia, that because the Banks did not receive independent financial statements for each of the entities during the negotiating process, they must have intended to deal with them as a unified whole. Because the Banks were unaware of the separate financial makeup of the subsidiaries, the argument goes, they could not have relied on their separateness.

This argument is overly simplistic. Assuming the Banks did not obtain separate financial statements for each subsidiary, they nonetheless obtained detailed information about each subsidiary guarantor from OCD, including information about that subsidiary's assets and debt. Moreover, the Banks knew a great deal about these subsidiaries. For example, they knew that each subsidiary guarantor had assets with a book value of at least $30 million as per the terms of the Credit Agreement, that the aggregate value of the guarantor subsidiaries was over $900 million and that those subsidiaries had little or no debt. Additionally, the Banks knew that Fibreboard's subsidiaries (including the entities that became part of ESI) had no asbestos liability, would be debt-free post-acquisition and had assets of approximately $700 million.

Even assuming the Plan Proponents could prove prepetition disregard of Debtors' corporate forms, we cannot conceive of a justification for imposing the rule that a creditor must obtain financial statements from a debtor in order to rely reasonably on the separateness of that debtor. Creditors are free to employ whatever metrics they believe appropriate in deciding whether to extend credit free of court oversight. We agree with the Banks that "the reliance inquiry is not an inquiry into lenders' internal credit metrics. Rather, it is about the *fact* that the credit decision was made in reliance on the existence of separate entities. . . ." Here there is no serious dispute as to that fact.

2. No Hopeless Commingling Exists Postpetition

There also is no meaningful evidence postpetition of hopeless commingling of Debtors' assets and liabilities. Indeed, there is no question which entity owns which principal assets and has which material liabilities. Likely for this reason little time is spent by the parties on this alternative test for substantive consolidation. It is similarly likely that the District Court followed suit.

The Court nonetheless erred in concluding that the commingling of assets will justify consolidation when "the affairs of the two companies are so entangled that consolidation *will be beneficial.*" *In re Owens Corning*, 316 B.R. at 171 (emphasis added). As we have explained, commingling justifies consolidation only when separately accounting for the assets and liabilities of the distinct entities will reduce the recovery of *every* creditor—that is, when every creditor will benefit from the consolidation. Moreover, the benefit to creditors should be from cost savings that make assets available rather than from the shifting of assets to benefit one group of creditors at the expense of another. Mere benefit to some creditors, or administrative benefit to the Court, falls far short. The District Court's test not only fails to adhere to the theoretical justification for "hopeless commingling" consolidation—that no creditor's rights will be impaired—but also suffers from the infirmity that it will almost always be met. That is, substantive consolidation will nearly always produce some benefit to some in the form of simplification and/or avoidance of costs. Among other things, following such a path misapprehends the degree of harm required to order substantive consolidation.

But no matter the legal test, a case for hopeless commingling cannot be made. Arguing nonetheless to the contrary, Debtors assert that "it would be practically impossible and prohibitively expensive in time and resources" to account for the voluntary bankruptcies of the separate entities OCD has created and maintained. In support of this contention, Debtors rely almost exclusively on the District Court's findings that

> it would be exceedingly difficult to untangle the financial affairs of the various entities . . . [and] there are . . . many reasons for challenging the accuracy of the results achieved [in accounting efforts thus far]. For example, transfers of cash between subsidiaries and

parent did not include any payment of interest; and calculations of royalties are subject to question.

In re Owens Corning, 316 B.R. at 171. Assuming arguendo that these findings are correct, they are simply not enough to establish that substantive consolidation is warranted.

Neither the impossibility of perfection in untangling the affairs of the entities nor the likelihood of some inaccuracies in efforts to do so is sufficient to justify consolidation. We find *R 2 Investments, LDC v. World Access, Inc. (In re World Access, Inc.)*, 301 B.R. 217 (Bankr. N.D. Ill. 2003), instructive on this point. In *World Access* the Court noted that the controlling entity "had no uniform guidelines for the recording of intercompany interest charges" and that the debtors failed to "allocate overhead charges amongst themselves." *Id.* at 234. The Court held, however, that those accounting shortcomings were "merely imperfections in a sophisticated system of accounting records that were conscientiously maintained." *Id.* at 279. It ultimately concluded that "all the relevant accounting data . . . still existed," that only a "reasonable review to make any necessary adjustments [was] required," and, thus, that substantive consolidation was not warranted. *Id.*

The record in our case compels the same conclusion. At its core, Debtors' argument amounts to the contention that because intercompany interest and royalty payments were not perfectly accounted for, untangling the finances of those entities is a hopeless endeavor. Yet imperfection in intercompany accounting is assuredly not atypical in large, complex company structures. For obvious reasons, we are loathe to entertain the argument that complex corporate families should have an expanded substantive consolidation option in bankruptcy. And we find no reason to doubt that "perfection is not the standard in the substantive consolidation context." We are confident that a court could properly order and oversee an accounting process that would sufficiently account for the interest and royalty payments owed among the OCD group of companies for purposes of evaluating intercompany claims—dealing with inaccuracies and difficulties as they arise and not in hypothetical abstractions.

On the basis of the record before us, the Plan Proponents cannot fulfill their burden of demonstrating that Debtors' affairs are even tangled, let alone that the cost of untangling them is so high relative to their assets that the Banks, among other creditors, will benefit from a consolidation.

3. Other Considerations Doom Consolidation as Well

Other considerations drawn from the principles we set out also counsel strongly against consolidation. First of all, holding out the possibility of later giving priority to the Banks on their claims does not cure an improvident grant of substantive consolidation. Among other things, the prerequisites for this last-resort remedy must still be met no matter the priority of the Banks' claims.

Secondly, substantive consolidation should be used defensively to remedy identifiable harms, not offensively to achieve advantage over one group in the plan negotiation process (for example, by deeming assets redistributed to negate plan voting rights), nor a "free pass" to spare Debtors or any other group from proving challenges, like fraudulent transfer claims, that are liberally brandished to scare yet are hard to show. If the Banks are so vulnerable to the fraudulent transfer challenges Debtors have teed up (but have not swung at for so long), then the game should be played to the finish in that arena.[27]

But perhaps the flaw most fatal to the Plan Proponents' proposal is that the consolidation sought was "deemed" (i.e., a pretend consolidation for all but the Banks). If Debtors' corporate and financial structure was such a sham before the filing of the motion to consolidate, then how is it that post the Plan's effective date this structure stays largely undisturbed, with the Debtors reaping all the liability-limiting, tax and regulatory benefits achieved by forming subsidiaries in the first place? In effect, the Plan Proponents seek to remake substantive consolidation not as a remedy, but rather a stratagem to "deem" separate resources reallocated to OCD to strip the Banks of rights under the Bankruptcy Code, favor other creditors, and yet trump possible Plan objections by the Banks. Such "deemed" schemes we deem not Hoyle.

IV. CONCLUSION

Substantive consolidation at its core is equity. Its exercise must lead to an equitable result. "Communizing" assets of affiliated companies to one survivor to feed all creditors of all companies may to some be equal (and hence equitable). But it is hardly so for those creditors who have lawfully bargained prepetition for unequal treatment by obtaining guarantees of separate entities. No principled, or even plausible, reason exists to undo OCD's and the Banks' arms-length negotiation and lending arrangement, especially when to do so punishes the very parties that conferred the prepetition benefit—a $2 billion loan unsecured by OCD and guaranteed by others only in part. To overturn this bargain, set in place by OCD's own pre-loan choices of organizational form, would cause chaos in the marketplace, as it would make this case the Banquo's ghost of bankruptcy.

With no meaningful evidence supporting either test to apply substantive consolidation, there is simply not the nearly "perfect storm" needed to invoke it. Even if there were, a "deemed" consolidation—"several zip (if not area) codes away from anything resembling substantive consolidation," *In re Genesis Health Ventures*, 402 F.3d at 424—fails even to qualify for consideration. It is here a tactic used as a sword and not a shield.

We thus reverse and remand this case to the District Court.

Study Question

Given that most complex cases end up with de facto consolidation, at least of intercompany claims, why should courts make such a big deal about formal substantive consolidation? Or framed differently, why don't courts make a bigger deal about de facto consolidation? Was the consolidation proposed in *Owens Corning* more like a de facto consolidation, in that it was to be for purposes of distribution only?

27. The same sentiment applies to the argument of the bondholders that, subsequent to the 1997 loan to OCD, the Banks defrauded them in connection with a prospectus distributed with respect to a sale of OCD bonds underwritten by some of the Banks. If the bondholders have a valid claim, they need to prove it in the District Court and not use their allegations as means to gerrymander consolidation of estates.

Problem Set 32

(1) Hades Mortuary Services is in Chapter 11 bankruptcy. Can either of the following claims be equitably disallowed or recharacterized?

    a. The $2 million general unsecured claim of Hades's CEO for a loan to the firm at a below-market rate of return. The CEO made false oral representations to several vendors on which the vendors relied when extending trade credit.

    b. The $1 million general unsecured claim of Hades's former CFO for a severance settlement. The former CFO was dismissed after an accounting and embezzlement scandal was discovered in which the CFO played a significant role. There are unresolved suspicions that the CFO embezzled significant funds from the company; it is known that he had company employees perform yardwork and remodeling work for him at company expense.

(2) Bacchus Investments Master Fund LLP had invested in bonds issued by Nationwide Mortgage Company, a large originator of subprime mortgages. Bacchus claims that the registration statement for the bonds contained numerous material misstatements and omissions, and has sued Nationwide for securities fraud seeking rescissory damages. Nationwide has filed for Chapter 11 bankruptcy.

    a. What is the status of Bacchus's claim against Nationwide if Bacchus obtained a judgment before the bankruptcy filing?

    b. What if Bacchus had not yet obtained a judgment? 11 U.S.C. §§ 501(c), 510(b).

    c. What is the status of other bondholders of the same issue who have not sued for securities fraud?

    d. Suppose Bacchus had instead invested in Nationwide's common equity and had brought a securities fraud claim seeking rescissory damages based on the material misstatements and omissions. What would be the status of Bacchus's claim if it had obtained a judgment pre-petition?

(3) The Hermes Investments LP hedge fund ran a major Ponzi scheme before its ignominious collapse and ensuing bankruptcy filing. Many of the largest charitable institutions and foundations in Los Angeles were heavily invested in Hermes Investments. These charities claim to have been unaware of the Ponzi scheme and that they were defrauded.

    a. What is the status of their claims in bankruptcy? 11 U.S.C. § 510(b).

    b. What is the status of a securities repo agreement made between Hermes Investments by Chaste Bank, N.A. wherein Hermes sells securities to Chaste and agrees to repurchase them on subsequent dates? The repo is at somewhat higher than market rates and is subject to a master netting agreement, but Chaste has no recourse to Hermes beyond those contracts subject to the master netting agreement. Chaste is Hermes's prime broker and therefore is in a position to see all of Hermes's trading activity. 11 U.S.C. §§ 101(47); 362(b)(6), (7), (27); 546; 555; 559; 561.

    c. What is the status of an arms'-length loan made by Mercutio Hermes, the founder of Hermes Investments and the mastermind of the Ponzi scheme, to the hedge fund? The loan?

(4) Your beloved aunt, Rhoda, invested her life savings in one of 20 hedge funds managed by famed fund manager Julius Makoff. Rhoda made the investment on the advice of her second cousin Maury, who told her that Makoff had been consistently producing 25% annual returns for investors in all his funds. Maury was so enthusiastic that he invested his small business's entire pension plan in another Makoff fund.

All of the Makoff funds are structured as limited partnerships with Julius Makoff Investments, LLC (JMI LLC) serving as the investment advisor (essentially manager) to the funds, as well as the general partner in the funds. The investors, like Rhoda and Maury, are the limited partners in the funds. The various Makoff funds are joint borrowers on a $700 million line of credit with Columbia National Bank, secured by all of the funds' investments. Columbia National also serves as the clearing bank for Makoff, so it is in a position to see all of Makoff's transactions.

Late last year rumors began to circulate that Makoff had been running a Ponzi scheme, and investors rushed to redeem their funds. Rhoda managed to redeem her funds before Julius Makoff was arrested while trying to flee the country, but Maury was too late. After Makoff's arrest, all of the Makoff funds as well as JMI LLC filed for Chapter 7 bankruptcy. The various Makoff hedge funds ended up in Chapter 7 bankruptcy, and the joint trustee appointed for all the funds' cases successfully brought an action to avoid Rhoda's redemption.

Rhoda and Maury, along with other Makoff investors, filed proofs of claim in the bankruptcies claiming that they had been defrauded by Makoff and that they are owed back their initial investments of $5 billion. The various investors' stated account balances (undistributed limited partnership interests) were nearly $20 billion at the time the pre-bankruptcy run started. It turned out that with the exception of his original fund, the Makoff Prime Fund (in which Rhoda is an investor), Makoff had made almost no investments, but just sent out false account statements. Few investors wanted to redeem funds that were performing so well, and those that did were paid out of funds from new investors. The Makoff Prime Fund has actually performed relatively well, although not as spectacularly as claimed, and its assets are worth $2.5 billion.

Columbia National filed a proof of claim for $700 million, claiming to be fully secured by the funds' investments. The Chapter 7 trustee for JMI LLC, the investment advisor to the various Makoff hedge funds, filed a proof of claim for $240 million for management fees owed by the funds. From behind bars, Julius Makoff himself filed a proof of claim for a $100 million market-rate unsecured loan he made to the funds on the eve of bankruptcy. JMI LLC has assets of $300 million, and other assorted liabilities of $150 million.

Makoff's loan to the funds was fully documented with careful legal work done by Howe, Dewey & Noughit LLP, a storied white shoe law firm. Howe, Dewey & Noughit filed proofs of claim totaling $10 million in the funds' bankruptcies for the work it did on the personal loan from Makoff. Makoff's accounting firm, Czech, DeNoume, Beers & Co. has also filed a proof of claim in JMI LLC's bankruptcy for $50 million in unpaid audit work for JMI LLC.

The Chapter 7 trustee for the various funds' cases thinks it will take years to sort through the actual Makoff accounting, but his estimate is that there will be perhaps $1 billion recovered on the funds other than the Makoff Prime Fund.

a. What is the status of Rhoda's claim? 11 U.S.C. §§ 502(a), 510(b). Of Maury's?
b. What will be the likely treatment of Julius Makoff Investments, LLC's claim? 11 U.S.C. §§ 502, 510(b)-(c).
c. What will be the likely treatment of Julius Makoff's claim? 11 U.S.C. §§ 502, 510(c).
d. What is the likely treatment of Columbia National's claim? 11 U.S.C. §§ 502, 510(c).
e. What is the likely treatment of Howe, Dewey & Noughit's claim? 11 U.S.C. §§ 502, 510(c).
f. What is the likely treatment of Czech, DeNoume, Beers & Co.'s claim? 11 U.S.C. §§ 502, 510(c).
g. Can the various Makoff funds be substantively consolidated? What effect would that have on Rhoda and Maury? Will Aunt Rhoda be able to retire?
h. Can the Makoff hedge funds also be substantively consolidated with Julius Makoff Investments, LLC?
i. Shortly before Julius Makoff attempted to flee the country, he sold half of his $100 million loan to Heliot Associates, a distressed investment fund. Heliot paid $1 million for the loan. One of the partners involved in the deal at Heliot had previously worked for JMI LLC as chief operating officer. Heliot then proceeded to sell half of its interest to Aegypius Investments for $3 million, the day before the bankruptcy. What is the likely treatment of the claims of Heliot Associates and Aegypius Investments?

CHAPTER 11
RESTRUCTURING

CHAPTER 33

CONSENSUAL PLAN CONFIRMATION

I. CHAPTER 11 COMPARED WITH CHAPTER 7

In the previous chapter we learned how a Chapter 7 liquidation occurs. The assets of the estate were marshaled while collection actions outside of bankruptcy were stayed. Meanwhile creditors filed claims (which might be challenged), and the trustee liquidated the estate's assets and then distributed them among creditors according to a complex statutory priority scheme. While the trustee in bankruptcy has some discretion about how to manage the assets of the bankruptcy estate, the trustee has no discretion about how to distribute the assets.

In some ways Chapter 11 works the same as Chapter 7. In Chapter 11 the assets are again marshaled. Collection actions outside bankruptcy are stayed, and claims are filed and potentially challenged. In Chapter 11, the assets of the estate are typically (but not necessarily) managed by a "debtor in possession," rather than an independent trustee in bankruptcy. The debtor in possession or DIP (not a pejorative term) has most of the same rights and powers as a trustee, 11 U.S.C. § 1107(a), but it is the pre-petition debtor managing the bankruptcy estate. Chapter 11, like Chapter 7, is ultimately working toward a distribution to creditors and equityholders. There are important differences in how the distribution works in Chapter 11, however.

First, the pool of assets available for distribution is Chapter 11 is potentially larger. In Chapter 11, the property of the estate is defined more broadly than in Chapter 7. In Chapter 7, the property of the estate includes whatever legal title or equitable benefits a debtor has in property as of the date of the filing. Income produced by the debtor post-petition through services is not property of the estate in Chapter 7. In Chapter 11, however, income produced post-petition through services is also property of the estate. 11 U.S.C. § 1115(a)(2).

Second, distribution in Chapter 11 is not always a distribution of assets, but might also or instead be a distribution of claims in the capital structure of a reorganized debtor. Thus, in Chapter 11, a distribution might be of cash or estate property, but could also be of notes owed by the reorganized debtor, equity in the reorganized debtor, or warrants (call options) to purchase equity in the reorganized debtor.

Third, the distribution in a Chapter 11 case is done according to a document called a **plan**. The plan is usually proposed by the DIP, which has an initial exclusive right to propose a plan. There are numerous statutory requirements regarding what a plan must and may not do, but plans may contain a multitude of discretionary terms, so there are important governance issues involved in having the DIP have initial plan proposal exclusivity.

Fourth, to the extent that a Chapter 11 plan is for a reorganization, rather than a liquidation, the distribution in Chapter 11 includes an allocation of the going-concern value of the firm. Accordingly, there are different rules for how that surplus over liquidation value may be distributed. Chapter 7's liquidation baseline is the starting point for a Chapter 11 distribution, but many other requirements apply.

For a plan to be put into effect, it must first be confirmed by the bankruptcy court. The plan is typically a negotiated document because confirmation usually requires a vote by creditors and equityholders. Confirmation may occur through two different methods, with different legal requirements, depending on the voting threshold achieved. One method is known as "consensual" confirmation, meaning that it has been approved by the requisite vote from all impaired classes of creditors or equityholders. The other method, known as "cramdown" confirmation, requires approval of only a single impaired class of creditors or equityholders, but substitutes greater substantive protections for creditors and equityholders in terms of the distribution of the going-concern surplus for the lower consent threshold. This chapter covers consensual confirmation. Cramdown is covered in subsequent chapters. After covering these procedures, we will turn to an alternative method of restructuring a debtor using the bankruptcy sale process.

II. YOU GOTTA HAVE A PLAN: CONTENTS OF A PLAN

With some exceptions that we will consider later, distributions in Chapter 11 occur according to a "plan." (Notably the Code does not refer to a "plan of reorganization," but simply to a "plan," which could also be a plan of liquidation.) A plan is a bespoke document detailing how the bankruptcy estate's assets will be handled. While a plan is highly customized, it must also conform to a number of statutory requirements.

Section 1123 of the Bankruptcy Code sets forth what must and what may be in a plan. Section 1123(a) details what must be included in a plan, while section 1123(b) further explicates on optional provisions, including the inclusion in a plan of "any other appropriate provision not inconsistent with the applicable provisions of this title." 11 U.S.C. § 1123(b)(6). The plan must classify claims into classes and specify how they will be treated, meaning what sort of distribution, if any, the class will receive. 11 U.S.C. § 1123(a)(1)-(3). A class of claims or interests can be left unimpaired, generally meaning that their rights are unaffected by bankruptcy. 11 U.S.C. § 1124 (defining impairment). We cover classification and impairment in detail in the next chapter.

One of the most important requirements of section 1123 is that the plan must also treat all claims in a class equally absent a claimant's consent. 11 U.S.C. § 1123(a)(4). The principle encapsulated here is a fundamental one of bankruptcy: Equity is equality. And yet, as the following excerpt makes clear, section 1123(a)(4) does not mean that all claimants must be treated equally solely because they have claims in the same class.

Section 1123(a)(4) merely mandates that the treatment *on account of a claim* be the same for those claims in the same class. It does not mean that all claimants holding a claim in a class must receive identical treatment. A claimant may have claims in multiple classes, and the claimant may recover on multiple claims in multiple classes. Moreover, some claimants may be entitled to additional rights by court order, including as part of the compensation for extending DIP financing.

In re Indianapolis Downs, LLC

486 B.R. 286 (Bankr. D. Del. 2013)

BRENDAN LINEHAN SHANNON, U.S. Bankr. J.

. . .

The [proposed] Plan provides for payment of the legal and professional fees of the Restructuring Support Parties, including Fortress [Investment Group, LLC ("Fortress"), which holds a substantial portion of the third lien debt (and second lien debt as well), and was one of the non-Debtor signatories of the pre-bankruptcy Restructuring Support Agreement or lock-up agreement in which it committed to supporting a Chapter 11 plan that met certain criteria]. Specifically, the Plan provides as follows:

> On the Effective Date, in full and complete settlement, release and discharge of their Allowed Administrative Claims pursuant to section 503(b) and 507(a)(2) of the Bankruptcy Code, the Debtors or the Reorganized Debtors shall promptly indefeasibly pay in full in Cash (pursuant to section 1129(a)(4) of the Bankruptcy Code or otherwise) all reasonable and documented fees, out-of-pocket costs, expenses, disbursements and charges incurred by the Restructuring Support Advisors in connection with the Chapter 11 Cases up to and including the Effective Date that have not previously been paid. . . .

Plan § 12.02.

The Oliver Parties object to payment of these fees and expenses[.] . . . [T]he Oliver Parties challenge the Debtors' contention that the professional fees are permissible under Bankruptcy Code § 503(b). Finally, they contend that the Plan provides for payments in derogation of Bankruptcy Code § 1123(a)(4)'s requirement that each member of the same class receive the "same treatment."

. . . [T]he Debtors contend that the Restructuring Support Parties have made a "substantial contribution" to these cases, such that the fees and expenses are entitled to priority treatment and payment under § 503(b). The Debtors next contend that the final financing order has already been approved by this Court. Finally, as discussed in detail below, the Debtors submit that the payment of fees and expenses at issue here is not being made on account of the Restructuring Support Parties' claim, but are independent of those claims, so that there is no disparate treatment of Class members.

The Court finds as a threshold proposition that the payments contemplated hereby have been previously authorized under the Final DIP financing order (the "Final DIP

Order") entered at the onset of these cases. [Fortress was one of the parties that provided funding for the debtor's post-petition operations.] Payment of these fees and costs was authorized under ¶19(d) of the Final DIP Order, and the record reflects that monthly invoices have been submitted and paid pursuant to that Order.

Equally important, the Court finds that the fees and expenses are allowable pursuant to Bankruptcy Code § 503(b). Section 503(b)(1)(A) provides that "[a]fter notice and a hearing, there shall be allowed administrative expenses . . . including . . . the actual, necessary costs and expenses of preserving the estate. . . ." 11 U.S.C. § 503(b)(1)(A). In determining whether a claim is entitled to administrative status, courts generally apply a two-part test: "(1) the expense must have arisen from a post-petition transaction between the creditor and the debtor, and (2) the expense must have been 'actual and necessary' to preserve the estate." *In re New Century TRS Holdings, Inc.*, 446 B.R. 656, 661 (Bankr. D. Del. 2011).

In the present case, the Debtors note that the consent of the Restructuring Support Parties at the onset of these cases made possible the use of cash collateral and post-petition financing. Further, in the absence of an official committee appointed in these cases, the Debtors contend that the Restructuring Support Parties performed a central role in the formulation of the confirmable Plan and to otherwise keep these proceedings moving forward. Allowance of the fees and expenses under § 503(b) is supported by the record in these proceedings and by the Court's own observations that, in the absence of the laboriously negotiated resolution built into the RSA and the Plan, these cases would either have either dragged on (expensively) for many more months or devolved (much more expensively) into ferocious litigation between and among the Debtors and their stakeholders. Accordingly, the Court finds that the Debtors have carried their burden to demonstrate that payment of the professional fees and expenses of the Restructuring Support Parties is permissible pursuant to Bankruptcy Code § 503(b).

The Oliver Parties' further opposition, on grounds of disparate treatment of Class 4 claims, fails upon close examination. Both Fortress and the Oliver Parties hold claims in Class 4. The Plan provides, at § 3.03, for treatment of Class 4 claims; whatever Fortress gets on account of its Class 4 claims, the Oliver Parties will likewise receive. However, the Court does not accept the Oliver Parties' contention that payment of Fortress' professional fees and expenses—admittedly a substantial sum—represents an enhanced distribution on account of Fortress' Class 4 claim. Rather, as discussed above, all Class 4 claimants will get what they get for their respect[ive] Class 4 claims under the Plan. These payments will occur under the imprimatur of the Final DIP Order and § 503; there is therefore no violation of § 1123(a)(4), and the Oliver Parties' objection to payment of these professional fees and expenses is overruled.

Questions on *Indianapolis Downs*

1. Why do you think the Oliver Parties are objecting to the disparate treatment? Is it the money that they are worried about or is their objection likely about something else?

2. Fortress's professionals' fees were incurred in respect to the Restructuring Support Agreement. Was that agreement "a post-petition transaction between the creditor and the debtor"? Wasn't it a pre-bankruptcy transaction? And how exactly was it "actual

and necessary to preserve the estate" as opposed to simply furthering a particular reorganization plan?

3. Why does the bankruptcy court need to justify the payment of the professionals' fees under section 503(b)? Shouldn't their approval in the DIP financing order have been enough?

Section 1123 also requires that the plan must detail how it will be implemented—how will the debtor manage to provide for the proposed treatment of the claims and interests? As section 1123(a)(5) indicates, this can include a wide range of actions: sales; mergers; modifications or satisfaction of liens; curing of defaults; changing of maturity dates, interest rates, or covenants; exchanges of securities for other new securities or cash or other property. And the plan must also set up certain corporate governance structures, creating corporate governance requirements beyond those that appear in state corporate law. 11 U.S.C. § 1123(a)(6)-(7).

III. WHO MAY PROPOSE A PLAN AND WHEN

Typically a plan is proposed by the debtor. The debtor may file the plan with the petition itself, as is common with "prepackaged bankruptcies" or "prepacs," or may file the plan subsequently. 11 U.S.C. § 1121(a). (We examine prepacs in Chapter 21.) The DIP initially has the exclusive right to file a plan. 11 U.S.C. § 1121(b). This exclusivity may be lost, however. Plan exclusivity is lost if a trustee is appointed to manage the estate's assets (rather than a DIP), if 120 days lapse without the filing of a plan by the debtor, or if 180 days lapse without a positive vote for the plan by all impaired classes of claims or interests. 11 U.S.C. § 1121(c). Thus, if a debtor proposes a plan on day 120, the debtor gains up to an extra 60 days of exclusivity, but will lose exclusivity if the plan is not confirmed within this 60-day window. The exclusive period may be extended or reduced for cause, but the 120-day exclusivity limit cannot be extended beyond 18 months and the 180-day limit cannot be extended beyond 20 months from filing. 11 U.S.C. § 1121(d).

Be careful about the counting of the dates—exclusivity lapsed in the bankruptcy of New World Pasta (the makers of Chef Boyardee) because of a miscalculation of dates by an associate. The mistake cost New World Pasta's law firm its engagement, and likely cost an associate his or her job.

Nathan Koppel
Bankruptcy Boo-Boo
The American Lawyer, Jan. 1, 2005

In recent years Kirkland & Ellis has been considered one of the top bankruptcy firms in the country. But its reputation took a hit this fall in the bankruptcy of New World Pasta Company.

The Harrisburg, Pennsylvania, maker of such pasta products as San Giorgio and Ronzoni filed for bankruptcy last May, claiming assets and debt of more than $100 million each. New World hired Kirkland, and the company at first enjoyed a significant advantage: exclusivity. The U.S. Bankruptcy Code grants debtors exclusive right for the first 120 days of a bankruptcy to file a plan of reorganization. "The debtor is surrounded by creditors who . . . are often asserting that they are entitled to their money now," says Harvey Miller, former head of bankruptcy at Weil, Gotshal & Manges and now a restructuring adviser with New York investment bank Greenhill & Co., Inc. "All that the debtor has is leverage given to it by the state to afford it a reasonable period of time to devise a plan. . . . Without exclusivity, the debtor is a bystander."

Kirkland took New World out of the driver's seat by failing to act in time. The company's exclusivity period lapsed on September 7, 2004. Kirkland failed, as required by law, to request an extension before exclusivity expired. Judges often grant such requests. On September 9 Kirkland realized its error and sought an extension. But bankruptcy court judge Mary France denied the request.

Matthew Kleiman, the Kirkland partner in charge of the case, did not return a call for comment. James Sprayregen, head of the firm's bankruptcy practice, said of the missed deadline: "It was pure inadvertence. No excuses." Sprayregen says it is too early to tell whether the mistake will hurt New World. And he will not comment on whether the firm might face a malpractice claim. A creditors' lawyer in the case, speaking on background, says missing a deadline would typically prompt a law firm to call its malpractice carrier. Still, the lawyer says, it would likely be hard for New World to quantify its damages, which would make a malpractice action unlikely.

New World's creditors can now file a reorganization plan, but none had as of early December. Cary Metz, New World's general counsel, did not return a call for comment. And none of the creditors' lawyers would cop to strategic advantages they might have gained. "I would hope and expect that [loss of exclusivity] will cause all parties to redouble their efforts to resume negotiations on the terms of a consensual plan," says creditors committee's lawyer Brad Scheler, a partner at Fried, Frank, Harris, Shriver & Jacobson.

Kirkland, at the very least, paid a price. In October, New World fired the firm, and replaced it with Weil, Gotshal. Since bankruptcy judges typically like to avoid taxing a debtor with duplicative costs, Judge France might require Kirkland to cover some of the cost of Weil preparing for the case. Judge France must also sign off on Kirkland's compensation; in early December she had not yet done so. Asked whether the firm should be docked, Sprayregen said: "We will deal with those issues in the fairest way possible to all parties."

Federal Rule of Bankruptcy Procedure 9006(a)

(a) COMPUTING TIME. The following rules apply in computing any time period specified in these rules, in the Federal Rules of Civil Procedure, in any local rule or court order, or in any statute that does not specify a method of computing time.

(1) *Period Stated in Days or a Longer Unit.* When the period is stated in days or a longer unit of time:

    (A) exclude the day of the event that triggers the period;

    (B) count every day, including intermediate Saturdays, Sundays, and legal holidays; and

    (C) include the last day of the period, but if the last day is a Saturday, Sunday, or legal holiday, the period continues to run until the end of the next day that is not a Saturday, Sunday, or legal holiday.

Exclusive plan filing rights give the debtor a power tool: doing nothing. The debtor can sit in bankruptcy for at least 120 days, and possibly more than a year and half without providing for any distribution to creditors and being protected by the automatic stay. This enables the debtor to play a waiting game. The debtor may be waiting under the aegis of the automatic stay to see if market conditions change, if it can improve its operations, or if the value of its assets increase. Delay can impose significant costs on creditors too and make them more willing to agree to concessions to the debtor.

At the same time, the limits on plan exclusivity give creditors a potential tool. A creditor that can delay plan confirmation until exclusivity lapses may be able to propose its own alternative plan.

If exclusivity lapses, then any party in interest may file a plan. Multiple plans may be proposed. Only one can be confirmed, however, even if multiple plans meet the confirmation requirements. 11 U.S.C. § 1129(c). It is rare to have competing plans, but when a competition arises, it is in the bankruptcy court's discretion which plan shall be confirmed, but the court is instructed by the Code to consider the preferences of creditors and equityholders (without any guidance as to how competing preferences should be weighed) in making its decision.

IV. PLAN CONFIRMATION REQUIREMENTS

A plan must be confirmed by the Bankruptcy Court to become effective and binding. Section 1129(a)-(b) of the Code sets forth the requirements for confirming a plan. Section 1129 is structured in a less than intuitive manner. Section 1129(a) lays out the requirements for so-called consensual plan confirmation, while section 1129(b) provides the requirements for "non-consensual" plan confirmation, also known as "cramdown." The non-consensual plan confirmation requirements include all but one of the consensual confirmation requirements, as well as additional requirements.

Section 1129(a) lays out the 16 basic plan confirmation requirements. 11 U.S.C. § 1129(a)(1)-(16). For a "consensual" plan confirmation, all of the applicable requirements must be met, but meeting one requirement, that of section 1129(a)(8), will also suffice for meeting another requirement, section 1129(a)(10). Additionally, two of these 16 requirements, 11 U.S.C. § 1129(a)(14)-(15), are inapplicable to business entity debtors.

Section 1129(b) provides the requirements for a "non-consensual" or "cramdown" confirmation of a plan. Section 1129(b) operates as an exception to one of those 16 requirements, section 1129(a)(8). Section 1129(b) is best thought of as a subsection of section 1129(a)(8). When section 1129(b) is invoked, however, then section 1129(a)(10) matters because it will not automatically be satisfied by meeting section 1129(a)(8).

Thus, to be confirmed, a bankruptcy plan must always comply with 14 of the section 1129(a) requirements: § 1129(a)(1)-(7), § 1129(a)(9), and § 1129(a)(11)-(16). The plan must also comply with either section 1129(a)(8) (consensual confirmation) or the section 1129(b) requirements plus the section 1129(a)(10) requirement.

Any party in interest has a right to raise, appear, and be heard on any issue, 11 U.S.C. § 1109(b), and may object to a plan, 11 U.S.C. § 1128(b), but only to the aspects of a plan or the confirmation requirements that affect it; to the extent that a particular confirmation requirement does not apply to a party in interest, it may not raise the issue. Additionally, the SEC has a right to appear and be heard on any issue, including plan confirmation, even though it is not a party in interest, and may not appeal from rulings. 11 U.S.C. § 1109(a).

We will examine the section 1129(b) exception in Chapters 37-40. For now let us concern ourselves with the main section 1129(a) requirements other than creditor voting. These are the Title 11 compliance requirements, 11 U.S.C. § 1129(a)(1)-(2); the good faith requirement, § 1129(a)(3); the requirements of reasonableness of fees paid in connection with the plan, § 1129(a)(4); the "best interests" test, § 1129(a)(7); the administrative cash payments requirement, § 1129(a)(9)(A); and the feasibility requirement, § 1129(a)(11). We will also consider section 1129(a)(5), a generally obscure provision that may have some potency. We will turn to the voting requirements of sections 1129(a)(8) and 1129(a)(10) in Chapter 34.

A. Compliance with Title 11 Provisions, Section 1129(a)(1)-(2)

Section 1129(a)(1) requires the plan to comply with all applicable provisions of Title 11. Section 1129(a)(2) contains a similar provision that requires compliance of the plan proponent, not just the plan. The effect of these requirements is to incorporate all of the other Title 11 provisions into a confirmation requirement. Section 1129(a)(1) and (a)(2) thus make denial of plan confirmation the remedy for other violations. For example, section 1123(a)(4) requires that a plan provide that all claims within a class be treated equally. Section 1123(a)(4) lacks a remedy provision, however. Absent section 1129(a)(1), a plan could be confirmed that violated the prohibition on disparate treatment within a class. Section 1129(a)(1) and (a)(2) operate to ensure the enforcement of other Code provisions.

B. Good Faith, Section 1129(a)(3)

Section 1129(a)(3) requires that a plan be "proposed in good faith and not by any means forbidden by law." 11 U.S.C. § 1129(a)(3). The good faith plan proposal requirement is distinct from the good faith filing doctrine. It is also distinct from the question of bad faith vote designation under section 1126(e). The Bankruptcy

Code does not define "good faith," and like most good faith requirements it would seem to involve a <u>totality of the circumstances</u>. The Seventh Circuit has given the most elaborate statement of what section 1129(a)(3) requires:

> Though the term "good faith," as used in section 1129(a)(3), is not defined in the Bankruptcy Code, . . . the term is generally interpreted to mean that there exists "a reasonable likelihood that the plan will achieve a result consistent with the objectives and purposes of the Bankruptcy Code." Thus, for purposes of determining good faith under section 1129(a)(3), . . . the important point of inquiry is the plan itself and whether such plan will fairly achieve a result consistent with the objectives and purposes of the Bankruptcy Code. . . .

> According to the good faith requirement of section 1129(a)(3), the court looks to the debtor's plan and determines, in light of the particular facts and circumstances, whether the plan will fairly achieve a result consistent with the Bankruptcy Code. The plan "must be 'viewed in light of the totality of the circumstances surrounding confection' of the plan [and] . . . the bankruptcy judge is in the best position to assess the good faith of the parties' proposals."

In re Madison Hotel Associates, 749 F.2d 410, 424-425 (7th Cir. 1984) (bankruptcy filing to avoid foreclosure and cure and reinstate the mortgage was not a bad faith plan proposal).

If no objections are filed on the issue of good faith, the court is permitted to conclude that the plan has been proposed in good faith and not by any means forbidden by law without receiving evidence on the issue. FED. R. BANKR. PROC. 3020(b)(2). In other words, there is a rebuttable presumption of good faith.

C. Reasonableness of Plan Fees, Section 1129(a)(4)

Section 1129(a)(4) requires that payments made in connection with the plan, including for plan expenses, be reasonable and subject to court approval. It does not cover distributions made under a plan to classes. Instead, it covers payments made in administering the case or implementing the plan. This is a wide-ranging provision designed to prevent payments made for administering the case or implementing the plan from being used as a payoff or from being padded as a way of engaging in individualized distributions in lieu of or in addition to those specified in the plan, which must be made without discrimination to all members of a class of claims or interests. 11 U.S.C. § 1123(a)(4).

D. Corporate Affiliations and Appointments, Section 1129(a)(5)

Section 1129(a)(5) requires disclosure of the identity and affiliations of any individuals who will serve as officers or directors of the reorganized debtor, as well as that of any insider to be employed or retained by the reorganized debtor and the nature of such compensation. 11 U.S.C. § 1129(a)(5)(A)(i), (B). Insider is a statutorily defined term in section 101(31), and it includes various corporate affiliates of the debtor, with affiliate defined as any "entity that directly or indirectly owns, controls, or holds" the voting power of 20% or more of the debtor's securities or in whom the debtor has such ownership or control. 11 U.S.C. § 101(2). This level of corporate disclosure is meant to make transparent to all stakeholders exactly who the parties in interest are in the reorganized debtor. Note that the 20% control threshold is a much higher disclosure threshold than that required under the securities laws, which require public disclosure upon obtaining a 5% ownership interest. 15 U.S.C. § 78m(d).

Section 1129(a)(5) is not merely a disclosure provision, however. It also contains a substantive requirement, namely that the appointments and continuations in office of officers and directors "[are] consistent with the interests of creditors and equity security holders and with public policy." 11 U.S.C. § 1129(a)(5)(A)(ii). This provision, like several other ones in the Code, points to a federal regulation of the governance of reorganized corporations that is distinct from state laws on corporate goverance. *See, e.g.,* 11 U.S.C. §§ 1123(a)(6) (prohibiting dual class stock); 1123(a)(7) (selection of officers and directors in accordance with public policy). There is little law on this provision, but the existing cases suggests that the requirement that officer/director appointments be in accord with public policy may create space for significant litigation over issues such as executive compensation packages. *See, e.g., In re Digerati Technologies, Inc.,* 2014 Bankr. Lexis 2352 (Bankr. S.D. Tex. May 27, 2014).

E. Best Interests, Section 1129(a)(7)

Section 1129(a)(7) contains what is known as the "best interests" test. The best interests test guarantees that every individual impaired, objecting creditor will receive at least as much under a Chapter 11 plan as under a Chapter 7 liquidation. That is, the best interests test sets the distribution in a Chapter 7 liquidation as the baseline for a Chapter 11 distribution. The implication is that only going-concern value—a firm's value above liquidation—is subject to negotiation and group vote; liquidation value is a right guaranteed to the individual creditor.

The best interests requirement provides that if a member of an impaired class who has not accepted (that is, voted for) a plan objects, the plan must provide that the objecting claimant or interest holder receive property with a present value equal to that the claim holder or interest holder would have received in a hypothetical Chapter 7 liquidation on the plan's effective date. In other words, a creditor can always opt to receive worse treatment than it would in a liquidation, but it cannot be forced to receive worse treatment. While the objection is raised by an individual, it cannot be solved simply by paying that single creditor more because of section 1123(a)(4), which requires a plan to treat all members of a class equally, unless a class member consents to less favorable treatment. (Query whether voting for a plan that does not provide best interests is in fact consenting to less favorable treatment than the rest of a claimant's class.)

The best interests test applies only to (a) objecting claim or interest holders in (b) impaired classes. Thus, if a class is unimpaired, a claim holder or interest holder cannot raise a best interests objection. Similarly, even if a class has rejected a plan, an individual claim holder or interest holder cannot raise a best interests objection. On the other hand, if an impaired class has accepted a plan, a claim holder or equityholder who has voted against the plan can still raise a best interests objection. (Bankruptcy voting is not by secret ballot, so individual claim holders' votes can be identified.)

Note, however, that best interests is based on an immediate hypothetical liquidation. That is not in fact what a creditor would receive if a plan were not confirmed and the debtor instead liquidated in Chapter 7. The creditor would receive the proceeds of a liquidation commenced some point in the future, rather than an immediate liquidation. Those future liquidation proceeds would probably be worth less both because of time value and because of depreciation of the debtor's assets. The best interests test, however, is based on a hypothetical, but impossible immediate liquidation.

The distribution valued for best interests can be of any type of property, such cash, debt (notes, bonds), stock, realty, personalty, intellectual property, etc. The present value requirement in the best interests test means that if the creditor is paid in new debt, such as a new note, the interest rate on the note must be sufficiently high so that present value is preserved.

As the result of the best interests test, disclosure statements for Chapter 11 plans typically contain liquidation analyses, although these analyses are, by their nature, hypothetical, with assumed liquidation values for the estate's assets.

F. Priority Claimants, Section 1129(a)(9)

requirement for plan to go thro(?)

Section 1129(a)(9) is a type of priority system for certain types of unsecured claims.

1. Administrative Priority and Gap Claims

First, section 1129(a)(9)(A) requires cash payment on the effective date of the plan for the full allowed amount of the claim for administrative claims under section 507(a)(2) and "gap" claims (the expenses incurred by a debtor between the filing of an involuntary bankruptcy petition and the granting of the order for relief). These administrative claims include the actual and necessary expenses of operating the estate post-petition, including attorneys' and financial advisor fees, and may also include the fees of attorneys employed by official committees or individual creditors that make a "substantial contribution" to the case. 11 U.S.C. § 503(b)(3)(D).

Recall that administrative priority claims are not classified, per section 1123(a)(1). This is because their treatment is not optional and cannot be specified by the plan. Accordingly, the cash payment requirement of section 1129(a)(9)(A) is the major protection for administrative and gap claims. They do not benefit from the best interests test or from the cramdown provisions because they are not classified nor do they vote. Instead, they are given an absolute protection that cannot be waived by a majority on behalf of all administrative or gap claimants.

Unstated in section 1129(a)(9)(A) is an exception for creditors that agree to less favorable treatment, essentially settling their claims. Attorneys and professionals involved with the bankruptcy sometimes will do this. Attorneys and professionals may receive interim compensation throughout the case, 11 U.S.C. § 331, so their unpaid claims at the conclusion of a case are typically a fraction of their actual costs.

The cash payment requirement means that the debtor must have sufficient cash on hand as of the effective date of the plan to be able to pay all of its unpaid administrative expenses. This can be quite burdensome in terms of the debtor's liquidity if there is significant post-petition trade debt, including from assumed executory contracts and unexpired leases, that receives section 507(a)(2) priority.

One solution is to arrange for exit financing that provides the debtor with new liquidity on the effective date of the plan. Other solutions are to delay the effective date of the plan until after many trade claims are payable. Alternatively, it is possible to provide in the plan that absent objection these claims will be paid in the ordinary course of business.

Section 1129(a)(9)(A) requires cash payment not only of the post-petition administrative expenses of the estate, but also of reclamation claims under section 503(b)(9) for goods sold to the debtor within 20 days of bankruptcy in the ordinary course of the debtor's business. These section 503(b)(9) claims have section 507(a)(2) priority and thus are covered under section 1129(a)(9)(A). The cash payment requirement of section 1129(a)(9)(A) can make reorganization very difficult for retailers with significant reclamation claims under section 503(b)(9).

Consider, for example, the now-defunct electronics retailer Circuit City. A retailer like Circuit City must be well stocked with state-of-the-art inventory. If the shelves are bare, customers will go elsewhere. Circuit City had over 6,500 vendors supplying everything from TVs and computers to furniture and telecommunications products. Circuit City had almost $350 million in reclamation claims. If all of those claims were allowed, it would have meant that Circuit City would have needed $350 million in cash on hand at confirmation. Such a staggering amount of cash is simply not feasible for most retailers. In such a situation, the case is "administratively insolvent," and cannot be confirmed. Because section 503(b)(9) claims must be paid in real dollars, it behooves debtors to challenge improper section 503(b)(9) claims more aggressively than improper general unsecured claims. The cost, however, of litigating the status of thousands of section 503(b)(9) claims may itself be prohibitive.

2. Other Priority Claims (Excluding Tax Claims)

Second, section 1129(a)(9)(B)(i) requires cash payments for any class of priority claims (excluding 507(a)(2), gap, and 507(a)(8) tax priority claims) that has not accepted the plan. The priority claims covered by this section include priority pre-bankruptcy wage and salary claims and employee benefit claims. If such a class accepts, however, it must receive deferred cash payments with a present value equal to the amount of the claim on the effective date of the plan.

3. Priority Tax Claims

Third, section 1129(a)(9)(C) provides for the treatment of tax claims with priority under section 507(a)(8) and those tax claims that would have such priority other than for being secured. 11 U.S.C. § 1129(a)(9)(C)-(D). Such claims are to be paid in cash in installments. The installments must have a present value equal to the amount of the claim on the effective date of the plan. 11 U.S.C. § 1129(a)(9)(C)(i).

Section 507(a)(8) claims must be paid over a period of no longer than five years from the date of the order for relief—meaning the time of a filing of a voluntary petition. 11 U.S.C. § 1129(a)(9)(C)(ii). This means that if the plan is confirmed in one year, the payments may be made over four years, but if the plan is confirmed after three years, then the tax claims must be paid over only two years.

What if the case is not confirmed until after five years have elapsed? The answer is not clear. It might mean that the payment must be made as a lump sum, but that conflicts with the installment requirement. Alternatively, section 1129(a)(9)(C)(ii) might mean that if a plan is not confirmed within five years from the order for relief, it cannot be confirmed if there are unresolved section 507(a)(8) claims. In other words, section 1129(a)(9)(C)(ii) may function as a sort of expiry date for confirming a Chapter 11 plan. Presumably, it is possible to settle section 507(a)(8) claims, but the time limit gives tax authorities significant leverage in that regard.

Finally, the payment structure of the tax claims must be at least as good as the most favorable one for nonpriority unsecured claims other than convenience claims. Thus, if a class of nonpriority unsecure claims was to be paid in six months, the tax claims would also have to be paid in six months.

G. Feasibility, Section 1129(a)(11)

Section 1129(a)(11) requires that a plan be feasible, meaning that confirmation will "not likely to be followed by the liquidation, or the need for further financial reorganization, of the debtor or any successor to the debtor under the plan, unless such liquidation or reorganization is proposed in the plan." The concern with feasibility is that the debtor will end up right back in bankruptcy, and the creditors' claims in that new bankruptcy will not be based on their original rights, but on their rights coming out of the old bankruptcy. The feasibility requirement does not mean that the plan must guarantee a successful reorganization, but that it appear to have reasonable prospects of success. *Kane v. Johns-Manville Corp.*, 843 F.2d 636, 649 (2d Cir. 1988).

Factors courts have considered include:

- the adequacy of the debtor's capital structure;
- the earning power of its business;
- economic conditions;
- the ability of the debtor's management;
- the probability of the continuation of the same management;
- any other related matters which determine the prospects of a sufficiently successful operation to enable performance of the provisions of the plan.

In re Greate Bay Hotel & Casino, Inc., 251 B.R. 213, 226-227 (Bankr. D.N.J. 2000).

The following case is an example of a relatively rare appellate decision on feasibility.

DISH Network Corp. v. DBSD North America Inc.

634 F.3d 79 (2d Cir. 2011)

GERARD E. LYNCH, Circuit Judge:

These consolidated appeals arise out of the bankruptcy of DBSD North America, Incorporated and its various subsidiaries (together, "DBSD"). The bankruptcy court confirmed a plan of reorganization for DBSD over the objections of the two appellants here, Sprint Nextel Corporation ("Sprint") and DISH Network Corporation ("DISH").

. . . DISH . . . argues that the bankruptcy court should not have confirmed the plan because the plan was not feasible. See 11 U.S.C. § 1129(a)(11).

. . . On DISH's appeal we find no error, and conclude . . . that the bankruptcy court did not err in finding the reorganization feasible. We therefore affirm . . . and remand for further proceedings.

BACKGROUND

. . .

ICO Global Communications founded DBSD in 2004 to develop a mobile communications network that would use both satellites and land-based transmission towers. In its first five years, DBSD made progress toward this goal, successfully launching a satellite and obtaining certain spectrum licenses from the FCC, but it also accumulated a large amount of debt. Because its network remained in the developmental stage and had not become operational, DBSD had little if any revenue to offset its mounting obligations.

On May 15, 2009, DBSD (but not its parent ICO Global), filed a voluntary petition in the United States Bankruptcy Court for the Southern District of New York, listing liabilities of $813 million against assets with a book value of $627 million.

. . . After negotiations with various parties, DBSD proposed a plan of reorganization which, as amended, provided for "substantial de-leveraging," a renewed focus on "core operations," and a "continued path as a development-stage enterprise." The plan provided that the holders of the First Lien Debt would receive new obligations with a four-year maturity date and the same 12.5% interest rate, but with interest to be paid in kind ("PIK"), meaning that for the first four years the owners of the new obligations would receive as interest more debt from DBSD rather than cash. The holders of the Second Lien Debt would receive the bulk of the shares of the reorganized entity, which the bankruptcy court estimated would be worth between 51% and 73% of their original claims. The holders of unsecured claims . . . would receive shares estimated as worth between 4% and 46% of their original claims. Finally, the existing shareholder (effectively just ICO Global, which owned 99.8% of DBSD) would receive shares and warrants in the reorganized entity.

. . . DISH[, a competitor of DBSD's that purchased claims in the bankruptcy postpetition, argues,] among other things, that the plan was not feasible under 11 U.S.C. § 1129(a)(11). . . .

. . . The court . . . rejected DISH's objections to the plan, finding that the plan was feasible. . . . DBSD I, 419 B.R. at 203, 208-09. . . . [T]he bankruptcy court confirmed the plan. The district court affirmed, and DISH . . . appealed to this Court.

. . .

B. The Feasibility of the Plan

To confirm a plan under Chapter 11, a bankruptcy court must find that the plan is feasible, or, more precisely, that "[c]onfirmation of the plan is not likely to be followed by the liquidation, or the need for further financial reorganization, of the debtor . . . unless such liquidation or reorganization is proposed in the plan." 11 U.S.C. § 1129(a)(11). DISH argues that the feasibility of this plan is "purely speculative" and that the bankruptcy court therefore should not have confirmed it. We review a finding of feasibility only for clear error, and we find none here.

For a plan to be feasible, it must "offer[] a reasonable assurance of success," but it need not "guarantee[]" success. Some possibility of liquidation or further reorganization is acceptable and often unavoidable. The bankruptcy court applied this standard and found this plan feasible based primarily on four factors.

First, the plan "dramatically deleverage[s]" DBSD. Before bankruptcy, DBSD owed over $800 million; the projected debt of the reformed DBSD would be as low as $260 million as late as 2013. Given the bankruptcy court's valuation of a reorganized DBSD as worth between $492 million and $692 million, this debt reduction makes a big difference.

Second, the court found it likely that DBSD would be able to obtain the capital it needs. DBSD has already received commitments for a credit facility to provide working capital for the first two years. After two years, DBSD would need further capital, but the court found "very reasonable" the possibility that DBSD will be able to secure either more financing or a strategic investor. *Id.* As evidence of this possibility, the court pointed to expert testimony, actual offers that had been made (including DISH's own offer), and the ability of similar companies to access the capital markets. The court also noted the likely attractiveness to future investors of DBSD's control over 20MHz of prime bandwidth, a "finite" and "very valuable" resource.

Third, the court found little risk of default on DBSD's secured obligations to DISH, and still less risk that any such default would lead to the liquidation or financial reorganization that § 1129(a)(11) seeks to avert. The plan makes the interest on DISH's First Lien Debt, which had been payable in cash, payable only in kind, with no cash due for four years. This feature buys DBSD breathing room to shore up its position before it becomes necessary to secure significant additional capital, as described above.

Fourth, and finally, the bankruptcy court noted that general credit markets at the time of its decision in October 2009 had improved from their low a year before. Although no one can predict market conditions two or four years down the road, the improvement the bankruptcy court noted was real, and increased the likelihood that DBSD will be able to repay its creditors.

Based on all of these factors, the bankruptcy court found the plan of reorganization feasible. We find the bankruptcy court's analysis thorough and persuasive. DISH's arguments to the contrary do not successfully identify any clear error in it.

First, DISH argues that the bankruptcy court employed the wrong legal standard. DISH claims that a bankruptcy court cannot confirm a plan unless the proponents prove "specifics . . . as to how the Debtors would be able to meet their repayment obligations at the end of the Plan period." That is true at some level of generality, but exactly how specific those "specifics" must be depends on the circumstances. In most situations, the time immediately following bankruptcy will call for fairly specific proof of the company's ability to meet its obligations—as here, where it was "undisputed that the Debtors have commitments for working capital financing for the next two years." As one moves further away from the time of confirmation, however, the proof will necessarily become less and less specific. Had DBSD's plan called for the issuance of 20-year notes, for instance, no one would expect specifics about the sort of financing it might get in year 19. When a court is dealing with an intermediate time frame like the four years after which the balloon payment comes due in this case, the level of proof required will be somewhere in the middle. In this context, the bankruptcy court based its feasibility finding on sufficiently specific proof to conclude that DBSD would be likely to avoid reorganization or liquidation even after four years. Overall, the bankruptcy court both stated and applied the correct standard in this case, dooming DISH's legal challenge.

Second, DISH argues that the district court clearly erred in its fact-finding. At most, DISH's arguments on this front demonstrate that there is some chance that DBSD might eventually face liquidation or further reorganization. But that small chance does not change the feasibility analysis, which requires only a "reasonable assurance of success," not an absolute "guarantee[]." A small or even moderate chance of failure does not mean that the plan is *"likely* to be followed by the liquidation, or the need for further financial reorganization, of the debtor." 11 U.S.C. § 1129(a)(11) (emphasis added). We therefore uphold the bankruptcy court's feasibility determination.

Sometimes feasibility is a matter of whether a firm will be able to service its post-bankruptcy debt. Other times, however, feasibility can depend on whether a firm can obtain the requisite regulatory approvals to operate. The following case addresses this issue.

In re Indianapolis Downs, LLC

486 B.R. 286 (Bankr. D. Del. 2013)

Brendan Linehan Shannon, U.S. Bankr. J.

Before the Court is the request of Indianapolis Downs, LLC and Indiana Capital Corp. (collectively, the "Debtors") for confirmation of their Modified Second Amended Joint Plan of Reorganization (the "Plan"). Confirmation is opposed by the Oliver Parties, who include senior management and holders of equity and debt instruments of the Debtors. . . .

The Debtors operate a combined horse racing track and casino—a "racino"—in Shelbyville, Indiana. They employ over 1,000 people and provide patrons a wealth of wagering and entertainment options. In addition to betting on horse racing, visitors to the racino can try their luck at roughly 2,000 electronic wagering games, including slot machines.

. . .

The Oliver Parties contend that the Plan is not feasible because transactions contemplated under the Plan are conditioned upon receipt of regulatory approvals and licensing by the Indiana Gaming Commission and the Indiana Horse Racing Commission. As discussed above, the Plan is built around the sale of the Debtors' business to Centaur. If the necessary approvals are not obtained, that transaction will fail and the Plan will likewise fail. The uncertainty of receipt of those approvals dooms the Plan, according to the Oliver Parties.

Pursuant to § 1129(a)(11) of the Bankruptcy Code, a court may confirm a plan of reorganization if "[c]onfirmation of the plan is not likely to be followed by the liquidation, or the need for financial reorganization, of the debtor or any successor to the debtor under the plan, unless such liquidation or reorganization is proposed in the plan." 11 U.S.C. § 1129(a)(11). As discussed in detail below, however, § 1129(a)(11) does not require a guarantee of the plan's success; rather the proper standard is whether the plan offers a "reasonable assurance" of success.

The purpose of the feasibility test is to protect against visionary or speculative plans. Just as speculative prospects of success cannot sustain feasibility, speculative prospects of failure will not defeat feasibility. The first, best indicator of feasibility is the position of the creditors whose economic interests are at stake. The support or opposition of creditors with skin in the game and an opportunity to study a debtor's proposal is more illuminating to the Court than any expert report or accountant's projections. Courts have identified a number of other factors relevant to evaluating the feasibility of a proposed plan of reorganization, including (a) the prospective earnings or earning power of the debtor's business; (b) the soundness and adequacy of the capital structure and working capital for the debtor's post-confirmation business; (c) the debtor's ability to meet its capital expenditure requirements; (d) economic conditions; (e) the ability of management and the likelihood that current management will continue; and (f) any other material factors that would affect the successful implementation of the plan.

As noted, the Oliver Parties contend that the closing of the sale to Centaur, which is the centerpiece of the Plan and provides a half-billion dollars of proceeds, is uncertain due to the need for regulatory approvals. If those approvals are not obtained, the sale will fall through and the Plan cannot be consummated.

It is not at all unusual for consummation of a Chapter 11 plan to be conditioned upon the expectation of approval by regulatory authorities, and courts have not typically held up confirmation of a plan to wait for issuance of such approvals. Rather, the plan proponent bears the burden of demonstrating that achieving the necessary approvals is not subject to "material hurdles" or readily anticipated, significant obstacles. *Id.* at 185 (finding plan feasible notwithstanding FCC licensing conditions); *In re TCI 2 Holdings, LLC*, 428 B.R. 117 (Bankr. D.N.J. 2010) (overruling feasibility objection relating to prospect of issuance of gaming license in casino case).

In the present case, the Court finds that the Debtors have carried their burden regarding feasibility. The entity requiring regulatory approvals in this case is Centaur; the record reflects that Centaur already operates the only other racino in Indiana and has been duly licensed to do so. Further, in approving the sale to Centaur, the Court has already made necessary findings regarding Centaur's ability to close the transaction, which is similarly predicated upon regulatory approvals. But beyond the evidence presented in the sale hearing—which was adequate for its purpose—there are also readily apparent and practical considerations that give the Court confidence that there is a reasonable assurance of success: Centaur is already in this business in the State of Indiana, and has thus already successfully gone through the licensing process. It has committed half a billion dollars to this deal. Absent compelling evidence to the contrary, it is almost inconceivable that Centaur, the Debtors and the other stakeholders in these cases would have headed down this path unless they were confident that the necessary licenses and approvals would be obtained.

The Debtors have demonstrated that the Plan is feasible, that the necessary approvals are reasonably likely to be obtained, and that the Plan is not likely to be followed by the need for further financial reorganization. The objection on grounds of feasibility is overruled.

Problem Set 33

(1) Bacchus Wineries has proposed a Chapter 11 plan. Which of the following provisions may be included in its plan? 11 U.S.C. §§ 1123, 1129(a)(3).

    a. Classification of Bacchus's creditors and equityholders into separate classes.

    b. Payment of Bacchus's Class 3 (general unsecured) creditors at 50 cents on the dollar on their claims.

    c. Payment of Bacchus's Class 3 (general unsecured) creditors at 50 cents on the dollar on their claims, except for insiders (as defined by statute), who will be paid 25 cents on the dollar on their claims.

    d. Payment of 50 cents on the dollar to those of Bacchus's Class 3 (general unsecured) creditors who vote in favor of the plan, and payment of 20 cents on the dollar to those Class 3 creditors who vote against the plan.

    e. Payment of Bacchus's Class 3 (general unsecured) creditors at 50 cents on the dollar, but only if the Class votes to accept the plan; otherwise, the Class will be paid 20 cents on the dollar.

    f. Payment of Bacchus's Class 3 (general unsecured) creditors at 50 cents on the dollar, but only if there are no objections raised to the plan by Class 3 creditors; otherwise, the Class will be paid 20 cents on the dollar.

(2) Titan Corp. has proposed a Chapter 11 plan. Which of the following provisions may be included in its plan? 11 U.S.C. § 1123.

    a. Settlement of Titan's antitrust suit against Tartarus Corp.

    b. Sale of Titan's mining products division (not separately incorporated).

    c. Sale of Titan's headquarter's building free and clear of the mortgage on the building.

    d. Distribution of the stock of Titan's subsidiary Atlas Corp. to three classes of unsecured creditors, thereby effectuating a spinoff of Atlas.

    e. The merger of Titan Corp. with the unaffiliated Rhea Corp.

    f. Elimination of a debt limitation covenant in a secured loan.

    g. Cure and reinstatement of a defaulted loan.

    h. Extension of the maturity date on a bond issue by five years without the consent of all bondholders.

    i. The amendment of Titan's charter to expand its board of directors by five seats.

j. Retention and post-confirmation enforcement by Titan of Titan's fraudulent conveyance suit against Olympian Corp.

k. Assignment of Titan's patent infringement suit against Prometheus, Inc. to a newly settled litigation trust in exchange for the shares of the litigation trust, which will be distributed to certain classes of Titan's creditors.

l. Issuance of new bonds by Titan Corp.

m. Issuance of new equity by Titan Corp.

n. The divorce decree, marital property settlement, and child custody arrangement for Titan's CEO.

o. The sale of all of Titan's property, with the liquidation proceeds to be distributed among the creditors and shareholders according to the priority system set forth in 11 U.S.C. §§ 725 and 726.

(3) Blackbeard Ventures, Inc. filed for Chapter 11 on January 1 of this year and has not yet proposed a plan. The Jolly Roger Fund is eager to propose its own plan.

a. What is the earliest date the Jolly Roger Fund can file such a plan? 11 U.S.C. §§ 1121(b)-(c); FED. R. BANKR. PROC. 9006.

b. What is the latest possible date that Blackbeard Ventures could file a plan without a competing plan being allowed? 11 U.S.C. § 1121(d).

c. If Blackbeard Ventures wished to extend its exclusivity window, what sort of evidence should it include in its motion to extend?

d. Suppose that Blackbeard Ventures did not file a plan until May 6. It is now May 7. Can the Jolly Roger Fund file a plan today? 11 U.S.C. §§ 102, 1121(c).

e. What are the consequences to Jolly Roger of filing a plan too soon?

(4) Figaro, Inc. is in Chapter 11 bankruptcy. Figaro's plan of reorganization has four classes, I-IV.

- Class I consists solely of Figaro's senior secured lender, Marcelinna Bank. Marcelinna Bank is owed $40 million and is secured by $60 million in collateral. Figaro has never defaulted on the loan, and Figaro's plan leaves the loan's maturity, payment schedule, and liens intact.

- Class II consists of unsecured trade creditors, including Cherubino Partners. Cherubino voted for the plan, but the majority of Class II members voted against it. The plan would pay Class II 20 cents on the dollar; in an immediate liquidation Class II would receive 25 cents on the dollar.

- Class III consists of unsecured bondholders, including Contessa Holdings. The plan would plan provide Class III with shares in the reorganized Figaro, Inc. worth 30 cents on the dollar of the Class III claims; in an immediate liquidation Class III would receive 32 cents on the dollar. Class III voted to accept the plan, but Contessa Holdings voted against it.

- Class IV consists of Figaro's shareholders. The plan would dilute the shareholders to owning 40% of the reorganized firm, valued at $35 million. Class IV has voted against the plan, as did Susanna d'Almaviva, a shareholder. In a liquidation, equity would get nothing.

Can Marcelinna Bank, Cherubino Partners, Contessa Holdings, or Suzanne d'Almaviva block confirmation of Figaro's plan under section 1129(a)(7)?

(5) Which of the following claims must be paid in full, in cash, on the effective date of the plan?

a. Pre-petition suppliers' claims. 11 U.S.C. § 502.

b. Post-petition suppliers' claims. 11 U.S.C. §§ 503(b)(1), 507(a)(2), 1129(a)(9).

c. Pre-petition tax claims. 11 U.S.C. §§ 507(a)(8), 1129(a)(9).

d. Post-petition tax claims. 11 U.S.C. §§ 503(b)(1)(B), 507(a)(2), 1129(a)(9).

e. The claim of the DIP's attorneys for post-petition work. 11 U.S.C. §§ 330(a), 503(b)(2), 507(a)(2), 1129(a)(9).

f. The post-petition expenses of an indenture trustee that did absolutely nothing in the case. 11 U.S.C. §§ 503(b)(5), 507(a)(2), 1129(a)(9).

(6) Panacea, Inc. is a pharmaceutical company in Chapter 11. Panacea has proposed a plan of reorganization in which it will be repaying various creditors over five years after the effective date of the plan. The plan calls for annual payments of $20 million to secured creditors for 5 years. Unsecured creditors will receive a 5-year $200 million note at 12.5% annual interest, payable in kind. Panacea currently has annual revenue of $50 million, and annual non-interest operating expenses of $15 million. Panacea believes its annual net revenue will increase substantially—by perhaps another $30 million annually, if it obtains "orphan" drug approval for a drug it is developing for treatment of Degenerative Personality Disorder. If the drug is approved and given "orphan drug" status, it will be granted FDA "exclusivity" for seven years, meaning that no other drug can be approved for the same indication unless the maker of the other drug can prove that it is therapeutically superior, a process that will likely take at least several years. Thus, orphan drug approval is functionally a grant of monopoly for several years. The results of the drug's Phase III clinical trial—the final stage of clinical trial prior to applying for FDA approval—are expected in six months. If the results are positive, FDA approval and orphan drug status could be secured within another 12 to 18 months. Panacea's competitor Chiron also has a drug in a Phase III clinical trial, the results of which are not expected for perhaps a year, but Panacea is convinced that Chiron's drug will have unpleasant side effects. If a majority of all impaired classes support Panacea's plan, is it confirmable? 11 U.S.C. § 1129(a)(11).

(7) Drusilla & Prunella, Inc. has filed for Chapter 11 bankruptcy. D&P's proposed plan of reorganization cancels D&P's existing equity and provides for the issuance of new equity. The new equity consists of a single class of non-voting preferred stock and dual classes of common stock: 100 shares of Class A stock with 30% of the voting power and 10,000,000 shares of Class B stock with 70% of the voting power. The plan further provides for a staggered board for the reorganized firm, a dual chairman/CEO structure, with a supermajority of vote of shareholders required to remove any director from office. The plan also provides for a corporate bylaw that shifts the costs of legal fees to shareholders for any action successfully brought against the corporation, either directly or derivatively. Additionally, the plan provides that upon any change of control or removal of a majority of board officers, the firm will issue an additional 10,000,000 shares of Class B stock to the Class A stock holders. A majority of all impaired classes have approved the plan. You represent Cinderella, a creditor in Class 7, who will receive shares of Class B stock under the reorganization plan. Are there any objections Cinderella can raise? 11 U.S.C. §§ 1123(a)(6)-(7), 1129(a)(5).

CHAPTER 34

PLAN VOTING

I. VOTING

In the previous chapter, we saw a number of statutory requirements for plan confirmation. But even if all of those requirements are met, there is still another that is arguably the most important of all consensual plan confirmation requirements: a vote of impaired classes of creditors and equityholders. The right of impaired creditors and equityholders to vote on a plan in Chapter 11 is one of their most important and fundamental protections because it provides a moment when they may exercise governance rights over the estate. 11 U.S.C. § 1126(a).

The right to vote on a plan exists only for *impaired classes* of allowed claims and interests. Thus, creditors whose claims are not classified—those with section 507(a)(2), (a)(3), and (a)(8) claims—do not vote. Instead, they are protected by the cash payment requirement of section 1129(a)(9). Likewise, creditors or equityholders whose claims or interests are unimpaired do not vote. (What constitutes impairment is discussed in the following chapter.) And, perhaps, obviously, disallowed claims or interests are not allowed to vote. 11 U.S.C. § 1126(a).

The additional governance right of a vote is only granted to those creditors or equityholders whose rights are affected by the bankruptcy. Thus, in the rare situation in which a plan does not impair any creditors or equityholders, there is no vote on the plan, as unimpaired classes are conclusively deemed to have accepted the plan, so their votes need not be solicited. 11 U.S.C. § 1126(f). Conversely, classes that receive nothing under a plan are conclusively deemed to have rejected the plan. 11 U.S.C. § 1126(g).

Most cases, however, have at least one impaired class and thus require a vote. The requirement for a vote is found in two separate provisions in section 1129(a). First, section 1129(a)(8) requires that every impaired class of claims or interest has "accepted the plan." Acceptance means voting in favor of a plan as specified in section 1126(c)-(d). The voting is by class, rather than by the entirety of the body of claims and interests. For a class of claims, this means dual majorities of over one-half in number of claims and at least two-thirds of the amount of claims in the class must support a plan. 11 U.S.C. § 1126(c). For a class of interests, acceptance requires only a single majority of at least two-thirds of the amount of interests in the class to support the plan. 11 U.S.C. § 1126(d).

The majority voting requirements raise questions about how claims are counted. Can a claim be split if half is sold to another party? Does that double the number of claims? Similarly, can claims be combined to reduce numbers? Are claims from five separate contracts between the debtor and a single party five claims or one? We will consider the counting issue in Chapter 41 when we examine claims trading.

Why does bankruptcy have these particular voting requirements? For classes of claims, the separate numerosity and amount requirements attempt to strike a balance in power between numerous creditors with small claims and a few creditors with large claims. The dual majority requirements effectively give each group a veto so that one large creditor cannot force acceptance on numerous small creditors or vice-versa. In effect the dual majority requirements mean that consensual confirmation requires a fair level of consensus within a class. Hence the amount requirement is larger than the numerosity requirement, lest a single creditor with a relatively large claim easily force acceptance by a class of creditors.

The two-thirds of the amount requirement for a class of equity interests is more perplexing. Currently, Delaware General Corporate Law does not have any supermajority requirements for any corporate transactions, although it does allow for corporate bylaws that impose such supermajority requirements. Historically, at common law, a sale or other disposition of all corporate assets required unanimous shareholder approval. Catherine L. Curran, *Shareholders' Rights in Short-Form Mergers: The New Delaware Formula*, 64 MARQ. L. REV. 687, 689 (1981). (An exception, existed, however, for situations when the firm was in financial distress. *Id*.) During the early twentieth century, however, most states adopted statutes permitting a two-thirds supermajority to authorize majority transactions, such as mergers and consolidations. A two-thirds supermajority requirement for mergers was the position that existed in most states' laws when the 1938 Chandler Act was passed. The two-thirds equity supermajority requirement of section 1126(d) is a carryover from the Chandler Act.

State law, however, has since changed. A trend toward simple majority merger requirements began with the 1962 Model Business Corporation Act. Today most states, including Delaware, have now adopted a simple majority requirement; only a few retain a two-thirds supermajority requirement. When the current Bankruptcy Code was drafted in 1977, the movement to simple majority requirements was not so pronounced as it is today. The result is that federal bankruptcy law currently imposes a greater shareholder consent requirement for a plan confirmed under section 1129(a) than would be required for similar transactions under state corporate law.

Confirmation under section 1129(a) is referred to as a "consensual" plan confirmation, but that name is misleading. It does not mean that every creditor supports the plan. All it requires is that there be requisite majorities accepting the plan in every single class. Because the vote is by class, 49.99% of the claims in each class, representing 33% of the dollar amount of the claims, could vote against the plan, and the plan would still be confirmable "consensually." Thus, in Chapter 11, majorities in each class can bind the minorities. Chapter 11 can thus overcome the holdout problem created by the Trust Indenture Act.

Chapter 11 still protects minorities, though, through pre-vote disclosure requirements and the other plan confirmation requirements, particularly, good faith, best interests, and feasibility. Likewise, some unimpaired or unclassified creditors may still be quite unhappy with the plan, but there is nothing they can do about it as they lack a right to vote. Thus, "consensual" here merely indicates a distinction with non-consensual confirmation under section 1129(b), a process known as "cramdown."

We will look at cramdown in much more detail in later chapters, but for now, you should know that it requires that all of the section 1129(a) provisions are met *other than section 1129(a)(8)*. In place of section 1129(a)(8), cramdown requires that in regard to impaired classes, a plan not discriminate unfairly and that it be "fair and equitable," which includes application of the absolute priority rule for unsecured creditors and equity, meaning that no claim may receive a distribution unless all claims senior to it have been paid in full. The result is that a cramdown plan places constraints on the distribution of the going-concern surplus among stakeholders that do not exist in a consensual plan confirmation.

Although a cramdown plan does not require that all impaired classes accept the plan, per section 1129(a)(8), it must still comply with the second voting requirement, that of section 1129(a)(10). Section 1129(a)(10) requires that if there is an impaired class under the plan, at least one impaired class must accept the plan, not counting the votes of insiders. For corporate or partnership debtors, insiders include directors, officers, control persons, general partners, partnerships in which the debtor is a general partner, and relatives (defined as relation via affinity or consanguinity, including adoptive and step relationships, to the third degree) of any insider. 11 U.S.C. §§ 101(31), (45). Insider also includes any affiliate of the debtor or insiders of affiliates. 11 U.S.C. § 101(31)(E). An affiliate is defined as any entity that controls or owns 20% of the debtor's voting securities or in which the debtor controls 20% of the voting securities. 11 U.S.C. § 101(2).

The section 1129(a)(10) requirement that one impaired class have the requisite majorities in favor of the plan, not counting insiders' votes, is an additional voting requirement to that of section 1126. In a consensual plan confirmation for a single debtor, section 1129(a)(10) rarely does any work—almost any plan that meets the requirements of section 1129(a)(8) will also meet the requirements of section 1129(a)(10). Section 1129(a)(10)'s meaning springs with cramdown or in multi-debtor cases.

Frequently a bankruptcy involves not simply one firm, but a number of related firms—parents, subsidiaries, and affiliates. Each entity files a separate bankruptcy petition and is a legally separate bankruptcy case. While the cases are usually jointly administered, absent substantive consolidation, discussed in Chapter 32, the entities remain legally separate, with separate creditors and assets. Nonetheless, it is typical to file one joint plan for all of the entities, even though creditors of each entity will usually vote separately by entity for section 1126 purposes.

The excerpt from a plan confirmation ruling in the Tribune Company's bankruptcy illustrates the difficulties that a joint plan can pose for voting on a single plan: Must section 1129(a)(10) be satisfied for all entities separately or just for the plan overall? Courts differ on whether the provision applies on a per-debtor or per-plan basis. *Cf. JPMorgan Chase Bank v. Charter Commc'ns (In re Charter Commc'ns)*, 419 B.R. 221, 266 (Bankr. S.D.N.Y. 2009) (per-plan basis) *and In re Enron Corp.*, 2004 Bankr. LEXIS 2549, at *234 (Bankr. S.D.N.Y. July 15, 2004) (per-plan basis) *with In re Tribune Co.*, 464 B.R. 126 (Bankr. D. Del. 2011) (per-debtor basis) *and In re JER/Jameson Mezz*

Borrower II, LLC (In re JER/Jameson), 461 B.R. 293 (Bankr. D. Del. 2011) (per-debtor basis). The difference in interpretation of section 1129(a)(10) can be significant—if it must be satisfied on a per-debtor basis, it may not be achievable for all affiliated entities given the exclusion of insider claims; the per-debtor basis may substantially increase certain creditors' blocking power. Yet it is also the effect of taking corporate separateness seriously; were affiliated debtor entities to be consolidated, the per-plan vs. per-debtor distinction would disappear.

The Bankruptcy Code itself specifies nothing regarding the form of plan votes or the method of solicitation, but Federal Rule of Bankruptcy Procedure 3018 prescribes the form of the vote. It requires that the vote be written and signed, identify the plan (or plans) accepted (and may indicate a preference among them), and conform to Official Form B14, a sample ballot provided by the Administrative Office of the U.S. Courts. Among other things, this form of voting means that voting is not done by secret ballot. Instead, it is an open vote, which is necessary to ensure the integrity of the franchise, to enable votes to be counted by classes, to enable votes to be counted by amount as well as number, and to allow enforcement of the Code's remedial provisions regarding designation of votes in certain circumstances. Typically the actual mailing and tabulation of ballots is not done by the DIP, but by a third-party claims agent that is retained by the estate. Given that the DIP is often the plan proponent (and that the DIP's management is not disinterested in the outcome, irrespective), does it seem strange that the DIP effectively controls the counting of the ballots?

Federal Rule of Bankruptcy Procedure 3018.
Acceptance or Rejection of Plan in a Chapter 9 Municipality or Chapter 11 Reorganization Case

. . .

(c) Form of Acceptance or Rejection. An acceptance or rejection shall be in writing, identify the plan or plans accepted or rejected, be signed by the creditor or equity security holder or an authorized agent, and conform to the appropriate Official Form. If more than one plan is transmitted pursuant to Rule 3017, an acceptance or rejection may be filed by each creditor or equity security holder for any number of plans transmitted and if acceptances are filed for more than one plan, the creditor or equity security holder may indicate a preference or preferences among the plans so accepted.

. . .

II. CLASSIFICATION

Section 1123(a)(1) of the Code requires that a plan classify claims and interests into classes other than administrative priority and priority tax claims and certain claims relating to involuntary bankruptcies, which are automatically treated as their own classes of claims and as nonimpaired on the basis of their mandatory treatment under section 1129(a)(9). Because the vote is by class, classification determines the shape of the electorate. Section 1122 sets forth the statutory rules governing classification. The statutory language itself merely provides that a class may contain only "substantially similar" claims or interests. 11 U.S.C. § 1122(a).

There is an exception to the "substantially similar" standard for unsecured claims, under a particular dollar threshold. 11 U.S.C. § 1122(b). These claims may be classified in an "administrative convenience claim." Such a class typically has a large number of small-dollar unsecured creditors, such as trade creditors. The ability to shift small unsecured claims into a single class can provide an important tool for plan proponents to obtain confirmation, as one of the confirmation requirements in section 1129 is that at least one impaired class must accept the plan. 11 U.S.C. § 1129(a)(10). A class dominated by small trade claims that are only superficially impaired is likely to support a plan because the trade creditors' interest in obtaining future business from the debtor may outweigh any resentment at the impairment.

The "substantially similar" language in section 1122 is a phrase open to interpretation, so it allows plan proponents some flexibility in classification. More significantly, the statutory language does not require that all "substantially similar" claims or interests be placed in the same class. This would appear to give plan proponents much more flexibility in classification. Case law has developed some different interpretations, however, as the case below explains.

In re Bloomingdale Partners

170 B.R. 984 (Bankr. N.D. Ill. 1994)

RONALD BARLIANT, U.S. Bankruptcy Judge:

I. INTRODUCTION

[The sole] secured creditor, John Hancock Mutual Life Insurance Company ("Hancock"), moved to strike the most recent plan of reorganization filed by Bloomingdale Partners (the "Debtor") and to dismiss the case. Hancock argues that the classification scheme in the Debtor's modified plan is improper. The Court agrees. After an examination of the language and legislative history of the Bankruptcy Code and an analysis of the many opinions addressing the issue of classification in a Chapter 11 plan, the Court adopts the "restrictive classification" standard: Taking into consideration legal and other relevant attributes, all claims that are found to be "substantially similar" must be placed in the same class. The Debtor's modified plan violates the "restrictive classification" standard because it places "substantially similar" claims in separate classes. Accordingly, the Debtor's modified plan is stricken.

Under the classification scheme formulated in the Debtor's previous plan, a tally of the ballots reveals that no impaired class has accepted the plan. Therefore, confirmation is denied. Further, since under the circumstances Hancock has demonstrated that the Debtor is unable to effectuate a plan of reorganization, the case is dismissed.

II. BACKGROUND

The Debtor is a limited partnership organized under Illinois law. Its primary asset is an apartment building. One Bloomingdale Place, located in Bloomingdale, Illinois. The property is the collateral of the John Hancock Mutual Life Insurance Company ("Hancock"), the sole secured creditor.

The Debtor failed in its first attempt to confirm a plan of reorganization. However, the Court gave the Debtor another opportunity to propose a plan. The Debtor subsequently filed a new plan, captioned "Third Plan of Reorganization" (the "Third Plan").

After the first confirmation hearing, creditors John and Jean Zarlenga filed a motion, pursuant to § 502(c)(1), for an order allowing and assigning a value to their contingent and unliquidated claim for the purpose of voting on the Debtor's Third Plan. The Zarlengas' claim is based upon a state common law private nuisance theory; the Zarlengas assert that the noise emanating from the air-conditioning units attached to the Debtor's apartment building interfered with their interest in the quiet enjoyment of their adjoining land and that they are entitled to damages. The Debtor strenuously objected to the Zarlengas' claim. After a lengthy hearing, this Court overruled the Debtor's objection and estimated and allowed the Zarlengas' claim in the amount of $40,000.

The Third Plan classifies all unsecured claims together so that the Zarlengas' claim is in the same class, Class 5, as the other unsecured claims. Three days before the close of voting, the Debtor filed its "Modified Third Plan of Reorganization" (the "Modified Third Plan"). This plan retains the Zarlengas' claim in Class 5, but it places all of the other unsecured claims in a separate class, Class 6.[3]

Hancock and the Zarlengas voted against the Debtor's plan.[4] The two unsecured creditors in Class 6 who were entitled to vote cast their ballots in favor of the plan.[5] Consequently, if the Zarlengas' claim is classified separately from the other unsecured claims (as the Modified Third Plan provides), then that plan may be confirmed if the

---

3. The entire classification scheme set forth in the Modified Third Plan is as follows:
   Class 1: administrative claims; unimpaired
   Class 2: Hancock's secured claim; impaired
   Class 3: priority claims (§§ 507(2)-(6)); unimpaired
   Class 4: tax claims (§ 507(7)); unimpaired
   Class 5: the Zarlengas' claim; unimpaired
   Class 6: all other unsecured claims; impaired
   Class 7: all equity interests; impaired.

4. The Zarlengas cast a ballot even though their vote cannot affect the confirmation of the Modified Third Plan. The Modified Third Plan provides that the Zarlengas are to be paid $40,000, the allowed value of their claim, on the effective date of the plan, rendering the class containing their claim unimpaired. *See* § 1124(3)(A) (providing that a class is unimpaired if each holder of a claim in that class is to receive the allowed amount of its claim, in cash, on the effective date of the plan). Unimpaired classes are conclusively presumed to accept the plan. § 1126(f). Accordingly, the Zarlengas' rejecting vote is immaterial with regard to the confirmation of the Modified Third Plan. Under the Third Plan, however, the Zarlengas' vote counts because their claim is classified with all of the other unsecured claims, and this class is impaired.

5. These two unsecured creditors, Holleb & Coff ($8,307.36 claim) and Katten, Muchin & Zavis ($6,490.00 claim), are law firms whose claims are based upon pre-petition work that they performed for the Debtor. All of the other unsecured claims are held by "insiders," *see* § 101(31)(C) (defining "insider" when the debtor is a partnership), whose votes are not considered for the purpose of plan confirmation, *see* § 1129(a)(10) (providing that the acceptance of a class is "determined without including any acceptance of the plan by any insider").

cramdown standards contained in § 1129(b) are met. However, if the Zarlengas' claim is classified together with the other unsecured claims (as the Third Plan provides), then the Zarlengas in effect have veto power over the plan because without their acceptance, no impaired class entitled to vote will have accepted the plan. *See* §§ 1126(c) (providing that a particular class accepts a plan only if at least two-thirds in amount of the claims in that class vote in favor of the plan) and 1129(a)(10) (providing that a plan may be confirmed only if at least one impaired class accepts the plan).[6]

In support of its motion to strike the Modified Third Plan and to dismiss the case, Hancock argues that the revised classification scheme established in the Modified Third Plan is improper because "the Debtor attempts to artificially classify the Law Firm Claims separately from the Zarlenga Claim for the purpose of gerrymandering an assenting impaired class of unsecured creditors in violation of [the Bankruptcy Code]."

The Court agrees with Hancock that the classification scheme set forth in the Modified Third Plan is improper, but its conclusion is not based upon an "artificial classification" nor a so-called "gerrymandering" theory. Instead, the Court applies the "restrictive classification" standard and concludes that its factual finding of "substantial similarity" between the Zarlengas' claim and the other unsecured claims compels its decision to strike the Modified Third Plan, to deny confirmation of the Third Plan, and to dismiss the case.

III. DISCUSSION

A. Determining the Appropriate Classification Standard

The classification standard articulated by this Court, which may be termed "restrictive classification," admittedly cannot be found in the plain language of the Code. Instead, this Court has settled upon this standard after examining the relevant sections of the Code and their legislative history and considering the approaches taken by other courts that have faced this issue.

1. Bankruptcy Code § 1122

The Code's primary provisions regarding classification are set forth in § 1122. Unfortunately, the Code does not expressly address the question of classification of "substantially similar" claims.

Subsection (a) of § 1122 addresses only claims that are *not* "substantially similar"; it prohibits their placement in the same class. Subsection (a) is silent as to the classification of claims that are "substantially similar."

---

6. This sort of conflict regarding the classification of claims in a Chapter 11 plan arises in many contested single-asset bankruptcy cases. Usually the dispute concerns the classification of the undersecured creditor's § 1111(b) deficiency claim. In the instant case, however, Hancock has become oversecured through the accrual of post-petition rents, so it has no § 1111(b) deficiency claim. Instead, in one of this case's unique twists, unsecured tort creditors with *de facto* veto power (the Zarlengas) have appeared, but the secured creditor (Hancock) is raising the standard classification argument. *See* § 1109(b) ("A party in interest, including . . . a creditor, . . . may raise and may appear and be heard on any issue in a [Chapter 11] case.").

Subsection (b) merely provides that a plan may separately classify one or more unsecured claims from the other unsecured claims under certain circumstances for administrative convenience. The Code contains no provision regarding the classification of "substantially similar" claims—either authorizing or prohibiting their separate classification.

Some courts, however, have discerned a restriction on the separate classification of "substantially similar" claims in the interplay between the two subsections of § 1122. Their reasoning is that if the plan proponent possesses the discretion to classify "substantially similar" claims separately, then § 1122(b), which permits a plan proponent to carve out a separate class of *de minimis* unsecured claims for administrative convenience, is superfluous—the plan proponent could create this administrative convenience class even without § 1122(b). Since one section of the Code should not be interpreted in such a way as to render another section superfluous, the "wholly permissive" view of classification must be incorrect.

This logic is flawed. Subsection (b) of § 1122 is not superfluous because it expressly authorizes the joint classification of claims that are not "substantially similar," notwithstanding the general prohibition on such joint classification contained in § 1122(a), provided only that the amounts of the claims are less than a certain amount. The first words of § 1122(a) are "Except as provided in subsection (b) of this section. . . ." Subsection (b) is explicitly an exception to the prohibition contained in subsection (a) against classifying claims that are not "substantially similar" in the same class.

Consequently, the plain language of the Code provides no express guidance concerning any restrictions on the separate classification of "substantially similar" claims.

2. Legislative History of § 1122

Similarly, the legislative history of § 1122 does not aid the Court in determining the appropriate classification standard to apply to a Chapter 11 plan. [Discussion omitted.]

3. Judicially Created Standards

. . .

a. *"Flexible Classification" Standard*

Several courts have interpreted the absence in the Code of an explicit prohibition on the separate classification of "substantially similar" claims as an implicit authorization for such separate classification. *See, e.g., In re ZRM-Oklahoma Partnership*, 156 Bankr. 67, 71 (Bankr. W.D. Okla. 1993).

ZRM is representative of the most permissive view of "flexible classification." That court employed what it denominated "The Correct Method of Statutory Interpretation," *ZRM*, 156 Bankr. at 68, to conclude that a plan proponent possesses absolute flexibility to classify "substantially similar" claims together or separately, as it sees fit, subject only to "other explicit protection mechanisms in the Code which Congress agreed to in sections 1111, 1123, and 1129." *Id.* at 71.

AG Consultants, another opinion adopting "flexible classification," took a slightly narrower approach by imposing some meager restrictions on a plan proponent's right to establish separate classes of "substantially similar" claims. That court granted the plan proponent the flexibility to classify "substantially similar" unsecured claims in separate classes "if [the classes as established in the plan] are in the best interest of creditors; foster reorganization efforts (ensure success); do not violate the absolute priority rule; and, do not uselessly increase the number of classes." *AG Consultants*, 77 Bankr. at 674.

Other courts and commentators have raised a fundamental objection to the application of the "flexible classification" standard: "Flexible classification" renders § 1129(a)(10), the Code provision requiring the assent of at least one impaired class, a mere ministerial requirement.

Section 1129(a)(10) requires that if any class is impaired under the plan, at least one impaired class must accept the plan. As pointed out by several Circuit Courts of Appeals, § 1129(a)(10) is in direct conflict with the "flexible classification" standard. The Third Circuit stated:

> Nevertheless, it seems clear that the Code was not meant to allow a debtor complete freedom to place substantially similar claims in separate classes. The critical confirmation requirements set out in Section 1129(a)(8) (acceptance by all impaired classes) and Section 1129(a)(10) (acceptance by at least one impaired class in the event of "cram down") would be seriously undermined if a debtor could gerrymander classes. A debtor could then construct a classification scheme designed to secure approval by an arbitrarily designed class of impaired claims even though the overwhelming sentiment of the impaired creditors was that the proposed reorganization of the debtor would not serve any legitimate purpose. This would lead to abuse of creditors and would foster reorganizations that do not serve any broader public interest.

Route 38, 987 F.2d at 158 (footnote added). Seven years earlier, the Sixth Circuit declared:

> There must be some limit on a debtor's power to classify creditors in such a manner. The potential for abuse would be significant otherwise. Unless there is some requirement of keeping similar claims together, nothing would stand in the way of a debtor seeking out a few impaired creditors (or even one such creditor) who will vote for the plan and placing them in their own class.

U.S. Truck, 800 F.2d at 586.

Moreover, in a recent decision, a district court stated:

> The policy underlying Section 1129(a)(10) is that before embarking upon the tortuous path of cramdown and compelling the target of cramdown to shoulder the risks of error necessarily associated with a forced confirmation, there must be some other properly classified group that is also hurt and nonetheless favors the plan. Allowing a debtor to manipulate the voting by creating a class that is certain to favor a plan effectively nullifies the threshold requirement that at least one impaired class accept the plan.

In re One Times Square Assocs. Ltd. Partnership, 165 Bankr. 773, 776-77 (S.D.N.Y. 1994) (internal citations omitted).

In other words, the "flexible classification" standard is flawed because it would permit the plan proponent to carve out a separate class for one friendly creditor who the plan proponent knows will vote for the plan.[13] Permitting this action would circumvent the requirement, set forth in § 1129(a)(10), of an assenting impaired class, rendering it, at best, a mere ministerial requirement. Since one section of the Code should not be interpreted in such a way as to render another section superfluous, the "flexible classification" standard must be rejected.

b. "Gerrymandering" and "Reasonableness" Standards

The recent trend, at least among the Circuit Courts of Appeal that have faced the issue of the propriety of a classification scheme in a Chapter 11 plan, is for the court to conduct an implicit two-pronged analysis. First, the court determines whether a particular claim is "substantially similar" to other claims in a different class under the plan. If not, the analysis ends; under § 1122(a), the claim is required to be classified separately from the other claims. See *Woodbrook*, 19 F.3d at 319 (following *In re SM 104 Ltd.*, 160 Bankr. 202, 221 (Bankr. S.D. Fla. 1993), in finding that a § 1111(b) deficiency claim is not "substantially similar" to other unsecured claims).

On the other hand, if the claim is found to be "substantially similar" to claims in another class, then the court next determines whether it is nevertheless appropriate for this claim to be classified separately. In the course of this analysis, courts have employed various non-Code-based tests, including "gerrymandering," *e.g., Greystone*, 995 F.2d at 1279, and "reasonableness," *e.g., Jersey City Medical Center*, 817 F.2d at 1061.

(1) "Gerrymandering"

"The term 'gerrymander' arose from an election district—that took the shape of a salamander—formed in Massachusetts by Governor Elbridge Gerry's[17] Jeffersonian or Democratic-Republican Party. The phrase was coined by Gerry's opponents, the Federalists." *Rogers v. Lodge*, 458 U.S. 613, 649 n.36 (1982) (Stevens, J., dissenting) (footnote added).

In the context of the classification of claims in a Chapter 11 plan of reorganization, to "gerrymander" is to create classes of claims in an artificial way with the purpose of ensuring that the plan will be confirmed. Perhaps the most influential case banning the practice of "gerrymandering" is *Greystone*, which states that "one clear rule . . . emerges from otherwise muddled caselaw on § 1122 claims classification: thou shalt not classify similar claims differently in order to gerrymander an affirmative vote on a reorganization plan." *Greystone*, 995 F.2d at 1279.

---

13. Indeed, the case at bar reflects precisely this risk. The two law firms who are the only non-insider unsecured creditors (other than the Zarlengas) are undoubtedly friendly creditors. Although this Court has previously held that the impairment of the class containing their claims is not "artificial impairment" such that their votes should not be counted, this is a different issue than whether their claims may be classified separately from the Zarlengas' claim. It is not inconsistent with the purposes of § 1129(a)(10) for the Court to consider the votes of creditors who support the plan even though their support may be based upon their non-economic relationships with the debtor, but it would be inconsistent to classify pro-debtor creditors separately from other creditors solely because of those relationships.

17. Elbridge Gerry is one of the signatories of the Declaration of Independence. He also served as Vice President of the United States from 1813 to 1814 under President James Madison. Mr. Gerry's name and the word "gerrymander" are properly pronounced with a hard "g" sound.

Greystone's "one clear rule" prohibiting "gerrymandering" has been soundly criticized on two grounds. First, at least some of the authorities cited in that opinion do not support the "one clear rule":

> For its "one clear rule" prohibiting gerrymandering of similar claims the [Fifth Circuit] cited three Circuit Court decisions, none of which found impermissible gerrymandering for an acceptance, and one of which *approved* it. The separate classification in *In re U.S. Truck Co.*, [800 F.2d 581 (6th Cir. 1986)], was approved on the basis that employee creditors had different interests in the debtor's survival than trade creditors, a rationale that is indistinguishable from the "gerrymandering" at issue in *Greystone*. *In re Holywell Corp.*, [913 F.2d 873, 880 (11th Cir. 1990),] denied confirmation not because of classification per se, but because of the discriminatory treatment in subordinating a claim solely because it was held by an insider; there was no gerrymandering for an affirmative vote because the plan was a creditor's plan that had "overwhelming support of creditors." *Hanson v. First Bank of South Dakota*, [(828 F.2d 1310 (8th Cir. 1987),] involved an attempt to reclassify claims at the confirmation hearing, which was deemed too late. The cases hardly provide a "clear rule" on what constitutes inappropriate efforts to "gerrymander an affirmative vote," and the holding of *U.S. Truck* is inescapably to the contrary. Indeed, so is the Fifth Circuit's own prior decision, which it never mentioned, holding in a Chapter XII case "The fact that bankruptcy courts are courts of equity . . . allows exceptions to any strict rules of classification of claims."

Randolph J. Haines, Greystone *Becomes Tombstone*, NORTON BANKR. L. ADVISOR, Jan. 1992 at 3 (emphasis in original).

Second, and more significantly, it is difficult or impossible for a court to apply the "gerrymandering" standard in the context of a Chapter 11 classification scheme because "gerrymandering" focuses upon the plan proponent's state of mind. *See Greystone*, 995 F.2d at 1279 ("If [the debtor's] proffered 'reasons' for separately classifying the [undersecured creditor's] deficiency claim simply mask the intent to gerrymander the voting process, that classification scheme should not have been approved."). "The 'one clear rule' is not easy to apply since it is not about 'classifying similar claims'; it is about the debtor's purpose."

Every plan proponent creates its classification scheme with the goal of maximizing the probability that its plan will be confirmed. The characterization of a plan proponent's efforts as "gerrymandering" is pejorative and falsely conclusive. In other words, every plan proponent "gerrymanders" to some extent; an examination of the plan proponent's intent is neither helpful nor feasible. Instead, the question remains: How far may the plan proponent go in drawing its class boundaries?

(2) "Reasonableness"

Similarly, opinions that employ a "reasonableness" standard to a plan proponent's classification scheme are not particularly illuminating or easy to apply. *See, e.g., Jersey City Medical Center*, 817 F.2d at 1061 ("The authorities recognize that the classification of claims or interests must be reasonable. . . . We immediately note the reasonableness of distinguishing the claims of physicians, medical malpractice victims, employee benefit plan participants, and trade creditors.").

This "standard" raises more questions than it answers: How is a court to determine whether a classification scheme in a Chapter 11 plan is reasonable? What aspects of a given classification scheme cause it to be reasonable or unreasonable?[18] The best way to answer these questions is to look to the Code itself.

c. "Restrictive Classification" Standard

As discussed at length in part III.A.1. above, the Code provides a test, "substantial similarity," to determine when a claim cannot be placed in a particular class; § 1122(a) provides that claims that are not "substantially similar" must be classified separately. It is logical to apply this Code-based test in a correlative manner to fill the void left by the amorphous "reasonableness" and "gerrymandering" standards. That is, the "restrictive classification" standard is not remarkably different from the "gerrymandering" and "reasonableness" standards that many courts have been applying; "restrictive classification" merely looks to the Code for a test to establish the bounds of "reasonableness." Under the "restrictive classification" standard it is reasonable for the plan proponent to classify claims separately only if these claims are not "substantially similar."

This Court, therefore, concludes that "restrictive classification" is the appropriate method for evaluating the classification of claims in a Chapter 11 plan. Instead of conducting a two-part analysis, the Court will determine, as a single finding of fact, whether the particular claim is "substantially similar" to the other claims in the class at issue.

If it is not "substantially similar," then, as under the two-pronged analysis, this claim must be classified separately pursuant to the plain language of § 1122(a). However, if this claim is "substantially similar" to other claims, then it must be classified together with these other claims. This analysis preserves the viability of § 1129(a)(10) without requiring an examination of a plan proponent's subjective motives.

The plan proponent has broad discretion in classifying claims. If the plan proponent can articulate differences among the claims—that is, if the plan proponent can demonstrate the lack of "substantial similarity"—then separate classification is proper. The differences may relate to legal rights or bankruptcy priorities or business reasons relevant to the success of the reorganized debtor.

As an example, it might be vital to a debtor to be able to treat customers' warranty claims differently than trade creditor claims, even though they are all general unsecured claims. In this instance, a court may reasonably find that warranty claims are not "substantially similar" to trade debt. The significant aspect of the "restrictive classification" analysis is that the inquiry focuses objectively upon the claims themselves, not upon the plan proponent's subjective intent.

---

18. Indeed, as Judge Ginsberg points out in *SM 104*, many courts that purport to apply the "gerrymandering" and "reasonableness" standards actually appear to be basing their decisions on equitable grounds: "While *Greystone* and the other cases have paid lip service to principles of statutory construction and the language of § 1122, they have turned more on notions of basic fairness and good faith." *SM 104*, 160 Bankr. at 217. Of course, Judge Ginsberg did not address the propriety of a Chapter 11 plan that classifies "substantially similar" claims separately because he ultimately held that a § 1111(b) deficiency claim is not "substantially similar" to general unsecured claims. *Id.* at 218 n.33.

B. Finding of "Substantial Similarity"

The Court's final task is to apply the "restrictive classification" standard to the facts of the instant case.

The Court finds that the Zarlengas' claim is "substantially similar" to the unsecured claims in Class 6 of the Debtor's Modified Third Plan. They are all unsecured claims with the same bankruptcy priority. Although the Zarlengas' claim is based upon a state common law private nuisance theory—that is, it is a tort claim—the Zarlengas' claim has the same non-bankruptcy legal status as the contract-based claims contained in Class 6. For the purposes of this bankruptcy case, the dispute regarding the Zarlengas' claim has been resolved, and their claim is liquidated in the amount of $40,000. *Bloomingdale III*, 160 Bankr. at 110-12. Outside of bankruptcy, the Zarlengas and the contract claimants may look to the partnership, then to the general partners, to satisfy their claims. None of these claims entitles its holder to receive punitive damages. Outside of bankruptcy, all of these claims share the same priority and "race to the courthouse" pressures; none is subject to equitable subordination. And finally, the Debtor has not articulated any business or economic difference among these claims. *Cf. In re Rochem, Ltd.*, 58 Bankr. 641, 642-44 (Bankr. D.N.J. 1985) (holding that it was not "unfair discrimination" for plan proponent to classify separately and to treat differently a $35 million unliquidated and disputed tort claim when all other unsecured claims totalled only $171,130).

The Debtor only asserts that the Zarlengas' claim is not "substantially similar" to the claims in Class 6 of the Modified Third Plan because the Zarlengas have a different motivation; the Zarlengas' attorney stated on the record that the Zarlengas will vote against any plan proposed by the Debtor because they do not agree with the Debtor's proposed solution to the noise problem that gave rise to their $40,000 pre-petition claim. Accordingly, the Debtor argues, the Zarlengas' claim should not be classified with the Class 6 claims, whose holders all favor the Debtor's reorganization.

The Court is not persuaded by the Debtor's argument. Different creditors will always have different motivations. The relevant issue is the similarity among the characteristics of the claims, not the motives of the holders of the claims. The way in which the holder of a particular claim is likely to vote is not a legitimate factor for a court to take into account when evaluating the issue of "substantial similarity." *See Route 37*, 987 F.2d at 161 ("Absent bad faith or illegality (see 11 U.S.C. § 1126(e) (1988)), the Code is not concerned with a claim holder's reason for voting one way or the other, and undoubtedly most claim holders vote in accordance with their overall economic interests as they see them.").

IV. CONCLUSION

For the reasons discussed above, the Court finds that the Zarlengas' claim is "substantially similar" to the claims in Class 6 of the Debtor's Modified Third Plan. Under the "restrictive classification" standard adopted by the Court, the Zarlengas' claim cannot be separately classified. The Debtor's Modified Third Plan violates this standard; therefore, the Modified Third Plan is stricken. *See* § 1127(a) (providing that a plan proponent may not modify a plan in a way that violates § 1122). Under the classification scheme set forth in the Debtor's Third Plan, no impaired class has accepted the plan, so confirmation is denied. *See* § 1129(a)(10) (providing that a plan cannot be confirmed if all impaired classes reject it). Finally, the case is dismissed because it is apparent to the Court that, without the support of either Hancock or the Zarlengas, the Debtor is unable to effectuate a plan of reorganization. See § 1112(b)(2) (providing that a court may dismiss a case for "inability to effectuate a plan"). An appropriate order has been entered.

Study Questions

1. How do the interests of a noise nuisance claimant differ from those of a tort claimant who was run over by a car? How do their interests differ from those of a supplier-claimant? From an unsecured bondholder? From a secured creditor?
2. What are the four different standards for classification courts have applied?
3. Why does the court adopt a "restrictive classification" standard?

III. DESIGNATION OF VOTES

Classification rules combined with the 1129(a)(3) good faith requirement police the manipulation of the bankruptcy electorate by the plan proponent (usually the debtor). The remedy for an improper classification—regardless of the plan proponent's motive—is to deny plan confirmation and send the plan proponent back to the drawing board. But what about manipulation of the electorate or other bad behavior by a creditor? There are both statutory and equitable remedies available. Among them is designation of a creditor's vote. A claimant or interest holder that misbehaves *in regard to voting* may find itself stripped of its voting right. Section 1126(e) provides for the designation of the vote of a party that has acted in bad faith regarding a vote. Notably, designation is not a remedy for other misbehavior vis-à-vis the debtor, such as pre-petition interactions, but what behavior relates to the vote could be read broadly. Section 1126(e) is not self-executing. Instead, a motion must be made for a vote to be designated as an acceptance or rejection, as the case may be. The following case, *DBSD North America*, illustrates the type of behavior that can result in designation of a vote.

DISH Network Corp. v. DBSD North America Inc.
634 F.3d 79 (2d Cir. 2011)

Gerard E. Lynch, Circuit Judge:
These consolidated appeals arise out of the bankruptcy of DBSD North America, Incorporated and its various subsidiaries (together, "DBSD"). The bankruptcy court confirmed a plan of reorganization for DBSD over the objections of the two appellants here, Sprint Nextel Corporation ("Sprint") and DISH Network Corporation ("DISH").
. . . DISH . . . argues that the bankruptcy court erred when it found DISH did not vote "in good faith" under 11 U.S.C. § 1126(e) and when, because of the § 1126(e)

ruling, it disregarded DISH's class for the purposes of counting votes under 11 U.S.C. § 1129(a)(8). . . .

. . . On DISH's appeal we find no error, and conclude (1) that the bankruptcy court did not err in designating DISH's vote, (2) that, after designating DISH's vote, the bankruptcy court properly disregarded DISH's class for voting purposes. . . . We therefore affirm in part . . . and remand for further proceedings.

BACKGROUND

. . .

ICO Global Communications founded DBSD in 2004 to develop a mobile communications network that would use both satellites and land-based transmission towers. In its first five years, DBSD made progress toward this goal, successfully launching a satellite and obtaining certain spectrum licenses from the FCC, but it also accumulated a large amount of debt. Because its network remained in the developmental stage and had not become operational, DBSD had little if any revenue to offset its mounting obligations.

On May 15, 2009, DBSD (but not its parent ICO Global), filed a voluntary petition in the United States Bankruptcy Court for the Southern District of New York, listing liabilities of $813 million against assets with a book value of $627 million. Of the various claims against DBSD, three have particular relevance here:

1. *The First Lien Debt*: a $40 million revolving credit facility that DBSD obtained in early 2008 to support its operations, with a first-priority security interest in substantially all of DBSD's assets. It bore an initial interest rate of 12.5%.

2. *The Second Lien Debt*: $650 million in 7.5% convertible senior secured notes that DISH issued in August 2005, due August 2009. These notes hold a second-priority security interest in substantially all of DBSD's assets. At the time of filing, the Second Lien Debt had grown to approximately $740 million. It constitutes the bulk of DBSD's indebtedness.

3. *Sprint's Claim*: an unliquidated, unsecured claim based on a lawsuit against a DBSD subsidiary. Sprint had sued seeking reimbursement for DBSD's share of certain spectrum relocation expenses under an FCC order. At the time of DBSD's filing, that litigation was pending in the United States District Court for the Eastern District of Virginia and before the FCC. In the bankruptcy case, Sprint filed a claim against each of the DBSD entities jointly and severally, seeking $211 million. The bankruptcy court temporarily allowed Sprint's claim in the amount of $2 million for voting purposes.

After negotiations with various parties, DBSD proposed a plan of reorganization which, as amended, provided for "substantial de-leveraging," a renewed focus on "core operations," and a "continued path as a development-stage enterprise." The plan provided that the holders of the First Lien Debt would receive new obligations with a four-year maturity date and the same 12.5% interest rate, but with interest to be paid in kind ("PIK"), meaning that for the first four years the owners of the new obligations would receive as interest more debt from DBSD rather than cash. The holders of the Second Lien Debt would receive the bulk of the shares of the reorganized entity, which the bankruptcy court estimated would be worth between 51% and 73% of their original claims. The holders of unsecured claims, such as Sprint, would receive shares estimated as worth between 4% and 46% of their original claims. Finally, the existing shareholder (effectively just ICO Global, which owned 99.8% of DBSD) would receive shares and warrants in the reorganized entity.

. . . DISH, although not a creditor of DBSD before its filing, had purchased the claims of various creditors with an eye toward DBSD's spectrum rights. As a provider of satellite television, DISH has launched a number of its own satellites, and it also has a significant investment in TerreStar Corporation, a direct competitor of DSDB's in the developing field of hybrid satellite/terrestrial mobile communications. DISH desired to "reach some sort of transaction with [DBSD] in the future if [DBSD's] spectrum could be useful in our business."

Shortly after DBSD filed its plan disclosure, DISH purchased all of the First Lien Debt at its full face value of $40 million, with an agreement that the sellers would make objections to the plan that DISH could adopt after the sale. As DISH admitted, it bought the First Lien Debt not just to acquire a "market piece of paper" but also to "be in a position to take advantage of [its claim] if things didn't go well in a restructuring." Internal DISH communications also promoted an "opportunity to obtain a blocking position in the [Second Lien Debt] and control the bankruptcy process for this potentially strategic asset." In the end, DISH (through a subsidiary) purchased only $111 million of the Second Lien Debt—not nearly enough to control that class—with the small size of its stake due in part to DISH's unwillingness to buy any claims whose prior owners had already entered into an agreement to support the plan.

. . . Separately, DISH proposed to enter into a strategic transaction with DBSD, and requested permission to propose its own competing plan (a request it later withdrew).

DBSD responded by moving for the court to designate that DISH's "rejection of [the] plan was not in good faith." 11 U.S.C. § 1126(e). The bankruptcy court agreed, finding that DISH, a competitor to DBSD, was voting against the plan "not as a traditional creditor seeking to maximize its return on the debt it holds, but . . . 'to establish control over this strategic asset.'" *DBSD II*, 421 B.R. at 137 (quoting DISH's own internal presentation slides). The bankruptcy court therefore designated DISH's vote and disregarded DISH's wholly-owned class of First Lien Debt for the purposes of determining plan acceptance under 11 U.S.C. § 1129(a)(8). *Id.* at 143; *DBSD I*, 419 B.R. at 206.[2] . . .

After designating DISH's vote and rejecting all objections, the bankruptcy court confirmed the plan. *See id.* at 221. The district court affirmed, *see DBSD III*, 2010 WL 1223109, and DISH and Sprint appealed to this Court. After oral argument, DBSD received approval from the FCC to transfer its spectrum rights to the reorganized entity—the last hurdle before consummation of the reorganization. We subsequently stayed consummation of the plan and then, on December 6, 2010, issued an order disposing of the case and vacating our stay so that the proceedings could continue below without further delay, indicating that an opinion would follow. *See In re DBSD North America, Inc.*, 627 F.3d 496 (2d Cir. 2010). This is that opinion.

---

2. The court did not designate DISH's vote on its Second Lien Debt claims, because DISH's stake in that class was too small to make any difference. *See DBSD II*, 421 B.R. at 137 n.12.

DISCUSSION

. . .

II. DISH's Appeal

. . . DISH contends that the bankruptcy court should not have designated its vote as "not in good faith," 11 U.S.C. § 1126(e), and that, even after the designation, the bankruptcy court should not have disregarded the entire class that DISH's claim comprised. . . .

A. The Treatment of DISH's Vote

1. Designating DISH's Vote as "Not in Good Faith"

To confirm a plan of reorganization, Chapter 11 generally requires a vote of all holders of claims or interests impaired by that plan. *See* 11 U.S.C. §§ 1126, 1129(a)(8). This voting requirement has exceptions, however, including one that allows a bankruptcy court to designate (in effect, to disregard) the votes of "any entity whose acceptance or rejection of such plan was not in good faith." *Id.* § 1126(e).

The Code provides no guidance about what constitutes a bad faith vote to accept or reject a plan. Rather, § 1126(e)'s "good faith" test effectively delegates to the courts the task of deciding when a party steps over the boundary. *See In re Figter Ltd.*, 118 F.3d 635, 638 (9th Cir. 1997); see also Revision of the Bankruptcy Act: Hearing on H.R. 6439 Before the House Comm. on the Judiciary, 75th Cong. 181 (1937) ["1937 Hearing"] (statement of Jacob Weinstein) (describing "good faith" test of predecessor to § 1126(e) as delegation to the courts). Case by case, courts have taken up this responsibility. No circuit court has ever dealt with a case like this one, however, and neither we nor the Supreme Court have many precedents on the "good faith" voting requirement in any context; the most recent cases from both courts are now more than 65 years old and address § 1126(e)'s predecessor, § 203 of the Bankruptcy Act. *See Young v. Higbee Co.*, 324 U.S. 204 (1945). Nevertheless, these cases, cases from other jurisdictions, legislative history, and the purposes of the good-faith requirement give us confidence in affirming the bankruptcy court's decision to designate DISH's vote in this case.

We start with general principles that neither side disputes. Bankruptcy courts should employ § 1126(e) designation sparingly, as "the exception, not the rule." *In re Adelphia Commc'ns Corp.*, 359 B.R. 54, 61 (Bankr. S.D.N.Y. 2006). For this reason, a party seeking to designate another's vote bears the burden of proving that it was not cast in good faith. See *id.* Merely purchasing claims in bankruptcy "for the purpose of securing the approval or rejection of a plan does not of itself amount to 'bad faith.'" *In re P-R Holding Corp.*, 147 F.2d 895, 897 (2d Cir. 1945). Nor will selfishness alone defeat a creditor's good faith; the Code assumes that parties will act in their own self interest and allows them to do so. *See In re Figter*, 118 F.3d at 639.

Section 1126(e) comes into play when voters venture beyond mere self-interested promotion of their claims. "[T]he section was intended to apply to those who were not attempting to protect their own proper interests, but who were, instead, attempting to obtain some benefit to which they were not entitled." *In re Figter*, 118 F.3d at 638. A bankruptcy court may, therefore, designate the vote of a party who votes "in the hope that someone would pay them more than the ratable equivalent of their proportionate part of the bankrupt assets," *Young*, 324 U.S. at 211, or one who votes with an "ulterior motive," 1937 Hearing, *supra*, at 180 (statement of SEC Commissioner William O. Douglas), that is, with "an interest other than an interest as a creditor," *In re P-R Holding*, 147 F.2d at 897.

Here, the debate centers on what sort of "ulterior motives" may trigger designation under § 1126(e), and whether DISH voted with such an impermissible motive. The first question is a question of law that we review *de novo*, and the second a question of fact that we review for clear error, *see In re Baker*, 604 F.3d at 729, recognizing that "a decision that someone did or did not act in good faith" hinges on "an essentially factual inquiry and is driven by the data of practical human experience," *In re Figter*, 118 F.3d at 638.

Clearly, not just any ulterior motive constitutes the sort of improper motive that will support a finding of bad faith. After all, most creditors have interests beyond their claim against a particular debtor, and those other interests will inevitably affect how they vote the claim. For instance, trade creditors who do regular business with a debtor may vote in the way most likely to allow them to continue to do business with the debtor after reorganization. *See John Hancock Mut. Life Ins. Co. v. Route 37 Bus. Park Assocs.*, 987 F.2d 154, 161-62 (3d Cir. 1993). And, as interest rates change, a fully secured creditor may seek liquidation to allow money once invested at unfavorable rates to be invested more favorably elsewhere. *See In re Landing Assocs., Ltd.*, 157 B.R. 791, 807 (Bankr. W.D. Tex. 1993). We do not purport to decide here the propriety of either of these motives, but they at least demonstrate that allowing the disqualification of votes on account of *any* ulterior motive could have far-reaching consequences and might leave few votes upheld.

The sort of ulterior motive that § 1126(e) targets is illustrated by the case that motivated the creation of the "good faith" rule in the first place, *Texas Hotel Securities Corp. v. Waco Development Co.*, 87 F.2d 395 (5th Cir. 1936). In that case, Conrad Hilton purchased claims of a debtor to block a plan of reorganization that would have given a lease on the debtor's property—once held by Hilton's company, later cancelled—to a third party. *Id.* at 397-99. Hilton and his partners sought, by buying and voting the claims, to "force [a plan] that would give them again the operation of the hotel or otherwise reestablish an interest that they felt they justly had in the property." *Id.* at 398. The district court refused to count Hilton's vote, but the court of appeals reversed, seeing no authority in the Bankruptcy Act for looking into the motives of creditors voting against a plan. *Id.* at 400.

That case spurred Congress to require good faith in voting claims. As the Supreme Court has noted, the legislative history of the predecessor to § 1126(e) "make[s] clear the purpose of the [House] Committee [on the Judiciary] to pass legislation which would bar creditors from a vote who were prompted by such a purpose" as Hilton's. *Young*, 324 U.S. at 211 n.10. As then-SEC Commissioner Douglas explained to the House Committee:

> We envisage that "good faith" clause to enable the courts to affirm a plan over the opposition of a minority attempting to block the adoption of a plan merely for selfish

purposes. The *Waco* case . . . was such a situation. If my memory does not serve me wrong it was a case where a minority group of security holders refused to vote in favor of the plan unless that group were given some particular preferential treatment, such as the management of the company. That is, there were ulterior reasons for their actions.

1937 Hearing, *supra*, at 181-82.[10] One year after Commissioner Douglas's testimony, and two years after the *Waco* case, Congress enacted the proposed good faith clause as part of the Chandler Act of 1938. Pub. L. 75-575, § 203, 52 Stat. 840, 894. The Bankruptcy Code of 1978 preserved this good faith requirement, with some rewording, as 11 U.S.C. § 1126(e).[11]

Modern cases have found "ulterior motives" in a variety of situations. In perhaps the most famous case, and one on which the bankruptcy court in our case relied heavily, a court found bad faith because a party bought a blocking position in several classes after the debtor proposed a plan of reorganization, and then sought to defeat that plan and to promote its own plan that would have given it control over the debtor. *See In re Allegheny Int'l, Inc.*, 118 B.R. 282, 289-90 (Bankr. W.D. Pa. 1990). In another case, the court designated the votes of parties affiliated with a competitor who bought their claims in an attempt to obstruct the debtor's reorganization and thereby to further the interests of their own business. *See In re MacLeod Co.*, 63 B.R. 654, 655-56 (Bankr. S.D. Ohio 1986). In a third case, the court found bad faith where an affiliate of the debtor purchased claims not for the purpose of collecting on those claims but to prevent confirmation of a competing plan. *See In re Applegate Prop., Ltd.*, 133 B.R. 827, 833-35 (Bankr. W.D. Tex. 1991).

Although we express no view on the correctness of the specific findings of bad faith of the parties in those specific cases, we think that this case fits in the general constellation they form. As the bankruptcy court found, DISH, as an indirect competitor of DBSD and part-owner of a direct competitor, bought a blocking position in (and in fact the entirety of) a class of claims, after a plan had been proposed, with the intention not to maximize its return on the debt but to enter a strategic transaction with DBSD and "to use status as a creditor to provide advantages over proposing a plan as an outsider, or making a traditional bid for the company or its assets." *DBSD II*, 421 B.R. at 139-40. In effect, DISH purchased the claims as votes it could use as levers to bend the bankruptcy process toward its own strategic objective of acquiring DBSD's spectrum rights, not toward protecting its claim.

---

10. Commissioner Douglas also described the Hilton claim-holders telling the other parties, in effect, "For a price you can have our vote." 1937 Hearing, *supra*, at 182. In this respect, Douglas's memory may have served him wrong, since at least the opinion of the court of appeals records nothing along these lines, unless one interprets "a price" broadly to include reinstatement of a lease or reassignment of management rights.

11. Based on a House committee report, some have cited a further case, *Aladdin Hotel Co. v. Bloom*, 200 F.2d 627 (8th Cir. 1953), as an example of what the authors of the 1978 Code meant to overrule when they reenacted the good faith requirement as § 1126(e). *See, e.g., In re Pleasant Hill Partners, L.P.*, 163 B.R. 388, 392-93 (Bankr. N.D. Ga. 1994), quoting H.R. Rep. No. 95-595, at 411 (1977). But the committee actually intended a different provision (originally designated § 1126(e), hence the confusion) to overrule *Aladdin Hotel*, not the good faith provision (which was originally designated § 1126(f)). When Congress removed the former provision, the latter became § 1126(e) in its place. *See In re Dune Deck Owners Corp.*, 175 B.R. 839, 845 n.13 (Bankr. S.D.N.Y. 1995). The relevant committee report provides no insight into the good faith provision that began as § 1126(f) and became § 1126(e), instead merely paraphrasing the statutory language. H.R. Rep. No. 95-595, at 411 (1977).

We conclude that the bankruptcy court permissibly designated DISH's vote based on the facts above. This case echoes the *Waco* case that motivated Congress to impose the good faith requirement in the first place. In that case, a competitor bought claims with the intent of voting against any plan that did not give it a lease in or management of the debtor's property. 87 F.2d at 397-99. In this case, a competitor bought claims with the intent of voting against any plan that did not give it a strategic interest in the reorganized company. The purchasing party in both cases was less interested in maximizing the return on its claim than in diverting the progress of the proceedings to achieve an outside benefit. In 1936, no authority allowed disregarding votes in such a situation, but Congress created that authority two years later with cases like *Waco* in mind. We therefore hold that a court may designate a creditor's vote in these circumstances.

We also find that, just as the law supports the bankruptcy court's legal conclusion, so the evidence supports its relevant factual findings. DISH's motive—the most controversial finding—is evinced by DISH's own admissions in court, by its position as a competitor to DBSD,[12] by its willingness to overpay for the claims it bought,[13] by its attempt to propose its own plan, and especially by its internal communications, which, although addressing the Second Lien Debt rather than the First Lien Debt at issue here, nevertheless showed a desire to "to obtain a blocking position" and "control the bankruptcy process for this potentially strategic asset."

The Loan Syndications and Trading Association (LSTA), as *amicus curiae*, argues that courts should encourage acquisitions and other strategic transactions because such transactions can benefit all parties in bankruptcy. We agree. But our holding does not "shut[] the door to strategic transactions," as the LSTA suggests. Rather, it simply limits the methods by which parties may pursue them. DISH had every right to propose for consideration whatever strategic transaction it wanted—a right it took advantage of here—and DISH still retained this right even after it purchased its claims. All that the bankruptcy court stopped DISH from doing here was using the votes it had bought to secure an advantage in pursuing that strategic transaction.

DISH argues that, if we uphold the decision below, "future creditors looking for potential strategic transactions with Chapter 11 debtors will be deterred from exploring such deals for fear of forfeiting their rights as creditors." But our ruling today should deter only attempts to "*obtain* a blocking position" and thereby "control the bankruptcy

---

12. Courts have been especially wary of the good faith of parties who purchase claims against their competitors. *See In re MacLeod*, 63 B.R. at 655; *see also In re Figter*, 118 F.3d at 640 (finding no bad faith in part because party was not competitor); *In re 255 Park Plaza Assocs.*, 100 F.3d at 1219 (same); *In re Pine Hill Collieries Co.*, 46 F. Supp. 669, 672 (E.D. Pa. 1942) (finding no bad faith even for a competitor, but only because competitor had a prior interest in the debtor).

13. The fact that DISH bought the First Lien Debt at par is circumstantial evidence of its intent, though we do not put as much weight on the price as the bankruptcy court did. *See DBSD II*, 421 B.R. at 140. It is certainly true, as the Loan Syndications and Trading Association points out in an *amicus* brief, that purchasers may have many good business reasons for buying debt at par, especially when, as in this case, the debt is well secured and interest rates dropped between the original issuance of the debt and its purchase. Buying claims at or above par therefore could not provide the sole basis for designating a creditor's vote. Nevertheless, a willingness to pay high prices may tend to show that the purchaser is interested in more than the claim for its own sake. The weight to be given to such evidence is primarily an issue for the finder of fact, and we see no clear error in the bankruptcy court's reliance on the factor in this case.

process for [a] potentially strategic asset" (as DISH's own internal documents stated). We leave for another day the situation in which a *preexisting* creditor votes with strategic intentions. *Cf. In re Pine Hill Collieries Co.*, 46 F. Supp. 669, 672 (E.D. Pa. 1942). We emphasize, moreover, that our opinion imposes no categorical prohibition on purchasing claims with acquisitive or other strategic intentions. On other facts, such purchases may be appropriate. Whether a vote has been properly designated is a fact-intensive question that must be based on the totality of the circumstances, according considerable deference to the expertise of bankruptcy judges. Having reviewed the careful and fact-specific decision of the bankruptcy court here, we find no error in its decision to designate DISH's vote as not having been cast in good faith.

2. Disregarding DISH's Class for Voting Purposes

DISH next argues that the bankruptcy court erred when, after designating DISH's vote, it disregarded the entire class of the First Lien Debt for the purpose of determining plan acceptance under 11 U.S.C. § 1129(a)(8). Section 1129(a)(8) provides that each impaired class must vote in favor of a plan for the bankruptcy court to confirm it without resorting to the (more arduous) cram-down standards of § 1129(b). Faced with a class that effectively contained zero claims—because DISH's claim had been designated—the bankruptcy court concluded that "[t]he most appropriate way to deal with that [situation] is by disregarding [DISH's class] for the purposes of section 1129(a)(8)." *DBSD I*, 419 B.R. at 206. We agree with the bankruptcy court. Common sense demands this result, which is consistent with (if not explicitly demanded by) the text of the Bankruptcy Code.

The Code measures the acceptance of a plan not creditor-by-creditor or claim-by-claim, but class-by-class. The relevant provision explains how to tally acceptances within a class of claims to arrive at the vote of the overall class:

> A class of claims has accepted a plan if such plan has been accepted by creditors, *other than any entity designated under subsection (e) of this section*, that hold at least two-thirds in amount and more than one-half in number of the allowed claims of such class held by creditors, *other than any entity designated under subsection (e) of this section*, that have accepted or rejected such plan.

11 U.S.C. § 1126(c) (emphasis added). For each class, then, the bankruptcy court must calculate two fractions based on the non-designated, allowed claims in the class. To arrive at the first fraction, the court divides the value of such claims that vote to accept the plan by the value of all claims that vote either way. For the second fraction, the court uses the number of claims rather than their value. If the first fraction equals two-thirds or more, and the second fraction more than one-half, then the class as a whole votes to accept the plan.

The arithmetic breaks down in cases like this one. Because the only claim in DISH's class belongs to DISH, whose vote the court designated, each fraction ends up as zero divided by zero. In this case, the plain meaning of the statute and common sense lead clearly to one answer: just as a bankruptcy court properly ignores designated *claims* when calculating the vote of a class, *see* 11 U.S.C. § 1126(e), so it should ignore a wholly designated *class* when deciding to confirm a plan under § 1129(a)(8). We agree with the bankruptcy court that any other rule "would make [the] designation ruling meaningless" in this context. *DBSD I*, 419 B.R. at 206.[15] We therefore affirm the bankruptcy court's treatment of DISH's class.

. . .

CONCLUSION

For the reasons set forth above, we . . . AFFIRM . . . and REMAND for further proceedings consistent with this opinion.

In re Adelphia Communications Corp.

359 B.R. 54 (Bankr. S.D.N.Y. 2006)

ROBERT E. GERBER, U.S. Bankr. J.

In this contested matter in the Chapter 11 cases of Adelphia Communications Corporation and its subsidiaries (the "Debtors"), I have before me the motion of a group of holders of ACC Senior Notes (the "ACC Bondholders Group") to designate the votes in the class of ACC Senior Notes of three creditor groups that voted to support the Plan now before me for confirmation:

> (1) the members of a "crossover committee" of holders of both ACC Senior Notes and notes of Arahova Communications Corp., an indirect ACC subsidiary (the "ACC II Committee");
> (2) accounts maintained or managed by W.R. Huff Asset Management Co., some or all of which are likewise holders of notes of each of ACC and Arahova (referred to, for simplicity, simply as "Huff"); and
> (3) those members of the Arahova Noteholders Committee who also hold ACC Senior Notes.

The three of them (the "Targeted Creditors"), joined by the Creditors Committee, oppose the motion, arguing, among other things, that even if the underlying factual contentions are true, there is no basis for disqualifying their votes.

The antagonists on both sides of the issue are predominantly or exclusively investors in distressed debt. . . . [M]otions to designate are within the discretion of the court. Here I conclude that even if all of the factual allegations asserted by the ACC Bondholders Committee were true, I would not disqualify the Targeted Creditors' votes. The ability to vote on a reorganization plan is one of the most sacred entitlements that a creditor has in a Chapter 11 case. And in my view, it should not be denied except for highly egregious conduct—principally, seeking to advance interests apart from recovery under the Plan, or seeking to extract plan treatment that is not available for others in the

---

15. DISH argues that "[t]he plain language of section 1126(c) dictates that in order for a class to be deemed to have accepted a plan of reorganization, it must have actively voted in favor of the plan," and that, because "the votes of any entity designated . . . are excluded from both the numerator and denominator in determining whether a class has accepted a plan," DISH's class cannot be found to have voted in favor of the plan. This makes no sense. A class with no qualifying members cannot be required to accept a plan by an affirmative vote.

same class. While creditor tactics, activities or requests (or plan provisions that result from them) may be objectionable, the Code provides for other ways to address concerns that arise from such (such as upholding objections to confirmation), without the draconian measure of denying one's franchise to vote. . . . Thus the motion is denied. Findings of Fact, Conclusions of Law and bases for the exercise of my discretion in this regard follow.

FACTS

The Plan

On October 17, 2006, I approved a supplement to the disclosure statement and authorized solicitation of votes on what is now the present Plan. A central feature of the Plan is the settlement of disputes relating to the intercompany relationships among the Debtors. Settling parties include Huff, the ACC II Committee, the Creditors' Committee, the ACC Settling Parties, the Arahova Noteholders Committee and certain other ad hoc committees of unsecured creditors. The Plan includes provisions for releases, exculpation and fee reimbursements for members of ad hoc committees and for individual creditors who signed onto the settlement and agreed to support the Plan, and for the same releases to go to any and all ACC Senior Noteholder creditors that support the Plan. The Targeted Creditors voted all of their claims, including any ACC claims, in support of the Plan. The ACC Bondholders vehemently oppose the Plan and the underlying settlement and, thus, voted against the Plan.

. . .

Earlier in this case, the Arahova Noteholders filed numerous motions and engaged in related acts (together, the "Arahova Motions") seeking to thwart the judicial determination of interdebtor issues that the Debtors proposed and that I had approved; seeking relief which, if granted, would have been devastating to creditor recoveries in these cases (including, most significantly, a motion seeking the appointment of a Chapter 11 trustee for the Arahova debtors, which would have been a breach of the Debtors' DIP financing facility and an event excusing Time-Warner and Comcast from closing on their purchase); and entering into an agreement to put their motions on hold pending the outcome of settlement negotiations. The ACC Bondholder Group asserts, and I take it as true for the purposes of this motion, that these were tactics on the Arahova Bondholders Group's part to improve its recovery. As the ACC Bondholders group appropriately notes, I "sharply criticized" the Arahova Bondholders' tactics, and was "understandably dismayed" by them. In a lengthy decision in January 2006 addressing Arahova Debtors' motions, I stated:

> [T]he Court further decides these motions in light of the compelling inference that the motions were filed as part of a scorched earth litigation strategy that would provide the Arahova Debtors with little benefit that they do not already have (trumped, dramatically, by a resulting prejudice to the Arahova Debtors themselves, along with all of the other Debtors), and which would have the effect (and, the Court believes, the purpose) of imperiling the pending Time Warner/Comcast transaction and the Debtors' DIP financing in an effort to extract a greater distribution, sidestepping the Court-approved process for determining the Intercreditor Dispute issues on their respective merits.

I stated at the conclusion:

> The bringing of motions like these is not unethical, or sanctionable, but neither should it be encouraged, or rewarded. Motions that would bring on intolerable consequences for an estate should not be used as a tactic to augment a particular constituency's recovery.

Huff's Rule 2004 Discovery

Huff sought and obtained Rule 2004 discovery to investigate the creation and dissemination of a letter sent by certain members of the ACC Noteholders Committee to the Board of Directors of ACC and to the Wall Street Journal on April 17, 2006. Huff sought discovery based on the premise that dissemination of the letter was an attempt to manipulate the market and an improper solicitation under section 1125(b) of the Code. The ACC Bondholders contend (and I must accept as true for the purposes of a demurrer) that this was not, in fact, Huff's true intent, and instead was an effort to improperly pressure ACC Noteholders.

Plan Agreement

The ACC Bondholders then contend that only two days after I expressed an adverse reaction to alleged activities on the part of certain ACC Bondholders which were the subject of the now-withdrawn motion directed at them, and "in the midst of Huff's coercive tactics," two other holders of ACC Senior Notes agreed to a term sheet embodying a plan settlement, including a settlement of the interdebtor issues. That term sheet, following further modifications, now serves as the basis for the Plan. "Among other egregious positions," the Plan included "thinly-veiled threats of litigation and continued discovery against ACC Senior Notes" who refused to join in the agreement, hire the counsel for the assenting ACC Bondholders, and vote to accept the proposed Plan, and provided broad release provisions for those who satisfied those conditions.

DISCUSSION

. . . Section 1126(e) of the Bankruptcy Code provides:

> On request of a party in interest, and after notice and a hearing, the court may designate any entity whose acceptance or rejection of such plan was not in good faith, or was not solicited or procured in good faith or in accordance with the provisions of this title.

Section 1126(e) is permissive in nature, and a bankruptcy judge has discretion in designating votes. The issue before me, then, is whether, assuming all of the ACC Bondholders' contentions to be true, I should (or would) disqualify, by "designation," any of the Targeted Creditors' votes.

While 1126(e) does not define "bad faith," the courts have designated votes as having been cast in "bad faith" in the following instances:

> (1) if the claimant is using obstructive tactics and hold-up techniques to extract better treatment for its claim compared to the treatment afforded similarly situated claimholders in the same class; or

(2) if the holder of the claim casts its vote for the ulterior purpose of securing some advantage to which it would not otherwise be entitled; or
(3) when the motivation behind its vote is not consistent with a creditor's protection of its own self-interest.

Some courts have held that some type of wrongdoing must be present to evidence bad faith.

. . . A right to vote on a plan is a fundamental right of creditors under Chapter 11. Designation of a creditor's vote is a drastic remedy, and, as a result, designation of votes is the exception, not the rule. The party seeking to have a ballot disallowed has a heavy burden of proof.

In his decision in *Dune Deck Owners*, in this district, Chief Judge Bernstein canvassed the law in this area, and noted that the "badges" of the requisite bad faith include creditor votes designed to (1) assume control of the debtor; (2) put the debtor out of business or otherwise gain a competitive advantage; (3) destroy the debtor out of pure malice or (4) obtain benefits available under a private agreement with a third party which depends on the debtor's failure to reorganize. A moment earlier, he capsulized the standards that would satisfy the requisite bad faith as (i) where a claim holder attempts to extract or extort a personal advantage not available to other creditors in the class, or (ii) where a creditor acts in furtherance of an ulterior motive, unrelated to its claim or its interests as a creditor.

Notably, a movant must demonstrate more than a mere selfish motive on behalf of a voting party in order for a court to designate that party's vote.[36] "[W]hen the voting process is being used as a device with which to accomplish some ulterior purpose, out of keeping with the purpose of the reorganization process itself, and only incidentally related to the creditor's status *qua* creditor," disqualification is appropriate.

[The ACC Bondholder Group asserts] that the Targeted Creditors extracted special consideration for themselves—releases, exculpation and fee awards—that was not awarded to other members of their voting classes who voted against the settlement (and used such as a coercive "carrot" to induce additional acceptances of the Plan), and, with respect to some of the Targeted Creditors, that they acted beyond the bounds of acceptable behavior in the process that led to the ultimate solicitation of the Plan.

The ACC Bondholders argue that the votes on the ACC claims of the Targeted Creditors should be designated because these creditors obtained special consideration in the form of releases, exculpation and reimbursement of fees expressly conditioned upon their acceptance of the settlement in the Plan, and used such as an enticement to others to support the Plan. Members of the same class who rejected the Plan did not secure those benefits.

These matters may support confirmation objections, but they are not matters of the type that warrant disqualification of the Targeted Creditors' votes. The factors identified above as badges of bad faith do not come even close to being applicable here. The Targeted Creditors did not seek to (1) assume control of the debtor; (2) put the debtor out of business or otherwise gain a competitive advantage; (3) destroy the debtor out

---

36. *In re Pine Hill Collieries Co.*, 46 F. Supp. 669, 671 (E.D. Pa. 1942) ("If a selfish motive were sufficient to condemn reorganization policies of interested parties, very few, if any, would pass muster.")[.]

of pure malice or (4) obtain benefits available under a private agreement with a third party which depends on the debtor's failure to reorganize. Taking the ACC Bondholders Group's allegations at face value, the Targeted Creditors whose behavior was challenged (*i.e.*, those other than the ACC II Committee) were overly aggressive, and/or stepped over the line, in taking action to benefit their economic interests in securing the confirmation of this Plan, and overreached, in particular, in benefiting themselves and using enticements to others to likewise support the Plan.

But to the extent complaints as to that conduct are justified, they can be addressed in the confirmation process. The disputed plan provisions will need to be examined, as part of the confirmation process, to evaluate their compliance with law, and to ascertain whether they are or are not appropriate benefits for those settle, and for those who choose to vote in favor of a Chapter 11 plan. And depending on the particular provision concerned, various measures might have to be taken as part of the confirmation process if the contested plan provisions turn out to be objectionable. But whether or not the disputed provisions pass muster at confirmation, they are in any event all variants of measures to advance one's interests in maximizing recoveries under a reorganization plan, which have consistently been held to be acceptable exercises of creditor power. Proposing them is not the type of conduct that warrants vote designation, especially when it is fully disclosed under the Plan.

Likewise, I do not believe that the conduct alleged on the part of the Arahova Bondholders and Huff, even taking the allegations with respect to that conduct as true, warrants designation. Without question, at least some of it was overly aggressive and overreaching. But it was, once more, an effort to maximize recoveries as a creditor under a prospective plan.

To be sure, a culture has developed in large Chapter 11 cases in which many consider it acceptable, and indeed expected, to use the litigation process as a means to assert or follow through on threats, and to seek various kinds of relief, to secure "leverage" in efforts to increase recoveries. I don't like it. And I particularly don't like it when supposedly critical concerns then somehow turn out to be not so critical, and threatened or filed motions are put on hold or withdrawn pending "negotiation." But aside from saying, in precatory terms, that I don't like such tactics and that they are a good way to irritate the judge, I don't think that I can or should do anything about them on a motion of this character. In particular, I don't think I should disenfranchise creditors from their statutory voting rights based on my personal views as to the way they should behave. My views as to acceptable behavior in Chapter 11 intercreditor disputes may be naive, or they may be right on the money, but in either event I believe that where, as here, creditors are acting to maximize their recoveries, their overly aggressive conduct in the Chapter 11 process is not a basis for disqualifying their votes.

Thus, assuming, as I do, that all of the allegations of the motion are true, they boil down to activities that, while distasteful and heavy handed, are sufficiently within what the law permits, and sufficiently tied to maximize creditor recoveries, that I should not disenfranchise creditors from their statutory rights.

. . . The motion of the ACC Bondholders to designate ACC votes of Huff, Arahova Noteholders Committee and ACC II Committee is denied.

Designation of votes is hardly an exclusive remedy for misbehavior. Federal Rule of Bankruptcy Procedure 9011 provides for sanctions in bankruptcy. Rule 9011 closely parallels Federal Rule of Civil Procedure 11. Additionally, equitable remedies, as discussed in Chapter 32, may apply.

Study Questions

1. If the facts alleged by the ACC bondholders in *Adelphia* were proven true, would sanctions be merited? If so, against whom? Why doesn't Judge Gerber mention this possibility in *Adelphia*? What does he suggest is the remedy? Does that ring correct to you?

2. Given Rule 9011, how comfortable do you feel counseling your client to undertake actions that will delay confirmation of a bankruptcy case? How about taking actions that will impose higher litigation costs on another party that might not have the funds to finance them?

Problem Set 34

1) Jobene Timber Products Corp. is in Chapter 11 bankruptcy. Jobene has proposed a plan of reorganization that classifies creditors into five classes. Class 1, consisting of four secured claims for $200 million each, is unimpaired. So too is class 2, consisting of 200 unsecured trade claims totaling $50 million. Class 3 consists of $300 million in claims of 60 unsecured noteholders and is impaired. Class 4 consists of $120 million in claims of three tort creditors, one of which is owed $60 million and the other two $30 million. Class 4 is also impaired. Class 5 is equity and is impaired. Jobene's CEO owns 10% of the company's shares. The CEO's wife owns another 10% of the company. Her nephew owns another 5% of the shares, as does her step-niece. The nephew's ex-wife owns another 10% of the shares. So too does the CEO's girlfriend. Can the plan be confirmed under section 1129(a) in the following scenarios?

a. Three of the four secured claim holders in Class 1 are opposed. 11 U.S.C. §§ 1126(c), (f).

b. Twenty of the claim holders in Class 3 vote against it. 11 U.S.C. § 1126(c).

c. Claims totaling $100 million in Class 3 vote against it. 11 U.S.C. § 1126(c).

d. The creditor with a $60 million claim in Class 4 votes against it. 11 U.S.C. § 1126(c).

e. One of the creditors with a $30 million claim in Class 4 votes against it. 11 U.S.C. § 1126(c).

f. The holders of 50 percent of the common equity shares vote against it. 11 U.S.C. § 1126(d).

g. All of the equityholders other than Jobene's CEO, his wife, her nephew, and her step-niece vote for the plan. 11 U.S.C. §§ 101(31)(B), 101(45); 1129(a)(8), 1129(a)(10).

(2) Centauri Shipping Co., as DIP, has proposed a Chapter 11 plan with the following classification:

Class I: A first lien loan secured by Centauri's equipment and receivables. The loan has a senior and a junior tranche.

Class II: A first lien loan secured by Centauri's real property.

Class III: A first lien loan secured by Centauri's real property, but subordinated to the Class II loan by an intercreditor agreement.

Class IV: The secured portion of an undersecured second lien loan secured by Centauri's equipment and receivables.

Class V: $100 million in fixed-rate bonds and $50 million in floating-rate bonds.

Class VI: $25 million in 10-year fixed-rate notes and $25 million in 6-month, fixed-rate commercial paper. The fixed-rate notes are guaranteed by Centauri's non-bankrupt parent company.

Class VII: Landlords' claims.

Class VIII: Unsecured trade debt and the unsecured deficiency on the Class IV claim.

Class IX: Unsecured domestic tort debt and an unsecured loan made by Centauri's controlling shareholder.

Class X: Unsecured foreign tort claims.

Class XI: All claims for less than $50,000.

Class XII: Intercompany claims.

Class XIII: Equity.

Is Centauri's plan confirmable if the plan is feasible, satisfies best interests, and all classes vote for the plan? 11 U.S.C. §§ 502(b)(6), 510(a), 1122, 1129(a)(1)-(3).

(3) Gemini Telecomm, as DIP, has proposed a plan of reorganization in its Chapter 11 bankruptcy. All of the classes have voted for the plan except for Class 3 and Class 6. Class 3 consists of a single creditor, Aquarius Investments, LLP, which is owed $50 million. The plan will pay $15 million to Class 3. Class 6 consists of 10 creditors with a total of $100 million in claims. Eight of the Class 6 creditors support Gemini's plan, but one of the objectors, Virgo Strategies, Inc., holds 40 percent of the amount of claims in the class. The plan will pay 10 cents on the dollar to Class 6.

    a. Is the plan confirmable under section 1129(a)? 11 U.S.C. § 1129(a)(8).

    b. Now suppose that Gemini discovered that Aquarius had taken out a $50 million total return swap on its position. Could that affect confirmability? 11 U.S.C. §§ 1126(e), 1129(a)(8).

    c. Now suppose that Gemini also discovered that Virgo Strategies holds a large equity stake in Gemini's competitor VegaOne. Could that affect confirmability? 11 U.S.C. §§ 1126(e), 1129(a)(8).

(4) Polaris-Ultra Corp. is in Chapter 11 bankruptcy and has put forth a plan of reorganization. The Official Unsecured Creditor's Committee (OUCC) has moved to designate the votes of four of the creditors on the plan:

    a. First, the OUCC has argued that the Ursa Major Fund is voting in bad faith against the plan because Ursa Major is hoping to block the plan in order to extract a higher payment for its class.

b. Second, the OUCC has argued that Orion Capital is voting in bad faith because Orion is hoping to block the plan to force reclassification (and better treatment of its claim) in the process.

c. Third, the OUCC has argued that the vote of Hydra Asset Management Co. should be designated because Hydra received under the plan releases and indemnification for its attorneys' fees in exchange for signing an agreement with the debtor to support any plan proposed by the debtor that met certain requirements.

d. Finally, the OUCC has argued that the vote of Andromeda Investments should be designated because Andromeda traded on insider information it gained during the plan negotiation process.

e. Is the Official Unsecured Creditors' Committee likely to succeed with any of these designation motions? 11 U.S.C. § 1126(e).

CHAPTER 35

IMPAIRMENT
AND THE RIGHT
TO VOTE

The treatment of a class of claims or interests depends on whether the claims or interests in the class are impaired or not, meaning whether the rights of the claimants are altered by the plan. Generally, if a plan provides for any alteration in the *legal* rights of a claimant or interest holder—the right to payment, the timing of payments, interest rates, covenants, etc.—it is an impairment. 11 U.S.C. § 1124(1). Thus, if a plan changed a shareholder's voting rights or extended the maturity date of a contract, the legal rights of the shareholder or contract counterparty would be altered.

Impairment is a term of art based on an analysis of legal rights, irrespective of economic rights. Legal impairment without economic impairment is still impairment, while economic impairment without legal impairment is not impairment. Thus, if a secured creditor were given additional collateral under a plan, but was required to give the debtor written notice prior to foreclosure, its economic position would have improved, but it would still be legally impaired. Even if a creditor's position is enhanced, it is still impaired if its rights are altered. *See In re Anaheim Assocs.*, 995 F.2d 940, 942-943 (9th Cir. 1993). Conversely, if a plan proposed a reorganized debtor with substantially lower annual revenue than the pre-petition debtor, it would constitute economic impairment for all creditors, but would constitute legal impairment only for creditors whose credit agreement included a covenant requiring the debtor to maintain a certain level of revenue. The application of bankruptcy law limitations on claim allowance, such as under sections 502(b)(6) and 502(b)(7) do not constitute impairment because there is no change to the creditor's legal rights—the creditor's legal rights have always been subject to the statutory limitation in bankruptcy. *Solow v. PPI Enterprises (U.S.), Inc., (In re PPI Enterprises (U.S.), Inc.)*, 324 F.3d 197 (3d Cir. 2002).

Impairment has several important implications. First, recall that only an impaired class has a right to vote on a plan. Unimpaired creditors or interest holders are conclusively deemed to have accepted the plan. 11 U.S.C. § 1126(f). Therefore, there is no need to solicit votes of unimpaired creditors or interest holders. Second, if there are any impaired classes, then plan confirmation requires approval of at least one class of impaired claims, if not all classes of impaired claims *and* interests. 11 U.S.C. § 1129(a)(8), (10). This makes determination of impairment critical because it essentially determines the size of the bankruptcy electorate. Thus, impairment or nonimpairment is, like classification, a critical tool for the debtor to manipulate the shape of the bankruptcy electorate. Sometimes a plan proponent will want to impair friendly creditors so that they can vote, while other times a plan proponent will want to leave certain unfriendly creditors unimpaired (and force them to continue their below-market-rate extensions of credit to the debtor). And third, certain plan confirmation requirements apply only to impaired classes: the best interests test and the cramdown requirements of no unfair discrimination and of fair and equitable treatment (discussed in the following chapter).

Because of the importance of impairment in determining the scope of the bankruptcy electorate, parties will often attempt to manipulate impairment to create a more favorable electorate. Thus, a plan proponent may want a class of claims that is likely to support a plan to be impaired to ensure that class can vote or, alternatively, attempt to leave plan opponents unimpaired so as to deprive them of their vote. Thus, what constitutes impairment is often contested, as the following cases illustrate.

I. ARTIFICIAL IMPAIRMENT

Connecticut General Life Insurance Co. v. Hotel Associates of Tucson

debtor

165 B.R. 470 (9th Cir. B.A.P. 1994)

MEYERS, Bankruptcy Judge.

Connecticut General Life Insurance Company ("Connecticut General") appeals from the orders confirming the First Amended Plan of Reorganization submitted by the Paragon Group (the "Paragon Plan") and denying confirmation of the competing Plan of Reorganization filed by C.R.H.C. of Tucson, Inc. (the "CRHC Plan").

FACTS

Hotel Associates of Tucson ("the Debtor") filed a voluntary Chapter 11 petition on February 28, 1992. The Debtor is an Arizona limited partnership whose sole asset is a 204-room hotel (the "Hotel") in Tucson, Arizona. The general partners of the Debtor are Lawrence Smira, Robert Ewing, Gary Wieser, Saliterman/Goldstein Investments (collectively, the "Paragon Group"), the Paragon Hotel Corporation and C.R.H.C. of Tucson, Inc. ("CRHC"). As a result of an objection to the petition and motion to dismiss filed by CRHC, an Amended Petition Commencing Involuntary Case Against Partnership was filed on April 1, 1992. An order for relief was entered on June 30, 1992.

Connecticut General is the Debtor's largest and only nongovernmental secured creditor. It holds a secured lien against the Hotel in the sum of $8,597,300 as of the petition date. Connecticut General's claim is evidenced, *inter alia,* by a promissory note dated December 5, 1981, in the original sum of $7,500,000 and a deed of trust and security agreement executed on the same date. The note provides for monthly install-ments of principal and interest calculated at the rate of 14 percent per annum, together with additional interest equal to 20 percent of the "gross annual room revenues" of the Hotel in excess of $3,100,000. The note further provides for payment of interest at a specified default rate following a default by the Debtor.

The Debtor defaulted on its obligation to Connecticut General in the summer of 1991. Since that time the Debtor has not made any payments of principal or interest to Connecticut General.

Both the Paragon Group and CRHC filed plans of reorganization. The Paragon Plan contains eight classes of claims and interests. It purports to capitalize all outstanding principal and non-default rate interest on Connecticut General's claim as of the effec-tive date of the Paragon Plan and to pay such claim over a seven-year period, with interest at the prime rate plus 1½ percent, based on a 25-year amortization schedule. It is undisputed that Connecticut General's claim is impaired under the Paragon Plan. Connecticut General voted to reject the Paragon Plan.

The Paragon Plan pays all other creditors in full. It pays all of the Class 6 general unsecured claims in cash, but delays payment for a period of 30 days, with interest paid on such claims at the prime rate.

The CRHC Plan also impairs Connecticut General's claim and proposes to pay all other creditors in full. It proposes to repay the Connecticut General loan at a base inter-est rate of 10 percent and offers Connecticut General a 40 percent participation in net cash flow and in the net proceeds of any sale or refinancing of the Hotel. The CRHC Plan proposes to remove the Paragon Group as the managing general partner of the Debtor, to install an affiliate of CRHC to operate the Hotel and to reduce the Paragon Group's aggregate ownership share in the Debtor from 45 percent to 22.5 percent. Connecticut General voted to accept the CRHC Plan.

Both plans propose to utilize all available cash of the estate as of the effective date. The Paragon Plan proposes to pay all creditors other than Connecticut General, imple-ment a capital improvement plan and distribute all of the excess cash to the Debtor's general and limited partners. The CRHC Plan proposes to use the cash to pay all credi-tors, implement a capital improvement plan and reinstate the claim of Connecticut General.

[T]he bankruptcy court entered an order confirming the Paragon Plan and denying confirmation of the CRHC Plan. Connecticut General [appealed].

DISCUSSION

Whether a Properly Impaired Class Has Accepted the Plan

On the merits, Connecticut General asserts that the Paragon Plan should not have been confirmed because no properly impaired class accepted it. Under Bankruptcy Code ("Code") Section 1129(a)(10), a plan cannot be confirmed unless at least one "impaired class" accepts the plan, excluding acceptance by any insider. Connecticut General contends that the only reason the Paragon Plan paid the Class 6 general unse-cured creditors 30 days after the effective date was to create an artificially impaired class[,] which would vote for the plan. Connecticut General maintains that the Debtor had sufficient cash on the effective date to pay Class 6 claims at that time. It cites several cases holding that an alteration intended only to create an impaired class to vote for a plan so that a debtor can effectuate a cramdown will not be allowed.

Although it appears that the 30-day wait was employed solely to create a slightly impaired class to vote on the plan, a recent Ninth Circuit Court of Appeals case found a similar action permissible. In *L & J Anaheim Associates*, 995 F.2d at 943, a secured creditor's rights and remedies under the Uniform Commercial Code were abrogated by that creditor's plan purporting to sell the creditor's collateral at public auction. The court in *L & J Anaheim Associates* noted that the plain language of Section 1124 states that a creditor's claim is "impaired" unless its rights are left "unaltered" by the plan. The court interpreted the language in Section 1124 as Congress's way of defining impairment in the broadest possible terms. The court found no suggestion that only alterations of a particular kind or degree can constitute impairment. The court concluded that the narrow question that arises is whether a creditor's legal, equitable or contractual rights were changed by the plan. If so, its claim is considered impaired.

The court then looked at the appellant's argument that the general rule defining impairment should not be used abusively, as where the plan proponent enhances its own position, then attempts to use this fact to show impairment and so cram down the rest of the creditors. The Court of Appeals held that abuses on the part of a plan proponent ought not affect the application of Congress's definition of impairment. Rather, such abuses should be addressed by the bankruptcy court by denying confirmation on the ground that the plan has not been proposed in good faith. The Court of Appeals concluded that the bankruptcy court's finding that the plan was proposed in good faith was not clearly erroneous. In sum, *L & J Anaheim Associates* holds that a plan proponent's motivations will not be questioned in determining whether a class is impaired under Section 1129(a)(10), but will be examined in deciding whether a plan was proposed in bad faith.

This Ninth Circuit case is binding on the Panel, while cases such as *Windsor on the River Associates, supra,* have persuasive authority only. Aside from our duty to follow Ninth Circuit precedent, we find the reasoning in *L & J Anaheim Associates* more convincing than that in the Eighth Circuit case of *Windsor on the River Associates.* The Eighth Circuit held that a claim is not impaired if the alteration of rights arises solely from the plan proponent's exercise of discretion. The court determined that two classes in the debtor's plan were not impaired, because the plan could have provided for these classes in full on the effective date if it had paid $100,000 less to the secured creditor.

We do not believe it is the bankruptcy court's role to ask whether alternative payment structures could produce a different scenario in regard to impairment of classes. Denying confirmation on the basis that another type of plan would produce different results would impede desired flexibility for plan proponents and create additional complications in the already complex process of plan confirmation. Moreover, nowhere does the Code require a plan proponent to use all efforts to create unimpaired classes. Such a requirement should not be imposed by judicial fiat.

The Paragon Plan provided that payment to the Class 6 general unsecured creditors would be delayed for 30 days. Therefore, based on *L & J Anaheim Associates*, the class was impaired. The ability of the Debtor to pay that class on the effective date does not alter that analysis. However, the necessity for the delay in payment may be considered in determining if Paragon proposed its plan in good faith.

Whether the Plan Was Proposed in Good Faith

Connecticut General argues that the Paragon Plan was proposed in a bad faith attempt to artificially impair the Class 6 claims and to benefit the Debtor's general and limited partners. The Debtor responds that because the issue of bad faith was not raised in the bankruptcy court, the issue should not be considered on appeal. Contrary to the Debtor's assertion, the issue was expressly raised in the bankruptcy court, on page 11 of Connecticut General's objection to the Paragon Plan. [The Panel goes on to find, however, that the Bankruptcy Court did not make any findings regarding good faith, and remands the case for such a finding.] On remand the court should recognize that the act of impairment in an attempt to gerrymander a voting class of creditors is indicative of bad faith.

Remanded.

II. CASE STUDY: *IN RE TEXAS RANGERS* BANKRUPTCY (OR "HOW NOLAN RYAN TRIED TO STEAL HOME, BUT WAS FORCED TO TAG UP ON MARK CUBAN'S SACRIFICE FLY")

What do you need if you want to play in the big leagues? You need a team. You need a stadium. And you need parking. (And as we'll see in some later cases, you need broadcast rights.) The story of the Texas Rangers bankruptcy is a tale of the problems that can arise when the team, stadium, and parking lots are held by different entities.

The Texas Rangers baseball club began life in Washington, D.C., in 1961 as the second incarnation of the Washington Senators franchise (the original Senators franchise having decamped for Minneapolis-St. Paul in 1960). In 1972, the new Senators franchise moved to Arlington, Texas, and was rechristened as the Rangers. The team went through a series of owners, including later president George W. Bush. In 1998, Bush and his partners sold the team to Thomas Hicks, a private equity mogul. Hicks acquired not only the Rangers franchise, but the lease on the stadium (the Ballpark in Arlington, owned by the City of Arlington, Texas), and the parking lots that sit between the Ballpark and the Dallas Cowboys AT&T stadium.

Under Hicks's ownership, the Rangers signed many long-term large-dollar contracts with players, including a record 10-year $252 million deal with shortstop Alex Rodriguez. Yet the Rangers were never profitable the entire time they were owned by Hicks, who advanced over $100 million to support the team. The result was that by 2010, the Rangers were the most indebted franchise in Major League Baseball and in violation of the League's debt service rules, which limit the level of team indebtedness.

Hicks's ownership of the Rangers was through a number of intermediate entities. Hicks owned the Hicks Sports Group (HSG), which owned a pair of partnerships, the Rangers Equity Holding General Partnership (REH GP) and Rangers Equity Holding Limited Partnership LP (REH LP) (collectively the "Rangers Equity Owners"). REHGP owned a 1% interest in the Texas Rangers Baseball Partners (TRBP), which held the franchise. REHLP owned a 99% interest in TRBP. TRBP in turn owned the Rangers Ballpark LLC, which held the lease to the Ballpark. HSG also owned the Dallas Stars National Hockey League franchise, the Liverpool FC soccer team, and an entity called Ballpark Real Estate LLC (BRE), which owned or leased 154 acres of parking lots near the Rangers stadium. Figure 35.1, below, illustrates the ownership structure.

HSG had borrowed some $525 million from a consortium of lenders led by JPMorgan (the Lenders). The loan was guaranteed by the Rangers Equity Owners, TRBP, Rangers Ballpark LLC, and the Stars. The loan was secured by first and second liens on all assets, including the equity of the HSG subsidiaries. The guaranty from TRBP was capped at $75 million per MLB regulations, and a similar cap existed from the Stars guaranty, but the guaranties from the Rangers Equity Owners and Rangers Ballpark LLC were uncapped. The loan agreement also gave the Lenders the right to veto any sale of the Rangers franchise.

The financial crisis in 2008 put strains on HSG's ability to service the loan while also funding the Rangers. HSG defaulted on the loan in May 2009. TRBP—not HSG—received a $18 million bridge loan from MLB via a third lien loan in order to enable it to make payroll. As a condition of the funding, MLB insisted that the team

Figure 35.1 Texas Rangers Corporate Structure

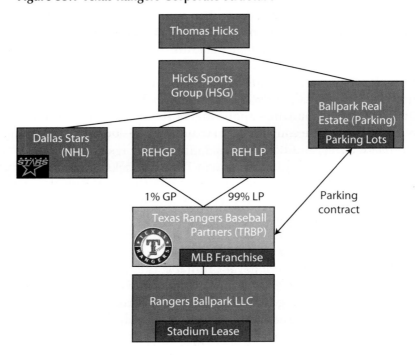

be put up for sale. MLB franchise rules required both the Commissioner of Baseball and the majority of MLB franchise owners to approve the new owner. Figure 35.2, below, shows the situation following the MLB loan.

In November 2009, the team was put up for auction. Rangers Baseball Express (Express), an entity led by former Rangers' star pitcher and current TRBP president Nolan Ryan, was mistakenly named the winner of the auction: A competing bid was actually higher, but its value was miscalculated. MLB, however, considered Ryan the winner and refused to back away from support of Ryan's bid. MLB believed that having a former star owning a team was good for baseball generally. The Lenders, led by JPMorgan, refused to consent to the sale to Express because they did not think the sale was producing the top price for the time. Hicks was proposing selling Express the Rangers together with the sale by BRE of a 47-acre parcel of land comprised of parking lots between the Rangers' ballpark and the Cowboys' stadium for $300 million, $270 million of which would go to the Lenders. Hicks argued that because the Lenders had no claim against BRE, they should not benefit from the proceeds of the sale attributable to the parking lots. The Lenders refused to consent to the sale because they thought Hicks was attributing too much value to the parking lots, and also giving Nolan Ryan a sweetheart deal on the team.

MLB, however, was playing hardball (what else?). In April 2010, MLB Commissioner Bud Selig threw a "brushback" at the lenders, publicly stating, "As part of the Texas Rangers sale process, Tom Hicks selected the Chuck Greenberg/ Nolan Ryan group as the chosen bidder on December 15, 2009, and entered into an exclusive agreement with that group. Major League Baseball is currently in control of the sale process and will use all efforts to achieve a closing with the chosen bidder. Any deviation from or interference with the agreed upon sale process by Mr. Hicks or any other party, or any actions in violation of MLB rules or directives will be dealt with appropriately by the Commissioner." Thus, at the end of the first it was all tied up: The Lenders would not agree on a sale to Ryan, and MLB would not agree on a sale to anyone else.

At this point, Hicks threw a change-up. Hicks decided to use bankruptcy to force a sale in the face of the Lenders' veto. On May 25, 2010, TRBP filed for bankruptcy with a "prepackaged" plan, not requiring post-bankruptcy solicitation of votes. TRBP's plan was to sell the team and the stadium lease—but not the parking lots—to Express in bankruptcy and distribute the proceeds: "The primary purpose of the Prepackaged Plan is to bridge the impasse between TRBP and the Lenders under the HSG Credit Agreement and to effectuate the sale of the Texas Rangers franchise and certain related assets to the Purchaser in order to satisfy TRBP's creditors in full."

Just before the bankruptcy filing, on May 23, 2010, TRBP engaged in a flurry of other transactions. Among them, TRBP caused the Rangers Ballpark LLC to assign its lease on the ballpark to TRBP in exchange for $10 and an assumption of lease liabilities. Thomas O. Hicks, Jr. signed for both parties.

The purpose of this transfer was to take advantage of TRBP's capped guarantee liability. Both TRBP and Rangers Ballpark LLC were guarantors of HSG's debt, but the guaranty from TRBP was capped at $75 million, while the guaranty from Rangers Ballpark LLC was uncapped. The TRBP cap did not much matter to the Lenders as

Figure 35.2 Texas Rangers Capital Structure

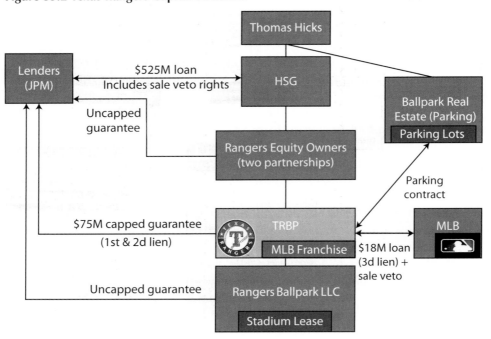

long as the Rangers Ballpark LLC's guaranty was uncapped because the Rangers could not play ball without a park. In late May the baseball season is already in full swing, so the Rangers could not easily find a replacement ballpark. Functionally, then, TRBP was uncapped, as TRBP had to make sure that Rangers Ballpark LLC could pay out on its guaranty in order for the ballclub to keep playing. Transferring the stadium lease from the uncapped guarantor Rangers Ballpark LLC to the capped guarantor TRBP meant that TRBP would formally *and functionally* be liable to the Lenders for only $75 million of the sale proceeds. Figure 35.3 shows the state of things if the sale to Ryan was consummated after the transfer of the stadium lease.

Hicks and Ryan thought the plan would slide through safely. TRBP obtained debtor-in-possession financing from MLB to provide liquidity during the bankruptcy, which was intended to be little more than a very fast sale of the team without an auction to Express, with the sale proceeds then doled out according to liquidation priority. According to the plan, *no creditors were impaired*, and thus no creditors had the right to vote on the plan. That meant that the Lenders would have little room to object. They would be paid the full $75 million of TRBP's capped guaranty from the sale proceeds, but they would not be able to exercise their sale veto, and would not be able to raise objections under sections 1129(a)(7) (best interests) or 1129(b) (cramdown). After the sale, there would be no other value left in Rangers Ballpark LLC or TRBP, and thus none in the Rangers Equity Owners.

Why would Hicks have offered Ryan this sort of sweetheart deal? One can only speculate, but the answer likely lies with the parking lots, the fate of which we shall return to later in our story. Suffice it to say for now that anything TRBP got for the ballclub and stadium was going to have to be paid to the Lenders, irrespective of

Figure 35.3 Texas Rangers Proposed Post-Transaction Structure

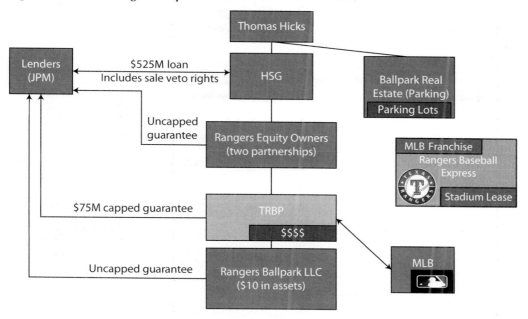

the capped guaranty, because the Lenders were guaranteed by the Rangers Equity Owners, which owned the stock in the ballclub. Unless the ballclub promptly spent the sale proceeds, the Lenders would be able to collect via the guarantor partnerships. But to the extent that Hicks recovered value from the sale of the parking lots, the Lenders had no claim on it. Hicks could keep it all. Hicks might have been willing to facilitate a sweetheart deal for Ryan for the ballclub with the understanding that Ryan would pay top dollar for the parking lots.

Of course, that deal would have been contingent on Ryan actually getting a sweetheart price on the Rangers, and the Lenders weren't throwing in the towel. First, they argued that they were in fact impaired and thus entitled to vote. The Lenders claimed impairment based on being denied their contractual right to veto the sale.

In re **Texas Rangers Baseball Partners**

434 B.R. 393 (Bankr. N.D. Tex. 2010)

D. MICHAEL LYNN, U.S. Bankr. J.

D. IMPAIRMENT

. . .

1. The Lenders

Debtor argues that, by providing in the Plan for payment of the capped amount of its guaranty ($75,000,000), it has left the Lenders unimpaired under Code §1124(1).

The Lenders, on the other hand, assert that, in order for them to be unimpaired under section 1124(1) they must retain all their rights under the Loan Agreement, the Pledge Agreement and their other credit documents, including their rights under sections 4.4.1(c)(i)(3) and 4.4.2(b)(i) of the Pledge Agreement. This, in turn, according to the Lenders, requires that, for them to be unimpaired, they must have the ability to veto sale of the Rangers under the APA.

Section 1124 defines impairment as being any treatment other than treatment as provided by section 1124(1) or (2). Prior to 1994,* payment in full and in cash of a claim also constituted unimpaired treatment. Since the 1994 amendment of section 1124, some courts have held that payment of a claim in full in cash constitutes unimpaired treatment so long as post-petition interest is also paid on the claim. [Citations omitted.]

The court in general agrees with these decisions. A claim is to be quantified "as of the date of the filing of the petition." Code §502(b). Thus, if a creditor receives under a plan everything to which the creditor would be entitled in a judgment entered immediately following the plan's effective date, the creditor is receiving treatment that, as required by section 1124(1), honors all the creditor's "legal, equitable, and contractual rights." For the typical unsecured creditor, those rights equate to payment of the debt owed with interest as allowed by law.

The Lenders, however, have rights *vis-à-vis* Debtor other than just payment of the $75,000,000 for which Debtor is obligated to them. Debtor is part of the HSG family of entities, and, as such, it has assumed obligations to the Lenders in addition to the guaranty.** In order for the Lenders to be unimpaired, their treatment under a plan must recognize and preserve those rights. In the context presented to the court, this, in turn, presents the question of whether a plan providing for the sale of the Rangers, to leave the Lenders unimpaired, must give effect to sections 4.4.1(c)(i)(3) and 4.4.2(b)(i) of the Pledge Agreement. In other words, must the plan grant the Lenders an effective veto over any proposed sale of the Rangers? The court concludes section 1124(1) does not so require.

First, unlike treatment under section 1124(2), section 1124(1) is prospective: section 1124(1) does not require that a plan provide for the cure of defaults—i.e., recreation of the situation as it was before default. Rather it requires that, as of the plan's effective date, an unimpaired creditor be able thereafter to exercise all its rights *vis-à-vis* its debtor. Under the Plan (presumably including any amended version), the sale of the Rangers will occur on the effective date. *See* Plan §§1.34, 6.1(a) and 10.1. Thereafter, the Lenders, if treated under section 1124(1), must be able to exercise their rights under their loan documents *vis-à-vis* Debtor (though those rights may have lost much of their usefulness) and other members of the HSG family.

As the sale of the Rangers will have been consummated at that point, however, the Lenders' rights under the Pledge Agreement will not affect the sale. As would be the

---

* Section 1124(3), which deemed a creditor unimpaired if it received full cash payment on the effective date of the plan equal to the allowed amount of the claim, was repealed in 1994.—ED.

** These obligations include the obligation to pay taxes and insurance, remain in existence, not change corporate form, etc.—ED.

case with a breach outside of bankruptcy, except to the extent the Code excuses such a breach as a matter of law, if the Lenders are damaged by the actions of Debtor or the Rangers Equity Owners or their parents through a pre-effective date failure to honor the Lenders' rights under section 4.4.1(c)(i)(3) or 4.4.2(b)(i), they may assert in this court a claim against Debtor for their damages or pursue its affiliates in an appropriate forum.

Secondly, the preceding analysis is supported by applying the ordinary rules of statutory construction to Code § 1124. . . .

When construing two provisions in such close proximity as subsections (1) and (2) of section 1124, the court must assume the legislature had good reasons for the differences between them. Thus, the fact that Congress provided in section 1124(2) that unimpaired treatment must include cure of most defaults but did not do so in section 1124(1) indicates that the intent of legislators was that unimpaired treatment under the latter provision would include, once that treatment became effective, allowing the class so treated to pursue remedies not otherwise in conflict with the Code, the plan or bankruptcy court orders for defaults existing as of the effective date.

Two illustrations will assist in explaining the court's construction of section 1124(1). A party to an agreement to purchase property of the debtor, which purchaser has a contractual right to specific performance as an alternative to damages, could be treated as unimpaired under section 1124(1) even if the property subject to the agreement were sold during the debtor's case or pursuant to the plan. That creditor would be entitled post-effective date to pursue a claim against the debtor just as it could have absent bankruptcy if the debtor defaulted such that specific performance of the sale agreement had become impossible.

Likewise, a party that is the beneficiary of an *ipso facto* clause, e.g., giving it rights upon commencement of a bankruptcy case, if treated under section 1124(1) could enforce the *ipso facto* clause after the plan's effective date to the extent the bankruptcy filing default survived under the parties' agreement. Enforcement of the clause post-effective date, however, could not affect transactions authorized by confirmation of the plan or that occurred in the debtor's case prior to the effective date. Likewise, that the plan provided treatment allowing post-effective date enforcement of the *ipso facto* clause would not mean its enforcement was allowed for any purposes prior to the effective date, including in connection with acceptance and confirmation of the plan.

Third, to permit [JPMorgan] Chase, acting [as agent] for the Lenders, to exercise the rights under section 4.4.1(c)(i)(3) or 4.4.2(b)(i) of the Pledge Agreement prior to the effective date, while Debtor and its owners are in the custody of the court, would give the Lenders a degree of control over the conduct of this case that is inconsistent with the Code and contrary to public policy. At the Hearing the Lenders agreed that a trustee appointed in this case could sell the Rangers without regard to the provisions of the Pledge Agreement. As a sale of the Rangers, whether under Code § 363 or under a plan, by Debtor acting as a debtor-in-possession is a transaction undertaken by Debtor in its role as a fiduciary, it would be inconsistent with the authority and responsibility conferred on that fiduciary by law to give effect to a contractual provision that would frustrate its performance of its fiduciary duties.

Fourth, in order for Chase to utilize section 4.4.1(c)(i)(3) prior to confirmation of the Plan, it would have to obtain relief from the automatic stay of Code § 362(a). Absent such relief, Debtor may deal with the Rangers as is consistent with the other provisions of the Code and court orders. To conclude that section 1124(1) requires allowing invocation of Pledge Agreement §4.4.1(c)(i)(3) or 4.4.2(b)(i) prior to the effective date of a plan would be tantamount to requiring, for compliance with section 1124(1), allowing enforcement by a creditor of its "legal, equitable, and contractual rights" prior to confirmation of the plan by the court and the binding effectiveness of that creditor's plan treatment.

Fifth, in the instant case, if the Lenders can utilize section 4.4.1(c)(i)(3) (or section 4.4.2(b)(i)) to block a sale, Debtor, a solvent entity, notwithstanding payment in full of all of its monetary obligations, could only confirm a plan that was acceptable to the Lenders or through cramdown by artificial impairment of another class of creditors. Given the impasse reached between the BOC and the Lenders, that would mean Debtor would have to artificially impair some class of creditors so that it satisfies the requirement for invocation of section 1129(b)(1) of the Code that one impaired class of creditors has accepted the proposed plan (Code § 1129(a)(10)). It would be inconsistent with public policy to construe the Code in a fashion that encourages debtors to deal with creditors by artificial impairment when such creditors could otherwise be left unimpaired.

For the foregoing reasons, the court concludes that treatment of the Lenders, to satisfy section 1124(1), must grant them their rights under their loan documents prospectively. While payment of the $75,000,000 plus interest will satisfy and discharge Debtor's monetary obligations as required by section 1124(1), in order for the Plan to be confirmed without the acceptance of the Lenders or satisfaction of Code § 1129(b)(1), the treatment of the Lenders must be modified to allow them to exercise their rights under their loan documents following the effective date.

Thus, the Bankruptcy Court gave the Lenders a Pyrrhic victory on the question of their own impairment. The Lenders were in fact impaired, but TRBP would be able to modify the proposed plan so that the Lenders' veto right would be reinstated . . . after the effective date of the plan, meaning after the sale. The Lenders would no longer be impaired, but their veto rights would be meaningless with the sale already completed. Not surprisingly, TRBP came back with an amended plan that provided: "On and after the Effective Date, the holders of Allowed [First or Second] Lien Holder Claims shall retain all existing contractual rights against the Debtor or its affiliates to which they are entitled under the [First or Second] Lien Credit Agreement and related documents." Fourth Amended Plan.

The Lenders had one more trick: They threw a spitball and filed involuntary bankruptcy petitions against the Rangers Equity Owners. The effect of the involuntary petitions was to trigger a shift in the fiduciary duties of the Rangers Equity Owners. Outside of bankruptcy, the Rangers Equity Owners owed fiduciary duties to their equityholders—other Hicks entities—but not to their creditors. Thus, outside of bankruptcy, the Rangers Equity Owners had no duty to maximize the value of assets for creditors. In bankruptcy, however, the Rangers Equity Owners picked up fiduciary duties to creditors as well. This meant that their assent to the TRBP sale had to be undertaken consistent with these duties. But the assent of the Rangers Equity Owners was only necessary to the extent *they* were impaired. Otherwise, they would have no vote on the plan.

In re Texas Rangers Baseball Partners
434 B.R. 393 (Bankr. N.D. Tex. 2010)

D. MICHAEL LYNN, U.S. Bankr. J.

. . .

D. IMPAIRMENT

. . .

2. The Rangers Equity Owners

Debtor takes the position that, as REHLP and REHGP will retain their interests in Debtor under the Plan, they are unimpaired. Even if the Plan impairs equity, however, Debtor points to the prepetition consent by REHLP and REHGP and urges that the court conclude this amounts to acceptance of the Plan.

Even if the Plan had not been modified, the court could not agree with Debtor. Under the Partnership Agreement, Debtor's governing document, sale of the Rangers is a "major decision." Partnership Agreement § 4.3(b). A major decision cannot be taken except with approval of a majority of the partners. Partnership Agreement § 4.3. Had a plan been proposed post-petition which called for sale of the Rangers, the plan would clearly have impaired the owners of Debtor's equity. As to the argument that the Rangers Equity Owners' prepetition consents satisfy the requirement of acceptance of the Plan, the requirements under the Code for counting a prepetition acceptance are different from the prerequisites for a consent under the Partnership Agreement.[38] For example, Code § 1126(b) sets disclosure requirements that must be met to count a prepetition acceptance in determining whether to confirm a plan.

In any case, in the case at bar, even if the court assumed that the prepetition approval of the Plan by the Rangers Equity Owners satisfied the requirement of their acceptance of it, the post-petition changes to the Plan require, at a minimum, affording the Rangers Equity Owners the opportunity to change their votes, as required by Code § 1127(d). As modifications already made to the Plan provide for payment of interest to both the Lenders and other unsecured creditors, the return to equity will necessarily be reduced by the amount of that interest not previously provided for in the Plan. As this change clearly "adversely change[s] the treatment [under the Plan] of . . . the interest[s] of . . .

---

38. Although the Partnership Agreement would permit approval of a sale of the Rangers by a simple majority of the partners, if the sale were to be accomplished pursuant to a plan, acceptance by the $2/_3$ majority required by Code § 1126(d) would be necessary.

equity security holder[s]," the modifications to the Plan cannot be "deemed accepted" under FED. R. BANKR. P. 3019(a). While under that rule effecting the modification, if it were accepted in writing by both REHLP and REHGP, would not require compliance with section 1127(d), such acceptance by REHGP and REHLP would be acts respecting property of their estates outside the ordinary course of business. As the court has made section 363 applicable in their cases, their acceptance of the modifications of the Plan will require court approval.

Because the Lenders and the Rangers Equity Owners are impaired, the Plan, even as modified on June 17, cannot be confirmed on the basis that no class of creditors or equity owners is impaired. Moreover, while the impairment of the Lenders may be cured, without significant changes to the Plan, that of the Rangers Equity Owners cannot be avoided and they must be allowed to elect whether to accept or reject the Plan. In making that election, the Rangers Equity Owners [being in bankruptcy] will have to seek court approval, acting in their fiduciary capacities outside the ordinary course of business.

Forced to act as fiduciaries for the Lenders, the Ranger Equity Owners were not able to approve the sale without an auction. Thus, the Lenders got what they wanted: an auction. MLB had wanted to avoid a real auction for the Rangers. MLB benefitted from having Ryan owning the Rangers, but got nothing from a higher sale price once the $75 million first lien guaranty was paid off and its $19 million loan was repaid. The Lenders, in contrast, needed an auction process to be confident that they were getting the best possible price from the Rangers. Even though their guaranty from the Rangers was capped, they could still look to the Rangers Equity Owners to collect any surplus (although that would come after TRBP's various debt obligations, including MLB's $19 million third lien loan, were repaid).

Thus, at 2:45 P.M. on August 4, 2010, the Texas Rangers, then in first place in the American League West, were placed on the auction block. Express was the stalking horse bidder at the auction, meaning that any bid had to top Express's to win. Express's opening bid was for $300 million. Only one other bidder showed up at the auction: billionaire Mark Cuban, the owner of the Dallas Mavericks, and the bad boy of American sports ownership. Cuban had been trying for some time to acquire a Major League Baseball team, but without success. Cuban came in with a higher bid . . . *financed by the Lenders!* The auction continued with repeated rounds of bidding until 12:45 A.M. on August 5. At that point, Cuban had bid the price up to $390 million. Ryan's top bid was only $385 million. Cuban's bid was discounted for various factors, however, including the possibility that his ownership would not be approved by the MLB Commissioner and MLB owners.

At the end of the season here were the standings:

In first place were the Texas Rangers. The Rangers used the DIP financing they obtained from MLB to trade for star pitcher Cliff Lee. The Rangers then went on to win the 2010 American League Championship, but lost to the San Francisco Giants in the World Series.

In second place was MLB. MLB got a financially healthy franchise and the baseball celebrity owner it wanted, and its loans were repaid in full.

Tied for third were Ryan and the Lenders. Nolan Ryan ended up owning the Texas Rangers and the stadium lease, but had to pay $85 million more than he had originally hoped, a 28% premium due to the auction. But Ryan still did not own the parking lots. The Rangers had had a land use agreement with BRE that required the Rangers to pay for security, property taxes, insurance, maintenance, and BRE's lease costs for those lots that BRE leased from the city of Arlington. Under the agreement, the Rangers would get the parking profits, and BRE would receive some profits from nonbaseball revenue (such as Dallas Cowboys game parking revenue). In February 2011, Hicks notified the Rangers that he was terminating the arrangement. Rangers parking prices had been kept artificially low to boost attendance, but with the team and lots under separate ownership, such a "loss leader" arrangement no longer made sense for Hicks. Hicks sought to increase his payments from the Rangers from $1.3 million annually to $3.5 million annually. The Rangers sued Hicks for wrongfully terminating the land use arrangement. By the beginning of the 2012 season, the litigation seemed to have settled, as the Rangers had reached a multi-year agreement for operation of the parking lots. In April 2013, Hicks sold the Rangers 55 acres of stadium parking lots, and a year later, Hicks sold the Rangers a 17.6-acre mobile home park near the stadium. To finance the purchase of the lots, the Rangers borrowed $60 million.

The Lenders recovered $75 million from the auction proceeds from TRBP. The Lenders also recovered all the excess cash from the sale—$197 million—via their involuntary bankruptcies against the Ranger Equity Owners. But the Lenders got caught in a structural subordination squeeze play. If TRBP's guaranty had not been capped, the Lenders would have received the full $385 million of sale proceeds. Instead, because of the cap, the Lenders had first dibs on $75 million, with MLB getting the next $19 million, and then TRBP's unsecured creditors—including its players—getting paid next before any distribution was made to the Rangers Equity Owners and thus to the Lenders on account of the Rangers Equity Owners' uncapped guaranty of the Lenders. The unsecured creditors of TRBP were paid some $94 million, so the Lenders lost out on $113 million because of the guaranty cap.

Or did they? MLB and Express would surely have insisted on payment to the players as part of the sale if there hadn't been the guaranty cap. Ryan surely wasn't going to buy a team of disgruntled, unpaid players. As with the *Chrysler* bankruptcy, the formal priority of labor (or any other critical supplier) may not matter as much as the leverage it can exert. Indeed, to extend the *Chrysler* analogy, MLB acted in the Rangers' bankruptcy much like the U.S. government in the Chrysler bankruptcy. Neither wanted a meaningful auction process because neither was interested in maximizing recoveries in the bankruptcy. Instead, both had outside, non-creditor interests that dictated their behavior—the economic stability of the United States or the "best interests of baseball."

Next comes Hicks. Hicks's sports empire disintegrated. In October 2010, Hicks sold Liverpool FC and Anfield stadium to a group that included former Boston Red Sox owner John Henry. In 2011, the Dallas Stars filed for bankruptcy and were sold.

And Mark Cuban? Cuban still does not have a MLB franchise. But he did appear on *Dancing with the Stars*.

III. CURE AND REINSTATEMENT

There is an important exception to the rule that any alteration in legal rights constitutes impairment. Section 1124(2) permits the debtor to unwind any acceleration of a defaulted debt, cure and reinstate the debt under a plan, and have the claim associated with that debt be treated as unimpaired. This statutory provision is separate and apart from any reinstatement terms that might be in a loan contract. Cure requirements are determined in reference to the applicable non-bankruptcy law, but with an important exception. No cure is required of defaults under *ipso facto* clauses—clauses triggered by the debtor's bankruptcy or insolvency. 11 U.S.C. §§ 1124(2)(A), 365(b)(2).

The ability to deaccelerate, cure, and reinstate provides debtors with a powerful tool, enabling them to use the time in bankruptcy, to cure defaults. Thus, a debtor with a liquidity problem can file for bankruptcy, and once its liquidity situation has been resolved, it can deaccelerate, cure, and reinstate an obligation under a plan. This means that the debtor can miss regularly scheduled debt payments during bankruptcy and catch up with a cure and reinstatement under a plan. Reinstatement also enables debtors to retain favorable pre-bankruptcy financing arrangements. Thus, if market interest rates have risen since the debtor's pre-bankruptcy financing, the debtor may want to cure and reinstate defaulted debts rather than find new market-rate financing (if it is available at all).

Reinstatement also enables the plan proponent to reshape the bankruptcy electorate. If a debt is cured and reinstated, then the creditor is deemed unimpaired and therefore is conclusively deemed to have accepted a plan. 11 U.S.C. § 1126(f). Cure and reinstatement can thus deprive a creditor of its vote, enabling the debtor to force a plan on the creditor.

Problem Set 35

(1) Which of the following creditors are impaired under a plan?

    a. The plan provides for a creditor to be paid $19,800 on a $20,000 claim. 11 U.S.C. § 1124.

    b. The plan provides for a creditor to be paid $20 million on a $20 million claim, but with payment made a week after the payment was due contractually. 11 U.S.C. § 1124.

    c. The plan provides for a creditor to be paid $20 million on a $20 million claim, but paid in euros, rather than in U.S. dollars, as the contract requires. 11 U.S.C. § 1124.

    d. The plan cures and maintains payments on the creditor's debt, but changes a choice of law provision. 11 U.S.C. § 1124.

e. The plan cures a default on a creditor's $30 million, 5-year loan, but a debt limitation covenant is changed to allow for greater borrowing. 11 U.S.C. § 1124.

f. The plan cures a default on a creditor's $30 million, 5-year loan, but a debt limitation covenant is changed to allow for less borrowing. 11 U.S.C. § 1124.

g. The plan cures and reinstates the creditor's debt, but provides for the issuance of new debt that is senior to the creditor's debt. The creditor's debt contract allowed for the issuance of senior debt. 11 U.S.C. § 1124.

h. The plan cures and reinstates the creditor's debt, but provides for the issuance of new debt that is junior to the creditor's debt. The creditor's debt contract is silent about debt limitations. 11 U.S.C. § 1124.

i. The plan provides for the creditor's lien on subdivision 13B to be replaced by a lien on subdivision 13C. Subdivisions 13B and 13C are all but identical, but subdivision 13B is contiguous with another plot of land (subdivision 13A) that the debtor owns free and clear and wishes to develop together with 13B. 11 U.S.C. § 1124.

j. The plan pays one-fifth of the former CEO's claim for wrongful termination of a five-year employment contract. 11 U.S.C. § 502(b)(7).

k. The plan cures and reinstates an unsecured note that includes a negative pledge clause that forbids the creation of any "additional liens." During the bankruptcy, the court approved a financing agreement under section 364(c) that gave liens on some of the debtor's assets to Alpha Corp. The plan includes an exit financing provision that calls for Alpha Corp.'s debtor-in-possession financing facility to roll over into a post-bankruptcy financing facility, with a renewal of the liens. 11 U.S.C. § 1124; *Texas Ranger Partners.*

(2) Is a common shareholder impaired in the following scenarios?

a. The shareholder's equity stake in the company is diluted under the plan. 11 U.S.C. § 1124.

b. The plan provides for the debtor to issue warrants that can be converted into common stock during a limited time period, but that will only be converted if the share price is favorable. 11 U.S.C. § 1124.

c. The shareholder's option to match any bid for the debtor's assets is suspended during bankruptcy. 11 U.S.C. § 1124.

d. A plan is confirmed with a two-thirds majority vote of a class of common shareholders when the debtor's corporate bylaws require a three-quarters majority vote for all major corporate transactions. 11 U.S.C. § 1124.

e. The plan issues new, longer-term debt securities of a face amount greater than the pre-petition debt of the firm. 11 U.S.C. § 1124.

j. The plan inserts a poison pill into the company's bylaws, such that if there is ever a change of control of the company, it will trigger a massive issuance of equity, thereby diluting existing shareholders. 11 U.S.C. § 1124.

(3) Siliconia Chemical Products, a specialty chemical manufacturer, is in Chapter 11 bankruptcy. Siliconia's debts include $1.1 billion in first lien notes. The first lien notes' Indenture permits Siliconia to redeem them prior to maturity, but includes a "make-whole" provision that provides that in the event of a pre-maturity redemption,

Siliconia is obligated to pay the first lien noteholders an amount that approximates the present value of the spread between a premium above an index interest rate and the interest rate on the first lien notes, applied to the outstanding balance on the notes for the remaining maturity of the Notes. At the time of the bankruptcy filing, there were seven years left before the maturity date of the first lien notes. Six months later, Siliconia has proposed a plan that would pay its first lien noteholders $1.16 billion in cash on the effective date of the plan—an amount equal to the full outstanding principal and all accrued and unpaid interest on the notes, but not including the make-whole, and treat the first lien noteholders as unimpaired. Are the first lien noteholders entitled to vote on the plan? 11 U.S.C. § 1124.

CHAPTER 36

SOLICITATION OF VOTES AND PREPACKAGED PLANS

I. SOLICITATION

Chapter 11 creates a process for parties to negotiate the allocation of going-concern value. Any proposal for the allocation must comply with a set of mandatory legal findings and must also either be approved by a stakeholder vote (conducted by classes) or meet additional legal findings. The stakeholder vote is done against the background of a disclosure regime designed to ensure that stakeholders have adequate information about the debtor. The vote is conducted through a solicitation of acceptances of a proposed plan.

In order to get a plan approved, a plan proponent must solicit "acceptances" (votes) for the plan. Acceptances need only be solicited from impaired creditors and interest holders. Accordingly, if no creditors are impaired, then no solicitation is necessary. As the *Texas Rangers* case shows, leaving a creditor unimpaired is a strategy for preventing that creditor from voting on a plan.

Acceptances may not be solicited absent certain written disclosures about the plan. 11 U.S.C. § 1125(b). What constitutes a "solicitation" is not defined in the Bankruptcy Code, but courts generally interpret the term quite narrowly.

The terms "solicits" and "solicitation," as used in section 1125(b) of the Code, must be interpreted very narrowly to refer only to a specific request for an official vote either accepting or rejecting a plan. The terms do not encompass discussions, exchanges of information, negotiations, or tentative arrangements that may be made by the various parties in interest in a bankruptcy case that may lead to the development of a disclosure statement or plan or information to be included therein. If these activities were prohibited by section 1125(b), meaningful creditor participation in Chapter 11 cases would cease to exist. *In re Snyder*, 51 B.R. 432, 436 (Bankr. D. Utah 1985). Similarly, the Third Circuit Court of Appeals has noted:

> We agree with the district court that "solicitation" must be read narrowly. A broad reading of § 1125 can seriously inhibit free creditor negotiations. All parties agree that [a creditor] is not barred from honestly negotiating with other creditors about its unfiled plan. . . . The purpose of negotiations between creditors is to reach a compromise over the terms of a tentative plan. The purpose of compromise is to win acceptance for the plan. We find no principled, predictable difference between negotiation

and solicitation of future acceptances. We therefore reject any definition of solicitation[,] which might cause creditors to limit their negotiations.

Century Glove Inc. v. First American Bank of New York (In re Century Glove Inc.), 860 F.2d 94, 101-102 (3d Cir. 1988).

In order for the solicitation to be meaningful, the holders of claims and interests require sufficient information about the debtor so that they can make an informed decision about whether to accept a particular plan. The disclosure statement must be approved by the court and must contain "adequate information." 11 U.S.C. § 1125(b). Adequate information is defined in section 1129(a)(1), and it must be sufficient to enable a hypothetical investor typical of a relevant class "to make an informed judgment about the plan." 11 U.S.C. § 1125(a)(1). The disclosure statement must, among other things, discuss the potential tax consequences of the plan. *Id.*

The disclosure statement is typically a major document—100+ pages is not uncommon—and its preparation and approval is a major step in a bankruptcy case. The disclosure statement also serves as a very detailed source of information about a firm: the factors behind its bankruptcy filing, the major events in the reorganization, its assets and liabilities, and its plans for the future.

Different disclosure statements may be made to different classes, given what would constitute "adequate information" for the class. 11 U.S.C. § 1129(c). Critically, solicitations and the adequacy of disclosure statements are governed solely by bankruptcy law and are exempt from federal and state securities laws. 11 U.S.C. §§ 1129(d)-(e).

In re Indianapolis Downs, LLC

486 B.R. 286 (Bankr. D. Del. 2013)

BRENDAN LINEHAN SHANNON, U.S. Bankr. J.

Before the Court is the request of Indianapolis Downs, LLC and Indiana Capital Corp. (collectively, the "Debtors") for confirmation of their Modified Second Amended Joint Plan of Reorganization (the "Plan"). . . . As a threshold matter, [the Oliver Parties, who include senior management and holders of equity and debt instruments of the Debtors, have filed a] motion to designate (the "Motion to Designate") and thus disregard the votes of any creditors that executed a post-petition (but pre-disclosure statement) restructuring support agreement with the Debtors. For the reasons that follow, the Court will deny the Oliver Parties' Motion to Designate. . . .

I. BACKGROUND

[The Debtors operate a racino, with horse track racing and electronic wagering games. The Debtors filed for Chapter 11 in 2011 and operated the business as DIPs. No official committee had been appointed.]

The Restructuring Support Agreement

Following months of negotiations and occasional litigation, the Debtors, Fortress [Investment Group, LLC ("Fortress"), which held a substantial portion of the debtor's second lien and third lien debt,] and the Ad Hoc Second Lien Committee ultimately achieved consensus on a process that provided for a "parallel path" approach to the Debtors' reorganization. The parties agreed on a plan that contemplated that the Debtors would test the market to determine whether bids would be made for their assets at a sufficiently high level that their major creditor constituents would support a sale. As an alternative simultaneous approach, these parties agreed that if the marketing effort failed to produce adequate offers, then the plan would permit the Debtors to proceed with a recapitalization. This "parallel path" approach was embodied in a Restructuring Support Agreement dated April 25, 2012 (the "RSA").

The RSA provides for (i) specific terms of the dual track plan of reorganization described above, including the financial terms of, and creditor treatment under, a potential sale or in the recapitalization transaction; (ii) the requirement that the Debtors propose a plan of reorganization within a time frame set in the RSA; (iii) a prohibition upon any party to the RSA proposing, supporting or voting for a competing plan of reorganization; and (iv) the requirement (enforceable by an order of specific performance) that parties to the RSA vote "yes" for a plan that complies with the RSA. Under its terms, the RSA was binding upon execution by its non-Debtor signatories (basically Fortress and the members of the Ad Hoc Second Lien Committee). The RSA would become binding upon the Debtors only upon approval by the Court of a disclosure statement.

The RSA was filed with the Court on April 25, 2012, immediately after it was executed. The Debtors also filed a proposed Disclosure Statement and accompanying Plan on April 25, 2012. The RSA was described at length in the Debtors' proposed Disclosure Statement.

. . .

III. DISCUSSION

A. The Motion to Designate

1. The Parties' Positions

The Oliver Parties contend that the RSA constituted a wrongful post-petition solicitation of votes on a plan prior to Court approval of a disclosure statement. As a remedy, the Oliver Parties request that the ballots of the parties to the RSA not be counted pursuant to Bankruptcy Code §§ 1125(g) and 1126(e). The result of such designation would be that the Debtors would lack sufficient votes to win confirmation of their Plan.

The Debtors and the Restructuring Support Parties, by contrast, dispute that developing and executing the RSA is a "solicitation" within the meaning of §§ 1125 and 1126. These parties point the Court to case law narrowly defining what constitutes solicitation. They also note that the RSA itself explicitly states that it is not intended to be a solicitation of a plan. RSA at § 6. Further, the Restructuring Support Parties argue that designation of votes is a rare and extreme sanction, which here would have the effect of disregarding ballots cast by the overwhelming majority of these Debtors' creditors in support of the Plan.

2. Analysis

The Court starts as always with applicable provisions of the Bankruptcy Code and Rules. The structure and timeline for the Chapter 11 plan process is well known: a debtor enjoys a limited exclusive period to develop and formulate a plan of reorganization. 11 U.S.C. § 1121(b). When that plan is filed with the Court, it is accompanied by a disclosure statement that is intended to provide stakeholders with "adequate information" to permit a creditor them an informed decision to vote for or against a proposed plan. The statutory scheme for solicitation is laid out in detail in Bankruptcy Code §§ 1125 and 1126:

> (b) An acceptance or rejection of a plan may not be solicited after the commencement of the case under this title from a holder of a claim or interest with respect to such claim or interest, unless at the time of or before such solicitation, there is transmitted to such holder the plan or a summary of the plan, and a written disclosure statement approved, after notice and a hearing, by the court as containing adequate information.

11 U.S.C. § 1125(b). Section 1126 goes on to articulate a potential consequence of failing to comply with § 1125(b), or a sanction for conduct found to be in bad faith:

> (e) On request of a party in interest, and after notice and a hearing, the court may designate any entity whose acceptance or rejection of such plan was not in good faith, or was not solicited or procured in good faith *or in accordance with the provisions of this title*.

11 U.S.C. § 1126(e) (emphasis added). It is the Court's understanding that the Oliver Parties are not contending that the Restructuring Support Parties have acted in bad faith. Rather, the Motion to Designate is premised on the final prong of § 1125(e), and the Oliver Parties' contention that the votes of the Restructuring Support Parties were not obtained "in accordance with the provisions of" Title 11.

The seminal case is this Circuit construing solicitation and the designation of votes is *In re Century Glove*, 860 F.2d 94 (3d Cir. 1988). In that case, the debtor filed a plan and disclosure statement; one of its major creditors, First American Bank ("FAB"), presented an alternative plan to the creditors' committee in hopes of garnering that body's support. *Id.* at 95. The committee decided to support the debtor's plan, and the bankruptcy court later approved the debtor's disclosure statement and permitted solicitation of votes on the plan.

Shortly thereafter, counsel for FAB directly contacted several large creditors "to find out what these creditors thought of the proposed reorganization, and to convince them to vote against the plan." *Id.* FAB later shared a copy of its proposed competing plan, marked "draft." *Id.* Ultimately, FAB and several of the creditors it contacted voted to reject the debtor's plan; the debtor sought to designate their votes, arguing that "FAB has acted in bad faith in procuring these rejections." *Id.* at 96.

The bankruptcy court granted the motion to designate, finding that FAB had violated Bankruptcy Code § 1125(b) when it circulated materials (*viz.*, its draft plan) that were not part of the court-approved disclosure and solicitation package. The district court reversed the bankruptcy court's designation of ballots, on the dual grounds that (i) FAB's circulation of the draft plan did not constitute bad faith and (ii) FAB's actions were more accurately characterized as "negotiations" rather than as a "solicitation" of votes. *Id.* at 97.

The Third Circuit affirmed the district court's ruling, holding that "solicitation must be read narrowly. A broad reading of § 1125 can seriously inhibit free creditor negotiations." *Id.* at 101. The court also rejected the debtor's contention that only court-approved statements could or should be communicated to creditors. *Id.* at 100-101.

The Debtors and the Restructuring Support Parties rely on Chief Judge Houser's comprehensive opinion *In re Heritage Organization, L.L.C.*, 376 B.R. 783 (Bankr. N.D. Tex. 2007). In that case, "after years of litigation," a Chapter 11 trustee and certain major creditors entered into a term sheet embodying key economic terms of a plan; the conforming plan was thereafter filed, and objecting creditors moved to designate the votes of the parties to the term sheet. *Id.* at 787. Citing to *Century Glove*, the court found that the term "solicitation" should be construed very narrowly, in deference to a clear legislative policy encouraging negotiations among creditors and stakeholders in Chapter 11 cases. *Id.* at 792-93.

The court in *Heritage* placed special emphasis on the fact that the creditors who signed the term sheet ultimately were co-proponents of the plan:

> [I]f a creditor believes that it has sufficient information about the case and the available alternatives to jointly propose [a] Chapter 11 plan with another entity (whether that co-proponent is another creditor, the debtor, or a trustee (who also believes that it has sufficient information)), it is absurd to think that the signing of a term sheet by those parties (that contains the material terms of their to-be-filed joint plan and states that the co-proponent creditor(s) will vote for their agreed upon joint plan) is an improper solicitation of votes in accordance with § 1125(b).

Id. at 791. While the Restructuring Support Parties are not co-proponents of the Debtors' Plan, given their significant respective stakes in the Debtors and the Court's own observation of these parties' involvement in these proceedings, precisely the same considerations pertain here as those found persuasive by the court in *Heritage*.

The Oliver Parties place significant weight on a pair of orders entered by this Court a decade ago in the context of two pre-packaged bankruptcy cases. *See In re Stations Holdings Co., Inc.*, Case No. 02-10882 (MFW), 2002 Bankr. LEXIS 1617 (Bankr. D. Del. 2002) (Order dated September 30, 2002); *In re NII Holdings., Inc.*, Case No. 02-11505, 2002 Bankr. LEXIS 2123 (Bankr. D. Del. 2002) (Order dated October 25, 2002). In these two cases, it appears that the Court designated votes of creditors that were received by the debtor after the filing of the bankruptcy petition. Noting first that (as far as the Court can tell) these two pre-packaged cases present a markedly different factual and procedural context than the case at bar,[4] the Court further observes that the two-page orders entered in those cases do not contain any legal analysis and, consistent with this Court's practice, are of only the most limited (if any) precedential value.

The Court finds the analysis and reasoning in *Heritage* dispositive. Congress intended that creditors have the opportunity to negotiate with debtors and amongst each other; to the extent that those negotiations bear fruit, a narrow construction of "solicitation" affords these parties the opportunity to memorialize their agreements in a way that allows a Chapter 11 case to move forward.

. . .

---

4. At a minimum, there was no question in those cases that the act in question was a "solicitation" of a specific ballot relating to a filed plan.

In summary, the Court observes that the filing of a Chapter 11 petition is an invitation to negotiate. Congress has carefully calibrated the Chapter 11 process—using the automatic stay, exclusivity, the right of secured creditors to adequate protection and a host of other statutory provisions—to provide stakeholders with leverage or bargaining chips to advance their respective agendas. The purpose, at bottom, is to permit parties to have a voice and to make their own economic decisions. Each case requires an analysis into its particular facts and circumstances to permit a court to determine whether there is material risk to the important interests sought to be protected by the Bankruptcy Code's disclosure requirements. But consistent with the holding in *Century Glove*, courts must be chary of construing those disclosure and solicitation provisions in a way that chills or hamstrings the negotiation process that is at the heart of Chapter 11. When a deal is negotiated in good faith between a debtor and sophisticated parties, and that arrangement is memorialized a written commitment and promptly disclosed, § 1126 will not automatically require designation of the votes of the participants. The Motion to Designate is denied.

II. PREPACKAGED BANKRUPTCIES

The typical bankruptcy involves solicitation and voting on a plan *after* the filing of the case. The Bankruptcy Code, however, does not require the solicitation and the vote to take place post-petition. Only plan confirmation must occur post-petition (otherwise the court would not have jurisdiction). Accordingly, it is possible to file a "prepackaged" bankruptcy (often called a "prepac") or a "prenegotiated" plan. A prepac involves the formulation of a plan and the solicitation of votes pre-petition, with the court merely confirming that the plan meets the requirements of section 1129 (including that it "complies with the applicable provisions of this title." 11 U.S.C. § 1129(a)(1)). The usual prepac has all or almost all intercreditor issues worked out before the filing, with the only procedural steps left being plan confirmation. Prepacs have become increasingly common.

To see the legal mechanism for how a prepac works, note that section 1121(a) provides that a plan may be filed along with the bankruptcy petition. 11 U.S.C. § 1121(a). Section 1125(g) provides that the votes may be solicited before the filing of the petition, so long as the solicitation complies with applicable non-bankruptcy law. What law might that be?

Federal securities laws may apply if there are solicitations of entities holding public securities, such as bonds or public equity. If there is no public debt or the public debt is unimpaired, federal securities laws would not apply. (Be aware that state securities laws sometimes define security more broadly than federal law, so as to encompass trade debt. *See, e.g.*, Ohio Rev. Code § 1701.01(B) (defining "security" to include "evidences of indebtedness").)

The shift from the bankruptcy disclosure regime to non-bankruptcy disclosure regimes has two important implications. First, non-bankruptcy disclosure regimes may simply not be as demanding. They may require some sort of disclosure of material facts, but that might be a lower threshold than "adequate information," as required by section 1125. Second, the bankruptcy disclosure system allows for objections, whereas non-bankruptcy disclosure systems do not. If a plan proponent fails to provide adequate information under section 1125, the disclosure statement may not be approved and votes may not be solicited. This provides creditors with some ability to hold up a bankruptcy. In contrast, if a debtor were to fail to provide sufficient information for the solicitation of votes under a prepackaged plan, it might incur securities law liability, but that would only be *ex post* liability (which might even be discharged by the plan); creditors would not have the ability to hold up the solicitation of votes because of complaints about inadequacy of information. Prepacs, then, unlike regular bankruptcies, are not subject to a creditor veto when there is insufficient disclosure.

If there is non-bankruptcy law, such as federal and state securities laws, governing the solicitation of consents, the disclosure requirements of section 1125(b) do not apply. 11 U.S.C. §§ 1125(b), 1126(b)(1). If there is no applicable non-bankruptcy law, however, then the Bankruptcy Code requires the provision of "adequate information," as defined by section 1125(a). 11 U.S.C. § 1126(b). That is, if there is no applicable non-bankruptcy law governing the adequacy of disclosure in connection with the solicitations, the adequate disclosure requirement of section 1125(a) springs back into place, per section 1126(b)(2). But do such situations exist? In many situations, federal or state securities laws will apply, but even when they do not, state unfair and deceptive trade practices acts might apply. In any event, a plan proponent must either file a disclosure statement with the court or file evidence of compliance with section 1126(b). Fed. R. Bankr. Proc. 3016(b).

Other Code provisions also facilitate prepacs. Section 1102(b)(1) permits pre-petition creditors' committees to continue serving as official committees in the bankruptcy, so long as their membership was chosen fairly and is representative. Section 341(e) permits a waiver of the initial creditors' meeting if the debtor has filed a prepackaged plan. Additionally, some bankruptcy courts even have local rules governing prepacs. *See, e.g.,* Amended Procedural Guidelines for Prepackaged Chapter 11 Cases in the United States Bankruptcy Court for the Southern District of New York, dated November 24, 2009 ("SDNY Prepack Rules").

In contrast to a prepac, a prenegotiated plan does not have a solicitation of acceptances before the filing of the petition. Instead, it merely has largely concluded negotiations regarding the terms of the restructuring, often combined with a "lock-up" or "plan support" agreement among the major creditors. (These lock-up agreements can be viewed as solicitations, however.) Unlike a prepac, a prenegotiated plan must comply with regular Chapter 11 procedures regarding the approval of a disclosure statement and solicitation of votes, and thus does not benefit from section 1125's exception to state and federal securities laws.

Why would parties ever do a prepac? The advantage of a prepac over a regular "free fall" bankruptcy is that it is faster and much more controlled. A prepackaged plan can be confirmed in around a month. Federal Rules of Bankruptcy Procedure 2002(b) and 3017(a) require 28 days' notice for a disclosure statement, and Rules 2002(b) and 3020(b)(2) require 28 days' notice for a plan confirmation hearing. The deadlines can run concurrently so that the hearing on the adequacy of the solicitation disclosure can be conducted together with the confirmation hearing. *See* Bankruptcy Court for the Southern District of New York Prepackaged Chapter 11 Guidelines, § XI. Even if the deadlines run concurrently, however, a prepackaged plan will still take at least 28 days to confirm. Confirmation orders are normally stayed for another 14 days (although the court may order otherwise). FED. R. BANKR. PROC. 3020(e). While a prepac can be very fast in terms of court time, it requires advanced planning. Laying the groundwork for negotiating a plan outside of bankruptcy and soliciting acceptances takes time, so the real time from when a debtor decides to undertake a prepac to confirmation can be substantially longer than the mandatory minimum procedural timetables.

The speed of a prepac means that many of the costs of bankruptcy may be avoided, such as the costs of attorneys' appearances at hearings, preparation and filing, and service of motions. Additionally, official committees of unsecured creditors are generally not appointed in prepac cases if the unsecured creditors are unimpaired. Bankruptcy Court for the Southern District of New York Prepackaged Chapter 11 Guidelines, § VIII.C. It also means that very few attorneys' and professionals' fees will come under court scrutiny. And with a prepac there isn't the uncertainty hanging over the reorganization process, as customers and vendors wonder whether the debtor will survive as a going concern and therefore possibly withhold business or demand more favorable terms.

Yet why file for bankruptcy at all then? A prepac provides an effective way of implementing out-of-court restructurings. First, the threat of a prepac can be used as leverage to encourage creditors to accept an exchange offer. Indeed, exchange offers are often coupled with solicitations of votes for prepacs. The exchange offer has the higher voting threshold—typically 90 percent or above—to become effective, whereas the prepac needs only two thirds of the amount and over one half of the number in each impaired class. If the restructuring terms in the bankruptcy are harsher than those in the exchange offer, creditors are incentivized to accept the exchange.

Second, a prepac can be used credibly when an exchange offer or other out-of-court restructuring fails. It is particularly useful when dealing with a minority of holdout creditors that for whatever reason (information problems, trust problems, valuation differences, etc.) are unwilling to agree to the restructuring. Dissenting creditors that are classified in a way that they cannot block a plan can be squeezed into submission via a prepac, whereas their rights could not be unilaterally altered outside of bankruptcy or even with majority consent in most cases.

While prepacs are quite useful in restructuring public debt obligations, trade obligations are usually left unimpaired in prepacs because of the difficulty in negotiating with numerous trade claimants pre-petition because of the numerosity of trade creditors (as opposed to a single bondholder trustee), the fluctuations in the amounts owed in trade debt (whereas bond debt remains constant), and the likelihood vendors would stop dealing with a firm they believed was about to file for bankruptcy. Tort creditors present similar problems for prepacs. Their claims may be contested or unliquidated, and there may be numerosity problems. All of this may make it hard to know whether a requisite majority have in fact accepted a plan.

A prepac also enables parties to capture value from some of the procedural tools bankruptcy provides. Releases and exculpations can be included in a plan, which, when confirmed, is a court order. Confirmation protects against litigation challenges from non-consenting holdouts. The confirmation order provides powerful protection for all parties involved. Assets may be sold "free and clear" under a bankruptcy plan. Such a sale enables the transfer of underwater collateral without the consent of the secured lender. It also ensures that successor liability or environmental liability does not attach to the purchaser. Such a limitation on liability may therefore increase the purchase price. The issuance of new securities can be accomplished in bankruptcy without complying with federal securities laws. And there may be tax advantages to a prepac. An exchange offer can result in cancelation of indebtedness income to the exchanging bondholders; bankruptcy losses do not. Moreover, in some circumstances, the debtor may be able to preserve net operating losses that can then be used to offset future income. This is possible only in bankruptcy.

Problem Set 36

(1) ERIS Investments is opposed to any plan of reorganization for Thetis Corporation; ERIS is determined that Thetis should liquidate. ERIS wants to reach out to other creditors to urge them to vote against any reorganization plan that might be proposed; no plan has yet been proposed. Is ERIS allowed to contact other creditors to urge rejection? 11 U.S.C. §§ 1121, 1125.

(2) Vulcan Foundries, as DIP, has filed a disclosure statement for its Chapter 11 plan. Vulcan has a range of creditors, including financial institutions and individual tort victims with asbestos claims. Can Vulcan file a single disclosure statement for all of them? Should it? 11 U.S.C. §§ 1125(a), (c).

(3) Io Beef Products, as DIP, has filed a disclosure statement for its Chapter 11 plan. The plan does not mention anything about the new packaging design and marketing campaign planned for Io's famous Chief-o'-Beef mega-beef product. Is the disclosure statement confirmable? 11 U.S.C. §§ 1125(a)-(b).

(4) The disclosure statement for Pharos Lighting Design's Chapter 11 plan says nothing about what will happen with Pharos's Net Operating Losses (NOLs), but provides that "all assets not specifically accounted for in the plan will remain property of the debtor following confirmation." Is the disclosure statement approvable? 11 U.S.C. §§ 1125(a)-(b).

(5) Chiron, Inc. is in Chapter 11. The firm's future depends heavily on the clinical trial performance of its new drug to treat Degenerative Personality Disorder. The final results of the clinical trial will not be available for at least six months and details on the product and its trial are a closely held trade secret. How can Chiron, Inc. get its disclosure statement approved without revealing its trade secrets? 11 U.S.C. §§ 1125(a)-(b).

(6) Pegasus Aeronauticars has been working hard on developing a flying car. It hasn't quite worked yet, and Pegasus needs to restructure its debt. Pegasus has been in talks with its secured lenders about a restructuring deal, and it has entered into an agreement with most of them to extend its financing. According to the agreement, the

interest rate on all of the secured debt will be increased, but it will be paid in kind for a couple of years and the term of the debt will be extended. The lenders will also extend Pegasus additional financing. Pegasus's unsecured trade debt and equity will be unimpaired. One of the secured lenders, the Medusa Fund, refuses to go along with a restructuring, so Pegasus has filed for bankruptcy to force a restructuring. The assenting lenders previously committed to support any plan Pegasus proposed that substantially conformed to the terms of the proposed restructuring agreement.

     a. Does Pegasus have to solicit votes on its restructuring proposal? 11 U.S.C. §§ 1126(b), 1129(a)(8).

     b. Does Pegasus have to file a plan of restructuring with the court? 11 U.S.C. §§ 1121(a), 1129(a).

     c. Does Pegasus have to file a disclosure statement with the court? 11 U.S.C. §§ 1125(b), (g); FED. R. BANKR. PROC. 3016(b).

     d. Might the SEC have something to say about Pegasus's agreement with its lenders? 11 U.S.C. §§ 1109(a); 1125(e), (g).

     e. What are the consequences for Pegasus if it improperly solicited votes? 11 U.S.C. §§ 1126(e), 1129(a)(1)-(3).

(7) Your client, famed toymaker Saturnalia, needs to restructure its debts. Saturnalia does not think it will be able to restructure outside of bankruptcy, but it thinks it can likely get a prepackaged bankruptcy plan approved. Saturnalia does most of its business during the holiday season that starts roughly at Thanksgiving. Saturnalia is very worried that if it is in bankruptcy during the holiday season, consumers will not purchase its toys because of concerns about warranties and reputation. Accordingly, Saturnalia puts a very high premium on being out of bankruptcy by Thanksgiving. It's now mid-October.

     a. Is it possible for Saturnalia to be out of bankruptcy before Thanksgiving? FED. R. BANKR. PROC. 2002(b), 3017(a), 3020(b)(2).

     b. Would you counsel Saturnalia that this is likely?

CHAPTER 37

CRAMDOWN CONFIRMATION

I. CRAMDOWN

A Chapter 11 plan can be confirmed either "consensually" or through "cramdown." A "consensual" confirmation means a plan that is confirmed by meeting all of the applicable requirements of section 1129(a), including section 1129(a)(8), which requires dual majorities approving the plan in *each* impaired class of claims and majorities approving the plan in *each* impaired class of interests. As we saw in the previous chapter, however, a "consensual" confirmation is somewhat of a misnomer. Consensual confirmation does not necessarily mean unanimous creditor consent, but merely that the requisite majorities in all impaired classes supported the plan. The plan might still be opposed by a significant minority in each class and by unimpaired creditors. Nonetheless, plan approval under section 1129(a) is premised on a certain quantum of creditor assent as required by section 1129(a)(8).

"Cramdown" is a non-consensual plan confirmation through section 1129(b). The colorful term "cramdown" never appears in the Bankruptcy Code, but the idea is that the plan is being crammed down the throats of non-accepting creditors. The holdouts are forced to accept the plan's terms. Section 1129(b) is reorganizational gavage. ("Cramdown" has a distinct meaning in Chapters 7 and 13, where it refers to reducing the allowed amount of a secured claim to the value of the collateral— what is more properly called strip-down or bifurcation.)

Section 1129(b) is an alternative to section 1129(a)(8). A cramdown confirmation must still comply with all other applicable provisions of section 1129(a). Good faith, best interests, and feasibility are all required for any plan. So too is the section 1129(a)(10) requirement of *one* impaired class (if any exist) approving the plan, not counting votes of insiders. But in lieu of the section 1129(a)(8) requirement of a majority vote in *all* impaired classes, section 1129(b) imposes a set of substantive requirements designed to ensure a modicum of distributional fairness in a plan, namely that the plan must not "discriminate unfairly" and that it must be "fair and equitable" in respect to impaired, non-accepting classes of claims and interests. The rest of this chapter explores what constitutes "unfair discrimination" and "fair and equitable" treatment regarding secured creditors. The next three chapters continue the consideration of what is "fair and equitable" in regard to undersecured, unsecured creditors, and equity interests.

Cramdown confirmation is not automatic if consensual confirmation fails; instead cramdown confirmation must be specifically requested by the plan proponent, in part because a cramdown plan is likely to result in pre-petition equityholders—with whom the DIP's management is likely affiliated—getting wiped out, meaning that their equity interests will be cancelled without any distribution.

Understanding cramdown is critical because not only does all of bankruptcy law operate in the shadow of cramdown, but all of financial restructuring. The ability to compel a reorganization through section 1129(b) sets the stage for restructuring negotiations. Outside of bankruptcy, a debtor generally cannot force restructuring terms on creditors who do not consent. Outside of bankruptcy, minority shareholders can be forced to accept a merger, but benefit from procedural protections such as *Revlon* duties for directors to shop the company for the best and highest price, *Revlon Inc. v. MacAndrews & Forbes Holdings*, Inc., 506 A.2d 173 (Del. 1986), and the "entire fairness" doctrine, including the duty to pay a fair price, for transactions with interested directors or controlling shareholders. Kahn v. Lynch Communc'n Syst., Inc., 638 A.2d 1110, 1115 (Del. 1994).

Bankruptcy provides legal authority for forcing holdout creditors and equityholders to accept a deal, either through the majority rule provisions, of section 1129(a)(8) or through cramdown. Like state corporate law protections for minority shareholders, section 1129(b) provides minimum standards for the treatment of impaired, non-consenting classes of creditors and equityholders.

There are two major differences, however, between corporate law protections for minority shareholders and cramdown protections. First, state corporate law protections for minority shareholders are standards-based—fair process, fair price. Cramdown protections for nonconsenting impaired classes are both standards ("no unfair discrimination" and "fair and equitable") *and* substantive rules.

Second, cramdown does not actually protect minority members of impaired classes. The special substantive requirements of a cramdown plan apply only to non-consenting impaired classes of claims and interests. Thus, if a majority of creditors in a class consents to a plan, the non-consenting minority cannot shelter in the substantive cramdown protections.

II. UNFAIR DISCRIMINATION

A cramdown plan may not "discriminate unfairly" in regard to an impaired, non-accepting class. If a class is unimpaired or accepts a plan, it cannot raise an "unfair discrimination" objection. *See Official Comm. of Equity Sec. Holders v. Official Comm. of Unsecured Creditors (In re Adelphia Communs. Corp.)*, 544 F.3d 420, 426 (2d Cir. 2008).

Unfair discrimination is not defined by the Code. The prohibition applies only to a class; section 1123(a)(4) requires identical treatment of members within a class absent their consent. Reading section 1129(b)(1) in conjunction with other Code provisions, however, the prohibition on unfair discrimination is clear that it is distinct from classification and instead relates to the distribution of the reorganization surplus over the liquidation value of the assets, which creditors are guaranteed under the best interests test. The prohibition on unfair discrimination indicates that the reorganization surplus in excess of liquidation value need not be allocated among creditors based on their liquidation priority. Instead, there can be some discrimination, so long as it is not unfair. There is not a standard test for unfair discrimination, but typically it involves a finding that the discrimination has no reasonable basis, is not necessary for the reorganization, or is not in good faith.

The scope of the prohibition is best understood by considering some types of discrimination. A plan might provide for different recoveries for similar classes of creditors. For example, one might be paid in cash, and another with a note. Or one class might recover a higher percentage of its claim than another, both over the liquidation recovery. Or there might be different recoveries based on contributions to the reorganization effort or on the basis of a class being composed of insiders. Depending on facts and circumstances, all of these types of discrimination might be acceptable. A trickier situation involves different treatment based on whether a class accepts or rejects a plan. This type of treatment, known as a "death trap" plan, may not be unfair discrimination, but it might raise good faith issues, analogous to coercive exchange offers.

In re Greate Bay Hotel & Casino, Inc.

251 B.R. 213 (Bankr. D.N.J. 2000)

JUDITH H. WIZMUR, U.S. Bankruptcy Judge.

. . .

The High River plan[, one of two competing plans for the reorganization of Greate Bay Hotel & Casino, Inc., which owns the Sands Hotel & Casino in Atlantic City, New Jersey,] is presented on behalf of [certain entities owned by Carl C. Icahn], hereinafter referred to collectively as "High River." . . . Collectively High River holds approximately $62,833,000 (or 34.4%) of the "Old Notes."

. . .

To fund the High River plan, High River proposes to buy 46.25% of the New Common Stock for $65 million in cash. The infusion of new capital will be used to consummate the plan and to implement the debtors "Global Development Plan 2000-2002." That plan envisions, among other things, the development of a hotel tower with 200 new rooms, additional casino space and 800 additional slot machines. Under the High River plan, the [undersecured] Old Noteholders [in Class 2] will receive a pro rata portion of $110 million in New Notes and 5,375,000 shares of New Common Stock (after the effect of the subordination of the Intercompany Notes). The shares of New Common Stock to be distributed to Old Noteholders represent 53.75% of the equity in the reorganized debtors. The general unsecured claims [in Class 4] will receive . . . 80% . . . of their allowed claims [in cash on the effective date of the plan]. . . . [Class 2 voted against the High River plan, while Class 4 voted for it.]

1. Unfair Discrimination.

The concept of unfair discrimination is not defined under the Bankruptcy Code. Various standards have been developed by the courts to test whether or not a plan unfairly discriminates. *In re Dow Corning Corp.*, 244 B.R. 705, 710 (Bankr. E.D. Mich. 1999). The hallmarks of the various tests have been whether there is a reasonable basis for the discrimination, and whether the debtor can confirm and consummate a plan without the proposed discrimination.

More recently, one court has adopted a modified test for unfair discrimination, which gives rise to:

> a rebuttable presumption that a plan is unfairly discriminatory . . . when there is: (1) a dissenting class; (2) another class of the same priority; and (3) a difference in the plan's treatment of the two classes that results in either (a) a materially lower percentage recovery for the dissenting class (measured in terms of the net present value of all payments), or (b) regardless of percentage recovery, an allocation under the plan of materially greater risk to the dissenting class in connection with its proposed distribution.

In re Dow Corning Corp., 244 B.R. 696, 702 (Bankr. E.D. Mich. 1999) (adopting the test proposed in Bruce A. Markell, *A New Perspective on Unfair Discrimination in Chapter 11*, 72 AM. BANKR. L.J. 227 (1998)).

In the High River plan, the general unsecured creditors in Class 4 are scheduled to receive an estimated 80% recovery. . . . To avoid unfair discrimination in this case, the recovery of the Old Noteholders on their [unsecured] deficiency claims must be consistent with the recovery of Class 4 general unsecured creditors. We must, therefore, evaluate the value to be received by Old Noteholders on account of their deficiency claims under the High River plan.

[Extensive discussion of valuation evidence regarding the treatment of the Old Noteholders' claims is omitted.]

By our calculations, the deficiency claims of Old Noteholders in Class 2 are receiving 76% of their claims, while the general unsecured claims in Class 4 are receiving 80%. While the difference is not large, the disparity is nonetheless discriminatory. The question is whether or not the difference constitutes "unfair" discrimination.

Courts that have rejected confirmation on the basis of unfair discrimination have confronted plans proposing grossly disparate treatment (50% or more) to similarly situated creditors. *See, e.g., In re Tucson Self-Storage, Inc.*, 166 B.R. 892 (9th Cir. BAP 1994) (providing for 100% for unsecured trade creditor and 10% to deficiency claim was unfair discrimination); *In re Barney & Carey Co.*, 170 B.R. 17 (Bankr. D. Mass. 1994) (denying confirmation where deficiency claim was to receive 100% and general unsecured 15%); *In re Caldwell*, 76 B.R. 643, 646 (Bankr. E.D. Tenn. 1987) (confirmation denied where 100% of credit card debt was proposed to be paid but only 22.7% of all other unsecured debt would be paid). *But see In re 203 N. LaSalle St. Partnership*, 126 F.3d 955, 969 (7th Cir. 1997) (paying unsecured trade creditors 100% and bank deficiency claim 16% not unfair because it was more than the bank would have received under a Chapter 7 liquidation); *Jersey City Medical Center*, 817 F.2d at 1057 (allowing payment of 100% of physicians' claims and 30% of other unsecured claims where source of repayment was an issue).

There is no bright line test which establishes whether a given difference in percentage recovery results in unfair discrimination. Under the *Dow Corning* test cited above, confirmation would be denied only if there was a "materially lower" percentage recovery for the dissenting class or a "materially greater risk to the dissenting class in connection with its proposed distribution." *In re Dow Corning Corp.*, 244 B.R. at 702. Like Judge Spector in *Dow Corning*, I adopt the test articulated [by Professor] Markell . . . because the test "effectively targets the kind of discrimination or disparate treatment that is commonly understood as being 'unfair,' namely that which causes injury or that unjustly favors one creditor over another." 244 B.R. at 702.

In this case, the dissenting class of Old Noteholders are not receiving a materially lower percentage recovery on their deficiency claim than the percentage recovery anticipated to be received by general unsecured creditors. The actual value being received by the Old Noteholders on their deficiency claims cannot be calculated with precision. There is substantial variation among the experts who testified at trial, including those who opined that the value received on account of the deficiency claims is higher than 80%. It is sufficient for these purposes to conclude that High River has met its burden to establish that the value being received on account of the deficiency claims is not "unfair."

Nor does the allocation of equity proposed by the High River plan on account of the deficiency claims of Old Noteholders impose a materially greater risk to the dissenting class. The disparity of risk imposed upon equally situated creditors may be evaluated by comparing the levels of risk accepted prepetition by each creditor with the levels of risk imposed in the plan. Markell, 72 AM. BANKR. L.J. at 253. For instance, it is generally recognized that "trade creditors have short-term maturities; debenture holders have long-term expectations." *Id.* at 252. Correspondingly, in this case, the trade creditors are receiving an immediate cash payout, while the Old Noteholders are receiving a package of securities that conform to prepetition long-term expectations. No "unfairness" is discerned in this necessary disparity in treatment.

Even if the more widely accepted tests of reasonableness and necessity for confirmation are applied, the disparity in treatment between the two classes of creditors would meet the requirement proscribing "unfair discrimination." In this case, the dissenting class of Old Noteholders is receiving all of the reorganization value of the debtors, in excess of $170 million, with a relatively minor carve-out for the cash payment of less than $6 million to trade. As noted in the classification discussion under § 1129(a)(1), the only opportunity for the proponent to offer the enterprise value of the debtors to the Old Noteholders is to offer them the equity in the reorganized debtors on account of their deficiency claim. The disparate treatment is necessary for reorganization, and the minor variation in recovery is reasonable.

   . . .

I conclude that the High River plan does not unfairly discriminate among dissenting creditors.

   . . .

III. FAIR AND EQUITABLE: TREATMENT OF SECURED CREDITORS

A cramdown plan must also be "fair and equitable" to impaired, non-accepting classes. 11 U.S.C. § 1129(b). If a class is unimpaired or accepts a plan, it cannot raise a "fair and equitable" objection. *Official Comm. of Equity Sec. Holders v. Official Comm. of Unsecured Creditors (In re Adelphia Communs. Corp.)*, 544 F.3d 420, 426 (2d Cir. 2008). The Bankruptcy Code defines "fair and equitable" to include specific treatments for secured claims, unsecured claims, and interests.

Section 1129(b)(2)(A) presents three alternative treatments of secured claims. A secured creditor must:

1. retain its liens and receive deferred cash payments totaling at least the allowed amount of its claim and adjusted (only upwards) to reflect the value of the secured claim as of the effective date of the plan, 11 U.S.C. § 1129(b)(2)(A)(i); or
2. receive the "indubitable equivalent" of its claim, 11 U.S.C. § 1129(b)(2)(A)(iii); or
3. have its collateral sold free and clear of their liens, with the liens instead attaching to the sale proceeds, and the secured claim then treated as under the other two options. 11 U.S.C. § 1129(b)(2)(A)(ii).

All three alternatives aim to produce the same result: that a secured creditor will recover the value of its claim. The result is meant to be the same that would obtain outside of bankruptcy, where the secured creditor would foreclose on its collateral and receive the value of the collateral. If the secured creditor were undersecured, it would have to pursue the deficiency (if there was recourse) as a regular unsecured debt.

In short, secured creditors are being guaranteed recovery of both the face amount *and* the present value of their secured claim as part of a section 1129(b) confirmation. This virtually always means that a secured creditor will receive payments with a face amount greater than that of the value of its collateral.

The debtor is given the flexibility of repaying the claims over time; there is no timetable set for the deferred cash payments, although the longer the timetable proposed, the less likely the plan will be found feasible. However long the timetable, the payments must compensate the creditor for time value. Does this make sense?

Consider what would happen in a liquidation. The creditor would get the collateral and would liquidate it, getting cash today. The creditor could then reinvest the cash and capture the time value of the money. Thus, section 1129(b)(2)(A) basically gives a secured creditor what the secured creditor would get outside of bankruptcy—the value of the collateral.[1] But because section 1129(b)(2)(A)(i) requires that the payments to the creditor equal face value of the allowed amount of the secured claim, the creditor is protected from the possibility of negative time value—that is, from a deflationary economy. Yet this protection makes some sense too. If the secured claim were a recourse debt, the creditor would be able to pursue not just the value of the collateral, but also the face amount of the claim to the extent it was not satisfied by the collateral.

---

1. Indeed, it might give more, as outside of bankruptcy there would be transaction costs for liquidation and reinvestment.

Importantly, secured creditors generally retain their liens. This means that if the debtor defaults on its payments under the plan, the secured creditor can proceed to foreclose on its collateral. As the automatic stay is lifted when the plan goes into effect, 11 U.S.C. § 362(c), there is no obstacle to foreclosure.

It is easy to miss what cramdown does *not* protect. Cramdown does not protect other contractual terms that ordinarily benefit a secured creditor, such as all of the covenants that might protect the right to payment. Those covenants can all be stripped away, and a cramdown plan can still be confirmed if the secured creditor retains its lien and is paid the value and amount of its secured claim. In other words, a secured creditor is not protected from all types of impairment, only from impairment of its lien and of its right to be paid. Thus, financial reporting covenants, leverage limitations, etc., can all be stripped out of a secured loan in a bankruptcy plan without jeopardizing cramdown confirmation. As with the Trust Indenture Act, these covenants are not inviolable. Conversely, cramdown can be combined with cure and reinstatement of a secured creditor's debt under section 1124(2), resulting in the debtor being able to retain a favorable pre-petition covenant package even in the face of the creditor's objections.

A. Retained Liens and Deferred Cash Payments

The first possible treatment of secured creditors in cramdown requires that the secured creditors retain their liens on the collateral and receive deferred *cash* payments. The cash requirement is important because it is what distinguishes section 1129(b)(2)(A)(i) from section 1129(b)(2)(A)(iii).

The deferred cash payments must total the *greater* of the allowed *amount* of the claim and the *value* of the claim as of the effective date of the plan. In other words, the secured creditor must receive a stream of deferred cash payments that give the creditor equal present value to the face amount of the claim. If a creditor is fully secured, then the amount of its claim will equal the value of the claim on the effective date of the plan. Accordingly, only the value requirement matters (except theoretically in a deflationary economy).

All of this raises a critical question: What is the discount rate to be used for determining the present value of a future stream of payments? The Bankruptcy Code itself provides no guidance on the issue. The courts, however, have explicated. The Supreme Court addressed the issue in a similar context in a Chapter 13 consumer case, *Till v. SCS Credit Corp. Till* provides guidance regarding Chapter 13, but, like *Rash* for valuation issues, it is not formally controlling in Chapter 11, and the Court has not addressed the issue directly in Chapter 11.

Till v. SCS Credit Corp.

541 U.S. 465 (2004)

Justice STEVENS announced the judgment of the Court and delivered an opinion, in which Justice SOUTER, Justice GINSBURG, and Justice BREYER join.

To qualify for court approval under Chapter 13 of the Bankruptcy Code, an individual debtor's proposed debt adjustment plan must accommodate each allowed, secured creditor in one of three ways: (1) by obtaining the creditor's acceptance of the plan; (2) by surrendering the property securing the claim; or (3) by providing the creditor both a lien securing the claim and a promise of future property distributions (such as deferred cash payments) whose total "value, as of the effective date of the plan, . . . is not less than the allowed amount of such claim." [11 U.S.C. § 1325(a).] The third alternative is commonly known as the "cram down option" because it may be enforced over a claim holder's objection. *Associates Commercial Corp. v. Rash*, 520 U.S. 953, 957 (1997).

Plans that invoke the cram down power often provide for installment payments over a period of years rather than a single payment. In such circumstances, the amount of each installment must be calibrated to ensure that, over time, the creditor receives disbursements whose total present value [meaning value as of the effective date of the plan] equals or exceeds that of the allowed claim. The proceedings in this case that led to our grant of certiorari identified four different methods of determining the appropriate method with which to perform that calibration. Indeed, the Bankruptcy Judge, the District Court, the Court of Appeals majority, and the dissenting Judge each endorsed a different approach. We detail the underlying facts and describe each of those approaches before setting forth our judgment as to which approach best meets the purposes of the Bankruptcy Code.

I

On October 2, 1998, petitioners Lee and Amy Till, residents of Kokomo, Indiana, purchased a used truck from Instant Auto Finance for $6,395 plus $330.75 in fees and taxes. They made a $300 down payment and financed the balance of the purchase price by entering into a retail installment contract that Instant Auto immediately assigned to respondent, SCS Credit Corporation. Petitioners' initial indebtedness amounted to $8,285.24—the $6,425.75 balance of the truck purchase plus a finance charge of 21% per year for 136 weeks, or $1,859.49. Under the contract, petitioners agreed to make 68 biweekly payments to cover this debt; Instant Auto—and subsequently respondent—retained a purchase money security interest that gave it the right to repossess the truck if petitioners defaulted under the contract.

On October 25, 1999, petitioners, by then in default on their payments to respondent, filed a joint petition for relief under Chapter 13 of the Bankruptcy Code. At the time of the filing, respondent's outstanding claim amounted to $4,894.89, but the parties agreed that the truck securing the claim was worth only $4,000. In accordance with the Bankruptcy Code, therefore, respondent's secured claim was limited to $4,000, and the $894.89 balance was unsecured. Petitioners' . . . proposed plan . . . provided that petitioners would pay interest on the secured portion of respondent's claim at a rate of 9.5% per year. Petitioners arrived at this "prime-plus" or "formula rate" by augmenting the national prime rate of approximately 8% (applied by banks when making low-risk loans) to account for the risk of nonpayment posed by borrowers in their financial position. Respondent objected to the proposed rate, contending that the company was "entitled to interest at the rate of 21%, which is the rate . . . it would obtain if it could foreclose on the vehicle and reinvest the proceeds in loans of equivalent duration and risk as the loan" originally made to petitioners.

At the hearing on its objection, respondent presented expert testimony establishing that it uniformly charges 21% interest on so-called "subprime" loans, or loans to borrowers with poor credit ratings, and that other lenders in the subprime market also charge that rate. Petitioners countered with the testimony of an Indiana University-Purdue University Indianapolis economics professor, who acknowledged that he had only limited familiarity with the subprime auto lending market, but described the 9.5% formula rate as "very reasonable" given that Chapter 13 plans are "supposed to be financially feasible." Moreover, the professor noted that respondent's exposure was "fairly limited because [petitioners] are under the supervision of the court." The bankruptcy trustee also filed comments supporting the formula rate as, among other things, easily ascertainable, closely tied to the "condition of the financial market," and independent of the financial circumstances of any particular lender. Accepting petitioners' evidence, the Bankruptcy Court overruled respondent's objection and confirmed the proposed plan.

The District Court reversed. It understood Seventh Circuit precedent to require that bankruptcy courts set cram down interest rates at the level the creditor could have obtained if it had foreclosed on the loan, sold the collateral, and reinvested the proceeds in loans of equivalent duration and risk. Citing respondent's unrebutted testimony about the market for subprime loans, the court concluded that 21% was the appropriate rate.

On appeal, the Seventh Circuit endorsed a slightly modified version of the District Court's "coerced" or "forced loan" approach. Specifically, the majority agreed with the District Court that, in a cram down proceeding, the inquiry should focus on the interest rate "that the creditor in question would obtain in making a new loan in the same industry to a debtor who is similarly situated, although not in bankruptcy." To approximate that new loan rate, the majority looked to the parties' prebankruptcy contract rate (21%). The court recognized, however, that using the contract rate would not "duplicat[e] precisely . . . the present value of the collateral to the creditor" because loans to bankrupt, court-supervised debtors "involve some risks that would not be incurred in a new loan to a debtor not in default" and also produce "some economies." To correct for these inaccuracies, the majority held that the original contract rate should "serve as a presumptive [cram down] rate," which either the creditor or the debtor could challenge with evidence that a higher or lower rate should apply. Accordingly, the court remanded the case to the Bankruptcy Court to afford petitioners and respondent an opportunity to rebut the presumptive 21% rate.

Dissenting, Judge Rovner argued that the majority's presumptive contract rate approach overcompensates secured creditors because it fails to account for costs a creditor would have to incur in issuing a new loan. Rather than focusing on the market for comparable loans, Judge Rovner advocated either the Bankruptcy Court's formula approach or a "straightforward . . . cost of funds" approach that would simply ask "what it would cost the creditor to obtain the cash equivalent of the collateral from an alternative source."

. . . We granted certiorari and now reverse.

II

The Bankruptcy Code provides little guidance as to which of the rates of interest advocated by the four opinions in this case—the formula rate, the coerced loan rate, the presumptive contract rate, or the cost of funds rate—Congress had in mind when it adopted the cram down provision. That provision, 11 U.S.C. § 1325(a)(5)(B), does not mention the term "discount rate" or the word "interest." Rather, it simply requires bankruptcy courts to ensure that the property to be distributed to a particular secured creditor over the life of a bankruptcy plan has a total "value, as of the effective date of the plan," that equals or exceeds the value of the creditor's allowed secured claim—in this case, $4,000. § 1325(a)(5)(B)(ii).

That command is easily satisfied when the plan provides for a lump-sum payment to the creditor. Matters are not so simple, however, when the debt is to be discharged by a series of payments over time. A debtor's promise of future payments is worth less than an immediate payment of the same total amount because the creditor cannot use the money right away, inflation may cause the value of the dollar to decline before the debtor pays, and there is always some risk of nonpayment. The challenge for bankruptcy courts reviewing such repayment schemes, therefore, is to choose an interest rate sufficient to compensate the creditor for these concerns.

Three important considerations govern that choice. First, the Bankruptcy Code includes numerous provisions that, like the cram down provision, require a court to "discoun[t] . . . [a] stream of deferred payments back to the[ir] present dollar value," *Rake v. Wade,* 508 U.S. 464, 472, n.8 (1993), to ensure that a creditor receives at least the value of its claim.[10] We think it likely that Congress intended bankruptcy judges and trustees to follow essentially the same approach when choosing an appropriate interest rate under any of these provisions. Moreover, we think Congress would favor an approach that is familiar in the financial community and that minimizes the need for expensive evidentiary proceedings.

Second, Chapter 13 expressly authorizes a bankruptcy court to modify the rights of any creditor whose claim is secured by an interest in anything other than "real property that is the debtor's principal residence." 11 U.S.C. § 1322(b)(2). Thus, in cases like this involving secured interests in personal property, the court's authority to modify the number, timing, or amount of the installment payments from those set forth in the debtor's original contract is perfectly clear. Further, the potential need to modify the loan terms to account for intervening changes in circumstances is also clear: On the one hand, the fact of the bankruptcy establishes that the debtor is overextended and thus poses a significant risk of default; on the other hand, the postbankruptcy obligor is

---

10. See 11 U.S.C. § 1129(a)(7)(A)(ii) (requiring payment of property whose "value, as of the effective date of the plan" equals or exceeds the value of the creditor's claim); §§ 1129(a)(7)(B), 1129(a)(9)(B)(i), 1129(a)(9)(C), 1129(b)(2)(A)(ii), 1129(b)(2)(B)(i), 1129(b)(2)(C)(i), 1173(a)(2), 1225(a)(4), 1225(a)(5)(B)(ii), 1228(b)(2), 1325(a)(4), 1228(b)(2) (same).

no longer the individual debtor but the court-supervised estate, and the risk of default is thus somewhat reduced.[12]

Third, from the point of view of a creditor, the cram down provision mandates an objective rather than a subjective inquiry. That is, although § 1325(a)(5)(B) entitles the creditor to property whose present value objectively equals or exceeds the value of the collateral, it does not require that the terms of the cram down loan match the terms to which the debtor and creditor agreed prebankruptcy, nor does it require that the cram down terms make the creditor subjectively indifferent between present foreclosure and future payment. Indeed, the very idea of a "cram down" loan *precludes* the latter result: By definition, a creditor forced to accept such a loan would prefer instead to foreclose.[14] Thus, a court choosing a cram down interest rate need not consider the creditor's individual circumstances, such as its prebankruptcy dealings with the debtor or the alternative loans it could make if permitted to foreclose. Rather, the court should aim to treat similarly situated creditors similarly, and to ensure that an objective economic analysis would suggest the debtor's interest payments will adequately compensate all such creditors for the time value of their money and the risk of default.

III

These considerations lead us to reject the coerced loan, presumptive contract rate, and cost of funds approaches. Each of these approaches is complicated, imposes significant evidentiary costs, and aims to make each individual creditor whole rather than to ensure the debtor's payments have the required present value. For example, the coerced loan approach requires bankruptcy courts to consider evidence about the market for comparable loans to similar (though nonbankrupt) debtors—an inquiry far removed from such courts' usual task of evaluating debtors' financial circumstances and the feasibility of their debt adjustment plans. In addition, the approach overcompensates creditors because the market lending rate must be high enough to cover factors, like lenders' transaction costs and overall profits, that are no longer relevant in the context of court-administered and court-supervised cram down loans.

Like the coerced loan approach, the presumptive contract rate approach improperly focuses on the creditor's potential use of the proceeds of a foreclosure sale. In addition, although the approach permits a debtor to introduce some evidence about each creditor, thereby enabling the court to tailor the interest rate more closely to the creditor's

---

12. Several factors contribute to this reduction in risk. First, as noted below, a court may only approve a cram down loan (and the debt adjustment plan of which the loan is a part) if it believes the debtor will be able to make all of the required payments. § 1325(a)(6). Thus, such loans will only be approved for debtors that the court deems creditworthy. Second, Chapter 13 plans must "provide for the submission" to the trustee "of all or such portion of [the debtor's] future . . . income . . . as is necessary for the execution of the plan," § 1322(a)(1), so the possibility of nonpayment is greatly reduced. Third, the Bankruptcy Code's extensive disclosure requirements reduce the risk that the debtor has significant undisclosed obligations. Fourth, as a practical matter, the public nature of the bankruptcy proceeding is likely to reduce the debtor's opportunities to take on additional debt. . . .

14. This fact helps to explain why there is no readily apparent Chapter 13 "cram down market rate of interest": Because every cram down loan is imposed by a court over the objection of the secured creditor, there is no free market of willing cram down lenders. Interestingly, the same is *not* true in the Chapter 11 context, as numerous lenders advertise financing for Chapter 11 debtors in possession. . . . Thus, when picking a cram down rate in a Chapter 11 case, it might make sense to ask what rate an efficient market would produce. In the Chapter 13 context, by contrast, the absence of any such market obligates courts to look to first principles and ask only what rate will fairly compensate a creditor for its exposure.

financial circumstances and reducing the likelihood that the creditor will be substantially overcompensated, that right comes at a cost: The debtor must obtain information about the creditor's costs of overhead, financial circumstances, and lending practices to rebut the presumptive contract rate. Also, the approach produces absurd results, entitling "inefficient, poorly managed lenders" with lower profit margins to obtain higher cram down rates than "well managed, better capitalized lenders." 2 K. Lundin, CHAPTER 13 BANKRUPTCY § 112.1, p 112-8 (3d ed. 2000). Finally, because the approach relies heavily on a creditor's prior dealings with the debtor, similarly situated creditors may end up with vastly different cram down rates.[17]

The cost of funds approach, too, is improperly aimed. Although it rightly disregards the now-irrelevant terms of the parties' original contract, it mistakenly focuses on the creditworthiness of the *creditor* rather than the debtor. In addition, the approach has many of the other flaws of the coerced loan and presumptive contract rate approaches. For example, like the presumptive contract rate approach, the cost of funds approach imposes a significant evidentiary burden, as a debtor seeking to rebut a creditor's asserted cost of borrowing must introduce expert testimony about the creditor's financial condition. Also, under this approach, a creditworthy lender with a low cost of borrowing may obtain a lower cram down rate than a financially unsound, fly-by-night lender.

IV

The formula approach has none of these defects. Taking its cue from ordinary lending practices, the approach begins by looking to the national prime rate, reported daily in the press, which reflects the financial market's estimate of the amount a commercial bank should charge a creditworthy commercial borrower to compensate for the opportunity costs of the loan, the risk of inflation, and the relatively slight risk of default. Because bankrupt debtors typically pose a greater risk of nonpayment than solvent commercial borrowers, the approach then requires a bankruptcy court to adjust the prime rate accordingly. The appropriate size of that risk adjustment depends, of course, on such factors as the circumstances of the estate, the nature of the security, and the duration and feasibility of the reorganization plan. The court must therefore hold a hearing at which the debtor and any creditors may present evidence about the appropriate risk adjustment. Some of this evidence will be included in the debtor's bankruptcy filings, however, so the debtor and creditors may not incur significant additional expense. Moreover, starting from a concededly *low* estimate and adjusting *upward* places the evidentiary burden squarely on the creditors, who are likely to have readier access to any information absent from the debtor's filing (such as evidence about the "liquidity

---

17. For example, suppose a debtor purchases two identical used cars, buying the first at a low purchase price from a lender who charges high interest, and buying the second at a much higher purchase price from a lender who charges zero-percent or nominal interest. Prebankruptcy, these two loans might well produce identical income streams for the two lenders. Postbankruptcy, however, the presumptive contract rate approach would entitle the first lender to a considerably higher cram down interest rate, even though the two secured debts are objectively indistinguishable.

of the collateral market"). Finally, many of the factors relevant to the adjustment fall squarely within the bankruptcy court's area of expertise.

Thus, unlike the coerced loan, presumptive contract rate, and cost of funds approaches, the formula approach entails a straightforward, familiar, and objective inquiry, and minimizes the need for potentially costly additional evidentiary proceedings. Moreover, the resulting "prime-plus" rate of interest depends only on the state of financial markets, the circumstances of the bankruptcy estate, and the characteristics of the loan, not on the creditor's circumstances or its prior interactions with the debtor. For these reasons, the prime-plus or formula rate best comports with the purposes of the Bankruptcy Code.

We do not decide the proper scale for the risk adjustment, as the issue is not before us. The Bankruptcy Court in this case approved a risk adjustment of 1.5%, and other courts have generally approved adjustments of 1% to 3%. Respondent's core argument is that a risk adjustment in this range is entirely inadequate to compensate a creditor for the real risk that the plan will fail. There is some dispute about the true scale of that risk—respondent claims that more than 60% of Chapter 13 plans fail, but petitioners argue that the failure rate for *approved* Chapter 13 plans is much lower. We need not resolve that dispute. It is sufficient for our purposes to note that, under 11 U.S.C. § 1325(a)(6), a court may not approve a plan unless, after considering all creditors' objections and receiving the advice of the trustee, the judge is persuaded that "the debtor will be able to make all payments under the plan and to comply with the plan." *Ibid.* Together with the cram down provision, this requirement obligates the court to select a rate high enough to compensate the creditor for its risk but not so high as to doom the plan. If the court determines that the likelihood of default is so high as to necessitate an "eye-popping" interest rate, the plan probably should not be confirmed.

V

The dissent's endorsement of the presumptive contract rate approach rests on two assumptions: (1) "subprime lending markets are competitive and therefore largely efficient"; and (2) the risk of default in Chapter 13 is normally no less than the risk of default at the time of the original loan. Although the Bankruptcy Code provides little guidance on the question, we think it highly unlikely that Congress would endorse either premise.

First, the dissent assumes that subprime loans are negotiated between fully informed buyers and sellers in a classic free market. But there is no basis for concluding that Congress relied on this assumption when it enacted Chapter 13. Moreover, several considerations suggest that the subprime market is not, in fact, perfectly competitive. To begin with, used vehicles are regularly sold by means of tie-in transactions, in which the price of the vehicle is the subject of negotiation, while the terms of the financing are dictated by the seller. In addition, there is extensive federal and state regulation of subprime lending, which not only itself distorts the market, but also evinces regulators' belief that unregulated subprime lenders would exploit borrowers' ignorance and charge rates above what a competitive market would allow. Indeed, Congress enacted the Truth in Lending Act in part because it believed "consumers would individually benefit not only from the more informed use of credit, but also from heightened competition which would result from more knowledgeable credit shopping." S. Rep. No. 96-368, p 16 (1979).

Second, the dissent apparently believes that the debtor's prebankruptcy default—on a loan made in a market in which creditors commonly charge the maximum rate of interest allowed by law, Brief for Respondent 16, and in which neither creditors nor debtors have the protections afforded by Chapter 13—translates into a high probability that the same debtor's confirmed Chapter 13 plan will fail. In our view, however, Congress intended to create a program under which plans that qualify for confirmation have a high probability of success. Perhaps bankruptcy judges currently confirm too many risky plans, but the solution is to confirm fewer such plans, not to set default cram down rates at absurdly high levels, thereby increasing the risk of default.

Indeed, as Justice Thomas demonstrates, the text of § 1325(a)(5)(B)(ii) may be read to support the conclusion that Congress did not intend the cram down rate to include *any* compensation for the risk of default. That reading is consistent with a view that Congress believed Chapter 13's protections to be so effective as to make the risk of default negligible.

Because our decision in *Rash* assumes that cram down interest rates are adjusted to "offset," to the extent possible, the risk of default, 520 U.S., at 962-963, and because so many judges who have considered the issue (including the authors of the four earlier opinions in this case) have rejected the risk-free approach, we think it too late in the day to endorse that approach now. Of course, if the text of the statute required such an approach, that would be the end of the matter. We think, however, that § 1325(a)(5)(B)(ii)'s reference to "value, as of the effective date of the plan, of property to be distributed under the plan" is better read to incorporate all of the commonly understood components of "present value," including any risk of nonpayment. Justice Thomas' reading does emphasize, though, that a presumption that bankruptcy plans will succeed is more consistent with Congress' statutory scheme than the dissent's more cynical focus on bankrupt debtors' "financial instability and . . . proclivity to seek legal protection."

Furthermore, the dissent's two assumptions do not necessarily favor the presumptive contract rate approach. For one thing, the cram down provision applies not only to subprime loans but also to prime loans negotiated prior to the change in circumstance (job loss, for example) that rendered the debtor insolvent. Relatedly, the provision also applies in instances in which national or local economic conditions drastically improved or declined after the original loan was issued but before the debtor filed for bankruptcy. In either case, there is every reason to think that a properly risk-adjusted prime rate will provide a better estimate of the creditor's current costs and exposure than a contract rate set in different times.

Even more important, if all relevant information about the debtor's circumstances, the creditor's circumstances, the nature of the collateral, and the market for comparable loans were equally available to both debtor and creditor, then in theory the formula and presumptive contract rate approaches would yield the same final interest rate. Thus, we principally differ with the dissent not over what final rate courts should adopt but over which party (creditor or debtor) should bear the burden of rebutting the presumptive rate (prime or contract, respectively).

Justice Scalia identifies four "relevant factors bearing on risk premium[:] (1) the probability of plan failure; (2) the rate of collateral depreciation; (3) the liquidity of the collateral market; and (4) the administrative expenses of enforcement." In our view, any information debtors have about any of these factors is likely to be included in their bankruptcy filings, while the remaining information will be far more accessible to creditors (who must collect information about their lending markets to remain competitive) than to individual debtors (whose only experience with those markets might be the single loan at issue in the case). Thus, the formula approach, which begins with a concededly low estimate of the appropriate interest rate and requires the creditor to present evidence supporting a higher rate, places the evidentiary burden on the more knowledgeable party, thereby facilitating more accurate calculation of the appropriate interest rate.

. . .

The judgment of the Court of Appeals is reversed, and the case is remanded with instructions to remand the case to the Bankruptcy Court for further proceedings consistent with this opinion. It is so ordered.

[Justice Thomas's concurrence, based on statutory interpretation grounds, is omitted.]

Justice SCALIA, with whom THE CHIEF JUSTICE, Justice O'CONNOR, and Justice KENNEDY join, dissenting.

My areas of agreement with the plurality are substantial. We agree that, although all confirmed Chapter 13 plans have been deemed feasible by a bankruptcy judge, some nevertheless fail. We agree that any deferred payments to a secured creditor must fully compensate it for the risk that such a failure will occur. Finally, we agree that adequate compensation may sometimes require an "'eye-popping'" interest rate, and that, if the rate is too high for the plan to succeed, the appropriate course is not to reduce it to a more palatable level, but to refuse to confirm the plan.

Our only disagreement is over what procedure will more often produce accurate estimates of the appropriate interest rate. The plurality would use the prime lending rate—a rate we *know* is too low—and require the judge in every case to determine an amount by which to increase it. I believe that, in practice, this approach will systematically undercompensate secured creditors for the true risks of default. I would instead adopt the contract rate—*i.e.*, the rate at which the creditor actually loaned funds to the debtor—as a presumption that the bankruptcy judge could revise on motion of either party. Since that rate is generally a good indicator of actual risk, disputes should be infrequent, and it will provide a quick and reasonably accurate standard.

. . .

Bank of Montreal v. Official Committee of Unsecured Creditors (*In re American HomePatient, Inc.*)

420 F.3d 559 (6th Cir. 2005)

RONALD LEE GILMAN, Circuit Judge.

In July of 2002, American HomePatient, Inc. (American) filed for relief under Chapter 11 of the Bankruptcy Code. Despite objections by a group of secured lenders to American's proposed plan of reorganization, the bankruptcy court imposed the plan on the lenders pursuant to the Bankruptcy Code's so-called "cramdown" provisions set forth in 11 U.S.C. § 1129(b). The bankruptcy court further concluded that the appropriate cramdown interest rate for the lenders was 6.785%, and it fixed their collateral value at $250 million.

Displeased with these rulings, the lenders appealed the order of confirmation to the district court. . . . The district court . . . concluded on the merits that the bankruptcy court had properly determined both the cramdown interest rate and the collateral value. Both parties appealed. For the reasons set forth below, we AFFIRM the judgment of the district court.

I. BACKGROUND

American is a publicly-held company based in Brentwood, Tennessee. It specializes in providing home healthcare services and products and has more than 280 affiliates and subsidiaries in 35 states. Over the course of its operations, American borrowed a significant amount of money. Most of this debt was incurred between 1994 and 1998, when American invested in dozens of new branch offices. The lenders in this case are 24 entities that loaned money to American during this time frame. Although the parties disagree as to the exact total owed to the lenders, both sides acknowledge that the principal balance is in the range of $278 to $290 million.

Following American's voluntary filing for bankruptcy protection under Chapter 11 of the Bankruptcy Code in July of 2002, the company and its affiliates filed a Joint Plan of Reorganization. American filed a Second Amended Joint Plan of Reorganization in January of 2003. This amended plan was approved by all but the lenders in the present case. American then sought to have the plan confirmed pursuant to the Bankruptcy Code's cramdown provisions set forth in 11 U.S.C. § 1129(b), which allow a reorganization plan to go into effect notwithstanding the fact that it has not been accepted by all of the impaired classes.

The bankruptcy court held a five-day hearing on the lenders' claims. During this hearing, the court heard from various witnesses who testified as to the appropriate cramdown interest rate to be applied to the lenders' allowed secured claim. The bankruptcy court was ultimately persuaded by the testimony of American's expert witness David Rosen, who opined that the appropriate cramdown interest rate was 6.785%, which was equal to the interest rate on a six-year Treasury note plus 3.5%. It determined that the lenders' proposed interest rate of 12.16% was inappropriate because it would result in a windfall to the lenders.

. . .

On May 14, 2003, the bankruptcy court overruled the lenders' objections and directed American to submit a proposed order confirming the amended reorganization plan. This confirmation order was entered by the bankruptcy court on May 27, 2003. The lenders subsequently appealed. . . .

II. ANALYSIS

. . .

C. The Cramdown Interest Rate

The lenders' first substantive argument is that the district court erred in applying the "coerced loan theory" to determine the appropriate cramdown interest rate. They further contend that the cramdown interest rate of 6.785% is too low. Instead, they submit that the bankruptcy court should have applied a blended interest rate of 12.16%. This complex issue is further complicated by the recent Supreme Court case of *Till v. SCS Credit Corp.*, 541 U.S. 465 (2004) (plurality opinion).

As an initial matter, a judicial cramdown is an available option when "one or more classes refuse to accept the plan." 7 COLLIER ON BANKRUPTCY ¶1129.04 (15th ed. 2005). The cramdown provisions set forth in 11 U.S.C. § 1129(b) allow courts, despite objections, to confirm a reorganization plan if "the plan does not discriminate unfairly, and is fair and equitable, with respect to each class of claims or interests that is impaired under, and has not accepted, the plan." This statutory provision, however, does not specify how bankruptcy courts are to calculate the appropriate cramdown interest rate for lenders. *Cf. Till*, 541 U.S. at 473 ("[Chapter 13] provides little guidance as to which of the rates of interest . . . Congress had in mind when it adopted the cram down provision.").

. . .

[In *Till*, a] Chapter 13 case, the Supreme Court evaluated the four widely used methods of calculating the cramdown interest rate (the coerced loan, presumptive contract rate, formula rate, and cost of funds approaches) and found that all but the formula rate suffered from serious flaws. . . .

Instead, the Court endorsed the use of the formula approach. Under this approach, the bankruptcy court

> begins by looking to the national prime rate, reported daily in the press, which reflects the financial market's estimate of the amount a commercial bank should charge a creditworthy commercial borrower to compensate for the opportunity costs of the loan, the risk of inflation, and the relatively slight risk of default. Because bankrupt debtors typically pose a greater risk of nonpayment than solvent commercial borrowers, the approach then requires a bankruptcy court to adjust the prime rate accordingly.

Id. at 478-79.

The Court further observed that adopting "the formula approach entails a straightforward, familiar, and objective inquiry, and minimizes the need for potentially costly additional evidentiary proceedings." *Id.* at 479.

Till, however, was a Chapter 13 bankruptcy case. So even though the plurality is clear that the formula approach is the preferable method for Chapter 13 cases, the opinion is less clear about cases in the Chapter 11 context. On the one hand, the plurality noted that "the Bankruptcy Code includes numerous provisions that, like the [Chapter 13] cram down provision, require a court to 'discount . . . [a] stream of deferred payments back to their present dollar value' to ensure that a creditor receives at least the value of its claim." *Id.* at 474. It further commented that "we think it likely that Congress intended bankruptcy judges and trustees to follow essentially the same approach when choosing an appropriate interest rate under any of these provisions." *Id.* Some commentators have taken this to mean that *Till*'s analysis of Chapter 13 cramdown interest rates might be applicable to Chapter 11 cramdowns as well. *See* 7 COLLIER ON BANKRUPTCY ¶1129.06[1][c][i].

In . . . footnote [14], however, the plurality noted that "there is no readily apparent Chapter 13 'cram down market rate of interest.'" *Id.* at 476 n.14. This follows from the fact that "because every cram down loan is imposed by a court over the objection of the secured creditor, there is no free market of willing cram down lenders." *Id.* But

> interestingly, the same is not true in the Chapter 11 context, as numerous lenders advertise financing for Chapter 11 debtors in possession. *Thus, when picking a cramdown rate in a Chapter 11 case, it might make sense to ask what rate an efficient market would produce.* In the Chapter 13 context, by contrast, the absence of any such market obligates courts to look to first principles and ask only what rate will fairly compensate a creditor for its exposure.

Id. (emphasis added). This footnote suggests that a formula approach like the one adopted by the plurality is not required in the Chapter 11 context.

At least one court that has examined cramdown interest rates post-*Till* has concluded that *Till* does not apply in a Chapter 11 context. *See In re Prussia Assocs.*, 322 B.R. 572, 585, 589 (Bankr. E.D. Pa. 2005) (holding that "*Till* is instructive, but it is not controlling, insofar as mandating the use of the 'formula' approach described in *Till* in every Chapter 11 case," and noting that "[*Till*'s] dicta implies that the Bankruptcy Court in such circumstances (i.e., efficient markets) should exercise discretion in evaluating an appropriate cramdown interest rate by considering the availability of market financing").

Several outside commentators, however, have argued that *Till*'s formula approach should apply to Chapter 11 cases as well as to Chapter 13 cases, noting that the two are not all that dissimilar. *See* 7 COLLIER ON BANKRUPTCY ¶ 1129.06[1][c][i] ("The relevant market for involuntary loans in Chapter 11 may be just as illusory as in Chapter 13."). . . . And at least one court has concluded that *Till* does apply in a Chapter 11 context. *See Official Unsecured Creditor's Comm. of LWD, Inc. v. K&B Capital, LLC (In re LWD, Inc.)*, 332 B.R. 543, 2005 Bankr. LEXIS 384, 2005 WL 567460 (Bankr. W.D. Ky. Feb. 10, 2005).

Taking all of this into account, we decline to blindly adopt *Till*'s endorsement of the formula approach for Chapter 13 cases in the Chapter 11 context. Rather, we opt to take our cue from Footnote 14 of the opinion, which offered the guiding principle that "when picking a cram down rate in a Chapter 11 case, it might make sense to ask what rate an efficient market would produce." *Till*, 541 U.S. at 476 n.14. This means that the market rate should be applied in Chapter 11 cases where there exists an efficient market. But where no efficient market exists for a Chapter 11 debtor, then the bankruptcy court should employ the formula approach endorsed by the *Till* plurality. This nuanced approach should obviate the concern of commentators who argue that, even in the Chapter 11 context, there are instances where no efficient market exists.

While we accept Footnote 14's recommendation that the appropriate rate here is the one that "an efficient market would produce," we must still reconcile this principle with the coerced loan theory employed by the bankruptcy court. Indeed, the lenders make two related arguments against the bankruptcy court's determination of the appropriate interest rate, which they contend demonstrate that the court did not apply the rate that an efficient market would produce. They first claim that the 6.785% rate fixed by the bankruptcy court is not a realistic measure of what an efficient market would provide. According to the lenders' experts, an efficient market would have produced a rate of approximately 12%. One of their experts opined that this is because it is not feasible, using conventional funding sources, to provide the $309 million in financing needed by the Company with 100% debt. There is, however, an established market that can provide financing of $309 million to the Company. This market would provide a combination of senior debt, mezzanine debt [that is, debt secured by a security interest in the Company's equity], and equity, with resulting yields priced in response to the inherent risks assumed by the holders of such instruments.

This dovetails with the lenders' second point of contention, which is that the bankruptcy court should have taken "loan-specific" criteria into account when adjusting the appropriate cramdown rate. In support of this argument, they cite to language in *Till* suggesting that the Supreme Court would look favorably on an analysis incorporating debtor-specific risks.

Our understanding of the bankruptcy court's methodology, however, is that it in fact sought to determine what an efficient market would have produced for the loan that the lenders provided, albeit under the rubric of the coerced loan theory. In its assessment of the coerced loan theory, the bankruptcy court accepted Rosen's testimony to the effect that the loan in question was "senior debt loan in the health care field . . . under a normalized capital structure." Rosen then proceeded to analyze the standard market rate for such a loan. The lenders' argument, on the other hand, is centered on the composite interest rate that a new loan (including "mezzanine" debt and equity) would command in the market, not what their loan to American (which was all senior debt) would require. But as the bankruptcy court properly noted:

> The Lenders' argument that the debtor could not obtain a "new loan" in the market place so highly leveraged might be so, but in actuality no new loan is being made here at all. Instead, the court is sanctioning the workout between the debtor and the Lenders. New funds are not being advanced without the consent of the claimants. Indeed, the only type of debt contemplated by American's reorganization plan was senior secured debt. The inclusion of other types of financing—mezzanine debt and equity—is a pure hypothetical suggested by the lenders.

In addition, the bankruptcy court commented that, in its opinion, the 12.16% interest rate called for by the lenders would result in a "windfall." The court observed that

> the lenders are not entitled to a premium on their return because the debtor filed for bankruptcy. The blended rate suggested by the Lenders goes beyond protecting the value of its claim from dilution caused by the delay in payment. . . . Any windfall because of bankruptcy is neither contemplated nor required under the Code. The court's role is not to reward the creditor for the "new loan" to a bankrupt debtor, but instead only to provide the creditor with the present value of its claim.

This observation, that the lenders' request would result in a windfall, is further highlighted by *Till*. In *Till*, the plurality acknowledged that lenders ought to be compensated for their risk. The opinion, however, cited with approval the fact that other courts starting from the prime rate "have generally approved adjustments of 1% to 3%." *Till*, 541 U.S. at 480. It also commented that if a bankruptcy court "determines that the likelihood of default is so high as to necessitate an 'eye-popping' interest rate, the plan probably should not be confirmed." *Id.* at 480-81 (citation omitted). The interest rate demanded by the lenders here—12.16%—is nearly eight percentage points higher than the 4.25%

prime rate in effect on May 27, 2003, the date that the confirmation order was entered by the district court. As such, the 12.16% rate appears to fall under the "eye-popping" category described unfavorably by *Till*.

In sum, *Till* provides the lower courts with the guiding principle that "when picking a cram down rate in a Chapter 11 case, it might make sense to ask what rate an efficient market would produce." *Till*, 541 U.S. at 476 n.14. Although the lenders argue that the rate chosen by the bankruptcy court was not the rate produced by an efficient market, this is a question that was fully considered by that court. Its conclusion that the appropriate market rate would be 6.785% was reached only after carefully evaluating the testimony of various expert witnesses. The fact that the bankruptcy court utilized the rubric of the "coerced loan theory" that was criticized in *Till* provides no basis to reverse the bankruptcy court's decision because *Till* pointed out that, if anything, the coerced loan theory "*overcompensates* creditors. . . ." *Till*, 542 U.S. at 477 (emphasis added). We therefore concur in the result reached by both the bankruptcy court and the district court on this issue.

. . .

III. CONCLUSION

For all of the reasons set forth above, we AFFIRM the judgment of the district court.

The Sixth Circuit's position in *American Home Patient* has subsequently been adopted by the Fifth and Second Circuits. *In re Texas Grand Prairie Hotel Realty, L.L.C.*, 710 F.3d 324, 337 (5th Cir. 2013); *Apollo Global Mgmt., LLC v. BOKF, NA* (*In re MPM Silicones, L.L.C.*), 874 F.3d 787 (2d Cir. 2017). These cases also give a little more guidance regarding what is an "efficient market," from which a market rate could be derived, namely one which "offer[s] a loan with a term, size, and collateral comparable to the forced loan contemplated under the cramdown plan." *In re Texas Grand Prairie Hotel Realty, L.L.C.*, 710 F.3d at 337. In other words, these circuits have reverted to something like the "forced loan" rate that *Till* rejected in the Chapter 13 context, but these circuits qualify their approach by allowing the use of the forced loan approach only when an efficient market exists.

It is important to recognize that the issue in *Till* and *American HomePatient* is not the interest rate that applies in bankruptcy, but rather the interest rate under a plan. The interest rate on interest that accrues during bankruptcy is either at the contract rate or at the statutory or judgment rate for non-contractual obligations entitled to interest under section 506(b). Thus, there are three separate periods during which different interest rates might apply, as Figure 37.1, below, illustrates.

B. Indubitable Equivalence

Section 1129(b)(2)(A)(iii) provides an alternative treatment of a secured claim in a cramdown plan—the secured creditor must be paid the "indubitable equivalent" of its claim. What on earth is the indubitable equivalent of a claim? The great

Figure 37.1 Interest Rates Before, During, and After Bankruptcy

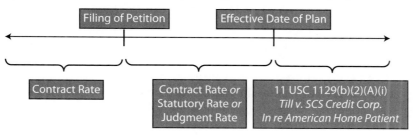

phrase, which comes from a Learned Hand opinion, *In re Murel Holding Corp.*, 75 F.2d 941, 942 (2d Cir. 1935), is best understood in contrast to section 1129(b)(2)(A)(i) and its provision for deferred cash payments. The indubitable equivalent of a claim must be something other than deferred cash payments, and it must be something other than the proceeds of the sale of the lender's collateral under section 1129(b)(2)(A)(ii).

So what could indubitable equivalence be? Payment in some form other than deferred cash. This could include immediate cash payment of the value of the claim, but it could also include payment in other forms of value—payment in the form of new debt, in stock, in land, etc. The statute itself doesn't provide any limit other than that it must be not just equivalent to the value of the claim, but indubitably equivalent. Thus, a secured creditor could be given third-party securities, such as Treasury bonds, on account of its claim. As risk-free securities, the interest rate on Treasury bonds should by definition ensure that the secured creditor is receiving the proper discount rate so that it gets the value of its claim over time.

More controversially, a "dirt for debt" plan will provide a secured creditor with payment in land. What's more, a "dirt for debt" plan need not even provide the secured creditor with land that is its collateral. Instead, the secured creditor with a lien on one parcel of land might receive a different parcel of land as payment. The question that a court must address to confirm such a plan is whether Greenacre or Blackacre or subdivision 13A or 100 acres of prime Florida swampland is the indubitable equivalent of the debt owed the secured creditor.

C. Sale of Collateral and Retention of Liens

Section 1129(b)(2)(A)(ii) provides a third alternative—the debtor may sell the creditor's collateral and pay the secured creditor the sale proceeds (up to the allowed amount of its secured claim). The sale works like a regular bankruptcy sale under section 363 of the Code. Among other things, such a sale normally allows for credit bidding by the secured creditor whose collateral is sold, but such credit bidding may be restricted "for cause."

Section 1129(b)(2)(A)(ii) functions like a foreclosure sale, but one forced by the debtor. The creditor might not want a sale: The creditor may have a favorable interest rate on the loan, or the market for its collateral might be temporarily depressed.

The debtor has the ability to "put" the collateral (or really its value) to the creditor under section 1129(b)(2)(A)(ii), even if the creditor does not want it. Thus, the debtor has a choice of (1) curing and reinstating, meaning paying per the original loan terms and payment structure, (2) paying off the secured creditor over time under section 1129(b)(2)(A)(i) at a new interest rate and with a new payment structure, (3) paying off the secured creditor in a lump sum via the sale of its collateral, or (4) paying the secured creditor the indubitable equivalent of (2) or (3).

IV. CRAM UP

Another possible treatment of secured claims in a cramdown is sometimes referred to through the colorful term "cram up." (Use your imagination.) A "cram up" is a non-consensual restructuring of secured debt that forces the creditor to accept repayment of the loan over time. Cram up is essentially a forced loan (or refinancing), which is particularly useful to a debtor if exit financing is hard to find on terms as favorable as the pre-petition secured debt.

While cram up would seem to be a parallel to cramdown, it's not. Cram up plans can be confirmed consensually or through cramdown, and not all cramdown plans involve cram up. More confusingly, there are actually two methods of cram up. One of these methods requires a cramdown; the other does not. The first method of cram up is to utilize section 1129(b)(2)(A)(i) to pay off the secured debt over time in deferred cash payments of a value equal to the debt or the indubitable equivalent of such deferred cash payments. This cram up method is available only in a cramdown, because the secured lender will be impaired and can therefore likely vote its class against the plan. The deferred cash payments (or equivalent treatment), however, deprive the secured creditor of a "fair and equitable" objection to cramdown, so if there is another impaired, accepting class (excluding insiders), cramdown confirmation is possible despite the negative vote by the secured creditor class.

Cram up through section 1129(b)(2)(A)(i) may make sense for a debtor if interest rates have fallen since the debt was originated. Courts apply current market rates to determine the discount rate for the deferred cash payments under section 1129(b)(2)(A)(i). Therefore, when rates have fallen, a cram up under section 1129(b)(2)(A)(i) forces a refinancing of the secured debt at lower rates without the lender's consent. The result can be considerable interest savings for the debtor. This is exactly what occurred in *DBSD*, where the secured debt was forcibly restructured to a four-year loan with payment in kind interest at 12.5%, which the court deemed to be the "indubitable equivalent" of deferred cash payments of a value equal to the face amount of the claim as of the effective date of the plan.

The other method of cram up is through cure and reinstatement of defaulted secured debt. Section 1124(2) allows for cure, deacceleration, and reinstatement of debts. Such debts are deemed unimpaired and therefore cannot vote on a plan. Thus, cram up can occur in the context of a consensual plan, as well as in a cramdown situation. Whereas a cram up through section 1129(b)(2)(A)(i) makes sense when interest rates have fallen since the origination of the debt, a cram up through reinstatement may make sense if interest rates have risen since origination; cure and reinstatement enables the debtor to retain the favorable financing. Similarly, cram up may be appealing to the debtor if the debt contains a favorable covenant package. Thus, Charter Communications saved over $500 million in annual interest expenses by cramming up its $11.8 billion in below-market rate debt.

The lesson to take is that neither consensual plan confirmation nor cramdown fully protect the rights of secured lenders; neither confirmation method gives them the ability to unilaterally exit the lending relationship other than by selling the debt.

V. RIGHTS OF UNDERSECURED CREDITORS

Undersecured creditors are given special protections in Chapter 11 (but not in Chapter 7) that run against the idea of Chapter 11 being a realization event and move toward relative priority. These special protections are found in section 1111(b). Section 1111(b) is one of the most opaque and hard to understand sections in the Bankruptcy Code, but it also provides undersecured creditors with very potent negotiating leverage. If some of the twists here are hard to follow at first, do not be frustrated—to understand section 1111(b) requires careful analysis and consideration.

Section 1111(b) provides creditors with two distinct rights. First, it provides that non-recourse debts are generally to be treated as if they were recourse for the purposes of calculating whether there is an allowed unsecured claim under section 502. Recourse treatment does not affect an oversecured creditor, but it matters if an undersecured debt is non-recourse. But for section 1111(b)(1)(A), the unsecured deficiency would be disallowed under section 502 as unenforceable against the debtor at state law, and indeed this is exactly the outcome that occurs in Chapter 7, where such an undersecured non-recourse creditor cannot receive a distribution on account of the unsecured portion of its claim.

Second, section 1111(b) allows a class of undersecured creditors to elect, in some circumstances, to have their claim treated as if the entire claim were a secured claim. In other words, by making the section 1111(b) election, a class of undersecured creditors opts out of having their claims bifurcated.

Opting out of claim bifurcation has a number of consequences, but most immediately it means that an electing class forgoes its section 1111(b)(1)(A) rights. It also means that the electing class forgoes any rights that would attend to the unsecured portion of the claim. Instead, under a cramdown plan it must receive payments that equal the greater of the present value of the collateral or the face amount of the entire debt. Recall that section 1129(b)(2)(A) provides that for a cramdown plan to be "fair and equitable" it must provide that secured creditors retain their liens "to the extent of the allowed amount of such claims" and that each secured claim holder receive "deferred cash payments totaling at least the allowed amount of such claim, of a value, as of the effective date of the plan, of at least the value of such holder's" lien. 11 U.S.C. § 1129(b)(2)(A)(i)-(ii). Thus, a secured creditor must (1) retain its liens for the amount of its secured claim, and (2) receive deferred cash payments equal to the greater of (a) the face amount of the allowed secured claim or (b) the value of the lien.

Accordingly, once a section 1111(b) election has been made, the creditor must receive the greater of deferred payments equal to the full amount of its allowed claim without including the time value of money, or payments with a present value as of the date of the plan equal to at least the value of the creditors' interest in the estate's interest in the collateral. A plan which proposes to pay an electing creditor only the value of its collateral is not confirmable when the proposed payments do not total at least the full amount of the creditor's claim.

The key to understanding the importance of the section 1111(b)(2) election is to understand that the "amount" of the claim is not the same as the value of the lien in all cases. If a creditor is fully secured, then the value of the lien is equal to the face amount of the secured claim. Likewise, if the creditor is undersecured and does not make the 1111(b) election, then the creditor's claim will be bifurcated and the face amount of the secured claim will be equal to the value of the collateral. If an undersecured creditor makes the 1111(b) election, however, then the entire face amount of the debt is treated as if it is a secured claim for section 1129(b)(2)(A) purposes, and that means that the face amount of the debt will exceed the value of the lien. Accordingly, the undersecured creditor must receive deferred cash payments equal to the face amount of the debt. By making the 1111(b) election, the undersecured creditor forgoes its unsecured deficiency claim and also forgoes the right to get the present value of the lien; it only has a right to receive the face value of the debt, and that can be paid over time without adjustment for present value.

Section 1111(b) was enacted as a reaction to a pre-Code case, *Great National Life Insurance Co. v. Pine Gate Associates, Ltd.*, 2 Bankr. Ct. Dec. 1478 (Bankr. N.D. Ga. 1976). *Pine Gate* involved a debtor whose sole asset was an apartment building. The debtor also had one debt: a non-recourse mortgage on the building. The debtor proposed paying the secured claim for the appraised value of the building in cash, after which the debtor would then own the building free and clear of all liens. The mortgage lender would get no payment on the deficiency because the loan was non-recourse. The result would be that the debtor would benefit from any undervaluation of the building or subsequent appreciation of the building.

Congress responded with section 1111(b) to prevent this forced cashing out of a non-recourse undersecured creditor at a judicial valuation. Section 1111(b)(1) treats a non-recourse debt as recourse, which means that there is an unsecured deficiency claim for the creditor. Even if the secured claim is paid in full, the creditor could still block consensual plan confirmation as the sole creditor voting and force payment in full in a cramdown plan if equity is to retain any property. At the same time, the section 1111(b)(2) election protects the undersecured creditor from having its lien stripped in bankruptcy, which matters if the secured creditor retains its lien after the bankruptcy and the debtor subsequently defaults. If the secured creditor retains its lien for the full amount of the debt, its recovery in a subsequent post-bankruptcy foreclosure would not be limited to the value of the collateral on the effective date of the plan, as would occur with lien stripping.

Why would a creditor ever make a section 1111(b)(2) election? First, the election protects a non-recourse undersecured creditor against a quick sale of the collateral.

Section 1111(b)(1)(A) provides that a non-recourse debt is to be treated as if it were recourse under section 502, which means that an undersecured creditor would be entitled to a section 502 unsecured claim for its deficiency even though it would not be able to collect such a deficiency at state law. Section 1111(b)(1)(A)(ii), however, provides that this deemed recourse treatment does not apply if the collateral is sold under a section 363 sale or a plan. If, however, the creditor makes the section 1111(b)(2) election, then the fact that the claim is non-recourse does not matter as the lien is for the full amount of the debt, not the value of the property. (Whether the property can still be sold under section 363(f)(3) is unclear.)

Second, the election provides protection to a secured creditor from a judicial under-valuation of its collateral and to potentially benefit from the future appreciation of its collateral. Under section 1129(b)(2)(A), the creditor retains its lien for the full amount of its claim. This is important if there is a subsequent default by the debtor under the plan. Suppose that the debt were $2 million and the court valued the collateral on the effective date of the plan at $1.3 million. If the creditor did not make the section 1111(b) election, the creditor would have a secured claim for $1.3 million and an unse-cured claim for $0.7 million. Let us also suppose that the plan were a cramdown plan in which general unsecured claims received nothing. The plan would, however, have to provide for the creditor to maintain its lien until it received the equivalent of $1.3 million in present value and $1.3 million in face amount.

Suppose that the debtor failed to make any payments to the creditor under the plan. The creditor could then foreclose on the collateral. But in the foreclosure sale, the creditor would be limited to recovering only $1.3 million. It could not recover the other $0.7 million, even if the property had appreciated in the interim (or if the judicial valuation were just low). If the property sold for $1.6 million, the creditor could keep $1.3 million, but the remaining $0.3 million would go back to the debtor. If, on the other hand, the creditor had made a section 1111(b)(2) election, the creditor would have retained a lien for the full $2 million, and would be able to keep the full $1.6 million generated by the foreclosure sale.

The section 1111(b)(2) election thus enables an undersecured creditor to protect itself from the risk of judicial undervaluation and to benefit from post-effective date appreciation. The effect of the section 1111(b)(2) election, then, is much like the effect of the Supreme Court's ruling in *Dewsnup v. Timm* that prevents lien stripping of allowed undersecured claims under section 506(d) in Chapter 7 of the Bankruptcy Code.

Third, the election may be used to force the debtor to propose plan terms that a court will find are not feasible and therefore will render the plan unconfirm-able. For example, in order to have payments equal the amount of the debt, not just the value of the collateral, the length of the payments may have to be extended. If the payment term extends beyond the life of the collateral, the court is unlikely to confirm the plan. Alternatively, the debtor could make payments at a higher inter-est rate, but if the rate is too high, the plan may not be feasible. Or perhaps the debtor will propose a plan with a balloon payment that the court believes is not feasible. Making the plan infeasible may be exactly what the undersecured creditor wants, as that provides it with significant negotiating leverage, including to force the surrender of the asset. One might reasonably ask if there is a problem with a secured creditor making a section 1111(b)(2) election for the purposes of making a plan infeasible—it raises questions of good faith and possible vote designation—but it would seem difficult to show an undersecured creditor's motives in this regard outside of unusual circumstances.

While there are benefits from a section 1111(b) election, there is also a cost. A creditor that makes the election loses the ability to vote its unsecured claim and to receive a distribution on account of it. While the distribution is unlikely to matter in most cases, the loss of the vote may mean that the creditor is forgoing a blocking position in another class.

The mechanics of the section 1111(b)(2) election also affect its strategic use. Under Federal Rule of Bankruptcy Procedure 3014, the election may be made at any point before the conclusion of the hearing on the adequacy of the disclosure statement or at a later time if the court allows, but obviously no later than the date on which ballots are due. This means that a class of undersecured creditors is able to evaluate the debtor's plan before making its election. Often courts require the debtor to explain in the disclosure statement the consequences of making the election and to propose an alternative plan if the election is made. This means that the debtor has to decide how it will treat an election before the election is made, which allows the creditors to evaluate the risks involved in the election.

The section 1111(b)(2) election is a class-wide election. It requires at least two-thirds of the amount of claims in the class and more than one-half of the number to make the election. 11 U.S.C. § 1111(b)(1)(A)(i). A class may not make the election if it is so heavily undersecured that the security interest is "of inconsequential value." 11 U.S.C. § 1111(b)(1)(B)(i). Case law has not elucidated where this line would be.

Similarly, a class may not make an election if any class member has a recourse claim and the property is to be sold under section 363 or under a plan. 11 U.S.C. § 1111(b)(1)(B)(ii). This is because section 1111(b)(2) also operates to protect *non-recourse* undersecured creditors from being forced to accept the proceeds of a section 363 sale in satisfaction of their entire debt, but if the creditor has a recourse claim, it needs no such protection, as the unsecured portion of its claim would be allowed under section 502 and eligible for distribution under a plan as an allowed unsecured claim.

Although section 1111(b) is conceptually important, it is rare to see a class of claims make the election. In part this relates to the interest rate environment since the early 1980s, but it is also because plans will typically specify a different, and less favorable, treatment for a class that makes the 1111(b) election.

Problem Set 37

(1) Polykrates Complex Systems has come to consult with you about the possible treatment of the claim by its secured creditor Xerxes Corp. Xerxes is owed $100 million on a 10-year 10% amortized note with 7 years remaining on the note. The loan is secured by all of Polykrates' real estate in Florida, worth around $115 million; Polykrates also owns substantial real estate in California, worth around $105 million, that is not subject to any liens. Interest rates have risen since Polykrates took out the loan. Polykrates

anticipates that it will have to confirm a cramdown plan, and wants to know which of the following treatments would enable Xerxes to successfully block plan confirmation:

a. Polykrates cures the defaults on the loan and reinstates the original loan for its original maturity.

b. Xerxes Corp. retains its existing liens and is given a new note for cash payments over five years with interest at the pre-bankruptcy contract rate.

c. Xerxes Corp. retains its existing liens and is given a new note for cash payments over five years with interest at a risk-adjusted market rate.

d. Xerxes Corp. retains its existing liens and is given a new note for cash payments over 10 years with interest at the risk-adjusted market rate.

e. Xerxes Corp. retains its existing liens and is given a new seven-year balloon note with interest paid in kind at a risk-adjusted market rate.

f. Polykrates Corp. will sell the Florida real estate with Xerxes Corp. being paid out of the sale proceeds.

g. Polykrates Corp. will sell the Florida real estate with Xerxes Corp. being paid out of the sale proceeds, but credit bidding will not be allowed.

h. Polykrates Corp. will give Xerxes Corp. substitute liens on its California real estate, but otherwise will pay off the loan per its original terms.

11 U.S.C. §§ 1124, 1129(b)(2)(A).

(2) Gemini Telecom, as DIP, has proposed a Chapter 11 plan that will cure and reinstate its secured debt; pay a class of trade creditors in full, in cash, on the effective date of the plan; and give the equity of the reorganized firm to a class of unsecured tort claimants, with no distribution made to pre-petition equity. If the tort claimants do not accept the plan, is it still confirmable? 11 U.S.C. §§ 1126(f)-(g), 1129(a)(10), 1129(b).

(3) Artemesia Petfoods, as DIP, has proposed a Chapter 11 plan with the following distributions:

Class I: Secured claims. Retain liens and paid with market-rate 5-year amortized note.

Class II: Unsecured note claims. Paid 30 cents on the dollar in the form of 40% equity in the reorganized debtor.

Class IIIA: Domestic tort claims. Paid 10 cents on the dollar.

Class IIIB: Foreign tort claims. Paid 5 cents on the dollar.

Class IV: Vendor claims. Paid in full.

Class V: Equity. Retains 60% of equity of reorganized debtor.

Is Artemesia's plan confirmable? 11 U.S.C. §§ 1122, 1129(a)(3), 1129(b).

(4) After Artemesia Petfoods failed to confirm the previous plan, it proposed a revised Chapter 11 plan with the following distributions:

Class I: Secured claims. Retain liens and paid with market-rate 5-year balloon note.

Class II: Unsecured note claims. Paid 60 cents on the dollar in the form of 40% of the equity in the reorganized debtor.

Class III: Tort claims. Paid 15 cents on the dollar if the class accepts the plan; otherwise paid 5 cents on the dollar.

Class IV: Vendor claims. Paid in full.

Class V: Equity. Retains 20% of equity of reorganized debtor.

Is Artemesia's new plan confirmable? 11 U.S.C. §§ 1122, 1123(a)(4), 1129(a)(3), 1129(b).

(5) Siliconia Chemical Products, a chemical manufacturer, is in Chapter 11 bankruptcy. Siliconia has $100 million in first lien notes outstanding. The first lien notes are secured by Siliconia's real estate. Siliconia has proposed a plan that would pay its first lien noteholders with new 7-year notes. The new notes would be secured by a first lien on the same collateral and bear an interest rate of 150 basis points above the rate of similar maturity (7-year) Treasury bonds. The debtor's expert, Professor Jan Pisher, who has appeared as an expert in over 400 cases in the past year alone, has testified that 150 basis points over Treasuries adequately compensates the first lien noteholders for the risks attendant to continuing to extend credit to the debtor.

   a. Do the first lien noteholders have a potential basis for an objection to the plan? And if so, is it likely to succeed? 11 U.S.C. § 1129(b)(2)(A)(i).
   b. Does this analysis change if the plan also provides for a $500 million 7-year exit financing facility secured by a *pari passu* first lien on the same collateral as the first lien notes and bearing an interest rate of 250 basis points above the rate of similar maturity Treasury bonds? What if the exit facility is being provided by the entity that also will own most of the reorganized debtor's equity?
   c. Suppose the plan provided that instead of receiving new notes secured by the same collateral, the first lien noteholders would receive a lien on Siliconia's equity in one of its operating subsidiaries, which Professor Pisher has testified is worth as much as the old collateral. Would that change your analysis? 11 U.S.C. § 1129(b)(2)(A)(iii).
   d. Suppose now the plan provided that instead of receiving new notes secured by the same collateral, the first lien noteholders would receive the stock of another of Siliconia's operating subsidiaries, which makes an experimental polymer. In effect, the plan would spin off the operating subsidiary. The indefatigable Professor Pisher has testified that based on his projected future sales of the polymer, the value of the stock of the operating subsidiary is equal to the amount of the first lien noteholders' claim. Recent news articles have noted that ingredients in the experimental polymer are highly carcinogenic, and the EPA has announced that it is considering regulations of those ingredients, including possibly banning them. Does this affect your analysis? 11 U.S.C. § 1129(b)(2)(A)(iii).

(6) Achilles Realty Corp. is in Chapter 11 bankruptcy. Achilles owns one asset, the enormous Olympian Arms apartment complex, which the court has valued at $80 million. The Olympian Arms is subject to a $100 million non-recourse first mortgage to First Bank of Illium. The mortgage contains a due-on-sale clause that accelerated the entire debt upon sale or encumbrance. Achilles also owes $1 million in unsecured pre-petition trade claims. Achilles has proposed a plan in which First Bank of Illium will retain its lien and receive deferred cash payments over 10 years under a new note. The unsecured claims will receive deferred cash payments over 5 years, and equity will retain ownership of the complex.

   a. How much must Achilles pay First Bank of Illium if the Bank does not make a section 1111(b) election? 11 U.S.C. §§ 1129(a)(7), 1129(b)(2)(A)(i).
   b. How much will Achilles have to pay First Bank of Illium if the Bank makes a section 1111(b) election? 11 U.S.C. §§ 1111(b), 1129(b)(2)(A)(i).

c. Can First Bank of Illium block plan confirmation if it makes the section 1111(b) election? What if it does not? 11 U.S.C. §§ 1111(b), 1126(c), 1126(g), 1129(a)(8), 1129(b).

d. Suppose that one year into the plan Achilles defaults on its plan obligations, having made $10 million in plan payments to First Bank of Illium. The value of the Olympian Arms has since soared to $95 million. When First Bank of Illium forecloses on the Olympian Arms, how much can it recover in the forclosure sale if it made the section 1111(b) election? If it did not? 11 U.S.C. §§ 1111(b), 1129(b)(2)(A)(i).

e. Suppose the First Bank of Illium has made the section 1111(b) election, and a year after the plan has become effective, Achilles sells the Olympian Arms for $120 million. Interest rates have also gone up considerably since plan confirmation. Can First Bank of Illium compel Achilles to pay off the entire debt immediately?

CHAPTER 38

THE ABSOLUTE PRIORITY RULE

I. THE ABSOLUTE PRIORITY RULE

Recall that section 1129(b) requires a cramdown plan to be "fair and equitable" to be confirmed. Section 1129(b)(2) not only specifies what "fair and equitable" includes in regard to a secured claim, as we saw in the previous chapter, but also what "fair and equitable" includes in regard to an unsecured claim or equity interest. For both unsecured claims and equity interests, "fair and equitable" generally means that the **absolute priority rule** will be applied. The Bankruptcy Code never uses the term "absolute priority rule," but the treatment that it prescribes is absolute priority, with which you are already familiar from our foreclosure sale exercise in Chapter 2 and the liquidation exercise in Chapter 28. Again, remember that the absolute priority rule only applies in a cramdown only for impaired, non-accepting classes, and only for unsecured claims and equity. A plan may violate the absolute priority rule in regard to a class if the class accepts the plan. *Official Comm. of Equity Sec. Holders v. Official Comm. of Unsecured Creditors (In re Adelphia Communs. Corp.)*, 544 F.3d 420, 426 (2d Cir. 2008). Likewise, the absolute priority rule, which protects the rights of general claimants on the firm, has no application to secured claims, which are asset-specific claims. Secured claims have priority only in their collateral, not generally.

A. Unsecured Creditors

For unsecured claims, section 1129(b)(2)(B) provides that to be fair and equitable a plan must provide for either

1. a distribution of property (not necessarily cash) with a value equal to the allowed amount of their claim, as of the effective date of the plan, 11 U.S.C. § 1129(b)(2)(B)(i); or
2. the application of the absolute priority rule, meaning that no junior class may receive any distribution unless the class has been repaid in full. 11 U.S.C. § 1129(b)(2)(B)(ii).

Thus, unsecured creditors either get the application of absolute priority or they get the present value (but not the face value) of their claims. This means that a cramdown plan does not have to invoke the absolute priority rule. Moreover, if absolute priority is not invoked, it is possible (and common) to pay unsecured creditors with new debt or with equity in the reorganized firm. Non-cash payments present valuation issues, of course, but the main point is that the payments need not be cash.

The invocation of absolute priority does not necessarily mean any recovery to unsecured creditors. It means only that no creditors junior to them (subordinated creditors) or equityholders can receive a distribution. If there is not enough money to pay unsecured creditors after the secureds and priority claimants have been paid, absolute priority can be invoked to confirm a plan that does not involve any distribution to the unsecureds. It is also important to recognize that absolute priority does not require sequential *cash* distributions. It can be satisfied as long as the *value* given to the senior claims fully satisfies those claims. *In re Penn Cent. Transp. Co.*, 458 F. Supp. 1234, 1283 (E.D. Pa. 1978).

The absolute priority rule also does not prevent a distribution to one class of unsecured creditors, but not to another. Instead, absolute priority prevents only distributions to junior classes. Indeed, some classes of identical priority could get property distributions, and others absolute priority per section 1129(b)(2)(B). Roughly equal treatment of different classes of unsecured creditors with the same priority is instead policed by the prohibition on unfair discrimination.

B. Equityholders

To be "fair and equitable," a cramdown plan must also provide that equityholders receive either

1. application of the absolute priority rule, 11 U.S.C. § 1129(b)(2)(C)(ii); or
2. the present value, as of the date of the plan, of the greatest of either the value of the interest, a fixed liquidation preference for the interest, or fixed redemption price for the interest. 11 U.S.C. § 1129(b)(2)(C)(i).

For equityholders, absolute priority might mean that they receive no recovery, if there is not enough value to spill down the priority waterfall to equity. If there is, then absolute priority would mean that preferred shares would have to be paid in full before common shares, and that senior preferred would have to be paid in full before junior preferred. If the company is insolvent, absent a fixed redemption price or liquidation preference, there will typically not be any value required to be distributed under section 1129(b)(2)(C)(i). (To be sure, there is always some option value in the stock of an insolvent company, but that assumes that option value is a type of value recognized in bankruptcy, which it is not for section 1129(b)(2)(C)(i) purposes.)

Absolute priority protects only *liquidation priority* (which includes structural priority). It does not protect priority derived from asset-based claims (liens), as those are covered under section 1129(b)(2)(A) and the best interest test. Nor does it cover temporal priority based on relative payment due dates. Absolute priority is based on a liquidation paradigm, and in liquidation all maturities are telescoped to the present. Indeed, the definition of "claim" in the Bankruptcy Code includes unmatured debt obligations. 11 U.S.C. § 101(5)(A). *But see* 11 U.S.C. § 502(b)(2) (disallowing otherwise allowable claims for unmatured interest). Likewise, covenant-based priorities, such as debt limitations or restrictions on asset-stripping or mergers or negative pledge clauses are disregarded, as covenant-based priorities are meaningless in a liquidation. Again, there is an exception—section 510(a) honors covenant-based subordination agreements, to the extent enforceable at non-bankruptcy law.

The following excerpt from the Third Circuit's decision in *Armstrong World Industries* is a recent example of just how absolute the absolute priority rule is: There are no *de minimis* value exceptions.

In re Armstrong World Industries, Inc.

432 F.3d 507 (3d Cir. 2005)

THOMPSON,* District Judge.

This matter is before the Court on Armstrong Worldwide Industries, Inc.'s ("AWI") appeal of the District Court's decision to deny confirmation of AWI's bankruptcy reorganization plan. In its decision, the District Court concluded that the plan could not be confirmed because the distribution of warrants** to AWI's equity interest holders over the objection of the class of unsecured creditors violated the absolute priority rule, as codified in 11 U.S.C. § 1129(b)(2)(B). AWI filed a timely appeal, contending that (1) the issuance of warrants does not violate the absolute priority rule. . . . For the following reasons, we affirm the judgment of the District Court.

I. FACTS AND PROCEDURAL HISTORY

AWI designs, manufactures, and sells flooring products, kitchen and bathroom cabinets, and ceiling systems. Due to asbestos litigation liabilities, AWI and two of its subsidiaries filed for Chapter 11 bankruptcy in the United States Bankruptcy Court for the District of Delaware on December 6, 2000. The United States Trustee for the District of Delaware appointed two committees to represent AWI's unsecured creditors: (1) the Official Committee of Asbestos Personal Injury Claimants ("APIC"), and (2) the Official Committee of Unsecured Creditors ("UCC"). . . .

Under [AWI's Fourth Amended Plan of Reorganization (the "Plan")], AWI's creditors were divided into eleven classes, and AWI's equity interest holders were placed into a twelfth class. Relevant to this appeal are Class 6, a class of unsecured creditors; Class 7, a class of present and future asbestos-related personal injury claimants; and Class 12, the class of equity interest holders who own AWI's common stock. The only member of Class 12 is Armstrong Worldwide, Inc. ("AWWD"), the parent company of AWI, which is in turn wholly owned by Armstrong Holdings, Inc. ("Holdings"). Classes 6 and 7 hold equal priority, and have interests senior to those of Class 12. All three are impaired classes because their claims or interests would be altered by the Plan. 11 U.S.C. § 1124.

---

* Sitting by designation.

** A warrant is a call option to purchase stock. A warrant differs from an option in two essential characteristics. First, warrants are issued by a private company, rather than by an options exchange, and are therefore dilutive of the company's stock when exercised. Second, a warrant is not a standardized instrument, so it can be readily exchange-traded.—ED.

The Plan provided that AWI would place approximately $1.8 billion of its assets into a trust for Class 7 pursuant to 11 U.S.C. § 524(g). Class 7's members would be entitled to an initial payment percentage from the trust of 20% of their allowed claims. Meanwhile, Class 6 would recover about 59.5% of its $1.651 billion in claims. The Plan would also issue new warrants to purchase AWI's new common stock, estimated to be worth $35 to $40 million, to AWWD or Holdings (Class 12). If Class 6 rejected the Plan, then the Plan provided that Class 7 would receive the warrants. However, the Plan also provided that Class 7 would automatically waive receipt of the warrants, which would then be issued to AWWD or Holdings (Class 12).

The Bankruptcy Court set September 22, 2003 as the deadline for voting on the Plan and for the parties to object to the Plan's confirmation. Because the Plan would distribute property to AWI's equity interest holders without fully paying off the unsecured creditors' claims, all impaired unsecured creditor classes were required to approve the Plan under 11 U.S.C. § 1129(a)(8). If any impaired class objected to the Plan, then the Plan could only be "crammed down" if it was "fair and equitable" to the objecting class. See 11 U.S.C. § 1129(b)(1).

UCC represented all of the classes of unsecured creditors, including Class 6, during the negotiations that led to the Plan. Although UCC initially approved of the Plan in May 2003, it later filed a conditional objection to the Plan's confirmation on September 22, 2003 based on . . . the possible applicability of the absolute priority rule, as codified in 11 U.S.C. § 1129(b), if the Plan was not accepted by all classes.

To accept the Plan, class members holding at least fifty percent of the number of claims and two-thirds of the amount of the claims would need to vote for the Plan. See 11 U.S.C. § 1126(c). Although 88.03% of Class 6 claim holders voted for the Plan, only 23.21% of the amount of the claims voted to accept the Plan. As a result, Class 6 rejected the Plan. Classes 7 and 12 accepted the Plan, but Class 12's acceptance was rescinded under the Plan due to Class 6's rejection.

. . .

The District Court found that . . . the issuance of warrants to the equity interest holders violated the absolute priority rule. . . . *In re Armstrong World Indus., Inc.*, 320 B.R. 523 (D. Del. 2005). AWI now appeals the District Court's decision. . . .

II. DISCUSSION

. . .

C. Confirmation of a Reorganization Plan

Confirmation of a proposed Chapter 11 reorganization plan is governed by 11 U.S.C. § 1129. A court will confirm a plan if it meets all of the requirements set out in section 1129(a). Only one of these requirements concerns us in this appeal, and that is the requirement that the plan be consensual, with unanimous acceptance by all of the impaired classes.[2] 11 U.S.C. § 1129(a)(8). If the plan is not consensual, a court may still

---

2. A class is impaired if its legal, equitable, or contractual rights are altered under the reorganization plan. 11 U.S.C. § 1124.

confirm as long as the plan meets the other requirements of section 1129(a), and "does not discriminate unfairly, and is fair and equitable" as to any dissenting impaired class. 11 U.S.C. § 1129(b)(1); *see Bank of Am. Nat'l Trust & Sav. Ass'n v. 203 N. LaSalle St. P'ship*, 526 U.S. 434, 441 (1999) [hereinafter *LaSalle*]. The latter type of confirmation is also called a "cram down," as the court can cram a plan down over the objection of a class of creditors.

1. The Absolute Priority Rule

The issues in this case require us to examine the "fair and equitable" requirement for a cram down, which invokes the absolute priority rule. The absolute priority rule is a judicial invention that predated the Bankruptcy Code. It arose from the concern that because a debtor proposed its own reorganization plan, the plan could be "too good a deal" for that debtor's owners. *LaSalle*, 526 U.S. at 444. In its initial form, the absolute priority rule required that "creditors . . . be paid before the stockholders could retain [equity interests] for any purpose whatever." *Id.*

The absolute priority rule was later codified as part of the "fair and equitable" requirement of 11 U.S.C. § 1129(b). Under the statute, a plan is fair and equitable with respect to an impaired, dissenting class of unsecured claims if (1) it pays the class's claims in full, or if (2) it does not allow holders of any junior claims or interests to receive or retain any property under the plan "on account of" such claims or interests. 11 U.S.C. § 1129(b)(2)(B)(i)-(ii).

At the heart of this appeal is the Plan provision that distributes warrants to AWI's equity interest holders (Class 12) through Class 7 in the event that Class 6 rejects the Plan. Appellant AWI argues that this provision does not violate the absolute priority rule because . . . the Plan did not give the warrants to Class 12 "on account of" its equity interests.

. . .

c. On Account of

. . . AWI argues that the warrants would not be distributed to Class 12 on account of their equity interests, but rather would be given as consideration for settlement of their intercompany claims. UCC disputes the existence of any such settlement, alleging that such an arrangement should have been brought to the attention of the Bankruptcy Court. In response, AWI indicates that the settlement was detailed in the Plan's Disclosure Statement, which the Bankruptcy Court approved on June 2, 2003. The relevant portion of the Disclosure Statement reads as follows:

> In the ordinary course of business, such intercompany claims have been recorded on the books and records of Holdings, AWWD and AWI, and, assuming that all such intercompany claims are valid, the net intercompany claim so recorded is in favor of Holdings in the approximate amount of $12 million. In consideration of, among other things, AWI's agreement under the Plan to fund the reasonable fees and expenses associated with the Holdings Plan of Liquidation, the treatment of Holdings, AWWD, and their respective officers and directors as PI Protected Parties under the Asbestos PI Permanent Channeling Injunction, the simultaneous release by AWI of any claims (known and unknown) AWI

has against Holdings and AWWD, and the issuance of the New Warrants to AWWD, and to avoid potentially protracted and complicated proceedings to determine the exact amounts, nature and status under the Plan of all such claims and to facilitate the expeditious consummation of the Plan and the completion of Holdings' winding up, Holdings and AWWD will, effective upon and subject to the occurrence of the Effective Date, release all such intercompany claims (known and unknown) against AWI or any of AWI's subsidiaries[.]

As stated earlier, section 1129(b)(2)(B)(ii) provides that holders of junior claims or interests "will not receive or retain [any property] under the plan *on account of* such junior claim or interest." 11 U.S.C. § 1129(b)(2)(B)(ii) (emphasis added). In *LaSalle*, the Supreme Court interpreted "on account of" to mean "because of," or a "causal relationship between holding the prior claim or interest and receiving and retaining property." 526 U.S. at 450-51. Although the Supreme Court did not decide what degree of causation would be necessary, its discussion on that topic revealed that the absolute priority rule, as codified, was not in fact absolute. First, it indicated that the "on account of" language would be redundant if section 1129(b) was read as a categorical prohibition against transfers to prior equity. *Id.* at 452-53. Second, it noted that a "less absolute prohibition" stemming from the "on account of language" would "reconcile the two recognized policies underlying Chapter 11, of preserving going concerns and maximizing property available to satisfy creditors." *Id.* at 453-54.

In keeping with these observations, we noted in *PWS* that the "on account of" language "confirms that there are some cases in which property can transfer to junior interests not 'on account of' those interests but for other reasons." 228 F.3d at 238 (discussing *LaSalle*, 526 U.S. at 451-52). In *PWS*, the debtors released their legal claims against various parties to facilitate their reorganization, including an avoidance claim that would have allowed them to avoid certain aspects of a previous recapitalization. *Id.* at 232-35. The appellants in *PWS* argued that releasing the avoidance claim resulted in a prohibited transfer of value to equity interest holders who had participated in the recapitalization. We held that "without direct evidence of causation, releasing potential claims against junior equity does not violate the absolute priority rule in the particular circumstance [where] the claims are of only marginal viability and could be costly for the reorganized entity to pursue." *Id.* at 242.

AWI would analogize AWWD and Holdings's release of intercompany claims in exchange for warrants to the release of claims in *PWS*. We disagree. According to the Disclosure Statement, the warrants have an estimated value of $35 to $40 million. In contrast, the intercompany claims were valued at approximately $12 million. This settlement would amount to a substantial benefit for Class 12, especially as the warrants were only part of the consideration for which the intercompany claims were released. Among other things, the intercompany claims were also ostensibly released in exchange for the simultaneous release of any claims by AWI against AWWD or Holdings and facilitation of the reorganization process. AWI gives no adequate explanation for this difference in value, leading us to conclude that AWWD or Holdings (Class 12) would receive the warrants on account of their status as equity interest holders. *See LaSalle*, 526 U.S. at 456.

III. CONCLUSION

We recognize that the longer that the reorganization process takes, the less likely that the purposes of Chapter 11 (preserving the business as a going concern and maximizing the amount that can be paid to creditors) will be fulfilled. Nevertheless, we conclude that the absolute priority rule applies in this case. We will accordingly affirm the District Court's decision to deny confirmation of AWI's Plan.

II. THE RELATIVE PRIORITY ALTERNATIVE

All restructuring deal-making in and outside bankruptcy operates in the shadow of the absolute priority rule. The absolute priority rule functions as the primary limitation on a plan proponent's ability to force unsecured or equity holdouts to accept the terms of a restructuring. Outside of bankruptcy, it is difficult for a debtor to legally force restructuring terms on its creditors. Section 1129(a)(8)'s majority approval requirement makes it possible for a majority of creditors to bind minority holdouts, but section 1129(b) makes it possible to bind holdouts even when they are a majority of creditors.

Because of the importance of the absolute priority rule, it is worthwhile understanding something of its history and rationale. The absolute priority rule is specified in sections 1129(b)(2)(B)(ii) and 1129(b)(2)(C)(ii), but it is never called such by name. Sections 1129(b)(2)(B)(ii) and 1129(b)(2)(C)(ii) are a codification of a judicially created absolute priority doctrine. The absolute priority doctrine is best understood in distinction to its alternative, relative priority.

Absolute priority requires that no junior priority creditor be paid anything until all senior creditors have been paid in full. Absolute priority is a liquidation paradigm based on the concept of payments flowing down the priority ladder, starting with the seniormost creditors until funds are exhausted. Absolute priority treats bankruptcy as a realization event similar to a foreclosure. All debts are accelerated to present, and payment is made in order of a liquidation priority on the basis of state law and any additional bankruptcy priorities. This means that there is no room for bargaining over the allocation of the going-concern surplus of the firm. Because absolute priority treats bankruptcy like a liquidation, any change in the future value of the reorganized firm inures to the benefit of the parties who receive the reorganized firm's equity.

In contrast, relative priority assumes a reorganization. Relative priority is a somewhat confusing concept because there has never been any clear judicial articulation of precisely what it requires. Indeed, the seminal Supreme Court case on relative priority isn't even a bankruptcy case. Instead, it involved a non-judicial restructuring through a foreclosure sale (not unlike the transaction that was executed in *Marblegate Asset Mgmt., LLC v. Educ. Mgmt. Fin. Corp.*, 846 F. 3d 1 (2d Cir. 2016), that you saw in Chapter 9) and was really a successor liability case that was decided on equitable grounds. *Northern Pac. Ry. Co. v. Boyd*, 228 U.S. 482 (1913).

Nonetheless, from reading between the lines in the case law, it seems that relative priority merely requires that the relative *liquidation* priorities of parties going into bankruptcy be preserved coming out of bankruptcy. The key to the relative priority approach is that it does not treat bankruptcy as a realization event—debts that were not yet due and owing do not have to be accelerated as long as their priority is preserved. Thus, as long as a senior party continued to have a senior interest in a debtor coming out of bankruptcy, the fact that a payment had been made to a junior party was acceptable, just as it is when a debtor is outside of bankruptcy. Relative priority treats priority as only a liquidation preference, not a payment preference. Relative priority thus allows for bargaining among claimants regarding the going-concern surplus of the firm when there is no liquidation. Under relative priority, the going-concern surplus can be divvied up in any number of ways so long as parties that had senior securities prior to bankruptcy were still senior in their position after bankruptcy.

To illustrate the difference between absolute and relative priority, imagine a firm with secured debt, senior unsecured debt, junior unsecured debt, and equity. Under an absolute priority regime, the secured creditors would get the value of their collateral. For simplicity's sake, let's assume that they are fully secured. Next, the senior unsecured debt would be paid. Let's assume it is paid in full. Then the junior unsecured debt would be paid. Let's assume it's only paid at 50 cents on the dollar. If so, the junior unsecured debt would also be given the equity in the firm (worth nothing), and the old equityholders would get nothing (and have their equity cancelled).

The problem with an absolute priority regime is that it is distributing the value of the firm as if the firm were frozen at a particular moment. Absolute priority does not account for the possibility that the firm's value at the moment of bankruptcy might be different than at some future state. Thus, absolute priority does not account for the "option value" that out-of-the-money claims or interests might have. Option value is the value of a claim or interest based on the possibility that it will be worth something in the future, making owning it equivalent to owning a call option—the option may be out of the money today, but it is still valuable because it could be in the money in the future.

To wit, let's return to the hypothetical firm described above. Imagine that the day following bankruptcy, the firm's value doubled (let's say it struck gold). Who would capture the gains? It would be the junior unsecureds, who received the firm's equity under absolute priority. They would capture a windfall, while old equity would still get nothing. If the absolute priority rule had been applied a day later, pre-petition equityholders would have retained the value of the firm beyond what was needed to pay off the creditors. Thus, absolute priority disregards option value. As a result, absolute priority encourages senior creditors to push for a quick liquidation or asset sale, while it encourages junior creditors to engage in delaying tactics in the hope that their claim will come back "in the money."

Relative priority potentially accounts for option value. Under a relative priority system, the secured creditors would either retain their liens or receive the value of their collateral. The senior unsecured debt would have to receive value equal to 100% of their claims, because under a liquidation they would have been paid in full. This value would have to be in a form that would retain their relative priority, meaning that the senior debt would have to remain senior. Thus, the senior debt could be given a new note, perhaps with a lower interest rate and a longer term, but the new note would have to be senior to the junior debt and the equity. Likewise, the junior unsecured debt would have to receive value equal to 50% of its claim, and it would have to be in a form that would remain subordinated to the senior debt and senior to the equity. And equity would retain some ownership stake in the firm. Thus, if the firm's value doubled the next day, equity, rather than the creditors, would capture the entire gain in value. Of course, if it turned out that the firm were overvalued, the old equityholders would still have a stake in the company—and control rights—even if they were out of the money.

Absolute priority puts different pressure on valuation than relative priority. In an absolute priority world, if the firm is overvalued, then equity may be able to retain an interest in the firm, and keep its option value. If the firm is undervalued, then equity may be wrongly deprived of its option value. But the whole issue hangs on valuation.

In a relative priority world, the polarity of valuation is reversed. If a firm is undervalued in a relative priority world, then creditors will receive less because their hypothetical liquidation share would be less, effectively shifting more value to old equityholders, who will retain rights even though they might be out of the money. If the firm is overvalued, then creditors will receive more based on a hypothetical liquidation, and going-concern value is effectively shifted away from equity.

We live in a world of valuation uncertainty. While courts routinely value assets and firms, there is no guaranty of the accuracy of those valuations, and valuations may fluctuate over time. So, as between relative priority, which is better for systematic undervaluation and absolute priority? Which is better for systematic overvaluation? Which should we prefer? Proponents of relative priority emphasize the ability of the parties to bargain over valuations in a relative priority system—the parties can agree to split the difference. In an absolute-priority world, there is no ability to bargain over valuations.

Whether we think this ability to bargain over valuations is a good thing depends on whether we think there is the possibility of frictionless bargaining or whether we think there are too many obstacles to ensuring an efficient allocation of rights. The difference between absolute and relative priority is essentially the difference between a property rights regime and a contract rights regime. In a property rights regime, parties have an absolute veto over transactions that would deprive them of their property rights. In a contract rights regime, rights are awarded to the highest bidder. Absolute priority, then, is a "property rule" that mandates a distribution of rights, whereas relative priority is a "contract rule" that lets parties bargain over the distribution of rights. (Both rules are built on a "property rule" edifice of best interests, as there is an unqualified entitlement for all parties to receive liquidation value.)

So which rule should we prefer? It depends on what we think about the parties involved in bankruptcies. Contract rules theoretically allow parties to bargain over the allocation of rights—the party that values the right the most will pay the other party for the right. That is what is called "Coasean bargaining" (after the economist Ronald Coase).

One of Coase's major insights, however, was that true Coasean bargaining was difficult to achieve because of transaction costs. *See* Ronald Coase, *The Problem of Social Cost,* 3 J.L. & ECON. 1 (1960). To the extent that it is costly for the parties to negotiate—including obtaining information, etc.—then rights might not get allocated to the party that value them the most. In other words, in a world—like the real world—with transaction costs, Coasean bargaining might be frustrated. If transaction costs are relatively small, we might not be so concerned, but if they are large, then we should be more concerned.

What do transaction costs look like in a bankruptcy? Recall that bankruptcy is not a simple bilateral negotiation. It is a multilateral negotiation typically involving several, if not thousands of parties. The procedural mechanisms of bankruptcy, such as plan exclusivity and the requirement of an approved disclosure statement for vote solicitation channel some of the negotiations, but the formal requirements also increase transaction costs.

Moreover, transaction costs are not all equally distributed. Repeat players that have experience with the bankruptcy system have much lower transaction costs than rookies because learning the system is expensive. Who is likely to be a repeat player in bankruptcy? Certainly some financial institutions. And also some trade creditors and tax creditors. But employees, retirees, and tort victims, as well as some trade creditors, and even some financial creditors (particularly bondholders) may not be experienced with bankruptcy. They are thus at a disadvantage relative to the more sophisticated, repeat players.

Similarly, to the extent that there are information asymmetries, they function much like transaction costs, as the cost of overcoming the information asymmetries falls on the informationally disadvantaged party. Are there likely to be information asymmetries in bankruptcy? Of course. Management probably knows more than anyone, and management is often affiliated with equity. Secured creditors also tend to have informational advantages, particularly if they are the DIP lender, as the DIP financing agreement will usually provide for the provision of a great deal of information about the debtor's ongoing operations to the DIP lender.

Bankruptcy law has features that are intended to counteract this information asymmetry problem: the requirement of dissemination of an approved disclosure statement prior to solicitation of votes, and the provision of information to the Official Committee of Unsecured Creditors. Neither device entirely rectifies information asymmetries, however.

Transaction costs are not the only factor that can frustrate Coasean bargaining. Wealth and liquidity constraints can also play a role. Party *A* might value a right more than Party *B*, but it will not matter if Party *A* does not have enough assets presently to buy out Party *B*'s interest in the right. Thus, if there are wealth or liquidity constraints, Coasean bargaining might not ensure that property ends up in the hands of the party that values it the most.

Do you think that creditors and equityholders might themselves ever suffer from wealth and liquidity constraints? Of course they do, although not all do so equally. Who is likely to be illiquid or wealth constrained? Employees, retirees, tort claimants, and trade claimants are the most likely candidates, but so too are some types of financial creditors, such as collateralized loan obligations (CLOs) and lending syndicates, which may have contractual impediments to raising new funds or achieving liquidity.[1]

Given these limitations on achieving true Coasean bargaining, the benefits of a contract rule like relative priority are suspect. Relative priority might not end up with the efficient allocation of resources, because they might not go to the party that values the resources the most, but instead to the party with the most wealth, most liquidity, most information, or lowest transaction costs.

This is not to say that a property rule like absolute priority is necessarily ideal. Absolute priority might well be an equally inefficient allocation of resources, in the sense that they might not be allocated to those who value them the most. But absolute priority has something to commend it that relative priority does not: There is no question of the fairness of absolute priority. Parties get the priority for which they bargained ex ante. We do not have to worry about whether some parties are getting ahead because they are richer or more sophisticated or have access to information that others do not. Absolute priority thus creates a protective floor for less sophisticated, less wealthy, less inside parties. Given that value in a relative priority system is allocated based on the parties' bargaining, rather than on an arms'-length market process such as a sale, there is good reason to be concerned that more sophisticated, more inside parties will systematically do better than less sophisticated ones. As bankruptcy is a judicial process involving the resources and authority of the state, there is a duty to ensure that the process has fundamental fairness to all parties, irrespective of their wealth, sophistication, or connections. Thus, absolute priority is not necessarily the optimal allocation of a firm's going-concern value, but assures a minimal level of fairness that relative priority cannot provide.

Indeed, this explains much of why Justice Douglas announced in *Case v. Los Angeles Lumber*, 308 U.S. 106 (1939), his first bankruptcy opinion after joining the Supreme Court, that the "fair and equitable" requirement for confirming a plan under section 77 of the Chandler Act of 1938 included a requirement of absolute priority. Indeed, Justice Douglas's opinion in *Case v. Los Angeles Lumber* arguably overturned the Supreme Court's functional (but not explicit) endorsement of relative

---

1. Liquidity constraints on certain types of creditors (particularly CLOs and lending syndicates) was one reason that some plans in the 2000s prohibited credit bidding and instead required cash bidding, as the cash bidding requirement effectively precluded certain parties from bidding at auctions.

priority in a case decided less than nine months prior.[2] To the extent that one does not trust the process of bargaining for the going-concern surplus, then a property rights regime like absolute priority makes sense. Justice Douglas had no confidence in the integrity of the pre-Chandler Act reorganization practice, as reflected in the multi-volume SEC report on reorganization practices compiled by Douglas (with future Supreme Court Justice Abe Fortas and future Second Circuit Judge Jerome Frank) starting in 1934. Douglas saw corporate reorganization practice as fundamentally corrupt, controlled by insiders and favored creditors, and used as a sword against outsiders, particularly "ma and pa" bondholders.

Both the Trust Indenture Act (as drafted by Douglas) and the Chandler Act (as interpreted by Douglas to require absolute priority) were a reaction to the perceived corruption of the reorganization process and inability to achieve fair, arms'-length bargaining among stakeholders. Douglas and Frank had argued in academic work that relative priority was effectively a fraudulent transfer if pre-petition equity retained an interest in the reorganized firm. *See* Jerome Frank, *Some Realistic Reflections on Some Aspects of Corporate Reorganization*, 19 VA. L. REV. 541-570, 698-718 (1933); William O. Douglas & Jerome Frank, *Landlords' Claims in Reorganizations*, 42 YALE L.J. 1003 (1933). Thus, the Chandler Act was meant to go hand in glove with the Trust Indenture Act of 1939 by creating a framework in which bondholders could not be forced to accept changes to their payment terms outside of bankruptcy, which then applied judicial oversight, disclosure, good faith, independent committee representation, supermajority voting requirements, and the fair and equitable requirement. (Curiously, there is no explicit bankruptcy exception to the Trust Indenture Act's prohibition of nonconsensual impairment of bondholders' right to payment, but this has always been understood to be the case.)

Notably, the Chandler Act required *both* creditor consent (through a class vote) *and* that a plan be fair and equitable, which Justice Douglas interpreted to require compliance with absolute priority. Thus, even if creditors approved a plan via their class vote, a plan could not be confirmed if it did not comport with absolute priority.

---

2. In February 1939, shortly before Douglas's nomination (and during a prior Supreme Court term), the Court had reversed a plan of reorganization that had transferred the debtor's assets to a new corporation, in which the majority of stock was awarded to the old common stockholder (the debtor's parent corporation), with a minority of the stock given to the preferred stockholders. *Taylor v. Standard Gas & Elec. Co.*, 306 U.S. 307 (1939) (the "Deep Rock" case). The Court held that "If a reorganization is effected, the amount at which [the parent corporation's] claim is allowed is not important if it is to be represented by stock in the new company, provided the stock to be awarded it is subordinated to that awarded preferred stockholders. No plan ought to be approved which does not accord the preferred stockholders a right of participation in the equity in the Company's assets prior to that of Standard, and at least equal voice with Standard in the management." *Id.* at 324. This ruling does not in fact comport with absolute priority, at least as expressed in 11 U.S.C. § 1129(b)(2)(C)(ii), as the parent corporation—a common stockholder—would receive a distribution without the preferred stockholders having been paid off in full at their fixed liquidation preference. Instead, it seems to have provided for a type of relative priority—the old common stockholders could retain an interest, but they had to remain subordinate to that of the preferred stockholders, both in terms of their liquidation preference *and* their governance rights. Writing in November 1939, Justice Douglas cited to the Deep Rock case in *Case v. Los Angeles Lumber*, 308 U.S. at 114, but for the point that it too required "fair and equitable" treatment. Justice Douglas elided over the fact that "fair and equitable" meant something entirely different in the Deep Rock case than what he interpreted it to mean in *Case v. Los Angeles Lumber*.

The resulting regime left little flexibility in reorganization plans, which were rare under the Act.

In contrast, the Bankruptcy Code requires *either* creditor consent (through a class vote) *or* that a plan be fair and equitable, which requires absolute priority. Thus, creditors must either strike a bargain regarding the allocation of the going-concern surplus or a reorganization can be forced through using a property rights regime. As the House Report on the 1978 Bankruptcy Reform Act noted, "When the extensive controls of the Chandler Act were adopted, the public interest was usually in senior bonds, and that Act was intended to protect the public holders in a senior position against the maneuverings of strong private groups in a subordinate position. Today, at least as frequently, the public interest is represented by public common stock or public subordinated debentures, while the persons in the driver's seat and under the strict priority rules are institutional private investors or strong trade creditors." H.R. REP. NO. 95-595, 95th Cong., 1st Sess. at 261 (1977). Accordingly, the Bankruptcy Code relaxed the absolute priority rule, applying it only when there was not the requisite creditor consent. Query how it should apply today with further changes in the composition of the market, particularly the development of a deep secondary market in bankruptcy claims.

Problem Set 38

(1) Bacchus Party Supplies, as DIP, has proposed a Chapter 11 plan. The plan will cure and reinstate its first lien secured loan. The second lien secured loan will be paid in full in cash on the effective date of the plan. Unsecured debt will be given new notes worth 30 cents on the dollar of their claims, and pre-petition equity will retain its interests. The first lienholder is opposed to the plan, but all the other creditors and equityholders support the plan.

   a. Does the plan comply with absolute priority? 11 U.S.C. § 1129(b)(2)(B)(2).
   b. Is the plan confirmable? 11 U.S.C. §§ 1124, 1126(f), 1129(b).

(2) Phoebus Technologies, a venture capital–funded start-up that makes Internet security software, is in Chapter 11. Phoebus, as DIP, has proposed a restructuring plan. Its creditors will be given 60% of the equity in the reorganized firm. Phoebus's preferred shareholders (who hold a liquidation preference) will be given 30% of the equity in the reorganized firm, and Phoebus's common shareholders will be given 10% of the equity in the reorganized firm. The creditors are supportive of the plan. If the preferred shareholders object, is this plan confirmable? 11 U.S.C. § 1129(b)(2)(C).

(3) Helios Solar, Inc., a venture capital–funded start-up that makes solar-rechargeable batteries, is in Chapter 11. Helios, as DIP, has proposed a restructuring plan that will pay its senior debt 90 cents on the dollar over 5 years, and will pay its subordinated debt 20 cents on the dollar over 2 years. If the senior debt objects, is the plan confirmable? Would your answer be different if the senior debt were paid in full? 11 U.S.C. § 1129(b)(2)(B)(2).

(4) You are counsel to a first-term senator serving on the Senate Judiciary Committee. A bipartisan coalition of senators has proposed bankruptcy reform legislation that

among other things would eliminate the absolute priority rule in Chapter 11 and replace it with a relative priority rule. The senator has asked for your thoughts on the matter. She'd like to know how you think it will affect reorganization practice and who will be the winners and losers; she'll figure out how to play the politics, but she needs to know the impact of the change. What do you tell the senator?

CHAPTER 39

THE LIMITS OF ABSOLUTE PRIORITY

The absolute priority rule constrains the ability to negotiate a plan. Oftentimes there are reasons why a plan proponent will want to provide some value to equityholders or junior creditors without having all senior creditors paid in full. What follows are a series of cases that have probed the possibility of exceptions to the absolute priority rule: an exception for "new value" given by junior claimants; a "gift plan" exception for senior creditors to gift some of the value that they would receive to juniors, while skipping over mezzanine creditors; and "cram up" plans that pay off senior creditors in full or cure and reinstate their loans (sometimes with financing from selective "rights offerings"), so that the seniors do not end up with equity of the reorganized firm.

I. NEW VALUE

creditor *debtor*

Bank of America National Trust & Savings Association v. 203 North LaSalle Street Partnership

526 U.S. 434 (1999)

Justice SOUTER delivered the opinion of the Court.

The issue in this Chapter 11 reorganization case is whether a debtor's prebankruptcy equity holders may, over the objection of a senior class of impaired creditors, contribute new capital and receive ownership interests in the reorganized entity, when that opportunity is given exclusively to the old equity holders under a plan adopted without consideration of alternatives. We hold that old equity holders are disqualified from participating in such a "new value" transaction by the terms of 11 U.S.C. § 1129(b)(2)(B)(ii), which in such circumstances bars a junior interest holder's receipt of any property on account of his prior interest.

I.

Petitioner, Bank of America National Trust and Savings Association (Bank), is the major creditor of respondent, 203 North LaSalle Street Partnership (Debtor or Partnership), an

Illinois real estate limited partnership.[2] The Bank lent the Debtor some $93 million, secured by a nonrecourse first mortgage[3] on the Debtor's principal asset, 15 floors of an office building in downtown Chicago. In January 1995, the Debtor defaulted, and the Bank began foreclosure in a state court.

In March, the Debtor responded with a voluntary petition for relief under Chapter 11 of the Bankruptcy Code, which automatically stayed the foreclosure proceedings, see § 362(a). The Debtor's principal objective was to ensure that its partners retained title to the property so as to avoid roughly $20 million in personal tax liabilities, which would fall due if the Bank foreclosed. The Debtor proceeded to propose a reorganization plan during the 120-day period when it alone had the right to do so, see 11 U.S.C. § 1121(b); see also § 1121(c) (exclusivity period extends to 180 days if the debtor files plan within the initial 120 days). The Bankruptcy Court rejected the Bank's motion to terminate the period of exclusivity to make way for a plan of its own to liquidate the property, and instead extended the exclusivity period for cause shown, under § 1121(d).

The value of the mortgaged property was less than the balance due the Bank, which elected to divide its undersecured claim into secured and unsecured deficiency claims under § 506(a) and § 1111(b).[6] Under the plan, the Debtor separately classified the Bank's secured claim, its unsecured deficiency claim, and unsecured trade debt owed to other creditors. See § 1122(a). The Bankruptcy Court found that the Debtor's available assets were prepetition rents in a cash account of $3.1 million and the 15 floors of rental property worth $54.5 million. The secured claim was valued at the latter figure, leaving the Bank with an unsecured deficiency of $38.5 million.

So far as we need be concerned here, the Debtor's plan had these further features:

(1) The Bank's $54.5 million secured claim would be paid in full between 7 and 10 years after the original 1995 repayment date.

(2) The Bank's $38.5 million unsecured deficiency claim would be discharged for an estimated 16% of its present value.

(3) The remaining unsecured claims of $90,000, held by the outside trade creditors, would be paid in full, without interest, on the effective date of the plan.

(4) Certain former partners of the Debtor would contribute $6.125 million in new capital over the course of five years (the contribution being worth some $4.1 million in present value), in exchange for the Partnership's entire ownership of the reorganized debtor.

The last condition was an exclusive eligibility provision: the old equity holders were the only ones who could contribute new capital.[11]

---

2. The limited partners in this case are considered the Debtor's equity holders under the Bankruptcy Code, see 11 U.S.C. §§ 101(16), (17), and the Debtor Partnership's actions may be understood as taken on behalf of its equity holders.

3. A nonrecourse loan requires the Bank to look only to the Debtor's collateral for payment. But see n. 6, *infra*.

6. Having agreed to waive recourse against any property of the Debtor other than the real estate, the Bank had no unsecured claim outside of Chapter 11. Section 1111(b), however, provides that nonrecourse secured creditors who are undersecured must be treated in Chapter 11 as if they had recourse.

11. The plan eliminated the interests of noncontributing partners. More than 60% of the Partnership interests would change hands on confirmation of the plan. The new Partnership, however, would consist solely of former partners, a feature critical to the preservation of the Partnership's tax shelter.

The Bank objected and, being the sole member of an impaired class of creditors, thereby blocked confirmation of the plan on a consensual basis. See § 1129(a)(8).[12] The Debtor, however, took the alternate route to confirmation of a reorganization plan, forthrightly known as the judicial "cramdown" process for imposing a plan on a dissenting class. § 1129(b).

There are two conditions for a cramdown. First, all requirements of § 1129(a) must be met (save for the plan's acceptance by each impaired class of claims or interests, *see* § 1129(a)(8)). Critical among them are the conditions that the plan be accepted by at least one class of impaired creditors, *see* § 1129(a)(10), and satisfy the "best-interest-of-creditors" test, *see* § 1129(a)(7).[13] Here, the class of trade creditors with impaired unsecured claims voted for the plan,[14] 126 F.3d at 959, and there was no issue of best interest. Second, the objection of an impaired creditor class may be overridden only if "the plan does not discriminate unfairly, and is fair and equitable, with respect to each class of claims or interests that is impaired under, and has not accepted, the plan." § 1129(b)(1). As to a dissenting class of impaired unsecured creditors, such a plan may be found to be "fair and equitable" only if the allowed value of the claim is to be paid in full, § 1129(b)(2)(B)(i), or, in the alternative, if "the holder of any claim or interest that is junior to the claims of such [impaired unsecured] class will not receive or retain under the plan on account of such junior claim or interest any property," § 1129(b)(2)(B)(ii). That latter condition is the core of what is known as the "absolute priority rule."

The absolute priority rule was the basis for the Bank's position that the plan could not be confirmed as a cramdown. As the Bank read the rule, the plan was open to objection simply because certain old equity holders in the Debtor Partnership would receive property even though the Bank's unsecured deficiency claim would not be paid in full. The Bankruptcy Court approved the plan nonetheless, and accordingly denied the Bank's pending motion to convert the case to Chapter 7 liquidation, or to dismiss the case. The District Court affirmed, as did the Court of Appeals.

The majority of the Seventh Circuit's divided panel found ambiguity in the language of the statutory absolute priority rule, and looked beyond the text to interpret the phrase "on account of" as permitting recognition of a "new value corollary" to the rule. According to the panel, the corollary, as stated by this Court in *Case v. Los Angeles Lumber Products Co.*, 308 U.S. 106, 118 (1939), provides that the objection of an impaired senior class does not bar junior claim holders from receiving or retaining property interests in the debtor after reorganization, if they contribute new capital in money or money's worth, reasonably equivalent to the property's value, and necessary

---

12. A class of creditors accepts if a majority of the creditors and those holding two-thirds of the total dollar amount of the claims within that class vote to approve the plan. § 1126(c).

13. Section 1129(a)(7) provides that if the holder of a claim impaired under a plan of reorganization has not accepted the plan, then such holder must "receive . . . on account of such claim . . . property of a value, as of the effective date of the plan, that is not less than the amount that such holder would so receive . . . if the debtor were liquidated under Chapter 7 . . . on such date." The "best interests" test applies to individual creditors holding impaired claims, even if the class as a whole votes to accept the plan.

14. Claims are unimpaired if they retain all of their prepetition legal, equitable, and contractual rights against the debtor. § 1124.

for successful reorganization of the restructured enterprise. The panel majority held that:

> when an old equity holder retains an equity interest in the reorganized debtor by meeting the requirements of the new value corollary, he is not receiving or retaining that interest "on account of" his prior equitable ownership of the debtor. Rather, he is allowed to participate in the reorganized entity "on account of" a new, substantial, necessary and fair infusion of capital.

In the dissent's contrary view, there is nothing ambiguous about the text: the "plain language of the absolute priority rule . . . does not include a new value exception." Since "the Plan in this case gives [the Debtor's] partners the exclusive right to retain their ownership interest in the indebted property *because of* their status as . . . prior interest holders," the dissent would have reversed confirmation of the plan.

We granted certiorari, to resolve a Circuit split on the issue. We do not decide whether the statute includes a new value corollary or exception, but hold that on any reading respondent's proposed plan fails to satisfy the statute, and accordingly reverse.

II

The terms "absolute priority rule" and "new value corollary" (or "exception") are creatures of law antedating the current Bankruptcy Code, and to understand both those terms and the related but inexact language of the Code some history is helpful. The Bankruptcy Act preceding the Code contained no such provision as subsection (b)(2)(B)(ii), its subject having been addressed by two interpretive rules. The first was a specific gloss on the requirement of § 77B (and its successor, Chapter X) of the old Act, that any reorganization plan be "fair and equitable." The reason for such a limitation was the danger inherent in any reorganization plan proposed by a debtor, then and now, that the plan will simply turn out to be too good a deal for the debtor's owners. Hence the pre-Code judicial response known as the absolute priority rule, that fairness and equity required that "the creditors . . . be paid before the stockholders could retain [equity interests] for any purpose whatever."

The second interpretive rule addressed the first. Its classic formulation occurred in *Case v. Los Angeles Lumber Products Co.,* in which the Court spoke through Justice Douglas in this dictum:

> It is, of course, clear that there are circumstances under which stockholders may participate in a plan of reorganization of an insolvent debtor. . . . Where the necessity [for new capital] exists and the old stockholders make a fresh contribution and receive in return a participation reasonably equivalent to their contribution, no objection can be made. . . .

We believe that to accord "the creditor his full right of priority against the corporate assets" where the debtor is insolvent, the stockholder's participation must be based on a contribution in money or in money's worth, reasonably equivalent in view of all the circumstances to the participation of the stockholder.

Although counsel for one of the parties here has described the *Case* observation as "'black-letter' principle," it never rose above the technical level of dictum in any opinion of this Court, which last addressed it in *Norwest Bank Worthington v. Ahlers,*

485 U.S. 197 (1988), holding that a contribution of "'labor, experience, and expertise'" by a junior interest holder was not in the "'money's worth'" that the *Case* observation required. Nor, prior to the enactment of the current Bankruptcy Code, did any court rely on the *Case* dictum to approve a plan that gave old equity a property right after reorganization. Hence the controversy over how weighty the *Case* dictum had become, as reflected in the alternative labels for the new value notion: some writers and courts (including this one, *see Ahlers, supra*, at 203, n. 3) have spoken of it as an exception to the absolute priority rule, while others have characterized it as a simple corollary to the rule.

[Consideration of the ambiguous legislative history is omitted.]

The upshot is that this history does nothing to disparage the possibility apparent in the statutory text, that the absolute priority rule now on the books as subsection (b)(2)(B)(ii) may carry a new value corollary. Although there is no literal reference to "new value" in the phrase "on account of such junior claim," the phrase could arguably carry such an implication in modifying the prohibition against receipt by junior claimants of any interest under a plan while a senior class of unconsenting creditors goes less than fully paid.

III

Three basic interpretations have been suggested for the "on account of" modifier. [The Court goes on to consider (1) a reading proposed by the Partnership, that "on account of" means "in exchange for." It then turns to (2) the government's suggestion as amicus curiae, that "on account of" means "because of," and then considers (3) a third position that "on account of" requires old equity to retain or receive property only if it contributed "the greatest possible addition to the bankruptcy estate" and more than someone else would have paid.]

IV

Which of these positions is ultimately entitled to prevail is not to be decided here, however, for even on the latter view the Bank's objection would require rejection of the plan at issue in this case. It is doomed, we can say without necessarily exhausting its flaws, by its provision for vesting equity in the reorganized business in the Debtor's partners without extending an opportunity to anyone else either to compete for that equity or to propose a competing reorganization plan. Although the Debtor's exclusive opportunity to propose a plan under § 1121(b) is not itself "property" within the meaning of subsection (b)(2)(B)(ii), the respondent partnership in this case has taken advantage of this opportunity by proposing a plan under which the benefit of equity ownership may be obtained by no one but old equity partners. Upon the court's approval of that plan, the partners were in the same position that they would have enjoyed had they exercised an exclusive option under the plan to buy the equity in the reorganized entity, or contracted to purchase it from a seller who had first agreed to deal with no one else. It is quite true that the escrow of the partners' proposed investment eliminated any formal need to set out an express option or exclusive dealing provision in the plan itself, since the court's approval that created the opportunity and the partners' action to obtain its advantage were simultaneous. But before the Debtor's plan was accepted no one else could propose an alternative one, and after its acceptance no one else could obtain equity in the reorganized entity.

At the moment of the plan's approval the Debtor's partners necessarily enjoyed an exclusive opportunity that was in no economic sense distinguishable from the advantage of the exclusively entitled offeror or option holder. This opportunity should, first of all, be treated as an item of property in its own right. While it may be argued that the opportunity has no market value, being significant only to old equity holders owing to their potential tax liability, such an argument avails the Debtor nothing, for several reasons. It is to avoid just such arguments that the law is settled that any otherwise cognizable property interest must be treated as sufficiently valuable to be recognized under the Bankruptcy Code. Even aside from that rule, the assumption that no one but the Debtor's partners might pay for such an opportunity would obviously support no inference that it is valueless, let alone that it should not be treated as property. And, finally, the source in the tax law of the opportunity's value to the partners implies in no way that it lacks value to others. It might, indeed, be valuable to another precisely as a way to keep the Debtor from implementing a plan that would avoid a Chapter 7 liquidation.

Given that the opportunity is property of some value, the question arises why old equity alone should obtain it, not to mention at no cost whatever. The closest thing to an answer favorable to the Debtor is that the old equity partners would be given the opportunity in the expectation that in taking advantage of it they would add the stated purchase price to the estate. But this just begs the question why the opportunity should be exclusive to the old equity holders. If the price to be paid for the equity interest is the best obtainable, old equity does not need the protection of exclusiveness (unless to trump an equal offer from someone else); if it is not the best, there is no apparent reason for giving old equity a bargain. There is no reason, that is, unless the very purpose of the whole transaction is, at least in part, to do old equity a favor. And that, of course, is to say that old equity would obtain its opportunity, and the resulting benefit, because of old equity's prior interest within the meaning of subsection (b)(2)(B)(ii). Hence it is that the exclusiveness of the opportunity, with its protection against the market's scrutiny of the purchase price by means of competing bids or even competing plan proposals, renders the partners' right a property interest extended "on account of" the old equity position and therefore subject to an unpaid senior creditor class's objection.

It is no answer to this to say that the exclusive opportunity should be treated merely as a detail of the broader transaction that would follow its exercise, and that in this wider perspective no favoritism may be inferred, since the old equity partners would pay something, whereas no one else would pay anything. If this argument were to carry the day, of course, old equity could obtain a new property interest for a dime without being seen to receive anything on account of its old position. But even if we assume that old equity's plan would not be confirmed without satisfying the judge that the purchase price was top dollar, there is a further reason here not to treat property consisting of an exclusive opportunity as subsumed within the total transaction proposed. On the interpretation assumed here, it would, of course, be a fatal flaw if old equity acquired or retained the property interest without paying full value. It would thus be necessary for old equity to demonstrate its payment of top dollar, but this it could not satisfactorily do when it would receive or retain its property under a plan giving it exclusive rights and in the absence of a competing plan of any sort. Under a plan granting an exclusive right, making no provision for competing bids or competing plans, any determination that the price was top dollar would necessarily be made by a judge in bankruptcy court, whereas the best way to determine value is exposure to a market. This is a point of some significance, since it was, after all, one of the Code's innovations to narrow the occasions for courts to make valuation judgments, as shown by its preference for the supramajoritarian class creditor voting scheme in § 1126(c), *see Ahlers, supra,* at 207 ("The Code provides that it is up to the creditors—and not the courts—to accept or reject a reorganization plan which fails to provide them adequate protection or fails to honor the absolute priority rule"). In the interest of statutory coherence, a like disfavor for decisions untested by competitive choice ought to extend to valuations in administering subsection (b)(2)(B)(ii) when some form of market valuation may be available to test the adequacy of an old equity holder's proposed contribution.

Whether a market test would require an opportunity to offer competing plans or would be satisfied by a right to bid for the same interest sought by old equity, is a question we do not decide here. It is enough to say, assuming a new value corollary, that plans providing junior interest holders with exclusive opportunities free from competition and without benefit of market valuation fall within the prohibition of § 1129(b)(2)(B)(ii).

The judgment of the Court of Appeals is accordingly reversed, and the case is remanded for further proceedings consistent with this opinion.

[Concurrence by Justice Thomas, joined by Justice Scalia, which endorses the reading that "on account of" means as a matter of plain language "because of," is omitted. Also omitted is a dissent by Justice Stevens arguing that new capital invested beyond the value of a party's interest in the reorganized firm is not "on account of" its prepetition claim or equity interest.]

Study Questions

1. What is the absolute priority violation at issue? Why does the plan violate absolute priority?

2. Is there a "new value" exception to absolute priority after *203 N. LaSalle*? If so, what does it require? Will "sweat equity" (labor) suffice? What if the labor contributed were some special talent that was not readily obtainable elsewhere?

3. What does *203 N. LaSalle* mean about the post-bankruptcy ownership of any bankrupt company that cannot pay all claims in full? If it is truly up for bid, should not bids be considered in all forms of value, ranging from cash to IP rights to labor?

4. Before *Case v. Los Angeles Lumber*, pre-petition equity was allowed to retain the company's equity post-petition provided that unsecured creditors' claims remained intact against the reorganized company. In other words, pre-petition debt could ride through the bankruptcy unimpaired, just as if the company were sold. In fact, the seminal Supreme Court case allowing this treatment was in the context of a foreclosure sale, rather than a bankruptcy. *See Northern Pac. Ry. Co. v. Boyd*, 228 U.S. 482 (1913).

II. GIFT PLANS

Creditor

debtor.

DISH Network Corp. v. DBSD North America, Inc.
(*In re* DBSD North America, Inc.)
634 F.3d 79 (2d Cir. 2011)

GERARD E. LYNCH, *Circuit Judge*:

These consolidated appeals arise out of the bankruptcy of DBSD North America, Incorporated and its various subsidiaries (together, "DBSD"). The bankruptcy court confirmed a plan of reorganization for DBSD over the objections of the two appellants here, Sprint Nextel Corporation ("Sprint") and DISH Network Corporation ("DISH").

Before us, Sprint argues that the plan improperly gave shares and warrants to DBSD's owner—whose interest lies below Sprint's in priority—in violation of the absolute priority rule of 11 U.S.C. § 1129(b)(2)(B). . . .

On Sprint's appeal, we conclude (1) that Sprint has standing to appeal and (2) that the plan violated the absolute priority rule. . . . We therefore . . . reverse . . . and remand for further proceedings.

BACKGROUND

. . .

ICO Global Communications founded DBSD in 2004 to develop a mobile communications network that would use both satellites and land-based transmission towers. In its first five years, DBSD made progress toward this goal, successfully launching a satellite and obtaining certain spectrum licenses from the FCC, but it also accumulated a large amount of debt. Because its network remained in the developmental stage and had not become operational, DBSD had little if any revenue to offset its mounting obligations.

On May 15, 2009, DBSD (but not its parent ICO Global) filed a voluntary petition in the United States Bankruptcy Court for the Southern District of New York, listing liabilities of $813 million against assets with a book value of $627 million. Of the various claims against DBSD, three have particular relevance here:

1. *The First Lien Debt*: a $40 million revolving credit facility that DBSD obtained in early 2008 to support its operations, with a first-priority security interest in substantially all of DBSD's assets. It bore an initial interest rate of 12.5%.

2. *The Second Lien Debt*: $650 million in 7.5% convertible senior secured notes that DISH issued in August 2005, due August 2009. These notes hold a second-priority security interest in substantially all of DBSD's assets. At the time of filing, the Second Lien Debt had grown to approximately $740 million. It constitutes the bulk of DBSD's indebtedness.

3. *Sprint's Claim*: an unliquidated, unsecured claim based on a lawsuit against a DBSD subsidiary. Sprint had sued seeking reimbursement for DBSD's share of certain spectrum relocation expenses under an FCC order. At the time of DBSD's

filing, that litigation was pending in the United States District Court for the Eastern District of Virginia and before the FCC. In the bankruptcy case, Sprint filed a claim against each of the DBSD entities jointly and severally, seeking $211 million. The bankruptcy court temporarily allowed Sprint's claim in the amount of $2 million for voting purposes.

After negotiations with various parties, DBSD proposed a plan of reorganization which, as amended, provided for "substantial de-leveraging," a renewed focus on "core operations," and a "continued path as a development-stage enterprise." The plan provided that the holders of the First Lien Debt would receive new obligations with a four-year maturity date and the same 12.5% interest rate, but with interest to be paid in kind ("PIK"), meaning that for the first four years the owners of the new obligations would receive as interest more debt from DBSD rather than cash. The holders of the Second Lien Debt would receive the bulk of the shares of the reorganized entity, which the bankruptcy court estimated would be worth between 51% and 73% of their original claims. The holders of unsecured claims, such as Sprint, would receive shares estimated as worth between 4% and 46% of their original claims. Finally, the existing shareholder (effectively just ICO Global, which owned 99.8% of DBSD) would receive shares and warrants in the reorganized entity.

Sprint objected to the plan, arguing among other things that the plan violates the absolute priority rule of 11 U.S.C. § 1129(b)(2)(B). That rule requires that, if a class of senior claim-holders will not receive the full value of their claims under the plan and the class does not accept the plan, no junior claim- or interest-holder may receive "any property" "under the plan on account of such junior claim or interest." *Id*. In making its objection, Sprint noted that the plan provided for the existing shareholder, whose interest is junior to Sprint's class of general unsecured claims, to receive substantial quantities of shares and warrants under the plan—in fact, much more than all the unsecured creditors received together. Sprint argued that "[b]ecause the Plan fails to satisfy" the absolute priority rule, "it cannot be confirmed."

The bankruptcy court disagreed. It characterized the existing shareholder's receipt of shares and warrants as a "gift" from the holders of the Second Lien Debt, who are senior to Sprint in priority yet who were themselves not receiving the full value of their claims, and who may therefore "voluntarily offer a portion of their recovered property to junior stakeholders" without violating the absolute priority rule. It held that it would permit such gifting "at least where, as here, the gift comes from secured creditors, there is no doubt as to their secured creditor status, where there are understandable reasons for the gift, where there are no ulterior, improper ends . . . and where the complaining creditor would get no more if the gift had not been made."

. . . [T]he bankruptcy court confirmed the plan. The district court affirmed, and DISH and Sprint appealed to this Court. After oral argument, DBSD received approval from the FCC to transfer its spectrum rights to the reorganized entity—the last hurdle before consummation of the reorganization. We subsequently stayed consummation of the plan and then, on December 6, 2010, issued an order disposing of the case and vacating our stay so that the proceedings could continue below without further delay, indicating that an opinion would follow. This is that opinion.

DISCUSSION

I. Sprint's Appeal

Sprint raises only one issue on appeal: it asserts that the plan improperly gives property to DBSD's shareholder without fully satisfying Sprint's senior claim, in violation of the absolute priority rule. *See* 11 U.S.C. § 1129(b)(2)(B). That rule provides that a reorganization plan may not give "property" to the holders of any junior claims or interests "on account of those claims or interests, unless all classes of senior claims either receive the full value of their claims or give their consent. *Id.* Because the existing shareholder received shares and warrants on account of its junior interest, Sprint argues, Sprint's class of general unsecured creditors had a right to receive "full satisfaction of their claims" or at least "an amount sufficient to obtain approval from the class." But the plan provided neither, and so Sprint asks us to vacate the order confirming it or to provide other relief that would satisfy Sprint's claim.

. . .

B. Gifting and the Absolute Priority Rule

Sprint argues that the plan violated the absolute priority rule by giving shares and warrants to a junior class (the existing shareholder) although a more senior class (Sprint's class) neither approved the plan nor received the full value of its claims. *See* 11 U.S.C. § 1129(b)(2)(B). The appellees respond, and the courts below held, that the holders of the Second Lien Debt, who are senior to Sprint and whom the bankruptcy court found to be undersecured, were entitled to the full residual value of the debtor and were therefore free to "gift" some of that value to the existing shareholder if they chose to. We recently avoided deciding the viability of this "gifting doctrine" in a similar context, *see In re Iridium Operating LLC*, 478 F.3d 452, 460-61 (2d Cir. 2007), but we now face the question squarely. . . .

Long before anyone had imagined such a thing as Chapter 11 bankruptcy, it was already "well settled that stockholders are not entitled to any share of the capital stock nor to any dividend of the profits until all the debts of the corporation are paid." *R.R. v. Howard*, 74 U.S. (7 Wall.) 392, 409-10 (1868). In the days of the railroad barons, however, parties observed this rule in the breach. Senior creditors and original shareholders often cooperated to control the reorganization of a failed company, sometimes to make the process go smoothly—to encourage the old shareholders to provide new capital for the reorganization or to keep them from engaging in costly and delaying litigation—or sometimes simply because the senior creditors and the old shareholders were the same parties. For their cooperation, the old owners would often receive or retain some stake in whatever entity arose from the reorganization. Junior creditors, however, often received little or nothing even though they technically stood above the old shareholders in priority. *See* John D. Ayer, *Rethinking Absolute Priority After* Ahlers, 87 MICH. L. REV. 963, 970-71 (1989).

In response to this practice, the Supreme Court developed a "fixed principle" for reorganizations: that all "creditors were entitled to be paid before the stockholders could retain [shares] for any purpose whatever." *N. Pac. Ry. Co. v. Boyd*, 228 U.S. 482, 507-08 (1913). "[A] plan of reorganization," the Court later stated, "would not be fair and equitable which . . . admitted the stockholders to participation, unless" at very least "the stockholders made a fresh contribution in money or in money's worth in return for 'a participation reasonably equivalent to their contribution.'" *Marine Harbor Props., Inc. v. Mfrs. Trust Co.*, 317 U.S. 78, 85 (1942), quoting *Case v. L.A. Lumber Prods. Co.*, 308 U.S. 106, 121 (1939). Courts came to call this the "absolute priority rule." *Ecker v. W. Pac. R.R. Corp.*, 318 U.S. 448, 484 (1943).

The Bankruptcy Code incorporates a form of the absolute priority rule in its provisions for confirming a Chapter 11 plan of reorganization. For a district court to confirm a plan over the vote of a dissenting class of claims, the Code demands that the plan be "fair and equitable, with respect to each class of claims . . . that is impaired under, and has not accepted, the plan." 11 U.S.C. § 1129(b)(1). The Code does not define the full extent of "fair and equitable," but it includes a form of the absolute priority rule as a prerequisite. According to the Code, a plan is not "fair and equitable" unless:

With respect to a class of unsecured claims—

(i) the plan provides that each holder of a claim of such class receive or retain on account of such claim property of a value, as of the effective date of the plan, equal to the allowed amount of such claim; or

(ii) the holder of any claim or interest that is junior to the claims of such class will not receive or retain under the plan on account of such junior claim or interest any property. . . .

Id. § 1129(b)(2)(B). Absent the consent of all impaired classes of unsecured claimants, therefore, a confirmable plan must ensure either (i) that the dissenting class receives the full value of its claim, or (ii) that no classes junior to that class receive any property under the plan on account of their junior claims or interests.

Under the plan in this case, Sprint does not receive "property of a value . . . equal to the allowed amount" of its claim. Rather, Sprint gets less than half the value of its claim. The plan may be confirmed, therefore, only if the existing shareholder, whose interest is junior to Sprint's, does "not receive or retain" "any property" "under the plan on account of such junior . . . interest." We hold that the existing shareholder did receive property under the plan on account of its interest, and that the bankruptcy court therefore should not have confirmed the plan.

First, under the challenged plan, the existing shareholder receives "property" in the form of shares and warrants in the reorganized entity. The term "property" in § 1129(b)(2)(B) is meant to be interpreted broadly. *See Ahlers*, 485 U.S. at 208. But even if it were not, there is no doubt that "any property" includes shares and warrants like these.

Second, the existing shareholder receives that property "under the plan." The disclosure statement for the second amended plan, under the heading "ARTICLE IV: THE JOINT PLAN," states:

Class 9—Existing Stockholder Interests

. . . In full and final satisfaction, settlement, release, and discharge of each Existing Stockholder Interest, and on account of all valuable consideration provided by the Existing Stockholder, including, without limitation, certain consideration provided in the Support Agreement, . . . *the Holder of such Class 9 Existing Stockholder Interest shall receive the Existing Stockholder Shares and the Warrants.*

(emphasis added). We need not decide whether the Code would allow the existing shareholder and Senior Noteholders to agree to transfer shares outside of the plan, for, on the present record, the existing shareholder clearly receives these shares and warrants "under the plan."

Finally, the existing shareholder receives its shares and warrants "on account of" its junior interest. The Supreme Court has noted that "on account of" could take one of several interpretations. *See Bank of Am. Nat'l Trust & Sav. Ass'n v. 203 N. LaSalle St. P'ship*, 526 U.S. 434, 449 (1999). The interpretation most friendly to old equity— which the Supreme Court rejected as "beset with troubles . . . exceedingly odd . . . [and] unlikely"—reads "on account of" as "in exchange for." *Id.* at 449-50. Even under this generous test, the existing shareholder here receives property "on account of" its prior junior interest because it receives new shares and warrants at least partially "in exchange for" its old ones. The passage from the plan quoted above states as much: the existing shareholder receives shares and warrants "[i]n full and final satisfaction, settlement, release, and discharge of each Existing Stockholder Interest."

The gift here even more easily satisfies the two less restrictive tests the Supreme Court examined (and viewed more favorably) in *203 North LaSalle*, both of which read "on account of" to mean some form of "because of." *Id.* at 450. The existing shareholder received its property "because of," and thus "on account of," its prior interest, for the same reasons set forth above.[6]

This conclusion is not undermined by the fact that the disclosure statement recites, and the district court found, additional reasons why the existing shareholder merited receiving the shares and warrants. First, a transfer *partly* on account of factors other than the prior interest is still partly "on account of" that interest. "If Congress had intended to modify ['on account of'] with the addition of the words 'only,' 'solely,' or even 'primarily,' it would have done so." *In re Coltex Loop,* 138 F.3d at 43. Upholding this principle in *203 North LaSalle*, the Supreme Court refused to characterize a benefit given to existing shareholders "merely as a detail of the broader transaction" in which those shareholders also contributed new capital. 526 U.S. at 456. Instead, receipt of property partly on account of the existing interest was enough for the absolute priority rule to bar confirmation of the plan.

Second, the other reasons that the appellees assert drove the award of warrants and shares to old equity here are themselves "on account of" the existing shareholder's prior interest. The existing shareholder did not contribute additional capital to the reorganized entity, *see, e.g., id.* at 443 (suggesting uncertainty about whether even new capital may suffice); rather, as the bankruptcy court explained, the gift aimed to ensure

---

6. We note that not all distributions of property to a junior class are necessarily "on account of" the junior claims or interests. For example, the Supreme Court has left open the possibility that old equity could take under a plan if it invests new value in the reorganized entity, at least as long as a "market valuation" tests the adequacy of its contribution. *203 North LaSalle*, 526 U.S. at 458. In such a situation, the party receiving the property may argue—though we do not now decide the correctness of such an argument—that it does not receive anything "on account of" its interest but only on account of its new investment. For another example, our decision does not stop a senior claim-holder from receiving property on account of its senior claim just because the claim-holder also happens to hold a junior claim on account of which it receives nothing. *See id.* at 452 n.24. There may well be other examples.

the existing shareholder's "continued cooperation and assistance" in the reorganization. The "continued cooperation" of the existing shareholder was useful only because of the shareholder's position as equity holder and "the rights emanating from that position," *In re Coltex Loop*, 138 F.3d at 43; an unrelated third party's cooperation would not have been useful. And "assistance" sounds like the sort of "future labor, management, or expertise" that the Supreme Court has held insufficient to avoid falling under the prohibition of the absolute priority rule. *Ahlers*, 485 U.S. at 204. Thus, notwithstanding the various economic reasons that may have contributed to the decision to award property to old equity here, it is clear that the existing shareholder "could not have gained [its] new position but for [its] prior equity position." *In re Coltex Loop*, 138 F.3d at 44.

In sum, we conclude that the existing shareholder received "property," that it did so "under the plan," and that it did so "on account of" its prior, junior interest.

The Supreme Court's interpretations of § 1129(b)(2)(B) give us confidence in ours. Although that Court has not addressed the exact scenario presented here under the codified absolute priority rule, its two post-Code cases on the rule are instructive. In both cases, the prior owners tried to avoid the absolute priority rule by arguing that they received distributions not on account of their prior interests but rather on account of the new value that they would contribute to the entity. *See 203 N. LaSalle*, 526 U.S. at 437; *Ahlers*, 485 U.S. at 199. In both cases, the Supreme Court rejected those arguments. Although dictum in an earlier case had suggested that contributing new value could allow prior shareholders to participate in the reorganized entity, *see Case*, 308 U.S. at 121, the Court refused to decide whether § 1129(b)(2)(B) permitted such new-value exchanges. Instead, the Court held that neither "future labor, experience and expertise," *Ahlers*, 485 U.S. at 199 (quotation marks omitted), nor capital contributions "without benefit of market valuation," *203 N. LaSalle*, 526 U.S. at 458, could suffice to escape the absolute priority rule, even assuming the ongoing validity of the *Case* dictum.

203 North LaSalle and *Ahlers* indicate a preference for reading the rule strictly. Given that the Supreme Court has hesitated to allow old owners to receive new ownership interests even when contributing new value, it is doubtful the Court would allow old owners to receive new ownership without contributing any new value, as in this case. As the Court explained in *Ahlers*, "the statutory language and the legislative history of § 1129(b) clearly bar any expansion of any exception to the absolute priority rule beyond that recognized in our cases at the time Congress enacted the 1978 Bankruptcy Code." *Ahlers*, 485 U.S. at 206. The Supreme Court has never suggested any exception that would cover a case like this one.

The appellees, unsurprisingly, see the case in a different light. They contend that, under the "gifting doctrine," the shares and warrants rightfully belonged to the secured creditors, who were entitled to share them with the existing shareholder as they saw fit. Citing *In re SPM Manufacturing Corp.*, 984 F.2d 1305 (1st Cir. 1993), the appellees argue that, until the debts of the secured creditors "are paid in full, the Bankruptcy Code's distributional priority scheme, as embodied in the absolute priority rule, is not implicated." DBSD was not worth enough, according to the bankruptcy court's valuation, to cover even the secured lenders' claims, much less those of unsecured creditors like Sprint. Therefore, as the bankruptcy court stated in ruling for the appellees, "the 'Gifting' Doctrine—under which senior secured creditors voluntarily offer a portion of their recovered property to junior stakeholders (as the Senior Noteholders did here)—defeats Sprint's Absolute Priority Rule objection." We disagree.

Most fatally, this interpretation does not square with the text of the Bankruptcy Code. The Code extends the absolute priority rule to "any property," 11 U.S.C. § 1129(b)(2)(B)(ii), not "any property not covered by a senior creditor's lien." The Code focuses entirely on who "receive[s]" or "retain[s]" the property "under the plan," *id.*, not on who *would* receive it under a liquidation plan. And it applies the rule to any distribution "under the plan on account of" a junior interest, *id.*, regardless of whether the distribution could have been made outside the plan, and regardless of whether other reasons might support the distribution in addition to the junior interest.

We distinguish this case from *In re SPM* on several grounds. In that case, a secured creditor and the general unsecured creditors agreed to seek liquidation of the debtor and to share the proceeds from the liquidation. 984 F.2d at 1307-08. The bankruptcy court granted relief from the automatic stay and converted the case from Chapter 11 to a Chapter 7 liquidation. The bankruptcy court refused, however, to allow the unsecured creditors to receive their share under the agreement with the secured creditor, ordering instead that the unsecured creditors' share go to a priority creditor in between those two classes. The district court affirmed, but the First Circuit reversed, holding that nothing in the Code barred the secured creditors from sharing their proceeds in a Chapter 7 liquidation with unsecured creditors, even at the expense of a creditor who would otherwise take priority over those unsecured creditors.

The first and most important distinction is that *In re SPM* involved Chapter 7, not Chapter 11, and thus involved a liquidation of the debtor, not a reorganization. Chapter 7 does not include the rigid absolute priority rule of § 1129(b)(2)(B). *See In re Armstrong*, 432 F.3d at 514. As the First Circuit noted, "the distribution scheme" of Chapter 7 "does not come into play until all valid liens on the property are satisfied." *In re SPM*, 984 F.2d at 1312; *see* 11 U.S.C. § 726(a). *In re SPM* repeatedly emphasized the "lack[]" of "statutory support" for the argument against gifting in the Chapter 7 context. 984 F.2d at 1313; *see id.* at 1313-14 (finding "no support in the Code for" rejecting gifting). Under Chapter 11, in contrast, § 1129(b)(2)(B) provides clear "statutory support" to reject gifting in this case, and the distribution scheme of Chapter 11 ordinarily distributes *all* property in the estate (as it does here), including property subject to security interests, *see* 11 U.S.C. § 1129(b)(2)(A).

Furthermore, the bankruptcy court in *In re SPM* had granted the secured creditor relief from the automatic stay and treated the property in question as no longer part of the estate. In a very real sense, the property belonged to the secured creditor alone, and the secured creditor could do what it pleased with it. Here, however, the relevant property has remained in the estate throughout, and has never belonged to the secured creditors outright. *See United States v. Whiting Pools, Inc.*, 462 U.S. 198, 203-04 (1983). For these reasons, therefore, assuming without deciding that the First Circuit's approach was correct in the context of Chapter 7—a question not before us—we do not find it relevant to this case. *See In re Armstrong*, 432 F.3d at 514 (similarly distinguishing *In re SPM*).

Even if the text of § 1129(b)(2)(B) left any room for the appellees' view of the case, we would hesitate to accept it in light of the Supreme Court's long history of rejecting such views. That history begins at least as early as 1868, in *Howard*, 74 U.S. (7 Wall.) 392. In that case, the stockholders and mortgagees of a failing railroad agreed to foreclose on the railroad and convey its property to a new corporation, with the old stockholders receiving some of the new shares. The agreement gave nothing, however, to certain intermediate creditors, who sought a share of the distribution in the courts.

The stockholders defended their agreement with nearly the exact logic the appellees employ here:

> The road was mortgaged for near three times its value. . . . If, then, these stockholders have got anything, it must be because the bondholders have *surrendered* a part of *their* fund to them. If the fund belonged to the bondholders, they had a right so to surrender a part or a whole of it. And if the bondholders did so surrender their own property to the stockholders, it became the private property of these last; a gift, or, if you please, a transfer for consideration from the bondholders. . . . What right have these complainants to *such* property in the hands of the stockholders?

Id. at 400. Even in 1868, however, the Supreme Court found that "[e]xtended discussion of that proposition is not necessary." *Id*. at 414. "Holders of bonds secured by mortgages as in this case," the Court noted, "may exact the whole amount of the bonds, principal and interest, or they may, if they see fit, accept a percentage as a compromise in full discharge of their respective claims, but whenever their lien is legally discharged, the property embraced in the mortgage, or whatever remains of it, belongs to the corporation" for distribution to other creditors. *Id*. Similarly, in this case, the secured creditors could have demanded a plan in which they received all of the reorganized corporation, but, having chosen not to, they may not "surrender" part of the value of the estate for distribution "to the stockholder[]," as "a gift." *Id*. at 400. Whatever the secured creditors here did not take remains in the estate for the benefit of other claim-holders.

As the Court built upon *Howard* to develop the absolute priority rule, it continued to reject arguments similar to the ones the appellees make before us. For example, in *Louisville Trust Co. v. Louisville, New Albany & Chicago Railway Co.*, the Court noted that "if the bondholder wishes to foreclose and exclude inferior lienholders or general unsecured creditors and stockholders, he may do so; but a foreclosure which attempts to preserve any interest or right of the mortgagor in the property after the sale must necessarily secure and preserve the prior rights of general creditors thereof." 174 U.S. 674, 683-84 (1899). The Court rejected another similar argument in 1913 in *Boyd*, where it finally set down the "fixed principle" that we now call the absolute priority rule. 228 U.S. at 507.

Those cases dealt with facts much like the facts of this one: an over-leveraged corporation whose undersecured senior lenders agree to give shares to prior shareholders while intermediate lenders receive less than the value of their claim. *See* Douglas G. Baird & Thomas H. Jackson, *Bargaining After the Fall and the Contours of the Absolute Priority Rule*, 55 U. CHI. L. REV. 738, 739-44 (1988). And it was on the basis of those facts that the Supreme Court developed the absolute priority rule, with the aim of stopping the very sort of transaction that the appellees propose here. *See In re Iridium*, 478 F.3d at 463 n.17. These old cases do not bind us directly, given that Congress has now codified the absolute priority rule. But if courts will not infer statutory abrogation of the common law without evidence that Congress intended such abrogation, *see United States v. Texas*, 507 U.S. 529, 534 (1993), it would be even less appropriate to conclude that Congress abrogated the more-than-a-century-old core of the absolute priority rule by passing a statute whose language explicitly adopts it.

We recognize the policy arguments against the absolute priority rule. Gifting may be a "powerful tool in accelerating an efficient and non-adversarial . . . Chapter 11 proceeding," Leah M. Eisenberg, *Gifting and Asset Reallocation in Chapter 11 Proceedings: A Synthesized Approach*, 29 AM. BANKR. INST. J. 50, 50 (2010), and no doubt the parties intended the gift to have such an effect here. As one witness testified below, "where . . . the equity sponsor is out of the money, . . . a tip is common to [e]nsure a consensual bankruptcy rather than a contested one." Enforcing the absolute priority rule, by contrast, "may encourage hold-out behavior by objecting creditors . . . even though the transfer has no direct effect on the value to be received by the objecting creditors." Harvey R. Miller & Ronit J. Berkovich, *The Implications of the Third Circuit's* Armstrong *Decision on Creative Corporate Restructuring: Will Strict Construction of the Absolute Priority Rule Make Chapter 11 Consensus Less Likely?*, 55 AM. U. L. REV. 1345, 1349 (2006).

It deserves noting, however, that there are substantial policy arguments in favor of the rule. Shareholders retain substantial control over the Chapter 11 process, and with that control comes significant opportunity for self-enrichment at the expense of creditors. *See, e.g.*, 11 U.S.C. § 1121(b) (giving debtor, which is usually controlled by old shareholders, exclusive 120-day period in which to propose plan). This case provides a nice example. Although no one alleges any untoward conduct here, it is noticeable how much larger a distribution the existing shareholder will receive under this plan (4.99% of all equity in the reorganized entity) than the general unsecured creditors put together (0.15% of all equity), despite the latter's technical seniority. Indeed, based on the debtor's estimate that the reorganized entity would be worth approximately $572 million, the existing shareholder will receive approximately $28.5 million worth of equity under the plan while the unsecured creditors must share only $850,000. And if the parties here were less scrupulous or the bankruptcy court less vigilant, a weakened absolute priority rule could allow for serious mischief between senior creditors and existing shareholders.

Whatever the policy merits of the absolute priority rule, however, Congress was well aware of both its benefits and disadvantages when it codified the rule in the Bankruptcy Code. The policy objections to the rule are not new ones; the rule has attracted controversy from its early days. Four Justices dissented from the Supreme Court's 1913 holding in *Boyd*, see 228 U.S. at 511, and that decision "was received by the reorganization bar and bankers with something akin to horror," James N. Rosenberg, *Reorganization—The Next Step*, 22 COLUM. L. REV. 14, 14 (1922). The Commission charged with reviewing the bankruptcy laws in the lead-up to the enactment of the Bankruptcy Code suggested loosening the absolute priority rule to allow greater participation by equity owners. *See* Bruce A. Markell, *Owners, Auctions, and Absolute Priority in Bankruptcy Reorganizations*, 44 STAN. L. REV. 69, 87-89 & n.117 (1991). Yet, although Congress did soften the absolute priority rule in some ways,[7] it did not create any exception for "gifts" like the one at issue here. *See also* H.R. Rep. 95-595, 1978 U.S.C.C.A.N. 5963, 6372 (1977) (noting that absolute priority rule was "to prevent a senior class from giving up consideration to a junior class unless every intermediate class consents, is paid in full, or is unimpaired"). We therefore hold that the bankruptcy court erred in confirming the plan of reorganization.

. . .

CONCLUSION

For the reasons set forth above, we REVERSE the order of confirmation on absolute-priority grounds . . . and REMAND for further proceedings consistent with this opinion.

___

III. RIGHTS OFFERINGS

Large bankruptcy cases commonly feature rights offerings as part of plans of reorganization. A rights offering is a short-term offer to a class or classes of creditors or equityholders to purchase newly issued securities or warrants of the reorganized debtor, typically at a discount, with pre-petition debt or equity interests providing part of the consideration for the new securities. The consideration paid in a rights offering thus provides new capital to the reorganized debtor, which can be used to fund plan distributions to other classes or fund asset purchases or provide working capital, all of which helps a plan meet the feasibility requirement. A rights offering also offers yet another way to "cram up" senior creditors, as it can provide the funding to pay off secured creditors' claims. Moreover, rights offerings can provide a strong signal to the market of creditor confidence in a reorganized firm, and can encourage acceptance of a plan by a participating class.

Traditionally, reorganized firms would turn to bond markets to provide their exit financing, as equity would be doled out to the juniormost classes in the money on account of their pre-petition claims. Absent a "new value" plan, the distribution of the equity of the reorganized firm would not raise fresh capital. Rights offerings can provide new funding either in tandem or in lieu of traditional exit finding. If capital markets are constrained (such as in 2008-2010), rights offerings present a way to take advantage of a type of "internal" capital market of existing creditors. Rights offerings also enable debtors to raise new funding in the form of equity, so they can remain deleveraged post-reorganization.

A rights offering is essentially the provision of an option to members of the recipient class. There is no requirement that the class members receiving a rights offering actually take up the offer. The debtor does not know, when it makes the

___

7. Most importantly, the Code now determines objections on a class-by-class basis, not creditor-by-creditor. *See* 11 U.S.C. § 1129(b)(2)(B); Markell, 44 STAN. L. REV. at 88.

offer, whether the offer will be "over-subscribed" or "under-subscribed," meaning whether there will be excess or insufficient demand for the offered securities. As a result, the debtor will often offer a discount on the securities offered in order to encourage subscription to the offering. (The discount might be in the form of issuance of preferred securities with favorable conversion terms to common stock.) The deeper the discount on the offered securities, the greater the likely demand for the offered securities, but the less capital the debtor will be able to raise from a rights offering.

A typical rights offering will offer each class member the right to purchase a pro rata share of the offered securities, assuming a full subscription. Thus, if all class members were to subscribe to the rights offering, there would be no dilutive effect. Rights offerings will, however, frequently have "over-allotment" rights, which will permit purchasers of the over-allotment rights the right to the purchase of additional securities in the event that the offering is fully subscribed.

In the event that the offering is undersubscribed, the proration is not adjusted. There is simply a shortfall in the funding. Two solutions exist to this problem. First, debtors will typically offer "oversubscription" rights, which allow parties to purchase beyond their pro rata share, to the extent there are available, unsubscribed securities. And second, a third party can commit to "backstop" (or "underwrite") the offering, meaning that it commits to purchase any unsubscribed shares. A backstopped/underwritten rights offering is one in which a third party—itself potentially a creditor with rights offering participation rights—will commit to purchasing any unsubscribed securities. No such commitment exists in an "uninsured" rights offering. The benefit of a backstop is that it guarantees that a minimum amount of capital will be raised by a rights offering; to the extent that the plan proponent is relying on this capital to fund the plan or post-bankruptcy operations, it need not worry about the take-up rate on the rights offering.

But the certainty that comes from a backstop is not free. The backstopping party assumes the risk that it will have to purchase more of the rights offering than it wants—and that will likely be in a situation in which there was an under-subscription because the terms of the offering were not appealing, namely that the risk on the securities was not favorable vis-à-vis their price. Thus, in Northwest Airlines's under-subscribed $750 million rights offering, backstop party JPMorgan Chase Bank found itself having to purchase $112.5 million of Northwest's securities, likely far more than JPMorgan wanted to purchase.

Backstopping parties will typically be paid a commitment fee of 2.5-7% of the total rights offering amount backstopped. They will also frequently get discounted over-allotment rights (with discounts of 12-60%) that ensure that the backstop party will get a minimum number of shares as part of the deal. Between the backstop obligation and over-allotment rights (which come into play only if the backstop is not triggered), backstopping parties can end up with a sizable share of the rights offered.

Backstop parties also typically receive break-up fees of 1-5%, professional fees, and releases. Backstopping parties will also sometimes be awarded governance rights in the reorganized debtor, such as guaranteed board seats and veto rights over certain corporate transactions. Between the share of securities and governance rights, a backstopping party may end up with control or at least significant influence over a reorganized debtor.

A key attraction of rights offerings is that they can be structured so that the securities issued may be freely sold without SEC registration. It is illegal for anyone—issuers, underwriters, and purchasers—to engage in the interstate sale of unregistered securities, unless a registration exemption applies. 15 U.S.C. § 77e(a). The registration requirement imposes costs on the registrant, both in terms of fees and legal expenses. It also carries with it strict liability for misstatements in the registration statement. 15 U.S.C. §§ 77k-77l. Thus, exemption from registration is quite valuable to a reorganizing company. The exemption from registration is not, of course, an exemption from the prohibition against securities fraud section 10(b) of the Securities Exchange Act and Rule 10b-5 thereunder, 15 U.S.C. § 78j; 17 C.F.R. § 240.10b-5.

Section 1145(a)(1) of the Bankruptcy Code creates an exemption from this requirement (and from state securities laws) for securities issued either (a) in exchange for a claim or interest or (b) "principally" in exchange for a claim or interest and "partly" in exchange for cash or other property. 11 U.S.C. § 1145(a)(1). Warrants, options, subscription rights, and conversion rights are also similarly exempt. 11 U.S.C. § 1145(a)(2). Section 1145(a)(1)(A) is what exempts the securities issued normally under a plan from registration requirements when the securities of the reorganized debtor are distributed to the holders of the "fulcrum" class of claims or interests—the juniormost in-the-money class. Section 1145(a)(1)(B) (in conjunction with section 1145(a)(2)) is what exempts rights offerings from registration. The exemption, however, is only if the rights are issued "principally" in exchange for the claim or the interest and only "partly" for cash or other property.

So what is "principally" and "partly" in this context? There is no bright line answer. The text of the statute suggests that the requirement is satisfied if the face amount of the cash/property is less than the face amount of the claim, meaning anything less than a 100% cash-to-claim ratio. A pair of SEC no-action letters approving of transactions with a 75% cash-to-claim ratio suggest that a lower cash-to-claim ratio may be required. *Jet Fl. Sys., Inc.*, SEC No-Action Letter, 1987 WL 107448 (Jan. 12, 1987); *Bennet Petroleum Corp.*, SEC No-Action Letter, 1983 WL 28907 (Dec. 27, 1983). These no-action letters only relate to SEC enforcement, not private enforcement of the Securities Act, and do not even formally bind the SEC, as the SEC does not have rule-making authority under section 1145.

Underwriters, like issuers, are subject to the registration requirement of the Securities Act of 1933. 15 U.S.C. § 77e(a). The section 1145(a) registration exemption does not apply to underwriters. Section 1145(b) further provides that an entity is an underwriter as defined in section 2(a)(11) of the Securities Act of 1933 if it purchases or offers to buy or sell securities offered or sold under the plan with a view to distribution of the securities and under an agreement in connection with the plan. Many backstop parties are thus underwriters and cannot shelter in the section 1145(a) exemption from the registration requirement, but they may still utilize the Securities Act's exemption from registration for private placements of securities.

15 U.S.C. § 77d(a)(2); 17 C.F.R. §§ 230.501-506. To the extent that such backstop parties wish to eventually offer the securities to the public, however, they will require the reorganized debtor to register the securities; backstop agreements will typically provide for a registration right in certain circumstances.

The requirements of section 1145(a)(1) mean that the securities offered without registration are not initially separable from claims—they cannot be offered to the general public, but only to the holders of claims and interests. Because underwriters cannot shelter in section 1145(a)(1), however, the right to backstop a rights offering is not necessarily restricted to pre-existing creditors and equityholders, but can still be done as long as a private-placement exemption is available.

Rights offerings are sometimes contentious, although few have resulted in published decisions. Generally, there are four issues that arise with rights offerings. The first is simply a valuation question. On the other hand, the right to participate in a rights offering can be auctioned off, thus creating a market test. Such a test will not satisfy parties that are incapable of participating in a rights offering, however, for reasons such as funding limitations and investment restrictions.

A second problem with rights offerings relates to the incentives provided to backstop parties. These incentives—commitment fees, break-up fees, discounted purchase prices, governance rights, professionals' fees, and releases—can appear excessive. For example, a backstopping party might receive the right to guaranteed seats on the board of directors of the reorganized debtor or the right to veto certain post-reorganization transactions. It might also secure releases for itself and certain insiders. Objections can be raised to any and all such terms. In particular, a backstop party's fees can be challenged under section 1129(a)(4), which requires that "Any payment made . . . by the debtor, or by a person issuing securities . . . under the plan, for services or for costs or expenses in or in connection with the case, or in connection with the plan and incident to the case . . . [is] reasonable." 11 U.S.C. § 1129(a)(4).

Third, rights offerings raise unfair discrimination problems when done within a cramdown context. Not all classes of creditors or equityholders are allowed to participate in a rights offering. This can give rise to an objection that the selection of participants is unfairly discriminatory.

Fourth, when the terms of a rights offering functionally discriminate between members of a class, by making participation impossible for some class members, there may be a problem of unequal treatment of members of a class under section 1123(a)(4). The proponent of a rights offering may argue that it is making the same opportunity available to all class members, but if that opportunity is obviously illusory for some or all class members, the equal terms of the offer may be insufficient.

Finally, rights offerings can raise absolute priority rule issues both in regard to the offering and the backstop rights. To the extent that a rights offering is awarding the equity in a reorganized debtor, it is necessary that the plan either be consensually confirmed or comply with absolute priority. *203 N. LaSalle Partnership* did not forbid new value plans, after all. Instead, it merely required that there be some sort of a market process (either auctioning off the right to contribute new value in exchange for equity or a surrender of plan exclusivity) *if a plan did not comply with absolute priority.* As long as a new value plan complies with absolute priority, awarding equity in the reorganized debtor in exchange for contribution of new value is fine.

Thus, if a class of equityholders was offered subscription rights when a class of unsecured creditors had not been paid in full, a rights offering would raise absolute priority issues. If, on the other hand, the rights offering was made solely to a class of unsecured creditors and equityholders received no distribution, then there would be no absolute priority issue. Thus, a rights offering could be made to a class of unsecured creditors, as long as all equityholders receive no distribution.

Rights offerings can also raise absolute priority issues in regard to the backstop. Suppose that a backstop is provided by a pre-petition creditor with a claim junior to that of the class given the rights offering. Is the compensation given to the backstop party on account of the backstop or on account of its pre-petition claim? Absent a market test for the backstop rights, it will generally be impossible to know, but there is a concern that a backstop party could receive overly generous compensation as a way of end-running absolute priority. Indeed, because the backstop party can easily end up with control over the reorganized debtor, the backstop rights may well be the controlling equity stake in the debtor. That would seem to require an auction process under *203 N. LaSalle Partnership* if the plan does not comport with absolute priority. Yet instead of being auctioned off in a process that ensures payment of the control premium, the backstop rights are sometimes awarded in a non-market process.

Rights offerings can also make absolute priority analysis quite difficult because they raise the question of whether the class that is given the option of participating in the rights offering has been paid in full or not. Much will depend on the valuation of the option to participate in the offering and the discount given. To the extent there is take-up on the rights offering, it is an indication that the market values the reorganized firm at no less than the debtor's valuation.

Rights offerings currently seem the primary method for avoiding the absolute priority rule, although it remains to be seen whether this will go unchallenged. The following case involves a number of challenges to a rights offering; absolute priority is not among them.

In re Washington Mutual, Inc.

442 B.R. 314 (Bankr. D. Del. 2011)

WALRATH, U.S. Bankr. J.

Before the Court is the request of Washington Mutual, Inc. ("WMI") and WMI Investment Corp. (collectively the "Debtors") for confirmation of their Sixth Amended Joint Plan of Affiliated Debtors Pursuant to Chapter 11 of the United States Bankruptcy Code, filed on October 6, 2010, as modified on October 29 and November 24, 2010 (the "Plan"). . . . WMI is a bank holding company, that formerly owned [Washington Mutual Bank ("WMB")]. WMB was the nation's largest savings and loan association, having over 2,200 branches and holding $188.3 billion in deposits. Beginning in 2007, revenues and earnings decreased at WMB, causing WMI's asset portfolio to decline in value. By September 2008, in the midst of a global credit crisis, the ratings agencies had significantly downgraded WMI's and WMB's credit ratings. A bank run ensued; over $16 billion in deposits were withdrawn from WMB in a ten-day period beginning September 15, 2008.

On September 25, 2008, WMB's primary regulator, the Office of Thrift Supervision (the "OTS"), seized WMB and appointed the FDIC as receiver. The FDIC's takeover of WMB marked the largest bank failure in the nation's history. . . . On September 26, 2008, the Debtors filed petitions under Chapter 11 of the Bankruptcy Code.

. . .

B. OTHER OBJECTIONS TO CONFIRMATION

. . .

3. Discriminatory Treatment of Creditors

One of the individual creditors, Nate Thoma, argued that he is being discriminated against in violation of the Code. Mr. Thoma is the holder of a PIERS claim[,]* which is less than the $2 million threshold necessary under the Plan for a PIERS claimant to participate in the rights offering to purchase stock in the Reorganized Debtor. Mr. Thoma argues that because he is precluded from participating in the rights offering, he is receiving less than others in his class, in violation of section 1123(a)(4) of the Code.

Section 1123(a)(4) provides that "a plan shall— . . . (4) provide the same treatment for each claim or interest of a particular class, unless the holder of a particular claim or interest agrees to a less favorable treatment of such particular claim or interest." 11 U.S.C. § 1123(a)(4).

The Plan Supporters argued that the offering was made only to the larger claimants to avoid the administrative burden of issuing stock to small holders. There is nothing in section 1123(a)(4), however, that would permit discrimination for administrative convenience.[46]

The Plan Supporters also contend that there is no discriminatory treatment because the rights offering is of no value. They argue that the rights offering does not provide for any discount in the purchase price of the stock. The Court is not sure this is correct. Under the rights offering, PIERS Claimants have the right to purchase $100 million in stock in the Reorganized Debtor (each can buy stock based on its percentage of total holdings of PIERS claims). Apparently only $31 million has been purchased through that offering. The Debtors presented testimony that the enterprise value of the

---

* A PIERS claim is a claim based on owning a Trust Preferred Income Equity Redeemable Security, a hybrid debt-equity instrument. While the characterization of PIERS as debt or equity was raised as an issue in *WaMu*, it is not germane to the discussion here.—ED.

46. A plan may provide for a "convenience" class of unsecured claims that are less than (or reduced to) a specific amount, but that class usually receives payment in full to avoid the administrative burden of calculating and paying very small amounts to creditors. 11 U.S.C. § 1122(b).

Reorganized Debtor was $157.5 million. Under the Plan, however, other creditors have the right to accept stock in lieu of cash for their claims. The Debtors were unable to advise how many creditors had chosen that option as the deadline to do so had apparently not passed. The Court, therefore, cannot determine if the value of the stock of the Reorganized Debtor to be held by the PIERS Claimants exceeds the price they will pay for it.

Even if the analysis showed that the PIERS Claimants were getting stock at par, the Court still could not conclude that the rights offering has no value. The right to buy into a company does have inherent value; it includes the "upside" if the company is successful.

Further, in this case the Court concludes that the reorganized company has value in excess of the enterprise value of $157.5 million set by the Debtors' expert. The expert acknowledged that his valuation was based only on the cash flows expected to be generated by the runoff of the insurance assets currently held by the Reorganized Debtor and did not consider that the Reorganized Debtor might start or acquire another business. The fact that the Reorganized Debtor is raising new capital through the rights offering suggests otherwise. *See, e.g., Exide*, 303 B.R. at 60 (committee's expert opined that fact that the senior creditors and management were taking stock in the reorganized company is a "strong indicator that the company is being undervalued"). *But see In re Mirant*, 334 B.R. 800, 832-35 (finding that "[t]he market is not the proper measure for the value of Mirant Group for the purpose of satisfying claims" because the market often undervalues companies in bankruptcy).

Further, the Reorganized Debtor may in fact be a public company (depending on the number of creditors who accept stock instead of cash or who participate in the rights offering). A public company has additional value in its ability to raise capital and acquire (or be acquired by) other businesses. *MicroSignal, Corp. v. MicroSignal Corp.*, 147 Fed. Appx. 227, 232 (3d Cir. 2005) (finding that a merger would result in a public company which is better equipped to raise capital); David N. Feldman, *Reverse Mergers + Pipes: The New Small-Cap IPO Reprinted and Updated from Pipes: Revised and Updated Edition—A Guide to Private Investment in Public Equity*, 3 Bus. L. Brief (Am. U.) 34, 39 (2007) ("It is easier to raise money as a public company than as a private company."). Finally, because the Debtors will not emerge from bankruptcy before December 31, 2010, the Debtors could potentially have the full use of their approximately $5 billion in NOLs. *See* Chaim J. Fortgang & Thomas M. Mayer, *Valuation in Bankruptcy*, 32 UCLA L. Rev. 1061, 1129-30 (1985) (noting that NOLs often are a debtor's largest asset).

Therefore, the Court cannot accept, as the Plan Supporters contend, that the rights offering is of no value. Mr. Thoma is correct. The Plan must be modified to allow all PIERS Claimants the opportunity to participate in the rights offering. *See, e.g., Combustion Eng'g*, 391 F.3d at 241, 248 (vacating confirmation order based on apparent disparate treatment of creditors within a class).

Problem Set 39

(1) Le Chef Geoff poured his heart and soul into his English haute cuisine restaurant, The Blood Pudding, which operates as wholly owned corporation. The Blood Pudding owns the Autumn Room, a magnificent space overlooking Central Park in New York City. The Autumn Room is mortgaged for $18 million, but is easily worth $20 million, if not much more. The Blood Pudding ran into trouble when a recession and a fad diet trend suppressed demand for its delicacies, resulting in a missed mortgage payment and an ensuing bankruptcy. Le Chef is very concerned about keeping the restaurant an operating concern; if it liquidates, he will face substantial personal tax liability. Le Chef has proposed a plan in which the mortgage on the Autumn Room will be cured and reinstated. The cure of the mortgage default will be funded through $1 million in new capital that Le Chef and some new partners will contribute to The Blood Pudding. Is Le Chef's plan confirmable?

(2) Dr. Sherman Klump founded Instathin, a promising biotech company that researched weight-loss drugs. Dr. Klump was the major shareholder in Instathin. The company borrowed heavily to fund its research. Instathin's drugs are all based on Dr. Klump's research, including a number of patents personally held by Dr. Klump. After one of its most hyped drugs failed in a clinical trial, Instathin's funding dried up and the company filed for bankruptcy. Instathin has proposed a plan which pays unsecured creditors only 10 cents on the dollar, but provides for Dr. Klump to retain a controlling equity interest in the company in exchange for continuing to serve as its CEO and Chief Science Officer and allowing Instathin to use his patents without royalties. The plan is supported by Instathin's secured lenders, who have liens on virtually all of Instathin's assets, as well as Instathin's vendors. However, it is opposed by a class of tort victims who were injured by various Instathin products. Is the plan confirmable? If so, what will Instathin be required to do? If not, is there an alternative solution for Instathin?

(3) San Remo Corp. (SRC) is in Chapter 11. SRC is proposing a plan in which secured claims will be paid deferred cash payments with a present value equal to the value of their collateral. Which of the following treatments of unsecured claims and equity will be confirmable?

    a. The unsecured claims will be paid 3 cents on the dollar and given warrants for up to 50 percent of the equity in the reorganized company (valued at 3 cents on the dollar of the claims), with the pre-petition equity retaining the rest of the equity in the reorganized company.

    b. The unsecured claims are given the equity in the reorganized firm (valued at 6 cents on the dollar).

    c. The unsecured claims are given all of the equity in the reorganized firm (valued at 6 cents on the dollar of the claims), but immediately following confirmation, the first lienholders give 5 cents on the dollar to the SRC's pre-petition equityholders.

    d. The unsecured claims are given all of the equity in the reorganized firm (valued at 6 cents on the dollar of the claims), but immediately following confirmation, the first lienholders give 5 cents on the dollar to the SRC's pre-petition equityholders in exchange for the equityholders proposing the plan? 18 U.S.C. § 152(6).

e. The unsecured claims are given all of the equity in the reorganized firm (valued at 6 cents on the dollar of the claims), but the first lienholders are deemed under the plan to gift 5 cents on the dollar of their claims to SRC's pre-petition equityholders.

(4) Omega Corp. is in Chapter 11 bankruptcy. Omega Corp., as DIP, has proposed a plan that contemplates a $1 billion rights offering to its unsecured noteholders. A group of shareholders, representing about 20 percent of the outstanding shares, objected to plan confirmation on the grounds that the unsecured creditors were receiving more than 100 percent on their claims based on the value of the equity being distributed. Omega Corp. feared that unless these shareholders were mollified, they would be able to block a consensual plan confirmation, and as part of a cramdown confirmation force a lengthy and costly valuation hearing. Accordingly, Omega Corp. offered to allow the objecting shareholders—but not other shareholders—to participate in the rights offering, which was allowable under the terms of the rights offering disclosed in the court-approved disclosure statement. Following this offer, the objecting shareholders drop their objection. You represent one of the shareholders not given the right to participate in the rights offering. Are there any objections you can raise?

CHAPTER 40

SALES VERSUS PLANS

I. SALES AND SUB ROSA PLANS

Chapter 11 of the Bankruptcy Code is built around the plan process—the assumption of the Code's drafters was that restructuring—or liquidation—in Chapter 11 would occur pursuant to a plan. That plan might involve asset sales under section 363, but the sales would be pursuant to the plan. Increasingly, however, Chapter 11 restructuring occurs instead through a pre-plan section 363 sale, with a liquidating plan as an afterthought used merely to distribute the sale proceeds according to absolute priority.

Pre-plan 363 sales can obviously be used as a type of "federal foreclosure" to liquidate a business: The buyer will buy the good assets, leaving behind the undesirable assets and the sale proceeds (cash, stock, etc.). The debtor can then simply liquidate those assets through further 363 sales, whether in Chapter 11 or Chapter 7.

Sales can also be used to reorganize a business. Imagine a debtor that operates two separate business lines. The debtor might decide that going forward it wants to focus on one business line. The other business line can be sold off under section 363. Likewise, suppose a buyer purchases the desirable operational assets of the debtor, possibly even including the debtor's name and trademarks. Those assets will continue to be operated, even under the same name—but by the buyer, which will have a new capital structure. The effect going forward is much the same as if the capital structure of the debtor were altered—the assets can be paired with a deleveraged capital structure.

The distributional effects, however, are quite different. If the buyer pays the fair value of the assets, there is no effect on creditors—$1 million of widgets have been swapped for $1 million cash, so the solvency of the debtor has not changed. If the sale price is too low, then creditors suffer—$1 million worth of widgets has been swapped for $700,000 in cash—but creditors have a potential protection: If the sale price is too low, they can (in theory) bid themselves. Thus, if bidding procedures are not distortive, the sale process should not in and of itself be distributionally problematic for creditors.

But what if the consideration paid for the sale were not cash or stock or the buyer's notes, but instead consisted in part of the buyer's assumption of certain liabilities of the debtor? Imagine that the buyer believes that the assets it's purchasing are worth $1 million. The buyer could pay $1 million in cash. Or the buyer could pay

$800,000 in cash and assume $200,000 of the debtor firm's debt. Economically, these transactions are equivalent, but distributionally they are not. The favored creditors whose debt is assumed can expect to be paid in full by the buyer (or at least have a greater chance of payment in full). But the disfavored creditors whose debts are not assumed will get only what they get in the debtor's subsequent liquidation—cents on the dollar or nothing at all. Moreover, because of the assumption of debts in the sale, the sale price has been lowered. There are fewer claims to pay . . . but also fewer dollars to pay them. If the assumed claims would not have been paid at 100 cents on the dollar, then the assumption of debts would harm the disfavored creditors who were left behind, just like a preferential payment. If the favored creditors whose debts are assumed by the buyer were of lower or equal priority to the creditors whose debts are not assumed, then the sale has effectively elevated their priority over the creditors whose debts are not assumed. A section 363 sale with assumption of select liabilities can effect a priority system that deviates substantially from that which would be required for a plan confirmation. Whether doing so is permissible was precisely the issue in the *Chrysler* bankruptcy appeal excerpted in Chapter 1.

The shift away from plan-based restructuring to sale-based restructuring is due to a couple of factors. First, section 363 lacks the mandatory procedural requirements that exist for plan confirmation. The debtor is able to control the sale process to a far greater degree than it can control the plan process, deciding what is sold and how, and through the use of stalking horses, breakup fees, bidder qualifications, and bidding procedures, a debtor can exert substantial control over who the bidders are. The greater flexibility of section 363 over a plan makes it inherently attractive to debtors as a method of restructuring.

Second, the institutional landscape of bankruptcy has changed since 1978. In the early years of the Bankruptcy Code, the paradigmatic large bankruptcy was a retailer's bankruptcy: The retailer would have a lot of unsecured debt, and little secured debt. The debt didn't trade, so the retailer would come out of the bankruptcy with the same creditors it had going in. The prevalence of unsecured debt gave debtors substantial flexibility in terms of their plans; section 1129(b)(2)(A) did not dictate the terms of a restructuring, and there were long-term relationships between debtors and creditors. Moreover, because debtors had substantial pledged assets, they had more flexibility when negotiating DIP financing, so the DIP lender had weaker control over the debtor.

Today, in contrast, the typical large debtor has liens on virtually all of its assets.[1] Not only will there be first lien debt, but there will also usually be second lien debt (often undersecured). This financial debt trades frequently, so the creditors are not in long-term relationships with the debtor, but are, instead, often repeat players in bankruptcy. The debtor has little flexibility in negotiating DIP financing; the debtor basically hands the keys over to the DIP lender, which as the senior secured lender

---

1. A revision of Article 9 of the Uniform Commercial Code that went into effect in 2001 facilitated this change. Prior to 2001, creditors had a jurisdictionally spotty and uncertain right to take and maintain a security interest in deposit accounts. Since 2001, the Uniform Commercial Code has expressly permitted security interests in deposit accounts. UCC § 9-104.

will usually push for a fast liquidation, done through a pre-plan 363 sale. Thus, one study has found a decline in absolute priority rule violations during the 1991-2005 period, which would be consistent with control in bankruptcy shifting from equityholders to secured creditors. Sreedhar T. Bharath *et al.*, *The Changing Nature of Chapter 11*, Fisher College of Business Working Paper No. 2008-03-003 (Nov. 2010).

Debtors' increased use of secured debt has limited their ability to maneuver in bankruptcy, which results in a transfer of control (and ultimately value) from unsecured creditors (particularly involuntary ones, but ultimately all non-adjusting ones) to secured creditors. Because there are fewer protections for dissenting creditors with a 363 sale than with a plan confirmation, bankruptcy has often become a vehicle for secured creditors to more efficiently foreclose on their collateral, if not take over the debtor firm's assets (and possibly selected liabilities) through a 363 sale and credit bid.

While section 363 does not itself deal with the allocation of the going-concern surplus over liquidation value, disposal of estate assets potentially changes the size of the going-concern surplus and can itself function as a type of backdoor allocation of value if the sale is not properly priced, which may in turn relate to the terms under which the sale occurs, namely whether there is an auction, who may participate in the auction, and the terms under which parties may participate in the auction.

Section 363's lack of procedural requirements gives debtors tremendous flexibility in the use of section 363. A section 363 sale may occur either under a plan or prior to a plan. To the extent that a sale occurs prior to a plan, it is not subject to the procedural requirements of section 1129.

The thinner creditor protections under section 363 make section 363 transactions a tempting alternative for undertaking the restructuring of the debtor's business outside of the more restrictive plan provisions of section 1129. The ability to use section 363 to effectively reorganize a debtor and to allocate going-concern value raises the concern of section 363 transactions functioning as "sub rosa" plans. The subsequent cases consider this problem. The difficulty in reconciling section 363 with section 1129 remains one of the most vexing issues in bankruptcy today.

In re The Lionel Corp.

722 F.2d 1063 (2d Cir. 1983)

CARDAMONE, Circuit Judge:

This expedited appeal is from an order . . . authoriz[ing] the sale by Lionel Corporation, a Chapter 11 debtor in possession, of its 82% common stock holding in Dale Electronics, Inc. to Peabody International Corporation for $50 million.

I. FACTS

On February 19, 1982 the Lionel Corporation—toy train manufacturer of childhood memory—[filed] for reorganization under Chapter 11 of the Bankruptcy Code. Resort to Chapter 11 was precipitated by losses totaling $22.5 million that Lionel incurred in its toy retailing operation during the two year period ending December 1982.

There are 7.1 million shares of common stock of Lionel held by 10,000 investors. Its consolidated assets and liabilities [had] a negative net worth of nearly $23 million. . . .

Lionel continues to operate its businesses and manage its properties [as a debtor-in-possession] pursuant to 11 U.S.C. §§ 1107-1108. . . .

Lionel's most important asset and the subject of this proceeding is its ownership of 82% of the common stock of Dale, a corporation engaged in the manufacture of electronic components. Dale is not a party to the Lionel bankruptcy proceeding. Public investors own the remaining 18 percent of Dale's common stock, which is listed on the American Stock Exchange. Its balance sheet reflects . . . shareholders equity of approximately $28.0 million. Lionel's stock investment in Dale represents approximately 34 percent of Lionel's consolidated assets, and its interest in Dale is Lionel's most valuable single asset. Unlike Lionel's toy retailing operation, Dale is profitable. . . .

On June 14, 1983 Lionel filed an application under section 363(b) seeking bankruptcy court authorization to sell its 82% interest in Dale to Acme-Cleveland Corporation for $43 million in cash. Four days later the debtor filed a plan of reorganization conditioned upon a sale of Dale with the proceeds to be distributed to creditors. Certain issues of the reorganization remain unresolved, and negotiations are continuing; however, a solicitation of votes on the plan has not yet begun. On September 7, 1983, following the Securities and Exchange Commission's July 15 filing of objections to the sale, Bankruptcy Judge Ryan held a hearing on Lionel's application. At the hearing, Peabody emerged as the successful of three bidders with an offer of $50 million for Lionel's interest in Dale.

The Chief Executive Officer of Lionel and a Vice-President of Salomon Brothers were the only witnesses produced and both testified in support of the application. Their testimony established that while the price paid for the stock was "fair," Dale is not an asset "that is wasting away in any sense." Lionel's Chief Executive Officer stated that there was no reason why the sale of Dale stock could not be accomplished as part of the reorganization plan, and that the sole reason for Lionel's application to sell was the Creditors' Committee's insistence upon it. The creditors wanted to turn this asset of Lionel into a "pot of cash," to provide the bulk of the $70 million required to repay creditors under the proposed plan of reorganization.

In confirming the sale, Judge Ryan made no formal findings of fact. He simply noted that cause to sell was sufficiently shown by the Creditors' Committee's insistence upon it. Judge Ryan further found cause—presumably from long experience—based upon his own opinion that a present failure to confirm would set the entire reorganization process back a year or longer while the parties attempted to restructure it.

The Committee of Equity Security Holders, statutory representatives of the 10,000 public shareholders of Lionel, appealed this order claiming that the sale, prior to approval of a reorganization plan, deprives the equity holders of the Bankruptcy Code's safeguards of disclosure, solicitation and acceptance and divests the debtor of a dominant and profitable asset which could serve as a cornerstone for a sound plan. The SEC also appeared and objected to the sale in the bankruptcy court and supports the Equity

Committee's appeal, claiming that approval of the sale side-steps the Code's requirement for informed suffrage which is at the heart of Chapter 11.

The Creditors' Committee favors the sale because it believes it is in the best interests of Lionel and because the sale is expressly authorized by § 363(b) of the Code. Lionel tells us that its ownership of Dale, a non-operating asset, is held for investment purposes only and that its sale will provide the estate with the large block of the cash needed to fund its plan of reorganization.

From the oral arguments and briefs we gather that the Equity Committee believes that Chapter 11 has cleared the reorganization field of major pre-plan sales—somewhat like the way Minerva routed Mars—relegating § 363(b) to be used only in emergencies. The Creditors' Committee counters that a bankruptcy judge should have absolute freedom under § 363(b) to do as he thinks best. Neither of these arguments is wholly persuasive. Here, as in so many similar cases, we must avoid the extremes, for the policies underlying the Bankruptcy Reform Act of 1978 support a middle ground—one which gives the bankruptcy judge considerable discretion yet requires him to articulate sound business justifications for his decisions.

II. DISCUSSION

The issue now before this Court is to what extent Chapter 11 permits a bankruptcy judge to authorize the sale of an important asset of the bankrupt's estate, out of the ordinary course of business and prior to acceptance and outside of any plan of reorganization. Section 363(b), the focal point of our analysis, provides that "the trustee, after notice and a hearing, may use, sell, or lease, other than in the ordinary course of business, property of the estate." 11 U.S.C. § 363(b).

On its face, section 363(b) appears to permit disposition of any property of the estate of a corporate debtor without resort to the statutory safeguards embodied in Chapter 11 of the Bankruptcy Code. Yet, analysis of the statute's history and over seven decades of case law convinces us that such a literal reading of section 363(b) would unnecessarily violate the congressional scheme for corporate reorganizations.

[An examination of the sales standard under prior bankruptcy statutes indicates that sales were generally permitted only of perishable or wasting assets.] . . . [T]he new Bankruptcy Code no longer requires such strict limitations on a bankruptcy judge's authority to order disposition of the estate's property; nevertheless, it does not go so far as to eliminate all constraints on that judge's discretion.

. . .

III. CONCLUSION

The history surrounding the enactment in 1978 of current Chapter 11 and the logic underlying it buttress our conclusion that there must be some articulated business justification, other than appeasement of major creditors, for using, selling or leasing property out of the ordinary course of business before the bankruptcy judge may order such disposition under section 363(b).

The case law under section 363's statutory predecessors used terms like "perishable," "deteriorating," and "emergency" as guides in deciding whether a debtor's property could be sold outside the ordinary course of business. The use of such words persisted long after their omission from newer statutes and rules. The administrative power to sell or lease property in a reorganization continued to be the exception, not the rule. In enacting the 1978 Code Congress was aware of existing case law and clearly indicated as one of its purposes that equity interests have a greater voice in reorganization plans—hence, the safeguards of disclosure, voting, acceptance and confirmation in present Chapter 11.

Resolving the apparent conflict between Chapter 11 and § 363(b) does not require an all or nothing approach. Every sale under § 363(b) does not automatically short-circuit or side-step Chapter 11; nor are these two statutory provisions to be read as mutually exclusive. Instead, if a bankruptcy judge is to administer a business reorganization successfully under the Code, then—like the related yet independent tasks performed in modern production techniques to ensure good results—some play for the operation of both § 363(b) and Chapter 11 must be allowed for.

The rule we adopt requires that a judge determining a § 363(b) application expressly find from the evidence presented before him at the hearing a good business reason to grant such an application. In this case the only reason advanced for granting the request to sell Lionel's 82 percent stock interest in Dale was the Creditors' Committee's insistence on it. Such is insufficient as a matter of fact because it is not a sound business reason and insufficient as a matter of law because it ignores the equity interests required to be weighed and considered under Chapter 11. The court also expressed its concern that a present failure to approve the sale would result in a long delay. As the Supreme Court has noted, it is easy to sympathize with the desire of a bankruptcy court to expedite bankruptcy reorganization proceedings for they are frequently protracted. "The need for expedition, however, is not a justification for abandoning proper standards." *Protective Committee for Independent Stockholders of TMT Trailer Ferry, Inc. v. Anderson*, 390 U.S. 414, 450 (1968). Thus, the approval of the sale of Lionel's 82 percent interest in Dale was an abuse of the trial court's discretion.

In fashioning its findings, a bankruptcy judge must not blindly follow the hue and cry of the most vocal special interest groups; rather, he should consider all salient factors pertaining to the proceeding and, accordingly, act to further the diverse interests of the debtor, creditors and equity holders, alike. He might, for example, look to such relevant factors as the proportionate value of the asset to the estate as a whole, the amount of elapsed time since the filing, the likelihood that a plan of reorganization will be proposed and confirmed in the near future, the effect of the proposed disposition on future plans of reorganization, the proceeds to be obtained from the disposition vis-à-vis any appraisals of the property, which of the alternatives of use, sale or lease the proposal envisions and, most importantly perhaps, whether the asset is increasing or decreasing in value. This list is not intended to be exclusive, but merely to provide guidance to the bankruptcy judge.

Finally, we must consider whether appellants opposing the sale produced evidence before the bankruptcy court that such sale was not justified. While a debtor applying under § 363(b) carries the burden of demonstrating that a use, sale or lease out of the ordinary course of business will aid the debtor's reorganization, an objectant, such as the Equity Committee here, is required to produce some evidence respecting its objections. Appellants made three objections below: First, the sale was premature because Dale is not a wasting asset and there is no emergency; second, there was no justifiable cause present since Dale, if anything, is improving; and third, the price was inadequate. No proof was required as to the first objection because it was stipulated as conceded. The second and third objections are interrelated. Following Judge Ryan's suggestion that objections could as a practical matter be developed on cross-examination, Equity's counsel elicited testimony from the financial expert produced by Lionel that Dale is less subject than other companies to wide market fluctuations. The same witness also conceded that he knew of no reason why those interested in Dale's stock at the September 7, 1983 hearing would not be just as interested six months from then. The only other witness who testified was the Chief Executive Officer of Lionel, who stated that it was only at the insistence of the Creditors' Committee that Dale stock was being sold and that Lionel "would very much like to retain its interest in Dale." These uncontroverted statements of the two witnesses elicited by the Equity Committee on cross-examination were sufficient proof to support its objections to the present sale of Dale because this evidence demonstrated that there was no good business reason for the present sale. Hence, appellants satisfied their burden.

Accordingly, the order appealed from is reversed and the matter remanded to the district court with directions to remand to the bankruptcy court for further proceedings consistent with this opinion.

[Judge Winter's dissent is omitted.]

Lionel includes a list of factors that a court might consider when evaluating a proposed section 363 sale. These factors are known as "the *Lionel* factors." To these factors, Judge Robert Gerber added four more in his decision approving the section 363 sale of a substantial part of General Motors assets. These additional factors have become known as "the *GM* factors."

In re GMC

407 B.R. 463 (Bankr. S.D.N.Y. 2009)

. . .

(h) Does the estate have the liquidity to survive until confirmation of a plan?

(i) Will the sale opportunity still exist as of the time of plan confirmation?

(j) If not, how likely is it that there will be a satisfactory alternative sale opportunity, or a stand-alone plan alternative that is equally desirable (or better) for creditors? And

(k) Is there a material risk that by deferring the sale, the patient will die on the operating table?

. . .

debtor

In re Continental Air Lines, Inc.

780 F.2d 1223 (5th Cir. 1986)

THOMAS GIBBS GEE, Circuit Judge:

The issue in this case is how far a debtor-in-possession can stretch the bankruptcy laws to undertake transactions outside a plan of reorganization. The district court did not consider whether the proposed transactions would effect an end run around the protection granted creditors in Chapter 11 of the Bankruptcy Code. For this reason, we vacate the district court order that affirmed the bankruptcy court decision authorizing the debtor to proceed with lease negotiations and remand for further consideration.

FACTS

Appellee, Continental Air Lines, Inc. ("CAL"), filed a voluntary petition under Chapter 11 of the United States Bankruptcy Code on September 24, 1983. During the period relevant to this case, CAL operated its commercial airline service as a debtor-in-possession, pursuant to 11 U.S.C. §§ 1107-1108. CAL owes appellants, its Institutional Creditors ("Institutional Creditors"), in excess of $30 million.

On March 16, 1984, CAL filed with the bankruptcy court a motion for authority to enter into lease agreements for two DC-10-30 aircraft. CAL represented that the leased aircraft would allow it to strengthen and enhance profitability and cash flow greatly and to increase the asset value of its Mid Pacific and South Pacific operations. In an accompanying motion to limit and restrict notice of the motion to enter into the leases, CAL further represented that the two aircraft were necessary in order for CAL to preserve its route authority in the Pacific, supposedly one of its most valuable assets.

The bankruptcy court granted CAL's latter motion; a three-day hearing on the proposed leases commenced on March 30, 1984. On April 6, 1984, the bankruptcy court signed an order authorizing the leases. The bankruptcy court amended this order on April 16, 1984. Under the terms of the amended order, the bankruptcy court authorized the leases subject to its approval of the final terms. The bankruptcy court found that if CAL did not implement new DC-10-30 service to its Mid-Pacific and South Pacific route system, CAL's revenue and profit forecast for 1984 and thereafter [would] be jeopardized, CAL [would] be unable to effectively compete over these routes, and CAL and its estate [might] not be able to protect and preserve these route systems for the benefit of CAL, its bankruptcy estate and the creditors thereof.

The bankruptcy court concluded that CAL had properly sought authority under 11 U.S.C. § 363 to enter into the leases, that the Mid and South Pacific route systems were extremely valuable assets of the bankruptcy estate under 11 U.S.C. § 541(a), and as a debtor-in-possession CAL "is under a duty to take reasonable steps to preserve, protect and enhance the assets of its bankruptcy estate which have value for the benefit of CAL and its creditors." The bankruptcy court further concluded that "this duty is subject to the overall impact of any proposed individual action on the existing financial condition of the Debtor and the attendant risks to creditors."

On appeal to the district court, the Institutional Creditors argued that the purpose of the proposed transaction was to avoid and shortcut the process that leads to a plan of reorganization, hence the bankruptcy court lacked the power to approve the leases in light of *In re Braniff Airways, Inc.*, 700 F.2d 935 (5th Cir. 1983). In rejecting the Institutional Creditors' position and affirming the bankruptcy court's order, the district court held that, unlike *Braniff*, CAL's proposed leases did not "dictate the terms of any future plan of reorganization, nor [would they] leave CAL with so few assets that reorganization [would become] unlikely." The leases did not have restrictions "on voting or any requirement for release of claims and [would] not alter any creditor's priority." Instead, "the proposed transaction by CAL is a 'use, lease or sale' of the debtor's assets as permitted under 11 U.S.C. § 363, and as such it was within the bankruptcy court's power to approve the agreement without submitting it to a vote of the creditors."

On appeal to this Court, the Institutional Creditors present us with two basic sets of issues. The first concerns the statutory authority for CAL's proposal to enter into a 10-year post-petition financial commitment in excess of $70 million. The second addresses the adequacy of the process the Institutional Creditors received in the approval of the leases. Because we are not yet convinced that there is authority for the leases, we decline to reach the second set of issues on this appeal.

11 U.S.C. § 363(B) TRANSACTIONS

Given the novelty of CAL's proposed use of 11 U.S.C. § 363(b), an overview of the relevant statutory and case law authority for the proposed transaction is in order. A debtor-in-possession under 11 U.S.C. § 1107 is authorized, absent court order otherwise, to operate the debtor's business. 11 U.S.C. § 1108. Such a debtor-in-possession, "after notice and hearing, may use, sell, or lease, other than in the ordinary course of business, property of the estate." 11 U.S.C. § 363(b).

When a proposed use, sale, or lease of assets is outside the ordinary course of business, § 363(b) requires that the assets be property of the estate. What is included in property of the estate is determined by 11 U.S.C. § 541. We also agree with the Second Circuit that implicit in § 363(b) is the further requirement of justifying the proposed transaction. *In re Lionel Corp.*, 722 F.2d 1063, 1071 (2d Cir. 1983). That is, for the debtor-in-possession or trustee to satisfy its fiduciary duty to the debtor, creditors and equity holders, there must be some articulated business justification for using, selling, or leasing the property outside the ordinary course of business. *Id.* Whether the proffered business justification is sufficient depends on the case. As the Second Circuit held in *Lionel*, the bankruptcy judge

> should consider all salient factors pertaining to the proceeding and, accordingly, act to further the diverse interests of the debtor, creditors and equity holders, alike. He might, for example, look to such relevant factors as the proportionate value of the asset to the estate as a whole, the amount of elapsed time since the filing, the likelihood that a plan of reorganization will be proposed and confirmed in the near future, the effect of the proposed disposition on future plans of reorganization, the proceeds to be obtained from the disposition vis-à-vis any appraisals of the property, which of the alternatives of use, sale or lease the proposal envisions and, most importantly perhaps, whether the asset is increasing or decreasing in value. This list is not intended to be exclusive, but merely to provide guidance to the bankruptcy judge.

722 F.2d at 1071. *See, e.g., Matter of Baldwin United Corp.*, 43 Bankr. 888, 905-906 (Bankr. S.D. Ohio 1984).

Use of property

. . .

Finally, as this Court recognized in *Braniff*, § 363 does not authorize a debtor and the bankruptcy court "to short circuit the requirements of a reorganization plan by establishing the terms of the plan *sub rosa* in connection" with a proposed transaction. 700 F.2d at 940. When a proposed transaction specifies terms for adopting a reorganization plan, "the parties and the district court must scale the hurdles erected in Chapter 11. *See, e.g.*, 11 U.S.C. § 1125 (disclosure requirements, *id.* § 1126 (voting); *id.* § 1129(a)(7), best interest of creditors test); *id.* § 1129(b)(2)(B) (absolute priority rule)." *Id.* at 940.

AUTHORITY FOR CAL'S PROPOSED LEASES

Applying the foregoing principles and our decision in *Braniff* to today's case, we must consider (1) whether the proposed transaction represents a use, sale, or lease of estate property; (2) whether the district court erred in finding that the business justifications offered for the transaction were sufficient to warrant authorization to proceed with lease negotiations; (3) whether the proposed transactions otherwise violate or are incompatible with the provisions of Chapter 11.

It is undisputed in this case that the proposed transaction is outside the ordinary course of business, thus invoking § 363(b). CAL argues that the asset it proposes to use under § 363(b) is estate funds. According to 11 U.S.C. § 541, property of the estate includes "proceeds, product, offspring, or profits of or from property of the estate," as well as "any interest in property that the estate acquires after commencement of the case." 11 U.S.C. § 541. Property of the estate therefore includes funds derived from airline operations or other sources. Hence the application of these funds to satisfy lease obligations is a use of estate property pursuant to § 363(b).

We further conclude that the district court did not err in affirming the bankruptcy court finding that the business justifications CAL offered in support of the leases are sufficient to authorize proceeding with lease negotiations, something the Institutional Creditors do not challenge at this point. The record shows that CAL's routes in the Mid and South Pacific are of significant economic value to it; that the new aircraft would allow CAL (1) to satisfy an increase in the quantity of airline services demanded as a result of a change in exchange rates; (2) to exploit an existing competitive advantage by offering new route combinations and by filling a void left by withdrawing carriers; (3) to take advantage of foreign governments' willingness to negotiate additional service requests; and (4) to increase cash flow as well as profits. These reasons were sufficient to warrant authorizing CAL to proceed with lease negotiations, subject to review of all considerations upon having the terms of the final agreement.

With respect to the other provisions of § 363 . . . the Institutional Creditors did not request the bankruptcy court to grant them adequate protection under § 363(e). Rather, the Institutional Creditors' primary argument is that the proposed leases represent pieces of a creeping plan of reorganization, incompatible with our holding in *Braniff*. In this regard, the Institutional Creditors assert that the district court fundamentally erred in confining the scope of our holding in *Braniff* to whether a transaction is a use, sale, or lease of estate property.

In *Braniff* we recognized that a debtor in Chapter 11 cannot use § 363(b) to sidestep the protection creditors have when it comes time to confirm a plan of reorganization. Likewise, if a debtor were allowed to reorganize the estate in some fundamental fashion pursuant to § 363(b), creditor's rights under, for example, 11 U.S.C. §§ 1125, 1126, 1129(a)(7), and 1129(b)(2) might become meaningless. Undertaking reorganization piecemeal pursuant to § 363(b) should not deny creditors the protection they would receive if the proposals were first raised in the reorganization plan. At the same time, we fully appreciate the post-petition, pre-confirmation transactions outside the ordinary course of business may be required and that each hearing on a § 363(b) transaction cannot become a mini-hearing on plan confirmation. Balancing these considerations, we hold that when an objector to a proposed transaction under § 363(b) claims that it is being denied certain protection because approval is sought pursuant to § 363(b) instead of as part of a reorganization plan, the objector must specify exactly what protection is being denied. If the court concludes that there has in actuality been such a denial, it may then consider fashioning appropriate protective measures modeled on those which would attend a reorganization plan.

The district court in today's case did not consider the Institutional Creditors' claims that they were being denied certain protection they would receive if the transaction were part of a reorganization plan. Because the bankruptcy court may have lacked statutory authority to authorize the leases if the Institutional Creditors could have defeated a plan of reorganization containing the leases or may have had to condition certain terms of any lease, we VACATE the district court's order and REMAND for consideration consistent with this opinion.

II. SETTLEMENT OF CLAIMS

Bankruptcy presents one of the few situations in which settlements must be approved by a court. Criminal plea bargains, class action settlements, and government settlements are the other major situations requiring court approval; in some situations, a trustee may also seek court approval of a settlement on behalf of a trust (*e.g.*, an Article 77 Proceeding in New York state court or a section 501B.16 Trust Instruction Proceeding in Minnesota state court).

The requirement of court approval for settlements involving the bankruptcy estate stems from the fact that a settlement affects the assets of the estate and thus the interests of parties other than the TIB/DIP. It also affects claimants and interest holders. Accordingly, they are given a chance to be heard regarding settlement. The approval of a settlement is not governed by section 1129, but the approval of a settlement may in fact be the major obstacle to plan approval, as a settlement can procure the support of key creditors or provide funding for a plan.

Federal Rule of Bankruptcy Procedure 9019 governs settlements. Curiously, there is no Code provision analogous to the Rule, although section 363(b) would seem to apply. The Rule provides no guidance as to the standard for approving a settlement, but courts have explicated standards, as discussed in the *Iridium* case below.

Federal Rule of Bankruptcy Procedure 9019.
Compromise and Arbitration

(a) **Compromise.** On motion by the trustee and after notice and a hearing, the court may approve a compromise or settlement. Notice shall be given to creditors, the United States trustee, the debtor, and indenture trustees as provided in Rule 2002 and to any other entity as the court may direct.

(b) **Authority to Compromise or Settle Controversies Within Classes.** After a hearing on such notice as the court may direct, the court may fix a class or classes of controversies and authorize the trustee to compromise or settle controversies within such class or classes without further hearing or notice.

(c) **Arbitration.** On stipulation of the parties to any controversy affecting the estate the court may authorize the matter to be submitted to final and binding arbitration.

Motorola, Inc. v. Official Comm. of Unsecured Creditors
(*In re* Iridium Operating LLC)
478 F.3d 452 (2d Cir. 2007)

WESLEY, *Circuit Judge*:

There is little doubt that settlements of disputed claims facilitate the efficient functioning of the judicial system. In Chapter 11 bankruptcies, settlements also help clear a path for the efficient administration of the bankrupt estate, including any eventual plan of reorganization. Before pre-plan settlements can take effect, however, they must be approved by the bankruptcy court pursuant to Bankruptcy Rule 9019.

This case requires us to determine whether a long-standing creditor protection—the Bankruptcy Code's priority scheme for reorganization plan distributions—applies to bankruptcy court approval of a settlement under Rule 9019. We hold that in the Chapter 11 context, whether a pre-plan settlement's distribution plan complies with the Bankruptcy Code's priority scheme will be the most important factor for a bankruptcy court to consider in approving a settlement under Bankruptcy Rule 9019. In most cases, it will be dispositive.

Iridium Operating LLC ("Iridium") is currently in Chapter 11 proceedings. A consortium of lenders represented by JPMorgan Chase Bank, N.A. (the "Lenders"), asserted liens over much of what is left of Iridium. The Official Committee of Unsecured Creditors (the "Committee") vigorously contested those liens; in particular, the Committee objected to the Lenders' claim to Iridium's remaining cash held in accounts at Chase. The Committee also sought to pursue claims against Motorola, Inc. ("Motorola"), Iridium's former parent company, but lacked money to fund the litigation. The Committee and the Lenders ultimately decided to settle their dispute and sought [and obtained] court approval [from the bankruptcy court] of their settlement (the "Settlement") under Bankruptcy Rule

9019. The Settlement concedes the liens and distributes the Estate's cash to the Lenders and to a litigation vehicle set up to sue Motorola. Motorola, also an administrative— and, therefore, priority—creditor, objects to the Settlement on the grounds that it takes a portion of estate property and distributes it to lower priority creditors (the litigation vehicle and the Committee) before any payments are made to Motorola.

BACKGROUND

lender
Motorola
Committee

. . .

The Settlement's Terms

The Settlement is lengthy and complex, but only a few of its provisions are in play here. First, the Settlement determines that the Lenders' liens are senior, perfected, and unavoidable and not subject to offsets, defenses, claims, or counterclaims by the Estate. The liens do not enjoy those concessions, however, until court approval of the Settlement.

Second, the Settlement divides up the Estate's remaining cash into three separate cash funds. Cash Fund Number One splits $130 million two ways: the Lenders get $92.5 million and $37.5 million will be distributed by the Estate directly to a newly-created entity, the Iridium Litigation LLC (the "ILLLC"). Cash Fund Number Two gets $5 million for professional expenses, including attorneys' fees. This fund is also split two ways: one-third goes to one of the law firms involved in negotiating the Settlement and two-thirds goes to the ILLLC for payment of professional expenses. Any interest accumulated in Cash Fund Numbers One and Two goes to the Lenders (approximately 71 percent) and to the ILLLC (approximately 29 percent). Cash Fund Number Three includes income from accounts receivable. Fifty-five percent of Cash Fund Number Three goes to the ILLLC, and the remainder goes to the Lenders on the effective date of the Settlement.

The ILLLC was created to serve as a funding vehicle for all Motorola-related litigation. A litigation trust, whose beneficiaries are the unsecured creditors, owns 99.9 percent of the ILLLC. Further, the ILLLC is controlled by Committee members and represented by Committee counsel. Should the Committee and the Estate prevail against Motorola, the Settlement provides that the proceeds, after the payment of any of the ILLLC's professional fees, will be split among the Lenders, administrative creditors, and the Estate. The Lenders would take 37.5 percent of any recovery. The other 62.5 percent of the recovery would go to the Estate, to be distributed according to a future, as-yet-unconfirmed reorganization plan, with administrative creditors—such as Motorola—taking first. Thus, a large portion of any monies recovered from Motorola as a result of the Motorola Estate Action will flow to the Estate and be distributed according to the Bankruptcy Code's priority scheme and creditors behind the Lenders will receive payment of their claims even if the Lenders' claims are not fully satisfied by the Motorola-related litigation. Any of the initial $37.5 million remaining in the trust at the end of the litigation will be paid by the ILLLC directly to the unsecured creditors. The Settlement further dictates that its signatories will only support a reorganization plan consistent with the terms of the Settlement.

From the Committee's perspective, the Settlement has a number of benefits. The Settlement (1) frees up cash from the Lenders' purported liens to fund the Motorola litigation; (2) allows creditors behind the Lenders to receive payment of their claims before the Lenders' claims are fully satisfied; (3) eliminates the Lenders' liens on any recovery from the Motorola cause of action; (4) coordinates litigation against Motorola; (5) allows the Estate to pursue causes of action that would normally belong to the Lenders, such as disputes over whether any of Motorola's administrative claims must be subordinated to the Lenders' claims; (6) frees other assets, such as non-Motorola causes of action (which it then ensures are funded), from Lenders' purported liens; and (7) results in an immediate payment of almost $7 million dollars to the Estate for resolution of other issues. In addition, the Lenders waive any rights they might have as unsecured creditors to receive any of the proceeds of the Motorola Estate Action. According to the Committee, the Settlement will help maximize the potential recovery against Motorola. The Committee also points out that if it lost its challenge of the purported liens, unsecured creditors would receive nothing unless and until the Lenders were paid at least the $800 million covered by the December 23, 1998 credit facility. The Committee was clearly concerned with the risk of litigating with the Lenders; the litigation process would be long and expensive and involve novel legal issues, and a loss would leave the Estate all but penniless.

. . .

DISCUSSION

. . .

B. Bankruptcy Rule 9019

Bankruptcy Rule 9019, unique in that it does not have a parallel section in the Code, has a "clear purpose . . . to prevent the making of concealed agreements which are unknown to the creditors and unevaluated by the court." *In re Masters, Inc.*, 141 B.R. 13, 16 (Bankr. E.D.N.Y. 1992). Courts have developed standards to evaluate if a settlement is fair and equitable, and, to that end, courts in this Circuit have set forth factors for approval of settlements based on the original framework announced in *TMT Trailer Ferry. Protective Comm. for Indep. Stockholders of TMT Trailer Ferry, Inc. v. Anderson*, 390 U.S. 414 (1968). Those interrelated factors are: (1) the balance between the litigation's possibility of success and the settlement's future benefits; (2) the likelihood of complex and protracted litigation, "with its attendant expense, inconvenience, and delay," including the difficulty in collecting on the judgment; (3) "the paramount interests of the creditors," including each affected class's relative benefits "and the degree to which creditors either do not object to or affirmatively support the proposed settlement"; (4) whether other parties in interest support the settlement; (5) the "competency and experience of counsel" supporting, and "[t]he experience and knowledge of the bankruptcy court judge" reviewing, the settlement; (6) "the nature and breadth of releases to be obtained by officers and directors"; and (7) "the extent to which the settlement is the product of arm's length bargaining." *In re WorldCom, Inc.*, 347 B.R. 123, 137 (Bankr. S.D.N.Y. 2006).

C. The "Fair and Equitable" Standard

Motorola does not contend that the Settlement fails under this multi-factor test. Rather, it argues that the Settlement should not have been approved because it provides for the transfer of money from the Estate to the ILLLC, and from the ILLLC to the unsecured creditors after the Motorola-related litigation. Motorola claims that a settlement can never be fair and equitable if junior creditors' claims are satisfied before those of more senior creditors.

The phrase "fair and equitable" derives from section 1129(b)(2)(B)(ii) of the Bankruptcy Code, which describes the conditions under which a plan of reorganization may be approved notwithstanding the objections of an impaired class of creditors, a situation known as a "cramdown." This provision codifies the judge-made "absolute priority rule," which provided that any plan of reorganization in which "stockholders [a]re preferred before the creditor, [is] invalid." *In re Armstrong World Indus., Inc.*, 320 B.R. 523, 533 (D. Del.), *aff'd* 432 F.3d 507 (3d Cir. 2005). In its current statutory form, the rule provides that "the holder of any claim or interest that is junior to the claims of such class will not receive or retain under the plan on account of such junior claim or interest any property." 11 U.S.C. § 1129(b)(2)(B)(ii).

Although the statute by its terms applies only to plans of reorganization, the Supreme Court has held that a settlement presented for approval as part of a plan of reorganization, because it constitutes part of the plan, may only be approved if it, too, is "fair and equitable" in the sense of conforming to the absolute priority rule. *See TMT Trailer Ferry*, 390 U.S. at 424 ("The requirements . . . that plans of reorganization be both 'fair and equitable,' apply to compromises just as to other aspects of reorganizations."). When a settlement is presented for court approval apart from a reorganization plan, however, the priority rule of 11 U.S.C. § 1129 is not necessarily implicated. Without the requirement that pre-plan settlements conform to the absolute priority rule, only the bankruptcy court's invocation of Rule 9019 factors would protect the interests of any nonsignatory intermediate or impaired creditors.

In response to this concern, the Fifth Circuit held that the absolute priority rule should also apply to pre-plan settlements, concluding that "a bankruptcy court abuses its discretion in approving a [pre-plan] settlement with a junior creditor unless the court concludes that priority of payment will be respected as to objecting senior creditors." *United States v. AWECO, Inc. (In re AWECO, Inc.)*, 725 F.2d 293, 298 (5th Cir. 1984). The pre-plan settlement in *AWECO* sought to resolve litigation involving the debtor and a junior unsecured creditor. The district court approved the settlement without considering proof from the senior secured creditors that the costs of the settlement could seriously deplete the estate and jeopardize the priority position of the senior creditors. The junior creditor argued that priority creditors' claims are often unresolved when settlements with individual creditors occur well in advance of approval of a reorganization plan. Thus it pressed that requiring conformity with the absolute priority rule would effectively preclude all settlements prior to a plan of reorganization. The Fifth Circuit rejected that argument and held that extension of the absolute priority rule to pre-plan settlements was necessary.

> As soon as a debtor files a petition for relief, fair and equitable settlement of creditors' claims becomes a goal of the proceedings. The goal does not suddenly appear during

the process of approving a plan of compromise. Moreover, if the standard had *no* application before confirmation of a reorganization plan, then bankruptcy courts would have the discretion to favor junior classes of creditors so long as the approval of the settlement came before the plan. Regardless of when the compromise is approved, looking only to the fairness of the settlement as between the debtor and the settling claimant contravenes a basic notion of fairness. An estate might be wholly depleted in settlement of junior claims—depriving senior creditors of full payment—and still be fair as between the debtor and the settling creditor.

Id. at 298. The Fifth Circuit accurately captures the potential problem a pre-plan settlement can present for the rule of priority, but, in our view, employs too rigid a test.

The Settlement here differs significantly from the facts in play in *AWECO*, and points out the shortcomings of the *AWECO* rule. The Settlement resolves claims of one group of *senior* creditors while at the same time compromising their preferred position by providing that they be paid only a portion of any monies received from the Motorola litigation. The Settlement also funds pursuit of the Estate's most significant asset - the Motorola claims. Lastly, many important facts are still in dispute. Motorola's claim as an administrative creditor is yet to be established, the costs of the litigation (and any balance remaining in the litigation fund at the close of the proceedings) are at best estimates, and the claims against Motorola are perhaps years from a sum certain judgment. It is difficult to employ the rule of priorities in the approval of a settlement in a case such as this when the nature and extent of the Estate and the claims against it are not yet fully resolved. In our view, a rigid *per se* rule cannot accommodate the dynamic status of some pre-plan bankruptcy settlements.

Rejection of a *per se* rule has an unfortunate side effect, however: a heightened risk that the parties to a settlement may engage in improper collusion. Thus, whether a particular settlement's distribution scheme complies with the Code's priority scheme must be the most important factor for the bankruptcy court to consider when determining whether a settlement is "fair and equitable" under Rule 9019. The court must be certain that parties to a settlement have not employed a settlement as a means to avoid the priority strictures of the Bankruptcy Code.

In the Chapter 11 context, whether a settlement's distribution plan complies with the Bankruptcy Code's priority scheme will often be the dispositive factor. However, where the remaining factors weigh heavily in favor of approving a settlement, the bankruptcy court, in its discretion, could endorse a settlement that does not comply in some minor respects with the priority rule if the parties to the settlement justify, and the reviewing court clearly articulates the reasons for approving, a settlement that deviates from the priority rule.

D. Application of the Rule 9019 Factors to this Settlement

The bankruptcy judge concluded that "[t]he terms of the Settlement Agreement are fair, reasonable and in the best interests of the Estate[]" and made a number of factual findings.   With respect to the first two factors for Rule 9019 approval—(1) the balance between the litigation's likelihood of success and the settlement's future benefits and (2) the chances that the litigation will be complex and protracted—the court concluded that "[i]n assessing the risk of establishing liability and damages at trial, the Court finds that the Estate[] would face serious obstacles in establishing that the Lenders' liens are invalid." The Settlement's benefits, however, were substantial, "including potentially providing significant recovery to the Estate['s] creditors, including administrative creditors [e.g., Motorola], priority creditors and general unsecured creditors." In short, avoiding the liens involved an expensive and complex lawsuit which, even if ultimately successful, offered little reward. On the other hand, acknowledging the liens while obtaining funding to pursue the Estate's claims against Motorola held out promise for all creditors. We agree with the bankruptcy court that these first two factors support approval of the Settlement.

The third factor asks the bankruptcy court to evaluate whether the settlement is in the interests of the creditors. The fourth factor looks to what extent other parties in interest support the settlement. Here, both of these factors weigh in favor of approval of the Settlement. As the bankruptcy court noted, "[e]xcept for one alleged administrative creditor, Motorola, who is also the primary defendant with respect to the Motorola Estate Action, no other creditors have objected to the [S]ettlement." Given the Settlement's funding of Motorola's litigation opponent, Motorola's objection is understandable. Nevertheless, it is telling that no other creditor objects to the Settlement.

With respect to the fifth and seventh factors, counsel on both sides, as well as the bankruptcy court judge, are competent and experienced. The bankruptcy court also found that the Settlement was "negotiated in good faith and at arms-length by the parties." No evidence points to the contrary.

What then of the Settlement's compliance with the Code's priority scheme? Motorola complains of the money transferred to the ILLLC, and focuses primarily on the distribution of what might remain of the $37.5 million in Cash Fund Number One at the conclusion of the ILLLC's litigation against Motorola. As previously noted, any residual money in the ILLLC will be distributed to unsecured creditors. As a result, that payment would violate the absolute priority rule if Motorola prevails in the litigation or its administrative claims exceed its liability in the litigation.

It is clear from the record why the Settlement distributes money from the Estate to the ILLLC. The alternative to settling with the Lenders—pursuing the challenge to the Lenders' liens—presented too much risk for the Estate, including the administrative creditors. If the Estate lost against the Lenders (after years of litigation and paying legal fees), the Estate would be devastated, all its cash and remaining assets liquidated, and the Lenders would still possess a lien over the Motorola Estate Action. Similarly, administrative creditors would not be paid if the Estate was unsuccessful against the Lenders. Further, as noted at the Settlement hearing, having a well-funded litigation trust was preferable to attempting to procure contingent fee-based representation.

The record does not explain, however, the Settlement's distribution of residual ILLLC funds to the Committee in violation of the absolute priority rule, and we will not speculate as to what reasons the Committee or the Lenders may offer for this deviation. Flexibility in crafting pre-plan settlements has its costs. The Committee has a fiduciary duty to maximize their recovery of the Estate's assets. If in pursuit of that duty, it reaches a settlement that in some way impairs the rule of priorities, it must come before the bankruptcy court with specific and credible grounds to justify that deviation and the court must carefully articulate its reasons for approval of the agreement. That has not happened here. Indeed, no reason has been offered to explain why any balance left in the litigation trust could not or should not be distributed pursuant to the rule of priorities. Thus, we remand this matter to the bankruptcy court for that court to assess the justification for providing for a distribution of ILLLC funds to the junior creditors at the completion of the Motorola litigation. The settlement has the overwhelming approval of almost all the parties involved. Our remand is not a repudiation of that support—it seeks only clarification of why the settlement need require a possible deviation from the rule in one regard.

E. The Settlement Agreement Is not a Sub Rosa Plan of Reorganization

The final issue is closely related to the parties' other arguments. Motorola contends that the Settlement Agreement is an impermissible *sub rosa* plan of reorganization. Under section 363(b) of the Code, "[t]he trustee, after notice and a hearing may use, sell, or lease, other than in the ordinary course of business, property of the estate." 11 U.S.C. § 363(b)(1). The trustee is prohibited from such use, sale or lease if it would amount to a *sub rosa* plan of reorganization. The reason *sub rosa* plans are prohibited is based on a fear that a debtor-in-possession will enter into transactions that will, in effect, "short circuit the requirements of [C]hapter 11 for confirmation of a reorganization plan." *Pension Benefit Guar. Corp. v. Braniff Airways, Inc. (In re Braniff Airways, Inc.)*, 700 F.2d 935, 940 (5th Cir. 1983). In this Circuit, the sale of an asset of the estate under § 363(b) is permissible if the "judge determining [the] § 363(b) application expressly find[s] from the evidence presented before [him or her] at the hearing [that there is] a good business reason to grant such an application." *Comm. of Equity Sec. Holders v. Lionel Corp. (In re Lionel Corp.)*, 722 F.2d 1063, 1071 (2d Cir. 1983).

Here, the bankruptcy court identified a proper business justification for the Settlement. By allowing the Lenders to take $92.5 million and redirect another $37.5 million to the ILLLC in exchange for the Committee dropping the challenge to the liens, the Committee has cleared the way for implementation of a reorganization plan. The Estate stands to gain significantly more from the action against Motorola than it might if it or the Committee were forced to fund the litigation themselves at some much later date. As the Lenders point out, Motorola did not object when other operational assets of the Estate were sold, including the entire satellite constellation. In short, the bankruptcy court did not err in concluding that the settlement of the dispute of the liens and other property had a proper business justification and was "a step towards possible confirmation of a plan of reorganization and not an evasion of the plan confirmation process."

CONCLUSION

The district court's order of April 4, 2005, which affirmed the bankruptcy court's order approving the Settlement Agreement, is hereby VACATED and the case is REMANDED to the district court with instructions to remand the case to the bankruptcy court for proceedings consistent with this opinion.

Normally a Chapter 11 case results in either a plan confirmation, a conversion to Chapter 7, or a dismissal. When a case is dismissed, everything normally returns to the prepetition status quo. The Bankruptcy Code, however, recognizes that conditions may make a restoration of prepetition status quo difficult or impossible and authorizes courts to alter the normal restorative effects of a dismissal "for cause." 11 U.S.C. § 349(b). When a court does this, it is known as a "**structured dismissal**." A structured dismissal is a "hybrid dismissal and confirmation order . . . that . . . typically dismisses the case while, among other things, approving certain distributions to creditors, granting certain third-party releases, enjoining certain conduct by creditors, and not necessarily vacating orders or unwinding transactions undertaken during the case." American Bankruptcy Institute Commission to Study the Reform of Chapter 11, *2012-2014 Final Report and Recommendations* 270 (2014). In 2018, the Supreme Court addressed the situation of a settlement that called for a structured dismissal that would have resulted in a distribution to creditors that did not conform to absolute priority. The Court held that such a deviation from absolute priority was not permissible. *Czyzewski v. Jevic Holding Corp.*, 137 S. Ct. 973 (2018). While *Jevic* only directly addresses structured dismissals, the structured dismissal in *Jevic* was approved as part of a settlement, raising questions about whether settlements must in all instances comply with absolute priority.

III. PRE-PLAN PAYMENTS TO CREDITORS

Finally, section 363 does not explicitly cover the use of estate assets, such as unencumbered cash, to pay creditors on account of pre-petition debt prior to the effective date of a plan. The Bankruptcy Code authorizes pre-plan payments on account of pre-petition debts in two circumstances: adequate protection payments and cure payments for assumed contracts and leases. Both provisions, though, can be seen as requiring the debtor to pay for continued use of property post-petition. To the extent an unsecured creditor is paid before the effective date of a plan, it is functionally elevated in priority, as it is paid in real dollars, not "bankruptcy dollars." Are there ever circumstances when this makes sense? The final case in the chapter address this issue and the question of what to do when there is urgency to making the payments prior to the effective date of the plan.

In the Matter of Kmart Corp.
359 F.3d 866 (7th Cir. 2004)

EASTERBROOK, Circuit Judge.

On the first day of its bankruptcy, Kmart sought permission to pay immediately, and in full, the prepetition claims of all "critical vendors." . . . The theory behind the request is that some suppliers may be unwilling to do business with a customer that is behind in payment, and, if it cannot obtain the merchandise that its own customers have come to expect, a firm such as Kmart may be unable to carry on, injuring all of its creditors. Full payment to critical-vendors thus could in principle make even the disfavored creditors better off: they may not be paid in full, but they will receive a greater portion of their claims than they would if the critical-vendors cut off supplies and the business shut down. Putting the proposition in this way implies, however, that the debtor must *prove*, and not just allege, two things: that, but for immediate full payment, vendors *would* cease dealing; and that the business will gain enough from continued transactions with the favored vendors to provide some residual benefit to the remaining, disfavored creditors, or at least leave them no worse off.

Bankruptcy Judge Sonderby entered a critical-vendors order just as Kmart proposed it, without notifying any disfavored creditors, without receiving any pertinent evidence (the record contains only some sketchy representations by counsel plus unhelpful testimony by Kmart's CEO, who could not speak for the vendors), and without making any finding of fact that the disfavored creditors would gain or come out even. The bankruptcy court's order declared that the relief Kmart requested—open-ended permission to pay any debt to any vendor it deemed "critical" in the exercise of unilateral discretion, provided that the vendor agreed to furnish goods on "customary trade terms" for the next two years—was "in the best interests of the Debtors, their estates and their creditors." The order did not explain why, nor did it contain any legal analysis, though it did cite 11 U.S.C. § 105(a). (The bankruptcy court issued two companion orders covering international vendors and liquor vendors. Analysis of all three orders is the same, so we do not mention these two further.)

Kmart used its authority to pay in full the pre-petition debts to 2,330 suppliers, which collectively received about $300 million. This came from the $2 billion in new credit (debtor-in-possession or DIP financing) that the bankruptcy judge authorized, granting the lenders super-priority in post-petition assets and revenues. Another 2,000 or so vendors were not deemed "critical" and were not paid. They and 43,000 additional unsecured creditors eventually received about 10 [cents] on the dollar, mostly in stock of the reorganized Kmart. Capital Factors, Inc., appealed the critical-vendors order immediately after its entry on January 25, 2002. A little more than 14 months later, after all of the critical-vendors had been paid and as Kmart's plan of reorganization was on the verge of approval, District Judge Grady reversed the order authorizing payment. He concluded that neither § 105(a) nor a "doctrine of necessity" supports the orders.

Thus we arrive at the merits. Section 105(a) allows a bankruptcy court to "issue any order, process, or judgment that is necessary or appropriate to carry out the provisions of" the Code. This does not create discretion to set aside the Code's rules about priority and distribution; the power conferred by § 105(a) is one to implement rather than override. Every circuit that has considered the question has held that this statute does not allow a bankruptcy judge to authorize full payment of any unsecured debt, unless all unsecured creditors in the class are paid in full. *See In re Oxford Management Inc.*, 4 F.3d 1329 (5th Cir. 1993); *Official Committee of Equity Security Holders v. Mabey*, 832 F.2d 299 (4th Cir. 1987); *In re B&W Enterprises, Inc.*, 713 F.2d 534 (9th Cir. 1983). We agree with this view of § 105. "The fact that a [bankruptcy] proceeding is equitable does not give the judge a free-floating discretion to redistribute rights in accordance with his personal views of justice and fairness, however enlightened those views may be." *In re Chicago, Milwaukee, St. Paul & Pacific R.R.*, 791 F.2d 524, 528 (7th Cir. 1986).

A "doctrine of necessity" is just a fancy name for a power to depart from the Code. Although courts in the days before bankruptcy law was codified wielded power to reorder priorities and pay particular creditors in the name of "necessity"—see *Miltenberger v. Logansport Ry.*, 106 U.S. 286 (1882); *Fosdick v. Schall*, 99 U.S. 235 (1878)—today it is the Code rather than the norms of nineteenth century railroad reorganizations that must prevail. *Miltenberger* and *Fosdick* predate the first general effort at codification, the Bankruptcy Act of 1898. Today the Bankruptcy Code of 1978 supplies the rules. Congress did not in terms scuttle old common-law doctrines, because it did not need to; the Act curtailed, and then the Code replaced, the entire apparatus. Answers to contemporary issues must be found within the Code (or legislative halls). Older doctrines may survive as glosses on ambiguous language enacted in 1978 or later, but not as freestanding entitlements to trump the text.

So does the Code contain any grant of authority for debtors to prefer some vendors over others? Many sections require equal treatment or specify the details of priority when assets are insufficient to satisfy all claims. *E.g.,* 11 U.S.C. §§ 507, 1122(a), 1123(a)(4). Appellants rely on 11 U.S.C. §§ 363(b), 364(b), and 503 as sources of authority for unequal treatment. Section 364(b) reads: "The court, after notice and a hearing, may authorize the trustee to obtain unsecured credit or to incur unsecured debt other than under subsection (a) of this section, allowable under section 503(b)(1) of this title as an administrative expense." This authorizes the debtor to obtain credit (as Kmart did) but has nothing to say about how the money will be disbursed or about priorities among creditors. Section 503, which deals with administrative expenses, likewise is irrelevant. Pre-filing debts are not administrative expenses; they are the antithesis of administrative expenses. Filing a petition for bankruptcy effectively creates two firms: the debts of the pre-filing entity may be written down so that the post-filing entity may reorganize and continue in business if it has a positive cash flow. Treating pre-filing debts as "administrative" claims against the post-filing entity would impair the ability of bankruptcy law to prevent old debts from sinking a viable firm.

That leaves § 363(b)(1): "The trustee [or debtor-in-possession], after notice and a hearing, may use, sell, or lease, other than in the ordinary course of business, property of the estate." This is more promising, for satisfaction of a pre-petition debt in order to keep "critical" supplies flowing is a use of property other than in the ordinary course of administering an estate in bankruptcy. Capital Factors insists that § 363(b)(1) should be limited to the commencement of capital projects, such as building a new plant, rather than payment of old debts—as paying vendors would be "in the ordinary course" but for the intervening bankruptcy petition. To read § 363(b)(1) broadly, Capital Factors observes, would be to allow a judge to rearrange priorities among creditors (which is what a critical-vendors order effectively does), even though the Supreme Court has cautioned against such a step. *See United States v. Reorganized CF&I Fabricators of Utah, Inc.,* 518 U.S. 213 (1996); *Noland, supra.* Yet what these decisions principally say is that priorities do not change unless a statute supports that step; and if § 363(b)(1) is such a statute, then there is no insuperable problem. If the language is too open-ended, that is a problem for the legislature. Nonetheless, it is prudent to read, and use, § 363(b)(1) to do the least damage possible to priorities established by contract and by other parts of the Bankruptcy Code. We need not decide whether § 363(b)(1) could support payment of some pre-petition debts, because *this* order was unsound no matter how one reads § 363(b)(1).

The foundation of a critical-vendors order is the belief that vendors not paid for prior deliveries will refuse to make new ones. Without merchandise to sell, a retailer such as Kmart will fold. If paying the critical vendors would enable a successful reorganization and make even the disfavored creditors better off, then all creditors favor payment whether or not they are designated as "critical." This suggests a use of § 363(b)(1) similar to the theory underlying a plan crammed down the throats of an impaired class of creditors: if the impaired class does at least as well as it would have under a Chapter 7 liquidation, then it has no legitimate objection and cannot block the reorganization. For the premise to hold true, however, it is necessary to show not only that the disfavored creditors *will* be as well off with reorganization as with liquidation—a demonstration never attempted in this proceeding—but also that the supposedly critical vendors would have ceased deliveries if old debts were left unpaid while the litigation continued. If vendors will deliver against a promise of current payment, then a reorganization can be achieved, and all unsecured creditors will obtain its benefit, without preferring any of the unsecured creditors.

Some supposedly critical vendors will continue to do business with the debtor because they must. They may, for example, have long term contracts, and the automatic stay prevents these vendors from walking away as long as the debtor pays for new deliveries. *See* 11 U.S.C. § 362. Fleming Companies, which received the largest critical-vendors payment because it sold Kmart between $70 million and $100 million of groceries and related goods weekly, was one of these. No matter how much Fleming would have liked to dump Kmart, it had no right to do so. It was unnecessary to compensate Fleming for continuing to make deliveries that it was legally required to make. Nor was Fleming likely to walk away even if it had a legal right to do so. Each new delivery produced a profit; as long as Kmart continued to pay for new product, why would any vendor drop the account? That would be a self-inflicted wound. To abjure new profits because of old debts would be to commit the sunk-cost fallacy; well-managed businesses are unlikely to do this. Firms that disdain current profits because of old losses are unlikely to stay in business. They might as well burn money or drop it into the ocean. Again Fleming illustrates the point. When Kmart stopped buying its products after the contract expired, Fleming collapsed (Kmart had accounted for more than 50% of its business) and filed its own bankruptcy petition. Fleming was hardly likely to have quit selling of its own volition, only to expire the sooner.

Doubtless many suppliers fear the prospect of throwing good money after bad. It therefore may be vital to assure them that a debtor will pay for new deliveries on a current basis. Providing that assurance need not, however, entail payment for pre-petition transactions. Kmart could have paid cash or its equivalent. (Kmart's CEO told the bankruptcy judge that COD arrangements were not part of Kmart's business plan, as if a litigant's druthers could override the rights of third parties.) Cash on the barrelhead was not the most convenient way, however. Kmart secured a $2 billion line of credit when it entered bankruptcy. Some of that credit could have been used to assure vendors that payment would be forthcoming for all post-petition transactions. The easiest way to do that would have been to put some of the $2 billion behind a standby letter of credit on which the bankruptcy judge could authorize unpaid vendors to draw. That would not have changed the terms on which Kmart and any of its vendors did business; it just would have demonstrated the certainty of payment. If lenders are unwilling to issue such a letter of credit (or if they insist on a letter's short duration), that would be a compelling market signal that reorganization is a poor prospect and that the debtor should be liquidated post haste.

Yet the bankruptcy court did not explore the possibility of using a letter of credit to assure vendors of payment. The court did not find that any firm would have ceased doing business with Kmart if not paid for pre-petition deliveries, and the scant record would not have supported such a finding had one been made. The court did not find that discrimination among unsecured creditors was the only way to facilitate a reorganization. It did not find that the disfavored creditors were at least as well off as they would have been had the critical-vendors order not been entered. Just so here. Even if § 362(b)(1) allows critical-vendors orders in principle, preferential payments to a class of creditors are proper only if the record shows the prospect of benefit to the other creditors. This record does not, so the critical-vendors order cannot stand. AFFIRMED.

Study Questions and Note

1. Why did Kmart have so many "critical" vendors? What kind of store is Kmart? Is any single vendor critical? A certain mass of vendors?

2. Pre-plan payments to creditors might also be made in an attempt to mitigate harms. In *Official Committee of Equity Security Holders v. Mabey*, 832 F.2d 299 (4th Cir. 1987), the Fourth Circuit denied the request of debtor A.H. Robins to make pre-plan payments to women who had been harmed by its Dalkon Shield IUD birth control device. A.H. Robins had wanted to make the payments to fund medical treatment (tubal reconstruction surgery or in vitro fertilization) to mitigate the harm to the women (as the passage of time would increase their chances of permanent infertility), but A.H. Robins equityholders objected. Despite the motivation for the payments, the Fourth Circuit sustained the objection because it found no statutory authority in the Bankruptcy Code for pre-plan payments to creditors.

Problem Set 40

(1) Hadley entered into a contract with Baxendale to make custom crankshafts for his milling operation with delivery in six months. Baxendale took great care to tell Hadley that if payment was not received on time, it would result in significant consequential damages of perhaps ten times the amount of the contract. Hadley filed for bankruptcy shortly after taking delivery of the crankshafts, but before having paid Baxendale. Can Hadley pay Baxendale outside of a plan? 11 U.S.C. §§ 363(b)-(c).

(2) Hadley entered into a contract with Baxendale to make custom crankshafts for his milling operation with delivery in six months. Hadley took great care to tell Baxendale that if the crankshafts were not provided in time, the mill would not be able to operate, resulting in significant consequential damages. Hadley prepaid Baxendale for the contract. Baxendale filed for bankruptcy four months later, without performing the contract. Can Baxendale perform the contract? 11 U.S.C. §§ 363(b)-(c).

(3) Facing ballooning pension and retiree health benefit liability and strict new environmental regulations, Bluegrass Coal filed for Chapter 11 after it was unable to roll over its financing. Bluegrass obtained $1.5 billion in DIP financing in exchange for a first lien on all of its assets and conditioned on Bluegrass completing a sale of its profitable

mining assets within 90 days. Bluegrass has subsequently proposed selling all of its profitable mines (the mineral rights, the equipment, and associated contracts). Under Bluegrass's accelerated bidding procedures, which allowed for minimal diligence, only one bid was tendered, a bid for $2 billion from Appalachian Acquisition Corp., a newly created acquisition vehicle that is wholly owned by the United Mine Workers. The UMW is Bluegrass's largest creditor, and is owed $10 billion in unfunded pension and health benefit obligations under the settlement of a collective bargaining agreement dispute. Bluegrass has indicated that following the completion of the sale, it will proceed to liquidate its remaining assets (worth perhaps $500 million) and distribute them according to absolute priority. Bluegrass's second lien creditors have a $3 billion second lien on most of the assets covered by the sale. The second lien creditors have objected to the sale, arguing that the price is too low by at least $6 billion, and that it is a de facto plan that violates the absolute priority rule. What is the likely outcome?

[handwritten margin notes: "should bid on it"; "Critical vendor doctrine"; "no P b/c this is a sale"]

(4) In Chapter 11, Napoleon LLC sued one of its lenders, Wellington Capital, for pre-petition acts that precipitated Napoleon's default and bankruptcy filing. Wellington had filed a claim for $100 million in the bankruptcy. Napoleon and Wellington have proposed a settlement wherein Wellington will release Napoleon from liability on its claims in exchange for $20 million and a release from Napoleon's claim against Wellington. Napoleon has recently filed a disclosure statement in which Wellington's class would be paid 2 cents on the dollar. Wellington's claim would have given it a blocking position in its class. Is the settlement confirmable? FED. R. BANKR. PROC. 9019.

(5) Your firm is preparing to file a Chapter 11 petition for Concord Automotive, a small auto parts supplier. Concord has several critical suppliers; if they refuse to ship to Concord without payment on their pre-petition debts, Concord will not be able to honor its own obligations and will lose business. The team working on the filing has met to talk through the issues. The lead partner on the team has just read the *Kmart* case and shakes her head. "I don't know how we're going to reorganize this company. We might as well file a Chapter 7. In *Kmart* Judge Easterbrook basically said 'no pre-plan payments to critical vendors.' But Concord's vendors aren't going to ship unless they know their past invoices will get paid. We're just not as important to them as they are to us." What do you say? Is there any way to get pre-plan payments to critical vendors approved? If so, what would you have to do?

(6) Facing massive environmental liability for an oil spill that contaminated much of Chesapeake Bay, destroying centuries-old oyster beds, Fraktal Energy filed for Chapter 11 bankruptcy. Among Fraktal Energy's assets is a pair of giant oil rigs anchored in the Arctic Ocean just outside of Russian territorial waters. Each oil rig costs over $1 billion to build, transport, and anchor. The oil rigs produce over $3 billion in annual petroleum extraction at current market prices. Fraktal owes several hundred million to a consortium of Russian banks and is worried that if it does not pay their claims in full that these Russian creditors will seize the oil rigs. Can Fraktal pay its Russian creditors prior to plan confirmation?

CHAPTER 41

CLAIMS TRADING

I. THE CLAIMS TRADING MARKET

Adam J. Levitin
Bankruptcy Markets: Making Sense of Claims Trading
4 Brook. J. Corp., Fin. & Com. L. 64 (2010) (excerpt)

INTRODUCTION

The creation of a market in bankruptcy claims is the single most important development in the bankruptcy world since the Bankruptcy Code's enactment in 1978. Claims trading has revolutionized bankruptcy by making it a much more market-driven process. Instead of serving as a forum for creditors to negotiate a restructuring of the debtor's finances with the goal of limiting their losses, bankruptcy is now a general investment opportunity. The development of a robust market for all types of claims against debtors has changed the cast of characters involved in bankruptcies. In addition to long-standing relational creditors, like trade creditors or a single senior secured bank or bank group, bankruptcy cases now involve professional distressed debt investors, whose interests and behavior are often quite different than traditional relational counterparty creditors.

The changes wrought by claims trading have placed tremendous pressure on the bankruptcy reorganization structure set forth in Chapter 11 of the Bankruptcy Code, which was drafted with a relational creditor world in mind. Because of the changes that claims trading has unleashed on the bankruptcy process, it arouses passions unlike any other issue in the bankruptcy world. Yet, in spite of this, claims trading remains a poorly understood and little studied area of bankruptcy. Although there are a fair number of legal decisions that touch on aspects of claims trading, only a few squarely address the key policy issues involved. Exacerbating this problem, only a limited number of scholarly articles . . . discuss bankruptcy claims trading. The existing literature tends to focus on doctrinal issues created by claims trading, contains no discussion of the market mechanisms for claims trading and rarely delves into the differences among the varied trading practices that fall under the rubric of "claims trading." Put another way, the limited literature on claims trading generally does not engage with claims trading's realities.

Instead, claims trading is often used as a totem for a larger normative debate about bankruptcy: What interests should be served by bankruptcy policy? What relative weight should be placed on concerns of efficiency and distributional fairness? Should bankruptcy merely be a procedural extension of the market or is it a safe-harbor from the market in which other values and interests are expressed? This Great Normative Bankruptcy Debate has focused on claims trading because it has been the leading factor in the marketization of bankruptcy.

This Article argues that it is unproductive to understand claims trading through the lens of the Great Normative Bankruptcy Debate. Burdening consideration of claims trading with the weight of this overarching policy debate has prevented a serious engagement with actual practice of claims trading. Instead, claims trading is frequently treated as a generic and stylized phenomenon, divorced from its more nuanced operation in practice.

This Article disaggregates the wide variety of investment practices that fall under the rubric of claims trading. It argues that claims trading is actually comprised of several overlapping and evolving markets that vary on dimensions of timing and asset class. These different markets have distinct mechanisms and distinct risks for buyers and sellers who are moved by a variety of motivations.

An examination of these markets shows that claims trading has cross-cutting impacts on the bankruptcy process with a net impact that is indeterminate on the available evidence. Accordingly, claims trading is not well-suited for broad policy reforms. Instead, at this point, we can merely identify several modest features of the claims trading market that can be improved.

. . .

I. CLAIMS TRADING AND THE GREAT NORMATIVE BANKRUPTCY DEBATE

A. A Taxonomy of Normative Views of Bankruptcy

Over a decade ago, Professor Douglas Baird mapped the world of bankruptcy scholarship as roughly divided into two loose camps: Traditionalists and Proceduralists. As Baird explained:

> The [T]raditionalists believe that bankruptcy law serves an important purpose in rehabilitating firms that, but for bankruptcy protection, would fail. Jobs would be lost and communities damaged, economically and otherwise, if the protections that bankruptcy law provides were unavailable. By contrast, the [P]roceduralists deny that bankruptcy can work any special magic. Firms must live or die in the market. All bankruptcy can do is ensure that fights among creditors and other investors of capital do not accelerate a firm's liquidation. For them, one does more harm than good by doing anything more to protect a firm from the forces of the market.

The division that Baird finds in the scholarship is also a different view of what bankruptcy's relationship to the market process should be. Should bankruptcy be a part of or apart from the market? Is bankruptcy merely an extension of the market or a safe haven from it?

Ultimately, the camps diverge on the question of whether markets can be relied upon to produce optimal outcomes. Are markets always the answer? Traditionalists are more skeptical of markets than Proceduralists. Part of this skepticism is both expressed in and a function of how optimal outcomes are defined. Traditionalists, who often work on consumer bankruptcy issues, look at net social outcomes, while Proceduralists, who tend to focus on corporate reorganizations, focus on the firm, in keeping with a long tradition of exclusively firm-focused corporate law scholarship. While many variations exist in these camps, it still remains a remarkably accurate intellectual cartography of the bankruptcy world.

B. Normative Views of Bankruptcy and the Claims Trading Debate

Baird's taxonomy has remarkable explanatory power for understanding the debate about claims trading. Arguments being made against claims trading are very much Traditionalist arguments, while arguments being made for claims trading are Proceduralist arguments. For example, Harvey Miller, perhaps the leading practitioner advocate of the rehabilitation view of business bankruptcy, has argued that:

> Distressed debt trading and changes in bankruptcy relationships have destroyed the symbiotic relationship of debtor and creditor. . . . Because Chapter 11 is premised upon a symbiotic relationship between debtor and creditor, it is becoming less effective in the context of distressed debt trading.

Miller contends that the failure rate of large Chapter 11 cases is due in part to claims trading, as "distressed debt traders may sacrifice the long-term viability of a debtor for the ability to realize substantial and quick returns on their investments." Similarly, Fredrick Tung has argued that claims trading upsets the community of interests involved in bankruptcy.

Others have maintained that claims trading merely provides a mechanism for creditors to move in or out of this community. They argue that "distressed-debt investors generally have a salutary impact on the residual actor problem of bankruptcy by expediting business reorganizations and protecting going-concern enterprise values" or that "courts should encourage, rather than interfere with, the market in order to facilitate the significant benefits claims trading offers in bankruptcy."

In this light, it is worth considering the standard arguments about claims trading. These arguments in favor of claims trading are about efficiency and markets:

- Claims trading allows an exit for those creditors who want to cut loose from the bankruptcy process because of liquidity constraints, administrative hassle and expense, regulatory risk, to avoid an adversarial relationship with the debtor, or to establish a tax loss. There are significant risks, costs, and delays inherent in bankruptcies. Payouts are speculative and can take years to receive. Selling a claim allows a creditor to "cash out" at a certain price.
- Claims trading permits an entrance to the bankruptcy process for those investors who want to take the time and effort to monitor the debtor and contribute expertise to the reorganization process.

- Claims trading increases liquidity overall in capital markets and lowers the cost of credit as the option of avoiding the uncertainty of being a creditor in bankruptcy increases the risk tolerance of originating lenders.
- Claims trading reduces transaction costs in the plan negotiation process by consolidating dispersed claimholders into a few large claimholders.
- Claims trading reduces the administrative costs of bankruptcies by speeding up the reorganization negotiation process through consolidation of claimholders.
- Claims trading creates a market for control in bankruptcy that might not exist absent a cramdown plan or a § 363 sale.
- Claims trading can result in a higher and/or quicker return for creditors because it imposes market discipline on debtors. If a reorganization is being run poorly, creditors will sell their claims, and the buyers will either push for a liquidation or attempt to take control of the reorganization.

Three more arguments not found in the literature might be added to the arguments above. First, claims trading ensures more efficient allocations of capital in the market by permitting entry and exit, which lets parties express their idiosyncratic valuations. Second, claims trading can facilitate reorganizations by bringing in parties who are willing and able to contribute the fresh capital needed to fund the reorganization process (Debtor in Possession (DIP) financing) and the newly reorganized company (exit financing). And third, claims trading may facilitate more sustainable reorganizations by enabling firms to emerge with lower leverage ratios.

Banks are generally prohibited from holding equity in non-financial operating companies. Therefore, bank creditors want their claims paid either in cash or in debt of the reorganized company. This either makes reorganization harder by requiring more cash on hand or adds to the debt burden of the reorganized firm, making the reorganization less sustainable and (all else being equal) increasing the likelihood of a refiling (a so-called Chapter 22).

Claims trading enables the replacement of bank creditors with hedge funds and private equity funds, which are able, and often eager, to take equity in the reorganized company. Thus, claims trading facilitates a shift in the composition of creditors that allows more flexibility in reorganizing and promotes more sustainable reorganizations.

These arguments emphasize efficiency gains both in bankruptcy and in the capital markets from claims trading. This contrasts with the arguments against claims trading, which raise countervailing efficiency concerns, as well as concerns about procedural and distributional fairness, not just within the bankruptcy, but also to a larger community of interests:

- Claims trading hinders bankruptcy plan negotiations by raising transaction costs of negotiation because the identity of creditors is churning, which makes it hard to lock in a deal. The delay imposes an externality on creditors who do not trade and reduces the value of the debtor's estate.
- Claims trading enables greenmail, insider trading, and other unfair practices that allow particular creditors to extract surplus rents.
- Claims trading hurts unsecured creditors by making it harder to find creditors willing and able to serve on committees. Many creditors will not serve on committees

because they wish to remain unrestricted for trading purposes, while others have purchased claims up and down the capital structure, and therefore, have conflicts of interest that preclude them from serving.

- Claims trading encourages participation of creditors who value short-term returns on trades and quick monetization over the long-term value and viability of the debtor company. This can lead to deadweight loss through the destruction of going concern value and can lead to recidivism among debtors. The loss often has externalities on non-creditor community interests affected by bankruptcies.
- Claims trading destroys the "symbiotic relationship of debtor and creditor" that is the premise of Chapter 11.

The arguments about claims trading roughly track the normative bankruptcy scholarship divide identified by Baird. Arguments in support of claims trading favor letting the market guide reorganizations, while the arguments against are skeptical of the market producing either efficient or fair results for the community of interests involved in a bankruptcy.

All of these arguments operate on a very high level of generality. The standard arguments about claims trading focus on whether claims trading should or should not be allowed. They are not arguments for regulating claims trading, but are instead arguments about it being either a positive or negative phenomenon.

This binary divide makes little sense, however. Are critics of claims trading really calling for an end to all claims trading or merely for some regulation of it? Are advocates of claims trading arguing for it to remain a virtually unregulated market, or simply arguing for claims trading to continue in some form? To date, no one seems to have called for an outright ban on claims trading. When pressed, proponents of claims trading will usually concede the need for some reforms in the market to curb such abuses as claims laundering, greenmail, insider trading, or to protect unsophisticated trade creditors.

When confronted with claims trading as an actuality, rather than as a way for expressing normative views on bankruptcy policy, the binary arguments collapse into a spectrum of more regulation to less regulation. This spectrum, however, contains relatively few regulatory proposals. To the extent that arguments about claims trading are really about claims trading, rather than a normative vision of bankruptcy, it has a thin evidentiary basis which forces claims trading to be addressed in a highly generalized manner. These features limit the debate to being little more than an imperfect battleground for the Great Normative Bankruptcy Debate.

C. The Thin Evidentiary Basis for the Claims Trading Debate

The debate over claims trading operates on a limited evidentiary base. Arguments about claims trading are based on theory, common sense, and anecdote, but not data. Empirically, we know relatively little about claims trading. What is the volume of claims trades in number? In amount? What percentage of claims change hands? How frequently do claims trade? Who buys and who sells? How many discrete buyers are there? How many are prepetition creditors? Does trading result in a consolidation or dispersal of holdings and to what degree? How much variation is there by case? By asset class? By timing within a case? By type of debtor? How does the pricing change over time? How accurate of a predictor of plan payouts is the claims market? And how does this all compare to distressed debt trading on the doorstep of bankruptcy?

No one has a handle even on the most elementary questions like the size of the bankruptcy claims trading market, either in terms of face value of claims trading hands or the volume of transactions. There is broad consensus that there is a large and growing market in claims. Academic articles place the market at hundreds of billions. One company attempting to create an exchange in trade claims estimates this piece of the market to be worth $75 billion. It is not clear what that number is actually measuring— total par value of claims, total amounts paid for claims, etc. Moreover, it is unclear how anyone could arrive at any number. The data simply does not exist.

The reason that we do not know the extent of the claims trading market is because it is largely invisible in court records. Claims trading is an over-the-counter (OTC) market, so there is no exchange that can provide information. The sole specific regulation of claims trading, Federal Rule of Bankruptcy Procedure 3001(e) (Rule 3001(e)), states that notice of claims trades be filed with the court, although no particular timeliness is required. The Rule 3001(e) filing requirement applies only when the actual claim changes hands, however, not when the beneficial interest represented by the claim changes hands. This means that many economic claims trades are not reported with the court.

In particular, two major categories of claims—bank debt and bond claims—do not show up in Rule 3001(e) filings. Bank debt is often syndicated; only the administrative agent for the syndicate (typically the lead bank) will file a claim in the bankruptcy. The syndicated interests (assignments or participations) might change hands, but it will not be reflected in a Rule 3001(e) filing.

. . .

For bonds, there will be only one claim filed per indenture, and it will be filed by the indenture trustee. Thus, there will be no Rule 3001(e) filings evident for trades in the debtor's bond debt. Trades in claims for two large slices of the capital structure of bankrupt companies are simply invisible.

The trades that are visible are primarily trades in unsecured trade debt. In large Chapter 11 cases (Mega-Cases), there is clearly an active market in such claims, as their case dockets are peppered with Rule 3001(e) filings. These trades will range from claims as small as a $40 claim by a locksmith (such a trade occurred in Footstar's bankruptcy) to multi-million dollar claims, but many are relatively small, under $1,000. While it would be possible to undertake an empirical study of claims trading based on Rule 3001(e) filings, it would necessarily be incomplete, and there is good reason to believe that the market in unsecured trade and vendor claims looks different from the market in bond claims or bank debt.

To the extent that claims trading has received scholarly attention, it is in the context of Mega-Cases, yet there are many smaller business bankruptcy cases, ranging from small businesses that file under Chapter 13 to small cap, middle market, and even sizeable Chapter 11's with publicly traded debt securities that are not Mega-Cases. We know almost nothing about claims trading dynamics in the medium and small business cases. For those small businesses in Chapter 13, the dynamics presumably resemble those of Chapter 13 consumer debtor cases. But for the smaller Chapter 11 cases, it is not clear how much claims trading there is or what its purpose is. Not surprisingly, given the epistemological limitations on any discussion of bankruptcy claims trading, the debate usually operates at a high level of generality, lumping all claims trading together.

The claims trading debate is hindered by this level of generality. At best, with a high level of generality, all we can say is that the net impact of claims trading is indeterminate. Unpacking the various practices that fall under the claims trading rubric is a necessary first step in advancing a more productive discussion about claims trading's impact on bankruptcy. The following section considers some of the key variations in the claims trading market and their likely impacts on the bankruptcy process.

II. THREE-DIMENSIONAL CLAIMS TRADING

Claims trading is a multi-dimensional and dynamic market that encompasses trades in claims based on a variety of types of debts and trading motivations. The market varies on three dimensions: temporally, regarding when claims trading takes place; qualitatively, regarding what is traded; and motivationally, regarding trading strategies. As an initial matter, however, it is necessary to define claims trading. We often speak of "bankruptcy claims trading," but what is it about a bankruptcy claim that distinguishes it from a regular debt claim? Answering this requires us to first consider the temporal dimension of claims trading.

A. The Temporal Dimension: Are Bankruptcy Claims a Distinct Market?

From a legal perspective, there are many possible distinctions between a bankruptcy claim and a regular debt. In an earlier work, I noted that the Bankruptcy Code's definition of "claim" was arguably broader than what might be commonly thought of as a debt because it included disputed, contingent, and unliquidated payment obligations. I also noted that not all debts were enforceable in bankruptcy, that a bankruptcy claim carries rights with it that are distinct from those that are part of a debt, and that bankruptcy endows a claim with a relational aspect that does not exist in a debt. Filing for bankruptcy can also accelerate debts that have not yet become due outside of bankruptcy.

Although there is a legal distinction between a bankruptcy claim and a regular debt, they are both rights to use the legal system to collect value from another. The value of those rights depends on legal distinctions, such as whether the collection takes place through state law or federal bankruptcy law, whether or not a claim is ultimately allowable, and, if so, in what amount, with what priority, and with what voting rights. Buying or selling either a bankruptcy claim or a regular debt is a gamble on this constellation of risks, but the market is concerned about these distinctions only to the extent that they are meaningful markers of risk and value. Yet, the market import of legal distinction between bankruptcy claims and distressed debt depends on whether it is in a consumer or a business context.

. . .

2. Business Debt

In the business context, in contrast, bankruptcy claims do not constitute a distinct market from distressed debt, in part because the collection efforts involved do not vary significantly depending on bankruptcy. Historically, there was a distinct "bankruptcy claims" market that was thin and highly specialized. Claims traders bought claims only after a plan was proposed. They assumed only plan vote and feasibility risk, which was *de minimis*. The plan was a public document, and investors looked to pick up claims on the eve of the vote.

Over the past two decades, however, investors began buying claims earlier and earlier. Now, investors trade in distressed debt well before bankruptcy. Instead of distinct markets based on whether the obligor is bankrupt or not, there is a general distressed debt market with a variety of investment strategies based on timing. The segmentation that exists in the market is not based on bankruptcy status, but rather on asset class.

The lack of temporal distinction between bankruptcy and non-bankruptcy claims trading in the business claims context is important because it suggests that regulatory cost spillovers would be much more severe in the business claims context. Because business bankruptcy claims are part of a broader market in business debt obligations, regulation of bankruptcy claims trading would also affect activity elsewhere in the broader market. While there might be good *bankruptcy* policy reasons to regulate bankruptcy claims trading in particular ways, the policy analysis has to consider the impact on *non-bankruptcy* claims trades in a way that it might not in the consumer claims context.

B. The Qualitative Dimension: Market Segmentation by Asset Class

2. Business Debt

Business debt claims fall into roughly four asset classes: bond debt, bank debt, trade debt, and tort debt. Some investors will purchase claims in any and all classes, while others limit themselves to particular classes. These types of debt differ not only based on where they are in the capital structure, but also based on the risks that a purchaser assumes.

a. *Bond Debt*

Claims based on bond debt are by far the most liquid type because bond debt is a commodity with relatively fewer risks attached to it than other asset classes. There is little risk about whether bond debt will be disallowed, subordinated, or subject to clawback actions. The validity and amount of the bonds are not in question and the bondholder and indenture trustee have no dealings with the debtor that would create equitable subordination grounds. Most bonds are unsecured, so there is no strong-arm risk. Moreover, because bond debt trades publicly, there is little counterparty risk involved in the trades because of the use of large financial institutions as broker-dealers; there is no question whether the party that is selling the claim actually owns it. There is minimal diligence involved in a bond debt trade, and the identity of counterparties is typically not known, making more serious diligence impossible.

There is also typically a rough symmetry of sophistication between parties in bond debt trades. Most corporate bonds are owned by financial institutions, not by individual investors. Accordingly, bond debt trades do not raise concerns of sophisticated investors fleecing naïve mom-and-pops.

b. Bank Debt

Bank debt is commonly syndicated, participated, or both and, trades in slices, rather than whole loans. The syndications now are written with an eye to trading, a contrast from a time when bank loan syndications were often restricted to banks, out of concerns about the different accounting rules and non-banks' ability to make further advances to the debtor.

Bank debt bears more risks for a claims purchaser than bond debt because it might be subject to disallowance due to clawback actions. Bank debt is almost always secured, but a lien might turn out to be unperfected and subject to avoidance. There is also risk of equitable subordination for misbehavior by the bank.

On the other hand, bank claims provide a purchaser with information and leverage that is not available to a bondholder. Bank loans typically have various reporting covenants beyond what exist in bond indentures. The access to the information is hugely valuable to an investor. Thus, bank debt is particularly attractive, especially to purchasers pre-bankruptcy, who will end up with a large informational advantage on the market.

Bank debt also provides a claims purchaser with far more leverage over the debtor, especially before bankruptcy. There are many more covenants in bank loans, which make defaults more likely, but which offer the purchaser of bank debt the possibility of forbearance fees, additional security, or forcing the debtor into bankruptcy by denying forbearance. Thus, the holder of bank debt, even if it is participated or syndicated, has greater influence over the relationship with the debtor than does a single bondholder. Additionally, because bank debt is usually sold in large denominations, if a seller breaches its sale warranties to the buyer, a lawsuit is economically viable and can likely cover the damages. Like bond debt, bank debt is almost always held by a financial institution and trades between sophisticated investors on both sides of the transaction.

c. Trade Debt

Trade debt offers even more challenges to a claims purchaser than bank debt. The counterparty risks, and therefore, the diligence requirements, are much higher. The defenses that a debtor might raise against a bank loan are fairly limited: There might be counterclaims against the bank or equitable subordination issues, but the validity of the loan itself is relatively easy to ascertain. This is not the case with trade debt.

For example, a vendor might have breached its contract with the debtor in any number of ways. The vendor might have delivered the debtor an insufficient quality or quantity of merchandise, failed to deliver it on time or failed to perform the services promised. Any of these breaches could provide the debtor with defenses to the enforcement of the contract, but would be quite difficult for a claims purchaser, with no right to inspect the debtor's books and records, to diligence. There might also be setoff rights based on other dealings between the vendor and the debtor, including other discrete contracts. A purchaser of trade claims has much greater uncertainty about how much, if any, of the claim will be allowed, and every trade claim presents distinct risks.

While the purchaser can protect itself via representations and warranties from the seller, many trade debt claims are in denominations that make litigation over misrepresentations on the sale uneconomic. This depresses the market for smaller trade claims, which is already limited because of the higher ratio of transaction costs to value, and because small claims are of little interest to buyers who are looking to gain influence over a plan. The market in smaller trade claims attracts buyers primarily looking to capture a spread, since small trade claims will probably be classified as convenience claims and likely paid in full. This means small claims are unlikely to have a vote on a plan, which makes them unattractive to buyers looking to gain control over a plan.

While trade debt offers investors many more diligence challenges than bond or bank debt, it also offers some advantages. Bondholders and bank lenders must lay out 100 cents to get a $1 allowed claim. Therefore, their "cost" of a claim is 100%. To the extent that the claim is sold for less than 100 cents on the dollar, there is an economic loss to the bondholder or bank lender.

A trade claimant, in contrast, likely has a much lower "cost" for its claim. If the trade claimant's markup on the goods it sold to the debtor was 50%, then the trade claimant will come out ahead economically (but not necessarily in accounting), by selling at 54 cents on the dollar. Additionally, trade creditors are more likely to place a premium on liquidity than bank lenders or bondholders, all of which means they are likely more willing to sell at lower prices. For a vulture fund looking to purchase unsecured debt in a bankruptcy, an allowed trade claim is just as good as an allowed bond claim, but the likely price spread produces an attractive arbitrage opportunity.

Trades in trade claims raise concerns about sophisticated traders taking advantage of ingénue vendors. It is important to remember that trade creditors include both incredibly sophisticated parties with extensive bankruptcy experience (e.g., Fortune 500 companies like OEM auto manufacturers) as well as sole proprietorship small businesses with no prior bankruptcy experience.

d. Tort Debt

Finally, there is a much smaller market for tort claims. Most investors are not interested in tort claims, in part because of the issues of proof involved in disputed claims and because champerty issues are particularly salient in the personal injury context.

3. Deal Mechanics and Documentation

Deal documentation and deal mechanics vary for claims depending on asset class. Bond debt and equity trade in bankruptcy just as it did outside of it (although exchange-traded equity will be delisted and trade OTC on the Pink Sheets), and with the same documentation. The same securities laws will apply in bankruptcy as outside, which presents another variation in asset class.

A claim's status under securities laws affects its attractiveness to investors. Federal securities laws will apply to bond claims and certificated equity interests, which sometimes trade as penny stocks. State securities laws might, in some cases, extend to bank or trade claims, as state law definitions of securities can be broader than federal law. Some investors are happy to comply with securities regulation regimes, while others do not want to be subject to it. This is another factor encouraging buyers toward bank and trade debt and away from bonds.

Bank debt trades OTC using standardized documentation from the Loan Syndication and Trading Association (LSTA), a trade association of syndicated loan broker-dealers. Large investment banks serve as the broker-dealers in this market, but a number of smaller firms such as Imperial Capital, Cantor Fitzgerald, The Seaport Group, and Pressprich & Co. also compete. Because bank loans are not treated as securities for federal law, the broker-dealers are not subject to federal broker-dealer regulation, including the duty of fair dealing and the 10b-10 trade confirmation rule.

Broker-dealer pricing depends on the size of the transactions and the liquidity in the claim type, but is typically in the range of a couple basis points on each trade. There is no direct contact between the buyer and the seller, and they receive separate trade confirmations. Thus, it is impossible to know if the broker-dealer is acting as a dealer engaged in a price arbitrage itself (trading for its own account and pocketing the spread between the buyer's offer and the seller's price) rather than as a broker (a fiduciary agent with compensation limited by contract).

Trade debt can also go through a broker-dealer, but its initial sale often involves direct contacts between the buyer and seller. As soon as schedules of claimholders or proofs of claims are filed, firms that specialize in buying trade claims rush to send offers to claimholders. As the website of Argo Partners, a firm that specializes in trade claims, explains:

> If you have received a letter from Argo Partners offering to purchase your claim, you are listed in papers filed in the bankruptcy court as a creditor in a bankruptcy proceeding. The letter you received extends an offer to buy your claim in exchange for the amount stated.
>
> To accept our offer, simply complete the Assignment Agreement and return it via mail, email or fax. Payment for your claim will be made pursuant to the terms of the offer letter you received. Argo Partners will file the necessary documents to effectuate the transfer with the U.S. Bankruptcy Court.

Documentation for trade claims is far from standardized, although there have been moves made in that direction. In 2002, a number of specialists in trade claims formed a Trade Claims Buyers Association (TCBA) with the goal of standardizing "the assignment, transfer and payment for such claims. This would not only clarify procedures among competitors in the trade claims market but, most importantly, would also act to bring additional confidence to creditors wishing to sell their claims."

It is unclear how much progress has been made in adoption of standardized procedures and documentation for trade claims. Trade claims can be subject to a range of contract defenses. Therefore, contracts for the purchase of trade claims typically have mechanisms to adjust for a disallowance, reduction or offset. Sellers often want to negotiate these terms carefully, which precludes standardization.

The differences in the asset classes of bankruptcy claims suggest that different types of regulation are necessary. Trade claims, for example, might require regulation with a greater eye to protecting sellers because of differences in sophistication. The differences in the asset classes also suggest that there should be different rules about transient liability with claims.

For example, consider the sorely confused district court ruling in *Enron*, the most important claims trading case to have emerged in recent years. The issue before the district court was whether a claim could be equitably subordinated or disallowed in the hands of a purchaser for malfeasance done by the seller unrelated to the claim. The district court held that the answer depended on whether the claim was "sold" or "assigned," a novel distinction that flew against the long-standing interchangeability of these terms in legal practice.

A rule that equitable subordination or disallowance follows a claim might make sense if there was a highly negotiated transfer, such as a trade claim with opportunities for the buyer to conduct diligence on the seller or negotiate warranties. It makes little sense, however, for a claim based on a bond, where counterparty diligence is impossible, as is the ability to negotiate separate warranties absent knowledge of the counterparty's finances. While it is true that *Enron* involved bank debt, which has a more complicated situation because it trades on standardized forms, there is a greater ability to negotiate terms and conduct diligence of the immediate seller (but not of upstream transferors) of bank debt. A rule that makes sense for one asset class of claim might not for another.

C. The Motivational Dimension: Trading Strategies

1. Sellers

A claims trade requires both a seller and a buyer, of course, but it is important to recognize the differences in their respective motivations, as well as the impact of their activity. Claims sellers have a variety of motivations. Parties want to get out of bankruptcy cases for a variety of reasons including liquidity constraints, administrative hassle, conflicts of interest with current customers (including the debtor), and expense or regulatory risk. Others wish to sell their claims to lock in a profit, limit a loss, or benefit from a tax advantage.

Additionally, there might be some creditors who want to get out of the bankruptcy case because they have done something nefarious that would cause the claim to be disallowed or subordinated in their hands and are looking to "launder" their claim through the sale. Unless there are grounds for an independent action against them for their conduct, once they cease to be a creditor in the bankruptcy, they have little to lose. Despite the celebrated *Enron* case, there is no evidence that this practice is widespread. Most likely, the vast majority of claims sellers are simply looking to disengage from the bankruptcy with no bad faith motivation.

Preserving exit opportunities for creditors is important because it affects the availability and cost of capital to all businesses, especially riskier ones. To the extent that creditors are worried about being trapped into a bankruptcy, it will reduce their willingness to lend, resulting in less credit availability and/or higher costs. This, in turn, might force marginal borrowers into bankruptcy.

Bankruptcy claims are the residual capital market, and as such are intimately linked with upstream markets. While the workings of this relationship depend on the ease of non-bankruptcy debt collection, there are indelible connections between bankruptcy markets and non-bankruptcy markets; with business debt, they are largely seamless.

From a policy perspective, however, it is very easy to view bankruptcy as a world in and of itself. The problem is that bankruptcy is not an end in and of itself, but a part of the market regulation system. It is an easy trap for those who work solely in the bankruptcy realm to focus only on the bankruptcy effects of claims trading (and often only through the prism of the case at hand); it is harder for them to see the indirect effects of claims trading on capital markets, much less the causal links. Nonetheless, evaluations of claims trading must account for the larger net social welfare impacts including liquidity.

To the extent that we believe there is value to protect in the exit opportunity from claims trading, it also means that we have to protect sufficient entry opportunities, as every claims trade requires a buyer and a seller. While claim purchases raise several problematic strategies, purchases are necessary for sales and vice versa.

2. Buyers

Claims buyers are a more complicated group than sellers. Every claims trader is looking to buy low and sell high, but beyond that, it is hard to generalize when and what, much less why, they are buying. Some of their activities are quite innocent while others raise serious policy concerns.

Some claims purchasers buy before the bankruptcy petition is filed, some at the beginning of the case, and some towards the end. For example, there are investors who look to purchase at low prices either when a business is failing or early in the bankruptcy and ride through the case until payouts are fairly certain. These investors might be hoping to buy at 30 cents on the dollar and get a payout at 70 cents on the dollar. Perhaps if they waited another six months, the payout would be 74 cents on the dollar, but the additional 4 cents on the dollar for six months might not be a worthwhile return for the time value of the investment.

Other investors might not want to assume the risk that exists in the early days of a case when the fate of the debtor is much less certain, but they would gladly purchase at 70 cents on the dollar at the end of the case to get a payout of 74 cents on the dollar six months later.

Some buyers focus on a particular asset class, while others buy up and down the capital structure, using one class of debt as a hedge on another. As for why they are buying, several different types of claims trading may be observed, at least in Mega-Cases.

As with consumer bankruptcies, there are simple passive arbitrageurs looking to make a spread between the price they pay for a claim and the ultimate payout, discounted for some time value. These buyers do not appear in court and are not active in the case. They are also often eager to purchase very small claims because these claims will likely be classified as convenience claims, which are frequently paid in full. Similarly, there are arbitrageurs who are not looking to make their spread based on the ultimate payout in the case, but rather as broker-dealers, earning a commission or markup on the claims. These passive investment types of activity are, by themselves, harmless, except to the extent claims trading volume overall is a problem.

Also, there are arbitrageurs, typically activist investment funds, who are active in the case, appearing in court, taking part in plan negotiations, and litigating to improve their payouts. These purchasers contribute to the reorganization process both through their expertise and ability to fund the reorganization, either through DIP lending or exit financing. These funds buy in because they want to impact the restructuring strategically. Sometimes this is simply with an aim to increase the payout. Other times it is because they see bankruptcy as an acquisition strategy.

Claims purchasing can also be a takeover strategy. There are claims purchasers who look to acquire the so-called "fulcrum security"—the class(es) of claims that will be paid with equity in the reorganized firm. Investors can purchase debt claims and end up as owners of the reorganized firm. This strategy is another type of arbitrage, because it uses claims trading as a way to acquire the reorganized debtor at a discounted price. Sometimes buyers will aim for the fulcrum security after a bankruptcy filing, but often they will get involved pre-bankruptcy, as part of a loan-to-own strategy with a distressed company.

There is reason to believe that bankruptcy might allow for cheaper acquisitions than outside of bankruptcy. First, there is uncertainty as to where in the capital structure the fulcrum security will lie. There might be reduced demand for what turns out to be the fulcrum security, and hence a lower price.

Second, bankruptcy claims can be acquired very quietly. There is no equivalent to the Williams Act [a federal securities law] provision requiring a public filing if a shareholder acquires more than 5% of a company's securities. As a result, a purchaser might avoid paying the control premium. This is not necessarily a problematic strategy from a policy perspective, but the ability to arbitrage regulatory regimes to gain a bargain raises the specter of companies being pushed into bankruptcy to facilitate cheaper takeovers that impose costs on other creditors and shareholders.

There are also claims traders who use claims as a method of shorting reorganizations. An entity might purchase bankruptcy claims because it is short on a reorganization due to another investment (such as an investment in a competitor), because it wishes to force an asset sale, or because they are competitors of the debtors. The purchaser's incentive in plan confirmation voting is to delay or block confirmation, and force a liquidation.

From a bankruptcy policy viewpoint, this looks quite bad, but it needs to be considered as part of the larger debate on shorting, which is essential for market discipline. The possibility of parties being short in reorganizations is typically part of the parties being long in other investments. By the same token, a party that is long on a bankruptcy reorganization might have hedged it with a short position on a competitor or index. If parties are to be encouraged to be long on reorganizations, they might need to be short elsewhere, and if shorting is acceptable outside of bankruptcy, it should be so in bankruptcy. Trading strategies that seem distasteful when viewed solely in a bankruptcy context can have a more neutral tone when the interconnectedness of bankruptcy markets to other markets is considered.

Additionally, there are claims purchasers who are seeking to acquire information about the debtor's operations and assets. The information might be valuable to a competitor of the debtor or to a party interested in purchasing a specific asset. Courts have begun to be more careful about this and restrict trading of parties with access to information, despite a very open-ended disclosure provision in the Bankruptcy Code.

Finally, there are greenmailers who accumulate enough claims of a particular impaired class to block plan confirmation. Greenmailers play on hostage value, using this blocking position to extract a greater payout in a plan of reorganization for their class of claims or to get bought out. The goal of the blocking position is not to force a better plan overall, in which the greenmailer will benefit, but to have value reallocated from other creditors to the greenmailer, either in the form of a direct buyout from the parties that have a strong interest in plan confirmation or via a shift in plan distributions.

To the extent the greenmailer uses bankruptcy's procedural requirements as a mechanism to extract value from other parties, it is an abuse of the process that undermines essential policy goals of efficiency and fairness and should be cause for vote designation or even equitable subordination. But determining whether an investor obtained a blocking position for greenmail purposes or to push an alternative vision of a reorganization could present difficult evidentiary challenges. Greenmail seems to be more a possibility to be dreaded and suspected than a clearly identifiable practice.

Claims trading strategies are not exclusive. A claims purchaser could be seeking the fulcrum security, but find itself with a simple dollar for dollar spread or a blocking position. Alternatively, an attempt to gain a blocking position might be unsuccessful, but a fallback would be making a simple spread. While a basic typology of claims trading is possible, we do not know how neat these categories are in practice.

The foregoing discussion of claims markets and claims trading strategies underscores that claims trading is comprised of dynamic, multi-motivational, and overlapping submarkets, which raise distinct policy concerns. Some claims trading is beneficial, and some is value eroding. The key value-added elements of claims trading are that it allows an exit for parties (which can have upstream effects on market liquidity, capital availability, and the cost of capital) and that it allows entrance to parties that can bring in the expertise and financing to speed along a reorganization. In other words, claims trading can help with efficient allocations of capital in the market. In order to preserve the essential exit opportunities, there must be sufficient entrance opportunities and vice-versa. Thus, greater liquidity in claims trading would appear to be beneficial to the bankruptcy process.

Yet, it is possible that distinctions in claims trading do not matter because the key issue is the impact on the bankruptcy process of trading volume (in terms of number of trades) and the creditor churn it produces.

The ability to buy into a bankruptcy case by purchasing distressed debt at a discount has substantially shaped the dynamics of the Chapter 11 process, as the following case excerpt shows.

Ion Media Networks, Inc. v. Cyrus Select Opportunities Master Fund Ltd. (*In re* Ion Media Networks, Inc.)

419 B.R. 585 (Bankr. S.D.N.Y. 2009)

JAMES M. PECK, United States Bankruptcy Judge

Cyrus Select Opportunities Master Fund Ltd. ("Cyrus") is an activist distressed investor that purchased certain deeply discounted second lien debt of ION Media Networks, Inc. ("ION," together with its affiliated debtors, the "Debtors") for pennies on the dollar. Throughout these cases . . . Cyrus has been vigorously challenging the rights of the First Lien Lenders to recover as secured creditors any of the enterprise value attributable to ION's FCC broadcast licenses. . . . Cyrus' motivations are easy enough to recognize. It has been using aggressive bankruptcy litigation tactics as a means to gain negotiating leverage or obtain judicial rulings that will enable it to earn outsize returns on its bargain basement debt purchases at the expense of the First Lien Lenders.

There certainly is nothing wrong with raising and pursuing opportunistic legal theories as a means to reap profits in connection with acquired, deeply discounted bankruptcy claims. Such activist strategies are an increasingly familiar part of the landscape in large chapter 11 cases.

II. TREATMENT OF PURCHASED CLAIMS IN BANKRUPTCY

There is surprisingly little law on claims trading despite the importance of the market. While claims trading appears in the background of many recent decisions and is necessary for understanding what is happening economically that is shaping the dynamics of the cases, the *Figter* decision below is one of the few that squarely deals with trading.

Figter Ltd. v. Teachers Insurance and Annuity Association of America (*In re* Figter Ltd.)

118 F.3d 635 (9th Cir. 1997)

FERNANDEZ, Circuit Judge:

Figter Limited, a Chapter 11 debtor and owner of Skyline Terrace, an apartment complex, appeals from the district court's affirmance of the bankruptcy court's decision that Teachers Insurance and Annuity Association of America (Teachers), the holder of a $15,600,000 promissory note secured by a first deed of trust on Skyline Terrace, bought twenty-one unsecured claims in good faith and that it could vote each one separately. We affirm.

BACKGROUND

Figter filed a voluntary petition under Chapter 11 of the Bankruptcy Code. It owns Skyline Terrace, a 198-unit residential apartment complex located in Los Angeles. Teachers is a creditor. It holds a $15,600,000 promissory note executed by Figter. The note is secured by a first deed of trust on Skyline Terrace and by $1,400,000 of cash on hand. In fact, Teachers is Figter's only secured creditor and is the only member of Class 2 in a reorganization plan proposed by Figter. The plan contemplates full payment of Teachers' secured claim, but at a disputed rate of interest. Thus, under Figter's plan, Teachers' claim is not impaired. The plan calls for the impairment of Class 3 unsecured claims by payment at only 80% of their face value.

Teachers has opposed Figter's reorganization plan from its inception because, among other things, that plan contemplates the conversion of Skyline Terrace Apartments into condominiums, with payment to and partial releases by Teachers as the units sell. That could easily result in a property that was part condominium and part rentals, if the plan ultimately fails in operation.

Teachers proposed a plan of its own, which provided for the transfer of Skyline Terrace and the cash collateral to Teachers in satisfaction of its secured claim, as well as a payment of Class 3 unsecured claims at 90%. Teachers' plan was premised on the assumption that its claim was partly unsecured. However, on May 31, 1994, before the purchases of other claims took place, the bankruptcy court determined that Skyline Terrace had a value of $19,300,000. Thus, Teachers' claim in the amount of $17,960,000 was fully secured. It did not thereafter pursue its plan. From October 27, 1994 until October 31, 1994, Teachers purchased twenty-one of the thirty-four unsecured claims in Class 3 at one hundred cents on the dollar, for a total purchase price of $14,588.62. Teachers had made the same offer to all of the Class 3 claim holders, but not all accepted it. The offer remained open. Teachers then filed notices of transfer of claims with the court, as is required under Bankruptcy Rule 3001(e)(2). Those notices were served on all affected parties, including Figter. No objections were filed by the unsecured creditors. The district court upheld the bankruptcy court's determination regarding Teachers' purchase of the unsecured claims. As a result, Figter's plan is unconfirmable because it is unable to meet the requirements of 11 U.S.C. § 1129(a)(10); there will not be an impaired, consenting class of claims. That will preclude a "cram down" of Teachers' secured claim under 11 U.S.C. § 1129(b). Figter has appealed in an attempt to avoid that result.

. . .

DISCUSSION

Figter asserts that Teachers should be precluded from voting its purchased Class 3 claims because it did not buy them in good faith. Figter also asserts that even if the claims were purchased in good faith, Teachers cannot vote them separately, but is limited to one total vote as a Class 3 creditor. If Figter were correct in either of its assertions, it could obtain Class 3 approval of its plan and enhance its chances of cramming down Teachers' Class 2 claims. But Figter is not correct.

A. Good Faith

The Bankruptcy Code provides that "on request of a party in interest, and after notice and a hearing, the court may designate any entity whose acceptance or rejection of [a] plan was not in good faith, or was not solicited or procured in good faith or in accordance with the provisions of this title." 11 U.S.C. § 1126(e). In this context, designate means disqualify from voting. The Bankruptcy Code does not further define the rather murky term "good faith." That job has been left to the courts.

The Supreme Court brought some clarity to this area when it decided *Young v. Higbee Co.*, 324 U.S. 204 (1945). In *Young*, the Court was discussing the predecessor to § 1126(e) when it declared that if certain persons "had declined to accept [the] plan in bad faith, the court, under section 203 could have denied them the right to vote on the plan at all." *Id.* at 210-11. It went on to explain that the provision was intended to apply to those "whose selfish purpose was to obstruct a fair and feasible reorganization in the hope that someone would pay them more than the ratable equivalent of their proportionate part of the bankrupt assets." *Id.* at 211. In other words, the section was intended to apply to those who were not attempting to protect their own proper interests, but who were, instead, attempting to obtain some benefit to which they were not entitled. While helpful, those reflections by the Court do not fully answer the question before us. Other courts have further illuminated the area.

If a person seeks to secure some untoward advantage over other creditors for some ulterior motive, that will indicate bad faith. But that does not mean that creditors are expected to approach reorganization plan votes with a high degree of altruism and with the desire to help the debtor and their fellow creditors. Far from it.

If a selfish motive were sufficient to condemn reorganization policies of interested parties, very few, if any, would pass muster. On the other hand, pure malice, "strikes" and blackmail, and the purpose to destroy an enterprise in order to advance the interests of a competing business, all plainly constituting bad faith, are motives which may be accurately described as ulterior.

That is to say, we do not condemn mere enlightened self interest, even if it appears selfish to those who do not benefit from it. *See id.*

Thus, if Teachers acted out of enlightened self interest, it is not to be condemned simply because it frustrated Figter's desires. That is true, even if Teachers purchased Class 3 claims for the very purpose of blocking confirmation of Figter's proposed plan. That self interest can extend even further without being an ulterior motive. It has been held that a creditor commits no wrong when he votes against a plan of a debtor who has a lawsuit pending against the creditor, for that will not, by itself, show bad faith. It has also been held that no bad faith is shown when a creditor chooses to benefit his interest as a creditor as opposed to some unrelated interest. And the mere fact that a creditor has purchased additional claims for the purpose of protecting his own existing claim does not demonstrate bad faith or an ulterior motive. "As long as a creditor acts to preserve what he reasonably perceives as his fair share of the debtor's estate, bad faith will not be attributed to his purchase of claims to control a class vote." *In re Gilbert*, 104 B.R. 206, 217 (Bankr. W.D. Mo. 1989).

Courts, on the other hand, have been sensitive to situations where a company, which was not a preexisting creditor, has purchased a claim for the purpose of blocking an action against it. They have seen that as an indication of bad faith. The same has been true where creditors were associated with a competing business and desired to destroy the debtor's business in order to further their own. And when the debtor had claims against itself purchased by an insider or affiliate for the purpose of blocking a plan, or fostering one, that was seen as a badge of bad faith. Figter would have us add that in a single asset bankruptcy, claim purchasing activities, like those of Teachers, are in bad faith. It cites no authority for that, and we see no basis for establishing *that* as a per se rule.

In short, the concept of good faith is a fluid one, and no single factor can be said to inexorably demand an ultimate result, nor must a single set of factors be considered. It is always necessary to keep in mind the difference between a creditor's self interest as a creditor and a motive which is ulterior to the purpose of protecting a creditor's interest. Prior cases can offer guidance, but, when all is said and done, the bankruptcy court must simply approach each good faith determination with a perspicacity derived from the data of its informed practical experience in dealing with bankrupts and their creditors.

Here, the bankruptcy court did exactly that. It decided that Teachers was not, for practical purposes, the proponent of an alternate plan when it sought to purchase the Class 3 claims. Nor, it found, did Teachers seek to purchase a small number of claims for the purpose of blocking Figter's plan, while injuring other creditors, even if it could do that in some circumstances. Rather, Teachers offered to purchase all Class 3 claims, and only some of those claimants' refusals to sell precluded it from doing so. Moreover, Teachers was a lender, not a competing apartment owner. It acted to protect its interests as Figter's major creditor. It reasonably feared that it could be left with a very complex lien situation, if Figter went forward with its plan. Instead of holding a lien covering the whole of the property, it could have wound up with separate fractured liens on various parts of the property, while other parts were owned by others. That could create a very undesirable mix of owners and renters and of debtors and nondebtors. Added to that was the actual use of cash, which was collateral for the debt owed to Teachers. It cannot be said that Teachers' concerns were irrational.

Based on all that was before it, the bankruptcy court decided that in this case Teachers was a creditor which acted in a good faith attempt to protect its interests and not with some ulterior motive. We cannot say that it erred in making that ultimate determination.

B. Voting

Figter's fallback position is that even if Teachers did act in good faith, it must be limited to one vote for its twenty-one claims. That assertion is answered by the language of the Bankruptcy Code, which provides that:

> A class of claims has accepted a plan if such plan has been accepted by creditors . . . that hold at least two-thirds in amount and *more than one-half in number of the allowed claims* of such class held by creditors . . . that have accepted or rejected such plan.

11 U.S.C. § 1126(c) (emphasis added). That language was interpreted in *Gilbert*, 104 B.R. at 211, where the court reasoned:

> The formula contained in Section 1126(c) speaks in terms of the *number of claims*, not the number of creditors, that actually vote for or against the plan. . . . Each claim arose out of a separate transaction, evidencing separate obligations for which separate proofs of claim were filed. Votes of acceptance . . . are to be computed only on the basis of filed and allowed proofs of claim. . . . [The creditor] is entitled to one vote for each of his unsecured Class X claims.

That same view was iterated in *Concord Square Apartments of Wood Cty, Ltd. v. Ottawa Properties, Inc. (In re Concord Square Apartments of Wood Cty., Ltd.)*, 174 B.R. 71, 74 (Bankr. S.D. Ohio 1994), where the court held that a creditor with "multiple claims, has a voting right for each claim it holds." We agree. It would not make much sense to require a vote by creditors who held "more than one-half in number of the allowed claims" while at the same time limiting a creditor who held two or more of those claims to only one vote. If allowed claims are to be counted, they must be counted regardless of whose hands they happen to be in.

Figter seeks some succor from the Supreme Court's indication in *Dewsnup v. Timm*, 502 U.S. 410, 419-20 (1992), that ambiguous language in the Code should not be taken to effect a sea change in pre-Code practice. However, that does not help Figter's cause. In the first place, as we have indicated, the present language is not ambiguous. In the second place, the old law to which *Figter* refers relied upon a code section which required voting approval by a "majority in number of all creditors whose claims have been allowed." Bankruptcy Act of 1898, ch. 541, § 12, 30 Stat. 544, 549-50 (*repealed* 1938). It is pellucid that "a majority in number of all creditors" is not at all like "more than one-half in number" of all claims. The former focuses on claimants; the latter on claims.

Nor is our conclusion affected by cases where other sections of the bankruptcy code, or other acts by creditors, were involved. For example, the predecessor to 11 U.S.C. § 702 indicated that a creditor could vote for the trustee. In *In re Latham Lithographic Corp.*, 107 F.2d 749 (2d Cir. 1939), there was an attempt to split a single claim into multiple claims for the purpose of creating multiple creditors who could vote in a trustee election. It is not surprising that the court did not permit that. *See id.* at 751. And in *In re Gilbert*, 115 B.R. 458, 461 (Bankr. S.D.N.Y. 1990), the court held that an involuntary petition in bankruptcy must be filed by three creditors, and a single creditor with three separate claims is still one creditor. *See also In re Averil*, 33 B.R. 562, 563 (Bankr. S.D. Fla. 1983). In fact, the involuntary petition section actually requires that there be three or more *entities*. *See* 11 U.S.C. § 303(b). Certainly, a creditor with three claims is still a single entity.

Of course, that is not to say that a creditor can get away with splitting one claim into many, but that is not what happened here. Teachers purchased a number of separately incurred and separately approved claims (each of which carried one vote) from different creditors. There simply is no reason to hold that those separate votes suddenly became one vote, a result which would be exactly the opposite of claim splitting. Therefore, the bankruptcy court did not err.

CONCLUSION

Figter hoped to obtain approval of a reorganization plan, which would require Teachers to thole what it saw as a diminution of its creditor's rights. Those hopes were dashed when Teachers bought up most of the Class 3 claims in an effort to protect its own Class 2 claim. Because the bankruptcy court determined that Teachers acted to protect its valid creditor's interest, rather than for ulterior motives, it held that Teachers had acted in good faith. That precluded designation of Teachers' purchased claims. The bankruptcy court also determined that Teachers could vote each of its twenty-one claims separately; it was not limited to a single vote. The district court affirmed those decisions. Because the bankruptcy court did not err in either its factual or its legal determinations, we agree with the district court and affirm the decision.

AFFIRMED.

Study Questions and Note

1. Does it matter that Teachers paid 100 cents on the dollar for the claims it purchased? If Teachers had purchased the claims at a discount, do you think the outcome would have been different? What if Teachers had purchased the claims *before* the bankruptcy? Would the outcome have been different if Teachers had not already been a pre-petition creditor?

2. Does it matter that Teachers made its purchase offer to all Class 3 claim holders?

3. The claims counting problem is more complex than *Figter* indicates because of the way ownership of debt securities works. Investors in debt securities are usually quite divorced from the actual debts. Typically, the actual bond is registered to CeeDee & Co., the nominee entity of the Depository Trust Corporation (DTC). DTC is the legal owner of the bond, and beneficial ownership is tracked in the DTC's book entry system. This structure, which is governed by UCC Article 8 and SEC regulations, was adopted to avoid the need to physically transfer bonds whenever a trade was made, as commonly occurred into the 1960s. The DTC's book entry system will typically track brokerages, which have a "security entitlement" with the DTC. The brokers' own book entry systems will then track the ultimate beneficiary of the bond, who holds a "security entitlement" with the broker. Thus, it is not even clear that a bondholder has a "claim." Instead, it likely has a security entitlement in a security entitlement in a bond. When ballots are sent out for voting on a bankruptcy plan, they are given to brokers, who then pass them along to the ultimate beneficiaries. The brokers then compile the votes of their clients and submit them for counting. Brokers, however, count votes by *account* not by beneficiary. One person or family could have numerous accounts with one or multiple brokers. Thus, a single creditor or affiliated group of creditors could end up with multiple votes based on no action of its own but on the technical workings of the securities holding system. In theory, a plan proponent could obtain the bondholder list directly from CeeDee & Co. under Federal Rule of Bankruptcy Procedure 1007(i), but the sole reported case on the issue declined to make the list available. *In re ITEL Corp.*, 17 B.R. 942 (9th Cir. B.A.P. 1982).

III. LOCK-UPS AND PLAN SUPPORT AGREEMENTS

Adam J. Levitin
Bankruptcy Markets: Making Sense of Claims Trading
4 Brook. J. Corp., Fin. & Com. L. 64 (2010) (excerpt)

. . .

There are also contractual mechanisms that can be used to counteract the problems created by the churn in creditors. Debtors "may negotiate provisions in its pre-petition credit agreements which restrict the lender's trading of its claims." Alternatively, a debtor can employ lock-up agreements that commit signing creditors to vote for the debtor's plan, place restrictions on their trading or require them to use their best efforts to see the plan confirmed. Lock-ups can be done in out-of-court restructurings or prepackaged plans without court approval. Lock-ups can also be done with the court's approval of a stipulation that settles a creditor's claim in exchange for the creditor agreeing to vote for the plan.

The way a lock-up agreement operates to restrict trading may be seen from the Plan Support Agreement (the Agreement) filed with the court in the Freedom Communications bankruptcy. The Agreement committed the debtor and certain creditors to "cooperate with each other in good faith and shall coordinate their activities in connection with (a) the implementation of the Restructuring and (b) the pursuit of the Restructuring and confirmation and consummation of the Plan." The Agreement applied to all claims purchased in the future by its creditor signatories, and prohibits the sale of claims by the signatory creditors unless the purchaser agreed to be bound by the Agreement or received the debtor's consent. . . .

Freedom Communications, Plan Support Agreement (exhibits omitted)

This PLAN SUPPORT AGREEMENT (as the same may be amended, modified or supplemented from time to time in accordance with the terms hereof, this "Agreement"), dated as of September 1, 2009, is entered into by and among (x) Freedom Communications Holdings, Inc., a Delaware corporation ("Holdings"), Freedom Communications, Inc., a Delaware corporation (the "Company"), each of the undersigned direct and indirect subsidiaries of the Company (collectively, with Holdings and the Company, the "Debtors") and (y) each undersigned lender (each a "Consenting Lender" and together, the "Consenting Lenders") under that certain Credit Agreement dated May 18, 2004 (as amended, modified or supplemented from time to time, the "Prepetition Credit Facility") among the Company, Holdings, the lenders party thereto (collectively, the "Secured Lenders") and JPMorgan Chase Bank, N.A., as administrative agent (in such capacity, the "Agent"). Each of the Debtors and the Consenting Lenders are referred to herein individually as a "Party," and collectively as the "Parties."

Recitals

WHEREAS, the Debtors and the Consenting Lenders have negotiated a transaction that will effectuate a financial restructuring of the debt and equity of the Debtors on the terms and conditions set forth in the Plan (as defined below) (the "Restructuring") that is to be implemented in voluntary cases commenced by the Debtors under Chapter 11 of the United States Bankruptcy Code, 11 U.S.C. §§ 101 et seq. (the "Bankruptcy Code"), before the United States Bankruptcy Court for the District of Delaware (the "Bankruptcy Court"), on a consensual basis pursuant to a plan of reorganization to be confirmed under Chapter 11 of the Bankruptcy Code, the terms and conditions of which will be substantially consistent with those described in the term sheet which is attached hereto as Exhibit A (including any annexes and schedules attached thereto, the "Term Sheet"), and, if not specified in the Term Sheet, that is otherwise in form and substance reasonably satisfactory to the Consenting Lenders (the "Plan").

WHEREAS, in order to implement the Restructuring, the Debtors have agreed, subject to the terms and conditions of this Agreement, (i) to prepare and file, in any case(s) filed under Chapter 11 of the Bankruptcy Code (the "Chapter 11 Cases"), (a) the Plan and (b) a disclosure statement that is substantially consistent with the Plan and the Term Sheet and otherwise is in form and substance reasonably satisfactory to the Consenting Lenders (the "Disclosure Statement") and (ii) to use commercially reasonable efforts to have the Disclosure Statement approved and the Plan confirmed by the Bankruptcy Court and consummated thereafter.

WHEREAS, the Debtors and the Consenting Lenders, who collectively hold more than fifty percent of the claims under the Prepetition Credit Facility, have agreed to support the Restructuring on the terms and subject to the conditions set forth herein.

Agreement

NOW, THEREFORE, in consideration of the premises and agreements set forth herein, and for other good and valuable consideration, the receipt and sufficiency of which are hereby acknowledged, the Parties, intending to be legally bound, agree as follows:

. . .

2. Implementation of the Restructuring.

Subject to the terms and conditions of this Agreement, the Parties agree severally and not jointly to use commercially reasonable efforts to complete the Restructuring through the Plan on terms and conditions consistent with those set forth herein. The Parties shall cooperate with each other in good faith and shall coordinate their activities in connection with (a) the implementation of the Restructuring and (b) the pursuit of the Restructuring and confirmation and consummation of the Plan. Furthermore, each Party shall take such action as may be reasonably necessary to carry out the purposes and intent of this Agreement, and each Party shall refrain from taking any action that would reasonably be expected to frustrate the purposes and intent of this Agreement and the Restructuring, including proposing a plan of reorganization that is not the Plan (or filing a disclosure statement with respect thereto). Each Party hereby covenants and agrees severally and not jointly . . . (i) to negotiate in good faith the definitive documents implementing, achieving and relating to the Restructuring, including, but not limited to, the order of the Bankruptcy Court confirming the Plan, the Disclosure Statement and other related documents, each of which are more specifically described in the Term Sheet and each of which shall contain terms and conditions substantially consistent in all respects with the Term Sheet and, if not specified in the Term Sheet, otherwise in form and substance reasonably satisfactory to the Consenting Lenders and the Debtors (collectively with the Plan and the Disclosure Statement, the "Definitive Documents"), and (ii) to execute (to the extent they are a party thereto) the Definitive Documents and otherwise support and seek to effect the actions and transactions contemplated thereby.

3. Consenting Lenders' Obligations to Support the Restructuring.

Subject to the terms and conditions of this Agreement, each Consenting Lender severally (and not jointly) agrees that, until this Agreement has been terminated . . . and in connection with the Restructuring and the Plan upon the terms set forth in this Agreement, it will (i) not object to, or otherwise commence any proceeding to alter or oppose, the Restructuring or the confirmation of the Plan; (ii) not take any action that is materially inconsistent with, or that would unreasonably delay the consummation of, the Restructuring or the Plan in accordance with the terms of this Agreement; (iii) . . . vote, and cause its controlled affiliates and funds, as appropriate, to vote to accept the Plan in the Chapter 11 Cases; (iv) not object to the approval of the Disclosure Statement; (v) not vote for, consent to, intentionally induce or participate directly or indirectly in the formation of any other plan of reorganization or liquidation proposed or filed, or to be proposed or filed, in the Chapter 11 Cases; (vi) not commence or support any action or proceeding to shorten or terminate the period during which only the Debtors may propose and/or seek confirmation of the Plan; (vii) not directly or indirectly seek, solicit or encourage any other plan, proposal or offer of winding up, liquidation, reorganization, merger, consolidation, dissolution, restructuring of any Debtor or the sale of any or all assets of any Debtor; (viii) not commence or support any action filed by any party in interest to appoint a trustee, conservator, receiver or examiner for the Debtors, or to dismiss the Chapter 11 Cases, or to convert the Chapter 11 Cases to cases under Chapter 7 of the Bankruptcy Code; (ix) not instruct the Agent to take any action that is inconsistent with the terms and conditions of this Agreement and if the Agent takes or threatens to take any such action, direct or cause the Agent to be directed not to take such action; and (x) subject to the terms of this Agreement, not withdraw, revoke or act inconsistently with any of the foregoing unless and until this Agreement is terminated in accordance with its terms. Nothing contained herein shall limit the ability of a Consenting Lender to consult with the Debtors, or to appear and be heard, concerning any matter arising in the Chapter 11 Cases so long as such consultation or appearance is not inconsistent with such Consenting Lender's obligations under this Agreement, the Plan and the Term Sheet.

4. Debtors' Obligations to Support the Restructuring.

The Debtors hereby agree (a) to file the Chapter 11 Cases with respect to the Restructuring with the Bankruptcy Court on or prior to 11:59 P.M. (Eastern) on September

3, 2009 (such filing date, the "Petition Date") and to file the Plan and the Disclosure Statement with the Bankruptcy Court on or prior to 11:59 P.M. (Eastern) on the date that is 60 days following the Petition Date; (b) not to assert or support any assertion by any third party that . . . a Consenting Lender shall be required to obtain relief from the automatic stay from the Bankruptcy Court (and hereby waives, to the greatest extent possible, the applicability of the automatic stay for the giving of such notice); (c) to prepare or cause the preparation, as soon as practicable after the date hereof, of each of the Plan, the Disclosure Statement and (in consultation with the Agent) the Definitive Documents; (d) to use all reasonable commercial efforts to consummate the Restructuring and Plan within the timeframe contemplated by this Agreement and take any and all necessary and appropriate actions in furtherance of the Restructuring and the confirmation and consummation of the Plan; (e) to use all reasonable commercial efforts to obtain any and all required regulatory and/or third-party approvals for such Restructuring, including any approvals or waivers (to the extent deemed advisable by the Debtors and the Consenting Lenders) required by the FCC to consummate the Restructuring; (f) not to seek to implement any transaction or series of transactions that would effect a restructuring on different terms from the Restructuring or propose or support any plan of reorganization or liquidation in the Chapter 11 Cases other than the Plan; (g) not to take any action that is inconsistent with, or that would unreasonably delay or impede approval or confirmation and consummation of the Plan or that is otherwise inconsistent with this Agreement; (h) not to directly or indirectly seek, solicit, support or encourage any other plan, sale, proposal or offer of dissolution, winding up, liquidation, reorganization, merger, consolidation, liquidation or restructuring of any of the Debtors that could reasonably be expected to prevent, delay or impede the confirmation and consummation of the Restructuring and the Plan; and (i) to provide written notice to the Agent and each Consenting Lender, within two business days of making such determination, if any Debtor determines that it would be inconsistent with its fiduciary duties to pursue confirmation and consummation of the Plan and the Restructuring contemplated by this Agreement; provided that nothing contained in this Agreement shall be deemed to prevent any Debtor from taking or failing to take any action that it is obligated to take (or fail to take) in the performance of any fiduciary or similar duty which such Debtor owes to any other person.

10. Restrictions on Transfer

(a) Except as set forth in Section 10(b), each Consenting Lender hereby agrees that, for so long as this Agreement shall remain in effect as to it, it shall not sell, transfer or assign all or any of its Secured Lender Claims, as the case may be, or any option thereon or any right or interest (voting, participation or otherwise) therein (each, a "Transfer") without the prior written consent of Holdings.

(b) Notwithstanding the foregoing, any Consenting Lender may Transfer any or all of its respective Secured Lender Claims, provided that, as a condition precedent, the transferee thereof agrees in writing, in the form attached hereto as Exhibit B, to be bound by the terms of this Agreement.

(c) Any Transfer of any Secured Lender Claim that does not comply with the foregoing shall be deemed void *ab initio*.

. . .

16. Specific Performance

It is understood and agreed by the Parties that money damages would not be a sufficient remedy for any breach of this Agreement by any Party and each non-breaching Party shall be entitled to specific performance and injunctive or other equitable relief as a remedy of any such breach, including, without limitation, an order of the Bankruptcy Court or other court of competent jurisdiction requiring any Party to comply promptly with any of its obligations hereunder.

. . .

23. Consideration.

It is hereby acknowledged by the Parties that no consideration shall be due or paid to the Consenting Lenders in exchange for their support of the Restructuring, in accordance with the terms and conditions of this Agreement, other than the obligations imposed upon the Debtors, the Consenting Lenders pursuant to the terms of this Agreement.

24. Acknowledgement.

This Agreement is not, and shall not be deemed to be, an offer of securities or a solicitation for consents to the Plan. Each Consenting Lender's acceptance of the Plan shall not be solicited until it has received the Plan contemplated by this Agreement, the Disclosure Statement in the form approved by the Bankruptcy Court in respect of the Plan contemplated by this Agreement and other solicitation material in connection therewith.

. . .

Study Questions

1. Who are the parties to the Plan Support Agreement (PSA)?
2. Why would they want to sign on to the PSA? *See In re Indianapolis Downs, LLC,* 486 B.R. 286 (Bankr. D. Del. 2013) (the "racino" case in Chapter 36).
3. What have the parties agreed to in the PSA? PSA ¶3.
4. Can the signatories to the PSA sell their interests? PSA ¶10.
5. What is the remedy if the PSA is violated? PSA ¶16. Is the remedy enforceable?
6. Can the PSA bind the debtor-in-possession?

saving association
(A Bank)

Problem Set 41

(1) Poor Richard's Thrift Society filed a proof of claim for $10 million in Caesar Rodney & Partners' Chapter 11 bankruptcy. Two months later, Poor Richard's sold the claim to John Hancock Strategies, LLP for $4 million.

 a. Why might Poor Richard's have sold the claim?
 b. Why might Hancock have purchased the claim?
 c. Is there anything that either Poor Richard's or Hancock needs to do to make the transfer of the claim effective?

    d. If the claim is allowed, how much will it be allowed for in Hancock's hand?

  (2) Your client, Mount Vernon Partners, holds a significant equity share in the Monticello Corp., which is in Chapter 11. Plan exclusivity is about to lapse for Monticello Corp., and your client would like to propose a plan. Your client would like to engage in some informal conversations with other key parties in interest to help it draft a confirmable plan. You've been asked to identify who holds the first lien senior loan debt, who holds the senior and junior bond debt, and who the largest five trade and tort creditors are. How will you do this?

  (3) You've been representing Robert Morris & Co. in its Chapter 11 bankruptcy. Bobbie, the firm's CEO, is on the phone with you. She's beside herself. She thought she had assembled a coalition of creditors that would vote for the reorganization plan she envisioned, and when she went for a meeting with them today to show them a draft of the disclosure statement that the firm had just submitted to the court, she found a totally different cast of characters. "There were all these dudes there I had never seen before," Bobbie explains. "They were all from various vulture funds. They wanted to renegotiate every point in the plan. They said they'd bought the claims from the creditors I negotiated with." Bobbie is worried that there's no way to form a stable coalition with a constantly churning cast of creditors. Is there anything she might do? Are there any concerns you have about your recommended strategy? 11 U.S.C. §§ 1125, 1126(e); Freedom Communications, Plan Support Agreement §§ 16, 23, 24.

  (4) Robert Morris & Co. (from question 3) is still in Chapter 11 bankruptcy. Morris has $100 million in junior unsecured notes outstanding. There are 100 notes, each for $1 million.

    a. Alexander Hamilton Special Opportunities Fund, LLP has purchased 40 of Morris & Co.'s junior notes with a total face amount of $40 million. Hamilton purchased the notes for 15 cents on the dollar on average. Hamilton has made it clear that it will not accept a plan of reorganization that does not pay the notes at least 30 cents on the dollar or a controlling share of Morris's equity. Morris has proposed a plan that would pay the junior unsecured notes 20 cents on the dollar. If Hamilton is the only unsecured junior noteholder opposed to the plan, is the plan confirmable without cramdown? 11 U.S.C. §§ 502; 1126(c), (e).

    b. Would the answer to (a) change if Hamilton proposed a plan that would pay the junior unsecured notes 40 cents on the dollar? 11 U.S.C. § 1129(a)(3).

    c. Suppose that Benjamin Franklin Investments, Ltd. held one of the Morris junior unsecured notes in the amount of $1 million. If Franklin sells a 50% interest in the note to Hamilton and a 10% interest in the note to Van Buren Partners and then another two separate 10% interests in the note to Hamilton, how many more notes would Hamilton have to purchase to be able to ensure that a class of unsecured junior notes would vote for the plan it proposes? 11 U.S.C. §§ 101(5), 1126(c).

    d. Would the answer to (c) change if Franklin sold the interests in the note pre-petition?

(5) Brandywine Distilleries, the maker of Old Federalist and other fine spirits, is preparing to file a prepackaged bankruptcy. As part of its preparations, Brandywine is seeking to get its creditors to sign a restructuring support agreement (RSA). Brandywine is offering to cover the legal expenses of the creditors that sign the RSA, and to pay an "early consent fee." The offer is available to all claimants who would have impaired claims under the plan.

    a. Do you have any concerns with this strategy? 11 U.S.C. §§ 1126(e), 1129(a)(3); 18 U.S.C. § 152(6).

    b. Now suppose that Brandywine Distilleries' prepackaged strategy was unsuccessful, and it is in Chapter 11. Brandywine is now seeking to get a core constituency of creditors to commit to an RSA. Brandywine is offering to ensure that the plan pays a "RSA fee" as an administrative expense of the case for those creditors who sign the RSA. Is your analysis different? 11 U.S.C. §§ 503(b)(3)(D), 503(b)(5), 1124(3), 1126(e), 1129(a)(3), 1129(b); 18 U.S.C. § 152(6).

CHAPTER 42

DISCHARGE AND POST-CONFIRMATION MATTERS

I. EFFECT OF PLAN CONFIRMATION

A bankruptcy case doesn't end with plan confirmation. A bankruptcy case only ends when the case is "closed." 11 U.S.C. § 350. This requires that the estate be "fully administered," *id.*, which requires that the plan be fully implemented, not just confirmed. There are often issues that remain unresolved post-confirmation, such as pending avoidance actions, any recoveries from which are allocated by the plan.

While there can be significant money at stake in post-confirmation litigation, the financial restructuring of a company is completed once a plan is confirmed. Confirmation of a plan "vests all of the property of the estate in the debtor," unless otherwise provided in the plan or confirmation order. 11 U.S.C. § 1141. The property administered under the plan becomes free and clear of all claims or interests of creditors or equityholders, except as provided by the plan. 11 U.S.C. § 1141(c). In other words, post-confirmation, the bankruptcy estate ceases to exist.

Confirmation also discharges almost all pre-confirmation debt if the debtor is reorganizing. 11 U.S.C. § 1141(d). (The discharge does not, of course, affect obligations created by the plan.) If the debtor is liquidating, there is no discharge. 11 U.S.C. § 1141(d)(3). Likewise there is no discharge in Chapter 7 for business entity debtors. 11 U.S.C. § 727(a)(1). With the discharge, the automatic stay is lifted. 11 U.S.C. § 362(c)(2)(C). In its place is the permanent discharge injunction that prohibits collection of any pre-confirmation debts discharged by the plan. 11 U.S.C. § 524. This injunction prevents collection of the debts as a personal liability of the debtor; it does not prevent a creditor from foreclosing on a lien. In other words, unsecured debts become uncollectible, but secured debts become non-recourse obligations.

Confirmation often results in a discharge, but the case remains open until the estate is fully administered. The Seventh Circuit has summarized the post-confirmation situation succinctly:

> Once the bankruptcy court confirms a plan of reorganization, the debtor may go about its business without further supervision or approval. The firm also is without the protection of the bankruptcy court. It may not come running to the bankruptcy judge every time something unpleasant happens. . . . Formerly a ward of the court, the debtor is emancipated by the plan of reorganization.

Pettibone Corp. v. Easley, 935 F.2d 120, 122 (7th Cir. 1991). As Judge Bruce Markell has noted, however:

> Emancipated or not, debtors often return to the bankruptcy court post-confirmation, seeking various forms of relief. Unfortunately for some of these debtors, relief may not be available, as the bankruptcy court's jurisdiction may be more limited after a plan is confirmed.

Bruce A. Markell & John Eggum, *Current Developments in Post-Confirmation Jurisdiction*, S.E. BANKR. L. INST. 2009.

Only after an estate is "fully administered" may the court enter a final decree that closes the case. FED. R. BANKR. PROC. 3022. Once the case is closed, the debtor is no longer a ward of the court, subject to the court's jurisdiction and the strictures of the Code.

The discharge injunction provides powerful protection for the debtor after plan confirmation. A discharge, however, applies only to the liability of the debtor, 11 U.S.C. § 524(e), and only to liability on claims that arose before the confirmation date of the plan. 11 U.S.C. § 1141(d)(1)(A). The reorganized debtor is thus still liable for claims that arise after confirmation. This issue often arises because a claimant might have a latent harm that manifests itself post-confirmation based on a pre-confirmation exposure. This situation creates a potential inequity in distribution between present and future claimants—the present claimants are paid in the bankruptcy, while the future claimants are paid by the reorganized debtor (or not paid at all if the debtor liquidates). The problem of future claimants often arises in mass toxic torts. Bankruptcy has developed a particular procedure for dealing with this problem in the context of asbestos claims; the procedure could be generalized to other claims, but the statutory provision is limited to asbestos claims.

II. ASBESTOS CHANNELING INJUNCTIONS

Asbestos is the name for a group of silicate minerals that were (and sometimes still are) widely used in a range of industrial products in part because of their flame retardant and insulating properties. In particular, asbestos has been used in roofing, insulation, mining, cement, and brake pads. While asbestos has many industrial benefits, it is also incredibly dangerous. Inhalation of asbestos fibers can lead to non-malignant conditions such as asbestosis (a non-cancerous scarring of the lungs that reduces lung capacity) and pleural plaque disease (a non-disabling scarring of the pleural membrane around the lungs). Asbestos exposure can also result in lung cancer and mesothelioma, a cancer of the pleural membrane. The probability and nature of asbestos diseases increases with the length and intensity of exposure. Smoking also compounds the likelihood of lung cancer in those exposed to asbestos. All asbestos diseases have long latency periods.

While the dangers of asbestos have been known in part since antiquity, asbestos was widely used by many different U.S. industries during the twentieth century without adequate worker or consumer protections. As a result, at least 27 million and possibly as many as 100 million workers and consumers were exposed to asbestos. GAO, *Asbestos Injury Compensation, The Role and Administration of Asbestos Trusts*, GAO-11-189, Sept. 2011 at 1. Because of the long latency period, not all of those exposed have or ever will exhibit asbestos diseases.

Despite the long knowledge of health risks related to asbestos, the first successful products liability suit for asbestos exposure resulted in a final judgment only in 1973. *Borel v. Fibreboard Paper Products Corp.*, 493 F.2d 1076 (5th Cir. 1973). *Borel* resulted in a veritable industry of asbestos litigation. From 1982 to 2000, asbestos claims ballooned from 1,000 against 30 companies to 730,000 against 8,400 companies. To date, around 100 of these companies filed for bankruptcy, but prior to 1994, bankruptcy law lacked a formal mechanism to address the future claims from those exposed to asbestos but in whom asbestos diseases were still latent. GAO, *Asbestos Injury Compensation, The Role and Administration of Asbestos Trusts*, GAO-11-189, Sept. 2011, at 2. As a result, companies with potential asbestos liability—especially manufacturers and their insurers—had enormous contingent, unliquidated liability hanging over them, and this debt overhang problem threatened their viability.

Attempts to settle asbestos liability outside of bankruptcy through global class action settlements have been unsuccessful. *See Amchem Prods. v. Windsor*, 521 U.S. 591 (1997) (affirming denial of class certification of a nationwide settlement class of absetos claimants); *Ortiz v. Fibreboard Corp.*, 527 U.S. 815 (1999) (reversing grant of class certification to class of asbestos claimants in a limited fund class action).

In 1982, the Johns-Manville Corporation, the world's largest miner of asbestos, filed for bankruptcy, seeking to deal with the 12,500 suits filed against it and the 50,000-100,000 additional suits it expected based on epidemiological studies. Johns-Manville's bankruptcy pioneered the use of a trust, funded by the reorganized company's securities, coupled with a "channeling injunction" that forced present and future asbestos claimants (represented in the bankruptcy by a "future claims representative") to look solely to the trust for payment.

The result was that Johns-Manville was free from its asbestos liability, but at the cost of the transference of most of the company's stock to the trust for the asbestos claimants. Johns-Manville could thus continue operating without the liability overhang from asbestos and to the extent it succeeded, it would benefit the asbestos claimants via their ownership of the company via the trust. The trust—managed by attorneys for asbestos plaintiffs—was, of course, free to sell the Johns-Manville stock and diversify its holdings. The trust was also responsible for managing payment of the present and future asbestos claims. The procedural fairness of the Johns-Manville trust plus channeling injunction was heavily litigated, but ultimately upheld by the Second Circuit Court of Appeals. *Kane v. Johns-Manville Corp.*, 843 F.2d 636 (2d Cir. 1988). Other cases repeated this structure. *See, e.g., In re UNR Indus., Inc.*, 46 B.R. 671 (Bankr. N.D. Ill. 1985); 71 B.R. 467 (Bankr. N.D. Ill. 1987).

The Johns-Manville trust plus channeling injunction solution became the model then for legislation that became section 524(g) of the Bankruptcy Code in 1994 with an aim at removing doubts about the validity of such channeling injunctions. Today there are around 60 such asbestos trusts. As of the end of 2010, they had paid out around $17.5 billion on 3.3 million claims and had assets of another $18 billion remaining. GAO, *Asbestos Injury Compensation, The Role and Administration of Asbestos Trusts*, GAO-11-189, Sept. 2011.

Section 524(g) contemplates the possibility of a trust plus statutory channeling injunction in connection with a plan. The section 524(g) injunction is of legal action to collect "any claim or demand that, under a plan of reorganization, is to be paid in whole or in part by a trust." 11 U.S.C. § 524(g)(1)(B). The term "demand" is defined in section 524(g)(5) as something that is not a "claim," but "arises out of the same or similar conduct or events that gave rise to the [asbestos] claim." A demand, then, is meant to refer to what would otherwise be a claim, but for arising after the bankruptcy is filed—in other words, latent harms that become patent or "future claims."

In order for a plan to be confirmed with a channeling injunction under section 524(g), the plan must comply with several additional legal requirements. First, the court must find that the debtor is likely to be subject to substantial future demands for payment on asbestos liability, that the amount, number, and timing of the demands cannot be determined, and that failure to deal with these claims under a plan would result in inequitable treatment of present and future claims. 11 U.S.C. § 524(g)(2)(B)(ii)(I)-(III).

Second, the plan must provide for the creation of a trust that assumes the debtor's asbestos liabilities. 11 U.S.C. § 524(g)(2)(B)(i)(I). Third, that trust must be funded with the securities of the debtor issued pursuant to the plan. 11 U.S.C. § 524(g)(2)(B)(i)(II). These securities must constitute a majority of the voting shares of the debtor or the debtor's parent corporation. 11 U.S.C. § 524(g)(2)(B)(i)(III). Fourth, the plan must be accepted by at least 75% of the claims (by number) in a separate class of asbestos claims. 11 U.S.C. § 524(g)(2)(B)(ii)(IV)(bb). Notably, the statute does not require that 75% of all asbestos claimants approve the plan, merely that 75% of *a* class of asbestos claimants approve the plan. It is possible to classify asbestos claimants into multiple classes, with domestic personal injury claims for malignant conditions in a different class than foreign personal injury claims, domestic personal injury claims for non-malignant conditions, environmental liability claims, or guarantor claims.

The 75% requirement, however, means that it is generally impossible to cram down an asbestos plan, unless the one impaired accepting class is an asbestos claim. Thus, a section 524(g) injunction cannot be forced on asbestos claimants without a class of such claimants accepting by a supermajority.

A plan that meets these requirements may be confirmed by the District Court, and may include an injunction that enjoins the entities specified in the plan from "taking legal action for the purpose of directly or indirectly collecting, recovering, or receiving payment or recovery with respect to any claim or demand . . . that is to be paid . . . by [the] trust" created by the plan. 11 U.S.C. § 524(g)(1)(B). (The plan must be confirmed by the District Court because, per 28 U.S.C. § 157, the Bankruptcy Court cannot hear personal injury or wrongful death claims.)

The injunction issued under section 524(g) does not protect just the reorganized debtor from future claims. It may also bar actions against third parties who are alleged to be liable for the asbestos harm caused by the debtor because of affiliation with the debtor, or management, insurance, or financing of the debtor. 11 U.S.C. § 524(g)(4)(ii). Notably, section 524(g) authorizes an injunction to bar claims and demands only against parties with *derivative* liability for the claims against the debtor, such as based on ownership, affiliation, management, insurance, or corporate transactions and financing. Section 524(g) does not authorize a release of *independent* liability. Thus, in Combustion Engineering's bankruptcy, the Third Circuit held that there was no authority under section 524(g) (or alternatively under section 105(a)) for a release of the debtor's subsidiaries that had "independent liability, wholly separate from any liability involving" the debtor. *In re Combustion Eng'g, Inc.*, 391 F.3d 190, 235 (3d Cir. 2004).

In order for the injunction to apply to third parties, however, there are two key requirements. First, future claimants must have been given representation during the bankruptcy process. 11 U.S.C. § 524(g)(4)(B)(i). The requirement of future claimant representation means that the court must appoint a "future claims representative" to advocate for the rights of future claimants who, by definition, are not present.

Second, the court must determine that the injunction is "fair and equitable . . . in light of the benefits provided or to be provided, to such trust on behalf of . . . such third party." 11 U.S.C. § 524(g)(4)(B)(ii). That requirement means that there is a price tag for third parties to benefit from such a channeling injunction. To benefit from the channeling injunction, a third party will have to make an appropriate contribution to the trust. How much will third parties have to pay? There's no black letter rule. In particular, they are not expressly required to put in a majority of their voting shares to the trust, as the debtor is. (Indeed, given that some third parties, such as insurers, could have derivative liability in multiple asbestos bankruptcies, there'd be no way to make such a requirement work.) Typically, a cash payment is accepted. Thus, the section 524(g) injunction does not inherently protect third parties from derivative liability absent particular procedures and findings.

A unique procedural feature of asbestos channeling injunctions is that the hearing takes place jointly before a bankruptcy judge and a district court judge (assuming that the district court has not withdrawn the reference to the bankruptcy court). Bankruptcy judges are forbidden from adjudicating wrongful death and personal injury claims. 28 U.S.C. § 157(b)(5). Those claims must be heard by the district court. Hence, if there are any individual asbestos victims (as there always are), a district court judge must be involved to implement the channeling injunction.

While asbestos bankruptcies are numerically a relatively small number of cases, they are noteworthy for their unique (but potentially replicable) approach to mass toxic torts and for what they show about the possibility of third-party non-debtor releases in Chapter 11 cases. Other mass toxic torts have been addressed outside of bankruptcy through specific legislation, most notably coal workers' pneumoconiosis (black lung disease).

The Federal Coal Mine Health and Safety Act of 1969 created a federal safety regime for coal mining and also established a system of federal payments (at taxpayer expense) to coal miners totally disabled by black lung disease and their survivors. 30 U.S.C. § 922. This is the only federal compensation program for victims of an occupational disease. It applied only to claims filed before 1974. Thereafter, existing coal companies (and their insurers) were once again directly liable for compensation and medical costs of their employees with black lung, but with liability determined administratively, rather than judicially. The Black Lung Benefits Act also provides for a Black Lung Disability Trust Fund to provide compensation to miners whose employers no longer exist, for miners who last worked in a mine before 1970, and in ongoing cases where a mine operator has failed to pay. This trust fund is financed by excise taxes on all existing coal mine operators. In other words, the entire coal industry now either self-insures or uses third-party insurers, but this system is backstopped through an industry-wide mutual insurance scheme operated through the Black Lung Disability Trust Fund, with the excise taxes serving as the insurance premia.

The legislative response to black lung disease is based around a trust fund and the channeling of claims, but it was coupled with federal assumption of most of the historical liabilities—over $29 billion to date, as compared to $16 billion paid by the Trust Fund—and does not utilize the bankruptcy system or result in a change in the ownership of the coal mines. Section 524(g) and the federal black lung legislation both provide models for treatment of mass toxic torts. Notably, however, both are confined to specific types of exposures. For other mass toxic torts, such as silicosis, silicon implants, the Dalkon Shield, etc., there is no pre-set statutory process to address the problem of how to distribute a limited pool of assets when faced with both present claimants and an uncertain number of future claimants with unknown claim amounts.

III. THIRD-PARTY RELEASES

Section 524(g) provides explicit statutory authority for enjoining suits against non-debtors, conditioned upon the third parties having made a fair and equitable contribution to the plan and future claimants having been adequately represented. Sometimes, bankruptcy plans will include provisions releasing non-debtors from liability to creditors and/or enjoining suits against these non-debtors. While releases and injunctions achieve much the same ends and are often used together as belt and suspenders, they are technically different. A release relieves the non-debtor from liability on claims. An injunction enjoins suits against the non-debtor. A released party can still be sued if there is no injunction, although the suit will be unsuccessful.

There is widespread agreement that temporary injunctions to shield third parties during the bankruptcy are permissible in certain circumstances, particularly when there is an "identity of interests between the debtor and the third party, usually an indemnity relationship, such that a suit against the non-debtor is, in essence, a suit against the debtor or will deplete the assets of the estate." *Class Five Nev. Claimants v. Dow Corning Corp. (In re Dow Corning Corp.)*, 280 F.3d 648, 658 (6th Cir. 2002). We have already seen this in Chapter 11 in *In re A.H. Robins Co., Inc.*, 880 F.2d 694 (4th Cir. 1989), where the court enjoined suits against the debtor's liability insurer during the bankruptcy under the automatic stay and section 105(a) of the Bankruptcy Code.

Permanent third-party releases and injunctions are more controversial and push against the jurisdictional limits of the bankruptcy court. Third-party releases and injunctions appear in bankruptcy plans, settlements, and DIP financing orders relieving variously insiders, affiliates, liability insurers, guarantors, and DIP or exit financiers from liability. While they are often a feature of plans in mass tort cases, they appear in non-mass tort cases as well.

The Bankruptcy Code neither expressly authorizes nor expressly prohibits third-party releases and injunctions. Section 524(g) expressly authorizes such injunctions in one situation, lending itself to an *expressio unius est exclusio alterius* interpretation, and section 524(e) provides that "discharge of a debt of the debtor does not affect the liability of any other entity on, or the property of any other entity for, such debt," which might be read as indicating that only the debtor is discharged.

On the other hand, section 524(e)'s phrasing is such that it refers only to the effect of discharge of a debt of the debtor, which is not the same as stating the effect of a separate plan provision or a settlement or financing order. Moreover, section 105(a) is often read as a broad authorization of any provisions that are not expressly prohibited, and section 1123(b)(6) provides that a plan may "include any other appropriate provision not inconsistent with the applicable provisions of this title."

Non-debtor releases and injunctions have been the subject of much disagreement between circuits and the issue remains unresolved by the Supreme Court.

In re Airadigm Communications, Inc.
519 F.3d 640 (7th Cir. 2008)

FLAUM, Circuit Judge.

Debtor-appellant, Airadigm Communications, Inc. is a cellular-service provider. In 1996, it successfully bid for fifteen personal communications services ("PCS") licenses [for large parts of Wisconsin, Iowa, and small parts of Illinois, Upper Peninsula Michigan, and Minnesota] as part of an FCC auction and opted to pay off the licenses under an installment plan set up by the FCC. For Airadigm, however, the airwaves were too turbulent, and by 1999 it had filed for Chapter 11 bankruptcy. Almost immediately, the FCC cancelled Airadigm's PCS licenses and filed a proof of claim in bankruptcy court for the remaining amounts owed under the installment plan. . . . In nearly identical circumstances, the FCC had cancelled [telecom licenses held by NextWave] after it had filed for bankruptcy. [In 2003, the Supreme Court held in *FCC v. NextWave Personal Communiciations, Inc.*, 537 U.S. 293 (2003),] that this action violated the bankruptcy code and set aside the FCC's decision [regarding NextWave]. After its own bankruptcy in 1999, Airadigm had filed a petition before the FCC seeking to reinstate its cancelled licenses. On August 8, 2003, the FCC denied this petition as moot, reasoning that, in light of *NextWave*, its cancellation of the licenses had been "ineffective." Airadigm thus had its licenses back as though they had never been cancelled.

Airadigm filed a second Chapter-11 petition in May 2006 to tie up the loose ends from the fairly significant legal developments that had come about since its first reorganization.

. . .

[Airadigm's 1999 bankruptcy] reorganization proceeded under the assumption that the FCC had properly cancelled the [PCS] licenses. The plan provided that the FCC had an allowed claim of $64.2 million and laid out several contingencies should the FCC reinstate the licenses. The reorganization hinged on financing by a third party, Telephone and Data Systems ("TDS"). Should the FCC reinstate the licenses by February 2001, TDS would pay the FCC's claim in full. If the FCC did not reinstate the licenses by February 2001, but did so by June 2002, TDS had the option of paying off the claim, but was not obligated to do so. But if the FCC never reinstated the licenses or "fail[ed] to act in a timely manner," the plan provided that TDS would obtain all of Airadigm's assets except the licenses.

. . .

Ultimately, on October 31, 2006, the bankruptcy court approved a second plan of reorganization, to which the FCC [objected]. . . .

. . .

[One of the FCC's objections] went to a [plan] provision that released the third-party financier, TDS, from liability for "any act or omission arising out of or in connection with the . . . confirmation of this Plan . . . except for willful misconduct." Airadigm owed TDS over $188 million in secured claims, debt that Airadigm would somehow have to finance [upon confirmation of the plan through other lenders] if TDS were not involved in the reorganization. In the bankruptcy court's estimate, there was "adequate" proof that TDS would not go forward [with the exit financing] without the limitation on liability ultimately contained in the plan. The court held that the release was reasonable given both TDS's centrality to the reorganization and the potential for liability should TDS engage in "willful misconduct."

The plan, as is relevant, states "[e]xcept as expressly provided . . . [TDS shall not] have or incur any liability to . . . any holder of any Claim . . . for any act or omission arising out of or in connection with the Case, the confirmation of this Plan, the consummation of this Plan, or the administration of this Plan or property to be distributed under this Plan, except for willful misconduct." The FCC argues that this violates the Bankruptcy Code and was therefore improper. For the reasons set out below, we disagree.

The question whether a bankruptcy court can release a non-debtor from creditor liability over the objections of the creditor is one of first impression in this circuit. *See In re Specialty Equipment Co.*, 3 F.3d 1043, 1046-47 (7th Cir. 1993) (approving of consensual non-debtor releases); *see also Union Carbide Corp. v. Newboles*, 686 F.2d 593, 595 (7th Cir. 1982) (holding under previous version of bankruptcy code that such releases are improper). And the circuits that have addressed the matter have set out a variety of approaches. Some have held that a non-consensual release of liability violates the Bankruptcy Code and is thus beyond the power of the bankruptcy court. *See In re Lowenschuss*, 67 F.3d 1394, 1401 (9th Cir. 1995); *In re Western Real Estate*, 922 F.2d 592, 600 (10th Cir. 1990). Others permit the releases but have splintered on the governing standard. *See, e.g., Deutsche Bank AG v. Metromedia Fiber Network, Inc.*, 416 F.3d 136, 142 (2d Cir. 2005) (permitting release if it is "important" to reorganization); *Gillman v. Continental Airlines (In re Continental Airlines)*, 203 F.3d 203, 214 (3d Cir.

2000); *In re A.H. Robins Co.*, 880 F.2d 694, 701-02 (4th Cir. 1989); *In re Dow Corning Corp.*, 280 F.3d 648, 658 (6th Cir. 2002) (setting out a seven-factor balancing test).

The nub of the circuits' disagreement concerns two interrelated questions, one of which we have already resolved and another that we answer here. The first is whether § 524(e) of the bankruptcy code bars a bankruptcy court from releasing non-debtors from liability to a creditor without the creditor's consent. *See, e.g.*, *Lowenschuss*, 67 F.3d at 1401 (yes); *Deutsche Bank AG*, 416 F.3d at 142 (no). Section 524(e) provides that the "discharge of a debt of the debtor does not affect the liability of another entity on, or the property of any other entity for, such debt." 11 U.S.C. § 524(e). The natural reading of this provision does not foreclose a third-party release from a creditor's claims. *Specialty Equipment*, 3 F.2d at 1047. Section 524(e) is a saving clause; it limits the operation of other parts of the bankruptcy code and preserves rights that might otherwise be construed as lost after the reorganization. *Id.* Thus, for example, because of § 524, a creditor can still seek to collect a debt from a co-debtor who did not participate in the reorganization—even if that debt was discharged as to the debtor in the plan. *Compare* 11 U.S.C. § 524(a)(2) *with* 11 U.S.C. § 524(e). Or a third party could proceed against the debtor's insurer or guarantor for liabilities incurred by the debtor even if the debtor cannot be held liable.

In any event, § 524(e) does not purport to limit the bankruptcy court's powers to release a non-debtor from a creditor's claims. If Congress meant to include such a limit, it would have used the mandatory terms "shall" or "will" rather than the definitional term "does." And it would have omitted the prepositional phrase "on, or . . . for, such debt," ensuring that the "discharge of a debt of the debtor *shall* not affect the liability of another entity"—whether related to a debt or not. *See* 11 U.S.C. § 34 (repealed Oct. 1, 1979) ("The liability of a person who is a co-debtor with, or guarantor or in any manner a surety for, a bankrupt shall not be altered by the discharge of such bankrupt.") (prior version of § 524(e)). Also, where Congress has limited the powers of the bankruptcy court, it has done so clearly—for example, by expressly limiting the court's power, *see* 11 U.S.C. § 105(b) ("[A] court may not appoint a receiver in a case under this title"), or by creating requirements for plan confirmation, *see, e.g.*, 11 U.S.C. § 1129(a) ("The court shall confirm a plan only if the following requirements are met. . . ."). As a result, for the reasons set out in *Specialty Equipment*, § 524(e) does not bar a non-consensual third-party release from liability.

The second related question dividing the circuits is whether Congress affirmatively gave the bankruptcy court the power to release third parties from a creditor's claims without the creditor's consent, even if § 524(e) does not expressly preclude the releases. A bankruptcy court "appl[ies] the principles and rules of equity jurisprudence," *Pepper v. Litton*, 308 U.S. 295, 304 (1939), and its equitable powers are traditionally broad, *United States v. Energy Resources Co., Inc.*, 495 U.S. 545, 549 (1990). Section 105(a) codifies this understanding of the bankruptcy court's powers by giving it the authority to effect any "necessary or appropriate" order to carry out the provisions of the bankruptcy code. *Id.* at 549; 11 U.S.C. § 105(a). And a bankruptcy court is also able to exercise these broad equitable powers within the plans of reorganization themselves. Section 1123(b)(6) permits a court to "include any other appropriate provision not inconsistent with the applicable provisions of this title." 11 U.S.C. § 1123(b)(6). In light of these provisions, we hold that this "residual authority" permits the bankruptcy court to release third parties from liability to participating creditors if the release is "appropriate" and not inconsistent with any provision of the bankruptcy code.

In this case, the bankruptcy court did not exceed its authority in granting the limitation on TDS's liability. Ultimately, whether a release is "appropriate" for the reorganization is fact intensive and depends on the nature of the reorganization. Given the facts of this case, we are satisfied that the release was necessary for the reorganization and appropriately tailored. First, the limitation itself is narrow: it applies only to claims "arising out of or in connection with" the reorganization itself and does not include "willful misconduct." *See Deutsche Bank*, 416 F.2d at 142 (noting that "potential for abuse is heightened when releases afford blanket immunity"). This is not "blanket immunity" for all times, all transgressions, and all omissions. Nor does the immunity affect matters beyond the jurisdiction of the bankruptcy court or unrelated to the reorganization itself. *See* 28 U.S.C. § 157(b); *Cf. In re Johns-Manville Corp.*, 517 F.3d 52 (2d Cir. 2008). Thus, should TDS have recklessly committed some wrong during the 2000 or 2006 proceedings, it would still be liable to the FCC or any other third party. Second, the limitation is subject to the other provisions of the plan, including one that expressly preserves the FCC's regulatory powers with respect to the licenses. Therefore, TDS cannot use this limitation as a way of skirting the FCC's regulations regarding the use, possession, or transfer of the licenses. Third, the bankruptcy court found "adequate" evidence that TDS required this limitation before it would provide the requisite financing, which was itself essential to the reorganization. *See Deutsche Bank*, 416 F.3d at 143. Airadigm owes TDS $188,264,000 for its secured claims, and it owes the FCC another $33 million in secured claims for the licenses. As the bankruptcy court found, without TDS's involvement, Airadigm would be on the hook for over $221 million in debt—an amount that some other would-be [exit] financier would not likely pay considering Airadigm's financial situation. Absent TDS's involvement, the reorganization simply would not have occurred. Given how narrow the limitation is and how essential TDS was for the reorganization, the release is "appropriate" and thus within the bankruptcy court's powers.

IV. FINALITY

The fundamental concept of bankruptcy is that it provides a single forum for determining the allocation of the debtor's assets, including its going-concern value. The allocation is done through a negotiated process that occurs pursuant to a disclosure regime under section 1125, the mandatory legal findings under sections 1129 and 1124, and a stakeholder vote by classes under sections 1122 and 1126. In order for this allocation process to work, it is first necessary to marshal all of the debtor's assets into the estate under sections 541 and 542 of the Bankruptcy Code and freeze all attempts to collect from the debtor or its assets outside of bankruptcy under section 362. Sections 541, 542, and 362 work together to ensure that the bankruptcy process all plays out in one forum.

Equally critical for bankruptcy process to work, however, is that it must be final. If parties are able to relitigate the allocation of value outside of the bankruptcy or to sit out the bankruptcy and then litigate in a different forum, the bankruptcy process will not work, and the race to the courthouse will reappear. Indeed, even within the bankruptcy process, there is limited ability to appeal some of the most important orders in the case, such as the DIP financing order and asset sale orders, because of detrimental reliance concerns. 11 U.S.C. § 363(m) (sales); § 364(e) (DIP financing). *But see* 11 U.S.C. § 502(j) (reconsideration of claims allowance decisions). Similarly, most valuation opinions are effectively unappealable because of their fact-intensive nature.

It is possible to appeal a confirmation order before it becomes effective, and sometimes the effective date will be stayed pending appeal. Once a plan becomes effective, however, and assets of the estate begin to be distributed, it becomes much more difficult to challenge or change the bankruptcy outcome. In particular, the doctrine of equitable mootness may be applied to dismiss an appeal "when, even though effective relief could conceivably be fashioned, implementation of that relief would be inequitable." *In re Chateaugay Corp.*, 988 F.2d 322, 325 (2d Cir. 1993). The term "equitable mootness" is somewhat misleading. As the Third Circuit has observed, "'Equitably moot' bankruptcy appeals are not necessarily 'moot' in the constitutional sense: they may persist in very live dispute between adverse parties . . . the term "prudential forbearance" more accurately reflects the decision to decline hearing the merits of an appeal because of its feared consequences should a bankruptcy court's decision approving plan confirmation be reversed." *In re Tribune Media Co.*, 799 F.3d 272, 277 n.3 (3d Cir. 2015). The Second Circuit has explained that:

> [e]quitable mootness is a prudential doctrine that is invoked to avoid disturbing a reorganization plan once implemented. *See, e.g., In re UNR Indus.*, 20 F.3d 766, 769 (7th Cir. 1994) ("There is a big difference between *inability* to alter the outcome (real mootness) and *unwillingness* to alter the outcome ('equitable mootness')."); *see also MAC Panel Co. v. Va. Panel Corp.*, 283 F.3d 622, 625 (4th Cir. 2002) ("Equitable mootness is a pragmatic principle, grounded in the notion that, with the passage of time after a judgment in equity and implementation of that judgment, effective relief on appeal becomes impractical, imprudent, and therefore inequitable."); *In re Envirodyne Indus.*, 29 F.3d 301, 304 (7th Cir. 1994) (defining the doctrine as "merely an application of the age-old principle that in formulating equitable relief a court must consider the effects of the relief on innocent third parties").

Deutsche Bank AG, London Branch v. Metromedia Fiber Network, Inc. (In re Metromedia Fiber Network, Inc.), 416 F.3d 136, 143-145 (2d Cir. N.Y. 2005). The equitable mootness doctrine was originally intended to protect parties that relied on a plan becoming effective—buyers, financiers, and recipients of distributions under the plan. Finality facilitates reorganizations by encouraging post-petition investment in the debtor. As one judge has observed:

> encouraging reliance on bankruptcy confirmation orders is critical to facilitating complex reorganizations. Once a third party . . . invests to improve the debtors' capital, to the benefit of creditors and debtors alike, it is much more difficult for it to walk away

if the terms of its bargain are altered on appeal. The rule the majority endorses ignores the realities of the marketplace, and creates strong incentives for investors to delay funding improvements until after the appeal is completed, which may take years. It has already taken approximately three years since [a new investor, SWVP,] funded the plan in this case. Had SWVP waited to fund improvements, the Debtors' hotels would still be depreciating in value, and perhaps might even have been abandoned for want of funding. This would have negatively impacted the Lender by decreasing the value of its collateral and impeding, or terminating, the ability of the Debtors to generate cash flow and service their debt. Worse, the majority approach discourages third parties from agreeing to make these kinds of post-confirmation investments in the first instance. This is likely to detrimentally impact both creditors and debtors by decreasing the value of debtors' estates *ex ante* and making it more difficult to facilitate workable reorganizations. . . . Once this plan was confirmed, and once the Lender's request for a stay was denied, the very success of the reorganization depended on SWVP promptly funding improvements in reliance on the confirmation order. Reliance should be encouraged here, not discouraged.

JPMCC 2007-C1 Grasslawn Lodging, LLC v. Transwest Resort Props. (*In re Transwest Resort Props.*), 801 F.3d 1161 (9th Cir. 2015) (Smith, J. dissenting). As a practical matter, however, equitable mootness is often used as a weaponized doctrine, a sword not a shield, deliberately used to foreclose appeals by making plans become effective as soon as possible after confirmation. The following case illustrates how the doctrine is applied.

Tribune Media Co. v. Aurelius Capital Mgmt., L.P.

799 F.3d 272 (3d Cir. 2015)

AMBRO, Circuit Judge

Aurelius Capital Management, L.P. ("Aurelius"), along with the Law Debenture Trust Company of New York and Deutsche Bank Trust Company Americas (the "Trustees"), appeal the District Court's dismissal as equitably moot of their appeals from the Bankruptcy Court's order confirming Tribune's Chapter 11 plan of reorganization. We agree with the District Court that Aurelius's appeal, which seeks to undo the crucial component of the now consummated plan, should be deemed moot. However, we reverse and remand with respect to the Trustees. They seek disgorgement from other creditors of $30 million that the Trustees believe they are contractually entitled to receive. As the relief the Trustees request would neither jeopardize the $7.5 billion plan of reorganization nor harm third parties who have justifiably relied on plan confirmation, their appeal is not equitably moot.

I. FACTS AND PROCEDURAL HISTORY

In December 2007, the Tribune Company (which published the *Chicago Tribune* and the *Los Angeles Times* and held many other properties) was facing a challenging business climate. Sensing an opportunity, Sam Zell, a wealthy real estate investor, orchestrated a leveraged buy-out ("LBO"), a transaction by which a purchaser (in this case, an entity controlled by Zell and, for convenience, referred to by that name in this opinion) acquires an entity using debt secured by assets of the acquired entity. Before the LBO, Tribune had a market capitalization of approximately $8 billion and about $5 billion in debt.

The LBO was taken in two steps: Zell made a tender offer to obtain more than half of Tribune's shares at Step One, followed by a purchase of all remaining shares at Step Two. In this LBO, as is typical, Zell obtained financing (called here the "LBO debt") to purchase Tribune secured by Tribune's assets, meaning that Zell had nothing at risk. The transaction took Tribune private and saddled the company with an additional $8 billion of debt. Moreover, as a part of the sale, Tribune's subsidiaries guaranteed the LBO debt. The holders of the debt that Tribune carried before Zell took it over (the "pre-LBO debt") had recourse only against Tribune, not against the subsidiaries. Thus the LBO debt, guaranteed by solvent subsidiaries, had "structural seniority" over the pre-LBO debt.

Unsurprisingly, Tribune, in a declining industry with a precarious balance sheet, eventually sought bankruptcy protection. It filed under Chapter 11 in December 2008, and at some later point Aurelius, a hedge fund specializing in distressed debt, bought $2 billion of the pre-LBO debt and became an active participant in the bankruptcy process. (We do not know how much Aurelius paid for this debt.)

Ten days after the filing, the U.S. Trustee appointed the Official Committee of Unsecured Creditors (the "Committee"), which obtained permission to pursue various causes of action (e.g., breach of fiduciary duty and fraudulent conveyance) on behalf of the estate against the LBO lenders, directors and officers of old Tribune, Zell, and others (collectively called the "LBO-Related Causes of Action," see In re Tribune Co., 464 B.R. 126, 136 n.7 (Bankr. D. Del. 2011)). As the Bankruptcy Court put it, "[f]rom the outset . . . the major constituents understood that the investigation and resolution of the LBO-Related Causes of Action would be a central issue in the formulation of a plan of reorganization." Id. at 142.

Various groups of stakeholders proposed plans of reorganization; the important ones for the purposes of this appeal are Aurelius's (the "Noteholder Plan") and one sponsored by the Debtor, the Committee, and certain senior lenders, called the "DCL Plan" (for Debtor/Committee/Lender) or simply the "Plan." The primary difference between the Noteholder and the DCL Plans was that the proponents of the former (the "Noteholders") wanted to litigate the LBO-Related Causes of Action while the DCL Plan proposed to settle them.

Kenneth Klee, one of the principal drafters of the Bankruptcy Code of 1978, was appointed the examiner in this case, and he valued the various causes of action to help the parties settle them. Professor Klee concluded that whether Step One left Tribune insolvent (and was thus constructively fraudulent) was a "very close call" if Step Two debt was included for the purposes of this calculation. Id. at 159. He further concluded that a court was "somewhat likely" to find intentional fraud and "highly likely" to find constructive fraud at Step Two. Id. He also valued the recoveries to Aurelius's and the Trustees' classes of debt under the various litigation scenarios and concluded that the DCL Plan settlement offered more money ($432 million) than all six possible litigation outcomes except full avoidance of the LBO transactions, which would have afforded the pre-LBO lenders $1.3 billion. *Id.* at 161. Given these findings for both steps of the LBO, full recovery was a possibility.

The DCL Plan restructured Tribune's debt, settled many of the LBO-Related Causes of Action for $369 million, and assigned other claims to a litigation trust that would continue to pursue them and pay out any proceeds according to a waterfall structure whereby the pre-LBO lenders stand to receive the first $90 million and 65% of the Trust's recoveries over $110 million (this aspect of the Plan we refer to as the "Settlement"). Aurelius objected because it believes the LBO-Related Causes of Action are worth far more than the examiner or Bankruptcy Court thought and that it can get a great deal more money in litigation than it got under the Settlement. The Bankruptcy Court's opinion on confirmation, thoroughly done by Judge Kevin Carey, discussed the parties' disagreement at length and ultimately concluded that it was "uncertain" that litigation would result in full avoidance of the LBO. *Id.* at 174. And full avoidance was the only result the Bankruptcy Court's opinion suggests could plausibly result in greater recovery than the Settlement. *See id.* at 161 (citing examiner's opinion that only full avoidance could exceed settlement value); 174 (rejecting contrary expert opinions). Thus the Court held that the Settlement was reasonable, and, on July 23, 2012, the DCL Plan was confirmed over Aurelius's objection.

Aurelius promptly moved for a stay pending appeal under Bankruptcy Rule 8007. The Bankruptcy Court held a hearing on the motion at which it considered whether to issue a stay and, if so, whether to condition it on a bond. Aurelius opposed posting a bond in any amount. The Court stayed its confirmation order, but it also considered how much an unsuccessful appeal by Aurelius would cost Tribune. As a result of this valuation, the Court conditioned its stay on Aurelius's posting a $1.5 billion bond to indemnify Tribune against the estimated costs associated with staying the order for the likely time to appeal. *In re Tribune Co.*, 477 B.R. 465, 482 (Bankr. D. Del. 2012).

With the threat of equitable mootness looming, Aurelius and the Trustees filed emergency motions to vacate the bond requirement and to expedite their appeals. The District Court, however, denied the motions and ordered that the briefing schedule for these appeals would be the same as for other appealing parties (who are not before us). Aurelius appealed the denial of the motions related to the bond requirement, but we dismissed the appeal for want of appellate jurisdiction (the denials were not final orders). Aurelius objected that the amount of the bond was prohibitively high, but it has never argued to any court that a lower amount would be reasonable; rather, it has consistently tried to eliminate the bond requirement altogether.

The appeals were fully briefed in the District Court on October 11, 2012 . . . and the Plan was consummated on December 31[, 2012]. On January 18, 2013, Tribune moved to dismiss the appeals as equitably moot. About 18 months later, the District Court granted that motion.

As all agreed, the plan was substantially consummated, and Tribune persuaded the District Court that it could not effectively afford relief without causing undue harm either to reorganized Tribune or to its investors. Aurelius appeals, arguing that the case is not equitably moot and that the Settlement was unreasonably low. The fund seeks modification of the confirmation order to reinstate the LBO-Related Causes of Action that the Settlement resolved so that the claims can be fully litigated or re-settled.

The Trustees also appeal. They represent certain pre-LBO debt treated as "Class 1E creditors" in the Plan. They argue that they had subordination agreements with the holders of two series of pre-LBO notes Tribune issued, called the PHONES Notes and the EGI Notes, worth a total of about $30 million. According to the subordination agreements, if Tribune went bankrupt, any recovery by the PHONES and EGI Notes would be payable to the Class 1E holders. However, the Plan provides that any recovery from those Notes will be distributed *pro rata* between Class 1E and Class 1F. The latter has about 700 creditors in it, the majority of whom "are individuals and small-business trade creditors." *In re Tribune Co.*, Nos. 12-cv-1072 *et al.*, 2014 U.S. Dist. LEXIS 82782, 2014 WL 2797042, at *6 (D. Del. June 18, 2014). Further complicating the intercreditor dispute is that under the Plan Class 1F members were allowed to choose one of two payment options: either they could receive a lump sum at the time of their election or they could participate in the Plan's litigation trust (the latter holding out a potentially greater, but more uncertain, recovery). The Trustees contend that the Plan gives Class 1F $30 million dollars that should go to Class 1E, and they propose several ways in which Class 1E could recover that money without fatally unravelling the Plan.

We have jurisdiction under 28 U.S.C. §§ 158(d) and 1291. We review the Court's equitable mootness determination for abuse of discretion.

II. DISCUSSION

A. The Doctrine of Equitable Mootness

"Equitable mootness" is a narrow doctrine by which an appellate court deems it prudent for practical reasons to forbear deciding an appeal when to grant the relief requested will undermine the finality and reliability of consummated plans of reorganization. The party seeking to invoke the doctrine bears the burden of overcoming the strong presumption that appeals from confirmation orders of reorganization plans—even those not only approved by confirmation but implemented thereafter (called "substantial consummation" or simply "consummation")—need to be decided. *In re SemCrude, L.P.*, 728 F.3d 314, 321 (3d Cir. 2013). Unless we can readily resolve the merits of an appeal against the appealing party, our starting point is the relief an appellant specifically asks for. And even "when a court applies the doctrine of equitable mootness, it does so with a scalpel rather than an axe. To that end, a court may fashion whatever relief is practicable instead of declining review simply because full relief is not available." *In re Blast Energy Servs., Inc.*, 593 F.3d 418, 425 (5th Cir. 2010).

We first recognized the doctrine of equitable mootness in *In re Continental Airlines*, 91 F.3d 553 (3d Cir. 1996) (*en banc*). . . . We explicitly held that it was the law of our Circuit but did not lay down any particularly clear guidance on how to decide whether an appeal was moot. Instead, the majority opinion noted certain factors theretofore considered in making a mootness call:

> Factors that have been considered by courts in determining whether it would be equitable or prudential to reach the merits of a bankruptcy appeal include (1) whether the reorganization plan has been substantially consummated, (2) whether a stay has been obtained, (3) whether the relief requested would affect the rights of parties not before the court, (4) whether the relief requested would affect the success of the plan, and (5) the public policy of affording finality to bankruptcy judgments.

Id. at 560 (citation omitted). This statement reveals that the doctrine was then, as far as our Court was concerned, in its infancy. Note, for example, that we listed "[f]actors that have been considered by courts" without specifying whether those factors are entitled to equal weight or whether any is necessary or sufficient. *Id.* Over the years, our precedential opinions have refined the doctrine to its current, more determinate state. As we recently put it,

> equitable mootness . . . proceed[s] in two analytical steps: (1) whether a confirmed plan has been substantially consummated; and (2) if so, whether granting the relief requested in the appeal will (a) fatally scramble the plan and/or (b) significantly harm third parties who have justifiably relied on plan confirmation.

SemCrude, 728 F.3d at 321.

This two-step inquiry reduces uncertainty from the factors of *Continental*, and this appeal reflects the importance of *SemCrude*'s step (2): in cases where relief would *neither* fatally scramble the plan *nor* significantly harm the interests of third parties who have justifiably relied on plan confirmation, there is no reason to dismiss as equitably moot an appeal of a confirmation order for a plan now substantially consummated. For example, reliance on consummation of a plan would not be justified if a third party obtained a benefit that was inconsistent with a contract, statute, or judgment, as any benefit from such an error would result in "ill-gotten gains."

While courts and counsel readily understand when granting relief on appeal would unravel a plan both confirmed and consummated, who are the "third parties" that equitable mootness is meant to protect? *Continental* singled out investors as the "particular" beneficiaries of equitable mootness, 91 F.3d at 562, while *SemCrude* discussed the interests of lenders, customers, and suppliers. 728 F.3d at 325. Likewise, *Philadelphia Newspapers* considered the interests of "other creditors" who were not equity investors. 690 F.3d 161, 171 (3d Cir. 2012). These cases teach that, although parties other than equity investors may rely on plan consummation and thus claim protection in the form of equitable mootness, they may not "merit the same 'outside investor' status as" those who make equity investments in a reorganized entity.

One reason some third parties have reliance interests more worthy of protection than others is that we want to encourage behavior (like investment in a reorganized entity) that contributes to a successful reorganization. *See Continental*, 91 F.3d at 564 ("[T]here was an integral nexus between the investment [by the parties urging mootness] and the success of the Plan."); *see also id.* at 563 ("[T]he Eastern claims were crucial to the willingness of the Investors to consummate the Financing Transaction." (internal quotation marks omitted)).

Also, in appropriate circumstances we further the free flow of commerce—a chief concern of commercial bankruptcy—when we decline to disturb "complex transactions undertaken after the Plan was consummated" that would be most difficult to unravel. *Charter*, 691 F.3d at 485 ("The Allen Settlement was the product of an intense multi-party negotiation, and removing a critical piece of the Allen Settlement—such as Allen's compensation and the third-party releases—would impact other terms of the agreement and throw into doubt the viability of the entire Plan."); *see also id.* at 486 ("[T]he third-party releases were critical to the bargain that allowed Charter to successfully restructure[,] and . . . undoing them, as the plaintiffs urge, would cut the heart out of the reorganization.").

At the same time, if funds can be recovered from third parties without a plan coming apart, it weighs heavily against barring an appeal as equitably moot, both in our Court and other circuits. *See In re PWS Holding Corp.*, 228 F.3d 224, 236-37 (3d Cir. 2000) (appeal not moot where appellant "seeks to invalidate releases that affect the rights and liabilities of third parties [and t]he plan has been substantially consummated, but . . . the plan could go forward even if the releases were struck"); *In re Paige*, 584 F.3d 1327, 1342 (10th Cir. 2009) ("The substantial consummation of a bankruptcy plan may make providing relief difficult, and may raise concerns about fairness to third parties, but '[c]ourts can and do order divestiture or damages in' situations where business deals or bankruptcy plans have been wrongly consummated." (quoting *In re Res. Tech. Corp.*, 430 F.3d 884, 886-87 (7th Cir. 2005) (alteration in *Paige*))). We agree with the Second Circuit that the disgorgement of "ill-gotten gains" is proper assuming that the disgorgement otherwise leaves a plan of reorganization not in tatters. *In re Charter Commc'ns, Inc.*, 691 F.3d 476, 484 (2d Cir. 2012).

In addition to the third parties (particularly investors) identified in our cases, equitable mootness properly applied benefits the estate, *In re Zenith Elecs. Corp.*, 329 F.3d 338, 346 (3d Cir. 2003), and the reorganized entity, *id.* at 344. All these players have a common interest in the finality of a plan: the estate because it can wind up; the reorganized entity because it can begin to do business without court supervision and can seek funding in the capital markets without the cloud of bankruptcy; investors because a reorganized entity will command a higher and more stable market value outside of bankruptcy; lenders because they can collect interest and principal; customers in certain industries who need parts or services; and other constituents for different context-specific reasons that may boil down to it is easier to do business with an entity outside of bankruptcy. Equitable mootness assures these stakeholders that a plan confirmation order is reliable and that they may make financial decisions based on a reorganized entity's exit from Chapter 11 without fear that an appellate court will wipe out or interfere with their deal.

The theme is that the third parties with interests protected by equitable mootness generally rely on the emergence of a reorganized entity from court supervision. When a successful appeal would not fatally scramble a confirmed and consummated plan, this specific reliance interest most often is not implicated, as the plan stays in place (with manageable modifications possible) and the reorganized entity remains a going concern. For example, the remedy of taking from one class of stakeholders the amount given to them in excess of what the law allows is not apt to be inequitable, as there is little likelihood it will have damaging ripple effects beyond the classes that the redistribution immediately affects. Consistent with our conclusion in *PWS*, 228 F.3d at 236-37, and as the Second Circuit reasoned in *Charter*, 691 F.3d at 484, when taking a payment to which one class is not contractually entitled, and giving it to the party contractually entitled to those funds, would not undermine the basis for other parties' reliance on the finality of confirmation, it makes little sense to deem an appeal equitably moot.

B. Aurelius's Appeal Is Equitably Moot.

Aurelius concedes that the DCL Plan is substantially consummated, but it argues that the relief it seeks would neither scramble that Plan nor harm third parties who have relied on consummation. Aurelius asks us to have the confirmation order modified to reinstate the settled LBO-Related Causes of Action. It argues that it should be allowed to pursue these claims or settle them on more favorable terms and that it can obtain relief from reorganized Tribune, from the LBO lenders themselves, or by redistributing the LBO lenders' future recovery from the litigation trust.

Aurelius's argument that the relief it ultimately seeks—further recovery on the LBO-Related Causes of Action—can be afforded (at least in part) misses the point of the equitable mootness inquiry. We must also ask whether the *immediate* relief Aurelius seeks, revocation of the Settlement in the DCL Plan, would "fatally scramble the plan and/or . . . significantly harm third parties who have justifiably relied on plan confirmation." *SemCrude*, 728 F.3d at 321. We believe it would do both.

To the first concern (fatal scrambling), the Bankruptcy Court noted the obvious: the Settlement was "a central issue in the formulation of a plan of reorganization." *Tribune*, 464 B.R. at 142. Though it is within the power of an appellate court to order the Settlement severed from the Plan and keep the rest of the Plan in place—thereby not attempting to "unscramble the eggs," *Continental Airlines*, 91 F.3d at 566, or turning a court into a "Humpty Dumpty repairman," *In re Pub. Serv. Co. of New Hampshire*, 963 F.2d 469, 475 (1st Cir. 1992), or any other ovoid metaphor—allowing the relief the appeal seeks would effectively undermine the Settlement (along with the transactions entered in reliance on it) and, as a result, recall the entire Plan for a redo.

Third-party reliance is related here to the problem of scrambling the Plan, as returning to the drawing board would at a minimum drastically diminish the value of new equity's investment. That investment no doubt was in reliance on the Settlement, as indeed was the reliance of those who voted for the Plan. Aurelius proposed a Noteholder Plan that didn't include a settlement of the LBO-Related Causes of Action, and it was overwhelmingly rejected by all but 3 of the 243 creditor classes (the remaining classes were Aurelius', the PHONES Notes', and a third "class in which a single creditor holding a claim of $47 voted in favor of both the DCL Plan and the Noteholder Plan"). Revoking the Settlement would circumvent the bankruptcy process and give Aurelius by judicial fiat what it could not achieve by consensus within Chapter 11 proceedings or, we can't help but add, if it had put up a bond.

On appeal, Aurelius proposes no relief that would not involve reopening the LBO-Related Causes of Action. Allowing those suits would "'knock the props out from under the authorization for every transaction that has taken place,'" thus scrambling this substantially consummated plan and upsetting third parties' reliance on it. *In re Chateaugay Corp.*, 10 F.3d 944, 953 (2d Cir. 1993) (quoting *In re Roberts Farms, Inc.*, 652 F.2d 793, 797 (9th Cir. 1981)). In this context, the District Court did not abuse its discretion in concluding that Aurelius's appeal is equitably moot.

When determining whether the case is equitably moot, we of course must assume Aurelius will prevail on the merits because the idea of equitable mootness is that *even if* Aurelius is correct, it would not be fair to award the relief it seeks. One might argue that holding the appeal moot is therefore by definition *in*equitable: if Aurelius prevails, that means the Bankruptcy Court committed legal error, and it could not be inequitable to correct the Court's mistakes. The reasons to reject this hypothesis are twofold.

First, bankruptcy is concerned primarily with achieving a workable outcome for a diverse array of stakeholders, and the reliable finality of a confirmed and consummated plan allows all interested parties to organize their lives around that fact. *See* Mark J. Roe, *Bankruptcy and Debt: A New Model for Corporate Reorganization*, 83 COLUM. L. REV. 527, 529 (1983) (identifying speed as one of "three principal characteristics desirable for a reorganization mechanism").

Second, and relatedly, an important reason we should forbear from hearing a challenge to the order before us is because of Aurelius's failure to post a bond to obtain a stay pending appeal. Courts may condition stays of plan confirmation orders pending appeal on the posting of a *supersedeas* bond. The purpose of requiring such a "bond in a bankruptcy court is to indemnify the party prevailing in the original action against loss caused by an unsuccessful attempt to reverse the holding of the bankruptcy court." *In re Theatre Holding Corp.*, 22 B.R. 884, 885 (Bankr. S.D.N.Y. 1982). Federal Rule of Civil Procedure 62(d) (made applicable to bankruptcy cases by Bankruptcy Rule 7062) provides for stays pending appeal as of right when a bond is posted in damages actions "or where the judgment is sufficiently comparable to a money judgment so that payment on a supersedeas bond would provide a satisfactory alternative to the appellee." 10 Collier on Bankruptcy ¶7062.06 (16th ed. 2015).

In this case, the Bankruptcy Court carefully calculated the likely damage to the estate of a stay pending an appeal from its confirmation order. In particular, it analyzed the following costs to Tribune and its creditors that a stay would cause: additional professional fees, opportunity costs to creditors who would receive delayed distributions from the DCL Plan or delayed interest and principal payments from reorganized Tribune, and a loss in market value to equity investors caused by the delayed emergence. *Tribune*, 477 B.R. at 480-83. We need not go through the opinion in detail, as Aurelius does not squarely argue that the bond requirement was an abuse of discretion, but we note that the valuation was well-considered and as convincing as the alchemy of valuation in bankruptcy can be.

As a result of its calculations, the Court determined that Aurelius should post a $1.5 billion bond to guarantee that the estate could be indemnified in the case of an unsuccessful appeal. *Id.* at 483. We repeat that Aurelius never challenged the bond amount, instead attempting unsuccessfully to modify the order to remove the bond in its entirety. But given the Bankruptcy Court's findings on the likely substantial loss to Tribune due to an appeal, a *supersedeas* bond in some amount was appropriate. Aurelius's failure to attempt to reduce the bond to a more manageable figure (assuming its representations are correct that it would be unable to finance such a large bond on short notice) leads us to conclude that it effectively chose to risk a finding of equitable mootness and implicitly decided that an appeal with a stay conditioned on any reasonable bond amount was not worth it. This risk-adjusted choice by such a rational actor makes a finding of mootness not unfair, as it appears from the record before us that Aurelius had the opportunity to obtain a stay that would have foreclosed the possibility of a moot-ness finding.[4]

C. The Trustees' Appeal Is Not Equitably Moot.

To reiterate, the Trustees contend that they are beneficiaries of a subordination agreement that guarantees that they will receive any recovery that goes to the holders of the PHONES and EGI Notes ahead of a class of trade and other creditors (Class 1F). This $30 million intercreditor dispute is not equitably moot. Indeed, there is no prudent reason to forbear from deciding the merits of the Trustees' appeal.

Again, it is conceded that the Plan has been substantially consummated. Thus we turn to *SemCrude*'s second question: "whether granting the relief requested in the appeal will (a) fatally scramble the plan and/or (b) significantly harm third parties who have justifiably relied on plan confirmation." 728 F.3d at 321. The answer is no.

The merits question presented by the Trustees' appeal is straightforward: does the Plan unfairly allocate Class 1E's recovery to 1F? If the answer is yes, disgorgement could be ordered against those Class 1F holders who have received more than their fair share, and the Litigation Trust's waterfall can be restructured to make sure that 1E gets its recovery to the exclusion of 1F. There's no chance that this modification would unravel the Plan: the dispute is about whether one of two classes of creditors is entitled to $30 *million* in the context of a $7.5 *billion* reorganization.

Nor, if the Trustees rightly read the subordination agreement, has anyone "justifi-ably relied," *id.*, on the finality of the confirmation order with respect to the $30 mil-lion. It is true that some of the money has been paid out, but it has gone to a readily identifiable set of creditors against whom disgorgement can be ordered, and, assuming the Trustees prevail on the merits, Class 1F members by definition cannot *justifiably* have relied on the payments. The Class 1F payouts are not "ill-gotten," *Charter*, 691 F.3d at 484, in the sense that the members of that class received them as a result of malfeasance, but the Trustees' argument is that the payments were not valid. Although the trade creditors and retirees who make up Class 1F are likely not sophisticated play-ers and may have understandably relied on any payouts they received, any reliance they have placed on the Plan confirmation and implementation—again, assuming the Trustees' argument on the merits is correct—is still not legally justifiable because Class 1F's claim of entitlement to the money is unlawful under the Trustees' interpretation of the relevant contract.

Moreover, disgorgement from Class 1F is not the only possible remedy here (though conceptually it is the most straightforward). On remand, if the Trustees prevail on the merits, the District Court could enjoin future revenue streams of the litigation trust from going to Class 1F until Class 1E is paid in full. To the extent this would result in

---

4. To the extent it could be argued that our approach endangers any low-value appeal in a large case (because the cost of a stay would overwhelm any potential recovery), we note that the lower a potential recovery is, the less likely an appeal is to be equitably moot because courts will be more willing to make minor changes to a plan of reorganization than big ones. *See Phila. Newspapers*, 690 F.3d at 170 (claim worth 1.7% of the price of debtor's assets not equitably moot); *Chateaugay*, 10 F.3d at 953 (claim worth up to 10% of a reorganized debtor's working capital was not equitably moot).

disparate initial distributions to the members of Class 1F who participated in the litigation trust and those who elected all cash distributions, the Court could allow payment of this difference to the Class 1F creditors who elected to participate in the trust first before diverting recoveries to Class 1E, thus effectively revoking the option to choose between an initial all-cash distribution and partial cash distribution plus participation in the litigation trust, as the Trustees suggest. Tribune's only response to this proposal by the Trustees is the unsupported statement that it "would be a logistical nightmare and would result in chaos." Tribune Response at 71 (internal quotation marks omitted). We fail to see the chaos and thus view this as a possible remedial option within the District Court's discretion.

The District Court held in a conclusory fashion that "[h]undreds of individuals and small-business trade creditors . . . were entitled to rely upon the finality of the Confirmation Order," 2014 U.S. Dist. Lexis 82782, 2014 WL 2797042 at *6, but that misses the point of equitable mootness and elevates finality over all other interests. The Plan has arguably deprived one prepetition lender class of $30 million. Requiring Class 1F to pay $30 million to Class 1E if the latter prevails on appeal would not affect Tribune's value and thus not any of its investors (nor would it harm the estate or new Tribune). It would be *unfortunate* from the perspective of the members of Class 1F to require disgorgement, but, if they were never entitled to that money in the first place, it is not *unfair*, and mootness must be fair (equitable in legalese) to be invoked.

Equitable mootness gives limited protection to those who have justifiably relied on the finality of a consummated plan, particularly new equity. No one is arguing that, if the Class 1F creditors lose, the consequences would be any worse than requiring them to forgo a windfall they never should have gotten in the first place. Because we disagree that this class of creditors was entitled to rely on the DCL Plan's finality (once again assuming that the Trustees should prevail on appeal), we hold that the District Court made an error of law and therefore abused its discretion in holding as it did.

. . .

IV. CONCLUSION

Aurelius's appeal is equitably moot: the DCL Plan is consummated; Aurelius spurned the offer of a stay accompanied by a bond; and it would be unfair to Tribune's investors, among others, to allow Aurelius to undo the most important aspect of the overwhelmingly approved Plan. By contrast, the Trustees' appeal is not equitably moot: assuming the Trustees prevail on the merits, Class 1F holders must forgo gains to which they were never entitled. Other third parties will not be harmed, nor is the Plan even remotely called into question. We thus affirm in part, reverse in part, and remand.

The Bankruptcy Code allows plans to be modified post-confirmation, but only if it has not been "substantively consummated," a statutorily defined term. 11 U.S.C. §§ 1101(2), 1127(b). The post-confirmation modification procedure again goes through the bankruptcy forum, but it is not easy. The modified plan must go through solicitation and confirmation procedures as if it were a new plan. 11 U.S.C.

§§ 1127(b)-(c). This means that there needs to be another disclosure statement, vote, and confirmation hearing making the requisite legal findings.

Additionally, the bankruptcy court may revoke its confirmation order, but only in the case of the confirmation order having been procured by fraud. 11 U.S.C. § 1144. Such revocation must occur within 180 days of the confirmation order creating what is effectively a very short statute of limitations. Note that revocation of a confirmation order is different from a confirmation order being overturned on appeal; revocation is done by the bankruptcy court itself, which typically retains broad continuing jurisdiction over the case pursuant to a plan rather than by a Court of Appeals. A confirmation order, of course, can be appealed, and formally the standards are for *de novo* review of questions of law, and substantial error review for questions of fact—which includes valuation determinations, but finality norms are very strong in bankruptcy. Lastly, there is a *res judicata* effect to a bankruptcy plan. If a plan is not timely appealed, it will still bind parties that received notice, even as to inappropriate provisions.

Problem Set 42

(1) Jefferson Tobacco, Inc. just confirmed its Chapter 11 plan. The plan assigned certain litigation claims to a litigation trust, with beneficial interests in the litigation trust distributed to some of Jefferson's pre-petition creditors. The plan also distributed the equity of the reorganized firm to Jefferson's subordinated unsecured noteholders. The plan provided that title to 5,000 acres of South Carolina upcountry tobaccoland would be sold to Rutledge Tobacco, Inc. for $50 million. The plan said nothing regarding the treatment of Jefferson's 20,000 acres of prime Virginia tobaccoland.

    a. Who now owns the 20,000 acres of prime Virginia tobaccoland? 11 U.S.C. § 1141(b).

    b. Pickney Tobacco, Inc., a pre-petition creditor for $10,000 that voted against the Jefferson Tobacco plan, has filed a quiet title action in South Carolina state court claiming that the South Carolina upcountry tobaccoland is actually its property. Madison Tobacco, Inc., which never filed a claim in the Jefferson Tobacco bankruptcy, has intervened in the quiet title action, claiming that it in fact owns the upcountry tobaccoland. What is the status of the South Carolina upcountry tobaccoland? 11 U.S.C. § 1141(a).

    c. What is the status of Jefferson Tobacco's pre-petition stock certificates held by Jefferson's pre-petition CEO? 11 U.S.C. § 1141(d).

(2) Samuel Adams Malting Company confirmed the Chapter 11 plan it proposed two years ago, and the plan went effective 22 months ago. The plan called for Samuel Adams to make periodic payments to Hancock Mercantile on its $40 million first lien debt for five years at an interest rate of 10%. The debt is secured by Adams's equipment and inventory. The plan also called for Samuel Adams to make periodic payments totaling $20 million on a $30 million unsecured debt owed to Knox Heavy Industries. A sudden surge in barley prices has put severe financial strains on Samuel Adams, which

failed to make its last periodic payment. Adams has paid off all of the other creditors receiving distributions under the plan. 11 U.S.C. §§ 362(c), 524(a), 1127, 1141(d).

    a. Is there anything Hancock Mercantile can do?

    b. Is there anything Knox Heavy Industries can do?

    c. Is there anything Adams can do?

    (3) The Franklin Press recently confirmed its Chapter 11 plan. The Franklin Press also owed the United States of America a $15 million False Claims Act judgment and the Commonwealth of Pennsylvania $5 million for unpaid taxes. The plan provided for installment payments of $3 million to the United States and a one-time immediate payment of $100,000 to the Commonwealth. After plan confirmation, the Franklin Press dutifully made its first two installment payments, but the United States Marshal for the Eastern District of Pennsylvania (a federal law enforcement officer) proceeded to levy on the Franklin Press's equipment and inventory on behalf of the United States as creditor. At the same time, the Commonwealth filed a tax lien against the Franklin Press's real estate for $4.9 million. 11 U.S.C. §§ 523(a)(2), 1141(d)(6).

    a. Can the Franklin Press force the Marshal to turn over the property?

    b. Can the Franklin Press avoid the Commonwealth's tax lien?

    (4) Gallatin Distilleries is in Chapter 11 bankruptcy after numerous consumers were sickened or died from ergot poisoning after consuming Gallatin's Old Federalist rye whiskey. While Gallatin issued a recall, Gallatin is concerned that there are many consumers still in possession of Old Federalist who may not be aware of the danger posed by the tainted spirit and who may be harmed by future consumption of contaminated bottles of "Ol' Fed." Gallatin has proposed a plan that would fund a trust with 51% of Gallatin's voting securities and would channel all present and future claims against Gallatin to the trust and enjoin the claimants from seeking recovery from Gallatin. Every class of Gallatin's creditors voted in favor of the plan by overwhelming majorities, including 90% of the class of consumer tort victims. One of the tort victims voting against the plan was Edmund Randolph. After the plan was confirmed, Randolph brought suit against Gallatin Distilleries for damages relating to his ergot poisoning injuries. A year later, Daniel Shays was blinded by the ergot poisoning from consuming an entire bottle of Ol' Fed at a single sitting. Shays has brought suit against Gallatin for his injuries. What is the result of the suits?

    (5) Valley Forge, Inc., a maker of industrial blast furnaces, is in Chapter 11. Valley Forge has significant unliquidated asbestos liability; for years, the firm used asbestos as a flame and heat retardant in its manufacturing process and in its products. Valley Forge has proposed a plan of reorganization. The plan contemplates the creation of a trust funded by 51% of the voting securities of Valley Forge, Inc., with beneficial interests in the trust to be distributed to four classes of asbestos claimants: a mesothelioma class, an asbestosis class, an exposure class, and an environmental damage class. Valley Forge has moved for an injunction in connection with the plan that would channel all of the current and future asbestos claims against Valley Forge to the trust.

    a. If 70% of each of the asbestos-related classes vote for Valley Forge's plan, can the plan and channeling injunction be confirmed? 11 U.S.C. § 524(g)(1)(A).

    b. If the sole member of a class of asbestos environmental damage claims votes for Valley Forge's plan, but all of the other asbestos-related classes vote against the plan, can the plan and channeling injunction be confirmed? 11 U.S.C. § 524(g)(2)(B)(ii)(IV).

   c. Valley Forge has also moved for the injunction to cover its non-debtor parent holding company, non-debtor subsidiaries and affiliates, officers and directors, products liability insurers, pre-petition lenders, and the post-petition purchaser of substantially all of Valley Forge's assets. May the court issue this channeling injunction? 11 U.S.C. §§ 524(e), (g)(4).

   d. Valley Forge's Chapter 11 plan was confirmed with a channeling injunction. After seven years, however, the Valley Forge section 524(g) asbestos trust ran out of money. You've been engaged by the United Steelworkers to represent a number of steelworkers who believe they were harmed by asbestos in Valley Forge products; these workers were unaware until recently that they were exposed to Valley Forge products, and many of have not yet shown any symptoms of asbestosis or mesothelioma. Is there any way for these steelworkers to recover for their harms?

  (6) Hamilton Island Sugar Refineries has just proposed its Chapter 11 plan. The plan includes a proposed release of Hamilton's corporate directors from their liability in pre-petition securities litigation. The litigation was stayed temporarily during the bankruptcy. The officers and directors are all covered by a D&O insurance policy purchased by Hamilton. Hamilton's corporate bylaws also call for Hamilton to indemnify its directors for any non-willful conduct. If the plaintiffs in the securities litigation object, can the plan be confirmed? 11 U.S.C. §§ 105(a), 524(g), 1129(a)(1)-(3).

  (7) Aquarius Industries, a major ship builder, has recently confirmed its Chapter 11 plan, which addressed some $2.5 billion of debt. Under Aquarius's plan, its old shareholders, members of the Capricorn family, contributed $100 million dollars in new capital in exchange for the stock in the reorganized firm. The Capricorn family's continued involvement with Aquarius was generally seen as essential for the reorganized firm's feasibility because Aquarius's shipyards are built on land leased from the Capricorn Family Trust. The Trust has historically leased the land at a nominal rate. The plan also provided for $500 million in exit financing from First Financial Bank, half as a term loan and half as a revolving line of credit. The plan was confirmed on Jan. 1, 2018, via cramdown, and over various objections that it was not proposed in good faith, that it fails to meet the best interest test for one class of creditors, and that it does not comply with absolute priority because of the retention of equity interests by Aquarius's old shareholders without a market test of the shares.

    • Gemini Capital Partners, LLP, a distressed debt investment fund that had invested in Aquarius's unsecured notes, claims that the plan does not meet the best interests test because it does not honor the make-whole clause in the notes. If Gemini is correct, another $20 million should be available for its class. Gemini also argues that the plan does not comply with absolute priority because of the Capricorn family's retained equity interest.

    • Zodiac Bancorp, agent bank for the syndicate of second lien lenders, argues that the interest rate on which it is paid for its secured claim under the plan is improperly low and that the plan is, therefore, not fair and equitable and not proposed in good faith. At the confirmation hearing, Whitman Holt, counsel to Aquarius, stated that the debtors intended to cause the plan promptly to become effective, both to proceed with much needed plant and equipment overhauls to make Aquarius competitive and to moot out any subsequent appeal.

Gemini and Zodiac both filed timely appeals of the plan's confirmation. Gemini moved to stay the plan pending appeal, and offered to post a supersedeas bond of $20 million, but the court indicated that a supersedeas bond of $2.5 billion would be required, which Gemini refused to post. Gemini has appealed the court's conditioning of the stay on the posting of the bond. Zodiac did not move to stay the plan pending appeal, but instead filed a statement with the court that doing so would be futile in light of the bond that would be required. The plan became effective while the appeals were pending.

Upon the effective date of the plan, Aquarius drew down on the revolving line of credit from First Financial to fund its daily operations. Aquarius also used the First Financial term loan plus the new equity contribution to upgrade its plant and undertake long-deferred maintenance. Aquarius also entered into new supply contracts with the orders personally guaranteed by Capricorn family members. Aquarius also entered into a new lease with the Capricorn Family Trust. The lease includes a "key man" provision that terminates the lease if family patriarch Joseph Capricorn or his heirs cease to continue to control at least 51% of Aquarius's voting stock.

When Aquarius argues that Gemini and Zodiac's appeals should be dismissed as equitably moot, what is the likely result?

CHAPTER 43

CONTRACTING AROUND BANKRUPTCY

Not everyone likes the possibility of bankruptcy. When a firm files for bankruptcy, its governance structure significantly changes: The court and creditors gain an important voice and sometimes a veto in the governance of the firm. Moreover, bankruptcy law dictates the way in which the firm's assets and/or future income will be divided: Bankruptcy law recognizes non-bankruptcy law priorities and supplements them with its own priorities both by virtue of statute and by virtue of accelerating the debtor's obligations. While bankruptcy law creates its own distributional rules, it also creates significant uncertainty about distributions. There is little certainty about the timing of and sometimes even the form of distributions. Furthermore, in Chapter 11, the distributional rules only set minimum requirements for treatment of creditors, but treatment above that minimum standard is heavily negotiated. The outcomes of a bankruptcy also depend a good deal upon the exercise of discretion by the trustee or DIP. And because bankruptcy provides a wealth of tools for examining and litigating past dealings with creditors, creditors may find themselves not only facing reduced recoveries, but actual liability.

Not every firm or its creditors would want to be subject to such a mandatory, yet uncertain governance and distribution regime or the possibility of having past dealings reexamined. Accordingly, some firms attempt to opt out of bankruptcy as a way of reducing their cost of financing by providing creditors with the ability to determine *ex ante* what will happen in the event of an insolvency.

Creditors will pay a premium (in terms of offering cheaper financing) to have the control and certainty over bankruptcy outcomes. There may be other creditors, however, who are not part of the contractual deal, which would affect their rights. They may not be happy with removal of the bankruptcy option, which limits a firm's ability to negotiate when it is in distress. Moreover, the firm may attempt to have its cake and eat it, by both capturing the lower cost of financing up front by agreeing to eschew bankruptcy, but then actually filing and taking advantage of bankruptcy relief when doing so is advantageous.

This chapter turns to the question of what is possible in terms of contracting around bankruptcy. To the extent that a firm can credibly present itself as unlikely or incapable of filing for bankruptcy, the dynamics of initial transaction structuring and of out-of-court workouts are fundamentally different. But is it really possible to credibly pre-commit not to file for bankruptcy? This is the Holy Grail of financial transaction design. Many have searched for it, but it is less clear whether any have truly found it.

Anna Gelpern & Adam J. Levitin

Rewriting Frankenstein Contracts: The Workout Prohibition in Residential Mortgage-Backed Securities

82 S. Cal. L. Rev. 1075 (2009)

. . . The quest for immutability in securitization design is consistent with contract theory's prediction that parties may commit to forgo ex post modification in exchange for savings ex ante. It is also consistent with a strain of bankruptcy theory, known as contractual bankruptcy, which predicts that parties to business contracts will seek to opt out of the Bankruptcy Code in favor of contractual ordering of the disposition of an insolvent firm's assets. Advocates of contractual bankruptcy argue that such private ordering is more efficient than the public ordering mandated by Congress. Private contracts can be drafted to reflect the idiosyncratic preferences of particular debtors and creditors as to the relative values of future bankruptcy protection and current cost of credit. The debate over the relative merits of public and private ordering has dominated bankruptcy scholarship for over a quarter century, beginning with [the] "creditors' bargain" theory of bankruptcy.

From the creditors' bargain theory, several proposals for contractual bankruptcy emerged. Early proposals did not advocate contracting out of bankruptcy per se (which was disfavored by the courts), but rather proposed using bankruptcy as a mechanism for enforcing the prebankruptcy, contractually determined priority scheme and for avoiding rent extraction by managers and "out-of-the-money" claimants. Thus, Baird envisioned a reformed Chapter 11 that would be used as a vehicle to conduct going-concern sales of firms free and clear of claims, with the sale proceeds then being divided among creditors according to absolute priority. Variations on the sale method [have been proposed that would add increased] flexibility to the sale process, but all envisioned a mandatory, judicially supervised process that enforced a contractually determined, nonbankruptcy priority system.

[Some scholars have taken] the idea of contractual bankruptcy a step further and proposed removing it from the courts. [Such proposals] merely followed the logic of making Chapter 11 a mandatory sale process. This process would allow creditors to bargain up front for where they would fit in the firm's priority structure, and the outcome would reflect the idiosyncratic preferences of any particular creditor/debtor pair. [Other scholars have] since proposed less drastic contract bankruptcy alternatives that contemplate a substantial degree of private autonomy for handling firm distress. While there are significant differences among various contractual bankruptcy proposals, they all require a degree of rigidity in their contractual design in order to ensure that creditors actually get the benefit of their bargain. This aspect of contractual bankruptcy is particularly stark in the proposals that stress mandatory, automatic implementation and minimize the role of the courts.

Contractual bankruptcy has been criticized on the ground that it fails to consider anything other than efficiency. Furthermore, its central efficiency claim has been called into question. Some scholars have questioned whether contractual bankruptcy would create new inefficiencies from redistribution, offsetting any efficiency gains. Others have asked whether the transaction costs involved in a contractual bankruptcy regime would outweigh the efficiency gains. . . .

Securitization offers a rare natural experiment for the contractual approach. The bankruptcy-remote SPV [(special purpose vehicle)] (the firm) functionally opts out of federal bankruptcy law. The rights of the creditors of the SPV are governed by the [securitization agreement], in particular its tranching and payment-schedule provisions. The senior/subordinate structure of tranching creates an absolute priority regime for the creditors of the SPV. Creditors are free to bargain for the terms of the securities that they buy—different SPVs have different tranching arrangements—and investors are free to purchase the position they wish to have in the SPV's capital structure. Securitization even deals with the problem of involuntary creditors who cannot "bargain": because the SPV is essentially a passive entity that merely holds assets, it is unlikely to incur liability to involuntary creditors. In sum, securitization effectively creates a self-executing contractual bankruptcy regime; this vast market shows that Schwartz was correct when he observed that "bankruptcy contracting would occur if it were permitted."

Securitization's natural experiment in contractual bankruptcy appears to be successful. Firms will securitize only if securitization offers a lower cost of capital than other methods of finance. Securitization will only offer a lower cost of capital than direct debt or equity financing if it offers creditors greater benefits. The very existence of securitization proves its efficiency, at least from the perspective of the firm. Of course, this efficiency is due to more factors than bankruptcy remoteness and the certainty of priority in distribution; however, as noted earlier, these two factors are central to securitization's design and are perhaps the most important features of securitization for investors.

Yet the experience with mortgage securitization also gives reason for skepticism about the efficiency claims of contractual bankruptcy. The mortgage crisis has revealed a third category of problems with contractual bankruptcy in addition to redistribution and transaction costs: this category comprises spillover effects from locking the parties into a precommitted resolution framework, or contract rigidity. Because contractual bankruptcy models limit themselves to the context of the firm, they do not consider spillovers beyond the firm. Contractualists leave the problem to the market. But thick markets are not always there to pick up the slack, and maximizing the value of a bankruptcy estate maximizes social welfare if and only if the marginal increase in welfare from the particular bankruptcy regime offsets the marginal decrease in welfare from the regime's externalities.

The debates surrounding contractual bankruptcy have all been in the context of business bankruptcy. There is an unspoken recognition that consumer bankruptcy policy is different. The transaction costs of contractual bankruptcy for consumers would be prohibitively high and would necessitate accounting for numerous involuntary creditors, as well as for creditors who cannot easily adjust their behavior for the many bespoke bankruptcy regimes that would be available to consumers. The efficiency benefits of a standardized bankruptcy regime for consumers are so manifest that there has been no attempt to apply contractual bankruptcy to them.

And yet that is precisely what securitization accomplishes. Securitization transforms consumer debt into business debt. The resulting transformation has profound implications for the application of a contractual bankruptcy regime, embodied in [private-label mortgage securitization contracts], designed to inhibit the reworking of the securitized consumer debts, forcing consumer debt out of the social policy world of the Bankruptcy Code and into the private ordering of securitization contracts.

In sum, securitization is the embodiment of contractual bankruptcy. For the device to work, its contracts must be rigid. Contractual bankruptcy theories, however, do not consider the full range of spillover effects created by rigidity

---

I. CONTRACTS WITH CREDITORS NOT TO FILE FOR BANKRUPTCY

How can a firm commit not to file for bankruptcy? One simple answer would seem to be contracting with a creditor not to file. Generally, contractual agreements prospectively prohibiting bankruptcy filings are unenforceable as against public policy. *See, e.g., Hayhoe v. Cole (In re Cole),* 226 B.R. 647, 651-652 (B.A.P. 9th Cir. Cal. 1998). Even if not void, such a contract would at best entitle a creditor to damages, not specific performance.

The public policy concern with contracts not to file is two-fold: Bankruptcy affects rights of creditors, including involuntary creditors, who may not have agreed to the contractual arrangement, and it also affects the rights of the debtor itself. The right to file for bankruptcy may simply not be the debtor's to bargain away.

II. DESIGNING BANKRUPTCY REMOTE FIRMS

While a simple contract with a creditor not to file for bankruptcy is unlikely to be effective, there are other ways in which a firm can commit not to file for bankruptcy. They all involve the use of so-called **bankruptcy remote** entities. (Such entities are often called "bankruptcy remote vehicles.")

"Bankruptcy remoteness" is a term with two distinct (and often confused) meanings. The first meaning refers to the inability of an entity to file for bankruptcy. The *entity* is itself bankruptcy remote.

The second meaning refers to the segregation of assets from an entity that can file for bankruptcy. In this usage, the *assets* are bankruptcy remote, even if the entity is not. For the assets to be remote from the bankruptcy risk of a firm, they need to be squirreled away in a legally separate entity. This is usually accomplished through a sale to an unrelated party. (See the *LTV Steel* case in Chapter 14 of this book for further discussion.) Transfers to related parties are more vulnerable to avoidance actions, as well as to substantive consolidation.

Our focus here is on the former meaning, namely how a firm can be structured so that it cannot or will not file for bankruptcy. Nonetheless, bear in mind that the two meanings can be combined, and frequently are: A firm can transfer assets to a bankruptcy remote entity. Such a transaction would ensure that the assets could not be clawed back into the transferor's bankruptcy estate and that the transferee's assets never could be part of a bankruptcy estate if it were ineligible to file for bankruptcy.

A. Entities Ineligible to File for Bankruptcy

Absolute bankruptcy remoteness for an entity can be achieved by using an entity that is per se ineligible to be a debtor under Title 11. What sorts of entities are ineligible to be debtors under Title 11? Section 109(b) allows any "person" to file for Chapter 7 bankruptcy excluding railroads, depositories, and insurance companies. Section 109(d) similarly provides that any "person" that may be a debtor under Chapter 7, as well as railroads and certain financial institutions, may be a debtor under Chapter 11. Both of these provisions turn on the term "person," which is defined in section 101(41) to "include[] individual, partnership, and corporation." The non-exclusive definition of "person" suggests that perhaps it is not limited to individuals, partnerships, and corporations. If so, however, what limits would exist on the term "person"? The Code does not define "individual" or "partnership," but it does define the term "corporation" as including an "unincorporated company or association," and also "business trust." 11 U.S.C. § 101(9).

One possible implication is that entities that do not fall under the definition of "corporation" and are not also individuals or partnerships are "persons" not eligible to file for Chapter 7 or Chapter 11. Thus, although a "business trust" is a corporation and hence a person and therefore eligible for filing of Chapter 7 or Chapter 11, a "nonbusiness trust" would be ineligible for filing. But what is a "business trust"? And by extension, what is a "nonbusiness trust," which would, arguably (if not a "corporation" and therefore not a "person"), be ineligible to file for either Chapter 7 or Chapter 11 relief? The Bankruptcy Code does not define either term (or even use the term "nonbusiness trust"). The following case considers this definitional problem.

In re General Growth Properties, Inc.

409 B.R. 43 (Bankr. S.D.N.Y. 2009)

ALAN GROPPER, U.S. Bankr. J.

ING Clarion . . . moves to dismiss the Chapter 11 case filed by Lancaster Trust, one of the . . . Debtors, on the ground [that Lancaster Trust] is an Illinois land trust and is ineligible to file. An Illinois land trust has been described as "a legal device whose primary function is to hold legal and equitable title to real estate," which "is not, and does not attempt to be, an active business or commercial entity." *In re North Shore Nat'l Bank of Chicago, Land Trust No. 362*, 17 B.R. 867, 869 (Bankr. N.D. Ill. 1982).

The facts are uncontested. Lancaster Trust was formed in 1979 and became a part of the [General Growth Properties] Group in June of 1998. It is the owner of the Park City Mall and the borrower under a loan serviced by ING Clarion, which is secured by the Park City Center. Lancaster Trust is described only as an "Illinois Trust" in its loan documentation, not as a "land trust." Nevertheless, ING Clarion contends that Lancaster Trust is ineligible to file for protection under the Bankruptcy Code because it does not maintain certain of the characteristics of a business entity, in that it lacks employees, independent managers, a governing board or officers, and the transferability of equity interests. The Debtors argue that the Lancaster Trust operates as a business trust because of its corporate attributes and because it transacts business for the benefit of investors, and thus that it is eligible to be a debtor under Chapter 11.

The Bankruptcy Code provides that a "person" may be a debtor under Chapter 11 and that the term "person" includes a "corporation." 11 U.S.C. §§ 109(d), 101(41). The term "corporation" in turn includes a "business trust." 11 U.S.C. § 101(9)(A)(v). However, neither the Bankruptcy Code nor its legislative history defines the term "business trust." *See Shawmut Bank Conn. v. First Fidelity Bank (In re Secured Equip. Trust of Eastern Air Lines)*, 38 F.3d 86, 89 (2d Cir. 1994). The question is whether the Debtors have met their burden of proof of establishing that the Lancaster Trust was eligible to file because it operates as a business trust.

In *Secured Equipment*, the Second Circuit addressed the question whether a "trust" should be considered a "business trust." The Court stated that "a basic distinction between a business trust and other trusts is that business trusts are created for the purpose of carrying on some kind of business, whereas the purpose of a non-business trust is to protect and preserve the res." *Id.* at 89. An important factor is whether the trust's purpose is to generate profit. *Id.* at 91. The Court concluded that each "inquiry must focus on the trust documents and the totality of the circumstances. . . ." *Id.* at 90-91, citing *In re St. Augustine Trust*, 109 B.R. 494, 496 (Bankr. M.D. Fla. 1990).[44] Other courts have recognized that a trust that conducts business activities directed at generating a profit is a business trust eligible to file under the Bankruptcy Code. *See Merrill v. Allen (In re Universal Clearing House Co.)*, 60 B.R. 985, 992 (D. Utah 1986) (court examined activity for which trust designed and authority granted to trustee); *Westchester County Civil Serv. E'ees Ass'n Benefit Fund v. Westchester County (In re Westchester County Civil Serv. E'ees Ass'n Benefit Fund)*, 111 B.R. 451, 456 (Bankr. S.D.N.Y. 1990) ("If a trust conducts some business or commercial activities for the benefit of the beneficiaries to the enterprise, it may qualify as a 'business trust.'"); *see also In re Cooper Properties Liquidating Trust, Inc.*, 61 B.R. 531, 536 (Bankr. W.D. Tenn. 1986) (trust created to wind up the affairs of a predecessor corporation was a business trust).

---

44. Because the trust in *Secured Equipment* was not created to run a business or to generate a profit, but only to act as a vehicle to facilitate a secured financing, the Court found the entity was not a business trust. *See id.* at 90. "Rather, it was established merely to secure the repayment of the certificateholders' loans to Eastern. As such, its purpose was to preserve the interest that the certificateholders had already been guaranteed, not to generate it." *Id.* at 90.

There is ample evidence in the record that Lancaster Trust is a profit-making enterprise and that its purpose goes beyond merely conserving a trust res or holding title to land. As the Park City Mall owner and operator, it is an active participant in various business activities aimed at earning a profit. It is the named lessor in leases with its tenants, the borrower under a loan agreement, party to various service contracts, and explicitly authorized to conduct business in Pennsylvania. ING Clarion argues that Lancaster Trust has no board, officers or stockholders, but these are characteristics of some closely-held business entities. ING argues that the Trust has an outside termination date and that the interest of Lancaster Trust's sole beneficiary is "non-transferable," but "restrictions on the transfer of shares, particularly in the case of close corporations, are also common." ING states that Lancaster Trust has no employees and is managed by a GGP Group entity, but this is also a characteristic shared by many, if not all of the project-level Debtors. Indeed, ING Clarion made no effort to distinguish the Lancaster Trust from any of the other Movants or from any of the other project-level Debtors in terms of its business characteristics, except that it was formed as an Illinois trust.

. . .

On the record as a whole, the Court finds that the Lancaster Trust is a business trust eligible to file under Chapter 11.

Despite the open-ended definition of "person," courts have treated nonbusiness trusts as bankruptcy remote. There is surprisingly little case law on what constitutes a "nonbusiness trust" for bankruptcy law purposes, and whether a court finds a trust to be a nonbusiness trust is fact specific. Nonetheless, it appears that if a trust is actively managed—meaning activities beyond simply collecting cash flows on obligations, but buying, selling, and transforming assets—it is likely to be a business trust. Some businesses can be operated with passively managed assets, but often active management is an important feature of a firm. Therefore, even to the extent that a nonbusiness trust is truly bankruptcy remote, there are limits on the use of nonbusiness trusts as bankruptcy remote entities.

B. Bankruptcy Remoteness Through Corporate Governance

While a contract with creditors not to file for bankruptcy will not be enforced, a firm may be able to commit itself to bankruptcy remoteness through corporate governance devices. It is axiomatic that for a corporate entity to voluntarily file for bankruptcy, the filing must be authorized under applicable non-bankruptcy law. *Price v. Gurney*, 324 U.S. 100, 107 (1945).

What does it take for a corporate entity to authorize a bankruptcy filing? The answer of course depends on the specifics of non-bankruptcy law, which also depend on the specific form of corporate organization involved.

For many corporations, Delaware General Corporation Law (DGCL) provides the statutory framework. The default rule under DGCL is that a simple majority vote of a board of directors will authorize corporate action unless the corporation's bylaws require otherwise. 8 Del. Code Ann. § 141(b). Therefore, unless a majority of a corporation's board of directors approve a bankruptcy filing, the filing is ineffective. Yet DGCL section 141(b) also allows for the majority threshold to be increased through corporate bylaws. Thus, bylaws could require unanimous consent of all directors. Such a requirement would make filing much more difficult, as a single hold-out director could frustrate a filing. Directors have potential personal liability, of course. Delaware General Corporation Law allows corporations to exculpate directors for breach of their fiduciary duty of care, but not for breach of their fiduciary duties of loyalty or good faith. 8 Del. Code Ann. § 102(b)(7). Thus, there are risks to a director for frustrating a bankruptcy filing if the director is conflicted or not acting in good faith.

Corporate bylaws can, of course, be changed. Delaware General Corporation Law section 109(a) provides that a corporation's bylaws may be amended by its shareholders or, additionally, if the certificate of incorporation so specifies, by the board of directors. 8 Del. Code Ann. § 109(a).

Similarly, directors can be removed or replaced. 8 Del. Code Ann. § 141(k). Thus, a corporate bylaw requiring unanimous consent to a bankruptcy filing does not create bulletproof bankruptcy remoteness, as the following case illustrates.

In re Kingston Square Associates

214 B.R. 713 (Bankr. S.D.N.Y. 1997)

BROZMAN, Chief Bankr. J.

INTRODUCTION

Fashion has a role not only in the garment industry but in the legal one as well. One of the newest fashions in commercial real estate financing is so-called "mortgage backed securitization" coupled with the presence of corporate governance provisions known as "bankruptcy remote provisions" designed to make bankruptcy unavailable to a defaulting borrower without the affirmative consent of the mortgagee's designee on the borrower's board of directors.

Here, a group of entities owning apartment complexes was stymied by such provisions from invoking the Chapter 11 process to prevent foreclosure despite the belief of their principal that the properties had value over and above the encumbrances against them. To prevent loss of this claimed value and the potential for reorganization, the debtors' principal paid a law firm to solicit creditors to file involuntary Chapter 11 petitions. Only one trade creditor for each debtor agreed; the other petitioning creditors came from the ranks of the debtors' professionals—attorneys and various consultants. At issue is whether the petitions ought therefore be dismissed as bad faith filings, relief which the mortgagees seek.

By agreement of the parties, the only issue at trial was whether there was collusion mandating dismissal, for it was the mortgagee's contention that, standing alone, collusion in their filing warranted dismissal of these petitions. The parties have not yet tried whether there is any possibility of reorganization. . . .

Each of the eleven debtors (the "Debtors") is or was controlled by Morton L. Ginsberg. The Debtors represent less than one-third of the thirty-eight Ginsberg-controlled entities that were restructured in 1991 or 1993 in transactions financed by The Chase Manhattan Bank, N.A. ("Chase") and REFG Investor Two, Inc. ("REFG") (the "Movants"). All thirty-eight properties, both debtor and nondebtor, are in receivership, with foreclosure proceedings pending against them. In one case, that of Lynnewood Associates, the Movants have foreclosed upon the property. The Debtors did not contest the filing of the involuntary petitions, with the result that orders for relief have been entered in all eleven cases.

Chase and REFG seek the dismissal of the Chapter 11 cases of the eleven Debtors for cause pursuant to section 1112(b) of the Bankruptcy Code. The Movants maintain that Ginsberg colluded with the petitioning creditors ("Petitioning Creditors") and their counsel, Pryor, Cashman, Sherman & Flynn ("Pryor Cashman"), to enable each Debtor to improperly avail itself of bankruptcy protection to thwart the Movants' ongoing efforts to foreclose on each of the Debtors' properties. Objections to the dismissal motion have been filed by the Debtors, the Petitioning Creditors, and the limited partners of the Florida Debtors, Lynnewood Associates, and Highland-Montgomery, L.P. . . .

The Debtors became indebted to the Movants pursuant to two loan transactions. In the first, known as MLG I, Chase lent slightly more than $132 million to twenty multi-family entities including the Florida and Metropolitan New York Debtors and took back a mortgage on each property. This transaction closed on August 30, 1991. Chase holds a single blanket mortgage containing cross-collateralization and cross-default provisions for fifteen of the twenty properties. Chase holds individual mortgages on the five remaining properties.

In the second loan transaction, known appropriately enough as MLG II, REFG lent nearly $145.25 million to eighteen multi-family entities including the Bronx Debtors and took back a mortgage on each property. This transaction closed on February 11, 1993. All eighteen properties are covered by one blanket mortgage with cross-collateralization and cross-default provisions. [The movants agreed that another entity, "DLJ," would act on their behalf to enforce the mortgages.]

Integral to the MLG I and II transactions was the inclusion in the charters of each corporate Debtor or the corporate general partner of each limited partnership Debtor of a bylaw, commonly referred to as a "bankruptcy remote" or "bankruptcy proof" provision, to prevent the Debtors from seeking voluntary bankruptcy protection without the unanimous consent of the board of directors of each Debtor or of its corporate general partner and the shareholders. Each board originally consisted of Ginsberg and two others, one of whom was his designee and the other of whom was a so-called independent director.

The independent director for each board of directors is Laurence Richardson. Richardson received his law degree from the University of Virginia in 1983 and was employed as an associate at Thacher Proffitt & Wood, a New York law firm, until 1986 in the residential mortgage backed securities area. After a two-year stint at E.F. Hutton beginning in 1986, Richardson worked at DLJ from February 1988 until April 1991 as a vice president. Upon his departure, he became a consultant to DLJ for the MLG I transaction as well as others. He was paid hourly for his consulting fees and received the sum of $25,000 per year for being a director for companies included in both the MLG I and II transactions. Richardson's director's fees were originally paid by the management companies handling the properties and then later by the receivers. At some point, the fees went into arrears; it was DLJ whom Richardson called to inquire about who was responsible for bringing the fees current. Richardson admits having received some of his director's fees from REFG, which at that time he did not know was a wholly-owned subsidiary of DLJ.

Richardson serves as an independent director for three other entities at the request of DLJ, receiving $10,000 per year per transaction. Therefore, Richardson receives the aggregate amount of $55,000 annually for serving on the various boards of directors created pursuant to DLJ-structured deals.

In 1994, the Movants issued notices of default and commenced foreclosure actions against each property, Debtor and nondebtor. With the consent of each borrower, receivers were installed at all thirty-eight properties. As of mid-1996, the Movants had obtained judgments totaling approximately $370 million and had commenced foreclosure proceedings against each of the thirty-eight properties. . . .

In the almost two years that the receivers have been in place, the Movants have advanced nearly $2 million to pay for repairs, taxes and insurance. No monies have been needed for salaries because the Debtors have no employees.

While no breakdown has been provided as to the number of apartment units for each of the Debtors, the thirty-eight Debtor and nondebtor properties in total aggregate nearly 11,200 units spread over approximately 41 garden apartment complexes. The only appraisal received into evidence . . . valued all the properties at $384 million. If the values contained in the appraisal were found to be correct, equity may exist in the properties. However, the appraisal was admitted for the limited purpose of rebutting the charge that the friendly involuntary petitions were filed in bad faith. As noted at the outset of this decision, the parties agreed in their pretrial order not to treat reorganization prospects initially, as a result of which there is no developed record regarding valuation. . . .

As each director, Kazarnovsky, Ginsberg and Richardson, testified, no meetings were held after the closing of the MLG I and II restructurings until December 16, 1996. At no other time was any meeting ever called, special or regular, to discuss the business activities of the Debtors, the defaults called by the Movants, or the commencement of the foreclosure actions. The directors conducted no business except to approve the $2.4 million loan to the Debtors to provide maintenance for the properties in June 1993. Other than this minor matter, they had little communication with each other, either by telephone or by letter until this motion was filed. No financial reports were circulated, nor were reports or updates on the legal proceedings distributed either by counsel or by Ginsberg, as president, to the other directors.

The directors testified as to the reasons for such inactivity, even in the face of the foreclosure actions, the installation of receivers and the filing of the involuntary petitions. Both Ginsberg and Kazarnovsky believed that involving Richardson in such meetings would prove fruitless because of their belief that Richardson was simply a pawn of DLJ and would not approve any course of action that would interfere with DLJ's plans. Because both Kazarnovsky and Ginsberg believed that Richardson was DLJ's agent on the board, they purposely ignored him. Significantly, the boards took no action in the face of foreclosure actions being commenced or receivers being installed. Although Ginsberg did retain counsel to contest the foreclosure proceedings in the state courts on behalf of the Debtors, there is no indication that the attorneys ever reported to anyone other than Ginsberg. Richardson learned in 1995 that the properties were being foreclosed, yet he took no action and did not seek any information from anyone as to what was happening although he assumed judgments would be entered against the properties. In any event, he never initiated communication with Ginsberg regarding these events nor did he ask for a directors' meeting.

Richardson's overall testimony at trial was enlightening on a number of topics including his perception of his fiduciary duty as a director, the purpose of the bankruptcy proof provision and his understanding of DLJ's status. Richardson seems not to have taken any interest at all in the properties. He testified that as a director he never reviewed any documents regarding any of the Debtors including rent rolls, judgments, or state court decisions. While apparently unaware of the foreclosure actions against all the properties until 1995, Richardson did acknowledge that he was certainly aware of the status of his directors' fees and made a number of inquiries of DLJ when his fees were in arrears.

According to his testimony, only long after the filing of the involuntary petitions did he become aware that a director has fiduciary duty not only to a corporation's shareholders but to its creditors when the corporation becomes insolvent. Nor did he comprehend his obligations to limited partners in those entities where he was on the board of directors of the corporate general partners. Richardson candidly admitted that from his appointment as a director to the Debtors' boards in 1993 until December 1996 he believed that his duty was to the shareholders whom he identified as Ginsberg. But Richardson's statement does not quite square with his later testimony when he described seeking DLJ's advice about resigning from the boards sometime in 1995. Richardson sought an answer from DLJ because he was under the impression that because DLJ had become the shareholder by virtue of its foreclosure of Ginsberg's equity interests and DLJ was now the owner of all the securities, "they became the investor who relied upon my independence to avoid a bankruptcy." In any event, Richardson had no idea until well into the midst of these cases that he had a fiduciary duty to anyone other than shareholders. . . .

Finally, Richardson gave his interpretation of what the bankruptcy proof provision was all about. As he read the bylaw, its purpose was to place an "independent" director on the corporate boards of directors to prevent, in the event that Ginsberg filed for personal bankruptcy, Ginsberg's filing from "sucking all of these properties into that proceeding," in order that, as Richardson further explained, "a creditor of Mort Ginsberg would not be able to say that somehow there was a corporate sham and therefore be able to pull these assets in." Interestingly, Richardson claims not to have known that DLJ had foreclosed on Ginsberg's equity interests, (at odds with other of his testimony) thereby making itself shareholder, but he did inquire as to whether he should resign as director after learning that DLJ had purchased all the bonds and was now foreclosing upon the properties. Obviously, Richardson clearly believed that the reason for his presence, as DLJ's guardian of the properties, had been mooted because DLJ was in complete control, having installed receivers at the properties and having started to foreclose on them.

The Movants argue that each of the eleven involuntary petitions was filed in bad faith and should be dismissed pursuant to section 1112(b) of the Bankruptcy Code. This conclusion is said to be warranted because Ginsberg, acting on behalf of the Debtors, initiated, funded and identified seven friendly creditors to prosecute the involuntary petitions so each Debtor could obtain improper leverage against the Movants by gaining access to the bankruptcy court without violating the bankruptcy restrictions in the bylaws of the various Debtors or their corporate general partners. The Movants point out that the filing of each petition was timed either to stay a scheduled foreclosure sale or to coincide with a particular Debtor's deadline to file an appellate pleading, which resulted, the Movants claim, in the frustration of their attempts to enforce their rights against each property. The Movants dismiss the Debtors' attempts to excuse such behavior by countering that there is no such doctrine as "justifiable collusion."

The Movants have centered their case around the Second Circuit decision, *Federal Deposit Ins. Corp. v. Cortez*, 96 F.3d 50 (2d Cir. 1996), which held that, in certain circumstances, a collusive filing of a bankruptcy case is a fraud upon the jurisdiction of the Bankruptcy Court and therefore susceptible to immediate dismissal. Because the Movants believe that the *Cortez* case is controlling, they did not offer initially any evidence regarding any of the Debtors' financial situations, their equity (or lack thereof) in the properties or their ability to reorganize. In other words, the Movants are of the opinion that if I were to find that collusion did occur, under *Cortez* I am bound to dismiss the cases. As an alternative, the Movants suggest that the facts warrant conversion of the cases to Chapter 7 or appointment of a Chapter 11 trustee. . . .

It is not appropriate for me to rule now on the myriad allegations about Ginsberg's dishonesty, mismanagement and the other horribles alluded to in the various court papers. All I know is that in the face of such behavior, the Debtors and limited partners continued to keep him on as chairman of the board and president of the Debtors, and the Movants accepted his presence without taking any action against him other than to slowly and inexorably close in on each property, notwithstanding that they say they acquired his equity interests and thereby the ability to oust him. In the meantime, the Movants ignore the fact that DLJ acts as lender and shareholder, while dominating the activities of the Debtors to the extent that its board designee, who was supposed to be "independent," abdicated his fiduciary role to the Debtors, creditors and limited partners in favor of the interests of DLJ.

While I find that the Respondents did orchestrate the filing of these cases, I conclude that their intention was to circumvent the inability of the Debtors to act in the face of the pending foreclosure proceedings by taking some action to preserve value for the Debtors' estates and creditors. I cannot find, as the Movants desire, that the petitions were filed solely to delay or frustrate the Movants' remedies for it is also undisputed that the Petitioning Creditors have introduced at least one third party, and as many as two others, to make proposals to purchase the properties as a package. The Movants may feel bruised because the Respondents outmaneuvered what the Movants thought was an iron-clad provision in the corporate by-laws preventing a bankruptcy filing, but this does not mean that, without more, the petitions must be dismissed.

I have previously held in another context that bad faith will not normally be found where the primary motivation of petitioning creditors was to prevent further dissipation of assets through foreclosure in an attempt to facilitate an orderly workout among all the creditors. *In re Reveley*, 148 B.R. 398, 408 (Bankr. S.D.N.Y. 1992). The fact that at least one third party has been brought forward early in this proceeding by the Petitioning Creditors certainly helps to establish that their intentions were not simply to stave off foreclosure at the last second and harass the Movants.

Thus, for all of the reasons just explained, I do not conclude that the Movants have proven that these cases were collusively filed.

Section 1112(b) requires consideration of what is in the best interests of creditors and the estates. On the record thus far developed I can draw no conclusion as to whether dismissal is in the parties' best interest. It appears that the only parties who would benefit from dismissal are the Movants, while unsecured creditors and limited partners would be left with nothing if the foreclosures were allowed to continue apace. Accordingly, I find that although the filings of the involuntary petitions were solicited at the behest of Ginsberg, they are an apparent attempt to salvage some value for these estates in the face of the pending foreclosures, which would have wiped out the opportunity for anyone other than the Movants to recover anything.

Because I have not found that the Debtors and the Petitioning Creditors acted collusively in filing these cases, I need not reach the merits of the Respondents' position request that I nullify the bylaw provision containing the bankruptcy proof provision as void against public policy. In any event, given that none of the Debtors observed corporate formalities and did not prior to the involuntary filings test the directors' mettle by calling a board of directors' meeting to ascertain whether bankruptcy would be authorized, I do not believe that the issue of validity of the bankruptcy proof provision is properly before me. . . .

The facts presented by these cases are quite troubling. The Debtors and the Petitioning Creditors orchestrated the filing of these involuntary cases to evade what they perceived to be an insurmountable restriction against the Debtors' filing voluntary petitions. The third director has engaged in transparent stalling tactics, the effect of which is to endanger the interests of all parties other than DLJ. Allegations circulate on the periphery that Ginsberg or his subordinates may have acted improperly in managing the properties.

Because of those concerns about Ginsberg and his asserted poor history of performing on a number of other real estate loan transactions, DLJ felt justified in structuring the two loans with Ginsberg to guarantee that it could avoid a bankruptcy filing and move to foreclose on the properties swiftly in case of default regardless of whether the default was based on lack of payment or performance. DLJ thereby put itself in the awkward position of financing the original restructuring transactions, then later assuming obligations toward the creditors and limited partners by acquiring Ginsberg's equity interests, while simultaneously pursuing and enforcing state court judgment rights (through the Movants) in order to minimize its loss on the original bonds it repurchased. As a result, DLJ essentially held veto power over the acts the Debtors could take and found itself walking a tightrope between looking out for its own interests and breaching its fiduciary duties. This is too fine a line to comfortably navigate.

Moreover, I am also concerned that the properties have been allowed to languish at a "mere survival level" while in receivership, without the Movants seeking to do anything except let the foreclosure process run its course. The record does not indicate that either DLJ or the Movants are expending much effort to sell the properties or authorize the expenditure of any more funds than the barest minimum necessary for upkeep (which could arguably make the properties more saleable). The parties have not agreed to a sale of the properties with a later determination of who is entitled to the proceeds. Of utmost concern to me is the fact that no one, the Movants, the Debtors, or the Petitioning Creditors, has even acknowledged the existence of thousands of residents living in these buildings, some of which have indisputably fallen into disrepair. The blame for this sorry state of affairs has to be shared by the Debtors and the Movants. . . .

To summarize, I hold that although the Movants have successfully demonstrated that the Debtors and Petitioning Creditors did orchestrate the filing of the eleven involuntary petitions commencing these cases, their behavior is not consonant with what is required by case law for collusion. As a result, the orchestration is not sufficient to warrant the dismissal of the cases without evidence that the Debtors have no chance at rehabilitation. . . .

In re General Growth Properties, Inc.

409 B.R. 43 (Bankr. S.D.N.Y. 2009)

ALAN GROPPER, U.S. Bankr. J.

Before the Court are five motions (the "Motions") to dismiss certain of the Chapter 11 cases filed by one or more debtors (the "Subject Debtors") that are owned directly or indirectly by General Growth Properties, Inc. ("GGP"). One of the Motions was filed by ING Clarion Capital Loan Services LLC ("ING Clarion"), as special servicer to certain secured lenders; one of the Motions was filed by Helios AMC, LLC ("Helios"), as special servicer to other secured lenders; and three of the Motions were filed by Metropolitan Life Insurance Company and KBC Bank N.V. (together, "Metlife," and together with ING Clarion and Helios, the "Movants"). Each of the Movants is a secured lender with a loan to one of the Subject Debtors. The primary ground on which dismissal is sought is that the Subject Debtors' cases were filed in bad faith. It is also contended that one of the Subject Debtors was ineligible to file. The above-captioned debtors (the "Debtors") and the Official Committee of Unsecured Creditors appointed in these cases (the "Committee") object to the Motions. Based on the following findings of fact and conclusions of law, the Motions are denied.

BACKGROUND

GGP, one of the Debtors, is a publicly-traded real estate investment trust ("REIT") and the ultimate parent of approximately 750 wholly-owned Debtor and non-Debtor subsidiaries, joint venture subsidiaries and affiliates (collectively, the "GGP Group" or the "Company"). The GGP Group's primary business is shopping center ownership and management; the Company owns or manages over 200 shopping centers in 44 states across the country. These include joint venture interests in approximately 50 properties, along with non-controlling interests in several international joint ventures. The GGP Group also owns several commercial office buildings and five master-planned communities, although these businesses account for a smaller share of its operations. The Company reported consolidated revenue of $3.4 billion in 2008. . . .

I. Corporate Structure

The corporate structure of the GGP Group is extraordinarily complex, and it is necessary to provide only a broad outline for purposes of this opinion. GGP is the general partner of GGP Limited Partnership ("GGP LP"), the company through which the Group's business is primarily conducted. GGP LP in turn controls, directly or indirectly, GGPLP, L.L.C., The Rouse Company LP ("TRCLP"), and General Growth Management, Inc. ("GGMI"). GGPLP L.L.C., TRCLP and GGMI in turn directly or indirectly control hundreds of individual project-level subsidiary entities, which directly or indirectly own the individual properties. The Company takes a nationwide, integrated approach to the development, operation and management of its properties, offering centralized leasing, marketing, management, cash management, property maintenance and construction management.

II. Capital Structure

As of December 31, 2008, the GGP Group reported $29.6 billion in assets and $27.3 billion in liabilities. At that time, approximately $24.85 billion of its liabilities accounted for the aggregate consolidated outstanding indebtedness of the GGP Group. Of this, approximately $18.27 billion constituted debt of the project-level Debtors secured by the respective properties, $1.83 billion of which was secured by the properties of the Subject Debtors. The remaining $6.58 billion of unsecured debt is discussed below.

A. Secured Debt

The GGP Group's secured debt consists primarily of mortgage and so-called mezzanine debt.* The mortgage debt is secured by mortgages on over 100 properties, each of which is typically owned by a separate corporate entity. The mortgage debt can in turn be categorized as conventional or as debt further securitized in the commercial mortgage-backed securities market.

(i) Conventional Mortgage Debt

The conventional mortgage debt is illustrated, on this record, by three of the mortgages held by Metlife. Each of the three mortgages was an obligation of a separate GGP

---

* Mezzanine debt is secured by a parent company's stock in its subsidiary, which usually holds real estate or operating assets. While a lender can foreclose on the stock much more quickly than on real estate, the mezzanine lender is structurally junior to the creditors of the subsidiary, and therefore functions as a type of subordinated debt with an accordingly higher return.—ED.

subsidiary. There is no dispute that some of the Subject Debtors that issued the Metlife mortgages were intended to function as special purpose entities ("SPE"). SPE's typically contain restrictions in their loan documentation and operating agreements that require them to maintain their separate existence and to limit their debt to the mortgages and any incidental debts, such as trade payables or the costs of operation. Metlife asserts, without substantial contradiction from the Debtors, that SPE's are structured in this manner to protect the interests of their secured creditors by ensuring that "the operations of the borrower [are] isolated from business affairs of the borrower's affiliates and parent so that the financing of each loan stands alone on its own merits, creditworthiness and value. . . ." In addition to limitations on indebtedness, the SPE's organizational documents usually contain prohibitions on consolidation and liquidation, restrictions on mergers and asset sales, prohibitions on amendments to the organizational and transaction documents, and separateness covenants.

The typical SPE documentation also often contains an obligation to retain one or more independent directors (for a corporation) or managers (for an LLC). . . ." The Company's view of the independent directors and managers is that they were meant to be unaffiliated with the Group and its management. It appears that some of the secured lenders believed they were meant to be devoted to the interests of the secured creditors, as asserted by a representative of Helios. In any event, this aspect of the loan documentation is discussed further below.

Although each of the mortgage loans was typically secured by a separate property owned by an individual debtor, many of the loans were guaranteed by other GGP entities. . . .

The typical mortgage loan for the GGP Group members had a three-to seven-year term, with low amortization and a large balloon payment at the end. Some of the mortgage loans had a much longer nominal maturity date, but these also had an anticipated repayment date ("ARD"), at which point the loan became "hyper-amortized," even if the maturity date itself was as much as thirty years in the future. Consequences of failure to repay or refinance the loan at the ARD typically include a steep increase in interest rate, a requirement that cash be kept at the project-level, with excess cash flow being applied to principal, and a requirement that certain expenditures be submitted to the lender for its approval. The Debtors viewed the ARD as equivalent to maturity and the consequences of a loan becoming hyper-amortized as equivalent to default, and historically sought to refinance such loans so as to avoid hyper-amortization.

(ii) Commercial Mortgage-Backed Securities

Many of the GGP Group's mortgage loans were financed in the commercial mortgage-backed securities ("CMBS") market, represented on these Motions by each of the loans serviced by ING Clarion and Helios, as special servicers. In a typical CMBS transaction, multiple mortgages are sold to a trust qualified as a real estate mortgage conduit ("REMIC") for tax purposes. The REMIC in turn sells certificates entitling the holders to payments from principal and interest on this large pool of mortgages. The holders of the CMBS securities typically have different rights to the income stream and bear different interest rates; they may or may not have different control rights.

The REMIC is managed by a master servicer that handles day-to-day loan administration functions and services the loans when they are not in default. A special servicer takes over management of the REMIC upon a transfer of authority. Such transfers take place under certain limited circumstances, including: (i) a borrower's failure to make a scheduled principal and interest payment, unless cured within 60 days, (ii) a borrower's bankruptcy or insolvency, (iii) a borrower's failure to make a balloon payment upon maturity, or (iv) a determination by the master servicer that a material and adverse default under the loan is imminent and unlikely to be cured within 60 days. While a master servicer is able to grant routine waivers and consents, it cannot agree to an alteration of the material terms of a loan or mortgage. A special servicer has the ability to agree to modify the loan once authority has been transferred, but often only with the consent of the holders of the CMBS securities, or in some cases the holders of certain levels of the debt.

   . . .

III. The Events of 2008-2009

Historically, the capital needs of the GGP Group were satisfied through mortgage loans obtained from banks, insurance companies and, increasingly, the CMBS market. As noted above, these loans were generally secured by the shopping center properties and structured with three to seven-year maturities, low amortization rates and balloon payments due at maturity. There is no dispute that the Company's business plan was based on the premise that it would be able to refinance the debt. The testimony of Thomas Nolan, the President and Chief Operating Officer of GGP, is that "[t]his approach was standard in the industry, so for many years, it has been rare to see commercial real estate financed with longer-term mortgages that would fully amortize."

However, in the latter half of 2008, the crisis in the credit markets spread to commercial real estate finance, most notably the CMBS market. This in turn affected the ability of the GGP Group to refinance its maturing debt on commercially acceptable terms. The GGP Group attempted to refinance its maturing project-level debt or obtain new financing, contacting dozens of banks, insurance companies and pension funds. It also contacted national and regional brokers and retained the investment banking firms of Goldman Sachs and Morgan Stanley to attempt to securitize and syndicate the loans. Despite these efforts, the only refinancing the GGP Group was able to obtain during this period was with Teachers Insurance, which is described above.

The GGP parent entities also attempted to find refinancing for their own mostly unsecured debt, but efforts to raise debt or equity capital were similarly unsuccessful.

The Debtors claim that the CMBS structure caused additional roadblocks to the Company's attempts to refinance its debt or even talk to its lenders. In January 2009, the GGP Group contacted the master servicers of those loans that were set to mature by January 2010, seeking to communicate with the special servicers regarding renegotiation of the loan terms. The response from the master servicers was that the Company could not communicate with the special servicers until the loans were transferred, and that the loans had to be much closer to maturity to be transferred. The GGP Group subsequently attempted to communicate with the master servicers regarding only those loans set to mature through May 2009, but received the same response. The Debtors then attempted to contact the special servicers directly, only to be referred back to the master servicers. Finally, in February 2009, the GGP Group attempted to call a "summit" of special servicers to discuss those loans due to mature through January 2010, but only one servicer was willing to attend and the meeting was cancelled.

Unable to refinance, the Company began to tap more heavily into its operating cash flow to pay both its regular expenses and financial obligations. This in turn left the Company short of cash to meet prior commitments towards development and redevelopment costs. As additional mortgage loans began to mature, the Company's liquidity problems grew worse. . . .

Based on the state of the markets, the GGP Group began to contemplate the necessity of a Chapter 11 restructuring. Several of the loans went into default and one of the lenders, Citibank, commenced foreclosure proceedings on a defaulted loan on March 19, 2009. On April 16, 2009, 360 of the Debtors filed voluntary petitions under Chapter 11 of the Bankruptcy Code. An additional 28 of the Debtors filed for protection on April 22, 2009, for a total of 388 Debtors in the above-captioned Chapter 11 cases.

Upon filing, the Debtors did not dispute that the GGP Group's shopping center business had a stable and generally positive cash flow and that it had continued to perform well, despite the current financial crisis. Specifically, they stated "[t]he Company's net operating income ('NOI'), a standard metric of financial performance in the real estate and shopping center industries, has been increasing over time, and in fact increased in 2008 over the prior year despite the challenges of the general economy." Despite this, faced with approximately $18.4 billion in outstanding debt that matured or would be maturing by the end of 2012, the Company believed its capital structure had become unmanageable due to the collapse of the credit markets.

The Debtors filed several conventional motions on the Petition Date. The only motion that was highly contested was the Debtors' request for the use of cash collateral and approval of debtor-in-possession ("DIP") financing. By the time of the final hearing on May 8, 2009, numerous project-level lenders had objected, based on concerns that the security of their loans would be adversely affected. Many of these parties argued that it would be a violation of the separateness of the individual companies for the Debtors to upstream cash from the individual properties for use at the parent-level entity. After hearing extensive argument, the Court ruled that the SPE structure did not require that the project-level Debtors be precluded from upstreaming their cash surplus at a time it was needed most by the Group. The final cash collateral order, entered on May 14, 2009, however, had various forms of adequate protection for the project-level lenders, such as the payment of interest at the non-default rate, continued maintenance of the properties, a replacement lien on the cash being upstreamed from the project-level Debtors and a second priority lien on certain other properties. DIP financing was arranged, but the DIP lender did not obtain liens on the properties of the project-level Debtors that could arguably adversely affect the lien interests of the existing mortgage lenders, such as the Movants.

At an early stage in the cases it became clear that several lenders intended to move to dismiss, and the Court urged all parties who intended to move to dismiss any of the cases to coordinate their motions. Six motions were filed (three by Metlife), with one party subsequently withdrawing its motion. ING Clarion and Helios, which hold CMBS debt, argued that their cases should be dismissed because they were filed in bad faith in that there was no imminent threat to the financial viability of the Subject Debtors. . . . Metlife, which holds conventional mortgage debt, similarly argued that the Subject Debtors were not in financial distress, that the cases were filed prematurely and that there was no chance of reorganization as there was no possibility of confirming a plan over its objection.

DISCUSSION

I. Bad Faith Dismissal

The principle that a Chapter 11 reorganization case can be dismissed as a bad faith filing is a judge-made doctrine. In the Second Circuit, the leading case on dismissal for the filing of a petition in bad faith is *C-TC 9th Ave. P'ship v. Norton Co.* (*In re C-TC 9th Ave. P'ship*), 113 F.3d 1304 (2d Cir. 1997). Under [*C-TC*] grounds for dismissal exist if it is clear on the filing date that "there was no reasonable likelihood that the debtor intended to reorganize and no reasonable probability that it would eventually emerge from bankruptcy proceedings." *In re C-TC 9th Ave. P'ship*, 113 F.3d at 1309-10, quoting *In re Cohoes*, 931 F.2d at 227 (internal citations omitted). One frequently-cited decision by Chief Judge Brozman of this Court has restated the principle as follows: "[T]he standard in this Circuit is that a bankruptcy petition will be dismissed if *both* objective futility of the reorganization process *and* subjective bad faith in filing the petition are found." *In re Kingston Square Assocs.*, 214 B.R. 713, 725 (Bankr. S.D.N.Y. 1997) (emphasis in original).

No one factor is determinative of good faith, and the Court "must examine the facts and circumstances of each case in light of several established guidelines or indicia, essentially conducting an 'on-the-spot evaluation of the Debtor's financial condition [and] motives.'" *In re Kingston Square*, 214 B.R. at 725. "It is the totality of circumstances, rather than any single factor, that will determine whether good faith exists." [*Id.*] Case law recognizes that a bankruptcy petition should be dismissed for lack of good faith only sparingly and with great caution.

  . . .

A. Objective Bad Faith: Prematurity

All three Movants support their contention that the Chapter 11 filings of these Debtors were, in effect, premature by reliance on the few cases that have dismissed Chapter 11 petitions where the debtor was not in financial distress at the time of filing, where the prospect of liability was speculative, and where there was evidence that the filing was designed to obtain a litigation advantage. The leading decision is *In re SGL Carbon Corp.*, 200 F.3d 154 (3d Cir. 1999), in which the debtors filed Chapter 11 petitions for the express purpose of protecting themselves from antitrust litigation. At the same time they published a press release touting their financial health, as well as their denial of any antitrust liability. The Third Circuit held that "the mere possibility of a future need to file, without more, does not establish that a petition was filed in 'good faith.'" *Id.* at 164. . . .

In *SGL Carbon* . . . the prospect of any liability from pending litigation was wholly speculative. By contrast, the Subject Debtors here carry an enormous amount of fixed debt that is not contingent. Movants argue nevertheless that none of the Subject Debtors had a mortgage with a maturity date earlier than March 2010, and that the Subject Debtors should have waited until much closer to the respective maturity dates on their loans to file for bankruptcy. Movants contend in effect that the prospect of liability was too remote on the Petition Date for the Subject Debtors, and that the issue of financial distress and prematurity of filing cannot be examined from the perspective of the group but only on an individual-entity basis. Accepting for the moment this latter proposition, the question is whether the Subject Debtors were in actual financial distress on the Petition Date and whether the prospect of liability was too remote to justify a Chapter 11 filing.

(i) The Financial Distress of the Individual Project Debtors

The record on these Motions demonstrates that the individual debtors that are the subject of these Motions were in varying degrees of financial distress in April 2009. Loans to four of the Subject Debtors had cross-defaulted to the defaults of affiliates or would have been in default as a result of other bankruptcy petitions. Of the loans to the remaining sixteen Subject Debtors, one had gone into hyper-amortization in 2008. Interest had increased by 4.26%. Five of the Subject Debtors had mortgage debt maturing or hyper-amortizing in 2010, two in 2011, and one in 2012. The remaining seven Subject Debtors were either guarantors on maturing loans of other entities or their property was collateral for a loan that was maturing, or there existed other considerations that in the Debtors' view placed the loan in distress, such as a high loan-to-value ratio.

The Debtors' determination that the Subject Debtors were in financial distress was made in a series of Board meetings following substantial financial analysis. . . . During these meetings, the Boards discussed general considerations applicable to the project-level companies, as well as specific facts relating to the individual properties, with both GGP personnel and the financial, restructuring and legal advisors available. The Boards specifically focused on: "the collapse of the commercial real estate financing market; the challenges facing the CMBS market and the practical difficulties of negotiating with CMBS servicers to meaningfully modify loan terms; integration of the project entities with GGP Group and requirements for securing DIP financing; and the consequences of filing an entity for bankruptcy individually, outside a coordinated restructuring with other GGP entities." . . .

In addition to these general considerations, the Boards discussed each project-level entity individually. . . . On April 15, 2009 the Boards separately voted to put most of the project-level Debtors into bankruptcy. Certain Subject Debtors acted by written consent of the directors or managers. Fourteen entities were left out of the filing [because the company did not believe a filing to be appropriate].

The foregoing is not to assert that every stand-alone company with ample cash flow would necessarily act in good faith by filing a Chapter 11 petition three years before its only debt came due. However, contrary to Movants' contentions, the Court is not required in these cases to examine the issue of good faith as if each Debtor were wholly independent. We turn to the interests of the Group as a whole.

(ii) The Interests of the Group

Movants argue that the SPE or bankruptcy-remote structure of the project-level Debtors requires that each Debtor's financial distress be analyzed exclusively from its perspective, that the Court should consider only the financial circumstances of the individual Debtors, and that consideration of the financial problems of the Group in judging the good faith of an individual filing would violate the purpose of the SPE structure. There is no question that the SPE structure was intended to insulate the financial position of each of the Subject Debtors from the problems of its affiliates, and to make the prospect of a default less likely. There is also no question that this structure was designed to make each Subject Debtor "bankruptcy remote." Nevertheless, the record also establishes that the Movants each extended a loan to the respective Subject Debtor with a balloon payment that would require refinancing in a period of years and that would default if financing could not be obtained by the SPE or by the SPE's parent coming to its rescue. Movants do not contend that they were unaware that they were extending credit to a company that was part of a much larger group, and that there were benefits as well as possible detriments from this structure. If the ability of the Group to obtain refinancing became impaired, the financial situation of the subsidiary would inevitably be impaired.

The reasoning in *U.I.P. Engineered Prods.* was largely adopted in *In re Mirant Corp.*, 2005 Bankr. LEXIS 1686 (Bankr. N.D. Tex. Jan. 26, 2005), where the Court addressed a motion to dismiss the case of one of more than 80 related debtors. The Court held that the standard for assessing the good-faith dismissal of a single stand-alone debtor is different from the standard applied to "a key operating affiliate placed in Chapter 11 in conjunction with necessary filings by its family of affiliates." 2005 Bankr. LEXIS 1686. The Court noted that if the subsidiary had not been included in the bankruptcy filing, it would have likely faced repercussions from the filings by its affiliates, and warned that "[a] failure to file for an entity that is a principal member of the family could prove disastrous if relief in fact was necessary." *See* 2005 Bankr. LEXIS 1686.

Movants do not contend that the parent companies acted in bad faith in filing their own Chapter 11 petitions. The parent companies depended on the cash flow from the subsidiaries, but much of the project-level debt was in default: from January 1, 2009 through the second week of April 2009, $1.1 billion of the GGP Group project-level debt had matured, none of which the Company had been able to refinance. As of the Petition Date, billions of dollars of project-level debt had also reached hyper-amortization, with several secured lenders having imposed cash traps. In March 2009, Citibank, a lender on one of the defaulted loans, had begun foreclosure proceedings against one property. In addition to the project-level debt, the Group had debt of more than $8.4 billion at the parent level. Much of this debt was in default and it, too, could not be refinanced. Beyond the unsecured debt of the parent companies were thousands of equityholders who depended, in large part, on the net cash flow of and the equity in the project-level Debtors as a principal source of protection for their investment.

Faced with the unprecedented collapse of the real estate markets, and serious uncertainty as to when or if they would be able to the refinance the project-level debt, the Debtors' management had to reorganize the Group's capital structure. Movants do not explain how the billions of dollars of unsecured debt at the parent levels could be restructured responsibly if the cash flow of the parent companies continued to be based on the earnings of subsidiaries that had debt coming due in a period of years without any known means of providing for repayment or refinance. That is not to conclude, as Movants imply, that the interests of the subsidiaries or their creditors should be sacrificed to the interests of the parents and their creditors. As further discussed below, there need be no sacrifice of fundamental rights. The point is that a judgment on an issue as sensitive and fact-specific as whether to file a Chapter 11 petition can be based in good faith on consideration of the interests of the group as well as the interests of the individual debtor.

Indeed, there is authority that under the circumstances at bar, the interests of the parent companies *must* be taken into account. The Operating Agreements of many of the project-level Debtors contained provisions that required the appointment of two "Independent Managers." The Operating Agreements do not enumerate the duties of the Independent Managers except in the following instance, which is obviously highly relevant to the instant Motions: "To the extent permitted by law . . . the Independent Managers shall consider only the interests of the Company, *including its respective creditors*, in acting or otherwise voting on the matters referred to in Article XIII(p)." Article XIII(p) requires the "unanimous written consent of the Managers of the Company, including both of the Independent Managers" before the SPE can take any action to file or consent to the filing, as debtor, of any bankruptcy proceeding. (*Id.*) The Operating Agreements further provide that, "in exercising their rights and performing their duties under this Agreement, any Independent Manager shall have a fiduciary duty of loyalty and care similar to that of a director of a business corporation organized under the General Corporation Law of the State of Delaware." (*Id.*)

The drafters of these documents may have attempted to create impediments to a bankruptcy filing; in considering a filing, the Independent Managers are directed to consider only the interests of the Company, including its "creditors"—meaning the lender as the only substantial creditor of the entity. However, it is also provided, appropriately, that the Independent Managers can act only to the extent permitted by applicable law, which is deemed to be the corporate law of Delaware. Delaware law in turn provides that the directors of a solvent corporation are authorized—indeed, required—to consider the interests of the shareholders in exercising their fiduciary duties. In *North American Catholic Educational Programming Foundation, Inc. v. Gheewalla*, 930 A.2d 92 (Del. 2007), the Delaware Supreme Court held for the first time that the directors of an insolvent corporation have duties to creditors that may be enforceable in a derivative action on behalf of the corporation.

. . .

But there is no contention in these cases that the Subject Debtors were insolvent at any time—indeed, Movants' contention is that they were and are solvent. Movants therefore get no assistance from Delaware law in the contention that the Independent Managers should have considered only the interests of the secured creditor when they made their decisions to file Chapter 11 petitions, or that there was a breach of fiduciary duty on the part of any of the managers by voting to file based on the interests of the Group.

The record at bar does not explain exactly what the Independent Managers were supposed to do. It appears that the Movants may have thought the Independent Managers were obligated to protect only their interests. For example, an officer of ING Clarion testified that "the real reason" he was disturbed by the Chapter 11 filings was the inability of the Independent Managers to prevent one:

> Well, my understanding of the bankruptcy as it pertains to these borrowers is that there was an independent board member who was meant to, at least from the lender's point of view, meant to prevent a bankruptcy filing to make them a bankruptcy-remote, and that such filings were not anticipated to happen.

However, if Movants believed that an "independent" manager can serve on a board solely for the purpose of voting "no" to a bankruptcy filing because of the desires of a secured creditor, they were mistaken. As the Delaware cases stress, directors and managers owe their duties to the corporation and, ordinarily, to the shareholders. Seen from the perspective of the Group, the filings were unquestionably not premature [and therefore in bad faith].

. . .

C. Subjective Faith

The second element in analyzing whether a Chapter 11 petition has been filed in good faith is whether the debtor has exercised subjective good faith. . . .

Movants do not contend that the Boards of the respective debtors did not act deliberately, or that they did not have an intent to reorganize the companies. In addition to their contentions relating to prematurity and lack of financial distress, they assert that the Subject Debtors acted in subjective bad faith because . . . the initial "Independent Managers" of several of the SPE's were fired and replaced shortly before the Petition Date.

. . .

(ii) The Discharge of the Independent Managers

The . . . principal bad faith charge against the Debtors is that they engineered the discharge of the original Independent Managers of some of the Subject Debtors and replaced them with other Independent Managers. The basic facts are not in dispute. As discussed above, the Operating Agreements of some of the SPE's required that there be two independent managers or directors. The organizational documents permitted these independent managers to be supplied by a "nationally recognized company that provides professional independent directors, managers and trustees." In the cases at bar, Corporation Service Company ("CSC") supplied at least two "independent managers" who served on the Boards of over 150 project-level debtors. It does not appear that these managers had any expertise in the real estate business and as mentioned above, some of the lenders thought the independent managers were obligated to protect their interests alone. As articulated by Debtors' counsel, "the assumption by the lenders was that the independent director was not really independent."

In any event, it is not disputed that the CSC-appointed independent managers were, prior to the Petition Date, terminated from the Boards of those of the Subject Debtors that maintained the independent-manager requirement. The terminations "came as a surprise" to the independent managers because there was "no prior indication such termination was being contemplated." Moreover, the managers did not learn of their termination until after the bankruptcy filings. It is also undisputed that the Debtors selected two "seasoned individuals," Charles Cremens and John Howard, to serve as successor independent managers or directors on the Boards. Cremens and Howard served on the Boards during the spring of 2009 when the Debtors reviewed their restructuring prospects and ultimately voted to file under Chapter 11. Nolan explained the decision to replace the independent managers as follows:

> Given the significance, complexity, and time-consuming nature of assessing potential bankruptcy filings involving numerous entities, the project entities' stockholders and members desired independent managers with known experience in restructuring environments and complex business decisions, who understood the capital markets, who could commit significant time to learning about the projects, and who would bring critical, independent thinking to the restructuring challenges these project entities were facing.

Nolan also asserted that the terminations were not disclosed to CSC or to the original managers themselves until after the bankruptcy filings due to concern that such information "could subject the company to publicity about potential restructuring strategies . . ." and because the Debtors had no contractual obligation to inform the managers.

On this record it cannot be said that the admittedly surreptitious firing of the two "Independent Managers" constituted subjective bad faith on the part of the Debtors sufficient to require dismissal of these cases. The corporate documents did not prohibit this action or purport to interfere with the rights of a shareholder to appoint independent directors to the Board. The new Independent Managers satisfied the requirements of that position. As discussed above, the Independent Managers did *not* have a duty to keep any of the Debtors from filing a bankruptcy case. As managers of solvent companies charged to act in the same fashion as directors of a Delaware corporation, they had a *prima facie* fiduciary duty to act in the interests of "the corporation and its shareholders." *Gheewalla*, 930 A.2d at 101. It may be for that reason that the two CSC-nominated Independent Managers voted in favor of the Chapter 11 filings of those debtors on whose boards they still served.

In *In re Kingston Square Assoc.*, the Court declined to grant motions to dismiss on bad faith grounds where the debtors' management, precluded from filing voluntary cases, colluded with creditors to engineer involuntary filings. The Court found that this far more egregious action was "suggestive of bad faith," but that the cases should not be dismissed as the collusion was not rooted in a "fraudulent or deceitful purpose" but designed "to preserve value for the Debtors' estates and creditors." 214 B.R. at 734, 736.[42]

---

42. Indeed, while the Movants, particularly Helios, devoted considerable attention to the independent manager issues in their papers and at trial, the precise basis for challenging the replacement of the independent managers remains unclear. As noted, Movants have conceded that the Debtors did not violate the corporate documents in firing the initial Independent Managers. Furthermore, ING has declined to ask the Court to find "that the way these entities landed into bankruptcy by replacing independent directors" was "wrongful" or indicative of bad faith.

The Debtors here have established that the filings were designed "to preserve value for the Debtors' estates and creditors," including the Movants. Movants are wrong in the implicit assumption of the Motions that their rights were materially impaired by the Debtors' Chapter 11 filings. Obviously, a principal purpose of bankruptcy law is to *protect* creditors' rights. Secured creditors' access to their collateral may be delayed by a filing, but secured creditors have a panoply of rights, including adequate protection and the right to post-petition interest and fees if they are oversecured. 11 U.S.C. §§ 361, 506(b). Movants complain that as a consequence of the filings they are receiving only interest on their loans and have been deprived of current amortization payments, and Metlife complains that it is not even receiving interest on its mezzanine loan, which is secured only by a stock interest in its borrower's subsidiary. However, Movants have not sought additional adequate protection, and they have not waived any of their rights to recover full principal and interest and post-petition interest on confirmation of a plan. Movants complain that Chapter 11 gives the Debtors excessive leverage, but Metlife [(which claimed a restructuring was futile in the face of its opposition)] asserts it has all the leverage it needs to make sure that its rights will be respected.

It is clear, on this record, that Movants have been inconvenienced by the Chapter 11 filings. For example, the cash flows of the Debtors have been partially interrupted and special servicers have had to be appointed for the CMBS obligations. However, inconvenience to a secured creditor is not a reason to dismiss a Chapter 11 case. The salient point for purposes of these Motions is that the fundamental protections that the Movants negotiated and that the SPE structure represents are still in place and will remain in place during the Chapter 11 cases. This includes protection against the substantive consolidation of the project-level Debtors with any other entities. There is no question that a principal goal of the SPE structure is to guard against substantive consolidation, but the question of substantive consolidation is entirely different from the issue whether the Board of a debtor that is part of a corporate group can consider the interests of the group along with the interests of the individual debtor when making a decision to file a bankruptcy case. Nothing in this Opinion implies that the assets and liabilities of any of the Subject Debtors could properly be substantively consolidated with those of any other entity.

. . .

CONCLUSION

For the reasons set forth above, the motions to dismiss are denied. . . .

Kingston Square and *General Growth Properties* show the limitations on using corporate bylaws requiring unanimous consent of directors as a bankruptcy remoteness device. It is vulnerable to involuntary bankruptcy filings, fiduciary duty suits, and removal and replacement of directors.

Corporations, however, are only a subset of corporate entities. Many businesses are organized as limited liability companies (LLCs) or limited partnerships (LPs), and different laws govern these entities. LLC operating agreements or partnership agreements, can, like corporate bylaws, require unanimous consent for actions, including bankruptcy filings. Moreover, Delaware and Texas LLCs and LPs are permitted by statute to waive *all* fiduciary duties. 6 Del. Code Ann. §§ 17-1101(d) (LPs), 18-1101(c) (LLCs); Tex. Bus. Orgs. Code §§ 7.001(d), 101.401 (LLCs), 153.152(a)(2) (LPs). For entities from these jurisdictions, member or partner voting may not be shaped by fiduciary concerns, making unanimous consent to a filing potentially harder to achieve.

There is scant law on the enforceability of such unanimous consent provisions in operating agreements or partnership agreements. The one case to take up the issue, however, has held that the members of a limited liability company (LLC) can agree *among themselves* as part of the LLC's operating agreement not to file for bankruptcy and have that agreement specifically enforced. *Capital Holdings, LLC v. Aspen HH Ventures, LLC (In re DB Capital Holdings, LLC)*, 2010 Bankr. Lexis 4176 (B.A.P. 10th Cir. Dec. 6, 2010). Given that LLCs can be actively managed, they are often a more attractive form of business organization than a nonbusiness trust. Yet if other courts were to adopt the ruling in *DB Capital Holdings*, it is important to note its limits are similar to that suggested by *Kingston Square*: It does not prevent an involuntary bankruptcy filing. In contrast, an entity that is per se ineligible for bankruptcy is not vulnerable to an involuntary filing.

C. Springing Guaranties and Bankruptcy Penalties

A final bankruptcy remoteness device is the use of provisions that functionally penalize bankruptcy filings by creating liability for the ultimate owner of the debtor. These provisions commonly appear in two contexts: commercial real estate lending and workout agreements.

Commercial real estate loans are frequently made on a collateralized, but non-recourse basis. This means that the lender can only look to the collateral, rather than to other assets of the borrower, for repayment. In other words, the borrower incurs *in rem*, not *in personam* liability.

Yet frequently, non-recourse commercial real estate loans are coupled with a so-called springing guaranty or bad boy guaranty. A springing guaranty is a guaranty from an individual or firm that controls the borrower that is contingent on certain conditions precedent besides a default on the loan itself. Typically, these conditions precedent are so-called bad boy conditions, such as fraud and malfeasance, but they also frequently include not just wrongful acts, but also the filing of a voluntary petition under Title 11 or failure to contest an involuntary Chapter 11 petition. Thus, the loan is non-recourse, unless there is a voluntary bankruptcy filing or uncontested involuntary filing, in which case the loan becomes recourse.

Workout agreements also often feature a springing guaranty of some sort in which a major stakeholder in the debtor will pledge its personal liability as a guaranty that the debtor will honor the workout agreement and not file for bankruptcy.

Springing guaranties function to disincentivize bankruptcy filings. The borrower firm's directors, members, or partners are the ones who must approve a bankruptcy filing. But the directors are appointed by the firm's equityholders, who may themselves be the springing guarantors. Alternatively, the members or partners may themselves be the guarantors. Such directors, members, or partners are unlikely to take action that would result in the guarantors incurring liability. Thus, springing guaranties function as a type of bankruptcy remoteness device. You've already seen one such springing guaranty. It lurked in the background of *Kingston Square Associates*. The guaranty received only passing mention in the case, but it was the motivation behind the directors' recalcitrance to undertake a voluntary bankruptcy filing.

Do springing guaranties conflict with bankruptcy policy? On some level, obviously yes, but it is difficult for bankruptcy courts to police them because of jurisdictional issues. The bankruptcy court does not have jurisdiction until there is a bankruptcy filing, and springing guaranties make such filings unlikely. Yet clearly the estate has an interest in the guaranty issue once it is created, as the guarantor normally has a claim against the estate based on principles of subrogation and sometimes based on explicit indemnification or contribution rights.

Springing guaranties also raise corporate governance problems. The directors of a firm may not want to incur the liability of a springing guaranty for the firm—or for the equity owners of a firm—but their fiduciary duties are owed to all shareholders, even if only a subset of the shareholders are on the springing guaranty.

Problem Set 43

(1) Mike "Rocky" Rollin is a director at Denver Investment Management Corporation (DIMCO), a ginormous institutional money manager. DIMCO has invested heavily in fixed income securities, including residential mortgage-backed securities. Unfortunately, many of these securities did not perform as hoped because many of the underlying mortgages defaulted. As Rocky has been reading the newspapers and government reports about the mortgage defaults, he's become convinced that few, if any, of the mortgages were underwritten according to the specifications presented to investors. Rocky has been pressing the trustees in the securitizations to enforce the representations and warranties that the securitization sponsors made about the underwriting of the loans. The representations and warranties require the sponsor to buy back non-conforming loans at original face value minus any payments that have been made on the loans.

Rocky is particularly concerned about securitizations of mortgages done by Nationwide Financial Corp. Nationwide was once the largest mortgage lender in the United States, but its assets were purchased in a distressed situation by Bank of Columbiana, leaving the Nationwide with $7 billion in cash. Nationwide is now winding down operations. Nationwide has over 700 securitizations still outstanding, representing over a trillion dollars in potential representation and warranty liability. DIMCO is invested in 20 of the Nationwide securitizations. Collectively, these deals had an original balance of $9 billion. There's still $6 billion in outstanding balances; losses have already been $2 billion on these deals. Rocky thinks that he's going to be able to get the securitization trustees for his deals to demand that Nationwide pay up on its representations and warranties. Does Rocky have anything to worry about?

(2) Medea Choi, the general counsel of Erymanthian Bancorp, is seeking your advice. Choi tells you that Erymanthian made a $20 million loan to Hesperides Chem-Agro Corp., a cutting edge producer of genetically modified seeds. Hesperides is in default on the loan. Hesperides is a Delaware corporation. The majority of Hesperides's stock is owned by Hippolyta Holding Corp., the stock of which is held by a partnership between the reclusive billionaire Leda brothers, Cass and Lux.

Erymanthian is willing to work with Hesperides to restructure the loan, but Choi is concerned that Hesperides will take any concessions made and then subsequently file for bankruptcy. She wants your advice as to what legal terms Erymanthian should request as a condition of any workout to protect Erymanthian from a future bankruptcy filing. She tells you that she's already told Hesperides that the only way Erymanthian will consent to a workout is if it agrees to the bankruptcy avoidance provisions you recommend.

     a. What advice do you give Medea Choi?
     b. How confident are you that it will work? What's the best attack on your proposal?

(3) Three years ago, an investor consortium led by commercial real estate developer Anya Gelfand through her portfolio company, Rondeau LLC, acquired Radpad, Inc., which owns and operates a large chain of mid-priced extended stay hotels across the United States. Following the acquisition, Gelfand became Radpad's president, CEO, and chairwoman. The acquisition was financed through approximately $3 billion in loans, consisting of a $2 billion syndicated senior mortgage loan, secured by Radpad's hotel properties, rents, and other receivables, and $1 billion syndicated junior mezzanine loan, secured by the equity of Radpad, Inc. The mezzanine loan is subordinated to the mortgage loan through an intercreditor agreement. In connection with the acquisition, Gelfand and Rondeau LLC jointly and severally guaranteed up to $50 million in aggregate for both loans in the event that Radpad, committed any "bad boy" acts, including the filing of a voluntary bankruptcy petition. The guaranty agreement also provides that Gelfand and Rondeau LLC have no right of offset or indemnity against Radpad. The guaranty was executed in separate documents for the senior mortgage loan and the junior mezzanine loan, and there's some ambiguity as to whether the guaranty is subject to the subordination clause in the intercreditor agreement.

A recent economic downturn has caused financial difficulties for Radpad and severely depressed the value of its properties, which were already highly leveraged. Radpad is in default on both loans, and the lenders in the mortgage syndicate are threatening to foreclose on the mortgaged properties; in the present market, there would be little, if any surplus from the foreclosure sales. The mezzanine lenders are urging Radpad to file for bankruptcy, and have indicated a willingness to provide DIP financing, as they believe the market will soon rebound.

   a. Anya Gelfand has retained you as counsel. What do you advise her?

   b. Suppose the senior mortgage syndicate indicates that it is amenable to a pre-packaged bankruptcy cramdown plan under which Radpad's junior mezzanine debt and equity (including Rondeau LLC's interest) will be wiped out without any distribution. Under the plan, the senior mortgage syndicate would take ownership of Radpad, Inc. and would indemnify Gelfand and Rondeau LLC for their liability under the bad boy guaranties. Do you counsel Gelfand to take this deal?

   c. You are counsel for the mezzanine debt. What's your best strategy once Radpad defaults?

(4) Pluto Investment Securities has retained your firm, Douthat, Forrest & Wheel-Paillou, LLP, to work on a new structured financial product. Pluto wants the product to be completely bankruptcy remote, but to also allow significant managerial discretion and a range of activities that go beyond passive holding of cash flow–producing assets.

   a. Can you design such a product? What would it look like?

   b. If you think you can design such a product, are you confident enough in your product to back it with an opinion letter?

   c. How much confidence should investors have in such an opinion letter?

(5) As a leading bankruptcy practitioner, you've been invited to testify before the Senate Judiciary Committee, which is considering various reforms to the Bankruptcy Code.

   a. At the hearing, the committee chair asks you about bankruptcy remoteness preventing firms from getting bankruptcy relief. "Who benefits from such bankruptcy remoteness?" she asks. "And who loses? Is this something we should be concerned with as a matter of federal bankruptcy law?" What's your response?

   b. The ranking minority member, formerly a philosophy professor, follows up by asking you, "If you put on the Rawlsian veil of ignorance—that is, you couldn't know in advance which party you would be—would you want to live in a world with bankruptcy remoteness? What is the bargain that creditors would make if they were all wearing the Rawlsian veil?"

CHAPTER *44*

CONCLUSION

Now that you've become a bankruptcy ninja, it's worthwhile stepping back and making sure that you have a framework in which to place your overflowing knowledge. This textbook is structured to provide that framework.

In the first part of this book, we saw the existence of a wide range of problems frustrating restructuring outside of bankruptcy:

- informational problems regarding the debtor's financial condition;
- informational problems about other creditors (their identity, actions, and ultimate motives);
- intercreditor coordination (race to the courthouse, difficulties identifying and communicating, empty creditor problems, free-riding);
- problems of uncertain rights (debt enforceability and priority);
- contractual restrictions on restructuring (majority vote requirements, negative pledge clauses, debt limitation covenants, penalty clauses, contract terminations);
- statutory restrictions on impairment of creditors' rights (Trust Indenture Act);
- transactional limitations (inability to conduct multi-state, multi-asset foreclosure sales; inability to transfer underwater property without creditor consent; inability to obtain new financing without creditor consent);
- debtors' ability to favor preferred creditors or dissipate assets resulting in an inequitable distribution among creditors;
- allocation of the costs of restructuring;
- incentive problems limiting value maximization in foreclosure sales by secured creditors.

In the subsequent parts of the book, we saw how bankruptcy addresses these problems, sometimes more successfully than others. For example, some provisions, such as the automatic stay and turnover provisions, work very well to address the race to the courthouse problem . . . except to the extent that they are hollowed out by carveouts for financial contracts. Likewise, determination of priorities depends, in part, on valuations of collateral and interpretation of subordination agreements, both of which are more an art than a science. And we've seen how priorities depend in no small part on structural separateness between affiliated debtors, which is honored inconsistently in and out of bankruptcy. Similarly, DIP financing does not really get around the problem of creditor veto rights over new financing because when a debtor has no unencumbered collateral that can be pledged as adequate protection for a primed lender, it cannot bring in new money absent its prepetition

consent. We've also seen how fraudulent transfer law has been gutted by
tlement payment defense of section 546(e), and how attempts to address the
creditor problem rely on an incomplete disclosure regime that applies only
itors working as groups—an easily circumventable trigger. And we've seen
how the section 363 sale process can function as a restructuring that is not subject
to bankruptcy's disclosure regime or creditor vote. Table 45.1 summarizes the out-
of-court restructuring problems we've seen, the bankruptcy solutions to those problems, and the limitations on the bankruptcy solutions.

Table 45.1. Bankruptcy Solutions to Restructuring Problems and Their Limitations

Restructuring Problem	Bankruptcy Solution	Limitations on Bankruptcy Solution
Informational Problems		
1. *Creditors possess limited information about debtor*	• Plan disclosure statement, § 1125. • Discovery in contested matters, FRPB 9014(c). • Feasibility analysis addresses redefault concern, § 1129(a)(11).	• Limitations on disclosure, especially beyond Official Committees because of trading issues.
2. *Creditors cannot identify and communicate with each other*	• Claims register enables identification of other creditors. FRBP 5003(b). • Official Committees as representatives.	
3. *Creditors possess limited information about each others' actions (e.g., acceleration, suit)*	• Common public docket. • Notice requirements. • Statutory acceleration, § 502(b)(2).	
4. *Unclear extent of debt obligations (enforceability)*	• Claim allowance rules, § 502(b).	
5. *Unclear priority of competing debt obligations*	• Eliminates temporal priority differences by accelerating all debts, § 101(5). • Elimination of covenant-based priority, § 1123(b). • Subordination agreements are honored to extent enforceable under nonbankruptcy law, § 510(a). • Guaranties and structural priority is honored to the extent enforceable under nonbankruptcy law.	• Valuation issues for secured claims. • Subordination agreement interpretation issues. • Guaranty interpretation issues. • High threshold for substantive consolidation.

Restructuring Problem	Bankruptcy Solution	Limitations on Bankruptcy Solution
	• Substantive consolidation unwinds blurred structural priority. • Subordination of securities-rescission claims, § 510(b). • Priorities in security interests are honored only if perfected, § 544(a). • Statutory *ipso facto* liens avoided, § 545. • Classification rules require clarification of priority, §§ 506, 1122. • Ch. 7 cashflow waterfall, § 726. • Preservation of lienholders' rights, §§ 725, 1129(b)(2)(A) • Absolute priority rule, § 1129(b)(2)(b)(ii)-(c).	
6. *Creditor concern about post-concession defaults*	• Feasibility requirement, § 1129(a)(13).	
7. *Empty creditor problem breeds intercreditor mistrust*	• FRBP 2019 and 3001(e) disclosures. • Equitable subordination, § 510(c). • Equitable disallowance. • Good faith voting requirement and vote designation, § 1126(e).	• Incomplete disclosure requirement. • Disclosures apply only to "groups."
Collective Action Problems		
8. *Race-to-the-courthouse*	• Single national forum, 28 U.S.C. § 157(b). • Nationwide service of process, FRBP 7004(d). • Automatic stay, § 362. • Property of the estate, § 541. • Turnover requirement, § 542. • Voidable preferences, § 547. • Setoff preference limitation, § 553.	• Automatic stay exceptions, §§ 362(b), 555-561. • Preference safe harbors for financial contracts, § 546.
9. *Creditors free-ride on each other's concessions*	• Pro rata distribution within all unsecured classes. § 726(b). • Equal treatment within classes, § 1123(a)(4). • Official Committees' funded by estate, § 1102. • Priority for creditors and indenture trustees who make a "substantial contribution, §§ 503(b)(3)(D), 503(b)(5).	

Restructuring Problem	Bankruptcy Solution	Limitations on Bankruptcy Solution
Property Rule Problems		
10. Creditors' ability to refuse to make concessions	• Plan can compel concessions over creditor objections (liability rule, not property rule). §§ 1126, 1129. • Ability to reject executory contracts and unexpired leases allows debtor out of bad contracts post-petition with pre-petition breach treatment, § 365.	
11. Trust Indenture Act protections for bondholders' payment rights, 15 U.S.C. § 77ppp(b)	• Trust Indenture Act protections not enforceable in bankruptcy. § 1123(a) ("notwithstanding any otherwise applicable nonbankruptcy law").	
12. Contractual requirements of majority vote for syndicated loan/ bond amendments	• Bankruptcy changes electorate, §§ 1122, 1126. • § 1123(a) ("notwithstanding any otherwise applicable nonbankruptcy law").	
13. Lienholder veto over free-and-clear transfer of collateral	• Free-and-clear sales, § 363(f).	• Dependent upon interpretation of §§ 363(f)(3) and 363(f)(5).
14. Lienholder veto over financing with higher lien priority.	• DIP financing with priming liens, § 364(d).	• Self-priming is only realistic possibility in most cases.
15. Landlord ability to refuse lease assignment	• Preemption of anti-assignment provisions and laws. § 365(f).	• Lease may not be assumable in "actual" jurisdictions.
16. Ipso facto clauses	• *Ipso facto* clauses are ineffective to prevent property entering the estate or preventing assumption of executory contract or unexpired lease. §§ 365(b), 541(c).	• Exception for financial contracts in § 362(b) and lack of clarity in law about effect on *ipso facto* clauses triggering penalty rates, etc.
Transaction Cost Problems		
17. Inability to foreclose on multiple assets in multiple jurisdictions in a single sale.	• Bankruptcy sales power preempts state law restrictions on sales and allows for national multi-asset sales, § 363.	
18. Cost of debtor's professionals ("Charon's obol")	• Prioritization of professionals' fees, §§ 503(b), 507(a)(2), 1129(a)(9).	

Restructuring Problem	Bankruptcy Solution	Limitations on Bankruptcy Solution
Equitable Distribution Problems		
19. *Debtor transfers value to preferred creditors (preferences)*	• Avoidance of preferential transfers, § 547. • Avoidance of preferential setoff rights, § 553(b). • Avoidance of fraudulent transfers, §§ 544(a), 548. • Exclusion of insider votes, § 1129(a)(10).	• Settlement payment safe harbor, § 546.
20. *Contractual penalty and termination provisions shift value to favored creditors (contractual preferences)*	• Unenforceability of *ipso facto* clauses and penalty provisions, §§ 365(b)(1)(A), 365(b)(2), 1124(2)(A). • Subordination of non-compensatory penalty provisions, §§ 507(a)(8)(G), 726(a)(4).	• *Ipso facto* clause prohibition applies only to executory contracts and unexpired leases
21. *Risk of dissipation of debtor's assets to third-parties (fraudulent transfers)*	• Avoidance of pre-bankruptcy fraudulent transfers, §§ 544(b), 548. • Trustee or DIP as fiduciary to protect assets in bankruptcy,	• Settlement payment safe harbor, § 546.
Secured Creditor Incentives		
22. *Secured creditor runs foreclosure sale has no incentive to maximize sale price*	• Sale is run by debtor, not secured creditor, and parties in interest can object to sale procedures. § 363.	• Secured creditor control via DIP financing may affect sales.

It's also worth considering how bankruptcy works, and how it doesn't, within the framework in which it was originally conceived. Although the Bankruptcy Code dates from 1978, its real structural framework lies in the New Deal securities laws. As originally envisaged by its New Deal crafters (W.O. Douglas first and foremost among them), the law of restructuring consisted of three pieces: a private contract regime for bilateral debts and the Trust Indenture Act regime for multilateral debts,[1] both backstopped by bankruptcy law.

Both private contract and the Trust Indenture Act gave creditors the ability to veto any restructuring of their payment terms and the right to sue for payment. In bilateral contracts, a creditor did not have to make any concessions it did not want to make, and in multilateral contracts, a majority could not compel a minority to make these concessions. Private contract and the Trust Indenture Act both functioned as a

---

1. The substantial Trust Indenture Act carveout for nonregistered debt securities that exists today, 15 U.S.C. § 77ddd(a)(4)(A), did not exist originally, and loan syndications were more rare.

property rule in this regard. A debtor that could not restructure in the face of these property rules regimes could, however, always file for bankruptcy, which substitutes a liability rule regime for a property rule regime.

In bankruptcy, a restructuring can be forced on creditors—provided certain minimum requirements are met. Cramdown confirmation requirements, then, are the strike price for this liability regime. Thus, if a debtor could not restructure based on reaching a voluntary deal with its creditors, it could restructure in bankruptcy, where the restructuring would take place under judicial supervision, subject to a disclosure regime, numerous substantive statutory requirements, a creditor vote, with unconflicted collective representation of unsecured creditors through official committees chosen by the United States Trustee, and a generous garnish of good faith requirements.

Bankruptcy law as often practiced today, however, bears only faint resemblance to this New Deal vision. The pillars of the New Deal bankruptcy system—judicial supervision, disclosure, substantive plan requirements, and a creditor vote—have all been undermined. There is judicial supervision, but often no meaningful appellate review, whether because of statutory limitations, such as sections 363(m) and 364(e), the deferential review of factual determinations such as valuation, doctrines such as equitable mootness, or procedural obstacles to obtaining stays pending appeal.

The disclosure regime only applies to restructurings that take place through plans. It has no bearing on pre-plan sales that are increasingly the favored method for restructuring. And even in the universe of restructurings that happen pursuant to a plan, the disclosure regime only applies to those plans where votes are solicited post-petition. Thus, the disclosure regime does not apply to pre-packaged bankruptcies.

The copious statutory requirements for plan confirmation—both regarding the substance of the plan and the creditor vote—obviously apply only to *plans*, but often the real restructuring in many bankruptcies occurs through a pre-plan asset sale, insisted upon by the DIP financier, which can then credit bid on the assets, leaving only a pool of cash for distribution pursuant to the best interests test, thereby rendering the creditor voting meaningless.

Official creditors committees do function as envisioned by the New Deal. While Official Committees play a key role in shaping a restructuring, they are inherently imperfect representatives of the creditor collective, and their judgment was never meant to substitute for substantive requirements, as shown by the fact that a creditor vote and judicial confirmation findings were still required, even if the Official Committee(s) supported a plan. And while good faith has more bite in bankruptcy than it does at state law, where it often receives little more than lip service, it is a gap filler that cannot replace the four pillars of judicial supervision, disclosure, substantive plan requirements, and a creditor vote.

This is not to say that bankruptcy has failed. But it is not working as intended, either by the New Deal designers or the 1978 editors. A substantial factor in why bankruptcy does not operate as designed is the greater prevalence of secured credit. Most firms today enter the bankruptcy operating room with almost no unencumbered assets. That was not true when the Bankruptcy Code was enacted in 1978. The fact that debtors file with few, if any, substantial, unencumbered assets means that those firms are entirely at the mercy of their DIP lender, which will usually push for a quick asset sale to lock in collateral value and at which it can credit bid. (That DIP lender, is, of course, typically the senior secured creditor with something like a blanket lien on almost all assets.)

The entire structure of bankruptcy law, however, is based around the plan process, and that process is increasingly disfavored for restructurings. The need to restructure through a plan is increasingly limited to two sets of cases. First, there are pre-packaged or pre-negotiated cases in which a plan is simply the tool for addressing holdouts or taking advantage of the free-and-clear sale power to convey cleansed title to assets to a buyer. And second, there are cases in which a key value component of the firm cannot be transferred through an asset sale, such as a non-transferrable gaming license or valuable tax attributes. For other cases, a firm can be restructured through a plan, but a sale will often be the simpler, quicker, and easier method for restructuring.

This is where the U.S. bankruptcy system sits today. Neither the bankruptcy system nor the out-of-court restructuring system is perfect. They are not working as originally conceived. But together, they are a restructuring regime that has proven quite flexible and that works remarkably well in terms of returning valuable assets to productive use and encouraging the economic risk-taking that has been the hallmark of American innovation.

Problem Set 44

Wait! We're not quite done. There's one more problem set left in this book. So far, you've learned a lot of law and a lot of transactional moves. But you've learned all of these moves in a piecemeal fashion, however, and that's not how the world generally operates. This problem set doesn't cover everything, but it brings together a lot of the pieces we've learned.

(1) Famed online magazine The Tinseltown Tabloid, Inc. was just hit with a $50 million judgment for libel in favor of wrestling superstar Sonny Samson. The tort judgment accounts for around 95% of The Tinseltown Tabloid's unsecured debts. Samson would like to be able to collect on the judgment because his lavish lifestyle has left him cash poor, but he also has a long-standing grudge against The Tinseltown Tabloid and has made clear that above all he wants to see the paper shut down.

The Tinseltown Tabloid's other obligations include a $60 million first lien security interest on most of its assets. The first lien debt is held by a syndicate led by California Credit Bank, but most of the syndicate members are distressed debt investment funds that have limited liquidity at any given moment. The syndication agreement requires individual syndicate members' consent to change of payment terms, but is majority rule otherwise. The Tinseltown Tabloid's assets are probably worth between $25 and $30 million in liquidation, and include a valuable photo archive, not all of which has been published. The photo archive contains embarrassing photographs of everyone who is anyone in Hollywood and is probably worth around $10 million to most buyers.

The Tinseltown Tabloid's current controlling shareholder, Eddie Electric, a Silicon Valley icon, is desperate to retain control of the photo archive, which contains some compromising photos of him, and he's willing to spend up to $40 million to do so. "If the photos get out, the divorce alone will easily cost me at least $40 million," he explains, "and that's not including the reputational damage to my brand." Eddie Electric has retained you to advise him. He is himself on the board of The Tinseltown Tabloid, and controls a majority of the directors. What do you suggest he do to retain control of the photo archive, and what are the risks of your proposal?

(2) Patriot Petroleum, Inc., securitized the revenues from its oil wells in Oklahoma using a common law trust as the securitization vehicle, with Banque Française serving as the trustee and backup servicer in the event of the default of the servicer. The securitization was backed by a true sale opinion from the law firm of Barrow & de Waalt LLP. As part of the securitization, Banque Française, as trustee, duly filed and perfected a prophylactic security interest in the Oklahoma oil wells.

As part of the securitization, Patriot Petroleum warranted that the wells would produce a minimum revenue stream of at least $50 million/year. Patriot Petroleum also retained the juniormost tranche in the securitization, which received any revenues in a given month in excess of those necessary to pay that month's obligations to the senior tranches.

Patriot also contracted with the securitization trust to provide all servicing of the oil wells in exchange for a monthly fee. As servicer, Patriot is responsible for providing maintenance of the oil wells as well as selling the oil and remitting the oil sales revenue

Class	Treatment Under the Plan	Voting Result
$40 million in Administrative Priority Claims	Paid in full in cash on effective date of plan.	Votes not solicited.
Class I: $500 million in Secured Claims	Cured and reinstated.	Votes not solicited.
Class II: $30 million in Unsecured Prepetition Vendor Claims	Given equity of the reorganized firm.	90% acceptance by number; 60% acceptance by amount.
Class III: $200 million in Unsecured 7-Year Noteholder Class	Given new, 10-year notes for the face amount of the debt at a market interest rate, with interest paid-in-kind.	5% acceptance by number; 3% acceptance by amount.
Class IV: $100 million in Unsecured 5-Year Noteholder Claims	Paid per original terms, but with final maturity date extended by 90 days.	100% acceptance by amount and number.
Class V: $150 million in Unsecured 3-Year Junior Noteholder Class	Given new 1-year notes for the face amount of the debt with no interest.	25% acceptance by number; 40% acceptance by amount.
Class VI: Equity Interests	Given the option to participate in rights offering for warrants to purchase the equity of the reorganized firm.	100% acceptance by amount.

to the trust on a monthly basis. Patriot's duties as servicer also include advancing any missed monthly payments to the trust. Such advances are reimbursable to Patriot off the top of any future monthly revenues, but without interest. Patriot is currently just breaking even on the servicing contract.

Patriot believes that the value of the Oklahoma oil wells themselves is currently anywhere between $1 billion and $1.1 billion, depending on valuation methodology and assumptions. $950 million remains outstanding on the securities issued by the securitization trust. Patriot has no significant unencumbered assets.

Patriot is hoping to fund its operations in Chapter 11 with revenue from the Oklahoma oil wells. Can it?

(3) Patriot Petroleum, Inc., is wholly owned by entities controlled by the Broch brothers. Patriot is in Chapter 11 and has proposed a plan of reorganization with the treatment of claims and interests indicated in the table below. The bankruptcy court has approved the disclosure statement for the plan, and votes have been solicited. The voting results for each class are indicated in the table below. What objections can be successfully raised against plan confirmation by the various creditors and equityholders?

TABLE OF CASES

Principal cases are indicated by italics.

INDEX